THE PEOPLEPEDIA

The Ultimate Reference on the American People

Les Krantz

and

Jim McCormick

A Henry Holt Reference Book
Henry Holt and Company
New York

Les Krantz & Jim McCormick
Coeditors in chief

Biography Editor: Adrienne Brown. *Senior Editor:* Mark Mravic. *Contributing Editors:* Mark Scheffler, Edith McCormick. *Senior Manuscript Editor:* Charles Fletcher. *Associate Manuscript Editors:* Jan Fletcher, Christine Nielsen-Craig.

Photo Editor: Lynn Lobell

Research Director: Steve Bittner. *Research Associate:* Cynthia Robertson

Contributing Writers: Oveda Brown, Jim Cavallero, Richard Chapman, Bill Frazier, David Linton, David Rosansky, Gus Venditto, Rosanne Welch.

Special Acknowledgment: Many thanks to Paula Kakalecik for her expert council, her good catches, and the congeniality we enjoyed while it took place. And to Ken Wright for skillfully juggling his list while I (Les Krantz) was convalescing.

A Henry Holt Reference Book
Henry Holt and Company, Inc.
Publishers since 1866
115 West 18th Street
New York, New York 10011

Henry Holt ® is a registered trademark
of Henry Holt and Company, Inc.

Library of Congress Cataloging-in-Publication Data
Krantz, Les.
The peoplepedia: the ultimate reference on the American people /
Les Krantz.—1st ed.
p.   cm.—(A Henry Holt reference book)
Includes index.
1. United States—Miscellanea. 2. United States—Statistics.
3. United States—Biography—Miscellanea. I. Title. II Series.
E156.K74 1996   95-8948
973'.092'2—dc20   CIP

ISBN 0-8050-3727-6

Henry Holt books are available for special promotions and premiums.
For details contact: Director, Special Markets.

First Edition—1996

Designed by Les Krantz

Printed in the United States of America
All first editions are printed on acid-free paper.

10 9 8 7 6 5 4 3 2 1

CONTENTS

OVERVIEW
OF THE PEOPLEPEDIA

The *Peoplepedia* is a new concept for a general reference. Rather than reporting on just one facet of the American people, it profiles them in three ways:

(1) *as a mindset*; that is, what Americans think about the issues and themselves. This is the subject of Part One, The American Mindset.

(2) *as a collective* with accompanying statistics and informative text. This is the subject of Part Two, The American Collective.

(3) *as individuals*; that is, the "influentials," both the celebrated and those who command behind-the-scenes power or special knowledge. Approximately 1,350 individuals are succinctly profiled with biographical highlights of their careers and achievements. Their mailing addresses and telephone numbers (where available) are also provided. This is the subject of Part Three, Notable Americans.

THE AMERICAN MINDSET—PART ONE

This portion deals with "Intuitive America;" that is, the national consensus (or lack there of) involving a variety of perceptions and emotions. The sources of data are wide-ranging including commercial pollsters such as the Gallup Organization or Louis Harris Associates as well as scholarly surveys conducted by the likes of the National Opinion Research Center or the Alan Guttmacher Institute. Some data is culled from a poll that was conceived by our editors, the Peoplepedia Opinion Poll, which was conducted by the National Opinion Registry and Media Artists. Many other nationwide surveys were drawn upon.

The subject of the entries in this portion generally deal with: (a) assessment of societal changes, (b) confidence in various institutions, (c) familial relationships (d) perceptions of public figures, (e) personal preference issues, (f) satisfaction levels, and (g) trust.

THE AMERICAN COLLECTIVE—PART TWO

This portion is subdivided into 11 chapters, each one in some way dealing with broad spheres of influence every American is exposed to: America's educational system, the subject of the chapter "Education;" familial situations, the subject of the chapter; "Families" and many other arenas and themes relating to life in the United States, each treated in separate chapters.

Data relating to the American collective is culled from many sources, including some pollsters, however, in the main, governmental agencies predominate. Sources such as the U.S. Bureau of the Census, the Bureau of Labor Statistics and others are frequently drawn upon. Many private sources are also cited, which are as diverse as the American Automobile Association and the *Yearbook of American and Canadian Churches*.

NOTABLE AMERICANS—PART THREE

For individuals to be included in this portion, they had to meet two basic requirements: they must have been active in their professions during the writing of the *Peoplepedia*, and at the same time, be either American citizens, or permanent residents.

While objectivity concerning who will be included was strived for, subjective decisions are part of the business of writing and publishing. In this case, the subjective decisions made by our editors involved a difficult question: who really influences the American way of life? Since it is our belief that America is a nation in which people define one another more by their occupations than any other characteristic, we selected certain professions as parameters for inclusion. We chose many broadly defined professions as being the most influential disciplines that shape our nation (See: Appendix on page 462). Knowing full-well that there are more fields to consider, several other categories served as "catch-alls." They include Cultural Influences, which include philosophers and religious leaders, to name just a few. The Authors category also takes in many professionals from the ranks of lawyers, radio personalities, cartoonists and many other persuasions. By including these lesser-defined genres, there is a diverse mix of professions represented among the biographees in Part Three.

In order to reduce the weight of our own subjectivity as to which individuals should be profiled, we deferred to many recognized organizations which purport to examine many individual achievements and select out the most worthy among them for awards such as the Pulitzer and Nobel Prizes and the Academy Awards. These were criteria for inclusion for many categories. Other criteria for inclusion include professional status within given professions; i.e. CEOs of the largest U.S. corporations, anchorpersons at the television networks, political figures with large constituents and other factors that would make one influential. An enumeration of these criteria is found in the Appendix.

Despite the obvious influences of sports figures, they are not included among Notable Americans. We felt that there are so many—hundreds, perhaps thousands—that it was a subject of a book unto itself and we therefore omitted the sports category. The *Peoplepedia,* however, does cover major sports subjects in Part Two in the "Pastimes" chapter.

OVERVIEWS

One easily overlooked highlight of the *Peoplepedia* is the twelve chapter overviews that are provided at the beginning of Part One and the beginning of each chapter in Part Two. For a fascinating and informative read, it is suggested that you read these overviews successively. In tandem, they provide a succinct picture of the American people today.

Les Krantz

part one:

THE
AMERICAN
MINDSET

THE AMERICAN MINDSET
OVERVIEW

The "American Mindset" portion of the *Peoplepedia* deals with how we feel about the issues that face us. Many are new issues that were not issues at all before a few years ago: retirement of the Baby Boomers, fatty foods, spousal abuse, to name a few. And old issues are rearing their ugly heads again: our consciousness of the Holocaust, race relations, equality of the sexes and others issues that Americans are reassessing for the first time in half a century.

At the outset of the century, the unbridled enthusiasm of the American people, coupled with the country's massive economic potential and promise of greatness, prompted social commentator Walter Lippmann to dub this "the American century." But as the 20th century comes to a close, the spirit of optimism implied by that coinage has given way to a mood of worry and concern. Crime, drugs, education, employment, race relations, political scandal, AIDS—the litany of problems that bother Americans seems to go on endlessly. And what emerges from a look at the mindset of the country in the mid-1990s is that these problems have soured the American spirit.

Social critics will point to events of the turbulent '60s and '70s as the prime cause for America's disillusionment. Vietnam and Watergate did much to harm America's faith in the moral virtues of its leaders and its policies. But today's distress goes much farther than the new-found political skepticism. As we head into the new century, Americans are concerned not so much about their leaders as about their jobs and whether they will be

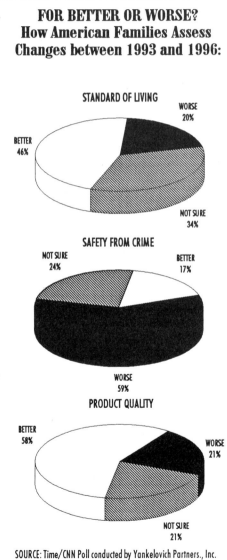

FOR BETTER OR WORSE?
How American Families Assess
Changes between 1993 and 1996:

STANDARD OF LIVING
WORSE 20%
BETTER 46%
NOT SURE 34%

SAFETY FROM CRIME
NOT SURE 24%
BETTER 17%
WORSE 59%

PRODUCT QUALITY
BETTER 58%
WORSE 21%
NOT SURE 21%

SOURCE: Time/CNN Poll conducted by Yankelovich Partners., Inc. Jan. 17-18, 1996.

victims of downsizing, or that they will suffer a job loss for other reasons. If so, will they find another job? A big "if," at least in their minds—and will that new job pay enough to maintain the standard of living to which they and their families are accustomed? A *Time* magazine poll in January, 1996 found that 70 percent of Americans worry about job-loss, more than any other issue.

Arguably, things aren't all bad. The environment is cleaner in the '90s, Americans are healthier and living longer. Technological advances have transformed our everyday life, making it easier to communicate and to entertain ourselves. And we are at peace with the world, though not with ourselves. This is perhaps the most revealing and certainly the most ironic disclosure of the data that follows.

Economic uncertainty taints America's outlook on a wide range of issues. For instance, the opinion polls on which the American Mindset portion are based, clearly point out that the social liberalism of the '60s has given way to a backlash against such programs as affirmative action. Recent polls demonstrate a wide rift in racial attitudes in the country: The entry on "Racial Equality" finds that while 60 percent of white Americans believe blacks and other minorities have the same opportunities as whites, a mere 27 percent of blacks feel they have reached a level of equality.

A souring mood can be seen even in our changing attitudes toward the rest of the world. Though the Cold War has ended with the U.S. and its allies victorious, we are uneasy. With our erstwhile enemies no longer a threat, we have changed our opinions of our friends. As the entry on "Allies" shows, Americans' goodwill toward Russia has improved dramatically since the early 1980s, when President Reagan referred to the Soviet Union as an "evil empire;" on the other hand, our regard for our Cold War partners and long-time allies—Britain, France, Germany, and Japan—has deteriorated. Opinions concerning the latter two countries especially, undoubtedly reflect the economic tensions between the U.S. and those two industrial powerhouses that over the course of the past decade have remained political allies but become serious economic rivals to the U.S. in the international marketplace.

On the whole, America's response to the uncertainty of the future has been marked by a return toward the old ideals—in everything from politics (to conservativism and the Republican Party) to our musical preferences (to country-western and mood music).

Finally there is an entertaining and revealing adjunct to the polls on which this chapter is based—the Peoplepedia Opinion Poll that concerns public and private persons and our opinions regarding them. The questions were formulated by the editors of the *Peoplepedia* and posed to the American public in late 1995 and early 1996 with the assistance of the National Opinion Registry on the World Wide Web (http://www.opinion-reg.com), which is where the questions were accessed and subsequently answered by anyone who desired to participate. The assembly of participants was then statistically adjusted to reasonably reflect a random sample of the American adult population. The results were tabulated by Media Artists of Chicago.

ADVICE

The traditional role of parent as advisor is still in tact, even in an age in which the nuclear family is declining as a percentage of familial situations. According to the Peoplepedia Opinion Poll, a survey that concerns public and private persons and our opinions regarding them, mothers ranked somewhat ahead of fathers as the best advisor.

One might surmise that this may be expected as women gain more power and equality in American society. The image of the all-knowing, omnipotent father gradually has given way to a more realistic, more fallible perception of the father as "human," rather than an all-knowing authority figure.

Another possible interpretation of the poll's finding is that there may be a bit of Oedipal influence at work: males named their mothers as the best advisors, while according to females, their mothers and fathers were in a dead heat for first place.

The tabulations below represent the percentage of poll respondents who gave the following answers to the question: **"Overall (meaning on most matters), which one family member is most likely to give you the best advice?"**

ALL RESPONDENTS

Mother	15.84%
Father	13.82
Wife	9.63
Husband	5.67
Sister	5.38
No Answer	5.35
Brother	4.08
Grandfather	2.55
Grandmother	2.34
Aunt	1.85
No One	1.85
Son	1.07
Self/Me	0.99
Cousin	0.87
Daughter	0.58
Equal	0.58
Uncle	0.58
Animal	0.29
Mother-in-Law	0.29
Niece	0.29

FEMALE RESPONDENTS

Mother	18.67%
Father	18.67
Husband	10.67
Sister	10.67
No Answer	6.67
Grandfather	5.33
Brother	4.00
Grandmother	4.00
Aunt	2.67
No One	2.67
Self/Me	2.67
Son	1.33

MALE RESPONDENTS

Mother	14.19%
Father	10.99
Wife	8.24
No Answer	4.58
Brother	4.12
Sister	2.29
Aunt	1.37
Cousin	1.37
Grandmother	1.37
No One	1.37
Daughter	0.92
Equal	0.92
Grandfather	0.92
Son	0.92
Uncle	0.92
Mother-in-Law	0.46
Niece	0.46
Animal	0.46

ALLIES

Among 13 countries named in an opinion poll conducted by Roper Starch International in 1993, only four were regarded as more friendly to the U.S. than they had been in the early 1980s: Mexico, Russia, Haiti, and Cuba. Japan took the biggest bashing in the survey, which polled 2,006 adults age 18 and older. In 1982 Japan was described as a friend or ally of the U.S. by 64 percent of Americans; but by 1993 only 38 percent of Americans felt the same way toward Japan. The pollsters cited tensions between the U.S. and Japan on trade practices as causing the decline.

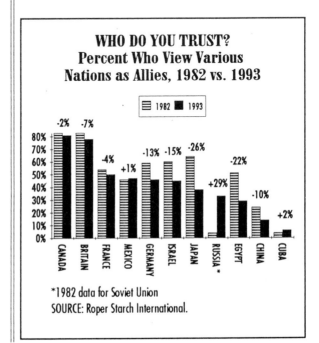

WHO DO YOU TRUST?
Percent Who View Various Nations as Allies, 1982 vs. 1993

*1982 data for Soviet Union
SOURCE: Roper Starch International.

Russia rose almost one-third in favorable responses from those polled. In 1982 only four percent regarded the Big Bear as friendly to the U.S. After the breakup of the Soviet Union, that climbed to 29 percent.

In 1982—just a few years after the U.S.-brokered Egyptian-Israeli peace agreement—51 percent of Americans regarded Egypt kindly, but in 1993 that percentage dropped to 29 percent. Israel fared little better, falling from 60 percent to 45 percent in favorability.

According to the pollsters, China's dismal record on human rights was reflected in a drop of 10 percentage points in the estimation of Americans, from 24 percent viewing the country as friendly in 1982 to 14 percent who did so in 1993.

A general feeling of growing animosity extended even to longtime ally Britain, which fell from 85 percent who regarded it as friendly to 78 percent. France, Poland, and Canada also slightly declined as friends or allies in the view of Americans.

Percentage of those polled who agreed that the given country was a friend or ally of the U.S., and percentage point change since 1982, according to Roper Starch International.

Country	1982	1993	Change
Canada	83%	81%	-2
Britain	85	78	-7
France	54	50	-4
Mexico	46	47	+1
Germany*	59	46	-13
Israel	60	45	-15
Japan	64	38	-26
Russia**	4	33	+29
Poland	33	30	-3
Egypt	51	29	-22
Haiti	7	16	+9
China	24	14	-10
Cuba	4	6	+2

*1982 data for West Germany

**1982 data for Soviet Union

ANXIETIES

The national mood is growing sullen and fearful as the decade of the 1990s progresses, according to pollsters in two surveys that show Americans' attitudes have become less compassionate toward the poor and minorities, less tolerant toward immigrants, and increasingly fearful of crime.

A *New York Times*/CBS News poll found that 23 percent of Americans identified crime as "the most important problem facing this country today." Economic concerns ranked second, with 18 percent seeing the economy as the nation's top concern. Health care, ranked second in an earlier poll, plunged to fifth place, behind drugs.

Twenty-five percent of the 1,429 adults surveyed feared a close relative would lose his or her job in 1995, while 40 percent worried about their safety from crime.

Seventy-five percent took Congress to task, saying it was not doing its job. Only 20 percent thought it was. This is in line with an earlier Gallup poll, which showed that only 18 percent approved of the performance of Congress. Almost three-fourths of respondents could not name their own U.S. representative, and 50 percent could not name one public official they admired. Sixty-six percent said they felt they did not have a say in what government did, and nearly 75 percent said most members of Congress did not understand their needs.

Those surveyed said they usually get most of their news from television (three to one), and about one in two said they listen to political talk shows on TV sometimes or frequently. Fifty-seven percent believe the country needs a new political party, while others (two to one) think the government should be less involved in solving national problems.

The second poll showed that 51 percent of whites believed the drive for equal rights for all has been pushed too far, an increase from 42 percent in 1992. Fifty-seven percent of the 4,809 respondents agreed that the government should help people who can't help themselves, a decline from 71 percent in 1987. Only 41 percent believed the needy should be helped if it added to the national deficit. The pollsters in the second survey, the Times Mirror Center for the People and the Press, said it was the first time since 1987 that the latter assertion failed to win a majority.

The poll registered a decline in Americans' views on immigrants. Eighty-two percent of those polled said the number of people coming to live in the U.S. should be restricted and controlled more than it is now. That represented a six percent increase from in 1992.

Financial insecurity was also evidenced by 40 percent of the respondents, who said they often can't make ends meet on their present incomes. Sixty percent said they cannot live the life they want because of lack of funds, and 50 percent of those think they never will. The pollsters commented that after five years of early retirements, downsizing by business, privatization, and the hiring of temporaries, the new wave of hirings as the economy expands offers lower wages, benefits, and pensions.

On a topic that held no threat to their jobs or finances the gloom lifted somewhat. To the question whether it was all right for blacks and whites to date each other, 65 percent—a record— approved, up from 43 percent in 1987.

Response to the question: Will the future of the next generation be better or worse than today (New York Times/CBS poll):

Opinion	Percent
Better	18%
Worse	57
Same	21
No opinion	3

How much trust can be put in the government to do what is right?

Opinion	Percent
Always or most always	22%
Sometimes or never	77
No opinion	1

Do you know the name of your representative in Congress?

Answer	Percent
Yes	28% correct
Yes	15 wrong
No	52
No answer	5

BABY BOOMERS AND RETIREMENT

Providing for retirement is the single most important aim for Americans age 45 to 59, in households with more than $50,000 annual income, made up of college graduates, executives, and dual-earner married couples. Among America's 80 million baby boomers, though, retirement is a distant third in their list of life priorities.

First on the list of boomer parents' priorities surveyed in a 1992 Roper poll was "making sure my children go to college," and second, cited by 46 percent, "having enough now." Yet a Gallup poll in 1993 showed that 34 percent of boomers expect their standard of living to improve after retirement, against 37 percent who believe it will stay the same and 29 percent who expect it to decline.

Though 65 percent of boomers say that having enough money to retire on is a major concern and 52 percent fear outliving their savings, a Merrill Lynch poll in 1993 shows that older members of the generation are saving only 34 percent of what they will need to keep up their standard of living after retirement.

Married-couple boomer households with incomes between $40,000 and $60,000 will need to save $200,000 by age 65 to maintain their standard of living, the pollsters say, and those without a pension will need $270,000. But in 1992 married-couple households had saved only $13,000, mostly (67.4 percent) in equity in their homes, although 79 percent of them say they are saving for retirement.

The average American retiree in the mid-1990s receives the largest part of his or her income—36 percent— from Social Security. Twenty-five percent is received from assets, 18 percent from pensions, 12 percent from wages, and nine percent from other sources, according to the Employee Benefit Research Institute.

When boomers retire, the average contribution from Social Security will likely be lower, and they will have waited longer for payments to begin. But pensions will be higher, according to the pollsters.

A Census Bureau study found that Twenty-one percent of boomers own stocks or mutual-fund shares with a median value of $4,563. About 23 percent own

U.S. savings bonds, valued at only $600. IRA and KEOGH accounts attract 25.8 percent of the boomers, their median value being $8,634. Seven percent have interest-earning asset in bonds, funds, or government securities valued at more than $9,000.

EBRI finds that 45 percent of Americans expect to live 11 to 20 years after the retirement age of 65. One-fourth expect one to 10 years of retirement, although the average number of years remaining at age 65 is 17.2 years, according to EBRI, which says that many boomers will live many years beyond even that, and will have to stretch their savings nest-egg from 10 years to 20.

Median value of assets held by baby boomers age 35 to 44, and percent of householders owning them, using Census Bureau statistics on household wealth and asset ownership, 1991:

Asset	Amount	Percent Owning
Equity in home	$31,082	67.4%
Rental property equity	30,114	9.3
Other real estate	18,284	10.8
IRA/KEOGH accounts	8,634	25.8
Equity in business/ professions	9,703	16.0
Other interest earning accounts	9,311	7.4
Stocks/mutual funds	4,563	21.3
Bank interest earnings	2,325	75.0
U.S. savings bonds	600	23.2
Checking accounts	481	48.8
Other assets	14,353	2.2
Total net worth	31,148	NA

BASEBALL

The major league baseball strike of 1994-95 is the chief cause of dissatisfaction among the game's fans, although there are a number of less-subtle dissatisfactions that were in place before the strike.

According to 42 percent of 305 volunteer *USA Today* "team members" — a group the newspaper formed to check out the general state of ball games — food is the biggest gripe and the priciest feature at the parks. Despite the beef, the ballpark dog has a noble history.

It was in 1850 that the butchers' guild introduced the spicy smoked pork sausage that would eventually captivate the American kid. It was introduced as "dachshund sausage." Harry Stevens, a vendor at the Giants' Polo Grounds in New York City, stuck one on a bun in 1906 and sold it in the bleachers as "a red-hot dachshund sausage." The rest is history. Today, 16.5 billion "dogs" are turned out every year, and baseball parks are still one of America's favorite places in which to buy them at any price. New York's Yankee Stadium has the top price for a hot dog: $3.00. Baltimore sells dogs for $2.75. The average around the league is $1.81. Cincinnati and Philadelphia fans have a bargain — $1.00.

Other complaints among fans about prices and the percentage that was irked about them were as follows:

Complaint	Percent
Tickets	31%
Souvenirs	14
Parking	12
Nothing	1

And Who's to Blame? For a change, it's not the umpire or the team's manager. The volunteer team members blamed the parties below in the following percentages:

Blame	Percent
Owners	51%
Players	35
Fans	7
Concessionaires	7

But What Are They Doing about It? The volunteers reported that their plans for future games are as follows:

Plans	Percent
Will attend more	28%
Will attend fewer	15
Will attend about the same number	41
Will not attend	16

BLACK CHILDREN

Fears for the future of black children in the U.S. are overwhelmingly felt among black adults, as violence, guns, drugs, and gangs proliferate in their communities, a 1994 national poll reveals.

The poll of blacks showed that more than three-fourths of the adults surveyed thought there was a crisis for black children in the country, and more than 70 percent said it was harder to raise their children than it was during the era of segregation.

Among 411 children age 11 to 17 included in the poll, 75 percent viewed the present without fear but saw major troubles ahead. More than three-quarters feared violence in school, 70 percent feared their peers who owned guns, and 64 percent feared the dangerous neighborhoods they lived in.

The poll was taken for the Children's Defense Fund and a fledgling group called Black Community Crusade for Children, which is training college students to become tutors and lobbying for government to recognize and help black children troubled by the turmoil of their times. Peter D. Hart Research Associates conducted the poll of 1,004 adults and the children.

Sixty-six percent of the adults polled said there are fewer opportunities than problems for black children. The vast majority of those believed that 50 percent of all black children will become teenage parents, will face racial prejudice, and will destroy their lives with drugs or imprisonment.

Second to health care, black parents adjudge job training and better schools as the strategy that can help their children the most. The youth above is getting both thanks to New York City's School Volunteer Program. Photo by Ken Levinson.

The poll also found that it was not the Michael Jordans of the black world who most influence black kids. Eighty-three percent said the biggest influences on their lives were their parents or other relatives, with religious leaders second. Basketball star Jordan was cited as an influence by only six percent of kids polled.

Asked who was most influential in their lives, the children answered:

Parents	58%
Churches	15
Local black leaders	5
National black leaders	4
Government	4
School	4

Asked what are acceptable strategies for helping black children, the parents answered:

More health care	81%
Job training	78
Better schools	78
Preschooling	75
Religious teaching	73
Activities/jobs	70
Gun controls	68
Parent counseling	65
Reduce teen pregnancy	64
Welfare reform	43

BUSING

Eighty-eight percent of whites in the country oppose busing black schoolchildren into their communities, and 64 percent of blacks agree with them. This is one revelation in a Gallup poll taken 40 years after the Supreme Court's landmark decision in Brown vs. the Board of Education of Topeka, Kan., which banned segregation in schools.

In the 1994 poll of 1,016 adults age 18 and over, including a balanced proportion of 230 blacks, 86 percent of whites and 94 percent of blacks agree with the part of the ruling calling segregated public schools illegal. While 74 percent of whites say their communities are all or mostly white, 71 percent believe the level of integration, without busing, in their neighborhoods is about right, as do 58 percent of blacks about their communities.

Among ways to improve minority education, 32 percent of respondents list integrating public schools, while 48 percent would direct resources toward improving schools in minority communities. Blacks rejected by 54 percent the idea that it would sometimes be better to let blacks attend all-black schools. Whites accept the notion, 56 percent to 36 percent.

Sixty-five percent of the public credits the Brown decision with improving black schooling; 48 percent of both whites and blacks credit it with easing tensions between them. Forty percent in 1971 saw improvement in race relations because of the decision; by 1988, that figure rose to 55 percent.

Among the 18-29 age group, 59 percent of whites were familiar with the Brown case; 52 percent of blacks the same age had never heard of it. Overall, 58 percent of whites were familiar with the decision, as were 57 percent of blacks.

The tables below repesent various opinions about segregation and the Brown decision.

APPROVE BROWN DECISION:

Opinion	Total	Blacks	Whites
Approve	87%	86%	94%
Disapprove	11	12	3
No opinion	2	2	3

HAS BLACK EDUCATION IMPROVED SINCE BROWN DECISION?

Opinion	Total	Whites	Blacks
Yes	65%	64%	70%
No	28	29	25
No opinion	7	7	5

HAS INTEGRATION IMPROVED WHITE EDUCATION?

Opinion	Total	Whites	Blacks
Yes	42%	39%	59%
No	50	52	33
No opinion	8	9	8

BROWN DECISION OPINION TREND:

Year	Approve	Disapprove	No Opinion
1994	87%	11%	2.0%
1961	63	32	5.0
1959	60	35	5.0
1957	59	37	5.5
1956	63	31	6.0
1959	57	39	4.5
1954	54	42	4.3

HAVE RACE RELATIONS IMPROVED SINCE BROWN DECISION?

Opinion	Total	Whites	Blacks
Better	48%	48%	56%
Same	21	20	21
Worse	29	30	17
No opinion	2	2	6

CAREER CHOICES, TEENS

The profession of physical therapist, the fastest-growing occupation in the health care field, was the top career choice of American teens. Jobs in physical therapy increased from 55,000 in 1983 to 115,000 one decade later, and are expected to grow 88 percent by the year 2005.

Seventy-three percent of physical therapists are women, down from 77 percent in 1983; 19 percent are men, up from 11 percent; 3 percent are black, down from 8 percent; and 5 percent are Hispanic, up from 2 percent. Annual salaries in the profession run an average of $35,643, with the top level at $52,468 and the bottom at $17,784.

Other careers in the teens' top 10 list, according to a teen survey by Careers & Colleges magazine, were FBI agent, accountant, lawyer, architect, veterinarian, environmental engineer, psychotherapist, business manager, and pharmacist, in that order.

CELEBRITIES AS PRESIDENT

In the last several congressional elections, candidates have tried to distance themselves from the Washington establishment, perhaps noting the success of Presidents Jimmy Carter, Ronald Reagan and Bill Clinton, all of whom had never occupied a national office before being elected President. With that as a backdrop, many non-politicians have entered their names in the ring for the highest office in the land. In this context, the Peoplepedia Opinion Poll—a survey concerning public and private persons and our opinions regarding them—asked what nonpolitician would be the best President. The answers were mixed—evangelists, talk show hosts, poets and basketball players all made the list. The surprising roster of potential White House inhabitants is led by Colin Powell, but also includes such unlikely candidates as Oprah Winfrey, David Letterman, Maya Angelou, and Charles Barkley.

The tabulations below represent the percentage of poll respondents who gave the following answers to the question: "What one public figure who is not a politician would make the best President of the United States?"

ALL RESPONDENTS

Colin Powell	13.74%

Rush Limbaugh	5.03
Oprah Winfrey	2.75
Robert Redford	2.55
David Letterman	2.26
Steve Forbes	2.22
Maya Angelou	1.97
Walter Cronkite	1.56
Bill Gates	1.44
Charlton Heston	1.44
Bill Cosby	1.27
Ross Perot	1.07
Billy Graham	1.07
Arnold Schwarzenegger	1.07
Ralph Nader	0.99
Hillary Clinton	0.99
Charles Barkley	0.87
Noam Chomsky	0.58
Harry Browne	0.58
Pat Buchanan	0.58

FEMALE RESPONDENTS

Colin Powell	20.00%
Oprah Winfrey	6.67
David Letterman	5.33
Robert Redford	5.33
Maya Angelou	5.33
Rush Limbaugh	2.67
Bill Cosby	2.67
Walter Cronkite	2.67
Hillary Clinton	2.67
Ralph Nader	2.67
Steve Forbes	1.33
Ross Perot	1.33
Billy Graham	1.33
Arnold Schwarzenegger	1.33

MALE RESPONDENTS

Colin Powell	10.07%
Rush Limbaugh	6.41
Steve Forbes	2.75
Bill Gates	2.29
Charlton Heston	2.29
Charles Barkley	1.37
Robert Redford	0.92
Ross Perot	0.92
Billy Graham	0.92
Walter Cronkite	0.92
Arnold Schwarzenegger	0.92
Noam Chomsky	0.92
Harry Browne	0.92
Pat Buchanan	0.92
Oprah Winfrey	0.46
David Letterman	0.46
Don't Know	0.46
Bill Cosby	0.46
None	0.46

AND THE WORST? "President Limbaugh" was the overwhelming nonchoice for President, according to the poll, which also asked who the worst President might be among nonpoliticians. Though Limbaugh,

Ross Perot (No. 2), and even Howard Stern (No. 3) have expressed interest in political office, it's highly unlikely that some other names that made the poll tally—O.J. Simpson, Courtney Love or Dennis Rodman—will be appearing on the ballot anytime soon.

The tabulations below represent the percentage of poll respondents who gave the following answers to the question: **"What one public figure who is not a politician would make the worst President of the United States?"**

ALL RESPONDENTS

Rush Limbaugh	7.61%
Ross Perot	5.93
Howard Stern	4.11
Babra Streisand	3.09
Madonna	2.34
Louis Farrakhan	2.26
Jesse Jackson	1.85
O.J. Simpson	1.65
Hillary Clinton	1.56
Charlton Heston	1.36
Pat Buchanan	1.27
Courtney Love	1.27
Pat Robertson	1.27
Steve Forbes	1.07
Dan Rather	0.99
Dennis Rodman	0.87
Jane Fonda	0.87
Jay Leno	0.87
Whoopi Goldberg	0.87
Don King	0.78
Don Rickles	0.78
Michael Jackson	0.78
Ted Turner	0.78
Al Sharpton	0.58

FEMALE RESPONDENTS

Rush Limbaugh	12.00%
Howard Stern	8.00
Ross Perot	6.67
Louis Farrakhan	5.33
Madonna	4.00
Pat Buchanan	2.67
Hillary Clinton	2.67
Jesse Jackson	2.67
Courtney Love	2.67
Dan Rather	2.67
Pat Robertson	2.67
Babra Streisand	1.33
O.J. Simpson	1.33
Charlton Heston	1.33
Don King	1.33
Don Rickles	1.33
Steve Forbes	1.33
Michael Jackson	1.33
Ted Turner	1.33

MALE RESPONDENTS

Ross Perot	5.49%
Rush Limbaugh	5.04
Babra Streisand	4.12

O.J. Simpson	1.83
Howard Stern	1.83
Madonna	1.37
Jesse Jackson	1.37
Charlton Heston	1.37
Dennis Rodman	1.37
Jane Fonda	1.37
Jay Leno	1.37
Whoopi Goldberg	1.37
Steve Forbes	0.92
Hillary Clinton	0.92
Al Sharpton	0.92
Pat Buchanan	0.46
Courtney Love	0.46
Louis Farrakhan	0.46
Don King	0.46
Don Rickles	0.46
Michael Jackson	0.46
Ted Turner	0.46
Pat Robertson	0.46

CHILD CARE

Among the list of employer benefits given workers is a growing trend of child-care assistance. More than 66 percent of adults believe it is about time.

Women are more likely than men to feel this way, given their traditional role of being more involved in families than men. Seventy-one percent of women support the view that employers should do more to help employees on child-care support, compared with 64 percent of men, according to a 1993 Gallup poll commissioned by the Employee Benefit Research Institute. There is no difference between the views of married and single people on the subject.

CHRISTMAS GIFTS

A Harris poll taken in 1992 suggests that parents are fighting back against Nintendo brainwashing, judging from the kinds of gifts they're giving their kids. Though the kids may clamor for electronic hypnosis, their parents would rather have them well-clothed and well-read.

When the poll asked 1,190 parents what they had in mind for the kids, clothing was the most popular selection of 77 percent of the respondents. Non-electronic games and puzzles scarcely beat out books, 70 percent going for the fun gifts and 69 percent for books. Dolls were on the shopping list for 48 percent of the parents, two percentage points above the mundane gift certificate or the gift that always fits, cash. Stuffed animals, at 41 percent, were popular, as was sports equipment, at 40 percent. In contrast, electronic games were considered by only 29 percent.

What are the most popular gifts for Mom and Dad or for a lover or friend? Clothing again, along with money and perfume or cologne.

True Believers: The average respondent in the poll think kids stop believing in Santa Claus around age eight. Nearly half thought of the holiday as a time for family gatherings rather than religious communion. Turkey is still considered the appropriate Christmas dinner — it's served by 50 percent of American households; 38 percent feast on ham.

CLASSICAL MUSIC

About 62 million Americans like classical, and 63.7 million like jazz. More women find classical agreeable than men, 35 percent to 32 percent, and whites enjoy it more than blacks, 35 percent to 18 percent, according to the 1992 National Endowment for the Arts survey.

People aged between 35 to 74 make up the preponderance of potential audiences for America's 90 symphony orchestras. Those between 65 and 74 enjoy classical music, with 43 percent of respondents in the age group expressing a preference for it. Sixty-five percent of people with graduate school educations listen to classical music, while only 16 percent of adults who have had just some high school do so.

The same trend is observed concerning family incomes and classical music. Forty-seven percent of people who earn $50,000 or more a year prefer classical. Thirty-five percent of those with incomes between $25,000 to $49,999 like that form of music. But only 23 percent of adults with annual incomes of $5,000 to $9,999 enjoy classical music.

Comparative salaries and pensions at top U.S. symphonies, according to the International Conference of Symphony and Opera musicians:

Orchestra	minimum salary	pensions
New York Philharmonic	$68,120	$40,000
Boston Symphony Orchestra	67,600	26,500
Chicago Symphony Orchestra	67,600	40,000
Philadelphia Orchestra	67,080	37,500
Cleveland Orchestra	65,000	27,000

CONFIDENCE IN U.S. INSTITUTIONS

Confidence in the U.S. presidency has declined steadily since March 1991, shortly after the Gulf War, when 72 percent of Americans expressed confidence in the office. In 1994 pollsters measured confidence at almost half that, 38 percent, a drop of five points from the 43 percent confidence registered in 1993.

The presidency is not the only American institution to suffer an erosion in national esteem. TV news, measured at a 46 percent confidence level in 1993, dropped a sharp 11 points to 35 percent in a year, the biggest plunge of all institutions in the Gallup poll of 1,036 adults age 18 and older.

Lowest-rated of all institutions listed in the poll is the nation's criminal justice system, with 49 percent of Americans showing very little or no confidence in it. This is six points worse than the 43 percent of 1993, and 17 points below the next lowest-rated institution, the U.S. Congress, of which only 18 percent of the people are convinced it is doing its job.

In 1981 Congress was viewed positively by 29 percent of Americans, but in 1991 only 18 percent felt that way, and the institution has not recovered since. Along with banking, Congress has lost 25 percentage points of respect in the eyes of the American people since 1973.

The most esteemed of American institutions, as it has been since the mid-1980s, is the military. Sixty-four percent of those polled are proud of the U.S. armed forces, as opposed to 8 percent who are not. In 1981 confidence in the military stood at only 50 percent.

The police and organized religion, at confidence levels of 54 percent, are second and third in esteem of the people, though religion has dropped 10 percentage points since 1971, as have the Supreme Court, at 42 percent; banks at 35 percent; and newspapers at 29 percent. The police, first included in the poll in 1993, gained two percentage points in a year.

Organized labor and the nation's schools are equally out of favor, the poll shows. Both registered confidence levels of only 26 percent, with 31 percent of those polled having very little or no regard for labor, and 30 percent for big business.

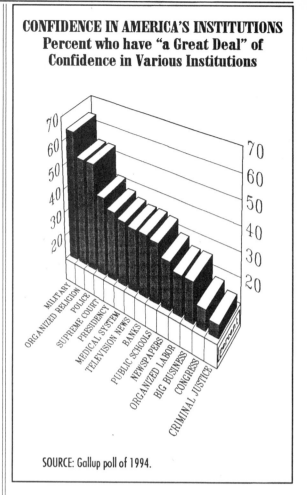

CONFIDENCE IN AMERICA'S INSTITUTIONS
Percent who have "a Great Deal" of Confidence in Various Institutions

SOURCE: Gallup poll of 1994.

Institutions	Great deal/ quite a lot	Very little or none
Military	64%	8%
Organized religion	54	16
Police	54	12
Supreme Court	42	17
Presidency	38	27
Medical system	36	26
Television news	35	27
Banks	35	17
Public schools	34	25
Newspapers	29	28
Organized labor	26	31
Big business	26	30
Congress	18	32
Criminal justice system	15	49

American's confidence in its institutions, as measured by a Gallup poll in 1994:

CONSUMERISM

The well-educated and wealthy are not the wisest shoppers. High school graduates and lower income people are. And women are smarter than men, blacks sharper than whites and Hispanics, according to a survey of how Americans approach the purchase of 27 different products or services.

Overall, women, the young, blacks, the least affluent, people age 55 to 64, and high school graduates show the most interest in researching a product before they buy. Men, people age 65 or older, whites, the well-off financially, and college graduates show the least interest.

Seventy-one percent of adults with incomes of $25,000 annually or less are greatly interested in prod-

uct research, compared to 60 percent of adults with household incomes of $50,000 or more.

Eighty-five percent of poor Americans—those with annual incomes of less than $15,000 a year—would research available information on auto and health insurance, 80 percent would look into prescription drugs, 71 percent would seek information on eyeglasses, and 67 percent on local telephone service.

The National Opinion Research Center (NORC), which conducted the survey of 1,021 adults in 1993 for the American Association for Retired Persons and the Consumer Federation of America, points out that these Americans spend proportionately more of their incomes on these products and services than do the affluent and college graduates. They also are less likely to browse for information on needs that are beyond their means, such as home loans, mortgage refinancing, airline tickets, and top-of-the-line appliances.

High school dropouts, with the lowest average income of all American adults, are only slightly less likely to look for more product information—66 percent, compared to 70 percent of high school graduates—though they may have more trouble reading and evaluating the information they dig up, NORC points out.

The respondents in the poll age 65 and over typically seek opinions on prescription drugs (75 percent) and hearing aids (56 percent). Those age 55 to 64 are the most vigorous in researching products—71 percent do so on items mostly related to health: prescription drugs (77 percent), eyeglasses (77 percent), nursing homes (73 percent), non-prescription drugs (64 percent), and hearing aids (63 percent). Fifty-seven percent also check up on funeral costs.

Only 61 percent of college graduates show great interest in looking for product information, because, according to ORC, they feel they "know it all." Predictably they show the greatest interest in a new car (85 percent), investments (82 percent), and air fares (61 percent).

Blacks (79 percent) have greater interest in product research than do Hispanics (72 percent) and whites (65 percent). The greatest difference relates to housing and health: home purchases (17 percentage points), funerals (28 percent), life insurance (25 percent), prescription drugs (19 percent), and nonprescription drugs (17 percent).

The pollsters point out a striking regional difference, that Americans in the South show a greater interest in product information than people in the other three regions, probably accounted for by the fact that there are more blacks in the South than elsewhere in the country.

Women in their traditional role as household caretakers are more likely than men to want independent opinions on products such as groceries (67 percent to 52 percent); checking accounts (69 percent to 54 percent); nonprescription drugs (61 percent to 48 percent); and long-distance and local telephone service (57 percent to 44 percent). They show little difference, however, on the subjects of homes, mortgage loans, and investments.

Percent of Americans interested in seeking the best deal when shopping for selected products or services, and average annual spending on the product or service, according to the National Opinion Research Center, for the Consumer Federation of America and the American Association of Retired Persons:

Product	Interest	Annual Spending
New car	83%	$1,218
Health insurance	80	537
Home purchase	79	NA
Investments	79	NA
Auto insurance	78	575
Homeowners insurance	76	151
Mortgage loan	75	1,741
Car repair	74	561
Mortgage refinancing	73	NA
Life insurance	72	346
Home repairs	71	369
Used car	69	1,051
Car loan	68	303
Home equity loan	68	NA
Prescription drugs	66	176
Nursing homes	65	NA
Savings account	63	NA
Checking account	62	25
Non-auto consumer debt	60	234
Food	60	2,390
Eyeglasses	58	51
Air fares	56	188
Nonprescription drugs	55	64
All phone service	51	567
Funerals	50	58
Hearing aids	49	NA

CONSUMER INTEREST BY INCOME

Under $15,000	71%
$15,000-25,000	71
$25,000-35,000	67
$35,000-50,000	67
$50,000 or more	60

CONSUMER INTEREST BY AGE

18-24	69%
25-34	63
35-44	65
45-54	68
55-64	71
65 and older	63

CONSUMER INTEREST BY EDUCATION

High school dropout	66%
High school grad	70
College incomplete	67
College graduate	61

CONSUMER SATISFACTION

Americans as a whole are satisfied with many of the products turned out by workers and management in the electronic, appliance, clothing, and prepared food products industries, but show dissatisfaction with those in the service sector, the fastest-growing area of the economy.

Nondurable manufacturing showed a satisfaction index of 81.6 in a 1994 survey that rated 200 companies in about 40 industries on a scale of zero to 100. Durable goods earned a rating of 79.2. Express delivery scored 81 and long-distance phone service 82, the highest in the service sector.

Other services such as motion pictures and hospitals, rated poorly, at a below-average 74.4. The U.S. Postal Service, included in the category of transportation, utilities, and communications, rated a score of only 60, lowest in that category. The Internal Revenue Service, included in the public administration group, scored lowest of all in the survey at 55.

Second to the service sector was manufacturers of durables such as autos, appliances, and computers, which scored 79.2, with appliances receiving the highest score in the sector, at 85. Restaurants and fast-food establishments rated only a 69, compared to 77 for department and discount stores in the retail sector. U.S. companies overall scored a satisfaction rating of 74.5, which survey organizers said was too low to protect U.S. business from foreign competition.

The new index, created by the business school at the University of Michigan and the American Society for Quality Control, surveyed 50,000 consumers on what they thought about various products and services of major companies and agencies, and whether, if they liked them, they would go along with them at current prices.

Below are index scores of various other products and services rated from zero to 100.

Nondurables

Apparel	82
Athletic shoes	79
Beer	83
Cigarettes	81
Canned foods	87
Chocolate, confectionaries	87
Milk, ice cream	86
Baked goods, bread, etc.	84
Cold meats, cheese	82
Cereal	83
Gasoline	78
Newspapers	72
Personal care	84
Soft drinks	86
OVERALL	**81.6**

Durables

Automobiles	79
Consumer electronics	83
Household appliances	85
PCs/printers	78
Transportation, communications, utilities	75.
Airlines	72
Broadcasting/TV	77
Electric service	75
Express delivery	81
Phone, local	79
Phone, long distance	82
U.S. Postal Service	60
Retailing	76
Department stores	77
Discount stores	77
Restaurants/fast food	69
Supermarkets	76
Finance, Insurance	75
Commercial banks	74
Life insurance	77
Property insurance	81
Services	74
Hospitals	74

Hotels	75
Motion pictures	77
Public Administration/ government	64
Garbage pickup, city	74
Garbage pickup, suburban	74
Police, city	61
Police, suburban	65
Internal Revenue Service	55
OVERALL	**79.2**

CORPORATIONS VS. THE ENVIRONMENT

Americans up in arms over environmental pollution are goading local governments into action to take up the slack left by slow-moving federal authorities, according to sponsors of a survey on the subject.

Local jurisdictions prosecuted 882 criminal cases in the first half of 1992 alone, the survey found. This is 42 more than the federal government pursued in the eight-year period from 1983 to 1991.

The 1993 survey by the National Environmental Crime Prosecution Center (NECPC) showed that in the 100 largest jurisdictions in the country, 381 corporations faced criminal prosecutions by local authorities in 1990, 756 in 1991, and a projected total of 1,764 in 1992, for a total of 2,901 cases. Over the same period 1,544 civil cases were pursued by those jurisdictions.

The NECPC pointed out that most federal suits are civil cases, while local authorities prosecute mostly under criminal law. Civil penalties often are treated by corporations as a "cost of doing business," said NECPC, an organization established in 1992 by local prosecutors to track environmental criminal prosecutions.

In a study by the Roper organization on teens' knowledge of environmental concerns, respondents answered three of 10 multiple-choice questions correctly, on average. Only 39 percent knew that biodegradable packaging put into landfills does not decompose within 10 years. Sixty-two percent did not know that the destruction of their wetland habitats is the leading cause of the decline in geese and duck populations, and about 33 percent incorrectly thought acid rain from the Midwest decimated rain forests in South America.

The numbers on environmental suits brought by the 100 largest local jurisdictions in the U.S:

Year	Criminal Cases	Civil Cases
1990	381	286
1991	756	318
1992	1,764	940

CORPORATE LARGESS

The U.S. public is watching the interest businesspersons show in the education of American youth, according to a 1994 survey, which found that 27 percent of adults polled say business should work hard to help solve educational problems. Ten percent say companies are not doing a good job.

On other issues that need national attention and help, such as AIDS, drug abuse, and the environment, the respondents gave business much better grades in their efforts to spread around its $300 million a year largess, a Roper Starch Worldwide poll for Cone Communications found.

One aspect of the survey showed that business stood to gain by contributing to causes. Examples: Red Lobster's efforts on behalf of children with physical disabilities, called "ironkids," and American Airlines' global geography course for schoolchildren and its program on the origins and cultures of various races. Seventy-eight percent of the adults in the poll said they would be more likely to buy a product linked to a cause they care about. Sixty-six percent would switch brands, and 62 percent would switch retailers to support the cause.

DRUG ABUSE

A survey of 1,001 randomly selected adults found that among all Americans age 12 and older, 45 percent believed occasional use of marijuana could be harmful, 5 percent below the figure in 1988. Sixty-eight percent of those polled said trying cocaine once or twice carried great risk of harm, down from 71 percent in 1988, while 75 percent saw heroin as risky, which was little changed from 77 percent in 1988. And 64 percent of Americans thought smoking a pack or two of cigarettes a day could be harmful, also barely changed from the 62 percent in 1988.

Analysis of the poll by Drug Strategies, a drug abuse organization, conducted by Peter D. Hart Research Associates, showed that the group that believed drug use was harmful included young people, men, and whites. Highly educated people perceived a great deal of risk in smoking cigarettes but not much risk in using illicit drugs.

Concerning the availability of drugs in society, 59 percent of respondents said marijuana was easy to obtain, and 40 percent found cocaine readily available. The groups reporting easiest access were the 18-to-25 and 26-to-34 age groups. Americans on the whole favored treatment and prevention programs for users, but prison time for drug peddlers.

A separate poll, taken in the first half of 1993 by the Drug Abuse Warning Network for the U.S. Substance Abuse and Mental Health Services Administration, found that drug-related hospital emergency room admissions increased by nine percent compared to the first half of 1993. Heroin-related admissions, accounting for more than half the total increase, increased by 44 percent, with cocaine admissions showing little change.

Though the percentage change seems large, the pollsters point out that drug-related emergency room admissions represent only 0.5 percent of drug use nationwide.

Seventy percent of Americans in 1994 saw drug abuse as worse than it was five years earlier, and agree that government money spent on drug interdiction outside the U.S. could be better spent at the local level in the "war on drugs."

Methods of control by strategies and respondents who advocate them:

Method	Percent
Treatment, education	77%
More community action	74
Needle exchange to curb AIDs	55
Prison for suppliers	51
Prison for users	33
More U.S. interdiction	26

EDUCATORS, PUBLIC

Seventy percent of first-time teachers in American public schools after two years of experience are "very satisfied" with their interaction with students, and 60 percent are content with their interactions with other teachers. But 75 percent are less than "very satisfied" about their experiences with parents, a poll of new teachers shows.

Of the group of teachers entering a given class, the survey found that two years later, 89 percent of the teachers were still counted among the 2.4 million public school teachers in the U.S. school system. Four percent had transferred to a private school, and seven percent had quit teaching. The poll, taken over the two-year period from 1990 to 1992 questioned 1,000 teaching college graduates—78 percent women and 22 percent men—about their aspirations and concerns as educators. Nationwide, the gender breakdown of public school teachers is 72 percent female and 28 percent male.

In 1990, 93 percent of the new teachers believed all students were open to learning. By 1992, this rate had dropped 7 percent. In 1990, 83 percent of the teachers believed they could have a positive effect on their students' lives; by 1992 this rate had dropped to 71 percent.

In the first year of teaching, 28 per cent of the teachers recognized that many children have non-school problems that make it hard for them to learn. Two years later this figure had jumped overall to 50 percent, according to the survey, which was conducted by Louis Harris and Associates for MetLife and published in the July-September 1993 issue of the journal *Statistical Bulletin*.

Sixty percent of teachers in inner city schools (a group that constituted 44 percent of those surveyed) and schools with all or many minority students (33 percent) were the most pessimistic about non-school-related problems and learning. More than half of the teachers in rural schools also recognized such problems among their students, up from 30 percent in 1990. For suburban teachers, the figure was 44 percent, up from 27 percent in 1990.

The proportion of junior high and high school teachers agreeing with this outlook increased from 38 to 59 percent. Almost half of the white teachers in the survey recognized the problem, as did 47 percent of the non-white teachers, vs. 29 and 15 percent, respectively, in 1990.

After two years of classroom work, 19 percent of the teachers said it was "very" or "fairly" likely that they would leave teaching within the next five years. Forty-nine percent said it was "not at all likely," and 31 percent said "not too likely."

The major reason for leaving their career was lack of parental support for the students, mentioned by at least 50 percent of high school teachers and those with large minority or low-income student bodies. Next were low pay, disappointment with school administrators, and social problems faced by students. The four reasons together accounted for 60 percent of all the reasons given for quitting the profession.

Below is the percent who answered they are "very satisfied with" various school characteristics, according to the Metropolitan Life Survey of the American Teacher, 1992:

SCHOOL LEVEL

Contacts	Elementary	Junior/Middle	High School
Students	78%	60%	60%
Other teachers	62	58	47
Principal	53	49	38

Administrators	34	33	28
Parents	34	16	11

WITH MINORITY STUDENTS

School Body	All/Many	Some	Few/None
Students	64	74	72
Other Teachers	55	57	60
Principal	41	52	51
Administrators	30	35	33
Parents	18	27	30

WITH LOW-INCOME STUDENTS

School Body	All/Many	Some	Few/None
Students	70	66	75
Other Teachers	56	54	68
Principal	45	45	61
Administrators	32	29	40
Parents	18	25	43

Selected characteristics of second-year public school teachers and schools:

BY SEX	
Male	22%
Female	78

BY RACE	
White	93
Black	4
Other Races	3

BY SCHOOL TYPE	
Elementary school	58
Junior high	19
High school	19
Junior/high school	4

BY LOCATIONS	
Inner city	14
Urban	12
Suburban	26
Small town	27
Rural	20

BY OTHER CHARACTERISTICS	
All low-income students	5
Many	39
Some	36
A few	18
None/not sure	2
All minority students	6
Many	27
Some	25
A few	36
None/not sure	7

FAITH

Personal faith in the power of religion to influence people's thoughts and actions stands at 64 percent among Americans, but on the whole, 69 percent believe religious groups in America face an image problem. A 1952 poll showed that 95 percent of Americans felt religion was very or fairly important to them personally.

Religion's skid began in the 1960s, when the percentage of the faithful dropped to 45 percent in 1962, and to its record low of 14 percent in 1969-70—coincidental with the Vietnam War, assassinations of political leaders, and turmoil over sexual, political, and cultural changes in the country.

Not surprisingly, baby boomers age 30 to 49 who reached adulthood during those turbulent years and who are the most populous age group in America today at roughly 81 million, give religion the lowest marks, with 16 percent seeing it on the upswing, and 83 percent seeing it losing strength. Sixty-one percent of boomers think religion is still relevant, however, while only 23 percent call it out of date.

On the other hand, Generation X—those born after 1965—give religion the highest marks in the 1994 Gallup poll of 1,014 American adults. Thirty-two percent view it favorably, while 59 percent see its power declining. Non-whites are less skeptical than whites, with 30 percent against 26 percent seeing its influence increasing. Catholics and Protestants view religion almost equally: 26 percent of both denominations regarding it as strong, against 72 percent of Catholics and about 70 percent of Protestants calling religious faith weak.

The Eastern section of the country caused a blip in the statistics—33 percent of those polled registered "no opinion," while "no opinions" voiced by those in the Midwest, South, and West amounted to no more than two to three percent.

Below are Americans' views on the relevance of religion, according to the Gallup poll:

Year	Provides answers	Out of date
1994	64%	20%
1991	60	22
1990	63	18
1989	61	18
1988	57	29
1986	58	23
1985	58	24
1985	61	22
1984	56	21
1982	60	22
1981	65	15
1974	62	20
1957	82	7
1952	75	5

OVERAL RELEVANCE BY GROUP CHARACTERISTICS

	Increasing	Losing	Same
Nationally	27%	69%	2%
By Groups:			
SEX			
Male	25%	70%	2%
Female	38	69	1
AGE			
18-29 years	32%	59%	5%
30-49	16	83	1
50-64 years	25	72	2
65 and older	27	64	2
RACE			
White	26%	71%	1%
Non-white	30	62	4
EDUCATION			
College pots-graduate	31%	61%	5 %
College grad.	28	67	5
Some college	27	69	2
No college	25	71	1
INCOME			
$50,000 and over	30%	67%	2%
$30,000 to 49,999	27	70	1
$20,000 to 29,999	28	69	3
$20,000 or less	21	75	1
AFFILIATION			
Catholic	26%	72%	1%
Protestant (Mainline)	24.5	71.5	1.5
Protestant (Baptist)	25.5	70	3

"BORN AGAIN" CHRISTIANS

Year	Yes	No	No opinion
1994	45%	48%	7%
1993	46	50	4
1992	42	52	4
1991	41	54	5

RELIGIOUS PREFERENCES

Religion	1992	1993	1994
Protestant	56%	57%	62%
Rom. Catholic	26	26	23
Mormon	1	1	2
Jewish	2	1	2
Greek Orthod.	1	2	1
Muslim	0.5 or less	0.5 or less	0.5 or less
Hindu	0.5 or less	0.5 or less	0.5 or less
Other	4	5	2
Undesignated	7	6	6
None	2	2	2

FAITH HEALING

Several studies since 1985 unanimously agree that doctors believe they should do the healing and let the clergy take care of the spirit. But those studies show that up to 40 percent of hospital patients believe medicine and faith should work together, and one study found that 48 percent of patients wanted their doctors to pray for them.

A report published in *The Journal of Family Practice* in 1994 supports and enhances the conclusions of the earlier studies. Seventy-seven percent of patients in two hospitals located in the North and South said physicians should consider patients' spiritual needs, 37 percent wanted frequent discussions with their doctors on religious beliefs, and 48 percent wanted their physicians to pray with them. Eighty percent said their doctors never or rarely talked about religion with them.

The report is based on two cross-sectional surveys of adults past age 18 taken in 1992 and 1993 by Drs. Dana E. King and Bruce Bushwick and carried out at the East Carolina University School of Medicine in North Carolina and York Hospital in York, Pa.

Ninety-eight percent of the respondents at the two sites said they believed in God, 58 percent "very strongly" and 35 percent "somewhat strongly." Seventy-three percent prayed daily, and 42 percent had attended at least one faith-healing service. Blacks were more likely to do so than whites, 54 percent to 34 percent, respectively.

Sixty-three percent of the patients who attended faith-healing services desired their physicians to pray with them, compared to 37 percent who had not. Opinions varied among blacks and whites on the value of faith healing. Sixty percent of the whites agreed that reliance on faith healers would likely impair medical treatment, compared to just 28 percent of blacks.

Though 77 percent of the patient respondents said physicians should consider their spiritual needs, and 37 percent wanted more discussion of religious beliefs with their doctors, 68 percent said their physicians never discussed religion with them, and 12 percent said they rarely had. This bore out findings in two studies in 1988 and 1991 that medical students are generally taught that their views on the relationship between religion and health are inappropriate to their work.

A study published in the *Southern Medical Journal* in 1988 found prayer effective in reducing medical complications in a coronary care unit. Two other studies, published in *Journal of Family Practice* in 1989 and the American Journal of Psychiatry in 1992, concluded that patient/doctor discussions on the subject of religion improved physical healing and the patient's general well-being, and resulted in fewer rehospitalizations among elderly men.

Comparisons of religious preferences and prayers among in-patients at York Hospital, York, Pa., and East Carolina University School of Medicine, Greenville, N.C., from statistics published in "One Nation under God: Religion and Contemporary American Society," B.A. Kosmin, S.P. Lachman (Harmony Books, New York: 1993):

	East Carolina	York
RELIGIOUS PREFERENCE		
Protestant	89.2	85.5
Catholic	0.8	9.6
Other	4.2	1.2
No religion	5.8	3.6

FEEL DOCTOR SHOULD DISCUSS RELIGIOUS BELIEFS		
More	31	47
Same amount	13	15
Less	1	6
Not at all	59	32

WANT DOCTOR TO JOIN IN PRAYER		
Strongly agree	17	10
Agree	37	30
Uncertain	16	34
Disagree	23	16
Strongly disagree	8	10

WANT DOCTOR TO SEND SOMEONE TO PRAY WITH		
Strongly agree	14	4
Agree	35	30
Uncertain	12	18
Disagree	29	42
Strongly disagree	10	5

"FAMILY FUNNIES"

Which member of the family is the most fun to be with? According to the Peoplepedia Opinion Poll wives topped the list. Various in-law relations were at the bottom, tied with the family dog.

The tabulations below represent the percentage of poll respondents who gave the following answers to the question: **"Overall, meaning on most occasions, which one family member is the most fun to be with?"**

ALL RESPONDENTS

Wife	11.68%
Brother	10.29
Sister	9.75
Husband	6.83
No Answer	5.64
Father	5.18
Son	5.18
Mother	5.06
Aunt	1.56
Cousin	1.44
Daughter	1.65
Self/Me	1.56
Uncle	1.65
Grandfather	1.07
Other Relative	1.07
Grandmother	0.78
No One	0.58
Stepfather	0.49
Nephew	0.49
Children	0.49
Animal	0.29
Mother-in-Law	0.29
Niece	0.29
Sister-in-Law	0.29
Grandson	0.29

FAMILY INTELLECT

According to a recent poll, women predominantly believe that their fathers are the most intelligent members of the family. In the Peoplepedia Opinion Poll, 25 percent of females polled believe that their father is the most intelligent one in the family. Male respondents, on the other hand, voted *themselves* as the smartest in the family. According to the tally of male responses, the top three votes for the "most intelligent family" member are males: self/me, father and brother respectively.

According to females polled, their mothers' intellect was not highly esteemed—mother ranked 14th among women who voted. Only 1.33 percent thought she was the smartest in the family which translates to fathers' rank in the family intelligence question as being almost 20-times higher than mothers'.

The tabulations below represent the percentage of poll respondents who gave the following answers to the question: **"Which one family member is the most intelligent?"**

ALL RESPONDENTS

Self/Me	15.30%
Father	15.13
Brother	6.67
No Answer	6.13
Sister	5.26
Husband	3.99
Mother	3.09
Son	2.63
Uncle	2.55
Grandfather	2.26
Wife	2.22
Cousin	1.36
Daughter	1.07
Grandmother	0.87
No One	0.87
Aunt	0.78
Other Relative	0.58
Children	0.49
Sister-in-Law	0.49
Stepfather	0.49
Animal	0.29
Niece	0.29

FEMALE RESPONDENTS

Father	25.33%
Self/Me	22.67
Sister	8.00
No Answer	8.00
Grandfather	5.33
Husband	5.33
Uncle	5.33
Brother	4.00
Son	4.00
Aunt	1.33
Children	1.33
Cousin	1.33
Daughter	1.33
Mother	1.33
Sister-in-Law	1.33
Stepfather	1.33
Don't Know	1.33

MALE RESPONDENTS

Self/Me	10.99%
Father	9.15
Brother	8.24
No Answer	5.04
Mother	4.12
Sister	3.66
Wife	2.75
Cousin	1.37
Grandmother	1.37
No One	1.37
Son	1.83
Animal	0.46
Aunt	0.46
Daughter	0.92
Grandfather	0.46
Niece	0.46
Other Relative	0.92
Uncle	0.92

FATTIE FOODS

Thirty-three percent of Americans adults rarely say no to fat in their food. Fifty-seven percent are ambivalent on the subject, leaving only 14 percent who conscientiously scan the labels at the supermarket for fat content.

Survey officials suggest that recession-weary consumers in the early 1990s resisted further punishment by denying themselves the foods they love, driving them to "fat nostalgia." As a result the ambivalents do watch the fat they eat, but, reluctantly, they do eat.

Fifty-seven percent are extremely or very concerned about fat in their diets, and 88 percent agree that they "really miss the taste of fatty foods." Seventy-three percent say fat-reduced foods taste funny, and 86 percent would prefer some fat if it made the food taste better.

About 50 percent of the ambivalents eat cheese, ice cream, yogurt, and baked goods, while about 25 percent regularly consume salad dressing, mayonnaise, and cream cheese.

Among the 33 percent who may be aware of the widely publicized health risks from too many fats in their diets but consume them anyway, 66 percent agree that "since fat-free foods are less appealing, I tend to eat less of them." Seventy-two percent say such foods "have a funny taste or aftertaste."

"Fat-free fanatics," as the D'Arcy Masius Benton & Bowles survey labels those who stringently try to avoid fats, seem oblivious to taste. Fourteen percent of American adults fall into this category. Only 11 percent of them miss the taste of regular food, and another 11 percent agree that they eat less reduced-fat food because it is less appealing. The remaining 88 percent are extremely or very concerned with fat intake, and 78 percent say they have cut down on fat drastically or a great deal. About 90 percent agree that the less fat in a product the more likely they are to buy it.

The survey points out that 37 percent of Americans aged 55 and older are most likely to fall into the "fat-free fanatic" category, compared to less than 20 percent in the ambivalent and the disinterested classes.

It also adds that 68 percent of the fat avoiders have some college education, compared with 58 percent of the ambivalents and 53 percent of the disinterested. In household income, 40 percent of the fanatics earn $40,000 or more annually, compared to 38 percent of ambivalents and 28 percent of the disinterested.

Still, about 50 percent of the "fat-free fanatics" indulge themselves in regular baked goods and ice cream, though not often.

A 1994 report on the ongoing National Health and Nutrition Examination Survey III, found that the proportion of overweight U.S adults age 20 to 74 remained around 25 percent from the 1960s through the 1980s. That figure jumped to 33 percent by 1991, with an average weight increase of eight pounds. The report was printed in the July 20, 1994, issue of the *Journal of the American Medical Association*.

The survey, headed by Dr. Robert J. Kuczmarski of the Centers for Disease Control and Prevention, found that 35.3 percent of women were overweight, as were 31.4 percent of men. Thirty-two percent of white men and 34 percent of white women were overweight, compared to 48.7 percent of black women and 30.9 percent of black men, and 46.7 percent of Hispanic women and 35.5 percent of Hispanic men. The age group 50 to 69 was the plumpest for both men and women—42 percent of males and 47 percent of females in the group are categorized as overweight.

Age-specific prevalence of overweight Americans, 1988-1991, in men and women in U.S. population 20 years of age and older, from Center for Disease Control and Prevention statistics:

Age	Men	Women
20-29	20.2%	20.2%
30-39	27.4	34.3
40-49	37.0	37.6
50-59	42.1	52.0
60-69	42.2	42.5
70-79	35.9	37.2
80-plus	18.0	26.2

PREVALENCE OF OVERWEIGHT PERSONS (by race and sex in population age 20 and older)

Population Group	Sample Size	Percent
Total	8260	33.4%
Men	4209	31.4
Women	4051	35.3

RACE/ETHNICITY

Non-Hispanic white men	1896	32.3
Non-Hispanic white women	1818	32.9
Non-Hispanic black men	1045	30.9
Non-Hispanic black women	1067	48.6
Hispanic men	1136	35.5
Hispanic women	1040	46.7

RACE/SEX

White men	3060	32.1
White women	2887	34.0
Black men	1057	30.9
Black women	NA	48.7

FEAR ITSELF

One possible interpretation of the results of the Peoplepedia Opinion Poll is that trust and distrust of national figures are tied to the perception of their moral character. The poll also possibly indicates that fear, on the other hand, is linked to a concern over the amount of power such figures wield or have the potential to wield, and what they may do with that power. The poll indicated that Hillary Clinton, who has no specific executive duties, is feared by a significant portion of the American populace. The first lady ranks fourth overall in the poll as the most feared public figures.

The poll's results differ widely from women to men. Women fear conservative Republicans who wield actual power over such issues as abortion rights and workplace equality much more than they do the first lady; in contrast, Ms. Clinton ranks third overall among male respondents in terms of their fear of her.

The tabulations below represent the percentage of poll respondents who gave the following answers to the question: **"What one public figure do you find the most frightening?"**

ALL RESPONDENTS

Newt Gingrich	11.02%
Bill Clinton	7.86
Pat Buchanan	6.83
Hillary Clinton	5.81
O.J. Simpson	4.11
Louis Farrakhan	3.70
Rush Limbaugh	3.12
Phil Gramm	2.63
Jesse Helms	2.63
Dick Gephardt	1.85
Pat Robertson	1.56
Ross Perot	1.36
Howard Stern	1.36
Bob Dole	1.36
Sadaam Hussein	1.07

FEMALE RESPONDENTS

Newt Gingrich	17.33%
Pat Buchanan	10.67
Bill Clinton	8.00
O.J. Simpson	8.00

Louis Farrakhan	5.33
Rush Limbaugh	5.33
Hillary Clinton	4.00
Phil Gramm	4.00
Jesse Helms	4.00
Dick Gephardt	2.67
Pat Robertson	2.67
Ross Perot	1.33
Howard Stern	1.33
Bob Dole	1.33
Sadaam Hussein	1.33

MALE RESPONDENTS

Bill Clinton	7.78%
Newt Gingrich	7.32
Hillary Clinton	6.87
Pat Buchanan	4.58
Louis Farrakhan	2.75
O.J. Simpson	1.83
Rush Limbaugh	1.83
Phil Gramm	1.83
Jesse Helms	1.83
Dick Gephardt	1.37
Ross Perot	1.37
Howard Stern	1.37
Bob Dole	1.37
Pat Robertson	0.92
Sadaam Hussein	0.92

FEMINISM

A survey conducted by the Ms. Foundation for Women and the Center for Policy Awareness shows that women have a broad range of views on some very important issues, feminism among them.

A New Label Needed: At one time, many a woman would proudly proclaim herself a "feminist." Today, many women who support women's issues don't like the label. Some 66 percent of the women surveyed said they would be likely to join a group seeking increased professional and educational opportunities, equal pay, and equal rights for women. When the question was rephrased to include the words "feminist group" seeking the same things, only half the respondents said they would be likely to join such a group.

When the women named the most important problem they faced today, only the issue of balancing work and family reached double digits, with 14 percent. No other subject got more than 7 percent response.

What would improve family life? Below are the women's answers and the percentage who gave them.

More flexible hours	25%
Higher-paying job	19
More help at home	12
More reliable day care	5
Nothing	13

FLAT TIRES

A little more than six out of ten American women—61 percent—will get somebody else to change a flat tire for them. Only a little more than one out of 10 men—13 percent—will seek help.

In a national survey by the Gallup poll on the confidence respondents felt about doing one of the basic repair jobs on autos, women trailed men in all categories but one. That category was in getting somebody to do the work for them. Overall, 38 percent of Americans would seek help, and 61 percent would change the tire themselves.

As to the question whether they had ever changed a tire, 96 percent of men said they had, while only about half as many women had (49 percent). Among all drivers, 72 percent had changed a tire at least once during their driving experience.

Concerning confidence about how to go about the job, 92 percent of men said they were very confident, but just 38 percent of women said so. One percent of men were not confident about such a job at all, while 26 percent of women were.

Opinions concerning confidence levels changing a flat, according to a 1994 Gallup poll:

Confid. level	Men	Women	Total
Very	92%	38%	64%
Somewhat	4	24	14
Not too	2	12	7
Not at all	1	26	14
No opinion	1	-1	NA

EVER ACTUALLY CHANGED A TIRE?

Respondents	Men	Women	Total
Yes	96%	49%	72%
No	4	51	28

CHANGING A FLAT TIRE

Method	Men	Women	Total
Get help	13%	61%	NA
Change it myself	86	38	NA
No opinion	1	1	1

FRESHMEN, VIEWS OF NEW ENROLLEES

"Politically disengaged" stood out in a snapshot of new college enrollees in 1994 taken by two national surveys, which found 68.1 percent of the students putting politics second to extracurricular interests. In 1966 only 42.2 percent of the incoming students were sour on politics.

The 1994 figure is the highest rate of disinterest in politics in the 29-year history of annual surveys conducted by the Higher Education Research Institute at the University of California.

A second survey in 1994, taken by the Study of the American Electorate, reported that except for a brief increase in political interest among students in 1992—the year of the George Bush-Bill Clinton presidential race—a steady decline in interest among 18- to 24-year-olds has occurred every year since 20-year-olds were granted the vote in 1972. Voter turnout for the age group in recent elections, according to that survey, has been under 16 percent, compared with a national average of 39 percent.

The biggest single issue among freshmen respondents in the University of California survey, published in *The Chronicle of Higher Education* in January 1995, was environmental pollution, with 79.4 percent of male respondents and 87.8 percent of female respondents saying the government was not active enough in controlling pollution. Eighty percent of the students favored gun control, 70.5 percent a national health care plan, and 67.3 percent raising taxes on the rich.

Opposition to homosexuality decline. The 33.9 percent who approved outlawing homosexuality represented the lowest such proportion ever recorded on the subject. Fifty-three percent of students supported antihomosexual laws in 1987.

Concerning law and order, 22 percent said they supported the abolition of capital punishment, a record low, against the record high of 57.6 percent in 1971, the year of the prison riots in Attica, N.Y. Seventy-three percent believed the courts are too concerned with the rights of criminals.

Among the life objectives the students thought essential or very important, being very well off financially rated highest, at 73.7 percent. Raising a family was second, at 70.6 percent overall. Becoming an authority in one's chosen field was third, at 65.2 percent. Becoming accomplished in one of the performing arts was deemed non-essential or very unimportant by 90 percent of the students.

Freshmen students' political views, according to UCLA's Higher Education Research Institute:

Position	Percent
Middle of the road	52.6
Liberal	22.7
Conservative	20.9
Far left	2.3
Far right	1.5

CURRENT RELIGIOUS PREFERENCES

Religion	Percent
Baptist	16.9%
Buddhist	0.5
Eastern Orthodox	0.4
Episcopal	2.0
Islamic	0.4
Jewish	1.9
Latter-Day Saints	0.5
Lutheran	6.1
Methodist	8.6
Presbyterian	4.0
Quaker	0.2
Roman Catholic	30.1
Seventh-Day Adventist	0.3
United Church of Christ	1.7
Other Christian	9.3
Other	4.0
None	13.1

BORN-AGAIN CHRISTIAN

Yes	29.2%
No	70.8

RACIAL AND ETHNIC BACKGROUND

American Indian	2.1%
Asian-American	4.2
Black	10.0
White	81.5
Mexican-American	2.3
Puerto Rican-American	0.7
Other Latino	1.3
Other	1.9

FRIENDS IN HIGH PLACES

Who is the "best friend" of your dreams? That is, what one public figure would you most like to have for a friend? That question was posed in the Peoplepedia Opinion Poll that concerns public and private persons and our opinions regarding them.

In terms of who more Americans said they would like to befriend, it is not the President, but the Speaker of the House of Representatives. By a small margin, more respondents said, if given the choice, they'd rather have Speaker Newt Gingrich as a friend than Bill Clinton. Responses differed significantly by gender: Hillary Clinton was tops among female respondents, followed by Oprah Winfrey. The President came in a distant third, with Gingrich behind him.

The tabulations below represent the percentage of poll respondents who gave the following answers to the question: **"What one public figure would you most like to have for a friend?"**

ALL RESPONDENTS

Newt Gingrich	5.31%
Bill Clinton	4.94
Rush Limbaugh	4.16
Oprah Winfrey	4.03
Hillary Clinton	3.94
Colin Powell	2.14
Tom Hanks	1.27
Mel Gibson	1.27
None	1.07
Pamela Anderson Lee	0.87
Ronald Reagan	0.87

FEMALE RESPONDENTS

Hillary Clinton	10.67%
Oprah Winfrey	9.33
Bill Clinton	4.00
Newt Gingrich	2.67
Rush Limbaugh	2.67
Colin Powell	2.67
Tom Hanks	2.67
Mel Gibson	2.67
None	1.33

MALE RESPONDENTS	
Newt Gingrich	6.87%
Bill Clinton	5.49
Rush Limbaugh	5.04
Colin Powell	1.83
Pamela Anderson Lee	1.37
Ronald Reagan	1.37
Oprah Winfrey	0.92
None	0.92
Tom Hanks	0.46
Mel Gibson	0.46

FURS

Though fur lovers have been going out of style in the U.S. for more than five years, the industry gives little credit to animal rights groups who have been protesting the wearing of fur since 1988, according to a 1993 poll.

The survey, by the Fur Retailers Information Council, (FRIC) showed only 15 percent of non-furbuyers credited concern about animals with why they remained furless. The recession and oversupply was blamed for the halt in 1988 to a 15-year growth in fur sales, the pollsters said, a period which saw the largest fur company in the U.S., Evans, close 42 of 84 department store salons in 1992.

Other polls vary widely on American's consciousness of fur. Sixty-three percent of 85 percent of the respondents to a *Parents Magazine* poll who disapproved of wearing furs objected in the name of animal rights. But a poll by *USA Today* found 74 percent felt it was OK to wear furs if people wish. The FRIC said its study found 25 percent urging the industry to speak out in its defense.

The future of furs? Fake furs, fur trims instead of all-fur garments, and furs sheared and dyed to look more like fabric.

GENDER EQUALITY

Macho American men and feminist women are not as far apart as the media would have the nation believe, a Gallup organization poll indicates. The poll showed that Americans of both sexes agree that a woman's life is harder than it was 20 years ago. Forty-seven percent of men think so in the 1990s, up from 32 percent in 1975 and 42 percent in 1989.

Another finding indicates that men and women are reaching an agreement about whether there is equal job opportunities among the sexes—60 percent of Americans overall say women are not treated fairly in that regard, up from 48 percent in 1975 and 56 percent in 1989. Fifty percent of men say women are not treated well, compared to 69 percent of women.

College graduates, especially women, go further than women in general on the debate, with 71 percent believing women are mistreated in the job market; 76 percent of college women show high dudgeon on the

Evans Furs, where this demonstration took place, closed half its stores nationally. Why? Industry sources say it was due to a lack-luster economy in the early 1990s, as well as an oversupply of fur garments. Photo courtesy of Animal Rights Mobilization.

subject. Whites and blacks agree, at 60 percent, that women are unfairly treated.

The largest point of agreement between men and women is on the subject of equal pay for equal work. Ninety-nine percent of men approve of the practice, as do 98 percent of women, up from 87 percent of Americans in 1954 and 88 percent in 1962.

Gallup pollsters in the 1993 survey of 1,065 persons spotted another step toward unity on a subject favoring women. When asked whether they approve or disapprove of a married woman working if her husband can support her, 86 percent of the respondents overall approved. In 1938 the idea was scoffed at by 78 percent of Depression-era Americans, in more affluent 1970, by 36 percent, in 1975 by 29 percent, and in 1993 by only 13 percent.

The women's movement over the last 20 years is met with a mixed reaction from women themselves. Fifty percent say the movement has made their lives easier, but 45 percent say it has made life harder. Fifty-four percent of both genders polled say the movement has made men's lives harder, while 33 percent say it has made their lives easier. In 1989, 36 percent of men thought the movement helped them, while 43 percent said it had made life harder.

Both sexes strongly disagree, men at 36 percent and women at 38 percent, with the statement that the man should be the achiever outside the home, while the woman tends to the family and to housework.

Forty-one percent of men believe they are more supportive of efforts to improve the status of women, compared to 58 percent of women. Forty-one percent of men and 35 percent of women think they are equally supportive.

After all the polling is done, women are only moderately satisfied, at 43 percent, with men's attitudes toward helping them achieve equality, and only 48 percent are moderately satisfied with their own sex's attitudes on the question. Forty percent of men are moderately satisfied that they are politically correct on the subject.

Selected Gallup poll results:

SOCIETY FAVORS:

Opinion	Total	Men	Women
Men over women	62%	52%	71%
Equally	24	30	18
Women over men	10	13	7
No opinion	4	5	4

SHOULD MEN BE THE ACHIEVERS?

Opinion	total	Men	Women
Strongly agree	26	22	29
Moderately agree	17	18	16
Moderately	19	23	15
Strongly disagree	37	36	38
No opinion	1	1	2

The tables below represent various attitudes on women's rights, according to the Gallup poll.

ONGOING EFFORTS TO IMPROVE WOMEN'S STATUS

Opinion	Total	Men	Women
Strongly satisfied	14.5%	46.0%	14.0%
Moderately satisfied	46.0	46.0	45.5
Moderately dissatisfied	21.5	23.0	20.5
Strongly dissatisfied	14.0	11.5	24.5
No opinion	4.0	4.0	4.5

ARE JOB OPPORTUNITIES FOR WOMEN EQUAL?

Groups	Yes	No	No Opinion
National	39%	60%	1%
Male	50	50	0+
Female	30	69	1
Age 18-29	43	57	0
Age 30-39	34	65	1
Age 50-64	42	58	0
Age 65 and older	45	51	4
East	34	65	1
Midwest	40	59	1
South	44	55	1
West	38	61	1
White	39	60	1
Black	39	60	1
College, postgraduate	28	71	1
College graduate	29	70	1
Some college	34	65	1
No college	46	53	1
College men	41	58	1
College women	24	76	0+
No college men	57	43	0
No college women	35	63	2
Liberal	38	62	0
Moderate	32	66	2
Conservative	47	53	0+
Earn $50,000 or over	36	63	1
Earn $30,000 to 49,999	33	67	0+
Earn $20,000 to 29,999	45	54	1
Earn under $20,000	44	56	0

GIFT PREFERENCES

Money is the preferred gift of 66 percent of American adults age 18 and older in post-recession America, a choice that runs through nearly every age group, educational attainment, and income status.

On a scale of one to five for preferences between 16 gift categories examined, money scored a high five for 66 percent of affluent people with household incomes of 75,000 or more annually, a survey on gift-getting shows. Overall, the average among survey respondents was a scale value of 4.2 in favor of money, the highest ranking for all categories of gifts.

Second highest on the "want" list in the 1993 survey was a gift of travel, ranked at 3.8 overall on the scale by both men and women. Eighty-six percent of the affluent ranked it 4.6 on the scale, 82 percent of the men and 91 percent of the women. At the low end of the income group—those earning less than $20,000 annually—gifts of travel appealed to 78 percent of men respondents and 73 percent of women, who ranked it 3.8 and 3.3, respectively, on the scale.

Gifts of jewelry please young women the most, according to the survey, especially 18-to-24-year-olds, almost 80 percent of whom value it as a gift, though it was only ranked 3.4 on their preference list. The 35-to-44 age group was next at 78 percent and 3.7 on the preference scale, and women aged 45 to 54 were third, at 76 percent and 3.6 on the scale.

Fifty-eight percent of men aged 18 to 24 liked jewelry but gave it only 2.8 on the preference scale, but they still were the age group liking jewelry the most. Overall, jewelry ranked eighth as a favorite gift of the respondents and ended up at 2.9 on the scale devised by the survey conductors, Discovery Research Group in Salt Lake City for Present Perfect Gift Consultants. The survey results were published in the journal *American Demographics* in December 1993.

Men preferred audio/video gifts more than women (3.5 vs. 3), sports equipment (3.3 vs. 2.1), tools (3.4 vs. 1.9), magazine subscriptions (2.4 vs. 2.2), and games (2.4 vs. 2.1). Women of all educational levels preferred books as gifts more than men, except among postgraduates, where men inched one percentage point above women, 69 percent to 68 percent and 3.9 and 3.8, respectively, on the scale. More women college graduates showed preferences for books than any other group, at 69.5 percent and 3.9 on the scale. Fifty-five percent of the men and 58 percent of the women with less than a high school education also preferred books, ranking them 2.5 and 2.8, respectively, on the scale.

Magazine subscriptions, food or candy, and games ranked last among preferred gifts, at 2.3, 2.3, and 2.25, respectively.

Selected gifts ranked by preference, one being least preferred and five most preferred, according to Discovery Research Group/Present Perfect Survey:

Gift	Total	Men	Women
Money	4.20	4.24	4.17
Travel	3.80	3.81	3.79
Clothing	3.42	3.19	3.64
Audio/video	3.27	3.56	2.98
Books	3.17	3.03	3.31
Photographs	2.99	2.71	3.28
Home accessories	2.98	2.75	3.20
Jewelry	2.94	2.46	3.41
Flowers/plants	2.77	2.17	3.37
Kitchen gadgets/appliances	2.73	2.50	2.96
Sports equipment	2.69	3.30	2.08
Fragrances	2.66	2.34	2.97
Tools	2.61	3.35	1.87
Magazine subscriptions	2.29	2.42	2.15
Food or candy	2.28	2.21	2.34
Games	2.25	2.37	2.14

GROCERY SHOPPING

Not taste, not price, not convenience, but *nutrition* is the chief consideration of supermarket shoppers when buying everything from cake mixes to a can of soup. So says a survey conducted by the Grocery Manufacturers of America, a trade association representing 85 percent of the food and nonfood grocery products sold in the U.S.

According to the survey, the first and second consumer priorities were as follows:

	First	Second
Nutrition	44%	65%
Price	19	26
Taste	17	20
Product safety	91	1

Photo courtesy Greater Miami Convention and Visitors Bureau.
A great gift? Travel, to this beach in Miami or elsewhere, is the second most preferred gift, according to a survey (see table at right). The most preferred gift is money.

Ease of preparation	5	8
Environmentally responsible packaging	3	11

And the label? Some 71 percent read the nutritional information all or most of the time, and 76 percent read the list of ingredients. The changes in packaged food products considered the most important in the last few years are reduced salt, fat, and cholesterol, according to 58 percent of the shoppers. The safety of the products satisfied 72 percent of buyers, but they were split on the value of additives, preservative residues, and toxic chemicals.

HMOs (HEALTH MAINTENANCE ORGANIZATIONS)

A new study suggests that Americans who belong to health maintenance organizations are more satisfied with their care than members of traditional health insurance plans.

HMOers cite less waiting time, less paperwork, and more quickly handled claims and billing problems than plans provided by large employers. Big companies negotiate with doctors and hospitals and urge employees to seek care from preferred providers organizations (PPOs) or conventional indemnity plans.

About 85 percent of HMO members say they are satisfied with their policies, compared to 72 percent with their PPOs, according to the Sachs Group of Evanston, Ill. The study weighed responses from 5,000 households enrolled in either an HMO or a PPO.

HMOs are the most common plan, enrolling 49 percent of all insured Americans, according to the American Medical Association, compared to 20 percent in PPOs. In a 1994 survey, the association found that 76 percent of the nation's physicians have a contract with a managed-care organization—either an HMO, a PPO, or another plan.

Of the two types of HMOs, the most common—in which members pick a doctor from among a panel of physicians at their HMO—is the Independent Practice Association (IPA). The second type is called a Staff HMO, which operates clinic-style at a standing facility. Members get the first doctor available.

Seventy-one percent of IPO members would recommend their plans to a friend, compared to 79 percent of Staff members, 57 percent of indemnity plan members, and 59 percent of PPO members. But InterStudy, a Bloomington, Minn., health care information company that specializes in HMOs, cautions that first entering an HMO with its new methods can be frustrating. It agrees with survey respondents that members quickly settle down to a broad approval.

Just 48 percent of indemnity plan members say they are satisfied with the waiting time they must spend to see their doctor. Sixty-seven percent of Staff HMO members are satisfied with their waiting time, against 59 percent of IPA HMO members with their single doctor, and 53 percent of PPO members.

HMO members, who typically pay only a small co-payment at the time of the visit, do not have to send bills to their insurer. Indemnity plan members do. Staff and IPA-HMO members agree that their claims and billing problems are handled quickly, 92 and 82 percent, respectively. But only 69 percent of indemnity plan members and 68 percent of PPO members say their claims are handled efficiently.

But HMO members are not totally satisfied with their health care arrangements. Sixty percent regret that their access to outside doctors is denied. PPO members, who generally can receive reimbursement for seeing a physician outside of their plans, approve of the arrangement by 71 percent.

HOLOCAUST CONSCIOUSNESS

A Roper poll released in 1992 found that 22 percent of Americans believed the Nazi Holocaust during World War II never happened. The finding elicited nationwide headlines that caused many to question the future of democratic ideals in the country. A survey taken in 1994 by Roper for the American Jewish Committee, found that only one percent of Americans doubted accounts of the Holocaust, and only two percent of those denied the Holocaust with any vigor.

The disparity was caused by a flawed question in the first poll that rested on a double negative and resulted in a misleading conclusion, Roper admitted in releasing results of the second poll. The question was, "Does it seem possible or does it seem impossible to you that the Nazi extermination of the Jews never happened?"

In the second poll Roper revised the question. It asked, "Does it seem possible to you that the Nazi extermination of the Jews never happened, or do you feel certain that it happened?"

Ninety-one percent in the second poll were certain it happened, eight percent did not know, and less than one percent thought the Holocaust was exaggerated or unbelievable. The poll also showed an overall awareness and a seven-point increase in correct definitions of the Holocaust.

The American Jewish Committee said that though 19 in 20 Americans knew about the Holocaust, their knowledge of it was "shallow, incomplete, and imperfect."

HOMOSEXUALITY

After 15 years of gay activism for full acceptance into American life, the gay community foresees a long fight ahead over civil and legal rights. A poll taken in 1994 indicates that activists may already be stretching

Though myths about homosexuality abound, so does intolerance according to a CNN/Time Poll (see following page).

the limits of tolerance. The survey by *Time* magazine and CNN indicated that 65 percent of those queried thought the gay rights issue was getting too much attention. Fifty-three percent believed homosexuality is morally wrong, exactly the same percentage as in a 1978 poll, before the widespread movement to "come out of the closet." A three percent increase—41 percent to 38 percent—was registered since 1978 in the percentage of Americans who saw nothing wrong with homosexuality so long as it was practiced between consenting adults.

Fifty-seven percent of the respondents said gays cannot be good role models, compared to 36 percent who said they can be. Service in the military was approved by 53 percent of those polled, and giving gays the same civil rights protection afforded racial and religion minorities was acceptable to 47 percent, as against 45 percent who disapproved.

Transferring a civil rights plurality from the people to the government is a major problems for gays. In 23 states homosexuality is illegal; 42 states allow employers to fire employees for their sexual preference. Though more and more businesses acknowledge the fact of homosexuality and have issued policies banning discrimination or have hired consultants to teach employees about sexual orientation, a Philadelphia poll in 1992 of 1,400 gay men and women found that 76 percent of gay men and 81 percent of gay women conceal their homosexual orientation at work. The most common reason was the fear that their sexuality might hurt their chances for promotion.

Gay-bashing continues to trouble the country from coast to coast. The FBI reported at least 750 assault or intimidation cases in 1992, a figure strongly disputed as too low by National Gay and Lesbian Task Force surveys. In Boston, Chicago, Denver, Minneapolis-St. Paul, New York, and San Francisco alone, the task force reported 2,103 episodes in 1992.

The list below indicates the percentage of Americans answering yes to the question of whether they would consent to social interaction with homosexuals, according to the *Time*/CNN poll:

Activity	% yes
Shop at a store owned by a gay	75%
Vote for a gay politician	48
Allow child to view gay character on TV	46
Attend church or synagogue with a gay minister or rabbi	42
Enroll child in preschool with gay staff members	42
See a gay doctor	39

INTELLIGENCE

America always has had the most respect for the kind of knowledge that expresses itself in practical terms and positive contributions to social, political, and cultural life. Thus when asked which public figures are the most intelligent, more Americans name

proven movers and shakers like Newt Gingrich, Colin Powell, and Hillary Clinton than such undoubted intellectual forces as astrophysicist Stephen Hawking and linguist/leftist Noam Chomsky, both having made the lists, however far down they were.

The tabulations below represent the percentage of poll respondents who gave the following answers to the question: "What one public figure is the most intelligent?"

ALL RESPONDENTS	
Newt Gingrich	9.10%
Colin Powell	5.50
Hillary Clinton	4.81
Bill Clinton	3.91
Rush Limbaugh	3.50
Bill Gates	3.21
Stephen Hawking	2.14
Jimmy Carter	1.77
Bob Dole	1.48
Al Gore	1.48
Noam Chomsky	1.07
William Bennett	0.87
William Buckley	0.87
Ralph Nader	0.58
None	0.58
FEMALE RESPONDENTS	
Colin Powell	13.33%
Hillary Clinton	10.67
Newt Gingrich	6.67
Bill Clinton	6.67
Rush Limbaugh	4.00
Bill Gates	4.00
Jimmy Carter	4.00
Bob Dole	4.00
Al Gore	4.00
Stephen Hawking	2.67
Noam Chomsky	1.33
MALE RESPONDENTS	
Newt Gingrich	10.53%
Rush Limbaugh	3.20
Bill Gates	2.75
Bill Clinton	2.29
Stephen Hawking	1.83
Hillary Clinton	1.37
William Bennett	1.37
William Buckley	1.37
DNK	1.37
Colin Powell	0.92
Noam Chomsky	0.92
Ralph Nader	0.92
Jimmy Carter	0.46

LIKABILITY

The more closely related a family member is to you, the more he or she is perceived as being the one who is liked the most by your friends, or so says the Peoplepedia Opinion Poll. The one modifier is that an older family member, such as a parent, outranked younger relations, such as a sibling, who is obviously more closely related to you than your parent. Overall, a mother or father is most likely to be perceived as the one your friends like the best among your family members.

The likability quotient, however, doesn't always follow bloodlines. A wife or a husband is perceived as being the most liked, almost as much as a parent. Next to parents and spouses, siblings outranked other family members. Sister, however, however outranked husband. The bottom line on the sister is that she is quite well-liked, or at least is perceived as being so by family members, according to the poll. Overall, sisters outranked brothers as being the most likable.

Among male respondents, sisters ranked fifth as the family member their friends like best. Brothers, on the other hand—though ranked high over all (5th for all respondents)—are not perceived as being especially well liked by friends of female family members. Brother was in 11th place according to how females perceive his likability quotient. Among males, however, an opposite sex sibling is perceived as being well-liked. According to the male's perception, sister ranked fifth, more than twice as high as how females perceive of their brother.

More distantly related family members, such as aunts, uncles, grandparents and cousins, uniformly ranked low on the list.

The tabulations below represent the percentage of poll respondents who gave the following answers to the question: "Which one family member do your friends like best?"

ALL RESPONDENTS

Mother	11.16%
Father	8.68
Wife	8.68
Sister	7.90
Husband	6.62
No Answer	6.13
Brother	5.89
Self/Me	3.41
Son	2.63
No One	2.34
Daughter	2.06
Grandfather	1.56
Animal (Dog)	1.27
Cousin	1.15
Brother-in-Law	1.07
Equal	0.58
Children	0.49
Grandmother	0.49
Nephew	0.49
Sister-in-Law	0.49
Stepfather	0.49
Aunt	0.29

FEMALE RESPONDENTS

Father	13.33%
Sister	12.00
Mother	10.67
Husband	9.33
No Answer	8.00
Self/Me	5.33
Daughter	4.00
No One	4.00
Son	4.00
Animal (Dog)	2.67
Brother	2.67
Grandfather	2.67
Brother-in-Law	1.33
Children	1.33
Grandmother	1.33
Nephew	1.33
Sister-in-Law	1.33
Stepfather	1.33

MALE RESPONDENTS

Mother	11.44%
Brother	7.78
Father	5.95
Wife	5.95
Sister	5.49
No Answer	5.04
Self/Me	2.29
Cousin	1.83
Son	1.83
No One	1.37
Brother-in-Law	0.92
Daughter	0.92
Equal	0.92
Grandfather	0.92
Animal (Dog)	0.46
Aunt	0.46

MARIJUANA

Of 51,797 respondents to a 1994 poll on whether marijuana should be made legal, three-fourths answered in the affirmative. Eighty nine percent said it definitely should be made legal for medicinal purposes, although habitual smoking of pot can be as harmful to the lungs and other parts of the body as cigarette smoking, according to medical experts.

Thirty five percent of those polled by *Parade* magazine said they use marijuana often. Only 20 percent had never used it. People of all ages took part in the poll, and female respondents outnumbered males by seven percent.

The Largest response was from persons age 36 to 50, accounting for 41 percent of respondents. The group least represented was those under age 18, accounting for less than 5 percent of respondents.

Facts on marijuana use, according to the *Parade* poll:

How often used

Never	19.9%
Once	8.0
Occasionally	31.6
Frequently	35.4

Age of respondents	
75-plus	0.8%
51-74	17.2
36-50	40.9
26-35	21.2
18-25	9.0
Under 18	4.4

MARITAL DISCORD

It's a toss-up as to who wins the battle over money between husbands and wives, but one thing a 1994 poll makes clear: finances are the most common source of quarrels between married couples. Twenty-nine percent of both husbands and wives cited money as a marital problem. What to watch on television runs a close second, at 28 percent.

Both men and women agree on who usually prevails in the money arguments. Overall, thirty-three percent of husbands say they settle matters, and 33 percent say they do not. Wives see things almost accordingly, with 30 percent saying they get their point across, and 32 percent saying they do not. Also, 34 percent of wives claim money disputes are never resolved, as do 28 percent of husbands.

Older husbands feel they win arguments, but only 16 percent of wives 60 and older say they do. With the younger set the roles are reversed. Forty-three percent of husbands aged 18 to 29 perceive their wives as dominant in money matters, while only 36 percent of wives the same age say they usually win.

Though the dispute about how to spend money is the most prevailing difference among married couples, separate bank accounts are no answer to the problem—at least, that's what 20 percent of those polled by Roper Starch Worldwide for *Worth* magazine said. On the other hand, a joint bank account serves very well for 71 percent of married partners overall.

The percentage of husbands and wives who say they usually win money arguments in the household, according to Roper Starch Worldwide statistics:

Age	Husbands	Wives
18-29	36	43
30-44	39	38
45-59	38	32
60 and older	38	16

MATERIALISM

Love of money does not conflict with the love of God in the estimation of a majority of Americans in a survey of working men and women, both believers and unbelievers, on the subject of materialism. In fact, 68 percent of the respondents agreed that "money is one thing, morals and values are another."

While 89 percent of those surveyed agreed that Americans are too materialistic, and 71 percent said society would be better off if it placed less emphasis on money, and 74 percent said materialism is a serious national problem, 84 percent wished they had more money. Sixty-eight percent would be willing to work longer hours for more money, as would nearly 50 percent in a less interesting and more stressful job. And 46 percent would play a lottery to make more money.

As to whether it is wrong to want a lot of money, 88 percent of 2,000 persons in the U.S. labor force said they had never been taught the desire was wrong; among regular church-goers, 84 percent said the same thing. The survey, conducted in 1992 by Princeton University and analyzed by editor Robert Wuthlow in the March 3, 1993, issue of *Christian Century*, found that 75 percent of the participants rejected the view that it is morally wrong to have when others are wanting, and 80 percent rejected the idea that the poor are closer to God than the rich.

Seventy-five percent of the respondents believed "God wants me to have the kind of job that makes me happy," and more than 50 percent believe "people who work hard are more pleasing to God than people who are lazy."

Seventy-eight percent said having a beautiful home and a new car were very important or fairly important to them. Seventy-one percent thought money brought freedom, and 76 percent agreed that "having money gives me a good feeling about myself." Eleven percent thought wealthy people are generally happier than other people.

As to giving more to the church if the church asked them to, 30 percent said they would give less; seven percent said they would give more. If the church were less materialistic, however, 31 percent said they would give more, nine percent said they would give less, while 60 percent said it made no difference. Forty-three percent thought "churches are too eager to get your money," and 36 percent said that eagerness annoys them. Seventy-five percent said they would like churches and synagogues to be less materialistic.

Though 51 percent of the respondents agreed that the Bible contained much valuable discussion about money, 71 percent said they had given little thought to the Bible's views on the subject in the past year, and 69 percent had given little thought to the broader and related issue of religious values and personal finance. Seventy-eight percent said they thought a lot about their values and priorities in life.

In a matter such as buying a car, however, 81 percent said they would think a lot about the dealer they buy from, 76 percent would consider the car's mileage, and 57 percent would not consider whether a car fit into their basic values. Only 20 percent would question whether owning an auto is consistent with protecting the planet.

Ninety-seven percent of those surveyed said they seldom discuss their personal finances with fellow church members, and 89 percent said they never or hardly ever discuss their family budget with persons outside the family.

Major annual nondurable consumer spending in 1993, with a national average income of $36,307 for whites and others and $23,355 for blacks, according to the Department of Labor's Consumer Price Survey:

Item	Whites	Blacks
Food at home	$4,517	$3,399
Food away from home	1,746	978
Alcoholic beverages	288	98
Household furnishings/ equipment	1,299	667
Apparel and services	1,681	1,638
Entertainment	1,734	772
Personal care products /services	393	310
Tobacco products	277	198
Cash contributions	1,029	436
Miscellaneous	751	434

MINORITY MEDIA COVERAGE

America's three major ethnic minorities are taking a close look at how the nation's media view them, and of the three—blacks, Hispanics, and Asian-Americans—blacks are the most upset by what they see; Asian-Americans the least.

Taking off from a *New York Times* study in August 1994 that concluded that "the mainstream news media's coverage of people of color is riddled with old stereotypes, offensive terminology, biased reporting, and myopic interpretation of American society," a Gallup Poll set out to survey samples of three minorities to see whether the respondents agree.

The national sample of 304 blacks, 302 Hispanics, and 310 Asians indicates that the paper's conclusion was harsher than the Gallup poll. The pollsters are 95 percent confident that any sampling error in the results could be only plus or minus six percentage points.

With 81 percent of blacks receiving their news from television, 83 percent say they are somewhat or very satisfied with both local and national coverage, compared with 80 percent of Hispanics and 81.5 percent of Asians. As to issues specifically related to the respondents' ethnic group, 55.5 percent of blacks are somewhat or very satisfied with overall television news, as are 73.5 percent of Hispanics and 69.5 percent of Asians.

Local daily newspapers gained less than half (48 percent) of the very satisfied or somewhat satisfied votes of blacks on issues specifically relating to them, compared to 72 percent of Hispanics and 61 percent of Asians. On a broader news level, 73 percent of blacks, 76 percent of Hispanics, and 80 percent of Asians were very satisfied or satisfied with what they read in their local papers.

However, only 16 percent of blacks are "very satisfied" with what the media serve up overall, compared to 19.3 percent of Hispanics, and 21.3 percent of Asians. Local papers' treatment of black issues please only 13 percent of blacks, compared to 21 percent of Hispanics and 10 percent of Asians, respectively. Local and national TV pleases only 17 percent of blacks on black issues, while 24 percent of Hispanics and 15 percent of Asians approve of the media coverage of their respective ethnic groups.

About 51 percent of blacks believe the media are unfair in its presentation of crime stories about African Americans, compared to 32 percent of Hispanics and 13 percent of Asians. Among blacks, 54 percent rank TV higher than local papers in unfairness in this regard. Hispanics and Asians agree, though more moderately. Thirty-two percent of Hispanics see unfairness in TV and 30 percent see it in papers; and 12.5 percent of Asians see unfairness on the tube, compared to 10 percent who see it in print.

Blacks are particularly concerned over the media's ability to affect race relations. Seventy-four percent say the media worsens or has no effect on race relations. Fifty-four percent of Hispanics agree as do 49 percent of Asians.

Preferred appellation of two racial groups, according to Gallup Poll results:

Group	% preferred
African-American	30%
Black	41
Doesn't matter	25
Other	3
No opinion	1
Hispanic	62
Latino	10
Doesn't matter	24
Other	4
No opinion	0 to .05

Exposure to news in days per week among the three groups, according to Gallup Poll results:

Group Days	Blacks	Hispanics	Asians
NATIONAL NETWORK TELEVISION			
Six, seven	55%	40%	45%
Four, five	23	21	25
One to three	18	36	26
Zero	4	3	3
No opinion	0	0	1
LOCAL TELEVISION NEWS			
Six, seven	56%	41%	42%
Four, five	25	28	25
One to three	17	24	24
Zero	2	7	7
No opinion	0	0 to .05	2
LOCAL DAILY NEWSPAPER			
Six, seven	34%	37%	33%
Four, five	17	16	13
One to three	37	31	34
Zero	12	16	20
No opinion	0	0 to .05	0 to .05
Does Ethnic Reporter Covering Ethnic Story Improve Story?			
Great deal	36%	34%	32%
Moderately	38	34	31

Not much	13	14	21
Not at all	11	14	13
No opinion	2	4	3

MORALITY

Sexual indiscretions lead the list of what shames Americans the most, even though more people admit to sins such as lying and stealing. The biggest change has been not just what we do, but what we find acceptable, even when they may be things we clearly recognize as unsavory.

The list below represents what Americans are most ashamed of (by percentage), according to Patterson and Kim's findings as reported in *The Day America Told the Truth.*

Adultery/affairs	18%
Fornication/premarital sex	14
Lying	11
Stealing	10
Cheating/taking advantage of others	6
Drunkenness	5
Abortion	3
Shoplifting	3
Wicked thoughts	3
Verbal cruelty	2
Masturbation	2
Stealing from work	2
Kinky sex	2
Pornography	2

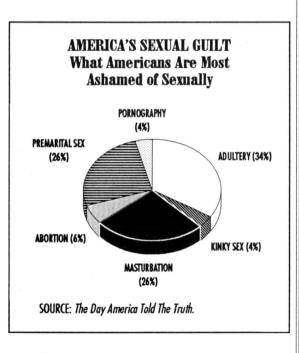

AMERICA'S SEXUAL GUILT
What Americans Are Most
Ashamed of Sexually

PORNOGRAPHY (4%)
PREMARITAL SEX (26%)
ADULTERY (34%)
ABORTION (6%)
KINKY SEX (4%)
MASTURBATION (26%)

SOURCE: *The Day America Told The Truth.*

MUSICAL TASTES

Fifty one percent of Americans like country-western music, and 21 percent like it best from among 20 cool sounds to choose from. Mood/easy-listening music is liked by 49 percent of Americans and liked best by nine percent. Rock is third at 44 percent, liked best by 14 percent of music fans.

Blues/R&B and hymns/gospel, at 40 percent, round out the top five favorite styles of music, all five of which drew the votes of 40 to 50 percent—representing between 72 and 96 million Americans— polled in a National Endowment of the Arts survey in 1992.

At the bottom of the popularity poll were opera and rap. Opera was liked by only 13 percent of the votes. Opera's highest proportion of likeability, 26 percent, came from persons with a graduate school education, the next, 21 percent, from persons aged 65 to 74. Seventeen percent of opera fans had an annual family income of $50,000. Rap drew a 12 percent likeability rating, but the survey did not include the genre in its breakdown.

Men and women were equally divided, at 52 percent, in their liking of bluegrass. The genre was liked by 57 of whites, but just 19 percent of blacks; 61 percent of persons aged 45 to 54; 59 percent of those with some high school; and 57 percent from fans with an annual salary of $15,000 to $24,999.

Seven in 10 younger adults aged 18 to 24 liked rock, and more than a third liked country, easy listening, and blues/R&B. Only 10 percent of the group expressed an affinity for folk music, and only 5 percent for opera.

Men liked rock more than women—48 percent to 39 percent—as did the better educated and more affluent. Between 53 percent and 55 percent of collegians and persons earning $50,000 or more annually said they rock.

Black listening tastes ran to blues/R&B (59 percent), jazz (54 percent), and easy listening (39 percent). African Americans showed the least affinity for opera (8 percent), folk and show tunes (15 percent), classical (18 percent), and bluegrass (19 percent).

Percent of adults who liked each of 20 types of music, according to a 1992 NEA poll:

Music	Percent
Country/western	51.7%
Mood/easy listening	48.8
Rock	43.5
Blues/R&B	40.4
Hymns/gospel	39.8
Big band	35.0
Jazz	34.2
Classical	33.6
Bluegrass	30.0
Show Tunes/operettas /musicals	27.8
Soul	25.0
Contemporary folk	23.1

Blues, as performed here at Chicago's Blues Festival, is enjoying the largest surge in popularity of all types of music, according to an NEA poll (see table below).

Ethnic	21.5
Latin/salsa	20.0
Reggae	20.0
Parade/marching band	18.0
New age	16.0
Choral/glee club	15.5
Opera	13.0
Rap	12.0

Percent, number in millions, and percent change, 1982 to 1992, in numbers liking selected forms of music:

Style	Percent	Number liking	Change
Country Western	52%	96.3	1%
Rock	44	81.1	41
Blues/R&B/ Soul	40	75.2	76
Jazz	34	63.7	49
Classical	34	62.5	36
Bluegrass	30	55.4	35
Show Tunes	28	51.8	37
Opera	13	23.5	43

NARCISSISM IN THE FAMILY

Vanity, we have long been told, is one of seven deadly sins. A more current theory espoused by psychologists is that a strong self-image is essential for good mental health. However, Americans may have taken self-image to heart too much. According to the findings of the Peoplepedia Opinion Poll, it may be so.

When asked who the most attractive member of the family is, the largest number of respondents among both sexes, 11 percent, maintained *they* were. Among female respondents, twice as many, 20 percent, answered that they were the best looking member of the family.

The tabulations below represent the percentage of poll respondents who gave the following answers to the question: **"Which one family member is the best looking?"**

ALL RESPONDENTS

Self/Me	11.14%
Brother	10.00
Wife	8.93
Sister	8.85
Daughter	7.32
No Answer	5.35
Cousin	4.89
Husband	3.82
Mother	3.50
No One	2.14
Father	1.94
Son	1.44
Brother-in-Law	1.07
Niece	0.58
Uncle	0.49
Children	0.49
Nephew	0.49
Equal	0.29
Grandmother	0.29
Other Relative	0.29
Sister-in-Law	0.29

FEMALE RESPONDENTS

Self/Me	20.00%
Daughter	12.00
Brother	10.67
Sister	10.67
Cousin	9.33
Husband	8.00
No Answer	6.67
Mother	4.00
No One	2.67
Brother-in-Law	1.33
Children	1.33
Father	1.33
Nephew	1.33
Uncle	1.33

MALE RESPONDENTS

Brother	9.61%
Wife	8.70
Sister	7.78
Self/Me	5.95
Daughter	4.58
No Answer	4.58
Mother	3.20
Cousin	2.29
Father	2.29
Son	2.29
No One	1.83
Brother-in-Law	0.92
Niece	0.92

Equal	0.46
Grandmother	0.46
Other Relative	0.46
Sister-in-Law	0.46

Pat Buchanan	0.46
O.J. Simpson	0.46

"PUBLIC DISTRUST"

When asked whom they distrust the most among public figures, Americans are divided fairly clearly by gender, according to the Peoplepedia Opinion Poll. According to the poll's overall rankings, President Clinton got the most votes for the "least trusted public figure"—more than 27 percent of respondents named him as the most distrusted. Women clearly find Clinton's Republican counterpart, Speaker of the House Newt Gingrich, less trustworthy than the President. Ironically, O.J. Simpson is less distrusted than many prominent politicians.

The tabulations below represent the percentage of poll respondents who gave the following answers to the question: "What one public figure do you trust the least overall?"

ALL RESPONDENTS

Bill Clinton	27.17%
Newt Gingrich	20.31
Bob Dole	4.11
Rush Limbaugh	2.14
Ted Kennedy	1.85
O.J. Simpson	1.77
Phil Gramm	1.56
Hillary Clinton	1.07
Dick Gephardt	1.07
Pat Buchanan	0.78
David Bonior	0.58
Kato Kaelin	0.58

FEMALE RESPONDENTS

Newt Gingrich	34.67%
Bill Clinton	26.67
Bob Dole	8.00
O.J. Simpson	4.00
Rush Limbaugh	2.67
Ted Kennedy	2.67
Phil Gramm	2.67
Hillary Clinton	1.33
Dick Gephardt	1.33
Pat Buchanan	1.33

MALE RESPONDENTS

Bill Clinton	27.46%
Newt Gingrich	11.90
Bob Dole	1.83
Rush Limbaugh	1.83
Ted Kennedy	1.37
Phil Gramm	0.92
Hillary Clinton	0.92
David Bonior	0.92
Dick Gephardt	0.92
Kato Kaelin	0.92

PUBLIC SCHOOL VIOLENCE

Pupils, teachers, and the police tell of their fears in a wide-ranging survey on violence in the nation's public schools, which finds that violence increases as the level of learning decreases as the proportion of minority and poor pupils increases, and is greater in city than in rural and suburban schools.

While 11 percent of teachers report having been a victim of violence in 1993 and 19 percent say violence has increased in the past year, 85 percent say their commitment to teaching keeps them in the profession. Twenty-nine percent of pupils report having been a victim of violence in the past year.

Teachers (72 percent) and the police (91 percent) blame the home situations of offenders and the lack of school involvement by parents for school violence. Violence in the media and gang or peer-group pressure is second, blamed by 35 percent of both pupils and teachers. Police see gang membership most starkly, 60 percent calling it one of the chief causes of school violence.

Pupils and the police are more likely to fear guns and knives brought to school than teachers, 50 percent of whom are unaware of weapons in their classes, against 21 percent of the pupils and 8 percent of the police. Nine percent of the pupils and 7 percent of the police think the percentage of pupils carrying a weapon into school exceeds 25 percent of the enrollment.

All three classes of respondents to the Louis Harris and Associates poll for Metropolitan Life Insurance Company agreed on the four major reasons weapons are brought into schools: to impress friends, for protection to and from school, for protection in school, and for self-esteem.

The police see protection to and from school and protection in school as the driving reasons. Pupils think impressing friends and feeling self-important are the reasons. Teachers pinpointed impressing friends and for protection going to and from school.

Overall, 59 percent of city police and 36 percent of suburban/rural police reported an increase in school violence in a select year, compared to 12 percent and 3 percent, respectively, who saw a decrease. Sixteen percent of city pupils and 14 percent of suburban/rural pupils saw an increase of violence, compared to 14 percent for both city and suburban/rural pupils who do not. And 22 percent of urban teachers see an increase, compared to 12 percent who do not.

The table on the following page represents perceived change by teachers, students, and police in the level of violence in U.S. schools by selected characteristics in 1993, according to the Metropolitan Life Survey of the American Teacher. In the left column (percent increase) is the percentage who perceived an increase; in the right column (percent decrease) is the percent who perceived a decrease. The remaining percentage of the whole perceived no change.

TEACHERS

Characteristic	Percent Increase	Percent Decrease
Urban	22	12
Suburban/rural	18	10
Elementary	14	8
Secondary school	21	12
In Quality of Education		
Excellent	12	11
Fair/poor	43	5
In Lower Income Enrollees		
All/many	24	12
Few/none	12	8

PUPILS

	Percent Increase	Percent Decrease
Urban pupils	16	14
Suburban/rural	14	12
Elementary school	11	16
Secondary school	18	11

POLICE

	Percent Increase	Percent Decrease
Urban	59	3
Suburban/rural	36	11

Teachers' and students' feelings of safety in school:

TEACHERS' VIEWS:

School Quality	Very Safe	Somewhat Safe	Not Very Safe
Excellent	88	11	1
Good	69	29	1
Fair or poor	44	53	2
on minorities			
All or many	61	36	3
Some	76	22	1
Few or none	90	10	0
on lower income pupils			
All or many	68	30	2
Some	80	18	1
Few or none	89	11	0
on school location/type			
Urban	64	35	2
Suburban/ rural	82	17	1
Elementary	80	18	1
Secondary	75	24	1

STUDENTS' VIEWS:

Location	Very Safe	Somewhat Safe	Not Very Safe
Urban	45	44	6
Suburban/ rural	53	37	3
Elementary	59	26	5
Secondary	44	50	1
on student grades			
Good/fair	52	40	4
Poor	34	48	11

PUBLIC TRUST

In the 1960s, the lies and misrepresentations concerning the Vietnam War drove a wedge between America's leaders and the man in the street. Generals and politicians were lumped together as equally worthy of mistrust. Although politicians are viewed in a skeptical light, the success of the Persian Gulf War, and the military's perceived openness concerning its operations, rehabilitated the image of the American military commander in the eyes of the civilian population. Hence, a quarter-century after the social upheaval of the Vietnam era, a retired general Colin Powell rates as the most trusted man in America, according to the Peoplepedia Opinion Poll that concerns public and private persons and our opinions regarding them. The poll also indicated that among both men and women President Clinton tops the list of the least trustworthy national figures.

The tabulations below represent the percentage of poll respondents who gave the following answers to the question: **"What one public figure do you trust the most overall?"**

ALL RESPONDENTS

Colin Powell	8.68%
Newt Gingrich	4.94
Rush Limbaugh	4.74
Oprah Winfrey	4.72
No One	3.99
Billy Graham	3.53
Bill Clinton	3.41
Bob Dole	2.63
Al Gore	2.06
Ralph Nader	1.85
Jimmy Carter	1.85
Hillary Clinton	1.77
Pat Buchanan	1.36
Janet Reno	1.07
The Pope	0.87
Dick Armey	0.87
Phil Gramm	0.87
Sandra Bullock	0.78
David Letterman	0.58
Lamar Alexander	0.58
Dan Quayle	0.58
Harry Browne	0.58

FEMALE RESPONDENTS

Colin Powell	13.33%
Oprah Winfrey	12.00
Billy Graham	8.00
No One	5.33
Bill Clinton	5.33
Newt Gingrich	4.00
Bob Dole	4.00
Hillary Clinton	4.00
Al Gore	4.00
Rush Limbaugh	2.67
Ralph Nader	2.67

Jimmy Carter	2.67
Pat Buchanan	1.33
Janet Reno	1.33
Sandra Bullock	1.33

MALE RESPONDENTS

Colin Powell	5.95%
Rush Limbaugh	5.95
Newt Gingrich	5.49
No One	3.20
Bill Clinton	2.29
Bob Dole	1.83
Ralph Nader	1.37
Jimmy Carter	1.37
Pat Buchanan	1.37
The Pope	1.37
Dick Armey	1.37
Phil Gramm	1.37
Billy Graham	0.92
Al Gore	0.92
Janet Reno	0.92
David Letterman	0.92
Lamar Alexander	0.92
Dan Quayle	0.92
Harry Browne	0.92
Oprah Winfrey	0.46
Hillary Clinton	0.46
Sandra Bullock	0.46

RACIAL EQUALITY

The percentage of whites who want blacks to be treated more fairly by society has undergone a dramatic change as the 1990s progress. In recent years surveys found that a majority of whites believed that way. But a 1994 poll showed that only 36 percent still do, a drop from 52 percent in 1992. Blacks and whites showed widely divergent views on the racial question in a telephone poll taken by the Associated Press of 1,113 adults in every state but Hawaii and Alaska.

Overall, 56 percent of those polled no longer see inequality between blacks and whites. Six out of 10 whites agree with that view; seven in 10 blacks disagree. One in five blacks think their situation has deteriorated in the last five years; one in 12 whites agree.

Concerning black gains, one in three Americans believe they have gained little since the civil rights movement of the 1960s, while half as many blacks, compared with a 1969 poll taken five years after "Freedom Summer," agree that little has been gained.

People under the age of 45 were more inclined toward skepticism about black gains, 45 percent saying the nation has done too little to help blacks, against 25 percent of the over-45s. But the poll also found that older white Americans are more likely to agree that on the whole they want to see blacks get a better break.

The most overwhelming response in the poll came on the question of hiring preferences for blacks and other minorities to redress past grievances. On this issue, 86 percent of those polled expressed negative sentiments, and 12 percent approved. Blacks were almost evenly divided on the question, with 46 percent supporting hiring preferences and 50 percent disapproving.

Poll results on the question of whether blacks and other minorities have the same opportunities as whites in the U.S.:

Group	Yes	No
Total	56%	41%
Whites	60	37
Hispanics	50	50
Blacks	27	71
Republicans	68	30
Democrats	45	53
Men	60	37
Women	52	45
Under $40,000	60	36
Over $40,000	51	47
Southern white	66	29
Southern black	31	67
College grads	44	53
No college	63	34

ROLE MODELS, FAMILIAL

Though he may be viewed in a little different light than in the past, the American father still serves as the top role model in the family unit, so says the Peoplepedia Opinion Poll.

More than 20 percent of the poll's respondents named their father as the family member who serves as their role model—though, interestingly, a larger percentage of women than of men view their fathers ias role models. The responses below amply indicate the existence of a male role model, even though he may not necessarily be living with his family.

The tabulations below represent the percentage of poll respondents who gave the following answers to the question: **"Which one family member is best identified as your role model?"**

ALL RESPONDENTS

Father	20.82%
Mother	13.53
No One	7.66
Grandmother	4.31
Sister	3.74
Grandfather	3.50
Brother	2.51
Husband	2.26
Aunt	1.65
Wife	1.65
Self/Me	1.48
Uncle	1.15
Other Relative	0.78
Father-in-Law	0.49
Animal	0.29

Daughter	0.29
Mother-in-Law	0.29
Niece	0.29
Parents	0.29
FEMALE RESPONDENTS	
Father	26.67%
Mother	18.67
Grandmother	9.33
Sister	9.33
No Answer	9.33
No One	6.67
Husband	5.33
Grandfather	4.00
Self/Me	4.00
Aunt	1.33
Brother	1.33
Father-in-Law	1.33
Other Relative	1.33
MALE RESPONDENTS	
Father	17.39%
Mother	10.53
No One	8.24
No Answer	5.49
Brother	3.20
Grandfather	3.20
Aunt	1.83
Uncle	1.83
Wife	1.83
Grandmother	1.37
Animal	0.46
Daughter	0.46
Husband	0.46
Mother-in-Law	0.46
Niece	0.46
Other Relative	0.46
Sister	0.46
Parents	0.46

ROMANCE

In spite of the well-publicized conflicts between the sexes, as the century winds down romance and courtship are blooming as strongly as when the century began, a recent survey on modern love indicates.

In a poll of 1,000 Americans, 78 percent said they are romantically involved. The survey tried to measure expressions of that involvement. Its number one finding: 94 percent of both men and women seniors and young adults in love believe flowers continue to be the universal sign of romance.

One twist to the time-honored tradition: Women increasingly are not only receiving flowers as a token of affection, they are also giving flowers. Fifty-four percent of men in the poll said they had received flowers from their sweethearts. The practice of women sending flowers received a 68 percent approval rating overall.

Another twist: Bringing or sending flowers was third on the list (46 percent) of what makes the biggest

impression when first dating, with being on time for the date and compliments on the date's appearance tying for first, at 52 percent. As the best "I love you" gift, 52 percent of the men chose flowers, compared to 42 percent of the women.

More than 75 percent of both men and women still believe it is the man's role to ask a woman out on the first date, pay the bills (82 percent), open the car door for her (83 percent), and, ultimately, pop the question (82 percent).

Seventy-eight percent of the women in the poll believed romance was more important to them than it is to men; 73 percent of men agreed. Only 10 percent of the women thought it was more important to men. Sixty-six percent of the women in the poll taken by Bruskin/Goldring Research for the American Floral Marketing Council thought they were better at romance than men, and 52 percent of the men agreed. Only 15 percent of women tipped their hats to men in this regard. The researchers said their sampling error is plus or minus three percent.

Twenty percent overall of those polled, 7 percent of the women and 34 percent of the men, said they had never received flowers from their lover, and 10 percent overall—12 percent of the women and 8 percent of the men—did not remember whether they ever had.

Survey results, from Bruskin/Goldring Research:

Is Romance More Important to Women or to Men?

Response	Total	Men	Women
Women	76%	73%	78%
Men	11	13	10
Equally	9	10	8
Don't know	4	4	4

Who Is Better at Romance?

Response	Total	Men	Women
Women	59%	52%	66%
Men	23	32	15
Equal	9	9	8
Don't know	9	7	11

When First Dating, Which Impresses Most?

Response	Total	Men	Women
Being on time	52%	47%	56%
Compliments on looks	52	51	53
Flowers	46	52	41
Making advance plans	39	37	40
Open door	39	38	39
Don't know	2	2	2

Which Adds Romance to Your Life?

Response	Total	Men	Women
Unexpected flowers	55%	38%	70%
Special outfit or perfume	33	45	23
Watch romantic movie	31	33	30
Write poem or love song	24	25	22
Feed grapes	13	16	11
Don't know	6	7	5

Which Is the Man's Responsibility?

Opening door	83%	87%	79%
Proposing	82	82	82
Paying on first date	82	89	75
Asking out on first date	77	78	76
Asking out on second date	74	75	73
Standing when date leaves table	59	65	59

Which Is Best "I Love You" Gift?

Flowers	47%	52%	42%
Jewelry	36	33	39
Fragrance	7	8	6
Tickets to an event	6	4	7
Candy	3	2	3
Don't know	2	1	3

Flowers Still the Best sign of Romance?

Agree	95%	95%	95%
Disagree	4	4	4
Don't know	1	1	1

Should Women Give Flowers?

Appropriate	68%	64%	70%
Inappropriate	31	35	28
Don't know	2	1	2

When Loved One Last Sent Flowers?

Three months ago	32%	23%	42%
Three months to a year	14	11	16
One year and three years	24	20	29
Never	20	34	7
Don't remember	10	12	8

ROMANCE ON HIGH

Romantic involvement with public figures is of surprisingly little interest to most people, according to the Peoplepedia Opinion Poll.

Surprisingly, "no one"—that is, no public figure at all—was the most common response to the question regarding what public figure they would be interesting in romancing. Among those named by female respondents, President Clinton tied for first with Brad Pitt and Mel Gibson, followed by many expected sex symbols including Pierce Brosnan, Kiefer Sutherland, Tom Cruise and Matt Leblanc.

The tabulations below represent the percentage of poll respondents who gave the following answers to the question: **"What one public figure would you most like to be involved with romantically?"**

FEMALE RESPONDENTS

None/No One	6.67%
Bill Clinton	4.00
Brad Pitt	4.00
Mel Gibson	4.00
Pierce Brosnan	4.00
Kiefer Sutherland	2.67
Matt Leblanc	2.67
Tom Cruise	2.67
Grant Hill	2.67
John Kennedy Jr.	2.67
Kenneth Branagh	2.67
Cindy Crawford	1.33

MALE RESPONDENTS

None/No One	7.78%
Sandra Bullock	2.75
Pamela Anderson Lee	2.75
Cindy Crawford	2.29
Anna Nicole Smith	1.37
Julia Roberts	1.37
Nicole Kidman	1.37
Kathy Ireland	1.37
Loni Anderson	1.37
Princess Diana	0.92
Alicia Silverstone	0.92
Jody Foster	0.92
Kate Moss	0.92
Meg Ryan	0.92
Michele Pfieffer	0.92
Shania Twain	0.92
Angela Bassett	0.92
Claudia Schiffer	0.92
Demi Moore	0.92
Winona Ryder	0.92

ANYONE BUT YOU! It's clear from the poll that women wouldn't want to be involved with someone they fear. The list of men that female respondents would least like to be linked with romantically contains many of the same names as the public figures women fear the most: Newt Gingrich, Rush Limbaugh, and O.J. Simpson top the list of least desirable men. The men polled made it apparent that they don't go for the outspoken type, be it a political figure such as Hillary Clinton, or wealthy celebrities like Madonna or Roseanne.

The tabulations below represent the percentage of poll respondents who gave the following answers to the question: **"What one public figure would you least like to be involved with romantically?"**

FEMALE RESPONDENTS

Newt Gingrich	14.67%
Rush Limbaugh	10.67
O.J. Simpson	8.00
Bob Dole	6.67
Phil Gramm	6.67
Pat Buchanan	2.67
Bill Clinton	2.67
Bob Packwood	2.67
Dennis Rodman	2.67
Michael Jackson	1.33

MALE RESPONDENTS

Hillary Clinton	14.19%

Roseanne	4.12
Janet Reno	3.66
Madonna	2.75
Babra Streisand	1.37
Phyllis Schlaffley	1.37
Jocelyn Elders	1.37
Pat Schroeder	1.37
Pamela Anderson Lee	0.92
Leona Helmsley	0.92

SENILE DEMENTIA

Intellectual decline and memory loss is not necessarily normal to aging as most people believe, according to several studies on aging. What often happens is that seniors believe the myth that younger people have a corner on brains and so lose confidence in their own. In a survey of 837 people age 29 to 95, which asked respondents to predict what they would do in a series of tests, people over 70 underestimated their potential.

In another study by the same scientists at Pennsylvania State University, 229 men and women were tutored for five hours in skills that seemed to be declining: where to put new books on bookshelves (spatial orientation) and finding patterns in bus schedules (inductive reasoning). Given a booster course seven years later and tested again, their skills still were sharp, while skills further deteriorated in another group who had not been given training. The study suggested that healthy, active seniors continuing to store information, make decisions, and solve problems can remain plugged in to what is going on around them throughout life.

Staying healthy-minded into old age may even help stave off Alzheimer's disease, which afflicts 15 percent of Americans in either its severe or mild form, according to a third study, this one at Columbia University in New York City. In the study of 593 well-educated achievers over 60 years of age it was found that subjects had about 33 percent less risk of developing the disease than did low-achievers with less than eight years of education.

SENIOR DRIVERS

Elderly people are unsafe drivers, according to 39 percent of the 9,866 respondents to a poll on the subject on driving safety. Sixty-five percent thought teens are unsafe drivers. Eighty-five percent of those polled carried driver's licenses, with the largest age group—39 percent—between 51 and 74. That group was followed by those aged 36 to 50 (27 percent) and 26 to 35 (11 percent).

The largest response—to the question as to whether a driver cited for a moving violation should be forced to pass a road test for license renewal—resulted in a split decision. Forty-four percent said yes, and 44 percent said no.

As to what age should drivers be required to take a road test to renew their licenses, 15 percent in the 1994 *Parade* magazine poll said age 70, followed by 14 percent who said age 65, and nine percent both age 60 and 75. Physical exams required for license renewal should be required at age 70, according to 16 percent of the respondents. Fourteen percent said age 65, and 10 percent said either age 75 or 80.

SENSE OF HUMOR

Father may not know best but he tells a good joke, at least according to the Peoplepedia Opinion Poll. Whereas the American dad once was viewed as the stodgy, serious-minded, breadwinner, the poll indicates that he takes his cue not from Ward Cleaver, but from Clifford Huxtable or Al Bundy, still leaders of their family unit, but just a bit off-center. The poll's respondents most often named dad as the funniest member of the family. Nearly the same percentage named themselves. Indeed, among female respondents, more thought themselves the funniest member of the family than any of their relatives.

The tabulations below represent the percentage of poll respondents who gave the following answers to the question: "Which one family member has the best sense of humor?"

ALL RESPONDENTS	
Father	12.50%
Self/Me	11.84
Sister	8.88
Brother	8.03
Mother	5.43
No Answer	5.35
Wife	5.15
Husband	3.50
Son	2.92
Uncle	2.34
Grandfather	1.56
Daughter	1.44
No One	1.07
Aunt	1.07
Cousin	0.87
Grandmother	0.78
Other Relative	0.58
Ex-Husband	0.29
FEMALE	
Self/Me	22.67%
Father	21.33
Sister	14.67
No Answer	6.67
Brother	5.33
Mother	5.33
Wife	5.33
Husband	4.00
Son	4.00
Uncle	4.00
Grandfather	2.67

Aunt	1.33
Grandmother	1.33
No One	1.33
MALE RESPONDENTS	
Brother	9.61%
Father	7.32
Mother	5.49
Self/Me	5.49
Sister	5.49
Wife	5.04
No Answer	4.58
Husband	3.20
Daughter	2.29
Son	2.29
Cousin	1.37
Uncle	1.37
Aunt	0.92
Grandfather	0.92
No One	0.92
Other Relative	0.92
Grandmother	0.46
Ex-Husband	0.46

SEX APPEAL

Dating has changed, namely in how singles meet. Surprisingly, bars are still a place to gather and pickup a date.

This list, from *Singles, the New Americans,* represents how single men and women meet dates and the relevant percentages.

	Men	Women
Friends	30%	36%
Social gatherings	22	18
Bars and discos	24	18
Singles functions	14	18
Work	10	9
Newspaper ads	1	1

What attracts women? American women are attracted by the upper torso and, most of all, by the most conspicuous physical characteristics, rather than the sexual anatomy of the male.

The following list from *Sex, A User's Manual* represents what women find most attractive in a man.

Face	55%
Hair	8
Shoulders	7
Chest	6
Hands	4

Women were also found to like men for their achievements, status, and intelligence. What attracts men? Though men are attracted by a pretty face, legs are high on their list.

This list, from the book cited earlier, represents what men find most attractive in women.

Face	27
Legs	24
Bust	18
Hair	5
Buttocks	4

Unlike women, men did not report a strong attraction to women's achievements or intelligence. They respond to physical appearance, the power to arouse them, and affection.

SIBLINGS AS LIARS

As in the Bible in which Jacob vied with Esau, sibling rivalry remains strong, or so it seems according to the findings of the Peoplepedia Opinion Poll.

The Poll asked which family member is most likely to tell you a lie. Brothers and sisters topped the list of both male and female respondents. Could it be due to battles over who broke the vase or put the dent in the family car? Perhaps it is not out of the realm of possibility. On a positive note, a good number of respondents—nearly nine percent—said no one member of the family is most likely to tell a lie, making it the third most frequent response regarding the issue of lies told among family.

The tabulations below represent the percentage of poll respondents who gave the following answers to the question: **"Which family member is most likely to tell you a lie?"**

ALL RESPONDENTS	
Brother	18.02%
Sister	10.04
No One	8.56
Mother	7.32
No Answer	6.13
Son	3.99
Father	3.82
Daughter	3.70
Self/Me	1.56
Cousin	1.44
Wife	1.36
Mother-in-Law	1.07
Sister-in-Law	1.07
Uncle	0.87
Brother-in-Law	0.78
Children	0.78
Equal	0.58
Ex-Husband	0.58
Husband	0.58
Animal	0.49
Nephew	0.29
Grandmother	0.29
Stepfather	0.29
Other Relative	0.29

FEMALE RESPONDENTS

Brother	25.33%
Sister	14.67
Mother	12.00
No One	10.67
Father	8.00
No Answer	8.00
Daughter	5.33
Son	5.33
Self/Me	2.67
Animal	1.33
Brother-in-Law	1.33
Children	1.33
Mother-in-Law	1.33
Sister-in-Law	1.33

MALE RESPONDENTS

Brother	13.73%
No One	7.32
Sister	7.32
No Answer	5.04
Mother	4.58
Daughter	2.75
Son	3.20
Cousin	2.29
Father	1.37
Uncle	1.37
Wife	1.37
Self/Me	0.92
Sister-in-Law	0.92
Mother-in-Law	0.92
Equal	0.92
Grandmother	0.46
Brother-in-Law	0.46
Children	0.46
Nephew	0.46
Other Relative	0.46
Stepfather	0.46

SMOKING

Smokers lost more ground in the last three years in their fight against total bans on smoking in restaurants, as 38 percent of Americans voiced their approval of making restaurants smoke-free. That is an increase of 10 points from the 28 percent in 1991, and more than double the 17 percent recorded in 1987.

In a 1994 poll, support for work place bans rose eight points, from 24 percent in 1991 to 32 percent, while support for banning smoking throughout hotels and motels remained unchanged at 20 percent.

Regarding smoking in their homes, 59 percent would not allow it, compared to 33 percent who would. In 1990, the figures were 47 percent and 39 percent respectively, according to a Gallup poll of 1,007 adults age 18 and older, including 261 smokers.

In those three categories, however, antismokers still are in the minority as they are on the subject of making smoking completely illegal, with only 11 percent in favor of the idea, down from 14 percent in 1990.

Most smokers accept the current restrictions on smoking in state and local government, business, and restaurant locations. Sixty percent do not feel discriminated against, and only 30 percent say they are smoking less because of curbs, while 70 percent say they are not. Sixty percent of all those polled felt sympathetic toward smokers because the habit is so addictive.

Percentage approval of smoking curbs in public places and characteristics of respondents according to the Gallup poll:

HOTELS AND MOTELS

Polled	Certain areas	Total Ban	No Ban
Nationally	**68%**	**20%**	**10%**
Sex			
Male	63	21	15
Female	72	19	7
Age			
18-29 years	70	15	14
30-49 years	69	21	9
50-64 years	68	23	8
65 and older	59	23	12
Race			
White	68	20	10
Non-white	66	20	12
Education			
College post-graduate	67	30	3
College graduate	65	29	5
College incomplete	69	21	9
No college	68	16	13
Income			
$50,000+	68	25	7
$30,000-49,999	68	21	10
$20,000-29,999	67	18	14
Less than $20,000	68	16	13
Smoking Status			
Never smoked	62	29	6
Ex-smoker	67	20	12
Smoker	77	18	4
WORKPLACES			
National	63	32	4
Sex			
Male	62	31	6
Female	65	32	2
Age			
18-25 years	65	30	5
30-49 years	62	34	3
50-64 years	65	33	2
65 and older	62	28	6
Race			
White	64	31	4

Non-white	59	37	4
Education			
College post-graduate	44	54	2
College grad-uate	46	51	3
College incom-plete	67	29	3
No college	69	24	5
Income			
$50,000+	57	40	3
$30,000-49,999	63	33	3
$20,000-29,999	66	30	4
ULess than $20,000	67	26	13
Smoking Status			
Never smoked	53	43	3
Ex-smoker	64	30	6
Smoker	81	13	5
Restaurants			
National	57%	38%	4%
Sex			
Male	55	38	6
Female	59	38	2
Age			
18-29 years	57	39	3
30-49 years	56	40	3
50-64 years	57	41	2
65 and older	57	32	7
Race			
White	58	37	4
Non-white	52	43	3
Education			
College postgraduate	39	57	4
College graduate	44	52	3
College incomplete	54	43	3
No college	64	30	4
Income			
$50,000 and over	50	46	4
$30,000-49,999	57	40	3
$20,000-29,999	56	37	6
Under $20,000	64	31	3
Smoking Status			
Never smoked	44	52	2
Ex-smoker	57	36	6
Smoker	80	16	3

SNACK FOOD

Each year Americans spend approximately $8 billion on snack food, much of it fried, high in fat, covered with gooey cheese, and absolutely delicious! So much so that it is often the staple when Mom and Dad are not there to curb the voracious appetites that are part of youth.

What are the favorites of our nutritionally misspent youth? According to a Gallup poll, they are the following, with the percentages of those who eat them regularly:

Pizza	82%
Chicken nuggets	51
Hot dogs	45
Cheeseburgers	42
Macaroni and cheese	42
Hamburgers	38
Spaghetti and meatballs	37
Fried chicken	37
Tacos	32
Grilled cheese sandwiches	22

SOCIAL CHANGE

Most Americans today believe social changes are happening faster than ever before and that the quality of those changes are low. Yet 60 percent agree they eventually will turn out for the best.

Especially hopeful and most willing to accept change are 68 percent of young adults under age 30, and 54 percent of people age 60 and older, in spite of admitting how increasingly hard it is to keep up with changes. Roper Starch Worldwide, which conducted the poll, suggests that most people believe the nation needs more change because so little so far has been of value.

On a personal level, the largest share of respondents, 49 percent, prefer to maintain the status quo in their lives. They would not change their name, friends, married partner, family, home, appearance, or social class. Forty percent, mostly the young, indicate they would change all or some of them. Eighty-four percent believe unhappiness can be overcome with personal effort.

The most difficult change people endure is the death of a spouse, 87 percent calling it very difficult or difficult. Divorce was second for 70 percent of respondents. The youngest child moving out of the house was third for 46 percent of the empty nesters left behind, and 41 percent of retirees listed leaving the working world behind as difficult. Thirty-six percent of movers listed relocating at that level.

First-time marriages fazed only 12 percent of Americans, but the second time around was very difficult to difficult for 27 percent. The coming of the first child was called difficult by 23 percent. Only five percent of elder Americans thought graduating from high school was difficult, but 13 percent of young adults admitted it was.

Percent of adults aged 18 and older whose first marriage or remarriage was very difficult or difficult, according to the Roper poll:

Age	First Marriage	Remarriage
18-29	16	30
30-44	15	26
45-59	10	31
60 and older	7	21

SOCIAL SECURITY, CONFIDENCE IN

UFOs are more credible to young American adults than the prospect of Social Security checks made out to them when they retire, a youth advocacy group poll indicates. The poll found that 72 percent of the 18- to 34-year-olds polled believe in UFOs, but only 28 percent believe in the efficacy of the commitment made to them by the Social Security Administration. Overall, 91 percent believe a Congressional Budget Office report that says the $300 billion Social Security program could be bankrupt by 2029 by the retirement of 76 million baby boomers.

Asked what solution they could offer, 82 percent of the young adults said they would rather use part of their Social Security contributions to build up a personal retirement account, according to the survey group Third Millenium.

SPOUSAL ABUSE

A nationwide outcry against wife battering has resulted in a double standard in Americans' view of marital violence, according to a poll measuring one degree of violence between husband and wife.

A Gallup poll in 1994 of 526 adults age 18 and older asked whether there were any occasions when slapping one's spouse could be condoned. Twenty-three percent of those polled approved of a wife slapping her husband if conditions warranted; only 10 percent could approve of a husband slapping his wife. A Harris poll in 1968 showed 20 percent of both sexes agreed slapping their mate was excusable under some circumstances.

The double standard was most noticeable among the 18-to-30 age group, 27 percent of whom approved of a wife slapping her husband, but not the reverse. Fifteen percent of men age 18 to 30 approved of a wife slapping her husband, but not the reverse.

Men approve slapping of either spouse more than women, 14 percent approving slapping a wife against 7 percent of women, and 27 percent of men and 18 percent of women approve of a wife slapping her husband.

Thirty percent of the women polled called themselves feminists. Of that number just over a half—16 percent—approved of a wife slapping her husband. Seventy percent of those polled called themselves nonfeminist. Among those polled, 18 percent approved of wife-slapping. Just 5 percent of the feminists and 6 percent of the nonfeminists approved of a husband slapping his wife.

Percentage who condone a wife slapping her husband, but not the reverse:

Sex	Approve
Men	14%
Women	13
MEN	
Age	Percent
18-30	15%
31-50	16
51 and over	11
WOMEN	
Age	Percent
18-30	27%
31-50	7
51 and over	17

The trend, according to the Harris poll, a National Alcohol and Family Violence Study by Glenda Kaufman-Kantor, and a National Family Violence Study by Richard Geles and Murray Straus:

Year	Husband slaps wife	Wife slaps husband
1994	10%	23%
1992	12	22
1985	13	21
1968	20	20

TEEN PRIORITIES

"Have fun now" is the major credo of Americans aged 12 to 19, according to a 1993 survey, which also finds "helping others" is on the decline—a two percent decrease. A similar survey in 1989 showed a 6 percent decrease from 1992.

Agreeing with the statement "I always try to have as much fun as I possibly can—I don't care what the future holds, and I don't care what people think," were 63 percent of the young people. That was a decrease from 65 percent in 1989 and 69 percent in 1993, but still the highest measurement in the survey of 2,000 young people taken by Teenage Research Unlimited of Northbrook, Ill.

Two of the four major categories touched upon in the survey showed a falling off from similar surveys taken in 1989 and 1992, an indication perhaps of a growing cynicism among the age group, according to TRU. Helping others was the highest measurement taken in 1989, beating out "having fun" by four percentage points at 65 percent to 61 percent. In 1993 helping others dropped two percentage points to 63 percent, after having climbed to 69 percent in 1992.

In the category of "first to try something new" in fashions and technology, 50.5 percent in 1989 said it was very important to them, compared with 46 percent in 1993, reflecting an attitude of "We've already done everything," according to TRU. In matters of religion and personal faith, 53 percent said such issues were very important to them in both 1989 and 1993, after climbing to 58 percent in 1992.

Focusing in on advertising awareness, the survey found that 60 percent valued honesty as the top rule advertisers should follow. Fifty percent like ads that have a clear message and use humor, 43 percent like originality, and 40 percent like music that thematically fits the commercial. Twenty-five percent say socially responsible advertising weighs heavily with them, and 60 percent say advertising helps them decide what to buy.

Dissatisfaction with the age bracket they are in and their apparent hurry to get on with life was shown across the board in the survey. On average, most teens would like to be one to five years older than they are, with this gap widest among the younger respondents in the survey.

Subject	1989	1993
Have fun now	61%	63%
Help others	65	63
Personal religion/faith	53	53
First to try something new	51	46

Percent of people aged 12 to 19 who agree at all with selected statements, 1989 and 1993, according to Teenager Research Unlimited statistics:

TEEN PRIORITIES

Added to the usual teenage cares of money, school grades, dates, borrowing dad's car, getting a job, and avoiding acne, the 1990s teen now has adult concerns such as violence, alcohol, and drugs. But according to poll of teens age 13 to 17, many cannot share these concerns with those who could help them the most: their parents.

The telephone poll of 1,055 teenagers conducted by *The New York Times* and CBS News showed that four out of 10 young people sometimes or often do not get help from their parents, although 40 percent said they knew somebody who had been shot in the last five years, and most of the attackers and victims were other teenagers.

Half of the students in their schools carried knives or guns, responded 13 percent of those polled, while another 16 percent said some students were armed. While four in 10 students said they worried about being the target of violence, 82 percent said neither they nor anyone in their immediate family had been a violent crime victim in the last two years.

The fears of violent attacks among black students, however, were based on reality. Seventy percent knew somebody who had been shot in the last five years, compared with 40 percent of the overall respondents.

Fifty three percent of those polled said at least half of the students they knew got drunk at least once a month. And 33 percent said at least some classmates had cheated on the last test they took, and most confessed to having cheated at some time.

TEENS, RACIAL VIEWS

Who's Who Among American High School Students polled 2,000 high-achieving high school students and found that 85 percent of blacks believe minorities have fewer opportunities, whereas only 30 percent of whites believe it to be true. By and large, whites were less aware of prejudices, actual or perceived. In addition, whites proved to be unaware that some of their actions are perceived as prejudice by people of color with whom they interact.

For example, as many as six in 10 blacks claim to have been victims of racial prejudice. Among whites, only one in 10 admitted to ever having acted openly prejudicial toward another racial or ethnic group.

Other findings include:

- Special educational opportunities: 60 percent of blacks and 10 percent of whites say blacks should have them.

- Confidence in police: 50 percent of blacks and 20 percent of whites do not trust the police.

- Interracial dating: 90 percent of blacks and 60 percent of whites approved of dating someone of a different race.

Today's youngsters have no first-hand memory of Dr. Martin Luther King, Jr., and the 1960s civil rights movement. As the inheritors of the changes brought on by that era, the teens of the 1990s interact with members of other races far more frequently and more readily than their parents. Yet 48 percent of today's teens describe U.S. race relations as "generally bad"; only 42 percent said they were good.

A detailed study by Peter Hart Research Associates for People for the American Way showed that blacks were more pessimistic about race relations than whites, with 57 percent calling them bad; 49 percent of Hispanic respondents said the same. Of the 1,170 young people polled, 71 percent had at least one "close personal friendship" with a member of another race. Among whites, 51 percent oppose colleges giving "special consideration to minority" students, and 65 percent are against giving "special consideration to minority job applicants." Almost half of the white youths, 49 percent, believe it is whites who are discriminated against, whereas 68 percent of blacks and 52 percent of Hispanics think their respective racial group is discriminated against.

The table below indicates the percentages of those polled who answered various questions in the following manner. (The numbers do not total 100 percent because some of those polled indicated they were "unsure" of their opinion.)

ARE RELATIONS GENERALLY GOOD OR BAD?

	Good	Bad
Whites	44%	48%
Blacks	35	57
Hispanics	82	16

IS DISCRIMINATION PREVALENT?

	Agree	Disagree
Whites	81%	18%
Blacks	82	17
Hispanics	82	16

TELEVISION

TV Guide posed the question to its readers: "How much money would it take to induce you to give up watching TV?" Enough people among the 1,007 persons polled took the question seriously enough to make their views into statistics.

The survey found that 23 percent would be willing to sell their viewing habits for $25,000; 46 percent demanded $1 million; and 25 percent were stalwart enough to refuse even a cool million.

Other results include:

- Male adults are twice as likely to control the remote box as women (41 percent to 19 percent respectively).

- Some 63 percent of adults often watch television while eating; three quarters of them are 18- to 24-year-olds.

- More viewers are offended by too much violence (37 percent) than too much sex (27 percent). Other points of dissatisfaction are lack of creativity (14 percent), too many reruns (11 percent), and too many commercials (seven percent).

- A higher proportion of younger (32 percent) than older viewers (22 percent) found explicit sex more objectionable than excessive violence.

TRADING PLACES

Would you rather be President of the United States, or the head of the most powerful computer software company in the world? According to the Peoplepedia Opinion Poll. Bill Gates, chairman of Microsoft, outpolled the president as the public figure Americans would most like to trade places with.

The tabulations below represent the percentage of poll respondents who gave the following answers to the question: "What one public figure would you most like to trade places with?"

ALL RESPONDENTS

Bill Gates	7.66%
Bill Clinton	5.11
Newt Gingrich	4.65
None	4.57
Hillary Clinton	2.75
Oprah Winfrey	1.97
Rush Limbaugh	1.73
Stephen King	1.27
Martha Stewart	0.99
Cindy Crawford	0.99
Courtney Cox	0.99
Janet Jackson	0.99
Bob Dole	0.87
Donald Trump	0.87
Michael Jordan	0.87
Peter Jennings	0.78
Colin Powell	0.78
Arnold Schwarzenegger	0.58
Harrison Ford	0.58
Dale Earnhardt	0.58
John Kennedy Jr.	0.58

Prince Charles	0.29
David Letterman	0.29

FEMALE RESPONDENTS

Bill Gates	6.67%
Hillary Clinton	6.67
None	5.33
Oprah Winfrey	5.33
Newt Gingrich	4.00
Stephen King	2.67
Martha Stewart	2.67
Cindy Crawford	2.67
Coutney Cox	2.67
Janet Jackson	2.67
Bill Clinton	1.33
Peter Jennings	1.33
Colin Powell	1.33

MALE RESPONDENTS

Bill Gates	8.24%
Bill Clinton	7.32
Newt Gingrich	5.04
None	4.12
Rush Limbaugh	2.75
Bob Dole	1.37
Donald Trump	1.37
Michael Jordan	1.37
Arnold Schwarzenegger	0.92
John Kennedy Jr	0.92
Harrison Ford	0.92
Dale Earnhardt	0.92
Peter Jennings	0.46
Prince Charles	0.46
Hillary Clinton	0.46
Stephen King	0.46
Colin Powell	0.46
David Letterman	0.46

TRUST, FAMILIAL

Mothers emerged as the most trustworthy members of the family, according to the Peoplepedia Opinion Poll.

Moms topped the list when survey participants were asked which member of the family could keep a secret the best, and which, overall, is the most honest. The poll also asked questions concerning lying, and mothers fared well (earning a fourth rank with brothers being perceived as the biggest liars in the family). Judging from the poll, in general, female members of the American family are perceived as more trustworthy than the males.

The tabulations below represent the percentage of poll respondents who gave the following answers to the question: "If you have a secret to share, which one family member would you trust the most to keep it confidential?"

ALL RESPONDENTS

Mother	12.75%
Wife	11.51

Sister	9.66
Brother	7.66
No One	6.38
Husband	6.17
No Answer	5.64
Father	5.47
Daughter	1.65
Son	1.07
Animal	0.87
Grandfather	0.78
Grandmother	0.78
Other Relative	0.58
Aunt	0.58
Father-in-Law	0.49
Self/Me	0.49
Sister-in-Law	0.49
Cousin	0.29
Niece	0.29

The tabulations below represent the percentage of poll respondents who gave the following answers to the question: "Which one family member is the most honest overall?"

ALL RESPONDENTS

Mother	16.05
Wife	10.41
Father	9.46
Husband	6.45
No Answer	5.64
Self/Me	5.55
Sister	4.40
Brother	3.87
Grandfather	2.55
Daughter	1.94
Equal	1.94
No One	1.07
Father-in-Law	0.99
Cousin	0.87
Grandmother	0.78
Stepfather	0.49

Animal	0.29
Mother-in-Law	0.29
Son	0.29
Uncle	0.29
Parents	0.29

WOMEN AND WORK

Forty-seven percent of American women say that balancing work and family is the greatest problem facing mothers today. And 83 percent agree with the statement, "Women work out of necessity, are having a hard time, and nobody cares."

Sixty-eight percent of women think equality in some part of their lives is the most important thing they lack, while 49 percent say they have no equality at all in any part of their lives. But only 25 percent said they would work hard to achieve equality, according to a survey conducted by EDK Associates, a research firm specializing in women's issues.

The survey found that 60 percent of women work outside the home, including 66 percent of mothers. Half of U.S. law school graduates are women, and 40 percent of medical school graduates.

In politics, women make up only 10 percent of Congress, and 23 states do not have a single woman representative in Washington. Four states have women governors.

Other findings include:

- 70 percent of women say the country would be different if more women held powerful positions.

- 74 percent say more women in politics would lead to greater equality.

- 26 percent say they would vote for a woman political candidate just because she is a woman.

- More American workers are employed by woman-owned businesses than work for Fortune 500 companies.

part two:

THE
AMERICAN
COLLECTIVE

EDUCATION
OVERVIEW

Americans still view education as a stepping stone to success. As more Americans achieve a higher education and reap its rewards, greater numbers are entering and graduating from college than ever before. Yet there is a large contingent of young Americans who do not have the traditional appreciation for education that the previous generation did. The quality of public education is a prominent factor in this alarming trend.

In an economy now reliant on high technology and the ability to comprehend, evaluate and manipulate advanced information, American schools produce an alarming number of scientifically and mathematically illiterate students. A mere 25 percent of American schoolchildren function at their grade level in math; 90 percent of the population does not understand fundamental scientific principles. This low level of achievement is at its worst among minorities, especially in the poorest inner-city neighborhoods.

Yet those who are coming out of the urban underclass still have an opportunity to compete, not just with our global neighbors, but with other Americans who have enjoyed better high school educations.

Thanks in part to many low-tuition community colleges and low interest college loans, today a college education is not the prize of a select few, as it has traditionally been. In 1940, 24.5 percent of Americans over age 25 had a high school diploma, and a mere 4.6 percent had completed four years of college. In 1994, nearly 81 percent of the over 25 crowd had finished high school, and 22.2 percent had earned a four-year college degree. College enrollment has more than doubled since 1960, from 758,000 to 1,559,000 in 1994. Women make up the largest proportion of the increase, from 350,000 in 1960 to 805,000 in '94. Indeed, women now outnumber men in American colleges, 53 percent to 47 percent.

Whether an individual's goal of higher education is learning or earning cannot be determined, but the efficacy of the latter has been calculated and drummed into the heads of millions of parents and their children. The median annual earnings for Americans age 25 and over with a four-year college degree is 78 percent higher than for those with just a high school diploma—$40,590 vs. $22,765.

The income gaps are even higher for minorities. Black women with just a high school degree earn a median income of $12,762; those with a college degree average more than twice that, $27,745. Over the course of a lifetime, the premium on a college education can be upwards of $1 million or more compared to a high school diploma.

The willingness to pay the high cost to attend colleges and universities are a gauge of the value Americans place on education. Despite soaring tuitions, each year colleges and universities grant more degrees than the previous year. According to *Time* magazine, aver-

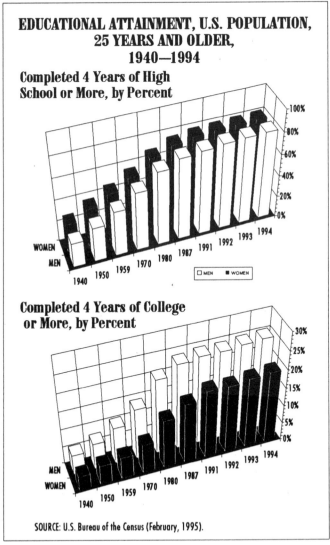

EDUCATIONAL ATTAINMENT, U.S. POPULATION, 25 YEARS AND OLDER, 1940—1994

Completed 4 Years of High School or More, by Percent

WOMEN
MEN

1940 1950 1959 1970 1980 1987 1991 1992 1993 1994

100% 80% 60% 40% 20% 0%

☐ MEN ■ WOMEN

Completed 4 Years of College or More, by Percent

MEN
WOMEN

1940 1950 1959 1970 1980 1987 1991 1992 1993 1994

30% 25% 20% 15% 10% 5% 0%

SOURCE: U.S. Bureau of the Census (February, 1995).

age tuition for a private four-year college in 1970 was $6,283, calculated in 1994 dollars. The cost in 1994 was $11,490—83 percent higher in real terms. Still, institutions of higher education granted an estimated 1,165,000 bachelor's degrees in 1994—nearly 400,000 more than in 1970. The increase is even greater for master's degrees: 370,000 in 1994 vs. 209,000 in 1970 (a 77 percent increase).

Despite Americans' thirst for education, an alarming tend is developing. Recent economic problems indicate that the trend toward more education may not continue. Rising tuitions have begun to squeeze people out in certain areas: Declines in higher education enrollments have been registered in a number of states, primarily those with fiscal problems, especially California. If, as some predict, the American states and the nation's largest cities head for fiscal crises, American education, at least for the masses, will be in jeopardy.

BLACK PH.D.s

A significant gain in Ph.D.s among blacks has been registered, mostly at black colleges, according to figures from the National Research Council. Its report showed a 13 percent increase in the number of doctorates issued to African Americans from 1989 to 1991, when 933 blacks earned the degree, 4 percent more than the 1990 figure of 897, which represented a 9 percent increase over the 821 black Ph.D.'s in 1989. In 1992, 18 out of every 1,000 white college students earned doctorates compared to eight out of 1,000 black college students. The largest number of black Ph.D.s, 1,047, came in 1982.

Education experts attributed the increase to college recruiting programs begun in the 1970s, because black students traditionally take eight or nine years to earn a doctorate. Frank Matthews, the publisher of *Black Issues in Higher Education,* noted that 12 black colleges graduate the most blacks, though three predominantly white schools are among the top twenty. He said, "Black colleges are still producing and carrying a disproportional share of the load."

COLLEGE COACHES, RACIAL COMPOSTION

Blacks make up 25 percent of the 58,398 student-athletes in the NCAA's Division I, yet in 1994 filled only 7.25 percent of athletic administrative positions. Staff jobs are defined in the NCAA's 1993 Minority Opportunity and Interests Committee four-year study as coaches, directors, business managers, and various support, information, promotion, and ticket sales areas.

A total of 5,889 positions in those categories became available between 1991 and 1994. Just over 10.1 percent of of those postions, 597 jobs, were filled by blacks or other minorities. That inched the overall percentage of black athletics administrators from 5.4 percent to 6.2 percent.

Nineteen blacks were hired as college athletics directors, among the 125 openings in that position. Four of those were at black institutions. Thus just 12.3 percent of AD openings at schools that were not primarily black were filled by African Americans.

In the three years 1991-93 a total of 1,109 head coach positions opened up among NCAA schools. Excluding black institutions, blacks earned 143 placements, or 12.9 percent of the jobs. Still, African Americans represented only 3.9 percent of the 10,176 head coaches in the network. Other minority (Asian, Hispanic, and Native American) and unknown categories lost 136 head coaching positions in the same period.

In the revenue sports of football and basketball, in which blacks make up 49.4 percent of student-athletes in 1993, 86 blacks, or 20.6 percent, serve as head coaches; in nonrevenue sports such as tennis, fencing, etc., blacks held 8 percent of those positions, or 57 of 692 head coaching positions.

Assistant coaching positions were similarly lacking in blacks and other minorities. Of the 2,394 assistant

The odds say that a disproportionally high number of blacks will be on an NCAA team such as this one, the Flames of the University of Illinois, Chicago. The odds, however, that an NCAA coach will be anything but white are dismal; only about 10 percent nationally are black.

positions that came open from 1991 to 1994, 213, or 8.9 percent, were filled by blacks. The committee said there had been no important percentage increase in the number of assistant coaches in that period.

Below is a breakdown by race of NCAA college athletic administrative positions the between 1991 and 94, in number and percent:

ATHLETIC ADMINISTRATORS

	1991-92	1992-93	1993-94
Black	387/6.17%	443/6.81%	494/7.25%
White	5,554/88.59	5,758/88.46	5,925/86.93
Other minorities	148/2.36	171/2.63	171/2.51
Unknown	148/2.36	171/2.63	171/2.51

ATHLETICS DIRECTORS (black institutions excluded)

	1991-92	1992-93	1993-94
Black	6/1.99%	6/1.97%	13/4.10 %
White	284/94.04	293/96.38	296/93.38
Other minorities	3/0.99	3/0.99	6/1.89
Unknown	9/2.98	2/0.66	2/0.63

HEAD COACHES (black institutions excluded)

	1991-92	1992-93	1993-94
Blacks	129/3.58%	166/4.15%	173/4.38%
Whites	3,280/90.91	3,659/91.45	3,591/90.98
Other minorities	82/2.27	96/2.40	94/2.38

Unknown	117/3.24	80/2.00	89/2.25
REVENUE-SPORT HEAD COACHES (black institutions excluded)			
	1991-92	1992-93	1993-94
Black	53/7.18%	68/8.72%	78/9.73%
Whites	654/88.62	689/88.33	693/86.41
Other minorities	9/1.22	9/1.15	10/1.25
Unknown	22/2.98	14/1.79	21/2.62

COLLEGE ENROLLMENTS

A college education has become an increasingly important indicator of young America's promise of comfortable lifetime earnings, but declining enrollments have been registered in 12 of 16 states that participated in a national survey. Another survey shows that public and private university costs soared.

An American Council of Education study, which the journal *American Demographics* says portends a nationwide trend, found that recession-troubled California leads the nation with a 7 percent decline in college enrollment between fall 1992 and fall 1993.

The Western Interstate Commission for Higher Education had predicted a 1992-93 enrollment increase because of growth in high school graduates in 13 of 15 Western states, but instead higher education enrollments fell in eight states. The commission points out that in spite of downsizing and budget cuts in California, tuition had doubled since 1988-89 at the University of California and in the California State University system, and community colleges have seen similar increases.

Overall, *Postsecondary Education Opportunity*, an Iowa-based newsletter, says that between 1981 and 1991 public university costs rose 27 percent and those at private uiniversities rose 54 percent, while median family incomes went up only 15 percent.

A Western Interstate commission official said the budget cuts and downsizing have hurt students still enrolled in California schools. San Francisco State eliminated nearly one in five class sections between 1989 and 1993. At the same time, available seats dropped by 11.5 percent, while students crowded into fewer but larger classes and continued to face double-digit tuition increases.

Among the 16 states overall, which account for more than 40 percent of the total U.S. college population, excluding California, enrollment dropped in Colorado, Connecticut, Illinois, Indiana, Louisiana, Maryland, Minnesota, Mississippi, New York, Ohio, Oklahoma, and Virginia. Modest gains were made in Georgia, New Jersey, Tennessee, and Texas, and Hawaii.

Dire consequences were seen in California's plight by some officials, which *American Demographics* says might be echoed by educational authorities across the country. A California Higher Education Policy Center official said, "We're starting to squeeze people out of the system," a statement seconded by San Francisco State's planning and analytic studies director, who

added, "We've lost people on the margin." The outlook is "scary" to Thomas Mortenson, publisher of the Iowa City education newsletter, because higher tuition rates mean poorer people have even less chance of getting ahead.

Percent change in higher education enrollment for selected states, 1992-93, compiled from statistics from the American Council on Higher Education and Western Interstate Commission for Higher Education:

State	gain or loss
California	-7.2%
Wyoming	-2.8
Mississippi	-2.5
Connecticut	-2.2
Oklahoma	-2.1
New Mexico	3.2
South Dakota	3.0
Hawaii	2.9
Idaho	2.7
Georgia	2.6

COLLEGE FOOTBALL PLAYERS, RACIAL COMPOSITION

Blacks comprise 49.4 percent of the 9,500 football players in NCAA Divisions I and IA. Off the field and in the classrooms, 61 percent of those in Division I scored low in their school work and failed to graduate in 1994, according to the NCAA. Four schools in the division failed to graduate any of their black players.

Fifty of the 107 schools in Division I graduated less than 33 percent of their black players, including major football-competing schools such Texas, Georgia, and Louisiana State.

All black players hoping to graduate at Boise State, San Jose State (which has never graduated a black football player under John Ralston in his 14 years as head coach), Southeastern Louisiana, and California State at Sacramento went back to their classrooms instead. NCAA rules allow an athlete to compete for six years if he fails to graduate in four.

Among the division's bottom 50 schools for graduating black football players in 1994, blacks who did graduate matched or outnumbered whites at two schools—26 percent of both blacks and whites at New Mexico State University graduated, and 26 percent of blacks and 20 percent whites at the University of Nevada at Las Vegas.

Four teams on the "bottom" list won bowl games in 1993: Louisville (the Liberty Bowl), Kansas State (Copper Bowl), Clemson (Peach Bowl), and Southern University (Heritage Bowl). Though overall black graduation rates in 1994 rose three points from the year before, 22 of the schools in the bottom 25 in 1993 were still on the 1994 list.

The University of Michigan, winner of the Hall of Fame Bowl in 1994 and second in rank for all-time victories, graduated 63 percent of its black and 70 percent of its white players in 1994. Penn State, 1994

Citrus Bowl winner, had 76 percent of its black players receive degrees within a six-year period, compared to 71 percent of its white players, and 1993 and 1994 Cotton Bowl winner Notre Dame, all-time NCAA Division I leader in games won (723 against 211 losses and 41 ties), graduated 79 percent of its blacks and 83 percent of its whites.

Under stricter academic guidelines for college athletes in school on athletic scholarships enacted by the NCAA in 1986 and affecting freshmen who entered college that year, blacks graduated four years later at an 8 percent higher rate than those who entered in 1985. Those who entered as freshmen in 1987 graduated at a 9 percent higher rate.

Below are the graduation rates in 1994 for black and white NCAA Division I college football players in the 20 schools with the lowest rates, according to NCAA figures:

School	Black	White
Boise State	0%	44%
San Jose State	0	36
Southeastern Louisiana U.	0	33
Cal State-Sacramento	0	8
University of Houston	2	39
Texas Tech	5	41
Southern Methodist	6	33
Texas Southern	6	0
Idaho State	10	45
Arkansas State	10	29
University of Montana	11	35
Nichols State	11	35
Lamar University	12	24
Wichita State	12	21
Louisiana State	13	53
Kansas State	14	56
Utah State	15	49
Northern Arizona	15	38

Below are the graduation rates for football players at black colleges:

BOTTOM 5

School	Percent
Texas Southern	6%
Tennessee State	22
Alabama State	24
Alcorn State, Loman Miss.	25
Southern University	25

COLLEGE STUDENTS, FRESHMEN

College-bound teens have their eyes set on professional or business careers, according to a 1994 survey of college freshmen across the U.S. Freshmen are least interested in physical sciences and the technical fields.

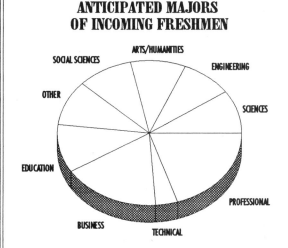

ANTICIPATED MAJORS OF INCOMING FRESHMEN

Professional careers attracted the most freshmen—18.7 percent— and business lured 15.9 percent. Nursing drew the most attention among those in the professions category, drawing 5.4 percent in the category and averaging out to 1.2 percent of all men and 9 percent of women. Medical, dental, and veterinary careers were eyed by 4.2 percent. Home economics interested only 0.2 percent, the least attractive pursuit in the professions, and aimed at only by women.

Among business professions, accounting drew the most interest among the 237,777 students at 461 institutions surveyed. Four percent liked this career, women outnumbering men, 4.5 percent to 3.4 percent, in expressing the preference. Next was business administration at 3.7 percent. Third was management at 2.8 percent. Secretarial studies (.6 percent) and finance (.9) were at the bottom of list.

The survey, conducted by the Higher Education Research Institute at UCLA, showed that after the professions and business, educational careers attracted 9.9 percent of freshmen—6.5 percent of men and 13.1 percent of women. Social sciences and the arts and humanities were the next most popular fields, at 9.1 percent and 9.0 percent respectively. Women again were attracted to those fields at a higher rate than men, 11.9 to 5.9 percent for social sciences, 9.0 to 8.8 percent in arts and humanities. Psychology was the most popular of the social sciences, with 4.1 percent of the men and 11.9 percent of the women surveyed expressing interest. Women's studies ranked last in popularity at 0.1 percent among all women.

English took a back seat to the fine and applied arts in the arts and humanities category, with 1.7 percent of the students in the survey expressing interest in a career in fine and applied arts, the percentages about the same for men and women. English was the expressed choice of 1.4 percent of freshmen, Journalism, music, and history followed at 1.3 percent. Least attractive were careers in philosophy and speech, both at 0.2 percent.

Of all categories of study, nursing drew the most attention overall, with 5.4 percent of the college-bound intending to major in the subject, and military and women's studies the least attention, both with far than .1 percent of the freshmen. Botany, astronomy, atmospheric science, and earth science were next lowest at 0.1 percent. Of the students polled, 7.6 percent were undecided which path to follow.

The largest percent of the students surveyed, 37.1 percent, intended to earn masters degrees; 27 intened to pursue doctorates; and 26.8 said they'd stop at a bachelor's degree.

What 1994 college freshmen students expect to choose as major, in percent of the poll overall, according to the Higher Education Research Institute:

Category	Percent
Professional	18.7%
Business	15.9
Education	9.9
Other fields	9.3
Social sciences	9.1
Arts and humanities	9.0
Engineering	8.1
Biological sciences	6.5
Technical	3.5
Physical sciences	2.4

Highs and lows in each category in percent by field of study and percent of men and women in various fields:

ARTS AND HUMANITIES

Field	Total	Men	Women
Art, fine	1.7%	1.8%	1.7%
Philosophy	0.2	0.3	0.2
Speech	0.2	0.1	0.2

BIOLOGICAL SCIENCES

Field	Total	Men	Women
Biology	2.9%	2.7%	3.1%
Botany	0.1	0.1	0.1

BUSINESS

Field	Total	Men	Women
Accounting	4.0%	3.4%	4.5%
Secretar'l study	0.6	0.0	1.0

EDUCATION

Field	Total	Men	Women
Elementary ed.	4.7%	1.3%	7.6%
Music or art appreciation	0.5	0.5	0.6

ENGINEERING

Field	Total	Men	Women
Electrical	1.9%	3.8%	0.3%
Industrial	0.2	0.4	0.1

PHYSICAL SCIENCE

Field	Total	Men	Women
Chemistry	0.7%	0.9%	0.6%
Astronomy	0.1	0.1	0.0
Atmospheric	0.1	0.1	0.0
Earth science	0.1	0.1	0.1

PROFESSIONAL

Field	Total	Men	Women
Nursing	5.4%	1.2%	9%
Home econ.	0.2	0.0	0.3

SOCIAL SCIENCES

Field	Total	Men	Women
Psychology	4.1%	2.1%	5.8%
Women's studies	0.0	~0.0	0.1

TECHNICAL

Field	Total	Men	Women
Data processing/ computer programming	1.0%	1.4%	0.6%
Mechanics	0.4	0.9	0.0
Law enforcem't	2.1	3.4	1.0
Military science	0.0	0.1	0.0

COLLEGE LANGUAGE STUDIES

In Japan, France, Germany, Italy, and the Scandinavian countries, many people know English well enough to get along, placing them some steps ahead of Americans in their ability to participate fully in today's global economy.

The Japanese have a strong advantage in dealing with the U.S. because of their widespread knowledge of English. Slowly, Americans are discovering that doing business in more than one language makes sense. However, the idea has not yet caught on among students who will soon be entering the business world.

According to the Modern Language Association, scarcely more than a million university students in the country are enrolled in the six principal language courses available.

Below is a breakdown of the languages and the number of students studying them.

Language	Students
Spanish	533,607
French	272,555
German	133,380
Italian	49,726
Japanese	45,717
Russian	44,384

DISABLED STUDENTS

Disabled students receiving help from the federal government reached a record high of 12 percent of all students enrolled in the nation's elementary and high schools in 1992, according to a government report. children with learning disabilities made up 5.3 percent of total school enrollment.

The proportion of children and youths with disabilities served by the Individuals with Disabilities Education Act, which mandates that every child in the U.S. have available to them a free education, has increased or remained the same in every year since 1977 to its 1992 record level, with learning-disabled children rising 50 percent or more each year since 1989 over all other disabled children conditions.

In 1992, the percentage of America's 4.6 million children and youths identified as speech-impaired fell 15 percent from 35.3 percent in 1977 to 20 percent in 1992. Mentally retarded students also fell 15 percentage points, from 26 percent in 1977 to 11.1 percent in 1992, while students with serious emotional problems rose from 7.7 percent to 8 percent. Enrollments of the speech-impaired and mentally retarded students have declined in every year since 1977.

Preschoolers participating in the federal program accounted for 10 percent of the program's enrollment in 1992. Hard-of-hearing and deaf, orthopedically handicapped, visually handicapped, deaf-blind, autistic, and brain-injured students all fell in the 1.3 percent to 0.5 percent range, except the multihandicapped, at 2.2 percent.

During the 1990-91 school year, according to the U.S. Department of Education's Annual Report to Congress on the subject, 94 percent of handicapped students with disabilities were taught in regular school buildings. Of these, 93 percent of those with speech impairments were taught in regular classrooms and/or resource rooms, as compared with 17 percent of deaf-blind students. Fifty-eight percent of the mentally retarded students were taught in separate classrooms, compared to 6 percent of students with speech impairments.

Since 1991, the government has spent $7.2 billion on education for the handicapped—$2.2 billion in 1991 and 1992, and $2.8 billion in 1993. Children aged six to 11 represent almost half of the handicapped total in school, at 2.2 million.

The following details children and youths from birth to age 21 who are served by IDEA, by type of disability in selected school years, in percent, from U.S. Department of Education's Annual Report to Congress on the Implementation of the Individuals with Disabilities Education Act:

Disability	1977	1985	1992
Learning	21.6 %	42.5%	45%
Speech	35.3	26.1	20.0
Mental retardation	26.0	16.1	11.1
Emotional disturbance	7.7	8.6	8.0

Number of children and youths served by IDEA as a percentage of total public elementary and high school enrollments by selected years; source, IDEA:

Disability	1977	1985	1992
All conditions	8.5	10.9	11.7
Learning	1.8	4.6	5.3
Speech	3.0	2.9	2.3
Mental retardation	2.2	1.8	1.3
Emotional disturbance	0.6	0.9	0.9
Preschoolers	N/A	N/A	1.2

EDUCATIONAL ATTAINMENT

One out of six American adults has gone to college but has not stayed around to earn a degree. These 27 million men and women age 25 and older, living in a gap between the high-school-only educated and college graduates, now have caught the attention of the Census Bureau and national survey companies such as Mediamark Research and Roper Starch Worldwide.

Their findings: In many ways the some-college crowd falls closest to the concept of "average" American: people with modest material comforts, a moderate budget, and a belief that the American Dream is still reachable for all.

Nearly 60 percent of the group are aged 25 to 44, according to a 1994 Census Bureau survey, compared to 51 percent of the population overall. Blacks with some college are even younger than whites, 71 percent of blacks and 74 percent of Hispanics in the category falling under age 45. Overall, the 17 percent of blacks with some college equals the percentage of whites, while Hispanics fall below the national average, at 13 percent.

Seventy-one percent of those with some college are married, the same share for all Americans age 25 and older. Thirty-five percent of the women are married to similarly educated men, as are 36 percent of the men to women. The rates for high-school-only men and women who marry mates with similar education, are , 56 percent of men and 66 percent of wives, respectively, and 51 percent for of spouses who both have advanced degrees. Men and women with bachelor's degrees are paired with educationally matched mates at a rate of 44 percent for men and 40 percent for women. All told, 48 percent of married couples in the U.S. are educationally matched.

In 28 categories at the spending level, high school graduates—the lowest in income among the three groups—outspend the some- college adults in seven instances, while the some-college person outspends the college graduate in only one: tobacco, $360 on average annually, to $165. In health care, high school graduates spend more than do the some-college people: $1,521 to $1,516. College graduates, on average, spend $2,035.

According to a 1992 survey conducted by the Bureau of Labor Statistics, the share of family income spent in restaurants increases steadily with education, from $1,460 annually by high school graduates to $1,844 in the some-college group, and $2,391 by college graduates.

A Roper poll in 1992 showed that 44 percent of high school graduates use regular savings accounts to put their money in, compared to 39 percent among some-college and just 31 percent of college graduates. The heaviest magazine readers and TV viewers are in the some-college group, at 28 percent, followed by 27 percent of high school graduates and 23 percent of college graduates.

Twenty-seven percent of the some-college group believe the American Dream is very much alive, compared to 26 percent of college graduates and 18 percent of high school graduates. It is only somewhat alive to 52 percent of the some-college group, and 51 percent of high school and college graduates. There is little faith in the dream among 26 percent of high school graduates and 19 percent of the some-college group and college graduates.

Outlooks on shopping among the three groups, with an index figure of 100 equaling the U.S. average, from Mediamark Research Inc. statistics:

Statement	High School	Some College	College Graduate
Buys by fad	78	117	77
Buys for quality	101	116	108
Buys influenced by neighbors	108	97	105
Buys for self-image	110	90	77

The percentage who put their money in various financial instruments, according to Roper Starch Worldwide:

Statement	High School	Some College	College Graduate
Savings account	41%	39%	31%
Home equity	26	28	29
Mutual funds	18	22	36
Life insurance	18	18	14
Money market funds	13	14	23

Median earnings for all Americans aged 25 and older and for full- time, year-round workers, by education; Census Bureau, Current Population Survey:

ALL MEN

Category	High school	Some College	College Grad
Age 25+	$22,765	$26,873	$40,590
White	24,086	27,563	41,239
Black	16,599	20,732	30,904
Hispanic	18,951	21,872	31,976

ALL WOMEN

Category	High school	Some College	College Grad
Age 25+	13,266	16,611	26,417
White	13,342	16,706	26,289
Black	12,762	15,606	27,745
Hispanic	12,710	16,192	24,542

MEN--FULL-TIME, YEAR-ROUND WORKERS

Category	High school	Some College	College Grad
Age 25+	$26,766	$31,413	$43,855
White	27,332	31,903	45,204
Black	21,311	26,762	33,388
Hispanic	22,163	26,997	34,811

WOMEN--FULL-TIME, YEAR-ROUND WORKERS

Category	High school	Some College	College Grad
Age 25+	18,648	21,987	31,378
White	18,953	22,271	31,441
Hispanic	17,789	22,066	31,197

EDUCATIONAL EXPENDITURES

University expenditures per student across the nation reached an average $15,078 in 1992, with 38.3 percent at public universities paid for by the state, down from about 75 percent in the 1970s. In comparison, U.S. Bureau of Justice statistics show that an average $10,680 is spent per capita on state prison populations, all paid by the state.

While state politicians scramble for money to support their colleges and universities, public school administrators are following the lead of private schools and going after rich benefactors themselves, an educational financial survey shows. They are putting the touch on corporations, however, while private schools mostly rely on wealthy alumni and on tuition increases.

The result is often good news for public school students, who have seen their average tuition, room, and board charges increase only $679 from 1991 to 1994, while the same charges at private schools increased an average $1,686, according to the National Center for Education Statistics (NCES). In 1991 on-campus resident charges at public colleges averaged $5,695, and in 1993 $6,374; in private colleges $14,273 and $15,959, respectively.

Targeting big business for education funds may be fracturing an ancient university tradition, the journal *Governing* says. It gives as an example Ohio State University, which in 1993 entered the exclusive $90 million to over $100 million annual donation club for the first time.

After snaring a $25 million gift from The Limited clothing stores, Ohio named its new Center for the Arts after The Limited's chairman, Les Wexler. It also renamed its business school for oil mogul Max Fisher who gave the school a gift of $20 million. Formerly, universities generally reserved such homage for campus luminaries, the journal points out. Ohio raised $89.2 million in 1993 from gifts.

Thus have eight public colleges and universities edged into the top 20 dean's donations list. The University of California at Berkeley, with $128 million in private donations in 1993, leads the group, behind seven private schools, all located in the East, according to Council for Aid to Education statistics. State funding at Berkeley has fallen off 15 percent since 1987 as its tuition doubled.

Berkeley is followed by the University of Minnesota, which secured $121.8 in gifts in 1993, and Indiana University, which raised $101.2 million. In contrast, Harvard raised $221.8 million to lead all schools in donations. Overall, according to the Council for Aid to Education, business donated $2.26 billion to higher education in 1992.

In 1992 public colleges and universities won gifts from individuals, alumni, and business of $3.6 billion, compared to $5.4 billion for private schools, NCES statistics show. In pre- corporate fund-raising America 1980, public school donations were only $856 million, as against $2.2 billion for private schools.

Below are the top 20 fund-raising colleges in the U.S., according to Council for Aid to Education statistics.

School	Millions raised
Harvard	$221.8
Univ. of Pennsylvania	191.3
Cornell	182.6
Stanford	182.4

Yale	156.3
Columbia	156.2
Duke	144.6
Univ. California-Berkeley	128.6
Univ. of Minnesota	121.8
Univ. of Southern California	110.0
Indiana Univ.	101.2
Univ. of Illinois	100.7
Univ. U of Washington	100.6
New York Univ.	98.6
Univ. of Michigan	98.0
MIT	94.0
Northwestern	93.0
Johns Hopkins	91.0
Texas A&M	90.1
Ohio State	89.2

MATH APTITUDE, STUDENTS

Math has never been as emphasized in U.S. schools as it has been in Europe and Asia, and this lack is showing up in poor math ability among U.S. students. According to the National Assessment of Educational Progress, a testing program for public school students, a dismal 25 percent of American children are proficient at their grade level in mathematical skills.

In 1992, the NAEP tested 250,000 fourth-, eighth-, and 12th- graders from 10,000 schools in 44 states. The results of the exams showed that:

- 82 percent of fourth-graders do not have a sufficient grasp of fractions and decimals.

- 80 percent of eighth-graders and 50 percent of 12th-graders cannot solve problems involving fractions, decimals, and percentages.

- 30 percent–40 percent of Asian American students are proficient in math.

- 20 percent–30 percent of white students are proficient.

- 10 percent of Native American, black, and Hispanic students are proficient.

Scores varied enormously from region to region. Highest were in the Midwest; lowest in the South.

Below are the top and bottom states in eighth-grade math ability (ties are ranked as equal):

Rank	State
1	Iowa
1	Minnesota
3	North Dakota
4	Nebraska
4	Wisconsin

Rank	State
38	West Virginia
38	Arkansas
39	Alabama
40	Louisiana
41	Mississippi

MINORITIES, AND EDUCATION

The number of black high school graduates dropped from a high of 438,000 in 1984 to 302,000 in 1993, while Hispanic graduates increased from 185,000 to 200,000 over the same period. Except for the figure in 1984, black high school graduates per year have remained in the 300,000 range from 1976 to 1993, U.S. Census Bureau reports show. Hispanic high school graduates have hovered in the 100,000 range in that span, reaching a high of 178,000 in 1989.

College-bound blacks increased by 34,000, from 134,000 in 1984 to 168,000, while Hispanics increased by 43,000, from 82,000 to 125,000, according to the American College Testing Program.

Mean monthly income for black high school graduates age 18-24 in 1990 was $1,009, compared to $1,405 for whites and $1,092 for Hispanics. For college graduates with a bachelor's degree the figure was $2,002, compared to $2,552 for whites and $1,895 for Hispanics.

PRESCHOOLS

Preprimary school enrollment in the nation has remained relatively stable since 1975, when five million children age three to five were enrolled in nursery schools or kindergarten out of a population of 10.2 million toddlers. In 1993 that total was 6.6 million of an under-age-five population of 11.9 million.

Nursery school enrollment was three million in 1993 and 1.7 million in 1975, broken down to 1.2 million in public preschools in 1993 and 1.8 million in private schools. Kindergartens handle 3.6 million children, up from 3.2 million in 1975.

Of the total number of children in preschools, 5.2 million are white, 976,000 black, and 726,000 Hispanic. In 1975 those figures were 4.1 million whites and 731,000 blacks. Hispanics were so few in number that any statistics on them were bound to be skewed.

At the age level, one million preschoolers are age three, 2.2 million age four, and 3.3 million age five.

The list below details preschool enrollment, 1970-93, in thousands; source, Census Bureau:

Characteristic	1975	1985	1993
U.S. population, 3-5 years	10,183	10,733	11,954
Total enrolled	4,954	5,865	6,581
Public nursery school	570	848	1,204
Private nursery school	1,174	1,631	1,779
Public kindergartens	2,682	2,847	3,020
Private kindergartens	528	541	577
White	4,105	4,757	5,252
Black	731	919	976
Hispanic	N.A.	496	726
3 years old	683	1,035	1,097
4 years old	1,418	1,765	2,197
5 years old	2,852	3,065	3,306

PRIVATE SCHOOLS

There were a total of 24,690 private schools in the U.S. in 1992, 15,636 elementary, 2,486 secondary, and 6,522 combined schools, educating 4.7 million students.

Average tuition for private secondary schools only was more than $8,000 in 1990-91, according to the U.S. Department of Education which updates its data on private schools less frequently than for public schools.

Of private schools, 35 percent, or 8,731 schools, are affiliated with the Catholic church, and 11,476 with other religious groups. Nonsectarian private schools numbered 34,483.

Private school enrollment is predominantly white. Though the majority of students come from central cities in 1991, a third of all private schools had less than 5 percent black students and another third had black enrollments below 20 percent. Black private school enrollment in 1993 breaks down thus: 107,000 in nursery schools, 69,000 in kindergarten, 266,000 in elementary schools, and 113,000 in high schools.

Almost equally divided between elementary and secondary private schools are 356,285 teachers, 328,624 of them white and 274,521 women. The average salary was $21,673, compared to $33,578 for public school teachers. Male teachers' average salaries were 36 percent higher than women teachers' pay, $27,196 to $19,999.

Private school elementary and secondary enrollment by grade, 1980-93, in thousands; source, Census Bureau:

Grade level	1980	1990	1993
Nursery school	1,354	2,188	1,788
Kindergarten	486	567	681
Elementary	3,051	2,676	2,911
High school	NA	906	970

Number of Catholic schools, pupils, and teachers, 1960-94; source, National Catholic Education Association:

Category	1960	1980	1994
ELEMENTARY			
Number	10,501	8,043	7,114
Pupils	4,373,000	2,269,000	1,992,183
Teachers	108,000	97,000	112,199
Religious teachers	79,000	25,000	10,982
Lay teachers	29,000	72,000	100,400
SECONDARY			
Number	2,392	1,516	1,231
Pupils	880,000	837,000	584,662
Teachers	44,000	49,000	45,002
Religious teachers	33,000	14,000	5,061
Lay teachers	11,000	35,000	38,345

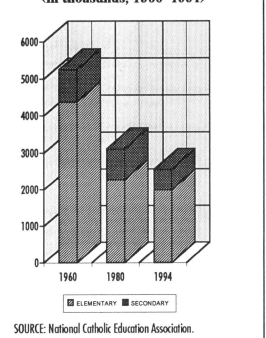

CATHOLIC SCHOOL ENROLLMENT (in thousands, 1960-1994)

ELEMENTARY ■ SECONDARY

SOURCE: National Catholic Education Association.

PUBLIC SCHOOL CONSTRUCTION

As the 1990s progress, American families are becoming less willing to spend big dollars for school construction, according to a 1994 school-bond survey of education construction reported in American School & University. But voter protests do not always doom such plans. Backed by new sources of funding, the nation's school systems spent $10.8 billion on construction in 1993, up 12 percent over 1990, and 43 percent of the $10.8 billion was spent for new schools.

Still, those protests are affecting the overall issuance of school bonds for elementary and secondary schools, the survey found. Total school bond volume in 1993 was $28.9 billion, down 10.9 percent from a record $39.8 billion in 1992 and up only $1.1 billion from $27.8 billion in 1991. In the first six months of 1994 bond issues totaled $11.4 billion, less than half the $23.3 billion during the first half of 1993. In 1989 school bond issues totaled $11.2 billion.

Residents in the southest corridor of the Sun Belt are the staunchest backers of school bonds for rehabilitation and expansio, an attitude necessitated by the population boom due to the economic growth in the area.

Together, Alabama, Florida, Georgia, Kentucky, Mississippi, North Carolina, South Carolina, and Tennessee spent $2.5 billion on education construction in 1993, over objections from some state leaders that education money should be spent on salaries, textbooks, and equipment. The Rocky Mountain region—Colorado, Montana, North and South Dakota, Utah, and Wyoming—spent the least on construction, $309 million.

California led all states with 206 school bond issues, accounting for a total of $3.6 billion. New York was second with 191 issues totaling $2.7 billion, followed by Pennsylvania with 204 issues totaling $2.4 billion. Sparsely populated Vermont was last with three issues worth $14 million.

Voters in Seattle are manning the battlements against school financial support. In February 1994 Seattle voters rejected a $339-million school construction bond proposal—the city's third bond failure since 1992. Similar worries confront school board members across the nation, in addition to contending with poor curriculum and standards, at-risk students, and parental lack of interest in education.

Below are the states with the five highest and lowest overall school bond issuances, ranked by value, and number, in 1993, according to the Securities Data Company:

HIGHEST

State	Value (billions)	Number issued
California	$3.6	206
New York	$2.7	191
Pennsylvania	$2.4	204
Florida	$2.3	31
Texas	$2.3	213

LOWEST

State	Value (million)	Number issued
Vermont	$13.8	3
West Virginia	$22.6	3
Maine	$28.5	3
North Dakota	$38.0	19
New Hampshire	$43.5	9

PUBLIC SCHOOLS SALARIES

Public school teachers in Connecticut on average are the highest paid in the nation, at $49,910 annually, and South Dakota teachers are the lowest paid at $25,059, according to statistics compiled by the National Education Association. The NEA also found that the average raise for teachers in 1993 was 2 percent, the smallest annual percentage increase for public school teachers since 1969.

Teachers in 18 states earn above the national average of $35,723. The average teacher has 15 years of experience. Public school teachers teach 43 million students, up 1.5 percent from 1992. Nevada, Arizona, and Florida had the highest new enrollments at 5.8 percent, 3.8 percent, and 3.1 percent, respectively.

The NEA study, which parallels an earlier survey by the American Federation of Teachers, also found that the percentage of male teachers in public schools has dropped sharply from 32 percent in 1983-84 to 27 percent in 1993-94.

For the first time in more than a decade, local taxpayers have assumed the largest share of keeping their schools running; 47 percent of all elementary and secondary school costs were borne by local taxes.

Below are the states that receive the most revenue from various sources, according to the NEA:

FROM LOCAL SOURCES

State	Percent
New Hampshire	88.8%
Vermont	62.5
Michigan	62.2

FROM STATE GOVERNMENTS

State	Percent
Hawaii	90.3%
New Mexico	75.3
Washington	71.5

FROM FEDERAL GOVERNMENT

State	Percent
Mississippi	17.9%
District of Columbia	12.9
New Mexico	12.8

The 18 states where teacher salaries are equal to or above the average national average, according to the NEA:

State	Avg. Salary
Connecticut	$49,910
Alaska	46,581
New York	45,772
New Jersey	44,693
Washington, D.C.	42,543
Michigan	42,500
Pennsylvania	42,411
Massachusetts	40,852
California	40,289
Maryland	39,463
Illinois	39,387
Rhode Island	39,261
Oregon	37,590
Delaware	37,469
Hawaii	36,564
Minnesota	36,146
Wisconsin	35,990
Washington	35,855

PUBLIC SCHOOL SUPPORT STAFF

Salaries of the nation's public school and college teachers grab the headlines every fall and serve as one measure of educational quality, while according to the National Education Association an army of 1.9 million full-time and 800,000 part-time support workers behind them receives little if any attention. In a historic two-year survey the NEA attempted to redress that oversight.

The NEA study of earnings among "educational support personnel" (ESP) disclosed that the highest-paid public school workers who are not full-time teachers or professors are those in the trades and crafts, and machine operators. The lowest-paid are library clerks.

Adjusted for hours worked per year, tradesmen, craftsmen, and machine operators earn an average $14.77 an hour. Second-highest paid are technical services workers at $13.8 an hour. Library clerks receive $6.90 hourly; cafeteria workers, at $7.72, are second-lowest paid group.

Full-time college ESPs earn an average of $10.10 an hour nationally. The biggest salary gap between ESPs is the average salary by gender. Men receive $11.72 an hour, women $8.04.

Asian Americans lead ESPs in average pay by ethnicity, earning $10.68 an hour. They are followed by whites at $9.45 an hour, blacks at $8.67, and Hispanics at $8.35. College graduates working as ESPs in public schools earn an average $11.12 an hour, those with some college $9.03, high school graduates $8.82, and less than 12 years schooling $8.22.

The following list details the states where salaries among educational support personnel in public schools and colleges, which includes maintenance workers, secretaries, food handlers, is highest and lowest, as estimated by the Educational Research Service:

HIGHEST

State	Est. avg. salary
Alaska	$25,893
District of Columbia	$24,267
California	$23,002
New Jersey	22,852
New York	22,750

LOWEST

Mississippi	12,194
Arkansas	13,162
South Dakota	13,550
Idaho	14,214
Louisiana	14,562

ESTIMATED SALARIES BY JOB GROUP

Job	
Machine operators	$29,488
Technical services	27,737
Security services	23,602
Health and student services	22,945
Maintenance, repairs	20,201
Secretarial, clerical, administrative	20,010
Transportation, delivery, mechanics	19,391
Paraprofessionals	12,425
Food services	11,031

Below are ESPs average hourly earnings, according to the NEA:

Job	1992-93	1993-94	Increase
Building secretary	$11.3	$11.68	3.2%
Bus driver	10.15	10.35	2.0
Cafeteria worker	7.56	7.72	2.1
Central office secretary	11.38	11.74	3.2
Clerk-typist	8.89	9.74	2.9
Instructional assistant	8.31	8.50	2.3
Library clerk	6.65	6.90	3.7
Noninstructional assistant	7.82	8.14	4.1
Payroll clerk	11.30	11.63	3.0

SCIENTIFIC ILLITERACY

Almost 50 percent of working Americans hold jobs requiring the use of advanced information technologies and a continual upgrading of skills, according to the American Association for the Advancement of Science. At the same time another survey estimates that nearly 90 percent of the population is scientifically illiterate.

About 30 percent of Americans believe radioactive milk can be made safe to drink by boiling it, the Congressional Clearing House of the Future found in a 1994 survey and reported in a March 1995 issue of the magazine *Society*. Less than 50 percent know the earth revolves around the sun once a year, and 75 percent do not know that antibiotics are ineffective against viruses.

Almost 60 percent of math courses offered in college in 1994 repeat material offered but which went unlearned in high school. Each year U.S companies spend $300 million to raise employees from their basic skills to a level of technical competence, the National Research Council reports.

The report adds that the average high school student takes one year of science, and more than half of all high school students take less than three years of mathematics. Internationally, the Council found, U.S. 13-year-olds stand near the bottom of industrial-nation students tested in mathematics and scientific ability. The National Science Foundation predicts a shortage of more than 400,000 bachelor degrees in science and engineering is predicted by year 2006.

STUDENTS, EDUCATIONAL ASSESSMENT

Academic skills in American schools in 1993 were only slightly above where they were in 1983, according to the findings of the National Assessment of Educational Progress study taken for the Department of Education. Stronger emphasis on science and mathematics resulted in general improvement in those subjects among nine-, 13-, and 17-year-olds, but reading and writing skills have slipped or remained stagnant, with nine-year-olds falling most sharply in reading. In science, 78 percent of nine- year-olds understood simple scientific principles in 1992, up from 68 percent in 1977. Sixty-one percent of 13-year-olds understood and could apply general informaton about the sciences, up from 49 percent in 1977.

Children nine years old also made gains in math, with 28 percent able to add, subtract, multiply, and divide, up from 20 percent in 1978. Seventeen-year-olds improved in that area, from 92 percent to 97 percent, while their skills at algebra remained constant. Student proficiency in reading achievement showed little change from 1971 to 1992, except in the 13 to 17 age group. The older group gained in understanding, summarizing, and explaining relatively complicated data. The study found that in general, students are reading more.

A sharp increase in writing skills was noted among eighth-graders from 1990 to 1992, but the department pointed out that it was of little significance because the group's size was statistically unusual.

Below are SAT mean scores of college-bound seniors, 1970, 1985, 1993, with a minimum score of 200 and a maximum of 800, according to a College Entrance Examination Board study:

VERBAL SCORES

	1970	1985	1992
Male	459	437	428
Female	461	425	420
Total	460	431	424

MATH SCORES

	1970	1985	1992
Male	509	499	502
Female	465	452	457
Total	488	475	478

SCORES OF 600 OR ABOVE

	1970	1985	1992
Verbal	NA	7%	7%
Math	NA	17	19

SCORES OF 400 OR BELOW

	1970	1985	1992
Verbal	NA	40%	42%
Math	NA	28	28

STUDENTS, PUBLIC SCHOOL

America's public elementary and high schools rolls continued climbing in enrollment in 1994, gaining almost 470,000 pupils to top off at 43.4 million youngsters, the highest level in two decades of steady enrollment growth.

Though the total enrollment is a gain from 1993's total of 43.3 million students, it falls 600,000 short of projections made concerning classroom growth in 1994 by the U.S. Center for Education Statistics.

The largest gains were found at sophomore/junior high schools, which picked up 183,000 students. Senior high schools gained 174,000 and elementary schools 113,000, according to a survey by Market Data Retrieval (MDR) of 250,000 educational institutions and libraries. The company supplies information to businesses that market educational materials.

MDR attributes the continued growth in enrollments to the increase in births beginning in 1977, continuing through the 1980s, and peaking in 1990 at just over 4.1 million. Though births are still above four million, a slow decline has set in, according to MDR, and is expected to continue until the end of the century.

Ken Levinson; courtesy, New York City School Volunteer Program.

The aid and support of the adult community, not just parents, has helped improve performance in many big city school districts such as the one in New York City where the youngster above attends.

Twelve states accounted for 58 percent of the nation's public shcool students below the university level, and in 1994 generated 64 percent of the enrollment growth. All 12 states serve more than one million students each. Florida grew the fastest with a 2.10 percent gain in students, from 2.02 million in 1993 to 2.06 million in 1994, though the increase in raw numbers was greatest in Texas among the 12 states, with a rise of 67,012, compared to Florida's 42,418.

California led the nation in school enrollments, serving 5.3 million students after gaining 44,832 new enrollees. Of 25 states where enrollments grew at a rate above the national average, most are located in the Mountain, Northeast, Midwest, South, and Southwest regions of the country.

The number of teachers reached 2.5 million in 1994, up from 2.4 million the year before; 1.5 million are at the elementary level and one million at the high school level. Average salaries are $35,388, up from $34,632 in 1993. The number of high schoolers graduating rose from 2.26 million to 2.37 million, more than 100,000 below the 2.38 million graduates of a decade ago—despite the fact that high school enrollments have since increased by 3.74 million students.

The following list details the top 12 states in public school enrollment in 1994, the gain from 1993, and the percent gain, from MDR statistics:

State	Enrollment	Gain	%
California	5,252,859	44,832	.86%
Texas	3,665,955	67,012	1.86
New York	2,752,796	34,675	1.28
Florida	2,062,585	42,418	2.10
Illinois	1,893,711	27,104	1.45
Ohio	1,849,561	3,480	.19
Pennsylvania	1,767,357	24,557	1.41
Michigan	1,624,043	2,794	.17
Georgia	1,264,366	25,721	2.08

New Jersey	1,160,777	11,422	.99
North Carolina	1,142,232	9,672	.85
Virginia	1,071,092	6,897	.65

WOMEN IN COLLEGIATE ATHLETICS

Young adult American women are on the march into college stadiums around the country, and a developing trend indicates they may be taking some over, according to a National Collegiate Athletic Association survey.

Backed by federal Title IX guidelines to colleges to increase support for women's sports, college women are taking their cases of neglect to court, and in 1994 they found sympathetic judges in discrimination suits against Brown University, California State, Colorado State, and Indiana University of Pennsylvania. Sixty-five other cases either had gotten to or were on their way to federal courts by late 1994

In addition, the threat of litigation has forced some NCAA schools to eliminate men's non-revenue sports to fund more women's sports. Notre Dame cut its wrestling team in 1994, and the University of Illinois axed its men's swimming team. In the same year, Western Michigan committed itself to spending $1 million a year to bring its women's athletic programs level with men's programs.

Measuring the current gender disparity among its Division I-A member schools, the NCAA survey found in 1992 that male athletes take 72 percent of athletic scholarships, and their programs command 80 percent of athletic operating budgets and 84 percent of recruiting budgets.

Women made up 29 percent of the division's athletes overall, men 71 percent. Women participated in 15 major collegiate sports, the men, 19—there is no female participation in baseball, ice hockey, water polo, or wrestling. Ninety-nine percent of the coaches in men's sports are men, as are 54 percent of the coaches in women's sports.

Total NCAA Division IA athletic program spending for selected years from 1972 to 1993, in thousands, according to NCAA statistics:

Year	Men	Women
1972	$1,300	$0
1981	4,500	300
1985	6,000	400
1989	7,900	1,800
1993	7,000	1,800

FACTS OF LIFE
OVERVIEW

American life is not a seamless tapestry of endless beauty, but a patchwork of conflicts, contentments, incredible highs and disturbing lows. This chapter attempts to paint the vast canvas of everyday life in the U.S. with a brush of statistical information.

While other chapters focus on specific issues, this one is about many things—from what we eat and drink, to the taxes we pay, and a vast array of often unrelated facts that shape our existence.

Some facts of American life eat away at the quality of our lives: late flight arrivals, crime in the streets, and welfare cheating, all of which are reported on in this chapter. Other facts of life are innocuous such as what color Americans choose their hair to be, which hand we prefer to use, or the strange things people see in the night sky. There are some fascinating facts provided about this too. And you will also read about some facts of life that are more than just a curiosity; they are the pleasures we live for—our weekend activities, our favorite foods, our reading habits.

Perhaps the only common denominator of all the data collected in this chapter is that most of it is unrelated and there is often little rationale for the facts being what they are. Dealing with the hodgepodge is part of American life. Knowing about them—and fathoming how we deal with them as successfully as we do—is essential to understanding the American character in all its great diversity.

Here is just a sampling of the curiosities you will find in the pages that follow:
- Americans drink nearly 50 million barrels of Budweiser in a given year, about one barrel for every couple in the U.S.
- Just 15 percent of American women and men are naturally blond, yet about one of every three have blond hair.
- We're eating more bagels and yogurt, and less peanut butter.
- Americans are smoking two-thirds fewer cigars than they were in the early '60s—but the cigars they are smoking are of better quality and are more expensive.
- There are nearly 800 comic book titles and 6,000 comic book stores in the U.S.
- The average sentence for murder in the U.S. is 18 years, 11 months; but the average murder convict serves just eight years, and one month, of his or her sentence.
- 18 percent of Americans have burglar alarms on their houses.
- An average American eats more than 200 eggs and 63 pounds of beef a year.
- One in 10 Americans uses food stamps.

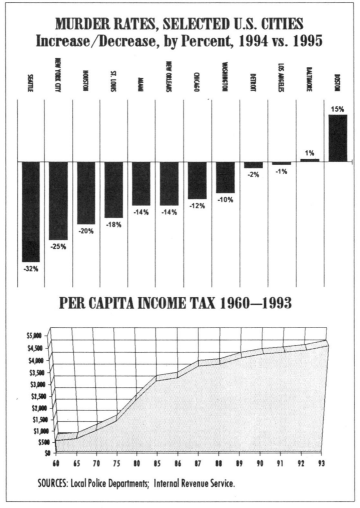

MURDER RATES, SELECTED U.S. CITIES
Increase/Decrease, by Percent, 1994 vs. 1995

SEATTLE -32%
NEW YORK CITY -25%
HOUSTON -20%
ST. LOUIS -18%
MIAMI -14%
NEW ORLEANS -14%
CHICAGO -12%
WASHINGTON -10%
DETROIT -2%
LOS ANGELES -1%
BALTIMORE 1%
BOSTON 15%

PER CAPITA INCOME TAX 1960—1993

$5,000
$4,500
$4,000
$3,500
$3,000
$2,500
$2,000
$1,500
$1,000
$500
$0

60 65 70 75 80 85 86 87 88 89 90 91 92 93

SOURCES: Local Police Departments; Internal Revenue Service.

- Americans throw away about eight times their body weight in garbage every year: 1,300 pounds annually, on average.
- Three million American households lack complete plumbing.
- 3.8 million tons of junk mail clog the nation's mailboxes each year.
- It's 10 times more lucrative to serve on a jury in New York than in New Jersey. New York state pays jurors $50 a day; head across the Hudson to Jersey, and jurors receive just $5 per diem.
- Men are more likely to lie than women; liberals more likely than conservatives.
- About 20 percent of Americans are highly literate; about the same percentage cannot perform simple literacy tasks such as totaling a bank slip or identifying a piece of information in a short news article.
- Forty million Americans change their addresses each year, about 10 times the number that say they've been abducted by aliens.

There's much more, of course. Read on.

ACCIDENTS

Accidents in the U.S. were the fifth leading cause of death in 1993 behind heart disease, cancer, strokes, and lung disease. But Americans are becoming less accident-prone. The death rate in 1993 from accidents was a record low 34.4 per 100,000 population. The total was 88,630. The National Safety Council reports that every 10 minutes two people die from unintentional injuries; about 2,080 persons are disabled every hour.

Auto accidents accounted for the most deaths in the year in question, with a total of 42,000, down from 54,673 in 1970. Second among the principal causes of accidental deaths were falls, totaling 13,500 fatalities in 1993, down from 16,926 in 1970. The number of poisoning deaths continued to climb, reaching 6,500 against a 13-year record low of 3,089 in 1980, at which point they continued to climb to the 1993 total.

Accidental deaths in the home totaled 22,500, with 3,500 resulting from falls, 5,300 from solid or liquid poisons, and 3,200 from fires and burns. Firearms accounted for 800 accidental deaths in the home and 1,600 overall.

The council estimates that the cost of all accidental injuries to Americans in 1993 was $407.5 billion, equivalent to 80 cents of every dollar individuals paid in income taxes or 62 cents of every dollar spent on food that year.

Motor vehicle accidents cost $167.3 billion, equivalent to 800 gallons of gasoline per registered vehicle in the country or a $19,200 rebate on each new car sold. Home injuries of $86.5 billion equaled a $76,800 rebate on each new single family home built in 1993, or 46 cents of every dollar paid in property taxes. Injuries occurring on public properties, such as swimming pools, in a public building, or due to natural disasters, amounted to $58.9 billion, equivalent to a $84,300 bonus for every police officer or fireman in the U.S.

The list below cites principal types of accidental deaths in 1970 and 1993, according to the National Safety Council:

Accident Type	1970	1993
Motor vehicle	16,926	42,000
Falls	16,926	13,500
Poison (liquid or solid)	3,679	6,500
Drowning	7,860	4,800
Fires, burns	6,718	4,000
Choking (food, object)	2,753	2,900
Firearms	2,406	1,600
Poison (gases)	1,620	700

AIR PASSENGERS

Where are all those people going who flood the airports? The facts are that the most traveled routes involve passage to or from the Big Apple—six of the 10 busiest airline routes have New York City as the point of arrival or departure.

This list below shows the most heavily traveled airline routes and the number of passengers who fly them annually, according to the *Travel Industry World Yearbook:*

DOMESTIC DEPARTURES

New York-Los Angeles	2,998,000
New York-Boston	2,948,000
New York-Washington	2,877,000
New York-Miami	2,590,000
Los Angeles-San Francisco	2,423,000
New York-Chicago	2,383,000
Dallas-Houston	2,306,000
Honolulu-Kahului (Maui)	2,055,000
New York-San Francisco	2,042,000
New York-Orlando	2,004,000

FOREIGN DEPARTURES

Mexico	2,696,000
United Kingdom	2,273,000
West Germany	1,209,000
Bahamas	979,000
Japan	973,000
France	845,000
Dominican Republic	655,000
Jamaica	578,000
Italy	458,000
Netherlands Antilles	408,000

AIRLINE SATISFACTION

Since the demise of People's Express, the airline industry has lacked an identifiable arch-fiend, but disgruntled travelers abound.

What's everyone grumbling about? Only one in every 4,000 passengers gets bumped due to overbooking, which translates into a paltry 125,000 travelers per year. Upon arrival, 99.55 percent get their luggage at the baggage claim; the other minute percentage (2.8 million passengers a year) is out of luck. About 80 percent of the flights are on time.

Each year 7,000 passengers complain to the U.S. Department of Transportation about some aspect of airline service. The list below indicates the proportions of consumer complaints, according to the *Air Travel Consumer Report:*

Flight difficulties	1 in 2
Baggage	1 in 5
Refunds	1 in 5
Ticketing problems	1 in 13
Overbooking	1 in 14
Smoking	1 in 35
Fares	1 in 42
Advertising	1 in 134
Credit	1 in 420
Tour problems	1 in 485

ALCOHOLIC BEVERAGE CONSUMPTION

Wine and wine coolers continue to creep up on beer as America's favorite alcoholic drink, with liquor a distant third. The overall drinking pattern in the country points to a more sober public.

Forty-seven percent of U.S. drinkers consume beer, as against 30 percent who prefer wine or wine coolers. Hard liquor is down to 18 percent. Seven in 10 men and six in 10 women call themselves drinkers—about the average for the 55-year history of Gallup polls on the subject.

The percentage of women who drink, which stood at 48 percent in 1989, has rebounded for the first time since 1985 to more than 60 percent.

In 1985, however, 11 percent of the respondents overall said they were drinking more over the previous five years; 10 years later only seven percent say their drinking has increased. The 41 percent who say they are drinking less is a significant increase over the 29 percent who said so in 1984, and whereas in 1984 only two percent planned to quit and 14 percent to cut down, 10 years later eight percent want to quit and 17 percent want to curb their intake.

Though 67 percent of Americans do not see alcohol as a major national problem—down from 81 percent in the early 80s—21 percent favor a ban on the sale of beer, wine, and liquor, up four points from the 1980s and marking the first time since 1966 that prohibitionists have exceeded 19 percent of the populace.

Drinkers outnumber smokers two-and-a-half to 1, but although 21 percent of the public supports outlawing alcohol, only one percent are for a total ban on cigarettes.

When Gallup first asked in 1950 whether drinking was a "cause of trouble" in their families, 14 percent of respondents said it was; in 1994, 27 percent acknowledged that it was—the highest percentage yet recorded.

The tables below represent significant facts from various Gallup surveys:

IS DRINKING A PROBLEM IN THE FAMILY?

Year	Yes	No
1994	27%	72%
1992	24	76
1990	23	76
1989	19	81
1987	24	76
1985	21	79
1981	22	78
1978	22	78
1976	17	83
1974	12	85
1966	12	88
1950	14	86

CAN ALCOHOL CAUSE BIRTH DEFECTS?

Opinion	1982	1987	1994
Agree strongly	57%	69%	81%
Agree somewhat	30	21	10
Disagree somewhat	3	4	3
Disagree strongly	2	1	3
No opinion	8	5	3

PERCENT WHO DRINK, BY GENDER

Year	Total	Men	Women
1994	65%	70%	61%
1992	64	72	57
1990	64	64	51
1989	56	64	48
1988	63	72	55
1987	65	72	57
1985	67	72	62
1984	64	73	57
1983	65	71	58
1982	65	69	61
1981	70	75	66
1979	69	74	64
1978	71	75	64
1977	71	77	65
1974	68	77	61
1966	65	70	61
1958	55	66	45
1957	58	67	50
1952	60	68	53
1949	58	66	49
1947	63	72	54
1945	67	75	60
1939	58	70	45

PREFERRED DRINK

Drink	1990	1992	1994
Beer	51	47	47
Wine	22	27	29
Liquor	23	21	18
All equally	4	4	3
Cordials	NR*	1	0
Wine coolers	NR*	NR*	1
No opinion	NR*	0	2

*No response

BEDROOM ACTIVITIES

Sex and sleep may be the all-time favorite activities in the bedroom, but what comes next? Eating? Entertaining? Surprisingly, slightly more than one in 6 people eat in the boudoir, and almost an equal number entertain there. But what else do most people do?

According to a recent survey of 1,020 men conducted by LDB Interior Textiles, the most popular activities and the percentages that engage in them are as follows:

Activity	Percent
Read	62%
Talk on the telephone	58
Listen to music	51
Watch television	42
Exercise	26
Work	22
Eat	18
Entertain	18

Arkansas	24.9
Oklahoma	25.6
Connecticut	26.6

BEER CONSUMPTION

Aging baby boomers and the health-conscious youth market increasingly turn toward diet soda and sparkling water as their liquid refreshments of choice; legislators plead for higher taxes on alcoholic beverages as a way of generating revenue; a public outraged at drunken driving cries for stricter penalties for violators; and minority groups and women express anger at being targeted by the alcohol industry. All of this adds up to a bear market for brewers. For only the second time in a decade, annual domestic beer sales saw a gain, a paltry one of 0.3 percent, up from 189.8 million barrels in 1991 to 190.4 million in '92.

By and large, beer drinkers are buying American; imported beers filled a negligible share of the market: 8.2 million barrels. A report in *Beverage Industry* magazine in January 1993, by John C. Maxwell Jr. of Wheat, First Securities, found only Anheuser-Busch increasing sales, by one million barrels, to 87 million in 1992. A-B's flagship Budweiser label remained the dominant domestic brand, although its sales slipped 3 percent, to 45.9 million barrels from 47.4 million in 1991. The top gainer was Miller Genuine Draft, up 19 percent, to 8.9 million barrels. Miller High Life dropped 14 percent, to 8.9 million barrels.

The list below shows barrelage (in millions) and the market share percentage of the five top domestic beer brands, according to *Beverage Industry*.

Brand	Barrels	Percent
Budweiser	45.9	24.1%
Miller Lite	18.0	9.7
Bud Light	13.5	7.1
Coors Lite	12.8	6.5
Busch	10.2	5.3

Beer sells better in some places than others. The Southern states have relatively low beer consumption rates—six of the 10 lowest-consuming states are below the Mason-Dixon Line (no doubt a result of many counties in the "Bible Belt" prohibit the sale of alcoholic beverages).

The following states have the highest and lowest annual consumption of beer per adult, according to the book, The Best and Worst of Everything.

HIGHEST CONSUMPTION (IN GALLONS)

State	Consumption
New Hampshire	52.4
Nevada	48.5
Wisconsin	46.7
Hawaii	45.0
Montana	43.3

LOWEST CONSUMPTION (IN GALLONS)

State	Consumption
Utah	21.6
Alabama	24.6

BLONDES

Though only some 15 percent of all American men and women are naturally blonde, according to a Clairol survey 18 percent of women artificially color their hair to various blonde tones. Roughly speaking, that means one in three American women are blondes.

Why blonde? Americans have had a love affair with flaxen hair since Mae West appeared on the silver screen in the 1930s. Blonde Betty Grable dominated the '40s, Marilyn Monroe the '50s. By the 1960s so many female stars had caught on to America's preference for the golden hue that the majority of women in the spotlight were blondes.

A 1991 CBS News story reported that 73 percent of all *Playboy* centerfolds were blondes, as were 70 percent of all magazine cover models, 65 percent of all Miss Americas, and 64 percent of all female TV news personalities.

Whether blondes have more fun, no one knows, but according to one study, they definitely have more publicity. Madonna, who until June 1991 adorned herself with blonde locks, received 42 percent more press coverage from 1986 to 1991 than the second-most popular female headliner, Jane Fonda (an "off-blonde"), followed by Marilyn Monroe (long-deceased

Dolly Parton, one of the seven in ten American celebrities who is blonde, is not just a singer and actress. She is also the owner of Dollywood, a country theme park in Pigeon Forge, Tenn. where she is pictured above.

blonde), Cher (a brunette, at one time a redhead), and Meryl Streep (blonde, of course).

BRAND NAMES VS. STORE NAMES

Highly advertised brand-name consumer products face a growing challenge from cheaper store-brand products at the supermarket in the 1990s, according to surveys of the buying habits of Americans, with milk, bread, and juices the favorite choices of consumers trying to save money.

Some store-brand products already outsell national brands, according to the Private Label Manufacturers Association. A $30 billion market in 1993, private-label purchasing represented seven percent of supermarket, drugstore, and retail outlet spending, up 2 percent from 1992.

Biggest buyers of store-brands—which a national survey dubbed "heavy buyers"—are most likely to be blue-collar workers who live in the South on a $20,000 to $40,000 annual income, typically age 35 to 44. Heavy buyers spend an average of $660 a year on store-brand goods, compared to $5,400 for all consumer packaged items, according to a 1992-93 survey by A.C. Nielsen Consumer Information Services.

The survey found that heavy buyers make up 17 percent of all shoppers in the nation but account for 42 percent of store-brand spending. A second segment, which the survey termed "occasional buyers," spends an average of $260 annually on private-label products, out of $3,800 on all packaged goods. The annual household income of this group ranges from $30,000 to $60,000, with the household head 45 to 64, high-school educated, working part-time, or retired. The largest numbers of occasional buyers are in the East or West. Forty-four percent of all shoppers fall into the "occasional" category; they account for 44 percent of spending on private-label products.

"Infrequent buyers," the third survey segment, are both low and high-income, earning between $20,000 and $60,000 annually, and most likely to be under age 35 or over age 65 and living in the Midwest, according to the survey, reported in the February 1995 issue of *American Demographics*. Infrequent buyers make up 39 percent of all shoppers in the country. They spend less than $90 on private-label products, out of $2,800 on all items, and account for only 14 percent of spending on store-brand products.

Forty percent of heavy buyers live in the South, 37 percent of occasional buyers, and 30 percent of infrequent buyers. About 25 percent of heavy buyers live in the West, 20 percent of the occasional buyers, and 19 percent of infrequent buyers, compared to 19 percent, 20 percent, and 22 percent respectively in the East, and 16, 24, and 28 percent in the Midwest.

Hispanics, who make up seven percent of the Nielsen survey's 40,000-member household panel, account for more than eight percent of heavy buyers, seven percent of occasional buyers, and six percent of infrequent buyers. Blacks, 11 percent of the survey group make up 7 percent of HBs, 10 percent of OBs, and 14 percent of IBs. The 0.1 percent of Asian-Americans on the panel broke down into 0.1 percent heavy purchasers, 0.3 percent occasional, and 1.5 percent infrequent purchasers.

Milk was the store-brand product most likely to be purchased; 70 percent of the heavy buyers, 59 percent of the occasional, and 28 percent of the infrequent buyers of store-brand items bought store-brand milk. Bread runs second at 28.5 percent, 24.5 percent, and seven percent, respectively, and juices third at 30 percent, 23 percent, and seven percent. Medications, remedies, and health aids were at the bottom of the list of 20 items for infrequent buyers, and were not mentioned among the heavy buyers or occasional buyers.

Among newer private-label items on the market, frozen pies gathered more dollars between 1992 and '93 than store-label such as like milk or baked goods, with dollar sales increasing 30 percent in the year. Frozen bagels (15 percent), and yogurt and cookies (about 12.5 percent) followed, while peanut butter dollar sales plunged 12 percent for the year.

Percent of dollars spent on store-brands for the top-10 packaged items purchased in each of the three segments, 1994; source, A.C. Nielsen Consumer Information Services: (Refer to the 3rd, 4th and 5th paragraphs respectively in the opposite for definitions of the various types of buyers listed in the table.)

Item	"Heavy Buyers"	"Occas'l. Buyers"	"Infreq't. Buyers"
Milk	70.0%	59.0%	29.0%
Bread	28.5	24.5	9.5
Juices	30.0	23.5	7.0
Paper products	26.0	8.5	7.0
Packaged meats	23.5	14.5	4.5
Pet foods	21.0	8.5	4.0
Cereal	16.0	6.0	2.5
Snacks	10.2	8.0	4.0
Carbonated drinks	10.0	5.5	3.0
Tobacco	6.0	1.0	N.A.

Top 20 private-label items in descending order purchased by the three segments of shoppers, 1994; source, A.C. Nielsen:

HEAVY BUYERS

Rank	
1	Milk
2	Bread/baked goods
3	Cheese
4	Vegetables, canned
5	Vegetables, frozen
6	Juices/drinks, shelf stable
7	Packaged meat
8	Paper napkins
10	Eggs, fresh

11	Cereal
12	Pet food
13	Sugar/substitutes
14	Juices/drinks, frozen
15	Tobacco/accessories
16	Fruit, canned
17	Snacks
18	Cottage cheese/sour cream
19	Jam/jellies/spreads
20	Packaged milk/modifiers

OCCASIONAL BUYERS

1	Milk
2	Bread/baked goods
3	Juices/drinks, shelf stable
4	Juices/drinks refrigerated
5	Cheese
6	Vegetables, frozen
7	Vegetables, canned
8	Eggs, fresh
9	Paper products
10	Sugar/substitutes
11	Pet foods
12	Packaged meats
13	Juices/drinks, frozen
14	Fruit, canned
15	Vitamins
16	Cereal
17	Cottage cheese/sour cream
18	Snacks
19	Wrapping materials/bags
20	Butter/margarine

INFREQUENT BUYERS

1	Milk
2	Bread/baked goods
3	Eggs, fresh
4	Vegetables, frozen
5	Juices/drinks, shelf stable
6	Paper products
7	Juices/drinks, refrigerated
8	Vegetables, canned
9	Cheese
10	Sugar/substitutes
11	Vitamins
12	Wrapping materials/bags
13	Juices/drinks, frozen
14	Fruit, canned
15	Packaged meat
16	Cottage cheese/sour cream
17	Pain remedies
18	Snacks
19	Butter/margarine
20	Medications/remedies/health aids

Percent change in selected newer private-label product dollar sales, 1992-93; source, A.C. Nielsen:

COMSUMPTION INCREASE/DECREASE

Item	% Change
Frozen pies	30.0%
Frozen bagels	15.0
Yogurt	12.5
Cookies	12.5
Ready-to-eat cereal	9.2
Carbonated soft drinks	9.2
Bread	7.5
Candy	6.5
Mustard	5.0
Frozen orange juice	3.0
Milk	3.0
Frozen mixed vegetables	1.5
Ice cream	1.5
American cheese	1.0
Frozen potatoes	-3.0
Frozen eggs	-4.0
Jams	-5.0
Peanut butter	-12.0

CIGAR CONSUMPTION

Cigar consumption in the U.S. took the plunge along with cigarettes after a Surgeon General's report in 1962 linked tobacco smoking with health problems such as heart disease, cancer, emphysema, high blood pressure, and fetal damage in pregnant women. Cigar Association of America data showed overall cigar consumption declining from an average of 6.1 billion a year in the U.S. to 2.2 billion in 1992. Even Cuban dictator Fidel Castro gave them up in 1985.

But in among the trendsetters, there's a definite move back to cigars, mainly among younger men who smoke more expensive but fewer stogies than their elders. Hand-rolled, premium cigars— usually made of tobacco rolled in a leaf, as opposed to cigarettes, made of fine-cut tobacco and rolled in thin white paper— that sell from $1 have become so popular that shortages appear. The most common price is $2 to $5, with some going as high as $8.50. Men in their 20s and 30s sometimes pay $6 to $7 for a cigar, but buy only a couple a week, tobacconists say. The heat of the cigar trend can be seen in the tony pages of the super-successful *Cigar Aficionado* magazine.

The growing optimism about a cigar revival is believed by some industry watchers to be based on the fact that President Clinton is an avid cigar smoker, as is Chicago's Mayor Daley and Hollywood star Arnold Schwarzenegger, once appointed head of Clinton's Council on Fitness and writer of a newspaper column on fitness. Nevertheless, Clinton has banned smoking in the White House and backs a sharp increase in the tobacco tax.

The optimism, however, does not extend to pipe tobacco, the smallest segment of the industry. According to the Pipe Tobacco Council of Washington, sales have dropped from 60 million pounds of cigar leaves in 1970 to about nine million pounds in 1994 of the total 1.7 billion pounds of tobacco produced in the 16 U.S. states that grow the product.

COMIC BOOK READERSHIP

The billion-dollar comic-book industry of 1992 and 1993 underwent a shakeout in 1994 that sent sales plunging to less than half the 1993 peak, as a proliferation of new titles produced chaos on bookstore shelves. Most sliced up were the large companies: Marvel Comics ("X-Men") and DC Comics (Superman/Batman). In 1991 the two companies controlled 80 percent of the comic-book market. In 1994 their percentage had dropped 50 percent, with Marvel falling 36 percent and DC 48 percent.

About 85 new comic-book companies have wrested sales away from the giants, and another 320 contribute to the 700 to 800 titles—up from about 70 titles 15 years ago and fewer than 50 in 1990— seeking sales in the nation's 6,000 comic-book stores.

The best-seller lists are filled with new-genre comics such as *Spawn, Wetworks, Gen 13, WildC.A.T.S.,* and *Pitt*—none of which are Marvel or DC productions. The two giants did place six entries among the top 10 sellers in one month of 1994. In that month newcomer Image Comics claimed 16 percent of the market with books such as *Spawn*, often a top draw in the market, and *Wetworks* and *Gen 13*.

Below are the 10 most popular comics in mid-1994:

Rank	Title	Publisher
1.	Spawn	Image
2.	X-Men	Marvel
3.	Uncanny X-Men	Marvel
4.	Wetworks	Image
5.	Batman	DC
6.	Gen 13	Image
7.	Wolverines	Marvel
8.	Superman	DC
9.	Superman Man of Steel	DC
10.	Wild C.A.T.S.	Image.

The list below represents the anticipated market share of various publishers in mid-1994:

Marvel	33.51%
DC	20.87
Image	16.58
Others	8.52
Dark Horse	6.93
Valiant	4.73
Malibu	3.94
Wizard	1.65
Defiant	1.11
Topps	1.11
Viz	1.05

Titles, mid-1994, by percent of market:

Non-top 20 publishers	52.6
Marvel	13.5
Other top 20 publishers	8.1
DC	7.3
Dark horse	5.5
Image	3.8
Malibu	3.8
Kitchen Sink	2.8
Valiant	2.2

CRIME

There are mixed reports about whether crime is up or down in America. The cover story of *Time Magazine*, January, 15, 1996 reported that crime was down significantly, however the statistics point to the decrease being mainly in America's largest cities.

A much graver view of crime in America than that presented in *Time* is evident in a separate government report that includes crimes the police never hear about. That survey concludes that violent crimes increased more than three times faster in 1993 than crime overall in America.

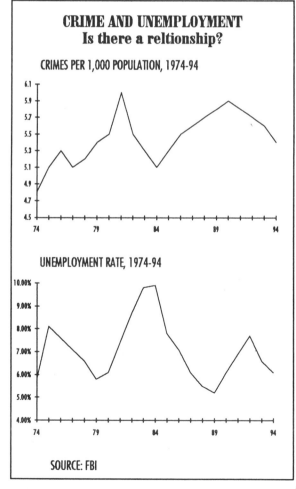

CRIME AND UNEMPLOYMENT
Is there a reltionship?

CRIMES PER 1,000 POPULATION, 1974-94

UNEMPLOYMENT RATE, 1974-94

SOURCE: FBI

Figures released by the FBI and the official figures used nationally in most assessments of the nation's crime rate show violent crimes—murder, forcible rape, robbery, and aggravated assault—decreased one percent in 1993, to 1.8 million from 1.9 million in 1992. A Justice Department survey, on the other hand, said violent crimes rose 5.6 percent, to 10.9 million from its figure of roundly 10.3 million the year before. That is a rate of 51.5 incidents per 1,000 population age 12 and older.

A 1994 FBI survey released at year-end showed a drop of 3.1 percent in crime overall between 1992 and 1993. Reassuring as that may be (and according to other statistics, it may not be), murder and manslaughter increased 2.2 percent. Since 1984 the rate has jumped 20.3 percent for those crimes. In 1965, about 31 percent of murder victims were killed by someone in their own family; by 1993, driven partly by random gang and drug killings, that number was just 11.6 percent.

The FBI, for its yearly Uniform Crime Reports, collects and compiles information submitted by the nation's 10,084 law enforcement agencies. According to the Justice Department, its Bureau of Justice Statistics for the annual Crime Victimization Survey interviews 100,000 Americans age 12 and older with both in-person and telephone contacts.

The total number of personal and household crimes rose about 1.7 percent from 1992 to 43.6 million, the victimization survey found. Adding such violations as purse-snatching and pick-pocketing to personal crimes increased that total to 11.4 million, a 6.7 increase from 1992, at a rate of 53.9 per 1,000 people.

Among violent crimes, there were 9.1 million aggravated assaults, seven million attempted and 2.1 million carried out, an increase of 8.2 percent at a rate of 43 per 1,000 people. FBI statistics found a zero increase in that category for 1993.

Robberies rose one percent and included 481,000 attempted and 826,000 carried out, for a rate of 6.2 per 1,000 people. FBI figures show a two percent decline in robberies in 1993.

Sexual attacks included 160,000 rapes, 152,000 attempted rapes, and 173,000 non-rape sexual assaults, according to the victimization survey. The category was down 20.1 percent, for a rate of 2.3 per 1,000 people. The FBI, which counts only rapes in its statistics, found that category had decreased four percent from 1992.

Property crimes, according to Justice Department figures, remained unchanged from 1992 at 32.2 million incidents, for an overall rate of property crimes of 322.4 per 1,000 people. Including drops in burglary and arson (six percent) motor vehicle theft (four percent), and larceny-theft (two percent), the FBI reported a three percent overall drop in property crimes.

The FBI Crime Index reported decreases in all population groupings in 1993. A five percent drop was recorded in cities with more than one million inhabitants. Rural county law enforcement agencies reported a three percent decrease, and suburban agencies a two percent decrease.

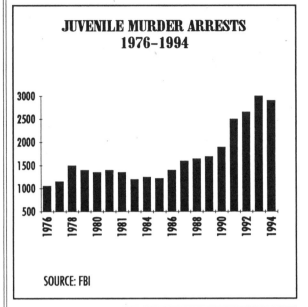

JUVENILE MURDER ARREST 1976–1994

SOURCE: FBI

The following list details average sentences vs. average time served in U.S. prisons for selected crimes, according to Bureau of Justice Statistics figures compiled in 1994 from 1991 data:

Offense	Sentence	Time Served
Murder	18 years, 11 months	8 years, 1 month
Rape	10 years	4 years, 9 months
Robbery	8 years, 10 months	3 years, 4 months
Burglary	6 years, 5 months	2 years, 2 months
Drug offenses	5 years	1 year, 6 months
Weapons offenses	4 years, 1 month	1 year, 9 months

The table below represents expenditures on the Omnibus Violent Crime Control and Prevention Act passed by Congress in 1994, according to federal data:

Agency	Amount
Bill's overall funding	$30.2 billion
LAW ENFORCEMENT	
Overall	$13.5 billion
State and local	10.8 billion
Community policing	8.8 billion
Rural law enforcement	245 million
Technical automation	130 million
Brady bill	150 million
Drug enforcement	1 billion
DNA testing	40 million
Courts, prosecutors, public defenders	200 million
Police Corps scholarships	200 million

FEDERAL

Overall	$2.6 billion
FBI	250 million
DEA	150 million
Border patrol	1.2 billion
U.S. Attorneys Office	50 million
Treasury Dept.	550 million
Justice Dept.	200 million
Federal courts	200 million

PRISONS

Overall	$9.7 billion
Grants for state prisons	7.9 billion
Jailing of criminal illegal aliens	1.8 billion

CRIME PREVENTION EXPENDITURES

Overall	$6.1 billion
Violence Against Women Act	1.6 billion
Crime Prevention Bureau	90 million
"Safe Haven" programs for children	567 million
In-school aid to children	243 million
Community crimefighters	1.6 billion
Model crime programs	626 million
Community job partnership	270 million
U.S., state drug treatment programs	383 million
Crime prevention grants	377 million
Drug courts	1 billion

CRIME, ADAPTATION TO

Americans are increasingly afraid to walk outdoors alone at night, fear being attacked while driving a car, frightened of home burglary, and scared of being beaten, knifed, shot, or sexually assaulted. Fifty-one percent of respondents in a Gallup Poll say they "have a gun in the house."

Persons among the 1,244 polled by Gallup who have been crime victims during the past year climbed from five percent in 1992 to 11 percent in 1993. Blacks and whites both see crime on the rise, blacks at 88 percent and whites at 87 percent. Thirty-four percent of blacks know someone who was a victim of crime in the past year, as do 31 percent of whites.

Black respondents perceive an increase in their neighborhood crime more than do whites, 51 percent to 42 percent, and in violent crimes, 41 percent to 30 percent. Thirty-five percent of women surveyed were in the poll's "most fearful" group, as were 15 percent of the men, 39 percent of blacks, and 23 percent of whites. Thirty-three percent of city people are in the group, and 24 percent of suburbanites and rural citizens.

According to the pollsters, fear is increasing demand not only for guns but for locks, guard dogs, burglar alarms, whistles, car alarms, auto wheel locks, and friendly neighbors to walk with at night.

The number of Americans who have installed special locks has increased from 13 percent in 1981, to 43

percent in 1993. Ownership of guard dogs is up to 38 percent, from 20 percent, of installed burglar alarms

With crime rates up, so is the growth of businesses like the Chicago firm above.

18 percent from five percent, and of whistles carrying 10 percent from five percent.

Below are various findings about how Americans adapt to crime according to a 1993 Gallup Poll. The right-hand colum represents the percentage of U.S. households that own guns.

IF GUN OWNED IN HOUSEHOLD

Belongs to	Men	Women	U.S.
Respondent	32%	52%	14%
Someone else	16	5	25
Both husband and wife	3	2	4
No gun in household	48	39	56
No opinion	1	2	1

SPECIAL LOCKS INSTALLED

	Yes	No
Male	40	60
Female	46	54
East	36	64
Midwest	39	61
South	50	50

West	45	55
Black	48	52
White	42	58

DO NOT WALK ALONE AT NIGHT

Male	23	75
Female	56	40
East	40	57
Midwest	35	61
South	43	54
West	42	55
Black	41	55
White	40	57

HAVE GUARD DOG

Male	35	65
Female	41	59
East	30	61
Midwest	29	71
South	40	60
West	44	56
Black	27	73
White	39	61

BOUGHT A GUN

Male	36	63
Female	25	75
East	18	82
Midwest	23	76
South	40	59
West	38	62
Black	31	68
White	30	69

OWN BURGLAR ALARM

Male	20	80
Female	16	84
East	17	83
Midwest	14	85
South	21	78
West	18	82
Black	25	75
White	16	83

CARRY WHISTLE

Male	4	96
Female	16	84
East	8	92
Midwest	10	90
South	10	90
West	14	86
Black	12	88
White	10	9

EGG CONSUMPTION

Nothing breaks easier than an egg, but American egg producers know how to keep the damage down and production up. Each year they supply the nation with about 68 billion eggs, almost all of which are perfect when the chickens lay them, but all that changes once the human hand enters the equation. As a result, you can expect to find one broken egg in every 24 cartons that leave the farm. By the time they get to the supermarket, one in 10 cartons will have a broken egg.

America is consuming fewer eggs, and egg production has been dropping precipitously in the last 10 years, presumably because Americans are increasingly aware of the cholesterol in egg yolks.

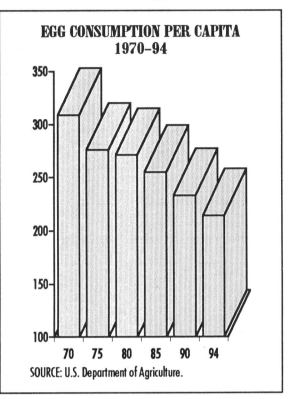

EGG CONSUMPTION PER CAPITA 1970–94

SOURCE: U.S. Department of Agriculture.

The list below, compiled by the Department of Agriculture, represents the per capita consumption of eggs in the U.S. between 1970 and 1990:

1970	309
1975	276
1980	271
1985	255
1986	254
1987	254
1988	246
1989	236
1990	233

According to the American Egg Board, of the more than 200 eggs the average American will eat this year, below is how they are eaten:

Scrambled	34%
Fried	31
Boiled	23

HOW AMERICA EATS ITS EGGS

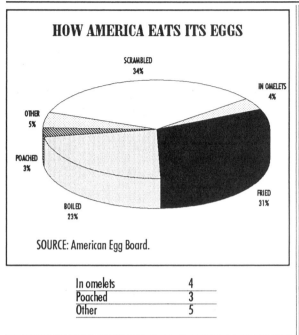

SCRAMBLED 34%

IN OMELETS 4%

OTHER 5%

POACHED 3%

FRIED 31%

BOILED 23%

SOURCE: American Egg Board.

In omelets	4
Poached	3
Other	5

EMERGENCY ROOM VISITS

Americans made at least 90 million visits to hospital emergency rooms in 1992, and 18 percent of the adult visitors could have been safely told to get help elsewhere, thus clearing the way for treatment of patients with devastating illnesses or injury. This same conclusion was reached in several other recently published studies.

Nearly 90 percent of the patients who visited a California ER for non-emergency treatment believed they needed immediate help, 44 percent making the visit on their doctor's orders, a 1994 study published in the March 1995 *Annals of Emergency Medicine* showed. Once those people safely arrived at the ER, 18 percent could have been sent elsewhere, a study in the same issue of the journal said.

None of 216 pregnant patients in a Medicaid managed-care program who arrived at the ER on their own volition and were sent to their regular pediatrician suffered ill effects, according to a study in the February, 1995, issue of the journal *Pediatrics*.

Nationwide, the cost of those who could have been turned away but were treated in the ER was between $5 billion and $7 billion, mostly because the care the patients received would have been cheaper had they seen their own doctor, according to the journal *Health Affairs*. An upper respiratory infection, for example, was estimated to cost $41 in a doctor's office and $113 in an ER because of expensive equipment and staff.

FASHION, WOMEN'S

More American women are favoring casual attire, and even business is getting the message, with many companies instituting "dress down Fridays" that allow employees are allowed to wear colored shirts and jeans.

Some companies, such as ALCOA of Pittsburgh, have found that letting employees dress as they wish had such a positive impact on morale and productivity that "dressing down" has become its rule, according to one survey.

In 1993, 75 percent of women had bought at least one pair of pantyhose in the past six months, a decline of seven percent from 1986, Mediamark Research of New York found. Another survey by Roper Starch Worldwide found that only 26 percent of women wore pantyhose every day in 1992. Most likely to still wear the hose every day are executive and professional women (49 percent) and other white-collar women (43 percent). Least likely are blue-collar women (22 percent) and homemakers (11 percent).

Along with the shift of women to tights, pants, or bare legs, other factors caused the makers of L'eggs and Hanes Hosiery to see a decline in sales of five percent in the last three months of 1992 and eight percent in the first quarter of 1993. These include the view at the International Apparel Mart in Dallas that women of the 1990s are thriftier than those of the '80s, and that pantyhose, while not expensive per pair, are run-prone and expensive ultimately because of frequent replacement. According to a survey by EDK Associates of New York City, 39 percent of women say pantyhose rip too easily, while 31 percent say they are hard to put on. Seventeen percent say that even if one gets them on without a run, the waist binding is the worst thing about them, and 17 percent say they itch.

The trend toward casual wear is causing a boom in the hosiery industry overall, according to *Women's Wear Daily*. From New York to California department stores and discounters are stocking colored tights, thigh-highs, boot, over the knee, and trouser socks as the decline in pantyhose sales extended into 1994.

Knee socks and thigh highs are popular in New York, cotton anklets, athletic socks, and "anything white," in the Midwest, and Hot Sox anklets, knee highs, colored tights, and trouser socks on the West Coast, where one chain, Gottschalk's, reported a 1994 increase of 12 percent in casual sock sales over 1993, while pantyhose were down four percent.

Women's dress shoe sales also are in a slump, according to Roper Starch. Between 1985 and 1992, the year experts say the casual trend began in earnest, the proportion of women who wore high-heeled shoes at least twice a week declined from 38 to 26 percent. And the share of professional women who had bought a pair of dress shoes in the past year had plunged from 57 percent to 30 percent.

FOOD, FAVORITES

Among the list of 10 favorite foods in the nation for lunch and dinner, pasta claimed two spots, according to a 1993 poll. Macaroni and cheese ranked No. 7, and spaghetti No. 9. In 1983, macaroni and cheese placed eighth, and spaghetti was not on the list.

Since 1984 the number of times Americans ate pasta in a two-week period rose 24 percent and placed the food in the No. 3 position in dinner foods that have shown increasing appeal to Americans. Tacos and burritos were tied for first, pizza was second, oriental food third, and rice fifth.

Meatless pasta dish choices increased to 55 percent of in-home pasta meals in 1993, up from 49 percent in 1984. Twenty-seven percent of in-home pasta meals were made Italian-style with meat, according to a survey made by the NPD Group, Inc., of Chicago, which follows U.S. eating trends.

Middle-income families eat pasta most often, the survey found, with 94 percent serving it at least once in two weeks, followed by affluent families at 92 percent and working-parent families at 88 percent. Children age six to 12 eat more pasta than any other age group, and an average of 73 percent of seniors eat pasta at least once every two weeks.

At the grocery, 36.2 percent of shoppers choose long pastas such as spaghetti and linguine over short goods such as elbows and twists, at 34.5 percent. Specialty pastas such as lasagna, jumbo shells, and manicotti are least chosen, at 12 percent of shoppers. Noodles with added egg are chosen by 17.3 percent.

Americans buy more dry pastas in package form at retail more than all other pasta products, purchasing 1.3 billion pounds in the period 1992-1993, up from 1.2 billion pounds in the period 1991- 1992, an increase of 4.5 percent, according to Information Resources, Inc. Dry salad and side-dish mixes are next favored, at 70.7 million pounds, up from 47.6 million pounds in 1991-1992, a 48.5 percent gain in a year. Pastas used in dry soup (193 million pounds) and canned soup (252 million pounds) are next- favored, followed by refrigerated salads (10.5 million pounds). These were up 6.3 percent, 2.4 percent, and 77.5 percent respectively. Biggest percentage leap from 1991-1992 to 1992-1993 to consumers was pasta used in frozen baby food— 52,022 pounds compared to 19,864 pounds, a change of 162 percent.

Meatless pasta dishes in percentage of all pasta eatings, according to NPD Group's National Eating Trends Service statistics:

Year	Percent
1984	49%
1985	50
1986	50
1987	49
1988	50
1989	50
1990	53
1991	53
1992	54
1993	55

With jobs in sanitation growing 200 percent through the year 2005, garbagemen like the one above have good reason to smile. Another reason may be their average salary, over $30,000 annually.

FOOD STAMP FRAUD

Since cuts in investigative staff of the Department of Agriculture's in the 1980s, food stamp waste and fraud cost taxpayers $3 billion annually, or more than 10 percent of the program's 1995 revenues of $26 million, according to the department. The program's growth has reached a point in 1995 where one in 10 Americans use the stamps.

Among perpetrators of fraud are sham retailers who operate without grocery inventories and buy food stamps for 50 cents to 70 cents on the dollar, the Agricultural Department says. These stamps then are traded in for merchandise from legitimate retailers who redeem them at face value from the government.

A case cited by the department before the House Agriculture Committee in February 1995 was a 1994 arrest of 29 persons charged with a $40 million money-laundering scheme involving food stamps.

GARBAGE

No nation in history has produced the volume of garbage that America has. We burn it, ship it cross-country on barges, bury it, recycle it, even catalogue it to analyze our way of life. Here is a profile of what we throw away:

Paper products	37%
Yard waste	18
Metal	10
Glass	10
Food waste	7
Plastic	6
Wood	4
Other	6

The average American throws away almost 1,300 pounds of garbage annually, about 100,000 pounds over a lifetime, which includes almost 15,000 pounds of food. In addition, the average American disposes of 10,370 aluminum cans, 67 tires, 487 pens, and 609 razors.

Below is a breakdown by pounds of lifetime garbage for the average American:

Disposition	lbs.
Sent to landfills	76,548
Recycled	10,525
Converted to energy	5,741
Incinerated	2,871

GARLIC CONSUMPTION

About one million 100-pound bags of garlic were sold on the fresh market for use in the home and in food service operations. An additional four million bags were dehydrated for use as salt, flakes, powders, in packaged foods, in the commercial preparation of catsup, mustard, and sausages, in pickles, sauces, and condiments, and for garlic powder pills and garlic oil perles sold in health food stores.

Twenty-one years later, in 1992, according to the Agriculture Department, California has 27,000 acres devoted to the bulb, producing 417 million pounds of garlic in five counties— Monterey, San Benito, and Santa Clara in the coastal regions, and in the internal counties of Fresno and Kern. That is more pounds than California produces in asparagus (151 million), snap beans (325 million), eggplant (100 million), honeydew melons (415 million), and radishes (150 million). In 1994, the price of garlic hovered between $2 and $3 a pound in the nation's supermarkets.

According to the Fresh Garlic Association, California produces approximately 90 percent of the domestic dry, paperlike-sheathed product, and its quality is rated the best in the world. An additional 540,000 bags are grown in Texas and Louisiana, and more is imported from Mexico, Argentina, Chile, Taiwan, Spain, Guatemala, and the Netherlands. Mexico accounts for 65 to 75 percent of the imports; Argentina and Spain about 20 percent; the rest 5 percent.

The association, explaining garlic's popularity in America today, says increased consumption began in the post-war years when home cookery included gingerly rubbing salad bowls with a clove of garlic, and when garlic bread first began to be served. As American travelers began invading Europe in the 1960s and '70s they learned about such treats as whole heads of baked garlic served with crusty bread as an appetizer or as an accompaniment to main dishes, in stuffed mushrooms, and in pesto and sauted scampi.

HATE CRIMES

In its first report ever on the subject of hate crimes, the FBI confirmed what everybody knows: This country still has a serious race relations problem. In a survey of 2,771 law enforcement agencies out of the 16,000 nationwide that report to it on murders, aggravated assaults, and robberies, the FBI found 4,558 hate crimes in the U.S. in one year. More than half of them — 2,963 in all — stemmed from racial bias. The racial violence was twice as likely to be directed toward blacks as toward whites. Fully 35.5 percent of all the hate crimes were directed toward blacks because of their race, 18.7 percent toward whites because they were white.

Flamboyant participants who go to gay libertion parades, such as the attendees above, don't necessarily contribute to homophobia. Hate crimes against gays are among the lowest of all assults on minorities.

But intolerance doesn't stop there. Of the remaining hate crimes, religious belief served as the reason in 27.4 percent of the crimes. Ethnic bias was next, at 9.5 percent, and sexual orientation (mostly directed against homosexuals) accounted for 8.9 percent.

Unlike other crimes, in which guns or knives are used, hate crimes are often perpetrated with psychological weapons. Intimidation was the most common weapon used; in 1,614 incidents, or 33.9 percent, it was the preferred means of torment. Vandalism was next, with 1,301 incidents, 27.4 percent of the total. Simple assault occurred 796 times and aggravated assault, 773 times. In 12 instances, the violence resulted in the victims' death. Seven forcible hate-rapes were reported. The Hate Crime Statistics Acts of 1990 required the FBI to compile the figures but did not require all law enforcement agencies to participate.

HIGHWAY MILEAGE

Each year Americans travel more than 1.4 trillion miles on the nation's major highways in about 190 million vehicles. Sometimes it seems as though everyone in the country is behind the wheel, and that you are on the most crowded stretch of highway of all. That may be the case, at least if you are on the Beltway around Washington, D.C.; it's the nation's most crowded road.

Following are the states with the most-traveled roads, and the number of cars per thousand residents.

Washington, D.C.	N/A
New Jersey	731
California	737
Hawaii	696
Maryland	754
Connecticut	798
Massachusetts	619
Florida	714

The list below cites the number of various kind of vehicles on the nation's roads, as determined by the Department of Transportation.

Automobiles	142,500,000
Trucks	43,000,000
Motorcycles	4,200,000
Buses	600,000

IN VITRO FERTILIZATION

Roughly 8.5 percent of U.S. married couples are infertile, and thus many seek children by in vitro fertilization, where the sperm is fertilized outside the body and the resulting embryo is later transplanted into the uterus for gestation.

Many couples, however, undergo several cycles of egg harvesting, test-tube fertilization, and embryo implantation before a baby is born, each cycle adding

to the cost, according to a study in the July 28, 1994, *New England Journal of Medicine*. In addition, in vitro babies often are premature, smaller and sicker, and require more extensive and expensive care.

The 1992 average cost of an in vitro-produced birth in one cycle was $67,000, another study showed. The cost climbed to $114,000 per delivery after the mother had gone through six cycles.

When the mother is age 40 or more and the husband infertile, delivery costs can climb even higher, from about $160,000 for one cycle of treatment to $800,000 for couples needing six cycles or more, according to a study from the HOPE Center for Health Affairs in Bethesda, Maryland, published in the August 6, 1994, issue of the journal *Science*.

HOUSING ARRANGEMENTS

The U.S. had about 93 million occupied housing units in 1993—out of a total of 105 million units nationwide—to house a U.S. Census population projection of 257 million Americans. Occupied dwellings house, on average, 2.7 persons. There has not been a significant change in household size since 1989.

Public water and sewer service is available in the vast majority of these units, and 51 million are heated by gas, 27 million by electricity. Fireplaces heat 1.3 million units, fuel oil and kerosene, 12.4 million, coal or coke 319,000, and wood or other fuel, 4.9 million.

Kitchen facilities are lacking in four million units, and complete plumbing facilities in three million. Telephones are available in 94.8 million units, air conditioning in 29 million, frost-free refrigerators in 75 million, and television sets in 90.3 million.

Sixty-four million Americans are homeowners living in 60 million owner units, 35 million of which have mortgages. Across the nation the median monthly cost for owner units is $455, for mortgage holders $761, and for wholly owned home owners $222. The average value of homes in the U.S. is $80,000.

Of the nation's total housing units, 33 million were occupied by renters in 1991, with rents at a median of $462 a month, according to the Bureau of the Census. Whites occupied 25.3 million rental units, a total that has increased steadily since 1970, when it was 19.6 million. Blacks occupied 7.9 million units, up from 3.9 million in 1970. Census figures from 1990 show that Hispanics occupied 3.4 million of the nation's rental units, Asians or Pacific Islanders 963,553, and American Indians, Eskimos, and Aleuts 273,371.

JUNK MAIL

Each year Americans receive over 60 billion pieces of "junk mail"—that is, advertisements from bulk mailers. The bulk mail industry in 1992 grossed $210 billion and sent out 3.8 million tons of mail, to 118 million addresses, all but 0.8 percent of American homes.

With the cost of disposing of U.S. garbage skyrocketing from $30 billion in 1992 to an estimated $45 billion in 1995, the issue is what to do with the mail after it is thrown away. "Trees are renewable," concluded an environmental task force of Direct Mail Association (DMA) members in 1989 looking into the proliferation of junk mail in America. "We see the real issue as landfills." It is estimated that only one or two percent of direct mail letters are answered, with the rest going into landfills. DMA is a Farmington, N.Y., association that purges names from most mailing lists for its members.

More than 42 percent of Americans want less junk mail, according to the U.S. Postal Service, and 2.5 million have joined the DMA, looking for relief. Yet junk mail is a $210 billion-a-year industry using 50,000 different mailing lists that sends out 3.8 million tons of mail to almost every home in the country. The services of 3.5 million people are involved in creation and distribution of the mailings. A Postal Service survey found that only 11 percent of the avalanche sent out remains unopened, and five percent of those surveyed want more. Fifty-five percent of Americans shop by mail or phone.

Recognizing the landfill crisis, some giant mailers, such as AT&T, which mails out 250 million pieces a year, are turning to recycled paper. According to a DMA Mail Preference Service survey, 50 percent of mailers bought recycled paper in 1992, and 85 percent planned to do so.

Catalog mailers, who send out 12 billion mailings of more than 10,000 different catalogs a year, also are taking the hint. Their trade magazine, *Catalog Age*, says recycled paper use for catalogs has more than doubled since 1992, and 38 percent of catalog mailers used it in 1994.

JURY PAY

Because of the low pay to jurors in the U.S. court system, hardship exemptions from long trials often lead to juries that are less than representative, according to experts. Jury pay throughout the country ranges from $5 to $50 a day, and if company policy is to cut off one's salary while the employee serves in what looms as a lengthy trial, exemption is asked for and most often given, leaving the selections from among the elderly, the unemployed, and government workers who are assured of continued salary while they serve.

Five states pay $50 a day: New York, Colorado, Wyoming, Connecticut, and Indiana. Alaska pays $25 for half a day of service. Two states pay the low of $5, New Jersey and California. One state, New Mexico, pays $4.25 an hour. All federal courts pay $40 a day.

Alabama and Nebraska are among the few states that require a company to continue paying full salary to an employee on jury duty, which rarely lasts longer than 10 days. Some companies pay the difference between jury pay and salary; the policy of most companies that continue full salary payments is to limit them to 10 to 30 days of jury duty.

While 27 states have eliminated occupational exemptions, and seven put limits on them, hardship exemptions are generally freely given. Federal and state laws forbid employers from firing workers chosen for duty on juries.

The following list details jurors' daily pay by states, plus the District of Columbia, according to the National Center for State Courts:

State	Pay
Alabama	$10
Alaska	25 (half-day)
Arizona	12
Arkansas	20
California	5
Colorado	50
Connecticut	50
D.C.	30
Delaware	15
Florida	15
Georgia	35
Hawaii	30
Idaho	10
Illinois	15
Indiana	50
Iowa	10
Kentucky	13
Kansas	10
Louisiana	12
Maine	10
Maryland	15
Massachusetts	15
Michigan	15
Minnesota	15
Mississippi	15
Missouri	6
Montana .	25
Nebraska	20
Nevada	30
New Hampshire	30
New Jersey	5
New Mexico	4.25 (hourly)
New York	50
North Carolina	30
North Dakota	25
Ohio	10
Oklahoma	13
Oregon	10
Pennsylvania	25
Rhode Island	15
South Carolina	10
South Dakota	40
Tennessee	10
Texas	30
Utah	17
Vermont	30

Virginia	30
Washington	25
West Virginia	15
Wisconsin	16
Wyoming	50

LAUNDRY

Men do almost a third of the 419 million loads of laundry Americans wash at home every week, but only seven percent of wives trust their husbands to do a good job of it, according to a detergent manufacturer's survey. Whom do they trust most? Themselves—that's what almost four fifths of the respondents (79 percent) said. Only six percent trust their mothers, and only three percent trust their grown kids.

The survey by detergent manufacturer Lever Brothers found that 43 percent of the women wash seven loads of laundry a week, while 19 percent of men do. Not all single men wait until disaster looms; 36 percent push the starter button four times a week, and 13 percent do seven or more loads a week.

Ignored in the statistics are the male "laundry haters," who do their three or four loads once every three or four weeks. One of these untallied respondents said he hadn't replenished his detergent supply in almost a year.

LEFT–HANDEDNESS

The Aristera Organization of Westport, Conn., has found that both the mentally retarded and the academically superior include more left-handers than the general population. But left-handedness brings its share of problems. A disproportionate share of lefties wind up in hospital emergency rooms. Why? Door injuries, one of the most common, affect left-handed people more because most doors open from the right.

Some one in 10 people are naturally left-handed. Among children, one in seven are; however, many are pressured to change and therefore go through a "clumsy" period while in transition.

When Dr. Charles Graham of the University of Little Rock studied 761 children treated at emergency rooms, he concluded that being a lefty carries a decided "risk factor." He found that accident patients were 1.7 times more likely to be lefties, and male lefties (who outnumber females two to one) were twice as likely to have accidents as females. Previous studies have found that lefties die younger, presumably from accidental deaths.

Once grown up, however, left-handers have a great advantage: They are less in danger from being incapacitated by a stroke because, unlike right-handers, they have speech control on both sides of the brain, so damage to one side can be offset.

LIES

When we don't lie, say the authors of *The Day America Told the Truth*, a book revealing some of America's darkest secrets, 45 percent of the time it is because we feel that lying is wrong; only 17 percent of the time do we refrain from lying for fear of being caught.

The book defines serious lies as those that violate trusts, hurt people, cause legal problems, or are totally self serving.

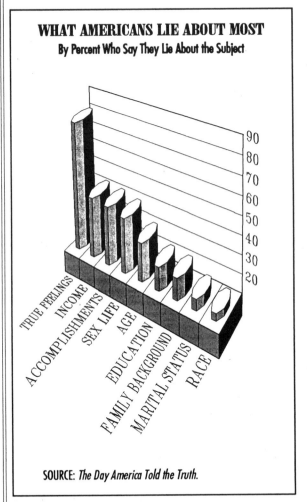

WHAT AMERICANS LIE ABOUT MOST
By Percent Who Say They Lie About the Subject

SOURCE: *The Day America Told the Truth.*

According to the findings, here is how serious liars break down:

- Men (40%) vs. women (31%)
- Homosexuals/bisexuals (52%) vs. heterosexuals (33%)
- Blacks (51%) vs. whites (33%)
- Catholics (36%) vs. Protestants (34%) vs. Jews (25%)

- Unemployed (42%) vs. employed (34%)
- Liberals (37%) vs. conservatives (29%)
- Ages 18—24 (50%)
- Ages 25—44 (34%)
- Ages 45—64 (29%)
- Ages 65 and older (19%)
- People earning less than $10,000 annually (49%) vs. those making $45,000 or more (31%)

Below are the dominant subjects Lied about in percent of respondents who say they have lied about the matter; source: The Day America Told the Truth:

True feelings	81%
Income	43
Accomplishments	42
Sex life	40
Age	31
Education	23
Family background	22
Marital status	16
Race	14

LITERACY

As America storms into an ever-broadening and deepening information society, the nation's literacy level is found wanting, according to a recent National Adult Literary Survey funded by the U.S. Department of Education. Complex data, comparisons, integrations, and arithmetical problems all are daily workplace challenges, yet the study shows that almost half the adult population is in the bottom two of five rankings for literacy.

Another report, "America's Choice: High Skills or Low Wages," from the National Center on Education and the Economy (NCEE), shows that already there is a widening division in earnings in the population.

Since 1980 the earnings gap between white-collar workers and skilled tradespeople has risen from two percent to 37 percent, and between the college-educated, whose earnings have climbed 10 percent, and high school graduates, whose earnings have declined nine percent, according to the NCEE report. Black family poverty is nearly three times that of whites. In the nation overall, one child in five is born into poverty; among minority families the figures are one in two.

The Department of Education studied 13,600 people aged 16 and over, plus 12,000 in 12 cooperating states, and 1,100 inmates of federal and state prisons in a separate prison population survey. All told, more than 26,000 adults were interviewed, a representative of the U.S. adult population of 191 million. The National Center for Education Statistics published its first report on the survey in 1994.

Literacy was rated in progressive stages from one to five in reading prose, understanding documents, and dealing with numbers, one being the lowest. At this level, 21 to 23 percent of the participants were unable perform simple tasks such as totaling an entry in a bank deposit slip, identifying a piece of information in a short newspaper article, or locating the time and place of a meeting on a form. Thirty-three percent of the participants in Level 1 were age 65 or older; 23 percent were black, 50 percent white, 22 percent Hispanic, three percent Asian, and one percent American Indian. The remainder were immigrants, high school dropouts, and the health-impaired.

The study defined level 2 as the ability to locate information in text, make minor inferences using printed material, calculate the total cost of merchandise, and locate an intersection on a street map. Twenty-one percent of the participants—representing 40 to 44 million of the 191 million adults in the nation, and 41 to 44 percent of those living in poverty—were found to be at this level. Level 2 breaks down as the elderly (16 percent), blacks (15 percent), whites (72 percent), Hispanics (10 percent), Asians (two percent), and American Indians (one percent).

Between 25 and 28 percent of the participants—representing about 50 million adults nationwide—showed higher skills but a still limited ability, placing them at level 3. Those who gained level 3 were asked to perform an arithmetical problem stated by inference rather than explicitly, read a bar graph, and find the time of bus travel from one location to another on a Saturday.

Of the nearly 33 percent of the original participants who remained through Level 3, representing 61 million adults nationwide, 55 percent were aged 25 to 44. The elderly made up 10 percent of level 3, blacks six percent, Hispanics six percent, and Asians and American Indians two percent and one percent, respectively. Whites made up 85 percent of the level 3 group, and the health-impaired dropped from 12 percent to seven percent.

Between 18 percent and 21 percent of the participants performed at the most difficult stages, levels 4 and 5, demonstrating an ability to contrast information in long and complex texts, calculate charges on a home loan, estimate the price per ounce of item at the supermarket, and rely on background knowledge to solve a problem.

MARCHES ON THE CAPITOL

Were there one million men who marched on the U.S. Capitol, October 16, 1995? Nation of Islam leader Louis Farrakhan thinks so and so do others—the "Million Man March, nonetheless was the biggest rally ever on the Capitol."

The Gay Rights March of April 25, 1993, may have been one of the largest marches on Washington — or one of the smallest, depending on who you listen to. The National Park Service estimated that 300,000 people attended; however, the local government in Washington estimated the crowd at one million—leaving 700,000 people possibly swinging in the wind around the Washington Monument. In April 1992, Park Service and D.C. police initially estimated a National Organization for Women abortion-rights crowd at 500,000. The Park police later lowered its estimate to 250,000, then returned to its original figure. In May 1992, local police estimated that a protest demanding more federal aid to cities drew 150,000 demonstrators; the Park police estimate was 600,000. And so it goes.

This is a list of the largest marches or rallies in Washington and the number of attendees, according to the National Park Service police.

- Million Man March (10/16/1995)—400,000*
- Vietnam War Moratorium Rally (11/15/69) — 600,000
- Abortion Rights March (4/5/92) — 500,000
- Vietnam War "Out Now" rally (4/24/71) — 500,000
- 20th anniversary of Martin Luther King Jr.'s civil rights march (8/20/83) — 300,000
- Abortion rights march (4/9/89) — 300,000
- Gay rights march (4/25/93) — 300,000
- Solidarity Day labor march (9/19/91) — 260,000
- Civil rights march (8/28/63) —250,000
- Solidarity Day labor march (8/31/91) — 250,000
- Anti-abortion march (4/28/90) — 200,000
- Abortion Rights march (11/12/89) — 200,000
- Gay Rights march (10/14/87) — 200,000
- King Holiday march (1/15/81) — 200,000

* A recount estimated the crowd to be 850,000 to 1,040,000, hence the Million Man March is generally regarded as the largest rally ever staged in Washington.

NEEDLE EXCHANGE PROGRAMS

Distributing clean needles free to drug abusers may cut the risk of AIDS infection by about 50 percent among the group, a New York-based study indicates. The study adds to scant data on the subject so far collected in 40 U.S. cities that have needle exchange programs.

With supplies provided by the American Foundation for AIDS Research, New York authorities use storefronts and mobile units in heavy drug areas to hand out color-coded syringes, which the addict must return to receive new ones.

About 22,000 users receive the needles, out of 200,000 needle drug abusers in the city, according to Dr. Don Des Jarlais of New York's Beth Israel Medical Center who presented the data at a meeting of the American Public Health Association in November 1994. Half of the city's drug addicts are already infected with HIV, the AIDS virus.

Attendance figures at a march on the U.S. Capitol is usually related to the politics of the organization responsible for the count.

The findings were based on a study of 350 users with an average of three injections a day, who were tested for HIV when they enrolled in the program and when they returned for clean needles. Des Jarlais calculated that their annual rate of infection was two percent, compared to five percent found in previous studies of addicts who are not in the program.

NEWS SOURCES

Sixty-six percent of the American public gets its news from television, contributing to a continuing decline in newspaper readership among the largest metropolitan papers in the country, a 1994 New York Times/CBS poll report showed.

A second poll, taken by America's Research Group in Charleston, N.C. following release of the latest figures on newspaper readership, found that 76 percent of those polled turned to television for national news, while just under 15 percent said they relied on newspapers. Sixty-nine percent said they chose TV for their political news, newspapers 27 percent.

Publishers said the 1994 decline was due to the major league baseball strike, price increases, and circulation cuts to distant areas that are costly to reach.

Leading the decline in the mid-year 1944 report by the Audit Bureau of Circulations was New York's *Newsday*, which lost 7.26 percent of its circulation from the year before, dropping from 747,890 readers to 693,556. *Newsday* was seventh in circulation among the nine major papers included in the report; it ceased publishing its New York City edition in mid-1995. The 10th paper on the list, *The Los Angeles Times*, did not report its figures for 1994. In 1991 its circulation was 1,177,253; in 1992 1,146,631; and in 1993 1,089,690.

Circulation of *The New York Times*, the third most widely read paper in the country, behind *The Wall Street Journal* and *USA Today*, dropped 2.32 percent, to 1,114,905 copies, from 1,141,366 in 1993. In September of the reporting year the paper raised the newsstand price of its metropolitan edition to 60 cents from 50 cents, and its national edition to $1 from 75 cents.

Some of the big dailies that showed losses for their Monday-to-Friday issues, such as the *New York Daily News* and the *Washington Post*, showed gains in their Sundays issues, but Sunday losses were felt by *The New York Times, Chicago Tribune, Newsday*, and the combined *San Francisco Chronicle* and *Examiner*.

USA Today lost readership of its five-day-per-week editions but gained overall due to an increase in bulk sales, mainly to hotels. Its 1994 circulation was 1,465,422, up 29,507 from 1993, including the bulk sales.

The most widely read paper in the nation, *The Wall Street Journal*, joined the other leaders in lost readership. From a 1,818,562 daily readership in 1993, it fell two percent to 1,780,422.

Among the country's 25 biggest papers, the only ones to gain circulation were the *Arizona Republic*, from 342,341 to 347,839, lifting it from 25th place to 24th among the nation's dailies; and the *Orange County* (Calif.) *Register*, from 332,164 to 343,906, lifting it from 28th place to 25th.

Despite declining newspaper circulations, U.S. retail and classified advertisers believe the American public still turns to newspapers for information on sales and business opportunities, another poll indicates.

Newspaper advertising spending rose to the highest in five years in 1994, to an estimated $8.4 billion in the third quarter of the year, up from $8.2 billion in 1993, according to the Newspaper Association of America, which represents about 1,500 papers in the U.S. and Canada. Retail advertising, the largest newspaper ad category, was up 4.9 percent to $4.3 billion; classified ad spending rose 12.3 percent to $3.1 billion; and national advertising was up 10.8 percent to $979 billion.

In the opposite Column is the percentage of change in the average weekday home delivery and newsstand circulation for the six months ended in September 1994 from the corresponding period in 1993, for the 10 largest papers in the U.S., from Audit Bureau of Circulation figures.

Newspaper	Circulation	% Change
USA Today	1,465,936	1.63%
Newsday	693,556	-7.26
San Francisco Chronicle	509,548	-6.38
Chicago Sun-Times	518,094	-3.30
New York Times	1,114,905	-2.32
Detroit Free Press	544,606	-2.07
Wall Street Journal	1,780,422	-2.00
Chicago Tribune	678,081	-1.85
Daily News (New York)	753,024	-1.13
Washington Post	810,675	-0.22

PROPERTY TAXES

California's Proposition 17 referendum in 1978 put a lid on property taxes. It also laid the foundation for a groundswell of anger against the tax among American homeowners that culminated in the 1990s in a nationwide outcry against the most hated tax people pay, according to a study by the national political journal *Governing*. Cutting property taxes will be easy; replacing the revenues they generate is the hard part, the journal concludes.

Governing noted that a balance was reached in Michigan in 1994, where property owners were paying $4.91 in property taxes per $100 of personal income, compared to the national average of $3.66. The state legislators merely increased Michigan's six percent sales tax—the least hated of all taxes—by two cents on the dollar to make up the difference. That allowed them to put through a 20 percent cut in property taxes, according to the journal. Since then, almost a dozen other states have moved to lower property taxes, with varying success.

In 1965, property taxes accounted for 87 percent of revenues raised by localities around the country. After Proposition 17, that average fell to 75 percent. In the early 1990s property taxes again increased in more than half the 50 states. That trend remained in effect through 1994, according to the journal, though revenues were by then flowing into the states at a rate 6.7 percent higher than in 1993.

School funding has become a target of tax reformers, with 25 states in litigation or under court orders to change their funding formulas for schools, decreasing the dependency on property taxes. One contention, the *Governing* article points out, is that under such formulas wealthier communities produce better schools than poor communities. New Jersey, Kentucky, Oklahoma, and Nebraska all have passed tax increases motivated by school finance problems.

State and local property taxes in the U.S. amounted to about $200 billion in 1994, up from $186 billion in

1992 and almost three times the $71 billion paid in 1980.

The table below indicates change in state and local property taxes, in billions (figures rounded), from 1980 to 1992, according to the Bureau of the Census, Government Finances:

Year	Total	State	Local
1980	$68	$3	66
1990	156	6	150
1991	168	6	162
1992	179	7	172

The table below shows national average per capita expenditures on state and local property taxes from 1980 to 1992, in dollars:

Year	State and Local
1980	302
1990	626
1991	666
1992	700

SNACK FOOD

Potato chips, once a dinner dish similar to french fried potatoes before they were popularized as a snack food by traveling salesman Herman Lay in the 1920s, are America's favorite munchie food, with almost seven pounds consumed by the average person a year. Americans eat more chips than any other people in the world.

The East Central U.S. and West Central regions consume the most—8.6 pounds and 7.8 pounds, respectively, per person. But as snack foods go, that's not the whole story.

The snack food industry is a $13.4 billion annual cornucopia of chips, cookies, crackers, candies, and cakes for snackers who ate more than five billion pounds of snack edibles in 1992, according to the 1993 statistical bible of the industry, the 1993 *Snack Food Association State-of-the-Industry Report*. Since that equals 21 pounds per person, potato chips are only a third of the market.

Potato chips (115 calories and eight grams of fat per 10 chips) are beginning to lose their crown in nationwide supermarket sales to tortilla chips made from corn (75 calories and 3.5 grams of fat per 10 chips), according to Information Resources International, which tracks supermarket sales. Introduced in the Pacific region over the years by Mexican immigrants and eventually made a health food snack by body-conscious Californians, tortilla chips are consumed at a rate of 5.4 pounds per capita along the Pacific Coast, compared to 5.1 pounds per capita of the potato chip variety, according to the industry survey. In the Southwest, with its large Hispanic population, consumers eat about six pounds of corn chips a year,

whereas the average for the whole of the U.S. is 4.2 pounds.

The mid-Atlantic states come to the fore with a central European favorite created in Italy in the seventh century and perfected in Germany in the 13th century: the pretzel (10 calories in 10 sticks, zero fat). The region consumes four pounds per capita a year, compared to the U.S. average of two pounds. Corn-chip lovers in the Southwest average less than a pound of pretzels each a year.

Fried pork rinds (25-plus grams of fat in a 2.7 ounce serving), once highly popular in the South and now sold in a microwaveable version, still lag far behind the big three. In 1994 consumers in the South ate only 0.3 pounds a year on average.

Despite the universality of popcorn as a snack in movie theaters and while watching TV, its annual consumption is far below that of potato chips and corn chips. Today the average American consumes less than two pounds of popcorn per year.

Below is the yearly consumption per capita, in pounds, of selected snack foods by region, 1992:

	Average	Potato chips	Tortilla chips	Pretzels
Total U.S.	20.6	6.6	4.2	2.0
Pacific	18.6	5.1	5.4	1.0
West Central	23.9	7.8	5.3	1.8
Southwest	21.3	6.5	5.9	0.9
Southeast	18.6	6.5	3.1	1.3
East Central	23.2	8.6	4.0	2.6
Mid-Atlantic	19.2	5.8	2.6	4.0
New England	20.5	7.0	3.2	2.0

SNUFF CONSUMPTION

In the late 1960s dipping snuff was looked down upon as low-brow and untidy, and a long decline in that part of the tobacco industry set in. Since the addition of cherry and wintergreen flavors in 1984 for users to suck on, snuff has surged into fashion among tobacco lovers and become a $1.1 billion-dollar industry.

Even children are using it, according to a 1992 Surgeon General's report, placing the age of initiation at just 9 1/2 years and the number of underage users at one million. Cherry-flavored snuff is the brand of choice among new users.

Nineteen percent of high school boys used snuff in 1991, up from two percent in 1970, according to the Centers for Disease Control and Prevention. United States Tobacco company says a 1993 report by the Substance Abuse and Mental Health Administration showed that the figure had declined to 4.8 percent of 12- to 17-year-olds in 1992. The resurgence has made U.S. Tobacco, makers of the popular Copenhagen brand and the company that enhanced snuff's taste with flavorings, dominant in the smokeless tobacco industry, which grew three percent in 1993.

U.S. Tobacco, located on Copenhagen Court in Franklin Park, Ill., sells 84 percent of the product used by 7.5 million people in the U.S.; its profits in 1993 were $349 million on its $1.1 billion sales, making it the most profitable American tobacco company on the basis of profit margins. The tobacco industry as a whole sells $22.5 billion in products annually.

Along with chewing tobacco, a coarser cut than fine-cut snuff, the smokeless tobacco industry's sales total $1.7 billion annually. Copenhagen and a sister brand, Original Fine Cut Skoal, hold a commanding 62 percent of the snuff market. Nicotine content of U.S. Tobacco's four products range from about nine milligrams of immediately absorbable nicotine per gram in Copenhagen, its strongest seller, down to 1.07 milligrams in its weakest brand, Skoal Bandits Wintergreen. Its 1.2 ounce packages of snuff sell for around $2.75.

According to the Centers for Disease Control, snuff users are four times more likely to develop mouth cancer than non-users, and 50 times more liable to contract cancers of the gum and inner-cheek lining. Tooth loss and gum lesions are also suffered more frequently by dippers than by non-users.

Below is the market share and amount of absorbable nicotine in U.S. Tobacco's four brands of snuff, according to the National Institute on Drug Abuse, the Maxwell Report, and industry estimates:

Brand	Market Share	Absorbable Nicotine
Copenhagen	42.0%	9.0 mg
Original Fine Cut Skoal	20.0	2.8
Skoal Long Cut Cherry	3.0	2.5
Skoal Bandits Wintergreen	2.0	1.1

SPOUSAL ABUSE IN THE MILITARY

Every week somebody dies at the hands of a relative of a U.S. serviceman, as spousal abuse increases in the military at double the civilian rate, according to a U.S. Army survey. The abuse occurs in one of every three military families each year. From 27,783 abuse cases reported in 1986, the rate increased to 46,287 cases in 1994, according to a study published in *Time* magazine.

In the civilian population, at least four million cases of domestic violence occur every year, according to the National Coalition Against Domestic Violence.

STEAK CONSUMPTION

Steak is making a comeback in the nation's restaurants after the healthy-eating binge of the 1980s and early '90s, when diners-out carefully selected the salad bar or chicken, turkey, pasta, or fish entrees.

From 1977, when beef consumption was 92 pounds per person, the century-old symbol of rich dining skid 29.2 pounds per person, down to 62.8 pounds per capita in 1993, according to a restaurant consulting group survey. The number of steakhouses in the U.S. fell from 7,900 in 1985 to about 6,600 in 1993.

Photo courtesy of Weber-Stevens Products.

Steak, whether ordered in a restaurant or cooked on a home grill like the above, is making a comeback.

The Recount Service of the Restaurant Consulting Group in Evanston, Ill., says the slide began in earnest in 1989 and budget or specialty restaurants—not the higher-priced locations—bore the brunt of disaffection for beef from diners.

Now heading the renewed taste for steak are a new type of restaurant called "casual-dining steakhouses," designed to fill the void between budget and high-end steakhouses, and whose dining tab averages close to $20, as opposed to the budget restaurants' $10. While patronage at budget steakhouses such as Ponderosa and Bonanza declined by five percent in the last five years, patronage at casual-dining spots like Outhouse and Lone Star increased 40 percent, according to a survey by NPD Crest, an industry-based research firm in Park Ridge, Ill.

The data shows that patronage at budget steakhouses dropped nine percent in 1992 and six percent in 1993, while casual steakhouse patronage climbed 19 percent. Business at high-priced steakhouses increased six percent in 1993, while the entire category of casual-dining restaurants rose four percent.

Sizzler International, which began as a budget steakhouse in the late 1950s, then switched to a family restaurant with a bigger menu, spotted the shift away from budget steak restaurants in 1992, company spokesmen say. Some of its 640 locations worldwide were converted from Sizzler to Buffalo Ranch casual steakhouses the same year, and the company had nine such units in place and plans for 12 more conversions in 1994.

TOLL-FREE TELEPHONING

American consumers are increasingly being urged to use 1.5 million toll-free services offered by U.S. businesses and government agencies, according to a 1993 survey. The reason? Many businesses use the line not only to take orders, but to gather personal information that they can use to sell goods.

Toll-free calls brought in $8.5 billion in 1993, 10 percent of all long-distance revenue. The amount was shared by three phone companies: AT&T gathered between 66 percent and 75 percent of that revenue, according to various estimates, and MCI and Sprint divided the remainder.

Toll-free revenues to the phone companies are projected to grow to $11.4 billion by 1997, as calls rise from 13 billion to 18 billion, according to Strategic Telemedia in New York City. The estimates were published in the December, 1993, issue of the journal *American Demographics*.

Almost half of AT&T business customers use the lines for sales and order-taking, about 19 percent are used for employees instead of customers, 21 percent for product inquiries, and the rest for reservations, customer reports, hotlines, and credit information, according to Strategic Telemedia.

Catalist, a directory of toll-free phone numbers, publishes 14,000 listings covering all carriers and is supported by advertising. The AT&T Toll-Free Directory-Shoppers Guide contains 60,000 entries.

UFOs

A very large number of credible witnesses have reported seeing UFOs. Each year there are approximately 10,000 reports of unidentified flying objects, 4,000 of them in the U.S.; Florida and New York State lead the list in sightings. About 25 million Americans say they have seen at least one UFO. At least one organization, the Center for UFO Studies in Chicago, investigates such reports with scientifically respected integrity. Most sightings, however, are not reported, and most are not investigated at all.

Many of the most incredible claims are those pertaining to abductions by space aliens. Sharon Sandusky, Ross's co-director on the film about UFO believers and researchers, said: "There is a belief that most abductees suffer from post-traumatic stress disorder, like rape victims and war survivors. They are ordinary, credible people who happen to be troubled by

a singular event in their lives. According to a recent Roper poll, at least 3.75 million people in this country believe that they've experienced abductions, and many more claim to have seen UFOs. Statistics show that UFO sightings cut across all socioeconomic strata, with as many men as women."

VITAMIN CONSUMPTION

Approximately 21 percent of Americans take vitamins. According to the National Health Interview Survey in the *American Almanac, 1992-1993,* the following percentages of demographic groups of Americans take vitamins:

Males	31.2%
Females	41.3
Whites	38.5
Blacks	21.5
Hispanics	28.7

Generally, the most educated and prosperous Americans take the most vitamins. Ironically, they are probably the group needing them least. Undernourished individuals in poor households, the group using vitamins the least, are those most likely to need nutritional supplements. Some 44 percent of households with incomes of more then $40,000 use vitamins compared to 27 percent of those with incomes of less than $7,000.

Most Americans who use vitamins prefer the pharmaceutical companies to mix and match the various kinds they take; hence, "multivitamins" are the biggest sellers.

The table below lists the most popular vitamins and their annual sales, according to the Council for Responsible Nutrition.	
Multivitamins	$1.2 billion
Vitamin C	350 million
Vitamin E	$75 million
B Complex	260 million

WAR DEATHS

The odds that American military personnel will die in combat have been reduced 200—fold over the last 130 years. In the Civil War (1861-65), one in 16 soldiers died; in World War II (1941-45), one in 55 died. By the time of the Korean conflict (1950-53), the fatality ratio had dropped to one in 170.

The dominant reason for this reduction is the introduction of the helicopter, which made it possible to move the wounded from the battlefields to nearby hospitals quickly. In the Vietnam conflict (1964-73), one in 184 who served died, and by the time of Operation Desert Storm, fatalities dropped to one in 3,156. The dramatic drop in fatalities in Desert Storm is generally attributed to the limited ground war made possible by the devastating U.S. air strikes before the ground action was begun.

The list below represents the number of war dead in U.S. military history, according to the Department of Defense.

World War II	291,557
Civil War*	140,414
World War I	153,402
Vietnam War	47,382
Korea	33,629
Revolutionary War	4,435
War of 1812	2,260
Mexican War	1,733
Spanish-American War	385

* Union casualties; Confederate deaths are estimated at about the same number, although accurate figures were not often kept by the Confederacy.

WEEKENDS

Only about half the world breaks on Saturday and Sunday; outside the Western world, the idea of the weekend has yet to catch on universally.

In 1908, the first five-day work week came to America, when a spinning mill in New England arranged its hours to accommodate its Jewish workers, who observed the Sabbath on Saturday. Unionism, which was on the rise in America, had many Jewish leaders, particularly in the garment industries of the manufacturing centers of the North. Hard-goods manufacturers soon followed suit. Henry Ford, an alleged anti-Semite and staunch anti-unionist, was the first industrial baron to launch a five- day week. In 1926 he closed his plants on Saturday. His motives were, however, less than altruistic. At that time the automobile was no less a recreational item than a mode of transportation, and Ford believed the practice would be a boon to the leisure industry. Ford got his way. America took to the weekend — and to the automobile — with a vengeance.

The list below, compiled by the American Automobile Association, reveals where we stay on our weekend jaunts. The average cost of a weekend for a family of two adults and two children is about $200.

Location	% of travelers
Hotels	54%
Friends or relatives	22
Campgrounds	17
Vacation homes	7

Michael Keating.

The Vietnam Memorial commemorates 47,382 war dead.

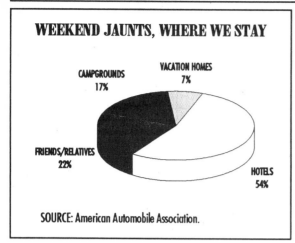

WEEKEND JAUNTS, WHERE WE STAY

CAMPGROUNDS 17%

VACATION HOMES 7%

FRIENDS/RELATIVES 22%

HOTELS 54%

SOURCE: American Automobile Association.

The list below details selected popular weekend pastimes, compiled from sources that include "Sports Poll" (conducted by *Sports Illustrated*), the National Recreation Survey (conducted by the Census Bureau), a Harris poll, and a Gallup poll. (The figures do not add up to 100% because many individuals reported several activities.)

Activity	% participating
Spectator outings	76%
Visit zoos and fairs	50
Flower gardening	47
Driving for pleasure	43
Photography	35
Sightseeing	34
Fishing	34
Boating	28
Running/jogging	26
Camping	24
Team sports	24
Tennis	17
Golfing	13
Skiing	9

WELFARE

In late fall 1991 the state of Michigan tackled a budget problem the rest of the nation would be debating in 1994. Facing a looming budget shortfall of $250 million, it cut 80,000 single adults from welfare payments to force them to find jobs. Two years later researchers found that relatively few were working.

The 43 percent of adults who found work represented approximately the same percentage who were getting off welfare two years before the cutoff. Also, in no quarter of 1992 did as many as 20 percent of the former recipients hold jobs—an employment rate the study finds has held constant since the cutoff.

Eighty-seven percent of the disabled who lost benefits were still jobless in 1944, as were 75 percent of the chronically ill, and 52.3 percent of the healthy recipients, according to the study, "The General Assistance Termination Project," which analyzed in detail what happens to people when welfare is cut off. Sixty-nine percent of the men and 67 percent of the women were still-jobless.

The Ford Foundation-funded study was conducted by professors Sandra Danziger and Sherrie Kossoudji of the University of Michigan School of Social Work, and Robert Lovell, director of the Planning and Evaluation Division of Michigan's Department of Social Services. A report on the study was published in *The Ford Foundation Report* in the fall of 1994.

As to what happens after aid is shut off, the researchers found that the average earnings of those who found jobs was $650 a month, plus food stamps. Sixty percent were in janitoring or food-service, where before they lost their jobs and went on welfare 33 percent of former recipients had worked in the manufacturing sector.

Almost 50 percent had health insurance in their previous jobs; 13 percent had health insurance in their new jobs. Thirty-three percent had been union workers, compared to 15 percent who were after the cutoff.

Seventy percent of the recipients had used their welfare money to pay rent. After the cutoff the transiency rate of former recipients overall increased from 5.9 percent to 17.7 percent. In the Detroit area, where 46 percent of those cut off from aid had lived, there was a similar increase in shifting from shelter to shelter.

Fifty percent of the aid recipients had a high school education; among the younger recipients 40 percent had a diploma. Fifteen percent of all those cut from aid were on disability the first year after the cut and 25 percent within the second year.

Seventy-four percent of blacks were still jobless after two years; among whites, 64 percent were.

Below is a breakdown of those still jobless after two years of being cut from welfare, by various criteria; source, GATP:

Respondents	Percent
Men	68.7%
Women	66.5
Blacks	74.1
Whites	63.7
Other	48.5
Age 41 and over	83.1
Age 26 to 40	58.7
Age 26 or less	34.9
Disabled	86.5
Chronically ill	75.1
Healthy	52.3

WRONGFUL CONVICTIONS

Celebrated cases of wrongful conviction for a crime make it appear that such cases are unusual. Not so. "It's endemic," says Dennis Cogan, the co-chair of the

National Association of Criminal Lawyers for the Convicted Innocent. Cogan has written a study on the issue with Michael Radelet, a sociology professor at the University of Florida.

Scouring newspapers, death penalty literature, libraries, and newsletters, Cogan and Radelet studied 420 capital cases since 1900 and found that 23 innocent people were executed. They also reported that since 1970, 46 persons on death row were eventually released, having been found innocent. The study said that most of those wrongfully convicted were poor and could not afford a defense attorney; half were black or Hispanic. The authors also concluded that the prisoners were convicted on "shoddy evidence," "unreliable testimony," and even coerced confessions.

FAMILIES
OVERVIEW

Many social critics maintain that the gradual dissolution of the America family unit as a conveyer of value and virtue is responsible for the prevalence of crime, drug abuse, and dropout rates. Elsewhere in this volume, the statistics confirm how commonplace these maladies are. In this portion that pretains to the American family, the dissolution of the family is also confirmed.

The statistics are staggering: millions of children live outside the nuclear family, cohabitation has replaced marriage for a large contingent of young adults, and among the underclass, the practice of having children out-of-wedlock outpaces births of married couples.

As such, the traditional American family of slightly more than four—a working father, a stay-at-home mother with an average of 2.3 children—is an increasingly obsolete.

Nearly one in three American children today live with a single parent who has never been married. The figures for minority single-parenthood are staggering: 66 percent of black children under the age of six—fully two out of three—live with just one parent.

The vast majority of single-parent households are headed by an unwed mother. Among them, 65 percent with a child under the age of six are less than 30 years old. One in three single mothers have no high school diploma. More than half are outside the labor force, reliant on public aid for basic subsistence. As if it's a symptom of our time, the term "unwed mother" or "single mom" is common in demographers' analyses of the 1990s. "Unwed fathers" and "single dads" are all but absent from the numerical data, as if they don't count in equation.

Economic and social realities are transforming even the traditional two-parent family. The number of women in the work force nearly tripled from 1960 to 1994—rising from 23,240,000 to 60,239,000—and women now make up nearly half of the American labor pool. While careerism undoubtedly has improved the overall status of women in society, it also has affected the family dramatically: Women are marrying later—the median age for a women's first marriage was 24.5 in 1993, compared to 20.3 in 1960—and, partly as a result of postponing marriage, are having fewer children. The arrival of children no longer removes mothers from the work force. Whether by necessity or desire, 70 percent of American women with children under the age of 18 remain in the labor force. The result is a whole new financial and social burden as well as a new term in the English language, "day care," which can consume 13 percent or more of a family's income and as much as 40 to 50 percent of the working mother's.

Those who espouse the importance of the family unit, will delight in one entry in this portion, "Dinner, with Children," which points out that children who regularly eat dinner with both parents are better students than those who eat with just one parent or dine infrequently with the rest of the family. From the demonstrable social importance of the family meal, we can add a host of other traditional family practices whose influence on child development is underestimated and undervalued.

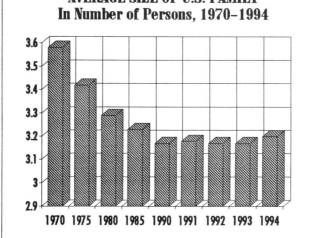

AVERAGE SIZE OF U.S. FAMILY
In Number of Persons, 1970–1994

Though the birth rate has dropped 17 percent, the size of American families has been further exacerbated by the following developments:

- The number of female-headed households with no husband increased from 5.5 million to 10.7 million.
- The percent of families without children increased from 44.1 percent to 51.2 percent.
- The number of single parent families has increased from 13 percent to more than 25 percent.

SOURCE: U.S. Bureau of the Census, Statistical Abstract, 1995.

ADOPTIONS

At any given time in the U.S., up to two million couples want to have children. Unfortunately, the difficulty in finding a child for those who must adopt has increased in the last two decades; the adoption rate peaked in 1970 at 89,200 and then started to decline. The rate leveled off to around 50,000 in 1992.

The shortage of adoptable infants can be attributed to a number of factors: later marriages, birth control, abortion, and publicly funded programs aimed at reducing unwanted pregnancies. Many Americans seeking to adopt have turned to foreign countries, but foreign adoptions also have decreased. in 1992 both South Korea and Romania restricted the number of adoptions of their children they would permit to U.S. parents.

The lists below show the number of adoptions in the U.S. in selected years, and the home country of foreign-born adoptees, as compiled by the National Council for Adoptions.

U.S.-BORN CHILDREN

Year	Number
1951	33,000
1961	61,600
1970	89,200
1975	47,700
1982	50,720
1986	51,157
1992	50,000

FOREIGN-BORN CHILDREN

1982	5,707
1984	8,327
1986	9,946
1987	10,097
1991	9,008
1992	6,536

Leading sources of foreign children adopted in 1992

Country	Number
Romania	2,552
Korea	1,787
Former Soviet Union	432
Guatemala	428
Colombia	403
Philippines	353

AFFLUENT HOUSEHOLDS, TAXES AND SPENDING

The Revenue Reconciliation Act of 1993 took an average of $23,500 from households where earnings were $200,000-plus annually, but surveys show that except for minor changes the tax increase will have little effect on the spending habits of the wealthy.

Most of the money generated by the one percent of Americans in the "plus" class goes toward maintaining an executive lifestyle and sending children to good schools—two spending habits members of the class are not likely to alter, according to the consulting firm Auricom Corporation in Bethesda, Md. The firm says wealthy households spend only two percent of their income on food, compared to 12 percent for the average U.S. household. In total, that one percent tax was estimated to contribute $2.2 billion to the federal budget in 1994.

The tax hike hit hard in Stamford, Conn., where 11.7 percent of households are in the plus class—the nation's highest concentration of the category—and in nearby Norwalk, Conn., where 8.9 percent are in the class. It is estimated that Stamford shelled out $214 million in taxes in 1994, and Norwalk $102 million.

It also is estimated that New York's Nassau and Suffolk counties, where three percent, or 25,000 households, are classed as rich, generates the most tax revenue of any area in the country: $593 million. That's due to the area's large population—2.64 million, compared to Stamford-Norwalk's 331,000. San Francisco is estimated to be second, producing $423 million, and Newark, N.J., third with $415 million, according to Donnelley Marketing Information Service of Stamford, in a survey reported by the journal *American Demographics* in November 1993.

Places with largest share of $200,000-plus householders in 1992, in percent, and estimated aggregate new federal income taxes in 1994, in millions:

Area	Percent rich	Taxes (millions)
Stamford, Conn.	11.7%	$214
Norwalk, Conn.	8.9	102
Lake County, Ill.	4.4	189
Naples, Fla.	3.4	55
Danbury, Conn.	3.0	49
Nassau-Suffolk, N.Y.	2.9	593
San Francisco	2.8	423
Newark, N.J.	2.7	415
Bergen-Passaic, N.J.	2.7	292
West Palm Beach, Fla.	2.3	217

BURGLARIES, RESIDENTIAL

The number of residential burglaries annually in the U.S. has increased steadily, from 1.5 million in 1982 to 2.1 million in 1993, meaning that about one in every 20 homes in the U.S. is burglarized every year. According to FBI statistics, intruders take an average of $1,018 in property from each burglary; the highest total came in 1991, when burglars got an average of $1,201 in valuables from every haul.

An increasing number of homeowners keep guns to protect themselves from intruders. A study conducted in Seattle, however, indicated that a gun in the home is 40 times more likely to kill a family member or friend than a criminal.

A home security system, a far safer route, is the choice of one million Americans annually. In 1992, Americans spent $1 billion on such systems. Ironically, the average cost—about $1,000—is close to the average loss in a burglary. The most basic home security systems cost about $500 to install and about $15 to $30 a month in monitoring fees for systems connected with a central station. Deluxe models can run as high as $4,000 for installation.

Police say that sturdy doors, deadbolt locks, secure windows, outdoor lighting, dogs, and neighborhood watch groups are effective in discouraging prowlers. Joe Mele, a loss prevention expert at the National Crime Prevention Institute at the University of Louisville and a police consultant in crime prevention, says studies prove that having a home security system in itself is a strong deterrent to burglars.

CHILD CARE

More white parents leave their children alone every day from the time school lets out until a parent returns home than Hispanic or black parents, and suburbanites and high-income and highly educated parents are more likely to do so, a Census Bureau survey found.

Basing its report on a survey of 13,600 households between October 1991 and January 1992, the bureau estimated that more than 1.6 million young Americans age 5 to 14 are left alone daily during the school week. Of the total, half a million are 11 or younger, and two-thirds are between the ages of 12 and 14. All told, 51 million American children under the age of 15 need care while their parents are at work.

Suburban "latch-key kids" total 9.3 percent, compared to 6.8 percent in cities and 5.3 percent in rural areas. Midwestern children, with 12.1 percent, lead those in other sections of the country. The West is second with 7.5 percent, the Northeast third with 5.7 percent, and the South last with 4.8 percent.

Only 3.6 percent of black parents leave their children alone, compared to 4.8 percent of Hispanics and 9.3 percent of whites.

The survey, entitled "Who's Minding the Kids?", looked into the child care arrangements for 21.2 million American children between the ages of 5 through 14.

Other findings include:

- An estimated 7.6 percent of grade-school children care for themselves at least part of the time while their parents are at work.

- Fathers care for children of 8.4 percent of married women, and less than one percent of unmarried working mothers.

- Child-care facilities care for 23 percent of preschoolers, while fathers care for 20 percent, and other family members 18 percent. The remainder either are cared for by nonrelatives or are taken to work by the mothers.

- Other relatives care for 10.2 percent of children of single mothers, compared with 3.8 percent for married working mothers.

- Seventy-six percent of the children remain at school while their parents work.

- The average cost of paid child care in an organized facility is $2.15 an hour; for nonrelative care at the nonrelative's home it is $1.93 an hour; and the cost is $2.73 an hour when a nonrelative comes to the child's home.

CHILD, SECOND, COST OF RAISING,

While conventional wisdom tells you a second child may be cheaper to raise than the first, the equation is more complicated than meets the eye.

According to the Department of Agriculture's Family Economics Research group, well-to-do married couples with a second child will spend $334,600 raising the child, compared to the single parent who spends just $1,100 more for a total of $335,500, assuming an average inflation rate of six percent. Schooling costs are not included in the projections because they vary widely based on region.

Single parents of a second child born in 1993 who earn $32,000 annually will spend more than married couples with incomes of $54,100 and above. The reason is the constantly increasing costs of child care that will confront the single parent.

Married couples with incomes between $32,000 and $54,100 will spend $231,100 to raise a second child born in 1993; those with incomes below $32,000 will spend $170,900; and single parents will spend $166,500.

Housing will account for 31 to 37 percent of the costs of raising the second child; this would include a share of rent, utilities, furnishings, and cleaning supplies. The share additionally spent on child care for the single parent will be between 13 and 17 percent.

Among the parental categories, single parents will spend the highest percentage of annual salary spent on the child: 22 percent to 39 percent. The proportion of income devoted to children falls as income rises. Higher-income single parents with incomes averaging $47,900 will spend 22 percent of income on the child; middle-income families earning $42,600 will spend 17 percent; affluent couples earning $79,400 will spend 13 percent.

For middle-class couples earning from $32,000 to $54,100, the child will be most expensive between ages 15 to 17, at a median of $8,300. The next most expensive age span is six to eight, at $7,460; followed by 12 to 14, at $7,390; three to five, at $7,220; and nine to 11, at $6,980. Excluding prenatal and delivery costs, such a family will pay $6,870 for the child's first two years.

The following lists detail the cost of raising a second child, born in 1993, to the age of 18, assuming a six percent rate of inflation; source, U.S. Department of Agriculture:

OVERALL COST

Parental status	Annual income	Cost
Single parent	$32,000+	$335,500
Married	54,100+	334,600
Married	32,000-$54,100	231,100
Married	32,000 or less	170,900

Single parents	below $32,000	$166,500

PROPORTION OF INCOME SPENT ON THE YOUNGER CHILD

Parental Status	Annual Income	Percent per child
Low income	$13,000	27%
Single parent	32,000	39
Single parent	47,900	22
Married	42,600	17
Married	79,400	13

EXPENDITURES BY CATEGORY, RANGE IN PERCENT

Housing	31-37%
Food	13-17
Transportation	13-17
Child care	8-13

CHILD SUPPORT

How tough is it to make dads pay child support? Plenty tough, according to a U.S. Census Bureau report, which indicates that nationwide, almost half of the women who deserve child support payments receive less than their due: 24.8 percent of the women receive no payments, and 23.8 percent receive only partial payment. Moreover, the total average expected annual payment is $3,292, but the total average received is just $2,252.

The women owed that money are not living in the lap of luxury. The average income for women who receive child support payments is $16,171; for those who do not get their money, the average income is $13,761. Neither figure is much above the national poverty level of $13,359 for a family of four.

CHILDREN, LIVING ARRANGEMENTS

The living arrangements of America's 66 million children under age 18 is as diverse as the race, color, and parents' age and education of the group.

According to Census Bureau studies published in the July- September 1993 issue of the journal *Statistical Bulletin*, nearly 71 percent of American children under age 18 live with both parents in 1992; of the rest, 27 percent live with one parent, and less than three percent live with a relative or nonrelative. Only one percent of the single-parent children live with the father.

Eighty percent of white children were found to live with both parents in all three age groups analyzed— under six years of age, six to 11, and 12 to 17. Approximately 66 percent of Hispanic children live with both parents in each of the three age groups. The figures are much lower for black children: 34 under age six and 42 percent over age six live with both parents.

Parental education levels were higher in two-parent households: 27.9 percent of the parents were college graduates, and 33.7 percent had a high school diploma but no college. College graduates accounted for 27.7 percent of the white parents, 18.5 percent of the black, and 7.5 percent of the Hispanic parents. Mother-only households included 40.3 percent high school graduates but only 4.4 percent college graduates—5.9 percent of white mothers, 2.1 percent of black, and 1.8 percent of Hispanic single mothers are college graduates.

Ninety-three percent of two-parent families had at least one parent employed in 1992. For the mother-only households, the figure was 81.6 percent, and for father-only households, 85.7 percent. Of the white households studied, 93.5 percent of the two-parent families were employed, as were 89.9 percent of the blacks, and 88.1 percent of the Hispanics. The highest joblessness was recorded among black, mother-only households, at 24.3 percent.

Twenty-two percent of Hispanic two-parent families had three or more children in 1992, compared to 19.1 percent of black families and 11.8 percent of white. Twenty-one percent of the mother-only Hispanic families had three or more children, as did 19.7 percent of black families and 11 percent of white families in the category. The largest number of households studied had one child- -42.6 percent of the white two-parent families, 35.9 percent of black, and 35.1 percent of Hispanic.

The following lists detail information concerning the homes of U.S. children in 1992, according to the U.S. Census Bureau.

CHILDREN UNDER AGE SIX

Parental Age	2-parent homes	Mother-only homes	Father-only homes
Under 25	7.3%	35.7%	20.3%
25-29	21.7	29.5	31.7
30-34	33.1	20.5	24.0
35-39	23.4	9.3	11.8
40-44	10.2	3.1	7.1
45 and over	4.3	1.9	5.1
Parental Educational Attainment			
No HS diploma	13.8	34.8	27.2
HS diploma	33.7	40.3	42.8
1-3 years college	24.6	20.5	21.5
College degree	27.9	4.4	8.5
Parents In Labor Force, in percent			
In labor force	92.6%	49.0%	88.7%
Employed	93.3	81.6	85.7
Unemployed	6.7	18.4	14.3
Not in labor force	7.4	51.0	11.3
number of siblings			
None	24.3	33.4	41.2
One	41.9	32.9	40.6
Two	22.0	19.0	12.9
Three or more	11.8	14.7	5.3
CHILDREN AGE SIX TO 11			
Parental Age			
Under 25	0.7%	4.3%	2.2%
25-29	7.7	26.2	10.8
30-34	25.0	30.6	25.6
35-39	30.7	22.8	29.7
40-44	22.6	10.9	16.0
45 and over	13.3	5.2	15.7

Parental Educational Attainment, by percent			
No HS diploma	14.7%	28.4%	21.5%
HS diploma	35.1	38.4	37.6
1-3 years college	24.4	24.4	25.1
College degree	25.8	8.8	15.8
Parents In Labor Force			
In labor force	93.4	63.7	86.8
Employed	94.2	85.6	89.6
Unemployed	5.8	14.4	10.4
Number of Siblings			
None	9.6	20.5	27.5
One	41.8	36.0	43.8
Two	30.2	25.6	19.3
Three or more	18.4	17.8	9.4

CHILDREN AGE 12 TO 17

Parental Age			
Under 30	1.4%	3.1%	1.5%
30-34	7.5	22.5	9.5
35-39	23.9	31.0	20.2
40-44	32.7	25.2	31.2
45-54	29.0	16.8	27.5
55 and over	5.5	1.4	10.1
Parental Educational Attainment, by percent			
No HS diploma	15.6%	28.6%	23.5%
HS diploma	35.0	35.9	33.5
1-3 years college	24.0	25.5	26.1
College degree	25.4	10.0	16.9
Parents In Labor Force, by percent			
In labor force	92.6%	71.1%	89.1%
Employed	94.5	89.2	94.5
unemployed	5.5	10.8	5.5
Not in labor force	7.4	28.9	10.9
Number Of Siblings			
None	14.4	24.6	42.8
One	42	35.1	37.8
Two	26.1	23.0	14.4
Three or more	17.5	17.3	5.0

CO-HABITATION

In the 1940s, living with a person of the opposite sex without the benefit of marriage was uncommon. By 1970, about 10 percent of American adults lived with an unmarried mate before their first marriage. Today, almost half of all young adults–45 percent–cohabitate before their first marriage, the incidence being slightly less among women than men.

The younger a woman is, the more likely she is to live with a male companion. Among unmarried women born in the 1940s, three percent have lived with an unmarried male. Among women born in the 1960s, approximately one third will live with a male before they are married.

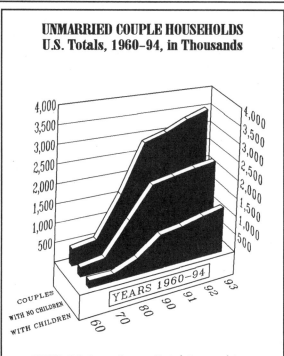

UNMARRIED COUPLE HOUSEHOLDS
U.S. Totals, 1960–94, in Thousands

SOURCE: U.S. Census Bureau, *Marital Status and Living Arrangements*, March 1993 (1994).

Below are Census Bureau figures on unmarried couples in the U.S. An "unmarried couple" is defined as two unrelated adults of the opposite sex who share the same household.

Characteristic	Number
Total	3,308,000
No children	2,187,000
At least one child	1,121,000
Under 25 years old	661,000
25 to 44 years old	2,026,000
44 to 64 years old	475,000
65 years old and over	146,000

DINNER, WITH CHILDREN

Students who eat dinner with one or more parents have higher grades, according to a nationwide survey of high school seniors performed by Louis Harris and Associates in 1993 for *Reader's Digest* and summarized in the July/August 1993 issue of the journal *Society*. And as with other aspects of child development, it helps to have both parents around.

Children who share dinner with both parents in a two-parent household tend to score higher than those who live with their mothers only, according to the survey. Sixty percent of those who ate meals with their parents frequently scored highly on a special academic test, while just 42 percent of those who ate with family three times or fewer a week scored well. The 53 percent who lived in America's 25 million two-parent families scored higher than the 41 percent who lived in America's eight million one-parent households, 5.4 million of those households being mothers only.

Girls performed worse than boys in two-parent households, scoring at a high level 51 percent of the time among frequent family diners and 32 percent of the time for those who joined the family meal three times or less a week. Twenty-two percent of blacks from two-parent families scored high, compared to nine percent of those living with a mother only. Among Hispanics, 45 percent who often joined parents at meals scored high, compared to 33 percent of those who did not often eat with parents.

Students from non-college-educated families who ate with mom and dad scored high 52 percent of the time, compared to just 36 percent of those who did not share the table.

In addition to questions on students' families and values, the survey also asked 2,130 seniors, a cross-section of seniors in the 20,120 U.S. public high schools, questions on math, science, literature, geography, history, and government.

Eighty percent of the students were optimistic about the future and confident they would "make things better for myself and for other people." Almost the same number described their home life as "pretty good" or "wonderful."

In general knowledge, more than 33 percent of the seniors did not know that the Great Depression happened in the 20th century, and unable to pinpoint France on a map. More than 90 percent knew the first 10 amendments to the Constitution of the United States are called the Bill of Rights, and 64 percent knew a rusting nail involved a chemical change, while melting ice did not.

DIVORCE

Though 1.2 million Americans obtained a divorce in 1993 and 287,000 couples in the first quarter of 1994, the rate of divorces in the country declined for the eighth straight year. Except for several glitches in the financially troubled early 1980s, when the number rose to a record high of 5.3 per 1,000 population (1981), the rate (4.6 in 1993) has hovered at the 5.0- to 4.4 level since 1975, when divorces broke the one million barrier for the first time at 1,036,000, or 4.8 percent.

In 1993, there were roughly 16.7 million divorced persons in the U.S., 9.9 million women (generally believed to be less likely to remarry), and 6.8 million men, according to the *Statistical Abstract of the United States* based on Census Bureau projections.

Divorce is more prevalent among the country's younger set. In 1988, the last year the Census Bureau shows final divorce statistics rather than estimates,

Las Vegas News Bureau.

Nevada, no longer the divorce capital of the U.S., is a mecca for quicky and budget weddings, similar to the one pictured above. For every divorce in Nevada, there are nine marriages, one of the highest marriage-to-divorce ratios in the U.S.

53 percent of divorcing men and 50 percent of women were under the age of 25. More than 33 percent of 1988 divorces were among couples that had been married less than five years; 66 percent were between couples married less than 10 years.

California led all states in divorces, according to the latest figures available, with 137,500 in 1985. It was followed by Texas with 89,000, according to 1992 figures, Florida with 71,600, and New York with 57,000. Nevada dissolved 13,300 marriages but married 114,200 couples. Reno and Las Vegas established themselves as the "divorce capitals of the nation" in 1931. Liberal divorce laws in many states have since ended that distinction for the two Nevada cities.

The divorce rate in the U.S. never has climbed above 5.3 per 1,000 since the year 1900. The highest rate occurred in 1981, when the rate was 5.3, with 1.2 million divorces. The lowest rate recorded was .7 in 1990, when 55,751 couples divorced.

The fewest number of divorces occurred in North Dakota (2,300), the District of Columbia (2,700), Wyoming (3,200), Delaware (3,400), and Alaska (3,700).

Divorced persons per 1,000 married persons, by sex and race, 1960-93; source, Census Bureau:			
Sex/Race	1960	1980	1993
BOTH SEXES			
All races	35	100	154
White	33	92	144
Black	62	203	296
Hispanic	NA.	98	136
MALE			
All races	28	79	125
White	27	74	119
Black	45	149	216
Hispanic	NA.	64	114
FEMALE			
All races	42	120	182
White	38	110	170
Black	78	258	378
Hispanic	NA	132	157

FAMILY FACTS

A total of 68.1 million families with children in the home resided in the U.S. in 1992. The median annual income for families was $36,812. About 52 million lived in metropolitan areas of the country and 15.8 million lived outside metropolitan areas, with the median income for metropolitan dwellers $39,471 and for those outside metropolitan areas $29,864.

The South is most heavily populated family section of the country, with 24 million units earning a median $33,028 annually. The highest median income is $40,824, earned by families in the Northeast, according to the U.S. Census Bureau's *Current Population Reports.*

Married-couple families totaled 53.2 million, with 31.4 million having a wife in the labor force. Families

with only a male householder present totaled three million. Those with only a woman present totaled 11.9 million, with a median annual income of $17,221.

White families total 57.8 million; black families 7.8 million; Hispanic families 5 million. American Indian, Eskimo, and Aleut families totaled 591,000 in 1990, 442,000 of them in family households. Asian and Pacific Islander families, 1.5 million in 1991, climbed to 1.7 million in 1993, 1.3 million of those in family households.

The median annual income of Hispanic families, $23,901, is greater than the black median income of $21,161, but Asians, who earned a median of $42,556 in 1992, topped them both. American Indian families earned $29,339 in 1990 and Eskimos $23,257, while the Aleuts topped them both at $36,472

Southern white families, at 19.2 million outnumber families in other sections of the country as do Southern blacks, at 4.4 million. Hispanic families are most numerous in the South and West, at 1.7 million and 2.4 million, respectively, earning most in the West at $25,682 annually, compared to $24,000 in the Midwest, $22,983 in the South, and $20,238 in the Northeast.

Half of 32.3 million American children in 1991 lived in non traditional families. These include single-parent families or families comprising a step-parent, a grandparent, another relative, or a nonrelative. White children were more likely to live in a traditional family of the same biological mother and father (whites: 56 percent, blacks: 26 percent, and Hispanics: 38 percent). About 4.7 million children lived with a grandparent, with 87 percent of that number living in the grandparent's home.

GRANDPARENTS AND GRANDCHILDREN

Interaction with grandchildren is a favorite pastime for America's 60.4 million grandparents, according to a survey that finds 90 percent involved with their grandchildren at least once a month. The 10 percent who do not interact with grandchildren represents a drop from the 16 percent reported in 1988.

More than 50 percent of grandparents invite their progeny over to eat with them once a month, and 40 percent ask them to spend the night. Almost 66 percent talk to them over the telephone at least once and a month, and 33 percent accompany them to a restaurant; about the same percentage goes shopping with them once a month, according to the Roper Organization in New York City.

Sixty-six percent of grandparents have three or more grandchildren, the survey shows, and among them 50 percent of the grandchildren will live out of state, according to Sunie Levin, editor of the newsletter *Today's Young Grandparents,* as told to the journal *American Demographics* which reported on the Roper survey in September 1993. Forty percent of grandparents age 45 to 59 have at least one grandchild aged 13 or older, according to Roper.

Grandparents spent 11 percent more on gifts for their grandchildren in 1992 than they did in 1988,

Roper says. Fifty percent spent more than $320, while grandparents in households with less than $15,000 spent an average of $210. More than 50 percent of all grandparents bought their grandchildren a gift in the month before the survey.

Households headed by persons age 55 to 64 spend an average of $900 a year on infant furniture, compared to $800 a year spent by persons age 25 to 34, according to the Bureau of Labor Statistics' Consumer Expenditure Survey.

Percent of grandparents with a grandchild aged three or younger, by age of grandparent; source, the Roper Organization:

Age	Percent
30 to 44 years	80%
45 to 59 years	73
60 and older	53

GUN SAFETY IN THE HOME

Keeping guns loaded, unlocked and within reach of children in the home contradicts what all firearm experts teach, according to a survey of gun-owner training, yet 14 percent of respondents to the survey say they do so. Also, despite the fact that 56 percent of respondents say they received formal training in the use and storing of guns, 21 percent kept a gun available in their homes unlocked and ready to fire.

Of gun owners formally trained in firearm storage, 48 percent were trained in the military, eight percent as part of law enforcement or security work, 11 percent in a program sponsored by the National Rifle Association (which has 32,000 certified instructors to teach basic gun skills and safety), and 33 percent received training elsewhere, according to the recent study, which was conducted by Fact Finders Inc. of Delmar, N. Y., for the Harvard Injury Control Center and reported in the January 4, 1995, issue of the *Journal of the American Medical Association*.

For 45 percent of those in the survey, training lasted 80 or more hours, and 30 percent had undergone training within the last five years. Gun storage was covered in the training 80 percent of the time.

A total of 232 gun owners, or 29 percent of the 800 randomly selected gun owners age 18 and over in the survey, kept a loaded gun in the house, despite the high risk of accidental shooting. Gun owners in households with children under age 18 were less likely to keep a loaded gun in the house than owners in households without children.

Seventy-four percent of the 492 male gun owners in the survey underwent formal training, as did 29 percent of the 308 women. Sixty-six percent of 198 college-educated respondents were trained, compared to 53 percent of the 598 respondents with less than a college education. Of the gun owners with incomes above $35,000, 61 percent underwent training, compared to 51 percent for those earning less than $35,000.

Of the 492 male gun owners in the survey, 24 percent stored their guns unlocked and ready to fire; of 308

National Shooting Sports Foundation.

According to a recent poll, more than half of U.S. gun owners undergo some form of formal training, ranging from military service requirements to private courses like the one pictured above.

females surveyed, 17 percent did so. Twenty-seven percent of the 224 Southerners surveyed kept their guns at the ready; the figure among those in the rest of the country was 19 percent. College-educated respondents were more likely to do so than the less educated by a factor of 30 percent to 19 percent. Handguns were the weapons mostly stored ready to use.

The authors of the "JAMA" report, Dr. David Hemenway, Sara J. Solnik, and Deborah R. Azrael of the Harvard School of Public Health, said results of the survey were subject to an error margin of plus or minus four percentage points when projected over the entire U.S. gun-owning population.

Here's what the survey of gun owners found concerning training of gun owners and their storage practices:

TRAINING CHARACTERISTICS

Group	Number in survey	Received training
Overall	800	56%
Men	492	74
Women	308	29
Age 50 and over	303	56
Under age 50	496	57
College degree	196	66

Less than college	53	NA
$35,000 income	435	61
Under $35,000 income	283	51
Southerners	224	50
Other	576	59
Urban	216	62
Nonurban	574	54
Have gun for protection	307	61
Other reason	490	54
NRA member	120	78
Handgun owner	486	61
Other gun owner	234	46

The following are statistics drawn from the 56% of respondents who had formal training in gun use:

SOURCE OF TRAINING

Military	217	48%
Law Enforcement/security	34	8
NRA	49	11
Hunting	46	10
Scouts/4-H	14	3
School	9	2
Other	82	18

TOTAL HOURS OF TRAINING

80 and over	182	45%
11-80	115	29
1-10	105	26

TRAINING TOPICS

Safe handling	131	97%
Firearm operations	125	94
Marksmanship	109	84
Firearm regulations	109	82
Safe storage	107	79

STORAGE PRACTICES (for all in survey)

Group	Number	unlocked/loaded	Loaded
Overall	800	21%	29%
Men	492	24	32
Women	308	17	27
Over age 50	303	25	32
Under age 50	19	27	NA
College degree	198	30	36
No college	598	19	37
$35,000+	435	23	30
Less than $35,000	284	21	27
Southerners	224	27	40
Other	578	19	25
Urban	216	23	34
Nonurban	574	21	27
For protection	307	34	48
Other	490	13	17
NRA member	120	33	43
Handgun	486	28	38
Other	234	8	9
Formally trained	451	27	35
Guns unlocked	399	N/A	39

HOMELESSNESS

A more recent 30-city survey by the U.S. Conference of Mayors in 1994 found that single men and families with children make up the largest groups of the homeless in the nation, The report showed total requests for shelter up an average 13 percent from 1993, and food requests up 12 percent.

Single men make up the highest group, at 48 percent of the total. Families account for 38 percent, single women 11 percent, and children—family-rejected or runaways—three percent. The family rate jumped 21 percent over 1993 for shelter and 14 percent for food, according to a report on the conference published in *USA Today.*

Steve Nozicka.

Streetwise, a newspaper sold primarily by the homeless, has helped thousands of individuals and families, such as this one in Chicago.

The Department of Housing and Urban Development maintains there are 50,000 homeless people in the United State. Advocacy groups say the number is more like three million. The Census Bureau has its own count.

Beginning on March 20, 1990, the Census Bureau undertook a two-day count of homelessness, visiting 11,000 shelters and 24,000 street sites. The census takers found far fewer homeless people to survey than others who have done head counts, such as those who work often with the homeless. The bureau's survey, however, is the best estimate we have of the nation's homeless population: 228,261—178,828 in emergency shelters and 49,793 at "preidentified street locations."

A 1991 survey by the Census Bureau said California led the way in homeless, with 48,887, with New York second with 43,793. Far behind in third was Florida with 10,299.

Blacks make up the highest percentage of the homeless population, at 53 percent, followed by whites at 31 percent, Hispanics at 12 percent, American Indians at three percent, and Asians at one percent.

The mayors gave as characteristics of the homeless: 43 percent substance abusers, an increase of three percent from a similar report by the mayors in 1991; 26 percent mentally ill, up from 24 percent in 1991; 23 percent veterans, down from 25 percent; 19 percent employed full- or part-time, up from 18 percent; and eight percent have AIDS or HIV, up 1 percent.

Minorities comprised the largest number of homeless in New York, Detroit, Chicago, Baltimore, and St. Louis, according to a study made by the National Academy of Sciences' Institute of Medicine. Milwaukee, Phoenix, Portland, and the state of Ohio accounted for the highest percentage of whites, according to the report, summarized in the *Universal Almanac*.

Below are the numbers of homeless people in select American cities, according to the official Census Bureau count on March 20–21, 1990.

Alexandria, Va.	220
Boston	3,613
Charleston, S.C.	600
Chicago	6,764
Cleveland	10,000
Kansas City	13,000
Los Angeles	31,000
Louisville	11,442
Nashville	942
New York City	55,000
Philadelphia	35,000
Phoenix	6,300
St. Paul	1,023
Salt Lake City	2,000
San Diego	7,000
San Francisco	3,000+
Santa Monica, Calif.	4,000
Seattle	1,350+
Trenton, N.J.	600
Washington, D.C.	7,500

INTERRACIAL MARRIAGES

Before the passage of the 1965 Civil Rights Act, many interracial couples lived in fear of being discovered by an intolerant public, and only some nine in 200 marriages were between couples of different races. By 1970, one in 145 marriages were interracial; by 1980, one in 75; and by 1990, one in 53. Today, slightly more than 20 percent of all interracial marriages are between blacks and whites; the others involve other races as well.

The list below represents various interracial marriage combinations, according to the Census Bureau, and the approximate proportions of them among interracial couples

("other" refers to Asians, Native Americans, and mixed races).

Characteristic	Percent
White man/woman, other	50%
White woman/man, other	25
Black man/white woman	16
White man/black woman	6
Black man/woman, other	3
Black woman/man, other	1

LANGUAGES, IN THE HOME

Not since World War II have so many Americans spoken a foreign language at home. Today, one in seven U.S. residents speaks a language other than English. Spanish is the leading tongue, spoken by 17 million Americans — 54 percent of whom do not use English at home. All told, 31.8 million American residents speak 329 foreign languages in their households. This represents an increase of 34 percent in foreign language usage in American households since 1980.

Asian languages are spoken by 14 percent of the foreign language speakers, reflecting the new wave of immigration from that region of the globe. The use of European languages have declined the most, as the descendants of the old immigrants abandon such languages as German, Yiddish, Polish, and Italian, and as immigration from Europe is supersede by that from Latin America, Asia, and Africa.

The list below indicates the 20 most common foreign languages in use in U.S. households, and states with the highest percentage of speakers, according to the U.S. Census Bureau.

Language	Households	State
Spanish	7,339,172	N Mexico
French	1,702,176	Maine
German	1,547,099	N Dakota
Italian	1,308,648	New York
Chinese	1,249,213	Hawaii
Tagalog	843,251	Hawaii
Polish	723,483	Illinois
Korean	626,478	Hawaii
Vietnamese	507,069	California
Portuguese	429,860	Rhode Is
Japanese	427,657	Hawaii
Greek	388,260	Mass.
Arabic	355,150	Michigan
Hindi	331,484	New Jersey
Russian	241,798	New York
Yiddish	213,064	New York
Thai/Lao	206,266	California
Persian	201,865	California
Creole	187,658	Florida
Armenian	149,694	California

Other languages spoken by more than 100,000 American residents, and the states in which they are chiefly used are: Navajo (New Mexico), Hungarian (New Jersey), Hebrew (New York), Dutch (Utah),

Mon-Khmer (Rhode Island), and Gujarathi (New Jersey).

Below are the five states with the most and the fewest foreign language speakers by percentage in the home, according to the U.S. Census Bureau.

MOST FOREIGN LANGUAGE SPEAKERS

State	Foreign Speakers
New Mexico	35.5%
California	31.5
Texas	25.4
Hawaii	24.8
New York	23.3

FEWEST FOREIGN LANGUAGE SPEAKERS

Kentucky	2.5
West Virginia	2.6
Arkansas	2.8
Alabama	2.9
Tennessee	2.9

Most of those who speak foreign languages at home—94.2 percent—speak some English. More than half of foreign language users—56.1 percent— speak English "very well," 23 percent speak it "well," and 15.2 percent speak it "not very well." Only 5.8 percent speak no English at all.

MARRIAGE

An estimated 2.3 million couples married during 1993, the smallest number since 1970, when 2.2 million couples wed. The marriage rate dropped to nine per 1,000 population, down from 9.2 in 1992, continuing a decline that began in 1985, when the rate dropped from 10.5 in 1984 to 10.1. The historical high rate since 1920 of 12.2 was reached in 1945—the year most World War II servicemen returned home.

In addition to fewer marriages, the nation is seeing an increase in the average age of marriage. About 40 percent of all 19-year-old women were married in 1960; by 1990 only 11 percent were. About 91 percent of all women in 1960 were married before reaching age 30; by 1990 the percentage had dropped to 81.

In the 20-year period 1970-90 Americans aged 30-34 who had never married tripled, from six percent for women to 16 percent, and for men from nine percent to 27 percent. For ages 35-39 the proportion doubled, from five percent to 10 percent for women, and from seven percent to 15 percent for men.

In 1988, the last year the Census Bureau showed final statistics for marriage and divorce, 54.1 percent of weddings were the first marriage of bride and groom, according to estimates by the U.S. Center for Health Statistics. In 1970 the figure was 69.6 percent. That same year, 16.5 percent of both bride and groom were getting remarried. By 1988 that had jumped about a third, to 23.4 percent. About 11 percent of 1988 marriages represented the first marriage for either the bride or groom.

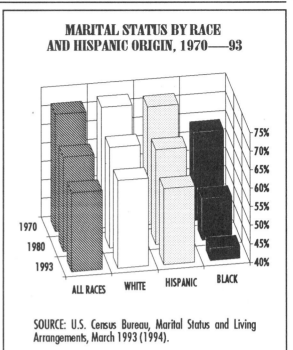

MARITAL STATUS BY RACE AND HISPANIC ORIGIN, 1970—93

SOURCE: U.S. Census Bureau, Marital Status and Living Arrangements, March 1993 (1994).

No state currently allows same-sex couples to marry. The Hawaiian Supreme Court in 1993 ruled three to one that a marriage ban on homosexuals may violate Hawaii's prohibition against sex discrimination. It sent the case back to the state's trial court for a determination of whether preserving the marriage ban was of "compelling state interest."

If Hawaii eventually permits same-sex couples to marry, the decision will be binding on the other 49 states, because marriages in one state are legally recognized by all states.

Texas led all states in marriages in 1992, with an estimated 183,000 (California figures not available; in 1985 the California total was 222,800), according to the National Center. Second was New York with 156,300, followed by Florida (138,100), Nevada (114,200), and Illinois (93,500).

Median age at first marriage by year and gender from 1890 to 1993 (years 1989-1993 estimated); source, U.S. Bureau of the Census.

Year	Male's Age	Female's Age
1880	26.1	22.0
1900	25.9	21.9
1910	25.1	21.6
1920	24.6	21.2
1930	24.3	21.3
1940	24.3	21.5
1950	22.8	20.3
1960	22.8	20.3
1970	23.2	20.8
1980	24.7	22.0

1985	25.5	23.3
1988	25.9	23.6
1989	26.2	23.8
1990	26.1	23.9
1991	26.3	24.1
1992	26.5	24.4
1993	26.5	24.5

MULTIPLE BIRTHS

Worldwide, about one in 100 pregnancies involves either the splitting of an egg, or two or more eggs being fertilized. About one in 90 births results in twins, and one in 9,000 yields triplets. In the U.S., the rate of multiple births is just about double the world average.

The reason is that in America, women are having children much later in life than women elsewhere, and as a woman ages, multiple births are more likely, due to the decreased regularity of menstruation. Often two or even three eggs are passed instead of one. In addition, many older women use fertility drugs to increase their chances of conceiving, which also increases the frequency of multiple births.

The following table, compiled by the American College of Obstetricians and Gynecologists, represents the proportions of various multiple births in 1990, the year for which the latest data are available, and for 1973.

Type	Rate, 1990	Rate, 1973
Twins	1 in 43	1 in 50
Triplets	1 in 1,341	1 in 3,500

Quadruplets and quintuplets are quite rare. In 1989, 229 quads and 40 quints were born in the U.S.; in 1990, there were fewer —185 quads and 13 quints.

NUCLEAR FAMILIES

Of 68.1 million families in the U.S. in 1993, less than half (33 million) had children under age 18 living in the home, the majority of which are "nuclear families," that is, households that consist of only the parents and their children.

Two children were the rule among 10 million of these couples. One-child families numbered 9.4 million, and those with three numbered 5.2 million. White couples made up 25 million of these families, black couples 4.6 million, and Hispanics 3.3 million.

The age groups 30 to 44 parented almost half of the 47,181 children in nuclear families (32.7 million), according to the *Statistical Abstract of the United States, 1994-95,* from unpublished Census Bureau data. Parents age 15-24 numbered 1.3 million; age 25-29 numbered 4.9 million, age 45-54 numbered 7 million, and age 55 and over numbered 1.1 million.

Most nuclear families owned their own homes in 1993 (39.9 million whites, 2.2 million blacks, and 2.3 million Hispanics). Renter nuclear families numbered 12.5 million (10 million whites, 1.6 million blacks, and 2.7 million Hispanics).

In 25.8 million nuclear families, both parents are employed (22.6 million whites, and 2 million both blacks and Hispanics). Families in which both parents' educational attainment is less than high school numbered 2.7 million; families where both parents have a college degree numbered 8.1 million. High school graduate parents were most predominant, at 15.6 million.

Sociologists recognize two subgroups of American families, "blended" and "extended." Blended families, composed of two parents and children from previous marriages or adopted children, numbered 8.2 million in 1990, up from 7.4 million in 1980. Children living with a half-siblings number 4.9 million—3.3 million white, 1.5 million black, and 593,000 Hispanic.

Extended families usually include one or two parents and children, and one or more grandparents, or parents and children living with grandparents. Those families totaled 6.1 million in 1993. Of these, 3.4 million lived in the grandparents' home. Extended families with only the mother present totaled 1.6 million; neither parent present numbered one million; both parents present 475,000, and with father only present, 229,000.

UNWED MOTHERS

With the diminishment of the stigma related to out-of-wedlock births, more professional women are having children without benefit of marriage, according to a 1995 Census Bureau report entitled "Fertility of Americans Women."

Overall, the report stated, one-fifth (20.2 percent) of never-married women bore children as of 1994, up from 18.1 percent two years earlier.

Twenty-seven percent of all American children under age 18 in 1993 lived with a single parent who had never married, and the total of such children had climbed by more than 70 percent from 1983 to 1993. The 1993 figure, 6.3 million children, is 2.9 million more than in 1983.

The report by the Census Bureau pointed out a sharp rise births to unwed mothers from 1960 onwards. In 1960 there were 243,000 children living with a single parent who had never married. Researchers say the increase in out-of-wedlock births in the 1960s can be traced to the policy that increased welfare payments to unwed mothers. Those payments continued to rise, though benefits declined because they were being outdistanced by inflation.

According to the Census Bureau report "Marital Status and Living Arrangements," 57 percent of black children were living with a never-married parent in 1993, compared to 32 percent of Hispanic children and 21 percent of white children. The comparable figures in 1982 were 49 percent, 16 percent, and 10 percent, respectively.

In 1992, about 65 percent of births overall to mothers age 15 to 19 were to unmarried mothers. Ninety-four percent of black teenage births were out of wedlock, 60 percent of Hispanic teen births, and 56 percent of white teen births.

WORKING MOTHERS

American mothers who work are more likely to be found in Midwestern cities than women with children in other cities around the country, according to U.S. Census figures. Eighteen Midwestern metro areas are among the top 25 in the country where mothers work, and almost half of those are in Wisconsin and Iowa.

Sioux Falls, S.D., on the western fringe of the Midwest, is the top employment city in the U.S. for working mothers, with 84 percent of its mothers working. Madison, Wis., is next, with 82.7 percent, followed by Sheboygan, Wis. (82 percent), Rochester, Minn. (82 percent), Springfield, Ill., and LaCrosse, Wis. (80.9 percent), and Des Moines, Iowa (80 percent).

Seventy percent of American mothers with children under the age of 18 are in the labor force. Eighty percent of working mothers in Sioux Falls have a child under age six, as do 75 percent of the working mothers in Madison. In that category, 13 metro areas in the Midwest are among the top 15 areas in the nation claiming the most working mothers of preschoolers, an average proportion of 73 percent.

Far down on the scale of metro areas where mothers work are Hispanic areas in Texas: Laredo (54.3 percent); McAllen- Edinburgh-Mission (56.6 percent); Brownsville-Harlingen (57.8 percent); and El Paso (58.9 percent). California metros with low percentages of working mothers include Yuba City (60.5), Visalia-Tulare-Porterville (62 percent); and Merced (62.8 percent) in California.

Mothers in the nation's labor force totaled six million in 1992, up from four million in 1978, according to Census Bureau figures evaluated in *American Demographics* in its November 1993 issue. Of those six million, 5.5 million held jobs, and 535,000 were looking for work. Mothers of preschoolers age three to five enrolled in nursery schools made up 26.8 percent of working mothers, up from 22.1 percent in 1978. Single married women with children, who totaled 14.6 million, made up 14.1 percent of working women in 1993, according to the Bureau of Labor Statistics.

White working mothers among the nation's 58 million working women age 22 and older totaled 6 million in 1992, compared to 874,000 blacks, and 623,000 Hispanics, according to the Labor Department. White mothers with children in nursery schools made up 28.1 percent of the working mother total, an increase from 21.1 percent in 1978.

Black mothers of preschoolers made up 19.7 percent of the working-mother total, down from 28 percent in 1978, and Hispanic mothers 17 percent, up from 16.3 percent.

The list below shows the top 15 and bottom 15 metropolitan areas ranked by women with childern in the labor force. The two right-most columns indicate the age of their children in 1990. Source, U.S. Bureau of the Census:

HIGHEST

	Rate	Under 6	6 to 17
Sioux Falls, S.D.	84%	80.3%	86.2%
Madison, Wis.	82.7	75.1	87.3
Bismarck, N.D.	82.7	75.6	85.7
Hickory-Morgan-town, N.C.	82.1	74.6	85.5
Sheboygan, Wis.	82.0	72.9	86.1
Lincoln, Neb.	81.7	76.6	84.8
Rochester, Minn.	81.0	75.8	84.4
Springfield, Ill.	80.9	70.6	85.8
LaCrosse, Wis.	80.9	70.5	85.8
Des Moines, Iowa	80.8	74.7	84.0
Columbia, Mo.	80.3	74.3	83.8
Fargo, ND–Moorhead, Minn.	80.1	73.2	84.1
Bristol, Conn.	80.0	70.3	85.8
St. Cloud, Minn.	79.9	75.2	82.2
Wausau, Wis.	79.8	72.6	82.9

LOWEST

	Rate	Under 6	6 to 17
Houma-Thibodaux, La.	52.2	47.3	54.3
Laredo, Texas	54.3	50.1	56.4
McAllen-Edinburg-Mission, Texas	56.6	51.7	58.7
Steubenville, Ohio-Weirton, W.V.	56.7	48.9	59.4
Huntington, W.V.-Ashland, Ky.	57.8	50.2	60.7
Brownsville-Harlingen, Texas	57.8	52.5	60.1
El Paso, Texas	58.9	51.6	62.4
Las Cruces, N.M	59.5	52.1	63.1
Yuba City, Ca.	60.5	47.5	68.5
Beaver County, Pa.	60.8	50.2	65.4
New York City	61.0	50.9	66.6
Fresno, Ca.	62.0	50.0	68.5
Visalia-Tulare-Porterville, Ca.	62.0	46.0	69.6
Lake Charles, La.	62.6	56.1	65.4
Stockton, Ca.	62.7	52.4	68.0

THE GENERATIONS
OVERVIEW

One thing U.S. history teaches us: Rebellion of our young is to be expected and perhaps it is even healthy for the nation. But the coming rift between the generations in the U.S. over the next several decades has all the signs that the "generation gap" of the '60s will prove mild compared to the coming one. It is likely to happen as early as the first decade of the new millennia.

All the facts and figures point to a disturbing possibility: The younger generation may fight to maintain the standard of living established by the group now reaching its senior years. In many ways, it will be fighting to fulfill the promises of the Baby Boomers, or to pull back some of those promises.

At the turn of the twentieth century, America is likely to be marked by tension and conflict between the aging Baby Boomers and their successors, "Generation X." Boomers, those born in the period between the end of World War II and the early '60s, number close to 80 million—more than one quarter of the population. Boomers were at the heart of the social transformation of the country as they came of age in the '60s and '70s, and as they reach their retirement years, they'll be taking increasing advantage of the programs they helped put in place or fund—namely, Medicare, Medicaid, and Social Security.

However, the sheer number of Baby Boomers will create an enormous drain on those programs and their resources. It will be up to Generation X—a smaller group—to keep the programs afloat. That most likely will mean higher taxes on fewer workers in a more uncertain economy, and that thought doesn't make the younger generation very happy. Neither does the gloomy but real prospect of the massive Baby Boom generation actually bankrupting the Social Security

system before the current working generation can enjoy its benefits.

The power of the aging Boomers can be seen in everything from the expanding rolls of the American Association of Retired People, at 32,000,000 already the largest non-profit association in the country, to Norman Lear's proposed new cable channel catering to older Americans. But even as society caters to the economic, political, and cultural clout of the Baby Boomers, it is desperate to figure out what Generation X wants and what it thinks. Like every new generation before it, Generation X confounds the establishment—the entry with this chapter about this age group, those Americans in their 20s and early 30s, characterizes them as combining unprecedented racial diversity and social tolerance with a financial conservatism unknown to the generation of the '60s and '70s.

Generation X is also growing up in a much more dangerous world: While overall crime statistics are down, rates of violent crime are up dramatically among younger people, both as perpetrators and as victims. Figures on teens and crime cited within this chapter indicate that the victimization rate is five times greater for juveniles than it is for those over 35. In addition, the lax social and sexual mores engendered in the '60s have resulted in widespread, and unforeseen problems, ranging from the drug abuse epidemic to higher divorce rates and the onslaught of sexually transmitted diseases. Social critics maintain that this is the darker side of the liberal legacy left by the Baby Boom—a mess left to the succeeding generations to cope with. The generation "gap" will be more like a canyon in the coming years.

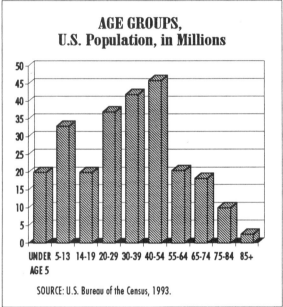

AGE GROUPS, U.S. Population, in Millions

SOURCE: U.S. Bureau of the Census, 1993.

AGE DISCRIMINATION

Call it downsizing, call it restructuring, or call it some other harmless-sounding euphemism, but American businesses continue to pare their workforce to contend with the economic climate of the 1990s. And though the job market is said to be difficult for new college graduates, older employers are taking more than their share of the hit.

According to the U.S. Equal Employment Opportunity Commission (EEOC), money awarded in job-related bias suits through either court action or out-of-court settlements totaled $65 million in 1992— the second-highest total ever. A record portion of that total, $50.7 million, or 77 percent, came in settlements of age discrimination suits, as employers attempted to reduce their payrolls by replacing higher-salaried, experienced employees with juniors whom they could pay less.

The EEOC found 70,339 complaints filed overall, the second- highest total since 1964, when the Civil Rights Act became law. That number was close to the all-time high set in 1988, when 70,749 complaints were filed. For the first time, the complaints included filings based on the new Americans with Disabilities Act—774, or 1.1 percent of the complaints—even though the law did not go into effect until November 1992.

Thus older employees now have joined minorities and women as those who suffer discrimination in the workplace. Racial discrimination, in fact, continues be the most frequent reason for equal opportunity complaints, at 40 percent of all complaints; that, however, represents a decline of three percent from 1991.

Charges based on sexual bias rose 2.2 percent from 1991, to 29.8 percent of all complaints. The EEOC attributed the increase in this category to a higher number of sexual harassment cases filed.

AGE DISCRIMINATION SUITS

The amount of money collected in age discrimination suits in the U.S. has far outdistanced that won in sex, racial, and disability suits, as corporate downsizing in the 1990s leaves a trail of older jobless people in its wake.

From 1988 through 1992, fired older workers who successfully sued their companies under the Age Discrimination in Employment Act of 1967 collected an average of $450,289. Litigants in successful sexual discrimination suits collected on average $255,734; those in racial suits $176,578; and in disability suits $151,421.

The 1967 act, which covers all workers age 40 or over, prohibits discrimination on the basis of age in hiring, promotion, firing, wages, and work conditions. The U.S. Department of Labor Statistics estimates that more than half of American workers will come under that protection within 10 years, a result of the aging of the baby boomer generation.

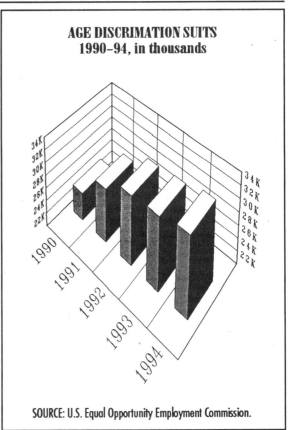

**AGE DISCRIMATION SUITS
1990–94, in thousands**

SOURCE: U.S. Equal Opportunity Employment Commission.

The number of age discrimination charges filed with federal and state agencies has climbed steadily since 1990. From 24,262 complaints filed in that year, they rose to 31,146 in 1993, according to the Equal Employment Opportunity Commission.

In the recession period 1990-91, workers past the age of 45 made up 26 percent of the unemployed. In another recession period, from 1981-82, workers in that age group made up just 16 percent of the jobless.

Among the largest amounts paid fired workers by companies in 1992 was $35 million to settle a suit brought by 32 dismissed division managers of IDS Financial Services of Minneapolis. McDonnell Douglas Corp., in the same year, shelled out $20.1 million in a settlement to 900 older employees laid off at one of its manufacturing plants.

Age discrimination suits filed from 1990 to 1993, in thousands, according to the EEOC:

Year	Suits
1990	24.3
1991	28.3
1992	30.6
1993	31.1
1994 (est.)	34.0

BABY BOOMERS

As World War II came to a close, the American homefront was experiencing a surge of optimism and a huge increase in birth rates. This period of skyrocketing fertility, commonly known as the "Baby Boom," occurred between 1946 and 1964, and led to an enormous boost in the U.S. population. Today the Baby Boom generation is estimated to number approximately 75 million, with the first wave of them turning 50 in 1996. Their storied history as a group thus far reached its apex in the 1960s, when the Civil Rights movement, the Vietnam War, effective oral contraception, and mistrust of the elder ruling class, all came to prominence. Their era saw the advent of hippies, psychedelia, and an increase in the kind of campus activism that played roles at Kent State and Montgomery, Alabama, as well as marches on Washington.

By the time the Boomers had hit the eighties, the term "Yuppie" had emerged out of the culture as a label predominantly attributed to those aging hippies who had allegedly "sold out" by joining the establishment and, in so doing, exchanged the ideals of 15 years earlier for the urban uniform of a suit and a tie. A "Yuppie" also came to signify the "young upwardly mobile professionals," a group of social climbers that included about one out of every 20 Boomers.

Boomers began placing less emphasis on money and more on meaning. Today the Boomers are the most spiritually-oriented living generation. Six out of every ten claim to have experienced an extrasensory force or presence, compared to four out of ten among older generations, and six times as many Boomers plan to spend more time in religious activities in future years as plan to spend less.

But the change-the-world mentality that was prevalent during the Boomer's coming-of-age years hasn't necessarily found the peace it worked so hard to foster. According to surveys from the Roper Center for Public Opinion Research, as the country inches toward the 21st century, 71 percent of the Baby Boomers claim to be dissatisfied with the way things are in the United States, with as many as 26 percent who say they are unhappy with their lot in life. And just as they find new challenges in terms of contentment and society, they are also now entering positions of power within corporations and various branches of the government. In their role as elder statesmen, they inherit a country that has slid in almost as many ways as it has prospered—gang violence, a huge federal debt, and racism are accepted as facts of life in the same way that baseball, apple pie and Chevrolets were 20 years ago.

As Boomers hit mid-life, and as the reality of retirement comes into view, they must contend with a Social Security fund that forecasters say will be depleted by the year 2036. As the tax rates are structured now, Baby Boomers are working to support the relatively small population of current retirees while they contribute to their own retirement funds. However, in the mid-eighties there were five people in their prime working years for every one person aged 65 or older, and as the Boomers near retirement, the ratio of beneficiaries to workers will lead to an increase in taxes to their generation. Whether or not the traditional transition from work to retirement will even apply to the Boomers remains to be seen, but for now the resulting tax burden will force many of them to re-plan for their golden years—a fact which has already led to increased financial prudence and pared-down lifestyles.

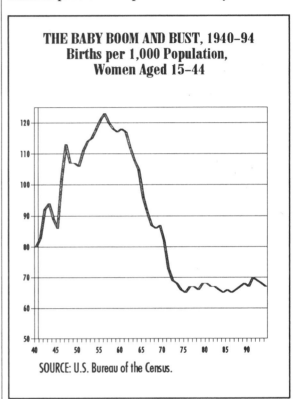

THE BABY BOOM AND BUST, 1940–94
Births per 1,000 Population,
Women Aged 15–44

SOURCE: U.S. Bureau of the Census.

Although in some respects the future holds unforeseen problems, the Boomers are a generation that will also look forward to staying active, both in the workplace on outside of it. Like no generation before them, they have benefited from jobs which were for the most part not confined to factories or fields—jobs which typically take their toll at a quicker rate. Since they are largely considered the twentieth century's showcase generation, they are in a position to alter age-old stereotypes about the elderly. As well, women's roles as decision-makers and leaders are expected to grow into the next millennium.

The Boomers are also now situated in a position to begin using the sheer clout of their numbers to swing political momentum or reverse their historically passive role as a generation prone to lobbyists and marketers. Should they choose to coalesce in the voting booths, they could have dramatic influence on the country's economic and political tides.

The Baby Boomer's impact on society has thus far been unprecedented: crucial Supreme Court rulings, the emergence of Playboy Magazine, and the arrival of the Beatles all helped usher America from one of its more innocent periods during the 1950s to one of its most mature and liberated. The Baby Boomers legacy can be felt throughout today's society, from the Boomer White House to the New Age movement and the health & fitness craze.

BIRTHS

In early 1994 the U.S. Census Bureau predicted that the baby boomlet that has produced 44 million children since the first baby busters began appearing in the early 1960s had reached its peak and was in decline. In late 1994 the bureau hastily altered its outlook.

Although births did decline for the whole of 1993, they still topped four million for the fifth year in a row. The bureau had predicted births would drop to just under that mark by the end of 1993. Instead a total of 4,039,000 busters were born—a drop from the 4,084,000 in 1992, but still above the significant four million mark. The peak in the boomlet was 4.2 million births, in 1990. From 1955 to 1963, the four million mark was passed each year.

The bureau had predicted in the middle of 1989 that births for that year would be 3.8 million. Instead, they topped the four million mark, and since then Census Bureau analysts have been playing catch-up with the baby-boom mothers who are confounding them, according to statistics from the National Center for Health Statistics and the Census Bureau. The bureau, in projections published in mid-year 1994, anticipated that births would remain above four million through 1995.

According to *American Geographics*, most births are to women in their 20s or younger, but women aged 30 to 49 may be catching up to that group, since many boomer women delayed childbearing until they were in their 30s.

The journal cites statistics from 1989 to 1991 showing that 29 percent of the 4,040,958 children born in 1989 were to women 30 and older. In 1990, births increased to 4,158,212, and so did the percentage of older women giving birth, to 30 percent. In 1980, just 20 percent of births were to women 30 and older. In 1991, the number of births in the U.S. declined to 4,110,907. The rates declined for younger women but increased per 1,000 women aged 35 to 39, to 32 percent. It also increased for teenagers, and held steady for women in their 40s.

The youngest boomer women still have at least a decade before their childbearing years end, the journal says—and new fertility procedures are being discovered that can extend childbearing past its natural limits.

The list atop the opposite column shows the number of births in the U.S., in millions, in selected years from 1970 to 1994, and projected to 2000, from the National Center for Health Statistics and the U.S. Census Bureau:

Year	Births (millions)
1970	3.7
1975	3.0
1985	3.6
1990	4.2
1994	4.0
2000	4.0

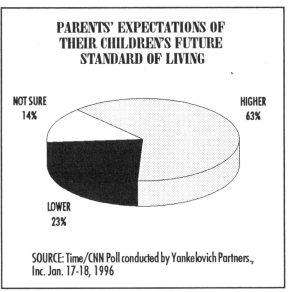

PARENTS' EXPECTATIONS OF THEIR CHILDREN'S FUTURE STANDARD OF LIVING

NOT SURE 14%

HIGHER 63%

LOWER 23%

SOURCE: Time/CNN Poll conducted by Yankelovich Partners., Inc. Jan. 17-18, 1996

CHILDREN, CHOLESTEROL LEVELS

It took nine years for researchers at the University of California at Irvine to conclude that poor diet and not enough exercise take their toll on young people, just as they do on adults. Their study involved 1,081 children between the ages of two and 20, television watchers all, and each with no family history of early heart attacks or cholesterol problems. Observed while watching TV, the kids mostly just sat there in front of the television set, munching on junk food.

The survey concludes that eight percent of the children had a cholesterol level of 200 milligrams or higher, which is considered dangerous for adults. Of those, 53 percent said they watched two or more hours of TV every day. If they watched TV for two to four hours a day, they were twice as likely to have high cholesterol levels, and they were four times as likely if they watched for more than four hours.

CHILDREN WITHOUT HEALTH INSURANCE

There are 8.5 million children without health insurance in the U.S., and the cause rests with businesses that have been slashing health care benefits and raising premiums because of runaway insurer costs, according to a Washington-based child lookout group. Mothers and fathers, children's health groups, and U.S. taxpayers are left to pick up the tab, a 1994 report by the Washington, D.C.-based Children's Defense Fund says.

In contrast to common perception, most uninsured young people are not urban minorities, children of single parents, or children of parents who have been displaced in the nation's workforce thus losing their health care benefits. More than 66 percent of the uninsured children are from families above the poverty line and from married-couple families, and 75 percent are white.

Between 1987 and 1992, at a time when 85 percent of Americans— primarily the elderly on Medicare and the fully employed—have some form of health insurance, the ratio of children covered by employer-based insurance dropped to less than 60 percent. If that trend continues, according to the report, entitled "The Health Insurance Crisis for America's Children," scarcely 50 percent of all children in America will by insured by the year 2000.

The South leads the nation in uninsured children; kids in the south are 50 percent less likely than children in other parts of the country to be covered in case of illness. That fact helps raise the average spending per consumer in the South on health care to the highest in the country, at $1,711 annually. Its 3.5 million uninsured children contrast with 4.5 million in the rest of the nation.

The national average for uninsured children is 10 percent, but every state in the South has a level higher than that. The percentage climbs from 12 percent in Tennessee and Georgia to 23 percent in Texas, yielding an average of 17 percent for the South as a whole. Texas alone has 1.1 million uninsured children, thus ranking dead last in the nation in caring for its kids, judged by this standard.

Below are the number and percentage of uninsured children in the South, by state, from the Children's Defense Fund report:

State	Children Insured	Percent
Texas	1,100,963	23%
Arkansas	130,275	19
Louisiana	211,133	19
Alabama	204,382	18
Florida	558,536	18
Mississippi	136,407	17
South Carolina	139,705	15
Kentucky	122,405	14
North Carolina	209,604	14
Virginia	229,804	14
West Virginia	64,017	14
Georgia	200,513	12
Tennessee	147,906	12

COLLEGE STUDENTS, BINGE DRINKING

A study by the Carnegie Foundation for the Advancement of Teaching concludes binge drinking is the No. 1 problem on college campuses across the country. Bearing out the foundation's report, the first major in-depth survey of binge drinking in colleges finds that among 17,096 students at 104 schools in 40 states and the District of Columbia, the problem seriously plagued anywhere from 35 to 51 percent of college students, depending on the school.

The survey found that non-drinkers made up just 16 percent of the American college population, drinkers who do not binge, 41 percent, and binge drinkers, 44 percent. The majority of binge drinkers were men. Among binge drinkers, 83 percent of the men and 82 percent of the women say they usually binge when drinking; 73 percent of the men and 68 percent of the women say the reason they drink is to get drunk; and 70 percent of the men and 55 percent of the women were drunk three or more times in the prior month.

The study, printed in the December 7, 1994 *Journal of the American Medical Association* and conducted by Drs. H. Wechsler, A. Davenport, G. Dowdall, B. Moeykens, and S. Castillo of the Harvard School of Public Health, found that 41 percent of the frequent-binge drinkers engaged in unplanned sexual activity, and 21 percent were more likely than non-binge drinkers to disregard using safeguards during sex.

Sixty-one percent of binge drinkers missed classes because of drinking, and 46 percent dropped behind in school work. Sixty-two percent of the men drove after drinking, as did 49 percent of the women; 53 percent of the men and 48 percent of the women rode with a driver who was high or drunk.

The Harvard group cites a 1994 Columbia University report reviewing other studies, which concluded that alcohol was involved in 66 percent of college suicides, 90 percent of campus rapes, and 95 percent of violent crime on campus.

Like alcohol abusers in general, few of the high-binge students surveyed believe they have a drinking problem—less than one percent of the total sample and only 0.6 percent of the high- binge drinkers, the study says. The Harvard group attributes this denial to the fact that binge drinkers see others on campus acting the same way, and to the sheltered life of the college community, which may make problem drinkers less likely to recognize their problem.

The following list details problems among students for non-binge drinkers occasional binge drinkers and frequent binge drinkers, according to the *JAMA* report:

Problem	Nonbingers	Occas. Bingers	Freq. Bingers
Hangovers	30%	75%	90%
Regret something done	14	37	63
Miss class	8	30	61
Forget what happened	8	26	54
Behind in school work	6	21	46
Quarrel with friends	8	22	42
Unplanned sexual activity	8	20	41
Get hurt or injured	2	9	23
Damage property	2	8	22
Engage in unsafe sex	4	10	22

Trouble with police	1	4	11
5 or more of above problems	3	14	47

Below are the effects of binge drinking at low-, middle-, and high levels:

Effect	Low	Middle	High
Insulted or shamed	21	30	34
Argued or quarreled seriously	13	18	20
Handled roughly or assaulted	7	10	13
Had property damaged	6	13	15
Cared for drunken student	31	47	54
Studying, sleep interrupted	42	64	68
Unwanted sexual advances	15	21	26
Sexual assault/rape victim	2	1	2
One or more of the above	62	82	87

Alcohol-related driving behavior of low-, middle-, and high-binge drinkers:

LOW LEVEL

Behavior	Men	Women
Drove after drinking	20	13
After five or more drinks	2	1
Rode with drunk driver	7	7

MIDDLE LEVEL

	Men	Women
Drove after drinking	47	33
After five or more drinks	18	7
Rode with drunk driver	23	22

High Level

	Men	Women
Drove after drinking	62	49
After five or more drinks	40	21
Rode with drunk driver	53	48

COLLEGE STUDENTS, DESIGNATED DRIVERS

One of the most important chores facing a majority of college students today earns no credits, gets no grades, and receives little thanks—yet 88 percent of men and women students surveyed on the subject have participated in the program. The chore is being selected designated driver.

Widely discussed in the late 1980s through a media campaign promoted by the Harvard Alcohol Project, the concept required one member of a partying group to stay sober and drive the other members of the group home safely. The benefits of the program relied on total driver abstinence, and planning ahead in drinking situations, thus avoiding the problem of having to know when to say when the person's judgment already is impaired by alcohol.

In 1991 the use of "DDs" (designated drivers) was called one of the most successful college campus programs for reducing the problems of drinking and driving by the U.S. Office for Substance Abuse Prevention. Certain provisos have been added to that estimation since 1991, however, according to a 1993 college DD survey of 288 men and women students at a public university in the Southeast, where 88 percent of the sample said they had been a DD and 82 percent said they had used one.

Doctors Mary A. Glascott, Sharon M. Knight, and Lisa K. Jenkins of East Carolina University in Greenville, N.C., found that 67 percent of the students, both men and women, drank while serving as a DD. Thirty-seven percent would allow the driver to have two drinks, and 53 percent said the availability of a driver increased drinking by other members of the group. Five percent would allow the DD to drink up to a certain time of evening, four percent to the point of intoxication, and two percent to the point of feeling a "buzz."

Forty-three percent of the drivers found their role rewarding, but 65 percent said it was also complicated and stressful. Nineteen percent said that more than two or three times when they drove they had to care for somebody who had passed out. Other stressful situations quoted in a report on the survey by the journal *College Health* included trying to monitor others' drinking during the binge; tending to passengers who vomited, passed out, or became unruly; putting passengers to bed; and checking on them the next day. Drinking activity of designated drivers by percent, from survey figures in *College Health*:

ABSTAINING WHILE DD

Frequency	Percent
Never	4.9
33% of the time	20.9
34-66% the time	8.4
67-99% of the time	32.9
100% of the time	32.9

WHEN LIMIT WAS SET

Never	32.4
1-33% of the time	20.4
34-66% of the time	11.2
67-99% of the time	23.6
100% of the time	12.4

MADE SURE TO STAY SOBER

Never	39.2
1-33% of the time	15.4
34-66% of the time	7.7
67-99% of the time	14.6
100% of the time	23.1

Drinking activity of designated drivers, from the users' viewpoint:

TIMES DRIVER ABSTAINED

Never	5.5
1-33% of the time	22.9
34-66% of the time	13.3
67-99% of the time	36.7
100% of the time	21.6

TIMES DRIVER SET A LIMIT

Never	21.1
1-33% of the time	24.3

34-66% of the time	15.6
67-99% of the time	29.4
100% of the time	9.6

TIMES DRIVER DRANK

(but made sure to stay sober)	
Never	26.1
1-33% of the time	22.0
34-66% of the time	13.8
67-99% of the time	35.4
100% of the time	2.8

Below are opinions concerning the DD program for students surveyed (not listed are those who neither agree nor disagree with the statement--median 22 percent--and those who strongly disagree--median 4.3 percent):

Statement	Strongly Agree	Agree	Disagree
Name DD before party	49.1	27.9	11.3
Rotate DD	52.9	35.8	1.4
Nondrinker usually selected	38.3	54.2	1.8
Pay for DD	20.6	36.1	13.5
DD often taken advantage of	14.1	40.8	16.6
DD job stressful	25.1	39.9	15.5
Job is rewarding	13.4	30.0	15.6
Some DDs cannot be trusted	33.7	52.1	3.9
On date, one should be DD	21.1	42.3	6.5
DD responsible for others	24.4	29.0	12.3
Prevent trouble in group	6.4	20.1	26.5
DD should never drink	35.2	24.9	15.0
Passengers drink more with DD	16.2	29.9	22.9
Men DDs face more trouble than women	17.0	23.4	17

ELDER CARE

Elderly Americans with disabilities requiring home care are tended to predominantly by women whose average age is 57.3 years, of whom 30.9 percent are employed and 8.9 percent have withdrawn from the labor market, according to a report on the allocation of labor in home caregiving in the summer 1992 issue of the *Journal of Consumer Affairs*. Twenty-one percent adjust their time schedules by working fewer hours, 29.4 percent rearrange schedules, and 18.6 percent take time off without pay.

About 48 percent of caregivers attend to a spouse, and 34 percent to a parent; nearly two million women care for children and parents simultaneously, according to the most recent data available, collected in a national survey by the Older Women's League in 1989. The league estimates that 37 percent of women over the age of 18 can expect to be caregivers during their lifetime.

GENERATION X

Perhaps no generation in America has been so aggressively pursued as a demographic, and yet so difficult to define as Generation X, the loosely applied moniker given to those born between the years 1965

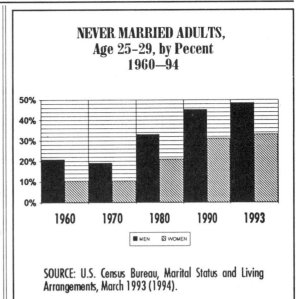

NEVER MARRIED ADULTS,
Age 25–29, by Pecent
1960—94

SOURCE: U.S. Census Bureau, Marital Status and Living Arrangements, March 1993 (1994).

and 1982. At approximately 75 million strong, they have already surpassed their predecessors, the Baby Boomers, in size, and during the second half of the decade will most likely come to outvote them. Though an MTV poll found that only one in ten young people would ever use the word "Generation X" to describe themselves, the sobriquet has stuck.

The term is taken from a Douglas Coupland novel by the same name which tells the story of three "twentysomething" protagonists who go from one "McJob" to another and, in the process, ostensibly reveal much about the lifestyles, realities and job circumstances that prevail in the twentysomething culture. Yet the Generation Xer's societal profile defies pigeonholes. For starters, their ethnic composition—70 percent white, 13 percent black, 12 percent Hispanic, 4 percent Asian and 1 percent Native American— situates them as the most racially diverse generation to date. This puts their world views at all notches of the philosophical spectrum, and contributes to the diversity of their social icons; their role models run the gamut from Robert Kennedy and the late Nirvana singer Kurt Cobain to Malcolm X and Pat Califia, a lesbian S&M writer.

Having come of age with the Brady Bunch, Watergate, the specter of AIDS, gangbanging, and a divorce epidemic that, throughout the '70s and 80's, affected a million children a year, theirs is a generation that manages to juggle a relative level of personal contentment with a clear-eyed skepticism of the government: The Roper Center for Public Opinion Research found that 25 percent of "twentysomethings" are unhappy with their lives, while 63 percent said they were dissatisfied with the way things were going in the U.S.

It was only as recently as 1990 that the Generation X'ers were thought of as "slackers," a term which is used to pinpoint what elder generations see as a lackadaisical, rudderless community of twentysomethings. Prior to that, they were regarded as cynical but ambitious entrants into the money-hungry 1980s, and social observers of that decade would go on to conclude that the greed- fueled mindset launched college grads into premature adulthood. All that changed at the dawn of the '90s as a recession forced about a million of those under thirty out of the workplace. Twenty years ago a typical 30-year-old male made 6 percent more than a typical 60-year-old male; today he makes 14 percent less. And while polls show that most teenagers expect to be earning in excess of $30,000 by the time they're thirty, the realities tell a different story: In 1990, the U.S. Census Bureau reported that among Americans aged 25-29, there were eight with total annual incomes of under $30,000 for every one making more than $30K.

Early on in the '60s, half of all adults agreed that parents in a bad marriage should stay together for the sake of the children. By 1980, only a fifth agreed. Yet among men 20 to 22 who are working full time, the numbers who marry is on the rise. Unsteady economic times have made the Gen Xers wary with their money, they are more financially conservative than they have been in 20 years. But falling mortgage costs have boosted the rate of home ownership among people in their 20s, though the average full-time salaries— $26,197 for males between the ages of 25 and 34; $21,510 for females in the same age range —still help explain why as many as 46 percent of single, twentysomethings are still living under their parents roof.

In 1993, 47 percent of 18- to 24-year-olds had at least a some higher education, better than the numbers from 1980, which were 16 points lower. Higher education for this generation translates into higher incomes and lower unemployment rates, though, as in generations past, a large percentage must work through a succession of lesser jobs en route to the vocation which matches their qualifications. Despite this, the Roper Center study recently showed that 87 percent of them were "somewhat or completely satisfied" with the conditions of their jobs; 87 percent had a "strong sense" of company loyalty; and 69 percent hold strong in the belief that "people get ahead by their own hard work."

One distinguishing characteristic prominent in Generation X's popular culture is the synthesis of disparate elements: In the nineties, punk rock meets folk, bell bottoms meet shaved heads, small towns have the identical "conveniences" as big towns, and multiracial couples walk the streets in larger numbers than ever before. This is a generation that has also seen the division between the cutting edge and mainstream vanish. Tattoos, earrings and anti-establishment musical groups have all become a part of the popular vernacular, making Generation X an unpredictable jumble of ideas and ideology.

MENOPAUSE

Troublesome symptoms commonly suffered by women at the onset, during, and after menopause can be eased by diet and exercise, according to a wide-ranging study of 15,000 women reporting on their experiences. Of those who found menopause "not bothersome," 64 percent exercised three or more times a week, compared with 39 percent who exercised two or fewer times a week.

The benefits of three-times-a-week exercise did not stop there. Of the 15 most common symptoms of a menopause, those who regularly worked out were nearly 50 percent more likely to report five or fewer symptoms than those who did not.

Fifty-eight percent of women in the survey of those just reaching menopause, in menopause, and just after menopause described the phases as "somewhat bothersome," or no more than annoying, according to the pollsters. More than 50 percent said for the most part the symptoms were mild. Hardest hit were respondents between the ages of 40 to 44, almost 33 percent of whom found the experience "very bothersome," compared to 21 percent of women 45 to 49 and 18 percent of women 50 to 54. Six percent of women who reached menopause at age 55 or older also found it "very bothersome."

Hot flashes were found not to be inevitable; 17 percent of the respondents experienced them in the stage before menopause began, at an average age of 48.7. On the other hand, 40 percent of the respondents overall and 46 percent of the women on the brink of menopause felt flashes, along with the other top troublesome symptoms: weight gain and sleep loss.

Sixty percent of the women reported taking on 10 pounds. Sixty-two percent of the women who reported hot flashes said the flashes awakened them at night.

Hormone-replacement therapy was tried by 39 percent of the women, usually prompted by the experience of hot flashes and other symptoms. Forty percent of younger women nearing menopause tried the treatment for as long as a year before they entered the stage, which is defined as the stoppage of the menstrual flow for at least one year. Sixty-nine percent of the younger women and 70 percent of women at the closing stage of menopause who had tried the therapy were still on it at the time of the survey.

Sixty-five percent of those in the therapy reported side effects, and 76 percent of those reported two or more effects. The chief effect was weight gain, reported by 60 percent of the women, 46 percent of those who took hormones for more than a year, gaining 16 or more pounds.

Excessive bleeding was the second-biggest side effect, at 46 percent; breast tenderness and water retention followed at 42 percent and 41 percent respectively.

Some of the alternative therapies to hormones include:

- Over-the-counter vaginal lubricants for vaginal dryness

- Reduced salt to ease water retention

- Reduced alcohol for hot flashes

- Yoga for joint pain

- Meditation for anxiety

Below are the most commonly reported symptoms during menopause, in percent of menopausal women who report the symptom, according to a *Prevention's* survey with the Center for Women's Health at Columbia-Presbyterian Medical Center, New York:

Symptoms	Percent
Weight gain	42%
Sleep problems	41
Hot flashes	40
Fatigue	37
Lost sexual desire	36
Forgetfulness	35
Joint pain	34
Mood swings	33
Water retention	31
Vaginal dryness	31
Frequent urination	31
Anxiety	26
Depression	26
Migraines/headaches	21
Heavy bleeding	15

Exercise and diet influences on menopause and percent who report five or fewer symptoms:

FREQUENCY

Times weekly	Percent
Three or more	47%
Two or fewer	35

DIET

Vegetarian	51%
Nonvegetarian	41

FAT INTAKE

Low	50
High	33

SOY INTAKE

Often	60
Rarely	41

Below are the side effects reported by those who underwent hormone-replacement therapy:

Side effect	Percent
Weight gain	60%
Excessive bleeding	46
Breast tenderness	42
Water retention	41
Headaches	22
Anxiety	19
Cramps	18
Nausea	14

Below are stress levels in troublesome menopause:

Stress levels	Percent
Low (6-10 symptoms)	16%
Low (11-15 symptoms)	4
Medium (6-10 symptoms)	7
Medium (11-15 symptoms)	33
High (6-10 symptoms)	20
High (11-15 symptoms)	35

PRESCHOOLERS, LITERARY AWARENESS

Every parent in America is a child's first teacher, and parents across the nation are doing a good job in getting their offspring ready to start school, according to a government survey. The analysis, based on National Center for Education Statistics surveys in 1991 and 1993 of an average 62,079 households, of which an average of 19,126 contained at least one pre-kindergarten child, showed that 78 percent of preprimary children were read to by a family member three or more times a week in 1993, an increase of eight percent since 1991.

Sixty percent of the children were regularly taught the alphabet, words, or numbers, 40 percent were told stories, 40 percent visited a library in the past month, 37 percent were taught songs or music, and 32 percent engaged in arts and crafts activities with a family member. All were increases from past figures, ranging from two percent for library visits to eight percent for those being read to.

Fewer children living in poverty were read to (68 percent) than those not in poverty (81 percent). Fewer poor children were told stories (37 percent vs. 42 percent), engaged arts and crafts activities (27 percent vs. 34 percent), or visited a library (29 percent vs. 43 percent). But poor children were more likely to have been taught songs or music (41 percent vs. 35 percent). The percentage of poor children being read to increased from 59 percent to 68 percent between 1991 and 1993; figures for children at or above the poverty level increased from 76 percent to 81 percent.

Blacks and Hispanics were more regularly taught letters, words or numbers than whites, Asians, or other groups (64 to 59 respectively), but were less likely to be read to (64 percent vs. 83 percent) or told a story regularly (38 percent vs. 41 percent). Blacks and Hispanics engaged in fewer arts and crafts activities (27 percent vs. 34 percent) and visited the libraries less frequently in the past month (30 percent vs. 43 percent).

Children in two-parent homes were read to more than children in one-parent homes (81 percent vs. 70 percent), participated with a family member in more arts and crafts (33 percent vs. 29 percent), and were more likely to visit a libraries (43 percent vs. 32 percent). High school and college-educated mothers read to their children more than mothers who had not completed high school (81 percent vs. 59 percent), and mothers who spoke English as the usual language in the home read more to their children than mothers who spoke a language other than English in the home (80 percent vs. 46 percent). Children in homes where English prevailed were more likely to be engaged in songs and music (38 percent vs. 32 percent), arts and crafts (33 percent vs. 24 percent), and library visits (41 percent vs. 28 percent).

Below are the percentages of preprimary children who have participated in literary activities three or more times in a given week in 1991 and 1993, in percent, from National Center for Education Statistics surveys:

Factor	1991	1993
PRESCHOOLERS READ TO		
Above poverty level	75.8%	81.1%
Below poverty level	58.5	67.6
White, non-Hispanic	76.7	82.9
Black or Hispanic	56.9	63.7
Two parents	74.1	80.5
None/one parent	62.2	70.0
Mother HS school grad	74.3	81.0
Less than HS	55.0	59.4
English-speaking home	73.9	80.3
Non-English-speaking	40.7	46.1
TOLD A STORY		
Above poverty level	36.5%	41.7%
Below poverty level	35.9	37.0
White, non-Hispanic	37.0	41.4
Black or Hispanic	34.6	38.0
Two parents	36.8	41.2
None/one parent	34.9	38.6
Mother HS school grad	37.1	41.5
Less than HS	32.9	35.4
English-speaking home	36.9	41.0
Non-English-speaking	32.0	35.4
TAUGHT LETTERS, WORDS, OR NUMBERS		
Above poverty level	61.0%	59.6%
Below poverty level	64.4	62.6
White, non-Hispanic	60.7	59.1
Black or Hispanic	65.0	63.7
Two parents	61.4	59.7
None/one parent	63.4	62.1
Mother HS grad	61.6	60.9
Less than HS	63.6	59.1
English-speaking home	62.0	60.9
Non-English-speaking	60.4	57.0
TAUGHT SONGS OR MUSIC		
Above poverty level	34.7%	35.4%
Below poverty level	37.4	40.7
White, non-Hispanic	34.9	35.1
Black, Hispanic	36.5	41.3
Two parents	35.5	35.8
None/one parent	34.9	39.4
Mother HS grad	35.6	37.0
Less than HS	33.8	37.8
English-speaking home	35.6	37.5
Non-English-speaking	32.2	32.0
PARTICIPATED IN ARTS AND CRAFTS		
Above poverty level	34.5%	34.0%
Below poverty level	29.5	27.0
White, non-Hispanic	34.8	34.2
Black, Hispanic	28.7	26.9
Two parents	34.3	33.4
None/one parent	29.3	29.2
Mother HS grad	33.8	33.7
Less than HS	30.0	23.9
English-speaking home	33.1	32.8
Non-English-speaking	34.2	24.4
VISITED A LIBRARY		
Above poverty level	40.9%	43.3%
Below poverty level	27.3	29.1
White, non-Hispanic	41.4	43.1
Black, Hispanic	26.5	30.2
Two parents	40.7	42.6
None/one parent	26.3	31.7
Mother HS grad	41.2	42.5
Less than HS	17.5	23.6
English-speaking home	39.2	40.7
Non-English-speaking	20.0	27.6

RETIREES, PENSIONS

Fifty-one percent of retirees today receive employer-paid or self-financed pensions, according to a 1994 study. By the year 2030 more than 80 percent of baby boomers, who will then be between age 66 and 84, will get pensions.

The study, entitled "Baby Boomer Pension Benefits," nevertheless predicts that because many boomers will continue to ignore saving habits, will squander lump-sum pension payments, and will neglect to buy a home while working, they will face troubled times in retirement.

Two scenarios for the future, a "good luck" scenario and a "bad luck" one, were drawn in the study sponsored by the American Association for Retired Persons. According to the first, which assumes steady economic growth, low inflation, and stable employment over the next 35 years, boomers will be receiving a median of $300 more a month in 2030—$6,900—than the median pension of $6,600 in the 1990s. All figures in the study are based on 1990 dollars.

Racial disparities are predicted to narrow in the future in regards to pensions. Fifty-one percent of retired whites received pensions in 1990, compared to 32 percent of blacks. Eighty-three percent of whites are expected to get pensions in 2030 and 79 percent of blacks. Also, 89 percent of married couples will be pensioned, vs. 73 percent of singles.

Experts caution that a lot of little pensions gathered from job- hopping can result in smaller pensions, since a federal law nullifies accumulated pension benefits unless the worker remains with the same company for more than five years.

The consulting firm, Lewin-VHI of Fairfax, Va., which conducted the study, said the luckiest boomers in 2030, as far as pensions are concerned, will be married full-time workers, white, male, and better-educated. Unluckiest will be single part-time and temporary workers, minorities, women, and the less-educated. A separate Congressional Budget Office report predicts that many poorly educated singles could wind up on public assistance, according to a 1993 article in *E* magazine.

The "bad luck" scenario is based on a weak economy, lower wages, high unemployment, and runaway inflation. In that scenario, rather than 82 percent of the 45 million boomers being retired with pensions, only 41 million, or 77 percent, would fall under that financial protection. Median pension benefits would plunge $1,500, from $6,900 annually to $5,400.

SENIOR CITIZENS

About 12 percent of the U.S. population (31.7 million) in 1993 was over age of 65, an increase of 6.3 million from 25.5 million in 1980 and 19.9 million in 1970. Eighteen million seniors were age 65 to 74, 10.5 million age 75 to 84, and three million age 75 to 84. In 1980 those figures were 15.5 million, 7.7 million, and three million, respectively. In 1950 the entire over-65 population totaled 9 million.

Of the 9.9 million aged 65 to 69, 4.5 million were males and 5.5 million females. Of 8.5 million in age group 70 to 74, 3.6 million were males, 4.8 million females. Women continue to outnumber men by almost 60 percent in the age group 75 to 100 and over. There were 10,000 men and 34,600 women at or past the century mark.

A total of 9.2 million seniors lived alone in 1993, up from 5.2 million in 1970. Of these, 1.9 million were men, up from 1.2 million in 1970, and 7.3 million were women, up from four million in 1970.

Among male seniors, 76.8 percent were married, 4.4 percent were single, 14.3 percent widowed, and 4.5 percent divorced, according to the Census Bureau. Among the women, 4.4 percent were single, 42.2 percent were married, 47.6 percent widowed, and 5.8 percent divorced. More than 81 percent of the men lived in families, compared to 57 percent of the women.

Still in the work force were 15 percent of the men and 7.9 percent of the women. Almost nine percent of the men and 15.7 percent of the women lived below the poverty level.

About 28 million of the nation's elderly were on Social Security in 1991, receiving an average of $643 in monthly benefits, for a disbursement of $194.3 million of Social Security funds, up from $172,042 in 1990. The highest number (2.7 million) live in California. Florida is second at 2.1 million.

Twenty-five million Social Security recipients are enrolled in Medicare, up from 16.2 million in 1970. They paid a premium of $41.10 a month in 1994 and $46.10 in 1995.

In 1993, the total number of deaths—16.3 million—among seniors from the ages 65 to 85 and older accounted for more than twice the number of deaths in all other ages combined. Included among the 30,810 suicides in the nation were 6,800 seniors (5,530 men and 1,250 women), according to the National Center for Health Statistics.

SENIORS AND DEPRESSION

Sadness and disappointment are normal experiences that no one escapes. Among the elderly, though, such psychological episodes can cause permanent debilitation. Of the more than 65 million seniors in the

U.S., 12 percent suffer from debilitating depression, and three percent are considered pathologically depressed, according a study by to the National Institute for Aging. The report went on to note that estimates for depression range as high as 25 percent for residents in nursing homes, who may feel alone, unhappy, and unstimulated.

The American Association for Aging adds that the suicide rate for people 65 and older is 50 percent higher than for the general population, making them the group most at risk in the American population. Depression is found to be more common in older women than in men and is the mental complaint most often reported by older women in physicians' offices and in outpatient clinics.

SENIORS, MEDICARE AND MEDICAID ELIGIBLE

Today's low-income seniors are the most secure group in America when it comes to receiving medical treatment for life-threatening illnesses. The combination of state and federal Medicaid programs and the national Medicare program have virtually guaranteed that medical attention is available to this group. Millions of seniors, however, are not taking advantage of the government programs that cover small items.

Nearly half of low-income seniors do not apply for out-of-pocket medical expenses, according to Families USA, a national health care advocacy group. These include such items as medicine and treatment for minor illnesses. For major medical expenses, most doctors and hospitals help seniors to get aid, but for lesser procedures, most must put in their own claims to be covered by Medicare and Medicaid.

Some 4.25 million people are eligible; however, about 42 percent of them—1.8 million seniors—fail to do the necessary paperwork. Administrators blame the problem on lack of public awareness of the specific programs. Seniors see it differently, however: The paperwork is so exhaustive that many of them simply find it more than they can handle. So far, the only answer has been local social service agencies, who help seniors wade through the paper jungle.

TEEN COURTS

Some 40 percent of the nation's two million juveniles who are arrested annually receive little more than a police record and a slap on the wrist. Thus authorities are looking for ways to dampen youthful criminal activity with something more than stern warnings and probation. Enter "Teen Courts," a mushrooming concept in smaller communities.

The Case of Bryan Couch: In Odessa, Texas, teen prosecutor Laurel Linde, 17, made short work of Bryan Couch, 16, who had been charged with driving under the influence. "How many beers were you drinking?" Linde asked. Couch replied eight to nine. "Did you know the legal drinking age?" Couch did. "Were you trying to impress your friends?" Linde asked. "I

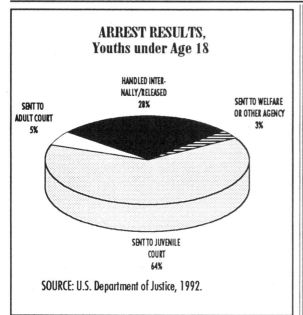

**ARREST RESULTS,
Youths under Age 18**

HANDLED INTER-NALLY/RELEASED
28%

SENT TO ADULT COURT
5%

SENT TO WELFARE OR OTHER AGENCY
3%

SENT TO JUVENILE COURT
64%

SOURCE: U.S. Department of Justice, 1992.

TEENS, CRIME

Federal reports show that the murder rate among youths aged 14 to 17 increased 68 percent between 1988 and 1992. Of 118,700 serious crimes committed by teens, aggravated assault cases increased the most, up 80 percent in the period to 77,900.

The victims, far from being from society at large, increasingly were young people between the ages 12 to 17, according to the Justice Department's Office of Juvenile Justice and Delinquency. Of 6.6 million violent crimes in the U.S. in 1992, 23 percent were perpetrated against juveniles, or 74.2 cases per 1,000 juveniles. Among persons 35 and older, the victimization rate was five times less: 13.9 per 1,000 population.

One juvenile in 13 was a violent crime victim in 1992, up 23 percent from 1987, when one juvenile in every 17 was a victim. Assaults accounted for 83 percent of the 1992 crime total, with 420,000 committed against 12- to 17-year-olds. Killings among teens increased 55 percent to 2,500; robberies climbed 52 percent to 32,900; and forcible rape cases rose 27 percent to 5,400. Past federal reports showed a 124 percent increase in the homicide rate among teens between 1986 and 1991.

The current report also noted an increase of 68 percent, or 11,700, in the transference of juvenile cases to adult courts since 1988. Offenses against persons were transferred in 68 percent of the cases, against property 45 percent, and 12 percent were drug violators.

Overall, juvenile court cases increased 26 percent to about 1.5 million in the period 1988 to 1992.

TEENS, GUN DEATHS

There are as many as 135,000 guns in American schools on any given day according to an estimate by *USA Today*. As many as two million teenagers carry guns, knives, clubs, or razors. According to the National Center for Health Statistics, 4,173 American teenagers were fatally shot in 1990, the year for which the latest statistics are available. Only automobile accidents kill more of our nation's youth.

Will guns replace the automobile as the nation's No. 1 killer of our young? We're moving in that direction. The figure 1990 was up by almost 600 (about 17 percent) over the previous year. In 1985, 2,498 teens were shot to death.

Racial Lines: The bullet knows no racial boundaries. Among black males 15 to 19 years old, fatal gunshot wounds have increased from 37 deaths per 100,000 in 1985 to 105 deaths per 100,000 in 1990. Among white males, the figure has nearly doubled, from five deaths per 100,000 to almost 10.

TEENS, PREGNANCY

Sixty-six percent of sexually active adolescents who have never used a contraceptive become pregnant

shouldn't have done it," Couch replied. The jury of two males and two females sentenced Couch to 20 hours of community service and three stints on a jury. "He should have gotten the max," Linde said, shaking her head.

Since 1983, Odessa has been a model for other cities that are experimenting with peer adjudication for teenagers. The Odessa court has passed judgment on 6,600 youths, issuing sentences on misdemeanor cases involving drugs or alcohol, traffic violations, shoplifting, or simple assault. Sentences can range up to 30 hours of community work four sessions to be served on a teen jury. At the completion of the sentence, charges are dismissed.

Is it working? "Kids are much tougher than any adult," said Natalie Rothstein, the program coordinator. "If the jury thinks the defendant is lying, they'll usually nail him to the wall."

The list below shows the leading juvenile offenses and the number of youths under 18 who were arrested in 1992, and the result of the arrest, as compiled by the Department of Justice.

Offense	Arrested
Runaways	174,000
Liquor violations	158,000
Assault	151,000
Burglary	143,000

COURT RESULTS

Sent to juvenile court	64%
Handled internally, released	28
Sent to adult criminal court	5
Sent to welfare or other agency	3

within the first two years of sexual activity; 25 percent become pregnant in the first month. And 75 percent of all unintended teen pregnancies occur to adolescents who do not use contraceptives, several 1994 national surveys found.

Of those sexually active teens aged 15 to 19 who do use birth control, 64 percent depend on the pill, 21 percent on condoms, eight percent on the rhythm method, six percent on a diaphragm, and two percent on mechanical devices (IUDs), according to studies reported in the May 24, 1994, edition of the *Chicago Tribune.*

More than 25 percent of unmarried teens who undergo abortions have never tried birth control, and most of those who did relied on withdrawal, the rhythm method, or douching—the three most unreliable types of contraception, according to the studies. For first intercourse, 38 percent of the males and 41 percent of the females reported using ineffective methods or no method, and for the most recent intercourse before the survey, 23 percent of males and 29 percent of females reported using ineffective methods or no method.

TEENS AND SMOKING

Smoking among teens, beginning with ninth-graders, hasn't declined for a decade; about 3,000 young people start the habit each day. This disturbing news was revealed by U.S. Surgeon General Dr. Antonia Novello, who adds a fact uncovered by the Centers for Disease Control: Camels were the preferred cigarettes for 30 percent of the ninth-graders who smoke—five times the market share for Camel among adult smokers. Dr. Novello blames Camels' "Joe Camel" campaign, which began in 1988.

Before Old Joe began, only 2 percent of young people smoked Camels. Now Old Joe is as familiar to American youngsters as Mickey Mouse. Nevertheless, according to the CDC, Marlboro is far and away the most popular brand-name cigarette among ninth-grade smokers, 43 percent of whom use it. Next in rank after Camels is Newport, with 20 percent. The three brands together account for almost 95 percent of the total youth market.

VETERANS

World War II veterans threw a salute to Vietnam veterans, who in 1993 passed them in numbers for the first time, according to a national tally of the 27 million military veterans from the four major wars the nation has fought in since 1917 and the Persian Gulf skirmish of 1991.

In 15 years, by 2008, WWII veterans are projected to drop to third and then fourth place in numbers as they yield to mortality, replaced by Korean and Gulf War veterans respectively. By 2010, providing there are no new conflicts, the share of peacetime-only veterans—those who served in the military between the Vietnam and Gulf wars—is expected to grow from 23 percent in 1993 to 32 percent.

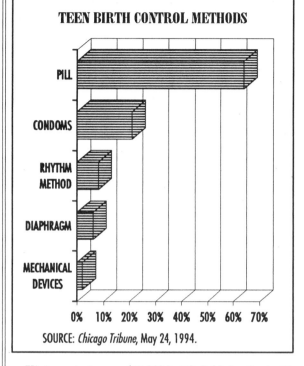

TEEN BIRTH CONTROL METHODS

PILL

CONDOMS

RHYTHM METHOD

DIAPHRAGM

MECHANICAL DEVICES

0% 10% 20% 30% 40% 50% 60% 70%

SOURCE: *Chicago Tribune,* May 24, 1994.

Vietnam veterans (47,369 battlefield deaths in 12 years) currently number 8.2 million; WWII vets 8.1 million (292,131 battlefield deaths in three and a half years). Peacetime-only vets number 6.1 million, Korean vets, 4.7 million (33,651 battlefield deaths in three years), Gulf war vets one million (148 battlefield deaths in 100 hours), and WWI vets 25,000 (53,513 battlefield deaths in 18 months), according to the U.S. Department of Veterans Affairs. Veterans are defined by the VA as those who have been separated from the service.

Since many in the military who served in Vietnam are still among the estimated two million men and women on active duty in the U.S. armed forces in 1995, the number of veterans of that war is expected to grow as those who began their military career in the Vietnam years retire. That growth will mean Vietnam vets will be the most numerous until at least 2010, when, though diminishing in numbers to 7.2 million through mortality, they may make up 36 percent of the total veterans, according to the VA.

By 2010 WWII vets are projected to drop from 8.1 million to 2 million, and Korean vets from 4.7 million to 2.8 million. The number of Gulf War veterans will increase from one million to 2.9 million (again due to retirements of those currently active in the military). The total veteran population is projected to drop from the current 27 million to 19.6 million.

About 31 percent of U.S. veterans are age 65 or older, according to a commentary on the VA figures published in *American Demographics.* Thirty-seven percent will be of that age by the year 2000. Twenty-five percent of Korean vets were of retirement age in 1993, and 60 percent of the eight million WWII vets were age 70 or older. About four percent of all veterans are women, but women make up 12 percent of newly discharged veterans.

The following table details disabled veterans receiving compensation, for selected years 1970 to 1993, in thousands, from the *Annual Report of the Secretary of Veteran Affairs*:

DISABLED

Military Service	1970	1990	1993
Peace-time	185	444	471
World War I	85	3	1
World War II	1,416	876	769
Korea	239	209	198
Vietnam	167	652	682
Persian Gulf	N/A	N/A	76

TOTALLY DISABLED

Military Service	1970	1990	1993
Peace-time	16	27	28
World War I	11	N/A	N/A
World War II	63	43	37
Korea	16	16	15
Vietnam	18	44	52
Persian Gulf	N/A	N/A	2

VA HEALTH CARE SUMMARY, 1980 TO 1993

Item	1980	1990	1993
Hospitals	172	172	171
Homes for aged and disabled	16	32	37
Outpatient clinics	226	339	353
Nursing home units	92	126	128
Employment (1,000s)	194	199	210
Obligations (millions)	$6,215	$11,827	$15,079
Prescriptions (millions)	37	59	59
Laboratory (millions)	215	188	N/A
Outpatient visits (millions)	18	22	24
Inpatients treated (1,000s)	1,359	1,113	1,043
Average on daily basis (1,000s)	105	88	84

YOUNG ADULTS AND DRINKING

Young Americans are not getting the message on drinking and driving, drunken-driving experts learned in a mid-1990s conference in Washington, D.C. The age group 21 to 34 remains the nation's deadliest drunken-driver group, and the conference sponsor says they are "a tough nut to crack."

While teens have marked the best 10-year drop (55 percent) in alcohol-related fatal crashes, the percentage of fatal wrecks among those aged 21 to 34 has

Michael Keating.

Slightly more military men and women served in Vietnam than in World War II (8.1 million vs. 8.2 million). Above, Vietnam veterans march on the nation's Capitol in commemoration of the twentieth anniversary of peace negotiations that ended the war.

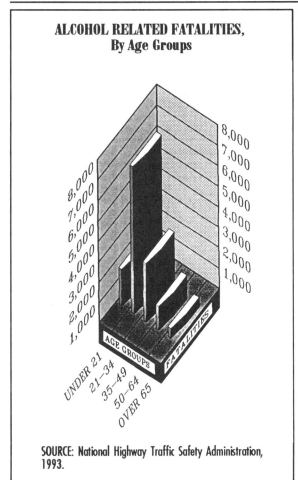

ALCOHOL RELATED FATALITIES, By Age Groups

SOURCE: National Highway Traffic Safety Administration, 1993.

Experts at the conference said these young drinkers of legal drinking age usually live away from home and are out of school, party a lot, and are free of rigid sobriety programs, unlike teens, who are the programs' captive audience.

Below are the ages of drinking drivers in fatal accidents in 1993, according to National Highway Traffic Safety Administration:

Age	Fatal crashes
Under 21	1,821
Age 21-34	7,221
Age 35-49	2,891
Age 50-64	1,177
Over 65	478

Below is the number of persons killed in car accidents in select years, from Department of Transportation figures:

Person	1980	1988	1992
Occupants	41,927	39,170	32,869
Drivers	28,816	27,253	22,583
Passengers	12,972	11,805	10,201
Other	139	112	85
Person	1980	1988	1992
Nonmotorists	9,164	7,917	6,366
Pedestrians	8,070	6,870	5,546
Bicyclists	965	911	722
Other	129	136	98

YOUTHS, DISADVANTAGED

A typical American disadvantaged youth is a high school dropout age 18 who reads at the seventh-grade level, comes from a poor family, belongs to a minority group, and has never held a full-time job. These youths are just what the Department of Labor wants in its Job Corps program.

For an average period of 7.5 months in nine regional offices and 81 centers across the nation, the department houses, disciplines, and trains these youths to become productive members of society. The cost to the government in 1994 was $1.04 billion, up from $966.1 billion in 1993, and was projected to increase to $1.1 billion in 1995. A study by Mathematica Policy Research, Inc., found that for every dollar invested to make the youths productive, $1.46 eventually is returned to society.

The federal government's Job Corps program, administered by the Labor Department in partnership with organized labor and the private sector, is a training and employment opportunity program for disadvantaged youth around the country, established in 1964. It accepts only U.S. citizens age 16 to 24 who are poor, high school dropouts, not on probation or parole, free of serious medical or behavioral problems, and living in a disruptive environment. In 1993, 39,387 new students were enrolled in the program with 102,098 overall participants. After an average stay of 7.5

improved only about one-third, 32 percent. That's the lowest sign of improvement of any age group. In 1993 those crashes killed 7,221 young Americans.

Over 10 years since a nationwide crackdown on drunken driving began in earnest, the age group has accounted for half of all alcohol-related fatal accidents: 54 percent in 1983 and 52 percent in 1993. By contrast, with only 478 fatal crashes in 1993, Americans 65 and older are the least likely to die in a car crash.

All 50 states and the District of Columbia have raised the legal drinking age from 18 to 21, and 31 states have "zero tolerance" laws that lower accepted alcohol levels for teen drinkers.

Experts at the conference, sponsored by the Century Council, which is composed of members of the alcohol industry, agreed on characteristics shown by young American drivers. They include the following:

- More likely to be drunk at the time of a crash;

- Twice as likely to have been in an earlier crash;

- And four times more likely to have had their licenses suspended or revoked.

months, seven days a week, in Job Corps dormitories, 63,117 made it through, 70 percent of whom were from minority groups (60 percent male, 40 percent female). Seventy-nine percent were high school dropouts, and 29 percent had never held a full-time job. At the end of training (which can last up to two years), 75.4 percent, or 40,536, of those contacted who completed the program in 1993 had found jobs or continued education on their own.

The Corps is the most expensive training and employment program run by the Department of Labor, costing $919.5 million in 1992. Thirty-seven percent of that figure was spent on student meals, lodgings, allowances, medical care, etc.; 18.8 percent was spent on administration; and 43.7 percent on student training. The program's cost rose to $1.04 billion in 1993 and $1.1 billion in 1994.

Unique to the Job Corps program is its residential aspect, where the student lives in one setting throughout his or her stay in the program. Approximately nine out of 10 students fall into this category, the remainder commuting daily to a center. An open-entry, open-exit, and self-paced program, it allows some students to stay as long as two years to earn a high-school equivalency diploma.

Below are the percentage of students served by Department of Labor's Job Corps, according to department statistics:

Race/Ethnic Group	Percent
Black	50%
Hispanic	30
Asian-Pacific islander	14
White	3
Native American	3
History	
High school dropout	79
Had prior full-time job	43
Family on welfare	29
Entry Reading Level	
Grades 0-4	15
Grades 4.1–7.4	28
Grades 7.5 to 10	28
Grades 10-plus	29
Average	**7.9**
AGE AT ENTRY	
Under 17	21.0
Age 17	19.8
Age 18	18.2
Age 19	15.9
Age 20	13.9
Age 20	11.3
Average	18.0

HEALTH AND BODY
OVERVIEW

The diagnosis is mixed for America's health as the century comes to a close. On the one hand, there is much to be pleased with. Americans on the whole are healthier than ever. The smoking rate among Americans age 18 and older is down from 39 percent in 1970 to 25 percent today. This has been a significant factor in bringing down the death rate from heart disease, which has dropped from 362 per 100,000 twenty-five years ago to 282 per 100,000 in the mid-1990s. Death rates from motor vehicle accidents are also down, from 26.9 per 100,000 in 1970 to 16.2 per 100,000 in 1995. Infant mortality, which stood at 20 per 1,000 births in 1970, has declined to 7.9 per 1,000.

A general rise in health consciousness has contributed to the improved physical well-being of the American population. Better exercise and nutrition have played a large role in the trend. Relative to it, 90 percent of American adults demand healthier foods as they scan the supermarket shelves. They are consuming less beef, more poultry, fewer additives and preservatives, lower sodium, less fat, and more natural ingredients. And it is paying off: Americans can expect to live five years longer today than they did in 1970. Life expectancy is up from 71 a quarter-century ago to 76 today.

But not all the news is good. No discussion of health in America can avoid the looming shadow of AIDS. More than 220,000 Americans have died from it since it surfaced in the early 1980s. Though HIV infection rates are falling among homosexual males, the hardest-hit and highest-profile group of AIDS sufferers, a disturbing increase in infection rates has been noted among intravenous drug users. AIDS is also striking hard at minorities: The AIDS rate among blacks is five-time higher than for whites, and for Hispanics, three times higher. Black women are 15 times more likely to contract AIDS than white women. AIDS now is the leading cause of death among Americans age 25 to 44.

Other data in this chapter also present cause for concern. Cancer is on the increase, rising from 130.9 deaths per 100,000 in 1950 to almost 160 per 100,000 in the 1990s among white males. Over the same time span, cancer rates nearly doubled for black males, from 126.1 to over 240. As with many diseases, from asthma to cancer, minorities suffer at a higher rate, and are less likely to survive after diagnosis. While 55 percent of white Americans diagnosed with cancer live for at least five years, only 39 percent of blacks do.

Though American infant mortality is down dramatically since 1970, it still is the highest registered among the top 10 industrial nations.

The advances in our health status have come with a price—the soaring cost of medical care. Despite this, people are going to the doctor more, and are therefore healthier. This drives up the number of medical procedures, boosting sheer overall expenditures and demand for health care. Related to this, as well as other factors, people are living longer and subsequently there is a greater need for elder care.

The AIDS epidemic has contributed to federal health care spending, searching for a cure. Unfortunately, rising costs are putting quality health care out of reach for a growing number of Americans. The continued national debate over health care primarily stems from this dilemma: The U.S. health care system is the best in the world, but many of its citizens simply cannot afford it. This issue will only become more intense as baby boomers age and require medical attention.

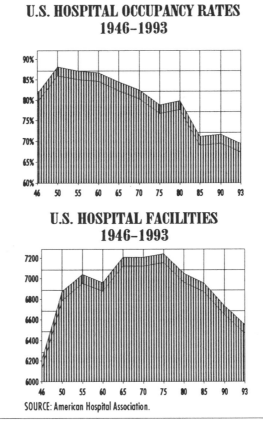

U.S. HOSPITAL OCCUPANCY RATES 1946–1993

U.S. HOSPITAL FACILITIES 1946–1993

SOURCE: American Hospital Association.

ABORTIONS

Abortions in the U.S. declined for the fourth straight year, and the number stands at its lowest level since 1979, with live births occurring three times as often as abortions, according to data from 1992, the latest year for which figures are available.

There were 1.529 million abortions among women age 15 to 44 years in 1992, a decrease of 28,000 from the year before. In 1979 the count amounted to 1.498 million, according to The Alan Guttmacher Institute in New York.

Almost half of the abortions took place during the first eight weeks of pregnancy, and 89 percent within 12 weeks. For each 1,000 live births, there were 379 abortions, a decrease from 422 in 1985, according to Guttmacher surveys of hospitals, clinics, and doctors identified as providers of abortion services. Government surveys on abortion rely only on reports sent in by the states.

The most abortions by region of the country occurred in the South. Southern totals reached 450,000, led by Florida, with 85,000. The next highest number occurred in the West, with 438,000 abortions, led by Arizona with 21,000 and New Mexico with 20,000.

The state with the highest number of abortions in 1992 was California with 304,000, almost 33 percent higher than the next highest state, New York, at 195,000. California has led all other states in abortions since 1980, according to the Institute. The Midwest registered the lowest abortion rate for the year, with 262,000, down from 318,000 in 1980, when it also was the region with the lowest abortion rate.

North and South Dakota's annual abortion rate was the lowest in the U.S., at 1,000 each. They were followed by Alaska and Idaho at 2,000, Vermont, West Virginia, and Montana at 3,000, and Maine, New Hampshire, and Utah at 4,000.

Abortions by selected characteristics, 1980 to 1990, compiled from *Statistical Abstract of the United States*, The Alan Guttmacher Institute, *Abortion Services in the United States, 1991 and 1992, Family Perspectives, 1994,* and unpublished data:

BY AGE GROUPS	Abortions (in thousands)		
Characteristic	1980	1985	1990
Total abortions	1,554	1,589	1,609
Under 15 years	15	17	13
15 to 19 years	445	399	351
20 to 24 years	549	548	532
25 to 29 years	304	336	360
30 to 34 years	153	181	216
35 to 39 years	67	87	108
40 years and older	21	21	29
BY RACE			
White	1,094	1,076	1,039
Black or other	460	513	570
BY MARITAL STATUS			
Married	320	281	284
Unmarried	1,234	1,307	1,325
BY NUMBER OF PRIOR LIVE BIRTHS			
None	900	872	780
One	305	349	396
Two	216	240	280
Three	83	85	102
Four or more	51	43	50
BY NUMBER OF PRIOR INDUCED ABORTIONS			
None	1,043	944	891
One	373	416	443
Two or more	138	228	275
BY WEEKS OF GESTATION			
Less than 9 weeks	800	811	850
9 to 10 weeks	417	425	418
11 to 12 weeks	202	198	185
13 weeks or more	136	154	155

AIDS

Since 1994, 376,889 persons have developed AIDS in the U.S., and almost three-quarters, 270,533, have died in what has been called the most alarming disease of our time. Worldwide, 30 to 40 million people are expected to contract AIDS by the year 2000.

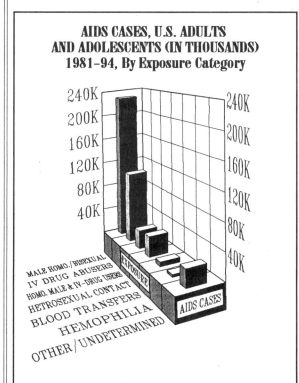

AIDS CASES, U.S. ADULTS AND ADOLESCENTS (IN THOUSANDS) 1981–94, By Exposure Category

SOURCE: U.S. Department of Health and Human Services, Centers for Disease Control and Prevention, HIV/AIDS Surveillance Report, 1994.

Since 1981, more than 14 million people, included about one million children, have been infected with HIV, or human immunodeficiency virus, the precursor to AIDS. New cases diagnosed in 1993 amounted to 104,468, contrasted to 49,799 from the previous year, though the sharp rise was called a one-time phenomenon by the Centers for Disease Control and Prevention.

According to the World Health Organization. 12 percent of U.S. AIDS suffers, or 43,999, were women; 10 percent were persons age 50 or older. AIDS is the fourth leading cause of death among American women age 25 to 44 and the eigth leading cause of death overall

About 54 percent of all adult and adolescent AIDS cases are among homosexual or bisexual males. Drug abusers made up 24 percent of the victims in 1994, but according to the CDC new infections are appearing at a higher rate among drug abusers than among homosexuals. AIDS is the leading cause of death among adults age 25 to 44.

AIDS cases among heterosexual men and women represent six percent of the total number of U.S. cases, but studies show that the disease is spreading faster among this group than among any other, due in large measure to women infected with HIV who pass it on to their children, according to the World Health Organization.

Men and women with AIDS, 1981-94; source, CDC:

Category	Males	Female
Homosexual/bisexual males	228,954	NA
Intravenous drug abusers	81,491	27,902
Homosexual male/ IV drug abusers	28,521	NA
Heterosexual contact	10,641	21,021
Blood transfusion	4,047	2,819
Hemophilia/coagulation disorder	3,545	97
Undetermined/other	19,690	6,589

Children under age 13 with AIDS, with number and percent of group infected, 1981-94; source, CDC:

Category	Number	Percent
Mother with/at risk	5,541	89%
Blood transfusion	357	6
Hemophilia/coagulation disorder	221	4
Undetermined	90	1

AIDS cases in selected U.S. cities, 1993; source, CDC:

New York	58,807
Los Angeles	22,803
San Francisco	18,135
Miami	10,920
Washington, D.C.	10,177
Chicago	9,797
Houston	9,538
Newark	8,248
Philadelphia	7,964
Atlanta	7,215

AIDS deaths in U.S., pre-1981 to 1993; source, CDC:

Year	Cases	Deaths	Deaths to Date
Pre-1981	92	31	31
1981	315	128	159
1982	1,156	461	620
1983	3,084	1,502	2,122
1984	6,198	3,478	5,600
1985	11,775	6,929	12,529
1986	19,042	12,021	424,550
1987	28,560	16,270	40,820
1988	35,267	20,903	61,723
1989	41,681	27,449	89,172
1990	46,075	30,649	119,821
1991	54,778	34,746	154,567
1992	67,306	36,941	191,508
1993	46,189	29,084	220,592

AIDS AMONG MINORITIES

Minorities continue to be hit hardest by the AIDS pandemic, rising to 55 percent of all victims in 1993 from 52 percent the year before and 51 percent in 1991. At the same time, the pace of the disease has slowed among white men.

The AIDS rate among whites in 1993 was 30 cases per 100,000 persons. Among blacks the rate was more than five times higher, at 162 cases per 100,000, and it was three times higher among Hispanics, at 90 per 100,000. The American Indian and Eskimo rate was 24 per 100,000, and the Asian and Pacific Islander rate was 12 per 100,000, according to the Centers for Disease Control and Prevention, based on reported cases in the U.S., Puerto Rico, Guam, and the Virgin Islands.

Black women had an AIDS rate of 73 per 100,000, making them about 15 times more likely to be victims than white women. Black men, with a rate of 266 per 100,000, were almost five times more likely to get AIDS than white men.

ALZHEIMER'S DISEASE

One of the greatest fears accompanying aging is that of dementia, through either stroke, Alzheimer's disease, or other nervous system disorders. The chief and most mysterious cause of senile dementia is Alzheimer's, an affliction for which there is no known cure. However, a vast amount of research on the disease has been done since 1980, when the disease began to capture the attention of the medical world. Today, according to the Alzheimer's Association, four million Americans suffer from Alzheimer's, and 100,000 die from it each year. The number of Alzheimer's sufferers in the U.S. is expected to rise to 14 million by the year 2040.

First diagnosed by a German neurologist in 1907, Alzheimer's affects five percent of the U.S. population over the age of 65 in its severe form; 10 percent of that age group suffers from the disease in its mild and moderate forms. Those 85 and older are at greatest risk from the disease. Alzheimer's, though, is not solely a disease of the elderly; it has been diagnosed in patients as young as their mid-40s.

Once the disease takes effect, symptoms including confusion, memory loss, and emotional dullness can be so severe that sufferers are a danger to themselves and require constant supervision. Patients frequently are confined to nursing homes, at an estimated average cost of $36,000 a year. As debilitating as the cost of medical care is the untold emotional hardship on the families of sufferers.

The following list represents the percentage of certain age groups that suffer from Alzheimer's disease, according to the Alzheimer's Association and the National Institute on Aging.

Group	Percentage
65-year-olds	6%
75-year-olds	20
85-year-olds	47

Given the aging of the baby boom generation, the sheer numbers of Alzheimer's sufferers will increase rapidly in the next two decades. Accordingly, money is speedily being infused into research on the disease and the search for treatment, and hopefully a cure.

The table below indicates how federal research funding for Alzheimer's research has risen in recent years:

Year	Funding
1989	$134 million
1990	$150 million
1991	$247 million
1992	$282 million
1993	$294 million

ASTHMA SUFFERERS

Sealed windows in high-rise office buildings and homes, locking in asthma-triggering substances such as wood dust, pesticide particles, printing chemicals, and chemicals in paint, may be partly responsible for a 42 percent increase in asthma cases since 1982, according to a government report that supports the findings of two earlier medical surveys.

From 1970 to 1980, annual deaths from asthma ranged from 2,000 to 3,000. By 1990 annual deaths from asthma had climbed to 4,800, and remained at nearly that level, 4,700, in 1993, according to the National Center for Health Statistics. An even higher total for 1993 deaths, 5,106, was announced by the U.S. Center for Disease Control and Prevention. The CDCP also reported an increase in asthma rates from 34.7 sufferers per 1,000 persons in 1982 to 49.4 per 1,000 in 1992.

The death rate was consistently higher among blacks, according to the CDCP. The asthma death rate among blacks stands at about 15 per million persons, while among whites it is three per million.

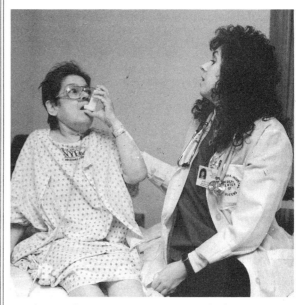

Asthma is on the rise, up over 40% since in 1982. Thanks to treatment centers like this one--New York City Hospital, Medical Center of Queens--death rates for sufferers are as low as three per million among whites. For blacks, however, the rate is 15 per million.

BREAST CANCER (FEMALE)

About one in every nine American women will suffer from breast cancer. Surgery is the most common but not always the prescribed treatment for breast cancer. Indeed, treatment varies widely across the nation. Women in some areas are five times more likely to have their breasts saved through conservation surgery.

In 1985, a consensus of cancer experts reported that breast-conserving procedures such as the removal of either a breast cyst or tumor (a lumpectomy) should be considered as alternatives to the removal of all or part of the breast (a mastectomy). One year later, acceptance of those recommendations varied widely from region to region: The rate of breast-saving surgery ranged from 21 percent of cases in Massachusetts to four percent in Kentucky. In general, women treated in large, urban teaching hospitals underwent fewer mastectomies. Dr. Ann Butler Nattinger, of the Medical College of Wisconsin in Milwaukee, isn't sure that this discrepancy still exists, but her group is studying the data from 1990 to find out.

The following list outlines the rates of breast-saving operations and number of overall breast cancer operation, by region, according to a 1992 Medicare study of patients aged 65–79:

- Middle Atlantic (N.J., N.Y., Pa.) — 20% of 6,334
- New England (Conn., Mass., N.H., R.I.) — 17% of 2,288
- Pacific (Alaska, Calif., Hawaii, Oreg., Wash.) — 13% of 5,000
- East North Central (Ill., Ind., Mich., Ohio, Wis.) — 11% of 6,436
- South Atlantic (Del., D.C., Fla., Ga., Md., N.C., S.C., Va., W. Va.) — 10% of 6,457
- Mountain (Ariz., Idaho, Mont., Nev., N. Mex., Utah, Wyo.) — 10% of 1,636
- West North Central (Iowa, Kans., Minn., Mo., Nebr., N.Dak., S.Dak.) — 8% of 3,225
- West South Central (Ark., La., Okla., Tex.) — 7% of 3,252
- East South Central (Ala., Ky., Miss., Tenn.) — 6% of 2,245

BREAST CANCER (MALE)

Though rarely appearing in national statistic tables, and almost never mentioned, breast cancer is suffered by men as well as women. About five percent of U.S. breast cancer cases involve men, according to a study from the Columbia University College of Physicians and Surgeons. The American Cancer Society (ACS) estimates 1,400 men will be diagnosed with breast cancer in 1995.

Male breast cancer likely is associated with genetics and increased levels of estrogen in the body, according to the ACS, though it is rare for several men in a family to develop the disease. Most men with breast cancer (90 percent) have localized or regional disease. The cancer usually does not spread to other parts of the body, as it often does in women.

Signs of breast cancer in men are a breast that swells and feels sore, and puckered, scaly, or irritated skin. A hard or firm lump may appear in the breast, and the nipple may become crusty. The nipple may also retract into the breast or develop a discharge. Seventy percent of men's breast cancers show these signs.

CANCER

The number of deaths from cancer nationwide is continuing a 44-year climb, according to estimates from the American Cancer Society, which predicted that 538,000 Americans would die of the disease in 1994. That's a rate of more than 1,400 each day.

At the same time the pattern of the nation's second biggest killer after heart attacks shows that the cancer death rate among children age 1 to 14 have declined markedly, from 18.4 in 1950 to 6.6 per 100,000 persons in the population. Declines also were registered by the age groups 15-55 years, while the rates for those over age 55 increased somewhat, partly affecting the over-

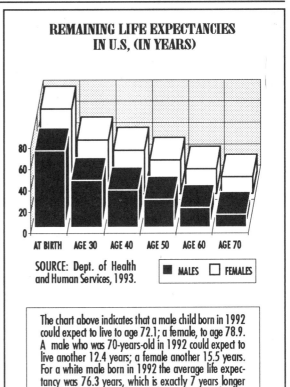

REMAINING LIFE EXPECTANCIES IN U.S. (IN YEARS)

SOURCE: Dept. of Health and Human Services, 1993.

■ MALES   □ FEMALES

The chart above indicates that a male child born in 1992 could expect to live to age 72.1; a female, to age 78.9. A male who was 70-years-old in 1992 could expect to live another 12.4 years; a female another 15.5 years. For a white male born in 1992 the average life expectancy was 76.3 years, which is exactly 7 years longer than for the average black child (not shown on chart).

all statistics, according to the National Center for Health Statistics.

The rate for white males rose from 130.9 cancer deaths per 100,000 in 1950 to 157.6 in 1992, according to the National Cancer Society. The rate among black males rose significantly, from 126.1 to 241. The white female rate dropped from 119.4 to 110, while it rose for black females from 131.9 to 135.8.

The Society also reported that the highest cancer death rates from 1986 to 1990 occurred in the District of Columbia (230 deaths per 100,000 population), Delaware (195), Maryland (193), and Louisiana (190). The lowest cancer rates were registered in Utah (124), Hawaii (138), Colorado (146), and New Mexico (146).

Survival rates show that more than eight million Americans with a history of cancer are still alive, the Society reports. Five million of them had diagnoses made five or more years ago. The Society predicts that four out of 10 persons who are diagnosed with cancer in 1994 will be alive after five years.

Five-year survival rate for cancer by race and site, 1960-89, in percent; source, National Cancer Institute, published by the American Cancer Society, 1994:			
Sites	1960-63	1970-73	1983-89
WHITES			
All Sites	39%	43%	55%

Bladder	53%	61%	80%
Breast (female)	63	68	81
Cervix	58	64	69
Colon	43	49	60
Leukemia	14	22	39
Liver	2	3	6
Lung and bronchus	8	10	13
Ovary	32	36	40
Pancreas	1	2	3
Prostate	50	63	79
Rectum	38	45	58
Stomach	11	13	17
Thyroid	83	86	94
BLACKS			
All sites	**27%**	**31%**	**39%**
Bladder	24	36	61
Breast (female)	46	51	64
Cervix	47	61	57
Colon	34	37	49
Leukemia	N/A	N/A	30
Liver	N/A	N/A	5
Lung and bronchus	5	7	11
Ovary	32	32	40
Pancreas	1	2	5
Prostate	35	55	64
Rectum	27	30	45
Stomach	8	13	18
Thyroid	N/A	N/A	92

The list below shows the highest and lowest cancer rates in the world, per 100,000 population, 1989-91; source, World Health Statistics Annual:

HIGHEST

Country	Rate
Hungary (1991)	119.0
Scotland (1991)	118.0
Belgium (1987)	105.0
England/Wales (1991)	104.0
Netherlands (1990)	102.3
Czechoslovakia (1990)	102.0
Denmark (1991)	99.8
Canada (1990)	96.5
U.S. (1989)	93.5
Italy (1989)	92.4

LOWEST

Country	Rate
Sweden	58.1
Norway	67.0
Japan	70.1
Finland	67.8
France	71.2
Spain	72.5
Bulgaria	73.6
Portugal	74.4
Australia	79.0
Switzerland	79.8

The list below shows cancer death rates by type per 100,000 persons, in highest and lowest groups in the world, by percent; source, WHSA:

HIGHEST

Country	Lung Area	Stomach	Female Breast
Hungary	61.8%	23.8%	33.4%
Scotland	67.4	12.8	38.2
Belgium	54.8	13.2	37.0
England/Wales	52.0	12.1	40.2
Netherlands	51.7	12.3	38.3
Czechoslovakia	53.2	20.1	28.7
Denmark	51.9	8.6	39.3
Canada	54.1	8.0	34.2
U.S.	56.1	5.5	31.9
Italy	43.3	19.3	19.8

LOWEST

Country	Lung Area	Stomach	Female Breast
Sweden	23.0	9.9	25.2
Norway	28.1	11.6	27.3
Japan	27.1	34.4	9.0
Finland	32.1	13.1	22.6
France	34.1	9.0	28.1
Spain	32.4	15.9	24.2
Bulgaria	31.2	20.9	21.5
Portugal	21.5	26.2	26.7
Australia	40.4	9.0	29.6
Switzerland	32.2	9.5	36.1

DEATH, CAUSES OF

Each year over 2 million Americans' leases on life expire—about .9 percent of those who were alive in the previous year. In 1994, 2,286,000 Americans died, 876.9 per 100,000 population.

This list below from the National Safety Council, indicates the 10 leading causes of death by percent in 1994.

Cause	Percent
1. Heart disease	32.1%
2. Cancers	23.5
3. Stroke	6.8
4. Pulmonary disease	4.5
5. Accidents	3.9
6. Pneumonia/influenza	3.6
7. Diabetes	2.4
8. AIDS	1.8
9. Suicide	1.4
10. Liver ailments	1.1

Death rates and causes vary enormously from city to city; they are more a matter of demographics than of geography. One of the most frightening reports came out in mid-1993: AIDS is the biggest killer of males between the ages of 18 and 44 in New York, Los Angeles, San Francisco, and more than 70 other met-

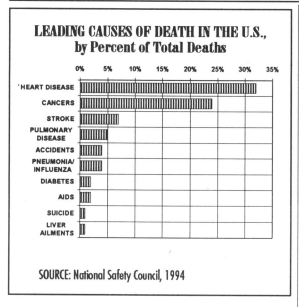

LEADING CAUSES OF DEATH IN THE U.S., by Percent of Total Deaths

	0%	5%	10%	15%	20%	25%	30%	35%
HEART DISEASE								
CANCERS								
STROKE								
PULMONARY DISEASE								
ACCIDENTS								
PNEUMONIA/ INFLUENZA								
DIABETES								
AIDS								
SUICIDE								
LIVER AILMENTS								

SOURCE: National Safety Council, 1994

ropolitan areas. In St. Petersburg, Fla., AIDS accounts for 1.8 percent of annual deaths; in St. Louis, 1.4 percent; in the Dallas suburb of Arlington, .41 percent; and in Anchorage, only .31 percent.

DEATHS, TIME OF

The psychological factor of an approaching birthday seems to precipitate death in men and prolong life in women, according to the largest study ever made on psychological factors and time of death.

The study of 2.7 million deaths by sociology professor David P. Phillips of the University of California at San Diego and published in the September 1992 issue of the journal *Psychomatic Medicine*, found that 3.03 percent more deaths than statistically expected occurred among all women within a week *after* a birthday; the number was a remarkable 10.8 percent for black females. For men, deaths peaked *just before* birthdays and showed no rise afterwards.

An earlier study by Phillips found that Jewish mortality dropped to 31 percent below normal before Passover, and rose by the same amount just afterward, and that the "dip-peak" pattern moved around with the variations in the date of the holiday. Chinese mortality similarly dips and peaks around the Harvest Moon Festival.

DEATH, TRANSPORTATION–RELATED

Nearly 1,400 more transportation-related deaths were recorded in the U.S. in 1993 than the year before. Declines were registered in aircraft and boating fatalities, and increases were registered in rail and road travel.

The National Transportation Safety Board reported total transportation-related deaths at 42,585 in 1993, up from 41,191 in 1992. That marked a reversal

in a four-year decline in transportation fatalities, principally due to a significant increase in highway deaths, from 38,722 in 1992 to 41,899 in 1993. Highway deaths account for 95 percent of all transportation deaths in the country, according to the Department of Transportation.

An Amtrak disaster in Alabama that killed 47 people helped account for the rise in railroad fatalities from 709 to 738. Marine fatalities decreased from 944 in 1992 to 832, and aviation deaths from 994 to 800.

Below are NTSB figures on the change in transportation fatalities from 1992 to 1993, by type:

MOTOR VEHICLE

Type	1993	1992
Passenger cars	21,494	21,366
Light trucks, vans	8,487	8,082
Pedestrians	5,638	5,546
Motorcycles	2,444	2,394
Pedalcycles	814	722
Medium, heavy trucks	610	584
Buses	18	28

RAIL

Type	1993	1992
Pedestrians	610	615
Passengers	58	3
Rapid transit	70	91

MARINE

Type	1993	1992
Recreational boating	800	816
Commercial fishing	32	84

AVIATION

Type	1993	1992
Private planes	715	860
Air taxis	42	65
Commuter	24	21
Foreign aircraft	18	15
Airlines	1	33

DENTAL CARE

American adults are keeping their teeth longer, and children and teenagers show fewer cavities since fluoridation of the nation's drinking water has become more widespread. The result: Though the number of dental institutions has declined since 1985 and so have the number of degrees issued, dentists have never been happier, a government assessment indicates.

Along with their regular patients, dentists are seeing more grandfathers and grandmothers, as the number of toothless Americans age 45 and older dropped from 18 million in 1986 to 16.5 million in 1989, according to the latest statistics available to the Centers for Disease Control and Prevention in Atlanta.

Fifteen percent of Americans without teeth age 65 or over see a dentist at least once a year, while 60 percent with teeth see a dentist at least once a year, according to a report on the CDCP findings in the September 1993 issue of the journal *American Demographics*. The national average for that age bracket is two visits a year, up from 1.1 visits in 1970, statistics from the National Center for Health Statistics (NCHS) show.

In the early 1970s, with fluoridation of water held back by widespread controversy over its safety, almost 75 percent of all nine-year-old children in the nation had cavities. By the late 1980s, when more than 50 percent of the nation lived in communities with treated water, that figure had dropped to 33 percent, according to CDCP. Plastic sealants applied to the surfaces of molars in children and teenagers, protecting them from decay for up to 15 years, contributed to the decline, according to *American Demographics*.

In 1970, Americans made 304 million visits to dentists; in 1989 they made 492 million visits, NCHS data show. From a record high of 5,339 dentistry graduates, 20.7 percent of them women, from the nation's 59 dental-degree institutions in 1985, a *Digest of Education Statistics* report shows a decline in graduates to 3,699, with 32.1 percent of them women, from 55 dental-degree institutions in 1991. The annual average income for general dental practitioners in 1992 was $98,140, up from $92,030 in 1991, and $153,410 for specialists, up from $143,030 in 1991, according to the 1993 American Medical Association *Survey of Dental Practices*.

Percentage of people who visted a dentist in the past year by selected characteristics, 1989; source, National Center for Health Statistics:

BY AGE BRACKETS	
All ages	57.2%
2 to 4 years	32.1
5 to 17 years	69.0
18 to 34 years	56.9
35 to 54 years	61.4
55 to 64	54.0
65 and older	43.2
BY SEX	
Men	54.9%
Women	59.4
BY RACE	
White	59.3
Black	44.5
BY ANNUAL FAMILY INCOME	
Less than $10,000	40.9%
$10,000 to $19,999	43.4
$20,000 to $34,999	58.3
$35,000 or more	73.0

DIET AND HEALTH CONSCIOUSNESS

Ninety percent of American adults are looking for healthier food choices when shopping at the market, according to two surveys taken by a health group. Survey results place persons between the ages of 30 to 39 as the group most highly committed to health against the multiple temptations on grocery shelves.

The 1990 and 1992 surveys by HealthFocus of Emmaus, Pennsylvania break down the 90 percent into five groups according to the consumers' dedication to

Though floridation of water in the U.S. has almost eliminated tooth decay in healthy individuals, many Americans opt for mineral waters like that offered by the vender above.

choosing the "right stuff": managers, investors, healers, strugglers, and disciples. Managers, who, for instance, eat less beef and more poultry, are the most numerous, at 50 percent. The total is up from 36 percent in 1990. Thirty-three percent of managers also eat ice cream on occasion.

Investors are the second largest segment, at 27 percent of the group, a decline from 45 percent in 1990. They have decreased their use of additives and preservatives and are most likely to eat with an eye on their future health. They also are the group least likely to be tempted by junk food.

Healers are eating more healthy food to repair the damage from the years when they ate less wisely. Nearly 75 percent of healers are aged 50 or older and show physical impairments such as arthritis, high blood pressure, diabetes, and high cholesterol. They have cut down on such items as pork, salt, and fat since 1990; 66 percent use low-sodium products once a week, while 68 percent have given up butter. Healers represented 11 percent of healthy food buyers in 1992, up from nine percent in 1990.

Strugglers would like to maintain a healthy diet but are eight times more likely than any of the other groups to call what they eat "healthy." Their ranks, 10 percent—up from 7 percent in 1990—are filled with the youngest of those surveyed, with more than 50 percent under age 40 and with the lowest incomes of those surveyed. Strugglers are most likely of all groups surveyed to eat white bread, spread it with butter, and drink nondiet sodas.

The smallest group in 1994 were the disciples, at two percent, down from 3 percent in 1990. These, according to the surveys recorded in the September 1993 issue of the journal *American Demographics,* shy away from all meats in favor of meat substitutes. They eat soy products, and 75 percent have increased their consumption of vegetables since 1992. Fifty-two percent, however, eat cookies at least once a week, and 62 percent use butter weekly.

DOWN'S SYNDROME

Down's syndrome, formerly referred to as mental retardation, limits intellectual capacity and leaves those afflicted with distinctive physical abnormalities and usually in need of a protective home or institutional environment. A new study shows that Down's syndrome strikes Hispanics more than white or black children.

A study by the Centers of Disease Control and Prevention followed 7.8 million American births from 1983 through 1990. The overall prevalence of Down's syndrome was 11.8 for Hispanics per 10,000 infants, 9.2 per 10,000 for whites, and 7.3 per 10,000 for blacks. The median for all three groups was 9.2 cases per 10,000 infants. The rate decreased from 9.5 per 10,000 in 1983 to 8.6 per 10,000 in 1990.

The group performing the study indicated that the results were a surprise in that previous surveys failed to show noticeable racial differences for the condition.

The syndrome is known to be more common as the age of the mother increases. The rate is one in 2,000 births when the mother is age 20; when she is 45 or older the rate is one in 20. In the case of Hispanics the overall rates were much higher than those for white or black infants in all age groups except ages 25-29.

The rate of Downs syndrome among white infants remained stable over the years of the study. The black rate dropped from 7.1 in 1983 to 5.3 in 1990, while the rate for Hispanics decreased from 9.4 to 6.4.

EXERCISE RISKS

A Harvard study on exercise and heart attacks concludes that only four percent of heart attacks occur during strenuous exertion, and 96 percent occur during rest. This shouldn't be as surprising as it appears: People who exercise generally improve their health and are less likely to suffer from a variety of illnesses, including heart disease. Nevertheless, while exercise clearly reduces the risk of heart ailment if done regularly and in moderation (at least three times a week), the study warns that for people out of shape, even occasional physical exertion such as sudden running or shoveling snow is risky.

Even walking across the parking lot or taking the stairs instead of the elevator is healthier than doing nothing, the study says. Ironically, sedentary persons who suddenly begin a strenuous exercise regimen (five to seven periods a week) increase their risk of a heart attack because the heavy exercise loosens plaque that can form a blood clot.

Below is relevant information from the *Mayo Clinic Health Letter.* "Heart attacks" refers to the percent of individuals who suffered from them.

Exercise rate	% Heart attacks
Sedentary	35%
1-2 times weekly	19
3-4 times weekly	11
5-7 times weekly	35

FOOT AILMENTS

Each year more than 80 million Americans have problems with one of the body's most complex and important features, the feet. Each foot has 26 bones and is laced with ligaments, muscles, nerves, and blood vessels. About three percent of Americans—more than seven million people—suffer from bunions, an excruciating and disfiguring foot problem. The cost of an operation to treat bunions ranges from $2,000 to $5,000, according to recent surveys.

The following list details the most common foot ailments in the U.S. and their occurrence per 1,000 population, according to Dr. Charles Kissel of APMA Public Opinion Research.

Affliction	Rate
Corns/calluses	70
Heel pain	41
Ingrown toenails	39
Bunions	28
Athlete's foot	27
Blisters	27

GULF WAR SYNDROME

While British, Saudi, and Iraqi soldiers who fought in the Persian Gulf War in 1991 remain unaffected by any mysterious ailments, thousand of American veterans continue to suffer from what has become known as Gulf War syndrome.

Among the health problems reported in relation to the baffling affliction are joint pain, rashes, shortness of breath, fatigue, and insomnia. Researchers are considering Gulf War syndrome a single affliction because no common denominator has been found, and they now are studying the subgroups of the ailment to assess whether common war experiences were shared by the sufferers.

At first the reports of Gulf War syndrome were brushed off by the Department of Veterans Affairs as stress-related, but a march by veterans on Capitol Hill forced the VA to take notice. The agency now has set up special referral centers for Gulf War veterans, and it has begun studies of the war's possible adverse health effects.

Because the syndrome is confined to American soldiers (fewer than 50 of the 42,000 Britons who served in the Gulf have reported similar ailments), a specific risk factor might have been the cause. The suspect is the drug, pyridostigmine bromide that the U.S. military supplied to 400,000 troops—ironically, to protect them from chemical weapons. The Senate Veterans Affairs Committee found that when the drug was tested by the Pentagon, adverse reactions were suffered by up to three percent of those receiving it. If that is indeed the rate of adverse reaction, 12,000 of the 400,000 soldiers who were supplied with the drug in the Persian Gulf would be at risk.

A survey of 166 syndrome sufferers by the Department of Veterans Affairs showed the following complaints:

Joint pain	59 %
Rashes	56
Shortness of breath	38
Chest pain	38
Insomnia	37
Poor cognition	35
Fatigue	33
Intermittent diarrhea	30
Nightmares	24
Hair loss	19
Bleeding gums	7

HAIR DYES, RISKS

Current estimates range from 20 percent to 60 percent of the population who wonder whether the use of hair dyes can cause medical risks up to and including cancer. Studies over the last two decades indicate that it may. Three recent reports, however, add information that may ease some fears.

Hair coloring products, readily absorbed through the skin and scalp during application, may contain chemicals that cause mutations or cancer in animals, according to the National Cancer Institute. Darker dyes are riskier than lighter dyes, the recent studies conclude, as are long-term or frequent use, and the use of permanent and semipermanent dyes rather than temporary rinses.

The latest study, by the American Cancer Society (ACS) and the U.S. Food and Drug Administration and published in the *Journal of the American Cancer Institute* in 1994, used information on 573,369 women enrolled in a cancer prevention study that was carried out over seven years.

The study shows that, overall, users of permanent dyes are not at increased risk of dying from cancer of the lymph system (non-Hodgkin's lymphoma), bone-marrow cancer (myeloma), or leukemia, as earlier reports indicated. However, women who use black hair dyes over a period of 20 years do have an increased susceptibility to such problems — though less than

one percent of the women in the survey had used permanent black hair dyes for more than 20 years. The ACS report looked only at cancer deaths, not cancers diagnosed, as previous studies had.

The National Cancer Institute points out that cosmetologists and other persons who apply the dyes are at risk no matter what the color, and it adds that the International Agency for Research on Cancer has classified cosmetology a hazardous occupation because of worker exposure to carcinogens.

An abstract published in the *American Journal of Epidemiology* in 1993 said that women or men who use permanent or semipermanent hair dyes for 16 or more years are at risk for leukemia. The survey at the National Institute of Environmental Health Sciences found that users of any type of hair dye had a 50 percent increased risk of developing the disease, compared with people who had never dyed their hair.

Most of the risk shown in the study concerned permanent and semipermanent dyes, the risk being factor 60 and 40 percent respectively, compared to 20 percent with temporary rinses.

Women who dye their hair one to four times a year have a 70 percent increased risk of ovarian cancer compared to women who never dye their hair, according to a 1993 report from the Harvard School of Public Health and the University of Athens Medical School, published in the *International Journal of Cancer* in 1993. Women who used hair dyes five times or more a year had twice the risk of ovarian cancer as nonusers of dyes, the report found.

A National Cancer Institute and University of Iowa report in 1992 said that women who use black, brown/brunette, and red hair-coloring products had two to four times the risk of developing bone marrow or lymph-system cancer, compared with zero risk from dyes among those who dyed their hair with lighter colors. The report also said the risk factor was increased 70 percent in the use of permanent hair-dyeing products, compared to 40 percent in the use of semipermanent or nonpermanent products. Risk increased with the number of years of use, but not with the frequency of use.

Studies concerning men have been less frequent in these reports because men's hair products tend to differ chemically from women's hair dyes. The NCI, however, cites a study it made in 1988 that showed that men who use hair dye have a twofold risk of developing lymph-system cancer and almost double the risk for leukemia compared men who do not dye their hair.

Below are overall statistic projections for 1994 for four types of cancer associated with hair dyes, compiled by the National Cancer Institute:

Cancer	Diagnosed	Deaths
Multiple myeloma	12,700	9,800
Non-Hodgkin's lymphoma	45,000	21,200
Leukemia	28,600	19,100
Ovarian	24,000	13,600

HEALTH CARE EXPENDITURES

In 1993, Americans spent a approximately $910 billion on health care. A cost update in 1994 showed the nation paid almost $1 trillion for health care in 1993, with an increase of 9.9 percent over 1992, 6.9 percent above the inflation rate as measured by the government's consumer price index.

The cost of health care has quadrupled since 1980, whereas the cost for all other goods and services has increased an average of 65 percent. Those who keep an eye on medical costs refer to the rate at which prices rise above general inflation as "excess medical inflation," and what they see is not a pretty picture.

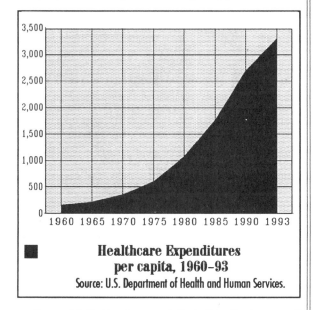

Healthcare Expenditures per capita, 1960–93
Source: U.S. Department of Health and Human Services.

General inflation has contributed to the increased cost of health care; in 1991, inflation was 4.2 percent. Another factor has been a one percent growth in the nation's population. Other factors have added a 3.5 percent increase to the cost of health care. Those factors include advances in medical technology and the aging of the population, the latter meaning simply that there are more people who need medical care.

Complicating the situation, Americans are more health conscious than ever and are seeking medical services at an increasing rate. In 1985, the average American saw a doctor five times a year. By 1991, the figure had grown to six times. The increased attention Americans are seeking leads to an increase in treatment— including expensive surgical operations and other procedures. According to the National Center for Health Statistics, between 1980 and 1991, coronary bypass operations for men increased almost threefold, from 108,000 to 296,000. The number of ultrasounds rose from 114,000 to 652,000, and the number of CAT scans rose from 306,000 to more than 1.4 million—a better than fourfold increase.

Does anyone escape these rising costs? Well, possibly the 37 million Americans who have no health insurance—simply because for a large percentage of that group, such expensive medical procedures are out of the question already. In addition, proposed changes in federal Medicaid policy put this group at even greater risk.

Annual health care costs in the U.S. outpace all other countries. But is all that money paying off in healthier Americans? According to comparative statistics in the Statistical Abstract of the United States, of 10 major industrialized nations in the world, the U.S. spends the most to stay healthy and get the least in return in two vital categories: infant mortality and longevity. Americans are the shortest-lived among the group of 10 nationalities, with an average life expectancy of 75.5 years in 1991; also the U.S. has the highest infant mortality rate, a distressing 8.9 per 1,000 births. Japan has the highest life expectancy among the 10 nations, at 79.3, and the lowest infant mortality rate—4.3 per 1,000 births.

In 1991 per capita spending on health care in the U.S. was $2,868, an amount more than double that in nations belonging to the Organization for Economic Cooperation and Development (OECD). Among that group of 24 industrial nations, average per capita health care spending was $1,305, according to the Statistical Bulletin. The U.S. share of gross domestic product spent on health care was 13.2 percent, outdistancing Canada at 10 percent, France 9.1 percent, and the OECD as a whole at 7.9 percent.

The $910 billion spent in the U.S. on health care amounted to 14.3 percent of the GDP—one-seventh of the U.S. economy. That figure was up from $828 billion in 1992 and more than double the $422.6 spent on health care a decade earlier. Leading in cost increases was hospital care, with a rise of 8.4 percent in 1993, and outpatient services climbing 9.2 percent, according to the consumer price index. The cost of physicians' services increased 5.6 percent, dental services 5.3 percent, and prescription drugs 3.9 percent.

Memberships in health maintenance organizations (HMOs) rose 7.3 percent in 1992, to 41.4 million participants, or 16.1 percent of the total population and 18.8 of all insured individuals. In 1980, only 4.7 of the nation's insured belonged to HMOs.

Federal tax exemptions to general medical and surgical, psychiatric, and specialty hospitals in 1992 amounted to $302 million, $278 million of that total going to general hospitals, according to the Statistical Abstract. Home health care services saw a $4.8 million reduction, and doctors' offices and clinics $15 million.

The Statistical Bulletin notes that a considerable gap remains between the CPI and the true medical care total because the CPI is not designed to capture all the different health care pricing systems. The Bureau of Labor Statistics currently has the medical component under review.

The tabel below indicates how Americans spent their health care dollars in 1993, according to the Bureau of Labor Statistics, Health Care Financing Administration:

Hospitals	$359 billion
Physicians	167 billion
Nursing homes	74 billion
Drugs	71 billion
Administration/Insurance	48 billion
Other services	45 billion
Dental services	41 billion
Public health	24 billion
Other personal health care	20 billion
Research and development	16 billion
Vision products	14 billion
Home health care	12 billion
Construction	12 billion

The following details national health care expenditures for the U.S. from 1970 to 1994, in billions, compiled by the U.S. Health Care Financing Administration; 1994 projection by the Metropolitan Life Insurance Company:

Year	Billions
1970	$74.4
1975	132.9
1980	250.1
1985	422.6
1990	675.0
1991	751.8
1992	828.0
1993	910.0
1994	995.0

Annual average percent change (increase) in costs, year by year, in selected areas of medical care; U.S. Bureau of Labor statistics; 1993 estimates and 1994 projections by Metropolitan Life Insurance Company:

Year	Drugs	Doctors	Hospitals
1984	9.6	6.9	8.7
1985	9.5	5.9	6.3
1986	8.6	7.2	6.0
1987	8.0	7.3	6.9
1988	8.0	7.2	9.3
1989	8.7	7.4	11.5
1990	10.0	7.1	10.9
1991	9.9	6.1	10.2
1992	7.5	6.3	9.1
1993	3.9	5.6	8.4
1994	3.5	5.3	7.9

Health expenditures in major industrial countries as percent of gross national product, and vital statistics on life expectancy and infant mortality per 1,000 births in 1991; (from *Health Affairs Statistics*, Summer 1993, and Statistical Abstract of the United States:

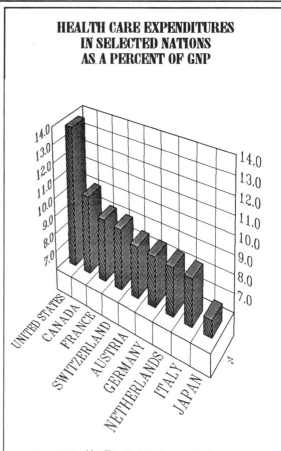

HEALTH CARE EXPENDITURES IN SELECTED NATIONS AS A PERCENT OF GNP

SOURCE: *Health Affairs Statistics*, Summer 1993.

Country	% GNP	Life Expectancy	Infant Mortality
United States	13.2	75.5	8.9
Canada	10.0	78.1	6.9
France	9.1	78.2	6.6
Sweden	8.6	78.3	5.7
Germany	8.5	76.3	6.5
Italy	8.3	77.6	7.6
Netherlands	8.3	77.8	6.1
Switzerland	7.9	78.3	6.5
Japan	6.8	79.3	4.3
United Kingdom	6.6	76.8	7.2

HEARING IMPAIRMENT

Sometimes the things you do the most often and think about the least can be the cause of serious medical problems. For instance, farmers who look over their right shoulder while plowing, leaving the left ear exposed to the sound from the tractor's engine, are susceptible to hearing loss.

In a national study of why 2.3 million Americans are hard of hearing, noise was found the chief cause of hearing loss; aging was second.

Of the 8.6 percent of hard-of-hearing Americans, 1.8 million are considered members of the deaf community

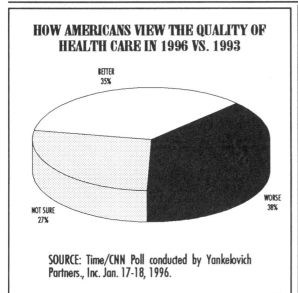

HOW AMERICANS VIEW THE QUALITY OF HEALTH CARE IN 1996 VS. 1993

BETTER
35%

WORSE
38%

NOT SURE
27%

SOURCE: Time/CNN Poll conducted by Yankelovich Partners., Inc. Jan. 17-18, 1996.

and communicate in sign language, according to a study published in the *Journal of the American Medical Association* in January 1995. The National Center for Health Statistics (NCHS) estimates that 552,000 persons in that community are completely deaf. Those figures are from the most recent survey on the deaf, made by the center in 1991. At that time the hard-of-hearing total had increased from 13 million to 20.2 million.

The U.S. Census Bureau dropped questions on hearing impairment in 1930 because, unlike with blindness, there is no legal definition of deafness. However, Gallaudet University in Washington, D.C., a liberal arts university for the deaf, uses three now-standard measures of deafness. They are: (1) deaf, both ears; (2) cannot hear or understand any speech; and, (3) at best, can only hear and understand words shouted in the better ear. The university's research center estimates there are 421,000 Americans in the first class, 552,000 in the second class, and 1.2 million in the third class.

Farmers, truckers, musicians, and workers in heavy industry who suffer hearing loss due to noise make up 33.7 percent of all hearing-impaired Americans, according to an NCHS evaluation of the 1991 survey made in 1994. The next most populous group of hearing-impaired Americans is age 65 and over, at 29.1 percent of the hard-of-hearing population. Those with hereditary hearing impairment, and those with ear infections or injury, make up 17.1 percent.

Of 51 million Americans age 55 and over, 44.5 percent suffer hearing impairment, compared to 16.6 percent of Americans aged 35 to 54, according to the NCHS. Men are more likely to be hearing- impaired in each of these groups. A total 4.2 million women and 4.5 million men age 65 and older are hearing-impaired; for the 45-to-64 age group, the numbers are two million women and four million men.

Whites and Asian Americans are more than twice as likely as blacks and Hispanics to be hard of hearing, the NCHS found. Overall, the rate of hearing impairment is 9.4 percent among whites, 9.1 percent among Asian Americans, and 4.2 percent among both blacks and Hispanics. Hearing impairment increases as the education level sinks; the rate of affliction is 16.6 percent for those with less than a high school education, compared to nine percent for those with high school and above. Those with family incomes of less than $10,000 annually are twice as likely as those with incomes of $50,000 and over to have hearing impairment—12.4 percent to 6.1 percent.

Of the hard of hearing who are employed, 78.7 percent are between age 18 to 44; 63.8 percent between age 45 to 64; and 11.4 percent age 65 years and older.

In a separate survey of U.S. students by Gallaudet University's Center for Assessment and Demographic Studies in 1992-93, heredity was found to be the major cause of hearing impairment, with 6,324 students afflicted. Next was meningitis, at 3,934, and then complications surrounding pregnancy and prebirth at 2,238. Maternal German measles, or rubella, afflicted 992 students, a significant decrease from 8,009 a decade before.

The following table shows the estimated prevalence of hearing impairment by age group, 1990-1991, in millions; data from the NCHS compiled in 1994:

Age Group	Total U.S.	Hearing Impaired	Percent
Overall	236.0	20.2	8.6%
3-17 years	53.3	1.0	1.8
18-34 years	67.4	2.3	3.4
35-44 years	38.0	2.3	6.3
45-54 years	26.0	2.6	10.3
55-64	21.0	3.2	15.4
65 and older	30.0	9.0	29.1

Below are statistics on hearing impairment among Americans, from sources discussed above, and broken down by gender, race/ethnicity, in millions, and percent among U.S. population:

GENDER /AGE

Age Group	Men	Women
Overall rate	12%	8.2%
3-17 years	0.5	.4
18-44 years	3.0	1.7
45-64 years	4.0	2.0
65 and older	4.5	4.2

Rate of hearing impairment, by race/ethnicity and age:

Total	White	Black	Hispanic
White	9.4%	4.2%	4.2%
3-17 years	1.9	1.2	2.0
18-44 years	4.9	2.1	2.9
45-64 years	13.4	7.2	8.4
65 and older	30.1	18.7	22.0

Estimate of hearing impairment by age groups and annual income (in thousands) by percent of U.S. population:

Age group	$10-$24.9	$25-$49.9	$50-plus
3-17 years	5.0 %	1.7%	1.5%
18-44 years	10.7	4.7	3.7
45-64 years	33.7	13.3	10.9
65 and older	61.9	28.8	26.2

Cause of hearing loss in the adult U.S. population, 1990-91, in percent; source, NCHS (compiled in 1994):

Cause	Percent
Aging	28.0%
Prolonged noise	23.4
Ear infection	12.2
Loud, brief noise	10.3
Ear injury	4.9
At birth	4.4
Other	16.8

Cause of hearing loss (at onset) for U.S. deaf and hard-of-hearing students, in percent, according to the Youth Center for Assessment and Demographic Studies, Gallaudet University, 1992- 93:

Cause	Percent
Total onset at birth	47.4%
Heredity	13.0
Pregnancy/birth complications	8.7
Maternal German Measles	2.1
Salivary gland infection	1.3
Not known	17.8
Other	4.5
Total onset after Birth	23.2
Meningitis	8.1
Infection, other than mid-ear	4.0
Mid-ear infection	3.7
Trauma	0.6
Other	1.5
Not known	5.3
Total onset not known	29.4

HMOs

By 1993, 19 percent, or 41 million Americans, belonged to an HMO, up from 11 million in 1982, nine years after the concept was approved by the Public Health Service Act.

Twenty-nine percent of Health Maintenance Organization members are women in the childbearing years of 15 to 44, although they compose 24 percent of the general population, according to an HMO trade group study in 1993. The study found that many pregnant women are turning to HMOs for care because they offer lower costs and more services than do hospitals.

Since members or employers prepay HMOs members who go into labor, a woman can have her baby at a cost ranging from $5 to $250, depending on the copayment stipulated in her policy, says the trade organization Group Health Association of America.

The largest HMO in the country is Kaiser Permanente, with 6.6 members in 16 states, many offering counseling for high-risk mothers, imunization for newborns, and pregnancy and sibling immunization classes.

HOSPITAL STAYS

At one time, surgical patients were almost certain to stay in the hospital for at least one night. That's no longer the case, according to the American Hospital Association.

AMA statistics indicate that the numbers of inpatient and outpatient operations are almost equal: of 24 million annual operations, 11 million are performed on an outpatient basis, 11 million on an inpatient basis, and somewhat more than 2 million at locations removed from hospitals.

That represents a vast increase in outpatient surgery. In 1980 only 16 percent of all hospital surgery was performed on an outpatient basis. By 1985, with the increasing scrutiny of hospital costs by insurers and the Medicare program, that figure jumped to 36 percent. New England leads the outpatient rate, with 42 percent; Illinois has the lowest rate, at 27 percent.

Jeff Goldsmith, president of Health Futures, Inc., estimates that by the end of the century 85 percent of all surgical procedures will be done on an outpatient basis.

The following are six surgical procedures that accounted for 2.4 million hospital days in 1990; all of them are rapidly becoming outpatient or very-short-stay procedures:

Gall bladder removal
Inguinal (above the testes) hernia repair
Hysterectomy
Prostatectomy
Appendectomy
Removal of part of the stomach

HOUSEHOLD INJURIES

Each year manufactured goods send almost five million Americans to the hospital. Some 15,000 of these injuries result from the ill-advised use of baby strollers, according to the Consumer Product Safety Commission. But despite their vulnerability, the young are not the most at risk from household injuries. Stairs and steps, used by normal adults, account for a million hospitalizations annually. Bicycle and bicycle accessories are the second leading cause of product injuries, with 600,000, followed by knives (500,000), tables (350,000), and chairs (300,000)

Many common objects that are not generally regarded as dangerous inflict serious injuries. Perhaps the greatest danger is in not realizing that certain things can be hazardous. Wheelchairs, for example, annually cause 50,000 injuries that require hospitalization, and bunk beds injure 40,000. Even the most innocuous items at home can be dangerous. Burns from hot water cause 40,000 trips to the hospital annually among Americans. Televisions injure 30,000; telephones, 16,000; and jewelry, 40,000.

Below is a list of household items and the estimated annual number of injuries they cause among Americans, according to data adapted from the CPSC:

Nails, screws, tacks	250,000
Bathtubs, showers	140,000
Drinking glasses	130,000
Ladders	130,000
Fences, fence posts	120,000
Drugs, medications	110,000
Bottles, jars	110,000
Metal containers	100,000

Other products that cause 50,000 or more injuries annually include carpets and rugs, footwear, lawn mowers, skateboards, sinks, toilets, and hammers.

MEDICAL MALPRACTICE

The current rates paid by surgeons for medical malpractice insurance add approximately $100 to the cost of every operation. Though the cost of liability insurance adds significantly to all health care costs, if every negligence lawsuit was dropped, only about one percent of America's health care costs would be saved. A significant movement is afoot to reform how medical malpractice cases are litigated, according to USA Today.

Are many doctors not operating up to snuff? One study in Florida indicated that a very small number of doctors is responsible for the vast bulk of bad medicine: only three percent of all doctors accounted for 85 percent of all the awards to plaintiffs in malpractice suits.

The real cost of medical malpractice to the consumer results from the preponderance of "defensive treatments"—that is, extra (and possibly unnecessary) tests performed by doctors in order primarily to protect themselves from possible court cases. According to the American Medical Association, the cost of such tests escalated from $4.8 million in 1982 to $15.5 million in 1990.

Doctors have good cause to be careful. Today's average award for patients who win malpractice suits is $1.17 million.

According to the AMA, the most frequent malpractice allegations and the number of suits filed in 1990 were:

Surgery/postoperative complications	922
Failure to diagnose cancer	498
Improper treatment/birth-related	416
Surgery/inadvertent act	283
Improper treatment/infection	232
Improper treatment during examination	202
Improper treatment/drug side effects	195
Failure to diagnose circulatory problems/thrombosis	181
Failure to diagnose fracture or dislocation	179

New Yorkers generally believe that they have the best health care facilities in the nation. That may be true of the *facilities*, but the *quality* of hospital care has been called into question by researchers from Harvard University. In 1990, a team studying cases at New York state hospitals from the year 1984 found an incredible 27,000 injuries and 7,000 deaths attributed to negligence. Surprisingly, only one in every eight victims of the purported negligence actually filed suit. The researchers concluded, "We do not now have a problem of too many claims; if anything, there are too few."

MENTAL RETARDATION

About three percent of Americans are children with deficits in intellectual capacity. Only half of those are diagnosed as such because the disease is difficult to diagnose in infancy and childhood. The ratio of mentally retarded boys to girls is three to two.

In almost 80 percent of mentally retarded cases the causes are unknown, according to the *Columbia College of Surgeons and Physicians Complete Home Medical Guide*. Usually, because of that difficulty, a diagnosis of retardation may not be made until the child's second or third year. Causes for the 20 percent of mentally handicapped children that are known include birth injuries, accidents, nutritional deficiencies, infections, chromosomal, hormonal, or metabolic disorders, and ingestion or exposure to toxic substances.

Ninety percent of retarded children fall into the mild range, meaning they have the ability to learn to read and perform arithmetic, and can be trained to function freely as adults. The remaining 10 percent fall into the moderate, severe, and profound range, where supervision of some kind is needed.

The number of state-operated residential facilities for the retarded increased from 190 in 1970 to 1,477 in 1991, as states developed a large number of community-based sites in the mid-1980s, even as admissions declined. The number of private facilities providing living quarters with 24-hour, seven-day-a-week responsibility increased at a much larger pace, from 10,219 registrations in 1977 to 45,309 in 1991.

Degrees of mental retardation, IQs, and special needs; adapted from *Nelson Textbook of Pediatrics*, and OHS.

Degree	IQ	Needs
Mild	52-67	Special classes
Moderate	36-51	Sheltered settings
Severe	20-35	Some supervision
Profound	Below 20	Total supervision

NURSING CARE

In many American hospitals, nurses' aides are taking the place of registered nurses. According to a national survey of nurses, that changeover is causing an increase in the workloads of the remaining RNs, in addition to medication errors, patients falling when left alone, occasions of oxygen loss, long waits for laboratory results and routine care, and increased infections.

In a survey performed under the auspices of the American Nurses Association (ANA), which represents the nation's 2.2 million registered nurses, more than 66 percent of 1,835 nurses nationwide reported reductions in the number of RNs in their facilities in a 12-month span. Forty-four percent said unlicensed aides with as little as four to six weeks of training were taking their places.

Twenty-seven percent of American hospitals planned more nursing layoffs in 1995, an increase from 19 percent in 1993, according to a 1994 survey by the journal *Modern Healthcare*. Sixty- six of the nurses in the ANA poll said their hospitals had reduced the nursing staffs, or had announced plans to do so. Seventy percent said the vacated positions were left unfilled, 53.7 percent said the remaining nurses were taking care of more patients than before, and 53.7 percent said they had less time to provide patient care. Forty-five percent reported increased use of nurses' aides to provide direct patient care.

An increase in errors made by the aides was reported by 17.5 percent of the respondents. Medication errors led the mistakes at 13.7 percent. Increases in falls and fractures were reported by 13.6 percent. A notable 78.6 percent believed the overall quality of patient care had been degraded by the cutbacks, and 64 percent thought patient safety had been adversely affected—2.3 percent reporting that situations attributed to nurse cutbacks led to the death or near death of a patient. One-fourth of the employing facilities had replaced RNs with aides or had announced their intentions to do so.

Sixty percent of the respondents whose facilities had reduced their RN staffs said the explanations given for the cuts were economic in nature. Forty-three percent gave a decrease in filled beds as the explanation given them.

Responses to the survey were received from all 50 states and the District of Columbia in rough proportion to population distribution. Still employed in hospitals were 73.4 percent of the respondents, with 64.7 percent staff nurses, 13 percent supervisors, and 6.3 administrators. Of those laid off, 58.3 percent had worked in nonprofit facilities, 23.6 in government-operated facilities, 19.8 in for-profit facilities, and 14.4 in HMOs.

Most frequently reported explanations for nursing cutbacks in 1994, according to the American Nurses Association:	
Reason	% Reported
Decrease in patients	58.2%

Profitability	43.0
Weak local economy	21.6
Mergers or acquisitions	16.4
Budget cuts	14.3
Managed care contract loss	11.2
Reorganization	6.6
To stay competitive	2.7

OUTPATIENT TREATMENT

Americans on Medicaid make up almost one third of the estimated 56.6 million visits to U.S. hospital outpatient departments, while Medicare patients total a little more than half that number, a first-ever survey of that component in health care shows.

Medicaid patients accounted for 31.2 percent of the visits and Medicare 16.3 percent. The private or work-insured were second at 23.8 percent, with patient-paid visits following Medicare visits at 13.7 percent, and HMO or other prepaid visits at 7.7 percent. The patient-paid category included patients' costs toward co-payments and deductibles, according to a 1992 National Hospital Ambulatory Medical Care Survey.

Women made up 61.4 percent of all visits and had a higher visit rate than males. Whites made up 74 percent of the visits; but the visit rate was significantly higher among blacks than among whites overall and in most age groups. There were no significant differences otherwise between age groups.

About 13 percent of the visits were referrals by doctors, and more than 50 percent were made by persons returning to a clinic for care of a previously treated problem. By region, the largest proportion of visits were made by patients in the Northeastern part of the country.

About eight percent of the visits involved surgical procedures, and about 70 percent of all visits included one or more diagnostic or screening services, with high blood pressure checkups involved in almost 50 percent of the visits. Laboratory testing, at 20.2 percent, and urinalysis, at 11.4 percent, were services that were also frequently mentioned.

Staff physicians were seen during most of the visits, a registered nurse in 38.3 percent of the visits, and a resident or intern in 32.4 percent. There were 63.3 million drug mentions, or an average of 1.1 drugs prescribed or ordered in each visit.

The following list details hospital outpatient visits (in thousand) in 1992, and the most frequently mentioned reasons, recorded in the patient's own words, according to the Centers for Disease Control and Prevention, the National Center for Health Statistics, and the National Ambulatory Medical Care Survey:		
Reason for Visit	Outpatient Visits (1,000s)	Percent
TOTAL	56,605	100.0 %
Progress visit	4,216	7.4
General examination	3,036	5.4
Routine prenatal	2,981	5.3

Well baby examination	1,497	2.6
Cough	1,169	2.1
Postoperative	1,037	1.8
Stomach pain, cramps, spasms	884	1.6
Earache or infection	844	1.5
Throat symptoms	836	1.5
Back symptoms	763	1.3
Medication	727	1.3
Skin rash	687	1.2
Diabetis melitus	668	1.2
Chest pains or related symptoms	641	1.1
Depression	639	1.1
Fever	638	1.1
Pain unspecified	632	1.1
Hypertension	556	1.0
Knee symptoms	535	0.9
Headache or pain in head	496	0.9
All other	33,124	58.5

PROSTATE CANCER

A little, walnut-sized male gland that secretes seminal fluid during ejaculation is the source of concern of men as they grow older. Located below the bladder, the prostate causes the second-most common cancer in men, according to the Mayo Clinic in Rochester, Minn.

In 1994 an estimated 200,000 American men will be diagnosed with prostate cancer, according to the American Cancer Society, and the Mayo Clinic estimates the disease will kill 38,000. That represents an increase of 8.5 percent since 1990, when 32,378 American men died from prostate cancer, and a more than 50 percent increase from 1960, when the death toll was 14,452, according to the clinic.

This form of cancer strikes fewer than one man in 10,000 from ages 40 to 50, but the rate increases to five in 10,000 among men their sixties. Among those diagnosed with prostate cancer, the average age is 73 at the time of diagnosis.

Once the disease is discovered, most men opt for treatment—but the side effects are troubling. According to Julian Whitaker, the editor of *Health and Healing*, removal of the prostate results in impotence in 25 percent of patients and incontinence in 30 percent. Radiation therapy also can result in impotence. Removal of the testicles to eliminate the cancer's stimulation by the male hormone testosterone can cause sterility and psychological trauma. Hormone therapy can lead to loss of sex drive and problems in developing an erection.

According to the Mayo Clinic, cancer specialists are hotly debating whether treatment for prostate cancer extends life and which treatment is best. Some urge treatment, while others counsel "watchful waiting." The clinic notes that a study in the journal *Cancer* in 1993 that analyzed prostate studies since 1980 concluded that only slightly more men who had their prostates removed were alive 10 years after surgery

than men who had radiation therapy or no treatment than all.

In several reports, the clinic notes, researchers determined that a man in his late 70s or 80s with a low-grade tumor may safely consider watchful waiting. However, men in their 50s or 60s who have a high-grade tumor are likely to live longer with treatment.

The Mayo Clinic adds a word of caution on early screening, which may or may not find a localized prostate cancer, again noting that experts are divided on the issue. It says that no large studies have indicated that early detection saves lives in the general population, but further tests, evaluations, and follow-ups are encouraged. That increases costs.

Demurring, Mayo urologist Joseph E. Oesterling comments, "Our finding makes PSA [prostate specific antigen, one test used] a significantly more sensitive indicator of prostate cancer, promoting more aggressive follow-up evaluation in younger patients and eliminating unnecessary tests in those who are older."

Another voice against screening with PSA, TRUS (transrectal ultrasound), or DRE (digital rectal examination) is the American Medical Association. An AMA study said that "screening may result in poorer health outcomes and will increase costs dramatically."

That study concluded that screening led to frequent aggressive treatment that does not substantially prolong life but markedly reduces the quality of the patient's remaining years by causing impotency and many other problems associated with conventional treatment of prostate cancer. The AMA essentially agrees with the Mayo Clinic statement that more men live with prostate cancer than die from it.

The list below indicates cancer deaths among males during various years, according to the American Cancer Society:			
Site	**1960**	**1990**	**1992**
Lung	31,257	91,091	96,800
Prostate	14,452	32,328	34,000
Colon/ rectum	19,127	28,635	28,900
Urinary	5,440	6910	12,700
Skin	1,194	3,844	4,100

SEXUALLY TRANSMITTED DISEASES

While AIDS is usally sexually transmitted, it is regarded in a class by itself and therefore it is not commonly thought of as a "STD" (sexually transmitted disease). Sexually transmitted infections—often refered to as "venereal diseases"—are commonly of five kinds: genital warts, genital herpes (blisters on the skin or mucous membranes), chlamydia (infections of the eyes, lung, and urinary tract), gonorrhea, and syphilis.

Of the five, chlamydial infections are the fastest-spreading STD in the U.S. in the 1990s, according to the Centers for Disease Control and Prevention, which estimates that about four million new infections occur every year. The CDC also estimates that genital warts

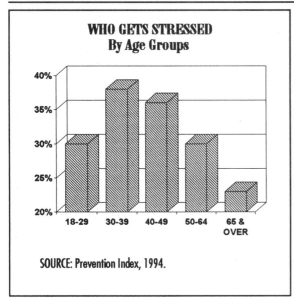

WHO GETS STRESSED
By Age Groups

SOURCE: Prevention Index, 1994.

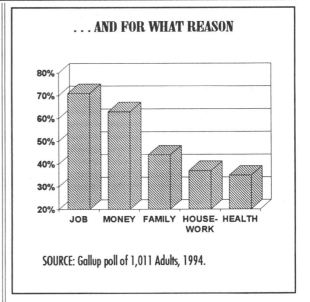

. . . AND FOR WHAT REASON

SOURCE: Gallup poll of 1,011 Adults, 1994.

attack about one million persons annually, and genital herpes, 500,000. Worldwide, chlamydial infections are also the dominant STD, with 50 million cases reported to the World Health Organization.

In a breakdown on reported cases of STDs from 1980 to 1992 (civilian only), the CDC reports that gonorrhea cases have declined steadily, from a little more than one million in 1980 to 500,000 in 1992. Syphilis increased from 69,000 cases in 1980 to 134,000 in 1990, but it declined to 113,000 in 1992.

REPRODUCTIVE HEALTH, MINORITIES

A survey sponsored by the Consortium Media Center and the National Council of Negro Women for the Women of Color Reproductive Poll, questioned 1,157 black, Asian American, Hispanic, and Native American women age 18 and older in 1992. Some 59 percent of the women surveyed did not practice birth control; 32 percent of the 302 black women questioned said they could not afford contraceptive devices, were afraid of them, or didn't like them. Some 22 percent of the Native American women reported having been sterilized, compared to 6 percent of respondents as a whole.

The survey also reported:

- More than 66 percent of black respondents said they had a gynecologist, compared to only 36 percent of the Native American women.

- 90 percent of black women had had Pap smears to screen for cervical cancer, compared to 71 percent of Asian American women.

- 52 percent of black women had undergone mammograms to test for breast cancer; 40 percent of Asian Americans and 32 percent of Native Americans had undergone the procedure.

STRESS

A mere 1 in 10 Americans never feel stressed out at the end of the working day, while twice that number feel great stress almost every day and six in 10 feel under great stress at least once a week. Sleep, exercise, and aging are the great stress relievers, according to a survey on the subject.

In a survey performed in late 1993 by *American Demographics* of 1,250 randomly selected adults, 15 percent said they feel great stress several days a week, and 27 percent feel it at least once or twice a week.

According to the 1994 Prevention Index survey, adults who sleep six or fewer hours each night are most likely to feel stress every day; 43 percent who get only that much sleep say they are stressed every day, compared to only 14 percent of adults who sleep seven to eight hours each night.

Sixty-six percent of the women in the study took stress-reducing steps, compared to 59 percent of the men. Adults who reported feeling little or no stress tended to be regular exercisers and nonsmokers.

While 62 percent of the respondents made conscious efforts to reduce stress, 36 percent did nothing about it. Sixty-eight percent of those who attended college attempted to ease the stress they feel, compared 59 percent who did not go to college. College-educated respondents also slept more than noncollegians, 70 percent sleeping seven to eight hours a night, compared to 60 percent of those who did not attend college.

Adults who live in the Western states were the most stressed out, according to a Gallup poll of 1,011 adults taken in 1994. Women were more likely to be stressed by child care than men, and at a time when people are annually working the equivalent of a month longer than their parents did, 33 percent of the respondents said they would take a 20 percent pay cut if they could reduce their hours at work. Seventy-six percent of all respondents said the amount of stress in their lives was under control.

Below is the percentage of individuals who feel stressed several times each week ("frequently stressed"), according to the Prevention Index, 1994:

Age	Frequently stressed
18 to 29	30%
30 to 39	38
40 to 49	36
50 to 64	30
65 and older	23

Below are the most frequent causes of stress, according to a Gallup poll of 1,011 adults in 1994:

Cause	percent
Job	71%
Money problems	63
Family	44
Housework	37
Health problems	35

SUDDEN INFANT DEATH SYNDROME

Fluffy bedding in a baby's crib is dangerous, according to a government study that concluded that suffocation caused by soft comforters and pillows contribute to as many as 1,800 deaths a year among infants younger than age one.

As a precaution, babies should sleep and rest on their backs on firm, flat surfaces, researchers say. The American Academy of Pediatricians, which began recommending the "tummy up" position in 1992, endorsed the study and its advice.

Officials of the Consumer Product Safety Commission, which sanctioned the two-year study, cautioned that the findings are not the last word on the mysterious Sudden Infant Death Syndrome, but they tend to agree with studies in Britain that showed that SIDS cases had decreased by more than half since 1991, when parents began to be urged to put infants to sleep on their backs.

Sleep position studies in New Zealand, Australia, and Norway also have shown that SIDS rates can be cut by up to 50 percent with the tummy up position.

TUBERCULOSIS

After declining in the U.S. for more than 30 years, the incidence of tuberculosis has increased among Americans by 20 percent, with 26,673 reported cases in 1992 alone. Another 10 to 15 million people are infected with the TB bacteria but are not sick; of those, 10 percent will go on to develop the disease in its possibly deadly form. These are the findings of a study of current scientific understanding of TB by the Congressional Office of Technology Assessment, which also found the emergence of TB strains that are resistant to the most commonly used drug treatments.

Particular concentrations of people are highly susceptible to TB: the poor, ethnic and racial minorities, immigrants from countries with high levels of the disease, and those diagnosed with HIV, whose chances of progressing to active TB are eight percent per year. Common-drug therapy is used successfully on HIV patients except during the most advanced stages of HIV, according to the OTA, as it is with high-risk people younger than age 35 and not infected with HIV.

The cost of drugs to treat TB have increased at an annual average rate of nine percent a year. Those costs are mostly paid by the government, acting through the Centers for Disease Control and Prevention. Some drugs used to treat drug-resistant TB have increased at a higher rate. To a CDC suggestion that it take over all TB drug purchases in the country to take advantage of volume buys, the pharmaceutical industry said such a move would disincline drug firms from continuing the search for new anti-TB drugs because of the loss of revenue needed to recoup research and development expenses.

On average, 75 percent of U.S. TB patients complete treatment within a year. One form of treatment, directly observed therapy, costs a patient $2,000 to $3,000 a year above that of unsupervised therapy.

PASTIMES
OVERVIEW

What does America do for fun? Just about anything you can imagine—from the old-fashioned pastimes like baseball, barbecues, and bowling to the Generation X thrill of snowboarding or bungeee jumping.

The following look at the pastimes in which Americans partake reveals the ways that we spend our leisure time, which are as diverse as the population itself. Nearly 50 million Americans take to the bowling lanes at least once a year; 2.7 million fit the category of "hardcore" bowler. Twenty-four million of us head for the greener pastures of the golf links, and 11 million call ourselves "core" golfers, with at least eight rounds of golf a year. Twenty-two million Americans enjoy the net gains tennis has to offer. There are 21 million piano players in country, three million drummers, and a million saxophonists—enough to make for an awesome national jazz combo. We fish, we swim, we knit and bowl, too. We ski and snowmobile, woodwork and walk. We gamble and merely gambol. Who says America isn't having fun anymore?

And when we aren't playing, we're watching. As this chapter indicates, attendance at NBA basketball and NFL football games is at an all-time high, and even beleaguered major league baseball draws out the fans in numbers far greater than it did 10 years ago. College sports, horse racing, and jai alai are just a few of the many other athletic events that bring America to the stadiums, racetracks, and other sports venues to enjoy the thrill of competition.

The arts, too, hold a strong place in American life. As this chapter reveals, more of us are attending art museums and galleries, arts and crafts fairs, plays, jazz performances, and even opera and ballet, than in the early '80s. Another unexpected sign reported in the following pages: Library usage is up dramatically since 1980—expenditures have risen 170 percent, and circulation 44 percent in the past 15 years.

So maybe we should all lighten up a bit. After all, there's still plenty to do, and some time left to do it.

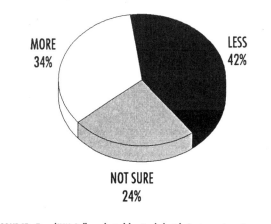

LEISURE TIME—MORE OR LESS?
How Americans regard the amount of free time they have.

When asked the following question:"Compared to three yeas ago, are you and your family better or worse off?" [regarding the amount of leisure time you

MORE
34%

LESS
42%

NOT SURE
24%

SOURCE: *Time*/CNN Poll conducted by Yankelovich Partners, Inc., January, 17-18, 1996.

ARTS PARTICIPATION

As the arts struggle against television viewing and family financial pressures, many artistic leisure activities in the American landscape are reeling from low rates of public participation. However, some arts activities are holding their own or increasing in popularity.

Art museums and galleries made the largest strides in attendance, according to surveys made for the National Endowment for the Arts (NEA) by the U.S. Census Bureau and a report on the arts in the journal *American Demographics*. Since 1982 the percentage of adults visiting museums and galleries increased four percent, from 22.1 percent of respondents to 26.7 percent, an increase of more than 12 million visitors a year.

Attendance at arts and crafts fairs was second, with a gain of almost two percent, from 39 percent to 40.7 percent, or seven million new participants. Drama was third in percent gain, almost 1.6 percent more people attending legitimate stage plays, from 11.9 percent to 13.5 percent.

These gains were offset by losses in visitors to U.S. historical sites, attendance at operettas and musicals, and in readers of fiction and poetry. Historic park sites were hardest hit, with a decline of 4.5 percent in the proportion of adults who visit them at least once a year.

Overall, 41 percent of American adults attended an arts event in 1992, compared to 39 percent in surveys taken in 1985 and 1982.

The survey found that in general blacks attend fewer art events than do whites or Asians—notably opera and ballet—but jazz was more popular among blacks than among those other groups. While 10.1 percent of whites attended at least one jazz event in 1992, the figure for blacks was 16.2; for other racial and culture groups, the rate was 4.9 percent. Blacks showed greater gains in attendance at live performances than did whites—perhaps, the NEA says, because of the growing black middle class.

Education level is a strong indicator of a person's likelihood of participating in the art: The survey found that 77 percent of adults with post-graduate degrees attend at least one arts event a year, compared to less than 10 percent of those with no high school education. But it also noted that the biggest decline in arts participation was among those who had at least some college.

The survey found that about 25 percent of American adults do needlework, and 4.5 million displayed their own artwork in public, though that's a decline of 32 percent in 1982. Almost eight percent of adults took up dancing in some form—modern, folk, or tap—and 22 million danced in a performance.

Forty percent of Americans have taken music lessons, down from 47 percent in 1982. The number of visual arts students is down from 24 percent to 18 percent, and figures for those who do pottery, metalwork, leather, or other crafts are down from 12 percent

to eight percent. But attendance at art appreciation classes increased by three percent.

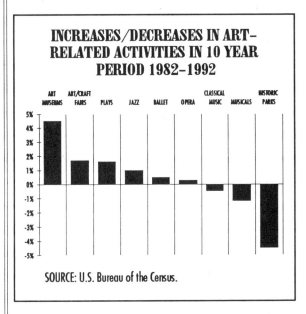

INCREASES/DECREASES IN ART-RELATED ACTIVITIES IN 10 YEAR PERIOD 1982-1992

SOURCE: U.S. Bureau of the Census.

The following list gives the percentage of adults attending major arts activities in 1982, 1985, and 1992, according to the U.S. Bureau of the Census and *American Demographics* magazine.

Activity	1992	1985	1982	Change
Art museums	26.7%	21.9%	22.1%	4.6%
Arts and crafts fairs	40.7	40.0	39.0	1.7
Plays	13.5	11.6	11.9	1.6
Jazz	10.6	9.5	9.6	1.0
Ballet	4.7	4.3	4.2	0.5
Opera	3.3	2.6	3.0	0.3
Classical music	12.5	12.7	13.0	-0.5
Musicals	17.4	16.6	18.6	-1.2
Historic parks	34.5	36.0	39.0	-4.5

Attendance rates by race for adults at selected arts events (at least once a month) in 1992:

Activity	Whites	Blacks	Asians*
Reading literature	55.6%	45.3%	39.0%
Arts and crafts fairs	43.6	22.7	27.6
Historic parks	37.1	17.6	21.6
Art museums	27.6	19.2	28.4
Musicals	18.1	14.2	10.5
Plays	13.8	12.2	8.0
Classical music	13.2	6.9	12.6
Jazz	10.1	16.2	4.9
Opera	3.4	1.9	4.9
Ballet	4.9	2.7	6.4

* Asians and others

BARBECUING

Americans fire up their barbecue grills 2.6 billion times a year. When they do, a majority of women call the shots and lay down the rules, but a majority of men do the cooking.

The pastime is practiced on a porch (12 percent of the time), in a yard (33 percent), or on the patio/deck (55 percent), not only on weekends but, increasingly, during the week as well.

According to an industry survey, 71 percent of American people partook of outdoor grilling in 1993, using their own grills, which they lighted up an average of five times a month. Fifty-seven percent of the time, women made the decision to barbecue and decided what should be grilled, but men did the grilling 61 percent of the time.

The average household—principally the younger, larger, higher-income families who live in houses—owns 1.4 grills. The regions with the highest grill ownership, amounting to 74 percent of barbecuers, are the Midwest, the Mountain states, and New England.

Of five basic types of grills—kettles and covered cookers, water smokers, portables or tabletops, braziers, and gas grills—kettles and covered cookers are the most popular, owned by 56 percent of the nation's barbecuers. Charcoal lighter fuel is used by 68 percent of grillers, while the rest opt for instant-lighting briquettes, electric starters, chimney lighters, and solid fuel lighters.

When grilled, respondents answered that distinctive taste in a variety of barbecue styles and sauces around the country is the top reason they like to cook outdoors, according to a biannual survey by the Barbecuing Institute of America. Other reasons: It's outdoorsy, it's a change of pace and fun, cleanup is easy, it's relaxing, and it's is an easy way to entertain.

Hamburgers are the favorite food to cook over coals, according to the survey, followed in order by steak, chicken, hot dogs, potatoes, and marshmallows. Ninety-two percent of grill owners use barbecue sauce at least some of the time. Hickory, tomato-based, mesquite, and spicy-hot are the top flavors.

The use of aromatic woods to enhance flavoring in barbecuing has increased 75 percent since 1983; hickory and mesquite are the most popular chips. Other woods gaining attention, the BIA says, are alder; fruitwoods such as apple, cherry, and peach; and grapevine cuttings, which are popular in some areas of France and Italy.

Of 15 regional barbecuing favorites from New England to California and from the Pacific Northwest to Texas, pork is the first choice in seven regions. Brisket of beef is preferred in four, followed by lamb, seafood, mutton, and vegetables. The BIA credits California with creating what it calls a "new classic" barbecue: the grilled vegetable. Heads of garlic, leeks, scallions and onions, eggplant, zucchini, peppers, avocado, turnip—if it's grillable, California has tried it, the report said.

Weber-Stevens Products Co.

Barbecuing is a pastime enjoyed by approximately 180 million Americans. A new trend in outdoor cookery, barbecuing with aromatic wood, has helped increase its popularity.

Barbecues in the U.S. by year, in billions, according to Barbecue Industry of America (BIA):

Year	Events
1983	1.1
1987	1.4
1991	2.3
1993	2.6

Charcoal briquette sales, in 1,000 of tons; source, BIA:

Year	Sales
1983	79
1987	78
1991	83
1993	83

Barbecue households, in millions; source, BIA:

Year	Households
1983	60
1987	63
1991	73
1993	71

Barbecue grill unit sales, in millions; source, BIA:

Year	Sales
1983	$13.0
1987	11.6
1991	10.7
1993	11.2

BASEBALL

The strike that curtailed the 1994 major league baseball season and delayed the start of the '95 campaign harmed the sport's national image and alienated fans. Prior to the labor dispute, big league baseball was booming. In 1993 the National League welcomed new teams in South Florida and Denver. In fact, the Colorado Rockies became a veritable "phenomenon" in the mountain states. Throughout the '93 season, fans from New Mexico to Montana trekked hundreds of miles to finally see big league baseball; the Rockies drew an astounding 4,483,350 fans to cavernous Mile High Stadium in Denver. The addition of the two new teams drove major league attendance from its 1992 level of 55,900,000 to more than 70 million in 1993. Those once-starved fans flocking to Denver and Miami helped boost average attendance at major league games from approximately 26,500 to nearly 31,000.

Inevitably, the big leagues couldn't cope with the success. The players and owners squabbled about how to divide the proceeds, and the players walked out in August 1994—in the midst of one of the most remarkable seasons in memory in which many of the most revered records were on the verge of being broken. But the excitement was washed away by the abrupt end to the season. The World Series, too, was canceled; not even World War II caused such catastrophic event.

When the 1995 major league season began—three weeks late— sentiments in the stands ranged from apathy to anger. Attendance dropped precipitously. The Pittsburgh Pirates saw average home attendance plummet 36 percent, from 20,345 in 1994 to a paltry 12,936. The Chicago Cubs suffered a 12 percent decline in home attendance at Wrigley Field in 1995. Overall, major league baseball drew 50,496,236 fans in 1995— about what it had attracted the previous year, when teams played an average of 32 *fewer* games each. Per game attendance dropped 21 percent leaguewide.

But American baseball fans don't remain angry forever. The same feelings of betrayal were voiced during the long strike of 1981. After the dispute was settled, major league baseball enjoyed the biggest boom period in its history. Indeed, even with the distressing 1995 turnout, average attendance only fell to its 1992 level—and it remains much greater than in the '60s and '70s. Moreover, television ratings, for the 1995 World Series, though low by traditional standards, were up 13 percent from 1993. Despite seeing CBS lose millions on its four-year deal to televise baseball, Fox and NBC jumped at the opportunity to pick up the sport.

To fully appreciate the popularity of big league baseball, consider how many American cities don't have a team, but are desperate to get one. Tampa and Phoenix will join the major leagues shortly, at an initiation fee of well over $100 million; Washington, D.C., is making an all-out effort to bring a team to the nation's capital.

Detroit mascot "Paws," leads cheers for the Detroit Tigers, which pulled 1.18 million fans in 1995. The Tigers drew over one million attendance for 31 consecutive seasons, the third best long-term record in the Major Leagues. The Dodgers have drawn over one million for 51 seasons (in Brooklyn and Los Angeles); the St. Louis Cardinals have done so for 33.

Though major league baseball may have its problems, the sport is booming at its lower levels. Minor league teams are enjoying enormous success; teams in Kane County, Ill., in St. Paul, Minn., in Riverside, Calif., and in hundreds of other American cities are drawing capacity crowds. In many ways, minor league baseball in small-town America presents the ideal image of the game, and its growing popularity represents the fans' desire to take the sport back to its pastoral roots.

Despite the hype that basketball is the new sport of America's youth, the percentage of boys playing baseball is higher than for basketball. According to the National Sporting Goods Association, 5,422,000 children age seven to 11 and 5,283,000 age 12 to 17 participated in organized baseball in 1993. A *Sports Illustrated for Kids* poll of 1,800 children found that 62 percent of boys and 34 percent of girls age eight to 12 play baseball. Organizations catering to youthful baseball players include Little League, Pony League, high school and college teams, the American Legion, and various lower echelons of the professional minors leagues.

Following is Major League baseball attendance, 1992-95:

Season	Games per team	Overall Att.	Average
1992	162	55,872,271	26,530
1993	162	70,256,459	30,977
1994	112	50,010,807	31,890
1995	144	50,496,236	25,047

BASKETBALL

On playgrounds from Brooklyn to Venice Beach, American youths who couldn't tell Newt Gingrich from Wayne Newton idolize basketball greats Michael Jordan, Shaquille O'Neal, and Charles Barkley. In many ways, basketball is the sport—indeed, the overriding interest—of young people today.

Basketball was floundering as a major professional sport in the late '70s and early '80s. As late as 1981, the NBA Finals were nationally broadcast on tape-delay after the late-night news. In addition, simultaneous reports of rampant drug abuse in the NBA presented an unseemly image. Compared to baseball and football, few Americans cared about professional basketball, and even fewer attended games.

To prop up the sport, David Stern , a savvy lawyer from New York, was brought in as commissioner of the NBA. He immediately recognized basketball's greatest asset—the incredible athleticism of its players—and set about to capitalize on that facet of the game. Luckily, he had two appealing stars in the fold, each playing on one of the two most storied and successful teams: Magic Johnson of the Los Angeles Lakers and Larry Bird of the Boston Celtics.

As the Lakers and Celtics squared off time and again in the Finals in the early and mid-'80s, through Stern's guidance the sport was promoted essentially as "Bird vs. Magic." America began to take notice.

The emphasis on star players paid off in earnest when Jordan entered the league in 1985. Armed with a Nike shoe contract and a talent unlike any other in the league, Jordan captured the attention of the nation. "Air Jordan" became the symbol of a high-flying, high-tech sport for modern America, and kids across the country wanted to "be like Mike."

Attendance skyrocketed—the NBA now plays to an average capacity of 91 percent and new attendance records are set every year. In addition, the price of network television contracts for basketball exploded, and advertisers climbed aboard the NBA bandwagon. The league now is the biggest marketing force in American sports.

Today, even for those who don't follow basketball, it's hard to avoid the NBA. Barkley pitches Big Macs and underarm deodorant, and argues that he shouldn't be forced to act as a role model for America's youth. O'Neal's $40 million face was seemingly everywhere before he played a minute of NBA basketball. The U.S. "Dream Team" Olympic squad was the most popular attraction at the 1992 Olympics in Barcelona. Jordan, its star, was described by Danny Ainge, a former NBA star himself, as the Elvis Presley of the new age.

Basketball's new-found hold on the nation is evident in participation rates among young people. According to a *Sports Illustrated for Kids* poll of 1,800 children nationwide, 62 percent of boys and 38 percent of girls age eight to 12 play basketball, or "hoops" as

Chicago Bulls

According to the city of Chicago, having Michael Jordan (above) playing for the city's team, the Bulls, contributes $4 billion in annual revenues to the local economy.

the game is known among youths. The American Basketball Council estimates that 12.5 million boys and eight million girls under the age of 17 play the sport formally or informally, as do 15.7 million men and 4.2 million women age 17 and older. According to the National Sporting Goods Association, youth participation in organized basketball in 1993 amounted to 5,751,000 children age seven to 11 and 9,361,000 children age 12 to 17.

The table below enumerates regular-season attendance at NBA games as counted by the NBA:

Season	Total	Average
1992-93	17,778,295	16,060
1993-94	17,984,014	16,246
1994-95	18,516,484	16,727

BOWLING

The number of hard-core bowlers in the U.S.—those who bowl 52 times or more a year—is falling, but the game still ranks fifth in the nation in "frequent" players among sporting pastimes, a 1994 for the Billiard & Bowling Institute of America shows. Fitness walking, camping, basketball, and billiards, in that order, are more popular.

Though the size of 52-plus group and of bowlers who call the game their favorite activity has decreased by 14 percent since 1987, the number of "infrequent" bowlers—those who participate one or more times a year—increased 2.5 percent. These include 3.7 percent more women, 29.7 percent more children age six to 11, 9.3 percent more adults age 35 to 54, and 70.6 percent more players with annual incomes of at least $50,000. The report was derived from an analysis of an American Sports Data Inc. survey of 15,000 U.S. households in 1994.

Those figures, the bowling association says, showed that overall, 49 million Americans bowled in 1993, making the game the most popular participatory sport in the country, ahead of basketball at 42 million and billiards at 40 million. The bowling figure, however, is down 2.4 percentage points from 1991.

In 1993 23.8 million females and 25.1 million males bowled at least once; 6.8 million six- to 11-year-olds; and 19.7 million 18- to 34-year-olds, who made up 40 percent of all bowlers. The study found 2.7 million hard-core participants, and 15.3 million bowlers with annual incomes above $50,000. The largest number of bowlers, 19.7 million in all, fall into the $25,000-50,000 income range of the study. Only 3.4 percent of persons 55 years or older participated in bowling, down 8.5 percent from 1987 but up two percent from 1991.

Thirty-four percent of bowlers played one to 11 times a year, down 2.4 percent from 1991; 12.1 percent played 12 to 51 times a year, up .02 percent; and 2.7 percent played more than 52 times a year, down .07 percent.

Bowlers in the North and South sections of the country who played once or more in 1993 make up the majority of players, at 29 percent each, or 58 percent of the total, compared to 21 percent in both the Northeast and West.

Below and in the opposite column are key findings compiled by National Bowling Participation Survey, in millions of players and percent change, 1987-93:

Demographics	Players	Change
Total players	49.0	2.5%
"Core" players	2.7	-28.3
Males	25.1	1.4
Females	23.9	3.7
Age 6-11	6.8	29.7
Age 12-17	7.5	4.3
Age 18-34	19.8	-6.3
Age 35-54	11.6	9.3
Over 55	3.4	-8.5

Income below $25,000	13.8	-32.9
$25-50,000	19.8	8.8
$50,000-plus	15.3	70.6
1-11 days played	33.7	8.6
12-24	5.4	4.0
25-51	6.7	-6.5
52-plus	2.7	-28.3
Average days played	14.6	-19.8

Number of players in select participatory sports, 1991-93, in millions who played once or more per year:

Sport	1991	1992	1993
Bowling	52.0	49.6	49.0
Basketball	39.3	40.4	42.1
Billiards	39.2	37.8	40.2
Volleyball (non-beach)	32.0	31.3	31.7
Softball	29.4	28.7	30.1

Bowling participation in days played 1991-1993, in millions:

Days played	1991	1992	1993
1-11	36.3	34.5	33.8
12-51	11.9	11.3	12.1
52-plus	3.4	3.3	2.7

Bowling participation once or more per year, by age, in millions, 1991-93:

Age	1991	1992	1993
Under 18	14.2	14	13.3
18-34	22.6	20.2	19.7
35-54	11.9	11.9	11.6
55-plus	3.2	3.5	3.4

CRAFTS

Americans who are deeply involved in arts and crafts are on average 48 years of age, have been crafting for 22 years, and have a median annual income of $32,100. On average, they're involved with 14.8 different crafts and spend 12.2 hours a week crafting. Eighty-eight percent work on their crafts for personal reasons rather than to sell their creations. On each visit to a crafts shop, they spend $22.65 on purchases.

This glimpse of the average dedicated crafter emerges from a survey taken by the Association of Crafts & Creative Industries, which in 1994 targeted on serious-minded workers in crafts with full-page ads in four large consumer crafts publications: *Crafts, Crafts and Things, Pack-O-Fun,* and *Decorative Arts Planning.* A total of 872 women readers of the magazines later completed survey forms and returned them to ACCI.

Most of the crafters—68 percent—were the only one in their household. When the husband also crafts, he averages 13.6 years of experience. Thirty-two percent of the respondents had children under age 18

Bead craft	42
Jewelry-making	41
Flower arranging	37
Quilting	36

living at home, averaging 1.3 child per household. Forty percent were homemakers, and 14 percent were retired. Of the 46 percent who had jobs, most were white-collar workers.

Sewing was favored by 69 percent of the respondents. The second choice was fabric painting, at 68 percent, followed by wearable arts at 54 percent, wreath-making at 52 percent, and plastic canvas at 50 percent.

Fabric painting, wearable arts, wreath-making, and painting showed significant drops in favor among crafters age 65 and older. Wearable arts were most favored in households with incomes above $45,000 annually. Crochet, at 46 percent, and embroidery, at 44 percent, appealed most to those age 55 and older. Jewelry making (41 percent) and bead crafts (42 percent) most attracted those age 35-44.

In households with children under age 18, beads were a favored craft, as were stenciling, rubber-stamping, ceramics, and candy-making. Stenciling was participated in by 31 percent of the respondents, rubber-stamping by 23 percent, ceramics by 27 percent, and candy-making by 20 percent.

Among those age 45 or older, favored crafts were doll-making, knitting, and tole-painting (enameled or lacquered metalware). Doll-making was named by 24 percent of the respondents (mostly by those age 65 and older), knitting by 23 percent, and tole-painting by 26 percent, mostly those age 55 to 64 and higher-income crafters.

The creation of personal gifts was the most frequent use for completed craft projects, at 91 percent. Other uses were home decoration (74 percent); personal satisfaction (68 percent); sale, but not as a business (37 percent); fashion accessories (37) percent; and as a business (12 percent).

About 60 percent of the crafters had taken classes, usually in a craft store. Eighteen percent went to a community college for lessons, and twenty percent reported taking a class every six months or more.

The most unusual of the 50 crafts mentioned in the survey were egguery (egg art), participated in by six percent of the respondents; tatting or lacemaking (seven percent); and wheat-weaving, bath products, and soaps and lotions (eight percent).

Below are the 15 most popular arts and crafts, according to the ACCI survey:

Craft	Percent
Sewing	69%
Fabric-painting	68
Wearable arts	54
Wreath-making	52
Plastic canvas	50
Cross stitch	48
Needlecrafts	47
Crochet	46
Embroidery	44
Painting	42
Applique	42

DINING OUT

Salads are creeping up on hamburgers as the favorite among Americans when dining out, according to a survey on what the nation eats away from home. French fries, steaks, and pizzas follow burgers and salads, in that order.

Fine dining continued its slide from 1993, when 59 percent of American adults chose a white-tablecloth restaurant, according to a February 1994 survey by Roper Starch Worldwide. A "Tastes of America" survey of 2,680 consumers on dining out, conducted in mid-1994 by National Family Opinion and published in the summer issue of the journal "Society," showed that the figure had dropped to 45 percent. Overall, 87.6 percent of the respondents felt their restaurant meal was not worth the price.

More than 32 percent of respondents ordered salads more frequently than in the past. Grilled chicken, fish, pizza, and baked potatoes followed, in that order, as 70 percent of the diners-out reported being more concerned with nutrition than they were in the past. Percentages concerned with nutrition were highest among working couples without children.

Fast-food restaurants were visited more than once a week by 27.4 percent of those surveyed, 98 percent of whom ate out in the last month, 85 percent in the last week, and 45 percent the day before the survey. Young singles, young couples, and married couples with children aged 13 to 17 were above-average in all three categories. Casual and family dining restaurants were visited by 15.3 percent of the respondents more than once a week, and fine dining restaurants by one percent. Almost 15 percent visited fine dining restaurants once a month, however.

Of the total number of meals eaten out in the average week, 40 percent were lunch, 29 percent dinner, 20 percent snacks, and 11 percent breakfast. The eating-out food bill of the respondents took a 2.6 percent dip from a 1992 Tastes of America survey, to $32.63. That median ranges from $19.88 for older singles to $41.23 for working couples with children aged 13 to 17.

Singles with children under age 13 made up 82.4 percent of the respondents who ate at a familiar restaurant, while 22.9 percent of more elderly couples were likely to try a new restaurant. About 28 percent of the respondents were eating out more often, compared to 26 percent in a 1992 Tastes of America survey. About six percent said they would eat out more in 1995, compared to nine percent in 1992.

About 75 percent of the respondents registered displeasure with what they encountered during their restaurant visits, with lack of cleanliness and rude and unfriendly service the most bothersome.

The 1993 Roper Starch survey found that 71 percent of Americans preferred home-cooked meals, though 56 percent said they ate dinner out during the week before the survey. Another 28 percent ate out sometime during the past month.

For 51 percent of Americans the decision to eat out was made at the last minute, with 64 percent of that total being young adults. Thirty-five percent of adults with household incomes of less than $15,000 planned their last dinner outing, compared with 49 percent of those with incomes of $50,000 or more. All told, 58 percent of dinners at full-service restaurants were planned, compared with 25 percent of trips to fast-food venues.

The most frequently given reason for dining out in the Roper survey was "just felt like going out," 42 percent. Next most popular was "socializing with friends," 14 percent.

FISHING

The number of fisherman has grown 20 percent since 1980, twice the rate of the U.S. population. One in four Americans go fishing at least once a year, outnumbering golfers and tennis players, according to an Alabama clearinghouse for the bass fishing industry. Between seasons, fishing fanciers can watch at least 10 network blocks of fishing shows and scores of regional and local shows, says the International Association of Fish and Wildlife Agencies in Washington, D.C.

Most of the shows are seasonal, according to the Bass Anglers Sportsman's Society (BASS), ballooning up in the winter and spring, so that on cable a viewer often can flip between three or more shows at one time. "Bassmasters," produced by B.A.S.S, runs 39 straight Sundays on the Nashville Network, along with a special episode on the national championship of largemouth bass fishing, the Bassmasters Classic, at the end of each year. Viewership has grown to more than 1 million households a week since the series began in 1985.

Through the season most of the shows portray an accurate depiction of a day on the water, according to pro anglers, although there are a few scenes where scuba divers catch the big one by net and then hook it while the camera is rolling. Pros easily spot this artifice and flip to another program.

Most "Bassmasters" viewers are middle-age men. "Bassmaster" magazine profiles its average reader as 39 years old, married, with an annual income of $45,000. He owns an average of one boat with a motor and a trailer to haul the it around, as well as 13 rods and reels made of space age materials, four tackle boxes filled with lures and lines, and perhaps a portable water temperature gauge. He spends an average $1,250 on fishing and goes fishing 59 days a year.

Fishing celebrities vie against each other in the year-long, multimillion-dollar Bassmaster Tournament Trail, which in 1992-93 paid out $3 million in

The number of recreational fisherman like the youths above has grown 20 percent in the U.S. since 1980, twice the rate of the U.S. population.

prize money. The tour winds up with the traveling Bassmaster Classic, which draws 80,000 spectators who spend $25 to $30 million in the host city.

Performers on almost all TV fishing shows and competitors in tournaments release the fish they catch, a practice called "catch and release" and initiated by Muskie, Inc., in the 1950s, when fishermen realized that the largest freshwater predator takes as long as 30 years to grow to large size. About 20 years later B.A.S.S. tournaments adopted the practice, which is now almost universal among professional fishers.

According to BASS, 80 percent of its members are married, and their spouses also fish. The South is the densest region for fishing fanatics, with more than 500,000 of those members living in the Southeast. A Midwest fishing stronghold is Indiana.

TV covers a wide variety of fishing, from largemouth bass in the South (though the species lives in most of the 50 states) to muskie and walleye in the North; trout, salmon, and walleye in the West; and saltwater species on both East and West coasts.

FOOTBALL

It is no coincidence that football's rise in popularity coincided with television's subtle intrusion into American life. The NFL had been around since its founding in 1920, but it remained in the sporting backwater for three decades, far behind baseball and college football in popularity. NFL teams began to draw crowds in substantial numbers in the '50s, when CBS picked up national television rights and began broadcasting games on Sunday afternoons.

In the 60s, forward-thinking NFL commissioner Pete Rozelle realized the potential of a captive audience for his sport, as Americans came in from the cold in the fall and spent their weekends indoors. Rozelle thus molded his game into TV-friendly entertainment, overseeing rules changes to boost scoring, marketing the sport in inventive new ways—"Monday Night Football," for instance—negotiating network contracts that practically amounted to partnerships with television, and merging his league with the upstart—and more exciting—AFL to create the force the NFL is today.

How great a force? NFL programming accounted for *eight* of the top-10 rated television broadcasts of 1995. Super Bowl XXIX between the San Francisco 49ers and San Diego Chargers was the most-watched show of the year, with a 41.3 rating and various play-off games accounted for seven of the other 10. Only the Academy Awards and a "Seinfeld" accompanied the football programs on the top-10 list. Indeed, there has been semi-serious talk from the NFL commissioner's office of efforts to make Super Bowl Sunday a national holiday. It already is, unofficially.

In 1995, for the third year in a row, the NFL set a regular-season attendance record, surpassing 15 million for the first time. Though that figure pales in comparison to the more than 50 million who attended major league baseball in '95, the NFL drew as many to its 240 regular-season games. NFL per game attendance was a remarkable 62,696 in 1995.

If fall Sundays are given over to the NFL, autumn Saturdays in America belong to college football. Intercollegiate football is played by more than 270 schools nationwide, 108 in the top-level Division IA. Massive stadiums such as those at the University of Michigan and UCLA pack in more than 100,000 fans for every game. For the big "football factory" schools, the gridiron team is as well known as major professional teams, and often has a greater following.

Football, however, is not quite the youth-sport that baseball and basketball are, perhaps because many mothers are wary of their children engaging in the dangerous sport, and perhaps because few girls play organized football. Nonetheless, the National Sporting Goods Association noted that 2,495,000 children age seven to 11 and 5,227,000 age 12 to 17 played organized football in 1993. The latter figure includes 334 girls who broke the gender barrier and played high school football.

Greater Miami Convention and Visitors Bureau.

For millions of Americans, from early September to late January, Sundays are a day of worship, not necessarily to God, but to the gods of the Gridiron.

The list below enumerates NFL regular-season attendance, according to the NFL.

Season	Total Attendance	Avg. Game
1994	14,030,435	62,636
1995	15,047,058	62,696

GAMBLING

Today in the U.S. gambling is permitted on riverboats, Indian reservations, at race tracks, off track, at church fund-raisers, and even at the grocery store where lottery tickets are sold.

Gambling is legal in one form or another in 48 of the 50 states, and Americans spend $300 billion on this recreation—about as much as the Department of Defense spends annually. The most recent mania began in the 1980s, when state lotteries became popular as a way of raising money without raising taxes. Thirty-four states now have lotteries, twice as many as did ten years ago.

Harrahs

Harrahs at Ak-Chin is one of the many Indian reservations that now offer casino gambling. Reservation gambling alone grossed $2.7 billion in 1994.

Las Vegas News Bureau.

With gambling now available in 48 states, vacation and convention capital Las Vegas offers two things most casinos don't: family activities and glittery shows like the one above.

Nevada casinos pulled in the most dollars as American's urge to gamble reached a new high in 1994. But the new kid on the block, riverboat gambling, is running a close second. Americans bet almost $51 billion on the tables and slots between 1989 and 1993, with an estimated $37 billion more in 1994-95, when the gambling rate will be almost three times what it was in 1989.

Nevada casinos will rake in $7.1 of the $20.4 billion expected to be spent on gambling in 1995. Riverboats will beat out Atlantic City casinos, $5.7 billion to $3.3 billion. Indian reservation casinos come next at $2.7 billion, followed by video and lotteries at $1.3 billion, and small stakes casinos, $300 million, as American spend an increasing amount of their disposable income on gambling.

The surge in popularity of riverboat gambling is attributed to their proximity to the gambler. According to Bala Subramanian, corporate director of two Harrah's riverboats in Joliet, Ill., "Convenience will always be the most important factor in terms of where people will go."

The list below ranks ways in which Americans wager their money, in order of popularity, according to *Gaming and Wagering Business* magazine (GWB):

1. Lotteries
2. Casinos
3. Pari-mutuel betting
4. Charitable games
5. Bingo
6. Card rooms
7. Sports bookmaking

U.S gaming revenues by year in billions of dollars, 1994 and estimated for 1995; source, GWB:

Year	Revenues
1989	$7.7
1990	8.8
1991	9.3
1992	11.3
1993	13.9
1994	17.4
1995 (est.)	20.4

Major convention cities, number of conventions, and gambling revenues, in billions; source, GWB:

City	Conventions	Revenue
Las Vegas	2,443	$2.3
New Orleans	1,446	1.6
Detroit	529	0.3
Atlantic City	60	N.A.

GOLF

Although golf's origins can be traced back to the Roman Empire, the game as Americans know it today was largely developed in 18th century Scotland when the first rules-of-play were established at the Company of Gentlemen Golfers, now known as the Honourable Company of Edinburgh.

The United States saw its first club and course take shape in 1888 at the Saint Andrews Golf Club of Yonkers, in New York. There are now 465 million rounds of golf being played annually on 15,000 golf courses

Greater Miami Convention and Tourist Bureau.

Golf in America is increasingly becoming a sport played by women as well as men; one of every three people who try golf for the first time are women.

across the country, 7,700 of which are public clubs. 68 percent of the nation's courses are open to the public, and 70 percent of all rounds are played on public courses.

According to the National Golf Foundation, there are 24 million golfers in the U.S. population. 11 million of those are classified as Core Golfers —those who are age 18 and older, and who play 8 or more rounds per years; 11.4 million are Occasional Golfers those 18 and older who play 1 to 7 rounds per year; and about 8 million Junior Golfers—those between that ages of 12 and 17 who play at least one round per year.

The typical golfer is a 40-year-old male with a household income of $56,200. He plays about 20 rounds per year, and will spend approximately $295 annually on golf equipment. The 5 million golfers who play more than 25 rounds annually will spend nearly double that amount on equipment per year.

Golf continues to attract new players, especially among women — who comprise 21 percent of all players — and younger people: Of the 2 million people who try the game each year, 55 percent are between the ages of 18 and 39, and 33.6 percent are women.

While golf has traditionally been a game for the rich, today its popularity spreads across the income spectrum. 38 percent of golfers come from homes headed by blue-collar and clerical workers to the 41 percent who come from homes headed by professionals or managers.

Golf continues to be popular among the over-50 section of the country, making up 40 percent of the golf population and playing over 36 rounds per year. Over 3.6 million seniors (60 years and older) are actively playing golf.

LIBRARY VISITS

Circulation at libraries rose every year from 1980 until 1993, when it decreased three percent relative to 1992. From 1980 to 1992 library circulation rose almost 50 percent.

Expenditures by libraries in 1993 rose eight percent from 1992, from an index level of 250 (1980 = 100) to 270, outdistancing inflation by five percent. Since 1980, expenditures per patron withdrawal have increased 96 percent, while circulation per capita has risen 36 percent.

According to the 1993 Index of American Public Library Circulation, 29 of the 53 libraries serving populations of more than 25,000 reported an increase of five percent in juvenile circulations over 1992, when it had declined five percent from 1991. The 1993 percentage brought juvenile library use back in line with 1991. The adult circulation index continued a three-year decline to 122, six points below 1991.

Library salaries increased six percent, from an index of 254 in 1992 to 269 in 1993. Expenditures for materials increased 10 percent, from 220 in 1992 to 242 in 1993. Salaries have registered a rise in every year since 1980, while the material index saw reductions in 1990 and 1992, to 217 and 220 respectively.

Circulation in public libraries per capita was down slightly from 1992, at 6.4. Expenditures per item withdrawn rose five percent from 1992, from $2.65 to $2.78. Expenditures per capita decreased 44 cents, from $18.27 per capita in 1992 to $17.83 in 1993, only the second time since 1980 that this index dropped.

Below are library circulation and expenditures from 1980 to 1993 (1980 levels=100); source, Index of American Public Library Circulation:

Year	Circulation	Expenditures
1980	100	100
1981	104	110
1982	107	121
1983	107	130
1984	109	145
1985	111	159
1986	111	176
1987	118	181
1988	121	196
1989	124	200
1990	124	223
1991	143	233
1992	148	250
1993	144	270

Change in adult and juvenile circulation:

Year	Adult	Juvenile
1980	100	100
1981	95	96
1982	108	106
1983	111	108
1984	114	112

1885	112	117
1986	109	120
1987	108	133
1988	108	140
1989	110	154
1990	119	168
1991	128	174
1992	124	165
1993	122	174

MOVIES

Projections by *American Demographics* magazine forecast smarter and less-violent movies in the later 1990s, as filmmakers are forced to cater to baby boomer audiences.

In short, because the cost of making a Hollywood movie and distributing and advertising it is so immense, moviemakers will begin to turn away from the declining youth market to which it has been catering in recent years. Gore and teenage angst and suffering will decrease on the screen, while family movies, animations, sophisticated fare, and adult themes will predominate, according to *American Demographics*.

Citing Motion Picture Association of America figures (MPAA), the journal says 24 percent of total movie admissions in 1981 were to those aged 16 to 20. Only 15 percent of admissions were in that category by 1992. During the same period attendance by 40- to-49-year-olds, many presumably accompanied by their children, climbed 10 percentage points, from six percent to 16 percent, and continued to climb in each of the next three years. This age group currently is the second largest segment of moviegoers, following the 30 to 39 category, which increased from 17 percent of the market in 1981 to 19 percent in 1992.

Every age groups from 30 years old to 60 and older showed an increase in moviegoing during the period: two percent in the 30-39 group, two percent in the 50-59 category, and four percent for those 60 and older. All age groups from 12 to 29 showed a decrease: 12-15, five percent; 16-24, nine percent, 21-24, four percent 25-29, two percent. Parents with children are more likely to go to the movies than childless couples, according to MPAA.

The following list details the percentage of yearly admissions of moviegoers, by age, in 1981 and 1992, compiled by Harold L. Vogel, "Entertainment Industry Economics: A Guide for Financial Analysis," and the Motion Picture Association of America:

Age Group	1981	1992
12 to 15	17%	12%
16 to 20	24	15
21 to 24	15	11
25 to 29	13	11
30 to 39	17	19
40 to 49	6	16
50 to 59	5	7
60 and older	4	8

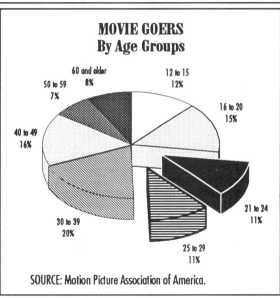

MOVIE GOERS By Age Groups

60 and older 8%
50 to 59 7%
40 to 49 16%
30 to 39 20%
25 to 29 11%
21 to 24 11%
16 to 20 15%
12 to 15 12%

SOURCE: Motion Picture Association of America.

MUSEUM VISITS

America's 64.5 million adult museum visitors in 1992 were predominantly white, affluent, well-educated, tourists, and suburbanites, as the nation's museum-goers traditionally are. Inner-city blacks, the poor, the homeless, and the uneducated scarcely knew museums existed, a national survey of U.S. cultural institutions indicates.

Nearly 27 percent of American adults visited art museums in 1992, an increase of 10 percent since 1982, making art museums America's most popular and rapidly growing cultural activity. Attendance at musicals over the period declined from 18.5 percent to 15 percent and classical music concerts from 13.7 percent to 13.5 percent, while attendance at plays increased from 12.5 percent to 14 percent and at jazz concerts from 9.7 percent to 10.5 percent.

Twenty-eight percent of whites made a visit to an art museum in 1992, compared to 19 percent of blacks; 46.1 percent of college graduates took in a museum, compared to just 3.8 percent of those with less than a high school education. Forty-four percent of people with incomes of more than $50,000 made visits vs. 17 percent with annual incomes below $25,000. Art museums attracted 31 percent of suburbanites, 29 percent of city dwellers, 21 percent of tourists.

Although both visits to art museums among both blacks and whites increased between 1982 and 1992, according to a National Endowment for the Arts survey conducted by the Census Bureau, blacks still make up just seven percent of visitors to all types of U.S. museums.

The survey, which interviewed 12,736 adults aged 18 and older, did not collect information from Hispanics, who represent nine percent of the population, or Asian-Americans, who represent three percent of the

Queens Museum. Photo by Rich Fahey.

The introduction of high-tech apparatus like the above has done much to make visits to America's museums the fastest growing cultural activity in the nation.

population, according to a report on the NEA survey in the journal *American Demographics*. Blacks, Hispanics, and Asians combined make up a majority of residents in New York, Los Angeles, St. Louis, and many other U.S. cities with important art museums, the journal points out.

Men and women were almost equally represented in art museum attendance; 26.5 of men and 26.9 percent of women attended an art museum. Those between the ages of 24 and 64 were much more likely than younger or elderly Americans to visit an art museum.

Visitation to museums in general, on the other hand, is gender-related. Women outnumbered men among all museum visitors by 56.4 percent to 43.6. The age group 25 to 44 made up 48.2 percent of visitors to cultural institutions as a whole; the 45-64 group accounted for 28.9 percent of visitors, and the 18-24 group 11.8 percent.

Museum directors are striving to make their museums less intimidating and more relevant to the changing demographics in their communities. The magzine *American Demographics* lists such efforts as hands-on activities and video-on-demand kiosks to view extensive museum holdings. Some also are recording the histories of "regular people" and a city's neighborhoods, recruiting local minority youths to work in a museum, explaining exhibits and the science behind them, and establishing "dollar nights," during which admission is reduced. The object, the journal says, is to begin building long-term relationships with their customers.

These lists below indicate the percentage of adults by selected characteristics who visited an art museum at least once in a given year, and distribution of attendees by age, sex, and education, and the visitors' share of all U.S. adults, 1992; NEA statistics:

	Art Museums	All Museums
SEX		
Men	26.5%	43.6%
Women	26.9	56.4
AGE		
18 to 24	28.7%	11.8%
25 to 34	29.4	24.1
35 to 44	29.7	24.1
45 to 54	29.3	16.9
55 to 64	24.7	12.0
65 and older	16.4	11.2
EDUCATION		
Less than high school	5.6%	3.8%
High school graduate	16.4	23.0
Some college	34.5	27.1
College graduate	51.8	46.1

Percent of adults age 18 and older attending art museums, by place of residence, 1982 and 1992, from NEA statistics:

Residence	1982	1992
Central city	25.5%	29.0%
Suburban	25.0	31.0
Tourists	15.3	21.0

MUSICAL INSTRUMENTS

Since 1980, not too many instrumentalists have made the popular music charts. Many who grew up during the 1960s and 1970s, however, cut their musical teeth on the music of greats as disparate as Al Hirt, Chet Atkins, and Liberace. Music lessons were a regular after-school activity for almost a quarter of all American kids.

More than 57 million adults play at least one instrument; half of them play two or more. Three-quarters of these musicians play music regularly. This list shows the various instruments Americans play and the numbers involved.

Piano	21.0 million
Guitar	19.0 million
Organ	6.0 million
Flute	4.0 million
Clarinet	4.0 million
Drums	3.0 million
Trumpet	3.0 million
Violin	2.0 million
Harmonica	1.7 million
Saxophone	1.0 million
Electronic keyboard	600,000

PLAYLOTS

Even the new "above standard" safety playlots beginning to dot the nation's neighborhoods—built with wood-chip surfaces, fall zones, and G-force testing—are not the safest places for children to play, according to two consumer protection groups.

Ninety percent of the nation's playgrounds still offer "hidden hazards that can injure and even kill," according to the Illinois Public Interest Research Group, which conducted a survey on playground safety with the Consumer Federation of America. The two groups checked 413 playgrounds nationwide. Their findings: 177,000 injuries to children a year from swing seats, cable walks, metal grab rings, climbing ropes, rope swings, and slides more than seven feet high.

Playground builders disagree with the findings, one citing the dropping of teeter-totters and merry-go-rounds in the 1970s to make playlots safer. But although the nation's playgrounds are safer than they used to be, builders still have not eliminated the dangers of strangulation and falls, the survey report said. Some of the "hidden hazards" still remaining in the nation's newest playlots, according to the survey:

- Hard surfaces under or near equipment
- Swing seats made of wood or metal
- Objects located in fall zones
- Equipment standing too high
- Equipment with sharp edges or protrusions
- Close spacing of swing seats that increases risk of them striking kids

SNOWMOBILING

There are more than 150,000 miles of designated snowmobile trails in the U.S., most of which are in three midwestern states: Wisconsin, Michigan, and Minnesota. Of 1.2 million one- and two- seat snowmobiles licensed in 31 states, 225,921 scurry around Michigan trails, 216,928 over Minnesota snowfields, and 216,928 over Wisconsin trails, according to a 1992-94 survey by the International Snowmobile Industry Association. The next-highest number of registrations is by snowmobilers in Maine, at 70,043.

Since 1989 snowmobile trail mileage lacing through the North American snowbelt has increased almost 40

Greater Miami Convention and Tourist Bureau.
Jai alai, a sport almost unknown to those who have never visited Florida, is the 9th most popular spectator sport in the U.S.

percent, the trails supported yearly by nearly $18 million in snowmobiler-generated fees and taxes and by volunteer labor. The high decibel level once associated with the machines has been reduced by 94 percent since 1980, and stringent safety features have multiplied.

Between 1990 and 1994, 429,000 new vehicles were sold in the U.S., and since 1989 annual sales have increased almost 35 percent, from $301 million to $389 million. The sport's enthusiasts include members of 2,200 snowmobile clubs across the country, who have raised $6.7 billion in five years for various charities. Snowmobilers annually spend more than $1.6 billion on machines, club memberships, tour guides, rented vehicles for one- day to three-week excursions, and accessories such as boots, snow suits, gloves, headgear, and helmets with face shields.

The average snowmobile owner is a male aged 35 to 39, married, and lives in a two- to four-member household. The snowmobiler is a skilled laborer, owner/manager of a business, or a professional, and a resident of a small town or a rural/farm area, with at least a nine to 12-year education. Average annual household income is $40,000-$45,000.

Top 10 states in registered snowmobiler ownership, according to ISIA survey statistics 1992-94:

State	Registrations
Michigan	225,921
Minnesota	216,000
Wisconsin	178,624
Maine	70,043
New York	62,110
Illinois	58,676
New Hampshire	37,761
Pennsylvania	35,300
Iowa	31,510
Washington	27,323

SPORTS, PARTICIPATORY

In our exercise-conscious culture, noncompetitive pastimes such as swimming, exercise walking, and bicycling garner far more participants than classic team activities like baseball, basketball, and football, perhaps because they can be done alone.

The table below represents the proportion of the U.S. population who engage in various sports regularly, according to the U.S. Bureau of the Census:

Sport	Percent
Swimming	32.8%
Exercise walking	28.7
Bicycling	24.8
Camping	19.5
Fishing (freshwater)	18.3
Bowling	17.5
Exercising with equipment	13.3
Aerobic exercising	11.2
Basketball	10.7
Running/jogging	10.6

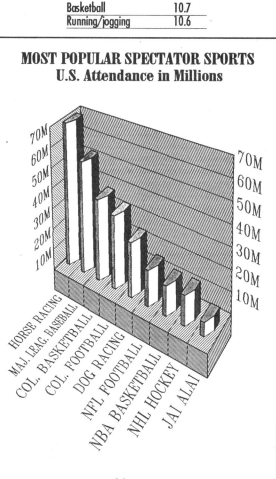

MOST POPULAR SPECTATOR SPORTS
U.S. Attendance in Millions

SOURCE: U.S. Bureau of the Census.

SPORTS, SPECTATOR

America's passion for gambling has overtaken its passion for baseball. Though the buying of lottery tickets is the most popular way to gamble when it comes to combining the urge to wager with an outing, the race track pulls in more fans than any other form of amusement.

The list below indicates the top spectator sports in the U.S., by annual attendance, according to the U.S. Bureau of the Census:

Sport	Spectators
Horse racing	69,946,000
Major league baseball	53,800,000
College football	35,581,000
Men's college basketball	32,504,000
Greyhound racing	26,477,000
NFL football	17,024,000

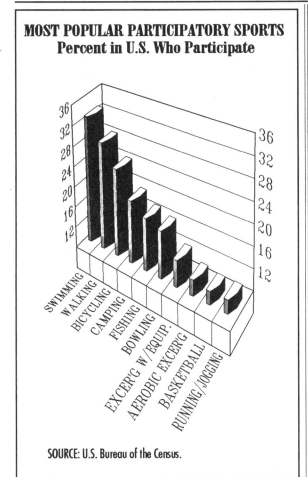

MOST POPULAR PARTICIPATORY SPORTS
Percent in U.S. Who Participate

SWIMMING, WALKING, BICYCLING, CAMPING, FISHING, BOWLING, EXERC'G W/EQUIP., AEROBIC EXERC'G, BASKETBALL, RUNNING/JOGGING

SOURCE: U.S. Bureau of the Census.

NBA basketball	14,051,000
NHL hockey	13,741,000
Jai alai	6,414,000
Women's college basketball	3,301,000

TENNIS

Twenty-two million Americans find the exercise, competition, fun, or social and outdoor aspects of tennis to their liking, according to a national survey, yet the general popularity of the game remains relatively stagnant. The problem: Aside from using a ball machine, tennis cannot be played alone.

Seventy-nine percent of the male and female racquet-swingers age 12 and over who do find partners and play at least once a year name exercise as one of the best things about the game. Fifty-five percent like the competition it affords, and 44 percent the fun. Just getting outdoors attracts 19 percent, and the game's social aspects draw 20 percent.

Since the middle 1980s, the growth of tennis clinics, training programs for teens, organized leagues, and better racquets, has not been matched by an increase

in players, according to the study, conducted by the research firm Audits & Surveys for the Tennis Industry Association (TIA).

In 1989 the number of Americans who played tennis at least once a year stood at 21.2 million; the figure increased by 1.4 million through 1992. The number who play four or more times a year decreased to 13.7 million from 14.2 million, while those who engage in 21 sessions or more declined to 5.9 million from 6.1 million.

TIA points out that 86 percent of the nation's tennis players participate in at least two other sports or exercise activities at least four times a year, an increase of eight percent since 1989. Also, the fad aspect of tennis in the 1970s, when the sport broke out from the wealthy enclaves where it had been confined, burned out in the 1980s. Its subsequent rebound has been slow but steady, according to TIA.

Two corollary studies tend to sharpen the tennis picture in the U.S. The number of tennis balls sold dropped from 100 million in 1992 to 91 million in 1993, according to the Sporting Goods Manufacturing Association, while the number of racquets sold dropped from 170,000 to 156,000. The percentage of Americans who play the game dropped 8.5 percent, to 19.3 million in 1993 from 21.1 million in 1987.

Thirty percent of "frequent" tennis players belong to private clubs, paying on average $426 annually for the privilege, according to the TIA survey. Seventy-one percent have played the game for six years or more, 26 percent attended a tennis match in the past year, and 20 percent are still taking lessons.

Sixty percent of those who play four or more times a year use public courts; 21 percent private clubs; six percent their apartment complex, and five percent resorts, company courts, or home. Since 1988, the percentage of players age 55 and older has almost doubled, from 7 percent to 13 percent, a growth TIA calls "dramatic."

Characteristics of Americans who played tennis four or more times in 1992, in percent, income in thousands, and players in millions, compiled by Tennis Industry Association:

Demographics	4-10 times	11-20	21+
Players	4.3	3.5	5.9
Male	56.0%	54.0%	63.0%
Female	44.0%	46.0%	37.0%
Household income	$52.6	$49.0	$60.8
Average age	29.6	29.0	34.6
Employed	67.0%	62.0%	66.0%
Professional/manager	35.0%	27.0%	39.0%
Supervisor	7	3	5
White collar	13	18	12
Blue-collar	12	14	10
Unemployed	33	38	34
Student	25	28	20
Housewife	2	3	5
Retired	2	3	7
Other	4	4	2

Major reasons players who like the game of tennis do not play more:

Reason	1992	1988
No time	52%	52%
Hard to find partner	27	26
Prefer other sports	27	25
Cold weather	22	16
Hard to get court	13	10
Injuries/health	10	10
Too costly	5	3
Hard to play	2	2

Other activities participated in by players of tennis four or more times a year, in percent:

MALES

Sport	Percent
Basketball	52%
Exercise machines	50
Bicycling	48
Running	48
Volleyball	39

FEMALES

Sport	Percent
Walking	61%
Bicycling	58
Aerobics	48
Exercise machines	45
Running	44

VACATION DESTINATIONS

Forty-eight percent of Americans prefer Florida as a domestic vacation site, putting it in first place as a U.S. vacation wonderland. California is second among 10 locations, with 34 percent liking it as a vacation spot. Hawaii is third at 26 percent.

The list below is based on a readership survey regarding favorite vacation spots by the *Chicago Tribune* in January 1995. It indicates the percentage of individuals who vacation at various destinations.

State	Percent
Florida	48%
California	34
Hawaii	26
Nevada	14
Colorado	11
Arizona	9
Texas	9
New York	8
District of Columbia	5
Louisiana	5

WINTER SPORTS

Overall, about 25 percent of Americans participate in the three major winter sports, skiing, ice hockey, and snowboarding. Skiing is far and away Americans' favorite winter participatory sport, and among skiers downhill is the way most want to go. Downhill skiing participation has remained almost constant since 1987, when 13.8 million skiers hit the slopes. In 1994 that figure was 14 million.

Cross-country skier numbers began to decline in 1987 when they totaled 7.1 million, according to the Sporting Goods Manufacturing Association. In 1994 they were down 13.7 percent from the year before, at 4.7 million, for a drop of 33 percent since 1987. Cross-country equipment sales grew only $11 million from 1993 to 1994, from $25 to $36 million, while downhill equipment sales increased $60 million, from $299 million to $350,000 million.

Ice hockey is a perennial favorite of winter sports lovers, reaching a high mark in 1993 with 2.5 million skaters participating. The figure dropped to 2.2 million in 1994, but the overall gain in players since 1987 has been 14.5 percent. Sales of ice skates and hockey skates rose $41 million in 1994, from $140 million in 1993 to $181 million in 1994.

The fastest-growing winter sport is snowboarding. The sport was statistically unimportant in 1987, but by 1990 1.8 million Americans were boarding their way down the slopes. In 1993 that figure had climbed to 2.2 million, and in 1994 to 2.4 million—an 84.7 percent increase in six years.

WOODWORKING

Almost 10 percent of the American population engages in woodworking as a leisure activity. The nearly 17 million hobbyists are more likely than the average adult to be married, white, college-educated, and in their mid-40s. They spend a combined estimated $10.4 billion a year on their work. The average woodworker spends $460 on tools and materials—beginners about $250, and experts more than $1,080. Beginners buy mostly tools, experts woods and veneers.

Twenty-five percent are beginners, age around 40, and 59 percent as yet have no workshop. Fifty percent are women. Woodworkers spend three hours a week on simple projects such as outdoor items, finishing, and carpentry and construction around the home. Their tools are mostly first-time purchases.

About 66 percent of woodworking hobbyists classify themselves as intermediate, which in terms of skill lies somewhere between simple carpentry and the ultimate in woodworking skill: cabinetmaking. They are in the average age bracket of all woodworkers, 44, and spend most of their money on first-time purchases of power tools.

Men predominate at the expert level, where they work as professionals as well as hobbyists. When experts consider power tools, it is usually as a replacement or an upgrade. They spend an average of 14 hours a week in workshops, which 79 percent of them own. There experts concentrate on activities such as lathe-turning (26 percent of their time), millwork such as finished moldings or latticework, and overlaying or facing wood with fine sheets of some material to give it a decorative appearance, called veneering (21 percent).

Eventually, 70 percent of the experts will turn to the crowning test of their skills: building a cabinet from scratch.

POPULATIONS
OVERVIEW

America continues to diversify, and to shift from the traditional population centers of the Northeast and Midwest to the booming South and West.

According to the U.S. Census, the population grew from 226.5 million in 1980 to 248.7 million in 1990, a growth rate of 9.8 percent. In the first quarter of 1996, the "middle series" population—a mid-range projection tabulated by Census Bureau statisticians—is estimated to be approximately 263 million. This unexpected slow rate of growth shades the fact that the black, Hispanic, and Asian American populations grew at significantly higher rates than the overall average, and much higher than the white population. Demographers thus see these groups as key to preventing a decline in population growth over the next several decades, as such, a decline would threaten the nation's economic potential and vitality.

U.S. Immigration and Naturalization Service data indicates that immigrants accounted for 32.8 percent of the total population growth between 1980 and 1990. The Immigration Act of 1990 dictates a complicated new formula for immigration. In sum, it allows approximately 800,000 new arrivals per year with emphasis on reuniting family members in the U.S. with their foreign-born relatives. Employment-related quotas annually attract 140,000 skilled workers. Arrivals have shifted from predominately Europeans to North Americans—primarily from Hispanic countries and the Caribbean—which account for slightly more than 50 percent of all immigrants. Asians account for approximately 30 percent of the total admitted and

Europeans now account for about 10 percent, down from 50 percent between 1955 and 1964.

The Baby Boom generation—about 75 million Americans, mostly white, born between 1946 and 1964—will soon be entering their retirement years. The aging of that group is driving the median age of America ever upward: In 1820 the median age of the U.S. population was 16.7; at the turn of the century it was still under 25; but in the 1990 census it stood at 32.4, and by 2030 it is projected to be an astounding 41.8. In contrast, the black and Hispanic populations have a much lower median age; and as the white population grows older, blacks, Hispanics, Asians, and other immigrants will become an even more integral part of working America.

In 1980, for the first time, more people lived in the South and West than the Northeast and Midwest. That trend continues today; in 1990, 55.6 percent of the population lived in the South and West, and those two regions provided 89 percent of the country's population growth from 1980 to 1990. Nevada, Alaska, Arizona, Florida, and California were the fastest-growing states. No Midwestern states enjoyed growth faster than the national average. The only states in the Northeast to do so were predominately rural New Hampshire and Vermont.

Increasingly, America has become an urban society. Three in four Americans live in an urban area, 187.1 million in all. California is the most urbanized state, with nearly 93 percent of its citizens living in a metropolitan area, though the state produces much of the nation's farm crops. Likewise, produce giant Florida has nine of the 11 fastest-growing cities.

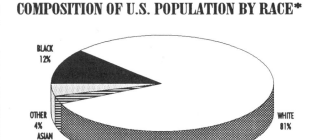

COMPOSITION OF U.S. POPULATION BY RACE*

BLACK 12%
OTHER 4%
ASIAN 3%
WHITE 81%

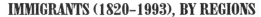

* There are 22.8 million Hispanics of all races in the U.S.

IMMIGRANTS (1820–1993), BY REGIONS

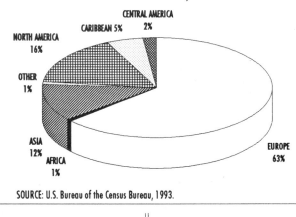

CENTRAL AMERICA 2%
CARIBBEAN 5%
NORTH AMERICA 16%
OTHER 1%
ASIA 12%
AFRICA 1%
EUROPE 63%

SOURCE: U.S. Bureau of the Census Bureau, 1993.

AMERICAN DEMOGRAPHICS

Age, race and gender are the most basic demographic data of a nation. Throughout this volume these are detailed in depth, however a snapshot of the nation is useful to view.

As detailed elsewhere, the median age of Americans has doubled, from 16.7 years-old in 1820 to an estimated 33 years-old in 1995. In a nation in which seniors are among the fastest growing age group, the largest segment of the population today could be described as "young adults;" that is the 25 to 45 age group.

The gender of America is basically the same as in other nations, primarily because gender is related to the basic physiology of the human reproductive system that produces an equal number of male and female embryo. Male fetuses, however are more prone to miscarry, and therefore there are slightly more girls born than boys. Additionally, women live longer than men, about 6.8 years longer according to 1993 data, and therefore the proportion of females in the U.S. is further exacerbated.

The following table lists various data relative to Americans, according to the latest available statistics which are broken down into the subcategories listed below. Source: U.S. Bureau of the Census (see footnote for 1995 estimate of U.S. total).

POPULATION BY RACE, 1990 *

Group	Population in U.S.	Percent
Total	248,709,873*	100.0%
White	199,686,070	80.3
Black	29,986,060	12.1
Hispanic	22,354,059	9.0
Asian, Pacific Islander	7,273,662	2.9
Native American	1,959,234	0.8
Other	9,804,847	3.9

1995 "middle series" estimate is 263,434,000
* Latest available data by race.

POPULATION BY SEX, 1993 *

Male	127,076,000
Female	133,265,000

* Latest available data by sex.

POPULATION BY AGE, 1994 *

Under 5	19,727,000
5 to 17	48,291,000
18 to 24	25,263,000
25 to 44	83,013,000
45 to 64	50,888,000
65 and older	33,158,000

* Latest available data by age.

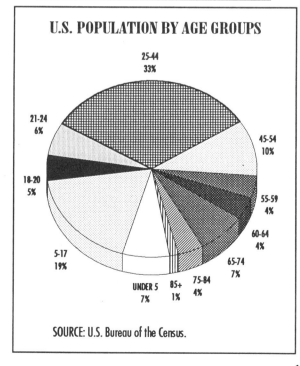

U.S. POPULATION BY AGE GROUPS

25-44 33%
21-24 6%
45-54 10%
18-20 5%
55-59 4%
60-64 4%
5-17 19%
65-74 7%
UNDER 5 7%
85+ 1%
75-84 4%

SOURCE: U.S. Bureau of the Census.

AMISH

Noted for their simple way of life, the value they place on family, church, and community, and strong beliefs in the rights of minorities, a stable family life, respect for the elderly, and religious freedom, the Amish are viewed by many as the "model minority" in the United States. A breakaway group from the Swiss Mennonites, the Amish began migrating to the U.S. in the

Illinois Department of Commerce.
These children from the Arthur area in Illinois, are from one of the westernmost Amish settlements in the U.S. Amish communitees began in Pennsylvania in the early 1700s and continue to slowly trickle westward.

early 1700s, settling first in Pennsylvania, then spreading principally to Ohio, Indiana, and Iowa. The 1990s population is an estimated 130,000 Amish in more than 720 church districts scattered through at least 20 states. The best-known Amish community is that in the region surrounding Lancaster, Pa., which has become something of a tourist attraction in the past several decades.

The Amish live in tightly knit rural farming communities. Their legal authorities are church leaders, backed by church members as arbitrators and consultants. Higher education is viewed as a waste of time, and, worse, an inculcator of "worldly ways" in the minds of the young. The Bible is interpreted strictly, and its teachings followed closely.

ARAB AMERICANS

The Census Bureau considers Arab Americans as those who come from Morocco, Tunisia, Algeria, Libya, Sudan, Egypt, Lebanon, Palestine, Syria, Jordan, Iraq, Saudi Arabia, Bahrain, Qatar, Kuwait, Yemen, and the United Arab Emirates.

A post-WWII flood of Arab immigration was characterized by influential families fleeing countries where the leadership had been overthrown. Immigration to the U.S. from the Mideast swelled in the 1960s, less a factor of political persecution than simply the lessening of constraints and quotas on immigration for those from around the world in search a better life. More than 75 percent of foreign-born Arabs currently living in the U.S. immigrated after 1964.

E.ghty-two percent of Arab Americans are citizens, according to the Census Bureau, and 63 percent were born in the U.S. Unlike the general population, men outnumber women among the Arab American community, 54 percent to 46 percent. Nearly half—47.5 percent—of Arab Americans are aged 18 to 44, Thirty percent are age 17 or younger.

Geographically, Arab Americans form a concentrated group, with 33 percent living in California, New York, or Michigan. Thirty-six percent live in metropolitan centers, chiefly Detroit (seven percent), New York City (6.7 percent), and Los Angeles-Long Beach, California, (6.5 percent).

Arab Americans generally are better educated than the average American. Of the U.S. Arab population 29.5 percent hold Master's degrees, three times the average of eight percent of Americans. Twenty-one percent have earned bachelor's degrees, compared to 18 percent of Americans. Not surprisingly, employment rates are high, with 80 percent of Arab Americans age 16 and over employed, compared with 60 percent of all American adults. Median household income for Arab Americans in 1990 stood at $39,100, significantly greater than the U.S. average of $30,000.

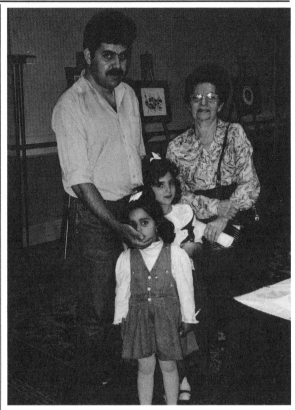

Over eighty percent of Arab Americans, such this family, are American citizens.

The list below represents the percent of Arab Americans by age groups and that of the U.S. population, according to the U.S. Bureau of the Census:

Age	Total U.S.	Arab Americans
17 and younger	26%	30%
18 to 24	10	11
25 to 44	33	37
45 to 64	19	15
65 and older	13	7

ASIAN AMERICANS

The arrival of growing numbers of Asians to the shores of the United States in the past 25 years has significantly altered the composition of the American populace, not only along the West Coast, where Asian immigrants traditionally have settled, but in most every community in the country.

The ranks of Americans of Asian and Pacific Islander ancestry grew from 1.5 million in 1970 to 3.5 million in 1980, a large portion of that growth— 400,000—accounted for by Southeast Asian refugees as a result of the fall of Vietnam and the institution of the Refugee Resettlement Act. Another 2.4 million Asians immigrated to the U.S. in the 1980s, and as a whole the number of Asian Americans increased by more than 100 percent, to 7.2 million in the 1990 census. Today, Asian Americans are such a part of the mainstream population that an act such as that which occurred during World War II, when Japanese Americans on the West Coast were forced into internment camps is unthinkable. Indeed, the strong family bonds and high sense of the importance of education that characterizes the Asian American community elicits a great deal of respect from fellow Americans.

Following is the Asian population of the U.S. in 1990, according to the U.S. Bureau of the Census.

Group	Asian pop.	% Asian pop.
TOTAL	7,273,662	100.0%
Chinese	1,645,472	22.6
Filipino	1,406,770	19.3
Japanese	847,562	11.7
Asian Indian	815,447	11.2
Korean	798,849	11.0
Vietnamese	614,547	8.4
Hawaiian	211,014	2.9
Samoan	62,964	0.9
Guamanian	49,345	0.7
Other Asian or Pacific Islander	821,692	11.3

Metro areas with the largest Asian and Pacific Islander population, 1980-1990:

Area	1980	1990	Change
Los Angeles-Anaheim-Riverside	561,876	1,339,048	138.3%
San Francisco-Oakland-San Jose	457,647	926,961	103.9
New York-New Jersey-Conn.	370,731	873,213	135.5
Honolulu	456,465	526,459	15.3
Chicago-Ind.-Wis.	144,626	256,050	77.0
Washington, D.C.,-Md-Va.	88,008	202,437	130.0
San Diego	89,861	198,311	120.7
Seattle-Tacoma	78,255	164,286	109.9
Houston-Galveston	53,056	132,131	149.0
Philadelphia-Wilmington-Trenton	53,291	123,458	131.7

BLACK AMERICANS

At the founding of the United States in 1776, nearly one in five inhabitants of the new country were African slaves. The black population of the U.S. has grown to more than 30 million in the years since, but due to waves of immigration from various parts of the globe over the ensuing years, the African American percentage of the total population never has been as high as it was in 1800. In the mid-19th century it dropped to below 10 percent, and in the most recent census was

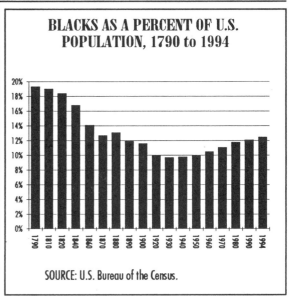

BLACKS AS A PERCENT OF U.S. POPULATION, 1790 to 1994

SOURCE: U.S. Bureau of the Census.

12.3 percent of the total population. The black population increased 18.6 percent from 1980 to 1990, twice the rate of white population growth. Nevertheless, by the year 2010, the Census Bureau projects that African Americans no longer will be the largest minority group in the country; Hispanics will outnumber blacks by that time.

The first two decades of the 1900s saw a large shift in black population from the South to the industrial cities of the Northeast and Midwest, but more than half of all blacks—52.4 percent—continue to live in the South. And the black population is predominantly urban: unlike whites, only 25.7 percent of whom live in central metropolitan areas, 56.3 percent of African Americans are city dwellers.

The black population is younger and poorer than the nation as a whole. The median age for African Americans in the 1990 census was 28.0, nearly six years below that for the white population. Thirty-three percent of black Americans are under the age of 18; only eight percent are older than 65. In 1993, 33.1 percent of African Americans were below the poverty level—almost three times the percentage of white Americans (12.2 percent) and higher than the Hispanic poverty rate (29.6 percent) as well. The African American struggle for social and economic equality has yet to improve the lives and fortunes of the black population as a whole; figures on life expectancy, crime rates, incarceration, single-parent families, and other social indicators remain significantly worse for African Americans than for the general population.

Black population of the U.S., selected years, 1800- 2000 (projected); source: U.S.Bureau of the Census.

Year	Population (000s)	Percent of U.S.
1800	1,002	18.9%
1850	3,639	15.7

1900	8,834	11.6
1920	10,463	9.9
1940	12,866	9.8
1960	18,872	10.5
1970	22,581	11.1
1980	26,683	11.8
1990	30,486	12.3
2000	35,006	13.1

Black population in thousands, by region and percent of total population in the region, 1990:

Region	Pop.	Percent
South	15,829	18.5
Midwest	5,716	9.6
Northeast	5,613	11.0
West	2,262	5.4

STATES WITH THE HIGHEST PERCENTAGE OF BLACKS

State	Black pop.	Percent of state
Mississippi	915,057	35.6%
Louisiana	1,299,281	30.8
South Carolina	1,039,884	29.8
Georgia	1,746,565	27.0
Alabama	1,020,705	25.3
Maryland	1,189,899	24.9
North Carolina	1,456,323	22.0
Virginia	1,162,994	18.8
Delaware	112,460	16.9
Tennessee	778,035	16.0

Ten cities with largest black populations in thousands, 1990; source: Population Reference Bureau:

City	Black pop.	Percent
New York, N.Y.	2,102.5	29%
Chicago	1,087.7	39
Detroit	777.9	76
Philadelphia	631.9	40
Los Angeles	487.7	14
Houston	458.0	28
Baltimore	435.8	59
Washington, D.C.	399.6	66
Memphis	334.7	55
New Orleans	307.7	62

CALIFORNIA

Though California is but one of the 50 American states, it is substantially different enough from the other 49—culturally, statistically and geographically—that many demographers consider it to be a unique population unto itself.

Recent Census Bureau projections show that despite overcrowding, natural disasters, fears of a water shortage, infrastructural problems, and an exodus of people, troubled California will grow in population by more than 50 percent—to 47.9 million—by the year 2020.

California's population in 1950 was 10 million; in 1970 it was 20 million; and in 1980 it was 25 million and by 1994 rose to 31.4 million.

The bureau estimates that over the next 25 years four million more California residents—most of them white—will move out of the state than are expected to move in from other parts of the country. This will place it at the bottom among states in net internal migration between 1994 and 2020. But more than making up for that emigration will be 10.3 million legal foreign immigrants, most of them Asians and Latin Americans. They will bring with them higher birth rates, lower educational attainment, and fewer skills than those leaving.

Census projections show that by year 2020 whites will be in the minority in California, with 34 percent of the state's population. Latinos, at 36 percent, will be the dominant group. Asians will make up 20 percent of the California population and blacks eight percent.

Below is the ethnic breakdown of the California population in 1993 and projected for the year 2020, according to the Census Bureau:

Group	1993	2020
Whites	52.8%	34.0.%
Hispanics	27.3	36.0
Asians and Pacific Islanders	11.2	20.0
Blacks	7.7	8.0
American Indians	0.9	0.8

CITIES, FISCAL CONDITION

Americans living in the growing Southern cities are faring best in the 1990s, while those in the rest of the country face higher taxes and curtailed services as cities trim already lean budgets, according to an annual survey by the National League of Cities.

Still mired in the recession of the early part of the decade, one in six U.S. cities postponed buying equipment or cut services in 1993. Kansas City stopped collecting yard waste for a $800,000 savings, only to see $200,000 of that trickle away when it was forced to deal with the problem of people turning to dumping leaves and trees on back roads, according to a city spokesman.

About 40 percent of the 688 cities surveyed in 1993 hiked taxes and trimmed city employees by layoffs or attrition. Sixty percent of city budget officials said the crisis was worse than in 1992, and 75 percent had predicted that the situation would worsen in 1994.

Cutting day care expenses, reducing services to AIDS patients, creating larger school classroom sizes, freezing wages, and reducing garbage pickups and the number of firefighters were some of the methods used by cities in their fight to hew to the budget line.

Philadelphia alone of the major cities in the North was on the track of recovering at the time of the survey, when it was in the first year of a five-year plan to save $1.1 billion. The cost to Philadelphians is a

Illinois Department of Commerce.
Pictured above, America's "Second City," Chicago, is now the third largest U.S. city. Its population dropped from a high of almost four million residents to its present 2.7 million population.

freeze on wages for city employees, cuts in health care spending, and layoffs of political appointees. The city has sought the help of local businesses and universities to bring efficiency to city hall.

New York City faced a $2 billion deficit in its 1994 budget of $31.3 billion and a $1.7 billion deficit in 1995. The city fathers planned to trim the force of 3,000 to 4,000 workers by attrition, sell off $215 million in property seized from delinquent taxpayers, and raise fees by $174 million.

CITIES, TAXES

Though cities and towns across the country reported improving economies in 1994, almost three-fourths were mapping further increases in taxes and user fees, a national survey of 551 municipalities found.

Who will the increases hit? Traditionally, property is the biggest target for municipal tax increases. In 1990 property taxes were the biggest source of income for U.S. cities, contributing $35 billion to municipal coffers, representing 17.3 percent of all revenues. Sales and income taxes brought in another $28.3 billion, or 14 percent. User fees for utilities such as gas, transit, water, and electricity contributed $32.9 billion, or 16.2 percent.

In 1994 one in four cities surveyed by the National League of Cities raised property taxes. Hardest hit were property owners in the Northeast, of whom 50 percent saw increases, as against 31 percent in the Midwest, 28 percent in the South, and less than 8 percent in the West. Half of the cities increased user fees, and 25 percent added new ones.

For the second straight year in 1994 a majority of municipal budgets had ended in the black after three years of budget woes during the recession of 1990-93. The survey found that 54 percent of the municipalities expected to collect more in taxes in 1994 than they would spend for services.

Spending required by federal and state governments, infrastructure rehabbing, and spiraling health care costs for city employees were the reasons given by city officials for more tax hikes. James Sharpe, the mayor of Newark, N.J., and the league president, said the taxpayer load for municipal workers' health care costs alone grew 250 percent from 1980 to 1994, and was cited by 42 percent of the cities as a major cause of tax increases.

CITIES VS. METROPOLITAN AREAS

Americans who move out of the cities aren't necessarily going very far; many are simply choosing the suburbs as their desired place of residence. Although the cities of the South and Southwest are growing quickly, the metropolitan areas—that is, the cities and with their suburbs—of the North continue to be substantial. For instance, while San Diego (6th ranked in population), Phoenix (9th-ranked), and San Antonio (10th-ranked) all pushed their way into the top 10 American cities by population in the 1990 census, they have yet to develop into the huge metroplexes that characterize the New York, Los Angeles, Chicago, and Washington-Baltimore areas. Thus they rank further down on the Census Bureau's list of "standard metropolitan statistical areas (SMSA):" There ranks as SMSA are as followings: San Diego 15th, Phoenix 20th, and San Antonio 30th.

The following lists represents the 10 largest cities in the U.S., compared to the 10 largest metropolitan areas, from Census Bureau figures:

TEN LARGEST CITIES

City	Population
New York	7,322,564
Los Angeles	3,485,398
Chicago	2,783,726
Houston	1,630,672
Philadelphia	1,585,577
San Diego	1,110,549
Detroit	1,027,974
Dallas	1,006,831
Phoenix	983,403
San Antonio	935,927

TEN LARGEST METRO AREAS:

City	Population
New York	19,640,175
Los Angeles	15,047,772
Chicago	8,410,402

Washington/ Baltimore	6,919,572
San Francisco/ Oakland/San Jose	6,409,891
Philadelphia	5,938,528
Boston	5,438,815
Detroit	5,245,906
Dallas/Fort Worth	4,214,532
Houston	3,962,365

EXPATRIATES

For some, living abroad is a right of passage and they will return eventually and live permanently within its borders. Some leave the U.S. to escape a country to which they feel no particular affection or allegiance. For others, it's necessitated by military service or career factors. Many expatriates simply choose the romance of another country and another culture as a means of enriching their life experience and expanding their horizons.

The following list represents the quantity of U.S. citizens residing abroad in 1994 in selected countries, according to the U.S. Bureau of the Census.

Nation	U.S. Citizens
Mexico	539,000
Germany	354,000
Canada	296,000
United Kingdom	259,000
Israel	112,000
Italy	104,000
Dominican Republic	97,000
Spain	79,000
Australia	62,000
France	59

FARM POPULATION

In 1945, the average net worth of an American farm was $12,502. In 1991, that figure was $326,215. One misconception, though, is that the family farm is dying, and that the boom in value is due to a boom in foreign ownership of the American bread basket.

Over the last 50 years the percentage of the population living on farms has plummeted, from 23.2 percent in 1940 to 2.5 percent in 1991. But the vast majority —90.7 percent—of America's 2.14 million farms, which average 467 acres each, still belong to families, accounting for some six million U.S. farmers. Giant corporations own only 3.2 percent of U.S. farms, and foreign corporations or individuals just 1.1 percent, according to the Department of Agriculture.

This list represents the top five types of farm by specialties:

Beef cattle	34.3%
Cash grain	22.0
Dairy	6.6
Field crops	6.1
Hogs	5.4

In 1940 3.4 percent of American farmers had been to college, and 10.2 percent had graduated from high school. By 1990 36.9 percent had been to college, and 81.8 percent were high school graduates. That rise in education levels among American farmers has been a necessity in a $1 trillion, increasingly high-tech industry in which new sciences search to boost yields, create hardier crops, and generally improve farming practices. "Farmers aren't rubes or hicks," says Calvin Beale, a senior demographer for the Department of Agriculture. "Farming is big business. People who don't want to be big can't make a living [at farming] without other income." The result is that many family farms are so large that they've incorporated, squeezing out the giants instead of the other way around.

Georgia Bureau of Industry and Trade.
With America's farms averaging 467 acres each and having a net worth of over $300,000, an "average acre" like the one pictured above is worth about $700.

The Census Bureau and the Department of Agriculture report the following farm facts:

- Blacks have largely abandoned the agrarian life. Just 1.1 percent of farmers are black, compared to 13 percent in 1900.

- Women are displaying more interest in farming. Female farmers total 131,641, or 6.3 percent of all farmers in 1987, up from 112,799 in 1978.

- Hispanics (.8 percent) and Asians (.3 percent) make up a tiny portion of farming households.

- Texas has the most farms, with 186,000.

- The average age of farmers is 52, up from 48 in 1940

- The average farm family had 3.20 persons in 1989, compared to 4.25 in 1940 and 5.20 in 1890.

- The number of people fed by each farm worker was 89 in 1989, 10.7 in 1940, 5.8 in 1890.

- The percentage of crops exported was 25 percent in 1990, compared to 3 percent in 1940, 19 percent in 1890.

Characteristics of American farmers, 1992, according to the aforementioned report	
Total operators	1,925,000
RACE	
White	1,882,000
Black	19,000
Native American	8,000
Asian or Pacific Islander	8,000
Hispanic	8,000
SEX	
Male	1,78,000
Female	145,000
AGE	
Under 25	28,000
25-34	179,000
35-44	382,000
45-54	429,000
55-64	430,000
65 or older	478,000
Average age	53.3

HISPANICS

In the broadest sense, anyone with a Spanish or Latin-American background comes under the umbrella term "Hispanic," and thus Hispanics in the U.S. comprise a wide range of cultures, ethnicities, and nationalities. Hispanics from Latin America might trace their origin directly to the Spanish settlers, or to the indigenous Indian population. A large number are "mestizo," or of mixed Spanish and Indian ancestry. Many Spanish-speaking countries of the Caribbean, and Central and South America—Cuba, Venezuela, and the Dominican Republic, to name three—have large black populations. Other Hispanics—for instance, those from Argentina and Chile—are predominantly of European extraction, traceable to large waves of immigration to South America from Germany and Italy. The U.S. Hispanic population reflects such diversity.

Nevertheless, the majority of U.S. Hispanics—64.3 percent, according to 1993 Census figures—are of Mexican descent. Central and South Americans constitute 13.4 percent of Hispanics, much of that population newly arrived from El Salvador and Nicaragua since 1980. Puerto Rican Americans account for 10.6 percent of the Hispanic population on the mainland (that is, not including Puerto Rico itself), and Cubans 4.7 percent.

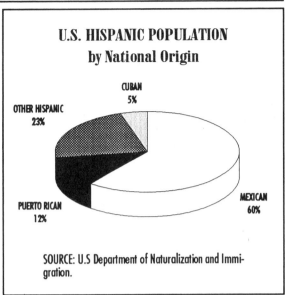

U.S. HISPANIC POPULATION
by National Origin

CUBAN 5%

OTHER HISPANIC 23%

PUERTO RICAN 12%

MEXICAN 60%

SOURCE: U.S Department of Naturalization and Immigration.

The Hispanic population is the fastest-growing in the U.S., thanks to continuing high rates of immigration from Latin American countries and much higher birth rates among Hispanics than among the U.S. population as a whole. The Hispanic population in 1970 was approximately nine million, or 4.5 percent of the U.S. By 1980 the numbers had climbed to 14.6 million and 6.4 percent. The 1990 census counted 22.4 million Hispanic Americans, nine percent of the population. Those figures represent a 10-year growth rate of more than 50 percent, five times that of the general population. Indeed, the Census Bureau projects that Hispanics will be the largest minority group in the U.S. by 2010, outnumbering African Americans 39 million to 38 million.

Reflecting their growing demographics, America's Hispanic population is increasingly being assimilated into mainstream America. English-only advocates notwithstanding, figures suggest that the strong Spanish-language presence in Hispanic communities is primarily attributable and for the benefit of recent, first- generation immigrants; in fact, 85 percent of Hispanic Americans speak English. Like the African American population, the Hispanic population is younger and poorer than the whole. The median Hispanic age in 1993 was 26.7, compared to 34.4 in the non-Hispanic population; 29.6 percent of Hispanics were below the poverty level in 1993.

With their long borders on Mexico, the states of California and Texas are the primary ports of entry for Hispanic immigrants to the U.S., and not surprisingly the place most such arrivals settle. In the 1990 census, 53.8 percent of all Hispanics lived in those two states, the large majority of those being of Mexican descent. New York's 2.2 million Hispanics (12.3 percent of the total) are primarily of Puerto Rican ancestry. Florida's Hispanic population, though variegated, is predominantly Cuban.

Growing numbers of Hispanics are joining the country's middle class, according to studies extending from 1990 to 1993. Sociologists and demographers call this well-educated, well-paid, and well-informed Hispanic population a "silent minority." A full 43.6 percent of the nation's Hispanics earn middle-class incomes between $30,000 and $104,000 annually, according to a November 1994 report in the magazine *Hispanic Business*. Between 1980 and 1990 the number of Hispanics in managerial and professional occupations grew by 190 percent, from 690,000 to 1.3 million.

Still, in spite of their gains, the advance of Hispanics into middle-class America falls short in private industry employment, education, and government. Hispanics make up only 2.9 percent of all officials and administrators in private industry, 3.1 percent of teachers and 2.5 percent of executives and administrators at institutions of higher learning, and 5.5 percent in the executive branch of the federal government.

Hispanic population of the U.S., by origin, 1993; source, U.S. Census Bureau:

Origin	Population	Percent
Mexico	14,628,000	64.3%
Central and S. America	3,052,000	13.4
Puerto Rico	2,402,000	10.6
Cuba	1,071,000	4.7
Other	1,598,000	7.0

Hispanic population in top five Hispanic states, and percentage of state population and total U.S. Hispanic population, 1990; source, U.S. Census Bureau:

State	Population	% of State	% Total
California	7.7 million	25.8	34.4
Texas	4.3 million	25.5	19.4
New York	2.2 million	12.3	9.9
Florida	1.6 million	12.2	7.0
Illinois	0.9 million	7.9	4.0

Occupations of Middle-Class Hispanics; source, U.S. Census Bureau:

Occupation	Percent
Technical	29.0%
Laborers	21.6
Managerial/professional	16.5
Service	16.3
Crafts	12.8
Farm/forest/fish	3.6
Military	0.2

IMMIGRATION

English and French settlers along the East Coast in the 17th and 18th centuries opened the doors for vast numbers from all over the world to seek their fortunes in the fertile soil of America.

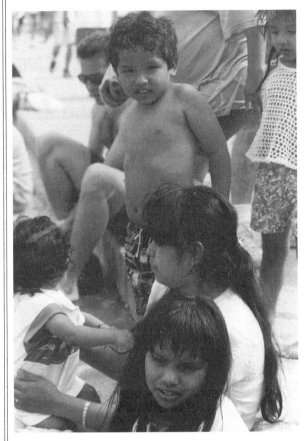

By the time these children are grown, Hispanics will be the largest ethnic minority in the U.S., outnumbering blacks 39 million to 38 million in the year 2010.

A great boom in immigration came as land to the West, taken from the Indians, became available for ranching and farming, and as the Northern and Midwestern cities developed their industrial base. Between 1880 and 1920 nearly 20 million European immigrants arrived in the United States—Scandinavians settling in the vast expanses of the Northern Plains, while Germans, Italians, and Poles found work in the mills and plants of Pittsburgh, Cleveland, Detroit, and Chicago.

The period after World War I saw a sharp decline in immigration, first from growing xenophobic sentiments, then due to the Depression and World War II. Immigration increased after 1960—both legal and illegal—and has continued at a high level since. This wave, of course, has been significantly more diverse than that from 1880 to 1920: Today's immigrants from Mexico and Cuba and Central America, from China and Philippines and India, from Egypt and Nigeria, are literally changing the complexion of the United States.

Such change can be troubling for some. Less enlightened Americans harbor a number of myths about immigrants, whom many use as scapegoats in a society undergoing drastic economic restructuring. Among those myths, studies say, are that immigrants impose burdens on the welfare system, drain public services, and grow up "un-American" because they refuse to speak English.

Surveys performed by the Urban Institute, the Chicago Coalition for Immigrant and Refugee Protection, and the Latino Institute paint a different picture. According to the Urban Institute, among nonrefugee immigrants who entered the U.S. in the 1980s, just two percent live on welfare, compared with 3.7 percent of working-age native-born Americans. In Illinois, a University of Texas study shows, nonimmigrant households are 40 percent more likely to receive welfare than immigrant households.

As for overuse of public services, the Urban Institute says immigrants pay more in taxes annually—$25 billion—than they use in government services.

Census figures show that immigrants' income and spending in the U.S. economy accounted for eight percent of all U.S. income in 1989, about equal to their 7.9 percent share of the population. In addition, immigrants are self-employed at a higher rate than native-borns, create more jobs than they fill, and on average earn as much as native entrepreneurs.

A major study in 1993 by two researchers, Alejandro Portes and Min Zou, reported that most immigrant children speak English fluently and prefer it to their parents' native language. For example, 99 percent of children in Miami and 90 percent of children in San Diego said they spoke English well or very well.

The researchers said that immigrant children were as likely to attend public schools, as unlikely to drop out, and as likely to graduate from high school as nonimmigrant children. Four-fifths expected to complete college and 70 percent aimed at professional or business careers.

Currently, more than 500,000 new immigrants arrive in the U.S. annually, with well over half Asians or Hispanics. This flow is needed for the health of the country, according to the Office of Population Growth at Princeton, which reports that the decline in American birth rates hints at a negative population growth by the year 2030.

Accordingly, the office contends that the U.S. will need 464,000 immigrants annually over the next century to keep U.S. population in year 2100 the same size it was in 1980, when it totaled 226.5 million. That still would be about 23 million less than the U.S. population in 1990. As always, immigrants to the U.S. will remain essential to the economic, social, and spiritual vitality of the country.

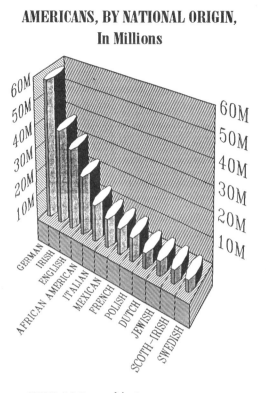

AMERICANS, BY NATIONAL ORIGIN, In Millions

SOURCE: U.S. Bureau of the Census.

Region of origin of immigrants to the United States, 1820-1993; source, U.S. Dept. of Justice, *1993, Statistical Yearbook of the Immigration and Naturalization Service (1994)*.

Region	U.S. Total
Europe	37,566,702
North America	9,478,377
Asia	7,051,564
Caribbean	3,035,898
South America	1,440,413
Central America	1,046,963
Africa	417,926
Oceania	223,821
Unspecified	267,639
Other America	110,147

Country of last residence of immigrants to the United States, 1820-1993; source, U.S. Dept. of Justice, *1993, Statistical Yearbook of the Immigration and Naturalization Service (1994)*.

Nation	Total U.S.
Germany	7,117,192
Italy	5,419,285
United Kingdom	5,178,264
Mexico	5,117,422
Ireland	4,755,172

Canada	4,360,955
Russia and USSR	3,572,281
Austria	1,837,232
Hungary	1,670,777
Sweden	1,288,763
Philippines	1,222,287
China	1,025,700
Austria-Hungary	846,076
Norway	803,281
France	800,016
Cuba	782,050
Greece	711,461
Korea	703,732
Poland	675,221
Dominican Republic	638,970

Country of last residence for immigrants to the U.S., 1991-93; source, U.S. Dept. of Justice, *1993, Statistical Yearbook of the Immigration and Naturalization Service (1994).*

Mexico	1,288,693
Philippines	195,634
Dominican Republic	128,834
Former USSR	128,675
India	116,201
China	111,324
El Salvador	99,794
Vietnam	77,913
Poland	68,885
Haiti	67,701
Canada	65,370
Korea	61,484
United Kingdom	59,114
Jamaica	58,018
Hong Kong	47,723

The following are estimated sizes of select ethnic groups in the United States; source, U.S. Bureau of the Census:

Group	Population
German	57.9 million
Irish	38.7 million
English	32.7 million
African-American	23.8 million
Italian	14.7 million
Mexican	11.6 million
French	10.3 million
Polish	9.4 million
Dutch	6.2 million
Jewish*	6.0 million
Scotch-Irish	5.6 million
Scottish	5.4 million
Swedish	4.7 million
Norwegian	3.9 million
Russian	3.0 million
French Canadian	2.2 million
Welsh	2.0 million
Spanish	2.0 million
Puerto Rican	2.0 million

Slovak	1.9 million
White	1.8 million
Danish	1.6 million
Hungarian	1.6 million
Chinese	1.5 million
Filipino	1.5 million
Czech	1.3 million
Portuguese	1.2 million
Greek	1.1 million
Swiss	1.0 million
Japanese	1.0 million

* About 80 percent of the Jewish population in the U.S. trace their ancestry to Central and Eastern Europe, chiefly Germany, Poland, and Russia.

MINORITY REPRESENTATION

Hispanics in the U.S. are fast closing the population gap between themselves and blacks. Statistics show, however, that Hispanic population growth in the U.S. is not translating into top positions in higher education, government, and private industry. The Census Bureau notes that blacks outnumber Hispanics by only 2.4 percent in the general population, and by 19 percent in the civilian labor force. But in higher education, private industry, and state, local, and federal government—a pool totaling 13.8 million workers—blacks outnumber Hispanics by 139 percent.

In the federal government, for instance, black employees outnumber Hispanics by more than 149 percent in all but three of the 14 executive departments, according to the National Association of Hispanic Federal Executives. At the Department of Housing and Urban Development the figure is 385 percent, and at the Department of Education 950 percent. Of the 2.17 million persons working in the federal executive branch, Hispanics hold 5.5 percent of these jobs, outnumbered by blacks by 201 percent. Of 200 jobs in the Democratic National Committee, Hispanics hold six positions, blacks 40, according to the magazine *Hispanic Business.*

The tables below show the gap reflected in U.S. population, employment in top jobs, and the total of blacks and Hispanics in the U.S. labor force of a projected 263.43 million by July 1995; source, U.S. Bureau of the Census, Department of Labor, and Hispanic Business. Inc.:

	Population in U.S.	Percent of U.S. Total
Hispanic	26,870,000	10.2%
Blacks	33,109,000	12.6
CIVILIAN LABOR FORCE		
Hispanics	12,000,000	9.2%
Blacks	14,350,000	11.0
TOP JOB INDEX		
Hispanics	.455	3.29%
Blacks	1.090	7.89

MOBILITY

The American populace always has been mobile. The willingness to pull up stakes and move on to something better, or at least different, has been part of the American tradition. Nevertheless, a smaller percentage of Americans than in the '50s and '60s—when the greatest migration to suburbs was in progress—are changing residences each year. Whereas in those decades fully 20 percent of the American population changed domiciles, just 16.8 percent did so from 1992 to 1993. By far the most mobile are those between the ages of 20 and 24 who are usually newly graduated or have recently moved away from their parents' homes.

The list below represents the characteristics of the U.S. population age-one and over that changed residence from 1992 to 1993, according to the U.S. Bureau of the Census.

1992-93	Total	% of U.S.
Movers	42,048,000	16.8%
U.S. residents	40,743,000	16.3
Different house, same county	26,212,000	10.5
Different county	14,532,000	5.8
Different house, same state	7,735,000	3.1
Different state	6,797,000	2.7
From abroad	1,305,000	0.5

NATIVE AMERICANS

The Native American population of the United States—including American Indians, Eskimos, and Aleuts—has been on a rebound in recent years. This rebound can be put both in population terms and in terms of economics.

The 1990 census counted a Native American population of 1,959,234. Given the 1980 population of 1,420,400, the 1990 figure represented a 37.9 percent increase in just 10 years (compared to a 9.8 percent increase in the U.S. population overall). Native Americans made up 0.8 percent of the U.S. population in the most recent census; that, too, was an increase from the 0.6 percent representation in the 1980 census. Indeed, the Native American population nearly quadrupled in the 30 years from 1960 (when it numbered 524,000) to the most recent complete census.

Native Americans are most populous in Oklahoma, numbering 252,089 in 1990. Three other states had 1990 populations of more than 100,000: California (236,078), Arizona (203,009), and New Mexico (134,097). About 340,000 Native Americans still reside on reservations or trust lands; by far the largest of these is the Navajo nation, 16 million acres spanning parts of Arizona, New Mexico, and Utah, containing a Native American population of 143,405 in 1990.

In recent years Native Americans have begun to realize the vast economic potential of their land hold-

Robert Belous; courtesy, U.S. National Park Service.

These Native Americans in Alaska's Kobuk Valley depend heavily on the Kobuk River's fish yield.

ings—which amount to about 2.5 percent of total U.S. acreage. As the mineral wealth— including large reserves of uranium, coal, and natural gas—and scenic beauty of these lands becomes utilized for the good of the inhabitants, the Native American population will grow as an economic force. One area where that already is apparent is in the incredible boom in casino gambling on Indian reservations throughout the country. Taking advantage of the legislative autonomy they enjoy on tribal lands, Native Americans from New England to California have set up gaming operations to rival those in Las Vegas or Atlantic City. The income from those establishments rapidly and dramatically has changed the fortunes of numerous American Indian tribes.

Most populous Native American reservations, 1990, from Census Bureau statistics:

Reservation	Native American Pop.
Navajo and trust lands, Ariz.-N. Mexico-Utah	143,405
Pine Ridge and trust lands, Nebraska-S. Dak	11,182
Fort Apache, Ariz.	9,825
Gila River, Ariz.	9,116

Pagago, Ariz.	8,480
Rosebud and trust lands, S. Dak.	8,043
San Carlos, Ariz.	7,110
Zuni Pueblo, Ariz.-N. Mexico	7,073
Hopi and trust lands, Ariz.	7,061
Blackfeet, Mont.	7,025

Distribution of U.S. Native American population, by region, 1990; source, U.S. Bureau of the Census:

Region	% of Native Americans
West	46.0
South	29.7
Midwest	17.8
Northeast	6.5

Cities ranked by Native American population, 1990; source, U.S. Bureau of the Census:

City	Native American Pop.
Tulsa, Okla.	48,196
Oklahoma City, Okla.	45,720
Los Angeles-Long Beach, Calif.	45,508
Phoenix, Ariz.	38,107
New York, N.Y.	29,711
Riverside-San Bernardino, Calif.	24,905
Minneapolis-St. Paul, Minn.	23,956
Seattle, Wash.	23,727
Tucson, Ariz.	20,330
San Diego, Calif.	20,066

Cities with two percent or more Native American population:

City	% Native American
Anchorage, Alaska	6.4%
Tucson, Ariz.	4.7
Oklahoma City, Okla.	4.2
Minneapolis, Minn.	3.3
Albuquerque, N.M.	3.0
Spokane, Wash.	2.0

POPULATION DENSITY

Despite the general shift of the population westward and southward, the densest populated states in the country are still primarily located in the Northeast and Mid-Atlantic areas.

The list below represents the 10 states with the densest populations in 1990, according to the U.S. Bureau of the Census.

State	Pop. per square mile
New Jersey	1,042.0
Rhode Island	960.3
Massachusetts	767.6
Connecticut	678.4
Maryland	489.2
New York	381.0
Delaware	340.8
Pennsylvania	265.1
Ohio	264.9
Florida	239.6

If you want to get far from the madding crowd, your best bet is the great white north: Alaska, with just one person per square mile, is the most sparsely populated state in the union.

The list below represents the 10 states with the least dense populations in 1990, according to the U.S. Bureau of the Census.

	Pop. per square mile
Alaska	1.0
Wyoming	4.7
Montana	5.5
South Dakota	9.2
North Dakota	9.3
Nevada	10.9
Idaho	12.2
New Mexico	12.5
Nebraska	20.5
Utah	21.0

POPULATION PROJECTIONS

The Census Bureau, forecasting what the American population will be like in 2050, confirms the projection of a dramatic rise in the Hispanic population, attributed in part to an influx of nearly 900,000 Hispanic immigrants a year (both legal and illegal).

The U.S. population is expected to grow by a staggering 50 percent — from 255 million to 383 million — by 2050, and with that increase will come a change in the makeup of the populace. The Hispanic population is expected to grow more than threefold, from its current 24 million to 81 million, eventually accounting for more than one in five Americans. The black population will nearly double, from its current 32 million to 62 million; however, its proportion of the overall population will rise only modestly, from 12 percent to 16 percent. The white population will increase just a fraction, from 192 million to 208 million. This means that whites as a percentage of U.S. population will drop from 75 percent of the population to 53 percent, a bare majority. In 1940, whites accounted for 90 percent of the population.

The tide of immigration from Asia and the Pacific islands will also swell. Asian Americans currently make up three percent of the nation's population, with 8 million people; by 2050 this group will grow to 41 million — 13 percent. And although the Native American population will remain at about one percent of the

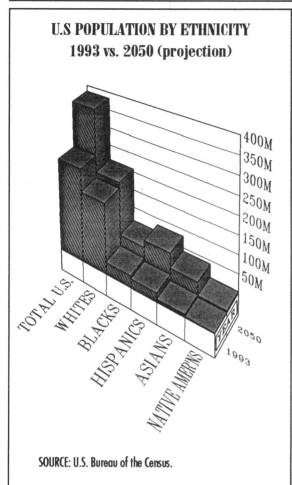

U.S POPULATION BY ETHNICITY
1993 vs. 2050 (projection)

400M
350M
300M
250M
200M
150M
100M
50M

TOTAL U.S.
WHITES
BLACKS
HISPANICS
ASIANS
NATIVE AMERNS

YEAR
2050
1993

SOURCE: U.S. Bureau of the Census.

populace, the number of Native Americans will more than double by 2050, from 2 million to 5 million.

PRISON AND JAIL POPUALTIONS

In 1994, the latest year for which data is available, almost 1.5 million persons were incarcerated, according to the U.S. Bureau of Justice. Two-thirds were in federal or state prisions, and the remainder were in local jails, where those awaiting trial or serving sentences of one year or less are usually held.

For the first time in U.S. history, the prison population exploded through the million mark in 1994, with drug offenders accounting for more than 30 percent of all newly sentenced inmates. In comparison, only seven percent of new prisoners in 1980 were drug offenders.

The number of men and women in state and federal prisons climbed to a record 1,012,851 in 1994, an increase of 63,970 over the 948,881 prison population in 1993. Nearly 40,000 of them imprisoned in the first half

of 1994, equivalent to 1,500 new prisoners a week. Women accounted for only 6.1 percent of the total.

State prisons held 919,143 inmates and federal prisons held 93,708, according to Bureau of Justice statistics. California's 124,813 inmates and Texas' 100,136 accounted for more than one-fifth of the total.

The rate for criminals sentenced to more than one year also set a record in 1994—373 per 100,000 Americans, up from 351 in 1993—as the U.S. continued to lock up prisoners at an astounding rate. It currently stands second in the world in prison rate, behind Russia. To give an idea of the figures, under the apartheid regimes, South Africa imprisoned 311 persons per 100,000.

Counting inmates both in prisons and those awaiting trial or serving short sentences in local jails, the U.S. incarceration rate was more than four times that of Canada, more than five times that of England and Wales, and 14 times that of Japan.

In 1994, drug offenders accounted for 60 percent of all federal prison immates, whereas in 1980, 25 percent did; in state prisons 25 percent of inmates were drug offenders. According to the *Chicago Tribune*(Oct. 13, 1995), approximately 25 percent of prisoners in state and federal prisons (234,000 offenders), were being incarcarated for drug offenses.

From 1980 to 1992, according to another Justice Department report, drug arrests more than doubled, from 471,200 to 980,700, and the likelihood of going to jail for a drug crime increased from 19 sentences per 1,000 arrests to 104 per 1,000—almost a five-and half-fold increase. The department attributed 50 percent of the growth in prison population from the 1980 total of 329,821 to drug traffic.

A racial breakdown of prisoners showed that at the end of 1993 1,432 out of every 100,000 blacks in the U.S. were in prison—more than seven times the rate of white imprisonment. There were 203 white inmates per 100,000 whites in the country.

Sexual assault, robbery, and aggravated assault also helped crowd the nation's prisons, as 50,000 more people were locked up in 1992 than in 1980. Tightened parole rules almost doubled prison admissions for violations, from 17 percent of total admissions in 1980 to 30 percent in 1992.

Below are the 10 states with the highest and lowest incarceration rates per 100,000 citizens, according to the U.S. Justice Department.

HIGHEST INCARCERATION RATES

State	Prisoners per 100,000
Washingoton D.C.	1,578
Texas	545
Louisiana	514
South Carolina	504
Oklahoma	501
Nevada	456
Arizona	448
Alabama	439

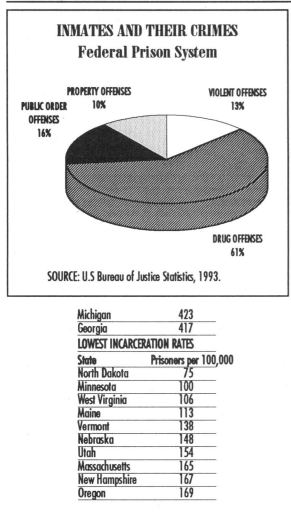

INMATES AND THEIR CRIMES
Federal Prison System

PROPERTY OFFENSES 10%

PUBLIC ORDER OFFENSES 16%

VIOLENT OFFENSES 13%

DRUG OFFENSES 61%

SOURCE: U.S Bureau of Justice Statistics, 1993.

Michigan	423
Georgia	417

LOWEST INCARCERATION RATES

State	Prisoners per 100,000
North Dakota	75
Minnesota	100
West Virginia	106
Maine	113
Vermont	138
Nebraska	148
Utah	154
Massachusetts	165
New Hampshire	167
Oregon	169

SEGREGATION

Older cities and suburbs are persisting in their ways despite the changing ethnic and racial makeup of the country. But the boomtowns of the 1990s are quickly getting in step with the emerging multiracial nature of the new America. That's the conclusion reached in a study of integration conducted by Reynolds Farley of the Population Studies Center at the University of Michigan at Ann Arbor.

When boomers were babies, there were 90 white Americans for every 10 who belonged to a minority group. In 1994 the minority rate had advanced to 25 for every 100 whites. When the boomers become senior citizens, minorities will make up 40 percent of the U.S. population. Yet, the older suburbs will still be predominantly white.

Using a demographic tool called a segregation index, which computes a score of 100 for complete segregation and 0 for a perfectly integrated neighborhood, Reynolds found that suburban developments built in

the last 15 years may be the most integrated neighborhoods in the nation. In addition, the paradises to which large numbers of Americans are moving—mostly in search of jobs—have shed the racial blinders of the past.

Rapidly growing cities have seen sharp drops in their segregation indexes since 1980. Dallas dropped from 81 in 1980 to 66 in 1990, Las Vegas from 64 to 51, and Orlando from 80 to 65. Meanwhile, slow-growth or no-growth metros such as Detroit, Chicago, Cleveland, and Newark persist in high segregation levels, according to the index. Detroit's index, at 89, is the same as it was in 1980. The study points out that in the Detroit metropolitan area 10 new homes were built in the 1980s for every 100 existing homes. In Orlando, 66 new homes were built for every existing 100 homes during the same period. the

Below are the 10 most integrated and 10 most segregated metropolitan areas relating to blacks and whites according to the segregation index:

MOST INTEGRATED

Metro. arae	Index
Jacksonville, N.C.	31
Lawton, Ohio	37
Anchorage, Alaska	38
Fayetteville, N.C.	41
Lawrence, Kans.	41
Clarksville, Tenn.-Hopkinsville, Ky.	42
Fort William Beach, Fla.	43
Cheyenne, Wyo.	43
Anaheim-Santa Ana, Calif.	43
Honolulu, Hawaii	44

MOST SEGREGATED

	Index
Gary-Hammond, Ind.	91
Detroit	89
Chicago	87
Cleveland	86
Buffalo	84
Flint, Mich.	84
Milwaukee	84
Saginaw-Bay City-Midland, Mich.	84
Newark	83
Philadelphia	82

URBANIZATION

At its founding, the U.S. was overwhelmingly agricultural. As the nation industrialized, the American population—both native-born and new immigrants—headed toward the cities. Now, more than three in four Americans lives in a metropolitan area, 187.1 million in all. Though it produces much of the nation's farm crop, California nevertheless is the most urbanized state, with nearly 93 percent of its citizens living in a metropolitan area.

POPULATIONS

Nine of the 11 fastest-growing cities were in Florida. The metro area with the greatest growth was Los Angeles-Anaheim-Riverside, Calif., which increased by nearly three million in just 10 years. The top 25 fastest-growing metro areas all were in Florida, Nevada, Texas, New Mexico, Arizona, and California. Las Vegas grew by 60 percent and Orlando by 53 percent; in comparison, Pittsburgh saw a 7.4 percent decline in population, and Duluth, Minn., fell by 10 percent.

The table at right details changes in the urban and rural populations of the U.S. since 1800, according the U.S. Bureau of the Census.

Year	Population	% Urban	% Rural
1800	3,929,214	6.1	93.9
1820	9,638,453	7.2	92.8
1840	17,069,453	10.8	89.2
1860	31,443,321	19.8	80.2
1880	50,155,783	28.2	71.8
1900	75,994,575	39.6	60.4
1920	105,710,620	51.2	48.8
1940	131,669,275	56.5	43.5
1960	179,323,175	69.9	30.1
1980	226,545,805	73.7	26.3
1990	248,709,873	75.2	24.8

POSSESSIONS
OVERVIEW

Owning a home, once the epitome of the American dream, is on the decline in the 1990s, an unfathomable trend in the eyes of the World War II generation and the Baby Boomers who grew up living in comfortable suburban homes that their parents purchased. In the '60s and 70's, approximately two-thirds of American householders lived in houses they owned. By 1982 homeownership dropped to 64.8 percent and by 1994, the latest available data, it dropped to 64 percent, up slightly from the 1988 low of 63.8 percent. Today's version of the American dream is focused on more realistic and affordable commodities other than homes.

The focus of this new "American Dream" is best-defined by a popular bumper sticker of the '80s that proclaimed, "The one who dies with the most toys, wins." Today, however, the "toys" of the '80s are generally regarded as practical necessities of the American household in the high-tech '90s.

According to a *Time* magazine survey in early 1996, the average American has more and better things now than he or she did 25 years ago. The average American household possesses 2.2 televisions, up from 1.4 in 1970; 94 percent of all houses have color TVs. More than half of all families own two cars; only 28 percent did so a quarter century ago. Sixty-nine percent of families own a clothes dryer. New houses being built today are bigger—by an average of 600 square feet—than they were in 1970. And although prices of cars, appliances, and other durable goods are far higher today, improved technology and better quality means those products are lasting far longer than they used to, bringing the overall costs to the consumer down. Despite the average cost today—more than twice as much as in 1970—a new car is a better value than it was then. In addition, it's much safer, equipped with features such as airbags, anti-lock brakes, and side-impact protection, which drive the price up but save lives.

Fax machines, cellular phones, VCRs, personal computers, modems, satellite dishes, central air conditioning—as this chapter illustrates, Americans now possess an array of high-tech devices their parents never could have dreamed of. Just 20 years ago, there was no such thing as a "personal" computer; now there are 33 million American homes that have at least one.

There's a flip side to material wealth in the eyes of American consumers: The more they have, the more they believe they need. Products such as PCs, cellular phones, and cable TV have gone from being novelties and curiosities owned by a select few to near requirements in the mid-'90s. Students without a home computer are at a learning disadvantage compared to their classmates who can do their homework and explore the Internet using the home PC. A car phone, once the symbol of luxury-living, now is touted as a safety feature on the average family car—a lifeline if you break down or are approached by unwelcome road guests in the middle of nowhere. Keeping up with the Joneses is becoming an expensive, and increasingly technological proposition.

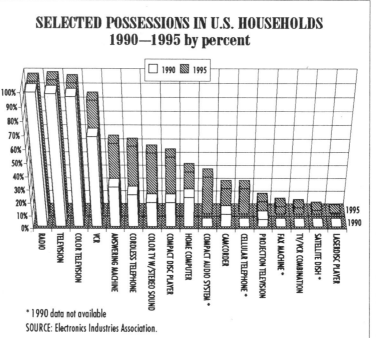

SELECTED POSSESSIONS IN U.S. HOUSEHOLDS 1990—1995 by percent

□ 1990 ▨ 1995

RADIO, TELEVISION, COLOR TELEVISION, VCR, ANSWERING MACHINE, CORDLESS TELEPHONE, COLOR TV W/STEREO SOUND, COMPACT DISC PLAYER, HOME COMPUTER, COMPACT AUDIO SYSTEM *, CAMCORDER, CELLULAR TELEPHONE *, PROJECTION TELEVISION, FAX MACHINE *, TV/VCR COMBINATION *, SATELLITE DISH *, LASERDISC PLAYER

* 1990 data not available

SOURCE: Electronics Industries Association.

ANSWERING MACHINES

Ten years ago answering machines were a rarity, and people were frequently unsure how to respond to them. Now, more than 50 million machines answer the nation's phones in 46 percent of all U.S. households.

The following list indicates the growth in sales of answering machines in the U.S., according to *Electronic Industries*.

1980 (est.)	1.0 million
1985	4.2 million
1990	13.8 million
1995	20.1 million

AUTOMOBILES

Today's American consumer no longer considers the automobile to be a luxury; rather it is a necessity, as crucial to their lifestyle as daily bathing and three square meals. Approximately 90 percent of American households have access to at least one car, van or light truck; just over half (53%) have two or more. Americans owned 146.3 million automobiles in 1993, the year for which the latest data is available. Per capita ownership of automobiles is .56 in the U.S., which roughly translates to each family owning 1.8 cars.

The primary use for automobiles in the U.S. is transportation to work—88 percent of all U.S. workers drive their cars to work.

In 1994, the Federal Highway Administration estimated that 175 million Americans had valid drivers licenses with men having slightly more, 89.0 million verses 86.1 million for women.

The list below represents the top selling passenger cars in the U.S. and the number registered between 1991 and 1994, according to the American Automobile Association.

Model	Registrations
1. Ford Taurus	397,031
2. Honda Accord	367,615
3. Ford Escort	336,967
4. Toyota Camry	321,979
5. Saturn	286,003
6. Honda Civic	267,023
7. Pontiac Grand Am	262,310
8. Chevrolet Corsica/ Beretta	222,129
9. Toyota Corolla	210,926
10. Chevrolet Cavalier	187,263

The colors American's choose for their automobiles are almost always a sign of the times. During the Great Depression, black was the most popular color. Green, the color of renewal, was in vogue after World War II. In the '60 and '70s, white dominated. In the late '80s and early '90s high-tech, cool colors reigned, with various shades of blue dominating. In the mid-nineties, green once again dominated, perhaps a function of Americans being once again renewed, after a disaster-ous recession in the early part of the decade. Green or white is among the top two colors Americans' pick for all types of vehicles from luxury cars to light trucks and vans.

Below are the most popular colors and the corresponding percentage of colors of all full size and intermediate cars, the most popular types of vehicles sold in the U.S., according the American Automobile Association, which compiled the list.

Rank	Percent
1. Green	19.4%
2. White	18.1
3. Light brown	11.8
4. Medium red	10.0
5. Black	5.7
6. Teal/aqua	5.5
7. Silver	4.6
8. Bright red	4.2
9. Medium blue	3.0
10. Dark red	3.3

BOAT OWNERSHIP

Americans ran into shortages and waiting lists in 1994 as they pushed the pleasure boat business into its strongest performance in four years, hitting $14 billion in sales—a 25 percent increase over 1993. The boom began after the 1933 repeal of a 10 percent luxury tax on big boats, according to the magazine *Boating Industry*, which published an industry survey sponsored by the powerboat magazine *Boating*.

With recreational boat harbors as crowed as the one above, power boat accidents have increased from approximately100,000 ten years ago to 500,000 today.

Water skis led all other categories of water crafts in sales, as Americans bought 142,000 units in 1994, an increase of 32.7 percent and the third year in a row in which skis have scored record sales. Inboard cruisers, the category hit that was hardest by the luxury tax, showed increased sales of 4,200 units, a gain of 24.4 percent. The average cost of such a boat was a hefty $212,067. Sales still were down more than 60 percent from the 1980s, when an average of 15,000 were bought annually.

Third choice for Americans hunting spaces in the nation's 10,000 marinas and boatyards in 1994 were inboard/outboard boats, a category in which sales increasing 20 percent to 90,000 units after hovering around 75,000 in 1992 and 1993. Average boat costs climbed 11.8 percent to $18,542, with most of the sales in the 17- to 18-foot and 20- to 21-foot range.

Boaters bought more outboards than any other type of craft, though the sale increase was only 7.3 percent, at 220,000 units, up from 205,000 in 1993. Buyers paid an average of a little more than $5,000. Within the outboard category, fiberglass boats were most popular, growing 25 percent in sales, while aluminum boat sales remained flat. Utility and other fishboats accounted for 48 percent of the aluminum market, while bass boats and pontoons and decks accounted for 24 and 22 percent, respectively. Bass boats and runabouts accounted for 30 and 24 percent of the glass boat market, respectively, and saltwater fish boats 22 percent.

Sailboats, the fourth largest category of boats after outboards, small craft, and inboard/outboard, in that order, showed an increase of 9.3 percent in sales, to 13,000 units. The survey estimates that 1.39 million sailboats dot the 50 states' 64,895 square miles of inland waterways, 60,178 square miles of Great Lakes, and 88,633 square miles of coastal shorelines, or 213,706 square miles of American sailing water.

Most popular among American sailboat buyers in 1993 were 20- to 29-foot craft, as production in that category increased 26 percent. Production of sailboats in the 41- to 45-foot class rose 12 percent, and 36- to 40-footers rose 11 percent. Novice sailors helped boost production of 12- to 19-footers by 10 percent.

Michigan boaters are the most numerous in the nation, at 874,818, representing 7.75 percent of 17 million American boaters. Californians are second at 820,219 and 7.27 percent, followed by Floridians at 719,071 and 6.3 percent, Texans at 591,879 and 5.26 percent, and Wisconsin boaters at 515,342 and 4.57 percent.

Of the top 50 participatory sports in the country, boaters account for five positions. Fishing is third in popularity (52.2 million) behind exercise walking (64.4 million) and swimming (61.4 million). Motor boating, with its 20.7 million participants, is ranked 12th, water skiing, at 8.1 million, is ranked 31st, canoeing (6.5 million) is 33rd, and sailing (3.8 million) is 39th.

At top right are facts and figures on boat and watercraft ownership in the U.S., according to the American Marine Manufacturing Association:

Vessels	Owned, 1994
Outboards	7,900,000
Small craft	4,600,000
Inboard/ outboards	1,600,000
Sailboats	1,400,000
Water skis	720,000
Inboards and jets	520,000

The following are boating accident and fatality figures for 1993, according to the U.S. Coast Guard:

Type of Accident	Number	Fatalities
Collision w/vessels	4,733	78
Collision w/objects	992	71
Falls/falls overboard	667	210
Capsizing	453	239
Swamping/flooding	415	90
Grounding	363	17
Fire/explosion	305	5
Fallen water skier	271	7
Struck by prop	183	10
Unknown	168	44
Sinking	139	29
Total	8,689	800

CATS AND DOGS

Over 4.5 million more cats sashay around American households than dogs, but dogs, at 52.5 million, remain

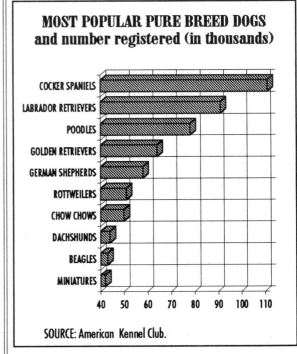

MOST POPULAR PURE BREED DOGS and number registered (in thousands)

COCKER SPANIELS
LABRADOR RETRIEVERS
POODLES
GOLDEN RETRIEVERS
GERMAN SHEPHERDS
ROTTWEILERS
CHOW CHOWS
DACHSHUNDS
BEAGLES
MINIATURES

40 50 60 70 80 90 100 110

SOURCE: American Kennel Club.

the most popular pet in the country, according to a veterinary survey.

Thirty-seven percent of U.S. households own at least one dog, down from 39 percent in 1987, according to the survey of 80,000 households by the American Veterinary Medical Association. Thirty-one percent of households own a cat, and often more than one, a figure unchanged since 1987.

Fifty-four percent of dog-owning households have one or more children, vs. 51 percent in cat-owning households. Thirty-two percent of those dog-owning families have two or more children, compared to 29 percent of cat owners.

Eighty-one percent of dog owners are homeowners. Forty-four percent of both dog-owning and cat-owning households have incomes of $40,000 or more; 34 percent of dog-owning and 35 percent of cat-owning households have incomes under $24,999.

Oklahoma tops all other states in dog owners, with almost 50 percent of the state's households owning canines, according to the Oklahoma Veterinary Association. Oklahoma is followed by Arkansas, Louisiana, and Texas, while the more crowded states of New England have the lowest share. California, Oregon, and Washington are the capitals for cats, according to the 1991 AVMA survey, the most recent the group has taken, reported in the September 1993 issue of the journal *American Demographics*.

The first table shows household pet ownership in millions, according to the American Veterinary Medical Association. The two tables below represent household data of pet owners by percent, according to *the Pet Ownership and Demographics Sourcebook.*, 1991.

DEMOGRAPHIC PROFILE

Item	Dog	Cat
Households	34.6	29.2
Total pet population	52.5	57.0
Total veterinary costs	$4.5	$2.3
Average visits per year (number)	2.6	1.8
Average annual cost (dollars)	$131.84	$79.75
ANNUAL HOUSEHOLD INCOME OF OWNERS		
Under $12,999	14%	15%
13,000 to $24,499	20	20
$25,000 to $39,999	24	23
$40,000 to 59,999	22	22
$60,000 and over	20	20
FAMILY SIZE		
One person	14%	18%
Two persons	32	33
Three persons	21	20
Four or more persons	33	29

CELLULAR TELEPHONES

Cellular telephones, a perk primarily for business executives scarcely 10 years ago, reached a level of popularity equaling videotape recorders by 1993 as nonbusiness consumers drove the phenomenal growth of the market.

A decade ago the instruments were bulky and cost between $2,000 and $4,000. By 1993, reduced in weight and size to a few ounces and able to fit into a purse or shirt pocket, cell phone prices had dropped to $75 to $300.

Seventy-one percent of cellular phone sales in 1987 were to business users and a mere 25 percent to general consumers, according to the Cellular Telecommunications Association, which represents America's wireless communications industry. In 1993, a preponderance were consumers: 46.7 percent of the industry's 16 million customers were personal users, and 45.6 percent business buyers; government and law enforcement agencies accounted for the rest. About five percent of U.S. households had a cellular phone in 1993, according to Mediamark Research of New York. Almost 14 percent of households with an annual income of at least $75,000 had two or more.

In the last six months of 1993, according to the CTA, 2.9 million new subscribers signed up for cellular phone service, a record for half-year growth in the market. Mediamark found that 55 percent of all cellular users are college graduates, and 27 percent are managers, professionals, or executives.

Cellular-phone ownership is most popular among householders aged 25 to 44 and least prevalent among those 55 or older, several surveys agree. Two-thirds of them are married, 78 percent own their own homes, and 65 percent have three or more members in their households.

The cost of using the service has been declining nine percent a year for five years, and in 1994 stood at an average of $61 a month, or $732 a year, down from more than $1,000 five years ago. A Bureau of Labor Statistics survey showed that the average U.S. household spent $620 a year on conventional home phone service in 1992.

The industry is dominated by Motorola Inc., which controls 40.9 percent of the $13.9 billion market for cellular infrastructure equipment. In 1993 that accounted for $5.2 billion for the company's cellular arm, representing about 33 percent of Motorola's $17 billion in company sales.

In 1990, the company had predicted a penetration of 2.5 to four percent for cellular phones by 1994. The penetration instead reached eight percent, double the optimistic projection.

The New Office: When AT&T invented cellular phones in 1947, it envisioned them principally as car phones for business use. Little did they anticipate that the cellular phone would turn the car into a veritable office on wheels for salespersons and that the portable phone would pervade everyday life, with corporate types chattering away on flip phones at ball games, on the beach, and on city sidewalks. Some parents reportedly even buy cellular phones for their children of dating age, and that disabled persons' lives have been saved by the phones.

The Underestimate of the Century? In the 1980s, surveys for AT&T projected the potential market for cellular phones at 900,000 by the year 2000. That kind of market apparently wasn't big enough for the communications giant, and it abandoned several of its cellular lines. Those surveys grossly underestimated the phones' potential. By 1991, there were 10 million cellular phones in use in the U.S. By decade's end there could be many-fold more. In a move that made headlines nationwide, AT&T offered McCaw Cellular Communications, one of the principal manufacturers of the instruments, $3.8 billion for a mere 33 percent of its business.

The booming cellular phone industry has created 100,000 new jobs. As prices drop, quality is up; demand keeps soaring. The U.S. market is the world's largest, with 10 million cellular phone subscribers who pay 50 to 75 cents per minute for each call. Now American companies are battling with their foreign competitors to build cellular systems in vast, untapped markets of Eastern Europe, South America, and India. Can the day be far off when everyone on the planet will be connected via the microwave transmitters of the cellular phone network?

The following charts sales of cellular phones in the U.S., according to data collected by the Electronic Industries Association and the Computer and Business Equipment Manufacturers Association:

1985 (est.)	200,000
1990	2,100,000
1995 (est.)	5,000,000

CHRISTMAS CLUB SAVING ACCOUNTS

Six million predominately small-town and rural-area Americans still cling to a savings plan concepts almost 100 years old: the Christmas or Hanukah Club, which became popular nationally during the Great Depression when children and adults deposited nickels, dimes, and quarters weekly in the local bank to fund their Christmas gift- giving.

More than 1,300 lenders across the country still market Christmas clubs, but these days they are more useful for customer relations than for profit-making, according to CC Direct Marketing Services in Easton, Pa., which prints coupon books, checks, deposit slips, and lobby displays for banks. One bank, First National Bank of Rochester, N.Y., reissued special holiday savings books in 1988, and in 1993 had a membership of 3,000 persons saving an average $500 a year each, according to First National.

In the economically depressed 1930s, club members—buying now and paying yesterday—came from all social groups and were major source of profit for savings and loans across the nation. In those days, doctors earned an average of $3,382 a year, professors $3,111, construction workers $907, and sleep-in domestic servants $260. A nation of 123 million suffered a net loss of $3.4 billion in their personal savings ac-

counts as more money was withdrawn from banks than was deposited.

In the 1980s credit cards and electronic banking—buying now and paying tomorrow—changed attitudes about savings and transformed holiday shopping patterns, according to CC Direct. A 1992 study by Simmons Market Research Bureau of New York City showed that Americans age 55 and older were most likely to have a club account, with 27 percent of all club members falling into the group. Only four percent of 18- to 24-year-olds were club members, and women were most likely to be joiners in the 1990s, when doctors earn an average of $118,400 annually, professors $58,000, construction workers $26,100, and live-in domestics $250 to $350 a week, and when a nation of 258 million people owned $189.9 billion in personal savings.

More than half of the nation's Christmas or Hanukah clubs are located in the Northeast, and only 10 percent in the West, according to Simmons Market Research, which adds that most of the club savings probably are no longer aimed at Christmas gifts to others but at vacations or home improvements for the saver.

Total personal savings deposits in U.S. national and state banks for selected years from 1980 to 1993, in billions, from the U.S. Bureau of Economic Analysis:

Year	Amount
1980	$153.8
1985	189.3
1989	152.1
1990	170.0

Jostens.

Some Americans buy a class ring, others earn one such as the NCAA final-four basketball ring pictured above.

1991	201.5
1992	238.7
1993	189.9

CLASS RINGS

With graduates facing monstrous college loans to pay off and the prospect of no job after graduation, class rings are no longer standard fare on the fingers of recent college grads. Like college tuitions, class ring costs have risen rapidly. A 14-karat-gold class ring that sold for $35 in 1949 will cost today's students between $300 and $400, and ringmakers are finding that only three out of 10 are buying rings at graduation.

Alumni with jobs buy 35 percent of all class rings, keeping the class ring market alive. Jostens Inc., one of the nation's largest makers of class rings, reported in 1992 that 11.5 percent of its customers had been out of school for three or more years. For example, a direct mail promotion by the University of Illinois Alumni Association for a "fine class ring" brought 500 responses. Lou Liay, director of the association, said there had been a steep downturn in sales to the college's senior class in the 1960s and a revival of interest in the late '70s and the '80s.

A Jostens spokesman said the 75 percent of the rings they sell annually through telemarketing are for alumni. Colleges and universities make a percentage on the sales of rings through their bookstores. Ring makers say they may or may not pay a percentage on sales made through direct mail and telemarketing, depending on whether a school's insignia is copyrighted.

But Are They Really Alums? Since proof of graduation is not required, no one knows how many bogus alumni buy a class ring. Mike Garvey, a spokesman for the University of Notre Dame, wondered how strict his school was on the question, so he asked at the campus bookstore. "If I wanted to buy a ring," he said, "they would not sell it to me until they verified that I had gone here and graduated." A Notre Dame alumnus himself, Garvey doesn't have a class ring.

COMPUTERS, PERSONAL

Nineteen years after introduction of the first personal computers by Apple, an estimated 16.5 percent of all American households owned a personal computer, up from eight percent in 1984. An increase in the number home computers of seven million a year is predicted by PC Data of Reston, Vt., which estimates 23.5 million home computers by 1996 and 30 million by 1997.

The National Science Foundation, which controls the Internet's core computer network, hazarded a guess in 1994 that 15 million people in the U.S. and 25 million persons worldwide access the network regularly, though the NSF admits a true count is impossible. In 1995, A.C. Nielsen, a highly respected auditing

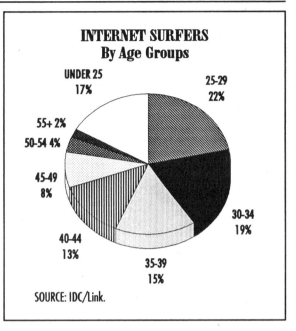

INTERNET SURFERS
By Age Groups

- UNDER 25: 17%
- 25-29: 22%
- 30-34: 19%
- 35-39: 15%
- 40-44: 13%
- 45-49: 8%
- 50-54: 4%
- 55+: 2%

SOURCE: IDC/Link.

firm, estimated the total number of Internet user to be approximately 35 million by years end.

A Census Bureau report on the growth of personal computer use showed that only 11 percent of black children had access to a computer at home, compared to 27 percent of whites and 28 percent of other races.

Forty-three percent of women use a computer at work, compared to 32 percent of men. Finance, insurance, and real estate workers are the most frequent business users of personal computers, with 71 percent of workers using them. The report was released in 1991, based on 1989 figures, the latest available.

Computer use is greater among children age 17 or under, 46 percent of those age three to 17 using a computer at home or at school, up from 30 percent in 1984. Fourteen percent of children between ages of three and five use a computer, 46 percent of six-year-olds, and 45 percent of children age seven to 17.

Most children have their first computer experience at school, where usage climbed from 18 percent of schools in 1981 to 97.2 percent in 1990, according to the National Center for Education Statistics and the Department of Education. Usage levels in elementary, junior high, and senior high schools are about equal, ranging from 97.2 in elementary school to 98.7 in senior high.

American householders owned 15 million personal computer in 1990s, according to a U.S. Energy Information Administration survey. By 1995, 69 million computers had been sold in the U.S., approximately half to consumers for use in the home.

Following is the penetration of computers in U.S. households, according to the Electronic Industries Association:

Year	% Households
1983	7%

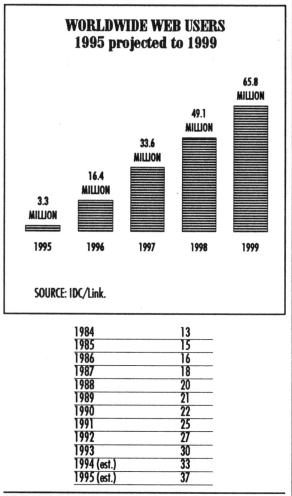

WORLDWIDE WEB USERS
1995 projected to 1999

- 3.3 MILLION — 1995
- 16.4 MILLION — 1996
- 33.6 MILLION — 1997
- 49.1 MILLION — 1998
- 65.8 MILLION — 1999

SOURCE: IDC/Link.

1984	13
1985	15
1986	16
1987	18
1988	20
1989	21
1990	22
1991	25
1992	27
1993	30
1994 (est.)	33
1995 (est.)	37

CREDIT CARDS

With more than 6,000 banks issuing Visa and MasterCard cards in the U.S., consumers have plenty of choices in credit cards. Making an intelligent choice can save big bucks in interest and annual fees.

According to the consumer group Bankcard Holders of America, bank card spending has soared like the national debt and is reaching an estimated $300 billion annually—about six times what it was in 1980. Average interest charges hovered at around 19 percent on unpaid balances, because there are few low-interest cards to bring down the average (the industry standard is 19.8 percent). That may explain why every mailbox in the country is flooded with "pre-approved" invitations from large banks—and small banks acting as agents for big ones—offering yet another card to pay off the balance on one's present and at a lower rate (the bait!), thus shifting the debt to a competing bank.

Indeed, competition among the proliferating issuers has nudged some banks to reduce their interest rates. Some nine million Citibank cardholders enjoyed that experience in the spring of 1993, when the bank

lowered its interest rate to 15.4 percent (from 19.8 percent) for its best customers. This translated to the bank's having 27 million cards—70 percent of its total— carrying rates below the 19.8 percent standard.

Credit cards users often plan to revolve charges or pay them off at their own pace, but they often wind up with thousands of dollars billed to the card, and many cannot pay off the principal, even in installments. Like the federal government, a significant number of cardholders pay only the interest charges plus a token installment toward the balance every month. The smarter consumers scan newspapers and business magazines to find the cards with the lowest interest rates.

In 1992, some states' usury laws—regulations to limit the amount of interest or fees that banks can charge on credit cards—allowed rates as high as 36 percent annually (Wyoming), and the national average in May 1993 was still a whopping 18.24 percent. But cardholders who do not pay off the principal each month can find variable rates of as low as eight percent, according to "Bank Rate Monitor".

The following list shows the increase in credit card spending (in millions), adapted from data from the Federal Reserve Board, Bankcard Holders of America, and credit card companies.

	Bank Cards	All Cards
1980	$54	$206
1983	80	240
1986	142	335
1989	216	529
1990	250	563
1991	260	659
1992	300	770

FAX MACHINES

When fax machines were invented in the 1960s, it took an average of six minutes to send a single page. As technological improvements brought the time down to seconds, fax machine sales soared—from 580,000 in 1987 to 11 million in 1992.

Jay Kaye, the author of *Light Your House with Potatoes*, a book about "totally off-the-wall solutions to life's little problems," reports a unique use of the fax machine, one that involves an Oklahoma convict who found jail to be relentlessly boring.

The Case of Jean Paul Barret: In Oklahoma, Barret was taken from the state prison to the Pima County Jail to await a hearing. He had a smart friend who apparently knew all about a new technique to finagle a way out of jail in the age of instant communication and document transfer. Barret's jailers received a fax ordering the inmate's release—the usual way they get orders to release prisoners, some 60 a day. Apparently Barret's friend got hold of an actual court document, and with a little typewriter white-out and some new names and dates, he faxed the forged release papers. It is therefore no longer true that bars and barbed wire may keep the criminals in jail, for telephone wires can get them out faster than a good lawyer.

Fax machines are changing the life of those outside jail, too; in fact, they are an addiction that is changing the face of office and home life. Today, Fortune 500 companies send an average of 49 documents a day, up from 40 a year ago. In 1992, corporate faxes averaged 4.6 pages; in 1993, 5.3 pages, mostly purchase orders and reports, as noted by a survey taken by Pitney Bowes, the office equipment giant.

A Gallup poll found that 75 percent of the Fortune 500 fax senders didn't know how much it cost to send a fax. It's cheap enough: averaging 15 to 18 cents a minute for a machine requiring 30 seconds to send a page.

FIREARMS

There are an estimated 30 million handguns in America, many times the number owned by the U.S. military. In 1990, more than 3.7 million firearms of all types were sold; in 1965, the year of the Watts riots in Los Angeles, 2.4 million were sold. Rifle sales decreased four percent and shotgun sales fell 16 percent—good news for wildlife—while human life was wearing bulletproof vests and uttering cries of anguish and pleas for sterner vigilance and harsh laws against handguns.

The list below shows U.S. sales of three types of firearms 1965 and 1990, compiled by the National Association of Federally Licensed Firearms Dealers.

	1965	1990
Handguns	28%	48%
Rifles	34	30
Shotguns	38	22

HOME OWNERSHIP

There are 61.2 million American families who live in homes they own, just under 90 percent of them are white (54.9 million), 8 percent are black (4.8 million) and 5 percent (2.8 million) are Hispanic. The average size in 1993, 1947 square feet, is considerably larger than it was in 1970, when the average size was 1,500 square feet. Central air conditioning was in 44 percent of all American homes in 1993, up from 17 percent twenty years ago. In the same time period, homes with two or more bathrooms has increased from 31 percent to 53 percent.

In the '60s and 70's, approximately two-thirds of American householders lived in houses they owned. By 1982 home ownership dropped to 64.8 percent and by 1994, the latest available data, it dropped to 64 percent, up slightly from the 1988 low of 63.8 percent. Today's "American Dream" is focused on more realistic, and affordable commodities.

At one time, to build a nest egg in America all you needed to do was buy a house, wait a few years for real estate inflation of 10 percent–15 percent to take effect, and count your money. Profits of $100,000 or more were

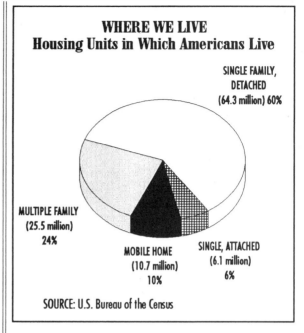

WHERE WE LIVE
Housing Units in Which Americans Live

SINGLE FAMILY, DETACHED (64.3 million) 60%

MULTIPLE FAMILY (25.5 million) 24%

MOBILE HOME (10.7 million) 10%

SINGLE, ATTACHED (6.1 million) 6%

SOURCE: U.S. Bureau of the Census

realized by average homeowners between 1970 and 1980, when the real estate boom was at its peak. That boom is over now, and house prices more or less keep pace with inflation.

The median price for an existing single-family home in America was $113,800 in January 1996, up 5 percent from the previous year, according to the National Association of Realtors. Considering that inflation in the 1990s has averaged 3.9 percent, that isn't too bad for homeowners looking for a profit. In the decade thus far, however, prices are up only 3.5 percent; therefore they are up only 0.4 percent over inflation. In the 1980s, home prices rose 4.8 percent and inflation averaged 5.1 percent—a *loss*, which would have seemed impossible at one time.

According to the NAR, the cities listed below witnessed the biggest increases and decreases in home prices in 1992 vs. 1993:

BIGGEST INCREASES

City	Change
Richland, Wash.	24.5%
Detroit	19.0
Syracuse, N.Y.	11.2
Spokane	10.9
Charleston, W.Va.	10.2
Fort Myers, Fla.	10.2

BIGGEST DECREASES

City	Change
Toledo	11.2%
Springfield, Mass.	9.1
Philadelphia	9.0
Los Angeles	8.0
Atlantic City	7.8

HOUSING UNITS BY YEARS BUILT
in millions

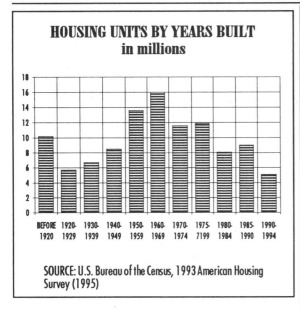

SOURCE: U.S. Bureau of the Census, 1993 American Housing Survey (1995)

The list below shows the approximte median price for a home in the 10 most and least expensive metropolitan areas during 1994, according to an estimate based on NAR data.

MOST EXPENSIVE

Honolulu	$345,000
San Francisco	250,000
Anaheim, Calif.	225,000
Los Angeles	200,000
Bergen-Passaic, N.J.	180,800
New York City	165,000
Boston	165,000
Middlesex County, N.J.	160,000
Nassau--Suffolk County, N.Y.	160,000
Washington, D.C.	155,500

LEAST EXPENSIVE

Waterloo, Iowa	$45,000
Davenport, Iowa	55,000
Peoria, Ill.	58,000
Youngstown, Ohio	59,000
Amarillo, Texas	60,000
Beaumont, Texas	60,000
Oklahoma City	61,000
Topeka, Kansas	64,000
South Bend, Ind.	63,000
Omaha	64,000

HOME MORTGAGE APPROVALS, BY RACIAL COMPOSTION

Of 15.4 million applicants for home mortgages in 1993, low-income blacks were turned down the most and Asians the least. Of applicants in the higher-in-come range, blacks also were turned down the most, while whites were turned down the least.

Banks, savings institutions, and credit unions rejected the applications of 34 percent of blacks applicants, 27.8 percent of American Indians, 25.1 percent of Hispanics, 15.3 percent of whites, and 14.6 of Asians.

In rates adjusted for income, low-income applicants—those with less than 80 percent of the median income in their areas—32.3 percent of blacks were rejected, 28.6 percent of Hispanics, 27 percent of American Indians, 19.3 percent of whites, and 16 percent of Asians.

The rejection rates for applicants with more than 120 percent of the median income were: blacks, 18.2 percent; Hispanics, 17.1 percent; Asians, 13.7 percent; American Indians, 13.6 percent, and whites, 7.9 percent.

The report, released by the Federal Financial Institutions Examination, a coordinating body for five federal regulatory agencies, did not take into account the applicants' previous indebtedness or credit records.

The overall rejection pattern in the fourth yearly study of its kind by the government follows closely the results in the first study, performed in 1990. In that analysis, 33.9 percent of blacks were turned down, 22.4 percent of American Indians, 21.4 percent of Hispanics, 14.4 percent of whites, and 12.9 percent of Asians.

For the study, home loan applications were compiled from 9,650 lending institutions by the Federal Reserve System, the Federal Deposit Insurance Corporation, the National Credit Union Administration, the Office of the Comptroller of the Currency, and the Office of Thrift Supervision.

INDIVIDUAL RETIREMENT ACCOUNTS

The popularity wanes but the pie is huge, even after the government changed the deductibility status. Nonetheless, the number of dollars currently invested in IRAs is still large enough to influence the stock market.

Money magazine estimates that $39 billion in fresh dollars was contributed to IRAs in 1992, down from $72 billion in 1991. Even so, the total IRA investment in 1993 was $725 billion, up from $199 billion in 1985, according to the Investment Company Institute.

Mutual Funds Soaking Up Dollars: From 1990 through 1992, stocks rallied briskly, as IRA holders began switching their savings into mutual funds. The giant Fidelity Investment group of mutual funds reported opening 60 percent more IRA accounts since January 1993. Vanguard Group said IRA accounts were up 35 percent over the levels of the year before.

The mutual fund industry claims to have 29.1 percent of those assets, double its share in 1985. According to Kathryn Hopkins, an executive vice president at Fidelity, 80 percent of the IRA money at Fidelity is targeted for stock funds. The most popular IRA choices, she says, are conservative stocks and Fidelity's Asset Manager funds, which emphasize stocks but include bonds and cash investments as well.

MOBILE HOMES

Today mobile homes not only are affordable—the average price is around $30,000—but they are livable, comfortable, and even have "ambiance." According to the Census Bureau, mobile homes are the fastest-growing type of housing nationwide. Their numbers increased 59 percent in 10 years, compared to 13 percent for all other types of homes.

Almost one in five houses built in the 1980s were mobile homes —now often called "manufactured housing" by those in the industry. Nearly half of the 195,000 sold in 1990 were double-wides, averaging 1,440 square feet in area. Additions such as porches are common; air conditioning is standard. Two-thirds of all mobile homes have three or more bedrooms. Nearly all are made in the U.S.

Mobile homes are primarily a post–World War II phenomenon. Starting in the 1950s, their numbers began to grow, more or less doubling every 10 years.

The table below shows the growth in mobile homes between 1950 and 1995, according to the U.S. Census Bureau:

1950	315,218
1960	766,565
1970	2,073,994
1980	4,663,457
1990	7,399,855
1993	10,732,000

MOTORCYCLES

More than four million Americans own motorcycles. Unlike prior decades, though, a growing white-collar crowd is taking to the road on motorcycles on weekends; in contrast, a large number of blue-collar riders, the traditional base of bikers, no longer can afford to buy bikes. (Check out the sticker price on a new Harley Davidson.) Due primarily to the poor economic climate for working class America, motorcycle registrations have dropped drastically— 25 percent since 1980.

The table below shows motorcycle registrations in given years as compiled by the U.S. Department of Transportation:

1980	5,694,000
1985	5,444,000
1989	4,434,000
1990	4,259,000
1992	4,065,118

Fatal motorcycle accidents also have declined sharply, down 45 percent between 1985 and 1991. Many attribute the drop to the new state laws that mandate the use of helmets. (The only states that currently do not require a helmet are Illinois, Iowa, and Colorado.) Most such laws went into effect in the 1970s, when motorcycle sales were booming and too many drivers and state legislators had witnessed ghastly accidents.

Americans are purchasing fewer motorcycles, but not necessarily riding them less. Older bikes, like the Harley Davidsons above, are as expensive as new ones from Japan and Germany. "Harley," one of three motorcycle manufacturers in the U.S., has a waiting list for their bikes, which retail for approximately twice the price of foreign makes.

The following table represents the number of motorcycle-related fatalities for select years, according to the National Highway Traffic Safety Administration.

1976	3,189
1980	5,144
1992	2,325

This dramatic drop in deaths also has been attributed to the following according to various sources.

- More riders are taking courses in motorcycle safety, possibly due to an increased percentage of better-educated riders than in the past. In 1992 alone, 105,000 cyclists attended courses given by the Motorcycle Safety Foundation.

- In the last fifteen years, the average age of motorcyclists has increased, and they are more experienced riders.

- The recession of the early 1990s has caused a decline in overall ridership.

MUTUAL FUNDS

In 1955, 82 percent of the outstanding shares on the New York Stock Exchange were owned by private citizens, most of whom were relatively unschooled in financial management. At the same time, institutional buyers held a meager 18 percent. In three tumultuous decades, those percentages have reversed, and as the 1990s dawned, institutionally managed stock funds proliferated.

In 1993, U.S. mutual funds manage more than $700 billion in negotiable securities. Before the debacle of Black October in 1987, more than 844,000 Americans had invested in funds offering shares in lucrative portfolios of stocks and bonds; the demand was so great that new funds were appearing at the rate of one each day. In the mid-1990s, that trend has returned. There are now 4,006 mutual funds, which translates to more funds than there are individual stocks on the New York Stock Exchange (2,726 stocks) and the American Stock Exchange (972 stocks) combined.

The table below shows some of the largest mutual funds now trading, according to the upcoming book *Who Really Owns America.* Values shown below represent approximate averages 1994-1995.

	Assets ($billions)	Shareholders
Fidelity Magellan	$16.0	1,000,000
Windsor Fund	8.0	250,000
Fidelity Puritan Fund	7.0	500,000
Investment Company of America	7.0	250,000
Templeton World Fund	6.5	350,000
Fidelity Equity Income	5.5	250,000
Pioneer II	5.0	650,000
Affiliated Fund	5.0	200,000
Merrill Lynch	4.5	350,000
American Capital Fund Pace	4.0	450,000

Below is a spectrum of the market choices that mutuals invest in, and their average annual profits from 1926 to 1992, as compiled by Ibbotson Associates of Chicago.

Small company stocks	17.6%
Common stocks	12.4
Long-term corporate bonds	5.8
Intermediate-term government bonds	5.3
U.S. Treasury bills	3.8
Inflation	3.2

PENSION FUNDS

Although they boast one of the world's largest pools of capital, with assets totaling $3.4 trillion, private sector pensions cover only about 50 percent of Americans in the workforce, leaving more than 35 million Americans uncovered. The Pension Rights Center of Washington, D.C., points out that the current law, the Employee Retirement Income Security Act, does not require employers to offer pensions, and it offers few incentives to expand coverage.

Another problem, according to the American Association of Retired Persons, is that ERISA allows pension fund managers to convert their funds to annuities. They then turn over administration of the plans to insurance companies, jeopardizing ERISA's insurance protection. About 33 percent of the 19.4 million private-sector retirees 55 and older receive these annuities, according to AARP. However, if an insurance company becomes insolvent, as eight did in 1991, retirees may lose their pensions even if the government intervenes.

A final argument in the looming debate is that over cost-of-living adjustments tied to company pensions. ERISA does not require this, although most public employee plans, many private sector plans, and Social Security do. In 1990, according to the Census Bureau, the average pension for Americans was $650 a month, which the AFL-CIO calls inadequate. Since 1990, inflation has eroded that amount by 15 percent, or $97, in real dollars.

PETS

The percentage of Americans owning at least one pet in year 2010 will decrease from 42.2 percent in 1993 to 40.6, the result of the growth of single-parent families and people living alone, those least likely to own a pet. In 1998, 44 percent of Americans owned some form of pet.

The 27.1 million dogs in the U.S. in 1993 outnumbered the nation's 20.5 million cats by almost seven million, according to Mediamark Research using Census Bureau 1993 figures and *American Demographics* magazine's household projections for the years 2000 and 2010. While the nation's general population is projected to grow from 250 million in 1993 to 294.3 million in 2010, an increase of 8.5 percent, ownership of cats will soar to 27 million, or 5.4 percent of U.S. households, while ownership of dogs will increase less than four million, or 4.8 percent. They still will be America's favorite pet.

Married couples with children under age 18 are most likely to own pets; 57 percent do. Couples with adult children living at home are next at 52 percent. Singles are about half as likely to own a pet, except for women in the 35 to 45 age group, who predominantly own cats.

Married couples with children under age 18 are the group most likely to own birds, horses, and other pets, at seven percent, two percent, and 13 percent, respectively. Couples without children are more likely to own horses.

The following table represents America's pet owners in 1993, and projections for the year 2010, according to Mediamark and Census Bureau surveys and *American Demographics* household projections (figures are in thousands):

OWNERS

	Any Pet	Dogs	Cats
1993	50,441	27,144	20,522
2000	58,000	30,095	22,861

2010	58,593	31,529	27,103
PERCENT CHANGE			
1993-2000	18.2%	10.9%	11.4%
2000-10	10.0	4.8	5.4
PERCENT OWNING			
1993	52.3	28.2	21.3
2000	50.6	27.3	20.8
2010	49.7	26.8	20.5

VACATION HOME OWNERSHIP

Vacation home buying is racing along at a boom level across the U.S., spurred by lower interest rates, tax breaks, investment appeal, and recession-battered home prices, realtors say. Industry sources think the demand will get hotter as the nation's 80 million baby boomers, now age 30 to 49, reach their second-home buying peak.

Currently, according to a survey by Ernest & Young, 7.5 million U.S. householders, with an average income of $46,000, own a second home. Stock and bond profits or refinancing of the primary home is the source of money for the purchase.

Century 21 Real Estate said prices in the top 21 vacation home markets rose an average 18 percent in 1993, the biggest increase being 44 percent for condominiums in the mountain and ski country of Ogden, Utah. Siren, Wis., led the increases in the Midwest at 39 percent; Mt. Vernon, Texas, in the South at 22 percent; and McHenry, Md., in the Northeast at 20 percent.

Home prices in the prime markets of Hawaii, California, Florida, Nevada, and much of the Northeast are climbing slowly after being hit hard by the recession and from overbuilding. Ernst & Young cites condos in Hawaii's Vista Waikoloa resort selling for $200,000 to $250,000, compared to a high of $650,000 in the late 1980s. Similarly, a three-acre home in the Pocono Mountain town of Milford, Pa., goes for around $95,000, compared to $145,000 in the late '80s.

Below are prices and percentage price increases in the top vacation home sections of the U.S., according to Century 21 Real Estate figures:

WEST

Location	1993 price	Increase from 1992
Ogden, Utah*	$98,000	44%
Jackson Hole, Wyo.	250,000	25
Kalispell, Mont.	93,300	24
McCall, Idaho	150,000	18
Vail, Colo.	350,000	17
Sedona, Ariz.	215,000	16
Bend, Ore.	117,000	4

MIDWEST

Location	1993 price	Increase from 1992
Siren, Wis.	$79,700	39%
Boyne City, Mich.	220,000	19
Lake of the Ozarks, Mo.	78,500	14
Grand Rapids, Minn.	42,000	9

SOUTH

Location	1993 price	Increase from 1992
Mt. Vernon, Texas	$110,000	22%
Hot Springs, Ark.	128,800	21
Key Biscayne, Fla.	300,000	20
Emerald Isle, N.C.	150,000	15
Amelia Island, Fla.	170,500	13
St. Simons Island, Ga.	172,500	5

NORTHEAST

Location	1993 price	Increase from 1992
McHenry, Md.	$187,900	20%
Nantucket, Mass.	375,000	15
Lake Placid, N.Y.	135,000	13
Penn Yan, N.Y.	178,400	10

*Condominium.

RELIGION
OVERVIEW

The vast scope and diversity of religious affiliation in the United States attests to one of this country's founding principles, the freedom of religious worship. Notwithstanding the concerned cries of fundamentalist groups, religion pervades American social life, and faith remains strong.

The 1995 *Yearbook of American and Canadian Churches* counts more than 163 million Americans—more than 60 percent of the total population—affiliated with a religion. This large figure, of course, doesn't take into account those who believe but do not belong to an organized church or choose to express their faith individually.

Even so, the incredible array of religious denominations within the predominant Christian faith also is testament to the diversity of character in America. This chapter presents an overview of the major religious groups in the U.S.—Catholicism, Protestantism, Judaism, Eastern Orthodox and Islam, along with various issues involving these faiths. Within the limited scope of the chapter it would be difficult to do justice to the numerous sub-denominations, branches, or smaller religious denominations. American Christians, for instance, break down into two major denominations, Catholicism, with about 60 million adherents, and Protestantism, with around 100 million. As the entry on Protestant churches points out, denominations divide into nine major subgroups: Baptist, Methodist, Pentecostal, Lutheran, Mormon, Presbyterian, Church of Christ, Episcopal, and Reformed.

Various other Christian denominations count significant adherents as well: the Orthodox (Eastern) Church, with 1,885,346, according to the yearbook; Jehovah's Witnesses, 926,614; Adventist churches, 794,859; Christians Scientists, 700,000; and numerous others. In all, more than 154 million of the nation's 163 million churchgoers are Christian.

Though that may indicate that the U.S. is de facto a Christian nation, the principles of religious tolerance and separation of church and state make this a welcome ground for those of other beliefs—Jews (nearly six million), Muslims (an estimated three million), and Buddhists (around 20,000) all can worship freely in this country, knowing that freedom is guaranteed to them by the Constitution.

An extreme shortage of Catholic clergymen now exists and is projected to get worse by the middle of the next decade. Ordinations are down 50 percent from the 1960s, and the increasing rate of retirement among a relatively older priesthood is further depleting the Catholic clergy; meanwhile, the number of parishioners—bolstered by a booming Hispanic population—is expected to grow rapidly in the coming decade.

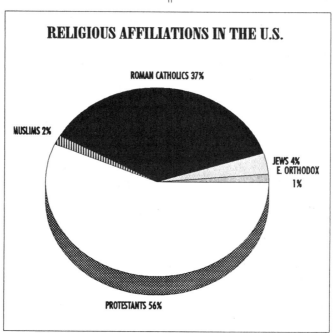

RELIGIOUS AFFILIATIONS IN THE U.S.

ROMAN CATHOLICS 37%
MUSLIMS 2%
JEWS 4%
E. ORTHODOX 1%
PROTESTANTS 56%

SOURCE: *Yearbook of American and Canadian Churches,* 1995.

BLACK CONGREGATIONS

Episcopal and Presbyterian churches in the U.S. have a higher profile in the media, but two African American churches have registered growth enough to place them among the five largest of 224 monitored Christian groups in the country, according to the statistical bible of the country's church leaders.

The National Baptist Convention U.S.A., was the fastest-growing religious body in the U.S. during the 1980s and in 1993 had a membership of 8.2 million, with 33,000 congregations, gaining 400,000 members and 3,000 congregations since 1992 to remain fourth in church membership in the country.

The Pentecostal Church of God in Christ, with an estimated membership of 6.3 million and 15,300 congregations, is fifth in size in the country, and in 1993 overtook the Evangelical Lutheran Church in America with 5.2 million members and 11,055 congregations. The black church gained 1.8 million adherents since 1991 and 5,318 congregations, while the Lutheran church gained 6,171 members and lost 32 congregations in the same period. The Catholic church, with 59.2 million members and 19,863 congregations, is the largest church in the country, followed by the Southern Baptist Convention, with 15.4 million members and 38,401 congregations, and the United Methodist Church with 8.8 million and 38,401 congregations. Members of the Presbyterians' largest body, Presbyterian Church U.S.A., totaled 3.8 million, with 11,456 congregations, and Episcopals 2.5 million with 7,367 congregations.

. Black church growth was highlighted in the 16th edition of the Yearbook of American and Canadian Churches 1993 and excerpted and published in an August 1993 issue of the magazine *Christian Century*. The yearbook pointed out that the Church of God in Christ averaged a gains of 200,000 members and 600 congregations per year since 1982. Between 1991 and 1993 it gained 1.8 million members and 5,318 congregations, according to updated figures in the 1994 Yearbook.

Underscoring the yearbook's point, the 1993 edition cited other examples of high growth in the African American church movement among revivalist churches that feature dancing and speaking in religious ecstasy:

- An independent church called World Changes Ministries in an Atlanta suburb of College Park grew by 3,250 members in 1990, to reach a total of 4,500.

- West Los Angeles Church of God accepted 2,000 new members in 1990, for a total of 8,000.

- Founded in 1960 in a house in Philadelphia, the Deliverance Evangelistic Church had 83,000 members in 1993 in 32 congregations in scattered major cities along the East Coast.

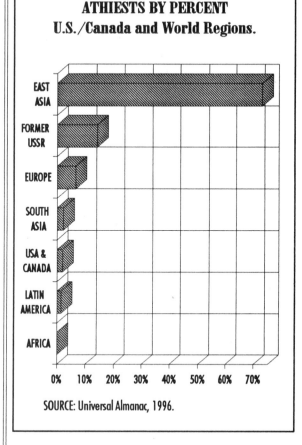

ATHIESTS BY PERCENT
U.S./Canada and World Regions.

SOURCE: Universal Almanac, 1996.

CATHOLICISM

Since 1850, Catholics have been the largest body of religious worshippers in the U.S. At 58.6 million in the U.S. in 1992, Catholics represent 36.6 percent of the U.S. church membership of 160 million, and 53,088 clergy, far ahead of Baptists, the second leader in U.S. church membership. Baptists total 32.8 million members, or 20 percent of total church membership, and 124,316 clergy.

Most Catholics (84.5 percent) are concentrated in metropolitan areas in the Northeast and Midwest, but large numbers of Hispanic Catholics are found in Florida, the Southwest, and California, according to the National Survey of Religious Identification, cited by Albert J. Menedez in the October 1993 issue of the journal *The Humanist*.

The median age of Catholics is 40.1 years, below than Protestants and Jews at 44. About nine percent of blacks are Catholic, a slight increase since 1960. The percentage of Hispanics who are practicing Catholics has declined to 66 percent, seven percent of whom have left the church to join Protestant congregations.

Since the Second Vatican Council of 1962-65, which contributed to major changes in Catholic opinions on church discipline, the church has lost 15 to 20 percent of those who were born to the faith. Catholics have reduced giving to the church from two percent of their income to one percent; weekly attendance at church also has fallen from close to 80 percent before the Council to 50 percent after it, and parochial school attendance has dropped from about 5.5 million in 1965 to 2.5 million in 1993, according to *The Humanist* essay. Fifty percent of Catholics now support admission of women to the priesthood, compared to 40 percent in the early 1980s.

Catholic hospitals total 16 percent of all hospital admissions, inpatient days, surgeries, payroll, and expenses, making the church the largest provider of private-sector health care in the U.S., according to a 1994 report in the journal *Conscience*.

CATHOLIC PRIESTS

The Catholic church is projected to lose 40 percent of its diocesan priests by the year 2005, while the number of parishioners grows 65 percent. The result will be that the number parishioners per priest will have more than doubled.

A study, using Census data on 36,000 priests in the 86 dioceses in the U.S., showed that the Church ordained only about 500 men per year in the 1980s, a 47 percent decline from about 1,000 per year in the late 1960s. The research of the period between 1966 and the forecast for 2005 was sponsored by the United States Catholic Conference and carried out by sociologists Richard A. Schoenherr and Lawrence A. Young.

Retirement of priests has grown from three percent annually in 1966 and is projected to reach 20 percent by 2005, when one out of every three priests is retired and 45 percent of diocesan priests will be past the age of 55.

The researchers point out that only 50 percent of priests who leave the ministry because of retirement, illness, resignation, or death will be replaced by ordination of new priests. To fill the places vacated by retirement alone would require an increase in ordination of 38 percent new ordinations a year, and chances of reaching this goal are minimal, the study concludes.

A vocal minority of bishops has attacked the study, arguing that it will be used to advance the ordination of women and married men. A majority of the USCC approved the research.

DONATIONS, RELIGIOUS

In a first-of-its-kind survey of 330,000 Catholics conducted for the Life Cycle Center of Catholic University in Washington, D.C., church leaders learned to their dismay that 60 percent of Catholic households in 1991 gave the church an average of less than a dollar a week. The study found that although many parishes asked their parishioners to contribute five percent of their annual income, the average donation was closer to 1.2 percent ($262 per year) — the lowest percentage of any faith, according to a further survey conducted by General Social Surveys from 1987 to 1989.

This study also revealed that Mormons gave the most: 6.2 percent of their income, or $1,713 a year. Baptists gave 2.9 percent, or $734 a year. Lutherans gave 1.3 percent, or $349 a year.

Of the total Sunday collections, 19 percent of Catholics gave an average of $950 a year, 19 percent gave an average of $294, and the remaining 62 percent gave just $42 on average. Churches with 10,000 or more members had household donations of $237 a year; in churches with 5,000 to 10,000 members, the average annual donation was $245. Those with 1,000 to 1,500 members got an average of $336 per member.

Single people and divorced or separated Catholics were the least generous, singles giving $175 a year, and divorced or separated Catholics $148. In contrast, married households gave $313 and widowed Catholics an average of $261.

The study, the first to ask data from parishes instead of individual Catholics, surveyed only those parishes with computerized accounting systems. Of 714 parishes contacted, 278 responded.

JUDAISM

Judaism, founded about 1300 B.C., is the largest non-Christian religious family in the U.S., with an estimated 4.7 million of America's 5.8 million Jews religiously affiliated or observant. Those belong to three main branches of Judaism: Reform, Conservative, and Orthodox. A fourth branch, Reconstructionist Judaism, is a 20th-century movement that accepts all forms of Jewish practice, regarding Judaism as a culture rather than a theological system.

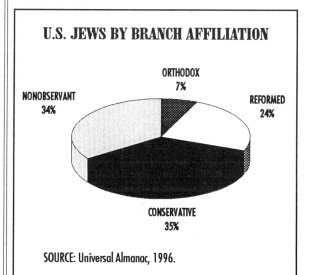

U.S. JEWS BY BRANCH AFFILIATION

ORTHODOX 7%

NONOBSERVANT 34%

REFORMED 24%

CONSERVATIVE 35%

SOURCE: Universal Almanac, 1996.

Conservative Jews (United Synogogue of America), with 800 congregations in the nation, make up the largest body of religious Jews, at two million, according to the American Jewish Yearbook in a 1990 report. They are followed by Reform Jews (Union of American Hebrew Congregations) with 848 congregations and 1.3 million members, and Orthodox Jews (Union of Jewish Congregations of America), with 1,200 congregations and one million members. Reconstructionist congregations and smaller, non-Rabbi-led groups ("havurots") number 80 nationwide, comprising 50,000 members.

Orthodox Judaism is the most traditional branch of the religion, strictly observing laws regarding food, purification, and ancient rituals. Reform Judaism, which call places of worship temples rather than synagogues, and which is strong in the U.S., is the most liberal of the three branches, following the spirit but not the letter of Orthodox practices. Conservative Judaism seeks a middle ground between the two.

Though Judaism is the oldest western religion, its adherents and practices in the U.S. have undergone more changes in the last 100 years, than any other religion. In 1985 the worldwide Conservative Rabbinical Association approved women in the clergy. By contrast, the Catholic church has been debating a similar move since woman's suffrage took hold early in the 20th century.

American Jewry in the 1990s is radically different from that of 30 to 50 years ago, when major Jewish organizations came into being, according to a study on Jewish institutions, which suggest that the institutions are not keeping up with the changes.

The result is that more Jews are distancing themselves from synagogues and reducing contributions, and from observances of Jewish customs and laws. The study also revealed a 50 percent intermarriage rate among Jews.

Furthermore, along with a shrinking synagogue membership is an aging one; 66 percent of the members in Hadassah, a Jewish women's social service organization are aged 50 and older, and just five percent age 34 or younger, according to the study by sociologist Gary Tobin in a booklet "Creating New Jewish Organizations and Institutions," reviewed in the magazine *Christian Century* in its January 18, 1995, issue.

Among Tobin's findings is the fact that the American Jewish Committee cut its staff by 33 percent in 1990 to offset a $4 million deficit after five years of financial difficulties.

Immigration of Jews to the U.S. from the former Soviet Union and the internal migration of Jews from smaller Midwestern communities continues to make the Northeast U.S. the bastion of Judaism in the country, though it is losing thousands of Jews to the South and West.

Jews made up 13 percent of the New York metropolitan population, compared to just two percent of the U.S. population, according to a 1991 survey by UJA-Federation of New York. A 1992 study by the American Jewish Year Book showed that three counties in New Jersey almost doubled their population of Jews in a decade, from 26,000 in 1982 to 49,000 in 1992.

Jewish-American population shifts clearly are following mainstream America to warmer climates, a trend noted by the Council of Jewish Federations in a 1990 nationwide survey. The council found that more than 50 percent of 838,500 Jews who left the Northeast moved to the South, and another 33 percent moved to the West. Of the Midwest's loss of 335,900 Jews, almost one-third went South, and just over 50 percent went West.

The UJA study showed that the Jewish population in Manhattan grew 15 percent between 1981 and 1991, but declined 8 percent in New York's five boroughs as a whole, and 14 percent in the metro area. The Yearbook estimated that the Chicago metropolitan area also registered a gain in Jewish population, from 248,000 in 1982 to 261,000 in 1992.

MUSLIMS

Since the early 1900s, when the first sizable group of Muslims arrived from Lebanon and Syria to settle in North Dakota, the third most-adhered to religion in the U.S. after Judaism and Christianity has grown to around three million members in the U.S. By year 2000 Muslims could outnumber Presbyterians and approach the number of Methodists, Lutherans, and Jews, according to Islamic sources.

The first American mosque was constructed by North Dakota immigrants in 1929. Later waves of

With alcoholic beverages forbidden to Muslims, coffee houses such as this one in Dearborn Michigan are meeting places where they congregate to play cards and converse.

Arabian, Iranian, East Indian, and Pakistani immigration has resulted in construction of 1,000-plus centers today, with at least one in every state. Roughly 80 percent are believed to have been founded since 1982, according to the Islamic Resource Institute in California.

The most elaborate is a $11 million mosque on the Upper East Side of Manhattan. In addition, a $4 million mosque accommodates 2,000 worshippers near the campus of the University of California, and a similarly sized center lies outside Toledo, Ohio.

Twenty-five percent of U.S. Muslims are American blacks, accounting for most of the native-born Muslims, following either the mainstream Islamic doctrine founded on the Koran or the black separatist Nation of Islam movement founded in the U.S. in 1930 by W.D. Fard, called Elijah Mohammed from 1925 until his death in 1975.

Nation of Islam members hold that Black Americans are descended from an ancient Muslim tribe. They call for a separate state in America for blacks and reparations for injustices of the past. Malcolm X was one of its foremost preachers, and Muhammad Ali perhaps its most well-known member. Most members of Islam today repute those doctrines and embrace instead orthodox Muslim beliefs.

Like Christians and Jews, Muslims believe in one God; Jerusalem is a holy place for all three religions. Muslims have their own publications and political lobbying groups in the U.S. Islamic social clubs, marriage service offices, and bookstores are proliferating around the country.

Conservatism rules Muslim life. Religious education and close-knit families—the ultimate authority for a Muslim and thus responsible for an individual's behavior—are of the highest importance, with the eldest man the head of the family.

ORTHODOX, EASTERN

Among religions that constitute one percent or more of America's religiously affiliated, Orthodox Christianity is the smallest in size, yet the fifth largest religious affiliation. Often referred to as Eastern Churches, or Eastern Orthodox, the denomination in the U.S. accounts for 1.2 percent of the nation's 163,471,391 religiously affiliated, according to the *1995 Yearbook of American and Canadian Churches.*

The Orthodox Church has its roots in Constantinople (today called Istanbul) in present day Turkey. In 1054 A.D., the schism between Rome's "Western Church," now commonly called Roman Catholicism, caused Christians in Greece and the Middle East to break away. In Russia the faith celebrated its 1,000th anniversary in 1988. Churches are hierarchically organized with exclusively male Bishops and Archbishops administering. The ancient traditions they perform in their services are elaborate, replete relig-

Bishops and archbishops of Orthodox churches are usually bearded and easily recogizable in their black flowing clerical robes. Above, various clerics meet for a convention at the Pittsburgh Airport.

ious feasts, including Easter, being calculating on different dates than Western churches.

The Orthodox churches serve as cultural centers for Americans of Greek decent, the largest Orthodox contingent in the U.S. The next largest are Russian, Armenian and Syrian, respectively. Together they account for eighty percent of the nation's Orthodox Christians. Most Orthodox churches are active in the National Council of Churches.

The following list represents the various denominations of Orthodox Christianity in the U.S., according to the *1995 Yearbook of American and Canadian Churches.*

	Congregations	Clergy	Members
All Orthodox	1,482	2,066	1,885,436
Orthodox Church in America	700	945	600,000
Armenian Diocese	72	70	414,000
Antiochian Archdioceses	178	350	350,000
Coptoic Church	85	68	180,000
Armenian Apostolic	32	27	150,000
Other (8 denominations)	415	606	191,346

PROTESTANTISM

Total membership in Protestant churches in the U.S. is approximately 101.4 million in 337,556 congregations. All told, about 220 Christian denominations exist in America. Twenty-one preach the Baptist faith, 14 the Methodist, 30 the Pentecostal, 14 the Lutheran, and four the Latter-Day Saints, according to the *1995 Yearbook of American and Canadian Churches.*

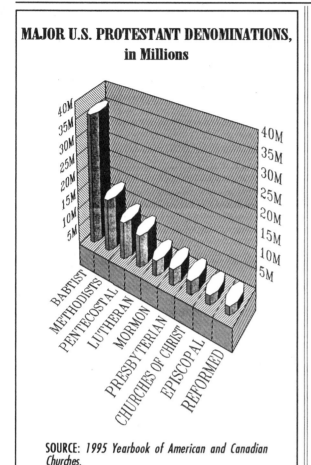

MAJOR U.S. PROTESTANT DENOMINATIONS, in Millions

SOURCE: *1995 Yearbook of American and Canadian Churches.*

The list below represents the largest Protestant denominations in the U.S. according to the yearbook.

Denomination	Membership
Baptist	36.4 million
Methodist	14.2 million
Pentecostal	10.3 million
Lutheran	8.3 million
Latter-Day Saints (Mormons)	4.7 million
Presbyterian	4.3 million
Churches of Christ	3.7 million
Episcopal	2.5 million
Reformed Churches	2.1 million

Among Baptist churches, the Southern Baptist Convention is the largest Protestant church in the country, with 15 million members. It has 37,922 local congregations and 124,316 clergy. Three of its churches—the National Baptist Convention, USA, Inc. (7.8 million members), the National Baptist Convention of America (7.8 million members), and the Progressive National Baptist Convention (2.7 million)—are predominately black churches. Together, the three black churches account for more black churchgoers than any other family of churches.

The United Methodist Church counts 8.9 million members, more than two-thirds of the family's total membership. Its two "African" churches with a total of 3.4 million members account for almost all of the remaining third of the group.

Because Pentecostal congregations tend to be small and many meet in storefronts or rented apartments, thousands of Pentecostal adherents are likely not to be counted in official records. Of its counted 9.9 million members, the Church of Christ in God, a predominately black church, is the largest with 5.5 million members. A second black Pentecostal church, United Pentecostal Church International, counts a 500,000 membership.

The cohesion of most Lutheran churches in America, once divided by language (German and Scandinavian, principally), custom, and theology, was brought about by the Evangelical Lutheran Church of America, which in the 1990s is made up of 11,087 local congregations, 17,402 clergy, and 5.2 million members, the largest in the denomination. The Lutheran Church-Missouri Synod, a conservative branch, is the only other sizable church in the group, with 2.6 million members.

Latter-Day Saints (Mormons) are located almost exclusively in Utah, but many adherents live in surrounding states. The Church of Jesus Christ of Latter-Day Saints is the bulk of the denomination, with 9,213 congregations, 31,059 clergy, and 4.3 million members. The Reorganized Church of Jesus Christ of Latter-Day Saints, headquartered in Independence, Mo., which the church's founder, Joseph Smith, had designated as the site of a great future temple, counts 9,213 congregations, 31,059 clergy, and 189,524 members.

Overall, in the matter of charity contributions and their allocation, churches were the prime beneficiary of all philanthropic monies given in 1992, benefiting by $56.7 billion of the total of $124 billion given by individuals, foundations, corporations, and charitable bequests.

RELIGIOUS ELITES

Despite a 33 percent drop in Presbyterian U.S.A. membership since 1960, a 29 percent loss of members in the Episcopal Church, and a 20 percent loss in United Church of Christ members, Protestants still cling to power in the U.S., forming what some scholars call a "post-Protestant age."

Episcopalians, in fact, are seven times more likely to be found in powerful positions than they are to be found in the general population, according to a study of religious affiliations listed in Who's Who in America editions of 1930 and 1992. Presbyterian and UCC members are three times as likely to be found in elite posts.

Ohio	131,000
Texas	107,000

Among other church groups studied by James D. Davidson, a sociologist of religion at Purdue University, Unitarian-Universalists—two groups that joined into one in 1953—took a large tumble in membership since 1960 yet hold a disproportionate number of positions for their 141,000-person membership, according to the study.

Underrepresented in the 1930 Who's Who, Jews are now six times more likely to be found among the elite compared to the general population, while synagogue membership grew only from 5.3 million in 1960 to six million in 1990. Catholic church membership rolls climbed from 41 million in 1960 to 59 million in 1991, but those gains were not reflected among the power elite in 1992, nor was the Mormon membership of 4.4 million, the study found.

RELIGIOUS ENCLAVES

Each Sunday (or Saturday), 147.5 million Americans—61 percent of the population—commune with some form of deity. Though no particular region in the U.S. has any particular affinity toward religion, some states have especially large concentrations of various faiths.

As one example, New York has almost two million Jews, as many as Israel did in 1970. Israel now has a population of approximately three million Jews. Utah is well-known to be bastion of Mormonism. Among Muslims, Detroit is known to be a major enclave of faithfuls to Mohammed.

The table below shows where most religiously affiliated Christians and Jews live, according to the Glenmary Research Center and *American Jewish Yearbook*.

TOP 10 CHRISTIAN STATES

State	Percent Christian	Number
Utah	75.0%	1,097,000
Rhode Island	75.0	710,000
North Dakota	73.8	482,000
South Dakota	66.9	462,000
Minnesota	64.9	2,644,000
Wisconsin	64.4	3,029,000
Massachusetts	64.0	3,669,000
Nebraska	63.1	990,000
Iowa	60.8	1,890,000
Connecticut	60.8	1,890,000

TOP 10 JEWISH STATES

State	Jewish Population
New York	1,844,000
California	909,000
Florida	585,000
New Jersey	411,000
Pennsylvania	346,000
Massachusetts	276,000
Illinois	258,000
Maryland	210,000

SMALL GROUP MOVEMENT

Seventy-two million Americans—67 percent of the nation's adult population—are engaged in five wings of a trendy movement that has no label, shuns publicity, limits its members, has few meeting places, and is backed by no one person or association, according to a Wuthnow/Gallup study.

Called "the small group movement," with most of its members churchgoers, it has a kinship to cottage prayer meetings and to evangelist John Wesley's class meetings in the 18th century, which usually met weekly and were later called "house churches." Going back to antiquity in religious history, some proponents liken the movement to the synagogue in Jewish culture, where 10 men with their families could form a synagogue.

Today small groups across the country are as diverse as they are disorganized, according to the Gallup survey taken with Robert Wuthnow, a *Christian Century* magazine editor at large. In addition to religion, they focus on literature and film, travel, exercise, current events, and help for psychological, physical, and emotional problems.

But far and away the largest in the category is religious, the survey shows. Religious groups cover the widest range of denominations, regions, social classes, and ethnicities, and make up 60 percent of the nation's small groups. Church-oriented cells include 800,000 Sunday-only meeting classes involving 18 to 22 million people, and 900,000 Bible-study groups involving 15 to 20 million people.

The magazine *Christianity Today*, reporting on the three-year Lilly Endowment-funded study, says revitalization of the old Christian movement is altering the landscape of the North American church. The magazine calls the movement pivotal to the church's sense of community, discipleship, evangelism, pastoral care, and the assimilation of newcomers.

Many church leaders agree, believing that much of the work of the church is best accomplished through a group, especially a small one.

But the definitions of "small" and "group" vary, according to *Christianity Today*. Some authorities say "small" is six or seven persons, others eight to 10, and others no more than 12. "Groups" are called "cell-church movements" by some and organized groups providing members with emotional and spiritual care by others.

George Gallup Jr., commenting on the three-year study, linked the resurgence of religious "cell" groups to turbulent social changes from the 1960s to the 1990s which, he says, have fragmented U.S. society. "If the 1960s represented the 'Movement Decade,' the 1970s the 'Me Decade,' and the 1980s the 'Empty Eighties,'" *Christianity Today* quotes him as saying, "then perhaps the 1990s will become known as "The Decade of Healing."

The list at right represents the prevelence of major small group movements in the U.S., in thousands of classes and millions of members; source, the Wuthnow/Gallup study:

Group	Number of groups	Number of people
Sunday church classes	800,000	18-22
Bible-study	900	15-20
Self-help	500	8-10
Political/current events	250	5-10
Sports/hobbyists	250	5-10

SEXUALITY AND GENDER
OVERVIEW

In the 1970s, America experienced two simultaneous phenomena: the sexual revolution and a new consciousness about the equality of the sexes.

Sometimes called the "golden age of sex," the 1970s catapulted researchers such as Alfred Kinsey and Masters and Johnson to almost celebrity status. Playboy's Hugh Hefner became a spokesman for the many pleasures of the flesh; Gloria Steinem, the harbinger of feminism.

In their wake, sexuality and equality of sexes became a prime topic in the media. With it followed scientific and sociological research into America's sexual practices that has allowed us to talk knowledgeably and rationally about birth control, sexually transmitted diseases, sexual abuse and assault, homosexuality, erotica, prostitution, and a whole host of formerly off-limits subjects. The copious data on these and other sex- and gender-related issues presented in this chapter is the "statistical aftermath" of it all.

Many social developments followed, most of which are detailed in the pages that follow. Among the many ramifications were that many once-alienated victims of past intolerances discovered they were not alone: homosexuals, lesbians, the abused and the casualties of oppressive sexism. Americans became aware that some "sexual problems," were also social problems. As a consequence, reports of abuse, discrimination, and harassment surfaced as never before. No one knows for sure if there was more of it before the reportage increased, but when it came out in the open, the American populace began to be educated about sex and gender issues, a learning experience never before afforded to so many.

In the '90s, education about these issues began to change attitudes. For example, without the gay rights movement that sprouted in the '70s, it would be extremely difficult to fully and openly address the issue of AIDS and provide widespread information about how to prevent or avoid it. But with AIDS came a backlash against homosexual tolerance and anti-gay legislation in a number of states.

The sexual revolution also is linked to the problems of teen pregnancy, especially the distressing rate of out-of-wedlock births among minority and inner-city women. The discussion about curbing it fostered programs that were once thought of as radical, including information on birth control that is aimed at young singles *who live with their parents*—an unthinkable situation in a previous era.

Though the pages that follow are merely the specific details behind everyday headlines, they would have had considerable shock value a few decades ago.

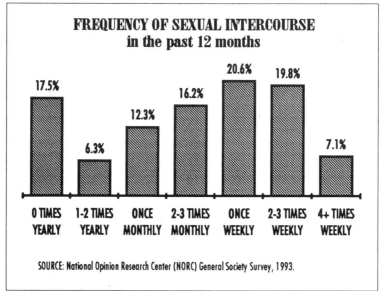

FREQUENCY OF SEXUAL INTERCOURSE in the past 12 months

- 0 TIMES YEARLY: 17.5%
- 1-2 TIMES YEARLY: 6.3%
- ONCE MONTHLY: 12.3%
- 2-3 TIMES MONTHLY: 16.2%
- ONCE WEEKLY: 20.6%
- 2-3 TIMES WEEKLY: 19.8%
- 4+ TIMES WEEKLY: 7.1%

SOURCE: National Opinion Research Center (NORC) General Society Survey, 1993.

ABUSE, SEXUAL AND OTHERWISE

One-fifth to 33 percent of all American women face physical abuse during their lifetime, with pregnancy being their most dangerous time, according to a 1933 report. Abuse occurs not only toward women, but toward men, elders, and children, and in gay and lesbian relationships. Overall, women are the most abused segment of the U.S. society.

Ten percent of cases of abused women require hospital treatment, either in emergency rooms or with hospital stays, according to Public Health Reports. Fifty percent of murdered women are killed by a current or former partner, and surveys in Texas and Kansas found that 34 to 85 percent of abuse calls were repeat offenses; 50 percent of the women were calling for help for at least the fifth time.

About 37 percent of abused women are carrying a child, and the abuse is directed mostly at the abdomen, with younger mothers-to-be the target more often than older pregnant women, PHR reports. Women commit 8 percent of all homicides in the country, but 51 percent of those are against a frequently abusive mate.

A report on gay-bashing by the Victim's Recovery Program at Fenway Community Center in Boston says that half of its phone calls from victims concern domestic violence, and suggests that power is as much an issue in domestic violence as gender.

A Boston study of 2,000 elderly persons showed that between 2.5 percent and 3.9 percent of the elderly interviewed were abused or neglected, either physically or emotionally. Projected nationwide, the study indicates that from 700,000 to more than one million elderly are abused or neglected in the U.S.

Most elderly abuse tends to be against the very old and the frail, and directed at those who live with an abuser who is financially dependent on the victim. Abusers of the elderly tend toward mental illness or alcoholism.

The "battered child syndrome," a designation for child abuse formally adopted by the medical profession in 1961, is on the increase in the U.S., with an estimated 2.4 million cases of suspected abuse, sexual abuse, and neglect reported to child protective agencies each year. That's more than quadruple the number of reports in 1980. Investigations in 1990 confirmed more than 1.5 million cases.

Studies among adults indicate that between 15 and 38 percent of women and about 10 percent of men report sexual victimization during childhood. As adults, however, a number of recovered accusers have recanted their memories of childhood abuse. As that number grows larger, the controversial subject of "False Memory Syndrome" is being studied by mental health experts.

The list atop the opposite column details substantiated child abuse cases, 1990-92; source, U.S. Department of Health and Human Services:

CHARACTERISTICS

	1990	1991	1992
Victims, total	801,143	819,922	918,263
Neglect	358,846	366,462	474,945
Physical abuse	205,057	206,057	212,281
Sexual abuse	127,853	129,425	129,982
Emotional maltreatment	47,673	46,334	48,929
Other, unknown	61,714	71,466	115,848

SEX OF VICTIM

	1990	1991	1992
Victims, total	775,596	816,223	951,312
Male	360,531	376,617	951,312
Female	409,286	434,729	498,952
Unknown	5,779	4,877	11,867

AGE OF VICTIM

	1990	1991	1992
Victims, total	788,338	813,057	950,333
1 year and younger	107,217	112,227	127,487
2 to 5 years	194,485	208,183	250,780
6 to 9 years	177,396	189,124	221,625
10 to 13 years	151,971	162,049	187,202
14 to 17 years	117,312	122,603	141,169
18 and over	7,184	6,327	8,009
Unknown	32,773	12,544	14,061

RACE, ETHNICITY OF VICTIM

	1990	1991	1992
Victims, total	775,409	818,527	952,620
White	424,470	454,059	525,399
Black	197,400	218,044	245,777
Hispanic	73,132	77,985	90,840
Asian, Pacific Islander	6,408	6,585	8,007
American Indian, Eskimo, Aleut	10,283	10,873	13,087
Other races	11,749	12,982	15,969
Unknown	51,967	37,999	53,541

ASSAULTS, SEXUAL

In addition to the humiliation and likely physical injury that women suffer from violent assaults, the attacks also lead many to alcoholism and substance abuse, according to a study by the National Crime Victims Research and Treatment Center at the Medical University of South Carolina. That in turn, sets up a cycle in which increased alcohol and drug use opens up the victims to being assaulted again, the survey of 4,008 women between the ages of 18 and 34 found.

Most of the women were interviewed twice, 75 percent of them one and two years after the initial interview. About one in 8 women in the first interview by phone of randomly selected households reported a rape prior to the interview; one in 10 cited violent attacks. Post-traumatic stress disorder was felt by 12 percent at some time in their lives, and by nearly five percent in the six months preceding the interview. Six percent of the interviewees had been alcohol-dependent during their lifetimes, and three percent in the prior year.

The study found that those who abstained from alcohol or drugs had fewer violent assaults during the two follow-ups than those who did not. The most new violent assaults were suffered by women who abused two or more drugs, and a history of violent assault and post-traumatic stress disorder were found more often in this group.

About nine percent of women in the study who had no history of alcohol abuse developed alcohol dependence after being assaulted. Women who developed stress disorders after the first interview also showed an increase of alcoholism.

BIRTH CONTROL

Some 41 percent of American women practice some form of birth control. Among American couples, approximately one third practice some form of contraception. The Guttmacher Institute, an organization that polls Americans concerning sexual behavior, reported in 1990 that a growing number of Americans voluntarily sterilize themselves—fully one-quarter of adults. In 1992, another survey commissioned by *Family Planning Perspectives*, called "Contraceptive Practices in the United States," reported that nearly 40 percent of couples have used sterilization; among them, 70 percent opt for female sterilization and 30 percent rely on vasectomies.

The increased incidence of sterilization among women can be attributed in some part to the aging of the female population—in the period from 1982 to 1988, the number of women aged 15 to 24 dropped by 1.5 million and those from 25 to 44 (the ones more likely to opt for non-reversible birth control methods) rose by nearly 5.4 million. The decline of the IUD, with its many potential dangers, also contributes to the higher number of women relying on sterilization.

The use of the pill, which declined in the late 1970s because of health concerns, has also become more popu'ar, due to its convenience and high rate of effectiveness. The condom, being the most effective method in guarding against sexually transmitted diseases (save abstinence), has increased in use rapidly among teenagers and single women, but the pill remains the method of choice for the younger set.

The list below cites the most common forms of contraception and the proportions of Americans who use them, according to the survey.

Method	Percent
Pill	34%
Condom	26
Sterilization	25
Diaphragm	6
Abstinence	2
Withdrawal	2
IUD	2
Foam	1
Other	2

CAESAREAN SECTIONS

Though the number of U.S. mothers receiving caesarean sections has declined slightly from a high of 24.7 percent in 1988, when doctors first got the mes-

sage that most C-sections were unnecessary, the word has not reached the South, according to Ralph Nader's Public Citizens' Health Research Group.

Nationally the rate for the nation's most common surgery six years later had declined a fraction over two percent, to 22.6 percent, compared to the 15 percent recommended by the Centers for Disease Control and Prevention, according to a CHRG study. In the South, C-sections range from a low of 22.3 percent of all births in Georgia to 28.4 percent in Arkansas. The rate was 5.5 in 1970, when caesareans were used chiefly in emergencies, the Nader group reported at the time.

Conventional wisdom has held that a woman who has had a caesarean must have subsequent babies by the same method. Though that notion is giving way to the medical recommendation that subsequent births should be delivered vaginally, in a method called VBAC (vaginal birth after caesarean), the South has fewer vaginal births after caesarean than the rest of the country. The U.S. average of VBAC births is 25.7 percent nationally for women who have had a C-section, while the South's average ranges from 23.6 percent in North Carolina to 10.9 percent in Louisiana, the study shows.

The five highest rates in the nation for C-sections were posted by Arkansas (28.4 percent), Louisiana (28.2 percent), Mississippi (27.7 percent), Texas (27 percent), and West Virginia (26.3 percent). The lowest C-section rates in the U.S., all under 18 percent, were in Colorado, Alaska, Minnesota, Idaho, Wisconsin, and Washington.

The Group points out that C-sections, though sometimes needed to save a baby's or a mother's life, add risk to the mother and costs $3,100 more than a vaginal delivery—$1.3 billion overall in 1990. The higher cost can be an incentive for doctors to recommend the procedure, and they are easier for the doctor to do, reduce the risk of lawsuits, and can be scheduled during day hours.

The study, which surveyed four million births from 1992, found that women with private insurance have the highest rate of C-sections. HMO members are next, followed by those with Medicaid, and then the self-paid.

Below is the percent of caesareans and VBAC births in the South in 1992 from Public Citizen Health Research Group statistics:

State	Caesarean	VBAC
Alabama	25.1%	17.5%
Arkansas	28.4	14.7
Florida	24.7	21.0
Georgia	22.3	20.5
Kentucky	24.3	16.1
Louisiana	28.2	10.9
Mississippi	27.7	13.5
North Carolina	22.8	23.6
South Carolina	23.4	18.1
Tennessee	23.4	19.0
Texas	27.0	13.6

Virginia	23.4	23.0
West Virginia	26.3	15.3

CONDOMS

Failure of condoms is not consistent across user groups, according to many studies on the subject of safe sex. Failure rates are highest among blacks and lowest among white men with high incomes.

Among studies of condom slippage and breakage, a *Consumer Reports* survey showed breakage rates of 0.6 percent during vaginal intercourse and 0.1 percent during anal intercourse, both at the low end of other reported clinical trials. A 1992 report published in *Family Planning Perspectives* said that among 70 couples using 405 condoms, 1.7 percent of the condoms broke during use, and 12.8 percent slipped off either during coitus or during withdrawal.

In that study, breakage and slippage rates for two brands of condoms, one twice as thick as the other, showed little difference, nor did normal applications of lubrication. When additional lubricant was used, however, the slippage rate reached 17 percent, compared to .6 percent when no additional lubricant was used.

The effect of personal characteristics on condom failure was measured in another study published in the magazine one year later. It found a breakage rate of 3.7 percent and a slippage rate of 3.5 percent. Age and race had no effect on the risk of condom failure, according to the study.

Slippage and breakage rates of 2.7 percent during intercourse were found in a 1991 national survey of 3,321 men aged 20 to 39, the ages when men are most subject to HIV-infection, according to authors William R. Grady and Koray Tanfer of the Battelle Centers for Public Health Research and Evaluation. Their findings were published in *Family Planning Perspectives* in 1994.

Blacks had a per-person breakage rate five times higher than men of other races, at 8.3 percent vs. 1.6 percent. The slippage rate was four times higher, 7.6 percent vs. 1.8 percent.

Men with an annual income of less than $10,000 were found to have a breakage rate of 5.8 percent, against one to 1.8 percent of men with higher incomes. The slippage rate also was higher, at 3.5 percent against 2.6 percent, for those earning between $10,000 and $20,000, and 1.5 percent for those earning $20,000-$40,000. Above $40,000, the breakage rate was the lowest of any group, at one percent, but the slippage rate of 3.2 percent almost equaled that for men earning below $10,000.

Users of non-spermicidal-lubricated condoms showed a higher breakage rate, at 3.2 percent, than those who used a spermicidal lubricant (1.3 percent) or no lubricant (0.9 percent). Men who stated no preference showed a breakage rate of 3.2 percent and a slippage rate of 3.3 percent.

Six percent of the survey participants who had two or more partners in the four weeks before his interview

Despite its location amid Chicago's singles bars on Division Street, this condom shop didn't last. The seemingly good idea of a store specializing in safe-sex paraphernalia has also failed to catch on elsewhere.

reported breakage rates of 11.5 percent, vs. 2.2 percent who had one partner; the slippage rate was 7.4 percent, vs. 2.8 percent.

Below are facts and figures on men aged 20 to 39 who used condoms in the six months before the survey, and percentage reporting breakage and slippage, according to National Survey of Men statistics:

Demographic	% in Survey	Breaks	Slips
Blacks	15.5%	8.3%	7.6%
Hispanics	12.3	2.4	3.8
Age 25 and under	34.5	3.6	2.1
Age 25-29	26.7	2.3	2.1
30-34	21.8	1.7	3.2
35 and over	16.9	2.4	4.1
Never married	52.2	3.0	2.5
Married	37.1	2.2	2.4
Formerly married	10.7	2.8	4.2
Non-HS grad	7.4	3.6	3.7
HS grad	41.0	2.6	2.9
HS-plus	51.5	2.5	2.3
$10,000-minus income	24.5	5.8	3.5
$10,000-$20,000	29.7	1.8	2.6
$20,000-$40,000	32.9	1.5	1.5
$40,000-plus	12.9	1.0	3.2
Catholic	35.6	1.8	1.9
Conservative Protestant	14.4	3.4	4.8
Other Protestant	32.0	3.4	4.8
Other/none	18.0	4.1	3.1
ALL CONDOMS USED*			
1-9	47.4	3.7	3.3
10-19	19.4	1.7	2.5

20-plus	33.2	1.7	1.9
USAGE FOR*			
Contraception	43.8	2.2	2.3
AIDS Prevention	8.6	2.8	3.4
Both	43.9	3.2	3.1
Neither	3.7	0.7	0.4
USAGE FOR VAGINAL INTERCOURSE **			
0	32.0	1.9	1.5
1	62.0	2.2	2.8
2-plus	6.0	11.5	7.4
USAGE FOR ANAL INTERCOURSE **			
Yes	11.1	5.0	7.0
No	88.9	2.9	2.2
PREFERENCES BY TYPES			
Spermicidal	10.8	1.3	3.2
Non-spermicidal	62.2	3.2	2.7
None	13.7	0.9	1.7
No preference	13.4	3.2	3.3
NON-LATEX			
Yes	5.9	1.8	2.0
No	94.1	2.7	2.7
RIBBING			
Yes	13.4	3.3	1.4
No	86.6	2.6	2.9
RESERVOIR TIP			
Yes	44.4	2.0	1.7
No	55.6	3.2	3.4

* Used in the last six months.

** Used in the last four weeks.

FERTILITY RATES

Women in the U.S. have far fewer children than those in other countries. The average American woman will have 1.9 children, well below the world average of 3.3. The highest fertility rates are in Africa, where women have an average of 5.1 children; the lowest in Western Europe, where the rate is 1.6 children per woman. Throughout the world, 80 percent of women bear children. In America, however, only 60 percent give birth. That's a decline from 1976, when the figure was 65 percent. By 1988, only 62 percent of American women were mothers.

The list below, compiled by the National Center for Health Statistics, represents the proportions of American women in different categories who will have a child in a given year.

Black	94 in 1,000
Hispanic	87 in 1,000
White	66 in 1,000

The list below represents the odds that a first birth will take place during various age periods in a woman's life.

Under 20	1 in 4
20--24	1 in 3
25--29	1 in 4
30--34	1 in 8
35+	1 in 25

CRIMINALS AND GENDER

Of the slightly more than 11 million Americans arrested annually, nine million (82 percent) are men, and two million (18 percent) are women. Just what is it that makes the criminal populace overwhelmingly male? Considering that crime costs the American public $300 billion annually, an explanation might prove cost-effective. Every imaginable academic discipline, from economics to psychoanalysis, offers answers. Recently, a related question has been raised: Should both sexes pay equally for the sins of criminals when they are so overwhelmingly male?

The list below represents the proportions of males vs. females who are arrested for various offenses in the U.S., according to the Department of Justice.

	Male	Female
Illegally possessing a weapon	93%	7%
Burglary	91	9
Robbery	91	9
Murder, manslaughter	90	10
Drunken driving	87	13
Arson	87	13
Aggravated assault	86	14

EROTICA CONSUMPTION

Sales of erotic paraphernalia in America are booming as men and women, young and old, try to escape the pandemic of sexually transmitted diseases (STDs) and still keep the joys of sex alive.

In 1993, STDs other than the AIDS virus were found in a nationwide survey by the Alan Guttmacher Institute to infect one in five sexually active persons in the country. An estimated four million new infections occur annually, according to the Centers for Disease Control.

Safe-sex erotic books and magazines are two of the beneficiaries of the boom, such as the magazine *Future Sex*, which features hard-core sex articles along with news of high technology in the erotic field. Launched in 1992, the magazine reports its circulation rose from 10,000 to 40,000 in one year.

A trade-interest journal, *Romantic Times*, reports the when it was started in 1981, romantic novels constituted 30 percent of all paperback sales. In 1993 they were 47 percent of the market. Sales at Condomania, a California-based chain of sex paraphernalia and erotic novelty stores that stretches from New York City to Los Angeles and sells hundreds of different condoms from around the world, are growing at 10 percent to 12 percent a year, according to Rubba Corporation, which owns the stores.

Rubba officials were surprised to find that most of their customers were women. Eighty to 85 percent of heterosexual men do not use condoms, the firm discovered, and the women were buying them for their partners who do use them.

According to surveys conducted by the Institute for the Advanced Study of Human Sexuality in San Francisco, single adults, who have 25 to 40 percent less sex than married persons, have to play the field and thus must to be more alert to protect themselves from STDs.

HOMOSEXUAL BOOKSTORES

At the time of the 1969 Stonewall riots in New York City, when gay men and lesbians rebelled against discrimination and began demanding equal rights and treatment, there was only one gay and lesbian bookstore in the U.S. In 1970 the first strictly lesbian bookstore in the country opened in Minneapolis.

By 1994 there were at least 45 gay and lesbian bookstores in the U.S., and 140 feminist bookstores in the U.S. and Canada, 98 of which had opened within the last 16 months. Feminist bookshops sell 40 to 60 percent of all lesbian books sold in America, according to *Feminist Bookstore News.*

The American Booksellers Association financial survey for 1993, which gives the norm of $290 as the average sales per square foot for general bookstores, and $283 for specialty shops, found that in 1993 the average for gay and lesbian stores was $455. An FBN survey was lower, but still above the ABA norm—gross sales of $356,569, and average sales per square foot of $296.

Well-known feminist bookshops fare much better, according to the ABA survey. In 1993, Lambda Rising reached $2.3 million in sales at its 1,750-square-foot store in Washington, D.C., for an average of $1,143 per square foot, plus $1.3 million from two of its other locations.

A Different Light, with locations in West Hollywood, San Francisco, and New York City totaling 4,200 square feet in 1993, grossed almost $4 million—up from $3.8 million the year before— for an average of $941 per square foot. In 1994 the New York City store was relocated to a 5,000-square-foot site in the Chelsea section, which A Different Light co-owner Norman Laurila calls the world's largest gay and lesbian bookstore.

In 1992 Laurila became the first gay or lesbian bookstore owner to be elected to the ABA's board of directors.

HOMOSEXUAL LIBRARIES

Along with proliferating sales of gay and lesbian literature in the bookstores that cater to the homosexual community is an increasing number of special collections of gay and lesbian material in North America and Canada.

There are 115 gay and lesbian special collections in North America, including 13 in Canada, one in Mexico, and 31 in scholarly institutions. That number was

With the stigma of homosexuality diminishing many gays are literally parading openly at events such as this "Gay Liberation Parade," an annual event in many cities throughout the U.S.

crowned in 1995 by the literature's first permanent home in a public institution: the Gay and Lesbian Center of the new main library of San Francisco. According to the Library Foundation of San Francisco, the center will house the largest collection of homosexual literature, film, and history in the world.

A 1994 survey shows that the Northeast houses the most gay and lesbian-operated archives and libraries in the U.S. Of the 20 in the area, New York City has seven. The West is next with 15, with San Francisco, the movement's symbolic home, housing five.

Twelve of the collections in scholarly institutions are located in the San Francisco area. The Northeast has with 10, according to a survey taken by the Gay and Lesbian Task Force of the American Library Association.

Below are the numbers of special collections of gay and lesbian material in the U.S., Canada, and Mexico, by sections, compiled by the Gay and Lesbian Task Force of the American Library Association:

Section	Number
Northeast	20
West	15
Canada	14
Southeast	13
Midwest	11

Southwest	7
Northwest	3
Mexico	1

COLLECTIONS IN SCHOLARLY INSTITUTIONS

West	12
Northeast	10
Midwest	10
South	2

HOMOSEXUAL MALES

Zoologist Alfred Kinsey was wrong in his 1948 report, which claimed that 10 percent of the U.S. population had flirted with homosexuality and four percent were lifelong homosexuals, according to surveys of what researchers say is one of the least-researched areas of human behavior.

The 1993 survey of 3,321 men between the ages of 20 and 39, on male sexual behavior, was financed by the National Institute of Child Health and Human Development, and conducted at the Battelle Human Affairs Research Center in Seattle. It was released by the Alan Guttmacher Institute in New York City. The survey found that two percent of American men and one percent of American women had tried gay sex, and only one percent of men and 0.5 percent of women were exclusively homosexual.

It determined that the number of men reporting sex with other men during the previous decade could be as low as 1.8 percent and as high as 2.8 percent, and the percentage of men reporting exclusively homosexual activity in the previous year could be as low as .7 percent and as high as 1.5 percent.

The conclusion closely agrees with a continuing survey concerning AIDS knowledge and attitudes conducted by the U.S. Census Bureau among 10,000 subjects since 1988. That survey had estimated that as of 1994 only two percent of American men have experienced gay sex, and one percent of women, for a mean of 1.5 percent for the general population.

Recent surveys using large samples from Canada, Britain, France, Norway, and Denmark support the Battelle survey, as do a series of surveys extending over four years by researchers at the University of Chicago. The Chicago survey of 1,537 adults found that of sexually active adults over age 18, 1.2 percent of males and females reported homosexual activity in the year preceding the survey. A total of 4.9 percent to 5.6 percent of both sexes had partners of both genders, and 0.6 percent to 0.7 percent exclusively homosexual partners.

The journal *Society* says the U.S. Center for Disease Control and Prevention has stopped using the Kinsey Report data for national projections.

Atop the opposite column are results from U.S., Canadian, and selected Western Europe nation surveys on prevalence of homosexuality, percent of men and women who had had a homosexual experience, gathered by Paul Cameron and

Kirk Cameron for their report *The Prevalence of Homosexuality*.

EXPERIENCED HOMOSEXUALITY

Country	Men	Women
United States	2.0%	1.0%
France	1.4	0.4
Britain	1.4	N.A
Canada (college students)	1.0	N.A
Norway	3.5	3.0
Denmark	2.7	N.A.

LIFETIME HOMOSEXUALS

Country	Men	Women
United States	1.0%	0.5%
France	0.7	0.6
Canada (college students)	1.0	N.A
Norway	0.9	0.9
Denmark	0.0-1.0	N.A.

HOMOSEXUAL PARENTS

Contrary to popular notions that gay parents groom their children to become gay, according to several studies neither the absence of a father nor the presence of homosexual parents unduly interferes with a child's emotional development.

In one study of 55 homosexual or bisexual fathers of 82 sons age 17 or older, 75 of whom were studied, just seven of the boys self-rated themselves as homosexual or bisexual. The nine percent rate in this study by J. Michael Bailey of Northwestern University exceeds the two percent to five percent rate of homosexuality thought to occur in Western societies, according to the study.

Healthy emotional and behavioral adjustments to their parents were found equivalent in three- to nine-year-old children of 15 lesbian couples and 15 heterosexual couples in a second study by psychologist David K. Flaks of St. Francis Medical Center in Trenton, New Jersey. The results were the same in a third study of 26 lesbian couples with four- to nine-year-old children by psychologist Charlotte J. Patterson of the University of Virginia, who found the children's psychological health similar to children of 11 heterosexual couples with the same backgrounds and incomes.

HOMOSEXUALS, INCOME

Undoubtedly, gay activists are disappointed that the most recent estimates of the gay population are lower than expected, but qualitatively, gay demographics are above-average. For example, according to a U.S. Census Bureau report released in 1993, 40 percent of the partners of homosexual couples have college degrees, compared to just 13 percent for heterosexual spouses.

The Homosexual Income Advantage: Gay male couples have higher incomes than any other co-habiting group, according to the Census Bureau report. One reason is that homosexual couples are more likely to have two working partners than are heterosexual ones, and gays are also more likely to live in big cities, where salaries are higher.

Furthermore, male homosexual live-in partners, which represent 56 percent of homosexual couples, have the advantage of the income gender gap. According to the Bureau of Labor Statistics, women's earnings nationwide are just 75 percent of men's. When sexual orientation and living status are taken into account, male homosexual partners have the highest annual average household incomes: $56,863. Households of unmarried heterosexuals have the lowest: $37,602. According to a poll of 1,000 adults age 25 and over conducted by the Wirthin Group, 46 percent of singles and 30 percent of married couples say homosexuals should have that right.

The list below represents a comparison of the average annual household incomes of heterosexuals and homosexuals, according to a 1993 Census report.

Married heterosexuals	$47,012
Unmarried heterosexuals	37,602
Male homosexuals	56,863
Female homosexuals	44,793

INTERCOURSE, SEXUAL

Some 150 million Americans (88 percent of adults) engage in sexual intercourse at least once each year. The average frequency is 57 times annually. Women have intercourse an average of 51 times annually, men, 66 times.

Some 85 percent of adults have participated in oral sex; 24 percent have participated in interracial sex, and 31 percent have had intercourse in public places.

The following list represents various situations involving sexual intercourse among American men and women. (The figures do not total 100 percent because of the variance in groups surveyed and multiple answers.) Sources: National Center for Health Statistics; Alfred Kinsey Report; *Singles, the New Americans*, by Jacqueline Simenauer and David Carroll.

ADULT PREFERENCES

With spouse	80%
With lights off	62
Missionary position	61
Woman on top	26

FOR FEMALES

Have any orgasm	92
Premarital	72
Before age 20	67
Regular orgasms	60
Orgasms while penetrated	37
Virgins	32
Anal penetration	32

FOR MALES

Premarital	81

Before age 20	78
Performed cunnilingus	76
Sex with prostitute	4
Virgins	29

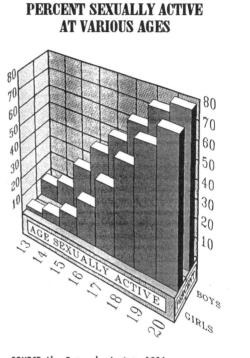

PERCENT SEXUALLY ACTIVE AT VARIOUS AGES

SOURCE: Alan Guttmacher Institute, 1994.

LESBIANS

Twenty-five years after the Stonewall Inn protest movement in New York City that launched the gay-rights movement, most women who have had lesbian sexual experiences do not proclaim themselves gay, a 1994 study by the University of Chicago indicates. Of 3,432 Americans surveyed, 8.6 percent of the women participants reported homosexual activity or desire, but only 1.4 percent identified themselves as lesbians.

Seven and a half percent of the women reported having felt same-sex desire, but only 3.5 percent reported consummation of the desire at least once since puberty, according to the study, *The Social Organization of Sexuality.*

In the 100 largest American cities, openly lesbian women amounted to 4.1 percent of the population; in the suburbs of 12 of those cities, the lesbian population totaled 1.2 percent.

College graduates and women with some college were most likely to report lesbian activity: 2.5 percent of college graduates and 1.1 percent women with some college did so. Professed gay men and lesbian women with less than high school education were more active than those with a high school education, 3.1 percent of such men and 0.9 percent of the women being active, compared to 1.4 percent and 0.8 percent of those with more education.

The Census Bureau keeps no count of the number of men and women homosexuals in the U.S. nor of those who head families, and the Bureau would need the approval of Congress to include such counts in the year 2000 census.

Lesbians in the U.S., in percent; source: *The Social Organization of Society* (University of Chicago Press).

CHARACTERISTICS	
Total reporting	8.6%
Self-identified	1.4
Felt desire	7.5
LOCATION	
12 largest cities	2.1%
Next 88 largest	2.0
Suburbs	2.0
Rural	0.6
EDUCATION	
College graduate	2.5
Some college	1.1
High school graduate	0.8
Less than high school	0.9

MALE IMPOTENCE

More than a million American males currently are being treated for sexual impotence, many of them relatively young. In addition to those who have been diagnosed as impotent, an estimated 30 million men have problems getting or maintaining an erection.

The most common treatment for impotence is self-injection with an erection-producing drug, which is used by about a million sufferers. Another 30,000 use a vacuum device to achieve an erection, while 20,000 choose penile implants. Researchers have found that the number of men seeking some form of treatment has increased five-fold in the last few years.

Twenty years ago, doctors thought impotence was caused by psychological problems in 95 percent of cases. Sleep research that monitors the penis has proved otherwise. Erections during sleep are natural in men. The average male's penis, even for many who claim to be impotent, is erect during periods of dreaming for about three hours each night, as the penis is filled with oxygen-rich blood. Only a small number of men cannot achieve an erection during sleep, usually the result of a vascular problem. Half the males who have undergone coronary bypass surgery are impotent.

According to Dr. Erwin Goldstein, a urologist at the Boston University School of Medicine and the author of *The Potent Male*, other reasons for impotence include the following:

- Many drugs used to treat heart disease interfere with blood flow, prohibiting erections.

- Smoking, lack of exercise, sleep deprivation, sexual abstinence, diabetes, and injuries prevent oxygen from reaching the penis.

- Diabetes or prostate surgery may cause nerve damage.

- Hormone imbalances and steroid overdoses can cause impotence.

MALE SEXUALITY

One of the most comprehensive surveys yet of male sexual behavior has found that the typical male under 40 years of age has had a total of seven sex partners and has both received and performed oral sex, though not nearly as often as he has had intercourse. Anal sex proved to be less common: 20 percent have tried it, most commonly with a woman.

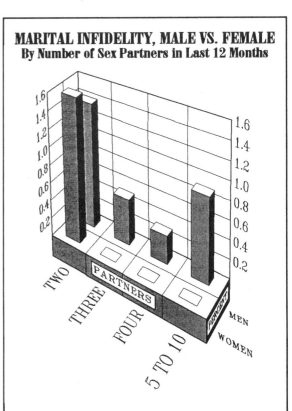

MARITAL INFIDELITY, MALE VS. FEMALE
By Number of Sex Partners in Last 12 Months

Married men report having more than two sex partners as shown above, while none of the women surveyed reported more than two. Who is being honest is unknown.

SOURCE: National Opinion Research Center (NORC), General Society Survey, 1993.

This $1.8 million study, funded by the federal government and conducted by the Battelle Human Affairs Research Center in Seattle in 1991, interviewed 3,321 men nationally age 20 to 39. It also found that:

- 23 percent of bachelors have had more than 20 partners in their lives.

- The typical married man has sex five times a month and does not cheat on his wife. He has had four other partners in his life.

- 75 percent of white males both perform and receive oral sex; only 43 percent of black men perform it, while 66 percent receive it.

- Anal sex has been practiced by 20 percent, but fewer practice it regularly.

- Anal sex is a mainly heterosexual activity; 90 percent who engaged in the act performed it the first time with a woman; 50 percent have done it with just one person, and 20 percent with more than four.

- Condoms are used by 50 percent of gay men.

- 75 percent agree that using condoms "shows you are a caring person"; the same number agree that condoms reduce sensation, while 27 percent admit they are embarrassed to buy them.

MALE VS. FEMALE MANAGEMENT STYLES

Women business owners show a distinct management style that differs from that of men according to a 1994 survey by the National Foundation for Women Business Owners. The study also concluded that both styles work equally well.

Thirty percent of women seek help from professional financial advisers in running their businesses, almost three times the number of men, according to the survey of 127 men and women entrepreneurs in six cities. This is in spite of the fact uncovered in the poll that 53 percent of women business owners emphasize intuitive thinking—creativity and sensitivity—in their management styles.

Seventy-one percent of men stress logical thinking, emphasizing analysis, disciplined processing of information, and development of procedures for getting the work out. Thirty-three percent of men turn to other business owners when they seek advice, and only 12 percent seek the help of financial advisers.

Women think in terms of networking and running their businesses like they would run a family, while men like to build hierarchies and establish strict company rules. Women found a man's ability to delegate tasks most admirable, while men admired women's skill in balancing priorities.

Below are the numbers on the business management gender gap, according to the NFWBO survey:

Seek advice from	Men	Women
Business owners	33%	42 %
Relatives	21	24
Financial advisers	12	30
Lawyers	18	24
Friends	13	20

MARRIAGE

Nearly a quarter of all adults—22.6 percent—have never been married, according to the Census Bureau, and the odds an individual will marry in the near future are dropping. The number of Americans over age 18 who have never taken a stroll down the aisle is 41 million, almost double the 21 million of 1970.

Some 72 percent of the adult population was married in 1970, but only 61 percent in 1991, according to the Census Bureau. It found that the median age for marrying is also rising. Today the median is 24, up from 21 in 1970. For men, the median age is 26 years, up from 23 in 1970. For women, the median age is 24, up from 21 in 1970. Today's median age at marriage for all adults is about the same as it was at the turn of the century, hence the trend toward getting married earlier in life has reversed itself.

Other significant changes in marriage trends, according to the Census Bureau, are as follows.

Status	1970	1991
Married	71.7%	61.4%
Never Married	16.2	22.6
Divorced	3.2	8.6
Widowed	9.0	0.4

The list below details the racial backgrounds of those individuals who have never married, according to the Census Bureau.

Race	1970	1980	1991
White	15.6	18.9	20.5
Black	20.6	30.5	37.1
Hispanic	18.6	24.1	27.3

One reason marriages are on the decline is the increasing incidence—and acceptability—of couples co-habiting. Twenty years ago, about 10 percent of adults lived with an unmarried mate before their first marriage. Today nine in 20— almost half—do. The younger a woman is, the more likely she is to live with her male lover. Among unmarried women born in the 1940s, three percent have lived with an unmarried male. Among women born in the 1960s, approximately one third will co-habitate.

PROSTITUTION

Each year about 100,000 individuals are arrested for prostitution or "commercial vice," according to the FBI's *Uniform Crime Reports*. One of every three prostitution arrests is of a man. Among women, who account for two in three prostitution-related arrests, one in 82 was under 18.

Taking a lead from the film *Indecent Proposal*, in which Robert Redford's character offered a man $1 million if the man would let Redford make love to his wife, *Men's Health* magazine conducted a survey of 3,000 men and women, which showed that nearly three

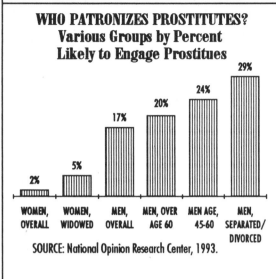

WHO PATRONIZES PROSTITUTES?
Various Groups by Percent
Likely to Engage Prostitues

2% WOMEN, OVERALL
5% WOMEN, WIDOWED
17% MEN, OVERALL
20% MEN, OVER AGE 60
24% MEN AGE 45-60
29% MEN, SEPARATED/DIVORCED

SOURCE: National Opinion Research Center, 1993.

Fathers or stepfathers	11
Boyfriends or ex-boyfriends	11
Husbands or ex-husbands	9
Refused to answer or were unsure	3

Other findings were as follows:

- Of 12.1 million women raped, 6.8 million were raped once and 4.7 million more than once; 600,000 were unsure of the number of times.

- Only 16 percent reported the crime to police; 69 percent feared being blamed for somehow causing the rape.

- About 66 percent said they would have reported the crime if there were a law prohibiting the media from disclosing their identity.

The courts are tougher on robbers than rapists. For six months a Senate Judiciary Committee compiled federal and state records on rapes and their aftermath. The panel also interviewed workers in rape crisis centers in 12 states. Experts on sexual assault and family violence appeared before the committee as well. Their

out of four male respondents said they would offer their services for only $100. Women asked a higher price for their favors: 82 percent wanted $1,000; nine percent, $500; nine percent, $100; and just one percent $50. Among the men, three percent would sell themselves for $50, 71 percent for $100, one percent for $500, and 26 percent for $1,000.

Despite the obvious dangers, one in three men admit to having had sex with a prostitute. Meeting men in bars is the most common way female prostitutes obtain clients. An increasingly frequent practice is to use classified ads. According to the noted sex researchers Masters and Johnson, women who run ads for sexual solicitation (for either fun or money) receive an average of 49 calls per ad. Men who advertise average 15 calls.

RAPE

Interviews with 4,000 women across the country revealed that 683,000 U.S. women were raped in 1990, and that 12.1 million adult women had been raped at least once in their lives. The government-funded study was performed in 1990 and released in 1993 by the National Victim Center and the Crime Victims Research and Treatment Center of the Medical University of South Carolina. About 62 percent of the victims said they were attacked when they were minors, with about 29 percent of that group saying they were 10 or younger at the time.

The list below represents the relationships of the victims and the offenders by percentage of cases, according to the study:

Relationship	Percent
Neighbors/friends	29%
Strangers	22
Relatives (other than immediate family)	16

Though almost eight in ten rapes are committed by relatives or acquaintances of the victim, bicycle patrols such as this one on Chicago's lake front have added a sense of security to public parks in major American cities.

conclusion: judges, prosecutors, and police throw up roadblocks to rape accusers and show too much leniency to those convicted.

Persons standing trial for murder or robbery are much more likely to be convicted than those accused of rape: Accused murderers face a conviction rate of 69 percent, robbers 61 percent, and rapists 46 percent. Of those ultimately convicted of rape, 25 percent are released on probation and *never serve prison time.* Only two percent of rape victims will ever see their attackers imprisoned.

RAPE, IN THE MILITARY

With men and women in the U.S. military now doing some of the same jobs and living in closer quarters than ever before, more Naval women are reporting assaults or are showing a heightened sensitivity about date rape.

Despite cuts in the number of sailors, rape is on the rise on navy ships and at bases around the world. In contrast, the incidence has decreased in the Army and Air Force. Documents obtained under the Freedom of Information Act and published by the *Orange County* (Calif.) *Register* show that rapes nearly tripled in the military in the last five years, and most rapists and victims were Navy personnel. This compares to a 10 percent increase in the general population, from 90,000 in 1987 to a little over 100,000 in 1992, according to the Justice Department.

Among other Naval findings:

- 46 alleged rapes took place in 1987, 134 in 1990, and 130 in 1991.

- 495 cases of reported rapes are "closed" due to charges being unsubstantiated or found false.

- 299 cases were "unresolved" after five years because no witnesses were found or there was no evidence.

SEXUAL PRACTICES

Monogamy is on the minds and in the hearts of a majority of Americans, according *The Social Organization of Sexuality: Sexual Practices in the United States*, a broad survey on the sexual activities of the average man and women in the U.S., which was released in 1994. Below are some of the issues the survey addressed and the findings:

Partners: The majority of respondents, 82 percent, had one partner or no partners in the preceding 12 months. Three percent had at least five partners in that time, 10 percent had a "one-night stand," and five percent had sex with a stranger. Fifty-three percent of those surveyed said they had had only one partner over the past five years. An additional 26 percent had had two to four partners, nine percent five to 10 partners, and four percent 11 or more; 12 percent of the men having five to 10 partners, and six percent of women. Eight percent of men and two percent of women reported having had 11 or more partners.

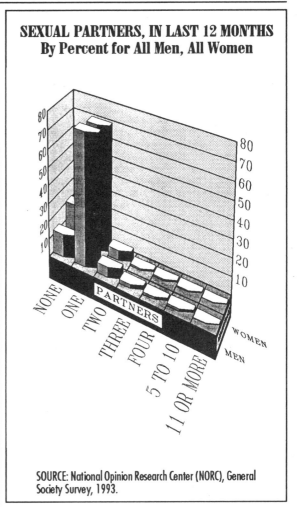

SEXUAL PARTNERS, IN LAST 12 MONTHS By Percent for All Men, All Women

SOURCE: National Opinion Research Center (NORC), General Society Survey, 1993.

"The first time:" Ninety-two percent of the men and 71 percent of the women said their first act of intercourse was voluntary. Of the 29 percent of women who did not desire sex in their first experience, four percent said they were forced to have intercourse. Eight percent of men responded similarly. Sixty-eight percent of the men initiated their first intercourse with someone they knew well, 37 percent with women they did not love, and 31 percent with women they loved. Seventy-five percent of the women had their first sexual experience with someone they loved, 53 percent with a premarital partner, and 22 percent with their spouse.

Religion: Twenty percent of the respondents who said religion had helped shape their sexual behavior had had no partners in the past year. Thirty percent had had just one partner since age 18, compared to 22 percent for the other respondents.

Contraception: Fifty-three percent of the men and 47 percent of the women said that over the past year they had always practiced contraception with their primary partner. Among 18- to 39-year-old women, 56 to 59 percent reported always using a method, while 62 percent of those aged 18 to 24 always used contraceptives, as did 39 percent of those age 30 to 34.

Sexually transmitted diseases: Eighty-three percent of the respondents reported never having had a sexually transmitted disease, and of the 17 percent who had, the most commonly reported were gonorrhea (seven percent), genital warts (five percent), and herpes, inflammation of the urethra, or pelvic inflammation disease (two percent).

AIDs-related behavior: Twenty-seven percent of the respondent had at some time been tested for HIV, the precursor to AIDS, the highest number being those with at least one homosexual partner in the last five years (65 percent), followed by those with 11 to 20 or more than 20 in the past five years (52 percent and 58 percent, respectively,) and those with more than 20 partners since age 18 (42 percent).

Thirty percent of those polled said the AIDS epidemic had changed their sexual behavior, including 35 percent of the men, 43 percent of those in the 18-24 age group, 45 percent of blacks, 52 percent of the never-married, 67 percent of those with five or more partners in the past five years, 68 to 77 percent of those with two or more partners in the past year, and 67 percent of those with at least one homosexual partner in the last five years.

Based on another study, "Sex in America" conducted by the University of Chicago and released in 1995, more findings on the sexual practices of Americans reveal the following.

- Americans are for the most part monogamous; 83 percent have one or zero sexual partners per year. During the course of a lifetime, a typical woman has two partners; men have six.

- Married couples have the most sex: 40 percent of married couples and 56 percent of those living together have intercourse twice a week.

- Opposites don't attract all that often: 93 percent marry the same race; 78 percent marry within 5 years in age; 82 percent have similar educations; 72 percent have the same religion.

- The study is a hands-down endorsement of marriage: 88 percent of spouses enjoy great sexual pleasure, 85 percent enjoy great emotional satisfaction; only 24.5 percent of males have been unfaithful, while 15 percent of women have. And in 1993, 94 percent of married people were faithful.

- Seventy-five percent of men always have an orgasm during sex, while 29 percent of the women do.

- Most sexual encounters last between 15 minutes and an hour; 20 percent of men and 15 percent of women spend over an hour. Married men are five times more likey than single men to spend 15 minutes or less on sexual intercourse.

- The top four turn-ons: 1) vaginal intercourse; 2) watching partner undress; 3) receiving oral sex; 4) giving oral sex. Other sexual activities, such as group sex and sex with a stranger were appealing only to a small percentage.

- 16 percent of men have paid for sex.

- 19 percent of women think about sex at least once a day; 54 percent of men do so.

- The survey reported that 1 out of 5 women and 1 in 10 men say sex is not pleasureable; 33.4 percent of women lack interest in sex, and 15.8 percent of men do.

- More than one quarter of men (28.5 percent) climax too early/ 10.3 percent of women do.

- Performance anxiety was more often prevalent among women, but men worry the most about the performances: 17 percent of men experience performance anxiety; 11.5 percent of women do.

SINGLE MEN

Whether by choice or by fate, almost one third of American men are bachelors, about double the percentage in 1970. Among age groups, 7.1 million, or 81 percent, of men age 20 to 24 are unmarried, according to the U.S. Bureau of the Census. This is a 27 percent increase since 1970.

Never-married men, at 23.6 million in 1993—almost exactly twice the number in 1970—accounted for the largest share of America's 32.9 million men living alone, out of 72.5 million American adult males. Ninety-five percent of 18-year-olds have never married. Overall, 7.3 percent of men between ages of 30 and 64 have never been married, nor have eight percent of men age 65 and over.

Divorced men numbered 6.8 million and widowers 2.5 million in 1993, according to Census Bureau estimates. In 1970, 1.7 million were divorced and 2.1 million were widowed.

Single U.S. males in 1993, by age groups, in thousands; source, U.S. Census Bureau:

Age Group	Single	Widowed	Divorced
20 to 24 years	7,113	7	91
25 to 29 years	4,727	11	435
30 to 34 years	3,333	15	822
35 to 39 years	2,085	33	1,189
40 to 44 years	1,008	51	1,148
45 to 54 years	951	142	1,602
55 to 64 years	670	380	904
65 to 74 years	389	765	458
75 years and older	180	1,24	1

Single U.S. males age 20-24 in 1970, 1980, and 1993, in millions; Census Bureau statistics:

Status	1970	1980	1993
ALL RACES			
Never married	11.8%	18%	23.6%
Divorced	1.6	3.9	6.8
Widowed	2.1	2.0	2.5
WHITE			
Never married	10.2	15	18.6

Divorced	1.3	3.4	5.8
Widowed	1.7	1.8	2.0
BLACK			
Never married	1.4	2.5	3.5
Divorced	0.6	1.4	2.2
Widowed	0.3	0.3	0.4
HISPANIC			
Never married	0.5	1.0	2.4
Divorced	0.1	0.2	0.5
Widowed	0.1	0.1	0.1

SINGLE WOMEN

Single women in the U.S. number 40 million in 1993, down four million from the year before but up 16 million since 1970, according to Census Bureau data for 1993. Never-married single women in the U.S age 18 and over numbered 19 million; divorced and never remarried women numbered 10 million; and widows numbered 11 million. Unmarried-couple households totaled 3.5 million, up from 523,000 in 1970.

Women in the age group 20 to 24 made up the highest number of never-marrieds, at six million of the nine million American women in that age group. Of the 9.8 million women age 25 to 29, 3.2 million were unmarried, and of the 11.1 million women age 30 to 34, 2.1 million were never married.

The dominant age group for divorced women is 45 to 54, at 2.4 million. Next is 55 to 64 (1.3 million) and 30 to 34 (1.2 million). There were 14,000 divorced women age 18 and 19; 194,000 age 20 to 24 group; and 789,000 age 25 to 29. A total of 57,000 of women over 65 were divorced.

Most widows, not surprisingly, were between the ages of 65 and 84: 7.2 million. Widows between ages 55 to 64 numbered 1.5 million; 85 and over 1.4 million. Seven thousand women between the ages of 20 and 24 were widows, as were 25,000 women aged 25 to 29, 58,000 women between ages 30 to 34, and 121,000 women age 35 to 39.

Percent of American women never married, by age and percent, from Census Bureau statistics:

Age	1970	1980	1993
15-17	97.3	98.5	98.7
18	82.0	88.0	89.9
19	68.8	77.6	*
20-24	35.8	50.2	66.8
25-29	10.5	31.1	33.1
30-34	6.2	9.5	19.3
35-39	5.4	6.2	12.5
40-44	4.9	4.8	9.0
45-54	4.9	4.7	5.4
55-64	6.8	4.5	4.3
65 and older	7.7	5.9	4.4

* Included with age 18

Never-married women, widows, and divorced women, by age, in thousand, 1993:

Age	Never Married	Widowed	Divorced
18-19	2,918	N/A	14
20-24	6,019	7	194
25-29	3,258	25	789
30-34	2,151	58	1,200
35-39	1,362	121	1,367
40-44	867	181	1,465
45-54	798	648	2,448
55-64	469	1,594	1,349
65-74	376	3,607	728
75-84	297	3,548	269
85-plus	122	1,424	57

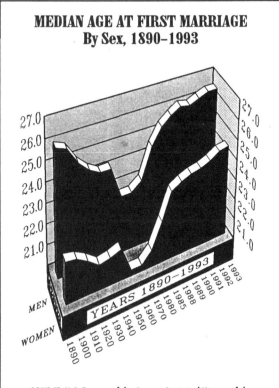

MEDIAN AGE AT FIRST MARRIAGE
By Sex, 1890–1993

MEN
WOMEN
YEARS 1890–1993

SOURCE: U.S. Bureau of the Census, Statistical History of the U.S. (1976) and Marital Status and Living Arrangements, March 1993 (1994)

THERAPIST–CLIENT SEX

It's been called "a growing crisis of ethical abuse" among doctors, lawyers, professors, and psychiatrists. Surveys estimate the incidence of sexual misconduct among professionals overall at between seven and 12 percent of practitioners, and a 1992 survey of family doctors, internists, gynecologists, and surgeons found as many guilty parties among them—nine percent— as have been found among therapists.

According to *Psychology Today*, 90 percent of the victims are psychologically damaged by such conduct, many severely. One survey found that 11 percent of victims had been hospitalized due to their abuse, and one percent committed suicide. Some therapists have been characterized as calculating, predatory professionals who may tell confused patients that their fear of sexual advances constitutes "resistance" to therapeutic change. Some therapists may leave a trail of 20, 50, or more victims, according to Dr. Glen Gabbard, director of the Menninger Clinic in Topeka, Kan. In 14 to 25 percent of the cases reported, patients initiated sex, according to *Psychology Today,* but every professional psychotherapy organization in America agrees that sex with clients is unprofessional—and in many states it is illegal. Nine states—California, Colorado, Florida, Georgia, Iowa, Maine, Minnesota, North Dakota, and Wisconsin—now classify sex with clients as felonies, with penalties that can include long prison terms.

One survey found that 7.1 percent of male psychiatrists admitted sexual misconduct, as did 3.1 percent of female psychiatrists. Another study found that 80 percent of the exploitation involved a male therapist and a female client, while 13 percent involved a female therapist and a female client. Therapists were female and clients male in five percent of the cases.

WIDOWS

A 1994 report by the House Select Committee on Aging found that more widows than widowers will be impoverished when they retire, because Social Security and private pension plans penalize women for living longer and earning less than men, for getting divorced, and for leaving the workforce to care for children or other family members.

The conclusions of the study are bolstered by a survey by Women Work!, which found 42 percent of divorced or widowed and four percent of single women living in poverty. Widows 65 and older make up the largest group of elderly poor, with 15 percent of them having annual incomes of less than $10,000. Overall, 11 percent of U.S. households lived in poverty in 1990.

According to a survey by Resource Financial Center, even taking into account Social Security, the median income of women 65 and older is $6,000; the 1991 poverty level for single persons was $6,932. And yet a woman age 65 may confidently expect to live another 20 years. That low median income is attributed to lower average lifetime pay scales for American women than for men, and to gaps in employment—often because of motherhood—which affect Social Security income.

A woman who has been married more than 10 years can receive half of her husband's benefits when he dies or 100 percent of her own, whichever is greater. Also, a divorced spouse who has not remarried is entitled to benefits starting at age 62 if she had been married for at least 10 years.

WOMEN AND DRUG CRIMES

The fastest growing crimes among women are drug-related. The percentage of women inmates jailed for drug crimes is greater than that of men inmates, according to a study of inmates in 424 of the nation's 3,316 jails, which held 37,383 women. One in three women were held on drug charges compared with one in four men. Ten years ago, about one in eight women inmates were held on drug charges.

Overall, drug crimes accounted for almost half of the 137 percent increase in the number of women jailed during the last decade, according to a Justice Department study. Women who were convicted were almost twice as likely as men to have used serious drugs daily in the month before their offense. About one in four of the women committed their crimes to get money for drugs.

According to the study, in the 1980s women were the fastest-growing segment of the U.S. jail population.

WOMEN IN THE MILITARY

In the mid-1990s, women have continued the gains they made in the military of the 1980s when presidents Jimmy Carter and Ronald Reagan both made four presidential appointments of women to Defense Department jobs that required Senate confirmation.

The number of such appointees more than doubled in the first three years of Clinton's term, at nine appointees. In mid-level Pentagon spots not requiring confirmation, 139 women were named by Clinton, compared to 77 for George Bush, 60 for Reagan, and 23 for Carter. All together, 148 women occupy powerful positions in the military under Clinton, compared to 84 under Bush, 64 under Reagan, and 27 under Carter.

Among important posts occupied by women in the Pentagon are procurement, research and engineering, and naval acquisition positions. One is secretary of the Air Force, and one each is an assistant secretary in the Navy and Air Force.

Women in the military, 1995, in percent; source, U.S. Department of Defense:

Service	Officers	Enlisted
Army	12.7%	12.9%
Navy	12.5	10.6
Marines	3.4	4.5
Air Force	15.0	15.4

WOMEN PHYSICIANS

Women made up 42 percent of medical school enrollees in 1992, 20 percent of practicing doctors, and 37 percent of first-year enrollments in the nation's dental schools in 1993-94, compared to 20 percent in 1984, according to a summary of women in medicine by a national journal. Twenty percent of U.S. physicians were women in 1990, up from 13 percent in 1980.

U.S. medical schools, a world leader in the training of women doctors in the 1890s, changed their rules in the early 1900s and virtually barred entry to women; by 1950 there were fewer women physicians in Boston than there had been in 1890, according to Mary Roth Walsh, author of a history of medical education.

The women's movement and affirmative active policies opened the doors to women again in the 1970s, and the number of U.S. women physicians jumped 310 percent by 1990, from 25,400 to 104,200, according to American Medical Association records. The AMA predicts that women will make up 33 percent of the profession by the year 2010.

But there still are gains to be made, according to an AMA report summarized in the November 1994 issue of the journal *American Demographics*. The average income of all women physicians in 1992 averaged 62 percent of that earned by all men physicians, at $117,500 and $188,600, respectively. Women with 20 or more years of medical experience earn 72 percent of what similarly experienced male doctors earn, with an average $125,300 in annual income, compared to $173,000 for men.

Women made up 54 percent of residents in pediatrics in 1990, the report says, but just five percent of residents in vascular surgery, one of the best-paying medical sub-specialties. Also, 43 percent of all women doctors are employed by hospitals, HMOs, group practices, or other organizations, compared to 22 percent of men doctors.

Fifty-seven percent of women doctors work as independent practitioners, while 79 percent of men doctors do. Overall, women doctors worked an average 55 hours a week in 1992, compared to 61 hours for men, and made 97 patient visits a week earning, an average $41.50 an hour, compared with 117 visits for men physicians at $52.40 an hour, according to the AMA. Women's median income was 27 percent less than men's in family practice, 29 percent less in internal medicine, and 34 percent less in pediatrics in 1991.

In medical academia, 50 percent of women doctors were at the assistant professor level in 1991, compared to 34.8 percent for male professors, while 9.6 percent of women were at the full professor level, compared to 31.5 of men, according to a study by the AMA's Council on Ethical and Judicial Affairs published in 1994. Two-hundred and one women were associate and assistant deans of medical schools in the 1989-90 school year; only one woman was a dean. In medical research,

Michael Keating.
While only 2.5 percent of the military was female during the Vietnam conflict, women in the military grew to 12.6 percent in 1995.

16 percent of the women and 30 percent of the men in the age group 40 to 59 won grant support in 1990 from the National Institutes of Health.

Three-fourths of women doctors experienced sexual harassment at some point in their careers, according to a 1993 AMA poll. Seventy-nine percent of those experienced it in medical school, 64.2 percent in residency training, and 41.8 percent in their practice, the majority of those polled saying the harassment was by either a colleague or member of management.

In approximately 80 percent of the harassment cases cited, respondents said no corrective action was taken. Of women who did not report experiences with harassment, 58.7 percent said they feared reprisal, 46.1 felt no action would be taken, and 34.8 percent said there was no sexual harassment policy at the institution where the harassment occurred.

Total per-hour and per-visit income for men and women physicians in non-federal positions by years of practice in 1992 from the AMA Socioeconomic Monitoring System Core Survey:

	Women	Men
YEARS OF PRACTICE		
All physicians	$117,500	$188,600
1 to 4 years	100,000	147,100
5 to 9 years	131,000	220,500
10 to 19 years	125,200	211,400
20 or more years	125,300	173,000
AVERAGE PER HOUR		
All physicians	$45.42	$65.93
1 to 4 years	41.50	52.40
1 to 9 years	52.10	73.20
10 to 19 years	49.30	73.10
20 or more years	48.60	65.50
AVERAGE PER VISIT		
All physicians	$25.34	$33.44
1 to 4	23.40	28.50
5 to 9	30.60	37.40
10 to 19	24.80	36.70
20 or more	28.80	32.80

Percent distribution of men and women doctors by type of practice in 1989:

Practice	Women	Men
Solo practice	29.2%	38.4%
Hospital employee	15.5	6.6
Group practice	12.5	25.5
Physician group	11.6	7.2
Independent contractor	8.3	5.7
Partnership	7.0	9.0
HMO	3.3	1.5
State/local government	3.0	1.2
University/medical school	2.4	1.0
Ambulatory-care center	1.7	.05
Other	5.5	3.5

WOMEN IN POLITICS

Twenty women have been or currently are presidents or prime ministers of their countries—Golda Meir of Israel, Margaret Thatcher of Great Britain, Gro Harlem Brundtland of Norway, and Mary Robinson of Ireland, to name a few. Will an American follow suit in the foreseeable future?

Things are looking up for women in state legislatures across the nation, often the stepping stone to higher office. In 1993, women held 20.2 percent of the seats in state legislatures, up from 18.4 percent in 1992, according to the Center for the American Woman and Politics. The increase is the biggest since 1981 and continues the trend of gains made every year since 1969.

Overall, women won 332 state senate seats and 1,171 state house seats, more than 50 percent of the open seat races, and a dominant number of redistricting races. Some 60 percent of women state legislators are Democrats, 38.5 percent are Republicans. Women made the biggest strides in the Western states and the least in the South.

The table below lists the states with the most and fewest women legislators, by percentage; adapted from data from the Center for the American Woman and Politics and Rutgers University:

MOST WOMEN	
Washington	38.1%
Arizona	35.6
Colorado	34.0
New Hampshire	34.0
Vermont	33.9
Idaho	31.4
Maine	31.2
Kansas	28.5
Nevada	27.0
Oregon	26.7
FEWEST WOMEN	
Kentucky	4.3%
Alabama	5.7
Louisiana	6.3
Oklahoma	9.4
Arkansas	9.6
Pennsylvania	9.9
Mississippi	10.9
Virginia	11.4
Tennessee	12.1
So. Carolina	12.4

WOMEN, VIOLENCE AGAINST

Increasingly, the targets of violent criminals are older women, who suffered more injuries each year than incur breast cancer, heart attacks, and strokes combined.

More than one million women past 65 are victimized by violence every year, at a time when violence against men in the same age group is in decline, the Older

Women's League reports. Nearly 400,000 more women living in nursing homes also are victims of physical or sexual violence.

The price the nation spends on medical care for injuries suffered by women through violence has reached the astronomical figure of $5 billion to $10 billion annually, plus another $3 billion lost to business because of absenteeism and sick time.

"Violence and fear of violence...shape older women's lives," the report says. "Far too many American women are living out their later years barricaded in their homes."

Yet the home is not always the safest place to be. According to the report, 700,000 women between the ages of 45 and 65 were physically abused by their spouses in 1993. These are the women least likely to seek a divorce or abandon the home. Even if they did, shelters often have no place for older women, being geared more toward younger women with children.

Among OWL's suggestions are a national data collection system, more U.S. funds for reporting abuse of elders, and the inclusion of assistance for family caregivers of women who have been victimized in health care reforms.

WOMEN'S WORKOUTS

Walking, the latest entry in the physical fitness revolution sweeping America, has far and away become the favored form of exercise among white-collar working women. Hardly thought of as an important exercise activity as the 1990s began, fitness walking experienced a boom as a groundswell of medical and therapeutic evidence indicated that the benefits of walking equal that of jogging, without less danger of injury. And 85 percent of white-collar working women agree.

In a 1992 survey by the Women's Sports Foundation for *Working Women* magazine, bicycling is the second favored exercise activity, and aerobics third. About a third of those who exercise work out at least three times a week. Fitness activities are more popular than athletic activities such as bowling, tennis, and other racquet sports, which draw more single mothers. More than half of these women bowled in the previous year, and almost a third played baseball or softball.

Although seven out of ten women who exercised stressed its physical benefits, an enhanced self-image was also an inducement, the survey indicated. Fifty-one percent of blacks, Asians, and Hispanics saw exercise as a help in "being accepted by co-workers," while 37 percent of white women believed so. Those figures are about equal in both categories to the number of women who believe exercising gives them "access to decision-making outside the office."

Below are the top 10 exercise activities for white-collar women who exercised at least once in 1993:

Activity	Percent
Walking	85%
Bicycling	63
Aerobics	61
Swimming	50
Bowling	33
Jogging/running	30
Calisthenics	30
Hiking/backpacking	26
Boating	22
Weightlifting	22

THE WORKPLACE
OVERVIEW

"What do you do?" That question has a particular significance in America where it means one, and only one thing: "What is your occupation?" Indeed, we are a nation in which our occupations define us more than any other characteristic.

The American workplace both reflects and shapes the social dynamics of some 260-million working and nonworking individuals. Not surprisingly, corporate policies are influencing once untouchable areas of our lives—child care, maternity leaves, pensions and insurance programs, to name just a few. In today's workplace where men and women often work at the same jobs—though not always for equal pay—even fraternization among co-workers of the opposite sex is influenced by unwritten company policies and government directives.

The movement toward women's equality has gone hand-in-hand with this relatively new and somewhat managed sexual integration of the workplace. Whereas men outnumbered women in the work force two to one in 1960, by 1994 nearly half of all the 125 million individuals in the labor force were women. Women have made their way into every segment of the workplace—from corporate boardrooms to the cockpits of jet liners and military jet fighters. For millions of women, working goes beyond just making a living. Their careers are their means of socioeconomic advancement, as well as a vehicle by which they prove their equality with men.

A newer development, the booming work-at-home sector of the economy, has the potential to further blur the lines between our social and our economic lives. The affordable personal computer—now packaged with modems and faxes—is creating the "virtual home office" whereby workers are linked, not by hallways and elevators, but by telecommunications lines. Fully one in five new jobs in 1993 was created by Americans working at home.

The data that follows documents the changing nature of work for millions of Americans. One pronounced aspect of it is the boom in temporary employment, once thought of as a catch-as-catch-can measure for employers and workers to fill occasional gaps. Instead, it has become fully integrated into the American working world. "Temps," as they are now known, aren't just fill-ins in at the typing pool, either. A growing number of professionals—managers, computer programmers, and even lawyers, accountants and CEOs—are temping. Some workers use temp jobs as stepping stones to full-time employment; others as an adjunct to freelance and consulting work. But more and more, many view it as a full-time occupation, one that allows them the freedom to work when and how much they want. More temp agencies are offering the kinds of benefits once only offered by major corporations to their most valued employees.

Another tide has come ashore, threatening to drown the American dream, at least as millions of workers see it— downsizing. One of the most successful adaptations to it has been the growth of small, often home-based businesses. Their clients are the same companies that downsized themselves, increasing their bottom line, but not their need for workers. Instead of having them on the payrolls and in their offices, they are contracted with small entrepreneurs who bailed out of corporate America voluntarily or involuntarily. Others are retraining, becoming entrepreneurs, or are re-evaluating their previous career choices and choosing other, less vulnerable ones. Still others remain in jeopardy; not being unemployed, but rather under-employed. As a result, real income—adjusted after inflation—has dropped 13.5 percent from 1970 to 1994.

ATTITUDES AMONG U.S. WORKERS

Are you satisfied with your job?

NOT SURE 1%

YES 85%

NO 14%

Do you worry about losing your job?

YES 29%

NOT SURE 1%

NO 70%

SOURCE: Time/CNN Poll conducted by Yankelovich Partners, Inc. Jan. 17-18, 1996.

BLACK-OWNED FIRMS

Some predicted that the 1990s would mean doom for many U.S. companies, but to date, black-owned businesses have fared better than many of the corporate giants, according to *Black Enterprise* magazine.

Revenue at the top 100 black businesses jumped 10.4 percent in 1991, to $7.9 billion, while revenue for the nation's top industrial corporations fell 1.8 percent.

Earl Graves, the publisher of *BE*, said that recession times means merely tightening the belt another notch. Black businesses have always lived in a "be ready" mode for bad economic times, he added. The report indicated that black businesses held down costs wherever possible; for example, while the revenues of the top 100 businesses rose significantly in 1991, employment rose a mere 3.9 percent, to 32,590 workers.

Below are the top 10 black-owned companies with their revenues (in millions), according to *Black Enterprise* magazine:

TLC Beatrice Int'l	$1,542.0
Johnson Publishing	261.4
Philadelphia Coca Cola Bottling	256.0
H. J. Russell	143.6
Barden Communications	91.2
Garden State Cable TV	88.0
Soft Sheen Products	87.9
RMS Technologies	79.9
Stop Shop and Save	66.0
Bing Group	64.9

BUSINESS ETHICS

A new growth industry is fanning across the U.S., that of "ethics consulting" to the business community. Practitioners of this new occupation come from the ranks of social activists, business school faculty, management consulting firms, and corporate leadership, as businesses address concerns about the image left behind by the corporate culprits of the past decade.

According to a survey taken by the Center for Business Ethics at Bentley College in Waltham, Mass., by 1994 about 90 percent of the largest corporations in the country had adopted codes of ethics to instruct employees about what are and what are not acceptable practices in their daily operations.

The Center itself is one of almost 50 percent of all public and private business schools that have at least one ethics course dealing with business. The percentage is slighly less in graduate business schools, but experts say the percentages for both groups have risen substantially since the survey was made in 1987.

According to the Bentley poll, almost 33 percent of all major U.S. firms have an ethics officer whose job it is to see that ethics directives are known and practiced. Twenty percent of those firms have established an entire department engaged in training employees in ethical behavior and monitoring compliance throughout the company.

A national Ethics Officers Association has been formed, drawing 50 sponsoring corporations and more than 100 practicing members. According to *Financial World* magazine, it is estimated that 24 management consulting firms in the U.S. derive a significant portion of their fees from advising companies on ethics policies, writing ethics codes, and establishing in-house systems for getting the message across. The magazine adds that there are about a hundred "solo practitioners" who work full time at helping companies avoid highly visible and embarrassing—and often costly—episodes of misconduct.

BUSINESS TRAVEL

American business executives who are inclined to inflate their expense accounts will find it tougher going as the 1990s progress, according to a 1994 survey of 2,000 companies that found only 17 percent of U.S. firms continue to give business-travel expenses in cash. The figure is down from 30 percent in 1991.

Instead, more business travelers will use corporate charge cards or credit cards, leaving a precise record of their expenses behind for scrutiny by company auditors. The cards pay for 100 percent of airline fares, rental cars, hotels, most trains, and even an increasing number of taxis. Out-of-hand expenses such as tips, tolls, and snacks on the road will be reimbursed from the cash drawer.

According to the survey, by American Express Travel Management Services, Hewlett-Packard is one company that has found the use of corporate credit cards cuts down on fraud and reduces administrative costs. HP has distributed 45,000 cards to its U.S. employees, at a cost of $20 a card to issue and process. In the period 1993-94 the move reduced cash advances from more than $1 million a month to less than $200,000. An official estimated that about 85 percent of the cash the company gave out came back with the expenses reported by the employee, cluttering up the administrative load.

Closing the cash drawer also frees corporate funds for other purposes, according to the survey, which points out that the average cash advance to employees who do not have a corporate card has fallen from $180 to $114 in the period because there is no need to hand out cash to somebody with a card.

Below are the average cash advances paid by companies for travel expenses, according to American Express:

Amount	Percentage
$250 or less	45%
$251-$500	42
$501-$1,000	12
More than $1,000	1

CHILD CARE IN THE WORKPLACE

In 1993, 63 percent of large employers offered parental leave from work. Ninety-seven percent of those companies offered unpaid leave, and three percent offered paid leave or a combination of paid and unpaid time off, according to Hewitt Associates of Lincolnshire, Ill., which made the survey.

A 1991 survey by the Bureau of Labor Statistics found that all told, only 37 percent of full-time employees in companies with 100 or more employees had unpaid leave available, and just 26 percent of the plans included leave for fathers. Eighteen percent of companies with fewer than 100 employees offered unpaid leave to mothers in 1992, and eight percent to fathers.

Company health insurance plans almost always cover prenatal care and delivery costs for employees. The BLS survey found that 83 percent of people working full-time in companies with more than 100 employees were covered for at least some of the cost in 1991, while the share of smaller companies was 71 percent in 1992. Thirty percent of workers in large companies were also given resource and referral services when parents returned to work, and more than 75 percent contracted with outside vendors to provide them, according to the Hewitt Associates poll.

Seventy-three percent of large organizations offered the most common benefit in 1993—a dependent-care spending and reimbursement account, wherein the employee sets aside non-taxable income for child-care expenses, the BLS survey found. Fourteen percent of those employed in small companies took advantage of this benefit in 1992.

Businesses' share in providing or subsidizing child care is small but growing. In 1989, five percent of full-time workers in medium and large organizations were able to take advantage of on-site care programs; by 1991 that figure had risen to eight percent. Two percent of workers in small enterprises participated in such programs in 1992, up from one percent in 1990.

CRIME IN THE WORKPLACE

Three to four bosses are killed in the nation each month by angry workers, more than double the number from 10 years ago. Yes, violent crime is moving from the streets, parking lots, and alleys into the nation's workplaces, according to a 1995 report on several national surveys. It's estimated that 10 percent of the almost one million violent crimes committed at work are carried out with handguns.

According to a Justice Department survey on criminal victimization in the United States, carried out from 1987 to 1992, an estimated four percent of the 22,540 murders nationally in 1992, eight percent of the 93,825 rapes by force, seven percent of the 1.2 million robberies, and 16 percent of the 1.8 million aggravated and simple assaults occurred at work. Bureau of Labor Statistics, Centers for Disease Control and Prevention, and National Institute for Occupational Safety and Health data also were used in the report, which was published in the January/February 1995 issue of the journal *Society*.

Two million personal thefts and 200,000 vehicle thefts occur each year while people are at work, according to the victimization survey. This accounts for about 11 percent of the 19 million personal thefts nationally and two percent of the 1.9 million vehicle thefts. From 1987 to 1992, according to the study, an average of 971,500 of the nation's 6.6 million violent crimes were committed in the nation's workplaces, as were 13,000 of the nation's 142,000 rapes. Workplace robberies averaged 79,100 over the period, of the 1.6 million nationwide, aggravated assaults 264,200 of the 1.6 million, and simple assaults 615,200 of the 3.2 million. An estimated $55 million was lost by more than 500,000 victims of violent crime at work, who lost an average of 3.5 work days per crime for injuries received there.

Below are crime incidents by percent, place, and time of occurrence, weapons used, and injuries suffered, in 1992, from *Criminal Victimization in the United States* and Justice Department statistics:

PLACE OF OCCURRENCE

Place	Rape	Robbery	Assault
Inside home	16.3%	10.1%	12.4%
Street near home	12.4	11.0	11.7
Friend, relative, neighbor's home	14.1	3.1	8.3
Inside commercial property	1.5	4.2	12.2
Parking lot or garage	6.5	13.6	7.3
School or on school property	7.9	3.9	14.1
Park or playground	8.5	6.4	4.4
Street not near home	25.9	39.7	20.6
Other	6.9	8.0	9.0

TIME OF OCCURRENCE

	Rape	Robbery	Assault
6 a.m.-6 p.m.	40.3%	39.5%	50.2%
Nighttime	59.7	58.9	49.5

WEAPONS USAGE AND INJURIES

	Rape	Robbery	Assault
Weapons used	27.6	54.0	31.8
Victims injured	N/A	35.7	29.7

DEATHS, WORK–RELATED

Cab drivers and workers in groceries, restaurants, and saloons made up 17 percent of on-the-job fatalities in 1993, a government report released in mid-1994 revealed. Robberies were the primary motive, the report said. The figure equaled the on-the-job fatalities in those categories in 1992.

Job-related deaths for the year amounted to 6,271, an increase from 6,217 in 1992. Highway accidents to or from work caused 20 percent of those deaths, and homicides accounted for another 17 percent. Other causes of worksite deaths included faulty machinery, electrocution, fires, suffocation, and falls. All told, the work-related death rate in the was 32 per 100,000 people—more than four times the death rate from firearms.

Ninety-two percent of fatalities in 1993 were to men, almost double their 55 percent share of U.S. employment. Differences in the type of industries and the work men do accounted for the preponderance of males on the lists of work-related male fatalities, the Labor Department report said.

Fifty percent of the 1,232 highway fatalities involved collisions between two or more trucks or cars driven by salespeople. Ninety percent of those accident victims were men. In 1982, highway accidents accounted for 18 percent of the year's on-the-job fatalities. In overall accident statistics, motor vehicle deaths in the U.S. lead all categories from infancy to age 74. From age 75, falls are the most common cause of accidental death, with 7,700 deaths in 1991 compared to 4,000 auto accident deaths in that age group.

Every Southern state except the two Carolinas exceeds the national death rate of seven percent for occupational deaths from injuries or diseases, according to the Centers for Disease Control. West Virginia ranks fifth in the nation, Mississippi is sixth, Arkansas is 10th, Kentucky 12th, and Louisiana 14th. These are all states with sizable mining, agriculture, construction, and textile industries.

Luckily these produce drivers have a relatively safe route in an affluent section of Chicago. For others at similar jobs, the possibility of trouble looms large. Transportation accidents are the number one killer on the job. To make matters worse, grocery stores and restaurants, where produce is customarily delivered, are the locations at which most on-the-job fatalities occur.

Below are the causes of accidental work-related deaths, in percent, for 1992, from Centers for Disease Control statistics:

Cause	Percent
Transportation accidents	40%
Assaults, violent acts	20
From objects and equipment	16
Falls	10
Harmful substances	10
Fires, explosions	3
DEATHS BY INDUSTRY:	
Transportation, public utilities	15
Construction	15
Agriculture, fishing, and forestry	13
Retail trade	12
Services	12
Manufacturing	12
Government	11
Other	10

DISPLACED WORKERS

Experienced workers were hardest hit by the recession of the early 1990s, which saw 5.6 million Americans who had been with their companies more than three years lose their jobs due to company closings, slack work, business downsizing, and privatization.

Workers age 35 to 54 accounted for 53 percent of that total, though the age group accounted for only 47 percent of the labor force of adults age 20 and older in 1992. Workers aged 55 and older accounted for 13 percent of the total labor force but 17 percent of the jobs lost. Together, those two groups of experienced workers, which make up for 60 percent of the American workforce, suffered 70 percent of the job loss.

Younger workers were much less likely to lose their jobs in the recent economic downturn. Just 5.9 percent of the lost jobs were among workers age 20 to 24, and 7.8 percent were among those age 25 to 34. Though they account for nearly 30 percent of total U.S. jobs, workers in those two age groups made up only 13.7 percent of the job loss totals.

On average, it takes 24 weeks for those under the age of 40 to land a new position, according to the Association of Outplacement Consulting Firms International; for those age 50 to 59, the wait is 36 weeks. Those earning less than $40,000 annually made connections in 26 weeks on average, while it took 34 weeks for those who had been earning $100,000 or more.

Those at the $100,000-plus wage level were the most likely to go into business for themselves—about 20 percent of displaced workers in that bracket did so, compared to just 11 percent among those earning less than $40,000. As for age groups, those 60 and older were the most likely to start their own businesses, at 45 percent, followed by those in their 50s, at 27 percent, and those under age 40, at 20 percent.

Seventy-eight percent of the businesses that cut their workforces from mid-1992 to mid-1993 used outplacement services to help the fired workers, according to the American Management Association. That represented a 14 percent increase from the year before.

Outplacement services were provided to 1.4 million people in 1993, compared to 800,000 in 1991. Revenues for outplacement firms reached $700 million in 1993, up from $500 million two years before, according to AOCFI, which said that 33 percent of their clients were women.

Below is an enumeration of recession victims age-20 or older who had three or more years with a company before losing or leaving their job (in thousands); source, U.S. Bureau of Labor Statistics:

AGE

	Displaced	Displacement rate
Total aged 20 and older	5,584	7.9%
20 to 24	203	5.9
25 to 34	1,447	7.8
35 to 44	1,742	8.4
45 to 54	1,227	8.2
55 to 64	750	7.9
65 and older	214	7.9
SEX		
Men	3,447	8.5%
Women	2,137	7.2
RACE		
White	4,828	7.9%
Black	626	8.8
Hispanic origin	511	11.8
INDUSTRY		
Managerial/professional	1,210	5.7%
Technical/sales, administration	1,559	7.5
Service	354	4.7
Production/craft/repair	1,021	11.2
Operator/fabricator/laborer	1,301	12.4
Farming, fishing, forestry	76	3.1

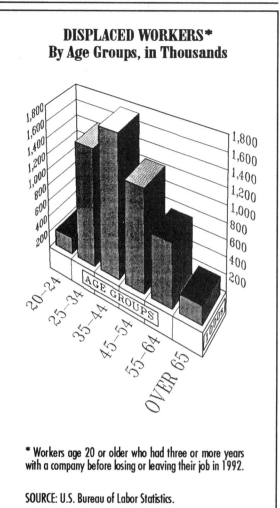

DISPLACED WORKERS*
By Age Groups, in Thousands

* Workers age 20 or older who had three or more years with a company before losing or leaving their job in 1992.

SOURCE: U.S. Bureau of Labor Statistics.

DOWNSIZING AND RE-EMPLOYMENT

With the stated purpose of helping relocate the nearly 5.6 million people who have lost their places in the nation's workforce after three or more years on the job, the U.S. Department of Labor has projected a future for them in a survey it calls *Getting Back to Work*, compiled in 1994.

Forecasting 18 million new jobs to be created between 1988 and the year 2000, the study surveys about 250 occupations, analyzing size, growth potential, and earnings, to give the displaced worker a target to aim at to avoid another job loss or a decrease in earnings as he or she makes a career change.

Because size, growth, and earnings fluctuate, the bureau has measured the jobs in comparative terms: in size, very large; large; average; small; and very small; in growth, very fast; fast; average; slow; and very slow; and in earnings, very high; high; average; low; and very low.

At the low end of the scale in size is rail transportation, with five out of six categories marked very

small in size and with very low expected growth, except among subway and streetcar operators, whose growth rate is seen as very fast.

The outlook is also bleak in three out of four categories in the printing field: typesetters, job printers, and bookbinders. Only lithographers and photoengravers can look forward to continuing high wages. Assemblers, hand sewers, and pattern and layout workers in the handworkers field, and machine operators in the textile and metal and plastic working fields will also fare poorly in the projections.

Booming in the size category will be food-related occupations including cooks and chefs, bartenders, counter clerks, busboys, and institutional cooks, all with a fast growth rate but dead last in earnings. Next is construction, six of very large size out of 19 occupations in the field, and 10 with a fast growth rate potential. None are in the large earnings category, however, and four of those are low to very low in earnings. They include carpet installers, painters and paperhangers, roofers, and construction helpers.

Protective service occupations, including policemen and guards, will average very fast growth and a high earnings rate. Other high earners will be engineering and science technicians, electronic home entertainment equipment repairers, office communication installers and repairers, tool and die makers, telephone repairers, installers, and central office frame wirers, millwrights, and aircraft mechanics.

Poorest paid jobs in addition to food-related occupations are in farming, forestry, and fishing; laboring; textile workers; packaging and filling machine operators; laundry and dry-cleaning machine operators and tenders; maids and servants, janitors and cleaners; dental assistants; and nursing aides and orderlies.

Of the 250 assorted occupations studied, the bureau was able to forecast worker earnings into the year 2000 for only 128. Nine job categories were ranked very high in earnings, 24 were rated high, 25 were rated average, 33 were rated low, and 37 were rated very low.

The Labor Department points out that most job openings are not publicly listed. They are found in the "hidden job market," it says, made up of people who know about a job opening and tell someone about it. The department said jobseekers should try to learn about jobs through "networking."

EDUCATION AND EARNINGS

American college students who earn professional degrees such as medical doctor or lawyer can expect to earn, on average, $3 million over their careers. Workers with just a high school diploma will earn $821,000 on average in a lifetime of work, according to a first-ever lifetime projection by the Census Bureau.

A college bachelor's degree means $1.4 million in lifetime earnings, on average, based on a typical 43.5-year career. A master's degree leads to $1.6 million, and a doctorate $2.1 million. People without a high school diploma can expect to earn $609,000 over their lifetimes.

The Census Bureau report found that the number of college graduates among young adults has remained around one in four since 1982. About 23 percent of Americans age 25 to 29 had a bachelor's degree in 1993. In 1982 the rate was 22.5 percent. The percentage of Americans in the same age group who had a high school diploma also barely budged, with 87.4 percent, compared to 86 percent a decade earlier.

Mitigating against an increase in Americans going to college, experts say, is the cost, which has doubled on average over the last decade and is increasing at roughly twice the rate of inflation. A student will spend an average of $9,876 a school year for tuition, fees, room and board, and supplies at a public university, the American Council on Education estimates.

Private universities cost an average of $23,704 in 1994, compared to $22,447 the year before.

Estimated lifetime earnings potential, in thousands of dollars:

Some high school	$609
High school graduate	821
Some college	993
Two-year degree	1,082
Bachelors degree	1,421
Masters degree	1,619
Doctorate	2,142
Professional degree	3,013

EMPLOYMENT BY INDUSTRIES

Service industries today dwarf those involved in the manufacture of durable and nondurable goods.

The list below cites the 10 largest industries in the U.S. today, and the number of workers they employ, according to the Department of Labor.

Health services	8.1 million
Eating and drinking establishments	6.5 million
Business services	5.9 million
Durable goods	3.8 million
Transportation	3.8 million
Food stores	3.8 million
Finance	3.4 million
Nondurable goods	2.6 million
General merchandise stores	2.4 million
Insurance	2.2 million

At one time or another, agriculture, manufacturing of durable and nondurable goods, and railroads were the largest U.S. industries. Now, a whole new class of smaller industries is emerging.

The following list shows the annual rate of increase of the fastest-growing subindustries in the U.S:

Industry	Annual percent growth
Electromedical equipment	9.0%
Surgical and medical	8.2
Medicinals and botanicals	8.0
Semiconductors and related devices	7.8
X-ray apparatus and tubes	7.8
Motorcycles, bicycles, and parts	7.7
Farm machinery and equipment	7.7
Oil and gas field machinery	7.7
Household audio and video equipment	6.8
Poultry slaughtering and processing	6.6

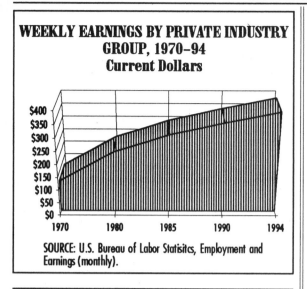

WEEKLY EARNINGS BY PRIVATE INDUSTRY GROUP, 1970–94
Current Dollars

SOURCE: U.S. Bureau of Labor Statisitcs, Employment and Earnings (monthly).

WEEKLY EARNINGS BY PRIVATE INDUSTRY GROUPS, 1970–94
Constant Dollars (1982)

SOURCE: U.S. Bureau of Labor Statisitcs, Employment and Earnings (monthly).

GENDER RELATIONS ON THE JOB

The bond between men and women in the workplace tends to strenghthen the longer they work together, but 54 percent of male executives who responded to a recent survey on workplace relations between the sexes say their jobs leave them too exhausted for the bonding to blossom into sex.

Twenty-seven percent of 3,000 men who worked less than 70 hours a week admitted finding more in common with their women colleagues than with their wives. The same bonding occurred among 35 percent of men who worked at least 70 hours a week, according to a reader survey by the magazine *Exec.*

Fifty-five percent of the respondents worked 60 hours or more a week and 29 percent 70 or more. The long hours and workplace pressures produced among 58 of the respondents at least one monthly quarrel with their wives, and among 28 percent accusations from their wives of having an affair.

INCOME, ANNUAL

Every state in the union reported workers receiving pay increases in 1993, ranging from 0.4 percent in New Hampshire to 3.3 percent in the District of Columbia and South Dakota, though the rates of increase were the smallest on record.

The 1.8 percent overall pay increases for American workers in 1993 represented the lowest recorded increase since the Labor Department began publishing such data in 1980. From 1980 to 1992, national average pay increases ranged from 3.2 percent to 9.4 percent annually.

The bureau points out that early bonus and lump-sum payments made to displaced employees during business downsizing in 1992 dampened the effect on pay growth for 1993, since those monies ordinarily would have shown up in 1993 reporting.

For workers on the whole, the average annual pay was $26,362 in 1993, a 1.8 percent increase over the 1992 national average. In the private sector, which accounts for 83 percent of the country's employment, the increase was an average of 1.5 percent, while government workers' pay rose 3.1 percent. In 1992 private sector pay outpaced that of government workers 5.7 percent to four percent. In industry overall, decreases were felt in some specific industries, notably mining, which saw average pay fall in 13 states. Construction pay dropped in 11 states.

The District of Columbia, as the seat of government, topped the states in average annual pay, at $39,199. Connecticut was second with $33,169, and New York third with $32,919.

South Dakota's average annual salary of $18,613 was the lowest among the states, followed by North Dakota at $19,382, Mississippi at $19,694, Montana at $19,932, and Arkansas at $20,337. The bottom 15 states in annual pay of workers remained the same as in 1992.

New Hampshire's 0.4 percent increase in average annual pay was the nation's lowest. Washington state was second low with 0.8, followed by West Virginia at 0.9 percent, Maine at 1.0 percent, and Arkansas at 1.1 percent.

New Mexico posted the third largest average pay increase at 3.2 percent, followed by Hawaii at 3.1 percent. Michigan, Montana, and Nevada tied for the next highest increases at 2.9 percent in the bureau's 1993 compilation of government statistics, which covered 109.4 million jobs, or 94.4 percent of the country's civilian employees.

In industry, mining, which accounts for less than one percent of private sector employment, showed the highest average annual pay, at $42,428, despite its pay falloff in some states. That figure was 15 percent higher than the next highest-paying industry— finance, insurance, and real estate, which registered $36,013 in average annual income. Retail trade, which employs a large proportion of temporary workers, was the lowest, at $13,997. In the three areas of government—local, state, and federal—the average annual salary was $28,495, making it eighth in pay if ranked with private sector industry.

Within the private sector, finance, insurance, and real estate led the way in pay increases for the second straight year, at 3.4 percent. Wholesale trade was second at 2.4 percent, and mining third at 2.1 percent. For the second year, construction almost dropped off the plus column, at just 0.7 in income growth for 1933.

The list below indicates annual pay and the percentage change for 1992 and 1993 by industries; source, U.S. Bureau of Labor Statistics:

Industry	1992	1993	Change
Total	$25,547	$25,935	1.5%
Mining	41,537	42,428	2.1
Finance/insurance/ real estate	34,822	36,013	3.4
Wholesale trade	32,931	33,717	2.4
Transport/communications/ utilities	32,862	33,451	1.8
Manufacturing	31,834	32,404	1.8
Government	27,628	28,495	3.1
Construction	27,379	27,560	0.7
Services	24,330	24,675	1.4
Retail trade	13,809	13,997	1.4

INCOME, CORPORATE VS. PERSONAL

American wage earners in the middle of the 1990s find their incomes continuing to decline in real dollars even as the business side recovers from the recession of the early part of the decade. A slide in median take-home pay of U.S. workers has occurred each year since 1991, according to Census Bureau data, and while the nation's total income expanded in 1993, the gains went mostly to the wealthiest 20 percent—the most highly trained and educated—of the national workforce.

In 1991 the median family income, adjusted for inflation, was $38,129. It fell to $37,668 in 1992, and to $36,959 in 1993. The percent decline was 2.2 for men and 1.2 for women from 1992 to 1993.

In the meantime, business downsizing and closings in the period idled 1.5 million workers, many of whom drifted into the 72 percent of new jobs that opened between 1988 and 1993 among below-average earnings employers areas such as restaurants and bars.

At the same time, managerial and professional job categories, which pay more than the median industry wage, increased by 1.3 million jobs in 1993, according

to Labor Department statistics. Technical positions also surged by 300,000 in 1994.

To better balance this earning and employment spread between the unskilled and skilled, business is increasingly turning to retraining programs. In 1991, 20 percent of people age 17 and older took part in adult education classes, according to the National Center for Education Statistics.

In 1993 U.S. businesses budgeted $48 billion for formal training, a survey by Lakewood Publications, Inc., of Minneapolis, showed. Seventy-two percent of that sum went to salaries to training staffs, eight percent went to facilities and overhead, and 20 percent for seminars, conferences, equipment, and materials. Ninety percent of employers offered employees basic computer training. Seventy-three percent of employer-sponsored retraining programs were offered to middle managers and executives.

Thirty-seven percent of lower-paying production workers also received employer-sponsored training, to help them rise from the unskilled to the skilled level as industries become more technologically advanced and demands increase for workers who can deal with high-tech tools.

Below is service industry employment as a percent of U.S. workforce, and growth of service industry jobs from 1989 to 1994; from Bloomberg Financial Markets:

Year	Percent	Job Growth
1989	25.1%	5 million
1990	25.6	10 million
1991	26.3	15 million
1992	26.9	20 million
1993	27.5	25 million
1994	28.2	30 million

INCOME, METROPOLITAN AREAS

The average worker in America's metropolitan areas is gaining ground in income but losing ground in purchasing power, a comparison of two Labor Department reports indicates. As pay rose 1.8 percent in 1993, prices rose three percent, following a 1.9 pay increase in 1992 when prices rose also by three percent. The result: a 2.3 percent drop in disposable income over two years.

From 1980 to 1991, pay hikes for the nation's workers averaged 6.3 percent, while prices rose 4.9 percent, according to the 1994 Consumer Price Index and Labor Department's Bureau of Labor Statistics. The 1993 figure on pay raises was the lowest the Labor Department has recorded.

The U.S.'s consumer-price inflation in 1993 placed it fourth-lowest among the 10 major industrial nations, behind Japan (1.3 percent), Britain (1.6 percent), Canada (1.8 percent), and France (2.1 percent).

Of 310 metropolitan areas reporting in the pay-level survey, 42 outdistanced inflation. These were led by Billings, Mont. (5.3 percent); Springfield, Ill., and

Kenosha, Wis. (five percent); Benton Harbor, Mich. (4.7 percent); and Great Falls, Mont. (4.4 percent). The Billings and Great Falls areas charted an inflation rate of 3.8 percent; the other three cities between 3.5 percent and 3.9 percent.

Eleven areas in the nation experienced pay growth of less than one percent. Among them, five cities saw annual pay declines. They were: Fort Smith, Ark. (2.5 percent), Sharon, Pa. (1.5 percent), Visalia-Tulare-Porterville, Calif. (1.1 percent), Beaumont-Port Arthur, Texas (one percent), and Hagerstown, Md. (0.9 percent). All these areas experienced inflation rates between 3.4 percent and 3.8 percent.

East Coast and West Coast cities led the nation in pay levels, at $39,381 in New York City, and $38,381 in San Jose, Calif., with inflation rates of 2.7 percent and 2.5 percent, respectively. San Jose is 11th in rankings for the fastest-growing American cities. Other top metros were Middlesex-Somerset-Hunterdon, N.J. ($35,573), San Francisco ($35,278), and Newark, N.J. ($35,129). These five metro areas ranged from 28 to 34 percent above the average for all metro areas in the nation.

Jacksonville, N.C., recorded the lowest average annual pay level among metro areas, at $15,919. It was followed by Myrtle Beach, S.C, at $17,012; McAllen-Edinburg-Mission, Texas, $17,173; Brownsville-Harlingen-San Benito, Texas, $17,757; and Yuma, Ariz., $17,759. These towns had average pay 36 to 42 percent below the national metro average. All had an inflation rates of 2.6 percent.

The average annual pay level in metro areas was $27,540, up from $27,051 in 1992. Thirty-eight areas reported pay levels above that average, 28 reported annual pay below $20,000, and 30 experienced pay growth levels below one percent. Average annual pay for the entire nation, metro and non-metro combined, was $26,362.

Below and at right are the 10 leading metropolitan areas in annual average pay, and percentage of pay increases in 1993, compiled by U.S.Bureau of Labor Statistics:

Area	1992	1993	Change
New York-Connecticut-New Jersey	$35,203	$35,799	1.7%
San Francisco-Oakland-San Jose	32,702	33,597	2.7
Washington, D.C.-West Virginia	30,447	31,156	2.3
Detroit-Ann Arbor	30,122	31,153	3.4
Boston-Brockton, N.H.	30,100	30,642	1.8
Chicago-Gary-Kenosha, Wis.	29,721	30,242	1.8
Los Angeles-Orange County, Calif.	29,688	30,199	1.7
Houston-Galveston	29,466	29,743	.9
Philadelphia-Atlantic City	28,940	29,414	1.6
Seattle-Tacoma-Bremerton, Wash.	28,061	28,159	.3

Ten lowest metropolitan areas in average annual pay, and percent of pay increases in 1993:

Area	1992	1993	Change
Jacksonville, N.C.	$15,624	$15,919	1.9%
Myrtle Beach, S.C.	16,320	17,012	4.2
McAllen-Edinburg-Mission, Tex.	16,583	17,173	3.6
Brownsville-Harlingen, Tex.	17,294	17,757	2.7
Yuma, Ariz.	17,438	17,759	1.8
Yakima, Wash.	17,211	17,816	3.5
Laredo, Tex.	17,660	18,082	2.4
Sumter, S.C.	18,157	18,345	1.0
Visalia-Tulare-Porterfield, Calif.	18,752	18,550	1.1
Rapid City, S.D.	18,505	18,820	1.7

INCOME, PROFESSIONALS, BY RACE

A three-tiered American professional class, with Asians at the top, whites in the middle, and blacks and Hispanics at the bottom: That's an indication of the future in a wide variety of professions in physical and social sciences, health services, teaching, the legal field, and in the arts, according to a Census-based study by the Center for Immigration Studies.

Foreign-born professionals in the U.S. total 1.3 million, and native-born 15.1 million. The report found that the median annual salary for foreign-born professionals is $35,363, compared to $31,008 for those born in the U.S. Native-born black professionals earn the lowest median salary of any group in the study: just over $26,000.

The highest paid foreign group is Korean doctors, with a median income of $101,000. East Indian doctors ranked second, at $82,205.

Though there are three times more blacks in the professions than Asians, only 4,000 black professionals earn more than $150,000 a year, while 14,000 foreign-born Asians earn that much.

In the $100,000-annual salary range, whites barely edge out Asians, 44 percent to 41 percent. Thirteen percent of Hispanic professionals earn that much, but only two percent of blacks.

The study found more foreign-born East Indian doctors working in the U.S. than native-born black doctors. It also cited a decline of blacks in graduate schools and the acceptance of more foreigners in advanced programs.

JOB GROWTH

From 1981 to 1993, about 17 million new jobs opened up to American workers, but 60 percent were temporary or part-time, and many were low wage, dragging down the overall real wages earned by Americans in 1992-93 by .06 percent.

The most dramatic job growth was in restaurants, bars, and health care services. The number of workers in restaurants and bars rose from 4.7 million to 6.6

million in the period. Health service workers, including insurance, increased from 5.6 million to 8.5 million, according to an Economic Policy Institute study conducted by Lawrence Mischel and Jared Bernstein.

Over the same period, manufacturing jobs declined among both durable and non-durable goods producers. Though the overall output of goods shot up almost 50 percent, the Bureau of Labor Statistics says jobs shrank from 25.1 million to 23.1 million because of widespread automation and industry downsizing. In durable goods manufacturing, the number of jobs dropped from 12.1 million to 10.2 million. In computer and office equipment manufacturing, the job loss was 19,000 in the period; in telephone communications, 19,000. Non-durable goods-producing industries from 1992 to 1993 lost 125,000 jobs of the total 2.4 million lost in this sector since 1981.

Defense cuts of $123 billion over the next four years are estimated by the National Commission for Economic Conversion and Disarmament to cost 1.8 million jobs. The effects are being felt in California, where employment in defense-related industries was expected to fall 17 percent in 1994. In 1993 aerospace employment in the state fell from 374,000 in 1988 to 220,000, and state officials expect another 125,000 jobs to be lopped off by 1998.

Though by winter 1993 unemployed Americans were buoyed somewhat by an increase of 11 points in the Help Wanted Index, which measures classified employment ads in 57 of the nation's major newspapers, the Conference Board survey concluded that the labor market improvement was minimal.

The South Atlantic region experienced the largest employment increase, up 11.3 percent. Next was East South Central, at 10.7 percent, followed by West South Central, at 9.2 percent, and New England, at 5.9 percent. Drops were recorded in the Mountain region (2.8 percent) and West North Central region (1.5 percent).

Alaska reports the highest median hourly wages in the country, at $12.26 an hour; Georgia, Alabama, and Louisiana report the lowest, at $6 an hour, according to a National Education Association Support Membership study by states in 1993.

The table below represents 1992 and projected 2005 employment, in thousands, in the 20 fastest-growing occupations in the U.S., according to the Bureau of Labor Statistics:

Occupation	1992	2005	Change
Home health aids	347	827	138%
Human services	189	445	136
Personal and home-care aids	127	293	130
Computer engineers/scientists	211	447	112
Systems analysts	455	956	110
Physical-corrective assistants and aids	61	118	93
Physical therapists	90	170	88
Paralegals	95	176	86
Teachers, special education	358	625	74
Medical assistants	181	808	71
Detectives, except public	59	100	70
Corrections officers	282	479	70
Child-care workers	684	1,135	66
Travel agents	115	191	66
Radiologic technologists/technicians	162	264	63
Nursery workers	72	116	62
Medical records technicians	76	123	61
Operations research analysts	45	72	61
Occupational therapists	40	64	60
Legal secretaries	280	439	57

Sentiment on the current financial situation, according to a 1994 Gallup poll of U.S. workers:

Condition	Rating
Excellent	5%
Good	42
Fair	42
Poor	10
No opinion	1

Economic news, good or bad, according to a 1994 Gallup poll:

Opinion	1993	1994
Mostly good	39%	42%
Mostly bad	48	46
Mixed	9	6
No opinion	4	6

JUDGESHIPS, BY RACIAL COMPOSTION

A landmark compilation by the American Bar Association has found that in the mid-1990s almost one-third of 7,860 judgeships in federal and state courts in the U.S. are held by minorities. African Americans account for 1,309 seats, or 16 percent of the total of 2,390 seats held by four minority groups.

The judgeships include, in addition, 210 Asian/Pacific Islanders, 848 Hispanics, and 23 Native Americans. (The list does not include Native American judges who preside over tribal courts.) The total minority representation is 30.4 percent of the judgeships in the entire U.S. and state justice systems. That system is made up in the federal judiciary of the U.S. Supreme Court, 90 district courts, 11 appeals court and the Courts of Appeal, and three special courts, claims, customs, and patent courts. State courts are justices of the peace, district, superior, circuit, and a supreme court.

California has more African American (149) and Asian/Pacific Islander (92) judges than any other jurisdiction in the country, and 390 minority judgeships overall. Texas has the most Hispanic judges (353), and most minority judges overall (403). Other states with large minority representation on the bench are New York (136), of whom 100 are African American; Michigan (115), of whom 111 are African American; Illinois (114), 85 African American; and New Mexico (100), 96 Hispanic.

Every state in the union but New Hampshire, North Dakota, and South Dakota, has at least one minority judge. Five—Idaho, Iowa, Montana, Nebraska, and Vermont—have only one. Idaho, Iowa, and Nebraska each have one African American judge, Montana has one Hispanic, and Vermont one Asian/Pacific Islander. Only three states have more than 10 Asian/American judges: California with 92, Hawaii with 59, and Washington with 14. Only two states have more than 100 of the 848 Hispanic judgeships: Texas with 353, and California with 146. Only three states have 100 or more black judges: California with 149, Michigan with 111, and New York with 100. Seven states have more than one Native American judge: California, Texas, and California, with three; and Oregon, Arizona, North Carolina, and New Mexico, with two.

Thirty-eight states have no Native American judgeships, 31 have no Asian/American judges, and 18 have no Hispanic judges.

The survey was taken by the ABA's Task Force on Opportunities for Minorities in the Judiciary, which published the first known directory of minority judges in the U.S. in 1994 to help facilitate an increase the number of minorities in the judiciary.

LAYOFFS

It turns out that there is yet another reason to hate Mondays. No longer are they just "blue;" some of them are the darkest shade of gray.

Employers announce more layoffs on Mondays than on any other day of the week, according to Challenger, Gray & Christman, a job placement consulting firm. Its report on the first three months of 1993 indicates that of 170,615 layoffs announced by 150 companies, 67,487, or 40 percent, were announced on a Monday, launching the now widely used label for the day: "Stormy Mondays." Tuesday came in second, with 55,168 layoffs (32 percent), Thursday third, with 18,514 (11 percent), and Friday fourth, with 16,935 (10 percent).

"Announcing layoffs on Monday makes more of a 'clean break' and gives the employee an opportunity to get an early start on planning his or her search for a new job," said James E. Challenger, the president of the consulting firm.

LABOR FORCE

Approximately 65 million men and women were employed in 1960; by 1995 that number reached 124 million, according to the Bureau of Labor Statistics.

About 66 percent of Americans age 16 and over had jobs or were seeking jobs in 1995. About 75 percent of the males in the group were working and about 65 percent of the females.

Since 1960 women have entered the labor force in rapidly increasing numbers. The increase was most dramatic for married women with children under age six, the number of whom were working more than tripled from 1960 to 1995 from approximately 29 percent to 60 percent. Of all married women, black women with children between the ages of six and 13 registered the highest employment rate between 1960 and 1995, 81.4 percent.

Women as a whole earn an average of 70 percent of men's median weekly pay.

Hispanics are the fastest growing population group in the labor force, rising from 5.5 million employees in 1980 to an estimated million in 1995. Hispanic workers on average earn about 75 percent of the median for all U.S. workers.

Membership in the most powerful labor organization in the country, the AFL-CIO, declined percipitiously since 1980, dropping from 19.8 million to 16.8 million in 1995. At its peak in the 1980s the AFL-CIO included 78 percent of the nation's organized workers and 18 percent of the U.S. labor force from 1979 to 1993.

The Census Bureau reports that 22.2 million persons are employed in the retail sales industry. The top three fields of employment are administrative support, including clerical; professional specialty; and executive, administrative, and managerial.

Seventy-two percent of employed persons drive alone to work; 13.4 percent join car pools. Commuting time nationwide averages about 22.4 minutes, according to the Census Bureau.

Average hourly earnings of American workers by industry group, 1985-1993; Source, U.S. Bureau of Labor Statistics:			
Industry Group	1985	1990	1993
Manufacturing	$9.54	$10.83	$14.60
Mining	11.98	13.68	14.35
Construction	12.32	13.77	11.76
Transportation, public utilities	11.40	12.97	13.64
Wholesale trade	9.15	10.79	11.71
Retail trade	5.94	6.75	7.29
Finance, Insurance, real estate	7.94	9.97	11.32
Services	7.90	9.83	10.81

MIDDLE–AGE WORKERS

Although middle-age Americans are for the most part economically and physically healthy at present, an uncertain future lies ahead for millions of such workers, a continuing study of those nearing retirement finds. Job insecurity is one of major reasons for the gloom.

Almost 50 percent of 13,600 persons age 51 to 65 polled in the study believe they will be cut loose from their jobs before retirement and think their chances of landing a new job are no better than 50 percent. About 33 percent of the people in the study group are locked in their jobs, and, though feeling insecure in their employment, are fearful of looking for another job. The "lock" that binds them is made up of the pension and health insurance benefits, which they would lose by switching employers. About 14 percent of persons age 51 to 65 lack health insurance, the study finds.

Other findings in the study sponsored by the National Institute on Aging, and being conducted through the year 2005 by the University of Michigan:

- About 40 percent of those surveyed will not receive pensions from their jobs.

- The average household in the group has an annual income of $37,000 and assets of $80,000.

- About 20 percent are nearing retirement without assets.

- Seventy-five percent hoped to phase down from full-time work to part-time when they retire.

OCCUPATIONS AND GENDER

Since at least the mid-1970s, women have been leaving homemaking and seeking a career in business or the professions. The fields in which they've made the biggest strides since 1975 have been electronics, law, economics, and dentistry. Even in careers almost exclusively male, women have begun to crack the glass ceiling. In 1975 not a single woman was a pilot with a commercial airplanes. In 1993, 3.9 percent of commercial airline pilots were female.

Men still outnumber women in most of the selected occupations studied by the Department of Labor's Bureau of Statistics, but the gap is closing. The percentage of women editors and reporters in 1993 was 48.5 percent, compared to 44.6 percent in 1975. Women climbed from 31.1 percent to 42.5 percent of college and university teachers and from 13.1 percent to 47.6 percent of all economists in the U.S.

Women dominate in social work, where they make up 68.9 percent of the workforce, and child care (97.2 percent). In 1975 the ranks of U.S. judges and lawyers were composed of 92.9 percent men and 7.1 percent women; in 1994 they were 67.2 percent male and 22.8 percent female.

About one third of the nation's bartenders in 1975 were women; in 1994 53.3 percent—more than half—were female. Women's share of computer programming jobs climbed from 25.6 percent to 31.5 percent; of computer systems analysts, 14.8 percent to 29.9 percent; of dentists, 1.8 percent to 10.5 percent; of mail carriers, 8.7 percent to 28.4 percent; and of bus drivers, 37.7 percent to 45.8 percent.

Over the same span, more men have entered traditional female jobs in child care (1.2 percent), dental assistance (2.2 percent), and registered nursing (2.6 percent).

Men dominated the ranks of college graduates from 1900 to 1980, but in 1981 women graduates outnumbered men for the first time, 480,000 to 473,000. Women college graduates annually have continued to

outnumber men; in 1992, the figures stood at 616,000 women to 529,000 men.

Males per 100 female college graduates by year, 1930-1990; source: Department of Commerce, Bureau of the Census.

Year	Men for every 100 women
1900	104.9
1910	106.6
1920	104.4
1930	102.9
1940	101.2
1950	99.0
1960	97.4
1970	95.3
1980	94.8
1990	95.9

Men and women college graduates, 1900-1992; Department of Education statistics:

Year	Men	Women
1900	22,173	5,237
1910	28,762	8,437
1920	31,980	16,642
1930	73,615	48,869
1940	109,548	76,954
1950	328,841	103,217
1960	254,063	138,377
1970	484,174	343,060
1980	570,000	465,000
1981	473,000	480,000
1982	479,140	490,370
1983	482,319	491,990
1984	482,528	496,949
1985	485,923	501,900
1986	480,854	510,485
1987	477,203	517,626
1988	483,346	535,409
1989	491,696	559,648
1990	504,045	590,493
1991	517,000	602,000
1992	529,000	616,000

PARENTS, WORKING

A survey conducted by the Families and Work Institute found that 33 percent of employees with children worry about the care their child receives while they are working; 25 percent with children under 12 have child care problems two to three times in three months. Such studies underscore the growing lament of working mothers, which have forced an increasing number of companies to create programs to help their workers merge job and family responsibilities.

The solution for many companies is to offer part-time or "flex-time" (flexible hours) for workers — both male and female. In the last 10 years, the number of companies offering such programs in the U.S. increased from 600 to more than 6,000; among them is Aetna Life & Casualty, in Hartford, Conn., which says it saves $2 million a year through a program benefiting high-performing women for a period of time after they have a child.

Part-time schedules are offered by 87.7 percent of the companies that have parenting programs, but there are drawbacks for employees who choose them: Often they must cover a larger portion of their medical and dental benefits. Flex-time — in which an employee might work the usual number of hours but not adhere to a five-day, 9-to-5 schedule — does not usually have this drawback. Flex-time began to grow in acceptance in the 1980s and is now the fourth most popular program, with 77.1 percent of the companies that have parenting programs offering it.

The list below shows the breakdown by percentage of the various programs offered by companies that have special programs for parents, compiled by the Families and Work Institute.

Part-time	87.7%
Employee assistance	85.6
Personal days	77.4
Flexible time	77.1
Leaves of absence	70.4
Child care resource referral	54.6
Spouse job assistance	51.9
Dependent care plans	49.5
Job sharing	47.9
Flexible place	35.1

POLICE HOMICIDES

Throughout American history, more than 13,500 police officers have been killed in the line of duty, dating from the first recorded U.S. police killing in 1794.

A total of 157 police officers were killed in the line of duty in 1994 (72 by guns) despite the passage by Congress in 1993 and 1994 of two laws aimed at curbing the proliferation of firearms across the country. The 1994 total represented a six percent increase over the 147 who lost their lives in 1993, and the highest number since 165 police officers were killed in 1980.

The Brady Bill, passed in 1993, requires gun purchasers to wait five days before taking possession of a firearm. The second law, passed in 1994, outlawed weapons that have no other purpose than to kill people quickly without taking aim. The Brady Bill was the first anti-firearm legislation passed by Congress since a ban on mail-order weapons in 1968. Between 1981 and 1991, 2.8 million assault weapons were manufactured in the U.S., and 720,657 were imported.

In addition to homicide, police face a great danger of assault. There between 60,000 and 80,000 assaults on offcers a year, according to the latest figures from the Federal Bureau of Investigation. In 1992, 81,252 assaults against police were registered; of those 66,098 were fights, 4,455 were firearm assaults, 2,095 were with cutting instruments, and 8,604 were by other means.

One in nine U.S police officers is assaulted each year, one in 25 is injured, and one in 4,000 is killed in the line of duty, according to a news release from the National Law Enforcement Officers Memorial Fund and the Concerns of Police Survivors. The FBI and the U.S. Justice Department's Public Safety Officer's Benefits program helped compile the data.

Of the officers killed in 1994, 76 were by assault from a person committing a felony, and were 81 from accidents while on duty, such as auto or aircraft crashes. More than 150 police lives were saved in 1994 by bullet-resistant vests; more than 1,800 police lives have saved by the vests since they started being worn in 1974, according to DuPont, which has a hand in manufacturing them.

Thirteen of the 1994 deaths were to federal officers. Five were Drug Enforcement Administration agents killed in a plane crash in Peru, and two were FBI agents, along with a Washington, D.C. homicide sergeant, gunned down when a man walked into a D.C. police station and opened fire.

The average age of the 1994 victims was 36. Six were women. The number of police officers killed by drunk drivers dropped from 16 in 1993 to four in 1944.

California had the most police fatalities at 13, with four occurring in Los Angeles, including Christy Lynne Hamilton, a 45-year-old rookie officer who was shot to death during her first month on the job. Texas suffered 12 police deaths, followed by Georgia with eight, Michigan and Ohio with seven, and New York and Virginia with six. Five of the killings in New York State occurred in New York City.

TECHNICAL GRADUATES

American college students graduating in one of the technical disciplines stand a better chance of landing a job in the service sector than in manufacturing or government, according to a survey on job trends for technical graduates.

The service sector of the U.S. economy is projected by the Bureau of Labor Statistics to account for 109.2 million jobs by year 2005, up from 85.9 million in 1992. At the same time, manufacturing jobs will decline by about three percent, added to a decline of nearly 14 percent between 1979 and 1992, while government jobs offerings will remain almost stagnant, according to BLS figures published by College Placement, Inc.

The service sector, as far as technical grads are concerned, is made up of those disciplined in fields such as marketing, teaching, personnel, recreation, construction management, therapies, and the like. In 1990 technical graduates received 22.1 percent of the total 43.3 percent of job offers given to new graduates by service-sector employers, an almost 50 percent ra-

Robert Gumpert, courtesy of UAW, Detroit, Mich.

These union members at a Rockwell plant may feel secure, but many aerospace workers are potential victims of the nearly $2 billion cuts in defense spending. Aerospace engineers, on the other hand, have numerous other avenues of employment (See table at right) that are outside the manufacturing sector.

tio. In 1994 service-sector employers made 57.3 percent of all job offers to new graduates, with technical graduates receiving 35.4 percent of those jobs, a ratio of 61 percent.

Consulting firms, classified in the service sector, accounted for the highest percentage of job offers to technical graduates, making up 10 percent of the grads' offers. In 1990 such firms made only 5.6 percent of offers to technical graduates. That year, electrical/electronic machinery and equipment manufacturers accounted for 10.7 percent of the offers, with chemicals, drugs, and allied products manufacturers next at 10.3 percent, and petroleum and allied products manufacturers third at 10.2 percent.

In manufacturing, technical graduates received 67.2 of their offers from manufacturers in 1990; in 1994 it was only 53.2 percent. BLS cited defense cuts, the early 1990s, as well as recession, downsizing, and pri-

vatizing by the government for the drop, which, ironically, increases the need for consulting organizations.

In government and non-profit organizations, 12.5 percent of the total reported job offerings were made to new college graduates, up from 11.4 percent in 1990. Technical graduates received 11.4 percent of these offerings in 1994, up only one-half a percent from 10.7 percent in 1990.

Most likely to extend job offers to 1994 technical graduates are consulting organizations (10 percent of technical grad offers), electrical/equipment manufacturers (8.4 percent), and automotive manufacturers (8.1 percent).

Below are the fastest-growing occupations requiring a bachelor's degree, from the BLS *Occupational Outlook Quarterly*:

Occupation	%
Marketing, advertising, public relations	36%
Personnel, labor relations specialists	36
Sports instructors, coaches, trainers	36
Vocational education	36
Secondary school teachers	37
Podiatrists	37
Recreation workers	38
Social workers	40
Recreational therapists	40
Management analysts	43
Construction managers	47
Psychologists	48
Speech-language pathologists/audiologists	48
Preschool, kindergarten teachers	54
Occupationasl therapists	60
Operations research analysts	61
Teachers, special education	74
Physical therapists	88
Systems analysts	110
Computer engineers/scientists	112

The table below shows the industries which will employ various technical graduates in the years to come:

Sector	1990	1994
AEROSPACE/AERONAUTICAL ENGINEERS		
Service	6.4%	37.8%
Manufacturing	82.0	37.2
Government/nonprofit	11.6	25.0
CHEMICAL ENGINEERS		
Service	3.4%	12.0%
Manufacturing	94.9	84.8
Government/nonprofit	1.7	3.2

CIVIL ENGINEERS		
Service	42.1	54.2
Manufacturing	31.9	23.5
Government/nonprofit	26.0	22.5

ELECTRICAL ENGINEERS		
Service	22.2	26.7
Manufacturing	69.2	66.2
Government/nonprofit	8.6	7.1

MECHANICAL ENGINEERS		
Service	13.2	17.9
Manufacturing	81.8	79.7
Government/nonprofit	5.0	2.4

COMPUTER SCIENCE		
Service	45.7	71.7
Manufacturing	47.4	21.4
Government/nonprofit	6.9	6.9

CHEMISTRY		
Service	11.2	23.7
Manufacturing	78.3	64.4
Government/nonprofit	10.5	11.9

BIOLOGICAL SCIENCE		
Service	23.1	26.0
Manufacturing	28.8	34.2
Government/nonprofit	48.1	39.8

AGRICULTURAL SCIENCE		
Service	12.4	35.0
Manufacturing	68.3	41.5
Government/nonprofit	19.3	23.5

TEMPORARY WORKERS

A business idea born half a century ago but which found little nurturing soil until the 1970s has grown into a $14 billion-dollar-a-year industry, and still is growing. It's the world of temporary workers, "just in time labor," where businesses call for just the help they need just when they need them.

Together with part-timers, independent contractors, freelancers, and consultants, temps in 1994 constitute up to 30 percent of the U.S. workforce, according to the National Planning Association. The National Association of Temporary Workers says the annual payroll of temps alone jumped from $3.5 billion in 1981 to its present level, and experts estimate that by the year 2000 half the U.S. workforce will be temporaries.

In new jobs created by the economic upturn of 1993 and 1994, 28 percent were temp jobs, and 26 percent were part-time. About 7.2 percent of the federal workforce is made up of contingency jobs, according to U.S. Office of Personnel Management. About 64 percent of temps are women, and 20 percent are black.

Older people increasingly are entering the ranks. NATS surveys in 1989 and 1994 show that among temps the age group 35-64 rose from 40 to 50 percent of the workforce. Seniors 65 and older remained unchanged at two percent.

Once looked down on as a transient, dead-end field of work, temporary employment since the early 1980s has become more attractive as temp agencies shift their message to client firms from "Keep your hands off our workers," to, "Try them, and if you like them, hire them," in an effort to build up long-term relationships with their customers.

Called "temps to perm," the new emphasis, according to a 1994 poll of 2,200 workers by NATS, showed that 38 percent of the five to seven million temp workers in the U.S. had been offered full-time jobs after testing the waters for 90 to 180 days at their temporary work sites.

Manpower Inc., the country's largest agency, with 640,000 temps, predicts that more than 33 percent of its people will go full-time in 1994, up from 25 percent in 1989. And in 1994 the second-largest agency, Kelly Services, launched KellySelect, a service that will cater solely to temps seeking full-time work.

Unlike part-time workers, seven percent of whom are unionized, temps have no union. Twenty-five percent of temp agencies offer health coverage for those who work a certain number of hours a year. Temps are not protected by the Equal Employment Opportunity Commission, nor are they covered by workers' compensation. Generally they receive no vacations, sick pay, or job guarantees.

Temps are treated better in Europe, many of whose businesses have taken up the idea. In Germany and Europe, temporary employees work through licensed agencies that contribute, along with the employee and the government, to national health care and workers' compensation funds. In Germany, temps are unionized, and through the union build up sick pay and vacation benefits.

WORKING AT HOME

Ninety percent of all home businesses in the U.S. are in the service sector, the Home Office and Business Opportunities Association in Irvine, Calif. reports. Other common work-at-home occupations are: consulting, construction, sales, and farming, according to authors Paul and Sarah Edwards in their book *Working from Home: Everything You need to Know About Working and Living Under One Roof.*

Americans working for themselves out of their homes in 1993 created one out of every five new jobs in the country, the Labor Department reports.

Hispanics are taking the lead in creating home-based businesses concurrently with the layoff of nearly five million employees of *Fortune* 500 companies in a decade, an equivalent of 1,500 jobs every day, according to surveys of what is called "the quiet revolution."

In California, five million self-employed individuals working from their homes in 1993 made up almost half of the 10.4 million in the nation who have created jobs for themselves, according to Link Resources, a research firm located in New York. Among them were an estimated 280,000 work-at-home Hispanics in the U.S. labor force of 10.4 million Hispanics, the magazine *Hispanic Business* reported in September, 1994, basing its figures on Census Bureau data.

The total is up from 109,266 Hispanic businesses in 1982 and 191,334 in 1987, a growth rate of 75 percent, compared to the non-Hispanic home-based businesses growth rate of 29 percent over the same period, Department of Commerce statistics show. Hispanic businesses overall grew 80 percent over the period, while non-Hispanic businesses grew by 32 percent.

part three:

NOTABLE
AMERICANS

ABDUL, PAULA JULIE

Third Rail Entertainment, Tri-Star Bldg., 10202 W. Washington Ave., #26, Culver City, CA 90232

BORN: 1963, Los Angeles. ACHIEVEMENTS: American Video Arts Award, Choreographer of the Year; National Academy Video Arts and Sciences, 1987; Emmy, Best Choreographer, Tracy Ullman Show, 1988-89, MTV award, Best Female Video, Best Dance Video, Best Choreographer in a Video, Best Editing in a Video for the hit Straight Up, 1989. STUDIED: California State University, Northridge; studied tap, jazz with Joe Tramine, the Bella Lewitzky Co.

As a former choreographer for the Los Angeles Lakers cheerleaders, Paula Abdul had plenty of practice in pleasing a crowd and getting people to notice her. After being noticed by the Jacksons, and asked to choreograph their music videos, Abdul was soon in high demand by such artists as Duran Duran, the Pointer Sisters and ZZ Top. Acquiring a taste for the music industry, Paula Abdul branched out on her own with a solo singing career in 1987. Abdul made a splash on the music scene with two back-to-back hit albums. Abdul is most noted for her catchy lyrics and grand music video productions.

ABELSON, ALAN

Barron's, 200 Liberty St., New York, NY 10281. (212) 416-2000

BORN: 1925, New York City. ACHIEVEMENTS: Barron's editor, NBC business commentator. STUDIED: City College of New York, B.S., English/chemistry, 1946, University of Iowa, M.A., creative writing, 1947.

After obtaining his master's in creative writing in 1947, Alan Abelson received his first full-time reporting job from the *New York Journal American* in 1949. He worked his way up through the ranks until *Barron's* stole him away in 1956. Abelson served there as a reporter for nine years when he was promoted to editor in 1965. He is best known for his weekly, front page column *Up and Down Wall Street*, which he began for *Barron's* in 1981. He is known for his ability to inject humor into the otherwise stale subject of the financial market, a factor that facilitated his "side" job as a business commentator for NBC *News at Sunrise.*

ABRAHIM, YOUSSEF M.

The New York Times, 229 West 43rd St., New York, NY 10036 (212) 556-1234

ACHIEVEMENTS: Paris correspondent, New York Times.

Youssef Abrahim's often offbeat dispatches while covering the factions vying for power in the Middle East are part of his success as Paris bureau correspondent for *The New York Times.* In his coverage of Muslim fundamentalists, he describes Al Salam Shopping Center for Veiled Women, and calls it the powerhouse for fundamentalism chic in Egypt. Abrahim suggests that there is waning Arab support for U.S. actions against Iraq because many Arabs see Americans rushing to use weapons against Muslims in Iraq, Libya and Somalia, but are reluctant to do so against Christian Serbs and Croats who massacre Muslim Croatians. The major issues of war and peace are strongly focused in Abrahim's dispatches.

ABRAMSON, JERRY

City Hall, 601 W. Jefferson St., 101, Louisville, KY 40202 (502) 625-3061

Abramson is a prominent political leader in Kentucky and the mayor of Louisville. For career credentials, consult the portion of this book entitled "Notable Americans by Profession" in the Appendix. Within this portion, the list "Political Leaders" describes requirements for inclusion in this volume.

ACKERMAN, JOHN G.

Cornell University Press, Box 250, Sage Hse., 512 E. State, Ithaca, NY 14851 (607) 277-2338

Ackerman is a prominent publisher and head of the Cornell University Press. For career credentials, consult the portion of this book entitled "Notable Americans by Profession" in the Appendix. Within this portion, the list "Publishers" describes requirements for inclusion in this volume.

AGNEW, SPIRO THEODORE

BORN: 1918, Baltimore. ACHIEVEMENTS: 39th vice president of the United States, author, The Canfield Decision, 1976. STUDIED: John Hopkins University; University of Baltimore, L.L.B.

Spiro Agnew served in the U.S. Army during World War II, from 1939 through 1945. He studied law at the University of Baltimore and became a practicing attorney in 1949. Agnew was elected as the Baltimore County executive in 1962, and served in the position until 1966, when he was elected governor of Maryland. He was elected vice president of the United States in 1968, and again in 1972, with President Richard Nixon. As vice president, he became known for his no-holds-barred speeches attacking liberals, dissidents, and the news media critical of the Nixon administration. In 1973 Agnew was charged by the U.S. Attorney General with accepting bribes while holding office as county executive, governor, and vice president. He resigned as vice president on Oct. 10, 1973. Agnew pleaded no contest to tax evasion charges, was sentenced to three years' probation, and fined $10,000.

AKROYD, DAN EDWARD

Atlantic Records, 75 Rockefeller Plaza New York, NY 10019.

BORN: 1952, Ottawa, Canada. ACHIEVEMENTS: Emmy, Best Writing in a Comedy, Variety, or Music Series, Saturday Night Live, 1977. STUDIED: Attended Carleton University.

Dan Akroyd is an original *Saturday Night Live* cast member. He is best known for his Blues Brothers character, which he created with John Belushi. Akroyd was a member of the Toronto Company of the Second City Theater. His major film appearances include: *Love at First Sight*, in 1975, *Mr. Mike's Mondo Video* and *1941*, in 1979, *The Blues Brothers*, in 1980, *Neighbors*, *in 1981*, *Doctor Detroit*, in 1983, *Trading Places*, in 1983, *Twilight Zone-The Movie*, in 1983, and *Ghostbusters*, in 1984. Akroyd is an avid police buff and has an interest in the supernatural. He is also one of the co-founders of the House of Blues and has regrouped the Blues Brothers Band to finance the John Belushi Memorial Fund, a program that provides scholarships for theater students and supports several drug-abuse organizations.

ALBEE, EDWARD FRANKLIN III

14 Harrison St., New York, NY 10013
Albee, III is a prominent dramatic artist. For career credentials, consult the portion of this book entitled "Notable Americans by Profession" in the Appendix. Within this portion, the list "Dramatic Artists" describes requirements for inclusion in this volume.

ALBERT, MARV

NBC Sports, Room 1411, 30 Rockefeller Plaza, New York, NY 10020
BORN: 1943, Brooklyn, N.Y. ACHIEVEMENTS: Global Ace Award and Emmy Award, both for play-by-play announcing, 1990. STUDIED: New York University, B.S., 1964.
Marv Albert, born with the name Marvin Philip Aufrichtig, practiced sportscasting as early as the third grade, when he created his own make-believe radio station and pretended to interview sports stars with his tape recorder. While still in junior high school, Albert was chosen by Howard Cosell to appear on the radio show *All-League Clubhouse*. In college Albert studied sportscasting and journalism, graduating from New York University in 1964. Albert went directly from college into broadcasting. By 1967 he was the play-by-play announcer for both the New York Knicks basketball team and the New York Rangers hockey team. In 1977 Albert became a sports announcer for NBC, covering basketball, football and boxing. He also hosts a baseball pre-game show on NBC Sports Network. Albert received both the Global Ace Award and an Emmy Award for play-by-play announcing in 1990, and has also received three Cable Ace Awards for play-by-play announcing.

ALDA, ALAN

Martin Bregman Productions, 641 Lexington Ave., New York, NY 10022
*BORN: 1936, New York City. ACHIEVEMENTS: Emmy Awards, Actor, Comedy Series M*A*S*H, 1974 and 1982; Emmy Award, Actor of the Year, Series, 1974; Golden Globe Awards, Best Actor in a Comedy Series, Musical/Comedy, all for M*A*S*H, 1975, 1976, and 1980 through 1983; Emmy Awards, Director, Comedy Series, for episode Dear Sigmund, 1977 and the episode Comrades in Arms—Part 1 (with Burt Metcalfe), 1978; Emmy Award, Writing, Comedy, Comedy-Variety, or Music Series, for episode Inga, 1979. STUDIED: Fordham University, B.S., 1956; studied at Cleveland Playhouse.*
To many, Alan Alda will always be remembered for his role as Hawkeye Pierce in the long running television series *M*A*S*H*, which originally appeared from 1972 until 1983 and continues in reruns. In addition to his work as an actor on the series, Alda wrote and directed numerous episodes. Alda began his acting career performing Abbott land Costello-style sketches with his father in 1945. His first appearance on television was

on the *Phil Silvers Show* in 1957. Alda got his first series role in *That Was the Week That Was* in 1964. He began acting in *M*A*S*H* in 1972, and continued with the series for 12 years. Alda also starred in, directed, or wrote a number of hit movies, including *Paper Lion*, in 1968, *California Suite*, in 1978, *The Four Seasons*, in 1981, *Sweet Liberty*, in 1986, and *Canadian Bacon*, in 1994.

ALDRIN, EDWIN "BUZZ" EUGENE JR.

c/o NASA, L.B. Johnson Space Center, Houston, TX 77058; (713) 483-0123.
BORN: 1930, Glen Ridge, N.J. ACHIEVEMENTS: Space Missions: Gemini 12 (pilot), Apollo 11 (lunar module pilot), second person to walk on the moon. STUDIED: U.S. Military Academy, B.S., 1951; Massachusetts Institute of Technology, Ph.D., astronautics, 1963.
Buzz Aldrin earned his Air Force pilot's wings in 1952 and flew 66 combat missions in the Korean War. He was selected by NASA as an astronaut in 1963, after earning a doctorate in astronautics. His first mission was Gemini 12, in 1966, with commander James Lovell. Aldrin made a record-setting, five-and-a-half-hour space walk where he solved the problem of space-walk exhaustion by using straps and pacing himself. His next mission was Apollo 11, in July 1969, where he flew to the moon with Neil Armstrong and Michael Collins. He piloted the lunar excursion module to the moon's surface, and was the second person to walk on the lunar surface, after Armstrong. Aldrin left NASA two years later to become the commander of the Air Force Aerospace Research Pilots School. He entered private business in 1972.

ANFINSEN, CHRISTIAN BOEHMER

Johns Hopkins University, Department of Biology, 34th & Charles Streets, Baltimore, MD
BORN: 1916, Monessen, Pa. ACHIEVEMENTS: Nobel Prize in Chemistry (shared with Stanford Moore and William Howard Stein), 1972; Public Service Award, Rockefeller Foundation; Myrtle Wreath, Hadassah. STUDIED: Swarthmore College; University of Pennsylvania; Harvard University.
Christian Anfinsen received his recognition from Stockholm while working as a researcher during the 1960s and 1970s at the National Institute of Arthritis, Metabolism, and Digestive Diseases. From that position he made many pioneering studies on enzymes and their uses as diagnostic aids in human diseases or for commercial use, for example as plant enzymes in meat tenderizers, clarifying beer, and in laundry detergents. It was that overall work the Nobel physics committee honored. Specifically mentioned in his citation, however, was his research on a class of enzymes that catalyzes the decay of RNA, breaking up its component parts with water for closer study.

ALICE, MARY

Ambrosio/Mortimer and Associates Inc., 9150 Wilshire Blvd., Suite 175, Beverly Hills, CA, 90212
BORN: 1941, Indianola, Miss. ACHIEVEMENTS: Drama Desk Award, Antoinette Perry Award, Best Featured Actress in a Play, both for Fences, 1987; Emmy Award, Outstanding Supporting Actress in a Drama Series, I'll Fly

Away, 1993. STUDIED: Chicago State University, B.Ed.; Negro Ensemble Company, New York, N.Y.; stage training with Lloyd Richards.

Although Mary Alice started out as a public school teacher in Chicago, her creative drive propelled her into acting. She shortened her name for the stage from Mary Alice Smith. Alice began acting professionally in 1967, making her Broadway debut as Cora Beasley in *No Place to Be Somebody* in 1971. She first appeared on film in 1974 as Moms in *The Education of Sonny Carson.* Her favorite role—also her television debut—came in 1974, when she played Alberta in *The Sty of the Blind Pig,* on *Hollywood Television Theatre.* She is best known on film for her 1976 portrayal of Ettie in the movie, *Sparkle,* and on stage for her portrayal of Rose, in the play, *Fences,* in 1987. More recently, she played opposite Danny Glover in the movie, *To Sleep with Anger,* in 1990 and appeared in the television series *I'll Fly Away.*

ALLAIRE, PAUL A.

Xerox Corporation, Lone Ridge Road, Box 1600, Stamford, CT 06904; (203) 968-3000
BORN: 1938, Worcester, Mass. ACHIEVEMENTS: Chairman, Council on Competitiveness; board member of Sara Lee Corp., the New York Stock Exchange, and SmithKline Beecham PLC. STUDIED: Worcester Polytechnic Institute, B.S., 1960; Carnegie-Mellon University, M.S., 1966.

As a boy, Paul Allaire worked for his father on the family truck farm. He was taught to make sure the fruit on the bottom of the basket was as good as the fruit on the top. He started work at Xerox in 1966, right after receiving his M.S. degree in industrial administration from Carnegie-Mellon University. Throughout his career with Xerox, Allaire earned a reputation as a cost cutter and department reorganizer, who increased market share in the process. As CEO, Allaire instituted what he calls the "total satisfaction" guarantee. If a Xerox product fails to satisfy a customer during the first three years of operation, the customer can exchange the machine for a replacement. Allaire has enabled Xerox to recover its position as a leader in document management.

ALLEN, MARTIN A.

Computervision Corporation, 100 Crosby Dr., Bedford, MA 01730 (617) 275-1800
Allen is a prominent business leader and CEO of Computervision Corporation in Bedford, Mass. For career credentials, consult the portion of this book entitled "Notable Americans by Profession" in the Appendix. Within this portion, the list "Business Leaders" describes requirements for inclusion in this volume.

ALLEN, JOAN

Brian Mann, International Creative Management, 8899 Beverly Blvd., Los Angeles, CA 90048
BORN: 1956, Rochelle, Ill. ACHIEVEMENTS: Antoinette Perry Award, Best Actress in a Play, Burn This!, 1988. STUDIED: Eastern Illinois University, Western Illinois University.

Joan Allen began acting professionally in 1983, and quickly received critical admiration. She is a founding member of the Steppenwolf Theatre Company of Chicago and made her stage debut with the company in the play *And a Nightingale Sang.* That appearance earned her a Theatre World Award, Clarence Derwent Award, Drama desk Award, and an Outer Critics Circle Award in 1984. She has continued to work on stage through the 1980s and into the 1990s and has also begun to develop her career on film. She has appeared in such films as, *Peggy Sue Got Married,* in 1986, and *Tucker: The Man and His Dream,* in 1988. Allen has also made a number of appearances on television, including the mini-series, *Evergreen,* in 1985.

ALLEN, GEORGE

Office of the Governor, State Capitol, Richmond, Virginia 23219 (804) 786-2211
BORN: 1952. ACHIEVEMENTS: National Federation of Independent Business Award; Council for Citizens Against Government Waste Award; National Taxpayers Union Foundation Award. STUDIED: University of Virginia, B.A. with honors, history, 1974, and Juris Doctor, 1977.

Gov. George Allen served nine years as a delegate to the Virginia House of Delegates, during which he led a successful effort to adopt a constitutional amendment to direct proceeds from the sale of confiscated drug dealer assets to local law enforcement agencies. In 1991, he was elected by a significant majority to the U.S. House of Representatives in a special election, which was a three-way contest. As a U.S. congressman Allen is best remembered for co-authoring a balanced budget amendment to the Constitution which limited tax increases, and which became the official Republican version of this legislation in Congress. On becoming governor of Virginia in 1993, he became the first gubernatorial candidate to receive more than a million votes in a general election. Allen intensified his career-long dedication to saving tax dollars. He has received many awards from bipartisan independent organizations for his efforts to reduce government spending and protect the interests of small business.

ALLEN, JR., GEORGE

Office of the Governor, State Capitol, Box 1475, Richmond, VA 23212 (804) 786-2211
Allen, Jr. is a prominent political leader in Virginia and governor of the state. For career credentials, consult the portion of this book entitled "Notable Americans by Profession" in the Appendix. Within this portion, the list "Political Leaders" describes requirements for inclusion in this volume.

ALLEN, WOODY

Rollins/Joffee/Morra/Brezner Inc., 130 W. 57th Street New York NY 10019.
BORN: 1935, Brooklyn, N.Y. ACHIEVEMENTS: Oscar, Best Director, Annie Hall, 1977; Oscar, Best Original Screenplay, Hannah and Her Sisters, 1986; Golden Globe, Best Screenplay, The Purple Rose of Cairo, 1986. STUDIED: Attended New York University, 1953; City College of New York, 1953.

Allan Stewart Konigsberg, (legal name Heywood Allen) began his career in high school, writing comic column-breaks for newspaper columnists Walter

Winchell and Earl Wilson. He later began writing gags for $25 a week. At the urging of the William Morris agency, Allen started writing comic sketches for Pat Boone, Buddy Hackett, Kaye Ballard, Peter Lindsay Hayes, Carol Channing and Stubby Kaye. He used his talents as a gag-writer on shows starring Ed Sullivan, Garry Moore, Sid Caesar, and Art Carney. Pushed by his agents, Allen began performing his own routines on stage. In 1961, he made his first appearance at the Duplex in Greenwich Village. Two years later, Allen wrote the script for *What's New Pussycat?*, in which he also made his film debut. Allen recycled a Japanese film, into the American movie *What's Up Tiger Lily?*, in 1966. Charles K. Feldman, the producer of *What's New Pussycat?* hired Allen again to write and perform in *Casino Royale*, in 1967. By 1969, his first plays ran on Broadway, *Don't Drink the Water* and *Play It Again Sam.* Next Allen turned his attention away from the stage and more toward the cinema, becoming devoted to writing, directing, and starring in his films. He directed *Take the Money and Run,* where he was the main creator. Other cinematic works include; *Annie Hall, Manhattan, Stardust Memories, The Purple Rose of Cairo, Hannah and Her Sisters, Radio Days, Crimes and Misdemeanors,* and *Bullets over Broadway.* Known for his neuroses, he plays clarinet every Monday night in Manhattan at Michael's Pub. He even missed the Academy Award ceremony, where he won one for *Annie Hall,* because it was on a Monday night.

ALLEY, WILLIAM J.

American Brands, Inc., 1700 E. Putnam Ave. #811, Old Greenwich, CT 06870 (203) 698-5000
Alley is a prominent business leader and CEO of American Brands. For career credentials, consult the portion of this book entitled "Notable Americans by Profession" in the Appendix. Within this portion, the list "Business Leaders" describes requirements for inclusion in this volume.

ALLEY, KIRSTIE

Barret/Benson/McCartt & Weston, 10390 Santa Monica Blvd., Los Angeles, CA 90025
BORN: 1955, Wichita, Kan. ACHIEVEMENTS: Emmy Award, Outstanding Lead Actress in a Comedy Series, Golden Globe Award, Best Actress in a Musical/Comedy Series, Cheers, 1991. STUDIED: Kansas State University, University of Kansas.
Kirstie Alley rose to fame in 1987 playing Rebecca Howe on the television series, *Cheers.* However, Alley's big break actually came in 1982, when she played Lieutenant Saavik in the movie, *Star Trek II: The Wrath of Kahn.* Alley, whose first career was interior decorating in the 1970s, has appeared in numerous television shows and movies throughout the 1980s and 1990s. Among her more popular movie appearances were: *Look Who's Talking,* in 1989, and *Look Who's Talking Too,* in 1990. Her many television appearances include: the movie, *The Prince of Bel Air,* in 1986; and

the mini-series, *North and South,* in 1985, and its sequel, *North and South: Book II,* in 1986.

ALMOND, LINCOLN

State House, Providence RI 02903 (401) 277-2080
BORN: 1936, Pawtucket, R.I. ACHIEVEMENTS: Historic Central Falls Hall of Fame; Dorothy Lohman Community Service Award, Rhode Island Bar Association; John Q. Stitely Distinguished Public Service Award, American Society for Public Administration; Brotherhood Award, Rhode Island/Southeastern New England Region of the National Conference of Christians and Jews. STUDIED: University of Rhode Island, B.A., science; Boston University, J.D., law.
A Republican, Gov. Almond brought to office in 1994 a dedication to the environment and school construction, and in fighting organized crime, drugs, white collar crime, and corruption in politics. At age 26, he supported an environmental program for open spaces in the state, and promoted purchase of water rights along several rivers, ponds, and marsh lands, a program still in effect. His platform in 1994 pledged to continue his early work, as well as to bring an economic resurgence to Rhode Island.

ALTMAN, SIDNEY

Yale University, Department of Biology, P.O. Box 6666, New Haven, CT 06520
BORN: 1939, Montreal. ACHIEVEMENTS: Nobel Prize in Chemistry (shared with Thomas Robert Cech), 1989. STUDIED: Massachusetts Institute of Technology; University of Colorado.
Contributing to the explosion of discoveries in biochemistry in the twentieth century, Sidney Altman, a naturalized American, along with Thomas Robert Cech, solved a problem that had eluded their peers for decades. It had long been known that DNA (deoxyribonucleic acid), the building block of life since it provides coded instructions of an organism's genes to enzymes, was master control over RNA (ribonucleic acids), which is involved in the synthesis of proteins in chemical cell reactions. Unanswered was the question of how RNA accomplished this. The coloaureates, working independently, proved that RNA molecules could actively aid chemical reactions in cells by rearranging themselves in the cell (becoming a ribozyme), producing different products while still under DNA's control (Altman). Cech proved that RNAs could also double as enzymes. Their work led to the discovery of many ribozymes, and also has potential application for treatment of disease states.

ALUM, MANUEL

c/o Manuel Alum Dance Company, 39 White Street, New York, NY 10013 (212) 925-5947
Alum is a prominent dancer. For career credentials, consult the portion of this book entitled "Notable Americans by Profession" in the Appendix. Within this portion, the list "Dancers" describes requirements for inclusion in this volume.

ANDERS, WILLIAM ALISON

General Dynamics Corp., Pierre Laclede Center, St. Louis, MO 63166 (703) 876-3000.

BORN: 1933, Hong Kong. ACHIEVEMENTS: Space mission: Apollo 8 (pilot). STUDIED: U.S. Naval Academy, B.S., 1955; Air Force Institute of Technology, M.S., nuclear engineering, 1962.

Prior to graduating from college with a master's in nuclear engineering, William Anders was an interceptor pilot in the U.S. Air Force. He went on to work at the Air Force Weapons Laboratory, and was chosen as an astronaut in 1963. Anders piloted Apollo 8, in December 1968, the first manned mission to fly around the moon, with Frank Borman and James Lovell Jr. The mission scouted for landing sights on the lunar surface, and on Christmas Day, the three astronauts read from the book of Genesis as a holiday greeting from the moon. From 1969 to 1973, Anders was executive secretary of the National Aeronautics and Space Council. Later positions included atomic energy commissioner, United States ambassador to Norway and corporate officer of General Electric, Textron, and General Dynamics.

ANDERSON, BILL

The Atlantic Monthly, 745 Boylston St., Boston, MA 02116-2603 (617) 536-9500

Anderson is a prominent magazine and publisher of the *Atlantic monthly*. For career credentials, consult the portion of this book entitled "Notable Americans by Profession" in the Appendix. Within this portion, the list "Publishers" describes requirements for inclusion in this volume.

ANDERSON, J. REID

Verbatim Corporation, 1200 W.T. Harris Blvd., Charlotte, NC 28262 (704) 547-6500

Anderson is a prominent business leader and CEO of the Verbatim Corporation of Charolette, N.C, a company that, among other things, developes and manufactures digital media. For career credentials, consult the portion of this book entitled "Notable Americans by Profession" in the Appendix. Within this portion, the list "Business Leaders" describes requirements for inclusion in this volume.

ANDERSON, PHILIP WARREN

Princeton University, Department of Physics, Princeton, NJ 08544

BORN: 1923. ACHIEVEMENTS: Nobel Prize in Physics (shared with John Van Fleck and Neville Mott), 1977; Oliver E. Buckley Prize; Guthrie Medal; National Medal of Science; Dannie Heineman Prize. STUDIED: Harvard University.

Philip Anderson was a research scientist at Bell Laboratories for 28 years, with time out for a teaching stint at Cambridge University in England. Later, he combined his job with teaching at Princeton University. Anderson was deeply involved in electricity and its effects and uses by the time he won his Nobel Prize (shared with John Van Fleck and Neville Mott) for work underlying computer memories and electronic devices. To the group's "theoretical investigation of the electronic structure of magnetic and disordered systems," Anderson contributed important new findings in superconductor metals, such as lead, magnesium, and zinc, and even some alloys, that overcome electrical resistance when they are cooled to absolute zero (the temperature at which substances possess no thermal energy, equal to -273.15 degrees Celsius, or -459.67 degrees Fahrenheit). He discovered that current in a superconducting circuit will continue to flow after the source of current has been shut off. Such current can be used in powerful electromagnets, which, once energized, retain their magnetic field, and in ultrasensitive electronic instruments and computer elements.

ANDREWS, M.D., MASON C.

Office of the Mayor, 1109 City Hall Bldg., Norfolk, VA 23501 (804) 441-2679

Andrews, M.D. is a prominent political leader. For career credentials, consult the portion of this book entitled "Notable Americans by Profession" in the Appendix. Within this portion, the list "Political Leaders" describes requirements for inclusion in this volume.

ANDRE, CARL

P.O. Box 1001, Cooper Station, New York, NY 10276

BORN: 1935. ACHIEVEMENTS: Collections: Museum of Modern Art, Art Institute of Chicago; exhibitions: Solomon R. Guggenheim Museum; Museum of Modern Art. STUDIED: Phillips Academy.

After studying with Hollis Frampton and Patrick Morgan, Carl Andre met Frank Stella and subsequently developed his own minimalist theories during the late 1950s. Wood and plexiglass, into which Andre carved geometrical patterns, were his media then. He emphasized architectural design until 1964, when, after working on a railroad, he decided to make his work "more like roads than like buildings." Considering himself a "post-studio artist," he placed bricks, metal strips and other industrial products of standard size in random arrangements on the floor. The identity of these pieces would change as the elements were stored and later rearranged elsewhere. Using only one medium in each piece, he leaves materials in their natural state, leaving time and the elements to change the surfaces. He questions the notion that art is unique and precious, and seeks to explore the interactions of space with the gravity, mass, weight and placement of forms.

ANDREAS, DWAYNE ORVILLE

Archer Daniels Midland Co., 4666 Faries Pkwy., Decatur, IL 62526

BORN: 1918, Worthington, Minn. STUDIED: Wheaton College, Wheaton, Ill.; Barry University, Miami Shores, Fla. (honorary degree).

After 20 years as chairman and chief executive officer of Honeymead Products (now National City Bancorp Company), in Cedar Rapids, Iowa, Dwayne Andreas turned his attention globally, and won national acclaim. Joining Archer Midland Daniels in Decatur, Ill., as CEO in 1970, he expanded the world's largest food processing company into international markets. The feat was so successful that he was called to Washington, D.C. to become a government adviser on international trade. Among his achievements: guiding the company to the number-two position in the Fortune 500 list ,and forging trade links between the U.S. and Russia.

ANFINSEN, CHRISTIAN BOEHMER

Johns Hopkins Univ., Dept. of Bio., 34th & Charles Streets, Baltimore, MD 21218-2685
Anfinsen is a prominent scientist. For career credentials, consult the portion of this book entitled "Notable Americans by Profession" in the Appendix. Within this portion, the list "Scientists" describes requirements for inclusion in this volume.

ANGELOU, MAYA

Wake Forest University, Department of Humanities, Winston Salem, NC 27106-4647
BORN: 1928, St. Louis, Mo. ACHIEVEMENTS: Obie Award for appearance in the revue Cabaret for Freedom and The Blacks; appointed by President Ford to the Bicentennial Commission; appointed by President Carter to the National Committee on Observance of International Women's Year; named Woman of the Year in Communications, 1976; Ladies Home Journal Top 100 Most Influential Women, 1983; The Matrix Award, 1983; The North Carolina Award in Literature. STUDIED: honorary degrees, Smith College, 1975; Mills College, 1975; Lawrence University, 1976; studied dance with Pearl Primus, N.Y.C.

During Maya Angelou's childhood, a traumatic event made her stop speaking for several years. Her years of silence led her to write to express her feelings. Her critically acclaimed autobiography *I Know Why the Caged Bird Sings*, 1970, is an account of this event and

Dancer Mary Anthony as Lady Macbeth.

other childhood experiences in segregated Arkansas. Her other novels include, *Gather Together in My Name*, 1974; *Singin' & Swingin' & Gettin' Merry Like Christmas*, 1976; *The Heart of a Woman*, 1981; and *All God's Children Need Traveling Shoes*, 1986. Also a poet, she wrote a poem for President Bill Clinton's inauguration. She read the poem *On the Pulse of Morning*, during the inauguration ceremony. Angelou's other books of poetry include: *And Still I Rise*, 1976; *Shaker, Why Don't You Sing?* 1983; *Now Sheeba Sings the Song*, 1987; and *I Shall Not Be Moved*,1990. In 1981 she received a lifetime appointment as the first Reynolds Professor of American studies at Wake Forest University.

ANGIER, NATALIE

The *New York Times*, 229 West 43rd St., New York, NY 10046 (212) 556-1234
BORN: 1958. ACHIEVEMENTS: Pulitzer Prize, Beat Reporting, 1991; International Biomedical Journalism Prize, 1990; Lewis Thomas Award for Excellence in Writing, Natural Obsessions: The Search for the Oncogene, 1988. STUDIED: Barnard College, B.A., magna cum laude English and physics, 1978.

Natalie Angier has been a science reporter for the *New York Times* since 1990. Before joining the *New York Times* staff she was a freelance science writer and editor as well as adjunct professor at New York University in the science and environmental reporting graduate program. She held these positions from 1986 until 1990. During this time she was a frequent contributor to the *Atlantic*, the *New York Times*, *Parade*, *American Health*, *Discover*, and other publications. Angier spent two years at *Time* magazine as science and environment writer. She also was senior associate editor of *Savvy* magazine from 1983 to 1984. Angier began her career at *Discover* magazine in 1980. She worked as a staff writer there until 1983.

ANTHONY, MARY

Mary Anthony Dance Theater, 736 Broadway, New York, NY 10003 (212) 674-8191

Anthony is a prominent dancer. For career credentials, consult the portion of this book entitled "Notable Americans by Profession" in the Appendix. Within this portion, the list "Dancers" describes requirements for inclusion in this volume.

APPEL, KAREL

c/o Martha Jackson Gallery, 521 W. 57th St., New York, NY 10019

BORN: 1921. ACHIEVEMENTS: Venice Biennale; First Prize for Painting, Guggenheim International Exhibition; collections: Museum of Modern Art, New York City; Museum of Fine Arts, Boston; exhibitions: Solomon R. Guggenheim Museum, New York City; Museum of Modern Art, New York City. STUDIED: Royal Academy of Fine Arts, Amsterdam (Holland).

As a founding member of the International Association for Experimental Art and of the COBRA group in 1948, this Abstract Expressionist created violent, forceful images with thickly applied paint. Often Karel Appel applied paint straight from the tube, making many layers of color. He said about his work: "The paint expresses itself. In the mass of paint, I find my imagination." For a while he applied objects to the canvases, but soon returned to two-dimensional work. Since COBRA disbanded, Appel has continued as a prolific artist, been active as a graphic artist and as a sculptor. His sculpture, large and bulky like the thickly applied paint of his canvases, and accented with lurid colors, is a three-dimensional counterpart to his paintings.

APPLEBAUM, IRWYN

Bantam Books, 1540 Broadway, New York, NY 10036 (212) 354-6500

BORN: 1955, Queens, N.Y. ACHIEVEMENTS: President of Bantam Books STUDIED: Columbia School of Journalism, B.A.

Irwyn Applebaum is the president and publisher of Bantam Books and senior vice president of the Bantam Doubleday Dell group. He moved to Bantam in 1985 from Simon & Schuster's Pocket Books, Bantam's chief rival in the paperback field. At Pocket Books for seven years, Applebaum guided the company to preeminence in the crowded industry by publishing more paperback best sellers than any other publisher in the period from 1987 to 1992. Applebaum worked at Bantam after graduation from Columbia, editing 21 books of the best-selling Western novelist Louis L'Amour among his other labors. His brother, Stuart Applebaum, is senior vice president and director for public relations of the Bantam Doubleday Dell group.

ARCHER, DENNIS

Office of the Mayor, 1126 City-County Bldg., Detroit, MI 48226 (313) 224-3400

Archer is a prominent political leader. For career credentials, consult the portion of this book entitled "Notable Americans by Profession" in the Appendix. Within this portion, the list "Political Leaders" describes requirements for inclusion in this volume.

ARLEDGE, DAVID A.

Coastal Corporation, 9 Greenway Plaza E., Houston, TX 77046 (713) 877-1400

BORN: 1945, El Dorado, Alaska. Achievements: President of Coastal Corporation STUDIED: University of Texas, B.A., business administration, J.D., New York University's Graduate Tax Law Program

David Arledge is the president and chief operating officer of the $10 billion energy holding company Coastal Corporation. He joined the firm in 1980, at age 35, as head of the corporate tax department. Three years later Arledge became a vice president, with the additional duties of chief financial officer. Elected to the board of directors in 1988 and named senior executive vice president in 1993, he assumed his present position in 1994. Coastal Corporation has subsidiary operations in natural gas marketing and power production.

ARMSTRONG, NEIL A.

AIL Systems, Inc., Commack Rd., Deer Park, NY 11729 (516) 595-5000.

BORN: 1930, Wapakoneta, Ohio. ACHIEVEMENTS: Space missions: Gemini 8 (command pilot), Apollo 11 (commander), first person to walk on the moon. STUDIED: Purdue University, B.S. aeronautical engineering, 1955; University of Southern California, M.S. aerospace engineering, 1970.

Neil Armstrong became a licensed pilot on his 16th birthday and joined the Naval Air Academy a year later. He studied aeronautical engineering, served in the Korean War, and then became a civilian research pilot for the National Advisory Committee for Aeronautics (now the National Aeronautics and Space Administration). Armstrong joined the Pilot-Astronaut program in 1962 and flew the North American X-15 as a test pilot, reaching an altitude of 207,500 feet. He commanded the Apollo 11 mission to the moon, in 1969, and piloted the lunar landing module, *Eagle*, to the lunar surface. Armstrong was the first person to set foot on the moon. As he stepped off the Eagle's ladder, he spoke the now famous words, "That's one small step for [a] man, one giant leap for mankind." He is now an aeronautical engineer.

ARNESON, ROBERT

110 East E. St., Benecia, CA 94510

BORN: 1930. ACHIEVEMENTS: Collections: Oakland Art Museum, San Francisco Museum of Modern Art; exhibitions: Whitney Museum of American Art, The Museum of Modern Art. STUDIED: California College of Arts and Crafts; Mills College.

For the last 20 years Robert Arneson has worked as a ceramic sculptor as well as in the inter-related fields of prints and drawings. A cartoonist as a youth, he later became interested in the glazed multi-part clay forms of Peter Voulkos. His skillful and rich color sense in his sculptural works has served him well in his drawings and prints. Even those in a single color tone have a richness about them which is seen still more fully in his color prints. Those prints employ anywhere from three to seven different hues.In the recent years, a good deal of his work has centered on the subject of the self-portrait and contemporary over-sized ceramic busts glazed in bright colors. Other major concerns in his work are the questions of identity and artistic persona which come so naturally to the subject of the self-portrait. His work pushes explic-itness to an absurd extreme. This is the core of his characteristic wit.

ARRINGTON, RICHARD JR.

Office of the Mayor, City Hall, 710 N. 20th St., Bir-mingham, AL 35203 (205) 254-2277
BORN: 1934, Livingston, Ala. ACHIEVEMENTS: Top 100 Most Influential Black Americans, Ebony magazine. STUDIED: Miles College, B.S., biology and chemistry; University of Detroit, M.S., biology; University of Oklahoma, Ph.D., zoology and biochemistry.

Richard Arrington, Jr. is the first African American mayor of Birmingham, Ala. He has taught at Miles College, the University of Alabama, and the University of Oklahoma. Arrington served on the Birmingham City Council from 1971 through 1979. In 1979 he was elected mayor of Birmingham, and has been re-elected to three additional terms. In 1989 Arrington promoted a new program called the "Birmingham Plan," a vol-untary program to help ensure that women and minori-ties share in the cities economic growth. Minority businesses now receive more than 30 percent of the city's contracts each year.

ARROW, KENNETH JOSEPH

Stanford University, Department of Economics, Stan-ford, CA 94305
Arrow is a prominent economist. For career creden-tials, consult the portion of this book entitled "Notable Americans by Profession" in the Appendix. Within this portion, the list "Economists" describes require-ments for inclusion in this volume.

ARTHUR, BEATRICE

c/o L. Auerbach, William Morris Agency, 151 El Camino, Beverly Hills, CA 90212
BORN: 1926, New York City. ACHIEVEMENTS: Antoinette Perry Award, Outstanding Musical Actress Supporting or Featured; Emmy Award, Out-standing Lead Actress in a Comedy Series. STUDIED: Franklin Institute of Sciences & Art; New School for Social Research

Beatrice Arthur is a product of the New York stage, but gained widest recognition when she played the brassy title role in the 1972-78 hit television sitcom *Maude*. She debuted in 1947 in Aristophanes' antiwar comedy *Lysistrata* at the Dramatic Workshop of the New School for Social Research, and the same year appeared professionally off-Broadway in *Dog Beneath the Skin*. Arthur was widely acclaimed for her por-trayal of Lucy Brown in a 1953 off-Broadway revival of

The Threepenny Opera (Die Dreigroschenoper) the gaily cynical production by German theatrical giant Berthold Brecht (music by Kurt Weill). She became a regular on *Sid Caesar's Comedy Hour* on television and made her film debut in *That Kind of Woman*. Arthur made several guest appearances as Cousin Maude on the television sitcom *All In the Family*. Those appear-ances spun off into *Maude*, Arthur's own long-running television show. She has since developed her uniquely forceful presence as Dorothy, the sarcastic member of *The Golden Girls*, which ran from 1985 to 1992.

ARTSCHWAGER, RICHARD ERNST

P.O. Box 99, Charlotteville, NY 12036
BORN: 1923. ACHIEVEMENTS: NEA Cassandra Award; collections: Whit-ney Museum of American Art, New York City, Museum of Modern Art, New York City; exhibitions: Venice Biennale; Whitney Museum of American Art, New York City. STUDIED: Cornell University.

After helping Claus Oldenberg put together *Bedroom Ensemble*, Richard Artschwager gained recognition with pseudo-furniture of formica on wood, such as *Table with Tablecloth*, and later with urban views, such as *High Rise Apartment*, made of liquitex on celotex with formica. These Pop works questioned the utility of art and its place in American culture. Recent paintings use photographs as their base: synthetic-looking hand execution distorts the photograph's de-scription of reality, and often the frame (the "furniture") becomes an integral part of the work, as in *Left Pinch*, in which space is expanded through the addition of a mirror to the frame.

ARTZT, EDWIN LEWIS

Procter & Gamble Company, 1 Procter & Gamble Plaza, Cincinnati, OH 45202 (513) 983-1100
BORN: 1930, New York City. ACHIEVEMENTS: Opportunity 2000 Award, U.S. Department of Labor; Martin Luther King Salute to Greatness Award. STUDIED: University of Oregon, B.A.

When Edwin Artzt took over as the guiding light of Procter & Gamble in 1990, the company was falling behind in market share in almost all of its multitudi-nous lines. At the end of his five-year term, sales had grown from $21 billion to nearly $32 billion, and earn-ings per common share increased from $1.78 to $3.40. Artzt accomplished this feat by introducing innova-tive new lines, such as *Pantene Pro-V*, the leading hair product in the world, stronger paper products (*Extra-Durable Bounty, Charmin Ultra*), and the world's num-ber one feminine protection product, *Always/Whisper*. Improving efficiency of operations by closing 30 plants and shedding 13,000 jobs—12 percent of Procter and Gamble's global work force—gave Artzt a reputation for ruthlessness but resulted in expected savings of $500 million by 1996. Artzt also added business in 10 countries including some in South America, Eastern Europe, and Asia, and bought 21 companies, among them Max Factor. In 1995 Artzt retired after 41 years with the company. He continues as director and chair-man of the company's executive committee.

ASH, MARY KAY

Mary Kay Cosmetics, 8787 Stemmons Freeway, Dallas, TX 75247 (214) 630-8787

BORN: 1915, Hot Wells, Texas. ACHIEVEMENTS: Dale Carnegie Leadership Award, Horatio Alger Distinguished American Citizen Award, National Sales Hall of Fame Award, Kupfer Distinguished Executive Award, Texas A&M University, Pathfinder Award, National Association of Women Business Owners, United Nations Environment Program recognition for a commitment to the environment and leadership in promoting sound environmental policies in the cosmetics industry. STUDIED: University of Houston.

Mary Kay Ash is the founder of Mary Kay Cosmetics, the largest direct seller of skin-care products and cosmetics in the country. The company has been on Fortune magazine's list of the 500 largest corporations in the United States since 1992. Her success is based on offering women opportunities in sales that were non-existent when she began Mary Kay in 1963. One well-publicized perk for top sales performers in her company is a pink Cadillac. Ash maintains that awards can be as motivational as money. In 1995 there were 325,000 Mary Kay consultants. According to company figures, three percent of American women earn more than $100,000 a year. Eighty percent of those, says the company, are associated with Mary Kay Cosmetics. Among her personal achievements was calling for a moratorium on animal testing for all 200 of its products and their ingredients in 1987. Ash is the author of four books, her autobiography, *Mary Kay*, a book on her management style, *Mary Kay on People Management*, a collection of brief inspirational essays aimed at women, *From My Heart*, and *Women Who Want It All*. In addition to her writings, she often does motivational speaking which is directed toward women.

ATWATER, JR., H. BREWSTER

General Mills, Inc., 1 General Mills Blvd., Minneapolis, MN 55426 (612) 540-2311

Atwater, Jr. is a prominent business leader. For career credentials, consult the portion of this book entitled "Notable Americans by Profession" in the Appendix. Within this portion, the list "Business Leaders" describes requirements for inclusion in this volume.

AUEL, JEAN MARIE

Jean V Naggar Literary Agency, 2117 E 75th St. New York NY 10021

BORN: 1936, Chicago. ACHIEVEMENTS: Friends of Literature Award, The Clan of the Cave Bear, 1980; Mensa, honorary vice president 1990-; Centennial Medal, Smithsonian Institute, 1990. STUDIED: Portland University, M.B.S., 1976, Lit.D. (honorary), 1984; University of Maine, HHD (honorary), 1986; Mt. Vernon College, L.H.D. (honorary), 1986.

Jean Auel did not start writing until the age of 40. While writing her adventure and historical novels, she does extensive research by visiting prehistoric sites and learning survival skills. Her novel *The Clan of the Cave Bear* 1980, won the Friends of Literature Award in 1980, and was a finalist for the 1980 Best First Novel National Book awards. This book was one in the Earth's children series. Other books in the series include: *The Valley of Horses*, 1982; *The Mammoth Hunters*, 1985; and *The Plains of Passage*, 1990. She is on the Board of Directors of the Oregon Museum of Science and Industry, and also contributes her time to various charitable and educational organizations.

AUGUSTINE, NORMAN R.

Martin Marietta Corporation, 6801 Rockledge Dr., Bethesda, MD 20817 (301) 897-6000

ACHIEVEMENTS: Undersecretary of the Army. STUDIED: Princeton University, B.S. and M.S. in aeronautical engineering.

Norman Augustine has spent his adult life working in the aerospace sector. He has extensive experience in both government bureaucracy and private business. He started his career at Douglas Aircraft Company in 1958. Later he held numerous government positions, first at the Defense Department from 1965 until 1970, and then as Army undersecretary in the 1970s. Augustine joined Martin Marietta in 1977 as vice president of aerospace technical operations. In 1987 he was promoted to chief executive, and then chairman in 1988. Augustine is slated to become chairman and chief executive of the merged Lockheed Martin companies upon the retirement of Daniel Tellep.

AUSTIN, ED

Office of the Mayor, Jacksonville, FL 32202 (904) 630-1776

BORN: 1926, Shenandoah, Va. ACHIEVEMENTS: Mayor, Jacksonville, Fla.; Florida State's attorney. STUDIED: Duke University (North Carolina), B.A., 1948; University of Florida, Law.

In 1954 Ed Austin entered the U.S. Army as a private. He was selected for Officer Candidate School, was commissioned a second lieutenant after graduation, and served until 1957, when he honorably discharged as a first lieutenant. After his discharge from the military, Austin continued his education and obtained a law degree. He was admitted to the Florida Bar and the Bar of the U.S. District Court for the Middle District of Florida in 1959. During the next 10 years, Austin ran a private practice, serving part time in the public sector as assistant county solicitor and as the Fourth Judicial Circuit's first public defender. Austin was appointed state attorney by Governor Reuben Askew in 1974. He was re-elected state attorney four times until his inauguration as mayor of Jacksonville, in 1991. Austin defined his priorities to be economic development, better opportunities for disadvantaged children, improved unity and communication among various groups in the community, and downsizing city government.

AUSTRIAN, ROBERT

3400 Spruce St., Philadelphia, PA 19104
Austrian is a prominent physician. For career credentials, consult the portion of this book entitled "Notable Americans by Profession" in Addendix A. Within this portion, the list "Physicians" describes requirements for inclusion in this volume.

AVEDON, RICHARD

407 E. 75th St., New York, NY 10021
BORN: 1923. *ACHIEVEMENTS:* President's Fellow, Rhode Island Institute of Design; Art Directors Club; collections: Metropolitan Museum of Art; Museum of Modern Art; exhibitions: Museum of Modern Art; Metropolitan Museum of Art. *STUDIED:* Columbia University; New School for Social Research.
From 1944 to 1950 Richard Avedon studied with fashion photographer Alexey Brodovitch at the Design Laboratory, New School of Social Research in New York City. He has been staff photographer for *Harper's Bazaar, Junior Bazaar* and *Vogue,* as well as a visual consultant for Paramount Studios. His early work was concerned with interpreting motion, and shooting subjects at slow shutter speeds. As his work evolved, he further refined the concept of arresting motion. Known for his portraits of notable people in the world of high

Bacharach Burt.

fashion, art and business, his success lies in his ability to let his subjects "get close to the camera," as he captures their response to being photographed. He has recently published several monographs and continues to enjoy his status as an interpreter of high style. His famous nude portrait of Nastassia Kinski surrounded by a giant python best typifies his expertise with sensual and erotic subject matter.

AZENBERG, EMANUEL

100 West 57th St., New York, NY 10019
Azenberg is a prominent dramatic artist. For career credentials, consult the portion of this book entitled "Notable Americans by Profession" in Addendix A. Within this portion, the list "Dramatic Artists" describes requirements for inclusion in this volume.

BABBITT, BRUCE E.

Department of the Interior, 1849 C St. N.W., Washington, DC, 20240 (202) 208-3100
BORN: 1938 Flagstaff, Ariz. ACHIEVEMENTS: Arizona attorney general, 1975-78; Arizona governor, 1978-87; U.S. secretary of the Interior, 1993-present. STUDIED: University of Notre Dame, B.S. (geology), 1960; University of Newcastle (England) M.S. (geophysics), 1962; Harvard Law School, LL.B., 1965.
After earning a bachelor's degree in geology from Notre Dame and a masters in geophysics from the University of Newcastle, in England, Bruce Babbitt began a career in geology. However, his geology career lasted only a few years. Babbitt went back to school, this time for a law degree at Harvard Law School. Upon graduating in 1965, he returned to Arizona, where he practiced corporate law until 1974. Babbitt joined the public sector in 1975 when he took office as Arizona's attorney general, a post he held until 1978. He took office as the governor of Arizona in that same year and served in that capacity until 1987. Babbitt ran for president in the 1992 Democratic primary. He was appointed secretary of the Interior by President Bill Clinton and confirmed by the Senate in 1993.

BABBITT, MILTON BYRON

Music Department, Princeton University, Princeton, NJ 08540
BORN: 1916, Philadelphia. ACHIEVEMENTS: Pulitzer Prize citation, 1982; George Peabody Medal, 1983; Madison Medal, 1986; Governor's Achievement Award, 1987; Music Award, Mississippi Institute Arts and Letters, 1988; Gold Medal in Music, American Institute Arts and Letters, 1988; award, Schoenberg Institute, 1988; William Schuman Award, 1992. STUDIED: NYU, A.B., 1935; Princeton University, M.F.A., 1942; Middlebury College, MusD, 1968; NYU, 1968; Swarthmore College, 1969; New England Conservatory, 1972; University of Glasgow, 1980; Northwestern

University, D.F.A. (honorable), 1988; Brandeis University, D.H.L., 1991; Princeton University, MusD, 1991, Ph.D., 1992.

After studying with composer Roger Sessions, Milton Babbitt realized he wanted total control of all musical elements in his compositions. Babbitt began his life-long work as a member of the faculty of Princeton University when he was 22. His work with the Columbia-Princeton Electronic Music Center, and with the journal *Perspectives of New Music*, has been much admired by music critics. His music is not aimed at the general public; instead of popularity, Babbitt has preferred the intellectual status of the mathematician, the scientist, or the philosopher. Works representative of Babbitt's musical interests include: *Composition for Four Instruments*, 1947-1948; *Philomel*, for voice and synthesizer, 1963-1964; *Relata II*, for orchestra, 1968; and *A Solo Requiem*, for soprano and two pianos, 1976-77.

BACHARACH BURT

Ernst Whinney, 1875 Century Pk E., Century City, Los Angeles, CA 90067
BORN: 1929, Kansas City, Mo. ACHIEVEMENTS: Grammy, Alfie, 1967; Grammy, (with Carole Bayer Sager) Song of the Year, That's What Friends Are For, 1986; Academy Award, Best Film Score, Butch Cassidy and the Sundance Kid, 1969; Academy Award, Best Film Score, Arthur, 1981; Drama Desk Award, 1968, and Academy Award, 1969, Best Music for a Play, Promises, Promises, which also won two Emmy awards and an Antoinette Perry Award. STUDIED: pupil of Henry Cowell, Music Academy, West Santa Barbara, Calif.; pupil of Darious Milhaud, New School; McGill University, Montreal, 3 years.

Working with lyricist Hal David since 1957, Burt Bacharach has written many popular songs, including two for Dionne Warwick, *Walk on By*, 1964; and *I'll Never Fall in Love Again*, 1969. Bacharach's stage and film scores include *Promises, Promises*, 1969, for which he won a Drama Desk ard and an Oscar; and *Butch Cassidy and the Sundance Kid*, 1969, whose Oscar winning *Raindrops* sold three million copies. Bacharach has won three Academy awards, four Grammys, two Emmys and a Tony award for his compositions. In 1970 he published a book of his compositions, *The Bacharach-David Song Book*.

BAKER, AL

Thomson Consumer Electronics, 600 N. Sheridan Dr., Indianapolis, IN 46201 (317) 267-5000
ACHIEVEMENTS: Co-developer of direct-satellite broadcasting system.
A giant leap for television watchers was made in 1994 when a large-scale direct satellite broadcasting system became operational. Developed by Al Baker, general manager of Thomson Electronics, and William Butterworth, senior vice president of Direc/TV, the system uses unobtrusive dish antennas only 18 inches across to pick up relays of television programs from two huge satellites 22,300 miles overhead. The picture clarity approaches the resolution of laser disc, the sound is of compact disc quality, and the small dish antenna will eventually put an end to the unsightly generation of huge satellite dishes dotting the coun-

trysides. Direct satellite broadcasting will ultimately offer viewers 150 channels. The innovation won *Discover* magazine's first place award in 1994 for best invention of the year.

BAKER, KATHY WHITTON

International Creative Management, 8899 Beverly Blvd., Los Angeles, CA 90048
BORN: 1950, Midland, Texas ACHIEVEMENTS: Emmy Award, Best Actress in a Drama Series, Picket Fences, 1993; Golden Globe Award, Best Actress in a Drama Series, Picket Fences, 1994. STUDIED: Attended University of California, Berkeley and California Institute of the Arts.

Kathy Baker has appeared on the stage, television, and in films. The success of the television series, *Picket Fences*, was largely influenced by her role in the series. She was raised in a Quaker household, and left stage acting at one point in the 1970s because she wasn't happy with the violent theater of that era. Baker has appeared in the films: *The Right Stuff*, in 1983, *Street Smart*, in 1987, *Permanent Record*, 1988, *Clean and Sober*, in 1988, and *Dad*, in 1989. Although she is a successful actress, Baker has also trained at the Cordon Bleu Cooking School, in Paris, as a Cordon Bleu cook, and founded her own catering service in San Francisco.

BAKER, HOUSTON A., JR.

Center for the Study of Black Literature and Culture, University of Pennsylvania, Philadelphia, PA 19104
BORN: 1943. Louisville, Ky. ACHIEVEMENTS: Guggenheim fellow, 1978 to 1979; Rockefeller Minority Group fellow, 1982 to 1983; director of Center for the Study of Black Literature and Culture. STUDIED: Howard University, B.A., 1965; University of California, Los Angeles, M.A., 1966, Ph.D., 1968.

Houston Baker, Jr., born and raised in Louisville, Ky., was one of just a few black students who graduated from a mainly white male college-prep high school for academically talented students. Baker earned his B.A. in English literature at Howard University. He continued his studies, earning his M.A. and Ph.D. at the University of California, Los Angeles. In the turbulent 1960s, Baker was an ardent supporter of Black Power, and admired the daring and defiance of the Black Panther Movement. After college, Baker took a teaching position at Yale University, New Haven, Conn. As an English professor, Baker has concentrated on black literature and black studies. Baker, an endowed-chair professor at the University of Pennsylvania, is also the director of the Center for the Study of Black Literature and Culture.

BAKER, RUSSELL

The New York Times, 229 West 43rd Street, New York NY 10036. (212) 556-1234.
BORN: 1925, Loudoun County, Va. ACHIEVEMENTS: Pulitzer Prize for Commentary, 1979, for his autobiography, Growing Up, 1983; author of several anthologies of columns and Growing Up, 1982. STUDIED: Johns Hopkins, B.A., English, 1947.

Truly an American institution, Russell Baker began his newspaper career in the all-American-boy way: by selling them. His first reporting job after college was with *The Baltimore Sun* from 1947 to 1954. He moved to *The New York Times* as a reporter in 1954, worked as a bureau chief overseas, and finally earned his own column, *The Observer*, in 1962. Anthologies of his columns have been published from 1964 through the present, with the most recent being *There's a Country in my Cellar*, in 1990. Baker won Pulitzer Prizes both for his column in 1979 and for his autobiography *Growing Up*, in 1983. In 1993 he followed Alistair Cooke as the host of *Masterpiece Theatre*, on PBS.

BALDESSARI, JOHN ANTHONY

3552 Beethoven St., Los Angeles, CA 90066
BORN: 1931. ACHIEVEMENTS: National Endowment for the Arts grants; collections: Museum of Modern Art; Los Angeles County Museum of Art; exhibitions: Museum of Modern Art; Documenta 5 and 7, Kassel (Germany). STUDIED: San Diego St. University; Otis Art Institute, Los Angeles.
Originally a painter, John Baldessari's work of the 1960s reflected an interest in Minimalism and the formal and semantic applications of words in the manner of Rene Magritte. *Work With Only One Property*, created in 1966, was a blank white canvas with only the title of the piece professionally lettered upon the pristine surface. As a conceptual photographer, his interests have been similar. He photographed words out of context from various pages of text, with an anonymous finger pointing to a phrase, as in *Scenario (Scripts)*, 1972-73. His film loops also repeat words, objects, or actions. In photography and in films, he hypothesizes about what art can be, expanding the definition of Conceptual Art.

BAQUET, DEAN

The Chicago Tribune, 435 N. Michigan Ave., Chicago, IL 60611 (312) 222-3232
ACHIEVEMENTS: Pulitzer Prize for Investigative Reporting, 1988. STUDIED: Columbia University.
Dean Baquet received his first Pulitzer Prize for investigative reporting while employed by *The Chicago Tribune*. In 1990 he moved to *The New York Times*. His first assignment was as an investigative reporter on the metropolitan staff. He covered a number of scandals in New York City, including the Bank of Credit and Commerce International (BCCI) abuses at the city's public hospitals, and at Empire Blue Cross and Blue Shield. He was nominated for another Pulitzer Prize for his Empire Blue Cross articles in 1994. In 1995 Banquet was promoted to national editor of the paper.

BARENBOIM, DANIEL

Chicago Symphony Orchestra, 220 S. Michigan Ave., Chicago, IL 60604 (312) 435-8122
BORN: 1942, Buenos Aires ACHIEVEMENTS: Beethoven Medal, Harriet Cohen Paderewski Prize, Legion of Honor, France. STUDIED: Mozartium, Salzburg, Austria, Accademia Chigiana, Siena, Italy, Santa Cecilia Academy, Rome.

Taught as a child by his mother and father to play the piano, Daniel Barenboim gave his first official recital at age 7 in Buenos Aires, Argentina. He received his early education in Israel, where the family moved two years later. At 10 Barenboim gave a recital in Vienna, at 13 in Rome, at 14 in London, and made his debut in the United States at 15, with Leopold Stowkowski. By age 16, after a tour of Australia in 1958, he was known as one of the most versatile pianists of his generation. Turning his attention to conducting in the 1960s, he performed in England, the U.S., and Japan. In 1970 he made his first appearance with the Chicago Symphony Orchestra, to which he would return as musical director in 1991. In addition to his position in Chicago, he is artistic and general music director of the Deutsche Staatsoper Berlin and often tours with the Vienna Philharmonic. Barenboim has made several videos, among them major works of Franz Liszt, and many recordings. His book, *A Life in Music*, has been published in the U.S. and Europe.

BARKER, ROBERT WILLIAM

Goodson-Todman Productions, 6430 Sunset Blvd., Hollywood, CA 90028
BORN: 1923, Darrington, Wash. ACHIEVEMENTS: Six Emmy Awards as host of television's The Price is Right, and one Emmy as producer of The Price Is Right. STUDIED: Drury College, Springfield, Mo., summa cum laude B.A., liberal arts.
After bouncing around radio and TV stations for 10 years in California, the Midwest, and Florida, smooth-talking, cheerful Bob Barker was discovered by television producer-personality Ralph Edwards in 1956. Edwards put him on NBC's *Truth or Consequences*, later a syndicated show, where he remained for 18 years. Beginning in 1975, he has also hosted his most successful game show, *The Price Is Right*, for years America's most watched game show and the only one to develop into an hour-long format. Barker hosted the *Miss America* and *Miss U.S.A.* pageants for 11 years. Since 1969 he has narrated *The Tournament of Roses Parade*. His refusal in 1987 to host a *Miss U.S.A.* pageant because, as an ardent animal rights activist, he learned that furs were part of the swimsuit competition, won him nationwide headlines. Headline splashes in the nation's tabloids in 1994 alleged that he was having an affair with one of the harem of models billed as *Barker's Beauties* on *The Price Is Right*.

BARRY, DAVE

Miami Herald, One Herald Plaza, Miami, FL 33132 (305) 350-2111
ACHIEVEMENTS: Pulitzer Prize for Commentary, 1988.
Dave Barry has worked as a columnist for the *Miami Herald* since 1983. His columns are syndicated nationwide and can be read in many hometown newspapers. Barry's columns are known for their portrayal of everyday situations taken to the extremely absurd. Besides his newspaper column, Barry is also the author

of numerous books, including *Dave Barry Slept Here*, Random House, 1989; *Dave Barry Turns 40*, Crown Publishers, 1990; and *Dave Barry Does Japan*, Random House, 1992. One of Barry's latest interests is playing in a rock-and-roll band with authors Stephen King, Amy Tan, Roy Blount Jr., Robert Fulghum, and Barbara Kingsolver.

BARRY, MARION, JR.

Government of the District of Columbia, Office of Communications, Rm. 218, District Building, Washington, DC 20004; (202) 727-6319
BORN: 1936, Itta Bena, Miss. ACHIEVEMENTS: Mayor of District of Columbia; . STUDIED: LeMoyne College; Fisk University, M.S.

Marion Barry's father died when he was young, and he was brought up by his mother, in Memphis, Tenn. where he became one of the first black Eagle Scouts in America. A good student, Barry attended LeMoyne College on a scholarship, obtained his master's degree at Fisk University, and entered a doctoral program in chemistry at the University of Tennessee. In 1960, while in graduate school, Barry helped form the Student Non-Violent Coordination Committee, a group dedicated to taking a moral stand against the forces of prejudice and segregation in the South. He served as the first national chairman of the committee he helped to create and moved to the District of Columbia as its director in 1965. Barry was elected mayor of the district in 1978, and was twice re-elected. During his third term, Barry was arrested on drug charges. Despite his difficulties, he ran for a fourth term as mayor, and was elected again in November 1994.

His Honor Marion Barry, Jr., mayor of Washington, D.C.

BARTHELEMY, SIDNEY

E-10, City Hall, 1300 Perdido St., New Orleans, LA 70112 (504) 586-4000
Barthelemy is a prominent political leader. For career credentials consult the portion of this book entitled "Notable Americans by Profession" in the Appendix.

Within this portion, the list "Political Leaders" describes requirements for inclusion in this volume.

BARTLETT, JENNIFER LOSCH

c/o Paula Cooper Gallery, 155 Wooster St., New York, NY 10012
BORN: 1941. ACHIEVEMENTS: Brandeis University Creative Arts Award, American Academy of Arts and Letters; collections: Museum of Modern Art; Metropolitan Museum of Art; exhibitions: Museum of Modern Art; Whitney Museum of American Art. STUDIED: Yale University School of Art.

Jennifer Bartlett's studies with Jim Dine, Al Held, James Rosenquist and Jack Tworkov, along with her interest in art history, has resulted in her work encompassing a variety of styles. Several series, such as *In the Garden*, a group of about 200 drawings of a certain garden in Nice, France, explore the processes of perception, impression and re-creation of one particular subject, each composition a small part of a continuous exploration of a single theme. Her media are also varied. *Up the Creek* is a series of 10 depictions of water, each one very different in approach from the other, recalling the works of Henri Matisse or Paul Cezanne, a Japanese screen or a computer's image.

BARTLETT, STEVE

Meridian Products Corporation, 14005 Stemmons Freeway, Dallas, TX 75234 (214) 484-7300
BORN: 1947, Los Angeles. ACHIEVEMENTS: Mayor of Dallas 1991-1995,; U.S. representative 1983-1991; founder, Meridian Products Corporation. STUDIED: University of Texas, B.A., 1971.

Steve Bartlett was the mayor of Dallas from 1991 until 1995. As mayor, Bartlett was credited with achieving the largest reduction of violent crime of any big city in the nation. He also initiated the nation's first one-stop construction permitting process for a large city, cutting the required number of permits and licenses by 42 percent. Bartlett began his political career as an at-large member of the Dallas City Council in 1977, where he served until 1981. He was elected to Congress in 1982, serving from 1983 through 1991. While in Congress he was GOP deputy whip, helping GOP whips, Trent Lott, Dick Cheney, and Newt Gingrich. He was widely recognized as a leader in banking reform legislation.

BARYSHNIKOV, MIKHAIL

c/o Edgar Vincent Association, 124 East 40th St., New York, NY 10016
BORN: 1948, Riga (USSR) ACHIEVEMENTS: Soloist with American Ballet Theatre, 1974–78; Artistic Director, New York City Ballet
Baryshnikov began his ballet career in the former Soviet Union where he was a member of the Kirov Ballet from 1969 to 1974, when he defected to the U.S. In 1976 he choreographed the *Nutcracker Suite* for the American Ballet Theatre. In addition to his dancing, he has appeared in two films: *The Turning Point* in 1976 and *White Nights* in 1985.

BATES, KATHY

Susan Smith & Associates, 121 North San Vincente Blvd., Beverly Hills, CA 90211
BORN: 1948, Memphis, Tenn. ACHIEVEMENTS: Academy Award, Best Performance by an Actress in a Leading Role, 1990, and Golden Globe Award, Best Actress in a Dramatic Film, 1990, for Misery. STUDIED: Southern Methodist University, B.F.A., 1969.
Kathy Bates began acting in the early 1970s after she earned a bachelor's in fine arts from Southern Methodist University. Early in her career, she worked as a singing waitress at a restaurant in the Catskill Mountains of New York but quickly moved on to more profitable work. She began working professionally on stage in 1973, when she appeared in *Virginia Folk Tales* at the Wayside Children's Theatre in Middletown, Va. After numerous stage appearances, she made her television debut on an episode of *The Love Boat* in 1977 and began appearing in movies in 1978. Her first film was *Straight Time*. Bates has many film roles to her credit but is best known for her portrayal of sadistic nurse, Annie Wilkes, in the 1990 film, *Misery*. Bates also received widespread recognition in 1991 for her role as Evelyn Couch in the film, *Fried Green Tomatoes*.

BATRA, RAVI

c/o Simon & Schuster, 1230 Avenue of the Americas, New York, NY 10020 (212)-698-7000
BORN: 1943, Punjab (India). ACHIEVEMENTS: Canada Council fellowship, 1971-1972; author of The Great Depression of 1990: Why It's Got to Happen—How to Protect Yourself, Venus Books, 1985. STUDIED: Punjab University, B.A., 1963; Delhi School of Economics, M.A., 1965; Southern Illinois University, Carbondale, Ph.D., 1969.
Ravi Batra immigrated to the United States in 1966 and entered Southern Illinois University to study for his Ph.D., graduating in 1969. Batra worked as an assistant professor of economics, first at Southern Illinois University, Carbondale from 1969 until 1970; next at the University of Western Ontario in London from 1970 until 1972; and finally at Southern Methodist University, Dallas, Texas, from 1972 until 1973. In 1973, Batra became a full professor of economics and department head at Southern Methodist University. Batra is best known for his books predicting a great depression in the United States during the 1990s. Batra predicts that when the disparity of wealth between the upper and lower classes widens beyond a certain point, the economy collapses and a depression occurs.

BATT, PHILIP E.

P. O. Box 1098, Boise, ID 83701 (208) 389-2288
BORN: 1927, Wilder, Idaho. ACHIEVEMENTS: Governor of Idaho; state chairman, Idaho Republican Party. STUDIED: University of Idaho.
Phil Batt entered public service in 1965, when he was elected to the Idaho Legislature. He served two years in the Idaho House and 14 years in the Idaho Senate. Batt held many leadership positions in the Idaho Senate, including, majority leader, president pro tempore, and caucus chairman. He served as lieutenant governor from 1978 to 1982. Batt, a Republican, ran for governor of Idaho in 1982, but was defeated. After a 10-year absence from elected office, Batt ran for governor again in 1992. His campaign emphasizing responsibility in government, struck a chord with the voters, and he won the election. Batt is a strong fiscal conservative who believes the private sector can do nearly anything better than the government.

BAUCUS, MAX

SH-511 Hart Senate Office Building, Washington, DC 20510 (202)224-2651
BORN: 1941, Helena, Mont. ACHIEVEMENTS: Montana state representative, 1973-75; U.S. representative, 1975-78; U.S. senator, 1979-. STUDIED: Stanford University, B.A., 1964; LL.B., 1967.
Max Baucus has represented Montana in the U.S. Congress for two decades, first as a two-term representative in the House starting in 1975 and, since 1979, as a member of the Senate where he is ranking member of the Environment and Public Works Committee. Prior to entering politics, Baucus practiced law in Missoula, Mont.

BAUER, VIRGINIA

The National Review, 150 East 35th St., New York, NY 10016-4178 (212) 696-0309
Bauer is a prominent publisher. For career credentials consult the portion of this book entitled "Notable Americans by Profession" in the Appendix. Within this portion, the list "Publishers" describes requirements for inclusion in this volume.

BAUMOL, WILLIAM JACK

Princeton University, Department of Economics, 108 Dickinson Hall, Princeton, NJ 08540
BORN: 1922, New York City. STUDIED: City College of New York, B.A., social science; London University, Ph.D., social science; London School of Economics, Stockholm School of Economics (honorary degrees).
After graduation from college, William Baumol taught at the London School of Economics from 1947 to 1949. However, a heavy professorial load has not kept him from significant achievements in original economic theory. While teaching concurrently since

1971 at Princeton University and New York University, he developed his best known work, distinguishing sales maximization from profit maximization in business. He also is known for transcribing the language used in business management and operations into economic terms.

BAYH, EVAN

Office of the Governor, Indianapolis, Indiana, 46204 (317) 782-6830
BORN: Terre Haute, Ind. ACHIEVEMENTS: Governor of Indiana; chairman, Democratic Governors Association. STUDIED: Indiana University, business economics, 1978; University of Virginia, law degree, 1978.
Evan Bayh, a fiscally conservative Democrat, began his political career as Indiana's secretary of state in 1986. Just two years later, he ran for governor of Indiana, won the election, and was re-elected in 1992. The *Wall Street Journal* has called Bayh "a genuinely fiscally conservative Democrat." He has made fiscal management, economic growth, and education his top priorities. Bayh has held the line on taxes, which have fallen, in per capita terms and as a share of personal income, during his term of office. In terms of economic development, Indiana is sixth in the nation for economic recovery since the 1990 recession, with new job creation being the highest in the nation. School funding has increased by over $1 billion dollars since Bayh took office. In 1994 Bayh served as chairman of the Democratic Governors' Association.

BEALL, DONALD R.

Rockwell International Corp., 2201 Seal Beach Blvd., Seal Beach, CA 90740 (310) 797-3311
Beall is a prominent business leader. For career credentials consult the portion of this book entitled "Notable Americans by Profession" in the Appendix. Within this portion, the list "Business Leaders" describes requirements for inclusion in this volume.

BEASLEY, DAVID M.

P.O. Box 11369, Columbia, SC 29211
BORN: 1959. ACHIEVEMENTS: Ex-officio member: Boards of Trustees University of South Carolina, College of Charleston, Francis Marion College, Lander College, Winthrop College, South Carolina State College, Educational Television Network of South Carolina, South Carolina Highway Commission and Aeronautics Commission. STUDIED: Clemson University, B.S., microbiology; University of South Carolina, J.D., law.
Having achieved a meteoric career in government since his election to the South Carolina House of Representatives at age 20, Gov. Beasley's career peaked with his election to the governorship in 1995. He brought to the job experience as House majority whip, speaker pro tem, and majority whip, occupying the latter two posts as the youngest ever to hold them in U.S. politics. His chief interests in the House were education and public works. A former athlete at Clemson University, he presently serves as a member of the South Carolina Board of the Fellowship of Christian Athletes, among several community and civic activities.

BECHERER, HANS W.

Deere & Company, John Deere Rd., Moline, IL 61265 (309) 765-8000
Becherer is a prominent business leader. For career credentials consult the portion of this book entitled "Notable Americans by Profession" in the Appendix. Within this portion, the list "Business Leaders" describes requirements for inclusion in this volume.

BECK, LEWIS WHITE

Department of Philosophy, University of Rochester, Dewy Hall, 351, Rochester, NY, 14627 (716) 275-4105
BORN: 1913, Griffin, Ga. ACHIEVEMENTS: Honorary degrees: DLitt., Hamilton College, 1974; L.H.D., Emory University, 1977; PhilDr., University Tubingen, Germany, 1977. STUDIED: Duke University, Ph.D., 1937, A.M., 1935; Graduated Emory University, A.B., 1934.
Lewis White Beck has been emeritus professor of Intellectual and Moral Philosophy at the University of Rochester since 1979. Beck is also currently a member of the Council of the American Academy of Arts and Sciences. He started as an instructor of philosophy at Emory University from 1938 to 1941 and then spent seven years at the University of Delaware, where he advanced from assistant professor to associate professor. At Lehigh University, he served as a professor, philosophy department chair, associate dean and dean of the graduate school, and Burbank professor, before moving on to Rochester in 1979. He has been a visiting lecturer at several institutes of higher learning including: Columbia University, 1950; Sir George Williams University, 1969; University of Western Ontario, from 1967 to 1968; University of California, Berkeley, 1973; and Yale University, 1974. Beck has also been a Guggenheim fellow, from 1957 to 1958, as well as an American Council Learned Society fellow, from 1965 to 1966.

BECKER, GARY S.

University of Chicago, Department of Economic Analysis, 1126 E. 59th St., Chicago, IL 60637
BORN: 1930, Pottstown, Pa. ACHIEVEMENTS: Nobel Prize in Economic Science, 1992; John Bates Clark Medal, American Economic Association; founding member, National Academy of Education; W.S. Woyrinsky Award, University of Michigan; Professional Achievement Award, University of Michigan; Frank E. Seidman Award in Political Economy; John R. Commons Award, Amicron Delta Epsilon. STUDIED: Princeton University, University of Chicago.
Four writings by Gary Becker have extended the boundaries of economics into sociology, anthropology, and psychology, and established him as one of the most original minds in the discipline. His first book, *The Economics of Discrimination*, a doctoral dissertation, sparked off debates on the persistence of wage disparity between whites and blacks. A second book, *Human Capital*, a theory of capital accumulation through schooling and on-job training, led in the 1960s to a revolution in economic thinking about the "human

investment" in the labor market. A third publication *Crime and Punishment: An Economic Approach*, called crime just another profession some people take up after weighing the expected benefits, the expected costs of possible arrest and punishment, and their risk preferences. *A Theory of the Allocation of Time* followed, exploring the divisions of labor within a family, a social institution then virtually neglected by economists. Two more books have extended the thoughts contained in the article while attempting to apply the theory of production to household behavior.

BECKMAN, ARNOLD O.

Irvine, Calif.
BORN: 1900 Chicago. ACHIEVEMENTS: Invented apparatus for testing acidity; inducted into the National Inventors Hall of Fame, 1986. STUDIED: University of Illinois, B.S., 1922; M.S., 1923; California Institute of Technology, Ph.D., 1928.
After earning his doctorate at California Institute of Technology in 1928, Dr. Beckman became an assistant professor at the institution, serving from 1928-1940. In 1935 he founded Beckman Instruments Inc., and resigned from teaching in 1940 to work full time in the development of scientific instruments used in chemical processes. His first instrument was the pH meter used for measuring acidity and alkalinity. Other inventions included the helical potentiometer, a precision electronic component, and the quartz spectrophotometer, an instrument used in automatic chemical analysis, which pioneered this process. Dr. and Mrs. Beckman contribute significantly to the educational and research efforts by the scientific community through their foundation. Their philanthropic efforts are responsible for auditoriums and laboratories located at the California Institute of Technology, University of Illinois, University of California-Irvine and the City of Hope Hospital and Medical Center, among others.

BEEBY, WILLIAM, JR.

Hammond Beeby and Babka, 1126 North State Street, Chicago, IL 60610
BORN: 1941. ACHIEVEMENTS: National Design Award, 1984; Distinguished Building Award, Chicago AIA; notable works: Malcolm X College, Chicago; World's Fair Plan, Chicago; Hewitt Associated Building, Lincolnshire, Ill. STUDIED: Yale University.
William Beeby Jr. is an "enlightened modernist" who has struggled to reconcile social and aesthetic iconography of the past modern movement with the structuralism and modularity of van der Rohe and the spatial fluidity of Le Corbusier. He is concerned with the expressive transparency of functional elements, as well with the identification and perpetuation of cultural and institutional gestalts. After graduation from Yale, Beeby accepted a position with C.F. Murphy, one of Chicago's leading Miesians. Predictably, his early designs adhered closely to the principles of Miesian structural geometry; and relied heavily on prefabricated elements and modular techniques. In his recent

efforts, he has continued his dependence on frame construction and prefabricating, but there is a movement toward freer plans, curvilinearity and super extra-functional showmanship.

BEIERWALTES, WILLIAM H.

22101 Moross-St. John Hospital, Detroit, MI 48236
Beierwaltes is a prominent physician. For career credentials consult the portion of this book entitled "Notable Americans by Profession" in the Appendix. Within this portion, the list "Physicians" describes requirements for inclusion in this volume.

BELLOW, SAUL

Committee on Social Thought, University of Chicago, 1126 E. 59th St., Chicago, IL 60637
BORN: 1915, Lachine, Quebec (Canada). ACHIEVEMENTS: Nobel Prize for literature, 1976; Pulitzer Prize, 1976. STUDIED: Northwestern University, B.S., 1937.
He was awarded the Nobel Prize for literature in 1976 "for the human understanding and subtle analysis of contemporary culture" in his writings. Bellow's work depicts modern man as "trying to find a foothold during his wanderings in our tottering world." Born in Canada, his family moved to Chicago in 1924, where he graduated from Northwestern University. The first of his novels to win critical praise was *The Adventures of Augie March*, 1953. It was followed by *Henderson the Rain King*, 1959; *Herzog*, 1964; *Mr. Sammler's Planet*, 1970; *Humboldt's Gift*, 1975; *The Dean's December*, 1982; *More Die of Heartbreak*, 1978; *A Theft*, 1989; and *The Bellarosa Connection*, 1989.

BELTON, SHARON SAYLES

Office of the Mayor, Room 331, City Hall, 350 South 5th Street, Minneapolis, MN 55415 (612) 673-2305
ACHIEVEMENTS: Mayor, Minneapolis; Minneapolis City Council president. STUDIED: Macalester College.
Mayor Sharon Sayles Belton can boast of a number of firsts in the city of Minneapolis. She was the first African American female Minneapolis City Council member. She was the first African American president of the Minneapolis City Council. And now she is the first African American and first female mayor of Minneapolis. Volunteering has become a way of life for Belton. She was a volunteer at Mount Sinai hospital while still a teenager. She attended Macalester college but chose to become a civil rights worker after graduation, and bused down to Jackson, Miss. to help with voter registration after graduation rather than begin her career. She worked as a parole officer for the Minnesota Department of Corrections, was assistant director of the Minnesota Program for Victims of Sexual Assault, and became a leading advocate for women's safety. Belton was elected mayor of Minneapolis and took office on January 1, 1994.

BENACERRAF, BARUJ

111 Perkins St., Boston, MA 02130

BORN: 1920, Caracas (Venezuela). ACHIEVEMENTS: Nobel Prize in Physiology or Medicine (shared with George D. Schell, U.S., and Jean Dausset, France), 1980; Rabbi Shai Schacknai Prize, Hebrew University of Jerusalem; T. Duckett Jones Memorial Award, Helen Jay Whitney Foundation; Waterford Award. STUDIED: Lycee Janson, France; Columbia University; Medical College of Virginia.

Baruj Benacerraf, a naturalized American, made a discovery which was heralded as a breakthrough in the search for controlling human immune responses. He and his colaureates' discovery explained how the structure of human cells relates to organ transplants and diseases, and won Nobel attention in 1980 for clarifying the body's mechanisms for accepting or rejecting transplants and for fighting off disease-causing organisms. Specifically, they found, in a complex of substances (antigens) that stimulate the production of antibodies and play a major role in transplant rejections, genes that control immune cell interactions responsible for immune responses.

BENGLIS, LYNDA

222 Bowery, New York, NY 10012

BORN: 1941. ACHIEVEMENTS: Fellowship, John Simon Guggenheim Memorial Foundation, National Endowment for the Arts; collections: Museum of Modern Art, Whitney Museum of American Art; exhibitions: Whitney Museum of American Art, Art Institute of Chicago. STUDIED: Newcomb College, Tulane University; Brooklyn Museum Art School.

Lynda Benglis' flowing plastic forms are made from such media as liquid rubber, latex, and polyurethane, often poured directly onto the floor of the exhibition space, creating "a freely twining mass...mixing fluorescent oranges, chartreuses, day-glo pinks, greens and blues, allowing the accidents and puddlings of the material to harden into a viscous mass." During the 1970s Benglis was involved in video productions; she also made wax paintings featuring oral and genital male and female symbols. Golden knots, which symbolize emotional states, have been included in her recent fiberglass sculptural. "My work contains an ironic self-parody of sexuality," she says.

BENNETT, WILLIAM JOHN

c/o Simon & Schuster, 1230 Avenue of the Americas, New York, NY 10020

BORN: 1943, New York City. ACHIEVEMENTS: Author, The Book of Virtues. STUDIED: Williams College, Williamsport, Mass., B.A., philosophy; University of Texas, Ph.D., philosophy; Harvard Law School, J.D., law.

An outspoken conservative, William Bennett left a decade of controversy behind him when he quit his government post in 1991. Named chair of the National Endowment for the Humanities in 1981, he promptly reversed the endowment's liberal policies. As U.S. secretary for education from 1985 to 1988, he cut federal student aid, and in its place urged schools to become a force for moral education. President Bush named him "drug czar" in 1989, a role he filled until 1991, when he quit Washington in frustration at the divergent forces opposed to his attempts to coordinate the war against drugs. Among his interests is the study of Greek, to which he says, "Read the Iliad the way Homer wrote it."

BENNETT, TONY

Tony Bennett Enterprises, Inc., 101 West 55th St., New York, NY 10019

BORN: 1926, New York, N.Y. ACHIEVEMENTS: Grammy, Best Pop Vocal-Male, and Grammy, Record of the Year, both for I Left My Heart in San Francisco, 1962, Grammy, Album of the Year and Traditional Pop Vocal Performance, MTV Unplugged, 1994. STUDIED: American Theatre Wing School.

As a teenager, Tony Bennett sang while waiting tables. Born Anthony Benedetto, Bennett first began his singing career using the name Joe Bari. During World War II he toured with military bands and then studied voice at the American Theater Wing school. He achieved major success in the early 1950s, with a long list of single hits. Twenty four of Bennett's songs made the Top-40 between 1950 and 1964. However Bennett's popularity dipped a bit when popular tastes turned toward rock style performers, such as Elvis Presley. Bennett shifted gears, at that point, and began to record more jazz numbers, making albums with Count Basie, as well as many other jazz greats. In the 60s and 70s, Bennett continued his success with recordings of jazz tunes and movie themes. He stayed out of the studio for many years, preferring to tour, but made a comeback in 1986 with his album, *The Art of Excellence.* In 1994 his career was given another boost when he appeared on MTV Unplugged.

BERG, PAUL

Stanford University, School of Medicine, Beckman Center, B062, Stanford, CA 94305

BORN: 1926, New York City. ACHIEVEMENTS: Nobel Prize in Chemistry (shared with Walter Gilbert, U.S., and Frederick Sanger, England), 1980; Eli Lilly Award; California Scientist of the Year; V.D. Mattia Prize, Roche Institute for Molecular Biochemistry; Albert Lasker Medical Research Award; Gairdner Foundation Award. STUDIED: Pennsylvania State University; Western Reserve University.

One of the leading scholars in studying the molecular biology of nucleic acids, Paul Berg was cited by the Nobel committee for those fundamental studies, particularly for his work on recombinant DNA (gene manipulation) and also for his development of so-called genetic engineering. Following further work on bacterial protein synthesis, he concentrated on gene expression in higher organisms, toward the goal of replacing defective genes in humans with functional genes. Ironically, he is also known for leading molecular biologists into calling a halt to gene manipulation until the possible risks can be evaluated.

BERGEN, CANDICE

William Morris Agency, 151 El Camino Dr., Beverly Hills, CA 90212

BORN: 1946, Beverly Hills, Calif. ACHIEVEMENTS: Emmy Awards, Outstanding Lead Actress in a Comedy Series, 1988 and 1989, Golden Globe Award, Best Actress in a Comedy Series, 1989 and 1992, for Murphy Brown. STUDIED: University of Pennsylvania.

Candice Bergen got her start as a model, but has achieved greater fame as an actress and photographer. She is the daughter of Edgar Bergen, a ventriloquist famous for his act with his puppet, Charlie McCarthy. Bergen's first film role was Lakey Eastlake in the 1966 movie, *The Group*. She has appeared in more than 20 films to date. Her first stage appearance was in 1967 when she appeared in the play, *Sabrina Fair*, at the Westbury Music Fair. Bergen is also an accomplished writer and photographer. She wrote a play in 1968, entitled *The Freezer*, which is included in *Best Plays of 1968*, and has been a contributor of articles and photographs for periodicals, including *Life, National Geographic, Esquire, Cosmopolitan, Interview,* and *Vogue*. However Bergen has attained her greatest fame on television. She began working on television in the late 1960s and has numerous appearances to her credit. Her most famous part has been the title role in the series, *Murphy Brown*, which began in 1988.

BERGSON, ABRAM

334 Marsh St., Belmont, MA 02178
BORN: 1912, Baltimore, Md. ACHIEVEMENTS: Member, National Academy of Science; authored seven major works on economics. STUDIED: Johns Hopkins University, B.A., economics; Harvard University, Ph.D. economics; University of Windsor, Canada, L.L.D., law; Brandeis University, D.H.L., humanities.

Currently one of the leading experts on Soviet economics, Abram Bergson gained early fame in his field when, at age 24, he published a much-talked-about article that established a new view of welfare economics. At age 31, he traveled to Russia as a member of the U.S. delegation to the Moscow Reparations Conference. Beginning in 1944, with Structure of Soviet Wages, he has written seven major works on economics, four of them with Russia as the subject. He teaches at Harvard and Columbia universities, is a consultant to the Rand Corporation in Santa Monica, Calif., and a member of the National Academy of Science.

BERLIN, SANFORD

Madrigal Audio Laboratories, Middletown, CT
ACHIEVEMENTS: Developed Proceed CD Library.

Sanford Berlin was the developer of a unique system of accessing individual tracks on an audio compact disk. The system, which is called *Proceed CD Library* provides flexible access to a track number, name of a song, or the musical category of 100 CDs at a time. It was developed under Berlin's direction by Madrigal Audio Laboratories, of which he is chief executive officer. The system also stores and organizes the user's CDs through a new style of infrared remote-control device. An audiophile-quality CD player/transport system is included in the Proceed CD Library.

BERNHARDT, MELVIN

c/o Steven C. Dunham, 123 West 74th St., New York, NY 10023

Bernhardt is a prominent dramatic artist. For career credentials consult the portion of this book entitled "Notable Americans by Profession" in the Appendix. Within this portion, the list "Dramatic Artists" describes requirements for inclusion in this volume.

BERRY, MARY FRANCIS

University of Pennsylvania, Philadelphia, PA 19104
BORN: 1938, Nashville, Tenn. ACHIEVEMENTS: Co-author, Long Journey STUDIED: Howard University, B.A., history; University of Michigan, Ph.D., history, J.D., law.

Mary Berry marched in civil rights protests while earning her law degree, and she has been marching upward ever since. Acting director of AfroAmerican studies at the University of Maryland, she also wrote, joined the District of Columbia bar, and became provost at Maryland's College Park campus. President Jimmy Carter brought her into politics as assistant secretary for education in the Department of Health and Welfare, and then appointed her a member of the Civil Rights Commission. Four years later she won a legal scrap from President Ronald Reagan who tried unsuccessfully to fire her from that post. Her most widely known writing is as co-author of a history of African Americans, *Long Journey*.

BIDEN, JOSEPH ROBINETTE, JR.

SR-221 Russell Office Building, Washington, DC 20510 (202) 224-5042
BORN: 1942, Scranton, Pa. ACHIEVEMENTS: Delaware legislator (Democrat). U.S. senator, 1973-. STUDIED: University of Delaware, B.A., 1965; Syracuse University, J.D., 1968.

Joseph Biden was second youngest person ever elected to the U.S. Senate, at age 29, in 1972. He was a candidate for the Democratic presidential nomination in 1987. As chairman of the Senate Judiciary Committee, Biden presided over the contentious hearings to confirm the nomination of Clarence Thomas to the U.S. Supreme Court. He is currently the ranking Democrat on Judiciary and a member of the Foreign Relations Committee. Before entering politics, he practiced criminal law in Wilmington, Del.

BINGAMAN, JEFF

110 Hart Senate Office Building, Washington, DC 20510-3102 (202) 224-5521.
BORN: 1943 ACHIEVEMENTS: Attorney general of New Mexico; chairman, Alliance to Save Energy. STUDIED: Harvard University, B.A., 1965; Stanford University School of Law, 1968.

Jeff Bingaman, a U.S. senator from New Mexico since 1982, is a proponent of "dual-use" technologies that can benefit national defense and the private sector. He helped develop the Technology Reinvestment Project, a government program that seeks to develop technologies with both commercial and military benefits through partnerships between industry, national laboratories and universities. Bingaman co-sponsored the Goals 2000: Educate America Act which includes a plan for establishing national academic standards in core subjects, such as math and English. Bingaman also proposed legislation that would establish a National Recreation Area, including 57,000 acres of land in the Santa Fe National Forest.

BINNIG, GERD KARL

IBM Research Division, One Old Orchard Rd., Armonk NY (1800) 426-4968
BORN: 1947, Frankfurt, Germany. ACHIEVEMENTS: Inducted into the National Inventors Hall of Fame, 1994; invented scanning microscope; Nobel Prize for Physics, 1986; King Faisal International Prize for Science; Hewlett-Packard Europhysics Prize. STUDIED: University of Frankfort, Ph.D., 1978.
Soon after earning his doctorate, Gerd Binnig began work with Henrich Rohrer on the scanning tunneling microscope, in IBM's Zurich Division. Five years after building the scanning tunneling microscope, Dr. Binnig and Dr. Rohrer received the Nobel prize for Physics. Prior to their invention, optical systems were limited by the wavelength of light. The scanning tunneling microscope allowed for individual atoms to be viewed. The fields of semiconductors, metallurgy, electrochemistry and molecular biology all benefited from this invention.

BISHOP, JOHN MICHAEL

University of California at San Francisco, 1001 Portrero Ave., San Francisco, CA 94110
BORN: 1936, York, Pa. ACHIEVEMENTS: Nobel Prize in Physiology or Medicine (shared with Harold E. Varmus), 1989; Biomedical Research Award, American Association of Medical Colleges; Albert Lasker Award; Armand Hammer Award; General Motors Foundation Award; Gairdner Foundation Award; Medal of Honor, American Cancer Society. STUDIED: Gettysburg College; Harvard University.
A discovery in cancer development that affected all future research on the normal growth of cells and the growth of tumors won the Nobel Prize for John Bishop and his colaureate. The pair discovered that the cancer-causing genes associated with a virus (oncogenes) did not come from the viral genes themselves, but resulted from altered cellular cells (proto-oncogenes) the virus had picked up.

BLAKE, PETER

Boston Architects Center, 320 Newbury Street, Boston, MA 02115 (202) 635-5188
BORN: 1920. ACHIEVEMENTS: FAIA; AIA Architecture Critic's Medal; notable works: Max Planck Institute, Berlin; Mental Hygiene Center, Binghamton, N.Y.; Roundabout Theatre Stage One, New York City. STUDIED: Pratt Institute of Architecture.
After paying homage to Wright, Le Corbusier and Mies van der Rohe in his 1960 book, *The Master Builders*, Peter Blake began a slow and painful reassessment of the goals and progress of Modernism. By the early 1970s he had broken completely with the hard-edged Miesian functionalism he once trumpeted. In his 1977 polemic, *Form Follows Fiasco: Why Modern Architec-*

ture Hasn't Worked, he charges that Modernism has lost touch with human needs; Modernism tells people what's good for them rather than recording and responding to their individual demands. The minimalist ethos, he says, produces merely functional buildings which provide truly minimal comfort and aesthetic nourishment. He has been increasingly attracted to the work of visionary humanists like Alvar Aalto, and has become a populist himself, trying to build as simply and modestly as he can while maintaining a formal, humane "softness." He has illustrated the economic viability of flexible, humanistic architecture in the construction of the Mental Hygiene Center in Binghamton, New York. By rejecting traditional prefabricated materials, and instead, custom-selecting materials from local distributors, he was able to bring the center in at nearly 10 percent under budget.

BLINDER, ALLAN

Council of Economic Advisors, Old Executive Office Bld., Washington, DC 20500
Blinder is a prominent economist. For career credentials consult the portion of this book entitled "Notable Americans by Profession" in the Appendix. Within this portion, the list "Economists" describes requirements for inclusion in this volume.

BLITZER, WOLF

CNN, 111 Mass. Ave., NW., Washington, DC 20001
Blitzer is a prominent journalist who first came into the national spotlight as the CNN correspondent covering the conflict in the Persian Gulf. Other assignments for CNN have included a recent stint as the White House. For career credentials consult the portion of this book entitled "Notable Americans by Profession" in the Appendix. Within this portion, the list "Journalists" describes requirements for inclusion in this volume.

BLOCH, HENRY WOLLMAN

H & R Bloch, Inc., 4410 Main St., Kansas City, MO 64111
BORN: 1922, Kansas City, Mo. ACHIEVEMENTS: Founder, H & R Bloch, Inc. STUDIED: University of Michigan, B.A., business administration.
Henry Bloch, and his brother Richard, saw a future for tax accountants and that future looked promising in the full-employment fifties. With the help of their lawyer father, they began the tax preparation firm H & R Bloch in their home town in 1955, and a year later branched out to New York City. Before the 1990s came around, they had 9,000 offices nationwide that prepared tax returns for 10 percent of all U.S. and Canadian taxpayers.

BLOEMBERGEN, NICHOLAAS

Harvard University, Division of Applied Science, Pierce Hall, Cambridge, MA 02138
BORN: 1920, Dordrecht (Netherlands). ACHIEVEMENTS: Nobel Prize in Physics (shared with Arthur Schawlow), 1981; Guggenheim Fellow; Buckley

Prize, American Physical Society; Morris Liebman Award and Medal of Honor, Institute of Electrical and Electronic Engineers; Ballantine Medal, Franklin Institute; National Medal of Science; Frederick Ives Medal, Optical Society of America; and other medals from the Netherlands, Germany, and Australia. STUDIED: University of Utrecht, Netherlands; Leiden University, Netherlands.

With Arthur L. Schawlow of the U.S., and Kai M. Siegbahn of Sweden, Nicholaas Bloembergen helped push back the boundaries of laser spectroscopy (measuring wavelengths and intensities of a spectrum of light, or radiation from any source), which permits the investigation of complex forms of matter not observed previously. Shortly after the first lasers were made, they were called "an invention looking for a use." Today the colaureates' work on the intricacies of the interaction of light with matter extended the uses of lasers in numerous areas of physics, chemistry, and biology, including pollution monitoring. Bloembergen also did pioneering work in development of the maser, the best amplifier of very faint signals from astronomical objects or deep space probes, which eventually found radiation coming equally from all directions of space as remnants of radiation. This supports the "big bang" theory— the dominant view among scientists of how the universe began.

Astronaut Charles Bolden.

BLUMBERG, BARUCH SAMUEL

7701 Burholme Ave., Philadelphia, PA 19111
BORN: 1925, New York City. ACHIEVEMENTS: Nobel Prize in Physiology or Medicine (shared with D. Carleton Gajdusek, U.S.), 1976; Albion O. Bernstein Award, Medical Society of the State of New York; Grand Scientific Award, Phi Lambda Kappa; Annual Award, Eastern Branch of the American Society of Microbiology; Eppinger Prize, University of Freiburg, Germany; Passano Award; Distinguished Achievement Award, Modern Medicine; Gairdner Foundation International Award; Karl Landsteiner Memorial Award, American Association of Blood Banks; Scopus Award, American Friends of Hebrew University; Strittmatter Award, Philadelphia County Medical Society. STUDIED: Union College, New York; Columbia University; Oxford University, England.

Career-long medical research in how and why people of different backgrounds respond differently to disease led Baruch Blumberg to multiple discoveries re-

lating to the mechanisms involved in the origin and spread of infectious diseases and ultimately to a Nobel Prize. Specifically, he discovered a substance in the blood that indicated the presence of hepatitisB, the more virulent of the two forms of hepatitis. The knowledge gained became the basis for screening out "B" carriers among blood donors and for vaccine work.

BLUMENTHAL, SIDNEY

The Washington Post, 1150 15th St. NW, Washington, DC, 20071 (202) 334-6000

BORN: 1948, Chicago, Ill. ACHIEVEMENTS: Author Pledging Allegiance: The Last Campaign of the Cold War, 1990. STUDIED: Brandeis University, A.B., 1969.

Sidney Blumenthal began his public career as a political commentator for the NBC morning program The Today Show in 1984. At the same time, Blumenthal was a national political correspondent for The New Republic until 1985, when he joined The Washington Post as a staff writer. In 1990 he became a senior editor for The New Republic and in 1992 he became a contributing editor for Vanity Fair. He became the Washington editor for The New Yorker in 1992 and currently can be found at The Washington Post. He has authored five books, including Pledging Allegiance: The Last Campaign of the Cold War, 1990.

BLY, ROBERT

1904 Girard Ave S., Minneapolis, MN 55403
BORN: 1926, Madison, Minn. ACHIEVEMENTS: Fulbright grantee 1956-1957; Recipient Award, National Institute Arts & Letters, 1968; 1990 best-selling book Iron John. STUDIED: St. Olaf College, A.B., 1947; Harvard, M.A., 1950; University of Iowa, 1956.

A poet, critic, translator and editor, Robert Bly's verse often evokes the atmosphere of his home state of Minnesota. His poetry collections include Silence in the Snowy Fields, 1962; Shadow-Mothers, 1970; Sleepers Joining Hands, 1972; and Talking All Morning, 1980. He became more widely known in 1990 with the his best selling book Iron John, which specified the need for young men to find "male mothers," or mentors to take them into true manhood. Other works include *Ten poems of Robert Bly Inspired by the Poems of Francis Ponge*, 1990 and *Remembering James Wright*, 1991.

BOLDEN, CHARLES FRANK, JR.

NASA, L.B. Johnson Space Center, Houston, TX 77058
BORN: 1946, Columbia, S.C. ACHIEVEMENTS: Colonel, USMC; commander, STS-45, 1992, and STS-60. STUDIED: U.S. Naval Academy, B.S. electrical science, 1968; University Southern California, M.S. systems management, 1977.
Charles Frank Bolden served during the Vietnam War as a combat pilot. Upon graduation from the U.S. Naval Test Pilot School, Colonel Bolden served as a test pilot at the Naval Air Test Center. In 1980, he was chosen as pilot-astronaut, piloting the STS 61-C and STS-31, which deployed the Hubble Space Telescope.

BOLTON, MICHAEL

Columbia Records, 51 West 52nd St., New York, NY 10019 (212) 975- 4321
BORN: 1953, New Haven, Conn. ACHIEVEMENTS: Grammy, Best Pop Vocal Male, How Am I Supposed to Live Without You, 1989; Grammy, Best Pop Vocal Male, When a Man Loves a Woman, 1991.
Bolton dons long flowing hair, often styled in a pony tail, adding, so says his fans, sex appeal to his appearance. He began his career by writing ballads for artists such as Laura Branigan, Cher, the Pointer sisters and Barbra Streisand. He made his recording debut in 1979 with the album *Blackjack*, which featured his band of the same name. In 1983 the band broke up, and he began recording solo and appearing as the opening act for artists Ozzy Ozbourne and Krokus. He was panned by critics who felt his vocals were pseudo rhythm and blues, but his female fans helped prove the critics wrong, and in 1989 he was named best male rhythm-and-blues vocalist for the Otis Redding classic *Sittin' on the Dock of the Bay*. Bolton has sold more than 20 million albums, due to the success of *Soul Provider*, in 1989, *Time, Love, and Tenderness*, in 1991, and *Timeless*, in 1992. The New York Medical College dedicated a research library to Bolton in 1993 honoring his work as honorary chairman of This Close for Cancer Research.

BOMBECK, ERMA LOUISE

c/o Universal Press Syndicate, 4900 Main St., Kansas City, MO 64112
BORN: 1927, Dayton, Ohio ACHIEVEMENTS: National Headliner Prize, Theta Sigma Phi; Mark Twain Award for Humor; many honorary degrees. STUDIED: Ohio State University, University of Dayton, B.A. English.
Twelve years of living the life of the average American mother and housewife with its minor triumphs and grievous vicissitudes, gave journalist hopeful Bombeck insights into women's woes. A mixture of humor, sarcastic jabs at housewives' fads and foibles, and her homemaking experience propelled her into national

fame when she exchanged the vacuum cleaner for the typewriter. As a high schooler Bombeck worked as a copy girl for the *Dayton Journal Herald*. In college she worked as a reporter on the same paper. After graduation she rose to the rank of feature writer. In 1953 Bombeck quit the paper to start a family, and, three children and 12 years later, began writing a column geared toward housewives in a local paper. The *Dayton Journal Herald* hired her and contracted with a syndicate to buy her columns, which are now syndicated in more than 900 newspapers.
Bombeck has also appeared frequently on television talk shows. In addition, she was a regular on ABC's "Good Morning America" show, on which she added her wit and wisdom about domestic problems women face daily. She has written 14 books whose raffish titles typify her style: *Family: The Ties That Bind . . . and Gag, If Life Is a Bowl of Cherries, What Am I Doing in the Pits?*, and many more. Bombeck also is creator, writer, and executive producer of the television series *Maggie*. She writes a column *Up the Wall* in *Good Housekeeping* magazine and is a frequent contributor to *Reader's Digest, Family Circle, Redbook, and McCall's*. In recent years she has been in ill-health and is seeking a kidn

BONIOR, DAVID E.

2207 Rayburn House Office Building, Washington, DC 20515 (202) 225-2106
BORN: 1945, Detroit, Mich. ACHIEVEMENTS: Michigan Democratic legislator. Michigan state representative, 1973-77; U.S. representative, 1977-; House Democratic whip, 1991-present. STUDIED: University of Iowa, B.A., 1967; Chapman College, M.A., 1972.
As Democratic whip, David Bonior is one of the party leadership's key strategists and parliamentary experts on the House floor. He is the co-author of the book *The Vietnam Veteran: A History of Neglect* and founded the Vietnam-era Veterans in Congress organization. Bonior served in the U.S. Air Force and worked as a probation officer and adoption caseworker prior to entering politics in 1972.

BOORSTIN, DANIEL JOSEPH

3541 Ordway St., Washington, DC 20016
BORN: 1914, Atlanta. ACHIEVEMENTS: Pulitzer Prize, The Americans. STUDIED: Harvard University; Oxford University; Yale University, J.S.D.
Though known by Americans generally as the long-time librarian of the treasure house Library of Congress, from 1975 to 1987, which honored him with the title Emeritus when he retired, Boorstin is at heart an historian. His most important work in the field is the three-volume, Pulitzer Prize-winning *The Americans*. Begun while he taught at the University of Chicago in the 1940s through the 1960s, it was not finished until 1973. The trilogy is noteworthy for its spare accent on politics and social movements in favor of revealing America through its people, their experiences, even their inventions.

BOOTH, LAURENCE

Booth/Hansen & Associates, 555 S. Dearborn Street, Chicago, IL 60605 (312) 427-0300
BORN: 1936. ACHIEVEMENTS: FAIA; Chicago AIA; Progressive Architecture Magazine Awards; notable works: Terra Museum of American Art, Chicago; Helene Curtis Industries Corporate Headquarters, Chicago; Krannert Art Museum Addition, Champaign, Ill.; Grace Place Church and Community Center, Chicago. STUDIED: Harvard University; Massachusetts Institute of Technology.

Laurence Booth calls for an architectural ideology rooted in the democracy of Thomas Jefferson which expresses "multiple concerns for energy and flexibility." His entry in the 1980 *Chicago Tribune* Tower competition is conceived as a metaphor for a free society. His light, open gothic detailing recalls attributes of the original Tower; a glassy membrane enclosing editorial offices opens its operations to public view. Critics praise his "handling of the basic geometries of architecture and allusion to the molecular structure of nature," and his "concern for proportion and color has been rightly called Palladian." He acknowledges a debt to Renaissance villas, because they were a "serious architecture genuinely appealing to people. Those buildings expressed cultural, historical and literary associations with many levels of meaning," said Booth.

Dr. Amar G. Bose.

BORMAN, FRANK

Patlex Corporation, Bldg. 4, 250 Cotorro Court, Rm. 4, Las Cruces, NM 88005
BORN: 1928, Gary, Ind. ACHIEVEMENTS: Space missions: Gemini 7 (commander), Apollo 8 (commander). STUDIED: U.S. Military Academy, B.S., 1950; California Institute of Technology, M.S., aeronautic engineering, 1957.
Frank Borman entered the U.S. Air Force after graduation from the U.S. Military Academy. In the Air Force, Borman was a test pilot. NASA selected him as an astronaut in 1962, and, in 1965, he commanded Gemini 7. He and pilot James Lovell Jr., set a 14-day endurance record during the mission in order to exceed the expected length of a lunar landing mission. Gemini 7 also served as a rendezvous target for Gemini 6. Borman flew with crew members Lovell and William

Anders on Apollo 8, the first manned mission to go around the moon to search for landing sites, and on Christmas day the three astronauts read from the Book of Genesis as a holiday greeting broadcast from the moon. He left NASA and the Air Force to join Eastern Airlines in 1970 and served as the company's president from 1975 until 1986.

BOSE, AMAR

Bose Corporation, The Mountain, Framingham, MA 01701 (508) 879-7330
BORN: 1929, Philadelphia, Pa. ACHIEVEMENTS: Invented the Direct/Reflecting speaker system, founded the Bose Corporation.
Amar Bose first became interested in the dynamics of sound while teaching at the Massachusetts Institute of Technology in the 1950s. He had purchased a highly rated record player and couldn't understand why the sound quality was so poor. Using the MIT labs for private research, Bose embarked on a quest to improve the sound quality of stereo speaker systems. Although initially a private project, Bose's studies soon became a university-authorized project involving electronics, acoustics, and psychoacoustics. Bose and five of his former students founded the Bose Corporation in 1964. In 1968 the first product was on the market, the 901 Direct/Reflecting loudspeaker system.

BOSKIN, MICHAEL

Council of Economic Advisers, Old Executive Office Building, Washington, DC 20500
BORN: 1943, New York City ACHIEVEMENTS: Distinguished Teaching Award, Stanford University; Abramson Award for Outstanding Research; Distinguished Fellow Award, National Association of Business Economists; Medal of the President of the Italian Republic for contributions to global economic understanding. STUDIED: University of California at Berkeley, A.B. with highest honors, M.A., economics, Ph.D., economics.
Michael J. Boskin is the author of more than 100 articles and books on world economic growth, taxes, United States savings, and the changing technology and demographics in the U.S. He is a professor at Hoover Institution at Stanford University. Boskin

also is a member of the board of the computer software company Oracle, and a research associate at the National Bureau of Economic Research. From 1989 to 1993, he chaired the Council of Economic Advisers, which was rated one of the five most respected agencies in the federal government by the Council for Excellence in Government. Boskin has held teaching positions at Stanford University, the University of California, Harvard University, and Yale University. Currently he is Adjunct Scholar at the American Enterprise Institute.

BOSLEY, FREEMAN R., JR.,

200 City Hall, Market & Tucker Streets, St. Louis, MO 63103 (314) 622-3201
Bosley, Jr. is a prominent political leader in Missouri and the mayor of St. Louis, where he is the first black elected to the office. For career credentials consult the portion of this book entitled "Notable Americans by Profession" in the Appendix. Within this portion, the list "Political Leaders" describes requirements for inclusion in this volume.

BOXER, BARBARA

112 Hart Senate Office Building, Washington, DC 20510-0501 (202) 224-3553
BORN: 1940 Brooklyn, N.Y. ACHIEVEMENTS: California legislator (Democrat). U.S. representative, 1983-92; U.S. senator, 1993-present. STUDIED: Brooklyn College, B.A., economics, 1942.
Barbara Boxer was elected to the U.S. Senate in 1992 and is a member of the Banking, Housing and Urban Affairs, and the Environment and Public Works committees. Her legislative concerns include anti-crime measures and immigration and environmental issues. Prior to her election to the Senate, she represented the San Francisco Bay area in the U.S. House of Representatives for 10 years. A former stock broker and journalist with a degree in economics, she served six years on California's Marin County Board of Supervisors and was its first woman president.

BRADFORD, BARBARA TAYLOR

450 Park Ave, New York, NY 10022-2605
BORN: Leeds, (England), came to U.S. 1964. ACHIEVEMENTS: Matrix Award, N.Y.; Women in Communications. STUDIED: Private schools in England; LittD (honorary), Leeds University, London, 1990.
After coming to the United States in 1964, Barbara Taylor Bradford worked as an editor at the *National Design Center Magazine* from 1965 until 1969. She has also been a national syndicated columnist with the *Chicago Tribune-N.Y.* (News syndicate N.Y.C.) from 1970 until 1975, and the *Los Angeles Times Syndicate* from 1975 until 1981. Bradford has written several interior design books, in addition to her best selling novels, which include: *A Woman of Substance*, 1979; *Voice of the Heart*, 1983; *Hold the Dream*, 1985; *Act of Will*, 1986; *To Be the Best*, 1988; *The Women in His Life*, 1990; *Remember*, 1991; and *Angel*, 1993.

BRADLEY, BILL

731 Hart Senate Office Building, Washington, DC 20510-3001 (202) 224-3224
BORN: 1943, Crystal City, Mo. ACHIEVEMENTS: Sullivan Award as the nation's outstanding amateur athlete, 1965; captain, U.S. Olympic basketball team, 1964. National Basketball Association Hall of Fame, 1983. STUDIED: Princeton University, 1965; Oxford University.
Bill Bradley is often cited as a potential candidate for the Democratic presidential nomination. An exceptional scholar and athlete, Bradley earned a Rhodes Scholarship in 1965 after he was named to the nation's All-American college basketball team. He went on to play professional basketball for the New York Knicks, playing forward on two championship teams. One year after retiring from professional basketball Bradley was elected to the Senate, where he became an expert on federal tax policy. His work led to the Tax Reform Act of 1986, which closed many loopholes in the tax code. A member of the Senate Finance Committee, Bradley advocated the line-item veto, which would give the president authority to remove spending programs from the federal budget. Bradley has also written legislation encouraging schools to stay open on evenings and weekends to provide community services.

BRADLEY, EDWARD

CBS News, 524 West 57th St., New York, NY 10019
BORN: 1941, Philadelphia, Pa. ACHIEVEMENTS: Six Emmy awards for television news documentaries. STUDIED: Cheney State College, B.A., journalism.
Bradley, a dropout newscaster from a CBS radio affiliate in New York City, was sitting around the cafes in Paris in 1971, writing poetry and dreaming of writing "the great American novel," as the last of his money slipped out of his pockets. To remain in Paris, he became a stringer for CBS' Paris bureau during the peace talks between the United States and North Vietnam. After a year on the job, he decided to return to the news business full time, a decision that sent him to Vietnam and Cambodia, where he covered the war for three years. He has since covered the White House, joined *CBS Reports* and *60 Minutes*, America's most popular television news show, and produced documentaries. His *60 Minutes* documentary, *Blacks in America: With All Deliberate Speed*, a 1979 look at race relations in the U.S., won him the first of the six Emmy Awards he has collected in his quarter of a century as a journalist.

BRADY, ROSCOE OWEN

U.S.P.H.S., Clinical Center, NIH, Room 3D04, Bethesda, MD 20892
Brady is a prominent physician. For career credentials consult the portion of this book entitled "Notable Americans by Profession" in the Appendix. Within this portion, the list "Physicians" describes requirements for inclusion in this volume.

BRAM, LEON LEONARD

Funk & Wagnalls Corp., 1 International Blvd., Mahwah, NJ 07495
BORN: 1931, Chicago, Ill. ACHIEVEMENTS: Vice president and editorial director of Funk & Wagnalls. STUDIED: DePaul University, 1931.
Bram is presiding over changes in publishing, coordinating his company's transition from being exclusively printed-media publishers to electronic publishers as well. He began in publishing in 1955 with the F.E. Compton Co., and has worked with both the Standard Educational Corporation and Encyclopedia Britannica. Bram has been vice president and editorial director of Funk & Wagnalls since 1974.

BRAND, VANCE DEVOE

c/o NASA, L.B. Johnson Space Center, Houston, TX 77058 (713) 483-0123.
BORN: 1931, Longmont, Colo. ACHIEVEMENTS: Space missions: Apollo-Soyuz Test Project, Space Shuttle orbital flight tests, STS-10 space shuttle mission. STUDIED: University of Colorado, B.S., business administration, 1960; University of California, M.B.A., 1964.
Vance Brand was a U.S. Marine fighter pilot from 1953 to 1957, and then went to work for Lockheed Aircraft Corporation as a test pilot in 1960. He joined NASA as an astronaut in 1966. Brand was the command module pilot of the Apollo-Soyuz Test Project in 1975, the first international joint space flight mission. In an Apollo space craft, he docked with a Soviet Soyuz spacecraft for a nine-day flight that included 44 hours of joint activities in orbit. He was the mission commander for the Space Shuttle orbital flight tests in 1978, and he commanded the Challenger on the 10th shuttle flight in 1984.

Astronaut Daniel Brandenstein.

BRANDENSTEIN, DANIEL CHARLES

Loral Space Information Systems, PO Box 58487, 2450 S. Shore Blvd., Houston, TX 77258
BORN: 1943, Watertown, Wis. ACHIEVEMENTS: Space missions: STS-8 space shuttle mission (pilot), STS-32 and STS-49 space shuttle missions (commander); Awards: decorated Legion of Honor (France); Yuri Bogarin Gold Medal (Federation Aeronautique Internationale, 1990). STUDIED: University of Wisconsin, B.S., 1965; U.S. Naval Test Pilot School, 1971.

Daniel Brandenstein joined the Navy in 1965 and flew 192 missions during his two tours of duty in Vietnam. He was chosen by NASA as an astronaut in 1978, and from 1987 until his retirement from NASA, in 1993, he served as chief astronaut. Brandenstein advanced in the Navy to the rank of captain and achieved 34 medals and military awards before his retirement from the Navy, in 1993. During his years with NASA he piloted the STS-8 space shuttle mission and commanded the STS-32 and STS-49 shuttle missions. In 1993 Brandenstein joined Loral Space Information Systems.

BRANDTNER, LT. GEN. M. L.

Office of the Secretary, Pentagon, Washington, DC 20301-1155 (703) 545-6700
Brandtner is a prominent military leader. For career credentials consult the portion of this book entitled "Notable Americans by Profession" in the Appendix. Within this portion, the list "Military Leaders" describes requirements for inclusion in this volume.

BRANSTAD, TERRY E.

Capitol, Des Moines, IA 50319; (515) 281-5211
BORN: 1946, Lake Mills, Iowa ACHIEVEMENTS: Governor of Iowa; Army Commendation Medal; chairman, Council of State Governments, 1991. STUDIED: University of Iowa, B.A., political science, 1969; Drake University Law School, J.D., 1974.

In 1969, after receiving a bachelor's degree from the University of Iowa, Branstad entered the U.S. Army. He received the Army Commendation Medal for his service, and left the military in 1971. Branstad was elected to the Iowa House of Representatives, representing District 8, in 1972. He was re-elected to the House for two additional terms. Branstad was elected lieutenant governor of Iowa in 1978. After a single term as lieutenant governor, Branstad ran for governor. He won his first term as governor in 1982, and has won three successive re-elections. Branstad served as chairman of the Rules Committee at the Republican National Convention in 1984, and was chair of the Iowa Delegation to the Republican National Conventions of 1988 and 1992. He is active in the National Governor's Association and Council of State Governments.

BRAUN, CAROL MOSELEY

SH-320 Hart Office Building, Washington, DC 20510
(202) 224-2854
BORN: 1947, Chicago, Ill. ACHIEVEMENTS: Illinois legislator (Democrat). U.S. Senator, 1993-present. STUDIED: University of Illinois, B.A., 1967; University of Chicago, J.D., 1972.
Carol Moseley Braun was the first black woman elected to the U.S. Senate, in 1992. A Chicago native, she was a low-profile Cook County Recorder of Deeds, from 1989 to 1992, prior to her successful senate campaign. She overcame an uneven start to her term to become an outspoken supporter of liberal issues. She was an assistant U.S. attorney in Chicago before running for the state legislature. Braun served in the House from 1979 to 1988 and was elected assistant majority leader in 1983.

BRAVER, RITA

CBS News, 524 West 57th St., New York, NY 10019
Braver is a prominent journalist. For career credentials consult the portion of this book entitled "Notable Americans by Profession" in the Appendix. Within this portion, the list "Journalists" describes requirements for inclusion in this volume.

BRAY, GEORGE AUGUST

6400 Perkins Rd., Baton Rouge, LA 70808
Bray is a prominent physician. For career credentials consult the portion of this book entitled "Notable Americans by Profession" in the Appendix. Within this portion, the list "Physicians" describes requirements for inclusion in this volume.

BREAUX, SEN. JOHN

516 Hart Senate Office Building, Washington, DC 20510-1803 (202) 224-4623
BORN: 1944; Crowley, La. ACHIEVEMENTS: Chairman, Democratic Leadership Council. STUDIED: University of Southwestern Louisiana, B.A. 1964; Louisiana State University, J.D. 1967.
Since his election to the Senate from Louisiana in 1986, John Breaux has worked to preserve wetlands. He now serves as the chairmen of the Merchant Marine Subcommittee of the Commerce, Science and Transportation Committee. He introduced the Managed Competition Act in the Senate, legislation to reform health care by allowing market forces to reduce costs. In the 103rd Congress Breaux was elected chief deputy whip, and sits on the Senate Finance Committee's Social and Family Policy Subcommittee. From 1988 to 1990 he served as the chairman of the Democratic Senatorial Campaign Committee.

BREDESEN, PHILIP

Office of the Mayor, 107 Metro Courthouse, Nashville, TN 37201 (615) 862-6000
BORN: 1943, Oceanport, N.J. ACHIEVEMENTS: Founded Health America, 1980, and Coventry Corporation. STUDIED: Harvard University, physics, 1967.

Philip Bredesen was elected mayor of Nashville, Tenn. in August, 1991. He grew up in Shortsville, N.Y., and graduated from Harvard University with a degree in physics in 1967. Bredesen founded the business, HealthAmerica, in his home in 1980. By 1986 the company had expanded nationwide to 39 cities, employed 6,500 people, and was sold. During his term Bredesen has instituted a strong public employee ethics policy, revised the cities procurement policies and procedures, and brought greater diversity to city government. Bredesen has been in the forefront of streamlining government through the combination of departments and consolidation of activities.

BLETHEN, FRANK

The Seattle Times, Box 70, Fairvica Ave., Seattle, WA 98111-0070 (206) 464-2111
Blethen is a prominent publisher. For career credentials consult the portion of this book entitled "Notable Americans by Profession" in the Appendix. Within this portion, the list "Publishers" describes requirements for inclusion in this volume.

BREYER, STEPHEN G.

Supreme Court of the United States, One First St. N.E., Washington, DC 20543 (202) 479-3000
BORN: 1938, San Francisco ACHIEVEMENTS: Associate justice, U.S. Supreme Court; chief judge, U.S. Court of Appeals for the First Circuit. STUDIED: Stanford University, A.B., 1959; Oxford University, B.A., 1961; Harvard University, LL.B., 1964.
Stephen Breyer served as clerk to Arthur J. Goldberg, associate justice of the U.S. Supreme Court from 1964 until 1965. In 1980 he was nominated judge in the U.S. Court of Appeals for the First Circuit by President Jimmy Carter. Breyer was chief judge of the Court of Appeals from 1990 until 1994. Breyer was nominated associate justice of the U.S. Supreme Court by President Bill Clinton, in 1994, succeeding Harry A. Blackmun.

BRINKLEY, DAVID

ABC News, 1717 DeSales St., NW., Washington, DC. 20036
BORN: 1920, Wilmington, N.C. ACHIEVEMENTS: Peabody Award; DuPont Award; Presidential Medal of Freedom, 1992.
David Brinkley began writing for his hometown newspaper, *The Wilmington Star-News*, before attending college and serving in the army during World War II. On his return in 1943, he was hired by NBC News, and in 1956 became co-anchor with Chet Huntley for the nightly *Huntley-Brinkley Report*. Brinkley hosted a variety of news specials across the years including *Our Man in Hong Kong* and *Boxing's Last Round*. When his partner, Huntley, retired in 1971, Brinkley remained on what was then retitled *NBC Nightly News* for another 10 years before a surprise switch to the ABC network.

BROADFOOT, ELMA

Office of the Mayor, 455 N. Main St., Wichita, KS 67202 (316) 268-4331

Broadfoot is a prominent political leader. For career credentials consult the portion of this book entitled "Notable Americans by Profession" in the Appendix. Within this portion, the list "Political Leaders" describes requirements for inclusion in this volume.

BRODER, DAVID S.

The Washington Post, 1150 15th St., NW, Washington, DC 20071 (202)334-6000

BORN: 1929, Chicago Heights, Ill. ACHIEVEMENTS: Author, The Man Who Would Be President: Dan Quayle, 1992; columnist, The Washington Post. STUDIED: University of Chicago, B.A., political science, 1947; M.A., 1951.

David Broder began his career in print journalism at *The Daily Pantagraph* in 1953, and by 1955 was already a political reporter for *The Congressional Quarterly*. He filled the same role for *The Washington Star* from 1960-1965 and for *The New York Times* from 1965-1966. It was at *The Washington Post* that he finally came into his own, rising in the ranks from associate editor, to national political correspondent and finally, to columnist. Along the way he had time to author several books, including one about Vice President Dan Quayle, *The Man Who Would be President*, which he co-authored with Bob Woodward in 1992.

Artist Frederick J. Brown.

BROKAW, THOMAS JOHN

NBC News, 30 Rockefeller Plaza, New York, NY 10020

BORN: 1940, Webster S.D. ACHIEVEMENTS: Anchor NBC Nightly News. STUDIED: University of South Dakota, B.A., political science, 1962.

Tom Brokaw started his career in Omaha as a morning news editor for KMTV from 1962-1965. He then moved to WSB-TV in Atlanta, where he was news editor and anchor. In 1966 he moved to Los Angeles, and worked as an anchor for KNBC until 1973, when he became a White House correspondent. As a White House correspondent for NBC, Brokaw covered such groundbreaking events as Watergate and President Nixon's resignation. He was then assigned the anchor position on the Saturday edition of *NBC Nightly News*. In 1974 he was offered a co-host position on the prominent *Today* show, but opted to continue with the hard news. It was two years later, when the show lost Barbara Walters, that he was finally willing to accept. He staffed the *Today* show desk for six years before being named co-anchor with Roger Mudd of the *NBC Nightly News*, where he is now sole anchor.

BROOKE, JAMES

The *New York Times*, 229 West 43rd St., New York, NY 10046 (212) 556-1234

BORN: 1955, New York City. ACHIEVEMENTS: Maria Moors Cabot Prize, 1994; IAPA-Pedro Joaquin Chamorro Award for Inter-American Relations, 1991. STUDIED: Yale University, degree in Latin American studies, 1977; spent a semester at Pontifica Universidade Catolica in Rio de Janeiro, 1976.

James Brooke has been the *New York Times* bureau chief in Rio de Janeiro since 1989. Previous to that he was bureau chief in Abidjan, Ivory Coast, since 1986. Brooke began at the *New York Times* in 1984 as a metropolitan reporter. Before coming to the *New York Times*, Brooke was a South American correspondent for the *Miami Herald*. While Brooke was at the *Miami Herald*, the paper won the 1983 Tom Wallace Award for best coverage of Latin America. Brooke began his career in journalism as a freelance reporter before taking an assignment with the *Berkshire Eagle* in Massachusetts.

BROOKS, JACK

U.S. House of Representatives, 2449 RHOB, Washington, DC 20515-4309 (202) 225-6565

Brooks is a prominent political leader. For career credentials consult the portion of this book entitled "Notable Americans by Profession" in the Appendix. Within this portion, the list "Political Leaders" describes requirements for inclusion in this volume.

BROWN, BOBBY

MCA Records, 70 Universal Place, Universal City, CA. 91608 (818) 777-4000

BORN: 1969, Boston, Mass. ACHIEVEMENTS: Grammy, Best R&B Vocal-Male, Every Little Step, 1989.

After leaving the singing group New Edition, Bobby Brown ventured out on a solo career. Brown hit it big in 1988 with *Don't Be Cruel*, a multi-platinum smash featuring the best of the New Jack sound. The album, which contains hits such as *Don't Be Cruel*, *Every Little Step*, and *Roni*, was the creation of the production wizards L.A. Reid and Babyface. With this effort, Brown reached the top of the Billboard charts, thus becoming the first teenager since Stevie Wonder to achieve such a feat. However, in 1992, despite a duet with his superstar wife, pop diva Whitney Houston, Brown's second effort *Bobby* was not as successful as his first.

BROWN, FREDERICK J.

Studio: 120 Wooster Street, New York, NY 10012
BORN: 1945 Greensboro, Ga. ACHIEVEMENTS: Recipient of an award from the New York State Council on the Arts. STUDIED: Southern Illinois University, B.A., art and psychology, 1968.

Frederick Brown grew up in a working class neighborhood on Chicago's South Side. His art, which ranges from the expressionistic style of his earlier work to his latter-day representational renderings is inspired by the Deep South blues and jazz traditions that surrounded him in his youth. In 1970, after a brief teaching stint at Southern Illinois University, he moved to New York's Soho district to establish a studio. It was there that he first truly integrated his appreciation of music with his love of the visual by creating a number of multimedia works with various jazz musicians. While in New York, he also met Willem de Kooning, who not only encouraged him as a painter, but also influenced him as an artist. Beginning most prominently in the early 1980s, religious themes began to play a large part in his work, culminating, perhaps, in *The Assumption of Mary*, a 1993 commission for Xavier University. At 33 feet by 28 feet, the work is one of the largest religious paintings in the world. Most recently he has put the finishing touches on *Echoes of New Orleans*, the second of a two-part homage to American music which began with *The Blues by Frederick Brown* at New York's Marlborough Gallery in 1989.

BROWN (BROVARNIK), HERBERT CHARLES

Purdue University, Department of Chemistry, West Lafayette, IN 47907
BORN: 1912, London. ACHIEVEMENTS: Nobel Prize in Chemistry (shared with George Wittig, Germany), 1979; Purdue Sigma Xi Research Award; Nichols Medal and Creative Research in Synthetic Organic Chemistry Award, American Chemical Society; H.N. McCoy Award; Linus Pauling Medal; National Medal of Science; Roger Adams Medal; Charles Frederick Chandler Medal; Madison Marshall Award; Chemical Pioneer Award; Scientific Achievement Award Medal; Elliot Cresson Medal; C.K. Ingold Medal; Priestley Medal; Perkins Medal. STUDIED: Wright Junior College, Chicago; University of Chicago.

Much bemedaled and awarded, Herbert Brown, a naturalized American, won his biggest award for developing a group of organic substances that facilitate extremely difficult chemical reactions. Ironically, he won the Nobel Prize in the very field in which two decades before he had participated as "Davy Crockett at the Alamo" in the longest dispute in the history of organic chemistry. The subject was recent research on ions having both a positive and a negative electrical charge, the method being developed for studying them so exciting the chemists involved decided to rename the ions they worked with "nonclassical ions" in recognition of their work. This angered Brown, who called the method typically "classic," and the argument raged on in seminars, meetings, papers, and books, but in virtual silence from the chemical community because it became so complicated. Brown finally backed down against his five distinguished opponents, known for their adept devising of new chemical vocabularies. But the upshot of the quarrel led to extended work on the "nonclassical ion" theory, revolutionized some organic chemistry procedures, and provided new insights into the reaction mechanisms in different solvents.

BROWN, JESSE

Department of Veterans Affairs, 810 Vermont Ave. NW, Room 1000, Washington, DC, 20420
BORN: 1944, Chicago. ACHIEVEMENTS: Vice president, Mayor's Commission on Employment of Handicapped, Chicago; executive director, Disabled American Veterans. STUDIED: Chicago City College, B.A., Roosevelt University, Catholic University of America..

Jesse Brown has been involved in the affairs of disabled Americans for most of his adult life. Born in Chicago, Brown served with the Marines from 1963 until 1965. Following military service, Brown began working with the Disabled American Veterans organization in 1967. His career with that organization took him first to Chicago, where he was a national service officer trainee from 1967 until 1972. He then moved to Washington, D.C., where he held various posts of increasing responsibility. He last held the post of executive director for the organization before he was appointed Secretary of the Veterans Affairs Department by President Bill Clinton in 1993.

BROWN, MICHAEL STUART

5323 Harry Hines Blvd., Dallas, TX 75235
BORN: 1941, New York City. ACHIEVEMENTS: Nobel Prize in Physiology or Medicine (shared with Joseph L. Goldstein), 1985; Pfiser Award, American Chemical Society; Passano Award, Passano Foundation; Lounsbery Award, National Academy of Sciences; Lita Annenberg Hazen Award; Louisa Gross Horowitz Prize, Columbia University; National Medal of Science. STUDIED: University of Pennsylvania.

All subsequent work on cholesterol has been based on what the Nobel Prize committee called the "revolutionary" discoveries of Michael Brown and Joseph Goldstein. Brown's earlier work had included the study of enzymes in the digestive system and of cholesterol production in the body, for which he had won many awards. While working with Goldstein on why some people tend to form excessive cholesterol buildup in their blood—which they found to be an inherited trait—they went on to discover that body cells have specific protein molecules on their surfaces whose function is to process bloodstream particles that carry cholesterol. Their work greatly expanded knowledge about the regulation of cholesterol metabolism and the treatment of diseases caused by abnormally high cholesterol levels in the blood.

BROWN, ROGER

c/o Phyllis Kind Gallery, 313 W. Superior St., Chicago, IL 60610

BORN: 1941. ACHIEVEMENTS: Collections: Museum of Modern Art, Whitney Museum of American Art; exhibitions: Museum of Contemporary Art, Chicago; Whitney Museum Biennial. STUDIED: American Academy of Art; School of the Art Institute of Chicago.

Roger Brown's paintings are both puzzling and whimsical depictions of rural landscapes and cityscapes. A Chicago Imagist, Brown creates tension between the composition and subject of the scenes, shifting scale and perspective. For example, in *Home on the Range*, patterning is used in a unique way to create a disorienting surface which simultaneously draws the viewer inside the picture's space. Skies are full of stylized clouds illuminated from an unknown source, which dwarf tiny silhouetted figures on the landscape, as in *Land of Lincoln* and *Buttermilk Sky*, and figures are engaged in mysterious encounters which the viewer can watch as if from above.

Architect C. William Brubaker.

BROWN, RONALD H.

Department of Commerce, 14th & Constitution Ave., Washington, DC 20230 (202) 482-2112

BORN: 1941, Washington, D.C. ACHIEVEMENTS: U.S. Secretary of Commerce; chairman, Democratic National Committee. STUDIED: Middlebury College, B.A., 1962; St. John's University, J.D., 1970.

Ron Brown was born in Washington, D.C., on August 1, 1941. With the help of a scholarship he attended Middlebury College in Vermont and received a B.A. degree. He earned his law degree from St. John's University in 1970, attending school at night and working by day. Brown served four years in the U.S. Army, stationed in both Germany and Korea. He is a member of the New York Bar, the District of Columbia Bar, and the U. S. Supreme Court Bar. Brown spent 12 years with the National Urban League, holding the positions of deputy executive director, general counsel, and vice president of its Washington operations. Brown, the first African American to hold the office of U.S. Secretary of Commerce, was nominated to the position by President-elect Bill Clinton in December 1992.

BROWN, TRISHA

Trisha Brown Company, 225 Lafayette St., #807, New York, NY 10012 (212) 334-9374

Brown is a prominent dancer. For career credentials consult the portion of this book entitled "Notable Americans by Profession" in the Appendix. Within this portion, the list "Dancers" describes requirements for inclusion in this volume.

BRUBAKER, C. (CHARLES) WILLIAM

Perkins and Will Architects, 123 North Wacker Street, Chicago, IL 60606 (312) 977-1100

BORN: 1926. ACHIEVEMENTS: FAIA; member, National Urban Planning and Design Committee; vice president, Chicago Architecture Foundation; notable works: National College of Agriculture, Chapingo (Mexico); First National Bank (and Plaza), Chicago; Woodbridge High School, Irvine, Calif. STUDIED: University of Texas at Austin.

The buildings that house educational institutions, Charles Brukaker believes, are the most important architecture in any property community. In the evolving American landscape, public schools have become de facto community centers, while colleges have become cultural touchstones. While he has concentrated his energy on spaces which promote and intensify the learning experience and its effects, the apogee of his humane, unmannerly modernist approach is his 1968 First National Bank and Plaza (with C.F. Murphy and Associates). The curving tower silhouette is an elegant response to the divergent needs of the bank's public service and executive departments. Large, open ground floors provide service space for the major metropolitan banking center, which then tapers up to smaller, more segmented upper floors which provide articulated space for managers and clerical support staff. To augment the spacious feeling of the lobby floors, elevator banks were separated and isolated against opposite walls. The granite and glass tower is set in a large sunken plaza, also with a slope-walled motif, which attracts constant foot traffic in fair weather. The plaza is built around a square fountain which subsumes nine square steps, and is highlighted by March Chagall's mural, *Pastoral Seasons*.

BRYAN JOHN HENRY, JR.

Sara Lee Corporation, 3 First National Plaza, Chicago, IL 60606 (312) 726-2600
BORN: 1936, West Point, Miss. STUDIED: Rhodes College, Memphis, Tenn., B.A., business administration and economics.
Bryan began his career at age 24 by working in his family's small business, Bryan Foods. Hardworking and ambitious, he built up the company to a level that caught the eye of executives at giant conglomerate Consolidated Foods Corporation, which purchased Bryan Foods. When Consolidated changed its name to Sara Lee Corporation, Bryan joined the company and rose through the ranks of president, chief executive officer, to chairman of the board in 1976.

BUCHANAN, JAMES M.

George Mason University, Department of Economics, 4400 University Ave., Fairfax, VA 22030
BORN: 1919, Murfreesboro, Tenn. ACHIEVEMENTS: Nobel Prize in Economic Science, 1986; founded Public Choice Society (with economist Gordon Tullock); fellow, American Academy of Arts and Sciences; Fulbright Research Scholar; Seidman Award. STUDIED: Middle Tennessee State College, University of Tennessee, University of Chicago.
While lecturing at universities all over the world, James Buchanan has produced a steady flow of books and articles on his public choice theory to where at present it forms a well-defined discipline within economics. With economist Gordon Tullock, Buchanan first propounded the theory in *The Calculus of Consent: Logical Foundations of Constitutional Democracy*, stating that people yield power to the government in self-interest, accepting in return a set of rules called a constitution. Why and how the rules are adopted, and whether some are better or worse than others is the subject of the book. In *The Power to Tax*, with C. Brennan, he uses his theory to attack public-sector economics and the establishment of governmental tax and spending levels. His further writings abound in demands for constitutional constraints on government and its mushrooming agencies, and he would be pleased with a "constitutional revolution" to re-examine the constitutional rights of citizens.

BUCHANAN, PATRICK J.

1017 Savile Lane, McLean, VA 22101
BORN: 1938, Washington, D.C. ACHIEVEMENTS: Special assistant to President Richard Nixon, 1968-74; director of communications for President Ronald Reagan, 1985; author Right From the Beginning 1992; co-host CNN's Crossfire. STUDIED: Georgetown, B.A., English, 1961; Columbia School of Journalism, M.A., Journalism, 1962.
Patrick Buchanan has been airing the highly conservative views for which he is known since his first editorials appeared in *The St. Louis Globe Democrat* in 1962. He was promoted to assistant editorial editor in 1964 but left the position in 1968 to become a speechwriter and special assistant for President Richard Nixon. Buchanan continued in that position through both of Nixon's terms and also continued briefly for President Gerald Ford. He began syndicating his columns in 1975 and broadcasting them in 1978 on radio. In 1985 he began co-hosting *Crossfire* and frequently commentating for *The McLaughlin Group*. President Ronald Reagan appointed him communications director, which led him to run for the Republican presidential nomination in 1992. He was unsuccessful in that bid.

BUCKLEY, WILLIAM F., JR.

The National Review Inc., 150 E. 35th St., New York, NY 10016-4178
BORN: 1925, New York City. ACHIEVEMENTS: Assistant instructor, Yale University, 1947-1951; founder, editor and publisher National Review, 1955; syndicated columnist On the Right; television host Firing Line; author of 33 books including God and Man at Yale, 1955, and Happy Days Were Here Again, 1993. STUDIED: Yale, B.A., political science/economics, 1950.
William F. Buckley Jr.'s career as one of America's foremost political conservatives began with a bang at the publication in 1955 of *God and Man at Yale*. After four years as associate editor of *American Mercury*, he founded *National Review* which he continued to edit and publish while also beginning his syndicated column, *On the Right*, in 1961 and hosting *Firing Line* for PBS, which debuted in 1966. Among the 33 books he has authored is *United Nations Journal*, 1974, which chronicled his experiences as a U.S. delegate to the United Nations.

BUGLIOSI, VINCENT T.

9300 Wilshire Blvd. #470, Beverly Hills, CA 90212
BORN: 1934, Hibbing, Minn. ACHIEVEMENTS: Deputy district attorney, Los Angeles, 1964-1972; Edgar Award, Mystery Writers of America for Till Death Us Do Part, 1979. STUDIED: University of Miami, Florida, B.B.A., 1956; University of California, LL.B., 1964.
Vincent Bugliosi was admitted to the California Bar in 1964 and served as a deputy district attorney for the Office of District Attorney in Los Angeles from 1964 until 1972. After leaving the Office of District Attorney, Bugliosi became a partner of the firm Steinberg & Bugliosi, Beverly Hills, Calif. With Curt Gentry, Bugliosi authored *Helter Skelter: The True Story of the Manson Murders*, Norton, 1974. As prosecutor of the famous case, Bugliosi was able to relate intimate details of the investigation and prosecution of the five members of the Manson family. Other books written by Bugliosi are *Till Death Us Do Part: A True Murder Mystery*, Norton, 1978 and *Shadow of Cain*, Norton, 1981. Both books were co-authored with Ken Hurwitz.

BURGEE, JOHN

John Burgee Architects with Philip Johnson, 375 Park Avenue, New York, NY 10152

ACHIEVEMENTS: Honor Award, AIA, 1975; Chicago Architecture Award, 1984, AIA Chicago Chapter; Reynolds Prize, 1978; notable works: O'Hare International Airport, Chicago; The Crescent, Dallas (with Philip Johnson); American Telephone and Telegraph Headquarters, New York City (with Philip Johnson). STUDIED: University of Notre Dame.

Although John Burgee has shared little of the attention that the popular media have given recently to his long-time partner, Philip Johnson, both men describe their working relationship as a true symbiosis. On a typical project, he prepares a detailed design "rebuttal" after Johnson completes initial conceptual work. Eventually a synthesis is reached, and the two prepare a broad consensus plan. Throughout the project, each freely edits the other's work. Ironically, his most frequent criticisms involve Johnson's excessive attention to "Miesian details," and his occasional tendency to cannibalize his own efforts. He is an adventurous geometer, whose formal flexibility is well displayed in his admixture of rectangular and cylindrical forms in his design for Boston's Fort Hill Square. His greatest contribution to contemporary architecture, however, is his reintroduction of ornamentation and vernacularism to large-scale commercial and institutional commissions. His "maximalist" gestures include his well-known crest to New York's AT&T Headquarters Building (modeled after the sinuous curves of a Chippendale cabinet), and the overscaled, cast metal, neo-Victorian lamps and crestings at Dallas' Crescent Center.

BUSCAGLIA, LEONARDO FELICE

LFB Inc., P. O. Box 5, Glenbrook, NV 89413

BORN: 1924, East Los Angeles. ACHIEVEMENTS: Author, columnist, and educator; California Governor's Award, 1965; Teaching Excellence Award, 1978; Appreciation Award, Public Broadcasting Service, 1981. STUDIED: University of Southern California, B.A., 1950, M.A., 1954, Ph.D., 1963.

Leo Buscaglia started his life as part of a large, Italian immigrant family. His father, Tulio Bartolomeo, described as a warm, loving patriarch who was not adverse to using corporal punishment when required, had an enormous, lasting influence on his life. Buscaglia served in the U.S. Navy during World War II from 1941 to 1944. After his military service, he became an educator for the Pasadena City School System from 1951 until 1965. Next he taught at the University of Southern California, first as an assistant professor, then as associate professor, and finally as professor of education. In his travels throughout Asia, Buscaglia was exposed to many disparate religions, and learned that all religions have one tenet in common, to love your neighbor, and by extension, yourself. Buscaglia is the author of many books, and has had as many as four titles on various bestsellers lists simultaneously. He is probably best known for *Papa, My Father: A Celebration of Dads*, Morrow, 1989.

BUSFIELD, TIMOTHY

c/o William Morris, 151 El Camino Dr., Beverly Hills, CA 90212 (310)859-4000

BORN: 1957, Lansing, Mich. ACHIEVEMENTS: Emmy, Best Supporting Actor in a Drama Series, Thirtysomething, 1991. STUDIED: East Tennessee State University, Actors Theatre of Louisville.

Timothy Busfield has acted in a wide variety of roles during his career on stage, screen and television. His stage debut was in the play, *Richard III* at the Circle Rep.'s Young Playwrights Festival. Busfield achieved widespread recognition for his portrayal of Arnold Poindexter in *Revenge of the Nerds* in 1984, and the sequel, *Revenge of the Nerds II: Nerds in Paradise*, in 1987. He played Dr. John "J.T." McIntyre Jr. on *Trapper John, M.D.* from 1984 to 1986. Several years later, Busfield found another popular role when he played Elliot Weston on the series, *thirtysomething*. Since then he has appeared in many made-for-TV movies including *Murder Between Friends* (1994) and *Birds of Paradise* (1995)

BUSH, GEORGE HERBERT WALKER

10000 Memorial Dr., Houston, TX 77024

BORN: 1924, Milton, Mass. ACHIEVEMENTS: Distinguished Flying Cross; Vice-President of the United States, 1981-1989; President of the United States, 1989-1993. STUDIED: Yale University, Economics, 1948.

George Bush joined the Navy at the start of World War II and became the its youngest commissioned carrier pilot. He fought 58 combat missions, was shot down once, and won the Distinguished Flying Cross. Bush attended Yale University and graduated with a degree in economics, in 1948. He moved to Texas and entered the oil business, with financial backing from his family. Bush first entered politics in 1964, when he failed in a bid for a Senate seat. In 1966 he won a seat in the House of Representatives and was re-elected in 1968. In 1970 he ran again for the Senate, and failed again. He spent the next eight years serving in various appointed positions within government, gaining experience in both domestic and foreign politics. He ran for the Republican presidential nomination in 1980, but was defeated by Ronald Reagan. Bush then became Reagan's running mate and was elected vice-president in 1980. In 1988 Bush won the Republican nomination for president. The Bush presidency was very strong on foreign policy, but was weakened domestically by a steady increase in unemployment and the budget deficit. Perhaps Bush's greatest error as president was to renege, in 1990, on his campaign pledge of no new taxes. During the conflict in the Persian Gulf, Bush led an international coalition of Western democracies, Japan, and Arab states that repelled an Iraqi invasion of Kuwait. In the 1992 presidential election Bush was defeated by Bill Clinton, the governor of Arkansas.

BUTLER, JOHN

360 East 55th St., #14H, New York, NY 10022 (212) 334-5149

Butler is a prominent dancer. For career credentials consult the portion of this book entitled "Notable Americans by Profession" in the Appendix. Within this portion, the list "Dancers" describes requirements for inclusion in this volume.

BUTTERWORTH, WILLIAM

Direc/TV, GM Hughes Electronics, 1230 Rosecrans Ave., 4238 Manhattan Beach, CA 90266 (310) 5366670
ACHIEVEMENTS: Co-developer of direct-satellite broadcasting system
William Butterworth is one of the main participants in the latest improvements in consumer electronics. He is the co-developer of a large-scale direct satellite broadcasting system, which became operational in 1994. Developed by Butterworth, senior vice president of Direc/TV, and Al Baker, general manager of Thomson Electronics, the system uses unobtrusive dish antennas only 18 inches across to pick up relays of television programs from two huge satellites 22,300 miles overhead. The small dish antenna will eventually put an end to the unsightly generation of huge satellite dishes dotting the countrysides. Yet in spite of the antenna's smaller size, the television picture clarity approaches the resolution of laser disc, the sound is of compact disc quality, and direct satellite broadcasting will ultimately offer viewers 150 channels. The innovation won *Discover* magazine's first place award in 1994 for best invention of the year.

BYRD, SEN. ROBERT C.

SH-311 Hart Office Building, Washington, DC 20510 (202) 224-3954
BORN: 1917, North Wilkesboro, N.C. ACHIEVEMENTS: West Virginia legisl or (Democrat). U.S. representative, 1953-59; U.S. senator, 1959-present. STUDIED: American University, J.D., 1963; Marshall University, 1994.
Robert Byrd was elected to the Senate from West Virginia in 1958 and served as Democratic majority leader from 1977 to 1981, minority leader from 1981 to 1987, and majority leader again from 1987 to 1989. Prior to running for the Senate, Byrd served in the West Virginia legislature from 1947 to 1953 and in the U.S. House of Representatives from 1953 to 1958.

CALDWELL, L. SCOTT

Bauman Hiller and Associates, 250 W. 57th St., New York, NY 10107
ACHIEVEMENTS: Antoinette Perry Award, Best Featured Actress in a Play, Joe Turner's Come and Gone, 1988.
L. Scott Caldwell began her professional career in the mid-1970s. Caldwell, a member of the Negro Ensemble Company, has primarily concentrated her efforts on the stage, appearing in such works as, *The Daughters of the Mock*, in 1978, and *A Season to Unravel*, in 1979. Her portrayal of Bertha Holly in *Joe Turner's Come and Gone* at the Ethel Barrymore Theatre, in New York City, won her a Tony award in 1988. Caldwell first played the role of Bertha Holly in 1985 at the Yale Repertory Theatre, in New Haven, Conn. Caldwell has appeared on several television shows, including *The Cosby Show*, in 1988; *Tour of Duty* and *L.A. Law*, in 1989. She also appeared in the television movie, *God Bless the Child*, in 1988. Among Caldwell's film appearances is *Without a Trace* in 1983.

CALLOWAY, WAYNE

Pepsico Inc., Purchase, NY 10577 (914) 253-2000
Calloway is a prominent business leader and CEO of Pepsico, Inc. For career credentials consult the portion of this book entitled "Notable Americans by Profession" in the Appendix. Within this portion, the list "Business Leaders" describes requirements for inclusion in this volume.

CAMERON, KENNETH D.

NASA, L.B. Johnson Space Center, Houston, TX 77058
BORN: 1949, Cleveland, Ohio. ACHIEVEMENTS: Colonel USMC; pilot for space flight STS-37, 1991; commander on flight STS-56, 1993. STUDIED: Massachusetts Institute of Technology, B.S. aeronautics and astronautics, 1978; Massachusetts Institute of Technology, M.S. aeronautics and astronautics, 1979.
Kenneth Cameron enlisted in the Marine Corps in 1969, serving as a platoon commander during the Vietnam War. In 1973 he served as a naval aviator, with tours of duty in Japan and other Pacific bases, after which he graduated from U.S. Navy Test Pilot School. In 1984 he was selected as an astronaut. He deployed the Gamma Ray Observatory on the STS 37 space flight, and carried the Atlas-2, an upper atmosphere research project, on the STS-56 mission.

CAMPBELL, BILL

Office of the Mayor, 68 Mitchell St., #2400, Atlanta, GA 30335 (404) 330-6100
Campbell is a prominent political leader and mayor of Atlanta. For career credentials consult the portion of this book entitled "Notable Americans by Profession" in the Appendix. Within this portion, the list "Political Leaders" describes requirements for inclusion in this volume.

CAMPBELL, ROBERT H.

Sun Company, Inc., 1801 Market St., Philadelphia, PA 19103 (215) 977-3000
Campbell is a prominent business leader. For career credentials consult the portion of this book entitled "Notable Americans by Profession" in the Appendix. Within this portion, the list "Business Leaders" describes requirements for inclusion in this volume.

CAMRAS, MARVIN

IIT, Dept. of Electrical and Computing Engineering, Chicago, Illinois 60616
BORN: 1916, Chicago. ACHIEVEMENTS: Developed method and means of magnetic recording; John Scott Medal; IEEE Consumer Electronics Award; Institute of Radio Engineers PGA Achievement Award; IIT

Alumni/Distinguished Service Award; H.M. Eta Kappa Nu Award; Inventor of the Year Award, Chicago Patent Law Association; inducted into the National Inventors Hall of Fame, 1985. STUDIED: Illinois Institute of Technology, B.S., 1940; M.S., 1942; Honorary Doctorate, 1978.

Marvin Camras has worked on campus at the Illinois Institute of Technology Research for most of his career, where he is currently a senior scientific advisor. He developed a wire recorder, and has been awarded over 500 patents in the field of electronic communications. During World War II, his wire recorders were used to train pilots. During the invasion of France in WW.II, battle sounds were recorded, amplified and placed in a false location, thereby misdirecting the Germans as to the exact location of the D-Day invasion. Today his inventions are used in magnetic tape and wire recorders for motion pictures, multi-track tape, stereophonic sound reproduction and video tape recording.

CAPERTON, GASTON

Office of the Governor, State Capitol, Charleston, WV 25305 (304) 558-2000
Caperton is a prominent political leader. For career credentials consult the portion of this book entitled "Notable Americans by Profession" in the Appendix. Within this portion, the list "Political Leaders" describes requirements for inclusion in this volume.

CAPONIGRO, PAUL

Astronaut Kenneth D. Cameron.

Rte. 3, Box 960, Santa Fe, NM 87501 (505) 270-1842
BORN: 1932. ACHIEVEMENTS: Guggenheim Fellowships; NEA; Boston Arts Festival; collections: Art Institute of Chicago; Metropolitan Museum, New York City; Museum of Fine Art, Houston; Museum of Fine Arts, St. Petersburg, Fla.; New Orleans Museum of Art; Smithsonian Institution; Philadelphia Museum of Art; Seattle Art Museum. STUDIED: Boston University.

Musical studies occupied Paul Caponigro throughout the late 1950s. Photographers Minor White and Benjamin Chin influenced his large scale images of nature. Close-up, abstract renderings of flowers, water and the French and English landscapes define the creative forces behind his work. "Through the use of the camera I must try to express and make visible the forces moving in and through nature—the landscape behind the landscape," said Caponigro. A founding member of the Association of Heliographers in New York City, he has taught at Minor White's Creative Photography Workshop and at Yale and other major universities.

CARAY, HARRY

WGN-TV, 435 N. Michigan Ave., Chicago, IL 60611
BORN: St. Louis. ACHIEVEMENTS: National Association of Broadcasters Hall of Fame Award, 1994; Ford Frick Award, 1989; American Sportswriters Association Hall of Fame, 1989; seven-time Sporting News Baseball Announcer of the Year.

Born Harry Christopher Carabina, Harry Caray has been a major league baseball broadcaster for 51 years. He currently is the play-by-play man, on WGN-TV and WGN Radio for the Chicago Cubs. Caray is famous for singing Take Me Out To The Ballgame with fans during the seventh-inning stretch of home games, and the line "Holy cow!". Caray got into the radio business at the age of 19 working radio stations in the Midwest for a few years. He began his broadcast career in 1945 with the St. Louis Cardinals. He also broadcast for the Hawks basketball team before they moved to Atlanta. For 24 years, he was the voice of the St. Louis Cardinals. He spent one year as the play-by-play announcer for the Oakland A's before coming to Chicago as the announcer for the Chicago White Sox television and radio broadcasts. Until 1981, he remained with the White Sox. During his tenure with the Chicago Cubs, Caray suffered a stroke. Due to the stroke Caray missed his first opening day in 41 years. He fought this setback, though, and returned to the Cubbies on May 19, 1987. Caray's son, Skip, is a broadcaster for the Atlanta Braves, and his grandson, Chip, is the play-by-play man for the Orlando Magic basketball team. This family of broadcasters marks the first time three generations have been announcers at the same time. Caray lives in Chicago during the baseball season and in Palm Springs, Calif during the break.

CARD, CLAUDIA

Dept. of Philosophy, UW Madison, 600 N. Park St., Madison, WI 53706-1475 (608) 262-0123

Card is a prominent philosopher. For career credentials consult the portion of this book entitled "Notable Americans by Profession" in the Appendix. Within this portion, the list "Philosophers" describes requirements for inclusion in this volume.

CAREY, MARIAH

Columbia Records, 51 West 52nd St., New York, NY 10019 (212) 975-4321
BORN: 1970, New York City ACHIEVEMENTS: Grammy, Best Pop Vocal-Female, Vision of Love, 1990; Grammy Best New Artist, 1990.
Mariah Carey made her solo debut in 1990 with her hit single *Vision of Love*. From there the singer, with her amazing multi-octave range, achieved crossover status on both the Pop and rhythm and blues charts. Her popularity was highlighted by her critically acclaimed *MTV Unplugged* performance. Married to Tommy Mattola, president of her record label, the former waitress spent a half million dollars on a storybook wedding reminiscent of the 1981 marriage of England's Prince Charles and Princess Diana.

CARLIN, GEORGE

Carlin Productions, 901 Bringham Ave, Los Angeles, CA 90049
BORN: 1937, New York City. ACHIEVEMENTS: Grammy, Best Comedy Recording, FM & AM, 1972; Jammin' in New York, 1993. Military: U.S. Air Force.
While some find Carlin's humor to be vulgar at times, few will deny that his witticisms are thought-provoking. Carlin worked as a disc jockey on several stations: KJOE, Shreveport, La; WEZE, Boston; KXOL, Fort Worth, Texas; and KDAY, Los Angeles. As a comedian, Carlin appeared in nightclubs, theaters, concert halls, and colleges throughout the United States. He has recorded over 10 comedy albums including; *Occupation: Fool*, 1973; *Indecent Exposure*, 1978; *A Place for My Stuff*, 1982; and *Playin' with Your Head*, 1986. He is probably best known for the "seven dirty words." Carlin's film appearances include: *With Six You Get Egg Roll, Car Wash, Outrageous Fortune,* and *Bill and Ted's Excellent Adventure.* In 1993 he returned to television in *The George Carlin Show.*

CARLSON, ARNE HELGE

Office of the Governor, 130 State Capitol, St. Paul, MN 55155 (612) 296-3391
BORN: 1934, New York City. ACHIEVEMENTS: Governor, Minnesota; Republican of the Year, 1993, National Ripon Society; Swedish American of the Year, 1994. STUDIED: Williams College in Massachusetts, B.A., 1957; University of Minnesota, post-grad, 1957-58.
Arne H. Carlson began public service in 1965 when he was elected to the Minneapolis City Council. He was elected to the Minnesota House of Representatives in 1970. During his tenure as a state representative, he was chief author of both the first state day-care bill and of legislation providing assistance centers for rape victims. From 1978 through 1990, Carlson worked as

Minnesota state auditor. He created a uniform accounting system for all levels of government in the state. Carlson was elected governor of Minnesota in 1991. He turned the budget around from a $2 billion deficit to a $600-million surplus. At the same time, he increased elementary and secondary school funding by 24 percent.

CARNAHAN, MEL

Room 216, State Capitol, Jefferson City, MO 65101 (314) 751-3222
BORN: 1934, Birch Tree, Mo. ACHIEVEMENTS: Governor of Missouri, lieutenant governor of Missouri. STUDIED: George Washington University, B.B.A.; University of Missouri-Columbia, law degree, 1959.
Mel Carnahan entered the U.S. Air Force, serving as an agent of the Special Investigations Office, after his graduation from George Washington University. After the Korean War, he entered law school, graduating with the highest scholastic honors, in 1959. Carnahan began public service at 26, when he was elected municipal judge in his hometown, Rolla, Mo. Next he served in the Missouri House of Representatives. Carnahan was elected majority floor leader of the House during his second term. In 1980 Carnahan was elected state treasurer. He modernized the treasurer's office by introducing up to date money management procedures, saving taxpayers millions of dollars. Carnahan was elected lieutenant governor of Missouri in 1988 and re-elected in 1992. he was elected Missouri's 51st governor by a landslide. As governor, Carnahan has focused on reforming welfare, job development, economic growth, and tough anti-crime laws.

CARNEY, FRANK L.

9111 E Douglas, Wichita, KS (316) 681-9000
BORN: Wichita, Kan. ACHIEVEMENTS: Founder, Pizza Hut Restaurants. STUDIED: University of Wichita.
Frank Carney started the Pizza Hut restaurant chain in 1958, while attending the University of Wichita as a freshman. His original goal was to earn enough money to pay tuition costs. Instead he began what was to become the largest pizza chain in the world. Pizza Hut was eventually sold to PepsiCo for $300 million, and Carney ran their food services division until 1980. Carney left PepsiCo and once again entered the franchise business, this time acquiring Chi-Chi's Mexican food restaurants. Again Carney increased his equity, until he was bought out by Chi-Chi's. In return for his restaurants, Carney received a major share of Chi-Chi's stock and a position on the companies board of directors. In his spare time, Carney is a professional sports car racer.

CARO, ROBERT A.

c/o Alfred A. Knopf, Inc., 201 East 50th St., New York, NY 10022 (212)-751-2600
BORN: 1935, New York City. ACHIEVEMENTS: Pulitzer Prize for biography, Francis Parkman Prize, Society of American Historians, and Washington Monthly Political Book Award, all 1975, all for The Power Broker, Knopf, 1974. STUDIED: Princeton University, B.A., 1957.

Robert Caro started his writing career in 1957 as a reporter for the *New Brunswick Home News*, New Brunswick, N.J. In 1959 he moved on to investigative reporting, working for *Newsday* in Garden City, N.Y. Caro's first book, *The Power Broker: Robert Moses and the Fall of New York*, Knopf, 1974, is said to have redefined the art of political biography as a form of writing. Caro relies heavily on extensive interviews with his subjects' contemporaries, and his investigative technique draws out many documents and facts that were previously unknown or hidden. Caro's current project is a four-volume biography of Lyndon Johnson. *The Years of Lyndon Johnson: The Path to Power*, Knopf, 1982, and *The Years of Lyndon Johnson: Means of Ascent*, Knopf, 1990, are the first two volumes in the ongoing work.

CARPER, GOV. THOMAS R.

Carvel State Office Bldg. Wilmington Delaware 19801 (302) 577-3210
BORN: 1947, Beckley, W.Va. ACHIEVEMENTS: Military decorations: Air Medal, Navy Commendation Medal, two Navy Achievement Medals, and three Vietnam Campaign Ribbons. STUDIED: Ohio State University, B.A. economics, 1968.
Delaware's 71st Chief Executive was elected in 1993, after serving five terms in the House of Representatives and six years as state treasurer. Thomas Carper grew up in Danville, Va., and spent five years as a Naval Flight officer and served during the Vietnam War. Following his tour of duty with the Navy, he moved to Delaware in 1973. At 29 he was elected state treasurer and was instrumental in improving the Delaware's credit rating from worst in the nation to a respectable "AA" rating in just five years. As a congressman, Carper played a key role in efforts to increase the availability of affordable housing, reform the welfare system, and combat drug money laundering. He served on the Banking Finance and Urban Affairs Committee and Merchant Marine and Fisheries Committee. Caper has chaired numerous fund raising efforts for Delaware organizations, including the United Negro College Fund, Big Brothers/Big Sisters, United Cerebral Palsy, the Special Olympics and the March of Dimes' Walk America.

CARR, GERALD PAUL

Arkansas Aerospace Education Center, PO Box 919, Huntsville, AR 72740-2966
BORN: 1932, Denver, Colo. ACHIEVEMENTS: Space missions: Skylab. STUDIED: University of Southern California, B.S., mechanical engineering, 1954; U.S. Naval Postgraduate School, M.S., aeronautical engineering, 1961.
Gerald Carr was flying as a pilot with the U.S. Marines when NASA selected him, in 1966, to be an astronaut. He was originally recruited to support the Apollo lunar landing missions but was later reassigned to the Skylab space station program. He commanded the last mission aboard Skylab in 1973-74. Carr and the other two members of the crew, Edward Gibson and William Pogue, set an endurance record of 84 days in space.

Carr later resigned from NASA and the Marines to pursue a civilian career. The orbit of the abandoned Skylab space station decayed sooner than expected and fell into the Earth's atmosphere in 1979, scattering debris across the Indian Ocean and Australia.

CARROL, PHILIP J.

Shell Oil Company, One Shell Plaza, Box 2463, Houston, TX 77252 (713) 241-6161
Carrol is a prominent business leader. For career credentials consult the portion of this book entitled "Notable Americans by Profession" in the Appendix. Within this portion, the list "Business Leaders" describes requirements for inclusion in this volume.

CARSON, JOHNNY

NBC, 3000 W. Alameda Ave. Burbank CA 91505.
BORN: 1925, Corning, Iowa. ACHIEVEMENTS: Emmy, The Tonight Show, 1977-80. STUDIED: University of Nebraska, B.A., 1949.
As host of *The Tonight Show* for 30 years, Johnny Carson is one of America's most durable television personalities. His career began as a radio comedy writer and television announcer in Omaha, Neb. After moving to California, he quickly got his own half-hour comedy show, *Carson's Cellar*, where comedians Groucho Marx and Fred Allen would make guest appearances. The show was short-lived but attracted the attention of Red Skeleton who hired Carson as a writer for his show. Once, Skelton injured himself hours before show time and Carson stepped in for him. His performance impressed network officials, and they gave him a prime-time television show of his own. However *The Johnny Carson Show* failed after 39 weeks. New York was Carson's next stop where he became the host of the daytime game show *Who Do You Trust?* It became a top-rated show on ABC, and led network executives to offer Carson *The Tonight Show* when Jack Paar quit, in 1962. Carson retired from *The Tonight Show* in 1992.

CARTER, ELLIOTT

Wacabuc, NY 10597
BORN: 1908, New York City. ACHIEVEMENTS: Pulitzer Prize, Second String Quartet, 1960, and String Quartet No. 3, 1973; New York Critics Circle Award, Double Concerto, 1961. STUDIED: Harvard University, B.A., 1930; M.A. in music, 1932; MusD (honorable) 1970; New England Conservatory, MusD (honorable), 1961; Swarthmore College, 1956; Princeton University, 1967; Boston University, Yale University, Oberlin college, 1970; Cambridge University (England), 1983; studied with Nadia Boulanger in Paris.
Carter is known as one of the premier composers of chamber music. His earliest works are neoclassical, while his later ones, including the two Pulitzer string quartets, are rhythmically more complex and often less accessible to the average listener. In 1939, Carter wrote the ballet *Pocahontas* for the American Ballet Caravan group, which he then served as musical director. Carter has written important works for orchestra as well, including *Variations for Orchestra*, 1955-1956; *Double Concerto*, 1961; and *A Symphony of Three*

Orchestras, 1977. He has also composed music for poems by Shakespeare, Robert Frost, and Hart Crane.

CARTER, JAMES EARL

The Carter Center, 1 Copenhill, Atlanta, GA 30307
BORN: 1924, Plains, Ga. ACHIEVEMENTS: Author, Why Not the Best, 1975, Keeping Faith, 1982, Negotiation, 1984, The Blood of Abraham , 1985, and An Outdoor Journal, 1988. STUDIED: U.S. Naval Academy, Annapolis, Md., 1946.

After graduation from high school in 1941, Jimmy Carter studied at Georgia Southwestern College for a year, and then another year at the Georgia Institute of Technology. He entered the Naval Academy in 1943 and graduated in 1946. Carter served in the Navy until 1953, when he resigned his commission to return home and run the family business, after the death of his father. He was elected to the first of two terms as a Georgia state senator in 1962. Carter was elected governor of Georgia in 1970 and served one term. He was elected president of the United States in 1976. His presidency was tumultuous at best. On the domestic front, inflation reached 20 percent a year. When interest rates were raised to combat inflation, unemployment exploded. Foreign policy under Carter didn't fare much better. He was accused of "giving away the Panama Canal" by some of his critics. The last years of his administration were overshadowed by the hostage situation in Iran, when Iranian militants seized the U.S. embassy in Tehran, Iran, and took the occupants hostage. His greatest success occurred when he obtained a historic peace treaty between Israel and Egypt at Camp David in 1979. Since his term as president, Carter has been active, teaching at Emory University, building housing for the poor under the banner of Habitat for Humanity, and has continued his interest in foreign affairs.

CARTER, STEVEN LISLE

Yale University Law School, PO Box 1303A, New Haven, CT 06520
BORN: 1954, Ithaca, N.Y. ACHIEVEMENTS: Author, Reflections of an Affirmative Action Baby. STUDIED: Stanford University Law School, B.A., history; Yale University, J.D., law.

Steven Carter has made an issue of affirmative action since winning his doctorate at Yale in 1979. Courted by Harvard University because he was black, and soured by the implied label "man of color" instead of "man of merit," he early came to believe that affirmative action programs denigrated blacks by categorizing them as "best black" instead of "best" in their field. He states in his 1991 book, *Reflections of an Affirmative Action Baby*, that affirmative action has helped only middle-class blacks while ignoring those who truly need help, where it should be eliminated or used to help the genuinely disadvantaged to enter the system. There, he believes, those blacks must move ahead based on their merit. Once that is achieved, he says, further preferential treatment for blacks is an insult to their capabilities. At Yale he was a member of *The Yale Law Journal*, then practiced with a prestigious law firm, served as a clerk for Supreme Court Justice Thurgood Marshall, and joined the faculty at Yale as a constitutional law professor. His devotion to religion also plays a large role in his life, inspiring his second book, *The Culture of Disbelief*, in which he writes that while growing up he had always sought the comfort of faith and a spiritual family.

CARVEY, DANA

NBC-TV, 30 Rockefeller Plaza New York NY 10112.
BORN: 1955, Missoula, Mont. ACHIEVEMENTS: Emmy, Best Individual Performance in a Variety or Music Program, The Saturday Night Live Presidential Bash, 1993. STUDIED: San Francisco State University, communication arts.

As a teenager, Dana Carvey honed his comedic talent by creating comic characters, which led to work as a stand-up comedian in local San Francisco comedy clubs. He was the winner of the San Francisco Stand-Up Comedy Competition. In 1981 he debuted in the film, *This is Spinal Tap*, and made his television debut as Mickey Rooney's grandson in the series, *One of the Boys*. Carvey joined the cast of *Saturday Night Live* in 1986 and became a favorite with his Church Lady character and impersonations of George Bush and H. Ross Perot. Carvey's Church Lady character was loosely based on several ladies at his Lutheran church, who expressed displeasure at his irregular attendance. Teaming up with another *Saturday Night Live* member, Carvey filmed *Wayne's World*, a sleeper hit. Other film credits include: *Halloween II, Racing With the Moon, Tough Guys, Moving, Opportunity Knocks*, and *Pleasure Island*.

CASH, JOHNNY

Agency for the Performing Arts, 900 Sunset Blvd., #1200, Los Angeles CA 90069
BORN: 1932, Kingsland, Ark. ACHIEVEMENTS: Grammy, Best Country Performance, Duo or Group, Jackson, with June Carter, 1967; Grammy, Best Country Vocal, Male, Folsom Prison Blues, 1968; Grammy, Best Country Vocal, Male, A Boy Named Sue, 1969; Grammy, Best Country Performance, Duo or Group, If I Were a Carpenter, with June Carter, 1970; Grammy, Best Spoken Word Recording, Interviews from the Class of '55, with others, 1986; Grammy, Legend Award, 1991.

The man in black has been a successful country singer since 1956, when he released the song *I Walk the Line*. Born J. R. Cash, he changed his first name to John when he entered the military because they wouldn't accept initials. Cash began to wear black while working with a group that wore only matching black outfits. Prison songs are a vital part of his repertoire, and he routinely performs in correctional facilities. Many of his songs are written with his wife, June Carter Cash. He has been featured in films, television and is a regular performer at the Grand Ole Opry. Cash has written two books, his 1975 autobiography *The Man in Black* and the 1986 novel, *The Man in White*. Cash was elected to the Country Music Hall of Fame in 1980, and to the Rock and Roll Hall of Fame in 1992.

CASPER, JOHN H.

NASA, L.B. Johnson Space Center, Houston, TX 77058
BORN: 1943, Greenville, S.C. ACHIEVEMENTS: Colonel, USAF; pilot, STS-36, 1990; commander, STS-54, 1993. STUDIED: U.S. Air Force Academy, B.S. engineering science, 1966; Purdue University, M.S. astronautics, 1967.

Casper was an Air Force pilot and a test pilot, serving in Vietnam. After the war, he served as a test squadron commander. Prior to being selected as an astronaut in 1984, he was deputy chief of the Special Projects Office at the Pentagon. The STS-36 space flight that he piloted was a classified Department of Defense mission.

CATTERSON, PAT

114 East 7th St., Apt. 6, New York, NY 10009 (212) 260-1834
Catterson is a prominent dancer. For career credentials consult the portion of this book entitled "Notable Americans by Profession" in the Appendix. Within this portion, the list "Dancers" describes requirements for inclusion in this volume.

CAVAGLIERI, GIORGIO

250 West 57th Street, Suite 2016, New York, NY 10107 (212) 245-4207
BORN: 1911. ACHIEVEMENTS: FAIA; Bard Award of Merit, City Club of New York; AIA; Distinguished Architecture Award, New York AIA; notable works: Restoration of Jefferson Market Branch Library, New York City; New York Shakespeare Festival Public Theatre, New York City; Renovation of New York Public Library, New York City; Renovation of National Museum of the Building Arts, Washington, D.C. STUDIED: School of Engineering, Milan (Italy); School of Architecture, Some (Italy).

In principle Giorgio Cavaglieri believes in the "modern moment," the "moment" that heralded rational, functional form. But as a technology and a way of life,

Vocalist Johnny Cash.

architecture can't be mere visual decoration. It should be valid and usable, at ease with its civilization. His restoration work has been marked by this civilized awareness that the best is eternal in every moment.His restoration of New York City's Jefferson Market Library, a former Greenwich Village courthouse, was an oft-cited example in the inauguration of the municipal Landmark Preservation Commission. He blends the old and the new in his design, so that both the "literature of architecture"—cut stone faces and flowers, spiral stairs, soaring stained glass windows—and new and necessary functions, are respected. The nineteenth century courthouse was inspired by a fourteenth century Venetian building. With a compelling frankness, he adds elements that in their contrast bring older forms, adornments and colors to new life: new fluorescent lighting is suspended in articulated black boxes, and a modern, austere railed catwalk crosses the main 37-foot hall without violence to Gothic stained-glass windows nearby. The entrance to a circular stair tower now passes through a sleek glass door which is set into the old carved limestone. A wheel of ornamented Victorian tie-rods is spotlighted at the top of the stairs. The low-vaulted basement chamber, with its softly aged salmon-pink brick columns and arches sandblasted clear of a century's accretions, is a bookworm's dream come true.

CAYETANO, BENJAMIN J.

State Capitol, Honolulu, Hawaii 96813 (808) 586-0034
BORN: 1939, Honolulu, Hawaii. ACHIEVEMENTS: Hawaii House, 1975-78; Hawaii Senate 1979-1986; lieutenant governor, 1987; governor, Hawaii

994. STUDIED: U.C.L.A., B.A., 1968; Loyola Marymount University, J.D., 1971.

Coming from a lucrative law practice before being elected to the office of Hawaii's governor, Cayetano moved his way up through the Hawaiian state government in a variety of positions. He first served as a state representative from 1975 until 1978 and enjoyed a distinguished career as a legislator. Later, he won a seat in the Hawaiian state senate, where he served from 1979 to 1986. The Democrat from Mililani won his seat defeating Republican Patricia F. Saiki to succeed Democrat John Waihee III.

CECH, THOMAS ROBERT

University of Colorado, Department of Chemistry & Biochemistry, Boulder, CO 80309
BORN: 1947, Chicago. ACHIEVEMENTS: Nobel Prize in Chemistry (shared with Sidney Altman), 1989; Passano Foundation Award; Harrison Howe Award; Pfizer Award; Steel Award; Mattia Award; Newcombe Cleveland Award; Heineken Prize. STUDIED: Grinnell College; University of California.

Contributing to the explosion of discovery in biochemistry, Cech, along with Sidney Altman, solved a problem that had eluded their peers for decades. It had long been known that DNA (deoxyribonucleic acids), the building block of life since it provide coded instructions of an organism's genes to enzymes, was master control over RNA (ribonucleic acids), which is involved in the synthesis of proteins in chemical cell reactions. Unanswered was the question of how RNA accomplished this. The colaureates, working independently, proved that RNA molecules could actively aid chemical reactions in cells by rearranging themselves in the cell (becoming a ribozyme), producing different products while still under DNA's control (Altman). Cech proved that RNAs could also double as enzymes. Their work led to the discovery of many ribozymes, and also has potential application for treatment of disease states.

Astronaut John Casper.

CERNAN, EUGENE ANDREW

Cernan Corp., Suite 300, 900 Town and Country Ln., Houston, TX 77024
BORN: 1934, Chicago, Ill. ACHIEVEMENTS: Space missions: Gemini 9 (pilot), Apollo 10 (lunar excursion module pilot), Apollo 17 (commander). STUDIED: Purdue University, B.S., electrical engineering, 1956; Purdue University and the U.S. Naval Postgraduate School, M.S., aeronautical engineering, 1961.

Cernan was the pilot of Gemini 9, in 1969, a mission with Thomas Stafford that included his space walk of more than two hours and a failed docking mission. In 1972 he was the lunar excursion module pilot on Apollo 10. He led the way for a lunar landing by the next Apollo mission by flying the lunar excursion module within 50,000 feet of the moon's surface. He was also the last person to set foot on the moon when he commanded Apollo 17, in 1972, after he and geologist Harrison Schmitt spent three days on the lunar surface. He became the deputy director of the Apollo-Soyuz Test Project, then retired from NASA and the Navy in 1976.

CHAFEE, JOHN H.

SD-567 Dirksen Office Building, Washington, DC 20510 (202) 224-2921
BORN: 1922, Providence, R.I. ACHIEVEMENTS: Rhode Island legislator (Republican); Rhode Island governor, 1963-69; U.S. senator 1977-. STUDIED: Yale University, B.A., 1947; Harvard University, LL.B., 1950.

John Chafee was elected to the U.S. Senate in 1976, where, as chairman of the Environment and Public Works Committee, he helped author the Clean Air Act of 1990 and other pollution control and wetlands conservation measures. A combat veteran of both World War II and the Korean War, he launched his political career in 1957 when he ran for the Rhode Island House of Representatives. Chafee served in the legislature for six years, and then three terms as governor, from 1963 to 1969. Following his defeat for re-election in 1969, he was appointed Secretary of the Navy where he served for three and one-half years prior to running for the Senate.

CHANDRASEKHAR, SUBRAHMANYAN

Dept. of Physics, University of Chicago, Chicago, IL 60637

BORN: 1910, Lahore (India). ACHIEVEMENTS: Nobel Prize in Physics (shared with William Alfred Fowler), 1983; Bruce Medal, Astronomical Society of the Pacific; Gold Medal, Royal Astronomical Society; Rumford Medal, American Academy of Arts and Sciences; Royal Medal, Royal Society; National Science Medal; Henry Draper Medal; Dannie Heineman Prize, American Institute of Physics; Copley Medal. STUDIED: Madras University, India; Cambridge University, England.

The Nobel citation noted a lifetime of scientific contributions by Subrahmanyan Chandrasekhar, a naturalized American, but specifically called attention to an early work as "possibly his best known achievement." It was a study of small stars, which he named "white dwarfs," defunct stars with the heat of the sun but collapsed to the size of the Earth, at which point they stabilize, representing one of the final stages of stellar evolution. The laureate's work has been used to explain neutron stars—dead stellar corpses remaining after a supernova explosion, and black holes—a collapsed star sealed off from contact with the outside world by the extreme curvature of space.

CHANNING, STOCKARD

International Creative Management, 8899 Beverly Blvd., Los Angeles, CA 90067

BORN: 1944, New York, N.Y. ACHIEVEMENTS: Antoinette Perry Award, Best Actress in a Play, Joe Egg, 1985. STUDIED: Radcliffe College, B.A., 1965.

Stockard Channing has appeared on the stage, silver screen, and television, but is primarily known for her work in the theater. Her stage debut was in the Theatre Company of Boston production of *The Investigation*, in 1966. She debuted in the off-Broadway production of *Adaptation/Next* at the Greenwich Mews Theatre, in 1969. Finally, in 1971, Channing appeared on Broadway in the chorus of *Two Gentlemen of Verona* at the St. James Theatre. Channing continued her stage career and, in 1985, won a Tony Award for best actress in a play as Sheila, in *Joe Egg*. Channing had two series on television: *Stockard Channing in Just Friends*, in 1979, and *The Stockard Channing Show*, in 1980. Neither show lasted more than a year.

CHAPMAN, MORRIS H.

Executive Committee, Southern Baptist Convention, Office of the President, 901 Commercial St., Suite 750, Nashville, TN 37203

BORN: 1940, Kosciusko, Mich. ACHIEVEMENTS: Memorial Award in Evangelism, Stella P. Ross; Honorary Doctor of Theology, Southwest Baptist University, Bolivar, Mo. STUDIED: Mississippi College, Clinton; Southwestern Baptist Theological Seminary, Fort Worth, Texas, M.D., Religion, D.M., Religion.

Chapman is president and chief executive officer of the Southern Baptist Convention, a post he assumed in 1992. He began his ministry in Albuquerque, N. M., where he pastored the First Baptist Church. Chapman served two terms as president of the Baptist Convention of New Mexico from 1976 until 1977. In 1979 he became pastor of the First Baptist Church of Wichita Falls, Texas, where he remained for 13 years. During that time, he successfully increased the Cooperative Program budget from 12 percent to 15 percent and tripled the Offering for State Missions for two years. During his pastorship his church averaged 168 baptisms annually. Chapman is the author of two books, most recently *Faith: Taking God at His Word*, in 1992, and is the compiler of two more.

CHARLIP, REMY

Remy Charlip Dances, 60 East 7th St., New York, NY 10003 (212) 777-6578

Charlip is a prominent dancer. For career credentials consult the portion of this book entitled "Notable Americans by Profession" in the Appendix. Within this portion, the list "Dancers" describes requirements for inclusion in this volume.

CHARNIN, MARTIN

c/o Richard Ticktin, 1345 Ave. of the Americas, New York, NY 10105

Charnin is a prominent dramatic artist. For career credentials consult the portion of this book entitled "Notable Americans by Profession" in the Appendix. Within this portion, the list "Dramatic Artists" describes requirements for inclusion in this volume.

CHASE, CHEVY

Creative Artists Agency Inc., 1888 Century Park East, Suite 1400, Los Angles CA 90067.

BORN: 1943, New York City ACHIEVEMENTS: Emmy, Best Supporting Actor in a Variety or Music Program, Saturday Night Live, 1976; Emmy, Best Writing in a Comedy, Variety, or Music Series, Saturday Night Live, 1975; Emmy, Best Writing in a Comedy, Variety, or Music Special, The Paul Simon Special, 1978. STUDIED: Bard College, B.A. (English); Massachusetts Institute of Technology, M.A.

Born Cornelius Crane Chase, he signed as a recording artist for Metro-Goldwyn-Mayer Records in 1968. A year later he was working as a writer for *Mad Magazine*. He also made appearances on the *National Lampoon Radio Hour*. During college he teamed up with Kenny Shapiro and Lane Sarahnson, collaborating on material for underground television. This collaboration became the off-off Broadway show and movie *The Groove Tube*. In 1975 Chase wrote for *The Smothers Brothers Show* and joined the cast of *Saturday Night Live*. His popularity on television converted to the big screen with movies such as *Foul Play, Caddyshack, National Lampoon's Vacation*, and *Fletch*. Trying his hand in the late-night arena was not as successful. His show on the FOX network was canceled after a few weeks, but he rebounded by poking fun at his show's demise in Frito-Lay commercials.

CHAVEZ, MARTIN J.

P. O. Box 1293, Albuquerque, NM 87103 (505) 768-3000
BORN: 1952, Albuquerque, N.M. ACHIEVEMENTS: Mayor of Albuquerque, N.M.. STUDIED: University of New Mexico, B.U.S., 1975; Georgetown University, J.D., 1978.
Martin Chavez, a native of Albuquerque, N.M., graduated from the University of New Mexico in 1975, earning a B.U.S. degree. Chavez obtained his Juris Doctor degree from Georgetown University Law Center in 1978. While at Georgetown College he also served as staff assistant at the U.S. Senate, in Washington, D.C. After he received his law degree, Chavez worked two years as a law clerk for the New Mexico attorney general, and then entered private practice as a civil trial attorney. Chavez's political career began when he was elected to the New Mexico Senate in 1988. He served two terms in the senate before he ran for mayor. Chavez was elected mayor of Albuquerque in 1993.

CHER

Bill Sammeth Organization, 9200 Sunset Blvd., Los Angeles, CA 90069
Born 1946, El Centro, Calif. ACHIEVEMENTS: Golden Globe Award, Best Actress in a Television Comedy or Musical, Sonny and Cher, 1974; Golden Globe Award, Best Actress in a Supporting Role in a Motion Picture, Silkwood, 1983; Academy Award, Best Actress, and Golden Globe Award, Best Actress in a Motion Picture Comedy or Musical, Moonstruck, 1987. STUDIED: Stage training with Jeff Corey.
Cher's career got started in the early 1960s, when she was a backup singer for the Crystals and the Ronettes. Born Cherilyn Sarkisian LaPiere, she began performing with Sonny Bono in 1964, first as Caesar and Cleo and later as Sonny and Cher. That same year Cher appeared with Bono on the television show *Shindig*. She has appeared in many television shows, including *The Sonny and Cher Comedy Hour*, from 1971 to 1975, and *The Sonny and Cher Show* from 1976 until 1977. She began working in movies in the late 1960s, winning an Academy Award nomination and a Golden Globe Award for *Silkwood*. Among her other movie credits are: *Mask*, in 1985, *The Witches of Eastwick*, in 1987, and *Mermaids*, in 1990. Cher has also continued her singing career and still records albums. She recently co-authored (with Robert Haas) *Forever Fit: the Lifetime Plan for Health, Beauty, and Fitness*, in 1991, and is the chief of Isis Productions, an independent film company.

CHICAGO, JUDY

938 Tyler St., P.O. Box 834, Benicia, CA 94510
BORN: 1939. ACHIEVEMENTS: collections: Brooklyn Museum, New York City; San Francisco Museum of Modern Art; exhibitions: ACA Galleries, New York City; Whitney Museum of Art, New York City. STUDIED: University of California, Los Angeles

Judy Chicago's art events center on women's experiences. *The Birth Project*, a recent five-year collaborative piece, involved needleworkers who donated their time to embroider large images of pregnant, birthing or nursing women. "I have approached the subject of birth with awe, terror, and fascination and have tried to present different aspects of this universal experience," says Chicago. In the 1970s, Chicago's *Red Flag* poster and *Menstruation Bathroom* used graphic images of menstruation to explore attitudes toward the female body. The needlework technique is precise, and the materials are opulent, honoring women's lives and experiences. Many people, especially women, have been mesmerized by Chicago's work, although she remains an outsider to the art world.

CHILDS, LUCINDA

Lucinda Childs Dance Company, 541 Broadway, New York, NY 10012 (212) 431-7599
BORN: 1940, New York City. ACHIEVEMENTS: Notable ballets: Street Dance; Museum Piece; Duplicate Suite; Cross Words; Figure Eights; Dance 15; Available Light; Premiere Orage; Formal Abandon. STUDIED: Sarah Lawrence College, B.A., dance, ca. 1962; Merce Cunningham, Hanya Holm, Helen Tamaris studios.
Ten years after debuting as a dancer with the Judson Dance Theatre in New York City, Lucinda Childs formed her own company for which she has choreographed more than 25 large-scale ensemble works and solos. Her early work, always performed in silence, shows her devotion to structure. After 1979, however, she began adding music and giant blowup projections of the live action on stage onto a stage-wide screen hung between audience and dancers. Her clean, cool, choreographic constraint is shown in elementary patterns where her dancers, wearing sneakers or jazz shoes, skip, canter, walk rhythmically, hop, and perform little jumps over and over, slowly revealing the pattern at their root.

CHILES, LAWTON

Executive Office of the Governor, Room 206, the Capitol, Tallahassee FL 32399-0001 (904) 488-5394
BORN: 1930, Lakeland, Fla. ACHIEVEMENTS: Healthy Start Program. STUDIED: University of Florida, B.A., J.D.
Lawton Chiles served first in the Florida House of Representatives, then in the Florida Senate. During his campaign for the U.S. Senate in 1970, he earned the nickname "Walkin' Lawton,"because of his unconventional campaign that was built around his walk of more than 1,000 miles across the state from the Panhandle to the Keys. Chiles was elected governor in 1990 and re-elected in 1994. During his term, he created a separate department of Juvenile Justice, moved to privatize many state services and launched the nation's largest welfare reform pilot program. His *Healthy Start* program screens every pregnant woman and newborn for health risks. Florida was the first state in the nation to do so. Chiles' health care plan,

unveiled in 1993, is considered a national model for free-market health care reform.

CHISHOLM, RODERICK MILTON

Department of Philosophy, Brown University, 54 College St., Providence, RI 02512
BORN: 1916, North Attleboro, Mass. STUDIED: Harvard University, Ph.D., Philosophy.
Chisholm earned his doctorate from Harvard and then joined the faculty at Brown University, where he has taught since 1946. Of the three traditional branches of philosophy—logic, epistemology, and metaphysics—he has made a specialty of epistemology, or the origins, nature, methods, and limits of human knowledge. He also writes and teaches on a modern sub-branch of philosophy, the philosophy of science. His book, *A Philosophical Study*, is most representative of his work.

CHOMSKY, AVRAM NOAM

Massachusetts Institute of Technology, 77 Massachusetts Ave., Cambridge, MA 02139
BORN: 1928, Philadelphia. ACHIEVEMENTS: Creator of revolutionary theory of linguistics. STUDIED: University of Pennsylvania, B.A., M.A., Modern Languages; Ph.D., Philosophy.
The public familiar with Chomsky's radical critiques of U.S. foreign policy during the Vietnam and Persian Gulf wars knows little about his theory of linguistics, which revolutionized the discipline. Called "transformational generative grammar," the theory holds that all human utterance is built on two structures, the superficial combining of words, and universal rules and applications. The process of building these structures is innate in all human beings, Chomsky posits, and is triggered in infancy. Son of a distinguished Hebrew scholar, Chomsky joined the faculty at MIT soon after obtaining his doctorate at the University of Massachusetts in 1995, and has remained there since.

CHRISTIAN, SPENCER

Good Morning America, 77 West 66th Street, New York, NY 10023
BORN: Charles City, Va. ACHIEVEMENTS:: Recipient of the Whitney M. Young, Jr. Service Award from the Greater New York Councils of the Boy Scouts of America; Member of the Virginia Communications Hall of Fame; Voted 1993's Virginian of the Year. STUDIED: Hampton University, B.A., English, MISSING DATE.
Morning viewers can see his national weather forecasts every half-hour on ABC's *Good Morning America*, where he has been a staple since 1986. He is also a feature reporter for the show and he frequently ventures out of the newsroom to cover special events and interview newsmakers as part of his weather report. He taught English at the Stony Brook School on Long Island before beginning his broadcasting career in 1971 as a news reporter for WWBT in Richmond, Virginia. By 1975 he had moved on to WBAL-TV in Baltimore where he became a weatherman and host of "Spencer's World," a weekly talk show. While in Bal-

timore, he also produced and narrated *Does Anyone Here Speak English?* an Emmy-Award winning, five-part report on declining verbal skills. Throughout his career, he has been involved in numerous activities outside the GMA studios. During 1988, he was the spokesperson for ABC Television's "Readasaurus" and is involved with several charities, including Up With People, the Girl Scouts of America, Special Olympics, and the United Negro College Fund among others. He is also the author of *Spencer Christian's Weather Book*, and, as a collector himself with over 1,000 bottles, he currently hosts *Spencer Christian's Wine Cellar*, for the Home and Garden Television Network.

CHRISTOPHER, WARREN

Office of the Secretary, 2201 C St. NW, Washington, DC 20520 (202) 647-5291
BORN: 1925, Scranton, N.D. ACHIEVEMENTS: Medal of Freedom, 1981; Harold Weill Award, New York University, 1981; Louis Stein Award, Fordham University, 1981; Jefferson Award, American Institute for Public Service; University of California at Los Angeles Medal; Thomas Jefferson Award in Law, University of Virginia. STUDIED: University of Redlands, 1942-43; University of Southern California, B.S. magna cum laude, 1945; Stanford University, LL.B., 1949; Occidental University, LL.D. (honorable), 1977; Bates College, LL.D. (honorable), 1981; Brown University, LL.D. (honorable), 1981; Claremont College, LL.D. (honorable), 1981.
Warren Christopher began his law career as a clerk for U.S. Supreme Court Justice William O. Douglas in 1949. After spending a year with Douglas, Christopher went into private practice with O'Melveny & Myers, a Los Angeles law firm. While in private practice, Christopher held many important posts, including special counsel to the governor of California, and member of the Board of Examiners of the California State Bar. Christopher returned to Washington, D.C., in 1967, when he was appointed deputy attorney general. He went back to practice with O'Melveny & Myers in 1969, but was called to Washington, D.C., again in 1977, when he was appointed deputy secretary of state, a post he held until 1981. Christopher was appointed secretary of state by President Bill Clinton in 1993. He has gained a reputation as an astute negotiator for his handling of the 1994 peace agreement between Israel and the Palestinian Liberation Organization and other Middle East peace issues.

CISNEROS, HENRY

Department of Housing & Urban Development, 451 7th St. NW, Washington, DC 20410-1047 (202) 708-0417
BORN: 1947, San Antonio, Texas ACHIEVEMENTS: Mayor of San Antonio, 1981. STUDIED: Texas A & M University, bachelor's, 1968, master's (urban planning), 1970; George Washington University, doctorate (public administration), 1976.
Born in San Antonio in 1947, Henry Cisneros began his career teaching urban studies at the University of Texas at San Antonio in 1974. Cisneros was elected to a seat on the San Antonio City Council in 1975, and went on to four terms as mayor, beginning in 1981. Cisneros was the first Hispanic mayor of San Antonio

since the 1840s, and the first Hispanic mayor of a major city in the United States. His political career in San Antonio was distinguished by his emphasis on economic development with an eye toward what he called the "politics of upward mobility." Cisneros opened an investment company in Houston in 1989. He was appointed by President Bill Clinton to serve as secretary of Housing and Urban Development in 1992.

CLANCY, THOMAS L. JR.

Putnam Berkeley Group, Inc., 200 Madison Ave, New York, NY 10016 (212) 951-8400
BORN: 1947, Baltimore. ACHIEVEMENTS: Best-selling author of military thrillers. STUDIED: Loyola College, 1969.
A former insurance agent, Tom Clancy popularized the realm of military technology and strategy, and gained a fan in President Ronald Reagan, with his best-selling novel, *The Hunt for Red October*, 1984. His other novels, all in the same genre, included *Red Storm Rising*, 1986; *Patriot Games*, 1987; *The Cardinal of the Kremlin*, 1988; *Clear and Present Danger*, 1989; *The Sum of All Fears*, 1991; *Without Remorse*, 1993; and *Debt of Honor*, 1994. He also wrote the nonfiction book *Submarine: A Guided Tour Inside a Nuclear Warship*, 1993.

CLAPTON, ERIC

Polygram Records Inc., 825 8th Ave, New York, NY, 10019-7416
BORN: 1945, Ripley (England). ACHIEVEMENTS: Grammy, Album of the Year, The Concert for Bangladesh (with George Harrison and Friends), 1972; Grammy, Best Rock Vocal-Male, Bad Love, 1990; Grammy, Record of the Year, Song of the Year, and Best Pop Vocal-Male, Tears in Heaven, 1992; Grammy, Album of the Year, Unplugged, 1992; Grammy, Best Rock Vocal-Male Tears in Heaven, 1992; Grammy, Best Rock Vocal-Male Layla, 1992. STUDIED: Attended Kingston Art School.
Eric Clapton was considered the premier blues guitarist of the 1960s. Born in England, he achieved widespread recognition for his technical prowess with blues bands such as the *Yardbirds*, *John Mayall's Bluesbreakers*, and *Cream*. Clapton set the stage for guitar greats Jimi Hendrix, Jeff Beck, and Jimmy Page, along with the many others who followed. When he finally began working solo in the early 1970s, however, the songs, not Clapton's guitar, were the primary feature of the music. Rather than the energetic blues of his early work, Clapton's solo work marked a shift towards a more relaxed style influenced by country, blues and reggae. This shift was characterized by his 1974 release, *461 Ocean Boulevard*, which formed the pattern for much of his later work. The album also represented the pinnacle of Clapton's popularity, his sales slowing somewhat in the 1980s. He has continued to record music with much success, though, winning a Grammy in 1992 for *Tears in Heaven*.

CLARK, STEVE

City Hall, 3500 Pan American Dr., Miami, FL 33133 (305) 250-5300

Clark is a prominent political leader. For career credentials consult the portion of this book entitled "Notable Americans by Profession" in the Appendix. Within this portion, the list "Political Leaders" describes requirements for inclusion in this volume.

CLARK, MARY HIGGINS

15 Werimas Brook Rd., Saddle River, NJ 07458
BORN: 1929, New York City. ACHIEVEMENTS: Grand Prix de Litterature Policiere; chair, International Crime Writers Congress; president, Mystery Writers of America. STUDIED: Ward Secretarial School; Pan Am Flight Attendant School; New York University, student, creative writing; Fordham University, summa cum laude B.A., philosophy, Ph.D. (honorary).
On the strength of 10 novels and a collection of short stories which sold more than 22 million copies, Mary Higgins Clark is known as "The Queen of Suspense," and "The American Agatha Christie." A one-time flight attendant, a widow with five children, an unsuccessful short story writer, a writer of four-minute-long syndicated radio programs and a failed biography of George Washington, Clark crashed to the top with her first suspense novel. The book, *Where Are the Children*, rejected by two publishing houses and picked up by Simon & Schuster became a best seller when it appeared in 1975. Paperback rights brought her $100,000, which led to an advance of $500,000 for her third book, *A Stranger Is Watching*. In 1988 Simon & Schuster gave her $11.4 million in advance for four novels and a short-story collection yet to be written, a record sale at the time. Her *A Stranger is Watching*, *A Cry In the Night*, and *Where Are the Children* have been made into movies, and *The Cradle Will Fall* and *Stillwatch* were aired as made-for-television movies.

CLAVELL, JAMES

c/o Foreign Rights, Inc., Rm. 1007, 200 West 57th St., New York, NY 10019
Clavell is a prominent author. For career credentials consult the portion of this book entitled "Notable Americans by Profession" in the Appendix. Within this portion, the list "Authors" describes requirements for inclusion in this volume.

CLAYBAUGH, DAVID

Noise Cancellation Technology, 800 Summer St., Stamford, CT 06091 (203) 961-0500
ACHIEVEMENTS: Co-developer of the NoiseBuster.
David Claybaugh, director of engineering development at Noise Cancellation Technologies, and engineer Roman Sapiejewski are the men behind the NoiseBuster, an invention that drowns out unwelcome noise. The setup is comprised of two microphones that sample background noise at the range of 30 to 1,200 hertz (cycles per second). What the mikes hear is relayed to a computer chip that signals the user's stereo headset speakers to generate noise exactly opposite to the offending waveform, thus cancelling the original sound. The equipment has a built in safety factor: The low range of sound the set picks up does not seal off

higher-pitched sounds such as phone calls, alarms, or voices. Also contributing to the NoiseBuster were engineers Dan Gaugher and Amar Bose.

CLAYTON, EVA

222 Cannon House Office Building, Washington, DC 20515-3301; 202 225-3101.
BORN: 1934, Savannah, Ga. ACHIEVEMENTS: North Carolina legislator. U.S. House of Representatives, 1992-. STUDIED: Johnson C. Smith University, B.S.; North Carolina Central University, M.S.
The first African-American woman to represent North Carolina in Congress, Eva Clayton was elected to the U.S. House of Representatives in 1992 and was elected president of the Democratic Freshman Class. She was the first woman to hold that office. Clayton is a member of the Agriculture Committee, and her legislative interests include housing and rural development. Prior to running for Congress, she was a member of the Warren County Board of Commissioners, serving as chairwoman from 1982 to 1990. In 1981, she founded Technical Resources International, Ltd., an organization specializing in economic development.

CLEAVER, EMANUEL II

29th Floor, City Hall, 414 E. 12th St., Kansas City, MO 64106 (816) 274-2595
BORN: Waxahachie, Texas. ACHIEVEMENTS: Governor's Award, Local Elected Official of the Year, 1993; James C. Kirkpatrick Excellence for Government Award, 1993.
Emanuel Cleaver II was elected mayor of Kansas City, Mo., on March 26, 1991. He also serves as Pastor of St. James United Methodist Church. Cleaver brings a long history of civic and community activism to the office of mayor. He has made it a priority to lobby the federal government for funds for law enforcement, and has spearheaded the community policing concept in Kansas City. He has promoted innovative programs such as evening basketball for city youth, a low-cost home financing program encouraging police officer to move into selected neighborhoods, and evening youth centers. Before winning the campaign for mayor, Cleaver served three terms on the City Council of Kansas City.

CLINES, FRANCIS X.

The *New York Times*, 229 West 43rd St., New York, NY 10046 (212) 556-1234
BORN: Feb. 7, 1938, Brooklyn. ACHIEVEMENTS: Deadline Writing Award of the American Society of Newspaper Editors, 1988; Meyer Berger Award, 1979. STUDIED: St. Francis College; Fordham University; St. John's University.
Clines started as a copy boy for the *New York Times* in 1958, and now is a national and metropolitan reporter for the same newspaper. He has held this position since February, 1992. Before that, he was Moscow bureau chief and a correspondent there from 1989 to 1992. Clines served as interim bureau chief in Jerusalem in April 1988. From 1986 to 1988, he was a correspondent in London. He covered politics as a reporter for the *New York Times'* Washington bureau from

1979 to 1986. After his initial job with the company, he eventually went on to become a news assistant for the metropolitan news, police reporter, and real estate news reporter. From 1968 to 1970, he covered the poverty found in New York City. In 1970, he became a reporter of the state's capitol in the Albany bureau. He remained there for five years covering the state government. The last two years there he was bureau chief. Clines was named City Hall bureau chief in 1976. During this time, he covered the city's fiscal crisis. That same year, he started writing the column *About New York*. His column was devoted to people and places around New York. In 1980 McGraw-Hill published a collection of his columns titled *About New York*.

CLINTON, BILL (WILLIAM) JEFFERSON

The White House, 1600 Pennsylvania Ave., Washington, DC 20500 (202) 456-1414
BORN: 1946, Hope, Ark. ACHIEVEMENTS: Rhodes scholar, 1968-1970. STUDIED: Georgetown University, 1968; Yale Law School, 1973.
Bill Clinton was named after his father, William Jefferson Blythe, who died shortly before he was born. His mother remarried, and he took his stepfather's last name after the birth of a stepbrother. Clinton graduated from Georgetown University, attended Oxford University, as a Rhodes scholar, and graduated from Yale Law School in 1973. After graduation from Yale, Clinton taught law at the University of Arkansas. In 1976 he was elected Arkansas attorney general. He was elected governor of Arkansas in 1978, lost the race for re-election in 1980, and then elected to serve as governor for the next four consecutive terms. Clinton's reputation was that of a pro-business centrist. He helped found the Democratic Leadership Council, a group of mainly southern moderates whose goal was to take control of the Democratic party from it's more liberal members. Clinton was elected president in 1992, with Albert Gore Jr. as his running mate. He campaigned for the interests of the middle class, such as tax cuts, reform of the health-care and welfare systems, and reducing the budget deficit. After taking office, in January 1993, Clinton expended tremendous amounts of political capital championing the rights of homosexuals in the military and the appointment of women and African Americans to high profile cabinet posts. At the same time he appeared indecisive dealing with the crises in Bosnia, Haiti and Somalia. When he failed to deliver on his middle-class tax cut, his popularity plummeted. In 1994 the Republican party gained control of the Congress for the first time in 40 years, and also won a majority of the governorships up for election.

CLOSE, GLENN

Creative Artists Agency, 1888 Century Park East, Suite 1400, Los Angeles, CA 90067
BORN: 1947, Greenwich, Conn. ACHIEVEMENTS: Antointette Perry Award, Best Actress, The Real Thing, 1984; Antointette Perry Award, Best

Actress, Death and the Maiden, 1992. STUDIED: College of William and Mary, B.A., drama, 1974.

Glenn Close is probably best known for her performances on film, however her experience extends to stage and television, as well. The daughter of William and Bettine Close, she has been performing professionally since the early 1970s. Early in her career she was a member of the repertory group, Fingernails, and also trained as a lyric soprano. Among her stage appearances is her performance as Angelica, in *Love for Love*, with the New Phoenix Repertory Company, in 1974, at Helen Hayes Theatre, in New York City. She debuted on film as Jenny Fields in *The World According to Garp*, in 1982, and has gone on to achieve many powerful screen performances. Close has narrated and hosted several television specials, including, *The Elephant's Child*, in 1987, on *Children's Storybook Classics*. Close was executive producer for *Sarah, Plain and Tall*, on *Hallmark Hall of Fame*, in 1991.

COHEN, STANLEY

Stanford University Medical Center, Stanford, CA 94305

BORN: 1922, Brooklyn, N.Y. ACHIEVEMENTS: Nobel Prize in Physiology or Medicine (shared with Rita Levi-Montalcini, dual U.S.Italy), 1986; William Thomson Wakeman Award; Earl Sutherland Research Prize; Albion O. Bernstein Award; H.P. Robertson Memorial Award; Lewis S. Rosentiel Award; Alfred P. Sloan Award; Louisa Gross Horwitz Prize; Lila Gruber Memorial Cancer Research Award; Bertner Award; Gairdner Foundation International Award; Fred Koch Award; National Medal of Science; Albert Lasker Award, Albert and Mary Lasker Foundation; Franklin Medal; Albert A.Michaelson Award. STUDIED: Brooklyn College; Oberlin College; University of Michigan.

In their work on substances that influence cells, Stanley Cohen and his colaureate, Rita Levi-Montalcini, made important fundamental contributions to understanding the mechanisms which regulate the growth of cells and organs. They first identified the proteins at work in controlling cell growth in the nervous system, then found a second growth factor, called the epidermal growth factor. They further purified that factor, discovered its amino acid sequence, and found the way it is bound to the surface of a cell. Many cellular control mechanisms depend on the way they grow, and understanding these mechanisms is one of the main problems facing cell biologists. Levi-Montalcini continued her work on nerve-cell growth and has made a strong impact in research on many diseases, including Alzheimer and Parkinson diseases, and cancer.

COHEN, WILLIAM S.

322 Hart Senate Office Building, Washington, DC 20510-1901 (202) 224-2523

BORN: 1940, Bangor, Maine ACHIEVEMENTS: Fellow, Harvard University's John F. Kennedy Institute of Politics, 1972; named one of America's 200 future leaders by Time Magazine, 1975. STUDIED: Bowdoin College, 1962; Boston University Law School, LLB, 1965.

William Cohen came to national prominence in 1974 as a member of the House Judiciary Committee, which conducted an inquiry on the impeachment of President Richard Nixon. After three terms in the House of Representatives, Cohen was elected to the Senator from Maine in 1984. He has twice won re-election. Cohen is chairman of the Special Committee on Aging and the Armed Services Committee's Seapower Subcommittee. In 1988 he collaborated with Sen. George Mitchell in writing *Men of Zeal*, a non-fiction book chronicling the Iran-Contra investigation. Cohen is also a poet and novelist. A collection of his poems, *A Baker's Nickel*, was published in 1986. His 1991 novel, *One-Eyed Kings*, is a spy-thriller set in the Middle East.

COLEMAN, CY

CC Enterprises, 161 W 54th St., New York, NY 10019-5322

BORN: 1929, New York City. ACHIEVEMENTS: Antoinette Perry Award, Best Original Score, On the Twentieth Century, 1978; Antoinette Perry Award, Best Original Musical Score, City of Angels, 1990; Antoinette Perry Award, Best Score, The Will Rogers Follies, 1991; Grammy award, Best Musical Show Album and Record Producer and Composer, The Will Rogers Follies, 1992; Emmy awards, Television Special, If They Could See Me Now, 1974, Gypsy in My Soul, 1975. STUDIED: High School of Music and Art; New York College of Music, diploma, 1948; student, Rudolph Gruen, Adele Marcus, Bernard Wagenaar, Hall Overton; L.I.U., MusD (honorable), 1994.

Cy Coleman's musical gifts appeared early in his life. He began playing the piano at the age of 4, performed in a recital at Steinway Hall at the age of 6, and was playing supper clubs in Manhattan at 17. In 1948, he formed a trio while still a student at New York College of Music. His compositions began to attract attention with *Try to Change Me Now* and *Witchcraft*, two 1950s hit singles sung by Frank Sinatra. He wrote *Firefly* for Tony Bennett in 1958. The 1960 musical, *Wildcraft*, written with lyricist Carolyn Leigh, starred Lucille Ball. Other stage successes included *Little Me, Sweet Charity, Seesaw*, and *Barnum*. His songs have been sung in motion pictures by Barbara Streisand, among many others, and he has occasionally recorded his own albums. Mark Murphy recorded an album of Coleman material in 1977. The 1985 film, *Pee Wee's Big Adventure*, opened up a successful career as a composer of television and film soundtracks. His credits include *Batman, Dick Tracy, The Simpsons, Edward Scissorhands, Scrooged, Beetlejuice*, and *Big Top Pee Wee*, among others.

COLEMAN, NORM

390 City Hall, 15 West Kellogg Blvd., Saint Paul, MN 55102 (612) 226-8510

BORN: 1949, Brooklyn, New York City. ACHIEVEMENTS: Founded the Minnesota chapter of D.A.R.E. STUDIED: University of Iowa College of Law, J.D. 1976

Prior to being elected mayor in November, 1993, Coleman spent 17 years with the Minnesota Attorney General's Office. In addition to his duties as chief prosecutor, solicitor general and legislative policy advisor, Mayor Coleman was instrumental in bringing societal issues such as drug abuse, domestic violence against women and children, and victims' rights to the attention of state lawmakers as well as the general public. He helped found the Minnesota chapter of Drug Abuse Resistance Education, known as D.A.R.E., a program to prevent the youth from turning to drugs.

COLL, STEVE

The Washington Post, 1150-15th St., NW., Washington DC 20071 (202) 334-6000
BORN: 1958, Washington, D.C. ACHIEVEMENTS: Pulitzer Prize, Explanatory Journalism; Gerald Loeb Award, University of California; Livingston Award, Molly Parnell Livingston Foundation. STUDIED: Occidental College, cum laude B.A.
Steve Coll is an international correspondent for the Washington Post. He is known for examining the political and economic forces behind events occurring in places such as Turkish bazaars and Kazakhstan oil fields. Among his notable dispatches were stories on the Mafia in Italy in which Mafia informant Tommaso Buscetta explained the organization's codes and provided organization and membership charts. Coll also dug into the threat of nuclear arms in Central Europe, pointing out that smugglers have moved nuclear weapons from states like Iran to nations bordering Russia, endangering the vision of a nuclear-free zone along those borders. News watchers rate Coll high among those correspondents who understand and interpret the international scene. His four books include *The Taking of Getty Oil* (with David A. Vise) and *The Deal of the Century.*

COLLIER, PETER

c/o Summit Books, 1230 Avenue of the Americas, New York, NY 10020 (212)-246-2471
BORN: 1939, Hollywood, Calif. ACHIEVEMENTS: National Endowment of the Arts, Literature fellowship, 1979; wrote with David Horowitz The Rockefellers: An American Drama, Holt, 1976; The Kennedys: An American Drama, Summit Books, 1984; and The Fords: An American Epic, Summit Books, 1987. STUDIED: University of California, Berkeley, A.B. 1961; University of California, Berkeley, M.A., 1963.
In 1964 Peter Collier became an instructor in English at his alma mater, the University of California, Berkeley. He began his journalism career as a staff writer for *Ramparts Magazine* in 1967. During the height of the Vietnam War, *Ramparts Magazine* was known as a champion of the anti-war movement. Collier was executive editor at the magazine from 1968 until 1969 and then as editor from 1969 until 1973. Collier, who has written and edited several books on literature and politics, began his career as a liberal, but in later years has adopted a more conservative viewpoint. He is best known for a series of multi-generational biographies co-authored with his best friend, David Horowitz.

COLTON, FRANK B.

3901 Lyons, Evanston, IL 60203-1324
BORN: 1923 (Poland). ACHIEVEMENTS: Developed oral contraceptives; Industrial Research Institute Achievement Award, 1978; Professional Achievement Award from the University of Chicago, 1978. Inducted into the National Inventors Hall of Fame, 1988. STUDIED: Northwestern University, B.S., 1945; M.S., 1946; University of Chicago, Ph.D., 1950.
Dr. Frank Colton made significant contributions in medicinal organic chemistry and steroid chemistry. As a research fellow at the Mayo Clinic, he worked with Nobel Laureate Edward C. Kendall in the development of an improved synthesis of cortisone. His research led to the development of Nilevar, the first orally active anabolic agent, and to the discovery of Enovid, the first oral contraceptive. In 1960 Enovid was introduced as a means of family planning, which ushered in the era of oral contraceptives. Dr. Colton retired from G.D. Searle and Co. in 1986, where he had worked for 35 years.

COMER, JAMES P.

Yale University, Child Study Center, New Haven, CT 06520
BORN: 1934, East Chicago, Ind. ACHIEVEMENTS: Distinguished Alumni Award, Howard University; Outstanding Service to Mankind Award, Alpha Phi Alpha E Region; Rockefeller Public Service Award; Vera Paster Award, American Orthopsychiatric Association; Solomon Carter Fuller Award, American Psychiatric Association; Harold W. McGraw, Jr. Prize in Education; Dana Prize in Education. STUDIED: Indiana University, B.A.; Howard University of Medicine, M.D., psychiatry; University of Michigan School of Public Health, M.P.H., public health.
After receiving his doctorate in medicine, James Comer interned at St. Catherine Hospital in his home town of East Chicago, Ind. One year later he broadened his internship at the U.S. Public Health Service where he found what would become a major part of his career work—education and public health. Ten years of psychiatry residency at Yale University School of Medicine was interrupted for a year of service as a lieutenant colonel with the U.S. Public Health Service. After his residency at Yale, he remained as associate professor and associate dean for six years, becoming a full professor in 1975. As a writer, he is a columnist for *Parents* magazine, author of two books, *Beyond Black and White*, in 1972, and *School Power* in 1980, and co-author of *Black Child Care* in 1975.

CONKLIN, WILLIAM

Conklin Rossant, 251 Park Avenue South, New York, NY 10010 (212) 777-2120
BORN: 1923. ACHIEVEMENTS: FAIA; notable works: Butterfield House, New York City; Myriad Gardens, Oklahoma City; STUDIED: Harvard University.
An architect, preservationist and archaeologist, William Conklin believes that architecture should integrate itself into the urban structure and fabric, providing space for social activities and meaning for human communities. His New York City Butterfield House is integrated into its street context by capturing neighborhood essences rather than copying surrounding building features. Adapting the classic bay-window design of a nearby cast iron building, the house offers streamlined bay windows in vertical formation, highlighted by bands of limestone that run between window columns. Narrow limestone spandrels mark the floors between the windows, but the

height of the windows dominates the spandrels, and in Modern fashion gives an effect of vertical columns of glass running the height of the seven-story structure. Within the building there is a landscaped interior garden. His Oklahoma City Myriad Gardens is a four-block park in the downtown areas which is sunken below grade to avoid strong winds. The excavated area provides civic facilities, plazas, waterways, and a lake. A cylindrical glass botanical bridge spans the lake. The overall effect of the park is of stylistically abstract buildings set in a modern oasis.

CONOVER, LLOYD H.

NCIPLA, Suite 203, 2001 Jefferson Davis Hwy., Arlington, VA 22202 (703) 415-0780
BORN: 1923, Orange, N.J. ACHIEVEMENTS: Invented the drug Tetracycline; inducted into the National Inventors Hall of Fame, 1992. STUDIED: Amherst College, A.B., 1947; University of Rochester, Ph.D., 1950.
Dr. Lloyd Conover's original plan to be a teacher evaporated when he took a position with the newly formed Chemical Research Department of Pfizer. He collaborated with Harvard professor R.B. Woodard to synthesize biologically active tetracycline antibiotic from molecular building blocks. His patent for tetracycline spent 27 years in court, with the final ruling in 1982 in favor of Dr. Conover. Along with W.C. Austin, and J.W. McFarland, he also patented the anthelmintic drugs pyrantel and morantel. Pyrantel is used in the treatment for intestinal worm parasites. These drugs are vital in the control of parasites in farm and other animals. He retired as senior vice president of Pfizer Central Research in 1984.

CONRAD, CHARLES "PETE" JR.

McDonnell-Douglas Space Systems Co., P.O. Box 516, St. Louis, MO 63166 (314) 232-0232
BORN: 1930, Philadelphia. ACHIEVEMENTS: Captain, USN; pilot, Gemini 5, 1965; command pilot, Gemini 11, 1966; commander, Apollo 12, 1969; third man to walk on the moon; commander of Skylab 2, 1973.
Charles "Pete" Conrad Jr. was among the second group of astronauts chosen in 1962. He piloted Gemini 11, and commanded Apollo 12 and Skylab 2. In February, 1974 he resigned from NASA, and the Navy, and became the vice president and chief operating officer of American Television and Communications Corporation, a cable firm in Denver, Colo. Conrad is now the vice president for International Business Development, McDonnell-Douglas Space Systems Co., in Huntington Beach California.

CONYERS, JOHN

U.S. House of Representatives, 2426 RHOB, Washington, DC 20515-2214 (202) 225-5126
Conyers is a prominent political leader. For career credentials consult the portion of this book entitled "Notable Americans by Profession" in the Appendix. Within this portion, the list "Political Leaders" describes requirements for inclusion in this volume.

COOK, LODWRICK M.

Atlantic Richfield Co., 515 S. Flower St., Los Angeles, CA 90071 (213) 486-3511
BORN: 1928, Amarillo, TEXAS. ACHIEVEMENTS: CEO, Atlantic Richfield. STUDIED: University of North Texas, B.A., M.A., business administration.
Lodwrick Cook helped steady a shaky ARCO when he took over the company as CEO in 1985 and chair of the board in 1986. He led the company through several reorganizations and an expansion overseas. He was a pioneer in the development of cleaner-burning gasoline. His biggest achievement, however, was the help he gave a privately run riot relief program after the Los Angeles riots in 1992. Taking the helm of RLA (Rebuild Los Angeles) with Linda Griego in 1994, the pair unseated a squabbling foursome of co-chairs and joined other corporations in helping 115,000 small business owners in Los Angeles county's neglected neighborhoods expand and create new jobs. After 39 years with ARCO, which began with Cook as an engineer trainee in 1956, at age 67 Cook stepped down as chair and CEO, retaining his connection to ARCO as a board member.

COOK, DAVID T.

The Christian Science Monitor, 1 Norway St., Boston, MA 02115-3195 (617) 450-2000
BORN: 1946, Boston. ACHIEVEMENTS: Fellow, Bagehot Fellowship in Business and Economic Journalism, Columbia University. STUDIED: Principia College, Elsah, Ill., B.A.; Michigan State University.
David Cook became editor of the *Christian Science Monitor* in 1994. Before assuming his current post he was the editor of Monitor Broadcasting, the broadcast arm of the newspaper. He oversees both print and broadcast activities of the *Monitor*. Cook began his career with the paper in 1969, specializing in business reporting. Previously he had worked for McGraw-Hill as a Detroit-based reporter for *Business Week*. While managing editor of Monitor Broadcasting's *World Monitor* his station won an Emmy. Earlier, as a reporter on the weekly television news program *Monitor Reports*, his program won a Peabody Award for international news coverage.

COOPER, LEROY GORDON JR.

5011 Woodley, Encino, CA 91436;
BORN: 1927, Shawnee, Okla. ACHIEVEMENTS: Space missions: Mercury 9, Gemini 5 (commander). STUDIED: Air Force Institute of Technology, B.S., aeronautical engineering, 1956.
Leroy Cooper joined the U.S. Air Force in 1949, and, after graduating from the Air Force Institute of Technology, he was trained as a test pilot. Cooper was chosen as one of the first seven U.S. astronauts, as part of Project Mercury. The Mercury 9 spacecraft took him into Earth orbit in 1963, where he circled the globe 22 times inside the space capsule Faith 7, in 34 hours, 20 minutes. He was the commander of the Gemini 5 space mission in 1965, with Charles Conrad Jr., and spent nearly eight days in orbit. Cooper left the

Air Force and NASA in 1970 for a position as vice-president of research and development with Walt Disney Productions.

COOPER, ROGER

Berkley Publishing Group, 200 Madison Ave., New York, NY 10016
BORN: 1953. ACHIEVEMENTS: Vice president, Doubleday Book and Music Clubs.
After two years as an executive with St. Martins Press, Cooper shifted to Doubleday Book and Music Clubs in 1995 as vice president and publisher. He was senior vice president and publisher of St. Martin's mass-market division. Cooper succeeded Arlene Friedman who moved up to president and publisher of Doubleday Publishing. He principally oversees the company's two general interest clubs, The Literary Guild and Doubleday Book Club. Also under his direction will be nine specialty clubs, among them mystery, military, health, large print, and audio. The clubs have an estimated membership of three million.

COOPER, LEON NEIL

Brown University, Department of Physics, Providence, RI 02912
BORN: 1930, New York City. ACHIEVEMENTS: Nobel Prize in Physics (shared with John Schrieffer and the late John Bardeen), 1972; Comstock Prize, National Academy of Science; Descartes Medal, Academy de Paris; John Hay Award, Columbia University. STUDIED: Columbia University.
Proving that electrical resistance in certain metals vanishes far above absolute zero (the temperature at which substances possess no thermal energy, equal to -273.15 degrees Celsius, or -459.67 degrees Fahrenheit), Leon Cooper and his colaureates, the late John Bardeen and John Robert Schrieffer, stimulated much work on superconductivity in physics. Their research showed that, at low temperatures, electrons in a conductor could act in bound pairs, called "Cooper pairs," an action which results in no electrical resistance to the flow of electrons through solids. The discovery that there are materials that are superconductive at hundreds of degrees above absolute zero has since revolutionized the production and transmission of electrical energy.

COPPLEY, JACK

Bell Atlantic Corporation, 1717 Arch St., Philadelphia, PA 19103 (215) 963-6000
ACHIEVEMENTS: Developed Thinx software package.
Software designer Coppley made life easier for computer number-crunchers in the 1990s with his creation of the Thinx software package. Thinx lets the user manipulate raw data in the form of images and graphics rather than numbers. For example, instead of a spreadsheet showing regional sales, Thinx generates a bird's-eye view of the totals by showing a map of the United States with each state sized to reflect the volume of its sales.

COREA, CHICK

ASCAP, 1 Lincoln Plaza, New York, NY 10023 (212) 595-3050
BORN: 1941, Chelsea, Mass. ACHIEVEMENTS: Grammy Awards, Best Jazz Group, Return to Forever, featuring Chick Corea, No Mystery, 1975; The Leprechaun, 1976; Friends, 1978; Duet (with Gary Burton), 1970; Chick Corea and Gary Burton in Concert—Zurich, October 28, 1979, 1979; Best Jazz Fusion Performance—Vocal or Instrumental, Chick Corea Akoustic Band, 1989.
Chick Corea was trained, as a child, by his father, who was himself a professional musician. The strong Latin influence in Corea's music comes from his early piano playing jobs with local Latin bands. Corea's work also shows the influence certain pianists had upon him, such as McCoy Tyner and Herbie Hancock. In 1968, Corea joined an electronic jazz-rock group headed by Miles Davis. From 1972 until 1978 he played with his own group, Return to Forever, known for its experiments with combinations of acoustic and electronic instruments, and for its collaborations with numerous jazz and classical musicians. Since 1978, Corea had led the Akoustic and the Elektric Bands.

COREY, ELIAS JAMES

Harvard University, Department of Chemistry, 12 Oxford St., Cambridge, MA 02138
BORN: 1928, Methuen, Mass. ACHIEVEMENTS: Nobel Prize in Physics, 1990; Intrascience Award; Harrison Howe Award; Ciba Foundation Medal; Evans Award, Ohio State University; Linus Pauling Award; Dickson Prize; George Ledlie Prize; Nichols Medal; Buchman Award; Franklin Medal; Kirkwood Award; Wolf Prize. STUDIED: Massachusetts Institute of Technology.
Elias Corey has been well rewarded for a professional life spent making substances or products such as plastics, artificial fibers, drugs, etc., by a synthesis of chemicals. His many honors were finally capped with the Nobel Chemistry Prize for developing the theory and methodology of organic synthesis. Cited by the Nobel committee were his synthesis of hydrocarbons found in plant oils, his synthesis of several hormones involved in human physiological functions, and the synthesis of a substance extracted from the ginko tree found useful for disorders of the blood system and in the treatment of asthma.

CORIGLIANO, JOHN PAUL

365 West End Ave., New York, NY 10014
BORN: 1938, New York City. ACHIEVEMENTS: Grammy Award, Best Contemporary Composition, Symphony No. 1, 1993; Composer of the Year, 1993, Musical America. STUDIED: Columbia University, B.A. cum laude, Music.
Corigliano's long dedication to symphonic composition bore fruit in 1987, when he accepted an invitation from the Chicago Symphony Orchestra to become composer in residence. Five years later his polished, avant garde, and popular Symphony No. 1 won a Grammy Award for Best Contemporary Composition. He was named composer of the year by Musical America, while the Chicago Symphony Orchestra, under Daniel Barenboim, won a Grammy for Best Orchestra Per-

formance. During his 25 years as a violinist with the New York Philharmonic, Corigliano composed 13 musical works from concertos to symphonies, and his score for the film *Altered States*, in 1981, won nominations for an Academy Award and a Grammy.

COSBY, BILL

The Brokaw Company, 9255 Sunset Blvd. Los Angeles, CA 90069
BORN: 1937, Philadelphia, Pa. ACHIEVEMENTS: Grammy, Best Comedy Recording, I started Out as a Child, 1964; Why Is There Air, 1965; Wonderfulness, 1966; Revenge, 1967; To Russell, My Brother, Whom I Slept With, 1968; Bill Cosby, 1969; Those of You With or Without Children, You'll Understand, 1986; Grammy, Best Recording for Children, Bill Cosby Talks to Kids About Drugs, 1971; Grammy, Best Recording for Children, The Electric Company (with Lee Chamberlin and Rita Moreno), 1972; Emmy, Best Actor in a Drama Series, I Spy, 1966, 1967, 1968; Emmy, Bill Cosby Special, 1969; Emmy, The New Fat Albert Show, 1981; Emmy, Best Comedy Series, The Cosby Show, 1985; Golden Globe, Best Actor in a Comedy Series, The Cosby Show, 1985, 1986; elected to the Emmy Hall of Fame, 1991. STUDIED: Temple University, 1961-62; University of Massachusetts, M.A., 1972, Ed.D., 1977.
One of Americas premiere entertainers, Bill Cosby has been making audiences laugh for more than 30 years, with his good-natured humor and rubber-faced expressions. He began his career as a stand-up comedian and has since recorded over 20 albums. Cosby was the first African-American actor to co-star in a prime-time television dramatic series. The series *I Spy*, ran from 1965 to 1968. He continued his success in 1972 as executive producer and host of the TV cartoon series *Fat Albert and The Cosby Kids*, which was based on one of his most popular comic characters. In the same year, he made his film debut in *Hickey and Boggs*. Teaming up with Sidney Poitier, Cosby made a series of successful films *Uptown Saturday Night*, and *Let's Do It Again*. In 1984, The Cosby Show debuted and became one of the most popular television shows in the United States, from 1984-1992. Returning to television in 1994, he created and produced the *Cosby Mysteries Series* for NBC. Cosby has also written several best-selling books: *Fatherhood* in 1986, *Time Flies*, 1987, and *Love and Marriage*, 1989. A jazz enthusiast, he is the president of the Rhythm and Blues Hall of Fame.

COSTAS, BOB (ROBERT) QUINLAN

NBC Sports, Room 1411, 30 Rockefeller Plaza, New York, NY 10020 (212) 664-4444
BORN: 1952, New York City. ACHIEVEMENTS: Sportscaster of the Year, National Association of Sportscasters and Broadcasters; 1988 Emmy Award, Outstanding Host of Play-By-Play Announcing (World Series). STUDIED: Syracuse University.
During Bob Costas' 21 years in television, he has broadcast the *Game of the Week*, the Winter and Summer Olympics, World Series, All-Star Game, the Super Bowl, plus many specials and host of many shows. At age 22 he switched from a Syracuse, N.Y., station to announcing sports on a St. Louis radio station for seven years, and finally landed with NBC

Sports in 1980 as sportscaster and program host. He is a past host of *Costas Coast-to-Coast* and the syndicated radio shows *Sporting News Report* and *Sports Flashback*. His video recordings include *The 500 Home Run Club*.

COSTNER, KEVIN

Michael Ovitz, Creative Artists Agency, 9830 Wilshire Blvd., Beverly Hills, CA 90212
BORN: 1955, Compton, Calif. ACHIEVEMENTS: Academy Awards, Best Picture (with Jim Wilson) and Best Director; Golden Globe Awards, Best Motion Picture—Drama (with Jim Wilson) and Best Director; all for Dances with Wolves, 1990. STUDIED: California State University, Fullerton, B.A., 1978; studied acting at South Coast Actors' Co-op.
Kevin Costner will always be remembered for his role as Lieutenant John J. Dunbar in the film *Dances with Wolves*, which he directed and also co-produced with Jim Wilson. His portrayal of a loyal cavalry officer abandoned at a lonely frontier outpost, and his subsequent adoption of Native American views and culture, was both haunting and educational. Prior to *Dances with Wolves*, Costner appeared in the hit movies *The Big Chill*, 1983, *Silverado*, 1985, *American Flyers*, 1985, *The Untouchables*, 1987, as Crash Davis in *Bull Durham*, 1988, *The Field of Dreams*, 1980, and the title role in *Robin Hood: Prince of Thieves*, 1991.

COURIC, (KATIE) KATHERINE

NBC, 30 Rockefeller Plaza, New York, NY 10112 (212) 664-4444
BORN: Washington, DC. ACHIEVEMENTS: Washington Journalism Review award "Best in the Business," 1993 STUDIED: University of Virginia
As the co-anchor since 1991 of NBC News' *Today*, she is one of the most instantly recognizable faces in television. She began with the show as its first-ever national correspondent, occasionally filling in as a substitute anchor. She first joined NBC News in 1989 as deputy Pentagon correspondent and has since interviewed numerous political figureheads including Ross Perot and George Bush. She was the first to conduct televised interviews with Hillary Rodham Clinton after the election victory; Anita Hill after sexual harassment charges were leveled against Clarence Thomas; and Norman Schwarzkopf upon the conclusion of the Gulf War. Her career began in 1979 at the ABC news bureau in Washington where she was a desk assistant. In 1980, she joined CNN and worked as an assignment editor before moving to associate producer, and by 1984, producer of *Take Two*, a two hour news program that would come to feature many of her reports on the 1984 Presidential campaign. In the mid-eighties, prior to joining NBC, she worked at WTVJ in Miami where she filed stories about crime and drugs as well as an award-winning series on child pornography.

COVEY, RICHARD OSWALT

NASA, L.B. Johnson Space Center, Houston, TX 77058
BORN: 1946, Fayetteville, Ark. ACHIEVEMENTS: Pilot of the STS 51-1, 1985, and STS-26, 1988, space flights; commander of the STS-38, 1990, space

flight. STUDIED: *U.S. Air Force Academy, B.S. engineering sciences, 1968; Purdue University, M.S. aeronautics and astronautics engineering, 1969.*
Originally an operational fighter pilot and weapons test pilot, Richard Covey was selected with the eighth group of astronauts in 1978. At the start of his career as an astronaut, he provided astronaut support in orbiter engineering development. He piloted the STS-26, the first flight after the Challenger accident, and was commander of the STS-38, a Department of Defense mission.

CRAIG, LARRY E.

302 Hart Senate Office Building, Washington, DC 20510-1203 (202) 224-2752
BORN: *1945, Council, Idaho*
ACHIEVEMENTS: *Co-founder, Senate Private Property Rights Caucus; member Board of Directors, National Rifle Association.* STUDIED: *University of Idaho, B.A. 1969; George Washington University, 1969-70.*

A third-generation Idaho rancher, Larry Craig came to the U.S. Senate in 1990, seeking to have a voice in federal management of natural resources. He is a member of the Senate Energy and Natural Resources Committee and is the ranking Republican on the Mineral Resources, Development and Production Subcommittee. Craig is also a member of numerous other subcommittees dealing with the use and conservation of the nation's

Astronaut Richard Oswalt Covey.

natural resources. In addition he is a member of the Agriculture Production and Stabilization of Prices Subcommittee, and the Agricultural Credit Subcommittee.

CRAIG, GEORGE

HarperCollins Publishers, 10 East 53rd St., New York, NY 10022 (212) 207-7000
ACHIEVEMENTS: *Successfully instituted $20 million annual cost reduction program at Harper & Row.*
Scotland-born George Craig, president and chief executive officer of HarperCollins Publishers, worked for Honeywell Computers in Scotland from 1965 to 1974. He entered publishing with struggling William Collins and in 13 years reorganized the British company's book manufacturing division, taking it into the high-tech age and profitability.

Craig moved to the U.S. in 1987 as president and chief executive officer of Harper & Row, a subsidiary of News Corporation. Instituting a $20-million annual cost-reduction program, he went on to revitalize the firm's general book publishing programs. In 1989, News International acquired Harper & Row and merged it with William Collins to form HarperCollins Publishers.

CRAM, DONALD JAMES

University of California at Los Angeles, Department of Chemistry, Los Angeles, CA 90024
BORN: *1919, Chester, Vt.* ACHIEVEMENTS: *Nobel Prize in Chemistry (shared with Charles J. Pedersen, U.S., and JeanMarie Lehn, France), 1987; American Chemical Society, 1953 and 1965; Herbert Newby McCoy Award, 1965 and 1975; Society of Chemical Manufacturers Award; Arthur C. Cope Award; Roger Adams Award; Willard Gibbs Award; Tolman Medal.* STUDIED: *Rollins College, Fla.; University of Nebraska; Harvard University.*

In his 1990 book, *From Design to Discovery,* Donald Cram writes that organic chemistry is like a "vast playground on which many new games could be invented, games whose players might engage in civil and international competition to discover the appropriate rules." In that world of "games," Cram spent a career inventing and designing molecules on paper and then thought up ways of making them in the laboratory. The result was the Nobel Prize at age 68, for broad-ranging research that included creation of the hand-drawn artificial molecules that mimic important chemical reactions in the processes of life. He also extended his co-laureate's work (Charles J. Pedersen) on problems of structuring compounds, problems the third co-laureate, JeanMarie Lehn, also worked on. Cram was one of the stream of graduating chemistry doctorates in the post-1945 period who would go on to spearhead the international domination of physical organic chemistry by Americans from the 1960s on.

CREIGHTON, JOHN W. JR.

Weyerhaeuser Company, Tacoma, WA 98477 (206) 924-2345
BORN: *1932, Pittsburgh.* STUDIED: *Ohio State University, B.S., science, J.D., law; University of Miami, B.A., business administration.*

John Creighton took over the helm of the pulp paper, container, and package manufacturer Weyerhaeuser in 1991. Twenty-one years earlier he had joined the company as general manager of its real estate development division, the Shelter Group, moving up to president and director in 1988, and chief executive officer in 1991. In addition to his position at Weyerhaeuser, he is director of the American Forest and Paper Association, MIP Properties Inc., the Civil War Trust, Washington Energy Corporation, Quality Food Centers Inc., Portland General Corporation, and the Local Initiatives Support Group. In 1995 he was elected to the board of Unocal Corporation.

CRICHTON, JOHN MICHAEL

Jenkins McKay, Inc., 2049 Century Park East, Los Angeles, CA 90067
BORN: 1942, Chicago, Ill. ACHIEVEMENTS: Author of many best-selling novels, including Jurassic Park, 1990; film director. STUDIED: Harvard University, Harvard Medical School, M.D.,
Trained as a physician with a degree from Harvard Medical School, Michael Chrichton soon turned to writing novels. His brand of fiction is distinguished by its realistic scientific and historical detail. His scientific suspense novels include his first best-seller, *The Andromeda Strain*, 1969, about an alien bacterium; as well as *The Terminal Man*, 1972, and *Jurassic*

Astronaut Robert Laurel Crippen.

Park, 1990. His 1975 historical novel, *The Great Train Robbery*, was set in the 1850s and included many particulars of the period. A number of his novels have been made into films, including the 1993 blockbuster *Jurassic Park*.

CRIPPEN, ROBERT LAUREL

NASA, Kennedy Space Center, FL 32899 (407) 867-7110.
BORN: 1937, Beaumont, Texas ACHIEVEMENTS: Space missions: STS-1 space shuttle mission (pilot, first space shuttle mission), STS-7, STS-11 space shuttle missions (commander). STUDIED: University of Texas, B.S., aerospace engineering, 1960.
While serving as a pilot with the U.S. Navy, in 1966, Robert Crippen was selected as an astronaut by the Department of Defense, as part of the Manned Orbital

Laboratory program. The Department of Defense canceled the program, in 1969, and Crippen transferred to NASA as an astronaut. He piloted the Columbia on the first space shuttle mission in 1981 under the command of John Young. He commanded the shuttle Challenger on its second space flight in 1983 on the STS-7 space shuttle mission, which carried Sally Ride, America's first woman in space. Crippen commanded the Challenger again on STS-11 in 1984 with a crew of six, the largest crew to fly a spacecraft. He later became the director of the John F. Kennedy Space Center in Florida.

CRISTOFER, MICHAEL

Joyce Ketay Agency, 334 W. 39th St., New York, NY 10024
BORN: 1945, White Horse, N.J. ACHIEVEMENTS: Pulitzer Prize and Antoinette Perry Award, The Shadow Box, 1977. STUDIED: Catholic University, 1962-1965; American University, Beirut, 1968-1969.
Originating from drafts of three one-act plays, Michael Cristofer's *The Shadow Box*, 1977, which won Pulitzer and Tony awards, concerns the state of mind of three characters in three cottages at an estate for the dying. His other plays include *Plot Counter Plot*, 1971; *Americomedia*, 1973; *Ice*, 1974; and *Black Angel*, 1982. He also wrote the screenplays for the films *Falling in Love*, 1985, and *The Witches of Eastwick*, 1987, and acted in a number of plays, including the title role in *Chinchilla*, 1979.

CRONIN, JAMES WATSON

University of Chicago, 5630 S. Ellis Ave., Chicago, IL 60637
BORN: 1931, Chicago. ACHIEVEMENTS: Nobel Prize in Physics (shared with Val Fitch), 1980; Research Corporation Award; Ernest Orlando Lawrence Award; John Price Wetherill Medal, Franklin Institute. STUDIED: Southern Methodist University; University of Chicago.
An early advance in the study of subatomic particles—what goes on inside an atom between its electrons, protons, and neutrons, the major interest of atomic scientists since the 1960s—won Nobel attention for Cronin and his colaureate in 1980. Previously it was thought that proton collisions within the nuclei of an atom obeyed the laws of symmetry observed in the

physical world. They found just the opposite, an important insight toward breaking up particles into their constituent parts for the study of their structure. As with Val Fitch, Cronin continues his work on the nature and characteristics of elementary particles.

CRUISE, TOM

Paula Wagner, Creative Artists Agency, 9830 Wilshire Blvd., Beverly Hills, CA 90212
BORN: 1962, Syracuse, N.Y. ACHIEVEMENTS: Golden Globe Award, Best Actor, Born on the Fourth of July, 1989.
A dyslexic, Tom Cruise had a difficult time in high school, and eventually dropped out to take up acting. His film career has been punctuated with a number of excellent roles. He appeared in *Taps*, 1981, *Losin' It*, 1983, *Risky Business*, 1983, and *Legend*, 1985. His first big hit was when he appeared as Lieutenant Pete Mitchell in *Top Gun*, 1986. He followed that success with a series of hits, including *The Color of Money*, 1986, *Cocktail*, 1988, *Rain Man*, with Dustin Hoffman, 1988, *Born on the Fourth of July*, 1989, *Days of Thunder*, 1990, *Interview With the Vampire*, and *A Few Good Men*.

CYRSTAL, BILLY

Rollins, Joffe, Morra, & Brezner, 5555 Melrose Ave. Los Angeles CA 90038.
BORN: 1947, Long Island, N.Y. ACHIEVEMENTS: Emmy, Outstanding Performance in Special Events, The Thirty-first Annual Grammy Awards, 1989; Emmy (co-winner) Best Writing in a Variety or Music Program, Midnight Train to Moscow, 1990: Emmy, Best Individual Performance in a Variety or Music Program, The 63rd Annual Oscars, 1991; Emmy, Best Writing in a Variety or Music Program, The 63rd Annual Oscars, 1991; Emmy, Best Writing in a Variety or Music Program, The 64th Annual Oscars, 1992. STUDIED: Attended Marshall University; graduated from Nassau Community College; New York University, B.F.A., television and film direction, 1970.
A former substitute teacher, Billy Crystal worked the comedy club circuit appearing at Catch a Rising Star, Playboy Clubs and the Comedy Store. His guest appearances on *Saturday Night Live* in 1976 brought him national attention. In 1977 he took a risk and played the part of the gay character, Jodie Dallas on the

Dancer/choreographer Merce Cunningham.

television series *Soap*. He remained on the series from 1977 until 1981. Crystal was on *Saturday Night Live* from 1984 to 1985, where he became known for his impersonations of celebrities, such as Sammy Davis Jr., Howard Cossell, and Mohammed Ali. His impersonation of Fernando Lamas, and the phrase, "You Look Mahvelous," turned into a song, a Grammy Award nominated comedy recording, *Mahvelous!*, and Crystal's autobiography *Absolutely Mahvelous*. He won American Comedy Awards for his films, *When Harry Met Sally*, and *City Slickers*, and for his work on the Academy Awards show.

CUNNINGHAM, MERCE

Merce Cunningham Dance Company, 55 Bethune St., New York, NY 10014 (212) 255-8240
BORN: 1919, Centralia, Wash. ACHIEVEMENTS: Notable ballets: Collage; Antic Meet; Summerspace; Sixteen Dances for Soloist; Suite by Chance; Variations V; Aeon; Winterbranch; How to Pass, Kick, Fall, and Run. STUDIED: George Washington University, Washington, D.C.; Cornish School of Fine and Applied Arts, Seattle, Wash.; Bennington College School of Arts, no degrees; School of the American Ballet.
A pioneer of post-modern dance, Cunningham is known for such antics as long silences while dancers move around the stage (*Runes*), or blinding white lights turned on the audience during the performance (*Winterbranch*). Nevertheless, his unpredictable work, freed from the ordinary dramatic baggage of ballet, has influenced two generations of dancers and choreographers, and has helped establish dance in the curriculum of higher education. In 1945, after five years with the Martha Graham School, Cunningham grew dissatisfied with modern dance's emphasis on story and character and set out to form abstract dances with the accent on movement itself. With the late composer John Cage, he adopted the custom of fashioning his steps independently of his composer and designer, who each in turn work independently, the elements meeting up for the first time on opening night. Dance is exquisitely existential, Cunningham believes, concerned only with the single instant that comes along; i.e. rigid dancers suddenly

becoming limp; haphazard entrances and exits by performers; dancers who seem totally preoccupied and unaware of anybody else on stage, all beautifully executed by highly disciplined dancers.

CURLEY, TOM

USA Today, 1100 Wilson Blvd., Arlington, VA 22234 (703) 276-3400

Curley is a prominent publishing executive and the publisher and president of *USA Today*, America's largest nationally circulated daily newspaper. His paper seeks to "serve as a forum for better understanding and unity to help make the USA truly one nation." The quote, credited to the paper's founder Allen H. Neuharth, set a precedent for their unique style of journalism—using national statistical data as an adjunct to standard news reportage. Other media, especially local broadcast media, frequently quote the statistical information, hence *USA Today*'s news coverage is frequently circulated over the air waves.

CURRIER, RUTH

425 Broome St., New York, NY 10013 (212) 966-7521
Currier is a prominent dancer. For career credentials consult the alphabetical index in the rear of this volume and go to the page indicated where they may be found atop the list entitled "Dancers."

D'AMATO, ALFONSE M.

U.S. Senate, 520 SHOB, Washington, DC 20510-3202 (202) 224-6542

D'Amato admits to a troubled childhood, a result of his crossed eyes and the ridicule resulting from it. He credits his parents and their support for carrying him through the difficult years and building his self-confidence. The Republican senator from New York has held many positions of prominence during his career of public service. He is head of the Senate Banking Committee as well as the head of the Senate team that is investigating the Whitewater controversy that is threatening President Clinton's administration.

DALEY, RICHARD M.

City Hall, 121 N. LaSalle St., Chicago, IL 60602 (312) 744-3300

BORN: 1942, Chicago. ACHIEVEMENTS: Illinois State Senate, 1972-1978; State's Attorney, Cook County, 1980-1988; while mayor, Chicago's bond rating was increased by Standard & Poor's, a distinction shared by no other major American city. STUDIED: DePaul University, B.A., J.D.

The eldest son of the late mayor of Chicago, Richard J. Daley, became mayor of the Windy City himself on April 4, 1989, when he was elected to complete the unexpired term of the late Mayor Harold Washington. Daley's public service career began in 1970, when he was elected to the Illinois Constitutional Convention. Two years later he was elected to the Illinois State Senate and was re-elected in 1976 and 1978. In 1980 Daley became State's Attorney of Cook County. He

was the first Cook County official to sign the Shakman decree, which eliminated political hiring and firing. He served as county prosecutor for eight years before being elected mayor.

DALY, MAYOR TOM

Public Information Office, Anaheim, CA (714) 254-5164

ACHIEVEMENTS: Member: Orange County Transportation Authority; El Toro Citizens Advisory Commission; Regional Advisory Planning Council of Orange County; Board of Directors, Urban Water Institute. STUDIED: Harvard University, B.A., arts.

Twice elected mayor of Anaheim, with the voters giving him 71 percent of the vote in 1994, increased Tom Daly's term from two to four years. During his first two years in office he concentrated on water supplies, air quality, transportation, highway planning, bus transit operations, a convention center and entertainment arena, and creation of a new airport serving Orange County at the site of the Marine Corps Air Station in El Toro.

DAMADIAN, DR. RAYMOND

NCIPLA, Suite 203, 2001 Jefferson Davis Hwy., Arlington, VA 22202 (703)415-0780

BORN: 1936, Forest Hills, N.Y. ACHIEVEMENTS: Apparatus and method for detecting cancer in tissue; founded the FONAR Corporation; inducted into the National Inventors Hall of Fame, 1989. STUDIED: Julliard School of Music; University of Wisconsin, B.S., 1956; Albert Einstein College of Medicine, M.D.; a fellow in nephrology at Washington University School of Medicine; a fellow in biophysics at Harvard University; studied physiological chemistry at the School of Aerospace Medicine in San Antonio, Texas.

Dr. Damadian served in the Air Force before joining the faculty at New York State University, Downstate Medical Center. Using his medical background, he developed the ION Exchanger Resin Theory, a theory of living cells. This led to the invention of the magnetic resonance imaging scanner, or MRI. The MRI produces images of the interior body more detailed than X-ray or CAT scanners. Using static and dynamic fields within the body, the MRI yields radio signals from body tissue that are transformed into images or analyzed, providing composition of the chemicals in the tissue examined. Since the Food and Drug Administration's approval of the scanner in 1984, there have been over 250 in use in medical institutions worldwide. In 1978, he founded the FONAR Corporation for the manufacture of the MRI, which is now sold globally.

DANFORTH, JOHN D.

U.S. Senate, 248 SROB, Washington, DC 20510-2502 (202) 224-6154

Danforth is a prominent political leader. For career credentials consult the portion of this book entitled "Notable Americans by Profession" in the Appendix. Within this portion, the list "Political Leaders" describes requirements for inclusion in this volume.be found atop the list entitled "Political Leaders."

DANGERFIELD, RODNEY

Dangerfields, 1118 First Ave. New York NY 10021
BORN: 1922, Babylon, N.Y. ACHIEVEMENTS: Grammy Award, Best Comedy Album, No Respect, 1980.
According to Rodney Dangerfield, he is the least respected person in the entertainment business. His classic line "I Don't Get No Respect" is the major theme he carries throughout his comedy routines. Born Jack Roy (informed sources say Jacob Cohen), he performed in night clubs under the name Jack Roy from 1941 to 1951. In 1963 he changed his name to Rodney Dangerfield. From 1972-1973 he was a regular on the *Dean Martin Show*. Film credits include: *The Projectionist, Caddyshack, Easy Money, Back to School, Moving, Rover, Dangerfield and Lady Bugs. Dangerfield has written two books:* I Couldn't Stand My Wife's Cooking So I Opened a Restaurant, and *I Don't Get No Respect*. He has also recorded four comedy albums: *The Loser, I Don't Get No Respect, No Respect,* and *Rappin' Rodney.*

DANIELL, ROBERT F.

United Technologies Corp., United Technologies Building, Hartford, CT 06101 (203) 728-7000
BORN: 1934, Milton, Mass. STUDIED: Boston University, Industrial Technology; University of Bridgeport, D.Sc., honorary; Trinity College, Boston, LL.D., law.
A 39-year veteran with United Technologies, Robert Daniell began his career with the company's Sikorsky division in 1956. He rose steadily through the ranks to become the division's president and chief executive officer, then vice president of the parent corporation in 1982 and finally president, CEO, and chair of the board. In 1995, Daniell relinquished all his duties except the chair to George Davids, CEO of the corporation, to devote the five years remaining before his retirement to strategic issues such as foreign collaborations and long-term relationships with key government and commercial customers.

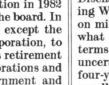

Houghton Mifflin President Nader Farhang Darehshori.

DANSON, TED

Creative Artists Agency, Suite 1400, 1888 Century Park East, Los Angeles, CA 90067.
BORN: 1947, San Diego, Calif. ACHIEVEMENTS: Golden Globe Award, Best Actor in a Motion Picture Made for Television, Something About Amelia, 1985; Emmy Award, Outstanding Lead Actor in a Comedy Series, Cheers, 1990 and 1993; Golden Globe Award, Best Actor in a Series-Musical/Comedy, Cheers, 1990 and 1991. STUDIED: Attended Stanford University and Carnegie-Mellon University; studied at the Actor's Institute.
Ted Danson made his television debut on the series *Somerset*, which ran from 1975 through 1976. He became a nationwide television star playing the lead character Sam Malone in the situation comedy *Cheers* from 1982 through 1993. His work on *Cheers* earned him two Golden Globe Awards and two Emmy Awards. Danson has also appeared in a number of movies, the most famous being *Three Men and a Baby*, 1987. Other films are *The Onion Field*, 1979, *Body Heat*, 1981, *Creepshow*, 1983, *The Music Box*, 1987, *Dad*, 1989, and *Made in America*, 1993.

DANTO, ARTHUR COLEMAN

Columbia University, Department of Philosophy, 708 Philosophy Hall, New York, NY 10027 (212) 854-3196
BORN: 1924, Ann Arbor, Mich. ACHIEVEMENTS: National Book Critics Award; Guggenheim Fellowship; Manufacturers/Hanover Prize for Distinguished Criticism; George S. Polk Award for Criticism; ICP Infinity Prize for Photography; Lionel Trilling Book Prize. STUDIED: Wayne University (now Wayne State), B.A., art and history; Columbia University, M.A., Ph.D., philosophy; University of Paris, student.
Discharged after serving three years in the Army during World War II, mostly in North Africa as a guard on military trains, Arthur Danto decided to attempt what he had never succeeded at before: coming to terms with life after an adolescence of confusion and uncertainty. Under the GI Bill that promised him a four-year education free with a living allowance he enrolled in Wayne State University, majoring in art and history. A superior learner, he earned his B.A. in

two years. With the two years still allowed him he enrolled in Columbia University, studying philosophy and earning his M.A. a year later. And a philosopher he would become, not the painter he had imagined while at Wayne State. In 1951 he was appointed an instructor of philosophy at Columbia. He completed his doctorate in 1952, became a full professor in 1966, and from 1976 until his retirement in 1992 was Johnsonian Professor of Philosophy at Columbia, where he is now professor emeritus. His major theme through 12 books and three collections of essays on art criticism concern the philosophy of art. He has also written on the study of history, knowledge, ethics, and religion. He is widely honored for his breadth of knowledge, the lucid presentations of his original ideas, and his constant daring in grappling with popular cultural movements and ideas.

DAREHSHORI, NADER FARHANG

Houghton Mifflin Company, 222 Berkeley St., Boston, MA 02116 (617) 351-5000
BORN: 1936, Shiraz, Iran. STUDIED: University of Michigan, B.A., economics; Postgrad.
The chairman, president, and chief operating officer of Houghton Mifflin publishing company was superintendent of schools in his home village of Shiraz, Iran, before he emigrated to the U.S. at age 26. Nader Darehshori, a naturalized American, took his first job in his new land as a salesman for Houghton Mifflin in Geneva, Ill., where he remained for nine years. In the next nine years he advanced to field manager, then Midwest sales manager. From general manager of the company's college division he advanced to senior vice president of the division and finally to vice president of the board of directors.

DARITY, WILLIAM A.

University of North Carolina, Department of Economics, 107 Gardner, 017A, Chapel Hill, NC 27599
BORN: 1924, Flat Rock, N.C. ACHIEVEMENTS: Fellowship, World Health Organization; Hildrus Poindexter Public Health Award; Distinguished Lecture/Chancellor's Award, University of Massachusetts; member and official of many civic organizations. STUDIED: Shaw University, Raleigh, N.C., B.S., Public Health; North Carolina Central University, M.S., public health; University of North Carolina, Ph.D., public health.
William Darity's dedication to public health has not only carried him to a top ranking in the field but has taken him to such faraway places as Nigeria and Egypt. A regional adviser to the World Health Organization from 1953 until 1964, he has also been a consultant to the Peace Corps and Headstart training programs, an examiner at the University of Thadan, Nigeria, and a senior associate of The Population Council posted in Cairo, Egypt. He directed and was chief investigator on a research study on cancer and smoking in black populations for the National Cancer Institute. As a professor, he has been on the faculty of the University of Massachusetts, the University of

North Carolina, and the School of Health Sciences at the University of Chicago.

DARLIN, DAMON

The Wall Street Journal, 200 Liberty St., New York, NY 10281 (212) 416-2000
Darlin is a prominent journalist. For career credentials consult the portion of this book entitled "Notable Americans by Profession" in the Appendix. Within this portion, the list "Journalists" describes requirements for inclusion in this volume.be found atop the list entitled "Journalists."

DAUB, HAL

1819 Farnam Street, Suite 300, Omaha, NE 68183 (402) 444-5000
BORN: 1941, Fayetteville, N.C. ACHIEVEMENTS: Decorated Army Commendation Medal with oak leaf cluster; mayor of Omaha, Neb.; U.S. Representatives (4 terms). STUDIED: Washington University, St. Louis, B.S., business administration, 1963; University of Nebraska, J.D., 1966.
After college, Hal Daub spent two years in the U.S. Army, serving in Korea. Before starting his career in politics, Daub practiced law for four years, and then worked as vice president of Standard Chemical Manufacturing Company. In 1981 Daub was elected to the U.S. House of Representatives. He was elected to four consecutive terms and served on the House Ways and Means Committee, Public Works and Transportation Committee, and the Small Business Committee. Daub was elected mayor of Omaha, Neb., and was sworn in Jan. 9, 1995.

DAVIDSON, GORDON

Center Theater Group, 135 North Grand Avenue, Los Angeles, CA 90012 (213) 972-7388
Davidson is a prominent dramatic artist. For career credentials consult the portion of this book entitled "Notable Americans by Profession" in the Appendix. Within this portion, the list "Dramatic Artists" describes requirements for inclusion in this volume.be found atop the list entitled "Dramatic Artists."

DAVIS, GEENA

Susan Geller and Associates, 335 N. Maple Dr., Rm. 254, Beverly Hills, CA 90210.
BORN: 1957, Wareham, Mass. ACHIEVEMENTS: Academy Award, Best Supporting Actress, The Accidental Tourist, in 1988. STUDIED: Boston University, B.F.A., 1979.
Geena Davis made her film debut as April in the film *Tootsie*, which starred Dustin Hoffman. She was a model for the Zoli Agency in New York City. At six feet tall, Davis found it difficult to land a modeling job, finally lying about her height before she was accepted. She received an Academy Award for best supporting actress for her part in *The Accidental Tourist*. She is probably best known for her performance as Thelma, in the near cult hit *Thelma and Louise*, in 1991. She has also appeared in *Beetlejuice*, 1988, *Earth Girls Are Easy*, 1989, *Quick Change*, 1990, and *A League of Their Own*, 1992.

DAY, COLIN LESLIE

University of Michigan Press, Box 1104, 839 Greene St., Ann Arbor, MI 48106 (313) 764-4394
BORN: 1944, St. Albans, England. STUDIED: Oxford University, B.A., M.A.; Stirling University, Scotland, Ph.D.
A career in the publishing world that began in England ended up in the U.S. for Colin Day, director of the University of Michigan Press. The one-time justice of the peace and chairman of the Labor Party in Perthshire, England, was senior economics editor for the Cambridge University Press in the United Kingdom. He moved to the New York City in the same position with the same press in 1976 at age 32. He was successively editor-in-chief and editorial director of the press from the years 1981 until 1987. He became director of the University of Michigan Press in 1988. Day co-authored *Company Financing in the United Kingdom* and has contributed many articles to professional journals.

DAYE, CHARLES EDWARD

University of North Carolina School of Law, Chapel Hill, NC. 27599
BORN: 1944, Durham, N.C. ACHIEVEMENTS: Lawyer of the Year, North Carolina Association of Black Lawyers; Civic Award, Durham. STUDIED: North Carolina Central University., B.A., cum laude, prelaw; Columbia University, J.D., cum laude, law.
Leaving an outstanding college career behind him, Charles Daye became a law clerk for a judge in North Carolina's sixth circuit court. Two years later he became a full professor at the University of North Carolina in Chapel hill, and has remained an educator ever since. After nine years in Chapel Hill he was appointed visiting professor at his alma mater, North Carolina Central University in Durham. Two years later he became dean of the school and a permanent professor. In 1985 he moved back to the University of North Carolina's School of Law, where he has remained since as Henry P. Brandeis distinguished professor. He is a member of the bar of the U.S. Supreme Court and the supreme courts of Connecticut, New York, North Carolina, and Washington, D.C.

Texaco CEO Alfred C. DeCrane.

DEAN, HOWARD

Office of the Governor, Pavillion Bldg., 5th Fl., Montpelier, VT 05602 (802) 828-3333
Dean is a prominent political leader. For career credentials consult the portion of this book entitled "Notable Americans by Profession" in the Appendix. Within this portion, the list "Political Leaders" describes requirements for inclusion in this volume.be found atop the list entitled "Political Leaders."

DEBREU, GERARD

University of California, Department of Mathematics, 787 Evans Hall, Berkeley, CA 94720
BORN: 1921, Calais, France. ACHIEVEMENTS: Nobel Prize in Economic Science, 1983; Chevalier of the French Legion of Honor; fellow, Rockefeller and Guggenheim Foundations, Erskine Fellowship for the Advancement of Science from the University of Canterbury, New Zealand; Senior U.S. Science Awardee, Alexander von Humboldt Foundation. STUDIED: University of Paris.
Existence of an Equilibrium for a Competitive Society, 1954, written with Kenneth J. Arrow, announced Frenchman Gerard Debreu's lifelong interest in the equilibrium systems of supply and demand (all forces pushing or pulling on one spectrum must be balanced by equal opposing forces, resulting in zero force). The article was epoch-making, in that it gave general equilibrium analysis a boost by providing mathematical proof that general equilibrium exists. Debreu published his masterpiece, *Theory of Value, An Axiomatic Analysis of Economic Equilibrium* in 1959, a slim work restating traditional results of competitive price theory in mathematically precise terms.

DECONCINI, DENNIS

U.S. Senate, 328 SHOB, Washington, DC 20510-0302 (202) 224-4521
DeConcini is a prominent political leader. For career credentials consult the portion of this book entitled "Notable Americans by Profession" in the Appendix.

Within this portion, the list "Political Leaders" describes requirements for inclusion in this volume."

DECRANE, ALFRED C.

Texaco, Inc., 2000 Westchester Ave., White Plains, NY 10650 (914) 253-4000
BORN: 1941, Cleveland, Ohio. STUDIED: University of Notre Dame, B.A., prelaw; Georgetown University, J.D., law.
Alfred DeCrane joined Texaco, Inc. in 1972 at age 31, and 11 years later was named president of the giant oil company, just preceding the biggest crisis in Texaco's history. His board of directors, in 1984, authorized the company to negotiate for acquisition of Getty Oil at the same time Pennzoil had an agreement with Getty on the same notion. The next year a Texas jury ordered Texaco to pay Pennzoil $10.5 billion for interfering with the agreement, an order later settled for $3 billion. Texaco filed for bankruptcy in 1987 despite assets of $35 billion, the largest bankruptcy filing in history up to that time. After that debacle the Texaco board underwent some changes, with DeCrane, who headed the company's legal and tax departments as one of his duties, emerging as board chairman. In 1994 he also became chief executive officer of Texaco and a member of the board of CPC International, rated among the 10 largest food companies in the U.S., and one of the largest industrial companies in the country.

DEDMAN, BILL

The Atlanta Journal & Constitution, 72 Marietta St., NW., Atlanta, GA 30303-2899 (404) 572-5151
Dedman is a prominent journalist. For career credentials consult the portion of this book entitled "Notable Americans by Profession" in the Appendix. Within this portion, the list "Journalists" describes requirements for inclusion in this volume.be found atop the list entitled "Journalists."

DE FOREST, ROY DEAN

P.O. Box 47, Port Costa, CA 94569
BORN: 1930. ACHIEVEMENTS: NEA Fellowship; La Jolla Art Museum Purchase Prize; collections: Art Institute of Chicago; San Francisco Museum of Modern Art ; exhibitions: Fuller Goldeen Gallery, San Francisco; Whitney Museum, New York City. STUDIED: California School of Fine Arts; San Francisco State College.
Several of Roy Dean De Forest's early series of drawings in marker or pastel on large paper depict the development of such themes as romance and friendship. He then turned to painting on large canvases in series alluding to pulp westerns or philosophy treatises. Whimsical, naive interpretations of the figure in landscapes characterize much of his recent work. He calls himself an "obscure visual constructor of mechanical delights" who seeks to depict the "phantasmagoric micro-world" in which he travels. Media have recently included ceramics, painted clay, and wood mounted on stretcher frames. He has worked with Robert Arneson in a project called "The Bob and Roys," a cooperative effort to create ceramic dishes and lamps.

DEHMELT, HANS GEORG

University of Washington, Physics Department, FM 15, Seattle, WA 98195
BORN: 1922, Gorlitz, Germany. ACHIEVEMENTS: Nobel Prize in Physics (shared with Wolfgang Paul, Germany); Basic Research Award, International Society of Magnetic Resonance. STUDIED: University of Gottingen, Germany.
The quest of atomic physicists to formulate a grand unification theory of the structure of matter grows more complex the more atoms are studied. For example, a gold wedding ring contains about sextillion atoms; 100 million atoms would fit on the period at the end of this sentence. Yet Hans Dehmelt and his co-laureate, Wolfgang Paul, successfully refined the methods used to trap particles so their measurements could be made more precisely, an advance honored by the Nobel physics committee in 1989. Dehmelt's major contribution was development of the "Penning Trap," where both a strong and a weak magnetic field isolated and trapped the particles. Though born in Germany, Dehmelt later became a naturalized American.

DE KOONING, WILLEM

c/o Fourcade Droll Inc., 36 E. 75th St., New York, NY 10021
BORN: 1904. ACHIEVEMENTS: President's Medal; Andrew W. Mellon Prize; collections: Metropolitan Museum of Art; Museum of Modern Art ; exhibitions: Museum of Modern Art; Whitney Museum of American Art. STUDIED: Academie voor Beeldende Kunsten en Technische Wetenschappen (Amsterdam).
While training in his native land of Holland for eight years, Willem de Kooning was influenced not only by the strict academic training, but also by the abstract art of the De Stijl group. Early works of the 1930s were untitled abstract works influenced by Arshile Gorky, with whom he shared a studio. Since the mid-1940s, he has rendered distorted figures, usually of women, in fragmented confusion. Bold brush strokes in vibrant colors, pastel tints and black areas outlined in white typify this abstract expressionist's work. Because he has never fully rejected the earlier influences, his work shows a passionate mixture of abstract expressionistic leanings and of the bold colorations of the C.O.B.R.A. School. Recently he has painted nearly abstract renderings of landscapes.

DELANY, DANA

International Creative Management, 8899 Beverly Blvd., Los Angeles, CA 90067
BORN: 1956, New York City ACHIEVEMENTS: Emmy Award, Outstanding Lead Actress in a Drama Series, China Beach, 1988. STUDIED: Phillips Andover Academy; Wesleyan University, Middletown, Conn.
Dana Delany started looking for acting jobs in the late 1970s. To pay the bills, she worked nights as a cocktail waitress—coincidentally at the same club as Bruce Willis. Her first television roles were on soap operas. She played Amy Russell on *Love of Life* from 1979 to 1980 and then went on to play Hayley Wilson on *As the World Turns* in 1981. That same year she debuted on film as Linda in *The Fan*. She worked in a variety of

parts on stage, screen and television through the mid-1980s and then hit it big in 1988. That year, Delany started playing Colleen McMurphy, an Army nurse in Vietnam during the war, in the television series, *China Beach*. The series ran until 1990 earning Delany an Emmy Award as well numerous other awards.

DELAP, TONY

225 Jasmine St., Corona Del Mar, CA 92625
BORN: 1927. ACHIEVEMENTS: NEA Fellowship; Purchase Prize, Long Beach Museum of Art; collections: Museum of Modern Art, New York City; Los Angeles County Museum of Art; exhibitions: Whitney Museum, New York City; Jan Turner Gallery, Los Angeles. STUDIED: California College of Arts and Crafts; Claremont Graduate School.

Tony Delap began as a painter, but turned to sculpture in the early 1960s. After working exclusively in sculpture for 10 years, he combined sculpture with painting to create "wall-hanging paintings" employing a variety of media, including wood, canvas and acrylics. One of his primary concerns is the edge: "I developed a hyperbolic, paraboloid, wooden edge that changed course as it continued around the canvas, much like a Mobius strip." In this way, the wall becomes an integral part of each work. In *Jaipur Jinnee*, the wall is also integrated into the work through experiments with different geometrical shapes and negative space.

DELL, MICHAEL S.

Dell Computer Corporation, 9505 Arboretum Blvd., Austin, TX 78759 (512) 338-4400

Dell is a prominent business leader. For career credentials consult the portion of this book entitled "Notable Americans by Profession" in the Appendix. Within this portion, the list "Business Leaders" describes requirements for inclusion in this volume.be found atop the list entitled "Business Leaders."

DELLUMS, RONALD V.

2108 Rayburn Office Building, Washington, DC 20515 (202) 225-2661
BORN: 1935, Oakland, Calif. ACHIEVEMENTS: U.S. Representative, 1971-present. STUDIED: San Francisco State University, B.A., 1958; University of California at Berkeley, M.S., 1962.

Ronald Dellums was a city councilman in Berkeley for five years before his election to the U.S. House of Representatives, in 1970, on a platform opposing the Vietnam War. He chaired the Armed Services Committee during the post Cold War period and advocated reversing the nuclear arms race and reducing military spending so the savings could be invested in social programs. Dellums is the ranking Democratic member of the National Security Committee. He also chaired the former District of Columbia Committee and served on a number of intelligence panels. He was a psychiatric social worker and a job training director in Oakland before he ran for the Berkeley Council.

DEMARIA, ROBERT, JR.,

Vassar College, Dept. of English, 124 Raymond Ave., Poughkeepsie, NY 12601-6121

DeMaria, Jr. is a prominent educator. For career credentials consult the portion of this book entitled "Notable Americans by Profession" in the Appendix. Within this portion, the list "Educators" describes requirements for inclusion in this volume.atop the list entitled "Educators."

DENIRO, ROBERT

Jay Julien, 1501 Broadway, New York, NY 10036;
BORN: 1943, New York City ACHIEVEMENTS: Academy Award, Best Supporting Actor, The Godfather Part II, 1974; Academy Award, Best Actor, and Golden Globe Award, Best Actor, both for Raging Bull, 1981. STUDIED: Dramatic Workshop, Luther James Studio, Stella Adler Studio, Actor's Studio.

Robert DeNiro grew up in New York City just a few blocks from his future friend and benefactor, Martin Scorsese. DeNiro later became known for the roles he played in Scorsese's films, such as: *Mean Streets*, 1973, *Taxi Driver*, 1976, *New York, New York*, 1977, *Raging Bull*, 1980, *The King of Comedy*, 1982, and *Goodfellas*, 1980. DeNiro won two Academy Awards, one for *Raging Bull* and the other for his part in *The Godfather, Part II*, 1974. DeNiro's other films include: *The Deer Hunter*, 1978, *True Confessions*, 1981, *Once Upon A Time in America*, 1984, *The Mission*, 1986, and *The Untouchables*, 1987.

DENVER, JOHN

John Denver Concerts, Inc., P.O. Box 1587, Aspen, CO 81612

Denver is a prominent vocalist. For career credentials consult the portion of this book entitled "Notable Americans by Profession" in the Appendix. Within this portion, the list "Vocalists" describes requirements for inclusion in this volume.be found atop the list entitled "Vocalists."

DERR, K. T.

Chevron Corporation, 225 Bush St., San Francisco, CA 94104 (415) 894-7700

Derr is a prominent business leader. For career credentials consult the portion of this book entitled "Notable Americans by Profession" in the Appendix. Within this portion, the list "Business Leaders" describes requirements for inclusion in this volume.be found atop the list entitled "Business Leaders."

DERSHOWITZ, ALLAN MORTON

Harvard University Law School, 1350 Massachusetts Ave., Cambridge, MA 02138
BORN: 1938, New York City. ACHIEVEMENTS: Author, Reversal of Fortune. STUDIED: Brooklyn College, B.A., magna cum laude, law; Yale University, L.L.B magna cum laude, law; Harvard University, M.A., law (honorary).

At age 28, Harvard's youngest tenured law professor would remain at the university throughout a brilliant career. Besides teaching, Allan Dershowitz has handled many celebrated cases having to do with free-speech issues. Among his clients have been Dr. Benjamin Spock for his antiwar actions; porn star

Harry Reems of *Deep Throat*; William Schockley, the racist genetic theorist; and boxer Mike Tyson. Dershowitz wrote the book *Reversal of Fortune* about the successful appeal and later acquittal of Claus von Bulow, a European aristocrat convicted in 1980 for attempting to murder his wife. He also wrote a syndicated column on the law, and has appeared on television programs dealing with the law. Dershowitz also served as part of the team of lawyers that successfully defended O.J. Simpson on murder charges.

DESIMONE, L. D.

Minnesota Mining & Mfg. Co., 3M Center, St. Paul, MN 55144 (612) 733-1110
DeSimone is a prominent business leader. For career credentials consult the portion of this book entitled "Notable Americans by Profession" in the Appendix. Within this portion, the list "Business Leaders" describes requirements for inclusion in this volume.be found atop the list entitled "Business Leaders."

DEVITO, DANNY

Fred Spektor, Creative Artists Agency, 1888 Century Park East, Los Angeles, CA 90067
BORN: 1944 Neptune, N.J. ACHIEVEMENTS: Golden Globe Award, 1979, Emmy Award, Outstanding Supporting Actor in a comedy or Variety or Music Series, 1981, both for Taxi. STUDIED: American Academy of Dramatic Arts.
Danny DeVito got his start in the entertainment business in 1969 on the Off-Broadway stage. The son of a small businessman from New Jersey, DeVito had numerous stage appearances under his belt by the time he played his first film role in 1972. He continued an active stage and screen career through the 1970s. In 1975, he played Martini in the film, *One Flew Over the Cuckoo's Nest*, a role he had originally played in the stage play of the same name in 1971. However, his career really took off in 1980 when he began playing Louie DePalma on the television series, *Taxi*. He landed much bigger parts in the 1980s, including Vernon Dahlart, in *Terms of Endearment*, in 1983, and Ralph, in *Romancing the Stone*, in 1984. In 1988 he directed his first film, *Throw Momma From the Train*, in which he also starred. DeVito then went on to act in and direct *War of the Roses*, in 1989, and *Hoffa*, in 1992. His most recent film was *Junior*, which was released in 1994.

DIAMOND, NEIL LESLIE

c/o Columbia Records, 1801 Century Park West, Los Angeles, CA 90067
Diamond is a prominent vocalist. For career credentials consult the portion of this book entitled "Notable Americans by Profession" in the Appendix. Within this portion, the list "Vocalists" describes requirements for inclusion in this volume.be found atop the list entitled "Vocalists."

DICKINSON, ELEANOR CREEKMORE

2125 Broderick St., San Francisco, CA 94115
BORN: 1931. ACHIEVEMENTS: National Society of Arts & Letters; Distinguished Alumni, San Francisco Art Institute; collections: National Museum of American Art; San Francisco Museum of Modern Art; exhibitions: Corcoran Gallery of Art; Smithsonian Institution STUDIED: University of Tennessee; San Francisco Art Institute; California College of Arts and Crafts.
Eleanor Dickinson is essentially a draftsman; although she works in a variety of media, these are usually linear, and color is employed for its value, not its hue. The act of drawing is most important, along with the excitement of unplanned composition and discovery. Her subject is always figurative, and her style is expressionistic realism. Among the subjects of her major series are old and young lovers, animals, revival meetings, models, and illness and death. Her recent exhibition, *Revival!*, comprised 2,000 objects interacting with each other in paintings, drawings, photographs, slides, holograms, artifacts and videotapes.

DICKMAN, JAMES

c/o *The Denver Post*, 650 15th St., Denver, CO 80202
BORN: 1949. ACHIEVEMENTS: Pulitzer Prize, 1983. STUDIED: University of Texas.
James Dickman's route to the Pulitzer Prize had as much to do with his social conscience as his photographic skills. In 1981, when he was a photographer for the *Dallas Times Herald*, he heard rumors that Salvadorean death squads were executing "enemies" and dumping the bodies in a lava field outside San Salvador. Dickman went down to investigate and found a graveyard horrific beyond his imagining. His photos of bullet-ridden skulls and other skeletal remains wrought an indelible image of brutality that shocked even the most callous observer. He left Dallas in 1986 and is currently a member of the photographic staff at the *Denver Post*.

DICHTING, DOUG

Coca-Cola, USA, 1 Coca-Cola Plaza, NW., Atlanta, GA 30313-2419 (404) 676-2121
Dichting is a prominent inventor. For career credentials consult the portion of this book entitled "Notable Americans by Profession" in the Appendix. Within this portion, the list "Inventors" describes requirements for inclusion in this volume.be found atop the list entitled "Inventors."

DIEBENKORN, RICHARD

c/o M. Knoedler, 19 E. 70th St., New York, NY 10021
BORN: 1922. ACHIEVEMENTS: Gold Medal, Pennsylvania Academy of Fine Arts; National Institute of Arts and Letters; collections: Metropolitan Museum of Art, New York City; San Francisco Museum of Modern Art; exhibitions: Whitney Museum, New York City; De Young Memorial Museum, San Francisco. STUDIED: California School of Fine Arts; Stanford University; University of New Mexico.

Richard Diebenkorn's early still-life, interior and figurative paintings during World War II were influenced by modern French painters such as Matisse and Bonnard. Contact with artists in California and New York transformed his work to a non-objective, energetic style that evolved quickly from geometric abstraction to a more expressionistic mode. In his large, expressionist canvases, such as in his *Ocean Park* series, he tends to use areas of color rather than line, arranging pictorial space asymmetrically into large open areas with smaller active areas, and abstracting specific elements from the landscape as a whole. In recent years, he has become increasingly independent from abstract expressionism, and has shown concern for more literal subject matter. He recently completed a set of prints at Crown Point Press.

DIEHL, GUY LOUIS

4161 Sacramento St., Concord, CA 94521
BORN: 1949. ACHIEVEMENTS: Purchase Award, Alameda County Art Commission; collections: City Hall Building, Oakland, Calif.; Alameda County Art Commission, Oakland, Calif.; exhibitions: Jeremy Stone Gallery, San Francisco; Oakland Museum. STUDIED: California State, Hayward; San Francisco State University.

Guy Diehl's acrylics and watercolors on canvas are realistic renderings of contemporary leisure activities, such as *Edge of Pool with Mondrian Towel*. Formal symmetrical compositions are full of the intense sunlight of summer, deep shadows and brilliant colors. Although figures are not present, personal belongings indicate their presence. His small-scale still lifes are classically painted with wit and humor. Subject matter consists of everyday objects: food, books, shells, flowers, paper airplanes, which are bathed in intense light and surrounded by painted shadow and reflection. These unpretentious works have been compared to the paintings of Bay Area artists Wayne Thiebaud and Mark Adams.

DIERDORF, DAN

ABC Press Relations, 7W-7, Avenue of the Americas, New York, NY 10019
BORN: Canton, Ohio. ACHIEVEMENTS: Emmy Nomination: 1987, 1988, 1989; six-time NFL All Pro; three-time NFL Offensive Lineman of the Year; 1970s NFL Team of the Decade; Pro Football Hall of Fame, 1996. STUDIED: The University of Michigan.

Currently a color analyst for *ABC's Monday Night Football*, providing analysis to complement the play-by-play, Dierdorf has been with ABC for eight years. For the past six years, he has been a ringside announcer for boxing on ABC Sports. Before joining ABC, Dierdorf was a play-by-play and color analyst for CBS Sports. He began his broadcasting career with KMOX-Radio St. Louis. While at KMOX he was a color analyst for the St. Louis Cardinals football and St. Louis Blues hockey broadcasts. He also hosted *Sports Open Line*, a two-hour sports talk show. Dierdorf had a highly awarded football career with the St. Louis Cardinals before entering the world of sports broadcasting.

DIETRICH, BILL

The Seattle Times, Box 70, Fairvica Ave., Seattle, WA 98111 (206) 464-2111
BORN: 1952, Tacoma, Wash. ACHIEVEMENTS: Pulitzer Prize; Nieman Fellow, Harvard University; Washington Governor's Writers Award; Pacific Northwest Booksellers Award. STUDIED: Fairhaven College at Western Washington University, B.A.

The Arctic Ocean and the South Pole are among the stops Bill Dietrich has made as he travels the world digging up stories. A science reporter for *The Seattle Times* and for wire services, he has also developed stories about the Pacific Northwest, Congress, and religious cults in the United States. In 1990, Dietrich was one of four *Seattle Times* reporters awarded the Pulitzer Prize for coverage the year before of the 240,000-barrel Exxon oil spill into Prince William Sound, off the coast of Alaska. His first book, *The Final Forest: The Battle for the Last Great Trees*, won two prestigious prizes. His second book, *Northwest Passage: The Great Columbia River*, was published in 1995.

DILL, GUY GIRARD

819 Milwood Ave., Venice, CA 90291
BORN: 1946. ACHIEVEMENTS: Theodoron Award, Guggenheim Museum; NEA Fellowship; collections: Museum of Modern Art, New York City; Museum of Contemporary Art, Los Angeles; exhibitions: Guggenheim Museum; Arco Center for the Visual Arts, Los Angeles. STUDIED: Chouinard Art Institute.

Guy Dill constructs architectonic structures in scale, from such materials as metal, marble, concrete and wood. Beginning in 1971, the circle served as a fulcrum for his compositions. Later he added the column as a "connection and icon." He preserved the natural colors and surfaces of the media in order to provide his works with "real energy." Now more interested in the combination of planes, surfaces and shapes, and in working with space and scale to create works of visual harmony, he seeks to unify his chosen forms: the circle, the beam and other elements, in order to create "an integrated icon or shape."

DILL, LADDIE JOHN

1625 Electric Ave., Venice, CA 90291
BORN: 1943. ACHIEVEMENTS: California Arts Council Grant; NEA Fellowship; collections: Los Angeles County Museum of Art; San Francisco Museum of Modern Art; exhibitions: Santa Barbara Museum of Art; Long Beach Museum of Art. STUDIED: Chouinard Art Institute.

An early influence on Laddie Dill's work was the environmental art of Robert Irwin. In 1986, Dill created light and sand pieces in a horizontal format: installations made of glass, neon and sand that appeared to be aerial views of landscape. Experiments with painting led him to a rectilinear format with the addition of architectonic shapes to the landscape imagery. In 1975, his format was vertical, suggesting "a figurative reference achieved by a more formal architectural structuring," and two years later he produced a vertical *Door* series. His latest paintings reflect both landscape and architectural imagery. His media are cement polymer, glass, silicone and oil on canvas; he has also made drawings in pastel, oil and graphite on rag paper.

DINGELL, JOHN D.

U.S. House of Representatives, 2328 RHOB, Washington, DC 20515-2216 (202) 225-4071

Dingell is a prominent political leader. For career credentials consult the portion of this book entitled "Notable Americans by Profession" in the Appendix. Within this portion, the list "Political Leaders" describes requirements for inclusion in this volume.be found atop the list entitled "Political Leaders."

DIONNE, JOSEPH L.

McGrawHill, Inc., 1221 Avenue of the Americas, New York, NY 10020 (212) 512-2000

BORN: 1935, Montgomery. Ala. STUDIED: Hofstra University, B.A., M.S., education; Columbia University, Ph.D., education

After holding positions in teaching, education administration, and consultant on many experimental educational projects, Joseph Dionne said goodbye to academia in 1967 and joined the publishing house McGraw-Hill. After steadily advancing in the company, 16 years later he became chief executive officer, and five years later chair of the board. In 1994 Harold McGraw III, 44, was named president and CEO of the house, a position second only to Dionne. The great-grandson of the founder of McGraw-Hill emerged as Dionne's heir apparent in 1993 when he took control of all the company's operations. Dionne, 59, was not expected to step down soon. He was elected a director of Ryder System, Inc., a rental and truck leasing company. in 1995.

DI SUVERO, MARK

c\o Oil & Steel Gallery, 3030 Vernon Blvd, New York, NY 11102

BORN: 1933. ACHIEVEMENTS: Longview Foundation Grant; Art Institute of Chicago Award; collections: Whitney Museum, New York City; Art Institute of Chicago; exhibitions: Los Angeles County Museum of Art; San Diego Museum of Art. STUDIED: University of California.

Mark Di Suvero synthesizes constructivist and baroque elements in his work in order to explore space, motion, gravity, balance and structure. His massive public works are spatial sculptures constructed out of wide-flange steel I-beams welded or bolted together. He invites viewer participation by including movable portions that can be climbed upon. His smaller, human-scale sculptures are comprised of balanced pieces and variable elements. The smallest works—puzzle pieces—are elaborate calligraphic shapes cut out of steel which the viewer can assemble.

DIXON, FRANK JAMES

10666 N. Torey Pines Rd., La Jolla, CA 92037

Dixon is a prominent physician. For career credentials consult the portion of this book entitled "Notable Americans by Profession" in the Appendix. Within this portion, the list "Physicians" describes require-

ments for inclusion in this volume.be found atop the list entitled "Physicians."

DJERASSI, CARL

Stanford University, Department of Chemistry, Palo Alto, CA 94305

BORN: 1923, Vienna, Austria. ACHIEVEMENTS: Involved in development of oral contraceptives. STUDIED: Kenyon College, A.B., summa cum laude chemistry, Doctor of Science. (honorary); University of Wisconsin, Ph.D., chemistry; and several other honorary degrees.

Carl Djerassi claimed to have developed "the pill" in 1951 while working for a little known company in Mexico City. Many in the scientific community disputed that he was the prime developer. Nevertheless he was involved in working on the contraceptive that has revolutionized birth control. The Austrian immigrant additionally has made important contributions in steroid research while at Stanford University, where he teaches chemistry, and he is noted for promoting international cooperation in the field.

DODD, CHRISTOPHER J.

444 Russell Senate Office Building, Washington, DC 20510-0702 (202) 224-2823

BORN: 1944, Willimantic, Conn. ACHIEVEMENTS: Peace Corps, Head Start Senator of the Decade, 1994. STUDIED: Providence College, University of Louisville School of Law, 1972.

Dodd has devoted much of his time in the Senate to family issues. First elected to the Senate to represent Connecticut in 1980, he founded the Senate Children's Caucus in 1983 and fought for passage of the Act for Better Child Care. In 1987, as chairman of the Children, Families, Drugs and Alcoholism Subcommittee, he mounted an effort to mandate 12 weeks of unpaid leave for workers facing a family emergency. In 1993 the measure was signed into law as part of the Family and Medical Leave Act. The son of the late Senator Thomas J. Dodd, he was the youngest person in Connecticut history elected to the Senate.

DOHNANYI, CHRISTOPH VON

The Cleveland Orchestra, Severance Hall, 11001 Euclid Ave., Cleveland, OH 44106-1713 (216) 231-7300

BORN: 1929, Berlin, Germany. Awards: 1992 Conductor of the Year, Musical America; Commandre's Cross, Republic of Vienna; Union Medal, Union Theological Seminary, New York; Commandeur de l'Ordre des Arts et Lettres, Republic of France; Commanders' Cross of the Order of Merit, Germany; and many other honors and honorary doctorates. STUDIED: University of Munich; Florida State University; Tanglewood Music Center, Massachusetts.

Christoph Von Dohnanyi has been conductor of the Cleveland Symphony for nine years. During his tenure, the orchestra has become the most frequently recorded in America and has made five tours through Europe and three to Eastern Asia. His guest conducting engagements in the 1994-95 season included concerts with the London Philharmonic Orchestra, the Munich Philharmonic, and the Vienna Philharmonic. He is only the third conductor in Vienna history to perform Richard Wagner's four-opera Ring of the Nibelung cycle, the last occurring in the 1970s under the direction of Herbert von Karajan. Since taking the position of music director in Cleveland, Dohnanyi's inventive and imaginative approach to the repertoire has resulted in an expansion of the subscription season to accommodate the largest audience in the orchestra's history. He has made many recordings with both the Cleveland Orchestra and the Vienna Philharmonic.

DOLE, ROBERT J.

U.S. Senate, 141 Hart Senate Bldg., Washington, DC, 20510 (202) 224-3135
BORN: 1923, Russell, Kan. ACHIEVEMENTS: Purple Heart (2), Bronze Star with 2 Oak Leaf Clusters; Horatio Alger Award, 1988. STUDIED: University of Kansas, 1941-43; University of Arizona; Washburn University, A.B., 1952; Washburn University, LL.B., 1952; Washburn University, LL.D. (honorary), 1969.
Robert Dole has spent most of his adult life in politics. Dole's college education was interrupted by World War II, where he received two Purple Hearts and a Bronze Star with two Oak Leaf Clusters. Dole served in the Kansas House of Representatives from 1951 until 1953. He was a practicing attorney from 1953 to 1961, when he took office in the U.S. House of Representatives. He was first elected to the Senate in 1968. Dole has three times run for president, in 1980, 1988, and 1996, and he ran for vice president with Gerald Ford in 1976. Dole became majority leader when Republicans gained control of the Senate after the 1994 elections, a post he had previously held from 1985 to 1987.

DOMAR, EVSEY DAVID

Massachusetts Institute of Technology, Department of Economics, E52391F, Cambridge, MA 02139
BORN: 1914, Lodz, Poland. ACHIEVEMENTS: Co-inventor of "Harrod Domar Model" of economic growth. STUDIED: Harbin University, Manchuria, China; University of California at Los Angeles, B.A., economics; University of Michigan, M.E., education; University of Chicago, M.A., economics; Harvard University, M.A., Ph.D., economics.
A professor at the Massachusetts Institute of Technology since 1958, Evsey Domar is co-inventor of the "Harrod Domar Model" of dynamic equilibrium in economic growth. In brief, equilibrium in economics occurs when all the forces involved—work force, lending rates, production, supplies, inflation, etc.—are working together in a stable fashion. The "Harrod Dolmar Model" measures these factors during periods of economic growth to keep that growth from spinning out of control, creating disturbances in all the forces involved. Dolmar taught at several universities before joining MIT.

DOMENICI, PETE V.

U.S. Senate, 427 SDOB, Washington, DC 20510-3101 (202) 224-6621
Domenici is a prominent political leader. For career credentials consult the portion of this book entitled "Notable Americans by Profession" in the Appendix. Within this portion, the list "Political Leaders" describes requirements for inclusion in this volume.be found atop the list entitled "Political Leaders."

DOMINIS, JOHN

252 W. 102nd St., New York, NY 10025 (212) 222-9890
BORN: 1926. ACHIEVEMENTS: Magazine Photographer of the Year, University of Missouri School of Journalism. STUDIED: University of Southern California.
In high school John Dominis studied photography under C.A. Bach and went on to take cinematography at the University of Southern California. In 1943 he joined the Air Force and, after his 1946 discharge, remained in Japan as a freelance photographer for *The Saturday Evening Post, Colliers,* and *Life.* While there, he also completed a book on Japanese children, *The Forbidden Forest.* After joining the staff of *Life* in 1950, he covered a wide variety of events including the Korean War, the beginning of the Laotian conflict, the early years of the Vietnam war and President Kennedy's term in office. In 1974 he became Picture Editor for *People* magazine, a position he held until 1978, when he moved to the same position at *Sports Illustrated.* He is now a freelance photographer, and in 1985 he photo-illustrated a 300-page cook book, *Giuliano Gugialli's Foods of Italy.*

DONAHUE, PHILIP JOHN

NBC, 30 Rockefeller Plaza, New York, NY 10020
BORN: 1935, Cleveland. ACHIEVEMENTS: Emmy Awards, Best Host of a Talk Show, Donahue, 1977, 1979, 1980, 1982, 1983, 1985, 1986, 1988; elected to the Emmy Hall of Fame, 1992. STUDIED: Notre Dame University.
The patriarch of the television talk show, Phil Donahue, has been in the broadcasting field for over 30 years and was the originator of the audience participation format for talk shows. The *Phil Donahue Show* originated in Dayton Ohio on WLWD-TV in 1967. The show became very popular, was moved to Chicago in 1974, and renamed *Donahue.* In 1985 the show moved to New York City, where it has remained. Donahue has written two books, *Donahue: My Own Story,* 1979, and *The Human Animal,* 1985. With the onslaught of more controversial talk shows, Donahue's popularity has been waning. Because of sagging ratings, his show has been dropped from WNBC in New York.

DONALDSON, SAMUEL

ABC, 1330 Ave. of the Americas, New York, NY 10019
Donaldson is a prominent journalist. For career credentials consult the portion of this book entitled "Notable Americans by Profession" in the Appendix. Within this portion, the list "Journalists" describes requirements for inclusion in this volume.DOUGLAS, NETTY
Christian Science Monitor, 1 Norway St., Boston, MA 02115-3195 (617) 450-2000
Douglas is a prominent publisher. For career credentials consult the portion of this book entitled "Notable Americans by Profession" in the Appendix. Within this portion, the list "Publishers" describes requirements for inclusion in this volume.be found atop the list entitled "Publishers."

DOUGLAS, MICHAEL

Creative Artists Agency, Inc., 1888 Century Park East, Los Angeles, CA 90067.

BORN: 1944, New Brunswick, N.J. ACHIEVEMENTS: Academy Award, Best Picture (with Saul Zaentz) for One Flew Over the Cuckoo's Nest, 1975; Academy Award, Best Actor, and Golden Globe Award, Best Actor, both for Wall Street, 1987. STUDIED: University of California, Santa Barbara, B.A., 1968; trained for stage at O'Neill Theatre Center's National Playwrights Conference three summers in 1960s; studied acting with Sanford Meisner at Neighborhood Playhouse, and with Wynn Handman at American Place Theatre, New York City.

Michael Douglas has enjoyed a long string of successes almost from the beginning of his show-business career. The son of the equally famous actor, Kirk Douglas, he began appearing in films, on stage, and on television just a year out of college. Within three years, he was the star of a television series, playing Steve Keller on *The Streets of San Francisco* from 1972 until 1976. In 1984 he rose to a new peak of popularity playing the swashbuckling adventurer Jack Colton opposite Kathleen Turner and Danny DeVito in *Romancing the Stone*. The three repeated their success in 1985 with the sequel, *The Jewel of the Nile*. Douglas was also the producer of both movies, as well as numerous others, including *One Flew Over the Cuckoo's Nest*, in 1975, and *The China Syndrome*, in 1979. Douglas's movie career continues to flourish with starring roles in movies such as *Fatal Attraction* and *Wall Street*, both in 1987, and *Basic Instinct* in 1992. His most recent film was *Disclosure*, which was released in 1994.

DREW, ERNEST H.

Hoechst Celanese Corp., Rte. 202206, Box 250, Somerville, NJ 08876 (908) 231-2000

BORN: 1937, Springfield, Mass. STUDIED: University of Georgia, B.S., chemistry; University of Illinois, M.A., Ph.D., organic chemistry.

Ernest Drew joined the United States Air Force the year of the Cuban missile crisis (1962) and served three years. His first job on leaving the service was as research chemist with Hoechst Celanese Corporation's chemical research company at Corpus Christi, Texas. In a series of rapid promotions he advanced from vice president and general manager of resins systems in 1974 to vice president sales, and vice president planning in 1975. Relocation to the company's corporate headquarters in New York City followed, where he was named director of strategic planning. In 1982 he became president and chief executive officer of Celanese Canada, Inc. and two years later director of Celanese Corporation. He moved upward to group vice president and corporate director and then president and CEO of Hoechst Celanese when Celanese merged with American Hoechst. Drew also serves as a member of the President's Advisory Committee for Excellence in Education for Hispanic Americans, and is on the board of trustees of the Junior Achievement National Board and two universities.

DUNCAN, DAVID DOUGLAS

Castellaras 53, Mouans-Sartoux, Alps Maritime 06, France

BORN: 1916. ACHIEVEMENTS: Overseas Press Club Award, Robert Capa Gold Medal. STUDIED: University of Miami.

A restless, inquiring photographer, David Duncan has recorded the violence and beauty of life on five continents. Beginning as a combat photographer in World War II and continuing through assignments in Korea and Vietnam, Duncan captured war at its most horrific. Wounded himself in World War II, and a recipient of the Legion of Merit, Duncan conveys a deep empathy for his subjects. From the eyes of a young soldier to more trivial aspects of clothing and appearance, his photographs are a haunting evocation of sadness and suffering. Duncan also has an eye for the idiosyncratic in life, capturing such details as painted sheep in Ireland or golfers teeing up amid Middle Eastern pipelines. His photographs of Picasso are perhaps the richest photographic record of any 20th century artist.

DUNN, DOUGLAS

c/o Pentacle, 104 Franklin St., New York, NY 10013 (212) 226-2000

BORN: 1942, Palo Alto, Calif. ACHIEVEMENTS: Notable ballets: Lazy Madge; Celeste; Suite de Suite, Pulcinella; Cycles, all commissioned by ballet companies in France; Gestures in Red; Secret of the Waterfall, a video dance. STUDIED: Princeton University; Jacob's Pillow summer workshop, American Ballet Center; Merce Cunningham Studio.

Known as a quixotic postmodern choreographer, Douglas Dunn was most influenced by the revolutionary antics of teacher/choreographer Merce Cunningham, in whose troupe he performed from 1969 to 1973. From Cunningham he evolved a style that shows bursts of sardonic wit as he explores the outer boundaries of dance. Many of his works are solos in which movements are visualized before they occur, and one, *Lazy Madge's Corruption* of Claude Debussy's *Les Images*, kept evolving in a series of concerts over several seasons with new material incorporated into each performance. Among his important choreographic works is *Gestures in Red*, an hour-long piece that explores movement from a slow crawl and builds dramatically to an explosive finale. *Gestures* was the opening performance of London's first Dance Umbrella festival in 1978. Dunn is cofounder of the improvisational ballet company Grand Union, and founder of Douglas Dunn & Dancers.

DURANT, DR. GRAHAM J.

Cambridge Neuroscience Inc., 1 Kendall Sq., Bldg. 700, Cambridge, MA, 02139

BORN: 1934. ACHIEVEMENTS: Inducted into the National Inventors Hall of Fame, 1990; invented antiulcer compounds and compositions; Medicinal Chemistry Award of the Royal Society of Chemistry. STUDIED: Birmingham University, B.S.; University of Iowa State, Ph.D.

Dr. Durant is an author and co-author of more than 70 publications, and inventor or co-inventor of more than 150 patents. He has been a U.S. resident since 1987, and he established the Center for Drug Design and Development at the University of Toledo. He currently serves as senior director of chemistry at Cambridge NeuroScience, Inc., and sits on the board of trustees of Inventure Place. Along with Drs. Emmett and Ganellin, Dr. Durant discovered the H2 receptor class of drugs, the most important being cietidine (Tagamet), which inhibits the production of stomach acid and helps heal stomach ulcers without surgery.

DURBIN, RICHARD

2463 Rayburn House Office Building, Washington, DC 20515-1320 (202) 225-5271
BORN: 1944, East St. Louis, Ill. ACHIEVEMENTS: Illinois legislator (Democrat). STUDIED: Georgetown University, B.S., 1966.
First elected to the U.S. House of Representatives in 1982, Richard Durbin is a member of two Appropriations subcommittees: Transportation, and Agriculture and Rural Development where he is the senior Democratic member. In addition to agriculture, his legislative interests include transportation infrastructure measures, and he authored the legislation that banned smoking on domestic airline flights. In 1991 prior to the Persian Gulf War,

Photographer Jack Dykinga.

Durbin introduced a House resolution that would have required Congress to approve in advance any offensive U.S. military action in the Gulf.

DUVALL, ROBERT

c/o Bill Robinson, Int. Creat. Mgt., 8899 Beverly Blvd., Los Angeles, CA 90048
BORN: 1931, San Diego, Calif. ACHIEVEMENTS: Academy Award, Best Actor, and Golden Globe Award, Best Performance by an Actor in a Motion Picture, both for Tender Mercies, 1984. STUDIED: Attended Principia College; studied acting at the Neighborhood Playhouse.
The son of a Navy admiral, Robert Duvall trained in New York City at the Neighborhood Playhouse and acted in off-Broadway theater productions before starting his film career. His first film appearance was as the character Arthur "Boo" Radley in *To Kill a Mockingbird*, in 1962. He continued with his career in a wide range of character roles, including Ned Pepper in *True Grit*, 1969, Major Frank Burns in *M*A*S*H*, 1970, the title role in *THX 1138*, 1971, and Tom Hagen in both *The Godfather*, 1972 and *The Godfather, Part II*, 1974. Duvall finally won both an Academy Award and a Golden Globe Award for his portrayal of Mac Sledge in *Tender Mercies*, in 1983.

DYKINGA, JACK

3808 Calle Barcelona, Tuscon, AZ 85716 (602) 326-6094
BORN: 1943. ACHIEVEMENTS: Pulitzer Prize in Feature Photography; Communication Arts Annual Award; New York Art Directors Award. STUDIED: St. Procopius College, Lisle, Ill.
What would come to be a distinguished career in photography began in high school with Jack Dykinga's winning the *Look* magazine National Snapshot Award. Next he worked with Mike Rotunno, photographing celebrities at O'Hare airport in Chicago, and taking shots that paved the way for a position with the *Chicago Tribune*. He was working across the street at the *Chicago Sun-Times* when he won the Pulitzer Prize in 1971 for his pictures of the living conditions of those in the state mental health institutions. Leaving Chicago for Tucson in 1976, he worked as the picture editor at the *Arizona Daily Star* until 1981. Shooting freelance, he has since concentrated on covering environmental issues. In 1985, in collaboration with author Charles Bowden, he published Frog Mountain Blues, a collection of photographs showing untouched color shots of wilderness landscape and black-and-white shots of torn open land. Currently, he is completing a book on the Sonoran Desert in Mexico. A collection of color shots, it will celebrate the beauty of the desert before it is appropriated for human use. He also publishes regularly in *Time, National Geographic*, and *Arizona Highways* magazine.

EADIE, BETTY J.

Eadie is a prominent author. For career credentials, consult the portion of this book entitled "Notable Americans by Profession" in the Appendix. Within this portion, the list "Authors" describes requirements for inclusion in this volume.

EASTWOOD, CLINT

Warner Brothers Studio, 4000 Warner Blvd., Burbank, CA 91522.
BORN: 1930, San Francisco. ACHIEVEMENTS: Academy Award, Best Director and Best Picture, Unforgiven, 1992. STUDIED: Los Angeles City College.
Clint Eastwood has starred in, directed, and produced films for more than 30 years. Early in his career he appeared in a number of forgettable films, mainly playing minor roles. In 1959 he was hired to play the second lead in the TV series *Rawhide.* During the seven-year run of the series, Eastwood became known to a much wider audience. In 1964 he made the first of three "spaghetti westerns," *A Fistful of Dollars,* directed by Sergio Leone. The films *For a Few Dollars More* and *The Good, the Bad, and the Ugly* followed shortly thereafter. The films were an international success. Playing the character, Harry Callahan, Eastwood brought a whole new meaning to the term rogue cop. Although his films were successful throughout the world, Eastwood was generally shunned by the critics. He finally won an Academy Award as Best Director for the film *Unforgiven,* in 1992. The film also won an Academy Award for Best Picture. In addition to his career as an actor, director, and producer, Eastwood served as the mayor of Carmel, Calif., from 1986 to 1988.

EATON, ROBERT J.

Chrysler Corporation, 1200 Chrysler Dr., Highland Park, MI 48288 (313) 956-5252
BORN: 1940, Buena Vista, Colo. STUDIED: University of Kansas, B.S. mechanical engineering.
Chrysler Corporation underwent a management style change in 1993 when low-key, no-nonsense Robert Eaton took over as chair of the board and chief executive officer, replacing flamboyant Lee Iacocca. An auto buff since age 11, when he bought a banged-up 1932 Chevy for $10 and made it run, he still drove dirt bikes for fun while one of 35 General Motors vice presidents. Eaton joined General Motors straight from college and for the next 29 years of hands-on leadership climbed steadily to the top in the high-stakes auto world. His biggest success came while head of GM European operations from 1988 to 1992. GM lost $4.5 billion in 1991. Under Eaton the Europe division netted $1.8 billion, marking its fifth straight year of profits. The same year, having induced Detroit to build a $650 million Opel plant in East Berlin, Opel out-sold even Volkswagon in the region. Eaton's biggest failure occurred in 1989 when he strongly backed GM's purchase of a $600 million stake in Sweden's Saab Automobile. The purchase backfired during 1990 and 1991 with GM forced to absorb $1.1 billion in Saab losses.

ECHIKSON, WILLIAM

The Christian Science Monitor, 1 Norway St., Boston, MA 02115 (617) 450-2000
Echikson is a prominent journalist. For career credentials, consult the portion of this book entitled "Notable Americans by Profession" in the Appendix. Within this portion, the list "Journalists" describes requirements for inclusion in this volume.

EDDINGS, DAVID

c/o Del Rey-Ballantine, 201 East 50th Street, New York, NY 10022
BORN: 1931, Spokane, Wash. ACHIEVEMENTS: Author of Belgariad and Malloreon fantasy series. STUDIED: Reed College, B.A., 1954, University of Washington, M.A., 1961.
David Eddings entered the U.S. Army in 1954 after he graduated from Reed College. After serving in the Army, Eddings worked as a grocery clerk, a college English teacher, and as a buyer for the Boeing Company. His first novel was *High Hunt,* by Putnam, published in 1973. In 1982 he published the first book of his *Belgariad* fantasy series, titled *Pawn of Prophecy,* by Del Rey. After promising reviews from *Publishers Weekly,* he followed the first book of the series with four others. In 1987 Eddings started his second series, titled the *Malloreon* fantasy series. Again he wrote five books for the series. Eddings has become one of the most popular writers in the fantasy genre, with his last four novels landing on the national best seller lists.

EDGAR, JIM

Office of the Governor Springfield IL 62706 (217) 782-7355
BORN: 1946, Charleston, Ill. ACHIEVEMENTS: As Illinois secretary of state he lead a drunk driving crackdown that earned national recognition and pioneered an adult literacy program that became a model for the nation. STUDIED: Eastern Illinois University, B.A., history.
Jim Edgar was the 38th governor of Illinois. He was first elected in 1991, and his first term was highlighted by success in holding the line on taxes despite inheriting severe budget problems. He has promoted an Illinois Teacher Corps, an alternative certification program that allows master professionals to teach in Illinois schools. Through his Project Success Initiative, he involves the entire community in the education process through a coordinated system for delivering social services at school. Edgar began his government service in 1968 and served for eight years as a key aide to leaders in both the Illinois House and Senate. In 1979 he was elected to the Illinois House of Representatives from the 53rd Legislative District. Between April 1979 and December 1980, he served as director of affairs in the Governor's Office. In 1981 he was appointed Illinois secretary of state. He was elected to the post the next year and was re-elected four years later. Edgar is the past chairman of the

Education Commission of the states, former president of the board of the Council of State Governments, and past chairman of the Governor's Ethanol Coalition.

EDSALL, THOMAS B.

The Washington Post, 1150 15th St., NW., Washington, DC 20071 (202) 334-6000

Edsall is a prominent journalist. For career credentials, consult the portion of this book entitled "Notable Americans by Profession" in the Appendix. Within this portion, the list "Journalists" describes requirements for inclusion in this volume.

EDWARDS, CHET

328 Cannon House Office Building, Washington, DC 20515-4311 (202) 225-6105
BORN: 1951. ACHIEVEMENTS: U.S. Representative, 1991-. STUDIED: Texas A&M, B.A., economics, 1974; Harvard University, M.B.A., 1981.
A Texas businessman who was elected to the U.S. House of Representatives in 1990, Chet Edwards is a member of the National Security and Veterans' Affairs committees. He is a strong supporter of, small business, veterans', and defense programs. His other legislative interests include passage of a constitutional balanced budget amendment. Along with a B.A. in economics from Texas A&M and an M.B.A. from Harvard Business School, Edwards gained valuable insight into American business when he worked in commercial real estate and was president of a radio broadcasting company prior to running for Congress. From 1974 to 1977, he was a legislative assistant to Texas congressman, Olin "Tiger" Teague, and served in the Texas legislature for eight years.

EGEN, MAUREEN MAHON

Warner Books Inc., 1271 Avenue of the Americas, New York, NY, 10020 (212) 522-7200
BORN: Philadelphia. STUDIED: Trinity College, Washington, D.C., B.A., biology.
Maureen Egen has been vice president of Warner Books and publisher of Warner Hardcovers since September of 1990. She began her career as a editorial director of science publishing at Doubleday and was promoted to associate editorial director of Anchor Press, a division of Doubleday. She then spent 11 years as editorial director of the Doubleday Book Clubs. At Warner Books, her primary responsibility is overseeing the Warner Hardcover List, beginning with the acquisition of a book and seeing that it makes its way to being published. Egen has edited and published *The Bridges of Madison County*, the bestselling novel of all time. In addition, she has edited and published the fastest selling novel ever, *Scarlett*.

EGGELSTON, WILLIAM

4382 Walnut Grove Road, Memphis, TN 38117
BORN: 1937. ACHIEVEMENTS: Guggenheim Fellowship, NEA. STUDIED: University of Mississippi.

One of the premier color photographers of his generation, William Eggleston was profoundly influenced by the work of Cartier-Bresson. Eggleston's bailiwick is the rural South, and he photographs it with a practiced and uncompromising eye. His images are simple, direct, and unadorned: they never allow the viewer the luxury of sentimentality. His colors are as rich and vibrant as his subjects are ordinary and unimportant. The result is a body of work that is accessible in a way that many more carefully wrought photographs are not. Today Eggleston lives and works in his native Memphis, where his photographs continue to inspire new generations of photographers.

EIGER, RICHARD WILLIAM

Funk & Wagnall Corp., 1 International Blvd., Mahwah, NJ 07495
BORN: 1933, New York City. ACHIEVEMENTS: Member of Pratt Institute Executive Committee; member of Brandeis University Publishers Committee. STUDIED: Pratt Institute, B.F.A. in Marketing, 1955; New York University Graduate School of Business, M.B.A., 1960.
Richard Eiger began his career with the Western Publishing Company in 1960 as an account executive in corporate sales. Two years later he was product director of Western's Golden Press, and in 1965 he became its publisher. By 1970, Eiger had ascended to vice president of publishing. In 1980, he left Western Publishing and moved to a position as both the senior vice president of the Macmillan Publishing Company and the president of the Macmillan Educational Company. He left Macmillan in 1991 for Funk & Wagnalls, where he is now the vice president of business development and the publisher of the World Almanac.

ELAHIAN, KAMRAN

Momenta, Mountain View, CA
ACHIEVEMENTS: Inventor of the Pentop portable computer.
It is only the size of an unobtrusive notebook binder, but Kamran Elahian's Momenta Pentop portable computer opens the computer world to the typing novice. Running on all DOS and Windows applications, the portable's electronic ink allows the owner to use either a pen or a keyboard as an input device, making it also handy at meetings where computers are not likely to be available. The Pentop also includes a fax machine.

ELFMAN, DANNY

MCA, 70 Universal City Plaza, Universal City, CA 91608-1022
BORN: 1953, Amarillo, Texas. ACHIEVEMENTS: Grammy Award, Batman, 1989.
As lead singer and songwriter for the band Oingo Bongo, Elfman enjoyed modest success with this alternative band, recording over ten albums. He was given the chance to score the 1985 Tim Burton film *Pee Wee's Big Adventure* which opened up a new career as a composer of films and TV soundtracks. He earned a Grammy for his film score of *Batman*, 1989, a Grammy nomination for *Dick Tracy*, 1990, and an Emmy and Grammy nomination for *The Simpsons*.

His other film credits have included: *Beetlejuice*, 1988; *Midnight Run*, 1988; *Scrooged*, 1988; *Edward Scissorhands*, 1990, *Batman Returns*, 1992; *The Nightmare Before Christmas*, 1993; and *Black Beauty*, 1994. Elfman also has written scores for television shows including, *The Simpsons, The Flash, Tales of the Crypt, Beetlejuice* (animated), *Pee Wee's Playhouse*, and *Alfred Hitchcock Presents*.

ELION, GERTRUDE BELLE

Burroughs-Wellcome Co., Research Triangle Park, NC 27709
BORN: 1918, New York City. ACHIEVEMENTS: Invented the leukemia-fighting drug 6-Mercaptopurine; Nobel Prize in Medicine, 1988; inducted into the National Inventors Hall of Fame, 1991. STUDIED: Hunter College, 1937 (summa cum laude); New York University, M.S., chemistry.
At the age of 15, Dr. Elion was a student at Hunter College, where she graduated summa cum laude. She taught high school before joining Burroughs-Wellcome in 1944. While at Burroughs-Wellcome, her research led to the development of several antileukemic drugs. Dr. Elion and her team also developed Zyloprim, a drug to treat gout, and Acyclovir, now marketed as Zovirx, a treatment for the herpes virus. Her name appears on more than 280 scientific publications and 45 patents. She retired from Burroughs-Wellcome in 1983 and is scientist emeritus. In 1988 she shared the Nobel Prize in Medicine with George Hitchings, and Sir James Black. Dr. Elion was inducted into the National Inventors Hall of Fame in 1991.

ELLETIN, MICHAEL

The Village Voice, 36 Cooper Square, New York, NY 10003-7149 (212) 475-3300
Elletin is a prominent publisher. For career credentials, consult the portion of this book entitled "Notable Americans by Profession" in the Appendix. Within this portion, the list "Publishers" describes requirements for inclusion in this volume.

ELSTER, ALLEN DE VANEY

300 S. Hawthorne Rd., RAD, Winston-Salem, NC 27103
Elster is a prominent physician. For career credentials, consult the portion of this book entitled "Notable Americans by Profession" in the Appendix. Within this portion, the list "Physicians" describes requirements for inclusion in this volume.

ENBERG, DICK

NBC Sports, Room 1411, 30 Rockefeller Plaza, New York, NY 10020
Enberg is a prominent television personality. For career credentials, consult the portion of this book entitled "Notable Americans by Profession" in the Appendix. Within this portion, the list "Television

Personalities" describes requirements for inclusion in this volume.

ENGEL, MORRIS

65 Central Park West, New York, NY 10023
BORN: 1918.
A disciple of New York's Photo League, Morris Engel was a particular admirer of Paul Strand. Engel's photographic essays of New York are justifiably famous: whether capturing lovers on a Coney Island beach or a street scene in Harlem, he invested his subjects with dignity and individuality. Strand wrote of Engel's show in 1939, "(he) sees his subjects very specifically and intensely. They are not types, but people in whom the quality of life they live is vivid—unforgettable." Engel served under combat photographer Edward Steichen in World War II before going on to further acclaim as a film producer and cinematographer.

ENGLER, GOV. JOHN

Office of the Governor, State Capitol Building, Lansing, MI 48913 (517) 373-3423
Engler is a prominent political leader. For career credentials, consult the portion of this book entitled "Notable Americans by Profession" in the Appendix. Within this portion, the list "Political Leaders" describes requirements for inclusion in this volume.

EPPS, EDGAR G.

Kimbark Ave., Chicago, IL 60637
BORN: 1929, Little Rock, Ark. STUDIED: Talladega College, Talladega, Ala., A.B, education; Atlanta University, M.A., Education; Washington State University, Ph.D., education.
Twenty-five years at the University of Chicago as Marshall Field IV Professor of Urban Education have given Edgar Epps a distinguished reputation as an educator and scholar. During that period he served as a member of the Chicago Board of Education for six years, and spent a year in Salzburg, Austria, as a faculty member of the Salzburg Seminar in American Studies. He has edited three books: *Black Students in White Schools*, 1972; *Current Perspectives*, 1973; and *Cultural Pluralism*, 1974. He has also co-edited *College in Black and White: African-American Students in Historically White and in Historically Black Schools*. In 1975 he co-authored the book *Black Consciousness, Identity and Achievement*. Before joining the University of Chicago faculty, he taught for three years each at Florida A&M University, the University of Michigan, and Tuskegee University.

ERDMAN, JEAN

c/o Theater of the Open Eye, 270 West 89th St., New York, NY 10024-1705 (212) 534-6363
Erdman is a prominent dancer. For career credentials, consult the portion of this book entitled "Notable Americans by Profession" in the Appendix. Within this portion, the list "Dancers" describes requirements for inclusion in this volume.

ERICKSON, JERRY

Hewlett-Packard Company, Inc., 3000 Hanover St., Palo Alto, CA 94304 (415) 857-1501
ACHIEVEMENTS: Developer of the HP 95LX Palmtop PC.
Hewlett-Packard research and development section manager Jerry Erickson developed an 11-ounce computer with all the processing power of a regular desktop model. Called the HP 95LX Palmtop PC, it contains built-in Lotus 1-2-3 spreadsheet software, a time management system, memo writing capability, and a phone book. Fitting in the palm of the hand, it can be used for information and analysis anywhere the user goes.

ESTEFAN, GLORIA MARIA

Estefan Enterprises Inc., 6205 Bird Rd. Miami, FL 33155
BORN: 1957, Havana, Cuba. ACHIEVEMENTS: American Music Award, 1987; Victory award, 1991; Songwriter of the Year Award, BMI, 1991; Humanitarian of the Year Award B'nai Birth, 1992; Casita Maria Gold Medal Award, 1993; Hispanic Heritage Award, 1993; Hearst Foundation Gold Medal Award, 1992; Ellis Island Congressional Medal of Honor, 1993; named Billboard's Best New Pop Artist and Top Pop Singles Artist, 1986. STUDIED: University of Miami, B.A., psychology, 1978, MusD (honorable), 1993.
In 1986 Estefan and the Miami Sound Machine was named Billboard's Best New Pop Artists and Top Pop singles Artist. With the release of the single *Conga*, they became the first group to cross-over to the pop, dance, Black and Latin charts at the same time. Born in Cuba, Estefan came to the United states in 1959, and attended the University of Miami. Along with her husband, Emilio, they founded the Miami Sound Machine, and in 1986, released their first album *Primitive Love*. At the height of Estefan's popularity, she was in a tragic accident and was never expected to walk or perform again. However, she miraculously recuperated from her injuries, and continues to perform.

ESTES, CLARISSA PINKOLA

c/o Ballantine, 201 East 50th Street, New York, NY 10022
BORN: 1943, northern Indiana. ACHIEVEMENTS: Las Primeras Award, MANA, National Latina Foundation, Washington D.C., 1993, for lifetime social activism and literature; Book of the Year Honor Award, American Booksellers Association, 1993, both for Women Who Run with the Wolves: Myths and Stories of the Wild Woman Archetype. STUDIED: Loretto Heights College, B.A., 1976; The Union Institute, Ph.D, 1981; Charter of Zurich, postdoctoral diploma, 1984.
Clarissa Estes was born in 1943 to mestizo parents of Spanish and Mexican lineage. She was later adopted by Hungarian immigrants to the United States. Throughout her childhood she was exposed to the art of oral storytelling as a means of relating family and cultural history. Estes is a psychoanalyst in private practice in Denver, Colo. She developed and teaches "Writing as Liberation of the Spirit," a program in state and federal prisons throughout the United States. She is also the co-founder and co-director of the Colorado Authors for Gay and Lesbian Equal rights. Estes is best known for her book, *Women Who Run with the Wolves: Myths and Stories of the Wild Woman Archetype*, Ballantine, 1992.

EVANS, ROWLAND JR.

The Chicago Sun Times, 401 N. Wabash, Chicago IL 60611-3593. (312) 321-3000.
BORN: 1921, White Marsh, Pa. ACHIEVEMENTS: Author (with Robert Novak) Lyndon Johnson: The Exercise of Power, 1966, Nixon in the White House: The Frustration of Power, 1971, The Reagan Revolution, 1981. STUDIED: Yale University, B.A., English, 1943.
Rowland Evans served in the Pacific Theater for two of the most harrowing years of World War II before returning home and beginning his career at the *Philadelphia Bulletin* in 1944. He joined the Associated Press in 1945 and spent 10 years in its Washington Bureau. Later he worked for the *New York Herald Tribune*, before teaming up with Robert Novak on their column *Inside Report* which began in 1963. The two conservative columnists also appear on television, especially CNN, and have collaborated on several books detailing American political history over the last 40 years. Evans also continues to be a roving editor for *Reader's Digest*, a position he's held since 1980.

EVANS, SLAYTON A.

University of North Carolina, Venable 045A, Chapel Hill, NC 27599
BORN: 1943, Chicago. ACHIEVEMENTS: Kenan Research Leave, University of North Carolina; Fulbright Fellowship; NATO Grant for Collaborative Research; Ralph Metcalfe, Jr., Lectureship; chair in Chemistry, Marquette University. STUDIED: Tougaloo College, Tougaloo, Mississippi, B.S., chemistry; Case Western Reserve University, Ph.D., chemistry; University of Texas at Arlington, Postdoctoral Fellow; University of Notre Dame, Postdoctoral Fellow; Illinois Institute of Technology.
After finishing his studies Slayton Evans spent a year as a research instructor at Dartmouth College. Offered the post of Kenan Professor of Chemistry at the University of North Carolina in 1974, Evans accepted, and began pouring forth what would amount to 70 scientific publications on organophosphorous (nerve gases, insecticides, and fire retardants) and organo sulfur compounds over a period of 20 years. He is a member of the Louisiana State Board of Regents; the New York Academy of Sciences, Alpha Xi Sigma; and chair, National Science Foundation Chemistry Division's Advisory Committee.

FABEL, GEORGE

CAChe Scientific, Beaverton, OR
ACHIEVEMENTS: Developer of the CAChe Work System.
George Fabel, of CAChe Scientific, developed a computer for chemists. The CAChe Work System allows chemists to model new compounds and test existing ones, slashing the time, expense, and danger in developing new products. It also allows chemists to predict and understand the molecular structure and chemical activity of substances without having to touch them, possibly exposing themselves to hazardous materials.

FALK, PETER

International Creative Management, 8899 Beverly Blvd., Los Angeles, CA 90048

BORN: 1927, New York City. ACHIEVEMENTS: Emmy Award, Outstanding Single Performance by an Actor in a Leading Role, The Price of Tomatoes, 1961; Emmy Awards, Outstanding Lead Actor in a Dramatic Series, Columbo, 1970, 1971, 1972, 1975, and 1976. STUDIED: Hamilton College, 1946-48; New School for Social Research, B.A., 1951; Maxwell School, Syracuse University, M.P.A., 1953; trained for acting with Eva Le Gallienne, White Barn Theatre, Westport, Conn., 1955, and with Sandford Meisner, Meisner Workshop, 1957.

Best known for his portrayal of Lt. Columbo on the television series, *Columbo*, Peter Falk's understated presence has graced stage and screen since the late 1950s. Falk once worked as an efficiency expert for the Budget Bureau of the state of Connecticut. His stage debut was in 1956 when he played Sagnarele in *Don Juan*. Falk worked actively on stage in the late 1950s, but infrequently in the ensuing decades, until his return in the late 1980s. He played Shelly Levene in *Glengarry Glen Ross* in 1985 when the production toured the major U.S. cities. His career in movies began in 1958 with *Wind Across the Everglades*. Falk has had a prolific film career with more than 30 movies to his credit, including *The Princess Bride*, in 1987. However his greatest success has come from television where his role as Lt. Columbo has made him immensely popular. The television series, *Columbo*, ran from 1971 until 1977, but it has been followed by numerous television movies featuring the same format.

FALWELL, REV. JERRY

Liberty Baptist Fellowship, Candler's Mountain Rd., Lynchburg, VA 24506

BORN: 1933, Lynchburg, Va. ACHIEVEMENTS: Founder, Moral Majority Inc. (Renamed Liberty Federation), 1979; named to National Religious Broadcasters' Hall of Fame, 1985; author: If I Should Die Before I Wake, 1986, Strength For the Journey (autobiography), 1987, and New American Family, 1992. STUDIED: Baptist Bible College, B.A., 1956; Temple University, D.D. (honorable), California Graduate School of Theology, LL.D. (honorable), Cen. U. (Seoul, Korea), LL.D. (honorable).

Jerry Falwell is perhaps most famous for founding the conservative political action group, Moral Majority Inc., in 1979. He started his career in 1956 when he became the pastor of Thomas Rd. Baptist Church, in his birthplace, Lynchburg, Va., a post he still holds. Falwell burst onto the broadcasting scene in 1971 with the national debut of his television show, *Old Time Gospel Hour*. He also founded Liberty University, in Lynchburg, that same year. Falwell expanded Moral Majority into a larger organization, Liberty Federation, in 1986. He is a leading proponent of religious conservatism and traditional morality. Falwell has been the author of numerous books, including his autobiography, *Strength for the Journey*, in 1987.

FAMIGHETTI, ROBERT JOSEPH

Funk & Wagnalls Corp., 1 International Blvd., Mahwah, NJ 07495

BORN: 1947, New York City. ACHIEVEMENTS: Author/Editor of best seller, the World Almanac. STUDIED: CCNY, B.B.A., 1967; Yale University Law School, 1967-68; New York University Graduate School of Education, 1968.

After brief stints in the late sixties with the New York City Council on Consumer Affairs and the New York City Board of Education, Famighetti worked from 1970 until 1975 in various editorial capacities for Macmillan Inc. In 1975 he become Macmillan's managing editor; the executive editor in 1982, and the editor-in-chief of yearbooks in 1991. In 1993 he was named editor of *The World Almanac* and *World Almanac Books* at Funk & Wagnalls Corporation. Throughout his career he has also served as editor for the *Collier's Encyclopedia Yearbook* and *Health and Medical Horizons* as well as serving as an editorial associate for the *Wharton Magazine*.

FARBER, VIOLA

Viola Farber Dance Company, 30 East 31st St., New York, NY 10016 (212) 679-4885

Farber is a prominent dancer. For career credentials, consult the portion of this book entitled "Notable Americans by Profession" in the Appendix. Within this portion, the list "Dancers" describes requirements for inclusion in this volume.

FARRAKHAN, REV. LOUIS

Nation of Islam, P.O. Box 50559, Atlanta GA 30302

BORN: 1933, New York, N.Y. ACHIEVEMENTS: Opened the $5 million dollar Salaam Restaurant in Chicago debt-free. STUDIED: Winston-Salem Teachers College.

As the leader of the Nation of Islam, Louis Farrakhan preaches economic empowerment, strict rules of discipline and diet, and separatism to his followers. Born Louis Eugene Walcott, he grew up in the Roxbury section of Boston. While working as a calypso singer, he was recruited by Malcolm X into the Nation of Islam. When Malcolm X moved to Harlem, N.Y., Farrakhan became minister of the Boston temple. He called himself Louis X until 1965 when Elijah Muhammad gave him the name Farrakhan. After Elijah Muhammad's death, in 1975, his son and successor, W. Deen Muhammad eventually disbanded the Nation of Islam in 1985. Farrakhan decided to remain loyal to the teachings of Elijah Muhammad and rebuilt the Nation's membership to over 15,000. Following his own theme of self-empowerment, Farrakhan opened the Salaam Restaurant and Bakery in February 1995, in an economically depressed area on Chicago's South Side.

FASI, FRANK F.

City Hall, 530 S. King St., Honolulu, HI 96813 (808) 523-4141

Fasi is a prominent political leader in Hawaii and mayor of the state's largest city, Honolulu. For career credentials, consult the portion of this book entitled

"Notable Americans by Profession" in the Appendix. Within this portion, the list "Political Leaders" describes requirements for inclusion in this volume.

FEINGOLD, RUSS

B40-1 Dirksen Senate Office Building, Washington, DC 20510-4904 (202) 224-5323
BORN: 1953, Janesville, Wis. ACHIEVEMENTS: Phi Beta Kappa, 1975; Rhodes Scholar, 1977. STUDIED: University of Wisconsin, 1975; Oxford University, 1977; Harvard University Law School, 1979.
At the age of 29, Russ Feingold won a seat in the Wisconsin State Senate. After winning re-election four times, he ran successfully for the U.S. Senate in 1992, defeating two-term incumbent Bob Kasten. Feingold serves on the Foreign Relations Committee, the Special Committee on Aging, and the Agriculture, Nutrition and Forestry Committee.

FEININGER, ANDREAS B.L.

18 Elizabeth Lane, New Milford, CT 06776
BORN: 1906. ACHIEVEMENTS: Robert Leavitt Award; Gold Medal, Art Directors Club of Metropolitan Washington; collections: Metropolitan Museum of Art; Museum of Modern Art . STUDIED: The Bauhaus, Weimar (Germany).
Son of painter Lyonel Feininger, Andreas Feininger graduated with high honors from the Bauhaus in 1925 and worked as an architect in Germany until 1931. In Sweden, two years later, he became a photographer, and after arriving in America in the 1940s became a staff photographer for *Life* magazine. Careful depictions of architectural forms and street scenes are documentary in their approach. He has done a great deal of work in telephoto and close-up photography, including intricate nature studies. Of greatest importance to him is "clarity of presentation." His works show a strong connection to Bauhaus, though it is often proclaimed as warm and intimate, very European in style and sensibility.

FEIST, GENE

Roundabout Theater Company, 100 East 17th St., New York, NY 10003
Feist is a prominent dramatic artist. For career credentials, consult the portion of this book entitled "Notable Americans by Profession" in the Appendix. Within this portion, the list "Dramatic Artists" describes requirements for inclusion in this volume.

FELD, ELIOT

Feld Ballets/NY, 890 Broadway, 8th Floor, New York, NY 10003
BORN: 1943, New York City. ACHIEVEMENTS: Notable ballets: West Side Story, Fancy Free, and I Can Get It for You Wholesale. STUDIED: High School of the Performing Arts, New York City; Juilliard School of Music, D.F.A., Fine Arts.
Founder of one of the most successful small dance companies in the country, the New York Feld Ballet,

Feld began as a dancer with the American Ballet Theater in 1963. He was lead soloist and choreographer for American Ballet Theater until he broke away and formed the unsuccessful American Ballet Company in 1968, and then the Feld group in 1974. His memorable performances as a dancer were in *West Side Story, Fancy Free,* and *I Can Get It for You Wholesale.*

FELDSTEIN, MARTIN

National Bureau of Economic Research, Inc., 1050 Massachusetts Ave., Cambridge, MA 02138
BORN: 1939, New York City. ACHIEVEMENTS: John Bates Clark Medal, American Economic Association; president, National Bureau of Economic Research; chairman, President Ronald Reagan's Council of Economic Advisers; George F. Baker Professor, Harvard; fellow, American Academy of the Arts and Sciences. STUDIED: Harvard University; University of Oxford.
In addition to his interests in old-age pensions, health insurance, and the effects of tax policies on private capital formation, again and again Martin Feldstein, in his work, has returned to the deteriorating effect the welfare state has on the American economy. For example, he argues that unemployment compensation raises unemployment by making not working preferable to searching for a job, and that half of temporary layoffs in the U.S. are attributed to the level of compensation, as laid-off workers sit back and wait to be recalled to their jobs. He proposes making jobless pay taxable-like income tax, at an increasing rate as the idle time lengthens. His astonishing array of publications is demonstrated by the fact that he wrote or co-authored articles on topics as varied as charitable donations, social security, medical and hospital care, inflation, unemployment, and the labor supply among a total of 14 produced in 1977.

FERGASON, JAMES

Optical Shields, Menlo Park, CA
ACHIEVEMENTS: Directed development of Optical Shields electronic windows.
Under the direction of company president James Fergason, Optical Shields developed electronic windows for office and automotive use that provide privacy, glare reduction, and security without the distraction of shutters and drapes. The effect is achieved at the flip of a switch which changes the windows from transparent to frosted glass, the opacity controlled by a layer of liquid crystals in a film sandwiched between two layers of glass.

FIELD, RON

5 West 19th St., New York, NY 10011
Field is a prominent dancer. For career credentials, consult the portion of this book entitled "Notable Americans by Profession" in the Appendix. Within this portion, the list "Dancers" describes requirements for inclusion in this volume.

FIELD, SALLY

Creative Artists Agency, Room 1400, 9830 Wilshire Blvd., Beverly Hills, CA 90212
BORN: 1946, Pasadena, Calif. ACHIEVEMENTS: Emmy Award, Outstanding Lead Actress in a Drama or Comedy Special, Sybil, 1976; Academy Award, Best Actress, and Golden Globe Award, Best Actress in a Dramatic Film, both for Norma Rae, 1980; Academy Award, Best Actress, and Golden Globe. Award, Best Actress in a Dramatic Film, both for Places in the Heart, 1985. STUDIED: attended Actor's Studio, 1968 and 1973-75.
Sally Field, a successful actress on both film and television, began her career when she starred in the TV series *Gidget*, beginning in 1965. Next she played the role of Sister Bertrille in the comedy *The Flying Nun*. Unfortunately, she found it difficult to obtain serious roles because of her part in *The Flying Nun*. She appeared in a few action comedies with Burt Reynolds, such as *Smokey and the Bandit*, 1977 and *Hooper*, 1978. But her part in *Norma Rae*, in 1979, brought her both an Academy Award and a Golden Globe Award. Her career has continued rise with the films: *Places in the Heart*, 1984, *Steel Magnolias*, 1989, *Mrs. Doubtfire*, 1993, and *Forest Gump*, 1994.

FIELDS, SUZANNE BREGMAN

The Washington Times, 3600 New York Ave. NE, Washington, DC 20002-1996
BORN: 1936, Washington, D.C. ACHIEVEMENTS: Author, Like Father, Like Daughter, 1983; editor of Innovations Magazine, 1971-79. STUDIED: George Washington University., B.A., 1957, M.A., 1964; Catholic University., PhD, 1970.
After receiving her masters Suzanne Fields became a freelance writer in her home town until 1971, when she was named editor of *Innovations Magazine*. Fields stayed in that position for eight years. She was given a column in *Vogue* in 1982 and then one in the *Washington Times* in 1984. In 1988 she began syndicating her columns through the L.A. Times Syndicate. Fields appears regularly as a panelist for *CNN & Co.* and also is a frequent commentator for the worldwide news network. Her first book, *Like Father, Like Daughter*, was published in 1983.

FINE, JUD

713 S. Gladys, Los Angeles, CA 90021
BORN: 1944. ACHIEVEMENTS: NEA Grant; Contemporary Art Council New Talent Grant, Los Angeles County Museum of Art; collections: Guggenheim Museum; Los Angeles County Museum of Art; exhibitions: Art Institute of Chicago; La Jolla Museum of Art. STUDIED: Cornell University.
During the 1960s, Jud Fine earned undergraduate and doctoral degrees in history; he did not receive a degree in sculpture until 1970. In his experimental mixed-media pieces, he parodies art and language, often with fragments of text or photographs in combination with stenciled images and colored shapes. *Discourse* is a booklet hung from a chain on the wall, containing a convoluted argument which ends where it begins. More recent sculptures continue an interest in history and language. The architectonic piece *Horizontal Pillar* is constructed from a 160-foot-long horizontal steel pillar with elements of straw and wood attached by string and wire. Accompanying drawings depict monolithic structures along with written explanations of man's existence and its relationship throughout history to the structures he has built.

FINK, TOM

Office of the Mayor, 632 W. 6th St., Rm. 812, Anchorage, AK 99501 (907) 343-4431
Fink is a prominent political leader. For career credentials, consult the portion of this book entitled "Notable Americans by Profession" in the Appendix. Within this portion, the list "Political Leaders" describes requirements for inclusion in this volume.

FINKBEINER, CARLETON S.

One Government Center, Suite 2200, Toledo, OH 46304 (419) 245-1001
Finkbeiner is a prominent political leader. For career credentials, consult the portion of this book entitled "Notable Americans by Profession" in the Appendix. Within this portion, the list "Political Leaders" describes requirements for inclusion in this volume.

FINLEY, JAMES

PPG Industries, 1 PPG Place, Pittsburgh, PA 15272 (412) 434-3131
ACHIEVEMENTS: Co-developer of thermal-controlled window glass.
Heat buildup in cars triggers the need for the air conditioner, which eats up gas and releases ozone-eating chlorofluorocarbons into the air. James Finley, and his associate, Joseph Gulotta, both of PPG Industries, solved those problems by developing thermal-controlled window glass. Embedded with a metal-oxide film that acts like a mirror, the glass reflects ultraviolet and infrared radiation, while allowing the light to come through. Reflecting the radiation can reduce the heat-buildup in a car by 60 percent.

FINN, RONALD JASON

4 Franklin St., Milton, MA 02186
Finn is a prominent physician. For career credentials, consult the portion of this book entitled "Notable Americans by Profession" in the Appendix. Within this portion, the list "Physicians" describes requirements for inclusion in this volume.

FISH, JR., HAMILTON

U.S. House of Representatives, 2354 RHOB, Washington, DC 20515-3219 (202) 225-5441
Fish is a prominent political leader. For career credentials, consult the portion of this book entitled "Notable Americans by Profession" in the Appendix. Within this portion, the list "Political Leaders" describes requirements for inclusion in this volume.

FISCHER, DAVID J.

City of St. Petersburg, Office of the Mayor, P.O. Box 2842, St. Petersburg, FL 33731

BORN: 1933, Evanston, Ill. ACHIEVEMENTS: Member, Board of Trustees, Eckerd College; Environmental Development Commission, chairman; St. Petersburg Chamber of Commerce, president; Community Alliance, co-chairman; Operation PAR, treasurer; United Way, treasurer. STUDIED: Duke University, B.A., business administration.

An Air Force pilot from 1956 to 1958, Mayor David Fischer began a 32-year career as a municipal financial consultant and municipal bond dealer after his separation from the service. Moving to St. Petersburg from the Midwest in the mid-sixties, he quickly became involved with community groups such as United Way, Community Alliance, and the Chamber of Commerce. He served in the City Council from 1975 to 1979, moved on to vice mayor in 1978 and to mayor in 1991. Reelected in 1993, he will serve until 1997.

FISHER, GEORGE MILES CORDELL

Eastman Kodak Company, 343 State St., Rochester, NY 14650 (716) 724-4000
BORN: 1940, Anna, Ill. STUDIED: University of Illinois, B.S., engineering; Brown University, M.A., Ph.D., applied mathematics.

After 18 years with Motorola Company, during which he succeeded in opening Japan to a percentage of Motorola products, George Fisher made a lateral move in 1993 to Eastman Kodak as chair and chief executive officer. The story behind the move from Motorola's top position to Kodak's is Fisher's success with Japan, whose giant Fuji Film controls 99 percent of a market which completely excludes Kodak. Besides his influence with the Japanese, which may jar open a door to Japan for Kodak, a second factor apparently also played a role in the move. Fisher reportedly was looking over his shoulder at the rapid rise through company ranks of the grandson of Paul Vincent Galvin, Chris Galvin, whose grandfather founded Motorola in his garage in 1928 after inventing the first car radio and heater. Fisher belongs to the American Academy of Arts and Sciences and is senior member of the Institute of Electrical and Electronics Engineers, Inc.

FITCH, VAL LOGSDON

Princeton University, P.O. Box 708, Princeton, NJ 08544
BORN: 1923, Merriman, Neb. ACHIEVEMENTS: Nobel Prize in Physics (shared with James Watson Cronin), 1980; Research Corporation Award; Ernest Orlando Lawrence Award; John Wetherill Medal, Franklin Institute. STUDIED: McGill University, Canada; Columbia University.

An early advance in the study of subatomic particles—what goes on inside an atom between its electrons, protons, and neutrons, the major interest of atomic scientists since the 1960s—won Nobel attention for Val Fitch and colaureate James Wason Cronin in 1980. Previously it was thought that proton collisions within the nuclei of an atom obeyed the laws of symmetry observed in the physical world. They found just the opposite, an important insight toward breaking up particles into their constituent parts for the study of their structure.

FLATT, ERNEST O.

c/o Becker and London, 30 Lincoln Plaza, New York, NY 10023

Flatt is a prominent dramatic artist. For career credentials, consult the portion of this book entitled "Notable Americans by Profession" in the Appendix. Within this portion, the list "Dramatic Artists" describes requirements for inclusion in this volume.

FLAVIN, DAN

P.O. Box 248, Garrison, NY 10524
BORN: 1933. ACHIEVEMENTS: Copley Foundation Grant; National Foundation of Arts and Humanities Award; collections: Museum of Modern Art, New York City; Whitney Museum, New York City; exhibitions: University Art Museum, Berkeley; Whitney Museum, New York City.

In 1961 Dan Flavin began a series of minimalist structures he called "blank, almost featureless square-fronted constructions with obvious electric lights." His later works employ fluorescent lights exclusively, without "constructions," sometimes rendering the light fixtures invisible. Most recently, he seeks to dissolve flat surfaces and restructure space. Artificial "installations" emphasize the characteristics of the rooms he works in.

FLETCHER, PHILIP B.

ConAgra Inc., One ConAgra Drive, Omaha, NE, 68102 (402) 595-4000
STUDIED: Massachusetts Institute of Technology, Sloan Fellowship, M.B.A.; graduated St. Lawrence University B.S., geology, 1954.

Chief executive officer of ConAgra since 1992, Fletcher was named chairman in May, 1993. He joined ConAgra in 1982 as president of Banquet Foods Co. Later, he was named president and chief operating officer of ConAgra Frozen Prepared Food Companies and a member of ConAgra's Office of the President. In 1989, he was named president and chief operating officer of ConAgra Inc. At this time, he became a member of the board of directors. Fletcher started in the food industry in 1958, with the Campbell Soup Company. He held various management positions with them around the country. From 1973 to 1978, he was general manager of operations and agriculture of Heinz, U.S.A. In 1978, he served as vice president of operations for Heublein, where he stayed until joining ConAgra. In addition to ConAgra, Fletcher is a director of the Grocery Manufacturers of America, Inc. and the U.S. Chamber of Commerce, and a member of the board of governors of Ak-Sar-Ben, a civic organization in Omaha.

FOGEL, ROBERT W.

University of Chicago, Graduate School of Business, 1101 E. 58th St., Chicago, IL 60637
BORN: 1926, New York City. ACHIEVEMENTS: Nobel Prize in Economics (with Douglass C. North), 1993; director of the Center of Population Economics; president, Economic History Association; president, Social Science History Association; program director, National Bureau of Economic Re-

search. *STUDIED: Cornell University; Columbia University; Johns Hopkins University.*

When Robert Fogel asked the conditional question, "At what rate would America have grown if railroads had never existed?" in his work, *Railroads and American Economic Growth: Essays in Econometric History,* he announced the arrival of the new field of economic history. His method of study, called "cliometrics"—the use of statistical data often computerized, to record a picture of the past—was further developed in *Reinterpretation of American Economic History,* with S.L.Engerman, and *"Scientific" History and Traditional History,* with G.R. Elton. Finally he turned his technique to re-examining the economics of American slavery, producing in *Time on the Cross: The Economics of American Negro Slavery,* again with Engerman, one of the most controversial books ever published on American history. In it they attacked the orthodox view that slave labor was inefficient and unprofitable, insisting instead that it was so efficient that only the Civil War could bring about its downfall. He has retrieved from historical archives data going back to the eighteenth century on such variables as birth and death rates, the role of women in the labor force, migration and mobility rates, and savings ratios.

FONDA, JANE

Fonda Films, P.O. Box 1198, Santa Monica, CA 90406
BORN: 1937, New York, N.Y. ACHIEVEMENTS: Academy Awards, Best Actress, Klute, 1971; Coming Home, 1968. STUDIED: Attended Vassar College; studied in Lee Strasberg's Actors Studio.
Renowned for her outspoken political views in the 1960s and her line of exercise books and videos in the 1980s, Jane Fonda has starred in many films including *Cat Ballou,* 1965; *Barefoot in the Park,* 1967; *They Shoot Horses, Don't They?,* 1969; *Klute,* 1971, for which she won an Oscar for best actress; *Julia,* 1977; *Coming Home, 1978, for a second best actress Oscar;* The China Syndrome, *1979;* Nine to Five, *1980;* On Golden Pond, *1981;* Agnes of God, 1985; and *Stanley and Iris,* 1990.

FORD, GERALD RUDOLPH, JR.

P.O. Box 927, Rancho Mirage, CA 92262
BORN: 1913, Omaha, Neb. ACHIEVEMENTS: Elected to U.S. House of Representatives; served 1949-73; U.S. House of Representatives, Republican Minority Leader, 1965-1973; Appointed Vice President of U.S., 1973; U.S. President, 1974-76. STUDIED: University of Michigan, B.A. 1938; Yale University, Law Degree, 1941.
Born as Leslie Lynch King, Jr., his parents were divorced while he was an infant. Soon after, his mother married Gerald Ford, Sr. and when he adopted young Leslie he changed his name to Gerald Rudloph Ford, Jr. At the University of Michigan, young Ford was a football star. His public life began in 1948 as the Republican candidate for Congressman from Michigan. After a nearly 25 year stint in Congress, President Richard Milhouse Nixon appointed Ford Vice President of the United States in 1973 to fill the position vacated by Spiro Angew who was forced to resign in a scandal involving allegedly taking a bribe while he was governor of the state of Maryland. Nixon, too, was forced out of office in a scandal that came to be known as "Watergate," in which he was alleged to have covered up the involvement of his staff in a burglary at the Watergate Hotel in Washington, D.C. When Vice President Ford succeeded him, Ford became the 38th President of the U.S. and the first U.S. president to never have been elected to the vice presidency or presidency. One month after his succession to the presidency, on August 9, 1974, he pardoned Nixon, hence paving the way for losing the 1976 presidential election. His brief presidency was marked by high inflation and a record number of vetoes; more than 50, 40 of which were sustained. In his final days in office he ordered an airlift of anticommunist Vietnamese refugees, bringing 237,000 new immigrants into the U.S. Ford is now retired and lives in California.

FORD, HARRISON

Pat McQueeny, McQueeny Management, 146 N. Almont Drive, Los Angeles, CA 90048
BORN: 1942, Chicago. ACHIEVEMENTS: Academy Award nomination, Best Actor, for Witness, 1985. STUDIED: Ripon College.
Harrison Ford has had a long and productive career. He began acting in films in 1966 with an appearance in the movie, *Dead Heat on a Merry-Go-Round.* After achieving widespread popularity during the 1970s with his portrayal of Han Solo in the *Star Wars* trilogy, Ford repeated the feat playing Indiana Jones in a series of three immensely popular movies in the 1980s. Along the way, Ford skillfully played numerous other roles, including John Brook in *Witness,* in 1985, for which he received an Academy Award nomination for best actor. Among his more recent films are: *Patriot Games,* released in 1992, and *The Fugitive,* which came out in 1994.

FORD, WILLIAM DAVID

239 Cannon House Office Building, Washington DC 20515
BORN: 1927, Detroit, Mich. ACHIEVEMENTS: Recipient of honorary degrees from 18 distinguished colleges and universities. STUDIED: Wayne University; University of Denver B.S., LL.B., JD.
David Ford's political career began in the 50s when he served as a township attorney and chairman for the Democratic party. Since 1952, he has juggled his public service work with a private law practice. As a U.S. representative, his activities include membership in the Northeast-Midwest Congressional Coalition, the Democratic Study Group, and the Congressional Steel Caucus.

FORDICE, KIRK

P O Box 139, Jackson, MS 39205 (601) 359-3741
BORN: 1934, Memphis, Tenn. ACHIEVEMENTS: Past president, Associated General Contractors; chairman, Southern Governor's Association. STUDIED: Purdue University, B.S.C.E., civil engineering, 1956; M.S., industrial management, 1957.

After college Kirk Fordice served in the U. S. Army for two years as an engineering officer. Prior to his election as governor of Missipippi, Fordice lived in Vicksburg, Miss. for over 30 years. He was a professional engineer and president of Fordice Construction Company. He was also president of the Associated General Contractors, the largest trade association in the construction industry. As governor, Fordice is known as a fiscal conservative. He has supported legislation that allows the state to budget just 98 percent of projected revenues, with the remainder going to a rainy-day fund to avoid budget cuts. He assured passage of the elimination of capital gains taxation on Missipippi investments. He has also supported an aggressive prison-building program, and Mississippi's first comprehensive welfare-reform legislation.

FOREMAN, LAURA

The Laura Foreman Dance Theater, 225 Lafayette St., #713, New York, NY 10012 (212) 925-3721
Foreman is a prominent dancer. For career credentials, consult the portion of this book entitled "Notable Americans by Profession" in the Appendix. Within this portion, the list "Dancers" describes requirements for inclusion in this volume.

FOSTER, JODIE

International Creative Management, 8899 Beverly Boulevard, Los Angeles CA 90048
BORN: 1962, Los Angeles. ACHIEVEMENTS: Emmy, ABC Afterschool Special, Rookie of the Year, 1973; Oscar, Best Actress, The Accused, 1988; Oscar, Best Actress, The Silence of the Lambs, 1991. STUDIED: Yale University, B.A., literature, 1985.
Born Alicia Christian Foster, she has been an actress since the age of 3 and was the original "Coppertone Girl" in suntan lotion ads. At age 8 she made her film debut in *Napoleon and Samantha*, (she still has faint lion-bite scars suffered during the filming of this movie). By the time she was 13 she had already won an Emmy and played the role of a hooker in *Taxi Driver*. Appearing in more than 27 films, she won an Oscar for *The Accused* and *The Silence of the Lambs*. Moving behind the camera, she made her directorial debut with *Little Man Tate*. In 1995 she was nominated for an Academy Award for her role in *Nell*.

FOSTER, DAVID

Gold Horizon Music Corporation, PO Box 80699, Los Angeles, CA 90080 (213) 469-8371
BORN: 1950, Victoria, British Columbia. ACHIEVEMENTS: 12 Grammys; on Billboard's Hot 100 Chart every week from 1984 to 1988; Order of Canada Metal for humanitarian efforts. STUDIED: University of Washington, student.
Pop guru David Foster started his music career on the piano at age 5, and quickly distinguished himself from other children his age. At 13 he enrolled in the University of Washington to study music, and three years later joined the backup band of rock legend Chuck Berry. His career was established when he moved to Los Angeles at age 21. He became a keyboard player working with John Lennon, George Harrison, Barbara Streisand, and Rod Stewart, eventually working his way into producing and writing his own songs. He won the first of his 12 Grammys in 1979 for best rhythm and blues song. Beginning in 1984 his singles recordings appeared on Billboard's Hot 100 chart every week for four years, and most of those weeks saw two or more of his records on the chart simultaneously. A solo album appearing in 1988 found Foster performing his compositions with the Vancouver Symphony Orchestra, including a duet with Olivia Newton-John. He continues to dominate the charts into the 1990s, holding the No. 1 spot for the years 1993 through 1994 more than 25 percent of the time, according to a 1994 report in *Time*. He joined Atlantic Records in 1994 as senior vice president of artists and repertoire with a three-year contract. In 1988 Canada awarded him its Order of Canada medal for his humanitarian efforts in establishing the David Foster Foundation to help families of children in need of organ transplants.

FOWLER, WILLIAM ALFRED

California Institute of Technology, Kellogg 106-38, Pasadena, CA 91125
Fowler is a prominent scientist. For career credentials, consult the portion of this book entitled "Notable Americans by Profession" in the Appendix. Within this portion, the list "Scientists" describes requirements for inclusion in this volume.

FRANCIS, LARRY

Two Civic Center Plaza, El Paso, TX 79901 (915) 541-4000
BORN: 1933, San Antonio. ACHIEVEMENTS: Mayor, El Paso, Texas, founder and president of SYT Corporation. STUDIED: Texas A & M University, B.S., electrical engineering, 1955, M.S., 1956.
Larry Francis served in the U.S. Air Force for three years after graduating from Texas A & M University in 1956. An electrical engineer, Francis founded and served as president of Francis Communications in 1959. In 1964 he started and was president of another business, SYT Corporation. After nearly 30 years of running successful companies, Francis retired from his business commitments in 1987. Francis was chairman of the El Paso Civil Service Commission for eight years and was chairman of the El Paso Sun Carnival Host Committee. He was elected mayor of El Paso in 1993.

FRANCIS, SAM

345 W. Channel Dr., Santa Monica Canyon, Los Angeles, CA 90402
BORN: 1923. ACHIEVEMENTS: Tamarind Fellowship; Dunn International Prize, Tate Gallery; collections: Guggenheim Museum, New York City; Museum of Modern Art, New York City; exhibitions: San Francisco Museum of Art; Albright-Knox Art Gallery, Buffalo, N.Y. STUDIED: University of California, Berkeley; Atelier Fernand Leger.
After prolonged formal study, Sam Francis had his first solo show in 1952 in Paris. This early work consisted of abstract paintings with large areas of color

light in tone. Soon his tones became more vivid, with areas of color bleeding into each other. Perhaps a trip around the world in 1957 influenced his artistic career most. Cool colors, thinly applied and arranged in asymmetrical segments on the canvas, seem to recall the Japanese tradition. During the 1960s he became increasingly occupied with lithography. His Oriental tendencies continue, with the clarity and starkness of form and composition related to the minimalists.

FRANKENTHALER, HELEN

173 E. 94th St., New York, NY 10028
BORN: 1928. ACHIEVEMENTS: First Prize, Biennale de Paris; Garrett Award, Art Institute of Chicago; collections: Whitney Museum of American Art; Metropolitan Museum of Art; exhibitions: Metropolitan Museum of Art; Solomon R. Guggenheim Museum. STUDIED: Bennington College; Art Students League.

After formal training in Cubism, Helen Frankenthaler developed an individual abstract expressionistic style influenced by the work of Arshile Gorky and Vassily Kandinsky. In 1951 she became interested in Jackson Pollock and the transformation of the unconscious into concrete artistic creations. She began to explore color-field combinations and the ways in which their accidental combinations are controlled. Progressing from small areas of color in oil to large areas in acrylic, she has painted on unsized, unprimed canvas, a technique developed from Pollock's method of dripping and staining the paints onto raw canvas. Paint actually soaks into the canvas to create a purely optical image, rather than a three-dimensional form.

FRANKLIN, ARETHA

8450 Linwood St., Detroit, MI 48206
BORN: 1942, Memphis, Tenn. ACHIEVEMENTS: Grammy, Best R&B, Respect, 1967; Grammy, Best R&B Vocal-Female, Respect, 1967; Grammy, Best R&B Vocal-Female, Chain of Fools, 1968; Grammy, Best R&B Vocal-Female, Share Your Love with Me, 1969; Grammy, Best R&B Vocal-Female, Don't Play That Song, 1970; Grammy, Best R&B Vocal-Female, Bridge Over Troubled Water, 1971; Grammy, Best R&B Vocal-Female, Young, Gifted and Black, 1972; Grammy, Best R&B Vocal-Female, Master of Eyes, 1973; Grammy, Best R&B Vocal-Female, Ain't Nothing Like the Real Thing, 1974; Grammy, Best R&B Vocal-Female, Hold On I'm Comin', 1981; Grammy, Best R&B Vocal-Female, Freeway of Love, 1985; Grammy, Best R&B Vocal-Female, Aretha, 1987; Grammy, Best R&B Duo or Group, I Knew You Were Waiting (For Me) (With George Michael), 1987; Grammy Legend Award, 1991.

The "Queen of Soul", Aretha Franklin has been one of the leading names in rhythm and blues music for over 30 years. She began singing at age 14 in the New Bethel Baptist Church choir in Detroit, where her father was the pastor. Her professional career began at age 18 and by the mid-1960s her records were million sellers. Franklin's vocal style was compared to the late gospel singer Mahalia Jackson, and she seemed the perfect choice to star in the Broadway musical *Sing, Mahalia, Sing*, but her fear of flying prevented her from appearing in the show. She has won over 10 Grammy awards, and in 1987, she was inducted into the Rock and Roll Hall of Fame.

FREDA, VINCENT J.

161 Fort Washington Ave., New York, NY 10032
Freda is a prominent physician. For career credentials, consult the portion of this book entitled "Notable Americans by Profession" in the Appendix. Within this portion, the list "Physicians" describes requirements for inclusion in this volume.

FREED, JAMES INGO

I.M. Pei & Partners, 600 Madison Avenue, New York, NY 10022 (212) 751-3122
BORN: 1930. ACHIEVEMENTS: FAIA; American Academy and Institute of Arts and Letters' Brunner Memorial Prize; New York AIA; Medal of Honor Associate, National Academy of Design; notable works: Jacob K. Javits Convention Center, New York City; U.S. Holocaust Memorial Museum, Washington, D.C.; First Bank Place, Minneapolis, Minn. STUDIED: Illinois Institute of Technology.

An urbanist by inclination no less than profession, James Freed enjoys working on large city projects that contribute to the transformation of urban areas. While solving the program needs of users he aims to act in the public interest as well, addressing the unarticulated need of every citizen to live in a meaningful and delightful world. He looks for large or difficult commissions (for example the Holocaust Museum) whose program requirements and contradictory constituencies commonly seem too unwieldy to be resolved "architecturally." Convention centers, a recent focus, require vast service, circulation and parking facilities in such controlled circumstances that to non-conventioneers they become "black boxes"—isolated across asphalt acres. His Los Angeles Convention Center is designed to enrich the experience of passers-by no less than users by addressing all comers on their own terms. While its pedestrian side is scaled to human contact, many more people experience the Center from the freeway curve in which it is situated. He counter-curves back to the freeway a wall of repetitive lights and canopies, offering a public identity that can be seized and remembered in freeway glances.

FREEDMAN, SANDRA W.

Office of the Mayor, 306 E. Jackson St., Tampa, FL 33602 (813) 223-8251
Freedman is a prominent political leader. For career credentials, consult the portion of this book entitled "Notable Americans by Profession" in the Appendix. Within this portion, the list "Political Leaders" describes requirements for inclusion in this volume.

FRIEDMAN, JANE

Vintage Books, 201 E. 50th St., New York, NY, 10022 (212) 572-2428
ACHIEVEMENTS: Founded Random House Publishing, 1985. STUDIED: New York University, B.A., English, 1967.

Jane Friedman has been an important force in publishing for more than 20 years. She started her publishing career in the publicity department at Knopf Publishing Group in 1967. In 1975, she founded the company's promotion department, expanding the coverage of personal publicity for Knopf authors. Friedman was named vice president and associate publisher in 1980. In 1985 she launched the company into the field of books on tape by founding Random House Publishing. She was promoted to senior vice president of publishing in 1987. Friedman has been publisher of Vintage Books since 1990. She was named executive vice president of the Knopf Publishing Group in 1994.

FRIEDMAN, JEROME ISAAC

Massachusetts Institute of Technology, Department of Physics, 77 Massachusetts Ave., Cambridge, MA 02139
BORN: 1930, Chicago. ACHIEVEMENTS: Nobel Prize in Physics (shared with Henry Way Kendall and Canadian Richard E. Taylor), 1990; Researcher, University of Chicago, Stanford University; Professor, Massachusetts Institute of Technology. STUDIED: University of Chicago.
Until the successful work of Jerome Friedman, and colaureates Henry Way Kendall and Richard E. Taylor, on the subject of quarks, the existence of the half-humorously named subatomic particles was only theoretically believed by physicists. The complexities of the theory were blamed on the failure of scientists to absolutely isolate a quark, on the one hand, and, on the other, actually observing them but believing they were another sort of matter or that they were seen but not recognized at all. Friedman and his cohorts broke through the reams of hypothetical theories on quarks by bombarding hydrogen and heavy hydrogen with a shower of high-energy electrons, at last revealing the existence of quarks. The experiment, however, opened another pandora's box of theories: first as to how many quarks there are, and second as to how they react with other elements within the nuclei.

FRIEDMAN, MILTON

Stanford University, Hoover Institution, Stanford, CA 94305
BORN: 1912, New York City. ACHIEVEMENTS: Nobel Prize in Economic Science, 1976; John Bates Clark Medal of the American Economic Association, 1951; Grand Cordon of the 1st Class Order of the Rising Sun, Japan; Presidential Medal of Freedom, and various other medals and awards. STUDIED: Rutgers University; University of Chicago; Columbia University.
That changes in a nation's money supply determine the direction of its economy is the doctrine of monetarists, and Friedman is their high priest. The only living economist probably everybody has heard about, through his columns in news magazines and appearances on television, as well as economic adviser to Barry Goldwater and former President Richard Nixon. Friedman does not worry about big business or unemployment, but only about competitive firms ruled by the market. Since the firms are competitive and ruled impersonally by market forces, he believes that limiting bank lending and money creation forces businesses to reduce prices or rein in price increases. Friedman's writings have grown monumentally since his doctoral dissertation, *Income of Independent Professional*

Practice (with Simon Kuznets) in 1946. Six years later, he won the prestigious John Bates Clark Medal, and with another book the same year, *A Theory of the Consumption Function*, established a national reputation at age 39. A spate of books followed, showing his genius for teaching applied economics, as he discussed a volunteer army, a negative income tax, educational vouchers and the like. In 1963 came the monumental *Monetary History of the United States*, with A.J. Schwartz. The book not only caused a sensation by blaming the Great Depression of the 1930s on the Federal Reserve System for bungling monetary policies, but helped win him the Nobel Prize for his work in analyzing U.S. consumption, for his monetary history and theory, and for demonstrating the complexity of money stabilization policies.

FRIEDMAN, THOMAS L.

The *New York Times*, 229 West 43rd St., NY 10036 (212) 556-1234
BORN: 1953. ACHIEVEMENTS: Pulitzer Prize 1983, 1988; National Book Award for Nonfiction; Marine Corps Historical Foundation Award; George Polk Award; Livingston Award for Young Journalists; Overseas Press Club Award for Best Business Reporting from Abroad. STUDIED: Brandeis University, B.A., Mediterranean studies; Oxford University, M.A., modern Middle East studies; American University, Cairo, student; Hebrew University, Jerusalem, student.
Two-time Pulitzer Prize winner Thomas Friedman joined the *New York Times* in 1981 as a business reporter. Qualified by his education in Middle East affairs and his former work with United Press International in London and Beirut, he became Beirut bureau chief of the paper just one year later. For the next two years he covered the hot spots in Lebanon, including the American Embassy and Marine bombings and the Israeli withdrawal from Beirut. Sent to Israel as bureau chief, he remained for four years before taking a leave of absence to write a book, *From Beirut to Jerusalem*, published in 1989, which won the National Book Award for nonfiction that year. Returning to the *Times*, he became chief diplomatic correspondent, chief White House correspondent, and chief economic correspondent. In 1994, the *Times* appointed him foreign affairs columnist, in charge of the oldest-running column on the op-ed page, which, since its inception, has included the bylines of Anne O'Hare McCormick, Cyrus Sulzberger, Flora Lewis, and Leslie H. Gelb, who left the paper in 1993.

FRIST, BILL

363 Russell Senate Office Building, Washington, DC 20510-4201 (202) 224-3344
BORN: 1952, Nashville, Tenn. ACHIEVEMENTS: Wilson Scholar, 1974; Distinguished Service Award, Tennessee Medical Association, 1992. STUDIED: Princeton University, 1974; Harvard Medical School, 1978.
An accomplished surgeon, Bill Frist is an expert in the practice of heart and lung transplants. He established the Vanderbilt Transplant Center at the Vanderbilt University Medical Center in 1986 and has published more than 100 articles and abstracts on medical re

FROST, MARTIN

2459 Rayburn Office Building, Washington, DC 20515
(202) 225-3605

BORN: 1942, Glendale, Calif. ACHIEVEMENTS: California legislator (Democrat). U.S. representative, 1979-present. STUDIED: University of Missouri, B.A., B.J., 1964; Georgetown University, J.D., 1970.

Elected to the U.S. House of Representatives in 1978, Martin Frost has long been concerned with national defense issues. He headed a special House task force to explore conversion of defense capabilities to peacetime applications and was the primary author of defense conversion legislation passed by the House in 1992. Frost has chaired a number other Democratic groups, including the party's redistricting organization from 1991 to 1994, and he is head of the Democratic Congressional Campaign Committee, making him the highest ranking Texan in the party leadership. He was a journalist in Texas before obtaining his law degree from Georgetown University. He practiced law in Dallas before running for Congress in 1978.

FULGHUM, ROBERT

c/o Villard (Random House Inc.), 201 East 50th St., New York, NY 10022 (212) 751-2600

BORN: 1937. ACHIEVEMENTS: Unitarian minister; author of All I Really Need to Know I Learned in Kindergarten, Villard Books, 1988. STUDIED: Attended the University of Colorado; Baylor University, B.A., 1957.

Author Robert Fulghum.

Robert Fulghum grew up in Waco, Texas. His childhood was marked by parents who fought frequently at home, and by his Southern Baptist upbringing. He attended the University of Colorado for two years, but had to return home during his junior year after his father became ill and could no longer afford the tuition. Fulghum graduated from Baylor University in 1957. He pursued a career as a Unitarian minister and was ordained in 1961. Fulghum is best know as the author of a series of books containing personal essays and homilies. His first book, *All I Really Need to Know I Learned in Kindergarten*, became a surprise best seller. When he published *It Was on Fire When I Lay Down on It*, Fulghum became the first author to have both the number one and two spots on the best-seller lists simultaneously.

FULLER, H. LAURANCE

Amoco Corporation, 200 Randolph Dr., #87703, Chicago, IL 60680 (312) 856-6111

Fuller is a prominent business leader and Chairman and CEO of Amoco Corporation, the parent company of Standard Oil.

FULLER, CHARLES H., JR.

William Morris Agency, 1350 Avenue of the Americas, New York, NY 10019

BORN: 1939, Philadelphia. ACHIEVEMENTS: Pulitzer Prize, A Soldier's Play, 1982. STUDIED: Villanova University, 1956-1958; La Salle College, 1965-1967.

A former bank loan collector and city housing inspector in his native Philadelphia, Charles Fuller's plays are dominated by self-destructive characters struggling within an environment of racism. He won the Pulitzer Prize for his 1982 drama *A Soldiers' Play*, which was based on an actual a murder in the segregated U.S. Army of World War II. His other plays include *The Brownsville Raid*, 1976; *Zooman and the Sign*, 1980; *We*, 1988; and *Jonquil*, 1990. He also wrote the screenplay for the film *A Soldier's Story*, 1984.

FULLERTON, CHARLES GORDAN

NASA/DFRF/ODF, Box 273, Edwards, CA 93523

BORN: 1936, Rochester, N.Y. ACHIEVEMENTS: Colonel, USAF; pilot of the STS-3, 1982 mission; commander of STS 51-F, 1985 mission. STUDIED: California Institute of Technology, B.S. mechanical engineering, 1957; California Institute of Technology, M.S. mechanical engineering, 1958.

Originally selected for the MOL program, Fullerton transferred to the NASA astronaut program in 1969. He participated in the shuttle landing test, and was the pilot of STS-3, the third shuttle test flight, and commander of the STS 51-F. After resigning from the astronaut program, he worked as a research pilot at NASA's Dryden Flight Research facility at Edwards Air Force Base in California.

GAINES, WILLIAM C.

The Chicago Tribune, 435 N. Michigan Ave., Chicago, IL 60611-4022 (312) 222-3232

Gaines is a prominent journalist. For career credentials, consult the portion of this book entitled "Notable Americans by Profession" in the Appendix. Within this portion, the list "Journalists" describes requirements for inclusion in this volume.

GAINES, BOYD

J. Michael Bloom and Associates, 9200 Sunset Blvd., #710, Los Angeles, CA 90069
BORN: 1953, Atlanta. ACHIEVEMENTS: Theatre World Award, A Month in the Country, 1980. STUDIED: Juilliard School.

Boyd Gaines has been acting professionally since the late 1970s. His off-Broadway debut was as Melchior Gabor in *Spring Awakening*, which played in 1978 at the New York Shakespeare Festival. Gaines appeared in numerous plays during the early 1980s, including: *A Month in the Country*, in 1980, and *Oliver Oliver*, in 1984. His movie career began with the film, *Fame*, in which he played Michael in 1980. Gaines has also appeared in the films, *Porky's*, in 1982, and *The Sure Thing*, in 1985. Gaines' television career began in 1981, playing Mark Royer on the series, *One Day At a Time*, a role he continued until 1984. He next played the part of Chris Bradford on the mini-series *Evergreen*, in 1985, and has continued to make regular appearances in television and movies.

GAJDUSEK, DANIEL CARELTON

National Institute of Health, Bethesda, MD 20205
BORN: 1923, Yonkers, N.Y. ACHIEVEMENTS: Nobel Prize in Physiology or Medicine (shared with Baruch Samuel Blumberg); E. Meade Johnson Award, American Academy of Pediatrics; Superior Service Award, National Institutes of Health; Distinguished Service Award, Department of Health, Education, and Welfare; Profesor Lucian Dautrebande Prize, Belgium; Cotzias Prize, American Academy of Neurology. STUDIED: University of Rochester; Harvard University.

Research into how and why people of different backgrounds respond differently to disease led Daniel Gajdusek and Baruch Blumberg to multiple discoveries relating to the mechanisms involved in the origin and spread of infectious diseases and ultimately to a Nobel Prize. Specifically, the pair discovered a substance in the blood that indicated the presence of hepatitis B, the more virulent of the two forms of hepatitis. The knowledge gained became the basis for screening out "B" carriers among blood donors and for vaccine work.

GALLAGHER, DENNIS

Magnavox, Nav-Com 1313 Production Rd., Fort Wayne, IN 46808 (219) 429-6000
ACHIEVEMENTS: Directed development of the MagnaPhone satellite telephone.

Reporters roaming the Iraqi desert during the Persian Gulf War used Dennis Gallagher's innovation to call their home offices. Expedition leaders at the North Pole used it to call for emergency help. Gallagher is director of advanced development at Magnavox, Nav-Com. His innovation, the MagnaPhone satellite telephone, allows phone calling from virtually any location on the planet. Complete with a compact satellite dish, the MagnaPhone is the most compact and portable satellite telephone ever made, and weighs 47 pounds.

GALLO, ROBERT CHARLES

U.S. Public Health Service, Building 37, 9000 Rockville Pike, Bethesda, MD 20892
BORN: 1937, Waterbury, Conn. ACHIEVEMENTS: Albert Lasker Award (with Luc Montagnier) for discovery of HIV virus. STUDIED: Jefferson Medical College, Philadelphia, D.M.S; 12 honorary degrees from universities in the U.S. and abroad.

In a 1984 paper, Gallo claimed to have discovered the HIV virus, and developed a test to detect the AIDS virus in the blood system. Two years later, he shared the prestigious Lasker Award for the discovery with French researcher Luc Montagnier, who claimed that he and his staff at the Pasteur Institute in Paris first discovered the virus and the test. A compromise between them was reached in 1987 which settled the matter until 1993, when a medical review committee found Gallo's promotion of himself in the dispute "scientific misconduct." Gallo continues to disagree with the committee's findings. Earlier, he had won his first Lasker Award for identifying the first retrovirus found in humans, and linked it to leukemia, a disease that had caused his sister's death in childhood.

GANDHI, HAREN

Ford Motor Company, American Rd., Dearborn, MI 48121 (313) 322-3000
ACHIEVEMENTS: Developed palladium-based catalytic converter.

Haren Gandhi revolutionized the technology of automotive catalytic converters. Catalytic converters transform carbon monoxide and other polluting auto emissions into less harmful compounds. The process originally used platinum to catalyze the chemical reactions in the converters. However platinum is only available from South Africa. Cleaner and cheaper catalytic converters for autos finally were achieved in 1990 when Gandhi developed a system that uses palladium instead of platinum. Not only is Gandhi's palladium converter more efficient than platinum converters, but the metal is widely available in the United States. Ford has used Gandhi's converter in all its new cars and trucks since 1993.

GANELLIN, DR. CHARON ROBIN

NCIPLA, Suite 203, 2001 Jefferson Davis Hwy., Arlington, VA 22202 (703) 415-0780
BORN: 1934, London. ACHIEVEMENTS: Invented antiulcer compounds and compositions; inducted into the National Inventors Hall of Fame, 1990; honored by United Kingdom Royal Society of Chemistry; American Chemical Society; La Societe de Chimie Therapeutique-France; Sociedad Espanola de Quimca Therapeutica-Spain. STUDIED: Queen Mary College, chemistry; M.I.T.

A professor of medicinal chemistry at University College London, Dr. Ganellin also served as director of the

Upjohn European Discovery Unit. Dr Ganellin and Drs. Durant and Emmett discovered the H2 receptor class of drugs. This work was done in collaboration with Sir James Black, a Nobel Laureate biologist. The most important discovery was cietidine (Tagamet), which inhibits the production of stomach acid. The drug cietidine is listed by the World Health Organization as one of the world's most essential drugs because it can heal stomach ulcers without the need for surgery. Dr. Ganellin is also co-author on over 120 scientific publications, and is listed as co-inventor on over 100 U.S. patents.

GARABEDIAN, CHARLES

c/o Ruth S. Schaffner Gallery, 128 W. Ortega St., Santa Barbara, CA 93101
BORN: 1924. ACHIEVEMENTS: NEA Fellowship; Guggenheim Fellowship; exhibitions: Whitney Museum, N.Y.; Rose Art Museum, Waltham, Mass. STUDIED: University of California, Santa Barbara; University of South Carolina.
Unswayed by current styles, Charles Garabedian employs a variety of media in innovative ways, including combinations of paper collage, watercolor, drawing and colored resins poured and hardened directly on the surface. His narrative works often suggest scenes of violence or eroticism, heightened by a melodramatic mood. Although his approach has gone through many changes, he has always dealt in some way with the figure and with the theme of freedom: the struggle to obtain it, what it means to possess it, and its limitations. In 1978 he began *Prehistoric Figures*, a series lasting several years, characterized by primitive-looking figures in enigmatic landscapes and similar to the earlier *Islands No.2*.

GARDNER, JOHN W.

Noise Cancellation Technologies, 800 Summer St., Stamford, CT 06901-1023 (203) 961-0500
Gardner is a prominent inventor. For career credentials, consult the portion of this book entitled "Notable Americans by Profession" in the Appendix. Within this portion, the list "Inventors" describes requirements for inclusion in this volume.

GARDNER, JOHN WILLIAM

Stanford University School of Business, Stanford, CA 94305
BORN: 1912, Los Angeles. ACHIEVEMENTS: President of Carnegie Corp. STUDIED: Stanford University, B.A., sociology; University of California, Ph.D.; honorary degrees from many colleges.
John Gardner was president of the Carnegie Corporation, the Carnegie Foundation for the Advancement of Teaching, and U.S. secretary of health, education, and welfare over a period of 14 years from 1955 to 1969. In those positions Gardner exerted a compelling force on the teaching of mathematics, on civil rights, and on children's television. Since then he has founded the citizens' lobby Common Ground, and a volunteer coalition called Independent Sector.

GARTH, MIDI

178 5th Avenue, New York, NY (10010) (212) 675-3795
Garth is a prominent dancer. For career credentials, consult the portion of this book entitled "Notable Americans by Profession" in the Appendix. Within this portion, the list "Dancers" describes requirements for inclusion in this volume.

GATES, BILL

One Microsoft Way, Redmond WA. 98052 (206) 882-8080
BORN: 1955, Seattle. ACHIEVEMENTS: Founder, Microsoft Corporation; created the MS-DOS operating system for the personal computer. STUDIED: Attended Harvard University.
Bill Gates showed an affinity for computer programming as early as the seventh grade. He wrote programs for TRW, in Vancouver, Wash., by his senior year in high school. At 17, Gates entered Harvard University, but he later dropped out to develop a version of the BASIC programming language for the MIT's Altair computer. This work later led to the development of the MS-DOS operating system, which was selected by IBM to run the IBM personal computer in 1981. Gates next strategic move was to agree to develop software for the Apple Macintosh computer before it was released. The Microsoft Corporation, which Gates founded, now develops and sells software for nearly every computer application imaginable. Gates is consistently acknowledged as one of the wealthiest men in the United States.

GATES, HENRY LOUIS JR.

Harvard University, Department of AfroAmerican Studies, 1430 Massachusetts Ave., Cambridge, MA 02138
BORN: 1950, Keyser, W. Va. STUDIED: Yale University, B.A. summa cum laude, education; Cambridge University, England, Ph.D., education; many honorary degrees.
Henry Gates has unearthed important African American texts, many from the slavery period, and compiled and edited them. He has also written and lectured on important issues regarding African Americans and their relations with the larger American society. He was the first African American to receive a doctorate from Cambridge University in England.

GAUGER, DAN

Bose Corporation, The Mountain, Framingham, MA 01701 (508) 879-7330
Gauger is a prominent inventor. For career credentials, consult the portion of this book entitled "Notable Americans by Profession" in the Appendix. Within this portion, the list "Inventors" describes requirements for inclusion in this volume.

GAULT, STANLEY CARLETON

Goodyear Tire & Rubber Company, 1144 E. Market St., Akron, OH 443160
BORN: 1926, Wooster, Ohio. ACHIEVEMENTS: CEO of Rubbermaid, Inc. and Goodyear Tire & Rubber Co. STUDIED: College of Wooster, B.A., business administration.

Stanley Gault instituted a major management shakeup and rigorous quality controls during the years 1980 to 1991, when he chaired the board and was chief executive officer of Rubbermaid, Inc. The shakeup would make the company a market leader. Previously, he specialized in consumer products and major appliances at General Electric, a firm he remained with for 31 years. In 1991 he took over as CEO of Goodyear Tire & Rubber Company after a controversial raid on the company by British financier Sir James Goldsmith five years before. When Goldsmith abandoned the fighting by accepting a $94 million payoff, the company was on the ropes. Gault's appointment signaled to the financial community that Goodyear was back on the way up.

GEHRY, FRANK O.

Frank O. Gehry and Associates, 11 Brooks Avenue, Venice, CA 90291 (213) 392-9771
BORN: 1929. ACHIEVEMENTS: FAIA; Brunner Memorial Prize; notable works: The Temporary Contemporary (Museum of Contemporary Art), Los Angeles; California Aerospace Museum, Los Angeles; Frances Howard Goldwyn Regional Branch Library, Hollywood, Calif. STUDIED: Harvard University.

Frank Gehry's approach to design is atypical. Ideas often result from the adaptation of building materials to cost constraints. For example, he has used materials which were not generally considered acceptable as serious design elements, such as corrugated iron, chain-link fence, asbestos shingles, and raw plywood,

Microsoft founder Bill Gates.

which he has left exposed. Unusual materials are also used for creating furniture from corrugated cardboard, and decorative lamps from broken chips of plastic laminate. Notable buildings include his own house, an ordinary bungalow surrounded by another house made of corrugated metal, plywood and glass. The Loyola Law School features a plaza defined by small structures variously clad in stucco, metal and prefinished "finn-loy" plywood, set against a three-story yellow stucco classroom building as a backdrop. The California Aerospace Museum is an 80-foot high building, characterized by a plain stucco box juxtaposed against a metal polygon joined by a wedge-shaped clerestory above, with an F-104 Starfighter thrusting upward on the facade. "The extreme end of unorthodoxy," is a term which has been applied to his unique approach to design, form, and especially to materials, be they "cheapskate," as one critic coined them, or very opulent when appropriate.

GELLMANN, MURRAY

California Institute of Technology, Department of Physics, Pasadena, CA 91125
BORN: 1929, New York City. ACHIEVEMENTS: Nobel Prize in Physics, 1969; Dannie Heineman Prize, American Physical Society and American Institute of Physics; Franklin Medal, Franklin Institute; Research Corporation Award. STUDIED: Yale University; Massachusetts Institute of Technology

Murray Gellmann's chase after the elusive quark began in 1963, when he and fellow physicist George Zweig formulated the concept to explain the wealth of particles then being discovered by particles researchers. He named the concept "quark," referring to a sentence in James Joyce's work *Finnegan's Wake*: Joyce's offbeat phrase "Three quarks for Muster Mark" set the tone for the offbeat names later given to hypothetical quarks as theories about them advanced: "up quarks, down quarks, strange quarks, charmed quarks, top quarks, and bottom quarks." Gell-mann's theoretical work in attempting to classify the mounting particle discoveries and their interactions—work which would lead to many other discoveries besides quarks—brought him the Nobel Prize and also the distinction of being one of the few physicist Nobel winners honored without the help of a colaureate.

GEORGES, JOHN A.

International Paper Co., 2 Manhattanville Rd., Purchase, NY 10577 (914) 397-1500

Georges is a prominent business leader. For career credentials, consult the portion of this book entitled "Notable Americans by Profession" in the Appendix. Within this portion, the list "Business Leaders" describes requirements for inclusion in this volume.

GEPHARDT, RICHARD A.

1432 Longworth Office Building, Washington, DC 20515 (202) 225-2671

BORN: 1941, St. Louis, Mo. ACHIEVEMENTS: Missouri legislator (Democrat). U.S. representative, 1977-present; House majority leader, 1989-94; House Democratic leader, 1995-. STUDIED: Northwestern University, B.A., 1962; University of Michigan, J.D., 1965.

As Democratic Leader, Richard Gephardt is the highest-ranking member of the party in the U.S. House of Representatives. From 1989 to 1994, he served as majority leader in the House and was the party's chief floor strategist and spokesman on legislative issues. Before that, he was chairman of the House Democratic Caucus and was a candidate for the party's presidential nomination in 1988. Gephardt is known for championing economic, trade and social legislation designed to improve the economic situation of working families. Prior to his election to Congress, in 1976, he served two terms as a St. Louis alderman.

GEHRELS, NEIL

NASA, L.B. Johnson Space Center, Houston, TX 77058

Gehrels is a prominent inventor. For career credentials, consult the portion of this book entitled "Notable Americans by Profession" in the Appendix. Within this portion, the list "" describes requirements for inclusion in this volume.

GERINGER, JIM

State Capitol Building, Cheyenne, WY 82002 (307) 777-7434

BORN: 1944, Wheatland, Wy. STUDIED: Kansas State University, B.S., mechanical engineering.

A career turnaround in 1977 carried Jim Gehringer to the Wyoming governor's chair in 1994. Becoming an Air Force officer after graduating from college, and assigned to space development programs in California,

he worked with space boosters, reconnaissance satellites, and on the Global Positioning Satellite System. In 1977 he and his wife, Sherrie, decided California was no place to raise a family, and they moved back to his home state. A fortuitous move as it turned out, for in 10 years they owned enough land for sheep and cattle grazing. In the interim he had been elected to the legislature, where he served six years each in the House and Senate. Among committees he worked with were Appropriations, Management Audit, and Judiciary, all of which made him a prime candidate to lead the state. He won the job in the 1994 Republican national takeover.

GERMAN, WILLIAM

San Francisco Chronicle, 901 Mission St., San Francisco, CA 94103-2905 (415) 777-1111

BORN: 1951, Brooklyn, N.Y. ACHIEVEMENTS: Fellow, Nieman Foundation. STUDIED: Brooklyn College, B.A.; Columbia University, M.A., journalism.

A 45-year veteran newspaperman, William German is the editor of the *San Francisco Chronicle*, with which he has been associated since entering the field in 1940. Starting as a copyboy, German moved up to reporter, assistant foreign editor, and copy desk chief. He served in the U.S. Army during World War II. After the war, he returned to the paper as news editor. During a newspaper strike in 1968, German helped establish a newspaper of the air, which pioneered the formats for many public service television news programs. In 1969 he was a consultant to the Ford Foundation on television news projects. German became editor of the *Chronicle* in 1993.

GERSTEN, BERNARD

Omni Zoetrope, 916 Kearny St., San Francisco, CA 94133

Gersten is a prominent dramatic artist. For career credentials, consult the portion of this book entitled "Notable Americans by Profession" in the Appendix. Within this portion, the list "Dramatic Artists" describes requirements for inclusion in this volume.

GERSTNER, LOUIS VINCENT

International Business Machines, Old Orchard Rd., Armonk, NY 10504 (914) 765-1900

BORN: 1941, Mineola, N.Y. STUDIED: Dartmouth College, B.A., engineering; Harvard University, M.A., engineering.

Anecdotes abound about the blue-collar worker who took over the top job at IBM in 1993 and brought the nearly ruined company back into the profit column one year later. In 1974 Louis Gerstner lost the tips of two fingers on his right hand in a lawnmower accident. He returned to work as usual the next day. Though known as a workaholic, when his two children, now collegians, were in grade school, he would leave work early on the days their report cards came out. On the day of his appointment as chief executive at white-shirted IBM, he appeared at work dressed in a blue shirt. Not long after he stunned the entrenched corporate leaders by abolishing the company's stiff dress code in favor of casual clothes for employees. He would further stun them by the drastic actions he took at once to return the company to the black. These included shaking up the company's top-heavy old guard who had precipitated IBM's decline by stubbornly relying on its mainframes and ignoring the boom in smaller and cheaper personal computers. He cut the workforce by about 86,000 and eliminated the company's lifetime employment practice. And he also dissolved the company's "Federation of Businesses," a plan which gave each of its businesses greater autonomy but which proved costly because each employed separate financial departments run by highly paid executives. The recovery in a year was remarkable, with a reported profit of $12.9 billion in 1994, against a $4.9 billion loss in 1992.

GERT, BERNARD

Dartmouth College, Hanover, NH 03755-3592 (603) 646-2022
BORN: 1934, Cincinnati. ACHIEVEMENTS: Fellow, National Endowment for the Humanities; National Endowment for the Humanities-National Science Foundation Sustained Development Award; Fulbright Grant, Israel; Fulbright Grant, Argentina; Principal Investigator, National Institutes of Health for "Ethical Issues Arising From the Human Genome Project" (inheritable traits of an organism). STUDIED: University of Cincinnati, B.A.; Cornell University, Ph.D, philosophy.
Bernard Gert has taught at Dartmouth College for 36 years. He presently is Eunice and Julian Cohen Professor for the study of Ethics and Human Values and Adjunct Professor of Psychiatry at Dartmouth Medical School. He has written two books, *The Moral Rules: A New Rational Foundation for Morality*, which was translated into German, and *Morality: A New Justification of the Moral Rules*. Gert co-authored, With Charles M. Culver, *Philosophy in Medicine: Conceptual and Ethical Issues In Medicine and Psychiatry*, which was translated into Japanese. This latter work led to Gert's appointment as investigator for the National Institutes of Health for a study of ethical issues in genetics.

GETTY, ESTELLE

Harris & Goldberg Talent Agency, 2121 Ave. of the Americas, Los Angeles, CA 90067
BORN: 1923, New York City. ACHIEVEMENTS: Golden Globe Award, Best Actress in a Comedy, The Golden Girls. STUDIED: New School for Social Research.
Estelle Getty is best known for her portrayal of Sophia Petrillo on the television series, *The Golden Girls*. She began her acting career on the Borscht Belt and also worked with the Yiddish Theatre. Her off-Broadway debut was in 1971 in the play, *The Divorce of Judy and Jane*. Getty has worked actively in the theater, with parts in many stage classics, including: *Arsenic and Old Lace, Glass Menagerie,* and *Death of a Salesman*. She began appearing in movies in the early 1980s. Some of her film credits include: *Tootsie*, in 1982,

Mask, in 1984, and *Mannequin*, in 1987. Besides *The Golden Girls*, Getty has appeared on many television shows and movies, among them: *Cagney and Lacey, One of the Boys,* and *Fantasy Island*.

GIAEVER, IVAR

Rensselaer Polytechnic Institute, Physics Department, Troy, NY 12180
BORN: 1929, Bergen, Norway. ACHIEVEMENTS: Nobel Prize in Physics (shared with Leo Esaki, Japan, and Brian D. Josephson, England), 1973; Oliver E. Buckley Prize, American Physical Society; Guggenheim Fellow; V.K. Zworykin Award, National Academy of Engineering. STUDIED: Norwegian Institute of Technology; Rensselaer Polytechnical Institute.
Ivar Giaever and his co-recipients of the Nobel Prize were cited for developing theories that have advanced and expanded the field of microelectronics. Giaever and Esaki's contribution dealt with their work on tunneling effects in semi-and superconductors, an effect occurring when normal electrons "tunnel through" theoretically insurmountable energy barriers. Their research in the late 1950s laid the foundation for Josephson, then a graduate student at Cambridge University, to predict in 1962 what is now termed the Josephson Effect, that supernormal electrons also could tunnel. The Josephson Effect, proven in laboratory experiments within a short time after Josephson's paper appeared, permits sensitive measurements of basic physical phenomena and has been widely applied in the computer and scientific instrument fields.

GIBBONS, SAM

U.S. House of Representatives, 2204 RHOB, Washington, DC 20515-0911 (202) 225-2276
Gibbons is a prominent political leader. For career credentials, consult the portion of this book entitled "Notable Americans by Profession" in the Appendix. Within this portion, the list "Political Leaders" describes requirements for inclusion in this volume.

GIBBONS, FRED

3165 Kifer Rd., Box 54983, Santa Clara, CA 95056 (408) 986-8000
BORN: Boston. ACHIEVEMENTS: Co-founder, Software Publishing Corporation. STUDIED: University of Michigan, computer science; Harvard University.
Fred Gibbons programmed his business education with the same care and skill used to craft a well-behaved, error-free, computer program. He attended the University of Michigan, where he received two degrees, one in the computer science field. He then worked at a small computer company to gain small business experience, while also enrolled in the Harvard Business School. Next, he went to work for the Hewlett-Packard Company, advancing to become one of their youngest marketing managers. At Hewlett-Packard, he teamed up with two co-workers, John Page and Janelle Bedke, to produce a database pro-

gram. Gibbons and Page worked at Hewlett-Packard while supporting Bedke, who wrote most of the new software program. The program was an immediate success, and the three co-workers were able to launch their own company, the Software Publishing Corporation.

GIBSON, CHARLES

Good Morning America, 77 West 66th Street, New York, NY 10023 (212) 456-7777
BORN: Evanston, IL. ACHIEVEMENTS: John Maclean Fellowship, 1992 (from Princeton University); Fellow, National Endowment for the Humanities, 1973. STUDIED: Princeton University
Gibson is the current co-host of *Good Morning America* and occasionally substitutes for Ted Koppel on *Nightline* as well as serving as a reporter on *ABC's World News Tonight With Peter Jennings*. In 1966 he entered broadcasting as a Washington producer for the RKO Network. He has also covered the Democratic handling of President Reagan's legislative agenda, a major investigation of the CIA, and Gerald Ford's 1976 Presidential campaign. Regarded as one of television's premier interviewers, he has interviewed Boris Yeltsin, Neslon Mandela, Yasir Arafat, President Clinton and other notables. Prior to joining ABC News in 1975, he worked as an anchor and a news director, and, as a reporter for Television News, Inc., where he covered the Nixon resignation. He has been with *GMA* since 1987.

GIBSON, ("HOOT") ROBERT LEE

L.B. Johnson Space Center, Astronaut Office, Houston, TX 77058 (713) 483-0123.
BORN: 1946, Cooperstown, N.Y. ACHIEVEMENTS: Space missions: STS-27 and STS-47 space shuttle missions (commander); Awards: Top Gun (Naval Fighter Weapons School). STUDIED: California Polytechnic State University, B.S., aeronautical engineering, U.S. Naval Test Pilot School; Naval Fighter Weapons School.
Robert Gibson entered the U.S. Navy in 1969 and became a combat pilot in the Vietnam War. After a tour of duty in Southeast Asia he instructed pilots in F-14 fighter aircraft. NASA selected him as an astronaut in 1978 for the Space Shuttle program. His first space flight was as commander of the STS-27 space shuttle mission which carried a secret military satellite into orbit aboard the shuttle *Atlantis*. Gibson was suspended from flying for one year after colliding with another aircraft during formation aerobatic flight. After his reinstatement, he served as commander of the STS-47 space shuttle mission with Spacelab J in cargo. In 1992 NASA promoted him to chief of the Astronaut Office.

GIFFORD, FRANK NEWTON

ABC-TV Sports Monday Night Football, 47 W. 66th St., New York, NY 10023
BORN: 1930, Santa Monica, Calif. ACHIEVEMENTS: Emmy award, Outstanding Sports Personality, 1977; National Football Foundation Hall of Fame, 1975; Pro Football Hall of Fame, 1977. STUDIED: Bakersfield Junior College, 1948-49; University of Southern California, B.A., 1952.
Gifford has been coming into American homes on Monday night as one of the commentators on *ABC Monday Night Football* for over 20 years. A former football player for the New York Jets from 1952 until 1965, his sports casting career spans four decades. Many consider Gifford to be the quintessential player-turned-journalist because of his in-depth commentary in which he combines the psychology of the on-field players and the inquisitiveness of the fans. He worked as a sports reporter for CBS Radio in New York from 1957 until 1959, then as the NFL pre-game host on CBS-TV, and from 1962 until 1971, he was the sports reporter on WCBS-TV in New York. In 1971 he switched to ABC, and was a sports correspondent and a correspondent for *Eyewitness News* before becoming an announcer on *Monday Night Football*. Gifford has also written several books, including: *Frank Gifford's NFL-AFL Football Guide*, 1968; *Frank Gifford's Football Guide Book*, 1966 (with Charles Mangel); *Gifford on Coverage*, 1976 (with Harry Waters Jr.); and *Gifford: The Whole Ten Yards*, 1993.

GILBERT, WALTER

The Biology Labs, 16 Divinity Ave., Cambridge, MA 02138
BORN: 1932, Boston. ACHIEVEMENTS: Nobel Prize in Chemistry (shared with Paul Berg, U.S., and Frederick Sanger, England), 1980; U.S. Steel Foundation Award, National Academy of Sciences; Ledlie Prize, Harvard University; Warren Triennial Prize, Massachusetts General Hospital; Louis and Bert Friedman Foundation Award, New York Academy of Sciences; Prix Charles Leopold Mayer, Academie des Sciences, France; Louisa Gross Horowitz Prize, Columbia University; Gairdner Prize; Albert Lasker Basic Science Award. STUDIED: Harvard University; Cambridge University, England.
One of the leaders in studying the molecular biology of nucleic acids, Walter Gilbert shared the Nobel Prize in Chemistry with Paul Berg and Frederick Sanger, particularly for their work on recombinant DNA (gene manipulation) and also for development of so called genetic engineering. Gilbert is also noted for his work on subverting a species of bacteria, often diseased, in the large intestines of humans and other animals.

GILES, ROBERT HARTMANN

The *Detroit News*, 615 Lafayette Blvd., Detroit, MI (313) 222-2300
BORN: 1933, Cleveland. AWARDS: Co-recipient Pulitzer Prize for Local Reporting; Scripps-Howard 1st Amendment Award; Nieman Fellow, Harvard University. STUDIED: DePauw University, B.A., journalism; Columbia University, M.S., journalism.
The editor and publisher of The *Detroit News* did his two-year hitch in the U.S. Army after graduation from Columbia. Robert Hartmann spent the next six years as a local reporter with the *Newport News Daily Press* and the *Akron Beacon Journal*. The *Beacon Journal* promoted him to editorial writer in 1963, city editor three years later, managing editor in 1969, and execu-

tive editor in 1973. Three years later he left Akron to become a special lecturer at the University of Kansas School of Journalism. He was a veteran of 29 years in the newspaper business when he joined the *Detroit News* as vice president and executive editor, which led to his current post. The author of *Newsroom Management: A Guide to Theory and Practice* is also president of Media Management Books, Inc.

GILROY, FRANK DANIEL

c/o Dramatists Guild, 234 West 44th St., New York, NY 10036

Gilroy is a prominent dramatic artist. For career credentials, consult the portion of this book entitled "Notable Americans by Profession" in the Appendix. Within this portion, the list "Dramatic Artists" describes requirements for inclusion in this volume.

GINGRICH, (NEWT) NEWTON LEROY

U.S. House of Representatives, 2428 Rayburn Bldg., Washington, D.C., 20515-1006 (202) 225-2800
BORN: 1943, Harrisburg, Pa. ACHIEVEMENTS: Co-author (with Marianne Gingrich) Window of Opportunity. STUDIED: Emory University, B.A., 1965; Tulane University, M.A., 1968, Ph.D. (European history), 1971.

Born in Harrisburg, Pa., Newt Gingrich began his professional

Conductor John Girodano.

career as a college professor. He received a doctorate in European history in 1971 from Tulane University and immediately began teaching at West Georgia College where he remained until 1978 when he was elected to Congress from Georgia's 6th District. Gingrich has been a highly vocal congressman, championing the cause of entrepreneurialism and many conservative topics. He became House Republican whip in 1989 and rose to speaker after Republicans captured a majority of the House in the 1994 elections.

GINSBURG, RUTH BADER

Supreme Court of the United States, One First St. NE, Washington, D.C. 20543 (202) 479-3000

BORN: 1933, Brooklyn, N.Y. ACHIEVEMENTS: Established Women's Rights Project of the American Civil Liberties Union, 1971; co-author, Civil Procedure in Sweden, 1965, and The Swedish Code of Judicial Procedure, 1968; author, Selective Survey of English Language Studies on Scandinavian Law, 1970, and Sex-Based Discrimination, 1974. STUDIED: Cornell University, B.A., 1954; Harvard Law School, 1956-58; Columbia Law School, 1959.

Ruth Bader Ginsburg began her law career in 1959 when she graduated from Columbia Law School. Born in Brooklyn, N.Y., Ginsburg is considered a trailblazer in the field of women's equality. In the 1970s, Ginsburg argued six cases having to do with women's rights before the Supreme Court, winning five. She was an associate professor at Rutgers School of Law from 1966 until 1969, and was a law professor at Columbia Law School from 1972 until 1980. Ginsburg was appointed in 1980 to the U.S. Court of Appeals by President Jimmy Carter. She is considered a prudent, erudite judge whose philosophy ranges from moderate to liberal. Ginsburg was appointed justice of the Supreme Court by President Bill Clinton in 1993 to replace Bryon R. White upon his retirement. She is the second woman to serve on the Supreme Court.

GIORDANO, JOHN

Fort Worth Symphony Orchestra, 4401 Trail Lake Dr., Fort Worth, TX, 76109 (817) 921-2676
BORN: Dunkirk, N.Y. ACHIEVEMENTS: First Western conductor to conduct an all-Chinese program. STUDIED: Royal Conservatory of Brussels, Fulbright Scholar; graduated Texas Christian University.

John Giordano is music director and principal conductor of the Fort Worth Symphony Orchestra and the Fort Worth Chamber Orchestra. He has been music director of the Fort Worth Symphony Orchestra since 1972, and founded the Fort Worth Chamber Orchestra in 1976. Under the direction of Giordano, the orchestra has achieved world-wide acclaim. His orchestra has toured the world, and appeared on television. It also has several recordings out. Giordano has conducted the London Philharmonic, the English Chamber Orchestra, the Belgian National Radio Orchestra, the

Amsterdam Philharmonic, and the Arena di Verona Orchestra, in addition to several other orchestras around the world. In 1980, he conducted the Pan-Asian Symphony, and became the first western conductor to conduct an all-Chinese program. He is currently a member of the Texas Christian University music faculty.

GIULIANI, RUDOLPH W.

Office of the Mayor, New York, NY 10007 (212) 788-3000
BORN: 1944, New York City. ACHIEVEMENTS: Mayor of New York City; associate U.S. attorney general. STUDIED: Manhattan College, A.B.; New York University Law School, J.D., 1968.

Giuliani, a lifelong resident of New York City, graduated from Manhattan College in the Bronx, and New York University Law School. He went to work for the U.S. Attorney for the Southern District of New York in 1970. In 1981 Giuliani was named associate attorney general, the third-highest position in the U.S. Department of Justice, in charge of 30,000 federal employees and a $1 billion budget. He was appointed the U.S. attorney for the Southern District of New York in 1983. He concentrated his efforts on jailing drug dealers, fighting organized crime, government corruption, and white collar crime. Giuliani ran for mayor of New York City in 1989 as an independent candidate. Although he lost, it was by the closest margin since 1905. Giuliani ran for mayor again, and on November 3, 1993 was elected as New York City's 107th mayor.

GLASHOW, SHELDON LEE

Harvard University, Department of Physics, Jefferson Laboratory, Cambridge, MA 02138
BORN: 1932, New York City. ACHIEVEMENTS: Nobel Prize in Physics (shared with Abdus Salam and Steven Weinberg), 1979; J.R.Oppenheimer Memorial Prize; George Ledelie Prize; Catiglione di Silica Prize. STUDIED: Cornell University; Harvard University.

Sheldon Glashow extended the Weinberg-Salam theory on electromagnetic interaction between elementary particles by defining a new characteristic to the unity they discovered between an electromagnetic force and a "weak" nuclear force—a feeble short-range force responsible for radioactive decay in some atomic nuclei. His concept, that both are facets of the same phenomena, a phenomena he named "charm," has been widely used since in work on the quark theory. Their work, however, has turned out to have accomplished only another milestone in the particles chase, which includes discovery of new particles so massive and highly charged that at present they surpass tools available to physicists to measure them.

GLASS, PHILIP

International Production Association, 853 Broadway, Rm. 2120, New York, NY 10003-4703
BORN: 1937, Baltimore. ACHIEVEMENTS: Recipient Broadcast Music Industry Award, 1960; Lado Prize, 1961; Benjamin Award, 1961-62; Young Composer's Award from Ford Foundation, 1964-66; Musical American magazine's Musician of the Year, 1985. STUDIED: University of Chicago, B.A.,

1956; Julliard School of Music, M.S. in composition, 1964; composition student with Nadia Boulanger, Paris, 1964-66.

This avant-garde musician has redefined traditional standards of musical composition. He was formally trained in musical composition, but after working with the Indian musicians Ravi Shankar and Alla Rakha in the 1960s, his interest leaned toward the synthesizing of the musical traditions of the East and West. Glass's music often features rhythmic repetition of short musical patterns that remind one of Indian ragas. His many instrumental compositions include: *Music in 5ths*, 1969, and *Glassworks*, 1982; operas *Satyagraha*, 1980, and *Akhnaten*, 1984; the four-and-a-half hour opera *Einstein on the Beach*, 1976 (with Robert Wilson); and the fifth act of the very large multimedia opera, *Civil Wars*, 1984. In a 1990 collaboration with poet Allen Ginsburg, Glass wrote the opera *Hydrogen Jukebox*, a multimedia exploration of the 1980s.

GLASSMAN, JAMES KENNETH

1150 15th St., NE, Washington, DC 20037
BORN: 1947, Washington, D.C. STUDIED: Harvard University, B.A., journalism.

The current *Washington Post* financial columnist has occupied many chairs in his 24 years of moving around the Fourth Estate. After Harvard, James Glassman edited and published the Provincetown, Mass., *Advocate* for two years, from 1971 to 1972. In New Orleans he was editor-in-chief and executive publisher of *Figaro* for six years, then executive editor of the *Washington Magazine* for two years. All told, he occupied the editor or publisher's chairs at three papers in 10 years. In the 1980s he was publisher of the *New Republic* for three years, president of the *Atlantic* magazine for two years, executive vice president of *U.S. News & World Report* for two years, and wound up the decade as editor-in-chief of *Roll Call*, a Washington, D.C., magazine, where he remained until 1993. He took on the *Post* job in 1993, where, in addition to being a financial columnist, he also is a contributing editor.

GLEASON, JOANNA

Agency for the Performing Arts, 888 Seventh Ave., New York, NY 10106
BORN: 1950, Toronto. ACHIEVEMENTS: Antoinette Perry Award, Best Featured Actress in a Musical, Into the Woods, 1988. STUDIED: University of California, Los Angeles.

Joanna Gleason has been performing since the late 1970s. The daughter of the television personality, Monty Hall, and his wife, Marilyn (Plottel) Hall, who is an actress, writer and producer, Gleason made her Broadway debut as Monica in *I Love My Wife*, in 1977. She played Morgan Winslow on the television series *Hello, Larry* from 1979 until 1980, and acted in several pilots and television movies. Gleason has appeared in two movies: *Heartburn*, in 1986, and *Hannah and Her Sisters*, in 1987. However, her greatest success thus far has come from the stage, where she has won numerous awards for her performances.

GLENDENING, PARRIS N.

BORN: Bronx, N.Y. ACHIEVEMENTS: Member, National Association of Counties; chairman, Urban County Caucus; member, Board of Visitors, University of Maryland's School of Public Affairs, National Forum for Black Administrators, Partners for Livable Places. STUDIED: Florida State University, B.A., M.A. Ph.D, political science.

The only Democrat east of Oregon to win a vacant governor's seat in 1994, Maryland's Gov. Glendening wielded an axe in his first legislative session. He cut the state's budget by $235 million and eliminated five business taxes, hoping to lure businesses to Maryland and stimulate the state's economy. A writer of textbooks used in more than 400 colleges and universities, Glendening taught for 27 years at the University of Maryland Park. Along with teaching he served as city councilman, county councilman, and county executive for three terms. His education initiatives and public safety and citizen involvement programs brought recognition to Prince George's County Council as the "All American City" from the National Civic League in 1986, and to Glendening as the "Most Valuable County Official" in the nation by the magazine *City and State* in 1990. Glendening plans to create and maintain good-paying jobs in Maryland during his term, improve public education, and make the state's communities safer.

GLENN, JOHN HERSCHEL JR.

United States Senate, 503 Hart Senate Bldg., Washington, DC 20510 (202) 224-3353
BORN: 1921, Cambridge, Ohio. ACHIEVEMENTS: Aviation: first person to fly from Atlantic Coast to Pacific Coast faster than Mach 1; space missions: Mercury 6, first American to orbit the Earth. STUDIED: Attended Muskingum, B.S., 1962.

John Glenn Jr. entered the U.S. Marine Corps in 1943. He served as a fighter pilot during World War II and also flew combat missions during the Korean War. Glenn later became a test pilot, which led to his historic flight in 1957 from New York to Los Angeles in 3 hours, 23 minutes, in an F8U Corsair. It was the first flight to cover that distance at a velocity greater than the speed of sound. Glenn was one of the original seven astronauts selected in 1959. The Mercury 6 spacecraft carried him into orbit inside the Friendship 7 space capsule. The 4-hour, 56-minute flight took him around the world three times, making him the first American to orbit the planet. He later resigned from the space program and the Marine Corps to pursue politics. He was elected to the U.S. Senate as an Ohio Democrat in 1974.

GLICKMAN, DAN

Department of Agriculture, 14th & Independence Ave., Washington, D.C. 20250 (202) 720-3631
BORN: 1944, Wichita, Kan. ACHIEVEMENTS: 26th U.S. Secretary of Agriculture; congressman, U.S. House of Representatives. STUDIED: University of Michigan, B.A., history, 1966; George Washington University, J.D., 1969.

Dan Glickman became the 26th secretary of agriculture of the United States on March 30, 1995. Prior to that achievement, Glickman was a congressman from Kansas' 4th Congressional District, a position he held for 18 years. Before his election to Congress, he practiced law, and served as a trial attorney for the U.S. Securities and Exchange Commission. In 1993, Glickman was appointed chairman of the House Permanent Select Committee on Intelligence. As chairman of this committee, Glickman pushed the intelligence community to publicly explain its functions in the post Cold War era.

GLIER, MICHAEL

Nestor, 12340-66th St., Largo, FL 34643 (813) 536-6505
ACHIEVEMENTS: Co-developer of the Ni1000 recognition accelerator computer chip.

Most standard computers operate in a serial fashion, carrying out instructional steps one at a time. A new computer chip developed by Michael Glier, of Nestor manufacturing, and Mark Holler, of Intel, is a breakthrough in robotics. The Ni1000 recognition accelerator chip is structured on a latticework of 1,024 silicon "neurons," each interconnected to communicate with its fellow neurons. Each neuron can store a tremendous amount of information. This storage capacity makes it possible for the Ni1000 to perform 17 billion simple operations a second, including identifying faces and spotting trends in stock market data. Unlike other neural systems, it need not be programmed and reprogrammed. The chip can also "learn" as it goes along, like the human brain, becoming increasingly skilled in recognizing the patterns it analyzes.

GOELLNER, J. G.

Johns Hopkins University Press, 2715 N. Charles St., Baltimore, MD 21218-4319 (410) 516-6900
Goellner is a prominent publisher. For career credentials, consult the portion of this book entitled "Notable Americans by Profession" in the Appendix. Within this portion, the list "Publishers" describes requirements for inclusion in this volume.

GOIZUETA, ROBERT C.

Coca-Cola Company, 1 Coca-Cola Plaza, NW., Atlanta, GA 30313 (404) 676-2121
Goizueta is a prominent business leader and CEO of Coca-Cola Company. For career credentials, consult the portion of this book entitled "Notable Americans by Profession" in the Appendix. Within this portion, the list "Business Leaders" describes requirements for inclusion in this volume.

GOLDBERG, BERTRAND

Bertrand Goldberg Associates, 800 S. Wells Street, Chicago, IL 60610 (312) 431-5200
BORN: 1913. ACHIEVEMENTS: Fellow, AIA; Silver Medal, Architecture League of New York, 1965; Award of Merit, Society of Registered Architects,

1982; notable works: Marina City, Chicago; River City, Chicago; Affiliated Hospital Center, Boston. STUDIED: Bauhaus, Berlin.

Bertrain Goldberg's work challenges the linear character of traditional spatial layout. Working with Edward Hall, anthropology professor at the University of Illinois, Goldberg pioneered the study of how people actually use space. This work has led to many design innovations. His Marina City, in Chicago, was the first mixed-use complex in the center of a large city, and the highest reinforced concrete structure at the time of its completion. Its adventurous use of concrete led him away from Miesian boxes toward more "biological" forms, first in Marina City spirals and circles, and more recently in his serpentine River City Complex, another mixed-use downtown development in Chicago. In health care too, his building forms are conceived as biological shells, within which human activities are free to evolve. His State University of New York Health Sciences Campus, at Stony Brook, is built on a million-square-foot megastructure of seven towers of various heights and forms, which interconnect with bridges as well as basements, and collect related and interconnected disciplines and services in a matrix of unrestricted open space for future use evolution.

GOLDBERG, WHOOPI

Solters, Roskin, and Friedman, Inc., 45 W. 34th Street, New York, NY 10001
BORN: 1949, New York City. ACHIEVEMENTS: Grammy, Best Comedy Recording, Whoopi Goldberg, 1985; Golden Globe, Best Actress, The Color Purple, 1986; Oscar, Best Supporting Actress, and Golden Globe, Best Supporting Actress, both for Ghost, 1991. STUDIED: graduated from the School for the Performing Arts.

Born Caryn Johnson, Whoopi Goldberg began performing at the age of 8 with the children's program at Hudson Guild and Helena Rubenstein Children's Theater in New York. Goldberg moved to San Diego, in 1974, and helped found the San Diego Repertory Theater. She created a solo act, *The Spook Show*, and toured the United States and Europe. An adaptation of this solo act was brought to Broadway, and Goldberg also won small roles in the Broadway productions of *Pippin*, *Hair*, and *Jesus Christ Superstar*. Goldberg toured in *Living on the Edge of Chaos*. In 1985, she made her film debut in *The Color Purple*, and was nominated for an Academy Award. She won an Oscar in 1990 for *Ghost*, making her the second African-American woman to win the coveted acting award. She also appeared in a recurring role on *Star Trek: The Next Generation*. As a founding member of Comic Relief, Goldberg continues to appear in many specials for the charitable organization.

GOLDING, SUSAN

Office of the Mayor, 202 C St., San Diego, CA 92101 (619) 236-6330
Golding is a prominent political leader. For career credentials, consult the portion of this book entitled "Notable Americans by Profession" in the Appendix.

Within this portion, the list "Political Leaders" describes requirements for inclusion in this volume.

GOLDSMITH, STEPHEN

Suite 2501 City-Council Building, 200 East Washington Street, Indianapolis IN 46204 (317) 327-3601
BORN: 1946, Indianapolis. ACHIEVEMENTS: Mayor of Indianapolis; President's Award, Council for Urban Economic Development, 1995. STUDIED: Wabash College, A.B., 1968; University of Michigan, J.D., 1971.

After receiving his law degree, Stephen Goldsmith, a lifelong resident of Indianapolis, entered private practice in Indianapolis. He became the chief trial deputy for the city of Indianapolis from 1976 through 1978. In 1979, Goldsmith became prosecuting attorney for Marion County, Ind., and served in the position until 1990. Goldsmith was elected mayor of Indianapolis in November, 1991. Since becoming mayor, Goldsmith has reduced government spending, bureaucracy, and regulation. He has also held the line on taxation. The money saved has been reinvested in law enforcement and infrastructure improvements.

GOLDSTEIN, JOSEPH LEONARD

University of Texas Southwest Medical School, Dallas, TX 75235
BORN: 1940, Sumter, S.C. ACHIEVEMENTS: Nobel Prize in Physiology or Medicine; Heinrich-Wieland Prize; Pfizer Award, American Chemical Society; Passano Award, Passano Foundation; Lounsbery Award, National Academy of Sciences; Gairdner Foundation Award; Award, New York Academy of Sciences; Lita Annenberg Hazen Award; Louisa Gross Horowitz Award, Columbia University; Mattia Award; National Medal of Science.

All subsequent work on cholesterol has been based on what the Nobel Prize committee called the "revolutionary" discoveries of Michael Brown and Joseph Goldstein. The team discovered that body cells have specific protein molecules on their surfaces whose function is to process bloodstream particles that carry cholesterol. Their work greatly expanded knowledge about the regulation of cholesterol metabolism and the treatment of diseases caused by abnormally high cholesterol levels in the blood.

GOLUB, LEON ALBERT

530 La Guardia Pl., New York, NY 10012
BORN: 1922. ACHIEVEMENTS: Ford Foundation Grant; Guggenheim Foundation Grant; collections: Museum of Modern Art; Art Institute of Chicago; exhibitions: Museum of Modern Art; Museum of Contemporary Art, Chicago. STUDIED: University of Chicago; Art Institute of Chicago.

In the 1940s Leon Golub earned degrees in art history as well as in studio art. In the following decade he criticized the popular Abstract Expressionists for destroying "the individualist of the Renaissance." Golub's subsequent paintings featured images of sphinxes and other figures from non-Western culture, and later of man's birth and struggle. Depictions of man took on mythological proportions in his representations of man versus the environment, created with tumultuous mixtures of thickly applied, garish colors. This method gave the huge figures a sculptured effect, and heightened the conflicts depicted. In 1965 he began a series which lasted for the next five years:

very large canvases called *Gigantomachies*, showing male nudes in combat. This series, and a large-scale series of *Assasins* in the 1970s, depicted violence and disorder. He has since painted portraits of contemporary figures.

GOMES, PETER JOHN

Harvard University Memorial Chapel, Cambridge, MA 02138

BORN: 1942, Boston. ACHIEVEMENTS: Fellow, Emmanuel College, Cambridge University, England, Royal Society of Arts; Trustee, Handel and Hayden Society, New England Conservatory. STUDIED: Bates College, Lewiston, Maine, A.B. religion; Harvard Divinity School, student; University of Alabama, student.

Much-honored divine Peter Gomes came from the cranberry bogs of Plymouth, Mass., where his Portuguese father labored as a bog hand. He worked in a public library and played the church organ to earn money enough to enroll in Bates College. After graduating from Bates in 1965 he enrolled in Harvard Divinity School and joined its faculty at age 28. He has authored Proclamation Series Commentaries, co-authored History of the Pilgrim Society, and edited the Harvard Divinity School History. He officiated at President Ronald Reagan's 1985 swearing in and delivered the sermon at Washington National Cathedral for President George Bush's

Vice President of the United States Albert Gore.

inauguration, at which he pleaded for his listeners to bring hope to those dying of AIDS.

GOMPERTZ, MARK

Simon & Schuster, 1239 Avenue of the Americas, New York, NY 10020

BORN: 1955. STUDIED: Boston University, B.A., summa cum laude, science.

After 18 years in the publishing business, Mark Gompertz, in 1993, was named vice president and publisher of Simon & Schuster Trade Paperbacks, a publishing arm of the global entertainment and publishing com-

pany Paramount Communications, Inc. He moved to his new position from Avon Books, where, for four years, he was responsible for a trade paperback program he helped conceive and carry out. His publishing career began with Overlook Books in 1976, where, from age 21 to 31, he held increasingly important mangerial and editorial positions. He moved to Crown Publishing as senior editor in 1986, and to Avon in 1989 as associate publisher. He held the position of publisher at the time he moved to Simon & Schuster.

GONZALEZ, HENRY B.

U.S. House of Representatives, 2413 RHOB, Washington, DC 20515-4320 (202) 225-3236

Gonzalez is a prominent political leader. For career credentials, consult the portion of this book entitled "Notable Americans by Profession" in the Appendix. Within this portion, the list "Political Leaders" describes requirements for inclusion in this volume.

GOODMAN, JOHN

The Gersh Agency, 232 North Canon Dr., Beverly Hills, CA 90210

BORN: 1952, Afton, Mo. ACHIEVEMENTS: Golden Globe, Best Actor in a Comedy Series, Roseanne, 1993. STUDIED: Southwest Missouri State University, B.F.A. theater arts, 1975.

As Dan Connor on television's *Roseanne*, John Goodman is known by millions of viewers. However, Goodman worked hard to achieve his celebrity status. After graduating from college, he made ends meet by acting in children's theater and dinner theater until he debuted on Broadway in the play, *Loose Ends*, in 1979. Goodman also acted in several television commercials for Coors Beer, Crest toothpaste and 7-Up. In 1983, Goodman got his first film role, as Herbert, in *Eddie Macon's Run*. Goodman appeared in numerous other movies in the 1980s, but really began hitting his stride in 1988 when he first began working on *Roseanne*. Among his recent hit movies are, *Arachnophobia* and *King Ralph*, in 1990, and *Barton Fink*, in 1991.

GORDON, IRVING

c/o ASCAP, 1 Lincoln Plaza, New York, NY 10023
(212) 261-6800
BORN: 1913, New York City. ACHIEVEMENTS: Grammy, Song of the Year, 1992, Unforgettable.

Forty-one years after writing the pop, rhythm, and blues classic Unforgettable, 72-year-old veteran songwriter Irving Gordon scored again with the same song. Then, in 1952, Nat (King) Cole turned it into a hit record. At the Grammy awards in 1992 it was a duet version of the song sung by Cole's daughter, Natalie, and, with the help of special effects, Nat Cole himself that won the prize for the song of the year. At the presentation, Gordon chastised pop songwriters and singers who "scream, yell, and have a nervous breakdown" while talking about tenderness. He said the award made him feel that a revolution was occurring in the music business, where people want to be able to sing a song without getting "a hernia when you sing it."

GORDONE, CHARLES EDWARD

17 West 100th St., New York, NY 10025
Gordone is a prominent dramatic artist. For career credentials, consult the portion of this book entitled "Notable Americans by Profession" in the Appendix. Within this portion, the list "Dramatic Artists" describes requirements for inclusion in this volume.

GORE, ALBERT JR.

The White House, 1600 Pennsylvania Ave., Washington, DC 20500 (202) 456-2326
BORN: 1948, Carthage, Tenn. ACHIEVEMENTS: Author, Earth in the Balance: Ecology and the Human Spirit. STUDIED: Harvard University, 1969.

Albert Gore Jr. was elected the 45th vice-president of the United States in 1992, with Governor Bill Clinton, of Arkansas, on the Democratic ticket. Gore graduated from Harvard University in 1969, and also attended Vanderbilt University, studying religion and law. He served in Vietnam with the U.S. Army from 1969 to 1971. Gore was first elected to the U.S. Congress in 1976. After winning re-election three consecutive times, he was elected to the U.S. Senate in 1984. He is strongly identified with environmental issues, and wrote the book *Earth in the Balance: Ecology and the Human Spirit*. Gore considers himself a "raging moderate," and places himself in the conservative wing of the Democratic party. His decision to run with Governor Clinton was considered a major asset to the 1992 Democratic presidential campaign.

GORMAN, JOSEPH T.

TRW, Inc., 1900 Richmond Rd., Cleveland, OH 44124
(216) 291-7000
Gorman is a prominent business leader. For career credentials, consult the portion of this book entitled "Notable Americans by Profession" in the Appendix. Within this portion, the list "Business Leaders" describes requirements for inclusion in this volume.

GORMAN, R.C.

Navajo Gallery, P.O. Box 1756, Taos, NM 87571
BORN: 1933. ACHIEVEMENTS: Grand Award, American Indian Art Exhibition, Oakland, Calif.; First Award, Scottsdale National Indian Exhibition; collections: Santa Fe Fine Arts Museum; Heard Museum; exhibitions: Muirhead Gallery, Costa Mesa, Calif. STUDIED: Northern Arizona University; Mexico City College.

The son of Navajo painter Carl Gorman, and an internationally known artist, R. C. Gorman produces Navajo figurative work. He was influenced by Mexican mural painters Jose Orozco and Diego Rivera. Simplified representations of women, with classic grace, are his trademark in paintings, sculptural ceramics, lithographs and serigraphs—all of which capture the tradition of Indian culture while using a contemporary style. Indian traditionalists say his precise and linear approach is too modern, others say his sketchiness is too primitive; but he continues his work, lives on a Navajo reservation and also owns a gallery, which represents Southwestern artists and modern Indian painters.

GORMAN, JOHN GRANT

550 First Ave., New York, NY 10016
Gorman is a prominent physician. For career credentials, consult the portion of this book entitled "Notable Americans by Profession" in the Appendix. Within this portion, the list "Physicians" describes requirements for inclusion in this volume.

GOROVITZ, SAMUEL

Department of Philosophy, Syracuse University, 541 Hall of Languages, Syracuse, NY, 13244 (315) 443-2245
BORN: 1938, Boston. ACHIEVEMENTS: Several invited presentations in the United States and worldwide; several invited testimonies in the U.S.; approximately 95 printed articles and reviews. STUDIED: Massachusetts Institute of Technology, B.S., humanities and science, 1960 Stanford University, Ph.D., philosophy, 1963.

Samuel Gorovitz has been professor of philosophy at Syracuse University since 1986. He was appointed professor of public administration in 1994. At Syracuse, he served as dean of the College of Arts and Sciences, from 1986 to 1993. Before coming to Syracuse, Gorovitz held positions at the University of Maryland at College Park, Case Western Reserve and Wayne State University. He has held visiting positions at Beth Israel Hospital in Boston, the National Center for Health Services Research, the U.S. Department of Health, Education and Welfare, and Stanford University. He is the author of six books, the last three covering morality and ethics in the medical field. Gorovitz has received funding for several research topics by the National Endowment for the Humanities and other bodies. He has consulted for several organizations such as the National Science Foundation, National Endowment for the Humanities, the National

Center for Health Care Technology, and the World Health Organization. Gorovitz is currently a member of the New York State Task Force on Life and the Law, to which he was appointed by Governor Mario Cuomo in 1988.

GORTON, SLADE

730 Hart Senate Office Building, Washington D.C. 20510-4701 (202) 224-3441
BORN: 1928, Chicago. ACHIEVEMENTS: Wyman Award, Outstanding Attorney General in the United States, 1980; colonel, U.S. Air Force Reserve, 1981. STUDIED: Dartmouth College, A.B., 1950; Columbia University, L.L.B., 1953.

In public office since 1958, Gorton served as majority leader of the Washington House of Representatives, and state attorney general, before running for the U.S. Senate. He was elected to the first of two terms in 1988 and has concentrated on issues affecting consumers and business in the state of Washington. He challenged airline fuel taxes so as to protect the local airline industry, and has fought for access to Japanese markets for apple farmers. A member of the Agriculture and Interior Subcommittees of the Appropriations Committee, Gorton has fought for equity for foresters in the Endangered Species Act.

GOSSETT, LOUIS JR.

Nancy Seltzer & Assoc., 845 Ashcroft Ave., Los Angeles, CA 90048
BORN: 1936, Brooklyn, N.Y. ACHIEVEMENTS: Emmy Award, Outstanding Lead Actor for a Single Appearance in a Drama or Comedy Series, Roots, 1977; Academy Award, Best Supporting Actor, An Officer and a Gentleman, 1983. STUDIED: New York University, B.A., 1959; stage training with Frank Silvera, Nola Chilton, Eli Rill, and Lloyd Richards.

Professor Samuel Gorovitz.

Louis Gossett Jr. is a man with many facets. A collector of African art, and also a composer, Gossett debuted on Broadway in 1953, at the age of 17, playing the part of Spencer Scott in the play *Take a Giant Step*. Gossett sang in New York City nightclubs in the 1960s, and played basketball for the New York Knicks. Richie Havens sang Gossett's anti-war song, *Handsome Johnny*, at Woodstock in 1969. Although Gossett appeared in many stage productions from the 1950s through the 1970s, he is best known for his work on television and in the movies. His portrayal of Fiddler in the mini-series, *Roots*, in 1977, earned him enor-mous praise. He also played the famous baseball pitcher, Satchel Paige, in the television movie, *Don't Look Back*, in 1981, and Egyptian President Anwar Sadat in the television movie, *Sadat*, in 1983. On film, Gossett received much praise for his role as Sergeant Emil Foley in *An Officer and a Gentleman*, in 1982. Among his more recent movies are, *Enemy Mine*, in 1985, and *The Principal*, in 1987.

GOTSCHLICH, JR., EMIL C.

Maine Medical Center, Department OBGYN, Portland, ME 04102

Gotschlich, Jr. is a prominent physician. For career credentials, consult the portion of this book entitled "Notable Americans by Profession" in the Appendix. Within this portion, the list "Physicians" describes requirements for inclusion in this volume.

GOULD, MORTON

Chappel & Company, 801 Seventh Avenue, New York, NY 10019
BORN: 1913, Richmond Hill, N.Y. ACHIEVEMENTS: Grammy Award, Best classical Record, 1966. STUDIED: attended New York Institute of Musical Art, New York University.

Morton Gould's blend of popular and serious music emphasizes Americana. He studied counterpoint and orchestration with Vincent Jones, and piano with Abby Whiteside. Whiteside's piano instruction introduced Gould to jazz as a serious component of musical composition. Gould has spent much of his professional life in radio: He conducted a program on contemporary American music for station WOR from 1934 to 1943, and he was a staff musician and conductor at NBC and CBS. Radio City Music Hall asked Gould to become their composer and conductor in 1965. He has written scores for Broadway musicals, films, ballets (including *Fall River Legend*), concertos, symphonies, and works with American themes such as *Symphony of Spirituals* and *Cowboy Rhapsody*.

GOULD, GORDON

RR Box 112, Kinsale, VA 22488
BORN: 1920, New York City. ACHIEVEMENTS: Inventor of the Year, 1978, Patent Office Society. STUDIED: Union College, New York, B.S. physics; Yale University, M.S., physics; Columbia University, M.A., physics.

Gordon Gould worked on the atomic bomb as a physicist for the Manhattan Project from 1943 until 1945, then, for various engineering firms while teaching at City College of New York, Columbia University, and Brooklyn Polytechnical Institute. It was at Columbia that he contributed to development of the laser by inventing the laser amplifier, for which he was named Inventor of the Year 1978 by the Patent Office Society. He also holds patents on many laser devices used in industry, medicine, and the field of optics. In 1974 he formed a company called Optelecom, Inc., from which he retired in 1985.

GRABE, RONALD JOHN

NASA, L.B. Johnson Space Center, Houston, TX 77058

BORN: 1945, New York City.
ACHIEVEMENTS: Colonel, USAF; pilot of the STS 51-J, 1985 and STS-30, 1989 space missions; commander on the STS-42, 1992 and STS-57, 1993 space missions. STUDIED: U.S. Air Force Academy, B.S. in engineering science, 1966; studied aeronautics as a Fulbright Scholar at the technische Hochschule, Darmstadt, West Germany, 1967.

A pilot during the Vietnam war, Colonel Ronald Grabe graduated from the USAF Test Pilot School in 1975. He served as a test pilot at the Air Force Flight test center and as an instructor at the USAF Test Pilot School at Edwards Air Force Base in California. In 1980 Colonel Grabe was selected as a pilot astronaut. As pilot of the STS-30, he deployed the Magellan probe. He commanded the STS-42 mission, the International Micro Gravity Laboratory, and the STS-57 mission, which retrieved the EURECA satellite.

Astronaut Ronald Grabe.

GRAHAM, BRUCE

Skidmore, Owings and Merrill 33 W. Monroe Street Chicago, IL

BORN: 1925. ACHIEVEMENTS: Fellow, AIA; member, Royal Architectural Institute of Canada; notable works: John Hancock Center, Chicago; Sears Tower, Chicago; Hyatt International Hotel, Cairo. STUDIED: University of Pennsylvania.

Bruce Graham is one of the most prolific and innovative high-rise designers of the post-war era. In his 25-year association with Skidmore, Owings and Merrill, he has been responsible for many of the nation's tallest and most visible buildings. He first attracted attention in 1958 when he led the team responsible for designing Chicago's Inland Steel Building, the first major office project in the heart of the business district since World War II. The Inland Building was the Midwest's introduction to the spare, functionalist style that Mies van der Rohe had made internationally popular. Chicago's commercial architecture of the next decade closely followed this prototype. In the mid-1960s he designed a number of skyscrapers in collaboration with SOM's Bangladesh-born engineer Faxlur Shan, which were primarily supported by revolutionary tubular steel exterior skeletons. Although the Sears Tower, the world's tallest building, is probably his most recognized project from that period, the John Hancock Center, also in Chicago, represents his most sensitive and harmonious use of the new technology. The building's fundamental form is an elongated pyramid. Six vertical tubular supports are superimposed on each of the structure's four nearly triangular exterior faces. These vertical supports are criss-crossed by pairs of intersecting diagonal supports, which form ever-narrowing diamonds and incidental quadrilaterals as they ascend.

GRAHAM, BILLY

Billy Graham Evangelistic Association, P.O. Box 9313, Minneapolis, MN 55440-9313

BORN: 1918, Charlotte, N.C. ACHIEVEMENTS: Founded the Billy Graham Evangelistic Association, 1950; author: Peace with God, 1953, World Aflame, 1965, How to be Born Again, 1977, and Answers to Life's Problems, 1988. STUDIED: Wheaton College, 1943.

Billy Graham began his career as the pastor of the First Baptist Church of Western Springs, Ill., after graduating from Wheaton College in 1943. Graham was also a leader of the Youth for Christ movement during the same period. He began a traveling revival team in 1947, with his first big success coming in 1949. That year, a number of famous Hollywood personalities converted to Christianity during Graham's revivals. Graham founded The Billy Graham Evangelistic Association in 1950. He has been an active proponent of radio, television and film, developing and producing many programs himself. He gave a prayer at the inauguration of President Richard Nixon, in 1969, and went on to become one of Nixon's closest advisors.

GRAHAM , BOB

524 Hart Senate Office Building, Washington, DC 20510-0903 (202) 224-3041
BORN: 1936, Dade County, Fla. ACHIEVEMENTS: St. Petersburg Times' Award for Most Valuable Legislator; Tropical Audubon Society's Conservation Award. STUDIED: University of Florida, 1959; Harvard Law School, 1962.

As a U.S. Senator from Florida, Bob Graham is best known for his work on behalf of environmental issues, especially for the protection of wetlands and coastlines. He serves on the U.S. Senate's Environment and Public Works Committee, and two subcommittees: Clean Air, Wetlands, Private Property and Nuclear Safety; and Transportation and Infrastructure. Graham's association with environmental issues began when he was governor of Florida, and created the Save Our Everglades program. He has also taken a leadership role in controlling illegal drug use. As governor of Florida, he instituted the stiffest sentences for drug use in the nation at the time, and as a senator, he co-authored the 1988 Omnibus Anti-Drug Act.

GRAHAM, DONALD EDWARD

The *Washington Post*, 1150 15th St., NW, Washington, DC 20071 (202)334-6000
BORN: 1945, Baltimore. STUDIED: Harvard University,. B.A.
Donald Graham joined the U.S. Army after graduating from Harvard After a two-year hitch, he went to work in 1968 for *Newsweek* magazine. Leaving *Newsweek* after three years he went to The *Washington Post* as assistant managing editor in the sports department and has remained with the paper for 24 years. From sports he became assistant managing editor of the paper in 1975, executive vice president in 1976, and publisher in 1979. He advanced to chairman, chief operating officer, and finally chairman of the board when his mother, Katherine Graham, stepped down in 1993. The *Washington Post* Company controls television stations, cable television systems, *Newsweek* magazine, and a subsidiary which focuses on electronic news dissemination.

GRAMMER, KELSEY

Mahoney/Wasserman Public Relations, 345 N. Maple Dr., Beverly Hills, CA 90210
BORN: 1955, St. Thomas, Virgin Islands. ACHIEVEMENTS: Emmy Award, Best Actor, Comedy Series, Frasier, 1993-94. STUDIED: Juillard School.
Despite his mild-mannered exterior, Kelsey Grammer is a man with a difficult past. Born on the Virgin Islands, Grammer's father and sister were murdered, and his two half-brothers died in a scuba-diving accident. However, the past has not kept Grammer from achieving success in his chosen profession. He began acting on television in 1983 when he debuted as Dr. Canard on the soap opera, *Another World*. Just a year later, Grammer got the part that made him famous: Frasier Crane, on the TV series, *Cheers*. Though that successful series ultimately came to an end, Gram-

mer's role lived on in the ensuing hit *Frasier*. Grammer has numerous stage appearances to his credit, including many roles in Shakespearean productions. He has also acted in several television movies, specials and pilots.

GRAMS, ROD

154 Russell Senate Office Building, Washington, DC 20510-2301 (202) 224-3244
BORN: 1948, Princeton, Minn. ACHIEVEMENTS: Freshman Republican Whip for the 103rd Congress, 1992. STUDIED: Carroll College.
For more than two decades, Rod Grams was a news reporter and producer on several television stations in the Midwest, serving as the senior news anchor at KMSP-TV in Minneapolis/St. Paul from 1982 to 1991. In 1992 he won a seat in the House of Representatives representing Minneapolis' south side, and played a key role in formulating the 1994 Republican deficit-reduction plan. In 1994 he won election to the U.S. Senate, advocating tax cuts and limits on government spending. Grams serves on the Banking, Housing, and Urban Affairs Committee, and chairs the newly established Senate Medical Device and Technology Caucus.

GRANGER, KAY

City Hall, 1000 Throckmorton St., Fort Worth, TX 76102 (812) 871- 6117
Granger is a prominent political leader. For career credentials, consult the portion of this book entitled "Notable Americans by Profession" in the Appendix. Within this portion, the list "Political Leaders" describes requirements for inclusion in this volume.

GRANN, PHYLLIS E.

G.P. Putnam's Sons, 200 Madison Ave., New York, NY, 10016 (212) 951-8400
ACHIEVEMENTS:
Phyllis Grann's career in publishing began in 1958 at Doubleday & Company, where she was an editor. She went to Simon & Schuster as senior editor and was editor-in-chief of Pocket Books, the company's paperback division, in 1974. Grann joined G.P. Putnam's Sons in 1976 as editor-in-chief, and in 1984 she was named president and publisher. In 1987, she became chief executive officer of the corporation and moved on to chairman in 1991.Grann is now chairman and CEO of the Putnam Berkley Group Inc., which includes The Putnam Publishing Group, The Berkley Publishing Group, The Putnam New Media, and the recently started Riverhead Books. Record profits have come under her leadership. The company has averaged 40 hardcover and paperback best-sellers annually and has ranked among the top five publishing houses in the industry repeatedly.

GRANT, AMY

A & M Records, 1416 N LaBrea Ave., Los Angeles, CA 90028-7563

BORN: 1961, Augusta, Ga. ACHIEVEMENTS: Grammy, Best Gospel Performance-Contemporary, Age to Age, 1982; Grammy, Best Gospel Vocal-Female, Ageless Medley Myrrh, 1983; Grammy, Best Gospel Vocal-Female, Angels, 1984; Grammy, Best Gospel Vocal-Female, Unguarded, 1985; Grammy, Best Gospel Vocal, Lead Me On, 1988. STUDIED: Furman University; Vanderbilt University.

Pop music singer Amy Grant began her musical career recording her debut gospel album. In 1982 she released her first big gospel album *Age to Age* for which she won a Grammy award. Her enormous success in gospel music has transferred to the pop music arena. Her decision to cross-over to pop music was met with much criticism from the gospel music community, but she survived the test of time, and has become a force in pop music. Her first pop album produced the hit single *Baby, Baby*, which she wrote for her daughter Millie. In addition to her Grammy awards, she has received three Dove awards from the Gospel Music Association.

GRASSLEY, CHUCK

135 Hart Senate Office Building, Washington, DC 20510-1501 (202) 224-3744
BORN: 1933, New Hartford, Iowa. ACHIEVEMENTS: Taxpayers Hero, National Taxpayers Union. STUDIED: University of Northern Iowa, B.A., 1955, M.A., 1956; University of Iowa, Ph.D., political science.

The only working family farmer in the U.S. Senate, Chuck Grassley is an advocate of free trade and open market policies. He is chairman of the International Trade Subcommittee, and serves on the Judiciary, Governmental Affairs and Budget committees, as well as the Senate Select Committee on Aging. Grassley wrote the Congressional Accountability Act, signed into law January, 1995. First elected to the Iowa House of Representatives at the age of 25, Grassley won a seat in the U.S. House of Representatives in 1974, and a Senate seat in 1980. In winning re-election, Grassley earned the biggest margin of victory up to that point in an Iowa Senate race.

GRAVES, BILL

Office of the Governor, State Capitol, 2nd Fl., Topeka, KS 66612- 1590 (913) 296-3232
Graves is a prominent political leader. For career credentials, consult the portion of this book entitled "Notable Americans by Profession" in the Appendix. Within this portion, the list "Political Leaders" describes requirements for inclusion in this volume.

GRAVES, MICHAEL

341 Nassau Street, Princeton, NJ 08540 (609) 924-6409
BORN: 1934. ACHIEVEMENTS: Fellow, AIA; Progressive Architecture Award, 1970, 1976, 1977, 1978, 1979; notable works: Municipal Services Building, Portland, Ore.; Whitney Museum Addition, New York City; Mezzo House, Princeton, N.J. STUDIED: Harvard University.

Michael Graves was one of the first young, prominent American designers who attempted to reestablish contextualism, wit and sculpturalism as virtues in center-city office architecture. His work reacts against the formal restrictiveness, material hardness and somewhat imperial presence of Modernist and International Style design. Yet he shuns the label of Postmodernism as he does any other doctrinaire categorization. His designs draw from Art Deco skyscrapers of the 1920s and 1930s, yet technically he is strongly indebted to his Miesian forebears. In many cases his designs have been selected to bring harmony to urban areas where reckless development in the 1950s and 1960s had created logistical and aesthetic chaos. The Municipal Services Building in Portland, Ore. was one of his first such efforts, and remains his most controversial. Portland's downtown is on a tight, square grid, situated between the Willamette River and a stretch of massive bluffs. A number of earlier International Style buildings had ignored the scale of the bluffs and the situation of their plazas disrupted the order of the street grid. His almost cubical design responds to these neglected site considerations: it imitates the scale of the bluffs and fits squarely within the established grid. The building conveys much of the whimsy and elegance of the high Deco period, while working within the technical and financial confines of a rather less spacious era.

GRAY, MITCHELL

145 W. 78th St., New York, NY 10024 212-362-9829
BORN: 1946. ACHIEVEMENTS: New York Art Directors Gold Award. STUDIED: University of Virginia.

Mitchell Gray specializes in commercial illustration with fashion overtones, such as the Gordon Gin "girl on the beach" ad, and the advertisements for Le Jardin de Max Factor featuring Jane Seymour. He published *The Lingerie Book*, St. Martin's Press, for which he has won several awards. His work has been described as "tastefully hot," and the photographs "honest without being offensive." He works in all formats, preferring 35mm and 2 1/4. By blending multiple sources of light, he creates highly conceptual images that are graphic and emotional His passion for athletics led to a series of photos on women athletes, which he plans to publish as a book.

GREATBATCH, WILSON

Greatbatch Genetic Aid, Inc., 10871 Main St., Clarence, NY 14031- 1707
BORN: 1919, Buffalo, N.Y. ACHIEVEMENTS: Invented the Medical Cardiac Pacemaker; inducted into the National Inventors Hall of Fame, 1986; New York State Society of Professional Engineers, Distinguished Service Award, 1985; National Society of Professional Engineers, Distinguished Service Award, 1984; Centennial Medal, 1984; AAMI Laufman prize, 1982; Niagara Frontier Patent Law Associations, Inventor of the Year Award, 1976; Buffalo-Niagara Technical Societies Council's Engineer of the Year, 1976. Institute of Electrical and Electronic Engineers, William J. Morelock Award, 1968; STUDIED: Cornell University, B.E.E. 1950; New York State University at Buffalo, M.S., 1957; honorary doctorates from Houghton College, 1970, and University of Buffalo, 1984.

Wilson Greatbatch invented the Medical Cardiac Pacemaker which has helped to increase human life expectancy. After serving in the Atlantic and Pacific theaters during World War II, Greatbatch studied electrical engineering at Cornell University. Using his engineering training, he focused his research on the interdisciplinary areas of engineering and medical electronics, agricultural genetics, electrochemistry of pacemaker batteries, and electrochemical polarization of physical electrodes. The original pacemaker patent was licensed to the Medtronic Company, and became the first implantable cardiac pacemaker device. In 1983, the pacemaker invention was chosen as one of most significant engineering contributions over the last 50 years. Greatbatch is one of two non-medical engineers to be elected to fellow grade by the American College of Cardiology. He has also received this honor from the Institute of Electrical and Electronic Engineers, and the British Royal Society of Health. His company, Greatbatch Enterprises, continues to manufacture or license pacemaker devices.

GREENBERG, ALLAN

31 High Street, New Haven, CN 06510 (203) 776-2006
BORN: 1938. ACHIEVEMENTS: First Prize, Art Center Competition, Thibodeaux, La.; notable works: Marshall Reception Room, Washington, D.C.; Bergdorf Goodman Facade, New York City; Trelis Room Proposal, White House, Washington, D.C. STUDIED: Cornell University.
Allan Greenberg's work marks a return to the neo-classicism of the late nineteenth century, which reached its apex in the public commissions of Englishman Sir Edwin Lutyens. Unlike Robert Venturi and Thomas Gordon Smith, who have attracted international attention with their highly selective and idealized use of classical idioms, Greenberg attempts to work wholly within the formal vocabulary that Lutyens distilled from his study of the high Renaissance. Appropriately, he has worked predominantly on major, authority-laden public commissions: courthouses, judicial buildings, war memorials, libraries, and recently, his design for the Trellis Room of the White House. But in 1984, he submitted a striking design for a monument to the victims of the Holocaust in New York City's Battery Park: a short, stout chimney rises from two mighty pairs of arches. The monument's eloquent evocation of tremendous forces—ponderous, crushing weight, and finally the wild upswept fire—all argue with him that the formal phrases of classical architecture provide mankind's most sensitive and complete language for symbolic expression.

GREENE, LEONARD MICHAEL

Safe Flight Instrument Corporation, 20 New King St., White Plains, NY 10604
BORN: 1918, New York City. ACHIEVEMENTS: Inventor flight safety instruments. STUDIED: City College of New York, B.S., M.S., engineering; Guggenheim School of Aeronautics, postgrad.
Leonard Greene's major invention is called as important a device for saving lives in air travel as the parachute. The invention was the airplane stallwarning device, developed during World War II for the Grumman Aircraft Company. Greene went on to invent and manufacture other flight safety instruments, and then, in 1974, founded the Institute for Socioeconomic Studies in White Plains, New York. Greene, father of eight children and stepfather of five, has won as many awards for his interest in social agencies as in aviation. He published *Free Enterprise without Poverty* in 1981.

GREENE, RICHARD E.

2014 Cross Creek Ct., Arlington, TX (817) 860-7171
BORN: 1943, Monroe, La. ACHIEVEMENTS: Texas Crime Coalition of Mayors, chairman; University of Texas at Arlington Development Board, director; Paul Harris Fellow, Rotary Clubs International; Good Scout Award, Boy Scouts of America. STUDIED: Northeast Louisiana University, B.S., business administration; Northwestern University School of Mortgage Banking, B.S., banking.
Richard Greene sells cars as a business, likes the creative arts, theater, and music, but his real interest since the mid-eighties lies in the civic affairs of Arlington, Texas. Named director of the University of Texas at Arlington Development Board in 1984, he went on to chair a crime coalition and a planning and zoning commission. From there the ladder led to the city council and then election as temporary mayor for two terms. He was elected mayor in 1987 and re-elected three times since.

GREENSPAN, ALAN

Federal Reserve, 21st & Constitution Aves. NW, Washington, DC 20551
BORN: 1926, New York City. ACHIEVEMENTS: Chairman, Federal Reserve System; Thomas Jefferson Award (with Arthur Burns and William Simon) for the Greatest Public Service Performed by an Elected or Appointed Official from the American Institute of Public Service; Public Service award, Claremont Men's College; Distinguished Alumni Award, New York University Graduate School of Business Administration; honorary Doctor of Commercial Science, Pace University; fellow, National Association of Business Economists, and director in several major U.S. corporations. STUDIED: Juilliard School; New York University; Columbia University.
In his own words a "free enterpriser," Alan Greenspan, in the eyes of his peers, is a notable economic forecaster. In 1975, after one of the worst declines in output since the end of World War II and two bad guesses on his part, he foresaw a flattening out of the economy and forecast to President Ford in his Economic Report to the President a recovery in the gross national product. The prediction was on target, as were his following forecasts in 1976 and 1977. By then, unemployment had fallen from 8.5 percent to 6.3 percent, and inflation from 12.1 percent to 6.3 percent, permanently silencing his detractors. One of Greenspan's biggest influences was the philosopher and novelist Ayn Rand, the champion of total laissezfaire capitalism, or "rational selfishness," whom he first met through his wife Joan Mitchell, a marriage annulled after one year. So it is not surprising that throughout his career he has steadfastly insisted that free enterprise and the marketplace should be free of

government interference, or, in his terms, should avoid a mixed economy. Excessive government spending brings the government into private capital markets, he believes, thus giving it prior right over private savers, who in turn pressure the banking system to accommodate their money and credit demands, resulting in inflation. On taxation, he believes the economy can be stimulated by tax reductions rather than by increased government spending. Since consumers will spend more freely if they expect the easing of taxes to be permanent, he recommends that they not be made temporary, and, likewise for business, which would look beyond a short-run incentive and decide their investment strategies on long-term consumer behavior, not on "tax rebates." An oft-quoted remark in *Business Week* in 1975 referred to Greenspan as a "one-man band," drawing on the fact that he had attended Juilliard School of Music and once toured with a dance band for a year, playing clarinet and saxophone.

GREER, THOMAS H.

Cleveland Plain Dealer, 1801 Superior Ave., Cleveland, OH 44114 (216) 344-4600
BORN: 1942, Nashville, Tenn. ACHIEVEMENTS: Nominating Jury Member, Pulitzer Prize; Walker/Stone Editorial Writing Award; Paul Miller Distinguished Journalism Lecturer, Oklahoma State University. STUDIED: Dillard University, B.A., journalism.
A former sports editor of the *Cleveland Plain Dealer*, Thomas Greer moved to the *Philadelphia Daily News* as sports writer and columnist for three years, and then to the *New York Daily News* for three years. In 1983 he returned to the *Plain Dealer* as sports editor. He successively advanced to managing editor of the paper, vice president, and senior editor in 1992. Among his many board memberships are the Greater Cleveland Roundtable, American Press Institute, Council for Sports Journalism, National Association of Black Journalists, and the American Society of Newspaper Editors.

GREGORY, DON

Sharome Enterprises, Inc., 165 West 46th St., New York, NY 10036
Gregory is a prominent dramatic artist. For career credentials, consult the portion of this book entitled "Notable Americans by Profession" in the Appendix. Within this portion, the list "Dramatic Artists" describes requirements for inclusion in this volume.

GREGORY, FREDERICK DREW

Office of Safety & Mission Quality, L.B.J. Space Center, Houston, TX 77058
BORN: 1941, Washington, D.C. ACHIEVEMENTS: Colonel, USAF; pilot on the STS 51-B mission, 1985; commander on the STS-33, 1989 and STS-44, 1991 missions. STUDIED: U.S. Air Force Academy, B.S.; George Washington University, M.S., information systems, 1977.
Colonel Gregory started out as both a helicopter and fighter pilot. Prior to being named as an astronaut in 1978, he attended the U.S. Navy Test Pilot School and

was a research/engineering test pilot for the Air Force and NASA. Since 1992, Colonel Gregory has served as the associate administrator of the Office of Safety and Mission Quality at NASA headquarters.

GRENIER, RICHARD

The Washington Times, 3600 New York Ave. NE, Washington, DC. 20002 (212) 636-3000
BORN: 1933, Cambridge, Mass. ACHIEVEMENTS: Author The Marrakesh One-Two, 1983. STUDIED: U.S. Naval Academy, B.S., engineering.
Richard Grenier's early work took him overseas, beginning with a job at the *Agence France-Presse* in 1962. From there he joined the Paris bureau of *The Financial Times* from 1962 to 1969, and Group W Broadcasting from 1968 to 1970, where he worked in the company's Paris office. He continued to contribute to various publications including *The New York Times* and *The American Spectator*, before landing his own column at *The Washington Times* in 1985. Grenier has authored several books, including *The Marrakesh One-Two*, 1983.

GRIFFIN, RODNEY

26 West 75th St., #1B, New York, NY 10023 (212) 595-1786
Griffin is a prominent dancer. For career credentials, consult the portion of this book entitled "Notable Americans by Profession" in the Appendix. Within this portion, the list "Dancers" describes requirements for inclusion in this volume.

GRISHAM, JOHN

c/o Doubleday, 666 Fifth Avenue, New York, NY 10103 (212) 765-6500
Grisham is a prominent author. For career credentials, consult the portion of this book entitled "Notable Americans by Profession" in the Appendix. Within this portion, the list "Authors" describes requirements for inclusion in this volume.

GROOVER, JAN

c/o Sonnabend Gallery, 420 W. Broadway, New York, NY 10012
BORN: 1943. ACHIEVEMENTS: Guggenheim Fellowship, NEA. STUDIED: Ohio State University; Pratt Institute.
Known primarily for her formalistic still lifes, Jan Groover brings a painterly eye and aesthetic rigor to all her subjects. From the diptychs and triptychs which established her reputation, to her more recent studies of plant forms and kitchen utensils, Groover's photographs represent a conscious departure from those of her more sociologically oriented contemporaries. By juxtaposing unlikely objects and using dramatic camera angles, she forces the viewer to examine spatial relationships. Light and shadow are carefully orchestrated: color serves to heighten tension rather than resolve it. Recently she has begun to explore new

venues for her talent, including black-and-white portraiture.

GROSSFELD, STAN

c/o The *Boston Globe*, Boston, MA 02107
BORN: 1951. ACHIEVEMENTS: Pulitzer Prize for Spot-News Photography, 1984; Pulitzer Prize for Feature Photography, 1985. STUDIED: Rochester Institute of Technology.
Stan Grossfeld is one of the few photographers who has managed to parlay his skills and experience into an editorial position on a daily paper. A two-time Pulitzer Prize winner for the *Boston Globe*, he is perhaps best known for his riveting 1984 photographs of the famine in Ethiopia. The photograph which earned him his second Pulitzer showed a group of refugees who had been denied permission to board a Sudanese food convoy. Rich Clarkson, the former president of the National Press Photographers Association, has called him "an excellent journalist who just happened to have picked up a camera." Grossfeld's most recent book, *The Whisper of Stars*, documents life in Siberia.

GROVE, ANDREW S.

3065 Bowers Ave., Santa Clara, CA 95051 (408) 765-8080
BORN: Hungary. ACHIEVEMENTS: CEO of Intel Corporation; author of High Output Management, New York: Random House, 1983. STUDIED: City College of New York, B.S.; University of California, Ph.D.
Andrew Grove was the son of a Hungarian dairyman. He came to the United States in 1957, and did not know the English language when he arrived, but graduated from City College of New York three years later. Grove obtained his Ph.D. at the University of California, and then went to work for the Fairchild Semiconductor Corporation. During the early 1960s, Fairchild was a hotbed of semiconductor innovation. In 1968 Grove and his two partners, Gordon Moore and Robert Noyce, left Fairchild to start their own company. With $2 million in seed money from venture capitalist Arthur Rock, the three partners launched Intel Corporation. Intel's primary product is the microprocessor. This little piece of silicon is now incorporated in nearly all consumer products Americans take for granted, from automobiles to washing machines.

GROVES, HARRY E.

Professor Emeritus, University of North Carolina, School of Law, Chapel Hill, NC 27599
BORN: 1921, Manitou Springs, Colo. ACHIEVEMENTS: Tun Abdul Razak Memorial Lecturer, Kuala Lumpur, Malaysia; Judge John J. Parker Award, North Carolina Bar Association. STUDIED: University of Colorado, B.A., prelaw; University of Chicago, J.D., law; Harvard University., LL.M.
Harry Groves served as a captain in the U.S. Army in World War II and in Korea. After completing his education, he became a professor and school administrator throughout a 38-year professional career, at one point becoming dean in the faculty of law at the University of Singapore. During his four years in the Orient, he gathered material for the *The Constitution of Malaysia*, the first of more than 30 books and articles he has written. Among the eight schools where he has taught are: Texas Southern University, the University of Minnesota, Memphis State University, and the University of North Carolina School of Law. He belongs to the North Carolina, Texas, and Ohio bar associations and is on the board of directors of the American Bar Association.

GRUSIN, DAVE

GRP Records Inc., 555 West 57th St., New York, NY 10019 (212) 245-7033
BORN: 1934, Littleton, Colo. ACHIEVEMENTS: Grammy Award, Best Arrangement on an Instrumental, 1983, 1985, 1989, 1992; Grammy, Best Instrumental Arrangement Accompany Vocals, 1989; Grammy, Best Original Instrumental Score, 1989; Grammy, Best Arrangement on an Instrumental, Mood Indigo, 1994; Academy Award, best original score, The Milagro Beanfield War, 1988.
Dave Grusin was music director for television's *Andy Williams Show* for seven years before beginning his spectacular career composing music for films. Since 1967, when his third film score that year was *The Graduate*, he has written music for over 50 films. Among the best known movies are *The Heart is a Lonely Hunter*, 1968; *Three Days of the Condor*, 1975; *The Goodbye Girl*, 1977; *The Electric Horseman*, 1979; *Absence of Malice*, 1981; *Reds*, 1981; and *Bonfire of the Vanities* and *Havana*, 1990. His Academy Award nominations were for *Heaven Can Wait*, 1978; *The Pond*, 1981; *Tootsie*, 1982; *The Fabulous Baker Boys*, 1989; and *The Firm*, 1993.

GUILLEMIN, ROGER C. L.

9894 Genesse Ave., La Jolla, CA 92037
BORN: 1924, Dijon, France. ACHIEVEMENTS: Nobel Prize in Physiology or Medicine (shared with Rosalyn S. Yalow and Andrew V. Schally, both U.S.), 1977; Bonneau and La Caze Awards, Academie des Sciences, France; Legion of Honor, France; Gairdner International Award; Albert Lasker Award, Albert and Mary Lasker Foundation; Dickson Prize; Passano Award, Passano Foundation.
Roger Guillemin and Rosalyn Yalow, with Andrew Schally working sometimes independently, produced a body of work on hormones in the brain that the Nobel committee saw as opening "new vistas within biological and medical research far outside the border of their own spheres of interest." Their combined research identified and synthesized three brain hormones used by the hypothalmus, which functions as the control center for the nervous system by regulating sleep cycles, body temperatures, appetite, etc. Their further understanding of the brain's role in body chemistry has enabled physicians to undertake successful therapy in many conditions where the body's hormones were in-

adequate. Though born in France, Guillemin is a naturalized American.

GULOTTA, JOSEPH

PPG Industries, 1 PPG Place, Pittsburgh, PA 15272 (412) 434-3131
ACHIEVEMENTS: Co-developer of thermal-controlled window glass.
Heat buildup in cars calls for the air conditioner, which eats up gas as well as releasing emissions of ozone-eating chlorofluorocarbons into the air. Joseph Gulotta, and his associate, James Finley, both of PPG Industries, solved those problems by developing thermal-controlled window glass. Embedded with a metal-oxide film that acts like a mirror, the glass reflects ultraviolet and infrared radiation, while allowing the light to come through. Reflecting the radiation can reduce the heat-buildup in a car by 60 percent.

GUMBEL, BRYANT, CHARLES

The *Today Show*, NBC, 30 Rockefeller Plaza, New York, NY 10020
BORN: 1948, New Orleans. ACHIEVEMENTS: Emmy award, 1976, 1977. STUDIED: Bates College, B.A., 1970.
Gumbel has interviewed perhaps more notables than anyone

Composer Dave Grusin.

in journalism, having hosted the *Today Show* since 1982. Prior to joining the *Today Show*, Gumbel was the host of *NFL 81*, a Sunday afternoon football show on NBC. He grew up in Chicago, and after college, he went to work as a writer, and eventually an editor, for *Black Sports* magazine. In 1972 Gumbel joined KNBC-TV as a sportscaster, becoming the sports director for the station in 1976. Gumbel's inimitable interviewing style has taken him around the world, conversing with the world's most influential people, and reporting on national and international news events.

GWATHMEY, CHARLES

Gwathmey Siegel and Associates, 475 Tenth Avenue, New York, NY 10018
BORN: 1938. ACHIEVEMENTS: FAIA; Design Award, Interiors magazine, 1983; Product Design Award, 1981; notable works: Francois de Menil House, East Hampton, N.Y.; Guggenheim Museum Addition, New York City; Museum of Moving Images, Astoria, N.Y. STUDIED: Yale University.
Charles Gwathmey's work is an indomitably American interpretation of the International Style of Le Corbusier. His formal vocabulary is almost exclusively limited to cylinders, semi-cylinders and most commonly close derivatives of the cube. His architecture is in many ways analogous to Cubism and Constructivism in art. His basic space-organizing unit—the cube—is invaded, adjoined and abridged by shooting columns, obtuse diagonal stairways and ribbon windows, creating an enormous geometric conflagration. Yet his work has unmistakable order and unity; its attraction is in its tension between movement and control. His materials of choice depart sharply from the International School's industrial-age standards. He borrows heavily from native crafts houses of early New England and the Shingle School, creating smooth, elegant wooden enclosures that belie the drama unleashed within.

GWINN, MARY ANN

The Seattle Times, Box 70, Fairvica Ave., Seattle, WA 98111 (206) 464-2111

BORN: 1951, Forest City, Alaska. ACHIEVEMENTS: Pulitzer Prize; C.B. Blethen Award; First Prize, Sigma Delta Chi, Northwest Chapter. STUDIED: Hendrix College, Conway, Ark., B.A., psychology; Georgia State University, M.Ed., special education/behavioral disorders; University of Missouri School of Journalism, M.A., news-editorial sequence.

After five years as a special education aide and teacher specializing in behaviorally disordered students, Mary Ann Gwinn entered the newspaper field in 1978 as a teaching assistant in the University of Missouri's news-editorial department and the next year became a reporter for the Columbia, Mo., *Daily Tribune*. In 1983 Gwinn joined *The Seattle Times* where she remains, gathering her share of honors including the Pulitzer Prize for her part of the *Times'* coverage of the Exxon oil spill. She also teaches non-fiction writing at the University of Washington and magazine and feature writing at Seattle University.search. In 1992 he organized a successful campaign to increase participation in Tennessee's organ donor program leading to an appointment from the governor to serve as chairman of the Tennessee Task Force on Medicaid. Two years later he ran for the U.S. Senate and defeated three-term incumbent Jim Sasser. Frist serves on the Budget Committee and is the Chairman of the Senate Labor and Human Resources Disability Policy Subcommittee.

HABER, STUART

Bell Communications Research, Inc., 290 W. Mt. Pleasant Ave., Livingston, NJ 07039 (201) 740-3000
ACHIEVEMENTS: Developed the Digital Time Stamp computer security system.
Stuart Haber has provided some security for computer users. Computer thieves, forgers, and counterfeiters are foiled when confronted with machines installed with the Digital Time Stamp, a creation of Haber and Scott Stornetta. Both men are researchers at Bellcore, a research and engineering company. The electronic notary system is based on cryptography, Haber's field, and enhanced with work by Stornetta. A small piece of a document is generated by a mathematical procedure that creates a unique digital fingerprint of the whole document based on a chain composed of the letters, numbers, graphics, and symbols in the document. Changing even one character in the original changes the chain's unique value. To check the authenticity of a document's time stamp needs only a recomputation of the values in the chain and comparing the results on file with the time stamper. Additional security is provided by altering the chain each week and publishing it in a garbled series of numbers and letters under "Public and Commercial Notices" in The New York Times.

HACKMAN, EUGENE ALDEN

Barry Haldeman, #2000, 1900 Avenue of the Stars, Los Angeles, CA 90067
BORN: 1930, San Bernardino, Calif. ACHIEVEMENTS: Academy Award, Best Actor, The French Connection, 1971; Golden Globe Award, Best Actor, The French Connection, 1972; Academy Award, Best Supporting Actor,

Unforgiven, 1992; Golden Globe Award, Best Supporting Actor, Unforgiven, 1993. STUDIED: Pasadena Playhouse; attended University of Illinois; School of Radio Technique in New York.

Gene Hackman and his classmate, Dustin Hoffman, were both voted least likely to succeed at the Pasadena Playhouse. Between acting jobs, he supported himself taking jobs as a doorman, truck driver, shoe salesman, and furniture mover. Although he played the role of Buck Barrow in the hugely successful film *Bonnie and Clyde*, 1967, it wasn't until he played the starring role of Popeye Doyle in *The French Connection* that he received widespread acclaim. Hackman has appeared in approximately 60 films during his long career. One of the most recent is *Unforgiven* for which he received both an Academy Award and a Golden Globe Award as Best Supporting Actor.

HAGELSTEIN, ROBERT

Greenwood Publishing Group, Box 5007, 88 Post Rd., W., Westport, CT, 06881 (203) 226-3571
BORN: Queens, New York. STUDIED: Graduated Long Island University, B.A., English.
Robert Hagelstein is president and chief executive officer of Greenwood Press. He has been with the publishing firm since 1970. By 1972, he was made CEO at the age of 30. Hagelstein restructured Greenwood completely by 1974. Hagelstein's company searched for markets that they feel no one is servicing, or that have not been serviced adequately in the past. Discography is an area in which his company has had success. Hagelstein is a piano enthusiast, and in the late 1970s his company started a reprint series that has made them the premier publisher in that area. He got the idea, while on a trip to Europe, when he saw a genuine discography in a bookstore. Before Greenwood, Hagelstein worked at the Johnson Reprint Company. He started there in 1964 and soon became a production manager. A few years later he was able to switch to editorial, and he started a series in the social sciences and humanities.

HALBERSTAM, DAVID

William Morrow and Company, 105 Madison Ave., New York, NY 10016
BORN: 1934, New York City. ACHIEVEMENTS: Pulitzer Prize for International Reporting, Columbia University, 1964; Political Book Award, 1986, for The Reckoning, 1986. STUDIED: Harvard University, B.A., 1955.
David Halberstam began his writing career as a reporter for the *Daily Times Leader* in West Point, Miss. from 1955 until 1956. In 1960 became a staff writer and foreign correspondent for the *New York Times*. As a war correspondent, Halberstam covered the Viet Nam War, often questioning the official version of events as related by the military public relations specialists. Halberstam is best known for a trio of non-fiction books, *The Best and the Brightest*, *The Powers That Be*, and *The Reckoning* which examine the acquisition and use of power in America. Halber-

stam's books combine exhaustive investigative reporting with a unique narrative style.

HALL, JOHN R.

Ashland Oil Corporation, P.O. Box 391, Ashland, KY 41114 (606) 329-3333
Hall is a prominent business leader. For career credentials consult the portion of this book entitled "Biographees by Profession" in the Appendix. Within this portion, the list "Business Leaders" describes requirements for inclusion in this volume.

HALL, R. E.

Citgo Petroleum Corp., P.O. Box 3758, Tulsa, OK 74102 (918) 495-4434
Hall is a prominent business leader. For career credentials consult the portion of this book entitled "Biographees by Profession" in the Appendix. Within this portion, the list "Business Leaders" describes requirements for inclusion in this volume.

HALL, ROBERT

Philadelphia Inquirer, 400 N. Broad St., Philadelphia, PA 19130-4015 (215) 854-2000
Hall is a prominent publisher. For career credentials consult the portion of this book entitled "Biographees by Profession" in the Appendix. Within this portion, the list "Publishers" describes requirements for inclusion in this volume.

HALPRIN, ANNA

Tamalpa Institute, 810 College Avenue, #10, Kentfield, CA 94914 (415) 461-9479
Halprin is a prominent dancer. For career credentials consult the portion of this book entitled "Biographees by Profession" in the Appendix. Within this portion, the list "Dancers" describes requirements for inclusion in this volume.

HAMILTON, CHARLES VERNON

Columbia University, Department of Political Science, 2960 Columbia Ave., New York, NY 10027
BORN: 1929, Muskogee, Okla. ACHIEVEMENTS: Alumni Award, University of Chicago; University Alumni Award, Roosevelt University; Lindback Teaching Award, Lincoln University, Oxford, Pa.; Van Doren Teaching Award, Columbia University; Great Teacher Award, Columbia University. STUDIED: Roosevelt University, Chicago, B.A., prelaw; University of Chicago, M.A., law; Loyola University School of law, J.D.
In 37 years as an educator, one-time U.S. Army private Charles Hamilton has won a spate of notable awards as he moved from assistant professor at Tuskegee University to a full professorship at Columbia University in 11 years. After a one-year hitch in the Army from 1948 to 1949 he enrolled at Roosevelt University in Chicago and worked up to his doctorate by studying while serving as assistant professor at Tuskegee and also at Rutgers University. He is a member of the Board of Trustees of the Twentieth Century Foundation, a board member of NAACP, and is on the Board of Editors of the Political Science Quarterly. He remains at Columbia where he has been a professor for 26 years.

HAMILTON, LEE H.

U.S. House of Representatives, 2187 RHOB, Washington, D.C. 20515-1409 (202) 225-5315
Hamilton is a prominent political leader. For career credentials consult the portion of this book entitled "Biographees by Profession" in the Appendix. Within this portion, the list "Political Leaders" describes requirements for inclusion in this volume.

HAMLISCH, FREDERICK MARVIN

c/o Allan Carr Enterprises, Box 69670, Los Angeles, CA
BORN: 1944, New York City. ACHIEVEMENTS: Academy Awards, The Way We Were, and for adapting Scott Joplin's ragtime music in The Sting, both 1973. STUDIED: Juilliard School of Music, student; Queens College, New York, B.A. music.
Juilliard, a giant among giants in American music schools, recognized the child prodigy in Hamlisch and admitted him to classes at age 7. He won Oscars for the title song and musical score for The Way We Were and for adapting Scott Joplin's ragtime music in The Sting, both 1973. He also composed the music for A Chorus Line, 1975, which won Pulitzer and Antoinette Perry awards in 1970, and holds the record for the longest-running musical in Broadway's history. He has performed and conducted with many large symphony orchestras.

HAMMER, SUSAN W.

Office of Mayor, 801 N. 1st St., Room 600, San Jose, CA 95110
BORN: 1938, Altadena, Calif. ACHIEVEMENTS: Member, President's Advisory Committee on Trade Policy and Negotiations, appointed by President Bill Clinton. STUDIED: University of California, Berkeley.
Two-term Mayor Susan Hammer looks out her window at San Jose's changing skyline and sees, among the major corporations that have established residence in her city, a revitalized downtown. Close by is one of the nation's premier sports and entertainment facilities. The city proper is one of the safest in the country, thanks to her community policing program and gang abatement strategy. Yet her work is not done. A "Recycle Plus" program is leading the city to increased recycling; a new pollution strategy protects San Francisco Bay, and her San Jose Education Network has been developed with the help of local schools and private business. These are some of the ways, Hammer says, that she is preparing San Jose to move into the 21st Century.

HANFORD, WILLIAM "BUTCH" EDWARD

NCIPLA, Suite 203, 2001 Jefferson Davis Hwy., Arlington, VA 22202 (703) 415-0780
BORN: 1908 Bristol, Pa. ACHIEVEMENTS: co-invented polyurethane with Donald Holmes; inducted into the National Inventors Hall Of Fame, 1991. STUDIED: Philadelphia College of Pharmacy, B.S., 1930; University of Illinois, M.S., Ph.D.
While working with Donald Holmes at E.I. du Pont de Nemours & Company, Butch Hanford co-invented and received a patent for polyurethane in 1942. Hanford got the nickname, Butch, for his crew cut hair style and red-stained lab coat he wore while a student at the University of Illinois. His invention is used as a heat insulator for homes and offices, in artificial hearts, and as safety padding in cars. After receiving the patent, Hanford left DuPont and joined GAF Corporation. In 1946 he became director of research for M.W. Kellogg, where he also served on the board of directors. In 1957 he joined Olin Industries as research and development vice president. Hanford and his son founded Water-Sure, Inc. in 1968, a company which develops equipment for sanitizing water supplies in third world countries.

HANKS, TOM

William Morris Agency, 151 El Camino Dr., Beverly Hills, CA 90212
BORN: 1956, Concord, Calif. ACHIEVEMENTS: Golden Globe, Best Actor in a Comedy, Big, 1989; Academy Award, Best Actor, Philadelphia, 1994; Golden Globe, Best Actor, Philadelphia, 1994; Academy Award, Best Actor, Forrest Gump, 1995; Golden Globe, Best Actor, Forrest Gump, 1995. STUDIED: Attended Chabot College, California State University, Sacramento.
Tom Hanks achieved his initial popularity with comedy. He played Buffy Wilson on the popular television series, *Bosom Buddies* from 1980 until 1982. But perhaps Hanks got his biggest break when he was noticed by *Family Ties* producer Ron Howard in 1983. Howard asked Hanks to read for a part in his upcoming film, *Splash*, which came out in 1984 with Hanks in the lead role. Hanks continued to star in one hit after another in the 1980s and early 1990s, for the most part sticking with his over-grown-boy persona. The peak of his success within this genre was in the movie, *Big*, in which Hanks played a pre-adolescent boy in an adult body. More recently, Hanks received tremendous praise for his portrayal of an attorney with AIDS in the film, *Philadelphia*. In 1994 Hanks managed to become a household word playing the title role in *Forrest Gump*.

HANSON, DUANE

6109 S.W. 55 Ct., Davie, FL 33314
BORN: 1925. ACHIEVEMENTS: Blair Award, Art Institute of Chicago; German Academy Exchange Services Grant, West Berlin (Germany); collections: Whitney Museum; Milwaukee Art Museum; exhibitions: Whitney Museum Biennial; Corcoran Gallery. STUDIED: Macalester College; University of Minnesota; Cranbrook Academy of Art
After graduate work, Duane Hanson lived from 1953 until 1961 in Germany, where he met George Grygo. Back in America during the 1960s, Hanson began working with polyester resin and fiberglass, the media of Grygo. From live models, he made negative molds of dental plaster bandages into which he poured a mixture of polyester resin and fiberglass. He painted figures in oil, and added real hair, clothes and objects. The figures illustrated themes of war, crime or violence. By 1970, instead of being ideographic, the pieces were satirical, such as *Tourists*. For a short time Hanson tried to present figures in movement, such as football players, but it proved unsuccessful. Super-realistic portrayals of lower- and middle-class Americans are disconcertingly lifelike, and it is common for an observer to mistake them for their living, breathing equivalents. He is interested not in human form but in capturing the "idiosyncrasies of our time" describes requirements for inclusion in this volume.

HARDYMON, JAMES FRANKLIN

Textron, Inc., 40 Westminster St., Providence, RI 02903 (401) 421-2800
BORN: 1934, Maysville, Ky. ACHIEVEMENTS: Corporation Development Award, American Society of Mechanical Engineers. STUDIED: University of Kentucky, B.S., science, M.S., science.
James Hardymon carved out a career for himself with St. Louis-based Emerson Electric Company when he joined the firm in 1961. He was successively vice president of planning and development of Emerson's Browning Division in 1970, president of the products division in 1976, and company president in 1988. In 1989 Textron, Inc.—builder of aerospace systems, helicopters, computers, and defense products Q lured him to Providence, R.I., as president and chief operating officer. He became chief executive officer and board chairman in 1991.

HARKIN, TOM

531 Hart Senate Office Building, Washington, D.C. 20510-1502 (202) 224-3254
BORN: 1939, Cumming Iowa. ACHIEVEMENTS: Wrote the Harkin Amendment which established criterion for dispersing foreign aid; principal sponsor of the Americans with Disabilities Act. STUDIED: Iowa State University, government and economics; Catholic University of America Law School, 1972.
Tom Harkin first came to national attention in 1970, while an aide to Iowa Congressman Neal Smith, when he exposed the "tiger cages" used in South Vietnam prison camps. As a U.S. Senator, he is best known for his efforts to reform the quality of health care in America, and he helped establish the Office of Alternative Medicine. In 1990 he became the first Iowa Democrat to win a second term as a U.S. Senator. In 1992 he lost his bid to become the Democratic Presidential candidate. Harkin currently sits on the Senate Agriculture Committee, and is known as a fierce advocate for family farmers.

HARRELSON, WOODY

Creative Artists Agency, Inc., 9830 Wilshire Blvd., Beverly Hills, CA 90212

BORN: 1961, Midland, Texas. ACHIEVEMENTS: Emmy Award, Outstanding Supporting Actor in a Comedy Series, Cheers, 1988. STUDIED: Hanover College, B.A. in theater arts and English.

Woody Harrelson achieved nearly instant success when he got the part of Woody Boyd on the television series, *Cheers*, in 1985. However, Harrelson has had many demons to fight. A hyperactive child prone to violence in his youth, he has been married and divorced numerous times, and arrested several times for cocaine possession. However, Harrelson has continued to build on his successes as an actor. He made the jump to movies in 1986 with the film, *Wildcats*, and appeared in *Casualties of War* in 1989. His portrayal of Billy Hoyle in *White Men Can't Jump* earned him extensive critical praise when it was released in 1991. Harrelson's most recent film was *Natural Born Killers*.

HARRIS, ELIHU MASON

1 City Hall Plaza, 505 14th St., Oakland, CA 94612 (510) 238-3141
Harris is a prominent political leader. For career credentials consult the portion of this book entitled "Biographees by Profession" in the Appendix. Within this portion, the list "Political Leaders" describes requirements for inclusion in this volume.

HATCH, ORRIN GRANT

SR-135 Russell Office Building, Washington, D.C. 20510 (202) 224-5251
BORN: 1934, Pittsburgh, Pa. ACHIEVEMENTS: Republican Utah legislator; U.S. Senator, 1977-. STUDIED: Brigham Young University, B.S., 1959; University of Pittsburgh, J.D., 1962.

A conservative Republican from Utah, Orrin Hatch is chairman of the influential Senate Judiciary Committee, and is a member of the Finance Committee. A proponent of reducing federal spending and restoring more power to the states, Hatch has been involved in the debate over school busing, school prayer and abortion issues. Prior to entering politics, he practiced law in Pittsburgh and Salt Lake City.

HATFIELD, MARK O.

U.S. Senate, 711 SHOB, Washington, D.C. 20501-0276 (202) 224-3573
Hatfield is a prominent political leader. For career credentials consult the portion of this book entitled "Biographees by Profession" in the Appendix. Within this portion, the list "Political Leaders" describes requirements for inclusion in this volume.

Astronaut Hank Hartsfield

HARTSFIELD, HENRY WARREN, JR.

NASA Flight Crew Operations, Code CA, L.B. Johnson Space Center, Houston TX 77058
BORN: 1933, Birmingham, Ala. ACHIEVEMENTS: Pilot for the STS-4, 1982 mission. Commander of the STS 41-D (1984), STS 61-A (1985) and the Spacelab D-1 missions. STUDIED: Auburn University, B.S. physics, 1954; , University of Tennessee, M.S. engineering science,1971.

In 1966 Henry Hartsfield began his career as an astronaut in the MOL program. He transferred to the astronaut program in 1969. A member of the ground support team for Skylabs 2, 3, and 4, Hartsfield piloted STS-4, the last shuttle test flight. After leaving the astronaut corps, he became manager of the Man-Tended Capability Phase, Space Station Freedom program at the Johnson Space Center.

HAUCK, FREDERICK "RICK" HAMILTON

Navy Space Systems, OP-943, Washington, D.C.
BORN: 1941, Long Beach, Calif. ACHIEVEMENTS: captain, USN; pilot, STS-7, 1983; commander on the STS 51-A, 1984, and STS-26, 1988. STUDIED: Tufts University, B.S., general physics, 1962; Massachusetts Institute of Technology, M.S., nuclear engineering, 1966.

While in the Navy, Frederick "Rick" Hauck served as a communications officer, pilot, test pilot instructor, and operations officer. In 1978 he joined the eighth group of astronauts and participated in the STS-26 mission, which was the first mission after the Challenger accident. In 1989 he resigned from NASA, and became the Director of the U.S. Navy Space and Naval Warfare command. He then resigned from the Navy, and became president and CEO for International Technology Underwriters of Bethesda, Maryland.

HAUPTMAN, JEROME A.

Medical Foundation of Buffalo, 73 High St., Buffalo, NY 14203
BORN: 1917, Bronx, N.Y. ACHIEVEMENTS: Administrator, Medical Foundation of Buffalo; Researcher, U.S. Naval Research Laboratory; Nobel Prize (shared with Jerome Karle), 1985; Belden Prize; Pure Science Award, Sigma Xi; American Crystallographic Association. STUDIED: City College of New York; Columbia University; University of Maryland.

"Unacceptable and controversial" was the verdict of his peers when Jerome Hauptman's Nobel Prize-winning work first appeared in a chemistry journal. And so it continued to be for 15 years until announcement of the prize for outstanding achievements in the development of methods for studying crystal structures for use in, for example, determining the structure of DNA. In almost all solids, the atoms are arranged in a certain order to form crystals, and finding the crystal structure of the solid is the first step in learning the solid's properties. One of Hauptman and Jerome Karle's remarkable achievements, scorned by crystallogists for a decade and a half, was to develop a way to quickly analyze the three-dimensional structure of the molecule, thus analyzing its intensity directly, even in complex molecules, in just a few days by using X-ray techniques. The work helped advance crystallography to a position of major importance in the development of other modern sciences, especially physical chemistry, physics, and biochemistry.

HAYES, JAMES B.

ACHIEVEMENTS: Pevious publisher, Fortune Magazine; president, Junior Achievement.
James Hayes is president and chief executive officer of the largest youth-serving organization in the world, Junior Achievement. The organization provides economic education to two million students in the U.S., and 500,000 students in 80 foreign countries. More than 57,000 business men and women volunteer their time to Junior Achievement each year. Hayes has been a board member of the organization for eight years and served as chairman of the board before his election to president in 1995. A one-time *Fortune Magazine* publisher, he also heads The New American Revolution, which has a mission of seeking business contributions to the social, economic, and educational needs of children. Hayes founded the non-profit organization after retiring from *Fortune Magazine* in 1994.

HAYWARD, CHARLES E.

Little Brown & Company, 34 Beacon St., Boston, MA 02108 (617) 227-0730
BORN: 1950. ACHIEVEMENTS: President, Little Brown & Co.
Charles Hayward has been president and chief operating officer of Little Brown & Co., a subsidiary of Time Warner, Inc., of Boston, since 1991. He began his career in publishing with Macmillan Company as vice president of marketing and sales. He then held various sales and marketing positions at St. Martin's Press and Houghton Mifflin, before moving on to president of HP Books, a subsidiary of KnightRidder Newspapers, Inc., in Tucson, Ariz. His last position before joining Little Brown was president of the trade division of Simon & Schuster.

HEALY, JANE E.

Orlando Sentinel, 633 N. Orange Ave., #2833, Orlando, FL 32802-2833 (407) 420-5000
Healy is a prominent journalist. For career credentials consult the portion of this book entitled "Biographees by Profession" in the Appendix. Within this portion, the list "Journalists" describes requirements for inclusion in this volume.

HEARNEY, GEN. RICHARD D.

Office of the Secretary, Pentagon,. Washington, D.C. 20301 (703) 545-6700
BORN: Penaluma, Calif. ACHIEVEMENTS: Defense Superior Service Medal; Legion of Merit with Gold Star; Distinguished Flying Cross; Bronze Star with Combat "V" for Valor; Purple Heart; Air Medal with Combat "V" and bronze numeral "39"; and Navy Commendation Medal with Combat "V". STUDIED: Stanford University, B.A.; Pepperdine University, M.A.; Naval War College.
Gen. Richard Hearney's 38-year career in the Marine Corps has included command positions at the squadron, air group, and air wing level. During Desert Storm he was deputy commander of the 1st Marine Expeditionary Force. His staff tours included deputy director, J-3, European command, as well as deputy chief of staff for Marine requirements, programs, and aviation at Marine headquarters in Washington. He assumed his present position as assistant commandant of the Marine Corps in 1994.

HEIMBOLD, CHARLES ANDREAS JR.

BristolMyers Squibb Company, 345 Park Ave., New York, NY 10154 (212) 546-4000
BORN: 1933, Newark, N.J. ACHIEVEMENTS: CEO, BristolMyers Squibb Co.; chair, Board of Overseers, University of Pennsylvania Law School; chair, Pharmaceutical Research and Manufacturers of America. STUDIED: Villanova University, cum laude prelaw; University of Pennsylvania, J.D., law.
Charles Heimbold was elected to his sixth board of directors position in 1995 when Mobil Corporation choose him to join 13 other members of its board. He retains his position as chairman of the board, president, and chief executive of Bristol Myers Squibb Company, formed in 1989 with the merger of BristolMyers and Squibb to create a pharmaceutical giant second only to Merck. He joined Bristol Myers in 1963, at age 30, and rose to president in 1994. He chairs the board of overseers of the University of Pennsylvania Law School and the Pharmaceutical Research and Manufacturers of America. His other board memberships include Sarah Lawrence College's Phoenix House and the board of the University of Pennsylvania. He also is a member of the Business Roundtable and Business Council.

HELLMUTH, GEORGE FRANCIS

Hellmuth, Obata and Kassabaum, 100 N. Broadway St., Louis, MO 63102 (314) 421-2000
BORN: 1907. ACHIEVEMENTS: FAIA; citation, Engineering News Q Record, 1977; notable works: Dallas/Fort Worth Airport; Married Student Housing, University of Alaska; National Air and Space Museum, Washington, D.C. STUDIED: Washington University, St. Louis, Mo.
Early in his career, George Hellmuth concluded that his skills as an organizer, motivator and administrator outstripped his considerable design abilities. As he worked in various offices for nearly a decade, he began to develop ideas for a more dynamic and efficient architectural practice. He noted that there are three broad phases to each commission: marketing/solicitation, design, and execution. He decided to assemble a firm of three principals, each with a special affinity and responsibility for one of these areas. In 1949 he established the firm of Hellmuth, Yamasaki and Leinweber. Though dissolved after six years, its innovative structure had proven viable. His second partnership, with Gyo Obata as designer and George Kassabaum as construction supervisor, has become one of the most enduring and productive collaborations in the history of American architecture. In their 25 years of enlightened cooperation, the firm has undertaken commissions in virtually every category of architectural endeavor, yet designs remain fresh, diverse and crisp.

HELMS, JESSE ALEXANDER

SD-403 Dirksen Office Building, Washington, D.C. 20510 (202) 224-6342
BORN: 1921, Monroe, N.C. ACHIEVEMENTS: North Carolina Democratic legislator; U.S. Senator, 1973-. STUDIED: Wingate College, 1938-1939; Wake Forest University, 1939-1940.
An outspoken conservative, Jesse Helms was elected to the U.S. Senate in 1972 after a career in newspapers and broadcasting. He is chairman of the powerful Foreign Relations Committee, and his legislative battles have ranged from opposition to the Panama Canal treaty and arms-control agreements, to controversies over federal funding of projects by the National Endowment for the Arts.

HENLEY, BETH

William Morris Agency, 1350 Avenue of the Americas, New York, NY 10019
BORN: 1952, Jackson, Miss. ACHIEVEMENTS: Pulitzer Prize, Crimes of the Heart, 1981. STUDIED: Southern Methodist University, B.F.A., 1974; University of Illinois, 1975-1976.
Beth Henley's plays feature strong female characters who explore their identities outside traditional relationships. Her writing combines a flair for humorous dialogue with an ear for colloquial speech. *Crimes of the Heart,* 1980, her first play to be produced in New York City, won the Pulitzer Prize. Her other plays include *The Wake of Jamey Foster,* 1982; *The Miss Firecracker Contest,* 1984; *The Debutante Ball,* 1988; and *Abundance,* 1990.

HENLEY, DON

Asylum Records, 75 Rockefeller Place, New York, NY 10019 (212) 484-7200
BORN: 1947, Gilmer, Texas. ACHIEVEMENTS: Grammy Awards (co-recipient with band The Eagles), Best Pop Vocal-Group, Lyin Eyes, 1975; Record of the Year, Hotel California, 1977; Best Arrangement for Voices, New Kid in Town, 1977; Best Rock Vocal-Group, Heartache Tonight, 1979; Grammy Awards (solo), Best Rock Vocal-Male, The Boys of Summer, 1985; Best Rock Vocal-Male, The End of the Innocence.
In 1982, after many years with The Eagles, Don Henley disbanded the successful group and started a solo career. In striking out on his own, Henley refined his song-writing abilities. Known for both biting political songs and songs of bittersweet love, his music showed a more sincere, focused quality than his previous work with The Eagles. During the 1980s, his work expanded into considerably more complex melodies and instrumentation. Henley sued Geffen Records in the early 1990s to end his contract with the company. They eventually reached an out-of-court settlement that left Henley free to work with another record company. In 1994, Henley got back together with The Eagles for a concert tour. It was expected that the band would record an album once the tour was over.

HENLEY, LARRY

c/o Atlantic Recording Corporation, 75 Rockefeller Plaza, New York, NY 10019 (212) 484-6000
Henley is a prominent composer. For career credentials consult the portion of this book entitled "Biographees by Profession" in the Appendix. Within this portion, the list "Composers" describes requirements for inclusion in this volume.

HEPBURN, KATHERINE H.

c/o William Morris Agency, 151 El Camino Dr., Beverly Hills, CA 90212
BORN: 1909, Hartford, Conn. ACHIEVEMENTS: Four Academy Awards: Best Actress, Morning Glory, 1933; Guess Who's Coming to Dinner, 1967; The Lion in Winter, 1968; and On Golden Pond, 1981. STUDIED: Bryn Mawr College.
The winner of an unprecedented four Academy Awards, Katherine Hepburn played high-comedy parts in her early films, later excelling in more dramatic roles. Often paired with actors Cary Grant or Spencer Tracy, her films, in addition to her Oscar performances, included *A Bill of Divorcement,* 1932, *Little Women,* 1933, *Bringing Up Baby,* 1938, *Holiday,* 1938, and *The Philadelphia Story,* 1940, all with Grant; *The African Queen,* 1952; *Summertime,* 1955; *Suddenly Last Summer,* 1959; and nine films with Tracy, including *Woman of the Year,* 1942, and *Adam's Rib.*

HERENTON, W. W.

City Hall, 125 N. Mid-America Hall, Memphis, TN 38103 (901) 576-6000
BORN: 1943, Memphis, Tenn. ACHIEVEMENTS: Horatio Alger Award, 1988. STUDIED: LeMoyne College, B.A.; Southern Illinois University, Ph.D.

W. W. Herenton is a native of Memphis, Tenn. He graduated from Lemoyne College and Memphis State University, and received his Ph.D. from Southern Illinois University. Dr. Herenton has a long history of public service, and has devoted time to the March of Dimes, the United Way, the Boy Scouts of America, and the Economic Club of Memphis. A member of the American Association of School Administrators and the American Management Association, Herenton served as superintendent of the Memphis City Schools prior to his election as mayor. Herenton was elected mayor of Memphis on Oct. 3, 1991.

HERSCHBACH, DUDLEY ROBERT

Harvard University, Department of Chemistry, 12 Oxford Street, Cambridge, MA 02138
BORN: 1932, San Jose, Calif. ACHIEVEMENTS: Nobel Prize in Physics (shared with Yuan T. Lee, U.S.), 1986; Pure Chemistry Award, American Chemical Society; Spiers Medal; Centenary Medal, British Chemical Society; Linis Pauling Medal; Polanyi Medal; Langmuir Medal. STUDIED: Stanford University; Harvard University.

In a chemical reaction, one compound is converted into another, the total mass of each remaining unchanged because no atoms have been destroyed or created but merely rearranged. The feat that won Herschbach and Lee their Nobel Prizes was for research that provided a more detailed understanding of how those reactions take place. The team developed two beams of molecules that accelerate and collide, at which point the results of the smashup are investigated. The process is a new and better way to study all types of chemical reactions.

HERZOG, DAVID BRANDEIS

55 Colbert Rd., East, West Newton, MA 02165
Herzog is a prominent physician. For career credentials consult the portion of this book entitled "Biographees by Profession" in the Appendix. Within this portion, the list "Physicians" describes requirements for inclusion in this volume.

HEWLETT, WILLIAM REDDINGTON

Hewlett Packard Company, 1501 Page Mill Road, Palo Alto, CA 94304
BORN: 1913, Ann Arbor, Mich. STUDIED: Massachusetts Institute of Technology, M.E., electrical engineering; many honorary degrees and awards in the U.S. and abroad.

In 1939, three years after graduating from college, William Hewlett and his friend, David Packard, then an engineer with General Electric, formed Hewlett Packard in Palo Alto, Calif. First producing resistance capacitance audio oscillators in a garage, they went on to manufacture a variety of electrical devices and a highly ranked line of computers. Packard served as U.S. deputy secretary of defense from 1969 to 1971. Hewlett was actively involved with the company until 1987, when he retired at age 74.

HEYMANN, C. DAVID

c/o Lyle Stuart/Carrol Publishing, 600 Madison Avenue, New York, NY 10022 (212) 486-2200
BORN: 1945, New York City. ACHIEVEMENTS: Author of Ezra Pound: The Last Rower, Viking, 1976; American Aristocracy: The Lives and Times of James, Russell, Amy, and Robert Lowell, Dodd, Mead, 1980. STUDIED: Cornell University, B.S., 1966; University of Massachusetts, M.F.A., 1969; State University of New York, A.B.D., 1976.

Although known for his writing, C. David Heymann is also an academician, lecturing in English, first at State University of New York at Stony Brook, and then at Antioch College in New York City. Heymann, a prolific contributor of articles and reviews to newspapers and magazines, is best known for his books, including *Poor Little Rich Girl: The Life and Legend of Barbara Hutton*, Random House, 1983 and *A Woman Named Jackie*, Lyle Stuart/Carol Communications, 1989. In addition to being successful books, both were adapted as television miniseries. *Poor Little Rich Girl: The Life and Legend of Barbara Hutton*, Random House, 1983, broadcast on NBC in 1987, won both a Golden Globe award and an Emmy award.

HICKEY, CARDINAL JAMES

Archbishop of Washington. Archdiocese of Washington, 5001 Eastern Avenue, P.O. Box 29260, Washington DC 20017
BORN: 1920, Midland, Mich. ACHIEVEMENTS: Former chairman of the Committee on Human Values; chairman of the Board of Governors of the Pontifical North American College; holds honorary degrees from eight colleges and universities. STUDIED: Sacred Heart Seminary College, 1942; Theological College; The Catholic University of America, License in Theology, 1946; Pontifical Lateran University (Rome), doctorate in Canon Law, ; Pontifical Angelicum University (Rome), doctorate in Moral Theology.

Cardinal James Hickey was ordained in 1946 at the Cathedral of St. Mary in Saginaw, Michigan. Following his ordination, Hickey spent a year at St. Mary's Cathedral as an associate pastor before he was assigned to Rome, where he earned two doctorate degrees. After returning to the United States in 1951, he served for nine years as secretary to the bishop of Saginaw. In 1959 he was named the first rector of St. Paul Seminary, in Saginaw. Hickey was appointed auxiliary bishop of Saginaw by Pope Paul VI in 1967. He was back in Rome by 1969 working as the rector of the North American College, where he oversaw seminarians from more than 80 dioceses in the United Sates. In 1974, he was installed as bishop of Cleveland. Pope John Paul II named him archbishop of Washington in 1980, and, in 1988, elevated him to the College of Cardinals.

HIJUELOS, OSCAR

211 West 106th St., New York, NY 10025
BORN: 1951, New York, N.Y. ACHIEVEMENTS: Pulitzer Prize, Best Fiction, The Mambo Kings Play Songs of Love; Pushcart Press, Outstanding Writer; Oscar Cintas Fiction Writing Grant, Creative Artists Program Service, Ingram Merrill Foundation; Creative Writers Award from National

Endowment for the Arts, American Academy in Rome from American Academy and Institute of Arts and Letters; Breadloaf Writers Conference scholarship. STUDIED: City College of the City University of New York, B.A., M.A.

A onetime advertising media traffic manager for a New York City display company after he left college, Oscar Hijuelos wrote stories in his spare time and very early was cited by Pushcart Press as an outstanding writer. His first novel, *Our House in the Last World*, which traces the life of a Cuban family after emigrating to the U.S., received wide critical approval, but it was his second novel, *The Mambo Kings Play Songs of Love*, that brought him fame. In *Mambo* two Cuban brothers leave Cuba for the U.S. and a career in the city's mambo clubs. The author follows them into a melancholy old age, where memory takes over and they lament missed connections and lost dreams. He won the Pulitzer Prize for best fiction with the book, and nomination for a National Book Award. Hijuelos' is represented in the 1978 anthology *Best of Pushcart Press*.

HILLER, JAMES

22 Arreton Rd. Princeton, NJ, 08540
BORN: 1915, Brantford, Ontario, (Canada) ACHIEVEMENTS: Invented electron lens correction device; Albert Lasker Award, 1960; inducted into the National Inventors Hall of Fame, 1980. STUDIED: University of Toronto, B.S., 1937; Ph.D., physics, 1941.

Dr. James Hiller contributed to the development of the electron microscope. While in graduate school he and a fellow student built a microscope model that magnified 7,000 times. A generation later his model was being used in labs throughout the world, some magnifying at least two million times. Originally a research engineer for RCA Laboratories from 1940 to 1953, he left to work for one year as research director at Melpar, Inc. In 1954 he then returned to the post of general manager at RCA Laboratories, retiring in 1978 as executive vice president and senior scientist.

HINES, GREGORY OLIVER

Fran Saperstein Organization, 9530 Wilshire Blvd., Suite 324 Beverly Hills, CA 90212
BORN: 1946, New York City. ACHIEVEMENTS: Antoinette Perry Award, Best Performance by a Leading Actor in a Musical, Jelly's Last Jam, 1992. STUDIED: Attended professional children's schools.

At the age of 2, Gregory Hines began his career as the junior member of a family dancing act. Three years later, he made his nightclub debut as the Hines Kids, with brother Maurice. At 8, Hines made his Broadway debut in *The Girl in the Pink Tights*. Later Gregory, and his brother Maurice, were joined by his father, and the act became Hines, Hines and Dad. He continued dancing with his brother until 1973. In 1988 he recorded a solo album *Gregory Hines*. He won acclaim in the movie *The Cotton Club*, and the Broadway show *Jelly's Last Jam*, for which he won his first Tony.

HIRSCH, JUDD

c/o Morton L. Leavy, 11 East 44th St., New York, NY 10017
BORN: 1935, New York City. ACHIEVEMENTS: Emmy Award, The Law, 1974; Emmy Award, Outstanding Lead Actor for a Single Performance in a Drama or Comedy Series, Rhoda, 1977; Emmy Award, Lead Actor in a Comedy Series, Taxi, 1981 and 1983; Antoinette Perry Award, Best Actor in a Play, I'm Not Rappaport, 1986; Golden Globe Award, Best Actor in a Television Musical or Comedy Series, Dear John, 1989; Antoinette Perry Award, Best Leading Actor, Conversations With My Father, 1992. STUDIED: DeWitt Clinton High School, Bronx, N.Y.; Cooper Union, 1957; City College of the City University of New York, B.S., physics, 1960; studied theater at American Academy of Dramatic Arts, Herbert Berghof Studios, and Gene Frankel Studio; studied acting with Bill Hickey, Viveca Lindford, and Uta Hagen.

Well known for his role as Alex Rieger on the television series, *Taxi*, Judd Hirsch didn't come at acting directly. In the 1950s Hirsch studied architecture at Cooper Union and then got a bachelor's degree in physics in 1960. However, two years later, Hirsch debuted in the play, *Crisis in the Old Sawmill*, at the Back Room Theatre, in Estes Park, Colo. He appeared in numerous plays during the 1960s, although his stage work has tapered off as he has devoted more energy to television and movies. Hirsch debuted on television in the movie, *The Law*, in 1974. That same year, he debuted in the movie, *Serpico*. Hirsch has had major roles in three television series. He appeared on *Taxi* from 1978 until 1982, on *Detective in the House* in 1985, and on *Dear John* in the late 1980s. His most memorable part on film was as Dr. Tyrone Berger in *Ordinary People*, in 1980, which won him an Academy Award nomination for best supporting actor. Hirsch returned to the stage for *I'm Not Rappaport*, in 1985 and 1986, and *Conversations with My Father* in 1991 and 1992, with both productions earning him Tony awards.

HITCHINGS, GEORGE HERBERT

BORN: 1905, Hoquiam, Wash. ACHIEVEMENTS: Nobel Prize in Physiology or Medicine (shared with Gertrude Ellon) 1988; Gairdner Award; Gregor Mendel Award; Passano Award; de Villier Award; Medicinal Chemistry Award; Bertner Federation Award; Mullard Award; Papanicalaou Award; C. Chester Stock Medal; Oscar B. Hunter Award; Alfred Burger Award; Lekow Medal, Poland; Albert Schweitzer Prize. STUDIED: University of Washington; Harvard University.

Designing drugs that selectively treat specific diseases won the Nobel Prize for the George Hitchings and Gertrude Ellon, who worked together for Wellcome Company, a pharmaceutical company in North Carolina. The two researched differences in the structure and actions of normal and abnormal cells to reach their findings, which were later used to operate against various disease states, including leukemia, malaria, gout, urinary and respiratory infections, and autoimmune disorders.

HOCKNEY, DAVID

c/o Andre Emmerich Gallery, 41 E. 57th St., New York, NY 10022
BORN: 1937 ACHIEVEMENTS: Graphic Prize, Biennial, Paris; Guinness Award, London; collections: Museum of Modern Art; Victoria and Albert Museum; exhibitions: Museum of Modern Art; Arts Council of Great Britain. STUDIED: Bradford College of Art; Royal College of Art, London.

Although this British artist was first identified with late Pop Art, David Hockney's stylistic tendencies came from Abstract Expressionism. Often his autobiographical works are known for their irony and humor, and a basic theme is the figure, in designs and surroundings which explain character. His acrylic paintings are bright and naturalistic, but flattened, with a strong sense of pattern. A versatile artist, Hockney has made photographic collages in which fragments are overlapped to create one image, such as *Desk, London, June 1984*. Other accomplishments include drawings and book illustrations, gouaches, lithographs, etchings and aquatints. His interest in the effects produced by moving water, and in reflections in glass, was evident in a series of paintings and in an autobiographical film, *A Bigger Splash. Hockney Paints the Stage* is a recent showing of paintings, drawings and displays depicting the various costume and stage designs he has executed for the theater.

HOFFMAN, DUSTIN LEE

Punch Productions, 75 Rockfeller Plaza, New York, NY 10019
BORN: 1937, Los Angeles. ACHIEVEMENTS: Academy Award, Best Actor, Kramer vs. Kramer, 1980; Golden Globe Award, Best Actor, Tootsie, 1982; Academy Award, Best Actor, Rain Man, 1989. STUDIED: attended Los Angeles Conservatory of Music; Santa Monica City College; studied acting at the Pasadena Playhouse and the Actor's Studio.

Dustin Hoffman originally aspired to be a concert pianist; acting was actually his third choice as a career. He has primarily applied the art of acting to the stage and the screen. The breadth of characters he has convincingly portrayed is probably unequaled by any other American actor. Hoffman made his film debut in *The Tiger Makes Out* in 1967, but it was another 1967 film that propelled him into stardom. He portrayed Ben Braddock in *The Graduate*, and established his status as a star. Hoffman continued his career in the films *Midnight Cowboy*, 1969; *Little Big Man*, 1970; *Straw Dogs*, 1971; *Papillon*, 1973; *Kramer vs. Kramer*, 1979; *Rain Man*, 1988; and many others.

HOFFMAN, ROALD

Cornell University, Department of Chemistry, Ithaca, NY 14853
BORN: 1937, Zloczow (Poland). ACHIEVEMENTS: Nobel Prize in Physics (shared with Kenichi Fukui, Japan), 1981; American Chemical Society Award; Fresenius Award; Harrison Howe Award; Annual Award of International Academy of Quantum Molecular Sciences; Arthur C. Cope Award, American Chemical Society; Linus Pauling Award; Nichols Medal; Inorganic Chemistry Award, American Chemical Society. STUDIED: Columbia University; Harvard University.

Developed between 1965 and 1969,—with Robert Burns Woodward, himself a Nobel winner in 1965—Hoffman's success in applying quantum mechanic theories to predict the course of chemical reactions won this naturalized American Nobel attention two years after Woodward's death. Their theory became known as the "Woodward-Hoffman Rules" and solved problems on heat and light contradictions in the bonding of molecules, a problem Woodward first encountered while working on the synthesis of vitamin B12, a 12-year research project. Meanwhile, the Japanese Kenichi Fukui, one of the new breed of scientists Japan desperately needed after World War II, was working along the same lines, and in 1950, published his progress report. Insights developed by Fukui, and finally rewarded in his sharing the Nobel Prize with Hoffman, became completely overshadowed, however, by the Woodward-Hoffman Rules developed 15 years later. Fukui is the first Japanese scientist honored with a Nobel.

HOLLAND, TOM

28 Roble Rd., Berkeley, CA 94705
BORN: 1936. ACHIEVEMENTS: Guggenheim Fellowship; NEA Fellowship; collections: Museum of Modern Art, New York City; San Francisco Museum of Modern Art; exhibitions: James Corcoran Gallery, Santa Monica, Calif.; Charles Cowles Gallery, New York City. STUDIED: University of California, Santa Barbara; University of California, Berkeley.

Tom Holland's paintings and sculptures are bright, three-dimensional geometric works, often in day-glo colors. *Helli*, in epoxy on aluminum, is one of the larger examples of what he calls a painting, even though it is two-sided and freestanding. He paints and works layer upon layer, each one referring to the structure of that underneath, so that these "stand-up" paintings, at times, take on an organic quality. Through this layering, he explores concepts of the substance underlying matter. He has also worked in fiberglass.

HOLLER, MARK

Intel, 2200 Mission Col. Blvd., Santa Clara, CA 95054
(406) 987-8080
ACHIEVEMENTS: Co-developer of the Ni1000 recognition accelerator computer chip.

Most standard computers operate in a serial fashion, carrying out instructional steps one at a time. A new computer chip developed by Mark Holler, of Intel, and Michael Glier, of Nestor manufacturing , is a breakthrough in robotics. The Ni1000 recognition accelerator chip is structured on a latticework of 1,024 silicon "neurons," each interconnected to communicate with its fellow neurons. Each neuron can store a tremendous amount of information. This storage capacity makes it possible for the Ni1000 to perform 17 billion simple operations a second, including identifying faces and spotting trends in stock market data. Unlike other neural systems, it need not be programmed and reprogrammed. The chip can also "learn" as it goes along, like the human brain, becoming increasingly skilled in recognizing the patterns it analyzes.

HOLLINGS, ERNEST F.

SR-125 Russell Office Building, Washington, D.C. 20510 (202) 224-6121
BORN: 1922, Charleston, S.C. ACHIEVEMENTS: South Carolina legislator; South Carolina Lieutenant Governor, 1955-59; South Carolina Governor, 1959-63; U.S. Senator, 1967-. STUDIED: The Citadel, B.A., 1942; University of South Carolina, LL.B., 1947.

A fiscal conservative, Sen. Hollings is the ranking Democratic member of the Commerce, Science and Transportation Committee, and the senior member of the Budget Committee. An advocate of pay-as-you-go spending, "Fritz Freeze" is a supporter of a balanced budget constitutional amendment. His other legislative concerns include trade and communications issues. Prior to his election to the Senate in 1966, he spent 18 years in state politics, serving in the South Carolina legislature from 1949 to 1955, as lieutenant governor from 1955 to 1963, and as governor from 1963 to 1966. During World War II, Hollings was an Army officer in North Africa and Europe, and was awarded the Bronze Star.

HOLMES, RUPERT

c/o ASCAP, 1 Lincoln Plaza, New York, NY 10023 (212) 595-3050
BORN: 1947, Northwich (England). ACHIEVEMENTS: Grammy Award, Best Original Score for A Star Is Born (with Kenny Ascher, Alan and Marilyn Bergman, Barbara Streisand, and others) 1977; Grammy Award, Best Cast Show Award for The Mystery of Edwin Drood; Record World, Cashbox, Performance, Most Promising Male Vocalist; American DJ Award, Best Male Vocalist; World Popular Music Song Festival Awards, Outstanding Song and Performance; Antoinette Perry Awards, Best Original Score and Best Book of a Musical, and Drama Desk Award, Best Music, Best Book, and Best Orchestration, all for The Mystery of Edwin Drood.

The composer of the popular *The Pina Colada Song* is the son of a band leader in the U.S. Army who was stationed in England and brought his son to America at age 1. Rupert Holmes won the first of two Grammys, with a medley of collaboraters, at age 29. Before that he had played bass with a rock band and performed as a backup vocalist. From that Grammy forward, Holmes' triple-play talents as composer, musician, and singer brought him a multitude of awards for music performed in stage plays, in films, on television, and on albums. He has arranged music for many top singers and groups, including the Platters and the Drifters. In film appearances he was the band leader in the comedy *No Small Affair*, featuring Demi Moore as a 23-year-old rock singer, and he appeared in the heartfelt drama *The Pursuit of Happiness*. Among other films he scored was *Jaws: The Revenge*. Holmes also composed the music and wrote the lyrics for three stage plays and for the New York Shakespeare Festival.

HOPE, BOB

c/o Eliot Kozak, 3008 Riverside Drive, Suite 100, Burbank, CA 91505
BORN: 1903, Eltham (England). ACHIEVEMENTS: Academy Award; Emmy Award; Congressional Gold Medal presented by President Dwight D. Eisenhower; Medal of Freedom, presented by President John F. Kennedy; Medal of Freedom, presented by President Lyndon B. Johnson.

Bob Hope's prolific career in the entertainment industry has spanned six decades, and has included appearances in more than 475 television programs and specials, 1,000 radio programs and 50 films. Born Leslie Towne Hope, he and his family emigrated to the United States in 1907 and settled in Cleveland, Ohio. Before entering show business, Hope tried amateur boxing. In 1927 he made his Broadway debut in *The Sidewalks of New York* and the next year he began using the name Bob Hope. His radio career started in 1935; 1938 he made his film debut in *The Big Broadcast of 1938*, the film in which the song *Thanks for the Memories* became his theme song. Teaming up with Bing Crosby and Dorothy Lamour in 1940, Hope filmed *The Road to Singapore*, the first of seven road pictures the trio made together. This movie made Hope a Hollywood celebrity. In 1950, he signed a contract with NBC, where he still appears in television specials. During World War II he entertained the U.S. troops overseas and established the annual Christmas tour from 1941-1972. The tours continued through the Korean and Vietnam wars and in Lebanon in 1983. Known for his humanitarian and philanthropic efforts, he has helped raise more than a billion dollars for hospitals, scientific research and other humanitarian organizations.

HOPE, FRANKLIN JOHN

Duke University School of Law, Durham, NC 27708
BORN: 1915, Rentiesville, Okla. ACHIEVEMENTS: Author of From Slavery to Freedom: A History of American Negroes; first African American president of the American Historical Association. STUDIED: Fisk University, B.A., history; Harvard University, M.A., Ph.D., history.

After teaching at colleges in North Carolina while he wrote on the side, Franklin Hope, in 1947, published a landmark historical study, *From Slavery to Freedom: A History of American Negroes*. He then taught at Howard College, Brooklyn College, University of Chicago, and Duke University, publishing three more studies which made him an important voice among all American historians. He became the first African-American president of the American Historical Association.

HORNER, JAMES

c/o MCA Records, Inc., 70 Universal City Plaza, Universal City, CA 91608 (213) 508-4000
Horner is a prominent composer. For career credentials consult the portion of this book entitled "Biographees by Profession" in the Appendix. Within this

portion, the list "Composers" describes requirements for inclusion in this volume.

HORNSBY, BRUCE

c/o RCA Records, 1133 Sixth Ave., New York, NY 10036 (212) 930-4000
BORN: 1954, Williamsburg, Va. ACHIEVEMENTS: Grammy, The Way It Is; Best New Artist, 1986. STUDIED: University of Miami, Berklee School of Music.
Bruce Hornsby spent years trying to break into the big-time arena of the music business before he finally made it. Born in Williamsburg, Va., he sent demo tapes to record companies for years while making a living playing piano in bars. In 1980, Hornsby and his brother, John Hornsby, moved to Los Angeles. The two worked at 20th Century Fox for three years. While there, Hornsby met Huey Lewis who later produced Hornsby's first album in 1986. *The Way it is*, by Hornsby and the Range, sold two million copies and earned the singer and his band a Grammy. He has continued his recording success with subsequent albums, and has written successful songs for other musicians, as well. *Jacob's Ladder*, written for Huey Lewis, and *The End of the Innocence*, for Don Henley, are two notable examples.

HOUSTON, WHITNEY

c/o Arista Records, 8370 Wilshire Blvd., Beverly Hills, CA 90211 (213) 655-9222
Houston is a prominent entertainer and Grammy-Award winning pop singer. She has also made several films in cluding *The Bodyguard* in which she starred with actor Kevin costner.

HOVING, LUCAS

Lucas Hoving and Company, 826 Adams St., Albany, CA 94706 (415) 824-5044
Hoving is a prominent dancer. For career credentials consult the portion of this book entitled "Biographees by Profession" in the Appendix. Within this portion, the list "Dancers" describes requirements for inclusion in this volume.

HUBEL, DAVID HUNTER

Harvard Medical School, Boston, MA 02115
BORN: 1926, Windsor, Ontario (Canada). ACHIEVEMENTS: Nobel Prize in Physiology or Medicine (shared with Roger Wolcott Sperry and Torsten N. Wiesel), 1981; Trustees Research to Prevent Blindness Award; Lewis S. Rosenstiel Award, Brandeis University; Friedenwald Award, Association for Research in Vision and Ophthalmology; Kark Spencer Lashley Prize, American Philosophical Society; Louisa Gross Horowitz Prize, Columbia University; Dickson Prize, University of Pittsburgh; Ledie Prize, Harvard University. STUDIED: McGill University, Canada.
The David Hubel team won their Nobel honor for vital work on "information processing in the visual system of the brain" describes requirements for inclusion in this volume. They discovered that every nerve carrier in the system (neurons) which codes and carries nerve impulses to the brain, responds best to certain stimuli In addition they discovered the complicated arrangement of the thousands or millions of photosensitive cells that operate to make vision work. The co-laureates in related work made discoveries in binocular vision (involving both eyes) and the importance of early stimulation of vision for its later development. Hubel is a naturalized American.

HUGHS, MARK

Herbalife International, Inc., 9800 La Cienega Blvd., Inglewood, CA 90301 (310) 410-9600
Hughs is a prominent business leader. For career credentials consult the portion of this book entitled "Biographees by Profession" in the Appendix. Within this portion, the list "Business Leaders" describes requirements for inclusion in this volume.

HUME, BRIT

ABC News, 1717 DeSales St., NW., Washington, D.C. 20036
Hume is a prominent journalist. For career credentials consult the portion of this book entitled "Biographees by Profession" in the Appendix. Within this portion, the list "Journalists" describes requirements for inclusion in this volume.

HUNT, JAMES B.

Office of the Governor, Raleigh, NC 27603 (919) 733-4240
BORN: 1937, Greensboro, N.C. ACHIEVEMENTS: Governor, North Carolina; Ford Foundation economic advisor to Nepal. STUDIED: North Carolina State University, B.S., agricultural education, 1959; M.S., agricultural economics, 1962; University of North Carolina-Chapel Hill, law, 1964.
James B. Hunt has a long history of public service in elective office. He was elected lieutenant governor of North Carolina in 1972. Next he served two terms as governor of North Carolina, from 1977 to 1985. During his first two terms, Hunt concentrated his efforts on education and economic development. He created, and still chairs, the National Board for Professional Teaching Standards, established to promote excellence in teaching through voluntary board certification of teachers. Hunt received the James B. Conant Award in 1984 as the public official in America who has contributed significantly to education. Hunt was elected to an unprecedented third term as governor in 1992. He has continued his focus on education, but is also working for tax relief, down-sizing government, and an overhaul of the state's welfare system.

HUNT, RICHARD HOWARD

1017 W. Lill Ave., Chicago, IL 60614
BORN: 1935. ACHIEVEMENTS: Collections: Museum of Modern Art; Metropolitan Museum of Art; exhibitions: Museum of Modern Art; Art Institute of Chicago. STUDIED: School of the Art Institute of Chicago.

Although his medium was welded sculpture during his study in Chicago, Richard Hunt has also made lithographs. By 1960 he included found objects and car parts, and assembled them into plant-like and insect-like pieces with textured linear extensions. In the late 1960s he constructed "hybrid figures," combining open and closed forms. He cast sculpture in aluminum in addition to the welded pieces. Since the 1970s Hunt has added flourishes to the constructions, so that they simultaneously magnify and are magnified by space.

HUNTER, HOLLY

c/o MSI, Inc, 370 Lexington, Suite 808, New York City, NY; (212) 481-5751
BORN: 1958, Conyers, Ga. ACHIEVEMENTS: Emmy, Best Actress in a Miniseries, Roe vs. Wade, 1989; Academy Award and Golden Globe, Best Actress, The Piano, 1993; Emmy, Best Actress in a Miniseries, The Positively True Adventures of the Alleged Texas Cheerleader-Murdering Mom, 1993. STUDIED: Carnegie Mellon University, B.A. 1980; acting training with Paul Draper.

The daughter of a sporting goods manufacturer's representative, Holly Hunter grew up on a cattle farm in rural Georgia driving a tractor. She is the youngest of seven children. Hunter first appeared on stage off-Broadway in 1981 in the play, *Battery*. That same year she also debuted on Broadway in *Crimes of the Heart*, and appeared in her first film, *The Burning*. Hunter appeared in numerous other stage, film and television productions during the mid-1980s, culminated by her role in *Broadcast News*, for which she received an Academy Award and Golden Globe nomination in 1988. Hunter won big in 1993, earning an Emmy, an Oscar and a Golden Globe award in the same year.

HURT, WILLIAM

c/o William Morris Agency, 151 El Camino Dr., Beverly Hills, CA 90212 (310) 274-7451
BORN: 1959, Washington, D.C. ACHIEVEMENTS: Academy Award, Best Actor, Kiss of the Spider Woman, 1985. STUDIED: Attended Tufts University, Julliard School of Music and Drama.

William Hurt made his initial mark as a stage actor, during his off-Broadway debut at the New York Shakespeare Festival in 1977. His first film appearance was in *Altered States* in 1980. In 1981 he played the part of Ned Racine in *Body Heat*, and became a star. His other principal films are *The Big Chill*, 1983; *Gorky Park*, 1983; *Kiss of the Spider Woman*, 1984; *Children of a Lesser God*, 1986; *Broadcast News*, 1987; and most recently, *Trial by Jury*, 1994.

HUSSEY, KEVIN

NASA Jet Propulsion Laboratory, L.B. Johnson Space Center, Houston, TX 77058
ACHIEVEMENTS: Inventor of Videos from Space.

While man may not yet be able to fly manned spacecraft over the surface of distant planets, Kevin Hussey has made it possible to create realistic, three-dimensional video simulations. Hussey is supervisor of the visualization and earth sciences application group at NASA's Jet Propulsion Laboratory. His system takes data from space probes and converts them into 3-D videos. The videos show overflights of Mars, Venus, asteroids, and even far-away Neptune, bringing them alive for scientists to study and children to learn from.

HUSTON, ANGELICA

William Morris Agency, 151 El Camino, Beverly Hills, CA 90212
BORN: 1951, Los Angeles. ACHIEVEMENTS: Academy Award, Best Supporting Actress, Prizzi's Honor, 1985. STUDIED: Trained for the stage at Loft Studio.

Angelica Huston, daughter of John Huston, comes from a family of movie actors and directors. After studying in Europe and training for the stage at the Loft Studio, she began her acting career debuting in the film *A Walk with Love and Death* in 1967. She followed with a number of appearances in films such as *Sinful Davey* in 1969, in 1976 *Swashbuckler*, *The Last Tycoon* in 1976 and *This Is Spinal Tap*, in 1984. It wasn't until 1985 when she played the part of Maerose Prizzi in *Prizzi's Honor* —directed by her father— that she received an Academy Award for best supporting actress. In 1991 she appeared in *The Addams Family* and in 1993 *The Addams Family Values*.

HUTTON, TIMOTHY

United Talent Agency, 9560 Wilshire Blvd., Beverly Hills, CA, 90212
BORN: 1960 Los Angeles. ACHIEVEMENTS: Academy Award, Best Supporting Actor, Ordinary People, 1981.

Timothy Hutton got started on the fast track. He won an Academy Award for his very first movie, *Ordinary People*, in 1981. Timothy is the son of Jim Hutton, also an actor, and Mayline Hutton, a teacher and printer. Prior to his initial movie appearance, Hutton acted in several television movies during the late 1970s, including *Zuma Beach*, in 1978, and *Young Love, First Love*, in 1981. Hutton's success in *Ordinary People* was no flash in the pan. He continued to appear in successful movies throughout the 1980s, including *Iceman*, in 1984, and *The Falcon and the Snowman*, in 1985. He has also tried out the director's chair, directing the video, *Drive*, performed by the *Cars* in 1984, and *Grandpa's Ghost* for the television series, *Amazing Stories*, in 1985. His film appearances in the 1990s were not as successful, but he did appear in the Broadway play *Prelude to a Kiss*, 1990 and *Babylon Gardens*, 1991.

IACOCCA, LIDO (LEE) A.

Bantam Books, 666 5th Ave., New York, NY 10103 (212) 765-6500
BORN: 1924, Allentown, Pa. ACHIEVEMENTS: Automotive executive, best-selling author. STUDIED: LeHigh University, B.S., 1945; Princeton University, M.E., 1946.

The son of Italian immigrants, Lee Iacocca joined the Ford Motor Company in 1946, and headed the team that created the best-selling Mustang model in the 1950s, subsequently working his way up to president in 1970. Abruptly fired by Henry Ford II in 1978, Iacocca moved to the foundering Chrysler Corp., where he served as president and then chairman, rescuing the automaker from bankruptcy. Later, he raised more than $265 million for the rehabilitation of the Statue of Liberty and Ellis Island. His inspirational biography, *Iacocca*, 1984, was a best-seller, and cemented his reputation as a corporate folk hero. He also wrote *Talking Straight*, 1988.

IBRAHIM, YOUSSEF

The *New York Times*, 229 West 43rd St., New York, NY 10046 (212) 556-1234

BORN: 1943, Cairo (Egypt). ACHIEVEMENTS: George Polk Award; Overseas Press Club Award; International Energy Economists Association Award. STUDIED: Columbia University Graduate School of Journalism, Cabot Scholarship; graduated the American University in Cairo, bachelor's degree, economics, political science, and journalism.

Youssef Ibrahim is a *New York Times* correspondent based in Paris who covers the Arab world. He is an expert in Middle East affairs and international energy. Ibrahim has been with the *New York Times* since 1977. Previously, he was an associate editor of the *Mideast Markets* newsletter, published by Chase World Information Corporation, from 1973 to 1977. Ibrahim was a bureau chief in Tehran and a correspondent in London. In 1981, he left the *Times* and joined the *Wall Street Journal* as a senior correspondent. In 1987, he returned to the *Times* and has been with them in Paris ever since. Ibrahim authored *Egypt*, a political and economic analysis.

IMPIGLIA, GIANCARLO

182 Grand St., New York, NY 10013

BORN: 1940. ACHIEVEMENTS: Collections: Museum of the City of New York; Museo Italo-Americano; exhibitions: Alex Rosenberg Gallery; Goldman-Kraft Gallery. STUDIED: Accademia di Belle Arti, Rome; Liceo Artistico, Rome.

Giancarlo Impiglia has worked in a variety of media, including assemblages, acrylics and oils on canvas, cut-out wood sculptures, and silkscreens. His education and training in Rome gave him a classical foundation, from which he has developed his own, highly personal imagery. His early pieces consisted of assemblages of clothes, canvas, and uniforms upon which he painted his images. His work was based on the conviction that clothes are costumes that reflect cultural values. In his current work, he still is questioning artistic and societal values. In these figurative works, the figures are faceless, suggesting the anonymity of urban life. There is a pronounced sense of isolation in his depictions of sumptuous interiors, where people supposedly gather to interact. Costume and posture are epitomized to the exclusion of content, communication, and emotion. These witty and humorous works satirically comment on the human condition.

INGRAM, JAMES

Warner Bros. Records, P.O. Box 6868, Burbank, CA 91510

BORN: 1956, Akron, Ohio. ACHIEVEMENTS: Grammy award, Best rhythm and Blues Vocal Performance, One Hundred Ways, 1981; Grammy award, Best Rhythm and Blues Duo (with Michael MacDonald), Yah Mo B There, 1984; Academy Award nomination, Best Original Song, The Day I Fall in Love (from Beethoven's 2nd), 1993.

James Ingram, a protegee of Quincy Jones, burst on the music scene in the 1980s with his Grammy-award-winning hit song *One Hundred Ways*. His smooth vocal styling made him an instant hit on both the pop and R&B charts. Ingram enjoyed great success in the 1980s, and teamed up with several pop-singers to produce hit duets, including *How Do You Keep the Music Playing*, 1983 (with Patti Austin); *Baby Come To Me*, 1982 (with Regina Belle); and *Yah Mo B There*, 1983 (with Michael MacDonald), which won a Grammy.

IRANI, RAY R.

Occidental Petroleum Corp., 10889 Wilshire Blvd., Los Angeles, CA 90024 (213) 879-1700

Irani is a prominent business leader. For career credentials consult the portion of this book entitled "Biographees by Profession" in the Appendix. Within this portion, the list "Business Leaders" describes requirements for inclusion in this volume.

IRVING, JOHN W.

c/o William Morrow & Co., 105 Madison Ave., New York, NY 10016 (212) 889-3050

BORN: 1942, Exeter, N.H. ACHIEVEMENTS: National Book Award, The World According to Garp, 1978; Fellow of the National Endowment for the Arts. STUDIED: University of Pittsburgh, University of Vienna, University of New Hampshire.

John Irving's fourth novel, *The World According to Garp*, 1978, a family saga about an eccentric feminist and her novelist son, earned him a National Book Award and a national following. His next novel, *The Hotel New Hampshire*, 1981, followed a similar vein in depicting 25 years in the life of a family that grew older in three hotels with the same name. His other novels included *Setting Free the Bears*, 1968; *The 158-Pound Marriage*, 1974; *The Cider House Rules*, 1985; and *A Prayer for Owen Meany*, 1989.

IRWIN, ROBERT

10966 Strathmore Dr., Los Angeles, CA 90024

BORN: 1928. ACHIEVEMENTS: Collections: Museum of Contemporary Art, Los Angeles; Whitney Museum, New York City; exhibitions: Museum of Modern Art, New York City; Matrix, Berkeley, Calif. STUDIED: Otis Art Institute; Jepson Art Institute; Chouinard Art Institute.

An abstract expressionist painter during the 1950s, Robert Irwin later abandoned personal expression for minimalism in the 1960s. He questioned the meaning of image and object in a series of dot paintings, followed by a series of spray-painted discs. In works circa

1968, aluminum convex discs protruded from the wall and were illuminated by floodlights, creating interior and exterior shapes in a composition of shapes and shadows. Installations during the 1970s explored varying arrangements of interior light and space, as in *Portal*. His recent work includes site/architectural sculpture in public spaces. His conceptual approach to art incorporates inquiries into philosophy, natural science and social science.

ISAAC, ROBERT M.

P. O. Box 1575, MS: 410, Colorado Springs, CO 80901
(719) 578-6600
BORN: 1928, Colorado Springs, Colo. ACHIEVEMENTS: Past president, U.S. Conference of Mayors. STUDIED: U.S. Military Academy, West Point, B.S., 1951; University of Southern California, J.D., 1962.
Robert Issac was born in Colorado Springs, Colo. in 1928. After spending two years as an enlisted member of the U.S. Army, he entered the U.S. Military Academy at West Point. He graduated a second lieutenant in 1951 with a B.S. degree. Issac served in the Army until 1957, after which he entered the University of Southern California and received his J.D. degree in 1962. After receiving his law degree, Isaac entered private practice. In 1965 he served as the assistant district attorney for the Fourth Judicial District. Isaac became the first popularly elected mayor of Colorado Springs in April, 1979. He has been elected to five consecutive terms as mayor, beginning his latest term in April, 1995.

IVEY, JUDITH

Triad Artists, 10100 Santa Monica Blvd., 16th Floor, Los Angeles, CA 90067
BORN: 1951, El Paso, Texas. ACHIEVEMENTS: Antoinette Perry Award, Best Featured Actress in a Play, Steaming, 1983; Antoinette Perry Award, Best Featured Actress in a Play, Hurlyburly, 1985. STUDIED: Illinois State University, B.S., 1973.
Judith Ivey began her stage career playing the part of Jilly in the play, *The Sea* in 1974. The daughter of Nathan Ivey, a college president, and Dorothy (Lewis) Ivey, a teacher, Judith Ivey has extensive stage work to her credit during the late 1970s and early 1980s. She debuted on Broadway as Kate in *Bedroom Farce*, in 1979, which ran for 140 performances at Brooks Atkinson Theatre. In 1982, Ivey debuted on television as Louise in *The Shady Hill Kidnapping*, on American Playhouse. She appeared in several more television movies, playing nuns in two: *Dixie: Changing Habits*, in 1983, and *We Are the Children*, in 1987. Ivey began her film career in 1984 with the movie, *Harry and Son*. Among her recent films are: *Brighton Beach Memoirs*, in 1986, and *Miles from Home*, in 1988.

JACKSON, JANET

A&M Records, 1416 N. LaBrea, Los Angeles, CA 90028
(213) 469-2411

BORN: 1966, Gary, Ind. ACHIEVEMENTS: Grammy, Best R&B Song, That's the Way Love Goes, 1993; Grammy, Best Music Video-Long form, Rhythm Nation 1814, 1989.
Born into one of America's most famous musical families, Janet Jackson stepped out of the shadow of her talented brothers and took control of her own career. After two mediocre attempts at a solo career, Jackson, the youngest sister of Michael, Marlon, Tito, Jermaine and Jackie, released her first successful effort in 1985. The album, *Control*, proclaimed Jackson's independent identity from her singing siblings. Masterminded by super producing duo, Jimmy Jam and Terry Lewis, *Control* produced five Top Ten hits and sold more than four million copies. Jackson's follow up effort, *Rhythm Nation 1814*, was even more successful, generating seven Top Ten hits including *Miss You Much*, *Escapade*, and *Black Cat*. Riding on a wave of successful hits and phenomenal record sales, Jackson made music history in 1991 by signing a $32 million recording contract with Virgin Records. With her hot dance moves, sensuous lyrics, spicy music videos, as well as sales and radio airplay success, Janet Jackson is second only to Madonna among the 1990s' hottest female pop singers.

JACKSON, KEITH JEROME

ABC Sports, 47 W 66th St., New York, NY 10023-6290
BORN: 1928, Carrolton, Ga. ACHIEVEMENTS: National Sportscaster of the Year, 1972-76; National Football Foundation (life); Seattle-Puget Sound Sportscaster of the Decade, 1978; American Legion Good Guy Award, 1983; Amos Alonzo Stagg Award, American Football Coaches Association, 1993. STUDIED: Washington State University, B.A. broadcast journalism, 1954.
A sportscaster for over 20 years with ABC Sports, Keith Jackson is known for his coverage of college football. In 1954, after graduation from Washington State University, he joined KOMO Radio-TV in Seattle, Wash. as a sports and special event director, eventually becoming associate news director. In 1964, he joined ABC Radio as a news correspondent, a position he held until 1969. From 1971 until 1974 Jackson was the sports director at radio station KABC in New York. He began his coverage of college football in 1974, a position he still holds today. Jackson has covered other sporting events for ABC including the *Wide World of Sports*, baseball, and the Olympic Games.

JACKSON, MICHAEL JOSEPH

Bob Jones, MJJ Productions, 10960 Wilshire Blvd., #2204, Los Angeles, CA 90024
BORN: 1958, Gary, Ind. ACHIEVEMENTS: Grammy, Best R&B Vocal Male, Don't Stop Till You Get Enough, 1979; Grammy, Album of the Year, Thriller, 1983; Grammy, Best Pop Vocal Male, Thriller, 1983; Grammy, Best R&B Song, Billie Jean, 1983; Grammy, Best Recording for Children, E.T. The Extraterrestrial, 1983; Grammy, Record of the Year, Beat It, 1984; Grammy, Best Pop Vocal Male, Beat It, 1984; Grammy, Song of the Year, We Are the World (with Lionel Richie), 1985; Grammy, Best Music Video, Short Form, Leave Me Alone, 1989; Grammy, Legend Award, 1993. STUDIED: private school; L.H.D. (honorary) Fisk University, 1988.

In the early 1960s, when Michael Jackson and his brothers were discovered by Motown and formed the Jackson Five, Jackson's talent was apparent from the start. The group became popular beginning in 1968, with numerous recordings and television appearances. The Jackson Five recorded a series of hits with Jackson as the lead singer. By the mid-1970s, the group suffered growing pains, and their appeal began to diminish. The Jackson Five left Motown and eventually Jackson left the group to go solo. In 1978, with the release of his solo album *Off the Wall,*, he created a new persona and grabbed the spotlight once again. His 1982 album, *Thriller*, broke sales records worldwide and energized the music business. His videos, which were mini-movies, boosted his record sales, and other groups began to copy this format. His other albums, *Bad*, 1987, and *Dangerous*, 1992, were not as successful, but were big sellers. In 1995 he released *History*, an album that sparked controversy as well as his record sales. Jackson's total record sales have made him one of the most phenomenal popular music successes since Elvis Presley and the Beatles.

JAHN, HELMUT

Murphy/Jahn Associates, 35 E. Wacker Drive, Chicago, IL 60611 (312) 427-7300

BORN: 1940. ACHIEVEMENTS: Distinguished Building Award, AIA, Chicago, 1984; Brunner Memorial Prize, 1982; Progressive Architecture Award, 1976, 1977, 1978; notable works: State of Illinois Building, Chicago; Board of Trade Annex, Chicago; One South Wacker Office Tower, Chicago. STUDIED: Illinois Institute of Technology

Helmut Jahn began his career as a functionalist, apprenticing at Chicago's Miesian mainstay, C.F. Murphy and Associates. Like many architects of his generation, he tired of the reducible, remote, "overplayed" Modernist credo. His straying from the party line at first was subtle: a secondary neo-Georgian facade for the University of Illinois' Agriculture School in Champaign/Urbana, Ill.; Deco accents and primary-color splashes for Chicago's Board of Trade high-rise annex. His imposing 1985 State of Illinois Building, however, was the first unambiguous signal of his arrival as major Postmodernist. Promoted as a prototype for the buildings of the next century, it has also been criticized as an exile from an alien land, marooned in an urban and historical context to which it bears no relation. Asymmetrical, ovoid, with his characteristic blue-glass banded curtain wall, the building drapes state offices around a huge glassed-in atrium. Its 75,000 square-feet of retail space, open rotunda and sunken, oval dining plaza have created the grand public meeting place he intended, but they also create unaccustomed noise and bustle which carries through open offices. Some have suggested he's succeeded too well in his goal of "opening up the government to the people" describes requirements for inclusion in this volume.

JAKES, JOHN

Rembar & Curtis, 19 W. 44th St., New York, NY 10036

BORN: 1932, Chicago. ACHIEVEMENTS: Best-selling author. STUDIED: De Pauw University, A.B., 1953; Ohio State, M.A., 1954; De Pauw University, doctorate (honorary) 1977; Wright State University, L.L.D. (honorary), 1976; Winthrop College, L.D.H. (honorary), 1985; University of South Carolina, L.D.H. (honorary), 1993.

John Jakes worked in the creative department of various ad agencies while pursuing his craft as an author. He wrote some 40 books in relative obscurity, in genres ranging from science fiction to children's literature, as well as plays and short stories, before publishing a series of novels known collectively as *The Kent Family Chronicles*, which follows the fortunes of the Kent Family from Revolutionary times to 1976. The books in this series are: *The Bastard*, 1974; *The Rebels*, 1975; *The Seekers*, 1975; *The Furies*, 1976; *The Titans*, 1976; *The Warriors*, 1977; *The Lawless*, 1978; and *The Americans*, 1980. His other well-known novels include the *North and South* Civil War trilogy: *North and South*, 1982; *Love and War*, 1984; and *Heaven and Hell*, 1987.

JAMES, ("FOB") FOREST HOOD, JR.

State Capitol, Montgomery, Alabama 36130 (334) 242-7150

BORN: 1934, Lanett, Ala. ACHIEVEMENTS: All-American halfback, Auburn University; CEO of Coastal Erosion Control Inc. and Escambia County Environmental Corporation; won the right for school prayer in Alabama's schools. STUDIED: Auburn University, B.S., 1955.

After serving in the United States Army, James became CEO of the Coastal Erosion Control Inc. and the Escambia County Environmental Corporation. He won his first term as governor in 1979. During his first term, Gov. James waged war on illiteracy, resulting in Alabama public school children exceeding California Achievement Test national average scores. He expanded industry by convincing industrial giants such as United States Steel and General Motors to open facilities in the state. He fought the federal courts and won the right for children to pray in Alabama's public schools. In November, 1994 he defeated James E. Folsom Jr., the incumbent, and began his second term as Alabama's 55th Governor. Gov. James is the only Alabamian to be elected governor as a Democrat and then switch parties and win the election as a Republican.

JAMES, SHARPE

City Hall, 920 Broad Street, Room 214, Newark, NJ 07102 (201) 733-8004

BORN: 1936, Jacksonville, Fla. ACHIEVEMENTS: Elected mayor of Newark, N.J.; ward councilman, Newark, N.J.; councilman at large, Newark, N.J. STUDIED: Montclair State College, Springfield College, masters degree.

Although Sharpe James was born in Jacksonville, Fla. in 1936, he spent most of his life in Newark, N.J. James served in the U.S. Army, was a Newark school teacher for seven years, and a professor at Essex County College for 18 years. James' political career began in 1970, when he became the South Ward Councilman for Newark. He was re-elected twice, and in 1982, was elected as councilman-at-large. In 1986 James ran as mayor, and was sworn into office on July 1, 1986. Under James' administration, the city of Newark has won numerous national awards, including Most Livable City, All-American City, and the Environmental Protection Agency Administrator's Award.

JANKLOW, GOV. WILLIAM J.

Executive Office, 500 E. Capitol, Pierre, SD 57501 (605) 773-3212

BORN: Chicago. STUDIED: University of South Dakota, J.D., law.

Son of a prosecutor at the Nuremberg Nazi war criminal trials, he dropped out of high school and joined the Marines. After a two-year enlistment, he returned to South Dakota, married, and tried to enroll in the University of South Dakota without a high school diploma. Rejected, he talked college officials into accepting him based on his Marine service record. After earning a law degree in 1973, Janklow started working in legal aid for the state's Native Americans. At the urging of Republicans he went on to the governorship for two terms, then retired from politics for eight years. In 1994 he was elected governor again. Among his successes: a 20 percent property tax reduction; elimination of more than 500 unnecessary education laws and rules; a new method of distributing state aid to public schools, reform of the workers' compensation system, and allowing previously uninsured people to obtain the insurance they need.

JARREAU, AL

c/o MCA Records, Inc., 70 Universal City Plaza, Universal City, CA 91608 (213) 508-4000

Jarreau is a prominent composer. For career credentials consult the portion of this book entitled "Biographees by Profession" in the Appendix. Within this portion, the list "Composers" describes requirements for inclusion in this volume.

JEFFORDS, MARION H.,

530 Dirksen Senate Office Building, Washington, D.C. 20510-4503 (202) 224-5141

BORN: 1934, Rutland, Vt. ACHIEVEMENTS: NAACP Legal Defense Fund Good Guy Award, 1990. STUDIED: Yale University, B.S.I.A. Degree, 1956; Harvard Law School, L.L.B., 1962.

During his tenure as Vermont's Congressman At Large from 1975 to 1986, Jeffords co-founded the Congressional Arts Caucus and was one of six founders of the Congressional Solar Coalition. While a congressman he also served on the House Agriculture Committee, and was the ranking Republican Member of the House Education and Labor Committee. In 1988, Jeffords was elected to the United States Senate, and is currently the ranking Republican member of the Senate Labor and Human Resources Committee, where he serves as chairman of the Subcommittee on Education Arts and Humanities. Jeffords is also a co-chairman of the Northeast- Midwest Senate Coalition.

JENNINGS, PETER CHARLES

ABC Press Relations, 47 West 66th St., New York, NY 10023

BORN: 1938, Toronto.(Canada) ACHIEVEMENTS: Named best anchor U.S., Washington Journalism Review, 1988-1989. STUDIED: Trinity College School, Port Hope, Ontario; Carleton University, Ottawa, Ontario; Rider (N.J.) College, L.L.D.

Peter Jennings' first on-air broadcast position was at age 9, when he hosted a CBC radio show *Peter's People*. A former bank teller, he worked in Canadian TV before starting with ABC News as an evening correspondent. In 1968 he went into the field as an international correspondent, and became chief ABC correspondent in London, and then foreign desk anchor for *World News Tonight*. In 1983 he became senior editor and anchor for the newscast. Jenning is also involved with producing network documentaries and serves as co-anchor on *the program Turning Point*.

JENNINGS, WILL

c/o Arista Records, 6 West 57th St., New York, NY 10019 (212) 489-7400

Jennings is a prominent composer. For career credentials consult the portion of this book entitled "Biographees by Profession" in the Appendix. Within this portion, the list "Composers" describes requirements for inclusion in this volume.

JEREMIAH, ADM. DAVID E.

Office of the Secretary, Pentagon, Washington D.C., 20301 (703) 545-6700

BORN: 1934, Portland, Ore. ACHIEVEMENTS: Distinguished Service Medal with three gold stars; Legion of Merit with gold star; Meritorious Service Medal with gold star; Achievement Medal with combat "V"; Presidential Citizens Medal, 1991. STUDIED: George Washington University, M.S., financial management; graduated University of Oregon, 1955; Officer Candidate School, 1956.

Currently the vice chairman of the Joint Chiefs of Staff, Adm. Jeremiah is the nation's second-highest ranking military officer. Jeremiah has served on seven Pacific Fleet destroyers. He commanded Cruiser-Destroyer Group Eight and Task Force 60 in the Mediterranean, and directed the capture of the Egyptian airliner carrying the hijackers of the Italian cruise ship Achille Lauro. He also was in charge of operations that sank two Libyan warships and an anti-air missile site in the Gulf of Sidra between January and March 1986. In June of 1986, he became director of Navy Programming Planning, and was promoted to vice admiral in July 1986. He was named 23rd commander-in-chief, U.S. Pacific Fleet in September, 1987, and became a four star admiral. In March, 1990, he was appointed vice chairman of the Joint Chiefs of Staff by President George Bush. He began his second term in March, 1992.

JETER, MICHAEL

Writers' and Artists' Agency, 11726 San Vincente Blvd., #300, Los Angeles, CA 90049
BORN: 1952, Lawrenceburg, Tenn. ACHIEVEMENTS: Antoinette Perry Award, Best Performance, by a Featured Actor in a Musical, Grand Hotel, 1990; Emmy Award, Outstanding Supporting Actor in a Comedy Series, Evening Shade, 1992. STUDIED: Memphis State University.

Michael Jeter got his start on stage. He debuted on Broadway in 1978 as the bellboy in *Once in a Lifetime* at Circle in the Square. He has continued his stage career, appearing in numerous productions, including *The Boys Next Door*, from 1987 until 1988, and the musical, *Grand Hotel*, in 1989. Jeter has roles in three television series to his credit. He appeared as Private Ridgely in 1980 on *From Here to Eternity*, as Art Makter on *Hothouse* (also known as *The Clinic*), in 1988, and as Herman Stiles on *Evening Shade* in 1990. In addition to a stage and television career, Jeter has appeared in several movies including, *Hair*, in 1980, *Tango and Cash* in 1989, and *The Fisher King* in 1991.

JOBS, STEVEN PAUL

3475 Deer Creek Rd., Palo Alto, CA 94304
BORN: 1955. ACHIEVEMENTS: Co-Founder, Apple Computer, Inc. and NeXT Inc. STUDIED: Reed College, Portland, Ore.

Steven Jobs was adopted as an infant by Paul and Clara Jobs. During his highschool years, he was a summer employee at Hewlett-Packard, where he met Stephen Wozniak, his future business partner. Jobs graduated from high school in 1972, and entered Reed College in Portland, Ore. He left college during his freshman year, and went to work for Atari, designing video games. In 1975 Jobs became reacquainted with Wozniak, who still worked for Hewlett-Packard and was also involved in a computer club. Jobs convinced Wozniak to work with him designing and marketing small personal computers. The first Apple computers were designed and built in Jobs' parents' garage. Jobs and Wozniak started the Apple Computer Company on April 1, 1976. In 1985 Jobs left Apple. His ensuing venture was a new computer company, NeXT, Inc. The NeXT computer is considered technically superior to many computers by industry analists, who have also criticized it as being too expensive.

JOEL, BILLY

Columbia Records, 51 West 52nd St., New York, N.Y. 10019 (212) 975-4321
BORN: 1949, Long Island, N.Y. ACHIEVEMENTS: Grammy, Record of the Year, Just the Way You Are, 1978; Grammy, Song of the Year, Just the Way You Are, 1978; Grammy, Album of the Year, Billy Joel, 1979; Grammy, Best Pop Vocal-Male, 52nd Street, 1979; Best Rock Vocal-Male, Glass Houses 1980; Grammy, Best Recording for Children, In Harmony 2 (with others), 1982; Grammy, Legend Award, 1991.

When Billy Joel first came onto the scene in 1973, he was compared to Elton John. Both performers tended toward the same complex piano tunes, but Joel's music was more forceful, and his singing was more assertive. Joel's approach is rooted in the Brill Building and Broadway style, with references to former-Beatle Paul McCartney's music. Joel's style has been too far from the rock-and-roll genre to please many critics, but his showmanship and compositional abilities have made him a crowd pleaser. His biggest hit, *The Stranger*, went multi-platinum and spawned a long list of hit singles and albums.

JOHNS, JASPER

225 E. Houston St., New York, NY 10002
BORN: 1930. ACHIEVEMENTS: Collections: Museum of Modern Art; Whitney Museum of American Art; exhibitions: Museum of Modern Art; Art Institute of Chicago. STUDIED: University of South Carolina

Jasper Johns reacted against Abstract Expressionism with a first solo show in 1958, which included paintings of targets, flags, numerals and alphabets. He chose everyday objects for the subjects, focusing attention not on the objects themselves but on the act of painting. An encaustic painting method turned ordinary images into thought-provoking works, which pointed to the ambiguity between object and image. His constant questioning of the nature of art brought him to the utilization of actual common objects. He cast in bronze the likenesses of beer cans, flashlights, and light bulbs, and affixed real objects directly to the paintings as well. Known for visual puns and contradictions, Johns has logically been compared to Marcel Duchamp. Unlike Duchamp, he has not renounced painting, but has continued to question the ways of seeing, maintaining the unique ambivalence of his creations.

JOHNSON, GARY E.

State Capitol Building, Santa Fe, NM 87503 (505) 827-3000
BORN: 1953, Minot, N.D. ACHIEVEMENTS: Governor of New Mexico; owner of Big J Enterprises, Inc. STUDIED: University of New Mexico, B.S. political science.

Gary Johnson moved to Albuquerque, New Mexico in 1966, where he attended public schools and then the University of New Mexico. In 1974 he began going door-to-door seeking work in the construction field to pay his college tuition fees. In 1976, with the assistance of his wife, Johnson formed Big J Enterprises, Inc. Over the ensuing years, the company became a full-service commercial and industrial construction company. Johnson has served on the board of the Albuquerque Chamber of Commerce and the board of advisors of the University of New Mexico Anderson School of Management Center of Entrepreneurship and Economic Development. The 26th governor of the state of New Mexico, Johnson has pledged that "people before politics" will define state government under his administration.

JOHNSTON, J. BENNETT

421 Russell Senate Office Bldg., Washington, D.C. 20510
BORN: 1932, Shreveport, La. ACHIEVEMENTS: Member of the Appropriations & Budget Committees; chairman of the Energy & Water Development

Subcommittee. STUDIED: Washington & Lee University; U.S. Military Academy; Louisiana State University Law School, LL.B., 1956.

J. Bennett Johnston has been a member of the U.S. Senate since 1972. Before his election to the Senate, he served a stint in the Army and spent several years as an attorney in private practice. Johnston has devoted the majority of his working life to the public sphere. He began his career in politics as a Louisiana state representative before moving on to the House in 1968, and to the Senate four years later.

JOHNSON, PHILIP CORTELYOU

John Burgee Architects with Philip Johnson, 885 3rd Avenue, New York, NY 10022 (212) 751-7440
BORN: 1906. ACHIEVEMENTS: FAIA; Pritzker Architecture Prize, 1979; Fellow, American Academy of Arts and Letters; notable works: AT&T Corporate Headquarters, New York City; Philip Johnson House, New Canaan, Conn.; Seagram Building (with Mies van der Rohe). STUDIED: Harvard University.

After a half-century of seminal involvement in the American Modern movement, Philip Johnson has radically shifted his stance, but remains a fundamental tastemaker and spokesman for contemporary architecture. As a wealthy young man he recognized the power and elegance of the International Style which he saw emerging in Europe. In 1930 he commissioned Mies van der Rohe to design his New York City condominium. Subsequently he styled himself as the first large-scale importer and interpreter of European Modernism, organizing van der Rohe's and Le Corbusier's first visits to the United States and later serving as director of the Museum of Modern Art's Department of Architecture. Though an early and key propagandist for the Modern movement, he didn't convey the social ideology of equality for all, which was the heart of the European movement. Modernism in his presentations was a new style and nothing else. Yet in Europe it was a social stance for which its foremost practitioners were driven into exile, most often in the United States, where Johnson was instrumental in finding them prestigious employment. He undertook his first major design, his own Glass House in new Canaan, Conn., after nearly 20 years of involvement in Modernism. By 1960 he was bored and disillusioned with Mies' rational, linear and homogeneous built environment. His New York City AT&T building, topped with a thirty-foot curled pediment fashioned after the ornate crest of a Chippendale cabinet, was an instant totem for the swelling Postmodernist camp, and an eloquent, if not precisely elegant, repudiation of his earlier approach to design.

JOHNSON, RICHARD J.V.

The Houston Chronicle, 801 Texas Ave., Houston, TX 77002 (713) 220-7171
BORN: 1930, San Luis Potosi (Mexico). ACHIEVEMENTS: Outstanding Philanthropy Award from the National Society of Fund Raising Executives, 1994; Communicator of the Year, University of Houston, 1994; Visionary of Houston, 1993; Houstonian of the Year, Houston School for Deaf Children, 1993; B'nai Brith Anti-Defamation League's Torch of Liberty Award, 1990; Houston Cultural Leader of the World, 1989; Texas Society to Prevent Blindness People of Vision Award, 1986; National Conference of Christians and Jews Brotherhood Award, 1984. STUDIED: Graduated University of Texas, B.B.A.

Chairman of the board and chief publisher of the Houston Chronicle, Richard Johnson serves as officer and director of numerous local civic and service organizations including: The state fair of Texas; Methodist Hospital, Houston; American General Corporation, and Mutual Insurance Company Limited, Bermuda.

JOHNSON, WILLIAM A. JR.

City Hall, Room 307-A, 30 Church Street, Rochester, NY 14614 (716) 428-7045
BORN: 1942, Lynchburg, Va. ACHIEVEMENTS: Mayor, Rochester, N.Y.; president and CEO, Urban League, Rochester, N.Y. STUDIED: Howard University, Washington D.C., B.A., political science, 1965; M.A., political science, 1967.

William A. Johnson Jr. exhibited his work ethic at an early age. While a young man attending college, he held a variety of part time and summer jobs, such as legislative analyst for the National Highway Users Conference, hospital orderly, seasonal mail carrier, and U.S. park ranger. After graduation from college in 1967, he taught political science at C.S. Mott Community College in Flint, Michigan. In 1971 Johnson became deputy executive director of the Flint, Mich. Urban League. Two years later he was chosen as president and CEO of the Urban League in Rochester, N.Y. Johnson took charge of an Urban League affiliate that was nearly bankrupt, and turned it around into one of the most successful Urban Leagues in the nation. In 1993 Johnson was elected the 64th mayor of Rochester, N.Y.

JONES BILL T.

BORN: 1951, Bunnell, Fla. ACHIEVEMENTS: Notable ballets: Negroes for Sale; De Sweet Streak of Loveland; Stories, Steps, and Stomps; Monkey Road Run, Blauvelt Mountain, Valley Cottage, a trilogy; Fever Swamp, Ritual Ruckus (How to Walk an Elephant). STUDIED: State University of New York at Binghamton; Brockport University, New York, B.A., dance, theater, ca 1974; improvisation techniques with almost a score of teachers.

Co-founder, with the late Arnie Zane of American Dance Asylum, and later as Bill T. Jones/Arnie Zane and Dancers, Bill Jones' smoothly coiling and uncoiling length expressed the complicated structures of his choreography. His demanding duets with Zane often had the free flow of contact improvisation as they taunted each other in dialogue about aspects of their personal lives, including the most private of confidences exchanged sotto voce. Their major talking-dance trilogy is ranked among the most evocative and autobiographical works of the era.

JONES, BRERETON C.

700 Capital Avenue, Frankfort, KY 40601 (502) 564-2611
BORN: June 27, 1939, Point Pleasant, W.Va. ACHIEVEMENTS: Dr. Nathan Davis Award, American Medical Association, 1994. STUDIED: University of Virginia, B.S., commerce.

Brereton Jones was born June 27, 1939 in Point Pleasant, W. Va. He graduated from high school with a straight-A grade point average, and attended the University of Virginia on a football scholarship. He graduated with a Bachelor of Science degree in commerce and went on to become a developer of residential and commercial properties. In 1987 Jones was elected lieutenant governor of Kentucky, and in 1991, governor. He won both elections by the largest margin in Kentucky history. His term has been marked by a determined effort to down-size government. Jones has eliminated more than 1700 permanent, full-time positions from the state government through attrition. Other steps taken to reduce the cost of state government include down-sizing the state vehicle fleet, reduced travel costs, and a reduced governor's budget. Another cornerstone of Jones' administration is a dedication to health care reform. The state's new Health Care Reform Law guarantees insurability, insurance rate review, and insurance portability from job to job.

JONES, JAMES EARL

Dale C. Olson & Associates, 292 S. La Cienega Blvd., Penthouse Suite, Beverly Hills, CA 90211-3326
BORN: 1931, Arkabutla Miss. ACHIEVEMENTS: Antoinette Perry Award, Best Actor, The Great White Hope, 1969; Golden Globe, New Male Star of the Year, The Great White Hope, 1971; Grammy (with Orson Welles, Henry Fonda, and Helen Hayes), Best Spoken Word or Non-musical Recording, Great American Documents, 1976; Antoinette Perry Award, Best Actor, Fences, 1987; Emmy, Outstanding Supporting Actor, Heatwave!, 1990; Emmy Award, Outstanding Lead Actor in a Drama Series, Gabriel's Fire, 1990. STUDIED: University of Michigan, B.A., 1953.

James Earl Jones, a brilliant actor with the recognizable voice, stuttered when he was a young boy in Michigan. By forcing himself to join debating teams and entering oratorical contests, he overcame this condition by the time he graduated from high school. He moved to New York and acted on and off Broadway, including major parts with Joseph Papps' New York Shakespeare Festival. In 1968 he was cast as Jack Johnson in *The Great White Hope*, for which he won a Antoinette Perry Award, and then went on to star in the film version. Other plays he appeared in were *The Iceman Cometh, Of Mice and Men, A Lesson from Aloes,* and *Othello.* For all the movies, plays and television shows Jones has appeared in, he is probably most famous for the voice of Darth Vader in *Star Wars,* and as the voice of CNN. He returned to television in 1995 starring in the dramatic series *Under One Roof.*

JONES, QUINCY DELIGHT

Eliot Sekuler, Publicist Rogers & Cowan, 10000 Santa Monica Blvd., Suite 400, Los Angeles, CA 90067
BORN: 1933, Chicago. ACHIEVEMENTS: Emmy award, Best Music Composition, Roots, 1977; 76 Grammy nominations, 26 Grammy awards; Hollywood Walk of Fame, 1980; Lifetime Achievement Award, National Academy of Songwriters, 1989; Grammy Living Legend Award, 1990; Grammy, Best Jazz Instrumental, Individual or Group, Miles and Quincy Live at the Montreaux, 1994. STUDIED: Seattle University, Berklee College of Music; private study with Nadia Boulanger; Boston Conservatory.

This multi-talented composer has penned music for recording artists, feature films and television shows. A trumpeter and arranger for the Lionel Hampton Orchestra in the 1950s Quincy Jones has worked with many pop and jazz heavyweights, including Frank Sinatra, Dinah Washington, Count Basie, Miles Davis, Ella Fitzgerald, Sarah Vaugh, Ray Charles and Dizzy Gillespie. In 1977 he scored the television mini-series *Roots,* for which he won an Emmy award. Michael Jackson chose him to produce his biggest selling albums: *Off the Wall,* 1980, *Thriller,* 1982 and *Bad.* Jones also produces television shows, including *The Fresh Prince of Bel Air,* and is the founder of *Vibe Magazine.*

JONES, TOMMY LEE

International Creative Management, 8899 Beverly Blvd. Los Angeles, CA 90048
BORN: 1946, San Saba, Texas. ACHIEVEMENTS: Emmy, Best Actor in a Miniseries, The Executioner's Song, 1983; Academy Award, Best Supporting Actor, The Fugitive, 1994; Golden Globe, Best Supporting Actor, The Fugitive, 1994. STUDIED: Harvard University, B.A., English, 1969.

His beginnings are rooted in the rolling hills of Texas, where he still lives on a ranch in his hometown of San Saba. This 18th-generation Texan worked in the oil fields during his youth. During college he once roomed with Vice President Al Gore, and played offensive guard on the football team. After graduation he moved to New York, and made his stage debut in *A Patriot for Me.* In 1970 he made his film debut as Ryan O'Neal's roommate in *Love Story.* Television movies provided him with his breakthrough roles. His performance in the television miniseries *The Executioner's Song* won an Emmy. The miniseries *Lonesome Dove* re-energized his career. His major film credits include; *The Fugitive, The Client,* and *Cobb.* In December, 1994, he received a star on the Hollywood Walk of Fame. A year later he made his directorial debut in the television movie *The Good Ole Boys.*

JORDAN, FRANK M.

Office of the Mayor, City Hall, 400 Van Ness Ave. Rm. 200, San Francisco, CA 94102 (415) 554-6141
BORN: 1935, San Francisco. ACHIEVEMENTS: 1992, elected mayor, San Francisco. STUDIED: University of San Francisco.

Frank Jordan's important strides in law enforcement during his administration reflect his previous career in the San Francisco Police Department. He served in the United States Army from 1954 until 1956. In 1957 he entered the San Francisco Police Academy as a cadet. His career included promotions from patrolman, through the ranks, to chief of police in 1986. In 1990 he retired from the Police Department. Jordan's accomplishments as mayor include a 26 percent reduction in major crime from 1993 through 1995; instituting a nationally-recognized Emergency Command Center and Emergency Response Plan to be used in the event of natural disasters, civil unrest or other emergency situations; and establishing the Safe Transit Enforcement Program. Jordan serves on the Executive Committee and co-chairs the Police Policy Committee of the U.S. Conference of Mayors.

JORDAN, JERRY L.

Federal Reserve Bank of Cleveland, 1455 E. 6th St., Cleveland OH 44114

BORN: 1941, Los Angeles. ACHIEVEMENTS: President, Council of Economic Advisers; president, National Association of Business Economists; CEO, Federal Reserve Bank, Cleveland; consultant, West German Central Bank; member, Economic Advisory Committee, American Bankers Association; Governing Council, National Association of Business Economists, and U.S. Chamber of Commerce, Council of Trends and Perspectives. STUDIED: California State University, University of California.

In 1967, after a brief flirtation with teaching at California State University, Jerry Jordan entered the Federal Reserve System in St. Louis, where, during the following eight years, his lifelong interest in the causes and effects of inflation were developed and nurtured. From the St. Louis bank, where he had risen to the position of senior vice president and director of research, he moved to the Pittsburgh National Bank as senior vice president and economist. His reputation by then as a tireless "Fed Watcher" and a spokesman for monetarism was built on articles published during his St. Louis years., In one, he laid down what would become the basis of modern monetarism: that the supply of money controls policy, and regulating the growth of money controls economic activity. From this he draws the conclusion that for a viable economy full employment, stable prices, and economic growth, the Fed should place less importance on adjusting interest rates than on letting the money supply grow at a moderate and steady rate over time. Though Jordan has moved successfully through several government, university, and banking positions, his views on monetarism have been consistent and effective. He shares part of the credit for changes in the Fed's emphasis on the use of the monetary policy to formalize money policy and to lay down rules for how that policy shall be enacted.

JORDAN, MICHAEL HUGH

Westinghouse Electric Corporation, 6 Gateway Center., WH Building, Pittsburgh, PA 15222 (412) 244-2000

BORN: 1936, Kansas City, Mo. ACHIEVEMENTS: chair, Center for Excellence in Education; certification, Westinghouse Bettis Atomic Power Laboratory. STUDIED: Yale University, B.S., chemical engineering; Princeton University, M.S., chemical engineering.

Building credentials which would finally make history at Westinghouse Electric Company, Michael Jordan spent 10 years at the highly regarded consulting firm McKinsey & Company. In 1974 he moved to Pepsico, Inc., where in 18 years he held several senior positions in its FritoLay division and corporate headquarters. In 1992 he joined Clayon, Dubilier & Rice, Inc., a leveraged buyout firm, and in 1993 he became the first outsider to head Westinghouse since 1929. As chairman of the board and chief executive officer of the faltering company, which had over-diversified into real estate, furniture, and even fancy wristwatches, he is best known for broadening the company's electronic systems business by buying Norden Systems. He also started a joint venture between Westinghouse and CBS in advertising and production. He serves on the board of the United Negro Fund and is chairman on the Center for Excellence in Education.

JUNKINS, JERRY R.

Texas Instruments, Inc., PO Box 6 Dallas, TX 75265 (214) 995-2011

BORN: 1937, Ft. Madison, Iowa. ACHIEVEMENTS: CEO, Texas Instruments; trustee, Southern Methodist University; member, National Academy of Engineering. STUDIED: Iowa State University, B.A., electrical engineering; Southern Methodist University, M.A., engineering administration.

As a 22-year-old, Jerry Junkins stored away his cap and gown from Iowa State University and traveled to Dallas, Texas, where he had been offered a job with Texas Instruments, Inc. Twenty-nine years later—in the interim studying at Southern Methodist University where he picked up a masters in engineering administration—he had climbed to chairman, president, and chief executive officer of the makers of semi-conductors, computers, and many other products. His first major promotion came in 1975, when he was named assistant vice president and manager of data systems and industrial systems. Six years later he became president of the company and chief executive officer, and in 1988 he achieved the top slot in the company. He serves on the board of Proctor and Gamble Company, Caterpillar, Inc., and Minnesota Mining & Manufacturing Company (3M). Junkins is a trustee of Southern Methodist University, serves on the board of the Dallas Citizens Council, and is a member of the National Academy of Engineering. @TITLE = KAHN,MICHAEL

c/o McCarter Theater, Box 526, Princeton, NJ 08540 Kahn is a prominent dramatic artist. For career credentials consult the portion of this book entitled "Biographees by Profession" in the Appendix. Within this portion, the list"Dramatic Artists," describes requirements for inclusion in this volume.

KAHN, MADELINE

Jeffrey Richards Association, Alwyn Court, 911 7th Ave., New York, NY 10019

BORN: 1942, Boston. ACHIEVEMENTS: Emmy Award, Wanted: The Perfect Guy, ABC Afterschool Specials, 1986; STUDIED: Hofstra University, B.A., 1964; trained for acting at the Warren Robertson Actors' Workshop.

Madeline Kahn burst onto the entertainment scene in 1968. The daughter of Bernard B. Wolfson and Paula (Kahn) Wolfson, she has worked on stage, screen and television throughout her career. Among her most popular work on stage has been her portrayals of Chrissy in *Boom Boom Room*, in 1973, and Mildred Plotka and Lily Garland in *On the Twentieth Century*, in 1978. Kahn has appeared many times on television. She has been on three series, including *Mr. President* from 1987 to 1988. Kahn has also appeared on many television specials. Her work on film has mostly been in the comedy genre, including *Blazing Saddles*, in 1974; *The Muppet Movie*, in 1979; and *Slapstick of Another Kind*, in 1984. In recent years, Kahn has done voice work on animated movies, the latest of which was *An American Tale*, in 1986.

KAISER, ROBERT G.

The Washington Post Company, 1150 15th St. NW, Washington, D.C. 20071
BORN: 1943, Washington, D.C. ACHIEVEMENTS: Author, Russia from the Inside and Why Gorbachev Happened. STUDIED: Yale University, B.A., journalism; London School of Economics, M.S., economics; Columbia University, postgrad.
Robert Kaiser joined the *Washington Post* as a summer intern in 1963, and one year later began what would become a distinguished career in foreign reportage with a two-year assignment in London. He wrote from Saigon and Moscow, then joined the national staff in 1975, advancing, in 1985, to assistant managing editor of national news, and in 1990 to deputy managing editor of the paper. Along the way, he authored several books on the former Soviet Union, notably *Russia from the Inside* and *Why Gorbachev Happened*.

KALIKOW, PETER

New York Post, 210 South St., New York, NY 10002
(212) 815-8000
Kalikow is a prominent publisher. For career credentials consult the portion of this book entitled "Biographees by Profession" in the Appendix. Within this portion, the list "Publishers," describes requirements for inclusion in this volume.

KANDEL, ERIC RICHARD

Howard Hughes Medical Institute, Columbia University, New York, NY 10017
BORN: 1929, Vienna (Austria).
Eric Kandel immigrated with his parents to the U.S. in 1939, fleeing the Nazis. His later schooling in neurobiology led him to specialize in cellular and molecular mechanisms. Concentrating on three basic forms of learning—habituation, sensitization, and classical conditioning—he found that the learning process produces changes in behavior by controlling the strength of neural connections in the brain. Kandel became a professor at Harvard University in 1983, and senior investigator at Columbia University's Howard Hughes Medical Institute in 1984.

KARLE, JEROME

U.S. Naval Research Laboratory, Structure Matter, #6030, Washington, DC 20375
BORN: 1918, Brooklyn, N.Y. ACHIEVEMENTS: Noble Prize in Physics (shared with Herbert A. Hauptman), 1985; Pure Science Award, Sigma Xi; Navy Distinguished Civilian Service Award; Hillebrand Award, American Chemical Society; Robert Dexter Conrad Award; A.L. Patterson Award,

American Crystallographic Association. STUDIED: City College of New York; Harvard University; University of Michigan.
In almost all solids, the atoms are arranged in a certain order to form crystals, and finding the crystal structure of the solid is the first step in learning the solid's properties. One of Jerome Karle's and Herbert Hauptman's remarkable achievements was to develop a way to quickly analyze the three-dimensional structure of the molecule, thus analyzing its intensity directly, even in complex molecules, in just a few days by using X-ray techniques. Their work helped advance crystallography to a position of major importance in the development of other modern sciences, especially physical chemistry, physics, and biochemistry.

KASSEBAUM, NANCY L.

U.S. Senate, 302 SROB, Washington, DC 20510-1602
(202) 224-4774
Kassebaum is a prominent political leader in the U.S. Senate, in which she represents the State of Kansas. She is one of the longer standing members in the Senate and considered to be one of the most influential women in government.

KATZ, VERA

303 City Hall, 1220 SW. 5th Ave., Portland, OR 97204
(503) 823-4120
Katz is a prominent political leader. For career credentials consult the portion of this book entitled "Biographees by Profession" in the Appendix. Within this portion, the list "Political Leaders," describes requirements for inclusion in this volume.

KAYE, JUDY

Bret Adams, Ltd., 448 West 44th St., New York, NY 10036
BORN: 1948, Phoenix. ACHIEVEMENTS: Antoinette Perry Award, Best Featured Actress in a Musical, The Phantom of the Opera, 1988. STUDIED: University of California, Los Angeles, Arizona State University.
Judy Kaye has been in show business since the mid-1960s. A versatile performer, she has not only performed on stage, in movies and on television, but has also appeared in concert with such orchestras as the London Symphony, the New York Philharmonic, and the Pittsburgh Symphony. Kaye has worked extensively on stage, debuting in 1967 in *Melodyland*. Her work includes, *Grease*, in 1977; *No, No, Nanette*, in 1986; and *The Phantom of the Opera*, for which she won a Tony award in 1988. Kaye appeared in the film, *Just Tell Me What You Want*, in 1980, as well as several television shows, including *The Doctors*, and *Kojak*.

KEATING, RICHARD

Skidmore, Owings and Merrill, 725 S. Figueroa Street, Los Angeles, CA 90017 (213) 488-9700
BORN: 1944. ACHIEVEMENTS: FAIA; Progressive Architecture design citations; Los Angeles AIA; Texas AIA; Award of Excellence, American Institute of Steel Construction; Houston AIA; notable works: Texas Com-

merce Bank Tower, Dallas; LTV Center, Dallas; Columbia Savings headquarters, Beverly Hills, Calif.; Memphis Brooks Museum, Memphis, Tenn.; Aichi Corporate Headquarters, Tokyo. STUDIED: University of California at Berkeley.

Despite several historical/contextualist projects, including his Milwaukee Theatre District Plan, which was inspired by the Flemish Renaissance-style Milwaukee City Hall, and an addition to the Brooks Art Museum in Memphis, Tennessee, Richard Keating considers himself a modernist. He says there's "a lot left in modernism as a word and as a design proposition that has gone untouched and needs more exploration," describes requirements for inclusion in this volume. His projects in Houston and Los Angeles endeavor to entertain the diversity of the human spirit, moving away from strictly structural-expressionist motifs. His collaboration with Edward C. Bassett in the Allied Bank Plaza of Houston resulted in a 70-story tower of green reflective glass issuing from a base of polished black granite. Giant trusses, housed in painted wood, counterpoint massiveness with the illusion of immateriality as they support "skylobbies" for an adjacent elevator core. In the Columbia Savings Headquarters in Beverly Hills, Calif., a Saarinenesque facade envelopes an interior with a central courtyard and a sculpture atrium,—a "Piranesi in glass"—replete with bridges and pools. Mechanical and service areas are located along the outer circumference, while access to the inner sanctum, housing a state-of-the-art kitchen, shooting gallery, gymnasium, art gallery and offices, is carefully controlled.

KECK, DONALD

Corning Inc. Sullivan Park, Corning, NY 14830
BORN: 1941, Lansing, Mich. ACHIEVEMENTS: co-invented optical fiber (with Peter Schultz and Robert Maurer); inducted into the National Inventors Hall of Fame, 1993. STUDIED: Michigan State University, B.S., 1962; M.S., 1964; Ph.D., 1967
After receiving his doctorate from Michigan State, Donald Keck joined Corning Inc. as a research physicist. Two years later, in 1970, Keck, along with Peter Schultz and Robert Maurer, designed and produced the first optical fiber that could be used on a wide scale in telecommunications. This was a breakthrough development which led to the commercialization of optical fibers, thus revolutionizing the telecom-munications industry. Keck is currently director of opto-electronic research at Corning Inc.

KEILLOR, GARRISON E.

Faber & Faber, 3 Queens Square, London, United Kingdom, WC1N 3AU
BORN: 1942, Anoka, Minn. ACHIEVEMENTS: Creator of A Prairie Home Companion on public radio. STUDIED: University of Minnesota, B.A., 1968.
Celebrated for his monologues that blended humor with nostalgia for small-town life, Garrison Keillor spun tales about the goings-on in fictional Lake Wobegon, Minn., "the town that time forgot and the decades cannot improve," on his live public radio program, *A Prairie Home Companion*, from 1974 until 1987, and in

his book *Lake Wobegon Days*, 1985. Raised according to the strict tenets of the Plymouth Brethren Church, he sold his first humor piece to *The New Yorker* magazine in 1969, and became a frequent contributor thereafter. His books include *Happy to be Here*, 1982; *Leaving Home*, 1987; *We are Still Married*, 1989; *WLT: A Radio Romance*, 1991; and *The Book of Guys*, 1993.

KELL, ERNIE

City Hall, 333 W. Ocean Blvd., Long Beach, CA 90802
(310) 590-6707
Kell is a prominent political leader. For career credentials consult the portion of this book entitled "Biographees by Profession" in the Appendix. Within this portion, the list"Political Leaders," describes requirements for inclusion in this volume.

KELLER, BILL

The *New York Times*, 229 West 3rd St., New York, NY
(212) 556-1234
BORN: 1949. STUDIED: Pomona College, B.A., journalism.
Bill Keller stepped into big shoes when he was named foreign editor of The *New York Times* in 1995. He succeeded Bernard Gertzman, who, in six years on the job, presided over the biggest run of foreign news since World War II: the fall of communism, the end of the Cold War, the Persian Gulf War, majority rule in South Africa, and widespread ethnic violence in Europe. Keller started at the *Times* in 1984 as its correspondent in Washington and moved to Moscow in 1986, becoming bureau chief in 1989, the year he won a Pulitzer Prize for his Soviet Union coverage. He was based in Johannesburg as bureau chief until his appointment as foreign editor. Previous to the *Times*, he worked for the *Dallas Morning Herald*, the *Congressional Quarterly Weekly Report*, and the *Oregonian* in Portland.

KELLEY, KITTY

c/o Simon & Schuster, 1230 Avenue of the Americas, New York, NY 10020; (212)-698-7000
BORN: 1942, Spokane, Wash. ACHIEVEMENTS: Author of Jackie Oh!, Lyle Stuart, 1978; Elizabeth Taylor: The Last Star, Simon & Schuster, 1981; and His Way: The Unauthorized Biography of Frank Sinatra, Bantam, 1986. STUDIED: University of Washington, B.A., 1964.
Kitty Kelley had a varied career prior to becoming an author. After graduating from the University of Washington, she was a VIP hostess for the General Electric exhibit at the New York City World's Fair. Next, she was a press assistant to U.S. Sen. Eugene McCarthy, in Washington D.C. She then went into writing, working for both the *Washington Post* and the *Washingtonian*. In 1973 she started her career as a free-lance writer. Her first book, *The Glamour Spas*, was published by Simon & Schuster in 1975. Kelley's latest book, *Nancy Reagan, the Unauthorized Biography*, was published by Simon & Schuster in 1991. Like her previous biographies, this book paints a sometimes

unflattering view of its subject, and immediately made the best-seller lists.

KELLY, ELLSWORTH

R.D.P.O. Box 170B, Chatham, NY 12037
BORN: 1923. ACHIEVEMENTS: Carnegie International Prizes; Flora Mayer Witowsky Prize, Art Institute of Chicago; collections: Metropolitan Museum of Art; Museum of Modern Art; exhibitions: Museum of Modern Art; Venice Biennale. STUDIED: Pratt Institute; Boston Museum School; Ecole des Beaux-Arts, Paris

Unconcerned with the spontaneity of Abstract Expressionism in the 1950s, Ellsworth Kelly painted preconceived, hard-edged silhouettes of shapes from nature in the manner of Henri Matisse's cutouts. The large-scale, simplified forms were often in two planes of black and white, so that it was difficult to distinguish figure from ground. His concern was with an observed object, its mass and shadow, distilled to its "telling shape," describes requirements for inclusion in this volume. In 1955, convinced that "a shape can stand alone," Kelly added sculpture to his media, freestanding, polychromed works that echoed his paintings, often consisting of connected planes, as in *Pony.* Wall reliefs and segmented pictures of the 1950s and 1960s portrayed effects of shadows upon fields of color. Some paintings resembled color charts, repeating rows of solid colors. His later works explore colorshape relationships, as in *Chatham XI: Blue Yellow.* Additional drawings are precisely outlined plants.

KELSO, ADM. FRANK B. II

Office of the Secretary, Pentagon, Washington, DC 20301 (703) 545-6700
BORN: 1934. STUDIED: U.S. Naval Academy.
A Tennessee native with 38 years service in the Navy, most of them in submarines, Adm. Frank Kelso retired in 1994, two months ahead of schedule following the "Tailhook" sexual harassment scandal, exposure of cheating in the Naval Academy, and charges that its top brass was insensitive to sexual harassment. He retired at full rank instead of two ranks below his present position. As head of the Sixth Fleet in the Mediterranean, Kelso helped capture four Palestinian terrorists implicated in killing an American citizen aboard the liner Achille Lauro in 1985. He also was in charge of American air strikes against Libya in 1986. In the wake of "Tailhook," Kelso initiated reforms to improve career opportunities and working conditions for Navy women, and strongly backed the Navy's decision to open combat aircraft and surface warships to women.

KEMP, JACK FRENCH

B40 Dirksen Senate Office Building, Washington, DC, 20510-1202; (202) 224-6142
BORN: 1935; Los Angeles. ACHIEVEMENTS: National Football League quarterback, politician. STUDIED: Occidental College, 1957.
Kemp was a quarterback in the National Football League for 13 years before becoming active in the Republican party. He was elected to Congress from upstate New York in 1971, and became a champion for the concept of supply-side economics, which eventually became a central theme for the reforms of the Reagan era. In 1988 Kemp mounted an unsuccessful campaign for the Republican presidential nomination. He was named U.S. Secretary of Housing and Urban Development by President Bush, and held the office until January, 1993. In that role he pressed for changes to federal policy to enable low-income residents of federal housing projects to buy their buildings.

KEMPTHORNE, DIRK

B40 Dirksen Senate Office Building, Washington, DC 20510-1202; (202) 224-6142
BORN: 1951. ACHIEVEMENTS: The United States Conference of Mayors' 1994 National Legislative Leadership Award; Distinguished Congressional Award from the National League of Cities. STUDIED: University of Idaho, Political Science, 1975.
Kempthorne began a crusade on behalf of local and state governments to remove unfunded federal mandates soon after he was first elected to the U.S. Senate in 1992. In 1995 his legislation was signed into law, prompting Republican leader Bob Dole to cite Kempthorne as one of the party's rising stars and to name him to the Senate Advisory Commission on Intergovernmental Relations. He is chairman of the Drinking Water, Fisheries and Wildlife Subcommittee of the Environment and Public Works Committee, where he is working on changes to the Endangered Species Act. Kempthorne also serves on the Helsinki Commission, a North American/European international human rights monitoring group.

KENDALL, HENRY WAY

Massachusetts Institute of Technology, Department of Physics 24514, 77 Massachusetts Ave., Cambridge, MA 02139
BORN: 1926, Boston. ACHIEVEMENTS: Nobel Prize in Physics (shared with Richard E. Taylor and Jerome Isaac Friedman), 1990; founder and chair: Union of Concerned Scientists. STUDIED: Amherst College; Massachusetts Institute of Technology.
Until Henry Kendall's successful work on the quark –along with Jerome Friedman's and Richard E. Taylor's—the existence of the half-humorously named subatomic particle was only theoretically believed by physicists. The complexities of the theory were blamed on the failure of scientists to isolate a quark and observing it. Kendall and his cohorts broke through the reams of hypothetical theories on quarks by bombarding hydrogen and heavy hydrogen with a shower of high-energy electrons, at last revealing the existence of quarks. The experiment, however, opened another pandora's box of theories: how many quarks there are, and how they react with other elements within the nuclei? The answer is still being studied.

KENNAN, GEORGE FROST

Institute for Advanced Study, Princeton University, Princeton, NJ 08540

BORN: 1904, Milwaukee, Wis. STUDIED: Princeton University, B.A. history; Berlin Seminary for Oriental Languages, diploma; many honorary degrees.

George Kennan was one of the formulators of the policy of "containment" toward the Soviet Union, first broached in his famous 1947 article in *Foreign Policy* called "The Sources of Soviet Conduct" and signed simply "Mr.X," describes requirements for inclusion in this volume. It effectively outlined what would become the West's policy toward Soviet Communism for the next 40 years. His subsequent publications often deviated from official U.S. policy, but just as often were vindicated by history, including his prediction of the demise of the U.S.S.R. He opposed the partition of Germany after World War II, the Korean Conflict and Vietnam War, the H Bomb, and reliance on nuclear weapons for national defense. In the foreign service for 27 years, from 1926 to 1956, he served in Geneva, Hamburg, Berlin, Estonia, Latvia, Moscow, Vienna, Prague, Lisbon, and London.

KENNEDY, EDWARD M. (TED)

315 Russell Senate Office Building, Washington, DC 20510-2101; (202) 224-4543
BORN: 1932, Boston. ACHIEVEMENTS: Democratic Whip, 1969-1971. STUDIED: Harvard University, 1956; University of Virginia Law School, 1959.
An articulate champion of liberal causes for over three decades, Kennedy won election to the Senate in 1962, taking the seat his brother, John, vacated when he was elected president. He served as chairman of the Labor and Human Resources Committee from 1987 to 1995, and chairman of the Judiciary Committee from 1979 to 1981. For many years Kennedy was considered an elder statesman of the Democratic party, and he fought for a number of liberal causes, including civil rights, fair housing and national health insurance. Often cited as a possible presidential or vice-presidential candidate, Kennedy's political career suffered in the wake of a 1969 car accident on the island of Chappaquiddick Island, Mass., which killed a campaign worker, Mary Jo Kopechne. Kennedy made a brief run for the Democratic presidential nomination in 1980.

KENNEDY, JOSEPH P. III

U.S. House of Representatives, 1210 LHOB, Washington, DC 20515-2108 (202) 225-5111
Kennedy, the son of the late Attorney General Robert (Bobby) Kennedy is a democratic Congressman from Massachusetts. He is considered a liberal in the tradition of his family, many members of which (including the late President John F. Kennedy) have been active in American politics since the 1940s when his namesake, Joseph Kennedy, Sr., was the U.S. ambassador to Great Britain. He has recently been plagued by allegations that he has used marijuana while in office.

KENNEDY, WILLIAM JOSEPH

State University of New York, Writers Institute, 1400 Washington Ave., Albany, NY 12222

BORN: 1928, Albany, N.Y. ACHIEVEMENTS: Pulitzer Prize, Ironweed, 1983. STUDIED: Siena College.
With the exception of his first novel, *The Ink Truck*, 1969, most of William Kennedy's fiction powerfully evoked the atmosphere of his home town, Albany, N.Y., through vibrant dialogue and vivid settings. His novels include *Legs*, 1975; *Billy Phelan's Greatest Game*, 1978; *Ironweed*, 1983, for which he won the Pulitzer Prize for literature; *Quinn's Book*, 1988; and *Very Old Bones*, 1992. He published a volume of essays, *O Albany!*, in 1983, and has written a number of short stories.

KENNELLY, BARBARA B.

U.S. House of Representatives, Room 110, Washington, DC 20515 (202) 225-7760
Kennelly is a prominent political leader. For career credentials consult the portion of this book entitled "Biographees by Profession" in the Appendix. Within this portion, the list "Political Leaders," describes requirements for inclusion in this volume.

KERREY, ROBERT

421 Russell Senate Office Building, Washington, DC 20510-2102: (202) 224-2742
BORN: 1943, Nebraska. ACHIEVEMENTS: Congressional Medal of Honor. STUDIED: University of Nebraska, 1966.
Robert Kerrey is known as a fiscally conservative Democrat, partly as a result of the austere budgets he instituted when he served as governor of Nebraska from 1983 to 1987. During his tenure Nebraska recovered from a deficit after Kerrey cut spending. In 1988 he was elected to the United States Senate, and made an unsuccessful bid for the Democratic presidential nomination in 1992, arguing for fiscal responsibility and a national policy on health care. Kerrey is a former member of the elite Navy SEAL Team, a highly decorated veteran of the Vietnam War, and the founder of a chain of restaurants and health clubs.

KILBY, JACK

7723 Midbury Dr., Dallas, TX 75230-3211
BORN: 1923, Jefferson City, Mo. ACHIEVEMENTS: Miniaturized electronic circuits; National Medal of Science, 1969, U.S. government; inducted into the National Inventors Hall of Fame, 1982. STUDIED: University of Illinois, B.S. electrical engineering,1947; University of Wisconsin, M.S. electrical engineering, 1950.
Jack Kilby spent 11 years with Centralab Division of Glob-Union, Inc., in Milwaukee, Wis.designing and developing thick-film integrated circuits. In 1958 Kilby joined Texas Instruments, where his work centered on integrated circuit development, and he invented the monolithic integrated circuit, which is now used in electronic systems. In 1970 he left the company to work on his own, developing a novel solar energy system. His work has been recognized by the Institute of Electrical and Electronic Engineers, the University of Illinois, and the Academy of Engineering. Kilby received the National Medal of Science in 1969, a

prestigious award given by the U.S Government for the advancement of science and engineering.

KINDLEBERGER, II, CHARLES P.

1010 Waltham St., A-406, Lexington, MA 02173
Kindleberger, II is a prominent economist. For career credentials consult the portion of this book entitled "Biographees by Profession" in the Appendix. Within this portion, the list "Economists," describes requirements for inclusion in this volume.

KING, ELEANOR

530 Garcia, Apt. 4, Santa Fe, NM 87501 (505) 989-7608
King is a prominent dancer. For career credentials consult the portion of this book entitled "Biographees by Profession" in the Appendix. Within this portion, the list "Dancers," describes requirements for inclusion in this volume.

KING, STEPHEN EDWIN

Viking Press, 625 Madison Ave., New York, NY 10022
BORN: 1947, Portland, Maine. ACHIEVEMENTS: Author of best-selling supernatural horror novels, short stories and screenplays. STUDIED: University of Maine, B.A., 1970.
As a boy growing up in Maine, Stephen King devoured horror tales and even made up his own stories and characters. After graduating from the University of Maine in 1970 with a degree in English, he taught at Hampden Academy in Maine for three years while trying to sell short stories to magazines. These early efforts were rejected, but the publication of his novel *Carrie* in 1974, and the success of the 1976 movie adapted from it, established him as a major horror novelist and screenwriter. His stories often featured young people caught up in supernatural situations. His books, many made into films, included *The Shining*, 1977; *Cujo*, 1981; *The Dead Zone*, 1979; *Pet Sematary*, 1983; *The Talisman*, 1984; *It*, 1986; and *The Stand*.

KING, LARRY

c/o Barbara S. Blaine, 700 13th St. NW, No. 1000, Washington, D.C. 20002
BORN: 1933, New York City.
Larry King began his popular, national late-night radio show in 1978 on the Mutual Network, and brought it to CNN TV as *Larry King Live* in 1985. The interview/call-in show's most famous occasion to date was Ross Perot announcing his presidential plans in 1992. King began his radio career in Miami, at age 25, and subsequently wrote entertainment columns for the *Miami Herald* in the 1970s.

KINSLEY, MICHAEL

The *New Republic*, 1220 19th St., NW., Washington, DC 20036; (202) 331-7494
BORN: 1951, Detroit. ACHIEVEMENTS: Author, Curse of the Giant Muffins and Other Washington Maladies; named one of 150 Journalists Who Make a Difference in American Politics, American Politics. STUDIED:
Harvard College, B.A., pre-law; Magdalen College, Oxford University, student; Harvard University Law School, J.D., law.
Michael Kinsley, known as a Washington outsider and a political contrarian, has worked for Ralph Nader as one of his "Raiders," the *Washington Monthly*, *Harper's Magazine*, and the *London Economist* during his 19-year on/off relationship with the centrist *New Republic*. Beginning while he was at Harvard Law School in 1976, he was *New Republic* managing editor or editor and wrote the TRB column until 1979, when he left in a battle with editor-in-chief Martin Peretz. Returning to the magazine in 1983 under Hendrik Hertzberg, where he remains as editor and TRB columnist, he also appeared on television on William Buckley's *Firing Line* and the *McLaughlin Group*. In 1989 CNN offered him a half hour in the liberal chair of its *CrossFire* debate show opposite Pat Buchanan. In 1986, Kinsley was listed in *American Politics* as among the "150 Journalists Who Make a Difference in American Politics," describes requirements for inclusion in this volume. Sixty-one of his articles from The *New Republic*, *Harper's*, the *Wall Street Journal*, and *Fortune* magazine have been published in book form in *Curse of the Giant Muffins and Other Washington Maladies*.

KLEIN, LAWRENCE R.

University of Pennsylvania, Department of Economics, Philadelphia, PA 19104
BORN: 1920, Omaha, Neb. ACHIEVEMENTS: Nobel Prize in Economic Science, 1980; John Bates Clark Medal of the American Economic Association, 1959; president of the Econometric Society, 1960; president of the Environmental Economics Association, 1975; president of the American Economic Association, 1977. STUDIED: University of California, Berkeley; Massachusetts Institute of Technology, 1944.
Long before computers were standard equipment in the nation's libraries, offices, and in millions of American homes, intrepid economists were among the first to utilize their formidable powers to demonstrate theories. In the forefront of this band of scientists was Lawrence Klein, a Keynesian economist who would devote his life to building statistical models describing activities in consumer spending, business and government saving, investments, the money supply, exports, imports, etc., all used simultaneously to forecast the nation's economy. His association with Brookings Econometric Model Project, the largest econometric model ever constructed for any economy, would lead him in 1980 to the Nobel Prize for developing models that would forecast economic trends, and also for shaping policies to deal with them. Klein reviewed some of the Brooking's projects findings and the models' performances over the last decade in *The Brookings Model*, co-edited with G. Fromm, in 1975.

KLEINFIELD, NATHAN RICHARD (SONNY)

c/o Bantam Books, 666 Fifth Avenue, New York, NY 10103; (212) 765-6500
BORN: 1950, Paterson, N.J. ACHIEVEMENTS: Author of The Traders, Holt, 1984. STUDIED: New York University, B.A., 1972.

Nathan Richard (Sonny) Kleinfield began his career as a reporter with the *Wall Street Journal* in 1972. Five years later he went to work for the *New York Times* as a business reporter. In addition to his newspaper work, Kleinfield has contributed to a number of popular magazines, including *Atlantic Monthly, Harper's,* and *Quest.* Kleinfield is best known for his investigative books of various American enterprises. In *The Biggest Company on Earth: A Profile of AT & T,* Holt, 1981, Kleinfield covers the operations of the telecommunication giant from the boardroom to the bathrooms. Kleinfield has also written *The Traders,* Holt, 1984, and *A Machine Called Indomitable,* Times Books, 1985.

KLINE, KEVIN DELANEY

Creative Artists Agency, Suite 1400, 1888 Century Park East, Los Angeles, CA 90067

BORN: 1947, St. Louis, Mo. ACHIEVEMENTS: Antoinette Perry Award, Best Supporting or Featured Actor in a Musical, On the Twentieth Century, 1978; Antoinette Perry Award, Best Actor in a Musical, The Pirates of Penzance, 1980; Academy Award, Best Supporting Actor, A Fish Called Wanda, 1988. STUDIED: Indiana University, B.A., 1970; Juilliard Drama Center, 1972.

Kevin Kline devoted most of his early career to acting on the stage. Much of his work was with New York Shakespeare Festival productions, early on in supporting roles, and after achieving success, in starring roles. Kline won his first Tony for his performance in the Broadway production of *On the Twentieth Century,* 1978. His performance of the pirate king in *The Pirates of Penzance,* 1980 earned him widespread fame and another Tony. Kline moved on to films, making his debut in *Sophie's Choice,* 1982, with Meryl Streep. He also appeared in *The Big Chill,* 1983; *Silverado,* 1985; *Cry Freedom,* 1987; *A Fish Called Wanda,* 1988, for which he won an Oscar; *The January Man,* 1989; and *Grand Canyon,* 1991.

KLUGH, EARL

c/o EMI/Liberty Records, 6920 Sunset Blvd., Los Angeles, CA 90028; (213) 461-9141

BORN: 1953, Detroit. ACHIEVEMENTS: Grammy Award, seven Grammy nominations.

Earl Klugh's affinity for selling records rather than just showing off his playing ability has not always won him high critical praise. After years of working with established artists, he continues playing the kind of music he likes. Practical wisdom has won him a Grammy and seven Grammy nominations. It also has allowed him to tour the U.S., Europe, and Japan, perform soundtracks for films, and reprise in "Sounds and Vision" songs from *Goldfinger, Tequila Sunrise, Calamity Jane,* and *The Thomas Crown Affair,* all enhanced by the London Royal Philharmonic Orchestra.

KNIGHT, PHILIP HAMPSON

One Bowerman Dr., Beaverton, OR 97005; (503) 671-6453

ACHIEVEMENTS: founded, Nike Inc. STUDIED: Stanford University, M.B.A., 1963.

Philip Knight proposed the idea that became NIKE, Inc. in a 1963 term paper he wrote for his Stanford M.B.A. program. After graduation he went to work for the CPA firm of Coopers & Lybrand. While employed as a CPA, he joined with his former running coach Bill Bowerman, and together they formed Blue Ribbon Sports, which imported and sold Japanese-made track shoes. In 1972 his supplier, Tiger shoes of Japan, demanded a 51 percent interest of Blue Ribbon Sports. Faced with the choice of losing control of his business, or losing his supplier, Knight choose to design and produce his own shoe. One of his employees came up with the name NIKE, the Greek goddess of victory. Through a combination of a superior quality shoe, reasonable cost, and product endorsements by professional athletes, NIKE has become one of the leading athletic shoe makers in the world.

KNIGHT, CHARLES FIELD

Emerson Electric Company, 8000 W. Florissant Ave., St. Louis, MO 63136; (314) 553-2000

BORN: 1936, Lake Forest, Ill. STUDIED: Cornell University, B.S., mechanical engineering, M.B.A., management engineering.

Charles Knight spent his first two years after graduation from college working for Goetzwerke A.G., in the town of Burscheid, West Germany, just northeast of Cologne. Returning to the States, he joined Lester B. Knight International Corporation in Chicago as president. In 1963 he became executive vice president of Lester B. Knight & Associates, Inc., and president and chief executive officer in 1967. In 1973 he joined Emerson Electric Company in St. Louis as vice chairman of the board, and that position led to chairman of the board in 1974. He also serves on the boards at Southwestern Bell Corporation, Caterpillar, Inc., Baxter International, and Anheuser Busch Companies, Inc.

KNIGHT, FRANKLIN W.

Johns Hopkins University, Department of History, 3400 N. Charles St., Baltimore, MD 21218

BORN: 1942, Jamaica. ACHIEVEMENTS: Fellow, National Endowment for Humanities, Center for Advanced Study in Behavioral Sciences, National Humanities Center. STUDIED: University College of London, B.A., (honors); University of Wisconsin, M.A., history, Ph.D., history.

Franklin Knight taught as an assistant professor at the State University of New York at Stonybrook while still working on his doctorate. That achieved, he became an associate professor until he moved to Johns Hopkins University in 1973, again as associate professor. He was made a full professor at Johns Hopkins in 1977, and has taught there since. He is the author of two books, *Slave Society in Cuba During the 19th Century,* and *The Caribbean, Genesis of a Fragmented Nationalism.*

KNOWLES, EDWARD FRANK

130 West 56th Street, New York, NY 10019 (212) 267-4459

BORN: 1929. ACHIEVEMENTS: fellow, AIA; First Prize, Boston City Hall Competition, 1962; notable works: Boston City Hall; Filene Center for the Performing Arts, Vienna, Virginia; Lowell Nesbitt Studio, New York City. STUDIED: Pratt Institute.

Edward Knowles first came to critical attention for his contribution to the design of the monumental New Boston City Hall, with Gerhard Kallmann and Noel McKinnell. Subsequently, he has been primarily known for his humane and often rustic designs for private residences and art institutions. Significant architecture, he now believes, must express the emotional states of its contributors as well as the pre-conditions of site, budget and function. So in his recent work, he has abandoned academic approaches to design, and instead proceeds piecemeal, attempting to "feel out" the emotional, aesthetic and practical textures of each project. His Filene Center for the Performing Arts in Wolf Trap Farm Park, Va. is a multi-story arts complex set amid a natural grassy amphitheater. Clear views of the main stage are offered both within the building and from the broad sloping front lawn. The structure's rough, unvarnished, red-cedar exterior evokes the long-weathered, gracefully sagging barns and water towers on the site's perimeter. Yet the smooth white paneling of the roof, and the building's strong planes, place it firmly in the modernist tradition.

KNOWLES, TONY

Office of the Governor, P.O. Box 11001, Juneau, AK 99811-0001 (907) 465-3500
BORN: 1943, Tulsa, Okla. ACHIEVEMENTS: Vietnam Veteran; served with the U.S. Army's 82nd Airborne Division. STUDIED: Yale University, B.A. economics, 1968.

In 1968, after graduating from Yale, Knowles moved to Alaska and worked as a roughneck in the Cook Inlet oil fields. One year later he started his first restaurant, the Grizzly Burgers, and quickly expanded to three locations. He spent four years on the Anchorage Assembly from 1975-1979. As the two-term mayor of Anchorage from 1982 to 1987, his administration was responsible for the conception and construction of the Alaska Center for the Performing Arts, the Egan Civic and Convention Center, and the 11-mile Tony Knowles Coastal Trail, a running/bike trail around the scenic Turnagain Arm. In 1984, under Knowles' leadership, the cost of government per person decreased, and Anchorage was named an All-American City. Knowles was elected governor in 1994, after campaigning on a "new directions" theme that focused on jobs for Alaskans, better schools and budget discipline. Knowles believes the fundamentals of business and state operations are similar. He says, "you give the customers what they want, you always live within your means, and you roll up your sleeves to do whatever needs to be done," describes requirements for inclusion in this volume.

KOCH, EDWARD I.

Robinson, Silverman, et. al., 1290 Avenue of the Americas, New York, NY 10104
BORN: 1924, New York City. ACHIEVEMENTS: Three-term mayor of New York City.

Outspoken, impetuous and combative, Edward Koch served three turbulent terms as the Democratic mayor of New York City, from 1978 to 1990. Despite serious economic and social problems during his mayoralty, he retained his popularity until support among minority voters eroded, and he was defeated in the 1989 Democratic primary election. His books included *Mayor*, 1984; *Politics*, 1985; *His Eminence and Hizzoner*, with John Cardinal O'Connor, 1989; and his autobiography, *Citizen Koch*, 1992.

KOHN, EUGENE A.

Kohn Persen Fox Associates, 111 West 57th Street , New York, NY 10019 (212) 977-6500
BORN: 1930. ACHIEVEMENTS: FAIA; Royal Institute of Architects Flame of Truth Award; notable works: Proctor & Gamble World Headquarters, Cincinnati; DG Bank, Frankfurt (West Germany); Four Seasons Hotel at Logan Square, Philadelphia. STUDIED: University of Pennsylvania.

Eugene Kohn is a contextualist guided by clear philosophical goals: he argues that urban commercial architecture, long dominated by bland functional design, has to attract the better architects away from traditional aesthetically oriented projects such as museums. He identifies with postmodernism because the movement's emphasis on tops and bases brings the perceived scale of a building back to street-level—the human level. While he is critical of extreme, pastiche design, he uses postmodern historical references and rich detailing in his architecture. "Contextualism"—a term his firm originally coined—is another of his dominant concerns. Contextualism is more than sensitivity to the surrounding buildings; it must express the history and spirit of the surrounding environment and more, it must add a "new thought": a design solution oriented toward the future of modern architecture. His 333 Wacker Drive in Chicago, co-designed with William Pedersen, is an office tower on a bend of the Chicago River, its curved skin of green-tinted glass reflecting the green weather, providing counterpoint and respite from the surround black and gray. His One Logan Square building in Philadelphia exemplifies a more traditional contextualism. While modern is design, it harkens to the colonial style of neighboring buildings.

KOLB, KEITH R.

Kolb & Stansfield AIA Architects, 628 Skinner Building, Seattle, WA 98101 (206) 622-0393
BORN: 1992. ACHIEVEMENTS: FAIA; AIA First Honor Award; J. F. Lincoln Arc Welding Foundation National Bronze Award; notable works: Forks Branch, Seattle First National Bank, Forks, Wash.; Puget Sound Blood Center, Seattle. STUDIED: Harvard University, University of Washington.

Suspicious of specialization, and the fads of the moment, Keith Kolb seeks to create environments in which the new is part of the old, and part of the future as well. Each of his buildings declare man's concern for his living, learning and working environment, clearly expressing the life and technology of a given time, place and culture. Expressing the rhythms of a given place and time in his hospital designs, Kolb begins with an awareness that most patients come and go from hospitals very quickly, and are encouraged to do so. Doctors, nurses and technicians, on the other hand spend their working lives inside his designs, so it is their needs and comforts, as well as their patients', which inform his designs. His Forks Bank also shows that awareness both for how people live, and how they want to live. This branch bank, in a small Washington coastal town, reflects the love of the local environment which keeps people in the area. Though often cloudy, the pulsing play of sun and cloud above is lighter and more beguiling than in inland Seattle. This suggested an energy-efficient skylight and window system that lets the spell of the constantly changing sky pass through the work environment.

KOLFF, WILLEM JOHAN

NCIPLA, Suite 203, 2001 Jefferson Davis Hwy., Arlington, VA 22202
BORN: 1911, Leiden (Holland). ACHIEVEMENTS: Invented kidney dialysis machine.
The inventor of the artificial kidney dialysis machine was born, raised, educated, and practiced medicine in Holland before immigrating to the U.S. in 1950 at age 39. His machine offers a technique for separating waste products or toxins from the bloodstream, and is used mainly in cases of kidney failure. Kolff also headed the team that invented and tested a soft-shell artificial heart. In 1967 he became a professor of surgery at the Utah School of Medicine.

KONER, PAULINE

263 West End Ave., 9F, New York, NY 10023 (212) 874-5621
Koner is a prominent dancer. For career credentials consult the portion of this book entitled "Biographees by Profession" in the Appendix. Within this portion, the list "Dancers," describes requirements for inclusion in this volume.

KOONS, JEFF

c/o Sonnabend, 420 West Broadway, New York, NY 10012
BORN: 1955. ACHIEVEMENTS: Exhibitions: Rena Bransten Gallery, San Francisco; Daniel Weinberg Gallery, Los Angeles. STUDIED: Maryland Institute College of Art; School of the Art Institute of Chicago
Jeff Koons reproduces consumer goods as symbols that confront moral and social issues. In 1980 he started encasing vacuum cleaners under plexiglas boxes to represent the new and to explore self-containment, display and preservation. He turned to the idea of submersion in 1985, in a show that featured tanks

in which basketballs floated in suspension, bronzes of scuba snorkels, and Nike posters of sports figures. In 1986 he created an edition of stainless steel, decorative Jim Beam decanters that were sent to the factory in Kentucky to be filled with liquor and officially sealed. Recent works include reproductions of kitsch gift items cast in steel, and an inflated rabbit made in Taiwan.

KOONTZ, DEAN R.

PO Box 5686, Orange, CA 92613
BORN: 1945, Bedford, Pa. ACHIEVEMENTS: author, 59 novels. STUDIED: Shippenburg State College (now Shippensburg University), Shippensburg, Pennsylvania, B.A.
Dean Koontz looks back on a tortured childhood, living in a motherless home with a brutal, alcoholic father as the impetus for his writing career. Author of 59 novels, with 30 still in print and selling an estimated 16 million a year, his genres include science fiction, fantasy, social commentary, writing, and journalism. In 1994 he published *Dark Rivers of the Heart*, the first in a three-book, $18.9 million deal with his publishers. In *Dark Rivers* he is still fighting the demons his father laid upon him as he delves into the ominous side of a relationship between a psychopathic father and his son. His books made into films include *Demon Seed*, one of his books that still pleases him, and *Shattered*. To get his 50 books on the shelves at bookstores without the omnipresence of his name driving potential buyers away, he uses seven pseudonyms: Deanna Dwyer, Brian Coffey, and Leigh Nichols are his favorites, each appearing on five novels; K.R. Dwyer are on three, Owen West, on two, and John Hill and David Axton are names used on the other two.

KOPPEL, TED

ABC Press Relations, 7W-7 1330 Avenue of the Americas, New York, NY 10019
BORN: 1940, Lancashire (England); immigrated to U.S., 1953. ACHIEVEMENTS: Anchor, Nightline, 1980-present; master of ceremonies for dedication of U.S. Holocaust Memorial Museum, 1993. STUDIED: Stanford University.
His crisp voice helped Ted Koppel enter his chosen career in radio news, and he was soon hired by ABC News. Koppel served as a war correspondent in Vietnam, a diplomatic correspondent in Washington, D.C., and as bureau chief in both Miami and Hong Kong before becoming anchor of the *ABC Saturday Night News*. Inspired by the Iranian hostage crisis of 1980, he began *Nightline*, a late night news broadcast, that provided solid competition to the usual fare of funny talk show hosts, and the show became a stalwart in the post prime-time market.

KOSUTH, JOSEPH

591 Broadway, New York, NY 10012
BORN: 1945. ACHIEVEMENTS: Cassandra Foundation Grant; collections: Museum of Modern Art, New York City; Whitney Museum; exhibitions: Leo Castelli Gallery, New York City; La Jolla Museum of Contemporary Art. STUDIED: Toledo Museum School of Design; Cleveland Institute of Art;

School of Visual Arts, New York City; School for Social Research, New York City.

A hard-core conceptualist, Joseph Kosuth explores the connections, relationships and analogies between visual perception and language. His early pieces are explicit investigations in which an object, its image and its verbal definition are juxtaposed. In the recent installation *Zero & Not*, Kosuth covered the walls of the entire gallery with wallpaper on which he photomechanically reproduced, enlarged and repeated a segment from Freud's *Psychopathology of Everyday Life*. The text was partially obscured by the addition of deletion bars; hence, the larger-than-life words presented were simultaneously repressed through the visual interference imposed upon them.

KRANTZ, JUDITH

c/o Warner Books, 665 5th Ave., New York, NY 10103
BORN: 1928, New York City. ACHIEVEMENTS: Best-selling novelist, authored Scruples, 1978. STUDIED: Wellesley College, English.
Judith Krantz was a journalist for 27 years, including a stint as an editor at *Good Housekeeping* magazine, before she launched her career as a popular novelist in 1978 with the best-selling *Scruples*. Like her later books, it portrayed the lives and loves of wealthy and glamorous international jet-setters. Her other novels included *Princess Daisy*, 1980; *Mistral's Daughter*, 1982; *I'll Take Manhattan*, 1987; *Till We Meet Again*, 1989; *Dazzle*, 1990; *Scruples Two*, 1992; and *Lovers*, 1994.

KRISTOF, NICHOLAS D.

The *New York Times*, 229 West 43rd St., New York, NY 10046; (212) 556-1234
BORN: 1959, Chicago. ACHIEVEMENTS: Pulitzer Prize, 1990; George Polk Award, 1990. STUDIED: Oxford University, Rhodes Scholar, graduated with first class honors; graduated Harvard, Phi Beta Kappa, 1981; studied Arabic at the American University in Cairo, 1983-1984.
The *New York Times* Tokyo bureau chief since December, 1994. Nicholas Kristof was also *New York Times* bureau chief in Beijing from 1988 to 1993, and Hong Kong in 1986. In 1990, he won a Pulitzer Prize, with his wife Sheryl WuDunn (also a *Times* correspondent), for coverage of Tiananmen Square. Kristof has been with the *New York Times* since 1984. At that time, he was an economics reporter. In 1985, he was a business correspondent, based in Los Angeles, for the *New York Times*.

KROO, ILAN

Dept. of Aeronautics & Astronautics, Stanford University, Stanford, CA 94305
Kroo is a prominent inventor. For career credentials consult the portion of this book entitled "Biographees by Profession" in the Appendix. Within this portion, the list "Inventors," describes requirements for inclusion in this volume.

KRULAK, GEN. CHARLES C.

Office of the Secretary, Pentagon, Washington, DC 20301 (703-6700)
BORN: 1942, Quantico, Va. ACHIEVEMENTS: Silver Star; Bronze Star with Combat "V" and two gold stars; Purple Heart with gold star; Combat Action Ribbon; Vietnam Service Medal with silver star and two bronze stars; Republic of Vietnam Cross of Gallantry; and the Kuwait Liberation Medal among his 16 military medals. STUDIED: U.S. Naval Academy, B.S., engineering; George Washington University, M.S., labor relations; Amphibious Warfare School; Army Command and General Staff College; Naval War College.
Before rising to his present rank, Gen. Charles C. Krulak headed a platoon and two rifle companies during two tours of duty in Vietnam. He subsequently held a variety of command positions in the Corps' special training and counter-guerilla warfare sections, at the U.S. Naval Academy, and at the Naval Air Station at North Island, Calif. Many staff positions followed, leading to Krulak's appointment as deputy director of the White House Military Office, in 1987, during which time he became a brigadier general. He advanced to major general five years later and in the same year, after serving as commanding general of the Marine Corps Combat Development Command, he stepped up to lieutenant general. He assumed his duties as the 31st commandant of the Marine Corps the day after he was promoted to full general in 1995.

KUNTMAN, DARYAL

Allied-Signal Aerospace, Columbia Rd. and Park Ave., Morristown, NJ 07692 (201) 455-2000
ACHIEVEMENTS: Developed the Forward-Looking Wind Shear Detection/Avoidance Radar System.
Wind shear is the unseen menace in air travel, its presence unknown until pilots feel dangerous downdrafts shaking the plane. It was a contributing factor in 26 civil aircraft crashes from 1965-1985, causing more than 500 deaths. Daryal Kuntman, manager of radar product design at Allied-Signal, developed the Forward-Looking Wind Shear Detection/Avoidance Radar System to solve the problem. His system measures the tiny drops of moisture always present in the air, and alerts the pilot to any dangerous area by determining the drops' velocity well ahead of the aircraft's approach to landing.

KURALT, CHARLES

119 W. 57th., Penthouse 1600, New York, NY 10019
BORN: 1934, New York City. ACHIEVEMENTS: Four Emmy Awards, Broadcaster of the Year, 1985, International Radio TV Society. STUDIED: University of North Carolina, B.A., journalism.
Breaking into newspaper work in Wilmington, N.C., Kuralt soon joined *CBS News*, and after two years on the staff, became a foreign correspondent in 1959 at age 25. He spent the next 10 years on foreign assignments, then began exploring his own country in an *On the Road* series. This was followed by the job of anchor on CBS's *Sunday Morning*. His memoirs, *A Life On the Road*, was published in 1990. Named Broadcaster of

the Year in 1985 by the International Radio TV Society, Kuralt also has won four Emmys during his career.

KUSHNER, TONY

c/o Joyce Ketay, 334 West 89th St., New York, NY 10024

Kushner is a prominent dramatic artist. For career credentials consult the portion of this book entitled "Biographees by Profession" in the Appendix. Within this portion, the list "Dramatic Artists," describes requirements for inclusion in this volume.

KYL, JON

328 Hart Senate Office Building, Washington, DC 20510-0302; (202) 224-4521

BORN: 1942, Oakland, Neb. ACHIEVEMENTS: Congressman and Senator. STUDIED: University of Arizona, B.A., 1964; University of Arizona, L.L.B., 1966.

Jon Kyl won election to the Senate from Arizona in 1994, after serving four terms in the U.S. House of Representatives. He has concentrated on issues affecting national defense, fiscal responsibility and ethics reform. His committee assignments include the Subcommittee on Immigration; Subcommittee on Constitution, Federalism and Property Rights; and the Subcommittee on Energy, Research and Development. He became a leader among the House's younger generation of aggressive conservatives, serving in his second term as chairman of the Conservative Opportunity Society.

LABELLE, PATTI

c/o MCA Records, 100 Universal City Plaza, Universal City, CA 91608-1022; (818) 777-4000

BORN: 1944 Philadelphia. ACHIEVEMENTS: Grammy, R&B Vocal-Female, Burnin, 1991.

Patti LaBelle has been singing professionally for more than 30 years. Born Patricia Holt, LaBelle got started in the 1960s singing with her band, the Bluebelles. After she changed her name, the band was renamed Patti LaBelle and the Bluebelles. Along with LaBelle, the group's members were: Cindy Birdsong, Sarah Dash and Nona Hendryx. The group had several successes in the rhythm and blues market between 1962 and 1967, when Birdsong left the group to sing with Diana Ross and the Supremes. LaBelle continued to sing with the band's remaining members during the late 1960s and early 1970s, but they didn't enjoy the same success of previous years. LaBelle started her solo career in 1977, and had scored several more R&B hits by 1983 with her fiery style and gospel-trained voice. In 1984, she released *If Only You Knew*, which finally gave her a number one hit.

LAKERVELD, HARRY

Philips Electronics Corporation, 100 East 42nd St., New York, NY 10017-5613 (212) 850-5000

Lakerveld is a prominent inventor. For career credentials consult the portion of this book entitled "Biogra-phees by Profession" in the Appendix. Within this portion, the list "Inventors," describes requirements for inclusion in this volume.

LAMHUT, PHYLLIS

Phyllis Lamhut Dance Company, 225 West 71st St., #31, New York, NY 10023 (212) 799-9048

Lamhut is a prominent dancer. For career credentials consult the portion of this book entitled "Biographees by Profession" in the Appendix. Within this portion, the list "Dancers," describes requirements for inclusion in this volume.

LANDERS, SAM

Goodyear Tire & Rubber, 1114 E. Market St., Akron. OH 44316 (216) 796-2121

ACHIEVEMENTS: Developed the Aquatred tire.

More than 20 percent of U.S. car crashes each year occur on wet roads. The main culprit in these accidents is a wedge of water buildup in front of the tires. This water buildup can cause a car to hydroplane on the road, potentially leading to loss of control. In the late 1970s Goodyear Tire & Rubber assigned Sam Landers to find a solution to hydroplaning, a job that took 13 years before the company's first Aquatred tire went on sale. His solution was to widen the grooves in tire-tread patterns from the traditional tiny grooves, and then build an inch-wide, half-inch deep channel in the center of the tire that gives water a place to go, so it doesn't build up in front of the tire. The 13-year project ran into many unforeseen complications such as vibration and noise problems. Solutions required chemical research on the composition of tire rubber. In the end, Landers found it necessary to set up an entirely new manufacturing process to produce large quantities of a synthetic rubber originally concocted during World War II.

LANG, PEARL

382 Central Park West, New York, NY 10025 (212) 866-2680

Lang is a prominent dancer. For career credentials consult the portion of this book entitled "Biographees by Profession" in the Appendix. Within this portion, the list "Dancers," describes requirements for inclusion in this volume.

LANGE, JESSICA

Creative Artists Agency, 1888 Century Park East, 14th Floor, Los Angeles, CA 90067

BORN: 1949, Cloquet, Minn. ACHIEVEMENTS: Academy Award, Best Supporting Actress, Tootsie, 1983. STUDIED: University of Minnesota; mime training with Etienne DeCroux, Paris.

Primarily an actress in film, Jessica Lange debuted in movies with her appearance in the remake of *King Kong*, in 1976. She has appeared in many popular movies, including *All That Jazz*, in 1979; *The Postman Always Rings Twice*, in 1981; and *Crimes of the Heart*; in 1986. Lange won an Academy Award for her portrayal of Julie in the movie, *Tootsie* in 1983. In 1984, she produced and starred in *Country*. On television, Lange played Maggie in the play, *Cat on a Hot Tin Roof* on Showtime, in 1984, and on *American Playhouse*, in 1985. She is the founder of Far West Pictures, and has been a dancer with the Opera Comique, of Paris, France.

LANIER, ROBERT C.

P. O. Box 1562, Houston, TX 77251-1562; (713) 247-2200

BORN: 1925, Baytown, Texas. ACHIEVEMENTS: Mayor of Houston, chairman, Texas Highway and Public Transportation Commission. STUDIED: University of New Mexico, B.A.; University of Texas, law, 1949.

Lanier served three years in the U.S. Navy before returning to school, graduating with honors in 1949. After completing school, Lanier opened his own firm, where he practiced law for 10 years. He then went into banking, and owned banks, and savings and loans, until 1981. Politically, Lanier served as chairman of the Texas Highway Commission from 1983 through 1987 and in April, 1988, chairman of the Metropolitan Transit Authority. On December 7, 1991 Lanier was elected mayor of Houston.

LANSBURY, ANGELA

William Morris Agency, 151 El Camino, Beverly Hills, CA 90212

BORN: 1925, London. (England) ACHIEVEMENTS: Golden Globe Award, Best Supporting Actress, The Picture of Dorian Gray, 1946; Golden Globe Award, Best Supporting Actress, The Manchurian Candidate, 1963; Golden Globe Award, Best Actress in a TV Series, Drama, Murder, She Wrote, 1985, 1987, 1990, 1992; Antoinette Perry Award, Best Actress, Musical, Mame, 1966; Antoinette Perry Award, Best Actress, Musical, Dear World, 1969; Antoinette Perry Award, best Actress, Musical, Gypsy, 1975, Antoinette Perry Award, Best Actress, Musical, Sweeney Todd, 1979. STUDIED: Webber-Douglas School of Singing and Dramatic Arts, 1939-40; Feagin School of Drama and Radio, 1940-42.

Angela Lansbury came to the United States from England in 1940 with her parents to escape the German bombing of London during World War II. She is the daughter of actress Moyna McGill. Lansbury is best known for her work on television, where she plays Jessica Beatrice Fletcher on the series, *Murder, She Wrote*, which began in 1984. She has appeared in more than 70 films. Her film debut was in *Gaslight*, in 1944. Two years later, she won a Golden Globe for her work as a supporting actress in *The Picture of Dorian Gray*. More recently, she has appeared in *The Mirror Crack'd*, in 1980, and *The Company of Wolves*, in 1985. Lansbury has worked the stage on Broadway, in London, and on tour. She has appeared in the title role of *Mame* in 1966, 1972 and 1983, as well as numerous other roles. She has worked extensively on television in movies, specials, and mini-series from the 1950s through the 1980s, including the mini-series, *Lace*, in which she played Aunt Hortense Boutin.

LAPINE, JAMES ELLIOTT

c/o Dramatists Guild, 234 West 44th St., New York, NY 10036

BORN: 1949, Mansfield, Ohio. ACHIEVEMENTS: Obie Award for Photograph; George Oppenheimer Playwriting Award for Table Settings; Pulitzer Prize (shared with Stephen Sondheim) for Sunday in the Park with George; Antoinette Perry Award for Into the Woods, Best Book of a Musical, and Falsetto, Best Book of a Musical; Drama Desk Award for Passion, Best Book of a Musical. STUDIED: Franklin and Marshall College, Lancaster, Pennsylvania, B.A., history.

James Lapine is a celebrated writer of texts for musical compositions, and one of the leading directors of the New York Stage. The former graphic designer for the Yale Repertory Theater and design teacher at Yale began his Broadway career by directing a production of Gertrude Stein's *Photograph*, which brought him his first award, an Obie. He continued his work as text writer and director until 1990, collaborating with playwright William Finn and later with composer Stephen Sondheim, with whom he directed the award-winning *Sunday in the Park with George* for the Public Broadcasting System. At that time he entered feature filmmaking by directing the screenplay *Impromptu*, written by his wife, Sarah Krenochan. The story tells of the tangled web woven from the lives and loves of 19th century artists George Sand (Lucile Aurore Dupia Dudevant), Frederic Francoise Chopin, and Franz Liszt. He also directed Michael J. Fox in *Life with Mikey*, a comic story about a child agent.

LAPINSKI, ANN MARIE

The Chicago Tribune, 435 N. Michigan Ave., Chicago, IL 60611-4022 (312) 222-3232

Lapinski is a prominent journalist. For career credentials consult the portion of this book entitled "Biographees by Profession" in the Appendix. Within this portion, the list "Journalists," describes requirements for inclusion in this volume.

LARROQUETTE, JOHN

NBC, 3000 Alameda, Burbank, CA 91523

BORN: 1947, New Orleans. ACHIEVEMENTS: Emmy, Best Supporting Actor in a Comedy Series, Night Court, 1985, 1986, 1987, 1988.

John Larroquette is well known for his portrayal of Dan Fielding, the assistant district attorney on the television series, *Night Court*, for which he has received numerous Emmy awards. Although he began acting on *Night Court* in 1984, his television debut occurred nine years earlier on the soap opera, *Doctors' Hospital*. He also played squadron member Robert Anderson, in the television series, *Baa Baa Black Sheep* from 1976 until 1978. Larroquette has numerous film appearances to his credit, too, including, *Altered States*, in 1980; *Cat People*, in 1982; and *Star Trek III: The Search for Spock*, in 1984. He has also acted on stage in Los Angeles in plays such as, *The Crucible, Enter Laughing*, and *Endgame*. He now stars *in the John Laroquette Show*.

LARSEN, RALPH S.

Johnson & Johnson, 1 Johnson & Johnson Pl., New Brunswick, NY 08933 (908) 524-0400

Larsen is a prominent business leader. For career credentials consult the portion of this book entitled "Biographees by Profession" in the Appendix. Within this portion, the list "Business Leaders," describes requirements for inclusion in this volume.

LASHUTKA, GREGORY S.

City of Columbus, Office of the Mayor, City Hall, Columbus, OH 43215 (614) 645-7671
BORN: 1944, New York City. ACHIEVEMENTS: 1993 Municipal Leader of the Year, American City & County magazine. STUDIED: Ohio State University, B.S., 1967; Capital University Law School, J.D. 1974.
Gregory Lashutka attended Ohio State University and was co-captain of the football team. After graduation from the Capital City Law School, he combined his knowledge of sports with his legal education to practice municipal and sports law. He was an aide to former Congressman Sam Devine, law clerk for former Probate Judge Richard Metcalf, and served eight years as city attorney. He was also an officer in the U.S. Navy for four years. Lashutka was elected mayor of Columbus, Ohio in 1992.

LAUPER, CYNDI

Portrait Records, 51 West 52nd St., New York, NY 10019; (212) 975-5283
BORN: 1950, Queens, N.Y. ACHIEVEMENTS: Grammy, Best New Artist, 1984.
Cyndi Lauper may be best known for her solo hit, *Girls Just Want to Have Fun.* Released in 1983, the song, with its timely feminist theme, made her an instant sensation on MTV and in record stores nationwide. It was preceded by years of guitar work with several different groups before she co-founded *Blue Angel* in 1977. *Blue Angel* put out a critically praised album in 1977 with Polydor. She also released *Time After Time* in 1983 and won a Grammy for Best New Artist in 1984 for her efforts. Lauper continues to record, although her more recent sales have not equaled her initial rise to popularity.

LAURER, MATT

NBC, 30 Rockefeller Plaza, New York, NY 10112 (212) 664-4444
Laurer began in television at Huntington, W. Vir.'s WOWK-TV in 1979. He has hosted many news and information shows including "PM Magazine" in New York in 1985-86 and "9 Broadcast Plaza" at WWOR-TV, also in New York. Currently he is the anchor at NBC's "Today Show" and co-anchor of "News4/Live at Five" with Susan Simmon's on WNBC-TV, New York.

LAUTENBACHER, REAR ADM. C. CONRAD JR.

Office of the Secretary, Pentagon, Washington, DC, 20301; (703) 545-6700
BORN: 1942, Philadelphia. ACHIEVEMENTS: Defense Distinguished Service Medal; Legion of Merit; Meritorious Service Medal; Navy Commendation Medal; Navy Achievement Medal; Combat Action Award; Navy Unit Commendation Award; Meritorious Unit Award. STUDIED: U.S. Naval Academy, B.S.; Harvard University, Ph.D., applied mathematics.
Rear Adm. Lautenbacher has been both a frontline warrior and a rearline planner. He has served at the Pentagon in jobs as varied as naval personnel, planning, and operations, and on the Joint Chiefs of Staff, and at sea as commander in the Atlantic, Pacific, and the Mediterranean. During Operation Desert Shield and Desert Storm, Lauterbacher, then age 50, commanded a destroyer cruiser group and the naval central command at Riyadh, Saudi Arabia. Redirected to the Pentagon following the operations, he directed an assessment of naval resources, joined the Joint Chiefs, and then became special assistant to the assistant secretary of the Navy, where he remains.

LAVENTHOL, DAVID

Los Angeles Times, Times Mirror Square, Los Angeles, CA 90012-3645 (213) 237-5000
Laventhol is a prominent publisher. For career credentials consult the portion of this book entitled "Biographees by Profession" in the Appendix. Within this portion, the list "Publishers," describes requirements for inclusion in this volume.

LAVIN, LINDA

Warner Brothers, 4000 Warner Bros. Blvd., Burbank, CA 91505
BORN: 1937, Portland, Maine. ACHIEVEMENTS: Antoinette Perry award, Best actress (Dramatic), Broadway Bound, 1987; Golden Globe Award, Best Actress in a Comedy Series, Alice, 1979. STUDIED: College of William and Mary, B.A., 1959.
Linda Lavin began her career in show business at the age of 5, playing the White Rabbit in the play, *Alice in Wonderland,* in 1942. She debuted on the New York stage in *Izzy, Oh, Kay!* in 1960 and has been busy on stage ever since. Her favorite stage roles have been, Elaine Navazio in *Last of the Red Hot Lovers,* Patsy Newquist in *Little Murders,* and the girl in *Cop Out.* In addition to her work on stage, Lavin is an accomplished television performer. She played detective Janice Wentworth in the series, *Barney Miller,* from 1975 to 1976, and Alice Hyatt in the series, *Alice,* from 1976 until 1985. Lavin has also worked as a producer on several television shows, including *Another Woman's Child,* in 1983, and *A Place to Call Home* in 1985.

LAWTON, HERBERT T.

Lawton & Umemura Architects, AIA, Inc., No. 1 Capitol District, Honolulu, HA 96813 (808) 529-9700
BORN: 1930. ACHIEVEMENTS: Notable works: Hyatt Regency Waikoloa, Kona Coast, Hawaii; Jimmy Carter Presidential Library and Museum, Atlanta; Hyatt Regency Maui, Hawaii. STUDIED: University of Cincinnati.
With longtime partner Robert Umemura, Herbert Lawton's practice has come to focus on resort design for the first great developer of mega-resort destinations, Chris Hemmeter. Hemmeter broke the mold of urban hotels for his sprawling destinations, which are shaped by the desires and fantasies of guests who seek

the adventure and romance of waterfalls, tropical vines, dolphins and the like. Hemmeter's hugely successful resorts are designed to give brief visitors to the Hawaiian islands precisely what they want in undreamt-of abundance. Lawton and Umemura came to work almost exclusively for Hemmeter, but as independent contractors they were reluctant to hire permanent staff for work that might disappear at any time. They eventually ironed out the uncertainties by selling their firm to Hemmeter. Lawton and Umemura have stayed on as principals in their unit of a larger Hemmeter corporation, which now creates turnkey resort communities. The design group grew from 30 to 80 employees in the first years following the sale. This unusual evolution highlights the unique role of the architect, which Lawton finds comparable to that of orchestra conductor.

LAYTON, JOE

c/o Roy Gerber Associates, 9200 Sunset Blvd., Los Angeles, CA 90069
Layton is a prominent dramatic artist. For career credentials consult the portion of this book entitled "Biographees by Profession" in the Appendix. Within this portion, the list "Dramatic Artists," describes requirements for inclusion in this volume.

LAZARUS, CHARLES

395 West Passiac St., Rochelle Park, NJ 07662; (201) 262-7800
ACHIEVEMENTS: First entrepreneur to build a chain of high-quality toy stores.
Charles Lazarus started his toy-store career in the early 1960s, when he changed his father's business from a bicycle shop into a children's furniture store, and then into a toy store. By 1966 he owned a total of four toy stores, and sold the business to Interstate Stores, Inc. for $7.5 million. Interstate increased the chain to 47 stores by 1974, but, due to poor management, filed for bankruptcy. To protect his investments, Lazarus took managing control of Interstate and sold off less profitable portions of the business, while retaining the toy store chain. By 1978 the chain had increased to 63 stores, all the creditors were paid, and Interstate changed its name to Toys 'R' Us. Lazarus has since started a children's apparel chain named Kids 'R' Us.

LEAHY, PATRICK

Russell Senate Office Building, 433 Washington, DC 20510-4502; (202) 224-4242
BORN:1940, Montpelier, Vt. ACHIEVEMENTS: U.S. Conference of Mayors Community Development Achievement Award; UNICEF's 1991 Congressional Award. STUDIED: St. Michael's College, B.A. 1961; Georgetown University, J.D. 1964.
Patrick Leahy has served as U. S. Senator from Vermont since 1974, and is the 12th most senior Democrat in the 104th Congress. As a result of this seniority, he is the ranking Democrat on several Senate committees, including the Appropriations Subcommittee on Foreign Operations and the Judiciary Subcommittee on Anti-trust, Business Rights and Competition. He is former vice-chairman of the Senate Select Committee on Intelligence, and served as chairman of the Agriculture Committee for eight years. His work on federal nutrition and farm policies resulted in the 1994 Leahy-Lugar bill which re-organized the U.S. Department of Agriculture, resulting in approximately $2 billion in spending cuts. In 1992 Leahy pressed for passage of the Children's Nutrition Improvement Act to ensure adequate nutrition for pregnant women and infants.

LEAVITT, MICHAEL O.

State of Utah, Office of the Governor, 210 State St., Salt Lake City, UT 841140601
BORN: 1951, Cedar City, Utah. ACHIEVEMENTS: Member, National Governors' Association Executive Committee, U.S. Advisory Commission on Intergovernment Relations, Republican Governors' Association; chairman, Western Governors' Association; president-elect, Council of State Governments,. STUDIED: South Utah State College School of Business.
High on the list of Republican Michael Leavitt's priorities is getting the states and the federal government to work together. He is one of the leading figures of three governmental associations in forming a Conference of States. This conference's aim is to write a State's Petition, pointing out the imbalance in federal-state relations. Among his other goals is better education, higher paying jobs, care for the needy, cutting waste in government, and protecting Utah's quality of life.

LEDERMAN, LEON MAX

Illinois Institute of Technology, Department of Physics, 3300 S. Federal St., Chicago 60616
BORN: 1922, New York City. ACHIEVEMENTS: Nobel Prize in Physics (shared with Melvin Schwartz and Jack Steinberger), 1988; National Medal of Science; Townsend Harris Medal; Elliott Cresson Medal; Wolf Prize. STUDIED: City College of New York; Columbia University.
For years Lederman worked with particle accelerators and with a device containing a vapor that condenses into droplets along the path of a particle, making the path of the particle visible. This led to studying the neutrino and subsequently sharing in the Nobel Prize. His team's discovery, which confirmed the reality of quarks, was based on the bombardment of the light metal beryllium with the subatomic particle proton, which produced neutrinos, elementary particles having little or no mass, but under the bombardment produced a beam. The beam in turn led the researchers to discovery of a second neutrino associated with the mumeson, one of the particles that glue all particles in an atom together. The team's "breakthrough" work had far-reaching effects on fundamental particle theories, and today the beams are routinely produced in machines called "meson factories."

LEDLEY, ROBERT

Georgetown University, 3900 Reservoir Rd., Washington, DC 20057

BORN: 1926, New York City. ACHIEVEMENTS: Invented the diagnostic x-Ray scanner; inducted into the National Inventors Hall of Fame. STUDIED: New York University, D.D.S., 1948; Columbia University, M.A., 1949.

Dr. Ledley holds over 20 patents, but he is best known for his invention of the whole-body computerized tomography (CT) machine or ACTA (Automatic Computerized Transverse Axial) diagnostic x-ray scanner. The ACTA scanner was the first to use three-dimensional imaging. Dr. Ledley formed Digital Information Sciences Corporation to manufacture the scanner and distribute it throughout Europe, Asia and the U.S. He eventually allowed Pfzier Inc. to take over his company's assets and manufacture the machine. In addition to his inventions, he authored the first textbook on digital computer engineering, and developed the computational methods in Boolean algebra, used in digital circuit design. Dr. Ledley has served the world of academia as a teacher and researcher at the National Institute of Standards and Technology, Johns Hopkins University, George Washington University and Georgetown University Medical Center.

LEE, TONY

National Business Employment Weekly, Route 1 at So. Ridge Road, Brunswick NJ; (609) 520-4304
BORN: 1959, Dallas. ACHIEVEMENTS: Published author in hundreds of publications. STUDIED: Northwestern University, M.S. journalism; graduated Regis University Denver, B.A. in political science and communications.

Lee is the editor of *National Business Employment Weekly*, a job search and career guidance publication from Dow Jones and Co., at which he is the editor. He is also editor of the quarterly *Managing Your Career*, a supplement of the *Wall Street Journal* that targets student subscribers of the *Journal* on college campuses, and military members in transition to civilian work. Lee has been on many television and radio programs produced by ABC, CNBC, and the *Wall Street Journal*. He has also been published in hundreds of national publications including the *Journal*, *American Banker*, *Omnibus*, and over 40 daily newspapers. Lee also oversees NBEW's premier guidebooks, a series of career guidance books published by John Wiley and Sons.

LEIBMAN, RON

Agency for the Performing Arts, 9000 Sunset Blvd., #1200, Los Angeles, CA 90069
BORN: 1937, New York City. ACHIEVEMENTS: Emmy Award, Outstanding Lead Actor in a Drama Series, Kaz 1979. STUDIED: Ohio Wesleyan University, stage training; American Academy of Dramatic Arts and the Actors Studio.

Ron Leibman began his acting career 1959 in the play *A View from the Bridge*. He debuted on Broadway as Peter Nemo in *Dear Me, the Sky Is Falling* in 1963. Leibman has appeared frequently on the stage throughout his career. He was highly praised for his work in *We bombed in New Haven*, in 1968, and for *Transfers* in 1970. He appeared in *Rumors*, at the Broadhurst Theatre, in New York City, in 1988. Leibman debuted on film in 1970 in the movie, *Where's*

Poppa?, also known as *Going Ape*. He has since appeared in numerous movies, including *Slaughterhouse-Five*, in 1972, and *Rhinestone* in 1984. Leibman starred in the television series, *Kaz*, from 1978 until 1979, which earned him an Emmy award. He has also acted in many television movies and pilots, including *Christmas Eve*, which earned him a Golden Globe Award nomination in 1987.

LEIBOVITZ, ANNIE

c/o Vanity Fair, 350 Madison Ave., New York, NY 10017
BORN: 1950. STUDIED: San Francisco Art Institute.

One of America's best-known photographers, Annie Leibovitz was *Rolling Stone's* "cover girl" for 13 years. Acclaimed for her dramatic portraits of the famous and infamous, Leibovitz's secret lies in her ability to strip celebrities of the affectation that usually accompanies their public personae. She achieves a rapport with her subjects that is playful and intimate. Her work is never marred by the self-consciousness which often affects less talented photographers. As a result even her most expressionistic work has an introspective quality. Leibovitz is currently a contributing photographer with *Vanity Fair* magazine.

LENO, JAY

General Management Corporation, 9000 Sunset Boulevard Suite 400, Los Angeles CA 90069.
BORN: 1950, New Rochelle, N.Y. STUDIED: Emerson College, B.A. speech communications, 1973.

Born James Leno, he once worked as a Rolls Royce auto mechanic and delivery man while seeking work as a stand-up comedian. Leno has opened for Perry Como, Johnny Mathis, John Denver, Henry Mancini, James Brown, Tom Jones, and others. In 1977 Leno made his TV debut on *The Marilyn McCoo & Billy Davis Jr. Show*. A year later, in 1978, he made his film debut in *Silver Bears*, and appeared in *American Hot Wax*. He hosted his own show, *The Jay Leno Show*, for NBC, in 1986. In 1992 he became the third host of the *Tonight Show*. A motorcycle enthusiast, he loves to ride his Harley Davidson and collect antique cars.

LEONTIEF, WASSILY W.

New York University, Institute of Economic Analysis, 269 Mercer St., New York NY 10003
BORN: 1906, St. Petersburg (Russia). ACHIEVEMENTS: Nobel Prize in Economic Science, 1973; French Legion of Honor, 1968; president, American Economic Association, 1970; Nobel Prize in Economics, 1973; Presidency of Section F of the British Academy for the Advancement of Science, 1976; Russian-American Hall of Fame, 1980. STUDIED: University of St. Petersburg; University of Berlin.

A "specialist's specialist," Wassily Leontief has made a life's work out of a single tool in the economists' bag of theories: input-output analysis, which requires "getting the hands dirty" by working with raw data. The son of a labor economics professor at the University of St. Petersburg, Leontief conceived his method of analysis as a youth, and has evangelized it ever since in countries around the world. The technique is simple: The economy is broken down into the movement of goods and services between industries, which are then recorded systematically to show their interrelationship. But in the days before computers, when these tedious calculations had to be carried out by hand with the help of desk calculators, the construction of tables was hard. In 1936, now living in the U.S., he began work on a table for the American economy. Five years later *The Structure of the American Economy, 1919-1939* appeared. When electronic computers first appeared in the 1950s, he forged ahead on two more books. While writing his two-volume classic, *Essays in Economics*, he learned he had won the Nobel Prize (1973) for devising the input-output technique of showing how different sectors of an economy interact. His method was used to calculate the resource costs of converting U.S. wartime production to peacetime production in 1945, to calculate the flow of trade between regions in a country, to analyze pollutants generated by a nation's industries, and to spell out relative factors in a nation's exports and imports.

LETTERMAN, DAVID

Rollins, Joffe, Morra, and Brezner, 801 Westmount, Los Angeles, CA 90069.
BORN: 1947, Indianapolis. ACHIEVEMENTS: Emmy, Writing in a Variety or Music Show, Late Night with David Letterman, 1984, 1985, 1986, 1987; Emmy, Best Host of a Daytime Variety Series, The David Letterman Show, 1981. STUDIED: Ball State University, B.A. radio and television broadcasting.

Letterman's career began in Indianapolis, where he worked at a local TV station as a weather reporter, host of a children's show and host of *Freeze Dried Movies*, a late night movie show. He also worked part-time as a radio call-in host. Letterman's irreverent style of humor emerged when once, on the movie show, he exploded a model of the television station where he worked. In 1975, he left for Los Angeles, and became a regular at the Comedy Store and wrote for television. He joined the cast of the *Mary Tyler Moore Variety Hour*, which led to guest spots on the *Tonight Show*. In 1980 *The David Letterman Show* debuted on NBCs mid-morning schedule, but was canceled after a few months, despite winning two Emmy Awards. *Late Night with David Letterman* premiered on NBC in 1982. Letterman moved the show to CBS in 1992, where the name changed to the *Late Show with David Letterman*

LEVI-MONTALCINI, RITA

BORN: 1909, Turin (Italy) ACHIEVEMENTS: Nobel Prize in Physiology or Medicine (shared with Stanley Cohen), 1986; William Wakeman Award; Lewis Rosenstiel Award; Louisa Gross Horwitz Prize; Albert Lasker Award. STUDIED: University of Turin, Italy.

Levi and his associate, Stanley Cohen, shared their Nobel prize for the discover of how cells regulate grow. (See Stanely Cohen entry for details of their work.)

LEWIS, DAVID LEVERING

Rutgers University, Department of History, New Brunswick, NJ 08903
BORN: 1936, Little Rock, Ark. ACHIEVEMENTS: Pulitzer Prize, Biography, W.E.B. DuBois: The Biography of a Race, 1994; grants: American Philosophical Society, Social Science Research Council, National Endowment for the Humanities; fellow, Woodrow Wilson International Center for Scholars. STUDIED: Fisk University, B.A., history; Columbia University, M.A., history; London School of Economics and Political Science, Ph.D. French history.

Author and college professor since 1963, Lewis has taught at the University of Ghana; Howard University, Washington, D.C.; Morgan State College; Federal City College and the University of the District of Columbia; the University of California at San Diego, and Rutgers University. Lewis' most successful of eight books is *W.E.B. DuBois: The Biography of a Race*, winner of a Pulitzer Prize, and nominated for a National Book Award. Eight years of research on the scholar, speaker, and writer led Lewis to 28 libraries and through more than 20,000 letters and other papers. He had to familiarize himself with DuBois' published writings which included 21 books, 15 books DuBois edited, and innumerable essays and articles. The finished book is only the first of a projected two-volume work. Another book by Lewis, *When Harlem Was in Vogue: The Politics and the Arts of the Twenties and Thirties*, is a study of wealthy, intellectual, and elite blacks and how they effected social change and the arts. Though praised, the book soon led to charges that Lewis cared to write more about American society's black upper crust than its masses. Lewis currently occupies the Martin Luther King chair in history at Rutgers University.

LEWIS, HUEY

c/o Chrysalis, 9255 Sunset Blvd., Los Angeles, CA 90069; (213) 550-0171
BORN: 1950, New York City. ACHIEVEMENTS: Hit songs: The Power of Love, Hip to Be Square; hit albums: Do You Believe in Love, Picture This, Sports.

Huey Lewis paid his dues in the music business with years of session work. Born Hugh Cregg, Lewis was a member of the San Francisco band, Clover, from 1976 to 1980. At the same time, he did session work with such notables as Nick Lowe on his album, *Labour of Lust*, and Dave Edmunds, on the album, *Repeat When Necessary*. After Clover broke up in 1979, Lewis took a day job and started jamming in the evenings at Uncle Charlie's, a Marin County bar. He formed his band, Huey Lewis and the News, from several of the musicians he played with at Uncle Charlie's. Although their first album did poorly, Huey Lewis and the News enjoyed many successful releases thereafter, including *Sports* which won several platinum records. While Lewis' sales slackened a bit in the late 80s, they picked up considerably in the mid-90s with their recordings of soul classics.

LEWIS, JOHN

U.S. House of Representatives, Room 114, Washington, DC 20515 (202) 225-7780
Lewis is a prominent political leader. For career credentials consult the portion of this book entitled "Biographees by Profession" in the Appendix. Within this portion, the list "Political Leaders," describes requirements for inclusion in this volume.

LEWIS, JOSEPH ANTHONY

The New York Times, 229 West 43rd Street, New York, NY 10036. (212) 556-1234.
BORN: 1927, New York City. ACHIEVEMENTS: Pulitzer Prize 1955, 1963; author Gideon V. Wainwright: A First-Hand Account of the Struggle for Civil Rights, 1966; The Supreme Court: How it Works, 1966; Make No Law: The Sullivan Case and the First Amendment, 1992. STUDIED: Harvard, B.A., English, 1948.
Lewis began as a desk man at *The New York Times*, collecting stories for the weekly review of news from 1948-52. He moved to Washington, D.C. in 1952, to write position papers for Adlai Stevenson, and joined the *Washington Daily News* as a reporter. Lewis earned his first Pulitzer Prize at the *Washington Daily News* in 1955 before returning to the *The New York Times*. There, he rose from legal reporter to Supreme Court reporter, then to London bureau chief, and, finally, in 1969, to columnist. He has written three books detailing events he witnessed while covering the civil rights struggle and the Supreme Court in America.

LEWITZKY, BELLA

Lewitzky Dance Company, 700 S. Flower St., #2000, Los Angeles, CA 90017-4207 (213) 627-9249
Lewitzky is a prominent dancer. For career credentials consult the portion of this book entitled "Biographees by Profession" in the Appendix. Within this portion, the list "Dancers," describes requirements for inclusion in this volume.

LICHTENSTEIN, ROY

P.O. Box 1369, Southampton, NY 11968
BORN: 1923. ACHIEVEMENTS: collections: Whitney Museum of American Art; Museum of Modern Art ; exhibitions: Solomon R. Guggenheim Museum; Whitney Museum Annual. STUDIED: Ohio State University; Art Students League.
As a young painter, Roy Lichtenstein's style was abstract expressionist, but in 1957, cartoon images from bubble-gum wrappers were his motifs, and during the early 1960s, he became increasingly concerned with making art from mass-produced merchandice. Huge reproductions of single frames from comic-strips using Ben Day dots (a simulation of the typographic technique) were his contributions to the Pop movement. In later years, his media included sculpture, reliefs which were representations of images borrowed from comic-strips, and art deco. His reproductions of advertising fragments, travel posters, romance characters, or stylized landscapes, make insipid what is already

trite. He avoids definition by continuing to make derivatives. Using an anonymous language, the sources are transformed, presenting new terms for understanding art.

LIEBERMAN, JOSEPH I

502 Hart Senate Office Building, Washington, DC 20510-0703; (202) 224-4041
BORN: 1942, Stamford, Conn. ACHIEVEMENTS: Conn. Senate, 1971-81 (majority leader, 1975-81); Democratic nominee for U.S. House, 1980; Conn. attorney general, 1983-89. STUDIED: Yale University., B.A. 1964, LL.B. 1967.
Joseph Lieberman has served as U.S. Senator from Connecticut since 1988, and was named Deputy Whip for the 104th Congress by the Senate Minority Leader. He was instrumental in passing the Congressional Accountability Act of 1995, which prevents legislators from enjoying special privileges. He has been involved in several initiatives to reduce waste in federal government, and has taken part in efforts to reduce filibusters on the Senate floor. He sits on the Armed Services and Small Business committees, and is pressing for legislation that will establish free-enterprise zones in order to re-build American cities. He also served as chairman of the Democratic Leadership Council.

LIFVENDAHL, HAROLD

Orlando Sentinel, 633 N. Orange Ave., #2833, Orlando, FL 32802-2833 (407) 420-5000
Lifvendahl is a prominent publisher. For career credentials consult the portion of this book entitled "Biographees by Profession" in the Appendix. Within this portion, the list "Publishers," describes requirements for inclusion in this volume.

LIGON, THOMAS

ARC Scientific Simulations, 1275 Bloomfield Ave., Fairfield, NJ 07004 (201) 575-0651
ACHIEVEMENTS: Developed Dance of the Planets software package.
Dance of the Planets is a software package showing a four-dimensional working model of the solar system. More than 16,000 night sky objects are shown in realistic animated graphics, along with detailed orbital simulations, making astronomy accessible to the ordinary person. The program, developed by Thomas Ligon, president of ARC Scientific Simulations, also generates a representation of the solar system at any time from 4600 B.C. to 10000 A.D.

LIMBAUGH, RUSH HUDSON

WABC, 2 Penn Plaza, 17th Fl, New York, NY 10023
BORN: 1951, Cape Giradeau, Mo. ACHIEVEMENTS: Best selling books including: The Way Things Ought to Be,.1992, and See, I Told You So, 1993. STUDIED: Southwestern Missouri State University.
The *Rush Limbaugh Show* is one of the most popular syndicated radio-talk shows, simulcast on over 480 stations, with a cumulative weekly audience of 18

million listeners or "ditto heads," describes requirements for inclusion in this volume. as his fans are known. Limbaugh has been credited with rejuvenating AM radio. Limbaugh gained notice in 1983, when he replaced Morton Downey Jr. on a Sacramento radio station. A year later he was the top radio host in the city. Limbaugh rose to national prominence during the Clinton Presidential campaign. His nightly half-hour television show was launched during this time.

LIPPENCOTT, JR., WALTER

Princeton University Press, Princeton, NJ 08540 (609) 258-4900

Lippencott, Jr. is a prominent publisher. For career credentials consult the portion of this book entitled "Biographees by Profession" in the Appendix. Within this portion, the list"Publishers," describes requirements for inclusion in this volume.

LIPSCOMB, WILLIAM NUNN JR.

Harvard University, Department of Chemistry, 12 Oxford St., Cambridge, MA 02138
BORN: 1919, Cleveland, Ohio. ACHIEVEMENTS: Nobel Prize in Physics, 1976; Harrison Howe Award and Distinguished Service Award, American Chemical Society; George Ledlie Prize, Harvard University; Peter Debye Award, Ohio State University; Remsen Award, American Chemical Society, Maryland Section; Alexander von Humboldt Foundation Award. STUDIED: University of Kentucky; California Institute of Technology.

Boranes are high-energy compounds of boron, a relatively rare element although found in large concentrations in borax and boric acid and hydrogen, and are sometimes used as rocket fuels. Chemical bonding occurs, for example, when electric forces link atoms in molecules like water, viruses, proteins, etc., with non-molecular solids like metals and diamonds, in which electrons are lost or gained so that the structure is held together by mutual attraction of the ions involved. Lipscomb's Nobel Prize feat was to explain both the molecular structure and the chemical bonding of the boranes, using a concept of two electrons binding together three atoms.

LIPSEY, STANFORD

Buffalo News, 1 News Plaza, Box 10, Buffalo, NY,14240; (716) 849-3434
BORN: 1927, Omaha, Neb. ACHIEVEMENTS: Pulitzer Prize, 1972. STUDIED: Graduated University of Michigan, 1948.

Since 1988, Stanford Lipsey has been the vice president of Berkshire Hathaway Inc. Before that, Lipsey served as publisher and president of the *Buffalo News*, owned by Berkshire Hathaway, from 1983. Lipsey has been associated with the *Buffalo News* since 1977, traveling to Buffalo as a consultant on a monthly basis. He is the former editor, publisher and owner of the *Sun Newspapers* of Omaha, Neb. which he sold to Berkshire Hathaway in 1969. During the Korean War, Lipsey served in the U.S. Air Force as editor of the newspaper for the Strategic Air Command Headquarters. While in Omaha, he founded and sat on the boards of many foundations such as the Nebraska Chapter of

Multiple Sclerosis Society, Strategic Aerospace Museum, United Way, and Boys Club of Omaha. Lipsey moved to Buffalo in 1980, and currently serves on the boards of Newspaper Association of America, Business Council of New York and Junior League Advisory Board. He is also the founding member and vice president of the Frank Lloyd Wright Darwin Martin House Restoration Corp.

LOGAN, ANDREW

McDonnell Douglas Helicopter, St. Louis Airport, #516, St. Louis, MO 63103 (314) 232-0232
BORN: 1943. STUDIED: Carnegie Institute of Technology, B.A., mechanical engineering; Pennsylvania State University, M.A., aeronautical engineering.

Andrew Logan went to McDonnell Douglas in 1974 from Sikorsky Aircraft, seven years after the corporation was created by a takeover of Douglas Aircraft by McDonnell Aircraft Corp., which then made only military aircraft. In 1992 Logan was involved in a shakeup of top management as McDonnell brought together the commercial and military helicopter engineering groups. Logan became vice president of the commercial programs division, a post he still holds. The division is in charge of program management for a series of McDonnell helicopters, an aircraft Logan has worked with since joining McDonnell.

LOGGINS, KENNY

Columbia Records, 51 West 52nd St., New York, NY 10019: (212) 975-1114
BORN: 1948, Everett, Wash. ACHIEVEMENTS: Grammy, Best Pop Vocal-Male, This is It and What a Fool Believes, 1980. STUDIED: Pasadena City College.

Loggins got his start as a songwriter in the early 1970s. Born in Everett, Wash., Loggins moved to Los Angeles as a teenager. He achieved early notoriety when he penned the hit, *House at Pooh Corner* in 1970 for the Nitty Gritty Dirt Band. His abilities brought Loggins to the attention of Jim Messina, a producer for CBS Records. Messina, formerly a member of the band, Poco, wanted to produce Loggins' first album. However, the two decided to make the album together, thus creating the successful duo, Loggins and Messina. The two enjoyed great success during the 1970s. The group broke up in 1976, and Loggins struck out on his own, as a solo performer. Although his album sales declined in the late 1980s, he found continuing success writing and singing songs for movie soundtracks.

LONG, ELIZABETH VALK

Time Inc., Time & Life Building, Rockefeller Center NY 10020 (212) 522-1217
BORN: Winston-Salem, N.C. ACHIEVEMENTS: Matrix Award, New York Women in Communications. STUDIED: Hollins College, B.A.; Harvard Business School, M.B.A.

Joining *Time* magazine straight from college, Elizabeth Long advanced from the circulation staff to director of circulation for *Fortune* magazine in three years. Moving around the Time Warner publishing empire, she next landed at *Sports Illustrated* as circulation director, and in 1985 returned to *Time* in the same position. She was named publisher of *Life* the next year, making her the first woman publisher of a Time Inc. magazine. She rose to vice president of The Time Inc. Company the next year. In 1988 Long became publisher of *People*, in 1989 senior vice president of The Time Inc. Magazine Company, and in 1995 executive vice president of Time Inc.

LONGO, ROBERT

c/o Metro Pictures, 150 Greene St., New York, NY 10012

BORN: 1953. ACHIEVEMENTS: Collections: Tate Gallery, London; Museum of Modern Art; exhibitions: Leo Castelli Gallery; Akron Art Museum

A versatile artist, Robert Longo has done performances which combine dance, sculpture, film and theatre, such as *Empire*. Large-scale, black-and-white drawings depict figures in urban attire and animated postures. His sculpted reliefs in bronze depict figures or imposing buildings. He has also made prints and paintings, and has employed such media as ink, acrylic, and charcoal on a variety of surfaces such as aluminum, wood and Masonite. His interest in the power of fascism, nostalgia and melodrama wield a strong influence upon his diverse creations.

LOUCKS, VERNON R., JR.

Baxter International, Inc., One Baxter Parkway, Deerfield, IL 60015 (708) 948-2000

Loucks, Jr. is a prominent business leader and CEO of Baxter International. For career credentials consult the portion of this book entitled "Biographees by Profession" in the Appendix. Within this portion, the list "Business Leaders," describes requirements for inclusion in this volume.

LOUIS, MURRAY

Murray Louis Dance Company, 38 East 19th St., New York, NY 10003 (212) 777-1120

BORN: 1926, New York City. ACHIEVEMENTS: Notable ballets: Triptych; Frenetic Dances; Harmonica Suite (Reflections); Junk Dances; Charade (Chimera); Hoopla; Index.(to necessary neuroses). STUDIED: San Francisco State, New York University; Ann Halprin, Alwyn Nikolais schools.

A unique muscular control is one of the qualities Murray Louis carried over from his dancing into his choreography. Studying under, and becoming the major dancer for the late Alwyn Nikolais, Louis developed a talent for moving his limbs and muscles in spasms and ripples in an isolated way that focused audience attention on those seemingly effortless movements. Long associated with the older Nikolais, Louis' works are a witty and more humane reflection of his master's style.

LOVELL, JAMES ARTHUR, JR.

Centel Corporation, 2004 Miner Rd., Desplaines, IL; (708) 768-6000

BORN: 1928, Cleveland. ACHIEVEMENTS: Space missions: pilot Gemini 7, commander Gemini 12, command module pilot Apollo 8, commander Apollo 13. STUDIED: U.S. Naval Academy, B.S., 1952.

James Lovell was a Navy test pilot when he was selected by NASA as an astronaut in 1962. He, and commander Frank Borman spent 14 days in space aboard Gemini 7. They participated in the first space rendezvous by meeting Gemini 6A in space. His next spaceflight assignment, as commander of Gemini 12, also included rendezvous tests. Lovell flew as command module pilot of Apollo 8, the first manned mission to orbit the moon. He also commanded the ill-fated Apollo 13, a mission originally intended to perform a lunar landing. The mission was aborted after an oxygen tank exploded, ripping through the service module. Lovell and the crew used the lunar excursion module as a lifeboat, and splashed down safely in one of the most tense near-disasters in aviation history.

LOVERIDGE, RONALD O.

Office of the Mayor, 3900 Main St., Riverside, CA 92522 (909) 782-5551

Loveridge is a prominent political leader. For career credentials consult the portion of this book entitled "Biographees by Profession" in the Appendix. Within this portion, the list "Political Leaders," describes requirements for inclusion in this volume.

LOWE, CHAD

William Morris Agency, 151 El Camino Dr., Beverly Hills, CA 90212

Lowe is a prominent actor. For career credentials consult the portion of this book entitled "Biographees by Profession" in the Appendix. Within this portion, the list "Actors," describes requirements for inclusion in this volume.

LOWRY, MIKE

Office of the Governor, P.O. Box 40002, Olympia, WA 98504-0002; (206) 753-6780

BORN: 1939, St. John, Wash. ACHIEVEMENTS: 20th governor of the state of Washington. STUDIED: Washington State University, 1962.

In 1975 Mike Lowry was elected to King County Council and three years later in 1977, he became chairman. He was elected to the U.S. House of Representatives in 1978 and re-elected four times, serving a total of 10 years. In 1992, he was elected governor of the state of Washington in a campaign free of special interest money and funded entirely by individual contributions under $1,500. Successes of his administration include: reducing the cost of state agencies by consolidation of agencies, streamlining operations, slashing the budget of the governor's office, and taking a sizable pay decrease himself. He spearheaded successes in state health care reform, updated the civil service system, and improved access to higher education.

LUBOVITCH, LAR

Lar Lubovitch Dance Company, 1517 West 18th St., New York, NY 10011 (212) 242-0633
BORN: 1943, Chicago. ACHIEVEMENTS: Notable ballets: Ecstacy; Whirligogs; Scherzo for Massa Jack; Marimba; Cavalcade; Big Shoulders; Of My Soul; Rhapsody in Blue; American Gesture; Concerto Six Twenty Two. STUDIED: Art Institute of Chicago; University of Iowa; Connecticut College, New London. Louis Horst, Anna Sokolow, Martha Graham, Jose Limon, Antony Tudor, Margaret Black, American Ballet Theatre schools.

A latecomer to ballet from the Art Institute in Chicago, where he studied in several college-level courses, Lar Lubovitch brought a new devotee's energy and originality first to his dancing, then to his choreography. During his dancing career in New York City, where his "ferocious determination" had brought him, he tried his hand at choreography for the Harkness Ballet, and from there formed a company of his own. He is noted for borrowing from both classical and modern dance, creating from the mix inventive pieces for his energetic troupe. His choreographic range even includes ice skating, in which he has created solos for Olympic gold medalists John Curry, Peggy Fleming, and Dorothy Hamill, plus an iceskating version of Tchaikovsky's *The Sleeping Beauty*.

LUDLUM, ROBERT

Henry Morrison, Inc., P.O. Box 235, Bedford Hills, NY 10507
BORN: 1927, New York City. ACHIEVEMENTS: Best-selling novelist. STUDIED: Wesleyan University, Middletown, CT, B.A., with distinction, liberal arts.

America's most prolific suspense novelist became a Broadway and television actor for eight years after his service in the Marine Corps during World War II. He then produced plays in New Jersey from 1957 until 1960, and in New York City from 1960 until 1969. He wrote his first novel, *The Inheritance*, in 1971, and has written 19 novels under his own name, many of them best sellers, in 24 years. He also writes under the pen names Jonathan Ryder and Michael Shepherd.

LUGAR, RICHARD G.

U.S. Senate, 306 SHOB, Washington, DC 20510-1410 (202) 224-4814
Lugar is a prominent political leader. For career credentials consult the portion of this book entitled "Biographees by Profession" in the Appendix. Within this portion, the list "Political Leaders," describes requirements for inclusion in this volume.

LUNDEN, JOAN

Good Morning America, 77 West 66th Street, New York, NY 10023 (212) 456-7777
ACHIEVEMENTS: Spirit of Achievement Award, Yeshiva University; Outstanding Woman's Award Speaker, YWCA ; National Women's Political Caucus Award; Outstanding Mother of the Year, 1982. STUDIED: American River College, Liberal Arts Degree; Universidad de Las Americas (Mexico City).

At 16 years running, she is the longest-standing co-host on early morning television. She began at *GMA* in 1976 as a consumer reporter before being named co-host in 1980. As part of the show, Lunden has rappelled glaciers, bungee-jumped off a bridge, whitewater rafted, and, in one of her most famous stunts, sat at the helm of an F-18 Jet and flew with the elite Air Force Thunderbirds. Her *GMA* itinerary has taken her to historic events, including the 50th Anniversary of D-Day and the 1984 and 1988 Olympic Games. Lunden is writing a new book, *Healthy Cooking For Your Family With Joan Lunden*. She has long worked as a spokeswoman for motherhood including making the highly acclaimed video *Your Newborn Baby: Everything You Need to Know*. She joined WABC-TV Eyewitness News in 1975 and a year later became co-anchor on the weekend newscasts. Her career in broadcasting began with KCRA-TV and Radio as co-anchor of the daily noon television news in Sacramento.

LURIE, ALISON

Cornell University, Ithaca, NY 14853
BORN: 1926, Chicago. ACHIEVEMENTS: Pulitzer Prize, Foreign Affairs, 1985. STUDIED: Radcliffe College, A.B., 1947.

Alison Lurie's novels explore the uneven relations between the sexes and draw on current events and fads. Her fiction includes *The Nowhere City*, 1965; *Imaginary Friends*, 1967; *The War between the Tates*, 1974; and *Foreign Affairs*, 1984, which won the Pulitzer Prize. Her nonfiction books include *The Language of Clothes*, 1984, and *Don't Tell the Grown-Ups*, 1990. She also edited *The Oxford Book of Modern Fairy Tales*, 1993. Lurie was a lecturer of English at Cornell University from 1969 until 1973, moving up to adjunct associate professor in 1973, associate professor from 1976 until 1979, then professor of English in 1979, a position she still holds.

LUTZ, JIM

General Motors Advanced Engineering, 3044 W. Grand Ave., Detroit, MI 48202 (313) 556-5000
ACHIEVEMENTS: Developed the Ultralite concept car.

As program manager at General Motors Advanced Engineering, Jim Lutz developed the Ultralite concept car. This 1,400-pound, four-passenger vehicle can achieve 100 miles per gallon on the highway thanks to its lightweight construction. The body is composed of carbon-fiber panels mated to low-weight components, and its tailpipe emission standards exceed the strictest on the market.

LYONS, DANIEL

NASA Jet Propulsion Laboratory, L.B. Johnson Space Center, Houston, TX 77058

ACHIEVEMENTS: Developed aerobraking maneuver for orbiting spacecraft.

A bonus from the spacecraft Magellan's radar-mapping of Venus is the Venusian gravity chart. This accomplishment was achieved through a seat-of-the-pants decision by Daniel Lyons and his NASA team. Magellan's mapping mission over, Lyons wanted to salvage the still operable spaceship to learn more about Venusian gravity. The ship, however, was not built for airbraking down to lower orbits to measure gravity at each level. So the Lyons team worked the ship through the unknown atmosphere with commands from earth, cautiously at first, allowing variations in Venus' gravity to alter its speed. The success of the maneuver, called aerobraking, has led mission planners to mark it for use in the Mars Global Surveyor probe, scheduled for launch in 1996.

MacARTHUR, JOHN

Harper's Magazine, 666 Broadway, New York, NY 10012-2394 (212) 614-6500

MacArthur is a prominent publisher. For career credentials consult the portion of this book entitled "Biographees by Profession" in the Appendix. Within this portion, the list "Publishers" describes requirements for inclusion in this volume.

MacHOVER, TOD

MIT Media Labs, Cambridge, MA 02139
ACHIEVEMENTS: Developed the Hyperinstruments system.

Tod Machover, a professor of music and media at the Massachusetts Institute of Technology Media Lab, uses technology to enhance and expand the power of musical instruments. His system, called Hyperinstruments, also uses the computer to blend human performances and various nuances. Machover also developed, with the help of Yamaha, a hypercello, viola, a glove that reads the motions of a conductor's hand and leads an electronic orchestra, and hyperpercussion.

MACKE, VICE ADM. RICHARD C.

Office of the Secretary, Pentagon, Washington, D.C. 20301 (703) 545-6700
BORN: 1938, Freeport, Ill. STUDIED: Naval Academy, B.S.; Naval Postgraduate School, M.S.

A veteran of more than 150 combat missions in Vietnam and one-time commander of the aircraft carrier Dwight D. Eisenhower, Vice Adm. Richard Macke was one of the first junior officers to command a carrier aviation squadron. Macke entered active duty as an ensign in 1960. His career record carried him through Battle Group Commander, Mediterranean, director of the Joint Staff, and director of Command, Control, and Communications of the Joint Chiefs of Staff. He was also a test pilot and a nuclear-trained engineer. In 1994 he was named vice chief of the Navy.

MACLAINE, SHIRLEY

Higher Life Seminars, #760, 1900 Avenue of the Stars, Los Angeles, CA 90067
BORN: 1934, Richmond, Va. ACHIEVEMENTS: Golden Globe Award, New Female Star of the Year (Film), 1955; Golden Globe Award, Some Came Running, 1959; Golden Globe Award, Most Versatile Actress, Ask Any Girl, 1959; Golden Globe Award, Best Actress in a Musical/Comedy, The Apartment, 1961; Golden Globe Award, Best Actress, Irma la Douce, 1964; Emmy Award, Outstanding Comedy-Variety or Music Special, Shirley MacLaine: If They Could See Me Now, 1974; Golden Globe Award, Outstanding Comedy-Variety or Music Special, Gypsy in My Soul, 1976; Emmy Award, Outstanding Writing of Variety or Music Program, Shirley MacLaine. . . Every Little Movement, 1980; Academy Award, Best Actress, Terms of Endearment, 1983; Golden Globe Award, Best Actress in a Drama, Terms of Endearment, 1984; Golden Globe Award, Best Actress in a Drama, Madame Sousatzka, 1989. STUDIED: Washington and Lee High School, Va.

Shirley MacLaine began her career as a chorus girl and dancer from 1950 through 1953. She became an actress, and earned her first Golden Globe Award in 1955 for New Female Star of the Year (Film). MacLaine is well regarded for her signing, dancing, and her ability to portray both dramatic and comedic characters. After receiving numerous nominations for Academy Awards in various films, she won the Oscar as Best Actress for her role in *Terms of Endearment*, 1983. In addition to her work in films, MacLaine has appeared on television as an actor and behind the scenes as a producer. MacLaine, the author of many books, has published *Out on a Limb*, Bantam, 1983; and *Going Within: A Guide for Inner Transformation*, Bantam, 1989.

MADDEN, EARL JOHN

Fox Broadcasting Company, 205 East 67th St., New York, NY 10021
BORN: 1936, Austin, Minn. ACHIEVEMENTS: Coach of the Year, American Football League and the Washington Touchdown Club; Vince Lombardi Dedication Award; Golden Mike Award, Touchdown Club of America; Sports Personality of the Year, American Broadcasters Association; Six Emmy Awards for Sports Broadcasting. STUDIED: University of Oregon, student; California Polytechnic State University, B.S., education, M.A., education.

Madden played college football and later profootball with the Philadelphia Eagles until he injured a knee in training, then became coach at Allan Hancock College. In 1967, Madden joined the Oakland Raiders as linebacker coach and two years later took over as head coach, a job he held for a decade. During that time his teams won Super Bowl XI, seven division championships, and more than 100 games, the first National Football League coach to hit those win numbers in his first decade of coaching. Soon after, suffering from a bleeding ulcer and burnout, he left the game for good. Next came weekly broadcasting for CBS, providing what critics described as common sense, a grasp of the game, and such plain speak as, "Boom!" "Whack!" and "Doink!," followed by national TV commercials. In one 30-second commercial, for Miller Lite's "tastes great, less filling" series, he broke through a sheet of paper. That simple feat led to instant fame and brought him contracts with almost a dozen marketers. CBS lost its exclusive TV rights to broadcast NFL games in 1993 when Rupert Murdock's Fox Broadcasting outbid it in a $1.6 billion, four-year deal with the NFL. After considering offers from CBS to take on its American Football League shows, and from ABC to broadcast *Monday Night Football*, Madden was lured to Fox Broadcasting by Murdock with a four-year, $8 million annual contract.

MADIGAN, JOHN

Chicago Tribune, 435 N. Michigan Ave., Chicago, IL 60611 (312) 222-3232
BORN: 1937, Chicago. ACHIEVEMENTS: President, Tribune Newspaper Co. STUDIED: University of Michigan, B.A., M.A., business administration.
The chairman and chief executive officer of a far-flung media and entertainment company began his career in 1960 as a financial analyst at Duff & Phelps, Inc., while serving in the Marine Corps Reserve. John Madigan then moved on to Arthur Andersen & Co., Paine, Webber, Jackson, and Curtis, and finally to Salomon Brothers, where he became vice president for corporate finance. In 1975 he joined the Tribune Company as vice president of finance and a board member. Frequently promoted in a company rapidly expanding from newspapers into multimedia ventures under aggressive CEO Charles Brumbach, whom he succeeds, Madigan became president of Tribune Newspaper Company in 1990, and in 1993, chief operating officer of Tribune Company, and Brumback's unofficial heir. He operates six daily newspapers, eight television stations, six radio stations, and the Tribune's stake in one of Canada's largest newsprint manufacturers.

"MADONNA," (CICCONE, MADONNA LOUISE VERONICA)

Sire Records, 75 Rockefeller Plaza, New York, NY 10019
BORN: 1958, Bay City, Mich. ACHIEVEMENTS: Grammy, Best Music Video, Long Form, Madonna: Blond Ambition World Tour Live, 1991. STUDIED: Attended Michigan State University.
Professionally known by just her first name, "Madonna," she is one of the most commercially successful pop-singers of the era. She pursued a career in dance prior to becoming a singer. Once dancing with the Alvin Ailey Dance Theater's third company in New York City. Her self-titled 1984 debut album produced the hit single *Borderline*, which reached the top 10. Madonna used the MTV explosion to her advantage, creating elaborate videos for hits such as *Like a Virgin*, 1984; and *Material Girl*, 1984. Her videos became more explicit with the song *Justify My Love*, 1990, which was banned from MTV. In 1990, she released *Vogue*, one of the most top-selling singles ever. Madonna's film career has been less successful. Her films include *Desperately Seeking Susan*, 1986; *Dick Tracy*, 1990; the documentary *Truth or Dare*, 1991; and *A League of Their Own*, 1992. Her book, *Sex*, was published in 1992, and was originally banned in Japan.

MAHONEY, RICHARD J.

Monsanto Company, 800 Lindbergh Blvd., St. Louis, MO 63167 (314) 694-1000
BORN: 1934, Springfield, Mass. ACHIEVEMENTS: CEO, Monsanto Co. STUDIED: University of Massachusetts, B.S., chemistry, LL. D., honorary.
After 33 years with Monsanto Company, chairman and chief executive officer Richard Mahoney stepped aside in 1994 to open the way for junior executives to have their chance. He retained his position as director of the company and chairman of the board's executive committee. Mahoney joined Monsanto in 1962 as a product development specialist, then held marketing, technical service, and management positions in plastics, agriculture, and foreign operations. He became executive vice president in 1977, took a board seat in 1979, was named president in 1980, CEO in 1983, and chairman in 1986.

MAILER, NORMAN

Rembar, 19 W. 44th St., New York, NY 10036
BORN: 1923, Long Branch, N.J. ACHIEVEMENTS: Pulitzer Prize, The Armies of the Night, 1968; Pulitzer Prize, The Executioner's Song, 1979. STUDIED: Harvard College, B.A. 1943.
Known for his brash personality and controversial views, Norman Mailer's popular first novel, *The Naked and the Dead*, 1948, drew on his World War II Army combat experiences in the Pacific, and set the tone for his later writings that dealt with conflict in American society. His other early novels included *Barbary Shore*, 1951; *The Deer Park*, 1955; and *An American Dream*, 1965. As a social critic, his essays and articles explored violence, politics and sexual conflict, including *The Armies of the Night*, 1968, about the 1967 peace march on the Pentagon; *Miami and the Siege of Chicago*, 1969, an account of the Republican and Democratic conventions of 1968; and *The Executioner's Song*, 1979, about the execution of murderer Gary Gilmore in 1977.

MAIMAN, THEODORE HAROLD

NCIPLA, Suite 203, 2001 Jefferson Davis Hwy., Arlington, VA 22202
BORN: 1927, Los Angeles. ACHIEVEMENTS: Constructed first operable laser. STUDIED: University of Colorado, B.S., engineering physics; Stanford University, Ph.D. physics. University of Cordoba, Argentina., Ph.D. (honorary).
Theodore Maiman joined the Hughes Electronics Research Laboratories the same year he won his doctorate, 1955. There, Charles Townes and his associates had constructed a working model of a maser, a device for amplifying electromagnetic waves, the previous year, and now were working on a laser. Maiman made improvements in the maser, then built the first operable laser in 1960. In 1975 he moved to TRW to work on computers, software, communication equipment, and military products.

MALKOVICH, JOHN

Phyllis Carlyle Management, 4000 Warner Blvd., Producers Building 7, Room 205, Burbank, CA 91522
BORN: 1953, Christopher, Ill. ACHIEVEMENTS: Emmy, Best Supporting Actor in a Made-for-TV Movie, Death of a Salesman, 1986. STUDIED: Eastern Illinois University.

Although he had originally enrolled in college to become an environmentalist, John Malkovich got into acting to be closer to a female drama student to who he was attracted. Malkovich began acting professionally in the late 1970s. His off-Broadway debut was in the play, *True West*, in 1982. In 1984, he played Biff, in *Death of a Salesman*, at the Broadhurst Theatre in New York City. Two years later, he won an Emmy playing the same role in a television version of the same play. Malkovich's film debut was in *The Killing Fields*, in 1984. Since that time he has starred in many other popular movies, including *Making Mr. Right*, *Empire of the Sun*, and *The Glass Menagerie* in 1987. He has also directed numerous stage productions, including *Coyote Ugly*, which was produced in Chicago and at the Kennedy Center in Washington, D.C., in 1986.

MALONE, DON

Dallas Morning News, Box 655237, Dallas, TX 75265-5237 (214) 977-8222
Malone is a prominent journalist. For career credentials consult the portion of this book entitled "Biographees by Profession" in the Appendix. Within this portion, the list "Journalists" describes requirements for inclusion in this volume.

MALTBY, RICHARD, JR.

Flora Roberts, Inc., 157 West 57th St., New York, NY 10019
For career credentials consult the portion of this book entitled "Biographees by Profession" in the Appendix. Within this portion, the list "Dramatic Artists" describes requirements for inclusion in this volume.

MAMET, DAVID ALAN

c/o Howard Rosenstone, 3 East 48th St., 4th Fl., New York, NY 10017
Chicago-born Mamet is a Pulitzer-Prize-winning playwright. His many hits include *American Buffalo*, *Edmund* and the movie *Magic*.

MANCHESTER, WILLIAM

Olin Library, Wesleyan University, Middletown, CT 06457
BORN: 1922, Attleboro, Mass. ACHIEVEMENTS: Decorated Purple Heart; recipient Dag Hammarskjold Prize, Association of Internationale Correspondents Diplomatiques, Rome 1967; citation for best book on foreign affairs, Overseas Press Club, 1968; University of Missouri Honor Award for distinguished service in journalism, 1969; Connecticut Book Award, 1975; President's Cabinet Award, University of Detroit, 1981; Frederick S. Troy Award, University of Massachusetts, 1981; McConnaughy Award, Wesleyan University, 1981; N.Y. Public Library Literary Lion Award, 1983; Distinguished Public Service Award, Connecticut Bar Association., 1985; Lincoln Literary Award, Union League Club N.Y., 1983; Blenheim Award, International Churchill Society, 1986; Washington Irving Award, 1988; Sarah Joseph Hale Award, 1993. STUDIED: University of Massachusetts, B.A., 1946; University of Missouri, M.A., 1947; University of Massachusetts, L.H.D. (Honorary), 1965; University of New Haven, L.H.D. (Honorary), 1979; Russell Sage College, L.H.D. (Honorary), 1990; Skidmore College, Littd (Honorary), 1987; University of Richmond, 1988.

After college Manchester worked as a reporter, foreign correspondent and war correspondent for the *Baltimore Sun* from 1947 until 1955. He then became managing editor of Wesleyan University Publications from 1955 until 1964. His book 1967 book, *The Death of a President*—written at the request of the family of John F. Kennedy—was a best-seller, but later was superseded by new evidence concerning the assassination. Many of his creative works were Book-of-the Month or Literary Guild selections including: *The Arms of Krupp*, 1968; *The Glory and the Dream, 1974;* American Caesar: Douglas MacArthur, 1880-1964, 1978; The Last Lion: Winston Spencer Churchill Visions of Glory 1874-1932, 1983; One Brief Shining Moment: Remembering Kennedy, 1983; and *The Last Lion: Winston Churchill Alone 1932-1940*, 1988. Since 1992, he has served as professor of history emeritus at Wesleyan University.

MANILOW, BARRY

Stilleto Ltd., P.O. Box 69180, Los Angeles, CA 90061
BORN: 1946, Brooklyn, N.Y. ACHIEVEMENTS: Grammy, Best Pop Vocal-Male, Copacabana (At the Copa), 1978. STUDIED: Attended New York College of Music, Juliard School of Music.

Barry Manilow's romantic ballads, combined with elaborate stage productions, have proven to be a hot combination all over the world. With sales of over 50 million records worldwide, Manilow has achieved remarkable success. In spite of his tremendous following, he has embittered some with his cynical remarks about the radio industry. However, if Manilow has been affected by the sarcasm of his detractors, he has met them with continuing success in record sales. Among his many hits are *Mandy, Could It Be Magic, I Write the Songs, Looks Like We Made It, Can't Smile without You*, and *Weekend in New England*.

MANN, BARRY

c/o MCA Records, Inc., 70 Universal City Plaza, Universal City, CA 91608 (213) 508-4000
Mann is a prominent composer. For career credentials consult the portion of this book entitled "Biographees by Profession" in the Appendix. Within this portion, the list "Composers" describes requirements for inclusion in this volume.

MANSFIELD, STEPHANIE

The Washington Post, 1150 15th St., NW., Washington, D.C. 20071 (202) 334-6000
Mansfield is a prominent journalist. For career credentials consult the portion of this book entitled "Biographees by Profession" in the Appendix. Within this

portion, the list "Journalists" describes requirements for inclusion in this volume.

MARCUS, RUDOLPH ARTHUR

311 S. Hill Ave., Pasadena, CA 91106
BORN: 1923, Montreal (Canada). ACHIEVEMENTS:Nobel Prize in Physics, 1992; Wolf Prize in Chemistry, and many others. STUDIED: McGill University, Montreal, B.S., Ph.D., chemistry; and many honorary degrees.
After working for the National Research Council of Canada for three years following his studies at McGill, Marcus emigrated to the U.S. in 1949. He served as research associate, and on the faculty, of several universities during the 1950s, and until 1965, while doing the work that would earn him the Nobel Prize in 1992. In that work, he mathematically analyzed how the energy in a system of molecules changes and induces an electron to jump from one molecule to another. It would be almost 30 years before chemists proved the validity of his conclusion and recognition would come from Stockholm.

MARK, REUBEN

Colgate-Palmolive Company, 300 Park Ave., New York, NY 10022 (212) 310-2000
BORN: 1934, Jersey City, N.J. ACHIEVEMENTS: CEO, Colgate-Palmolive Co. STUDIED: Middlebury College, B.A.; Harvard Business School, M.A.
The chairman and chief executive officer of Colgate joined the company after graduating from Harvard. Mark found his stride in the business world by taking on a series of domestic and foreign assignments, then in 1984 he was named chief executive officer, and in 1986 chairman of the board. Mark, who is also on the board of Toys 'R' Us, is chairman of the New York City Partnership's Education and Youth Employment, a trustee of Bank Street College, a member of the board of The Fund for New York City Public Education and the women's organization Catalyst. His other educational activities are as trustee of the National Center for Learning Disabilities and co-chairman of the School and Business Alliance of New York.

MARKOWITZ, HARRY MAX

Baruch College, City University of New York, 155 E. 24th St., New York, NY 10010
BORN: 1927, Chicago. ACHIEVEMENTS: Nobel Prize in Economic Science (with William F. Sharpe and Merton Miller), 1990. STUDIED: University of Chicago, B.A., M.A., Ph.D., economics.
Harry Markowitz began his career with IBM, and moonlighted in academia. He finally settled at Baruch College as the Marvin Spieser Distinguished Professor of Economics and Finance in 1982. His main interest has been in the theory of intelligent behavior in financial portfolios and in investment analysis and planning. The Nobel award specifically mentions his and his co-awardees' work in providing new tools for weighing the risks and rewards of different investments, and for valuing corporate stocks and bonds. Among computer programs he has designed and developed are SIMSCRIPT and EASE.

MARSALIS, WYNTON

Agency for Performing Arts, 9000 W Sunset Blvd., West Hollywood, CA, 90069-5801
BORN: 1961, New Orleans. ACHIEVEMENTS: Grammy Awards, Best Jazz Soloist, Think of One, 1983, Hot House Flower, 1984, Black Codes from the Underground, 1985; Best Jazz Group, Black Codes from the Underground, 1985, J Mood, 1986; Marsalis Standard Time—Volume 1, 1987; Best Solo Classical Performance with Orchestra, 1984-1985. STUDIED: New Orleans Center of Performing Arts, Berkshire Music Center, Julliard School of Music, 1979-1981.
The son of jazz pianist and teacher Ellie Marsalis, Wynton got his first trumpet from bandleader Al Hirt. At age 14 he played with the New Orleans Philharmonic. His musical abilities became known to jazz fans in the 1980s when he joined Art Blakely and the Jazz Messengers. Wynton and older brother Branford, a brilliant tenor saxophonist, formed their own band in 1982; a year later he released his first classical album, *Trumpet Concertos*. In 1984, Wynton became the first artist to be nominated and win Grammy awards for both classical and jazz recordings, in a single year. Since then, he has been recognized with many more awards for his work in jazz. His recent recordings include 1991's three-volume *Soul Gestures in Southern Blue*.

MARTIN, ANDREA

The Artists' Agency, Suite 305, 10000 Santa Monica Blvd., Los Angeles, CA 90067
BORN: 1947, Portland, Maine. ACHIEVEMENTS: Emmy Award, Best Writing for a Comedy Program, SCTV Network 90, 1982 and 1983. STUDIED: Emerson College, graduate.
Andrea Martin, an actress, comedienne, and writer, is best known for her acting and writing on the syndicated series *Second City TV*, 1977 to 1981, and then *SCTV Network 90* on the CBS network from 1981 to 1983. She won an Emmy Award for her writing on *SCTV Network 90* in both 1982 and 1983. In addition to her comedy work, Martin has a number of forgettable film appearances to her credit, such as *Cannibal Girls*, 1973; *Black Christmas*, 1974; *Wholly Moses!*, 1980; *Club Paradise*, 1986; and *Worth Winning*, 1989. She has also appeared on the stage, making her debut with the New York Shakespeare Festival production of *Hard Sell* in 1980. She also appeared in the production of *Sorrows of Stephen* in 1980.

MARTIN, STEVE

Agency for the Performing Arts, 9000 Sunset Boulevard, Suite 1200, Los Angeles, CA 90069
BORN: 1945, Waco, Texas. ACHIEVEMENTS: Emmy, Best Writing in a Comedy, Variety, or Music Program, The Smothers Brothers Comedy Hour, 1969; Grammy, Best Comedy Recording, Lets Get Small, 1977, and Wild and Crazy Guy, 1978. STUDIED: Attended Long Beach State College and the University of California, Los Angeles.
A self proclaimed "wild and crazy guy," Steve Martin parlayed his comedic talents from a writer on *The Smothers Brothers Comedy Hour*, to sold-out performances across the country, many television appearances, two Grammy Award-winning albums, a

best-selling book of comic sketches, *Cruel Shoes*, and eventually his first feature film, *The Jerk*. He got his start at Disneyland, where he performed magic tricks and played the banjo. His national break came when he hosted *Saturday Night Live*, where he and Dan Akroyd created the Czechoslovakian Playboys, the Festrunk brothers. While at the height of his popularity, he stepped away from stand-up comedy to concentrate on films. His cinematic efforts were met with mixed reviews, but his films *All of Me* and *Roxanne* were highly praised.

MARTINS, PETER

New York City Ballet, 20 Lincoln Center Plaza, New York, NY 10023 (212) 877-4700
Martins is a prominent dancer. For career credentials consult the portion of this book entitled "Biographees by Profession" in the Appendix. Within this portion, the list "Dancers" describes requirements for inclusion in this volume.

MARX, RICHARD

C/O EMI America/Liberty, 6920 Sunset Blvd., Los Angeles, CA 90028 (213) 461-9141
BORN: 1963, Chicago. ACHIEVEMENTS: Hit song: Don't Mean Nothing, 1987.
Richard Marx developed his skills singing on television and radio commercials, and doing back-up vocals for Lionel Richie. Using his timely mixture of commercial pop skills, Marx got his first hit in 1987. Marx's rock and roll tune, *Don't Mean Nothing*, quickly put him on the map, but, over the next several years, he achieved his greatest popularity singing ballads. His songs, *Right Here Waiting* and *Hold on to the Nights* were stock fare in the adult contemporary and pop music genres of the late 1980s and early 1990s. Marx rode the wave of popularity with his precise, complex blend of pop for several years. By the time he released his third album in 1991, his sales began to slow. However, he still remains a significant force in the pop music industry.

MACHASKEE, ALEX

Plain Dealer Publishing Co., 1801 Superior Ave., NE., Cleveland, OH 44114-2198 (216) 344-4600
Machaskee is a prominent publisher. For career credentials consult the portion of this book entitled "Biographees by Profession" in the Appendix. Within this portion, the list "Publishers" describes requirements for inclusion in this volume.

MASIELLO, ANTHONY M.

City Hall, 65 Niagara Square, Buffalo, NY 14202 (716) 851-4841
Masiello is a prominent political leader. For career credentials consult the portion of this book entitled "Biographees by Profession" in the Appendix. Within this portion, the list "Political Leaders" describes requirements for inclusion in this volume.

MASLIN, RABBI SIMEON J.

Central Conference of American Rabbis, 21 East 40th St., New York, NY 10016 (212) 684-4990
BORN: 1931, Boston. STUDIED: Chicago Theological Seminary, D.Min., pastoral counseling 1979; University of Pennsylvania, M.A., government administration, 1954; graduated Harvard University, B.A., cum laude, modern history, 1952; Boston Hebrew Teachers College, 1946-1949; Hebrew Union College-Jewish Institute of Religion; B.H.L., 1956; Rabbi, 1957; D.D., 1982.
Rabbi Maslin is currently the president of the Central Conference of American Rabbis, and sits on the Executive Board of the World Union for Progressive Judaism. He has been president or chairman of several Jewish organizations, such as the Philadelphia Board of Rabbis from 1989 until 1991, Hyde Park-Kenwood Council of Churches and Synagogues from 1972 until 1974, Chicago Association of Reform Rabbis from 1975 until 1977, Committee on Reform Jewish Practice from 1981 until 1984, and the Association of Caribbean and Middle-American Jewish Congregations from 1966 until 1967. In addition, he has been a board member of several other organizations. Maslin has given lectures around the U.S. and the Caribbean since 1961, and has taught at Beaver College, Pa., Chicago Theological Seminary and Spertus College of Judaica. He has authored several publications that cover topics of Jewish history, Reform Judaism and a book of sermons.

MASLOW, SOPHIE

c/o Sophie Maslow Dance Company, 51 West 88th St., New York, NY 10024 (212) 874-1467
Maslow is a prominent dancer. For career credentials consult the portion of this book entitled "Biographees by Profession" in the Appendix. Within this portion, the list "Dancers" describes requirements for inclusion in this volume.

MASON, MARSHALL

165 Christopher St., New York, NY 10014
Mason is a prominent dramatic artist. For career credentials consult the portion of this book entitled "Biographees by Profession" in the Appendix. Within this portion, the list "Dramatic Artists" describes requirements for inclusion in this volume.

MASSER, MICHAEL

c/o Arista Records, 6 West 57th St., New York, NY 10019 (212) 489-7400
Masser is a prominent composer. For career credentials consult the portion of this book entitled "Biographees by Profession" in the Appendix. Within this portion, the list "Composers" describes requirements for inclusion in this volume.

MATALON, VIVIAN

STE Representation, Ltd., 888 Seventh Ave., New York, NY 10019

Matalon is a prominent dramatic artist. For career credentials consult the portion of this book entitled "Biographees by Profession" in the Appendix. Within this portion, the list "Dramatic Artists" describes requirements for inclusion in this volume.

MATTINGLY, THOMAS KENNETH

Martin Marietta Corp., Space Systems Div., PO Box 85990, Kearney Mesa Plant, San Diego, CA 92186 (619) 573-8000

BORN: 1936, Chicago. ACHIEVEMENTS: space missions: command module pilot Apollo 16, commander STS-4. STUDIED: Auburn University, B.S., aeronautical engineering, 1958.

Thomas Mattingly was flying as a Navy test pilot when NASA picked him as an astronaut in 1966. He was scheduled to fly on Apollo 13, but the agency barred him from the mission after an accidental exposure to measles. In 1972 he served as the command module pilot on Apollo 16, during which he retrieved film magazines during a one-hour space walk. He was assigned to space shuttle development, and commanded the fourth space shuttle mission aboard the shuttle Columbia in 1982. He is now the vice president and program director of the Atlas Space Launch Vehicle for Martin Marietta.

MAUCERI, JOHN

Columbia Artists Management, 165 W. 57th St., New York, NY 10019

BORN: 1945. ACHIEVEMENTS: Antoinette Perry Award, On Your Toes, 1982. STUDIED: Yale University, B.A., 1967, M.A. philosophy, 1969.

A widely traveled orchestra conductor, John Mauceri won a Tony Award as music director of On Your Toes in 1982. He was the music supervisor and director of Candide, 1973; of Song and Dance, 1985, which he also produced; and of Leonard Bernstein's Mass on television in 1973. He conducted numerous operas, including productions at La Scala, Milan; the Metropolitan Opera, New York; Covent Garden, London; and the San Francisco Opera. His orchestral conducting includes concerts with the Israel Philharmonic, Los Angeles Philharmonic, Boston Pops, and San Francisco Symphony.

MAURER, ROBERT

Corning Inc., Sullivan Park, Corning, NY 14830

BORN: 1924, St. Louis, Mo. ACHIEVEMENTS: Fused Silica Optical Waveguide. STUDIED: University of Arkansas, B.S., 1948; M.I.T., Ph.D., 1951.

Dr. Maurer began working at Corning Glass Works in 1952 after earning his Ph.D. from M.I.T. Dr. Maurer retired from Corning in 1989 as a research fellow. While at Corning he worked with Peter Shultz and Donald Keck, and helped invent optical fiber, which is used today in telecommunications. Optical fibers are the backbone of the telecommunications industry, and nearly 90 percent of U.S. long distance communications are carried over optical fibers, with nearly all of it using Maurer's and the group's original design.

MAX, PETER

Peter Max Enterprises, 118 Riverside Dr., New York, NY 10024

BORN: 1937, Berlin (Germany) ACHIEVEMENTS: American Institute of Graphic Arts Award; Award, International Poster Competition, Poland; collections: U.S. postage stamp, World's Fair, Spokane, Wash.; World's Fair, Knoxville, Tenn.; exhibitions: Smithsonian Institution; Corcoran Gallery of Art. STUDIED: Art Students League; Pratt Institute; School of Visual Arts

Max spent his early years in China and Israel before coming to America in 1953. During the mid-1960s he gained wide attention when he became the primary protagonist of psychedelic art. Combining random and improvisational imagery, he painted posters for airlines, television, libraries, musicians and moon shots, eventually branching out to design such products as clocks, pillows, sheets and dinnerware. The exotic and eclectic images were referred to by some as composites of Art Nouveau, Pop and Op. Beginning in the 1970s, Max wanted to portray an art that was "superoptimistic, looking with great foresight towards a supercivilization, highly technologically oriented" describes requirements for inclusion in this volume. Adhering to the principles of Yoga, he is committed to "producing lots of beautiful things for everybody and turning everybody on to beautiful things" describes requirements for inclusion in this volume. The official artist of the 1982 World's Fair, he produced the Statue of Liberty series. He has also published his work in books.

MAYER, PETER

Penguin USA, 375 Hudson St., New York, NY 10014 (212) 366-2000

Mayer is a prominent publisher and head of Viking Penguin USA of New York City. For career credentials consult the portion of this book entitled "Biographees by Profession" in the Appendix. Within this portion, the list "Publishers" describes requirements for inclusion in this volume.

MAYS, LYLE DAVID

BMI, 320 West 57th St., New York, NY 10019 (212) 586-2000

BORN: 1953. ACHIEVEMENTS: Grammy nomination for North Texas State University Lab Band album.

Lyle Mays is associated with the jazz fusion septet N.Y. L.A. DreamBand. He won recognition and a Grammy nomination for composing and notating an album for the North Texas State University Lab band, the first college band to win a Grammy nomination. Apart from that, Mays is best known through his long musical relationship with Pat Metheny. Through the 1970s and early 1980s, Mays worked exclusively with Metheny. Mays' occasional forays on acoustic piano reveal his background in classical bop, but it's his electronic support on synthesizer that has earned him respect with Metheny. Mays has released recordings on ECM since the mid-1980s, including Lyle Mays,

1985; *Street Dreams*, 1988; and *Fictionary*, 1992 and 1993.

MAZEL, JUDY

c/o Macmillan Publishing Company, 866 Third Avenue, New York, NY 10022 (212) 702-5574
Mazel is a prominent author. For career credentials consult the portion of this book entitled "Biographees by Profession" in the Appendix. Within this portion, the list "Authors" describes requirements for inclusion in this volume.

McCAFFREY, GEN. BARRY R.

Office of the Secretary, Pentagon, Washington, D.C., 20301 (703) 545-6700
BORN: 1942, Taunton, Mass. ACHIEVEMENTS: Distinguished Service Cross with oak leaf cluster; Defense Distinguished Service Medal; Distinguished Service Medal; Silver Star with oak leaf cluster; Bronze Star Medal with "V" device; Purple Heart with two oak leaf clusters; Meritorious Service Medal. STUDIED: American University, M.A., civil government; graduated United States Military Academy, West Point, B.S.
McCaffrey began his military career as a platoon leader of the 325th Infantry, 82nd Airborne in December 1964 and finished as company executive officer in March 1966. He was an advisor from 1966 to 1967 and a company commander from 1968 to 1969 in Vietnam. As a brigadier general, he served as deputy United States Military representative, NATO, from 1988 to 1989. In September of 1990 he was commanding general, 24th Infantry Division, during Operation Desert Storm in Saudi Arabia. Gen. McCaffrey has been commander-in-chief of the United States Southern Command in Panama, since February 1994. Prior to this appointment, he was director of strategy, plans and policy for the Joint Staff, from May 1993 and assistant to the chairman of the Joint Chiefs of Staff. McCaffrey has also been an instructor at the United States Military Academy, West Point.

McCLANAHAN, RUE

Witt/Thomas/Harris Productions, 846 North Cahuenga, Hollywood, CA 90038
McClanahan is a prominent actor. For career credentials consult the portion of this book entitled "Biographees by Profession" in the Appendix. Within this portion, the list "Actors" describes requirements for inclusion in this volume.

McMURTRY, LARRY

c/o Simon and Schuster, 1230 Sixth Ave., New York, NY 10020
McMurtry is a prominent author. For career credentials consult the portion of this book entitled "Biographees by Profession" in the Appendix. Within this portion, the list "Authors" describes requirements for inclusion in this volume.

McCUTCHEON, JAMES WILLIAM

J. Michael Bloom, 223 Park Avenue South, New York, NY 10003
BORN: Russell, Ky. ACHIEVEMENTS: Antoinette Perry Award, Best Featured Actor in a Musical, Anything Goes, 1988; three Emmy Awards for Sesame Street. STUDIED: Ohio University, B.F.A., 1948.
Bill McCutcheon has been a regular on the stage and screen for over 40 years. He won a Tony Award for his role as Moonface in *Anything Goes*, in 1987, at the Vivian Beaumont Theatre. He has also appeared in *The Man Who Came To Dinner*, 1980; *You Can't Take It With You*, 1983; *The Marriage of Bette and Boo*, 1985; *The Front Page*, 1986; and *Light Up the Sky*, 1987. Besides his work on the stage, McCutcheon has won numerous awards for playing the part of Uncle Wally on the Public Broadcasting System series *Sesame Street*.

McDIVITT, JAMES ALTON

Rockwell International Corp., 1745 Jefferson Davis Hwy., Arlington, VA 22202 (703) 553-6600
BORN: 1929, Chicago. ACHIEVEMENTS: Space missions: commander, Gemini 4, commander, Apollo 9. STUDIED: University of Michigan, B.S., aeronautical engineering, 1959.
James McDivitt started his Air Force career in 1951 and flew 145 combat missions in the Korean War. He became a test pilot and NASA selected him as an astronaut in 1962. He commanded Gemini 4 in 1965, and watched as crewman Edward White left the spacecraft to become the first American to walk in space. In 1969, he commanded Apollo 9, and along with Russell Schweikart, flew the first lunar excursion module in Earth orbit. He left NASA and the Air Force for a civilian position as president of the Pullman Standard Corp., and is now a senior vice president with Rockwell International Corp.

McDONNEL, JOHN FINNEY

c/o Sun Distributors, 150 N. Wacker Dr., Chicago, IL 60606 (312) 236-3340
BORN: 1938. ACHIEVEMENTS: President, Sun Distributors. STUDIED: Loyola University.
An expert with 15 years experience in the field of distribution, John McDonnell is president of Sun Distributors. He oversees 13 divisions of the firm's operations in the fluid power, glass, and maintenance fields, and 3,000 employees in the U.S., Canada, and Mexico. McDonnell joined Sun in 1981 as president of a major distributor of fluid power, Sun's Walter Morris Division based in Rosemont, Illinois. He formerly held top marketing positions at Hydroline Manufacturing and Commercial Shearing Corp.

McEWEN, MARK

CBS-TV, 524 West 57th Street, New York, NY 10019
BORN: San Antonio, Tex. ACHIEVEMENTS:: Electronic Journalist of the Year, 1992 (presented by the CMA); TV GUIDE'S top-ten most trusted TV News Personalities. STUDIED: University of Maryland

McEwen has been reporting weather for *CBS This Morning* since it first began in November in 1987, and was named entertainment editor in 1992, after having served as the pop music editor. Before joining CBS in 1986, he was a co-host for the morning drive slot at WNEW-FM. Since joining the CBS morning show, he has covered the Academy Awards, the Cannes Film Festival, and the Rock and Roll Hall of Fame Inductions. As a reporter, McEwen has joined the Atlanta Falcons for a scrimmage, gone hang-gliding in North Carolina and participated in batting practice with the L.A. Dodgers. As entertainment editor, he has interviewed a multitude of super stars. He also contributes to the CBS show *48 Hours,* and periodically substitutes for Harry Smith. He was trained at Second City, the famous improvisation school in Chicago, and has performed as a stand-up comedian at many famous comedy clubs, including Catch A Rising Star and The Improv.

McFERRIN, BOBBY

EMI America/Liberty, 6920 Sunset Blvd., Los Angeles, CA 90028 (213) 461-9141
BORN: 1950, New York City. ACHIEVEMENTS: Hit Song, Don't Worry, Be Happy, 1983.
Bobby McFerrin's hit song, *Don't Worry, Be Happy,* made him an instant success in 1983. McFerrin used his captivating a cappella singing to create an entirely new style of song. He frequently sang not only the vocal parts, but also imitated the sounds of accompanying instruments, as well. He started performing in the early 1980s, mostly singing a variety of jazz tunes. Jon Hendricks caught one of McFerrin's early performances. Hendricks was impressed with McFerrin's talent and encouraged him. After his big hit in 1983, McFerrin did many solo performances. His repertoire has strayed away from jazz in recent years.

McGINNISS, JOE

c/o Morton L. Janklo, 598 Madison Ave., New York, NY 10022
BORN: 1942, New York City. ACHIEVEMENTS: Author of Fatal Vision, Putnam, 1983; Blind Faith, Putnam, 1988. STUDIED: Holy Cross College, B.S., 1964.
Joe McGinniss began his career as a journalist, working as a reporter for the *Port Chester Daily Item* in Port Chester, N.Y. McGinniss worked for a number of different newspapers until 1968, when he turned to free-lance writing as a full-time career. With the publication of *The Selling of the President*, Trident, 1968, McGinniss gained the distinction of becoming one of the youngest authors of nonfiction with a book on the best-seller list for seven months. McGinniss' next two books, *The Dream Team*, Random House, 1972, and *Heros*, Viking, 1976, were only moderately successful. In 1983 *Fatal Vision*, Putnam, was a huge success. Chronicling the arrest and conviction of Dr. Jeffrey MacDonald, *Fatal Vision* resulted in a four-year of legal battle between McGinniss and MacDonald.

McGinniss finally settled the case out of court after the first trial ended in a deadlocked jury.

McGOWAN, WILLIAM G.

1133 19th St. NW, Washington, D.C. 20036 (202) 872-1600
BORN: Wilkes-Barre, Pa. ACHIEVEMENTS: Challenged the AT&T monopoly, thus causing the deregulation of the phone industry. STUDIED: Harvard Business School.
William McGowan worked nights for the railroad while attending both high school and college. After college he worked for movie executive Mike Todd and the Shell Oil Company. The corporate life did not suit him, so he went into business for himself as a financial consultant to troubled businesses. It was in his consultant capacity, in 1968, that he met John Goeken, owner of Microwave Communications. Goeken was attempting to establish a microwave system between Chicago and St. Louis, but regulatory approval from the FCC had been held up for five years because of hostility from AT&T. McGowan bought the business for $50,000 and received FCC approval for the venture one year later, renaming the company MCI Communications Corp. It took nearly nine years for MCI to post its first profit. Throughout that period, McGowan was a master at raising the funds necessary to keep the business solvent. Today MCI is one of the leading competitors in the field of long distance telecommunications.

McGRAW, MIKE

Kansas City Star, 1729 Grand Avenue, Kansas City, MO 64108 (816) 234-4141
McGraw is a prominent journalist. For career credentials consult the portion of this book entitled "Biographees by Profession" in the Appendix. Within this portion, the list "Journalists" describes requirements for inclusion in this volume.

McKAYLE, DONALD

3839 Davana Rd., Sherman Oaks, CA 91423 (818) 784-5228
BORN: 1930, New York City. ACHIEVEMENTS: Notable works: Games; Rainbow 'Round My Shoulders; District Storyville; Blood of the Lamb; Incantation; Songs of the Disinherited; Raisin. STUDIED: City College of New York; a variety of modern dance teachers.
Donald McKayle usually assembles dancers for specific seasons rather than maintaining his own company, as he first attempted to do in 1951, when he created *Games*. As a teacher, he has taught at the Juilliard School, among others, and has appeared at the Festival of Two Worlds in Spoletto, Italy. The black experience is reflected in much of his work, such as black city life in *Games*, and prison life in *Rainbow 'Round My Shoulder.*

McKERNAN, JOHN R., JR.

Office of the Governor, State Hse., Station One, Augusta, ME 04333 (207) 289-3531

McKernan, Jr. is a prominent political leader. For career credentials consult the portion of this book entitled "Biographees by Profession" in the Appendix. Within this portion, the list "Political Leaders" describes requirements for inclusion in this volume.

McMILLAN, LARRY

Eastman Kodak, 343 State St., Rochester, NY 14650 (716) 724-4000
ACHIEVEMENTS: Developed Kodak Digital Camera System.
Professional photographers who are loathe to part with their expensive conventional equipment, can still use their cameras while taking advantage of the advances made by electronic imaging. Kodak's Digital Camera System, developed by Larry McMillan, starts with a standard Nikon F3 and converts it into a high-resolution digital camera, which, instead of using film, captures the shot electronically. The image can be accessed immediately on a display screen, transmitted over a phone line, or compressed for easy storage on a separate unit that comes with the system.

McMURTY, LARRY

Simon & Schuster, 1230 6th Ave., New York, NY 10020
BORN: 1936, Wichita Falls, Texas. ACHIEVEMENTS: Academy Award, Best Screenplay, The Last Picture Show, 1971; Pulitzer Prize, Lonesome Dove, 1986. STUDIED: North Texas State College, Rice University.
The son of a Texas rancher, Larry McMurty's novels contrasted the simple values of the American frontier with those of the modern era. His epic novel *Lonesome Dove*, 1986, for which he won a Pulitzer Prize, portrays compelling characters on a gritty cattle drive from Texas to Montana in the 1870s. He won an Oscar for his 1966 screenplay based on his novel *The Last Picture Show*, which portrayed life in a dying Texas town. His other novels include *Terms of Endearment*, 1975; *Cadillac Jack*, 1982; *Texasville*, 1987; *Anything for Billy*, 1988, and *Streets of Larado*, 1993.

McPEAK, GEN. MERRILL A.

Office of the Secretary, Pentagon, Washington, D.C. 20301-1155 (703) 545-6700
McPeak is a prominent military leader in the United States Air Force. For career credentials consult the portion of this book entitled "Biographees by Profession" in the Appendix. Within this portion, the list "Military Leaders" describes requirements for inclusion in this volume.

McPHERSON, JAMES ALAN

c/o Carl Brandt, 1501 Broadway, New York, NY 10036
BORN: 1943, Savannah, Ga. ACHIEVEMENTS: Pulitzer Prize; Fellowships: Guggenheim, MacArthur Foundation; Award for Excellence in Teaching, University of Iowa. STUDIED: Morris Brown College, B.A., English/history; Morgan State University, Baltimore, Student; Harvard Law School, LL.B, Law; University of Iowa, M.F.A.; honorary Bachelor of Law, Morris Brown College, Sumter, N.C.
James McPherson has been a contributor to the *Atlantic Monthly* for 27 years, winning many awards. He has been a judge for the National Endowment for the Humanities, the Loft McKnight Award, and General Electric Writing Awards. He is a member of the ACLU, NAACP, PEN, and the Authors Guild. McPherson has taught at the University of California at the teacher level, and at Morgan State University in Baltimore and the University of Virginia as associate professor. In 1981 he joined the University of Iowa as a full professor, where he remains.

McPHERSON, JAMES MONROE

Princeton University, Department of History, Princeton, NJ 08544 (609) 258-4159
BORN: 1936, Valley City, N.D. ACHIEVEMENTS: Pulitzer Prize; nominations: National Book Critics Circle, National Book Award; fellowships: Danforth, Proctor & Gamble, Guggenheim, Huntington-Seaver Institute, National Endowment for the Humanities, Huntington; Ainisfield Wolff Award in Race Relations. STUDIED: Gustavus Adolphus College, B.A., American history; Johns Hopkins University, Ph.D., American history.
James McPherson stunned the book world in 1988 when his *Battle Cry of Freedom: The Civil War Era* appeared. The sixth volume in the *Oxford History of the United States* was on The *New York Times* best seller list for five months, prompting Ballantine Books to make a record bid of $504,000 for the paperback rights. The shock the book produced was not in anything new McPherson said about what one critic called "the most worked-over topic in American history" describes requirements for inclusion in this volume. It was that McPherson expertly synthesized the era's political, social, economic, and military factors in a single volume, where heretofore the best historians could do ran from three to eight volumes. Secondly, he reassessed the outcome of the war. The North is generally believed to have been preordained to win. In his one volume, McPherson points out how many times contingency played a role in the outcome—the element of chance in every general's move, in every battle fought, in every decision made. All of which, according to critics, McPherson integrated perfectly to make his point: that neither side was preordained to win. The historian has taught at Princeton University since 1972, written three books and co-edited three more, and has contributed numerous articles to historical journals.

MEARS, LT. GEN. GARY H.

Office of the Secretary, Pentagon, Washington, D.C. 20301-1155 (703) 545-6700
Mears is a prominent military leader affiliated with the United States Air Force. For career credentials consult the portion of this book entitled "Biographees by Profession" in the Appendix. Within this portion, the list "Military Leaders" describes requirements for inclusion in this volume.

MEDLEY, BILL

c/o RCA Records, 1133 Sixth Avenue, New York, NY 10019 (212) 930-4000

Medley is a prominent vocalist. For career credentials consult the portion of this book entitled "Biographees by Profession" in the Appendix. Within this portion, the list "Vocalists" describes requirements for inclusion in this volume.

MEEHAN, NANCY

Nancy Meehan Dance Company,463 West Street #A1111, New York, NY 10014 (212) 929-2143
BORN: 1940, San Francisco. ACHIEVEMENTS: Notable ballets: Whitip; Hudson River Seasons; Bones Cascades Scapes; Yellow Point; Threading the Wave; White Wave; Seven Women. STUDIED: University of California at Berkeley, B.A., dance, ca 1962; Martha Graham, Erick Hawkins schools.
Nancy Meehan first trained in her home town of San Francisco before moving to New York City and her important studies at the Martha Graham School. Throughout the 1960s and early 1970s she danced with the American-Indian dancer/choreographer Erick Hawkins, one of the first classically trained ballet performers to switch to the modern style, and known as a maverick of modern dance. She established her own school in 1970 and choreographed for it for 11 years, winning the signal honor of having her archives placed in the Harvard Theatre Collection. Her best known dance, *Whitip*, performed by six dancers, is a 15-minute series of stage crossings performed in silence and widely acclaimed for revealing new schemes and even dimensions of movement possibilities.

MEIER, RICHARD ALAN

Richard Meier and Partners, 136 E. 57th Street , New York, NY 10022 (212) 967-6060
BORN: 1935. ACHIEVEMENTS: Fellow, AIA; Award of Merit, Concrete Industry Board, 1974; Bard Award, City Club of New York, 1977; Firm Award, AIA, 1984; notable works: Smith House, Darien, Conn.; Douglas House, Harbor Springs, Mich.; High Museum of Art, Atlanta. STUDIED: Columbia University.
Architecture, believes Richard Meier, is a wholly artificial, rational and inorganic activity. In his view, the alteration or destruction of nature is the invariable consequence of any construction. He shuns the pursuit of naturalism in his commissions; any material that has been refined and reformed by human agency, he argues, is already inherently unnatural. To highlight the contrasts between his buildings and natural environment, he sheathes them in white paint. This accentuates the artificial sharpness of their faceting, and so creates the greatest possible counterpoint to more amorphous and textually diverse geological and biological forms. To distinguish the horizontal plane from the vertical, he generally selects lightly-stained wood flooring as a foil to his prim white walls and window banks. In his residential commissions—i.e. the Smith House in Darien, Conn., the Douglas House, in Harbor Springs, Mich.—he has extended the flooring through a glass wall to form exterior deck areas, which give the effect of ramps only recently declared off-limits to pedestrian traffic.

MELLENCAMP, JOHN COUGAR

c/o Champion Entertainment, 130 West 57th St., #12B, New York, NY 10019
Mellencamp is a prominent vocalist. For career credentials consult the portion of this book entitled "Biographees by Profession" in the Appendix. Within this portion, the list "Vocalists" describes requirements for inclusion in this volume.

MENINO, THOMAS M.

Government Center, 1 City Hall Square, Boston, MA 02201 (617) 635-4000
Menino is a prominent political leader. For career credentials consult the portion of this book entitled "Biographees by Profession" in the Appendix. Within this portion, the list "Political Leaders" describes requirements for inclusion in this volume.

MERRIFIELD, ROBERT BRUCE

Rockefeller University, 1230 York Ave., New York City, NY 10021
BORN: 1921, Fort Worth, Texas. ACHIEVEMENTS: Nobel Prize in Chemistry, 1984; Albert Lasker Award; Gairdner Award; IntraSci Award; Award for Creative Work in Synthetic Organic Chemistry, American Chemical Society; Nichols Medal; Alan E. Pierce Award, American Peptide Symposium. STUDIED: University of California, Los Angeles.
A "simple but ingenious" technique that revolutionized the study of proteins through automated laboratory techniques won Robert Merrifield the Noble Prize. His method rapidly synthesizes, on a routine basis and in large quantities, the up to 50 amino acids in a peptide chain, enabling a researcher to quickly form longer polypeptide chains of a protein than heretofore. Benefits from his technique have been remarkably broad, ranging from the treatment and prevention of many of the more than 2,000 identified genetic diseases, and stimulating progress in genetic engineering as a way to treat diseases.

MERRILL, STEPHEN

State House, Concord, NH 03301 (603) 271-2121
BORN: 1946, Hampton, N.H. ACHIEVEMENTS: Governor, State of New Hampshire; chairman, Coalition of Northeast Governors and the New England Governors Association. STUDIED: University of New Hampshire.
Merrill is the first graduate of the University of New Hampshire to become governor of the state of New Hampshire. Elected governor in November, 1992, he made few promises during his campaign, but filled those he made during his first term of office. As a result, the people of New Hampshire returned him to a second term as governor in 1994. During his first term Merrill introduced the most sweeping changes to the states tax structure in 20 years. He closed tax loopholes, and at the same time reduced a number of key taxes while entirely eliminating others. Merrill also successfully introduced a comprehensive reform of the states workers' compensation laws, leading to a 20 percent rate reduction, saving New Hampshire businesses millions annually.

METCALF, LAURIE

William Morris Agency, 151 El Camino Drive, Beverly Hills, CA 90212

BORN: 1955, Edwardsville, Ill. ACHIEVEMENTS: Best Supporting Actress, Comedy Series, Roseanne, 1991-94. STUDIED: attended Illinois State University.

Laurie Metcalf is best known as Jackie Harris, the mentally confused, well meaning sister of Roseanne, in the on-going comedic series *Roseanne*. Prior to her role on *Roseanne*, Harris was a regular on the popular comedy series *Saturday Night Live*. In addition to her television work, Harris has appeared on both the stage and in films. Her stage credits include *Who's Afraid of Virginia Woolf?*, 1982; *Coyote Ugly*, 1985; *Bodies, Rest, and Motion*, 1986; *Educating Rita*, 1987; and *Killers*, 1988. Film credits encompass films such as *Desperately Seeking Susan*, 1984; *Making Mr. Right*, 1987; *Starts and Bars*, 1988; and *Miles From Home*, 1988.

METHENY, PATRICK BRUCE

Ted Kurland Associates Inc., 173 Brighton Ave, Allston, MA 02134-2003

BORN: 1954, Lee's Summit, Mo. ACHIEVEMENTS: Grammy Awards, Jazz Fusion Performance, Pat Metheny Group, Offramp, 1982; Pat Metheny Group, Travels; 1983, Pat Metheny Group, First Circle; 1984, Pat Metheny Group, Letter From Home, 1989, Pat Metheny, Secret Story, 1992. STUDIED: University of Miami, Fla.

Pat Metheny was gifted at an early age. While still in his teens, he joined a quartet headed by vibraphonist Gary Burton and, with Burton, taught at Boston's Berklee College of Music in the early 1970s. In the mid-1970s Metheny formed his own group, and has successfully toured throughout the United States and abroad ever since. With influences in his background ranging from country and western to Ornette Coleman, Metheny is more lyrical in his approach to the guitar than most. In recent years, he has produced music with a solid Latin flavor.

MEYEROWITZ, JOEL

817 West End Avenue, New York, NY 10025

BORN: 1938. ACHIEVEMENTS: Guggenheim Fellowship; NEA Fellowship.
Early work as an art director and designer spawned Meyerowitz's interest in photography. Seeking out scenes from urban and rural life, he instantly captures the spectacles of human activity. Early black-and-white work, which depicted social situations from the vantage point of a moving car, explored coincidental occurrences, and this theme continues to be his trademark. His aim is not social commentary; instead he asks the viewer to explore a way of seeing. Asymmetrical images display contrasts between color, light and shadow, space and activity. He often employs flash to create sharp profiles, deep shadows and glaring surfaces, providing information that the observer would normally not notice. Recently, his style has shifted to include large-format, highly detailed landscapes of Cape Cod in the manner of Walter Evans.

MFUME, KWEISI

2419 Rayburn House Office Building, Washington, D.C., 20515 (202) 225-4741

BORN: 1948. ACHIEVEMENTS: Chairman's 1993 Leadership Award for Civil Rights, NAACP; Chairman, Congressional Black Caucus. STUDIED: Morgan State University, Bachelor's Degree; Johns Hopkins University, Masters Degree, Liberal Arts.

Mfume is a four-term member of Congress, representing Maryland's Seventh Congressional District. In Congress, he has served on the Banking, Finance, and Urban Affairs Committee and the Small Business Committee. As a member of the Small Business Committee, he chaired the Subcommittee on Minority Enterprise, Finance, and Urban Development. Mfume authored the Minority Business Development Act, and the Minority Contracting and Employment Amendments to the Financial Institutions Reform and Recovery Act. He has consistently supported minority business and civil rights legislation. His civic activities include serving on the Advisory Board of the Schomburg Commission for the Preservation of Black Culture, and being a member of the Board of Visitors for the United States Naval Academy, and the Morgan University Board of Regents. Prior to serving in Congress, Mfume was a member of the Maryland state Central Committee and a member of the Baltimore City Council.

MICHEL, ROBERT HENRY

U.S. House of Representatives, Room 230, Washington, D.C.

BORN: 1923, Decatur, Ill. ACHIEVEMENTS: Two Bronze Stars and a Purple Heart. STUDIED: Bradley University, B.S.; Lincoln College, Illinois Wesleyan University, L.H.D., liberal arts.

Rep. Robert Michel entered politics working for seven years for Illinois Rep. Harold Velde after graduation from college in 1949. He was then elected to the House in 1957, and re-elected through 1994. He has served in the House as Minority Whip from 1975 until 1979 and Minority Leader from 1981 until 1995. In World War II, as a combat infantryman in Europe from 1943 until 1946, he received two Bronze Stars and a Purple Heart.

MICHENER, JAMES ALBERT

Barker Library, University of Texas, Austin, TX 78731

BORN: 1907, New York City. ACHIEVEMENTS: Pulitzer Prize, Tales of the South Pacific, 1948; Medal of Freedom. STUDIED: Swarthmore College.

Best known for his epic novels that presented immense amounts of information about the geography, history and culture of exotic regions, people and places, Michener's best-sellers include *Hawaii*, 1959 *Source, 1965; Centennial*, 1974; *Chesapeake*, 1978; *The Covenant*, 1980; *Alaska*, 1988; and *The Novel*, 1991, a work about novel writing. He won the Pulitzer Prize for his collection of stories, *Tales of the South Pacific*, 1947, which was made into the Broadway musical *South Pacific* in 1949. His nonfiction includes *Literary*

Reflections, 1993, and his autobiography, *The World Is My Home*, 1992.

MIDLER, BETTE

Creative Artists Agency, 1888 Century Park East, Suite 1400, Los Angeles, CA 90067
BORN: 1945, Honolulu. ACHIEVEMENTS: Grammy Award, Best New Artist, 1973; Emmy Award, Outstanding Special, Bette Midler: Ol' Red Hair Is Back, 1978; Golden Globe Award, Best Actress in a Musical/Comedy Film and Female New Star of the Year in a Film, The Rose; Grammy Award, Best Pop Vocal Performance by a Female, The Rose, 1980; Grammy Award (with others), Best Recording for Children, In Harmony/A Sesame Street Record, 1980; Grammy Award, Record of the Year, Wind Beneath My Wings, 1989; Emmy Award, Best Individual Performance in a Variety or Music Program, The Tonight Show Starring Johnny Carson, 1992. STUDIED: University of Hawaii, Berghof Studio of Acting.

Midler began her singing career in the chorus of *Fiddler on the Roof* playing at the Imperial Theatre in 1966. Starting in 1972, she worked as a singer-comedienne throughout the United States. Among her many credits is an appearance with Johnny Carson in Las Vegas in 1972. By 1973 she won her first Grammy Award as Best New Artist. She is best known for her portrayal of Rose, a fictional character many believe to be based on the singer Janis Joplin, in the film *The Rose*, 1979. Her performance earned her an Academy Award nomination, two Golden Globe Awards, and a Grammy Award. She has appeared in numerous comedy films including *Down and Out in Beverly Hills*, 1986; *Ruthless People*, 1986; and *Outrageous Fortune*, 1987. She also acted in dramas, staring in *Beaches*, 1988; and *For the Boys*, 1991. Midler is a partner of the production company All-Girl Pictures in Burbank, Calif.

MILES, MICHAEL A.

c/o Gulfstream Aerospace Corporation, PO Box 2206, Savannah, GA 31402 (912) 964-3000
BORN: 1939, Chicago. ACHIEVEMENTS: CEO, Philip Morris. STUDIED: J.L. Kellogg Graduate School of Management, Northwestern University; Northwestern University, B.A., journalism.

Michael Miles, chairman and chief executive officer, until 1994, of Philip Morris, one of the largest U.S. consumer products companies, is a member of the board of Thompson Miniwax, a wood stains and sealants company controlled by Forstmann Little. He is also a special limited partner and sits on the Advisory Committee of the private investment firm that owns or controls eight companies, with total revenues of more than $6 billion. Among those companies are ZiffDavis Publishing Company, the General Instrument Corporation, and the Gulfstream Aerospace Corporation. Miles sits on the board of directors of Dell Computer Corporation.

MILLER, ARTHUR

International Creative Management, 40 W. 57th St., New York, NY 10019

BORN: 1915, New York City. ACHIEVEMENTS: Antoinette Perry Award, 1947; 1949; and 1953; Pulitzer Prize, 1949, Death of a Salesman. STUDIED: University of Michigan, A.B., 1938.

Miller's works primarily concern man's relationship to society and struggles within and against it. His masterpiece, *Death of a Salesman*, 1949, which won a Tony Award and Pulitzer Prize, concerned the gap between the promise of success and the reality of failure as exemplified in the life of tragic hero Willie Loman. Miller's other major plays of the period include *All My Sons*, 1947; *The Crucible*, 1953; *A Memory of Two Mondays*, 1955; and *A View from the Bridge*. He wrote primarily short stories and essays from the mid-1950s to the mid-1960s, as well as the screenplay for the film *The Misfits*, 1961, which he later expanded into a novel. His later plays included *After the Fall*, 1964; *Incident at Vichy*, 1964; *The Price*, 1968.

MILLER, BARRY

William Morris Agency, 1350 Avenue of the Americas, New York, NY 10019
BORN: 1958, Los Angeles. ACHIEVEMENTS: Antoinette Perry Award, Best Featured Actor in a Dramatic Role, Biloxi Blues, 1985.

An actor on the stage, film, and television, Barry Miller is best known for his acting in the Broadway production of *Biloxi Blues*, 1985-86. Miller earned a Tony Award as best actor in a dramatic role for his portrayal of Arnold Epstein. He is a veteran of many other stage productions, including *The City at 4 a.m.*, 1979; *My Mother, My Father, and Me*, 1980; *Forty-Duece*, 1981; and *Festival of One-Act Comedies*, 1989. Miller is also a regular in films, appearing in *Lepke*, 1975; *Saturday Night Fever*, 1977; *Voices*, 1979; *Fame*, 1980; *The Chosen*, 1982; *Peggy Sue Got Married*, 1986; and *The Last Temptation of Christ*, 1988.

MILLER, MERTON HOWARD

University of Chicago, GSB, 1101 E. 58th St., Chicago, IL 60621
BORN: 1923, Boston. ACHIEVEMENTS: Nobel Prize in Economic Science (with Harry M. Markowitz and William F. Sharpe), 1990. STUDIED: Harvard University, B.A., economics; Johns Hopkins University, Ph.D., economics.

Merton Miller had a brush with Nobel Award fame when he worked with Franco Modigliani in establishing the controversial "Modigliani-Miller Theorems," which applied economic theory to the field of finance. Modigliani alone received the prize, however, on the basis of another important study he made earlier on national household saving rates. Five years later Miller himself won a trip to Stockholm as one of three awardees. Their work supplied new tools for economists in weighing the risks and awards of investments, and for valuing corporate stocks and bonds.

MILLER, PAM

200 East Main Street, Lexington, KY 40507 (606) 258-3194
BORN: 1938, Cambridge, Mass. ACHIEVEMENTS: Women of Achievement YWCA, 1984; Outstanding Woman of Blue Grass, AAUW, 1984; mayor of

Lexington, Ky.; Urban County councilwoman. STUDIED: Smith College, B.A., history, 1960.

Pam Miller graduated Magna Cum Laude from Smith College in 1960, majoring in history. She was the owner and operator of a small advertising firm, giving her the background required to understand the needs of small business operators. She began her career in politics when she was elected to the Urban County Council in 1973. In all, she served a total of 15 years on the council. Miller became Lexington's first woman mayor on Jan. 3, 1993. As a public servant, Miller has done much to improve the quality of life in Lexington. She played a key role in founding the city's farmers' market, starting a recycling program, and revitalizing downtown Lexington.

MILLER, ROBERT L.

Time Magazine, 1271 Avenue of the Americas, New York, NY, 10020 (212) 484-8000
BORN: May 22, 1949, Los Angeles. STUDIED: Columbia Business School, M.B.A., 1974. Graduated Williams College, B.A., American civilization, 1971.
President of Time Inc. Ventures since July 1991, Miller is responsible for all of Time Inc's non-New York-based magazines as well as the magazine division's international operations. As of October 1993, he has been president of television for Time Inc, which he joined in 1974. He worked in the Controller's Department, and two years later, he was named international operations manager of Time-Life Books Inc. Transferring to *Sports Illustrated* in 1979, he served as business manager and general manager in 1982 before becoming publisher in 1983. In February of 1986, Miller was elected a vice president of Time Inc. He was appointed publisher of *Time* magazine in 1987 and worldwide publisher in 1989. At this time, he supervised the publication of *Time, People* and *Sports Illustrated*. In addition to worldwide publisher, he also became group publisher and executive vice president. In 1990, while holding all these positions, he was made responsible for news, sports, and business and money. This action put him in charge of *Time, Life, Sports Illustrated, Sports Illustrated for Kids*, and *Fortune* and *Money* magazines.

MILLER, ROGER

c/o MCA Records, Inc., 70 Universal City Plaza, Universal City, CA 91068 (213) 508-4000
Miller is a prominent composer. For career credentials consult the portion of this book entitled "Biographees by Profession" in the Appendix. Within this portion, the list "Composers" describes requirements for inclusion in this volume.

MILLER, STEVE

Capitol Records, 1750 N Vine St., Hollywood, CA 90028
BORN: 1943, Milwaukee, Wis.
Although it was characterized as psychedelic rock, Steve Miller's brand of music was heavily based in blues. His group, the Steve Miller Band, achieved broad recognition in the 1960s. Lumped in with the San Francisco bands of the period, Miller's band actually was based in Texas. Boz Scaggs, lead vocalist for the group in its early stages, shared Miller's enthusiasm for blues. The two found success flavoring their tight blues sound with the popular psychedelic forms of the period. In the 1970s, Miller found his meter, and scored hit after hit with his unique style. His popularity waned in the 1980s, although he continues to record.

MILLER, ZELL BRYAN

Office of the Governor, State Capitol, Atlanta, GA, 30334 (404) 656-1776
BORN: 1932, Young Harris, Ga. ACHIEVEMENTS: Torch of Liberty Award, Anti-Defamation League; author of the books: The Mountains Within Me, Great Georgians, and They Heard Georgia Singing. STUDIED: University of Georgia, Masters Degree.
Zell Miller was born in the northern mountains of Georgia on February 24, 1932. Both his mother and father were teachers at Young Harris College. Miller, a historian, has taught at Young Harris College, The University of Georgia, and other institutions of post-secondary education. He began his political career as mayor of Young Harris, Georgia. In 1960 Miller was elected to the Georgia State Senate. He served his first term as lieutenant governor in 1974, and held that position for the next 16 years. In 1990 Miller was elected governor of the State of Georgia, and was re-elected in 1994. Education has been the centerpiece of Miller's administration. He has championed educational programs such as a voluntary pre-kindergarten for at-risk 4-year-olds, the HOPE scholarship program, and a technology initiative program that ensures computer technology is available in Georgia's public education systems.

MILLMAN, IRVING

BORN: 1923 New York City. ACHIEVEMENTS: Test and vaccine for Hepatitis B; inducted into the National Inventors Hall of Fame, 1993. STUDIED: City College of New York, B.S., 1948; University of Kentucky, M.S., 1951; Northwestern University Medical School, Ph.D., 1954
In 1963, along with Dr. Baruch Blumberg, Dr Millman discovered an antigen that led to a blood test and vaccine for Hepatitis B. Dr. Millman joined the Fox Chase Cancer Center in 1967 after working for Armour & Company, the Public Health Research Institute in New York City, and the Merck Institute for Therapeutic Research. He is a fellow of the American Academy of Microbiology, and a former member of the New York Academy of Sciences, the American Association for the Advancement of Science, and the American Society of Microbiology.

MITCHELL, ANDREA

NBC News, 30 Rockefeller Plaza, New York, NY 10020
Mitchell is a prominent journalist. For career credentials consult the portion of this book entitled "Biographees by Profession" in the Appendix. Within this portion, the list "Journalists" describes requirements for inclusion in this volume.

MITCHELL, GEORGE J.

BORN: 1933, Waterville, Maine. *STUDIED:* Bowdoin College, B.A., prepaw; Georgetown University, LL.B., law.

Mitchell's career in politics, which would carry him to the highest post in the U.S. Senate, began after a two-year hitch with U.S. Army Intelligence in Germany. Back home he finished college, and two years later became executive assistant to Sen. Edmund Muskie (D-Maine), then an aide in two Muskie campaigns. The association led to his appointment as U.S. Attorney for Maine, during which he cracked down on pornography peddlers and marijuana smugglers. When Muskie became secretary of state under President Jimmy Carter, he recommended that Mitchell fill his vacancy. In the campaign of 1982, Mitchell won the seat on his own in an upset by concentrating on environmental issues, especially acid rain, and he would keep the seat until he retired in 1994. As chairman of the Democratic Senatorial Campaign Committee in 1986, he steered thousands of dollars to helping 11 new Democratic senators get elected, returning the Democrats to the majority for the first time since 1980. He went on to win national fame during the Iran-Contra hearings when he bucked a tide of sympathy for Colonel Oliver North. After the hearings he co-authored, with Sen. William S. Cohen, from Maine, a book on the investigation called *Men of Zeal*. Mitchell went on to become president of the Senate and majority leader in 1988.

MODIGLIANI, FRANCO

Massachusetts Institute of Technology, Sloan School of Management, Cambridge, MA 02139

BORN: 1918, Rome (Italy) *ACHIEVEMENTS: Nobel Prize in Economic Science, 1985; consultant, Board of Governors, Federal Reserve System; senior adviser, Brookings Panel on Economic Activity; president, American Econometric Society, American Economic Association, American Finance Association, and vice president International Economic Association. STUDIED: University of Rome; New School of Social Research, New York City.*

A blip on the economic screen in regard to patterns of individual behavior in national savings had bothered economists since the mid-1930s. According to John Maynard Keynes, the demigod of economists in the Depression years and the antihero of conservatives today, the average ratio of savings to income increases as household income increases. Yet statistics show no evidence that the national saving rate rises as all households become more affluent. It was not until Franco Modigliani, an important contributor to the codification of the Keynesian system in the 1940s, developed a "lifecycle hypothesis" that a constant historical ratio between savings and income finally was reached. He hypothesized that individuals save during their earning years and use the savings after retirement and this affects the positive amount of total saving. This trend, he maintains is exacerbated when youthful savers are more numerous than the retired. Modiligiani's second contribution to economics involved the financial markets, and led, with his "lifecy-cle hypothesis," to a Nobel Prize in 1985. With Merton Miller, Modigliani developed a way to assess the worth of a company in contradiction to the then prevailing theory, that a firm with few debts would be worth more than one with heavy debts, and thus could pay less to borrow funds. The Modigliani-Miller theorems showed that the worth of a firm and its cost of raising capital are independent of the firm's ratio of bonds and stocks, as well as its dividend-payout ratio. The theorems, which provoked endless arguments, eventually led to creation of a new sub-specialty in economics, Financial Analysis.

MONAGHAN, THOMAS STEPHEN

Domino's Pizza, Inc., P.O. Box 997, Ann Arbor, MI 48105

BORN: 1937, Ann Arbor, Mich. ACHIEVEMENTS: Launched Domino's Pizza chain. STUDIED: Ferris State University, Big Rapids, Mich., student; many honorary degrees.

Thomas Monaghan and his brother bought a failing Ypsilanti, Mich., pizzeria in 1960. Changing the pizzeria's name, Dominic's, to Domino's, they began building a Domino's Pizza chain, which by 1988, had become the nation's second-largest franchisee, with 4,200 in operation. Among his other interests and philanthropies are owning the Detroit Tigers baseball team from 1983 until 1992, classic cars, and collecting Frank Lloyd Wright furniture and memorabilia.

MONDALE, WALTER FREDERICK

Dorsey & Whitney, 2200 First Bank Pl. E., Minneapolis, MN 55405

BORN: 1928, Ceylon, Minn. ACHIEVEMENTS: Appointed ambassador to Japan, 1993. STUDIED: University of Minnesota, law.

Walter Mondale, a graduate of the University of Minnesota Law School, served as state attorney general of Minnesota from 1960 to 1964. In 1964, he was appointed to fill the seat of Hubert H. Humphrey, when Humphrey was elected to vice president. Mondale was elected to the U.S. Senate again in both 1966 and 1972. He was known for his concern for federal aid to urban areas, housing problems, and civil rights. Jimmy Carter selected Mondale as his running mate for the presidency in 1976. As vice president, Mondale was a close advisor of President Carter, who was a Washington outsider. After losing re-election in 1980 to the Reagan/Bush ticket, Mondale returned to his law practice. He ran again for the presidency in 1984, but lost by an overwhelming margin, again to Reagan and Bush. In 1993, Mondale was appointed ambassador to Japan.

MOORE, JACK

126 East 10th St., New York, NY 10003 (212) 477-1193

Moore is a prominent dancer. For career credentials consult the portion of this book entitled "Biographees by Profession" in the Appendix. Within this portion, the list "Dancers" describes requirements for inclusion in this volume.

MOORE, JOHN D.

Columbia University Press, 526 West 113th St., New York, NY 10025 (212) 316-7100

Moore is a prominent publisher. For career credentials consult the portion of this book entitled "Biographees by Profession" in the Appendix. Within this portion, the list "Publishers" describes requirements for inclusion in this volume.

MOORE, THOMAS

Stanford University, Hoover Institution, Stanford, CA 94305

BORN: 1930, Washington, D.C.. ACHIEVEMENTS: Director and senior fellow, Hoover Institution's Domestic Studies Program; honorary research fellow, University of London; member, Council of Economic Advisers; author of six books, his first being The Economics of the American Theater. STUDIED: George Washington University, University of Chicago, Massachusetts Institute of Technology.

Thomas Moore launched his professional career writing about the theater. His first book, *The Economics of the American Theater*, examined costs of Broadway shows, as well as the subsidies, taxes, and other government policies that touch on the performing arts. Since then his work has covered a broad range of subjects, particularly the effects of government regulations; with early journal articles focused on licensing and electric utility regulations. His second book, *Freight Transportation Regulation*, proclaimed his dedication to a free market and a lifelong advocacy of deregulation. While deregulation hurts some, he argues after studying the pros and cons of deregulation in trucking, railroads, and airlines, it ultimately increases competition and reduces prices, its advantages far outweighing the disadvantages of government regulation. While scolding President Reagan for favoring big business at the expense of greater competition, he strongly supported Reagan's deregulation efforts, and applauded the dismissal by the Federal Trade Commission of three antitrust cases against cereal manufacturers, arguing that antitrust laws are regulatory statutes. He also approved of Reagan's decontrolling of oil prices and lifting auto passive resistant regulations. In the 1990s, he continues his support of deregulation, focusing much of his attention on energy and environmental regulation.

MOORE, THOMAS H. (TOM)

William Morris Agency, 1350 Avenue of the Americas, New York, NY 10019

BORN: 1943, Meridian, Miss. ACHIEVEMENTS: Fellowship, Yale School of Drama; Golden Eagle Award, Cine, and Golden Knight Award, Malta Film Festival, for Journey; Antoinette Perry Award, best director of a musical; Designated Old Master, Purdue University; six Dramalogue Awards, Humanitas Prize; Emmy Award, Best Director. STUDIED: Purdue University, B.A., Yale University School of Drama, M.F.A., drama; Honorary Doctorate of Fine Arts, Purdue University

Versatile Tom Moore has directed stage plays, films, television shows, lectured on American Studies in Salzburg, Austria, and taught drama at the State University of New York and the Yale School of Music. His production of *Grease*—with two national companies, bus and truck companies, and two London companies—was the longest-running show in the history of Broadway until its record was broken by *A Chorus Line*. Previous to its Broadway debut, *Grease* had run through 128 performances at an off-Broadway theater. Drama goers find his most representative work in *Oh What a Lovely War, Once in a Lifetime, Knock Knock, The Little Foxes,* and *The Octette Bridge Club.* In films, he directed *Journey* for the American Film Institute and *'night Mother* for Universal. But it is for his television work that he may be most widely known by the public. He directed many episodes of *thirtysomething, L.A. Law, The Wonder Years, Cheers, Northern Exposure, Picket Fences,* and *Class of '96.* He is a member of 40 Stage Directors and Choreographers, the Writers Guild, Directors Guild, and the American Film Institute.

MORGAN, WILLIAM

William Morgan Architects, 220 E. Forsyth Street, Jacksonville, FL 32202 (904) 356-4195

BORN: 1930. ACHIEVEMENTS: Fellow, AIA; Design Award, Progressive Architecture, 1975; Graham Foundation Grant, 1973; notable works: Dunehouse Apartments, Atlantic Beach, Fla.; Trident Submarine Base Headquarters, Kings Bay, Ga.; Riverfront Esplanade, Norfolk, Va. STUDIED: Harvard University.

After completing a 10-year inquiry into the evolution of prehistoric architecture in North America and Micronesia, William Morgan's work changed dramatically. In the early 1960s he designed a series of luxury houses which showed a boxy, Miesian face to the outside world but featured airy, two-story central atriums with integral balconies and unexpectedly intimate and earthy fireplace nooks. After his immersion in the organic forms of ancient vernacular architecture, he took up a series of commissions through which he hoped to prove that architecture could be an extension of traditional landscaping. One of his most striking designs, the 1975 Dunehouse Apartments in Atlantic Beach, Fla., is a multi-unit duplex built into the slope of a natural sand dune. The structure so closely follows the natural contours of the dune and the adjacent shoreline that its presence is only betrayed by a pair of small oval patios and a modest entrance way.

MORGANTI, STEVEN

E.I. du Pont de Nemours & Company, 1007 N. Market St., Wilmington, DE 19898 (302) 774-1000

ACHIEVEMENTS: Developed the Brailstat system for printing in braille. For those who read braille, fingers constantly moving over raised letters traditionally have worn out books and magazines after a few readings. Steven Morganti solved this problem by developing *Brailstat*, a polyester film for printing in braille. A non-tear, long-wear substance, polyester is also thinner and more resistant to static and mildew than conventional paper.

MORRICONE, ENNIO

c/o ASCAP, 1 Lincoln Plaza, New York, NY 10023
(212) 595-3050
Morricone is a prominent composer. For career credentials consult the portion of this book entitled "Biographees by Profession" in the Appendix. Within this portion, the list "Composers" describes requirements for inclusion in this volume.

MORRISON, TONI

Random House, 201 E. 50th St., New York, NY 10022
BORN: 1931, Lorain, Ohio. ACHIEVEMENTS: Pulitzer Prize, Beloved, 1987; Nobel Prize, 1993. STUDIED: Howard University, B.A., 1953; Cornell University, M.A., 1955.
Toni Morrison taught literature for ten years before joining Random House publishers as an editor in 1965. Her novels explore the lives of people in black communities that range from poor Southerners to rich New Yorkers in terms of their own cultures and pressures from the white world outside. Her novels include *The Bluest Eye*, 1969; *Sula*, 1973; *Song of Solomon*, 1977, which won the National Book Critics Circle Award; *Beloved*, 1987, which won the Pulitzer Prize; *Tar Baby*, 1981; and *Jazz*, 1992. She was awarded the Nobel Prize for literature in 1993.

MORROW, JOHN HOWARD JR.

University of Georgia, Department of History, Athens, GA 30609
BORN: 1944, Trenton, N.J. ACHIEVEMENTS: Lindsay Young Professorship; Outstanding Teacher, University of Tennessee National Alumni Association; University of Tennessee Macebearer, University Distinguished Service Professorship. STUDIED: Swarthmore College, with honors, B.A., history; University of Pennsylvania, Ph.D., history.
John Morrow began his teaching career as associate professor at the University of Tennessee in Knoxville and advanced to full professor and department head in 1971. In 1989 he became Lindbergh Professor of History at the National Aerospace Museum in Washington, D.C., after writing two of his three books, *Building German Airpower, 1909-1914*, and *German Airpower in World War I*. A third book, *The Great War in the Air* was published in 1993. He also joined the faculty at the University of Georgia in 1989, and became department chairman in 1991. Among his memberships is the History Advisory Committee to the secretary of the Air Force, of which he is chairman.

MOSEL, TED

400 East 57th St., New York, NY 10022
Mosel is a prominent dramatic artist. For career credentials consult the portion of this book entitled "Biographees by Profession" in the Appendix. Within this portion, the list "Dramatic Artists" describes requirements for inclusion in this volume.

MOSELEY–BRAUN, CAROL

SH-320 Hart Office Bldg., Washington, D.C. 20510
202-224-2854
Moseley-Braun is the U.S. Senator from Illinois. She is a democrat and one of the few black women to serve in the Senate. Her first term is therefore closely followed by the media. She is considered a liberal, and a close ally of the President.

MOSKOS, CHARLES C.

Northwestern Univ., Dept. of Soc., 1810 Chicago Ave., Evanston, IL 60201-3806
Moskos is a prominent. For career credentials consult the portion of this book entitled "Biographees by Profession" in the Appendix. Within this portion, the list "Educators" describes requirements for inclusion in this volume.

MOUNTCASTLE, VERNON B. JR.

725 N. Wolfe St., Baltimore, MD 21205
Mountcastle, Jr. is a prominent physician. For career credentials consult the portion of this book entitled "Biographees by Profession" in the Appendix. Within this portion, the list "Physicians" describes requirements for inclusion in this volume.

MOYERS, BILL D.

Pubic Affairs TV Inc., 356 W 58th St., New York, NY 10019-1896
BORN: 1934, Hugo, Okla. ACHIEVEMENTS: Recipient 22 Emmy awards; Ralph Lowell Medal for contribution to Pubic TV; George Peabody Award, 1976, 1980, 1985-86, 1988-90; DuPont/Columbia Silver Baton Award, 1979, 1986, 1988; Gold Baton Award, 1991; George Polk Award, 1981, 1986. STUDIED: University of Texas, B.J. (with honors), 1956; University of Edingburgh, Scotland, 1956-1957; Southwestern Baptist Theological Seminary, 1959; American Film Institute, honorary doctorate.
In the 1960s, Bill Moyers served as the personal assistant to then Senator Lyndon B. Johnson, eventually becoming his special assistant when Johnson became president, from 1963 to 1967, and then his press secretary from 1965 to 1967. His weekly public affairs program on public TV, *Bill Moyers Journal*, ran for eight years from 1971 until 1976, and 1978 to 1981. Moyers also served as chief correspondent for *CBS Reports* from 1976 to 1978, senior news analyst for CBS News from 1981 to 1986, and executive editor of Public Affairs TV, Inc. from 1987, a position he still holds. Moyers has written several books including: *Listening To America*, 1971; *Report from Philadelphia*, 1987; *The Secret Government*, 1988; *Joseph Campbell and the Power of Myth*, 1988; and *A World of Ideas*, 1989.

MOYNIHAN, DANIEL PATRICK

SR-464 Russell Bldg., Washington, D.C. 20510-3201
(202) 224-4451
BORN: 1927, Tulsa, Okla. ACHIEVEMENTS: Arthur S. Flemming Award, 1965; International League of Human Rights Award, 1975; John LaFarge Award for Interracial Justice, 1980; Thomas Jefferson Medal for Distin-

guished Achievement in the Arts or Humanities, 1993; first recipient of Hubert Humphrey Award for notable public service by a political scientist. STUDIED: B.A. Tufts University, 1948; Ph.D. Fletcher School of Law and Diplomacy, 1961.

Elected in 1976, and after a lifetime of public service, Moynihan is now the senior senator from New York serving on committees for Finance, Environment and Public Works, and Rules and Administration. His college career was interrupted by active duty in the Naval Reserve from 1944 to 1947. Moynihan was the first man to serve in four successive political administrations (Kennedy—Ford) and has held positions ranging from director of the Joint Center for Urban Studies at MIT in 1966, and ambassador to India from 1973 to 1975, to regent of the Smithsonian Institution in 1995.

MUDD, ROGER HARRISON

NBC News, 30 Rockefeller Plaza New York, NY 10020
BORN: 1928, Washington,D.C. ACHIEVEMENTS: professor, Princeton University; co-host Meet the Press. STUDIED: Washington & Lee University.

Mudd began his career in print journalism with the Richmond News Leader, and entered television as the news director of a local station as well (WRNL). In 1956 he transferred to the Washington affiliate of CBS, and in 1961 he was made a network correspondent, specializing in politics. As the designated substitute for Walter Cronkite on the CBS Evening News, it was expected that he would take the chair permanently when Cronkite retired in 1981. When that failed to happen, he moved to NBC, co-hosting Meet the Press and co-anchoring the NBC Evening News with Tom Brokaw. In 1987 he made his final network switch, opting for PBS and the MacNeil-Lehrer News Hour.

MULLER, JENNIFER

Jennifer Muller and The Works, 131 West 24th St., New York, NY 10011 (212) 691-3803
BORN: 1949, Yonkers, N.Y. ACHIEVEMENTS:Notable ballets: Nostalgia, Rust-Giocometti Sculpture Garden; Sweet Milkwood and Blackberry Bloom; Biography; Clown; Predicament for Five; Lovers. STUDIED: Juilliard School of Music, B.A., dance.

Considered a brilliant performer, she also demands high standards for her dancers as the choreographer of her own company, formed in 1973. She has produced works for the Netherlands Dance Theatre and the Repertory Dance Theatre of Utah. As a dancer, she performed for Jose Limon, a modern-dance company that was especially active in the 1960s. She later performed with fellow Limon dancer Louis Falco, becoming associate director of his troupe.

MULLIS, KARY BANKS

6767 Neptune Pl., Apt. 5, La Jolla, CA 92037
Mullis is a prominent scientist. For career credentials consult the portion of this book entitled "Biographees by Profession" in the Appendix. Within this portion, the list "Scientists" describes requirements for inclusion in this volume.

MUNDY, GEN. C. E.

Office of the Secretary, Pentagon, Washington, D.C. 20301-1155 (703) 545-6700
Mundy, USMC is a prominent military leader affiliated with the United States Marine Corp. For career credentials consult the portion of this book entitled "Biographees by Profession" in the Appendix. Within this portion, the list "Military Leaders" describes requirements for inclusion in this volume.

MURDOCH, RUPERT

News Corporation Limited, 1211 Avenue of the Americas, New York, NY, 10036 (212) 852-7000
BORN: 1931, Melbourne (Australia). ACHIEVEMENTS: Companion of the Order of Australia, 1984. STUDIED: graduated Oxford University, 1953.

Rupert Murdoch is chairman and chief executive of the News Corporation Limited, a newspaper, magazine, and book publishing, as well as major motion picture and television production and distribution operation. Murdoch took control of News Limited in 1954. From there, he acquired the Daily Mirror in Sydney in 1960, and started a national newspaper called the Australian, in 1964. In 1969, Murdoch acquired the British Sunday paper, News of the World and the Sun. During the 1980s, the company purchased Times Newspapers and HarperCollins publishing. The New York Post and TV Guide are also publishing interests of the News Corporation Limited. Murdoch purchased Twentieth Century Fox Film Corporation in 1985. A year later, six television stations were purchased from Metromedia, and Fox Television was created. The satellite broadcaster, Star Television, is also a holding of Murdoch's. Through Hong Kong-based Star, Newscorp transmits 11 channels to 53 countries in Asia. Over 20 channels are in the works for viewers in Europe. In 1993, Fox acquired the rights to broadcast the NFL's National Conference games for four years. Less than a year later Fox announced an alliance of 12 VHF stations that changed their network affiliations from ABC, CBS, and NBC to Fox Broadcasting.

MURKOWSKI, FRANK H.

SH-706 Hart Bldg., Washington, D.C., 20510-0202 (202) 224-6665
BORN: 1933, Seattle. ACHIEVEMENTS: Commissioner, Alaska Department of Economic Development, 1967; president, Alaska National Bank, 1970. STUDIED: Seattle University, B.A. Economics, 1955.

Murkowski was reared in Alaska, and spent his post-college years stationed in Ketchikan, serving on the Coast Guard Cutters Sorrel and Thistle. After a successful career in banking in his adopted state, Murkowski won his Senate seat in 1980. His Senate career has involved service on several key committees including Senate Intelligence, Veterans Affairs, Foreign Relations, and the Energy and Natural Resources Committee. He was the first Senator from Alaska to chair a full congressional committee, the Senate Veterans Affairs Committee.

MURPHY, CARLYLE MARIE

The *Washington Post*, 1150 15th St., NW, Washington D.C. 20037 (202) 334-6000
BORN: 1947, Hartford, Conn. ACHIEVEMENTS: Pulitzer Prize for International Reporting. STUDIED: Trinity College, B.A.; Johns Hopkins University, M.B., international public policy.

A woman wearing a black robe and veil among the throngs fleeing Kuwait after the 1990 Iraqi invasion made national headlines in the U.S. nine months later. The woman was Carlyle Murphy, the last remaining American newspaper reporter to leave the emirate before the Iraqi slaughter of civilians began. The headlines announced her winning the Pulitzer prize in 1991 for dispatches she wrote from Kuwait and smuggled out of the country. Cairo bureau chief for the *Washington Post*, Murphy began as a freelance reporter for the paper, writing dispatches from Angola before she was expelled by the Communist government in 1976. She subsequently became a *Post* staff member, with Virginia her beat, until she was moved back overseas to South Africa before taking over at Cairo.

Actor/Comedian Eddie Murphy.

MURPHY, EDDIE REGAN

Eddie Murphy Productions, Inc., 232 E. 63rd Street, New York, NY 10021
BORN: 1961, Brooklyn, N.Y. ACHIEVEMENTS: Grammy, Best Comedy Recording, Eddie Murphy Comedian, 1983; Golden Globe, Trading Places, 1984. STUDIED: Attended Nassau Community College.

Eddie Murphy is among the most popular comedians for the past decade, primarily due to his role as Alex Foley in the *Beverly Hills Cop* films. He began his

career as a stand-up comic at the age of 15. At 19, he was a regular on *Saturday Night Live*, and became known for characters such as Gumby, Buckwheat and Mister Robinson. At 22, he became a millionaire with the hit film *48 Hours*. His first solo-starring role was in *Beverly Hills Cop*. This film brought in three times as much money as other films released that year. Other film credits include *Another 48 Hours*, *Trading Places*, *Beverly Hills Cop 2*, *Beverly Hills Cop 3*, *Coming To America*, *Boomerang*, and *The Distinguished Gentleman*. He also created and produced the TV series *The Royal Family*, which was short-lived due to Redd Foxx's sudden death. Murphy has recorded several albums, donating part of the profits to charitable organizations through his Yeah Foundation.

MURPHY, THOMAS SAWYER

77 West 66th St., New York, NY 10023 (212) 456-7777
BORN: Brooklyn, N.Y. STUDIED: Cornell University, B.S.M.E., 1945; Harvard University, M.B.A, 1949.

Thomas Murphy was born and raised in Brooklyn, N.Y. He graduated from Cornell University in 1945 with a B.S.M.E. degree. Prior to entering Harvard University, where he earned an M.B.A. degree in 1949, Murphy served in the U.S. Armed Forces and worked for Texaco. In 1954 he joined Capital Cities Communications as general manager of their Albany, N.Y. television station. In three years Murphy became a director of Capital Cities Communications, and in 1964, president. Under Murphy's leadership, Capital Cities has undergone immense growth, entering television, radio, and print media markets nationwide. In 1985 Capital Cities announced its intent to purchase 100 percent of ABC, Inc., giving stations owned by or affiliated with Capital Cities access to one fourth of the nation's inhabitants.

MURPHY, TOM

City-County Building, 414 Grant St., Pittsburgh, PA 15219 (412) 255-2626

Murphy is a prominent political leader. For career credentials consult the portion of this book entitled "Biographees by Profession" in the Appendix. Within this portion, the list "Political Leaders" describes requirements for inclusion in this volume.

MURRAY, ALLEN E.

Mobil Corporation, 3225 Gallows Rd., Fairfax, VA 22037 (703) 846-3000

Murray is a prominent business leader. For career credentials consult the portion of this book entitled "Biographees by Profession" in the Appendix. Within this portion, the list "Business Leaders" describes requirements for inclusion in this volume.

MURRAY, BILL

Creative Artists Agency, 1888 Century Park E., Suite 1400, Los Angeles, CA 90067.

BORN: 1950, Evanston Ill. ACHIEVEMENTS: Emmy, Best Writing in a Comedy Series, Saturday Night Live, 1977. STUDIED: attended Regis College; studied comedy at Second City Workshop, Chicago.

A former pre-med student, Murray left school to join his brother in the Second City Improvisational troupe in Chicago. In 1975 he began appearing with his brother on radio in the *National Lampoon Radio Hour*, and in the off-Broadway revue, *The National Lampoon Show*. He also provided the radio voice of Johnny Storm, the Human Torch, on *Marvel Comics Fantastic Four*. ABC hired him in 1976 for *Saturday Night Live with Howard Cossell*. NBC then hired him in 1977 for *Saturday Night Live*, where he remained a cast member until 1980. In 1976 he made his film debut in *Jungle Burger*. Other major film credits include *Meatballs, Caddyshack, Stripes, Tootsie, Ghostbusters, Little Shop of Horrors*, and *Ground Hogs Day*.

MURRAY, JIM

The Los Angeles Times, Times Mirror Square, Los Angeles, CA 90012-3645 (213) 237-5000

Murray is a prominent journalist. For career credentials consult the portion of this book entitled "Biographees by Profession" in the Appendix. Within this portion, the list "Journalists" describes requirements for inclusion in this volume.

MURRAY, JOSEPH EDWARD

108 Abbott Rd., Wellesley Hills, MA 02181

Murray is a prominent physician. For career credentials consult the portion of this book entitled "Biographees by Profession" in the Appendix. Within this portion, the list "Physicians" describes requirements for inclusion in this volume.

MURRAY, PATTY

B34 Dirksen Senate Office Building, Washington, D.C. 20510-4704 (202) 224-2621

BORN: 1950, Seattle. ACHIEVEMENTS: Washington State Legislator of the Year, 1990. STUDIED: Washington State University, B.A., 1972.

Patty Murray has taken an unusual route to the U.S. Senate. She began her public service career as an activist for environmental and educational issues while serving on the Board of Directors for the Shoreline School District in the state of Washington. She was elected to the Washington State Senate in 1988, and was named Democratic Whip in 1990. In 1992 she was elected to the U.S. Senate, and serves on the Appropriations, Banking, Housing and Urban Affairs, and Budget committees.

MUSBURGER, BRENT

ABC Press Relations, 7W-7, 1330 Ave. of the Americas, New York, NY 10019

BORN: 1939. ACHIEVEMENTS: 16-time Super Bowl coverage participant. STUDIED: Northwestern University, Medill School of Journalism.

One of the top all-around sports broadcasters, Brent Musburger joined ABC Sports in May 1990. He does play-by-play for both college basketball and football, and he hosts the halftime report for *ABC's Monday Night Football*, and golf coverage. Before joining ABC, Musburger was at CBS Sports since 1975. While there, he hosted *The NFL Today*. Musburger's wide-ranging abilities also included lead play-by-play announcer for the NCAA Final Four Basketball Tournament, host of the NBA Finals, the Masters Golf Tournament, the U.S Open Tennis Championships, and *CBS Sports Saturday/Sunday*. He also hosted many special events, such as the Super Bowl and the Pan American Games. Musburger started his career as a sports writer for the *Chicago American*. He then joined WBBM Radio Chicago as sports director and eventually was given the same job at WBBM-TV.

MUSGRAVE, RICHARD ABEL

Crown College, University of California at Santa Cruz, Santa Cruz, CA. 95064

BORN: 1910, Koenigstein (Germany). ACHIEVEMENTS: Developer, Theory of Public Finance. STUDIED: University of Heidelberg, diploma; Harvard University, M.A., Ph.D., economics.

An emigre from Nazi Germany in 1933, Musgrove studied at Harvard and remained on the faculty after earning a doctorate. Among his achievements was providing the most complete text that incorporates public finance into economic theory as a whole. The text was published in 1959 as The Theory of Public Finance.

NAEF, DERICK

Group Technologies Corporation, 10901 McKinley Dr., Tampa, FL 33612 (813) 972-6000

ACHIEVEMENTS: Developed "Aspects" a document conferencing system. Aspects, a hybrid of the conference call and electronic mail, enables several users connected to a Macintosh computer network to work together on the same project, be it a document, design, or painting. Each user's input is immediately transmitted to all other users' screens, eliminating costly conference calls, travel, organized meetings, and overloads of electronic mail.

NAGLE, JAMES L.

Nagle Hartray and Associates, 230 E. Ohio Street, Chicago, IL 60602 (312) 266-2800

BORN: 1937. ACHIEVEMENTS: Henry Adams Award, AIA; Fulbright Traveling Fellowship; notable works: City Houses, Chicago; Cook Residence, Minneapolis; Oaks Housing Remodeling, Oak Park, Ill. STUDIED: Stanford University.

His projects range from minor institutional remodelings to full-scale commercial and residential high-rises. Critics maintain they betray the cool eye and steady hand of a builder, as well as portray a sublime vision of a sculptor and veteran civic planner. His recent projects included the design of a dormitory complex for Illinois' Northwestern University, and the renovation of the University of Chicago's School of Business, but his clean, functional approach is best seen in his recent commercial mid-rise on Chicago's Lake Shore Drive. Its strong rectilinear symmetry, simple masonry construction, atrium core and bay windows strongly recall the solid, utilitarian efforts of the first Chicago school.

NAGRIN, DANIEL

208 East 14th St., Tempe, AZ 85281 (602) 968-4063

BORN: 1917, New York City. ACHIEVEMENTS: Notable ballets: Strange Hero; Man of Action; Indeterminate Figure; Jazz, Three Ways; A Dancer Prepares; Volpone; The Peloponnesian War; Dance Portraits, and several Broadway musicals. STUDIED: City College of New York, B.S., education, ca 1939; Helen Tamaris, Hanya Holm, Martha Graham, Anna Sololow schools.

A jazz-oriented style filled with sinewy energy characterizes Nagrin's dancing, as it does his choreography. Many of his solo works emphasize social commentary, such as the glorification of the gangster type in *Strange Hero* and the ironic *Man of Action*, in which the busy principle gets nowhere. His work has also explored expositions of modern dance in *Jazz, Three Ways, Spanish Dance, Dance in the Sun,* and *A Dancer Prepares,* a program he has collected under the title *Dance Portraits,* and has shown across the country.

NAISBITT, JOHN

c/o Megatrends Ltd., 1901 Pennsylvania Ave., NW, Suite 500, Washington, D.C. 20006

BORN: 1929. ACHIEVEMENTS: Author, Megatrends.

One-time special assistant to the U.S. Commissioner of Education and aide to the U.S. Secretary of Health, Education, and Welfare, Naisbitt is most known as a trend spotter. *Megatrends, Megatrends 2000,* and *Megatrends for Women* are three of the eight books he has written since 1970. He also is president of the Naisbitt Group, a publisher of periodicals which include *Trend Report, Bellwether Report, John Naisbitt's Trend Letter,* and the *60-Year Ahead* annual. In 1975 he established the Center for Policy Research in Washington, D.C.

NALDER, ERIC

The Seattle Times, Box 70, Fairvica Ave., Seattle WA 09111 (206) 464-2111

BORN: 1946, Coulee Dam, Wash. ACHIEVEMENTS: Pulitzer Prize; Investigative Reporters and Editors Book Award; Thomas Stokes Award; Associated Press Managing Editors Award, the Goldsmith Prize, Worth Bingham Prize, Headliner Award, Investigative Reporters and Editors Award for investigation of U.S. Sen. Brock Adams; Associated Press Sports Editor Award; Sigma Delta Chi Distinguished Service Award, among more than 40 journalism awards. STUDIED: University of Washington, B.A.

The chief investigative reporter for *The Seattle Times,* Nalder has lived abroad in such varied places as Norway, Lebanon, and Afghanistan. In addition to being a frequent speaker, his notable journalistic work includes *Tankers Full of Trouble,* a book reporting one the Exxon oil spill. The book received the 1995 Investigative Reporters and Editors Award, the second award he garnered for his investigation of tankers. The first award was a share in the Pulitzer Prize in 1990 for his reporting on the spill for his paper. He has also investigated nuclear weapons plants, environmental dangers, and University of Washington football infractions. Before joining *The Times,* he was employed by the *Seattle Post-Intelligencer* and the *Everett* (Wash.) *Herald.*

NATHANS, DANIEL

2227 Crest Ave., Baltimore, MD 21209

BORN: 1928, Wilmington, Del. ACHIEVEMENTS: Nobel Prize in Physiology or Medicine (shared with Hamilton Othanel Smith, U.S., and Werner Arber, Switzerland), 1978; Guggenheim Fellow. STUDIED: University of California; Washington University, St. Louis.

Nathans and Hamilton Smith, working cooperatively—and progressing as a result of work done earlier by the Swiss researcher Werner Arber—developed enzymes that can be used to study genetic organization and to manipulate DNA for genetic engineering. The enzymes, or "chemical knives," can cut certain DNA chains carrying viruses, perhaps, thus curbing their activity. Nathans also described a DNA technique, later to be the subject of much controversy about the future role of genetic engineering. Smith purified and characterized the first "chemical knife" from a form of influenza, and applied the knife in experiments.

NEDERLANDER, JAMES

1564 Broadway, New York, NY 10036 (212) 765-3906

Nederlander is a prominent dramatic artist. For career credentials consult the portion of this book entitled

"Biographees by Profession" in the Appendix. Within this portion the list "Dramatic Artists" describes requirements for inclusion in this volume.

NELSON, CRAIG T.

Writers' and Artists' Agency, #300, 11726 San Vincente Blvd., Los Angeles, CA 90049.
BORN: 1946, Spokane, Wash. ACHIEVEMENTS: Emmy Award, Best Actor, Comedy Series, Coach, 1991-92. STUDIED: Attended University of Arizona; studied at Oxford Theatre, Los Angeles.
Before his acting career, Nelson was a security guard, a security analyst, and made appearances in local television advertising. He wrote comedy for *The Tim Conway Comedy Hour* and *The John Byner Comedy Hour*, both in the early 1970s. Nelson appeared in many movies, both on film and television, including *And Justice for All*, in 1979, *Private Benjamin*, in 1980, *Stir Crazy*, 1981, *Poltergeist*, 1982, *All the Right Moves*, 1983, *The Killing Fields*, 1984, *Poltergeist Two*, 1986, and *Turner and Hooch*, 1989. Nelson is best know for his role, Hayden Fox, a male chauvinistic, insensitive college football coach in the television series *Coach*, which he has been playing since 1989.

NELSON, E. BENJAMIN

P. O. Box 94848, Lincoln, NE 68509 (402) 471-2244
BORN: 1941, McCook, Neb. ACHIEVEMENTS: Governor of Nebraska, Schrader-Nelson award, Insurance Regulatory Examiners Society. STUDIED: University of Nebraska, logic, philosophy, and law.
A lifelong Nebraskan, Nelson began his law practice in 1970. He was named general counsel, president, and chief executive officer for a national insurance group, was executive vice president of the National Association of Insurance Commissioners, and was Nebraska's director of insurance. In 1985 Nelson joined the law firm of Kennedy, Holland, DeLacy & Svoboda, as attorney-of-counsel. Nelson was elected the 37th governor of Nebraska in November, 1990. His priorities have been education, the environment, and economic development. Nelson has controlled the budget by instituting plans to make government more efficient and effective. He proposed a state lottery to raise funds for the Governor's Environmental Trust Fund, used to finance for environmental projects. Nelson was re-elected to a second term as governor in November, 1994.

NEUWIRTH, BEBE

NBC, 30 Rockefeller Plaza, New York, NY 10112
Neuwirth is a prominent actor. For career credentials consult the portion of this book entitled "Biographees by Profession" in the Appendix. Within this portion the list "Actors" describes requirements for inclusion in this volume.

NEVILLE, PHOEBE

Phoebe Neville Dance Company, 12 St. John St., New York, NY 10038

BORN: 1941, Philadelphia. ACHIEVEMENTS: Notable ballets: Untitled Duet; Memory; Triptych; Passage in Silence; Cartouche; Ladydance. STUDIED: City College of New York; Joyce Trisler, Daniel Nagrin schools.
Phoebe Neville earned her stripes as a dancer with the Tamaris-Nagrin Company, where her first tentative steps in choreography were taken. She traveled on to Studio Nine and then to the Judson Dance Theater, slowly fashioning what would become her contribution to ballets-mall, careful pieces that could be called "ballet miniatures," influenced by her study of the stylized, meditative Chinese exercise regimen tai-chi chuan. She has deliberately maintained that pace throughout her career, refusing to show her works until she felt they were perfect. Her *Memory* is a construct in seven parts, each illuminated by a flame carried by the dancer, the most unusual and intimate work she has done.

NEWHART, BOB

David Cappel, Suite 1240, 2121 Avenue of the Stars, Los Angeles, CA 90067
BORN: 1929, Oak Park, Ill. ACHIEVEMENTS: Emmy Award, Outstanding Lead Actor in a Musical/Comedy Series, The Bob Newhart Show, 1961; Grammy Award, Best Comedy Performance (Spoken Word), The Button-Down Mind Strikes Back, 1962. STUDIED: Loyola University, B.A., 1952.
An actor and comedian, Newhart is best remembered for his dry, straight-faced brand of humor. In the early 1960s he won an Emmy for his series *The Bob Newhart Show* and a Grammy for his comedy recording *The Button-Down Mind Strikes Back*. Newhart has four television series to his credit, beginning with *The Bob Newhart Show*, 1961-62, then *The Entertainers*, 1964, *The Bob Newhart Show*, 1972-78, and finally *Newhart*, 1982-90. In between his weekly television appearances, Newhart found time to appear in a number of films, including *Hell Is for Heroes*, 1962, *Hot Millions*, 1968, *Catch-22*, 1970, *On A Clear Day You Can See Forever*, 1970, and *Little Miss Marker*, 1980.

NEWMAN, PAUL

Creative Artists, 1888 Century Park East, Los Angeles, CA 90067
BORN: 1925, Shaker Heights, Ohio ACHIEVEMENTS: Golden Globe Award, World Film Favorite, Male, Hud, 1967. STUDIED: Kenyon College, B.A., 1949; attended Yale University School of Drama, 1951.
Paul Newman appeared on Broadway in the stage production of *Picnic* in 1953. His first principal film appearance was in *The Silver Chalice*, in 1955, but he didn't achieve stardom until he appeared in *The Long Hot Summer* and *Cat on a Hot Tin Roof*, both in 1958. He went on to star in a number of "tough guy" roles, including *The Hustler*, 1961, *Hud*, 1963, *Cool Hand Luke*, 1967, *Butch Cassidy and the Sundance Kid*, 1969, *The Sting*, 1973, and *The Color of Money*, 1986. Newman is married to actress Joanne Woodward and spends his spare time as a professional race car driver. He is also an advocate of the antinuclear movement and child welfare issues.

NEWMAN, RANDY

Renaissance Management Corporation, 21241 Ventura Blvd., Suite 251, Woodland Hills, CA 91364
BORN: 1943, Los Angeles. ACHIEVEMENTS: Grammy, Best Instrumental Compositions, 1984. STUDIED: Graduated from the University of California.

In 1961 Randy Newman made his first attempt as a singer with the single *Golden Gridiron Boy*, produced by Pat Boone. The song went nowhere, but he went on to become a successful songwriter, writing songs for the Fleetwood, Jerry Butler, Cilla Black, Judy Collins, Manfred Mann, Nilsson, and Three Dog Night, among others. As he developed artistically, Newman used a blend of seductive melodies and styles to lure listeners into the unusual mind sets of the people who populate his songs. His 1978 tongue-in-cheek single *Short People* was thought mean-spirited by many. Even his fans began to worry about the literalness of his sentiments in the 1979 album *Born Again*, because of the way in which Newman mercilessly skewered each of the protagonists in his songs. In 1981, he began a successful career in film, scoring with the movie *Ragtime*, but not at the expense of an occasional new album. Titles include *Paper* and *Maverick*, produced in 1994; *Parenthood*, 1989; *Trouble in Paradise* and *I Love L.A.*, produced in 1983; and *Little Criminals*, 1977. Newman is a nephew of Lionel Newman and Alfred Newman, Hollywood composers and arrangers.

NEWMAN, ROSALIND

Rosalind Newman and Dancers, 124 Chambers St., New York NY 10007 (212) 962-1327
BORN: 1946, Brooklyn, N.Y. ACHIEVEMENTS: NEA grant; notable ballets: 4: Stories, Parts I, II, and III; Moorings; Juanita; Map: In a Green Place; Modern Dance; Free Speech; Mirror Lake; Heartbeat. STUDIED: University of Wisconsin at Madison; Connecticut College School of Dance; Martha Graham, Merce Cunningham, Dan Wagoner, Viola Farber, and a variety of ballet teachers.

The second generation of her family to become a dancer and choreographer, Newman performed for Viola Farber, one of her teachers who had formed her own company. In 1972 she presented her first dance, *Anne and Susanne*, and three years later formed her own company, for which she has created many works. Her company won several awards, including a National Endowment for the Arts grant for herself, and for Rosalind Newman and Dancers. Her popular dances showcase her ability to use props and to raise commonplace movements to the level of art.

NICHOLS, MIKE

International Creative Management, 40 West 57th St., New York, NY 10019
Nichols is a prominent producer and director. He began his career in the early 1950s as an announcer at Chicago radio station WFMT, one of the first classical-format radio stations on the FM dial. Eventually he tried out for the Second City Players—now a nationally famous theater company that discovered many comedic talents—and earned a position in the cast. Soon after, he teamed with Elaine May as a nightclub comedy duo. The two achieved fame on national television as well. His most acclaimed production is the 1967 film *The Graduate*, for which he won an academy award for best director. Today he is considered one of nation's most acclaimed film-makers.

NICHOLSON, JACK

Bresler, Kelley, and Associates, 15760 Ventura Blvd., 1730, Encino, CA 91436
BORN: Neptune, N.J., 1937 ACHIEVEMENTS: Academy Award, Best Actor, 1975; Best Supporting Actor, 1983.

Today a prominent actor, Nicholson played roles in Hollywood's B- movies during most of the 1960s. His first major role was in the 1971 film *Five Easy Pieces* in which he played opposite Karen Black. Has been cited for numerous motion picture achievements including two Academy Awards—for the lead role in *One Few over the Cuckoos Nest* in 1975 and for Best Supporting Actor in *Terms of Endearment* in 1983.

NIKOLAIS, ALWIN

Nikolais and Murray Louis Dance, 276 Riverside Dr., New York, NY 10025 (212) 662-7256
Nikolais is a prominent dancer. For career credentials consult the portion of this book entitled "Biographees by Profession" in the Appendix. Within this portion the list "Dancers" describes requirements for inclusion in this volume.

NISKANEN, WILLIAM A.

Cato Institute, 1000 Massachusetts Ave., Washington, D.C. 20001
BORN: 1933, Bend, Ore. ACHIEVEMENTS: Member, Council of Economic Advisers; Office of Management and Budget; Institute for Defense Analysis; Office of Secretary of Defense; and the Rand Corporation. Outstanding works include, Bureaucracy and Representative Government, Bureaucracy: Servant or Master? Lessons from America, and Structural Reform of the Federal Budget Process. STUDIED: Harvard, University of Chicago.

Two issues concern Niskanen: bureaucracies and budgeting. He maintains that bureaucracies need to be reduced, or privatized, and they should use profit-like incentives and internal competition to improve their efficiency. The federal budget, he maintains, grows too fast and includes many programs benefiting only small sectors of the economy. At the beginning of his career, Niskanen held established beliefs, including the simplistic view of the technocrats of the time: that efficiency could be achieved by placing qualified, hard-working people in places of power. In 1971, after eight years at the Pentagon, a hardened Niskanen published *Bureaucracy and Representative Government*, a theory of the behavior of bureaus, in which he points out that usually two, and often three, services spend parts of their budgets on the same military missions. After a second book on the subject, *Bureaucracy, Servant or Master? Lessons from America*, Niskanen turned his attention to the budget process. and was often criticaly of it.. He has since lectured in Tokyo on the growth of government due to increases in the costs of government services, a rise in the U.S. population, and an increase in the per capita gross national income.

NOLAND, KENNETH C.

South Salem, NY 10590
BORN: 1924. ACHIEVEMENTS: Collections: Museum of Modern Art; Metropolitan Museum of Art ; exhibitions: Solomon R. Guggenheim Museum; Metropolitan Museum of Art. STUDIED: Black Mountain College; Zadkine School of Sculpture, Paris
In the early 1950s Noland was introduced to Helen Frankenthaler's method of staining unprimed canvases with acrylic. With this technique he developed a geometric coloristic style. In the next decade, he presented in his works motifs such as circular or ellipsoid rings, and later, chevrons and targets. He first exhibited with the Minimalist group called The Washington Color Painters in 1965. Colors were sometimes juxtaposed with areas of raw canvas, or with other colored forms, creating an ambiguity between image and ground. His work moved from symmetry to asymmetry; from motifs to mere bands of color. Later experiments with shaped canvases and vertical and horizontal stripes ("plaids") led to the use of diagonals to create irregular compositions involving the space outside of the paintings.

NORICK, RONALD J.

Office of the Mayor, Oklahoma City, Okla. 200 N. Walker, Oklahoma City OK 73120.
BORN: 1941, Oklahoma City, Okla. ACHIEVEMENTS: president of Norick Brothers, Inc.; President of the United Satellite Antenna Television Corp. STUDIED: Oklahoma City University, B.S.
A lifelong resident and businessman in Oklahoma City, Ronald Norick was elected mayor in 1987. Now, a national figure as a result of the 1995 bombing of the city's federal building, he is attempting to rebuild a sense of security in his shaken community.

NORMAN, MARSHA

Tantleff Agency, 375 Greenwich St., New York, NY
BORN: 1947, Louisville, Ky. ACHIEVEMENTS: Pulitzer Prize, 'Night Mother, 1983; Antoinette Perry Award, Best Book Made into a Musical, The Secret Garden, 1991. STUDIED: Agnes Scott College, B.A., 1969; University of Louisville, M.A., 1971.
Marsha Norman's early work with disturbed children at the Kentucky Central State Hospital, from 1969 to 1971, influenced her plays in which her characters search for the true nature of their inner selves. Her drama 'Night Mother, 1983, about a woman's decision to commit suicide, won a Pulitzer Prize, and The Secret Garden, 1991, won a Tony Award. Her other plays include Getting Out, 1978; The Holdup, 1983; and Traveler in the Dark, 1990.

NORQUIST, JOHN O.

City Hall, 200 E. Wells Street, Milwaukee, WI 53202 (414) 286-2200
BORN: 1949. ACHIEVEMENTS: Mayor, Milwaukee, Wisc; chairman, National League of Cities Task Force on Federal Policy and Family Poverty. STUDIED: University of Wisconsin, B.A., M.A.
From 1971 to 1977, John Norquist served in the Army Reserves. He was elected to the Wisconsin State Legislature as both a state assemblyman and a state senator, representing Milwaukee's south and west sides. While serving in the state legislature he was elected to Democratic leadership positions in both the state Senate and the Assembly. Norquist was elected mayor of Milwaukee in 1988 and was re-elected in 1992. As mayor, Norquist has focused on streamlining city government, fighting crime, and creating new jobs. He has won recognition for his role in promoting a reduction in the cost of government.

NORTH, DOUGLASS C.

Washington University, Department of Economics, Box 1203, St. Louis, MO 63130
BORN: 1920, Cambridge, Mass. ACHIEVEMENTS: Nobel Prize in Economic Science (with Robert W. Fogel), 1993; Director of the Institute of Economic Research; co-editor Journal of Economic History; president, Economic History Association and the Western Economic Association, visiting director of the Centre de Recherche Historique at the Ecole Practique des Hautes Etudes in Paris. STUDIED: University of California, Berkeley.
Douglass North is a leader in the "new wave" of economic historians, who bring the tools of statistical and mathematical techniques (econometrics) to bear on problems of American history. After writing three books exploring the theory of property rights, economic growth in the U.S. from 1790 to 1860, and welfare in the American past, he broadened his reach in 1971 with The Rise of the Western World: A New Economic History, with R.P. Thomas. The oft-maligned book won North much attention and helped lead him to a Nobel Prize in 1993, which he shared with Robert W. Fogel. In The Rise of the Western World, North views the centuries 1600 to 1900 in a new perspective. Economic history, including Marxist dogma, holds that under feudalism, serfs worked as slaves to the lord of the manor, contributing free a number of days of labor and production each week to his table and needs. One of the many applications of North's ideas in his opus is that the feudal system worked instead to benefit the serfs, who exchanged their labor to gain their lord's protection of life and property when law and order were nonexistent. Thus the transition of society to capitalism led to the rise of national states and the development of laws establishing property rights in both human and physical assets. His contrarian view of economic history in The Rise of the Western World overall presents a broad survey of western economic history from the early phases of the Stone Age to the present.

NOVAK, ROBERT D.

The Chicago Sun Times, 401 N. Wabash, Chicago IL 60611-3593 (312) 321-3000.
BORN: 1931, Joliet Ill. ACHIEVEMENTS: Author (with Rowland Evans) Lyndon Johnson: The Exercise of Power, 1966, Nixon in the White House: The Frustration of Power, 1971, The Reagan Revolution, 1981. STUDIED: University of Illinois, B.A., English, 1952.
Robert Novak spent two years in the Army right out of college before beginning his career as a reporter at his hometown *Joliet Herald-News*. In 1958 he joined *The Wall Street Journal*, becoming their chief Congressional correspondent in 1961. In 1963 he teamed up with Rowland Evans on their column *Inside Report* and on their CNN interview show *Evans and Novak*. He can also be seen as a panelist on *Capital Gang*, of which he is also co-executive producer. Together with Evans, he has authored several books detailing American political history from Lyndon Johnson to Ronald Reagan.

NUGENT, NELLE

1501 Broadway, New York, NY 10036
Nugent is a prominent dramatic artist. For career credentials consult the portion of this book entitled "Biographees by Profession" in the Appendix. Within this portion the list "Dramatic Artists" describes requirements for inclusion in this volume.

NUNN, SAMUEL AUGUSTUS JR.

SD-303 Dirksen Bldg., Washington, D.C. 20510-1001 (202) 224-3521
BORN: 1938, Perry, Ga. ACHIEVEMENTS: Haiti mediation mission, 1994. STUDIED: Emory University, A.B., 1960; Emory University, L.L.B., 1962.
As the chairman of the Senate Armed Services Committee, it should come as no surprise that Sam Nunn, a traditional conservative Democrat, has been a steady supporter of defense spending. He is credited for salvaging from proposed budget cutbacks many high-tech weapons, among them the Stealth bomber. He was elected as a member of the House of Representatives in his home state in 1968 and entered the Senate in 1972, becoming so recognizably popular that he ran unopposed in 1994. In that same year he accompanied former President Jimmy Carter on the Haiti mediation mission, meeting with the ruling junta and forging an agreement for the junta to relinquish power.

NYREN, NEIL S.

G.P. Putnam's Sons, 200 Madison Ave., New York, NY, 10016 (212) 951-8400
BORN: Boston. ACHIEVEMENTS: Editor-in-chief, G.P. Putnam's Sons. STUDIED: Brandeis University, B.A.
Nyren is vice president, publisher and editor-in-chief of G.P. Putnam's Sons. He came to Putnam as senior editor in 1984. In 1986, he was named vice president and editor-in-chief; in 1989, he became publisher. Before Putnam, he was executive editor at Atheneum Publishers. He also held various positions in the publishing field with Random House, Arbour House, Little Brown and E.P. Dutton. At Putnam, Nyren has worked with authors such as Tom Clancy, Charles Kuralt, W.E.B. Griffin, Andy Rooney, Linda Ellerbee, James A. Baker, Pat Riley, and Larry King.

OBATA, GYO

Hellmuth, Obata & Kassabaum, Inc., 1831 Chestnut Street ,St. Louis, MO 63103 (314) 421-2000
BORN: 1923. ACHIEVEMENTS: General Services Administration Honor Award; Urban Land Institute Award; Society of American Registered Architects Distinguish Building Award; Twenty-Five-Year Award, Construction Products Manufacturer's Council; notable works: St. Louis Union Station, St. Louis; Levi's Plaza, San Francisco; National Air and Space Museum, Washington, D.C.; The Galleria, Dallas. STUDIED: Washington University; Cranbrook Academy of Art.
Gyo Obata is purported to design from the inside out. He is influenced by the micro-to-macro approach of Eliel Saarinen, and aiming to enhance the lives of the people who work and live in his designs. He frequently emphasizes natural lighting, using glass to form atriums and skylights, and then stressing the interplay between strong architectural forms and light. His instructor, Eliel Saarinen, used to say, "First you design a chair, then you design a room, then you design a house, then you design a street, then you design a city. You always ask, what's the next relationship?" By this standard, the ultimate test of a building is how it relates to its users and surroundings. His National Air and Space Museum on the Mall in Washington, D.C. is the world's most popular museum, having received more than 100 million visitors since its opening in 1976. Impressive without overwhelming either its neighbors or its exhibits, it features huge display bays, glass fronts and skylights which open the museum to the Mall. Inside, suspended aircraft are seen against the natural backdrop of open sky. *Smithsonian* magazine said of it, "Thirty years in the planning, four years in the building, the National Air and Space Museum can possibly be called the finest building of its kind ever erected. It is pretty safe to call it unique. And there is no quibble with calling it extraordinary" describes requirements for inclusion in this volume.

OBERNDORF, MEYERA E.

5404 Challedon Dr., Virginia Beach, VA 23462 (804) 427-4581
ACHIEVEMENTS: President-elect, Virginia Municipal League; member, National League of Cities Advisory Board, U.S. Conference of Mayors, Virginia Transportation Board, American Association of University Women; 1994 "Woman of the Year," Hampton Roads Business Community. STUDIED: Old Dominion University, B.S., elementary education.
Meyera Oberndorf's election to the city council on an independent ticket in 1976 marked a milestone in Virginia Beach history: the first woman to hold public office in the state's largest city. After two more terms, she became vice mayor in 1986 and mayor in 1988, winning a second term in 1992. Her strongest emphasis as mayor has been on economic development and— as the wife of 27 years to a U.S. Coast Guard captain—in furthering the city's ties to local naval air stations.

OBEY, DAVID R.

2462 Rayburn Bldg., Washington D.C. 20515-4907
(202) 225-3365
BORN: 1938; Okmulgee, Okla. ACHIEVEMENTS: Co-edited, with Senator Paul Sarbanes, The Changing American Economy; chairman, House Appropriations Committee. STUDIED: University of Wisconsin, B.S. Political Science, 1960, M.A., 1962.
While maintaining a successful career as a real estate broker David Obey also served in the Wisconsin Assembly from 1963 until 1969, before voters elected him to represent the 7th Congressional District in the House of Representatives. Obey has been continuously re-elected ever since. He has the distinction of being the only House member to serve on each of the three major Congressional committees on economics: the Budget Committee, the Joint Economic Committee and the Appropriations Committee. Obey has won the adoption of 20 amendments strengthening health services and has won awards for his work in both health and education.

O'BRIEN, CONAN

NBC Rockefeller Plaza, New York, NY 10038
BORN: 1963, Brookline, Mass. ACHIEVEMENTS: Emmy, Best Writing in a Variety or Music Program, Murders Among Us, 1989. STUDIED: Harvard University.
During college Conan O'Brien was the president of *The Harvard Lampoon* for two years, the first person to serve that long since Robert Benchley in 1912. He made his television debut in 1985 on the show *Not Necessarily the News*, and has written for *Saturday Night Live* and *The Simpsons*. O'Brien made his television producing debut in 1991 with *Lookwell*, a sitcom pilot starring Adam West as a television detective who becomes a real-life detective. In 1992 he replaced David Letterman as host of the *Late Night* show. The show was renamed *NBC's Late Night with Conan O'Brien*.

OCEAN, BILLY

Jive Records, 1348 Lexington Ave., New York, NY 10128 (212) 410-4774
BORN: 1950, (Trinidad) ACHIEVEMENTS: Grammy, Best R&B Vocal-Male, Caribbean Queen (No More Love on the Run), 1984.
Billy Ocean was popular in the United Kingdom for nearly 10 years before he received widespread recognition in the U.S. Born in Trinidad, Ocean immigrated to the U.K. as a young boy. In the 1960s, Ocean, a tailor by profession, pursued music in his off hours. In 1976, he scored his first big hit in the U.K., *Love Really Hurts Without You.* He continued to develop his popularity in the U.K. through the late 70s and early 80s, finally achieving mass appeal in the U.S. in 1984 with his number-one hit, *Caribbean Queen (No More Love on the Run).*

O'CONNOR, CARDINAL JOHN JOSEPH

Archbishop of New York, 1st Ave., New York, NY 10002
BORN: 1920, Philadelphia. STUDIED: St. Charles College, B.A., M.A.; Catholic University, Ph.D., religion; Georgetown University, Ph.D., religion; Villanova University, D.R.E., religion.
The conservative and influential archbishop of New York City, John O'Connor, spent 27 years as a U.S. Navy chaplain, serving in both the Atlantic and Pacific fleets, before retiring as a rear admiral and chief of chaplains in 1979. For the next four years he served as auxiliary bishop of New York, then as bishop of Scranton, Pa. Named archbishop of New York in 1984, he became a cardinal the next year. He has severely reprimanded politicians who are "prochoice" on the issue of abortion.

O'CONNOR, SANDRA DAY

Supreme Court of the United States, One First St. N.E., Washington, D.C. 20543 (202) 479-3000
BORN: 1930, El Paso, Texas. ACHIEVEMENTS: Associate justice, U.S. Supreme Court; senate majority leader, Arizona Senate, 1972. STUDIED: Stanford University, B.A., 1950, magna cum laude; Stanford University, LL.B., 1952.
O'Connor, the first woman supreme court justice, was assistant attorney general for the state of Arizona from 1965 through 1969. In 1969, she was appointed an Arizona senator. She was subsequently re-elected to two consecutive terms, and was senate majority leader in 1972. She married John Jay O'Connor III, in 1952, and is the mother of three sons. She was nominated as associate justice, U.S. Supreme Court in 1981 by President Ronald Reagan.

OLDENBURG, CLAUS THURE

556 Broome St., New York, NY 10013
BORN: 1929. ACHIEVEMENTS: Collections: Museum of Modern Art; Whitney Museum of American Art; exhibitions: Metropolitan Museum of Art; Museum of Modern Art. STUDIED: Yale University School of Art; School of the Art Institute of Chicago
Born in Sweden, Claus Oldenburg's early life was spent shuttling between America and Scandanavia. By the time he moved to New York in 1956, he rendered his figurative works with a loose brush stroke. Four years later he was involved with a group of artists, including Jim Dine, who started a new kind of participatory art called "happenings" describes requirements for inclusion in this volume. During the next decade, numerous happenings, with crude costumes, cardboard props, all kinds of objects, and crowds of people were his media. Later he imitated Pop Art by painting and selling plaster replicas of food and other merchandize. Monumental stitched pieces in soft vinyl or canvas and stuffed with kapok, such as *Soft Toilet*, are collapsible objects which rely on gravity and chance for their ultimate shape. The similarity of these pieces to human forms serves to lessen their potential irony, for this artist's main goal is to delight the senses.

O'LEARY, HAZEL R.

Department of Energy, 1000 Independence Ave. SW, Washington, D.C. 20585 (202) 586-6210

O'Leary is a prominent political leader. For career credentials consult the portion of this book entitled "Biographees by Profession" in the Appendix. Within this portion the list "Political Leaders" describes requirements for inclusion in this volume.

OLENDORF, BILL

9 E. Ontario, Chicago, IL 60610

BORN: Chicago, Ill., 1924. ACHIEVEMENTS: Grant, Rockefeller Foundation; Collections include: Tiffany & Co.; Vincent Price Collection, J.D. McArthur Collection: The Art Institute of Chicago; Galerie Marcelle Bernheim, Paris, the White House. STUDIED: Harvard University; School of the Art Institute of Chicago, Washington and Lee University.

Oil paintings and prints of European and American urban landscapes make up the majority of subjects in Olendorf's work. Paris rooftops, Spanish villages, and urban America ared depicted in his medium-to-large scale oil-on-canvas paintings and prints. The representational landscapes are executed in a painterly impressionistic vein. Olendorf describes his style as "realism without being naturalistic." His prints of Chicago's LaSalle Street, Wall Street in New York and London's financial district have been popular among the financial communities of the world. Olendorf has penned several sketchbooks, including the *Chicago* Sketchbook and the *Paris Sketchbook*. Other notable works are in the White House Collection including his portraits of Presidents Nixon, Reagan, Bush and Clinton.

Artist Bill Olendorf.

OLMOS, EDWARD JAMES

Artists' Agency, Suite 305, 10000 Santa Monica Blvd., Los Angeles, CA 90067.

BORN: 1947, East Los Angeles ACHIEVEMENTS: Emmy Award, Best Supporting Actor in a Drama Series, Miami Vice, 1985. STUDIED: East Los Angeles City College, A.A; attended California State University, Los Angeles.

Before becoming an actor, Edward Olmos founded and performed in the rock band Eddie James and the Pacific Coast. He gained a certain measure of fame playing the part of El Pachuco, first in the stage production of *Zoot Suit*, from 1978 to 1979, and then in the film of the same name, in 1981. Olmos also appeared in the films *Aloha Bobby and Rose*, 1975, *Virus*, 1980, *Wolfen*, 1981, *Blade Runner*, 1982, *The Ballad of Gregorio Cortez*, 1983, *Saving Grace*, 1986, and *Stand and Deliver*, 1988. Besides playing the starring role, Olmos also helped produce both *The Ballad of Gregorio Cortez* and *Stand and Deliver*. Olmos is probably best remembered as Lt. Martin Castillo, in the television series *Miami Vice*.

OLSEN, KENNETH HARRY

Digital Equipment Corporation, 40 Old Bolton Rd., Stow, ME 01775

BORN: 1926, Bridgeport, Conn. ACHIEVEMENTS: Founder, Digital Equipment Corp. STUDIED: Massachusetts Institute of Technology, B.A., engineering, M.S., electrical engineering.

Olsen, the founder of Digital Equipment Corp., contributed to the development of two early computers, the WHIRLWIND in 1950 and SAGE in 1957. He also supervised the building of transistorized computers including TXO, TX2, and VAX. Under his leadership Digital grew into one of the largest computer manufacturers in the world. Olsen left the company during the 1980s.

O'NEILL, LT. GEN. MALCOLM R.

Ballistic Missile Defense Organization, Pentagon, Washington, D.C., 20301 (703) 697-4040

BORN: March 25, 1940, Chicago. ACHIEVEMENTS: Defense Distinguished Service Medal; Defense Superior Service Medal; Bronze Star Medal with "V" device with 3 oak leaf clusters; Purple Heart with oak leaf cluster; Meritorious Service Medal. STUDIED: Rice University, Ph.D. and M.A., physics; graduated DePaul University, B.S., physics.

Currently the director of the Ballistic Missile Defense Organization, since November 1993, Lt. Gen. Malcolm O'Neill began his military career with the 1st Airborne Battle Group, 187th Infantry. From 1965 to 1966, he served as an advisor in Vietnam. He has also served as a senior instructor, Ammunition Service Maintenance and aide-de-camp to the commanding general at the Redstone Arsenal, Alabama from 1966 to 1967. McCaffrey was assigned as assistant chief of staff, United States Army Support Command, Vietnam, from 1970 to 1971. From January 1977 to June 1980, he was research and development program manager for the Strategic Technology Directorate. During this time he rose through the ranks of major and lieutenant colonel. He also has been a student of several Army training schools.

O'REILLY, ANTHONY F.J.

H.J. Heinz Company, 600 Grant St., Pittsburgh, PA 15219 (412) 456-5700
O'Reilly is a prominent business leader. For career credentials consult the portion of this book entitled "Biographees by Profession" in the Appendix. Within this portion the list "Business Leaders" describes requirements for inclusion in this volume.

O'ROURKE, P. J.

The Atlantic Monthly, 8 Arlington St., Boston MA 02116 (617) 536-9500.
BORN: 1947, Toledo, Ohio ACHIEVEMENTS: Author Give War a Chance, 1992. STUDIED: Miami University, B.A., English, 1970; Johns Hopkins, M.A., English, 1970.
P. J. O'Rourke began his career right out of college as an editor for Harry in 1971 and became feature editor of The Herald in 1972. In 1973 he joined The National Lampoon where he rose from associate editor, to managing editor, to editor-in-chief, a position he held from 1975 until 1981. Rolling Stone snagged him in 1981, and in 1995 he joined The Atlantic Monthly. While he is most known for his irreverent humor, he has also reported on some of the more tragic political stories of his time, including wars in Yugoslavia and Somalia.

OSBORNE, BURL

Dallas Morning News, #655237, Communications Center, Dallas, TX 75265 (214) 977-8222
ACHIEVEMENTS: Publisher and editor of the Dallas Morning News; board member, Associated Press. STUDIED: Marshall University, B.A., journalism; Long Island University, M.A., business.
Burl Osborne began his journalism career soon after college, when he took a position with the Associated Press wire service as a correspondent in Bluefield, W.Va. In 1980, after 20 years of working his way through the ranks to the position of managing editor, based in New York City, Osborne left the Associated Press. He went to work for the Dallas Morning News, filling the position of executive editor. Osborne advanced steadily while at the Dallas Morning News, filling positions as vice president, senior vice president

a
nd editor, and then president and editor by 1985. In 1991 Osborne was named publisher and editor of the paper. Osborne was elected to the board of directors of the Associated Press in 1993.

OSTOVICH, MAJ. GEN. RUDOLPH, III

Office of the Secretary, Pentagon, Washington, D.C. 20301-1155 (703) 545-6700
Ostovich, III, USA is a prominent military leader. For career credentials consult the portion of this book entitled "Biographees by Profession" in the Appendix. Within this portion the list "Military Leaders" describes requirements for inclusion in this volume.

OZAWA, SEIJI

Boston Symphony Orchestra, Symphony Hall, Boston, MA 02115 (617) 266-1492
BORN: 1935, Shenyang (China) ACHIEVEMENTS: First Prize, International Competition of Orchestra Conductors, Besancon, France; Koussevitsky Prize for Outstanding Student Conductor; Emmy, Evening at Symphony; Emmy, Individual Achievement in Cultural Programming; Inouye Award, Inouye Sho, Japan; Honorary Doctorates, University of Massachusetts, New England Conservatory of Music, Wheaton College, Norton, Massachusetts. STUDIED: Toho School of Music, Tokyo.
As the 13th music director of the Boston Symphony Orchestra, Seiji Ozawa's 22 seasons in Boston represent the longest of any musical director currently active with an American orchestra. During that time he has led the orchestra throughout the United States, Europe, Asia, and South America. He is widely acclaimed for commissioning new works, for recording more than 130 works with the orchestra— representing more than 50 composers—and as founder of the Saito Kinen Festival in Matsumoto, Japan. Ozawa appears regularly with the Berlin Philharmonic, the New Japan Philharmonic, London Symphony, Orchestre National de France, the Philharmonic of London, and the Vienna Philharmonic.

PACE, ARROW KENNETH

Stanford University, Department of Economics, Stanford, CA 94305
BORN: 1921, New York City. ACHIEVEMENTS: Nobel Prize in Economic Science (with John Hicks), 1972; president, Econometric Society, Institute of Management Sciences, American Economic Association, Western Economic Association; John Clark Bates Medal, American Economic Association; Guggenheim Fellow; Von Neuman Prize; vice president, American Academy of Arts and Sciences; recipient of honorary degrees from 16 universities worldwide. STUDIED: City College, New York; Columbia University.
In his doctoral thesis, Social Choice and Individual Values, Pace postulated that under the majority rules concept, it is impossible to determine a clear-cut social choice without "rigging" constitutions to limit choices to two, and only two, options. This "impossibility theorem" startled political philosophers and welfare economists when it first appeared in 1951. Since its publication, hundreds of papers have since been written to refute it. His subsequent work has dealt with the "mathematics" of subjects including price-demand

factors (equilibrium), inventory and production, and economic growth.

PACINO, ALFREDO JAMES

Actors Studio, 432 W. 44th St., New York, NY 10036
BORN: 1940, New York, N.Y. ACHIEVEMENTS: Antoinette Perry Award, Best Supporting Actor, Dramatic, Does A Tiger Wear a Necktie?, 1969; Tony Award, Best Actor, The Basic Training of Pavlo Hummel, 1977; Golden Globe Award, Best Actor, Serpico, 1974; Academy Award, Best Actor, and Golden Globe Award, Best Actor, both for Scent of a Woman, 1993. STUDIED: High School of the Performing Arts, New York City; Actor's Studio, 1966.

As a high school student, Al Pacino was determined to become an actor. He proved himself as an actor on both the Broadway stage and the silver screen, winning an Obie Award in 1968 for his role in *The Indian Wants the Bronx* and a Tony Award for his Broadway debut in *Does a Tiger Wear a Necktie?*. His portrayal of Michael Corleone in the popular film *The Godfather*, in 1972, insured his popularity with the movie public. He followed this success with the films *Serpico*, 1973, *The Godfather, Part II*, 1974, *Dog Day Afternoon*, 1975, and a number of others. After more than 20 years as an actor, Pacino won his first Oscar in 1993, for best actor for his role in *Scent of a Woman*.

PAGE, CLARENCE

The Chicago Tribune, 435 N. Michigan Ave., Chicago IL 60611-4022 (312) 222-3232
BORN: 1947, Dayton, Ohio. ACHIEVEMENTS: articpant Chicago Tribune Task Force Series on Vote Fraud, which won a Pulitzer Prize, 1972; Pulitzer Prize for commentary, 1989; editorial board member, Chicago Tribune, 1981-present. STUDIED: Ohio University, B.S., journalism, 1969.

Clarence Page left his home state right after college graduation for his first job as assistant city editor of the *Chicago Tribune*, a position he held until 1980. Then he joined WBBM-TV as a the director of their Community Affairs Department. He returned to the *Chicago Tribune* in 1984 as a columnist and member of the editorial board, a position he still holds. He has also appeared as a panelist on *Lead Story* for BET, and as a biweekly commentator for National Public Radio's *Weekend Sunday* program.

PAGE, ROBERT

Chicago Sun Times, 401 N. Wabash, Chicago, IL 60611-3593 (312) 312-3228
Page is publisher of Chicago's second largest newspaper, the *Chicago Sun Times*.

PAINTER, NELL IRVIN

Princeton University, Department of History, Dickinson Hall, Princeton, NJ 08544
BORN: 1942, Houston, Texas ACHIEVEMENTS: Coretta Scott King Award, American Association of University Women; fellowships: American Council of Learned Societies, Charles Warren Center for Studies in American History, Harvard University, Radcliffe Institute, National Humanities Center. STUDIED: University of California at Berkeley, B.A., history; University of California at Los Angeles, M.A., history; Harvard University, Ph.D., history; University of Bordeaux, France; University of Ghana.

Nell Painter has been a history professor at the University of Carolina at Chapel Hill for 15 years. She is also the author of seven historical works. Concentrating on aspects of black American life in the late nineteenth and early twentieth century, Painter won acclaim for stirring Afro-Americans to re-examine grass-roots black protest movements. In one of her two most important books, *Exodusters: Black Migration to Kansas after Reconstruction*, she concludes that the reason for the exodus of blacks from the South in the 1880s was the rural tyranny of landlord over farmer, not, as many believe, the response of ignorant people to unscrupulous speculators and agitators. In *The Narrative of Hosea Hudson* she traced a 20th century black union organizer's road from bondage to freedom. Compiling oral memoirs of the unionist, taped over several years, Painter was widely praised not only for coaxing the moving story out of Hudson but for shaping a coherent whole from the mountain of tapes.

PALANCE, JACK

15301 Ventura Blvd., #345, Sherman Oaks, CA 91403
BORN: 1920, Lattimer, Pa. ACHIEVEMENTS: Emmy Award, Best Single Performance by an Actor, Requiem for a Heavyweight, 1957; Academy Award, Best Supporting Actor, City Slickers, 1991. STUDIED: Attended University of North Carolina and Stanford University.

Before becoming an actor, Jack Palance was a professional boxer. During World War II, he served in the U.S. Army Air Corps. and was severely burned, requiring extensive plastic surgery. His long acting career includes numerous appearances on film, television, and the stage. In 1950 he performed on Broadway in the play *Panic in the Streets*, and also a film released under the same name. In addition to his Academy Award winning role in a film, other movies include: Palance can be seen in *The Halls of Montezuma*, 1950, *Sudden Fear*, 1952, *Second Chance*, 1953, *The Lonely Man*, 1957, *Ten Seconds to Hell*, 1959, *They Came to Rob Las Vegas*, 1969, *Chato's Land*, 1972, and many others. Palance was also a regular on television, acting in the series *The Greatest Show On Earth*, from 1963 to 1964, and *Bronk*, from 1975 to 1976.

PALERMO, PETER M.

JASON Foundation for Education, 395 Totten Pond Rd., Waltham, MA 02154
BORN: 1941, Rochester, N.Y. ACHIEVEMENTS: Catholic Media Award presented by Pope John Paul II. STUDIED: Bowling Green University, B.A., psychology and English; University of Rochester Graduate School of Business, M.B.A., economics.

Peter Palermo took the reins of the JASON Foundation for Education in 1993 after a 30-year career at Eastman Kodak Company, a sponsor of JASON. In 1990 Palermo, then general manager of the Consumer Imaging division of Eastman Kodak Company, developed Ektar color negative films which are thinner than those in other color negative films. The technique allowed more light to enter the imaging layers, providing greater clarity. In his post with JASON, his consortium of private industry, scientific research facilities, and educational and non-profit institutions collaborate to spread science and technology education to students throughout the nation. Founded in 1989, it has expanded its teaching sites to Canada, England, Bermuda, and Belize in North Central America. Palermo has served as a director of the Photographic Society of the Philippines, the Association of Photographer Manufacturers of Mexico, and the Health Industry Manufacturers Association of the United States. He was named one of the Outstanding Young Men of America in 1973.

PALMER, ROBERT B.

Digital Equipment Company, 111 Powdermill Road, Maynard, MA 01754 (508) 493-5111
BORN: 1941 ACHIEVEMENTS: Implemented MOS integrated circuit production process. STUDIED: Texas Tech University, B.S., mathematics, with high honors, M.S., physics.
Robert Palmer is the chairman of the board, president, and chief operating officer of Digital Equipment Corporation, one of the world's biggest computer companies. He left a position as an executive vice president of United Technologies Corporation to join Digital in 1985 as manager of its semiconductor operations. After being appointed to vice presidencies of various divisions throughout 1991, in 1992 he was given responsibility for all elements of Digital's worldwide manufacturing, as well as the engineering and manufacturing of semiconductors, personal computers, terminals, and printers. Later that year Ken Olsen, founder and president of the company, retired. Palmer succeeded him as president and chief executive officer. Among his achievements at Digital was the development and implementation of a groundbreaking MOS integrated circuit production process, hailed by the Semiconductor Equipment Manufacturing Institute as one of the most significant technology developments in the integrated circuit industry. In 1995 he became the first chairman in the company's 29-year history.

PANETTA, LEON

The White House, 1600 Pennsylvania Ave., Washington, D.C., 20500 (202) 456-6796
BORN: 1938, Monterey, Calif. ACHIEVEMENTS: U.S. congressman (Calif.), 1976-1992; director, Office of Management and Budget, 1993-present. STUDIED: University of Santa Clara (Calif.), B.A., 1960, J.D., 1963.
Leon Panetta began his political career as a Republican but switched to the Democratic party when he became disenchanted with the Republican stance on civil rights. As a Republican, Panetta served in many appointed positions in the late 1960s. He was President Richard Nixon's Civil Rights Office director, a part of the Health, Education, and Welfare Department, when he got into a disagreement with the administration over the application of the Civil Rights Act of 1964. Panetta disagreed with the administration's position on school integration in the South and

resigned his position in protest in 1970. Panetta was elected to Congress as a California Democrat in 1976. He was chairman of the House Budget Committee from 1989 until 1992. He was appointed by President Bill Clinton to serve as the director of the Office of Management and Budget in 1993. However the very next year he took over the post of White House chief of staff, replacing Thomas F. "Mack" McLarty III.

PARKER, LOUIS

c/o NCIPLA, Suite 203, 2001 Jefferson Davis Hwy., Arlington, VA 22202
BORN: 1906, Budapest (Hungary). ACHIEVEMENTS: Founder, Parker Instrument Co. STUDIED: City College of New York.
Louis Parker's most famous invention, an inexpensive television sound system, was a boon to viewers worldwide. Previous to that, he had worked on radio direction finders for aircraft and portable transmitters for military use. He founded Parker Instrument Company which produced some instruments used in the Apollo moon project. Parker immigrated to the U.S. in 1923.

PARKINSON, ROGER

Globe and Mail, Toronto, Canada.
BORN: 1942 STUDIED: Dartmouth College, B.A.; Harvard University, M.A., business administration.
Parkinson began his career at the business side of newspapers and magazines beginning with *Newsweek* magazine in 1969. He moved to the *Washington Post* six years later where he became vice president of administration. In 1980 he joined Cowles Media Company as president and publisher of the *Buffalo Courier-Express*. Cowles moved him to the *Minneapolis Star-Tribune* in 1982 where he became publisher and president from 1983 to 1992, at the same time serving as executive vice president and a member of the board of Cowles. Parkinson researched public policy issues as an executive fellow at the University of St. Thomas, in Minneapolis, from 1992 to 1994, when he was appointed publisher and chief executive officer of the *Globe and Mail*, Canada's national newspaper.

PARSONS, JOHN T.

NCIPLA, Suite 203, 2001 Jefferson Davis Hwy., Arlington, VA 22202 (703) 415-0780
BORN: 1913, Detroit. ACHIEVEMENTS: Invention of numerical control of machine tools; National Medal of Technology Award; inducted into the National Inventors Hall of Fame, 1993 STUDIED: University of Michigan, Ph.D. (honorary) engineering.
Dr. Parsons' numerical control invention combined his milling machine to a punch card system developed by Frank L. Stulen. The marriage of these two inventions marked the beginning of the second industrial revolution. An innovator, Parsons used adhesive bonding in aircraft building and then built the first all-composite airplane. Dr. Parsons' technology helped revolutionize various industries. He produced the fuel liens for the Saturn booster that helped propel U.S astronauts to the moon. He also brought computers to

aircraft designs, manufacture and management reporting.

PARTON, DOLLY

Creative Artists Agency, 1888 Century Park E., Los Angeles, CA 90067

BORN: 1946, Locust Ridge, Tenn. ACHIEVEMENTS: Grammy, Best Country Vocal-Female, Here You Come Again, 1978; Grammy, Best Country Vocal-Female, 9 to 5, 1981; Grammy, Best Country Performance, Duo or Group, Trio (with Linda Ronstadt and Emmylou Harris), 1987.

Dolly Parton's career comprises the quintessential rags to riches story. Born in a poor area of Tennessee, she began performing on Knoxville television at 12. A year later, Parton was appearing on the Grand Ole Opry and making her first records. In 1967, Parton released her hit album, *Dumb Blonde*. The record attracted the attention of Porter Wagoner, who hired her to perform on his television show. Parton and Wagoner earned a large following for their duets. With the release of her #1 album, *Joshua* in 1970, she achieved popularity as a solo performer. Parton began acting in movies in 1980 with her prominent role in *9 To 5*. She has continued her acting career and has many starring roles to her credit.

PASCHKE, EDWARD F.

1927 E. Estes, Chicago, IL 60626

BORN: 1939. ACHIEVEMENTS: Logan Medal, Art Institute of Chicago; Cassandra Grant, Cassandra Foundation; collections: Art Institute of Chicago; Museum of Contemporary Art, Chicago; exhibitions: Art Institute of Chicago; Whitney Museum Annuals. STUDIED: School of the Art Institute of Chicago.

In a biting style aided by acid colors, this Chicago Imagist presents disturbing events and enigmatic people from real life in order to provoke "emotive responses" from the viewer. Edward Paschke began as part of the Pop movement, and is well-known for sometimes grotesque figures which question sexual identity, such as *Nueva Yorka* and *Tropicale*. Current work includes figures which look as if they have been electronically produced in a "high-tech" surrealism of neon colors. A recent collaboration with Lyn Blumenthal and Carole Ann Klonarides resulted in the video *Arcade*.

PATAKI, GEORGE E.

State of New York, Executive Chamber, Albany, NY 12224

BORN: 1945, Peekskill, N.Y. ACHIEVEMENTS: Member, Assembly Environmental Conservation Committee, Ranking Minority Member; Assembly Education Committee; Named "Friend of the Taxpayer," Change New York; Top State Senator for Performance, New York State Conservative Party; "Environmental Champion in the State Senate," New York State League of Conservative Voters Education Fund. STUDIED: Yale University, B.A.; Columbia University School of Law, D. J., law.

The youngest mayor in Peekskill's history at age 37, Pataki, after three terms, moved on to the state senate where he served his fourth term before becoming New York's Governor. His committee assignments currently are Ethics, Environmental Conservation, Housing and Community Development, Social Service, Banks, and Codes. He is considered strongest on the subject of the environment, having served on the Senate committee as ranking minority member since 1991.

PATTEN, JOHN W.

Business Week, 1221 Avenue of the Americas, New York, NY, 10020 (212) 512-2000

ACHIEVEMENTS: STUDIED: Harvard Business School, Marketing Management Program; Dartmouth College; St. John's University, honorary doctoral degree, commercial science; Westminster College, honorary doctoral degree, humane letters.

John Patten is president emeritus of the Business Week Group of the McGraw-Hill Companies. He started at McGraw-Hill in 1954 as a trainee. In 1958, the first regional marketing office in the Rocky Mountain area for the company. He was regional manager in Denver until 1965. That year, he was sent to London as European director. In 1977, he returned to the United States and was named vice president of the Atlantic region and vice president of marketing for McGraw-Hill Publications the next year. Patten became associate publisher of *Engineering News-Record* in 1981. He went on to become publisher of *Aviation Week & Space Technology* in 1982 and was appointed vice president and publisher in 1983. In 1985, he was named publisher of *Business Week* and executive vice president and publisher of the Business Week Group in 1989. He was named president in 1992. Patten is also chairman of the Disability 2000-CEO Council, a director of the Business Council for the United Nations, and a director of The Conservation Fund.

PATTERSON, JIM

Office of the Mayor, 2600 Fresno St., Fresno, CA 93721 (209) 498-1516

Patterson is a prominent political leader in California and mayor of Fresno. For career credentials consult 'Biographees by Profession" in the Appendix. Within this portion the list "Publishers" describes requirements for inclusion in this volume.

PEARLSTEIN, PHILIP

163 W. 88th St., New York, NY 10024

BORN: 1924. ACHIEVEMENTS: National Endowment for the Arts Grant; Fellowship, John Simon Guggenheim Memorial Foundation; collections: Whitney Museum of American Art; Museum of Modern Art; exhibitions: Whitney Museum Biennial; Carnegie Mellon University. STUDIED: Carnegie Institute; Institute of Fine Arts, New York University

A realist figurative painter, Philip Pearlstein presents human bodies as forms arranged in the compositional limits of a rectangle. He works on specific parts of a figure, one at a time, so that even he is not sure about the final outcome of a painting. Thus, because his progress is not structured in accordance with the canvas edges, cropping is characteristic of the work. He calls the configurations of nude figures "a sort of stilled-action choreography" describes requirements for inclusion in this volume. The directional movement of the figures structures the paintings and expresses the innate dignity of the human body.

PEARSON, DURK

c/o Warner Books, Inc., 666 Fifth Avenue, New York, NY 10103 (212) 484-2900
Pearson is a prominent author. For career credentials consult the portion of this book entitled "Biographees by Profession" in the Appendix. Within this portion the list "Authors" describes requirements for inclusion in this volume.

PEDERSEN, WILLIAM

Kohn Pedersen Fox Associates PC, 111 W. 57th Street, New York, NY 10019 (212) 977-6500
BORN: 1938. ACHIEVEMENTS: Rome Prize in Architecture; AIA; notable works: 333 Wacker and 225 Wacker Drive, Chicago; Proctor & Gamble Headquarters, Cincinnati. STUDIED: University of Minnesota; Massachusetts Institute of Technology.
As chief design architect at Kohn Pedersen Fox, William Pedersen takes prime credit for many of the firm's award-winning projects. His buildings achieve contextual solutions by "explaining" the geography of their site. But "contextualizing" a building doesn't consist simply in blending it into surrounding structures; the building might instead strike a stylistic counterpoint to its environment to provide aesthetic relief. His 333 Wacker Drive is an office high-rise sited at a dramatic bend of the Chicago River. It faces away from the downtown Loop and toward the expanse of the city. Matching the river's bend, the outward face of the building is broadly and strikingly curved; its green-tinted glass sheet reflects the setting sun as well as the green of the river in a contextual play of color. The side of the building facing the Loop is a broad plane which extends above the opposite side's curve, as though intersecting it, while the base, several stories of horizontal marble and granite bands, adjusts the bold expanse of the building to the scale of the street. His Cincinnati Proctor and Gamble headquarters is an 800,000-square-foot addition to the company's 1960s headquarters which was designed by Skidmore, Owings and Merrill. The addition, joined to the original structure by a covered bridge which jointly forms an L-shape, stands at the edge of Cincinnati and symbolizes at once the city's outer boundry and, from the building's front, its gateway. The addition's limestone surface carries on the limestone and white marble elegance of the original. Its principal design feature is two octagonal towers which, together, with the "void" between them, create the symbolic gateway.

PEI, IEOH MING ("I.M.")

I.M. Pei & Partners, Madison Avenue, New York, NY 10022 (212) 751-3122 600
BORN: 1917. ACHIEVEMENTS: FAIA; Pritzker Architectural Prize; AIA Gold Medal; Chevalier de la Legion d'Honneur, France; American Academy and Institute of Arts and Letters' Brunner Memorial Prize; notable works: Le Grand Louvre, Paris; Bank of China, Hong Kong; Fragrant Hill Hotel,

Beijing; East Building, National Gallery of Art, Washington, D.C. *STUDIED: Massachusetts Institute of Technology; Harvard Graduate School of Design.*
Since completing his National Center for Atmospheric Research in Boulder, Colo. in 1967, and even more after his 1978 project, the East Wing for the National Gallery of Art in Washington, D.C., Pei has been known for his monumental, yet essentially simple stereometric forms. Recently these forms have expressed their underlying architectural complexity, most famously in the three eccentric glass pyramids—admitting light to a new underground visitors center—which he placed in the grand courtyard of Frances' most famous and historic museum, the Louvre. His Bank of China tower in Hong Kong responds to challenging program requirements quite apart from its freeway-tangled, hilly site. He was to create a strong architectural presence for the mainland state bank just a few blocks from the enormously expensive new headquarters of the Hong Kong and Shanghai Bank, with a slender fraction of their building budget. The largest building outside of North America, his tower is designed to withstand Hong Kong harbor's typhoon winds, which are twice the velocity of New York winds, and which create shear forces four times more powerful than those anticipated in the earthquake codes of Los Angeles. Yet the composite structural geometry of his design created for this building actually reduce by half the structural steel required for the 1034-foot structure.

PELL, CLAIBORNE

U.S. Senate, 335 SROB, Washington, D.C. 20510-3901 (202) 224-4642
BORN: 1919
A senator since 1960 serving his sixth term, Pell is one of the longest standing members in the U.S. Senate. The Democratic Senator from Rhode Island is a ranking member of the Senate Foreign Relations Committee and the Education, Arts, and Humanities Committee. He is also a board member of the Democratic Policy Committee and has served on numerous other committees.

PELLI, CESAR

Cesar Pelli and Associates, 1056 Chapel Street, New Haven, CT 06510 (203) 777-2515
BORN: 1926. ACHIEVEMENTS: First Prize, United Nations City Competition, 1969; Brunner Prize, National Institute of Arts and Letters; Design Award, Progressive Architecture, 1966; notable works: World Financial Center, New York; Northwest Center, Minneapolis; Pacific Design Center, Los Angeles. STUDIED: University of Illinois, Champaign/Urbana.
Rejecting the massive inorganic forms and materials of Modernism, he wants his buildings to be light, changeable and humane. In his mature work, most notably the World Financial Center in New York City's Battery Park, he has sheathed his skyscrapers in thin curtain walls to achieve a sometimes disconcerting effect of lightness and freedom of form. The Financial Towers sympathetically bridge the old landmarks of

the Manhattan skyline with the new. Their pointed tops recall the Chrysler Building, the RCA and the Empire State Building, but their vertical sweep and simple massing associate them firmly with the towers of the World Trade Center, which they adjoin.

PENA, FEDERICO F.

Department of Transportation, 400 7th St., SW., Washington, D.C., 20590 (202) 366-1111

BORN: 1947, Laredo, Texas ACHIEVEMENTS: U.S. secretary of transportation; mayor of Denver. STUDIED: University of Texas, B.A., 1969; J.D., 1972.

Pena's hands-on experience in transportation issues was acquired during his service as mayor of Denver, a job he held from 1983 until 1991. One of his most notable achievements was winning approval for the construction of Denver International Airport— one the world's largest. Pena views transportation as a key to reviving America's economy. He was nominated as secretary of transportation by President-elect Bill Clinton, and confirmed by the United States Senate on January 21, 1993.

PENDERECKI, KRZYSTOF

ICM Artists Ltd., 8942 Wilshire Blvd., Beverly Hills, CA, 90211

BORN: 1933, Debica (Poland). ACHIEVEMENTS: Three Grammy awards, 1988. STUD-

Secretary of Transportation Federico Pena.

IED: State Academy of Music, Krakow, 1958; Doctor honoris causa., University of Rochester, St. Olaf College, Cath U., Leuven, Belgium, University Bordeaux, France, Georgetown University, Belgrade University, Madrid University, Spain, Adam Mickiewicz University, Warsaw University, 1993.

Krzysztof Penderecki is known for treating instrumental and vocal sounds as independent elements of composition. His works for large numbers of strings are particularly striking: *Threnody for the Victims of Hiroshima*, for 52 strings, 1960, and *Polymorpha*, for 48 strings, 1961. Penderecki is also known for developing many notational devices to clarify his sound effects. His significant contributions to choral and dramatic music include the widely acclaimed and monumental *St. Luke Passion*, which premiered in

1966, his first opera, *The Devils of Loudun*, 1968. Other important works include: *Utrenya*, for solo voices, chorus, and orchestra, 1971; the sacred drama *Paradise Lost*, 1978; the choral piece *Polish Requiem*, which made its U.S. premier in 1986; and the opera *Black Mask*, 1986.

PENDERGRASS, HENRY P.

Vanderbilt University Hospital, CCC1108, Nashville, TN 37232

Pendergrass is a prominent physician. For career credentials consult the portion of this book entitled "Biographees by Profession" in the Appendix. Within this portion the list "Physicians" describes requirements for inclusion in this volume.

PENN, IRVING

Irving Penn Studios, Box 934, F.D.R. Station, New York, NY 10150

BORN: 1917. ACHIEVEMENTS: Collections: George Eastman House, International Museum of Photography; Museum of Modern Art; exhibitions: Metropolitan Museum of Art; Museum of Modern Art. STUDIED: Philadelphia Museum School of Industrial Art.

First a part of revolutionary fashion photographer Alexey Brodovitch's famed "design laboratories" in Philadelphia in the late 1930s, Penn then painted for a year in Mexico before going to New York City in 1943 to accept a job as cover designer for *Vogue* magazine. He gained recognition when he photographed the covers himself, and for over 40 years he has remained an editorial contributor to the magazine. His clients are in industry and advertising throughout America and Europe.

PENNIMAN, NICHOLAS G.

St. Louis Post-Dispatch, 900 N. Tucker, St. Louis, MO 63101 (314) 622-7000

Penniman is a prominent publisher. For career credentials consult the portion of this book entitled "Biographees by Profession" in the Appendix. Within this portion the list "Publishers" describes requirements for inclusion in this volume.

PENZIAS, ARNO ALLAN

AT&T Bell Labs, Box 400, Holmdel, NJ 07733
BORN: 1923, Munich (Germany). ACHIEVEMENTS: Nobel Prize in Physics (shared with Robert W. Wilson and Piotr L. Kapitsa of Russia), 1978; Henry Draper Medal; Herschel Medal; Townsend Harris Medal; Newman Award, City College of New York; Joseph Handleman Prize. STUDIED: City College of New York; Columbia University.

Two scientific theories about the creation of the universe have been hotly debated since Edwin Hubble first proposed, in 1929, that we live in a constantly expanding universe. In one, the "big bang" theory, Hubble and other radio astronomers postulated that all matter and all energy were once a single primeval atom, from which it has been expanding since an explosion 20 billion years ago. In the contrary "Steady State" theory, scientists believe the universe has continually expanded until it collapsed upon itself; the collapse is compensated for by the constant creation of new universes. Arno Penzias and Robert Wilson laid the "Steady State" theory to rest with their work in microwave radio detection, which found for the first time—and by accident—a hundredfold excess of radiation than that coming from all known scientifically measured sources, which would support the "big bang" theory. If further evidence develops along this line, scientists believe the team's discovery will have been as important as Hubble's theory itself. The Russian Kapitsa shared in the 1978 Nobel awards for basic inventions and discoveries in low-temperature physics, or cryogenic temperatures, where conditions such as superconductivity and superfluidity prevail.

PEREIRA, WILLIAM LEONARD

William L. Pereira Associates, 5657 Wilshire Blvd., Los Angeles, CA (213) 933-8341
BORN: 1909. ACHIEVEMENTS: Fellow, AIA; Honor Award, AIA Southern California Chapter, 1963; fellow, Academy of Motion Picture Arts and Sciences; notable works: Transamerica Building, San Francisco; Marine Land

Businessman/political activist H. Ross Perot.

of the Pacific, Palos Verde, Calif.; Citicorp Building, San Francisco. STUDIED: University of Illinois, Urbana.*

Although born and educated in the Midwest, William Pereira has contributed heavily to the development of a district style for large-scale commercial architecture on the West Coast. His major goal has been to give digestible and immediately recognizable silhouettes to each of his buildings. His pyramid-like Transamerica Building has become a national symbol for the Transamerica corporation, and a landmark of Eiffel Tower-like stature on the San Francisco skyline. His forms derive from the Modernist ethos, but his commitment to distinguishing them is more suggestive of the Beaux-Arts tradition. He also designs large projects that spread masses of people horizontally, with great sensitivity to crowd dynamics. His Marineland of the Pacific in Palos Verdes, Calif., and his Los Angeles International Airport, are sensitive to the human scale and comfortably master automotive and pedestrian traffic logistics.

PEREZ, RUDY

Rudy Perez Performance Ensemble, P.O. Box 36614, Los Angeles, CA 90036 (213) 931-3604
ACHIEVEMENTS: Notable ballets: Countdown; Bang, Bang; Center Break; Loading Zone; Transit; Arcade (revised as Match). STUDIED: Martha Graham School.

Social dancing led Rudy Perez to ballet, where, at the relatively late age for a dancer, 21, he threw his energy and drive into developing his inborn talents. Turning quickly to choreography, he allied himself with freelance groups of dancers who were welcomed to show their talents at a church in Washington Square in Manhattan. His pieces, consisting of simple gestures projected with power, move at a dreamlike, timeless pace that draws audiences to pay attention to their smallest details. A powerful influence on his career was Martha Graham, who drew out of him a dramatic power like her own.

PERLMAN, RHEA

Creative Artists' Agency, 9830 Wilshire Blvd., Beverly Hills, CA 90212
BORN: 1948, Brooklyn, N.Y. ACHIEVEMENTS: Emmy Award, Outstanding Supporting Actress in a Comedy, Variety, or Music Series, Cheers, 1984, 1985, and 1986. STUDIED: Hunter College.

Rhea Perlman has appeared on the stage, film, and television. Perlman is probably best known for her role as Carla Tortelli, a short, not terribly attractive, over-sexed waitress on the television series *Cheers*. Her acting in the series has netted Perlman three Emmy Awards as outstanding supporting actress. She is also a founder, with her husband actor Danny DeVito, of New Street, a production company. In addition to *Cheers*, Perlman has appeared on television in *The Tortellis*, 1987, and *Taxi*. She also performed in the TV movies *Mary Jane Harper Cried Last Night*, 1977, *Drop-Out Father*, 1982, *The Ratings Game*, 1984, and *Dangerous Affection*, 1987.

PEROT, HENRY ROSS

12377 Merit Dr., #1700, Dallas, TX 75251
BORN: 1930, Texarkana, Texas ACHIEVEMENTS: Founded, EDS Corporation STUDIED: U. S. Naval Academy, 1953.
Perot was appointed to the U. S. Naval Academy in 1949, receiving his commission in 1953. He was discharged from the Navy in 1957 and went to work for the IBM Corporation, selling computers in Dallas. Perot founded Electronic Data Systems (EDS) in 1962, with only $25,000 raised from his own savings and loans from family members. EDS was founded on the principle that an outside company could manage the data processing departments of large corporate and government clients more efficiently than they could themselves. In just six years, Perot increased his holdings in EDS from $25,000 to $1 billion. Perot sold EDS to General Motors in 1984 for $2.5 billion. In 1992 Perot ran for the United States presidency as an independent candidate. He garnered nearly 19 percent of the popular vote. Although Bill Clinton went on to become president, Perot emerged as an independent voice for nearly a fifth of the nation's population.

PERRY, WILLIAM J.

Department of Defense, The Pentagon, Washington, D.C., 20301 (703) 695-5261
BORN: 1927, Vandergrift, Pa. ACHIEVEMENTS: James Forrestal Memorial Award, 1993. STUDIED: Stanford University, B.S., 1949; M.S., mathematics, 1950; Pennsylvania State University, Ph.D., mathematics, 1957.
Perry served in the Army Corps of Engineers from 1946-47 as a commissioned officer. He is a founder of ESL Inc., and served as its president until 1977. He also worked for Sylvania/General Telephone as director of their Electronic Defense Laboratories. Perry was deputy secretary of defense from March, 1993, until his confirmation as secretary in March, 1994.

PESCI, JOE

The Artists' Agency, Rm. 305, 10000 Santa Monica Blvd., Los Angeles, CA 90067
BORN: 1943, Newark, N.J. ACHIEVEMENTS: Academy Award, Best Supporting Actor, Goodfellas, 1991.
Joe Pesci began his career in entertainment when he appeared on the *Star Kids* radio show in 1947. At just 5 years of age he appeared in Broadway musicals and Eddie Downing plays. By the time he turned 10 he was a regular on the television show, *Star Time Kids*. Pesci also played guitar for the band Joey Dee and the Starlifters. Between acting jobs he worked as a stand-up comic, nightclub singer, postal worker, delivery boy, and restaurant manager. It was during a stint as a restaurant manager that he was called by Robert DeNiro and Martin Scorsese and asked to play the part of Jake LaMotta's brother in the film *Raging Bull*, in 1978. Pesci won an Academy Award for Best Supporting Actor in the film *Goodfellas*, 1991.

PETERS, BERNADETTE

Richard Grant and Associates, 8500 Wilshire Blvd., #250, Beverly Hills, CA 90211
BORN: 1948, Jamaica N.Y. ACHIEVEMENTS: Golden Globe Award, Best Film Actress in a Musical/Comedy, Pennies from Heaven, 1981; Antoinette Perry Award, Best Actress in a Musical, Song and Dance, 1986. STUDIED: Attended Quintana School for Young Professionals.
Bernadette Peters, an accomplished stage actress, studied acting with David Le Grant, tap dancing with Oliver McCool III, and song with Jim Gregory. She began her career at the age of 11, appearing as Tessie in the New York City Center Theatre production of *The Most Happy Fella*, 1959. Her preparation and professionalism landed her a steady series of stage parts, mostly in the Broadway theater. She appeared in *George M!*, 1968; *Dames at Sea*, 1968-69; *On the Town*, 1971-72; *Tartuffe*, 1972-73; *Sunday in the Park with George*, 1984-85; *Song and Dance*, 1985-86; and *Into the Woods*, 1987-89. Her film appearances include *The Longest Yard*, 1974; *Vigilante Force*, 1976; *The Jerk* with Steve Martin, 1979; *Pennies from Heaven*, 1981, and *Pink Cadillac*, 1989.

PETERS, THOMAS J. (TOM)

c/o Harper, 10 E. 53rd St., New York, NY 10022
BORN: 1942, Baltimore. ACHIEVEMENTS: Co-author, In Search of Excellence.
Co-author of the business bible, *In Search of Excellence*, published in 1982, which analyzed the successful methods of many corporate practices, Tom Peters went on to form his own company, The Tom Peters Group. The Group, along with Peters' popular writings and lectures, has helped formulate a broad array of competitive American management systems.

PETERSDORF, ROBERT G.

1 Dupont Circle, NW., 200, Washington, D.C. 20036
Petersdorf is a prominent physician. For career credentials consult the portion of this book entitled "Biographees by Profession" in the Appendix. Within this portion the list "Physicians" describes requirements for inclusion in this volume.

PFAFF, WILLIAM

The Los Angeles Times, Times Mirror Square, Los Angeles, CA 90012-3645 (213) 237-5000
Pfaff is a prominent journalist. For career credentials consult the portion of this book entitled "Biographees

by Profession" in the Appendix. Within this portion the list "Journalists" describes requirements for inclusion in this volume.

PFEIFFER, ECKHARD

Compaq Computer Corporation, PO Box 69-2000, Houston, TX 77269 (713) 370-0670
BORN: 1941, Lauban, (Germany -now Poland) STUDIED: Kaufmaennische Berufsschule, business degree; Southern Methodist University, M.B.A., business.
After 20 years with Texas Instruments, Eckhard Pfeiffer joined Compaq Computer Corporation in 1983 as vice president, Europe. He subsequently directed the openings of wholly owned Compaq subsidiaries in Germany, France, and England. Basing the international headquarters in Munich, Germany, he eventually directed all Compaq business outside North America, including dealers in 65 countries as well as manufacturing facilities in Singapore and Erskine, Scotland. The company's international operations accounted for 54 percent of Compaq's overall revenue, with sales of almost $2 billion while Pfeiffer was in charge. In 1991 he was appointed president and chief executive officer of Compaq, responsible for directing the company's corporate strategies and operations worldwide.

PFEIFFER, MICHELLE

William Morris Agency, 151 El Camino Dr., Beverly Hills, CA 90212
BORN: 1957, Santa Ana, Calif. ACHIEVEMENTS: Golden Globe Award, Best Actress, The Fabulous Baker Boys, 1990. STUDIED: Golden West Junior College, Golden West College.
Michelle Pfeiffer started her acting career on television in the late 1970s. One of her early parts was so small she only had one line. However, she quickly rose through the ranks and, in 1982, played the lead role in the film production of *Grease 2.* Pfeiffer has found her greatest success in film, acting in such movies as, *The Witches of Eastwick,* in 1987, and *The Fabulous Baker Boys,* in 1989, which earned her a Golden Globe for Best Actress. Pfeiffer's personal life recently overshadowed her professional career, when she adopted a baby girl as a single mother. She later married David Kelley, and changed the baby's name from Pfeiffer to Kelley.

PHELPS, ASHTON JR.

The Times-Picayune, 3800 Howard Ave., New Orleans, LA 70125-1429 (504) 826-3279
Phelps, Jr. is a prominent publisher. For career credentials consult the portion of this book entitled "Biographees by Profession" in the Appendix. Within this portion the list "Publishers" describes requirements for inclusion in this volume.

PHILIPSON, MORRIS

University of Chicago Press, 5801 Ellis Ave., Chicago, IL 60637 (312) 702-7700
Philipson is a prominent publisher and head of the University of Chicago Press, considered one of the nation's most prolific university presses. The press, under Philipson's direction, has produced many bestsellers, rather than scholarly books, the usual output for most of the nation's institutional publishing houses.
volume.

PHILLIPS, JULIA MILLER

c/o Writers' Guild, 8955 Beverly Blvd., Los Angeles, CA 90048
BORN: 1944, New York City. ACHIEVEMENTS: Academy Award (with Tony Bill), The Sting; Palme d'Or, Taxi Driver; Katherine McFarland Short Story Award. STUDIED: Mt. Holyoke College, B.A.
Julia Phillips was an Academy Award-winning director at age 29, three years after she, her then-husband Michael Phillips, and actor Tony Bill formed the production company Bill/Phillips. The team followed that success with *Taxi Driver, Close Encounters of the Third Kind,* and *The Beat,* the last produced after her divorce and the beginning of her eclipse as a Hollywood meteor at age 47. In 1991 came her devastating personal memoir in the book *You'll Never Eat Lunch In This Town Again,* recounting her cocaine addiction and the disintegration of her career in films and writing, a career that began as a production assistant at *McCall's* magazine in 1965. On her path to Hollywood and celebrity status she was an East Coast story editor for Paramount Pictures, head of Mirisch Productions in New York City, and creative executive at First Artists Production at age 26. Her first film as a producer was *Steelyard Blues* in 1973. She made her directorial debut with *The Estate of Billy Buckner.*

PICARD, DENNIS J.

Raytheon Company, 141 Spring Street, Lexington, MA 02173
BORN: 1932. ACHIEVEMENTS: Chief executive officer of Raytheon, served in the United States Air Force 1951-53; Member NAE. STUDIED: Northeastern University, B.B.A., 1962.
Dennis Picard, at the helm of a $10 billion dollar international enterprise, is the chief executive officer of Raytheon, the nation's fourth largest defense contractor. Raytheon is a high technology company that focuses on commercial and defense electronics, engineering and construction, and aviation. School trained as an engineer, Picard began his career with Raytheon in 1955 and rose through the ranks of the electronics divisions. After working as the general manager of the company's Missile Systems Division, the makers of the Patriot air defense missile system, he was named the CEO in 1990.

PISCOPO, JOSEPH CHARLES

NBC Press Relations, 30 Rockefeller Plaza, New York, NY 10020
Piscopo is a prominent comedian. For career credentials consult the portion of this book entitled "Biographees by Profession" in the Appendix. Within this

portion the list "Comedians" describes requirements for inclusion in this volume.

PITTMAN, H. DOYLE

The Tampa Tribune, 202 Parker St., Tampa, FL 33606-2308 (813) 272-7711

Pittman is a prominent publisher and head of the *Tampa Tribune*, the state's second largest newspaper.

PLATT, LEWIS EMMETT

Hewlett-Packard Company, 3000 Hanover St., Palo Alto, CA 94304 (415) 857-1501
BORN: 1942, Johnson City, N.Y. ACHIEVEMENTS: president, chief operating officer and chairman of Hewlett-Packard Company. STUDIED: Cornell University, B.A., mechanical engineering; Wharton School of Business, University of Pennsylvania, M.B.A., business administration.

Lewis Platt joined Hewlett-Packard's medical division in 1966, soon after graduation from Wharton School of Business. Six years later he became general manager of the division, and since then his climb has been steady through the company's medical, analytical, and manufacturing operations. In 1990, he was named head of the Computer Systems Organization, which includes the company's multi-user systems and workstation businesses. When David Packard, one of the founders of the company, retired in 1993, the board elected Platt chairman to go with his titles of president and chief operating officer.

POOLE, RONALD

Mobil Oil, 3225 Gallows Rd., Fairfax, VA., 22037 (703) 846-3000
ACHIEVEMENTS: Developed organic, vegetable-based hydraulic oil.

Ronald Poole, research associate at Mobil Oil, developed an organic, virtually nontoxic vegetable-based hydraulic oil. Mobil FAL 22411 is useful for operating equipment on farms, in drinking reservoirs, forests, and ocean platforms, all areas sensitive to toxic oils. FAL, derived from common plant seeds, performs as well as hydrocarbon-based oils in lubrication, wear protection, and overall strength.

POOLE, WILLIAM

Brown University, Department of Economics, 64 Waterman St., Providence, RI 02912
BORN: 1937, Wilmington, Del. ACHIEVEMENTS: Staff, Board of Governors, Washington, D.C.; visiting economist, Reserve Bank of Australia; chief, Federal Reserve Special Studies Section; member, Council of Economic Advisers; books, Monetary Growth and the Economy, Money Growth and Inflation. STUDIED: Swarthmore College, University of Chicago.

William Poole's reputation for level-headedness, fairness, competency, and honesty emerged intact from two of the most bitter fights American economists have ever fought. In one, President Reagan turned his back on his Council of Economic Advisers, which included Poole, for views more favorable to his notions that cutting taxes, especially for the rich, would encourage business investment and stabilize the economy. In the second, the economics profession as a

whole was being blamed in the nation's financial markets in the late 1970s for its inability to accurately predict the economic variables market participants needed as signals of economic growth and interest rate movements. Poole at this time, as throughout his career, moved back and forth between government and academia to improve the quality of life for the average American. He achieved this by studying wage-price controls, inflation, and the monetary policy of the Federal Reserve Bank System, with which he would have a long and distinguished tenure. One of his signal departures from his peers was on the matter of money growth. While it is the general rule, which Poole accepted, that long-run cycles in money growth would produce similar results in long-run cycles of economic growth and inflation, he also said there were no beneficial effects from not controlling it closely. From that radical stance, Poole took on the Fed in the 1970s and became an advocate of steady money growth. Poole has continued writing papers on the Fed and has helped to fine tune the public's focus on the system, which he believes should adopt a less activist policy on money growth and instead foster a "steady as she goes" position. In the meantime, he also actively pursues one of his chief tenets: If policy is to be vivid and real, it must not only be economically sound, but understandable to the whole citizenry.

POPE, NORRIS

Stanford University Press, Stanford, CA 94305 (415) 723-9434

Pope is a prominent publisher. For career credentials consult the portion of this book entitled "Biographees by Profession" in the Appendix. Within this portion the list "Publishers" describes requirements for inclusion in this volume.

POPOFF, FRANK PETER

Dow Chemical Co., 2030 Dow Center, Midland, MI 48674
BORN: 1935, Sofia (Bulgaria). ACHIEVEMENTS: Recipient of the Rene Dubos Environmental Award; member of the President's Commission Environmental Quality; member, Chemical Manufacturers Association. STUDIED: Indiana University, B.S., 1957, M.B.A, 1959.

Frank Popoff left Bulgaria and came to America in 1940, joining Dow as a chemist in 1959. Throughout his 34 years with the company, he has held a variety of duties, including stints in the sales, marketing and business management divisions. Prior to becoming chief executive officer in 1987, he was the executive vice-president, with responsibility for all of the company's international operations.

POSIN, KATHRYN

Kathryn Posin Dance Company, 20 Bond St., New York, NY 10012 (212) 777-1515
BORN: 1945, Butte, Mont. ACHIEVEMENTS: Notable ballets: The Closer She Gets...The Better She Looks; Flight of the Baroque Airship; The Black Dance; The White Dance; Ladies in the Arts; Nuclear Energy, I, II, III; Tales from the Dark Wood; Saks Fifth Avenue Suite; Close Encounters of the

Third Kind. *STUDIED: Bennington College, Vermont ; Dance Theater Workshop; Maggie Black, Merce Cunningham studios.*

Newly out of college with a choreographer's grant from Bennington and a fellowship from the American Dance Festival at Connecticut College, Kathryn Posin first danced for the dour Anna Sokolow, the American Dance Center, and the Dance Theater Workshop. Turning to choreography in 1967 she formed her own company and has written for it since. She also contributes works for both ballet and modern dance troupes, and stages musical numbers for stage productions. A talent for high satire is shown in *The Closer She Gets...The Better She Looks*, where three men and three women of the TV commercial era impulse shop in a supermarket, finally heaping one another into the carts to be pushed around like so many boxes and jars of advertisized products.

POST, MIKE

c/o Polydor Records, Inc., 810 Seventh Avenue, New York, NY 10019 (212) 399-7075

Post is a prominent composer. For career credentials consult the portion of this book entitled "Biographees by Profession" in the Appendix. Within this portion the list "Composers" describes requirements for inclusion in this volume.

POTTER, MICHAEL

U.S.P.H.S., Department of Medicine, Bethesda, MD 20814

Potter is a prominent physician. For career credentials consult the portion of this book entitled "Biographees by Profession" in the Appendix. Within this portion the list "Physicians" describes requirements for inclusion in this volume.

POVICH, MAURICE (MAURY) RICHARD

Fox Broadcasting Company, 205 East 67th St., New York, NY, 10021

BORN: 1939, Washington, D.C.. STUDIED: University of Pennsylvania, B.A., journalism.

Talk show host Maury Povich emulated his father, a sports writer for the *Washington Post*, and became a journalist. After graduation Povich hosted the Washington, D.C., talk show *Panorama* and later moved to Chicago and worked at NBC affiliate WMAQ. His next position was as an anchorman in Los Angeles where he shared the newscast with Connie Chung who he later married. Fired because of low ratings, Povich put in a short stint with a station in San Francisco and one in Philadelphia, and then returned to Washington where *Panorama* welcomed him back. In 1986 Rupert Murdock hired Povich to host the sensationalist talk show, *A Current Affair*, allowing him to move to New York. Povich remained on *A Current Affair* for five years, while sneered at by many journalists for the often rakish subject matter he presented. In 1991 he gave up the show and jumped into the crowded daytime arena, already dominated by Oprah Winfrey, Phil Donahue, Montel Williams, and Jenny Jones. The *Maury Povich Show* faced a tough time ahead, trying to distinguish itself from the pack. Meantime, he and senior *People* magazine writer Ken Gross crafted a memoir of Povich's experiences on the Murdoch show. Eventually Povich's show became one of the most successful in the crowded talk show field.

PRESLEY, PRISCILLA BEAULIEU

c/o Putnam Berkley Group, 200 Madison Ave., New York, NY 10016 (212) 951-8400

BORN: 1945, Brooklyn, N.Y. STUDIED: Patricia Stevens Finishing and Career School; Steven Peck Theatre Arts School; Chuck Morris Karate School.

Presley's first enterprise after six years of marriage to Elvis Presley—which ended in divorce in 1973—was designer dress boutique. Named Bis and Beau, with designs by Presley's partner and designer Olivia, sold designer dresses to Barbara Streisand, Cher, Julie Christie, and others notable celebrities for seven years before she sold her share of the boutique to Olivia. As manager of Graceland after Elvis' death she showed further business acumen by opening the estate to the public, and charging a fee for entry. She became a spokesperson for beauty products before turning to acting. Between 1980 to 1990, she produced *Elvis and Me* for television based on her book. Presley also co-produced the television series *Elvis*. As a television actress, she made her debut in the documentary series *Those Amazing Animals*, going on to the role of Jenny Wade in the television soap opera *Dallas*. Her films include *Comeback/Love is Forever*, *The Naked Gun: From the Files of Police Squad* plus its sequel, *Naked Gun 2 1/2: The Smell of Fear*, a spoof on her sexy persona.

PRESSLER, LARRY

SR-283 Russell Bldg., Washington D.C. 20510-4101 (202) 224-5842

BORN: 1942; Humboldt, S.D. ACHIEVEMENTS: Rhodes scholar, Vietnam veteran, author U.S. Senators from the Prairie, 1982; Star Wars: The Strategic Defense Initiative Debates in Congress, 1986. STUDIED: University of South Dakota, B.A. 1964; Oxford University, 1965; Harvard University, M.A. 1971, J.D., 1971.

After three years as a lieutenant in the Vietnam War, serving in Saigon and on the Mekong Delta, Larry Pressler returned to the United States to complete his education at Harvard Law School. He entered the field of law in 1971, only to leave it three years later for a post in the U.S. House of Representatives. He was re-elected in 1976. In 1978 Pressler ran successfully for the U.S. Senate from South Dakota. There he has served on the Finance Committee, the Special Committee on Aging and as chairman of the Commerce, Science and Transportation Committee, while still finding the time to write two books.

PRINCE, "THE ARTIST FORMERLY KNOWN AS"

Paisley Park records, 3300 Warner Blvd., Burbank, CA 91510 (818) 846-9090

BORN: 1959, Minneapolis, Minn. ACHIEVEMENTS: Grammy, Best Rock Performance Duo or Group, Purple Rain (with The Revolution), 1984; Grammy, Best Rhythm and Blues Song, I Feel For You, 1984; Grammy, Best Soundtrack Album, Purple Rain (with The Revolution, John L. Nelson, Lisa & Wendy), 1984; Grammy, Best R&B Duo or Group, Kiss (with The Revolution), 1986; Academy Award, Original Score, Purple Rain, 1984. STUDIED: High School dropout.

Orignally known as Prince Rogers Nelson, he now uses only a symbol as a moniker and is usually referred to as "the artist formerly known as Prince." He began his career at the age of 19, writing, performing and producing all of his 1978 debut album, *Prince For You*. His 1984 film "Purple Rain and its soundtrack album won an Oscar and three Grammys. He tried to re-create the success of Purple Rain with the sequel, *Under the Cherry Moon*, and another movie, *Graffiti Bridge*, but they were both box-office disasters. He left his first band the Revolution and recorded the solo albums *Lovesexy*, 1989 and *Batman*, 1989. In 1991 he introduced his new band, the New Power Generation, and released the album *Diamonds and Pearls*. He now lives in Minneapolis where he is in semi-retirement.

PRINCE, FAITH

211 East 53rd Street, New York, NY 10022
STUDIED: Attended Cincinnati Conservatory of Music, 1980.
Faith Prince has made an enduring career on the stage. She performed in the ensemble of *Scrambled Feet* in 1979. She then went on to many other stage appearances, including: *Little Shop of Horrors*, 1983; *Guys and Dolls*, 1985; *Groucho: A Life in Revue*, 1986; *Carousel*, 1986; *Olympus on My Mind*, 1986-87; and many others. In addition to her work on the stage, Prince played the role of Angela in the film, *The Last Dragon*, 1985.

PRINCE, HAROLD S.

1270 Ave. of the Americas, New York, NY 10020 (212) 399-0960
Prince is a prominent dramatic artist. For career credentials consult the portion of this book entitled "Biographees by Profession" in the Appendix. Within this portion the list "Dramatic Artists" describes requirements for inclusion in this volume.

PULIDO, MIGUEL A.

Mayor's Office, City of Santa Ana, CA
BORN: 1956, Mexico City. ACHIEVEMENTS: Member, Santa Ana Re-development Agency; Santa Ana Business Association, and Senate Select Committee on Small Business Enterprises. STUDIED: California State at Fullerton, B.S., mechanical engineering.
Pulido, mayor of Santa Ana, Calif., is fluent in English, Spanish and French. Having been a consult working

with city government, he saw an opportunity to try his hand in city government. He therefore ran for a council seat and won election in 1986. Twice elected temporary mayor in 1990 and 1992, he became mayor on a nonpartisan ticket in 1994.

PULLIAM, EUGENE

Indianapolis Star, 307 N. Pennsylvania St., Indianapolis, IN 46204-1811 (317) 633-1240
Pulliam is a prominent publisher. For career credentials consult the portion of this book entitled "Biographees by Profession" in the Appendix. Within this portion the list "Publishers" describes requirements for inclusion in this volume.

PURCELL, PATRICK J

The Boston Herald, 1 Herald Square, Boston, MA 02118 (617) 426- 3000
ACHIEVEMENTS: CEO, News America Publishing. STUDIED: St. John's University, B.A.; Hofstra, M.B.A.
Patrick Purcell started his publishing career with the *Daily News* working as a supervisor and in advertising sales. After ten years with the *Daily News*, Purcell moved to News America Corporation. His first position with News America was as associate publisher of the *Village Voice*. His next job was with the *New York Post* as president of advertising sales. In 1984 he was appointed as president of the *New York Post* in addition to his advertising sales position. Purcell was promoted to president of News America/Newspapers in 1990. He assumed responsibility for both the *Boston Herald* and the *San Antonio Express News*. In 1993 Purcell was named president and CEO of News America Publishing, and is responsible for the U.S. publishing operation of News Corporation, including *TV Guide* and *Mirabella* magazines and *The Boston Herald* newspaper.

PUZO, MARIO

Simon & Schuster, 1230 Avenue of the Americas, New York, NY 10020 (212) 614-1300
BORN: 1920, New York City ACHIEVEMENTS: Best-selling author, The Godfather, 1969; Academy Awards, Best Screenplay, The Godfather, 1972, and Godfather II, 1974. STUDIED: New School for Social Research; Columbia University,
Mario Puzo is achieved national recognition for his best-selling novel *The Godfather*, in 1969. The novel portrays the saga of an organized crime family that encompassed themes of loyalty and betrayal and power, both benevolent and ruthless. He also won Oscars for his screenplays of the film version of *Godfather* and its sequel, *Godfather II*. Puzo also wrote the screenplays for *Earthquake, Superman*, and *Superman II*. In addition to his Godfather novels, he has also written, *Fools Die*, 1978; *The Sicilian*, 1984, and the nonfictionwork *Inside Las Vegas*.

QUALLS, ROXANNE

Room 150, City Hall, 801 Plum Street, Cincinnati, OH 45202 (513) 352-3250
ACHIEVEMENTS: Mayor of Cincinnati. YWCA Woman of Achievement Award, 1994.
Before being elected to public office, Roxanne Qualls served the community as director of the Cincinnati Office of Citizen Action, executive director of Women Helping Women, and director of the Northern Kentucky Rape Crisis Center. She also was the owner of her own company, Re: Crafters. Qualls was elected to the Cincinnati City Council in 1991. She served on the City Council for two years, and was elected mayor of Cincinnati in November, 1993. She is the first woman to win the seat of mayor in Cincinnati in a popular election.

QUAYLE, ("DAN") JAMES DANFORTH

7 N. Jefferson St., Huntington, IN 46750-2839
BORN: 1947, Indianapolis ACHIEVEMENTS: Published autobiography Standing Firm, 1994. STUDIED: DePauw University, political science, 1969; Indiana University, law degree, 1974.
Quayle was elected to the U.S. House of Representatives in 1976, and re-elected in 1978. In 1980 he won a seat in the U.S. Senate, and won re-election in 1986. Quayle was considered a fiscal and social conservative, and was identified with the New Right, a wing of the conservative movement. In 1988 Quayle was vice-presidential nominee on the Republican ticket. Quayle was excoriated by both the press and Democrats for being too young, and too inexperienced to be vice president. Despite the charges, Bush and Quayle defeated Governor Michael Dukakis and Senator Lloyd Bentsen in the election. As vice- president, Quayle headed the Council of Competitiveness, a cabinet-level body that sought to end government regulatory rules. In 1992 Quayle and President George Bush lost their bid for re-election.

QUINDLEN, ANNA

c/o The *New York Times*, 229 West 43rd Street, New York, NY 10036 (212) 556-1234
BORN: 1953. ACHIEVEMENTS: Pulitzer Prize for commentary, 1992. STUDIED: Attended Barnard College.
The former *New York Times* columists joined the paper in 1977 as a reporter, and wrote the *About New York* column, and soon became metro editor. In 1986 she began *Public and Private*, a column of observations about life, love and the pursuit of happiness. In her column, she has dealt with subjects ranging from the banning of gay marchers in the traditional St. Patrick's Day Parade, to the fallout from the Clarence Thomas/Anita Hill revelations. Quindlen has authored several books including; *Living Out Loud*, 1986, *Object Lesson*, 1991, *The Tree that Came to Stay*, 1992, and *Thinking Out Loud*, 1993.

QUINSON, BRUNO ANDRE

c/o Henry Holt & Company, 115 West 18th St., New York, NY 10011 (212) 886-9200
BORN: 1938, Norwich, Conn. ACHIEVEMENTS: STUDIED: Williams College, B.A.; New York University.
Bruno Quinson entered the business side of publishing in 1961. Beginning as a product manager for Simon & Schuster, he became publisher and general manager of the Golden Books division of Western Publishing Company from 1965 to 1970. Later he served as president of Larousse & Company, primarily a publisher of reference books. Quinson joined Macmillan Publishing Company in 1982 as a member of the board and president of the trade and reference division. In the next five years the company's net sales in the division increased from $17 million to $68 million. A reorganization in 1988, which removed some of Quinson's responsibilities while adding others, led to his exodus from Macmillan. Quinson moved to Henry Holt, Inc., where he served as president, chief executive, and later member of the board. Quinson is chairman of the board of the National Book Foundation and a member of the Manhattan Theater Club board and holds many other board positions.

QUINTERO, JOSE

SSD.C., 1501 Broadway, New York, NY
Quintero is a prominent dramatic artist. For career credentials consult the portion of this book entitled "Biographees by Profession" in the Appendix. Within this portion, the list "Dramatic Artists" describes requirements for inclusion in this volume.

RACICOT, MARC

State Capitol, Helena, MT 59620 (406) 444-3111
BORN: 1948, Thompson Falls, Mont. ACHIEVEMENTS: governor of Montana; Montana attorney general. STUDIED: Carroll College, B.A., English, 1970; University of Montana Law School, J.D., 1973.
Marc Racicot is a native of Montana. He worked his way through college finding employment with the Montana Highway Department, the Capitol print shop during the legislative sessions, and as a dishwasher/cook in the college cafeteria. After he received his law degree from the University of Montana, Racicot entered the U.S. Army and was assigned to the Judge Advocate General's Corps. He was discharged from the Army in 1976. From 1976 through 1988, Racicot served in a number of state and local positions, including Missoula County deputy county attorney, Montana Special Prosecutor, handling major cases for county attorneys, and as assistant attorney general. Racicot was elected Montana attorney general in 1989. He intended to run for a second term when the current governor, Stan Stephens, fell ill and dropped out of the race. Racicot was elected governor in November 1992. He is an advocate of reducing government wherever possible.

RAFFAEL, JOSEPH

c/o Nancy Hoffman Gallery, 429 W. Broadway, New York, NY 10012

BORN: 1933. ACHIEVEMENTS: Tiffany Foundation Fellowship; Fulbright Award; collections: Metropolitan Museum of Art, New York City; Smithsonian Institution; exhibitions: Whitney Museum, New York City; San Francisco Museum of Modern Art. STUDIED: Cooper Union; Yale University School of Art.

In the 1960s, Joseph Raffael produced photorealistic paintings that were depictions of nature taken from photographs: animals, ponds and foliage. His large-scale close-ups of animal faces, such as *Lizard's Head*, and human faces, such as *African Lady*, were sensuous replications reflecting a deep concern for nature, for "observing fertile and fantastic things that have within them the power to erupt, like Vesuvius". This interest in nature's mystical qualities made Raffael's approach quite different from that of other photorealists. His media changed from oil to watercolor, pastel and lithography, when renditions of natural phenomena became less photographic and more impressionistic, as in the watercolor *Luxembourg Gardens: Memory*." I like to think I paint feeling," said Raffael. "I am interested in spirit as expressed in nature, the invisible made visible".

RAINES, HOWELL

The *New York Times*, 229 West 43rd St., New York, NY 10036 (212) 556-1234

ACHIEVEMENTS: Pulitzer Prize, 1991; editorial page editor of The New York Times. STUDIED: Birmingham-Southern College, B.A., 1964; University of Alabama, M.A., 1973.

Howell Raines grew up in Birmingham, Ala. in the 1940s. He started his journalism career in Alabama in 1964, where he worked for both a television station and a number of newspapers. In 1971 he became the political editor of The *Atlanta Constitution*. He filled the same position at The *St. Petersburg Times* from 1976 until 1978. He was hired by The *New York Times* in 1978, first as a national correspondent in Atlanta, then as bureau chief. In 1992 Raines became the editorial page editor of The *Times*, just one year after receiving a Pulitzer Prize for an article describing his life growing up in Birmingham, Ala.—a white boy in a segregated community.

RAITT, BONNIE LYNN

P.O. Box 626, Los Angeles, CA 90078

BORN: 1949, Cleveland. ACHIEVEMENTS: Grammy, Album of the Year and Best Rock Vocal-Female, In The Nick of Time, 1969; Grammy, Best Rock Performances-Duo or Group, Good Man, Good Woman (with Delbert McClinton), 1991. STUDIED: Attended Radcliffe College.

Bonnie Raitt labored for nearly 20 years before striking it hot with her number-one album, *Nick of Time*. Although she had achieved a sizable cult following with her unique combination of seductive lyrics and potent slide guitar playing, Raitt had difficulty appealing to a mass audience. After 15 years of disappointing sales, Warner Bros. terminated Raitt's contract after the release of *Nine Lives*, in 1986. However, three years later, she signed a contract with Capitol Records and finally hit number one.

RAMOS, MELVIN JOHN

5941 Ocean View Dr., Oakland, CA 94618

BORN: 1935. ACHIEVEMENTS: NEA Fellowship; collections: Museum of Modern Art, New York City; Guggenheim Museum; exhibitions: James Corcoran Gallery, Santa Monica; Oakland Museum. STUDIED: California State, Sacramento.

After he studied with Wayne Thiebaud in the 1950s, Melvin Ramos' early works focused on the female figure in a precise and straightforward manner. In the early 1960s, he turned to Pop art paintings of comic-strip heroes, borrowing and inventing characters to comment on the mass-media images in energetic, distorted compositions. Later he became known for "pin-up" girls accompanied by exotic animals, as in *Aardvark*. *Chiquita* was a picture of a peeled banana with a woman inside. In the 1980s, his attention has turned to the iconography of the California landscape, and recently he has returned to investigations of the human figure.

RAMPERSAND, ARNOLD

c/o Alfred A. Knopf, 201 East 50th St., New York, NY 10022 (212) 751-2600

BORN: 1941, Trinidad (West Indies). ACHIEVEMENTS: Anisfield-Wolf Award in Race Relations, Cleveland Foundation; Clarence J. Holte Prize, Phelps Stokes Fund; American Book Award, Before Columbus Foundation. STUDIED: Bowling Green State University, B.A., M.A.; Harvard University, M.A., Ph.D.

Arnold Rampersand is best known for his two-volume biography of Langston Hughes, the leading black poet in the Harlem Renaissance of the 1920s. The first volume, *The Life of Langston Hughes: I, Too, Sing America*, covers the first 40 years of the radical poet's life, a six-year effort during which Rampersad traveled across the U.S., to the Soviet Union, and through southwestern Europe seeking material. He also combed through 6,000 papers housed at Yale University. The second volume, subtitled *I Dream a World*, follows the poet through the height of the civil rights movement as the author candidly represents the nation's tumultuous racial and political environment of the time. Among other works of Rampersad is the *Art and Imagination of W.E.B. Dubois*, a prominent civil rights leader, educator, and philosopher. Rampersad has contributed to many books and periodicals, and edited and co-written two books to add to his own production of three. He has taught at Columbia University and Princeton University, where he has been Woodrow Wilson Professor of History since 1990.

RAMSEY, NORMAN FOSTER

Harvard University, Lyman Laboratories, Cambridge, MA 02138

BORN: 1915, Washington, D.C. ACHIEVEMENTS: Nobel Prize in Physics (shared with Hans G. Dehmelt and Wolfgang Paul, Germany), 1989; E.O. Lawrence Award; Medal of Honor, Institute of Electrical and Electronics

Engineers; Rabi Prize; Monie Ferst Award; Compton Medal; Oersted Medal. *STUDIED: Cambridge University; Columbia University.*

Ramsey's Nobel citation honored him for "inventing a method of measuring time" on which all current time in the world is based. It is accurate a hundred times or more than any other method used—to 4 seconds in a million years. His research led to development of the hydrogen maser, which creates and amplifies high-frequency radio waves with a razor sharp, constant signal, and, as a byproduct, he elaborated details of the hydrogen atom structure. Also, in his long career, he played an important role in the development of radar. His colaureates were cited by the Nobel physics committee for developing methods to isolate atoms and subatomic particles.

RANDOLPH, JOHN

Gores/Fields Agency, Suite 700, 10100 Santa Monica Blvd., Los Angeles, CA 90067.
BORN: 1915, Bronx, N.Y. ACHIEVEMENTS: Antoinette Perry Award, Best Featured Actor in a Play, Broadway Bound, 1987. STUDIED: City College of N.Y., 1935; attended Columbia University, studied at American Theatre Wing, 1947, and Actors' Studio, 1948-54.

John Randolph, born Emanuel Hirsch Cohen, probably has more stage, screen, and television appearances to his credit than any three other actors combined. His stage debut occurred in 1935, at the East Houston Street Theatre production of *Ghosts*, in New York City. Shortly thereafter, in 1937, he made his Broadway debut, playing the role of Tuff in the play *Revolt of the Beavers*. Randolph continued his stage career, ranging from Shakespeare to modern, culminating in a Tony Award for his performance in *Broadway Bound*, 1986-87. Randolph was also a regular actor in films. His first principal appearance was in *The Naked City*, 1948. He played parts in two of the *Planet of the Apes* series of movies and had character parts in films such as *Prizzi's Honor*, 1985, and *National Lampoon's Christmas Vacation*, 1989. Randolph was also prolific on television, playing parts in series, television movies, and episodic appearances.

RANGEL, CHARLES B.

2252 Rayburn Bldg., Washington D.C. 20515-3215 (202) 225-4365
BORN: 1930; New York, N.Y. ACHIEVEMENTS: Cited for bravery, Korean War; first black member of Ways and Means Committee. STUDIED: New York University, B.S. 1957; St. John's University, LL.B., 1960.

As a high school dropout he served in the Korean War and was cited for bravery due to wounds received when he slipped behind enemy lines and helped rescue over 40 fellow soldiers. He returned to his native Harlem, N.Y., finished high school and obtained a law degree in 1960. In 1966 he was elected to the New York State Assembly and in 1970 to the U.S. House of Representatives. He headed the Health Subcommittee of the House Ways and Means Committee, served as chairman of the Select Committee on Narcotics and is a leader of the Congressional Black Caucus.

RAOS, JOHN G.

Hanson Industries, 99 Wood Ave., S. Iselin, NJ 08830 (908) 603-6600
ACHIEVEMENTS: Played guiding role in major capital acquisitions at Hanson Industries.

John Raos is president and chief operating officer of Hanson Industries, a $15 billion British-American industrial management corporation. Raos also sits on the board of Dataflex Corporation, a provider of desktop computing solutions and services. Raos joined Hanson Industries as corporate comptroller in 1976. After holding various positions he assumed his present titles in 1992. He is known for having played a guiding role in Hanson's important acquisitions in the chemical, coal, and cement fields.

RAPHAEL, SALLY JESSY

510 West 57th St., New York, NY 10019
BORN: 1943, Easton, Pa. ACHIEVEMENTS: Bronze Medal, International Film and Television Festival of New York; Emmy Award, Outstanding Talk Show Host. STUDIED: University of Puerto Rico, student; Columbia University, B.F.A.; Actors Studio, New York, student.

In addition to her television work, she has been part-time owner of a perfume gallery and owner of an art gallery, a wine bar, and a bed-and-breakfast business in Bucks County, Pa. She co-authored two books: *Finding Love: A Practical Guide for Men and Women*, with H.J. Abadie, and an autobiography, *Sally: Unconventional Success*, with Pam Proctor. As an actress Raphael played herself in *Fatal Flaw*, a talk show host in *Resident Alien*, additionally appearing in the *Addams Family*. Besides working in both radio and television in New York City, she has hosted many award and anniversary shows, including the *16th Annual Daytime Emmy Awards*, a *Jerry Lewis Telethon*, the 50th anniversary show honoring Bugs Bunny, and a 25th anniversary show honoring Phil Donahue.

RASPBERRY, WILLIAM J.

The Washington Post, 1150 15th St. NW, Washington, D.C., 20071 (202) 334-6000.
BORN: Okalona, Miss. ACHIEVEMENTS: U.S. Army photographer. STUDIED: Indiana Central College, B.A., History.

In 1956 William Raspberry began his journalistic career as both a reporter and photographer for the newspaper in his college town, the *Indianapolis Recorder*. After a two-year stint in the Army from 1960 until 1962, he became a columnist for *The Washington Post*, a position he still holds today. He is known for his balanced approach to commentary, carefully considering the myriad points of view surrounding controversial topics in his column.

RATHER, DAN

CBS News, 524 West 57th St., New York, NY 10019
BORN: 1931, Wharton, Texas. ACHIEVEMENTS: News anchor, CBS, author, he Camera Never Blinks. STUDIED: Sam Houston State College, Huntsville, Texas, B.A. journalism, 1953.

During college Dan Rather worked as a writer and sportscaster at KSAM-TV. After graduation he worked for the *Houston Chronicle*, United Press International and radio station KTRH in Houston. In the late 1950s he became director of news and public affairs at KHOU-TV, the CBS Houston affiliate. Rather gained nationwide attention during his in-depth coverage of President Kennedy's assassination. In 1964 CBS named him White House correspondent, a position he held though the Johnson and Nixon years. Ten years later, in 1974, he became an anchor and correspondent for *CBS Reports*. He co-anchored *60 Minutes* from 1975 until 1981, then went on to replace Walter Cronkite, in 1981, as anchor and managing editor of the *CBS Evening News*. In 1988 he became an anchor for *48 Hours*. Rather has also written several books including; *The Camera Never Blinks*, co-written with M. Herskowitz, 1977; *The Palace Guard*, co-written with G. Gates, 1974; and *I Remember*, 1991.

RAUSCHENBERG, ROBERT

c/o Leo Castelli Gallery, 420 W. Broadway, New York, NY 10012
BORN: 1925. ACHIEVEMENTS: Grand Prix D'Honneur, Thirteenth International Exhibition of Graphic Art, Ljubljana, Yugoslavia; Venice Biennale; collections: Whitney Museum; Museum of Modern Art; exhibitions: Whitney Museum of American Art; Museum of Modern Art. STUDIED: Kansas City Art Institute; Art Students League.
After working with de Kooning in 1955, Robert Rauschenberg exhibited his "mixed media" paintings that combined painted elements with found objects in an effort to break down the boundaries between art and life. He also participated at Black Mountain College with composer John Cage, and dancer Merce Cunningham, in some of the first performances that later came to be called "happenings". His new methods opened the way for Pop Art. Combinations of disparate images through photo-transfer, silkscreen, incorporation of found objects, and painted forms resulted in striking juxtapositions. Since 1966 he has experimented with disks, motors, plexiglass, sound, and variations in technique such as the transfer of photographs to silkscreen in the manner of Andy Warhol. Recent work includes a silkscreen-like collage of photographic images on the surface of the Talking Heads' plastic record album, *Speaking in Tongues*.

RAYMOND, LEE R.

Exxon Corporation, Irving, TX
BORN: 1938, Watertown, S.D. ACHIEVEMENTS: trustee Southern Methodist University; partner emeritus New York City; member of the American Petroleum Institute. STUDIED: University of Wisconsin, B.S., 1960; University of Minnesota, Ph.D., 1963.
Trained as a chemical engineer, Lee Raymond joined Exxon in 1963 as a production research engineer. He made his way through the company and served in Latin America and the Caribbean, eventually reaching the corporate pinnacle as the chairman and chief executive officer in 1993.

REAGAN, RONALD WILSON

11000 Wilshire Blvd., Los Angeles, CA 90024
BORN: 1911, Tampico, Ill. ACHIEVEMENTS: Governor of California, 1966-74; author of Where's the Rest of Me?, 1965, The Creative Society, 1968, Abortion and the Conscience of the Nation, 1984, Speaking My Mind, 1989, and An American Life, 1990. STUDIED: Eureka, College, B.A., 1932.
Ronald Reagan has deep roots in small-town, middle America. He graduated from Eureka College in 1932, where he was active in drama and sports. Reagan worked as a sportscaster after college until a screen test landed him a contract at Warner Brothers in 1937. He appeared in about 53 films, taking a break from acting to serve in the U.S. Army from 1942 until 1945. Reagan married actress Jane Wyman in 1940, but they divorced in 1948. He was president of the Screen Actors Guild for two terms during the 1950s. In 1952 he married his present spouse, Nancy Davis. In the 1950's Reagan moved to television, hosting the series *Death Valley Days*, and worked as a public relations speaker for the General Electric Company. Following the path of many of his contemporaries, Reagan leaned toward a New Deal orientation in his early years. As he matured, Reagan developed values that were decidedly more conservative. In 1966 Reagan defeated California's incumbent Democratic governor, Edmund "Pat" Brown. He served two consecutive four-year terms, gaining prominence as a national conservative political force. Reagan was considered a presidential contender in every election from 1968 until 1980, when he won the Republican nomination and defeated Jimmy Carter in the presidential race. He campaigned primarily against Carter's foreign policy, which included returning the Panama Canal Zone to Panama, SALT treaties with the Soviet Union, and coupling human rights considerations with the national interest in diplomacy. Reagan believed in a strong national defense, combatting the evils of Communism, downsizing the government, and built-up of the national defense infrastructure. The Soviet Union and its Eastern European satellites could not compete with the economic strength of the United States and eventually collapsed, leaving the United States as the only economic and military superpower in the world.

REDFIELD, JAMES

c/o Warner Books, 666 Fifth Ave., New York, NY 10103
(212) 484-2900
BORN: 1950, Birmingham, Ala. STUDIED: Auburn University, M.A., psychology.
After 15 years as a therapist for disturbed children in Alabama, New Age cult hero James Redfield himself published and distributed his *Celestine Prophecy: An Adventure*, in 1992. After a year of traveling through the South and West with copies of the *Prophecy*, his sales of 100,000 books to independent book stores shook up the New York Publishing world, which had universally rejected it. A "spiritual thriller" about a man in search of mysterious Peruvian texts which promise nine transcendental insights, the book was a chart-topper when finally brought out by Warner

Books in 1994. Spinoffs from the book include a newsletter, a sound recording, and *The Celestine Prophecy: An Experimental Guide*, with Carol Adrienne, also published by Warner Books. According to Marci McDonald in a *Maclean's* magazine article in 1995, Redfield is working on another *Prophecy* book entitled *The Tenth Insight*, and expects there will be 12 insights before the spigot is tapped.

REDFORD, ROBERT (CHARLES ROBERT)

Wildwood Enterprises, 100 Universal City Plaza, Universal City, CA 91608
BORN: 1937, Santa Monica, Calif. ACHIEVEMENTS: Golden Globe Award, New Male Film Star of the Year, Inside Daisy Clover, 1966; Golden Globe Award, Male World Film Favorite, 1975, 1977, and 1978; Academy Award and Golden Globe Award, Best Director, Ordinary People, 1980. STUDIED: Attended University of Colorado, Pratt Institute, and American Academy of Dramatic Arts.

Roles such as the Sundance Kid in *Butch Cassidy and the Sundance Kid* and Johnny Hooker in *The Sting* established Redford as a winning, knavish bad guy. He continued to star in many other films, including *The Way We Were*, 1973; *The Great Gatsby*, 1974; *All the President's Men*, 1976; *The Electric Horseman*, 1979; *Out of Africa*, 1985; and *Havana*, 1990. He won an Academy Award as Best Director for the film *Ordinary People*, in 1980. In 1988 he directed the film *The Milagro Beanfield War*, which didn't do quite as well at the box office. Redford, an active environmentalist, has narrated the documentaries *Broken Treaty at Battle Mountain*, 1974, and *To Protect Mother Earth*, 1989. His most current film (1996) is *Up Close and Personal*.

Author James Redfield.

REDLICH, DON

156 West 72nd St., New York, NY 10023 (212) 874-7156
BORN: 1933, Winona, Minn. ACHIEVEMENTS: Notable ballets: Electra and Orestes; Mark of Cain; Passin' Through; Four Sonatas; Salutations; Forgetmenot; Eight and Three; Oddities; Alice and Henry; Pocourante. STUDIED: University of Wisconsin. B.A., dance, ca.1955; Hanya Holm Dance Studio.

Don Redlich started dancing professionally in Broadway musicals and graduated to choreographing off-Broadway and television productions. He formed his own company in the late 1950s soon after presenting the first concert performance of his own work in 1958, and has since choreographed primarily for his troupe, but also for students at his alma mater, the first institution in the U.S. to develop a full-degree program in dance. His work is included in the repertory of the BatDor Company in Israel, and he teaches at Adelphi University in Garden City, New York, and Sarah Lawrence College.

REGAN, DONALD T.

11 Canal City Plaza #301, Alexandria, VA 22314
BORN: 1918, Cambridge, Mass. ACHIEVEMENTS: U.S. Treasury secretary and White House staff chief in the Reagan administration. STUDIED: Harvard, B.A., 1940; Hahneman Medical College Hospital, L.L.D. (Honorary), 1968; University of Pennsylvania, L.L.D. (Honorary), 1972; Pace University, L.L.D. (Honorary), 1973; Colegate University D.H.L. (Honorary).

After 35 years at Merrill Lynch and Co., where he rose to the presidency of the New York brokerage firm, Donald Regan was appointed secretary of the treasury by President Reagan in 1981. He moved to the White House during Reagan's second term to head the president's White House staff. However, his executive skills were said to be stronger than his political instincts in the position, and he resigned under pressure in 1987 amid the tumult of the Iran-Contra affair. He published his memoirs, *For the Record*, in 1988.

REHNQUIST, WILLIAM HUBB

Supreme Court of the United States, One First St. N.E., Washington, D.C. 20543 (202) 479-3000
BORN: 1924, Milwaukee, Wis. ACHIEVEMENTS: Chief justice, U.S. Supreme Court; Phi Beta Kappa. STUDIED: Stanford University, B.A., M.A., 1948; Harvard University, M.A., 1948; Stanford University, LL.B., 1952.
Rehnquist served in the Army Air Corps, both in the U.S. and overseas, during World War II, attaining the rank of sergeant. He spent his first year after graduation as clerk to Justice Robert H. Jackson, at the U.S. Supreme Court. He then went on to a private law practice in Phoenix. Rehnquist was appointed assistant attorney general, in the Legal Counsed Office, by President Richard Nixon in January, 1969. He served

in this position until January 7, 1972, when he was confirmed and sworn in as associate justice of the Supreme Court. In 1986, President Ronald Reagan nominated Rehnquist for the position of chief justice. He was sworn in September 26, 1986.

REICH, ROBERT B.

Department of Labor, 200 Constitution Ave. NW, Washington, D.C. 20210 (202) 219-9271
BORN: 1946, Scranton, Pa. ACHIEVEMENTS: solicitor general, U.S. Department of Justice, 1974-76; director of Policy Planning, Federal Trade Commission, 1976-81; U.S. secretary of Labor, 1993- present. STUDIED: Dartmouth College, B.A., 1968, Oxford University, M.A., 1970; Yale Law School, J.D., 1973.
Robert Reich developed an interest in politics, law and economics while studying at Oxford University. A Rhodes scholar, Reich began working in government right after graduating from Yale Law School, in 1973. He began his career at the Justice Department. Reich started lecturing at the Kennedy School of Government, at Harvard University, in 1981 and developed a reputation for forward thinking ideas on labor relations and economics. Soon after, he began publishing theoretical works on labor, putting forward ideas such as: the importance of vigorous investment in high-technology enterprises, and improving relations between labor and management. Reich was appointed secretary of labor by President Bill Clinton in 1993 and, in that post, has been a major player in the passage of several important pieces of legislation, including the Family and Medical Leave Act.

REICH, STEVE

Helen Cann, 175 Fifth Ave., Suite 2396, New York, NY 10010- 7703
BORN: 1936, New York City. ACHIEVEMENTS: recipient Koussevitsky Legend Award, 1981; Rockefeller Foundation grantee, 1975, 1978, 1981, 1990; National Endowment for the Arts grantee, 1974, 1976, 1991. STUDIED: percussion studies with Roland Kohloff, 1950-53; Cornell University, B.A., 1957; Julliard School of Music, 1968-61; Mills College, M.A.. music, 1963.
Steve Reich is known for experimental compositions built on repetitious and short, overlapping melodic rhythmic patterns. These compositions lead some to describe him as a minimalist, trance, or steady state structuralist composer. His attraction to musical abstraction has led him to the study of African tribal drumming, Balinese gamelan music, and traditional forms of Hebraic chanting. His music demonstrates his belief that structure can be transferred from one culture to another; his sounds are rich blends of vocal and acoustic instrumentation. Some of his notable compositions include: *Drumming*, 1971; *Music for Mallet Instruments, Voices, and Organ*, 1973; *Music for 18 Musicians*, 1979; and *Tehillim*, 1981. Reich has performed extensively in the United States and Europe.

REILLY, JACK

12720 Washington Blvd., 2nd Fl. Los Angeles, CA 90066

BORN: 1950. ACHIEVEMENTS: NEA Artist Residency/Exhibition Touring Grant; Best of Show, Bellair National Exhibition; collections: Oakland Museum; Fresno Metropolitan Museum; exhibitions: Stella Polaris Gallery, Los Angeles; Mission Gallery, New York City. STUDIED: Florida State University.
Extreme opposing forces at work typify the essence of Jack Reilly's paintings. His works have always demonstrated a responsibility to art history in the particular issues and stylistic tendencies he chooses to explore. During recent years, a clear-cut and logical development has taken place. From stark illusionism dealing with pictorial space, to the multilayered, shaped canvases, artistic options such as movement/stillness, thin/thick, color/neutrality, and edge/amorphic have been prevalent in his paintings. Recent pieces incorporate built-in sound that he composes and records for specific pieces.

REIMER, GEN. DENNIS J.

Office of the Secretary, Pentagon, Washington, D.C. 20301 (703) 545-6700
BORN: 1939, Medford, Okla. ACHIEVEMENTS: Defense Distinguished Service Medal; Distinguished Service Medal; two Legions of Merit; Distinguished Flying Cross; six Bronze Star medals, one with "V" device for valor, and the Purple Heart among his many Army citations. STUDIED: U.S. Military Academy; Shippensburg State University, M.S., science.
From his position as commanding general of the U.S. Army, Reimer became the 33rd Army chief of staff in 1995. During his 33 years in the service he has held command positions from company to division level, and served on several staffs leading to headquarters staff in the Department of the Army. Reimer served two combat tours in Vietnam, one as an adviser to a South Vietnamese battalion, and the other as an executive officer for a U.S. Army infantry division. In Korea, Reimer was assistant chief of staff of a combined Korean/U.S. force, and chief of staff of a combined field army. He held the post of deputy chief of staff for operations and plans for the Army during Desert Storm.

REITMAN, IVAN

c/o CAA 9830 Wilshire Blvd., Beverly Hills, CA (310) 289-2000
BORN: 1946, Czechoslovakia. ACHIEVEMENTS: NATO Director of the Year, National Association of Theater Owners; Genie, Special Achievement. STUDIED: McMaster University, Hamilton, Ontario, Canada, B.A., music.
Ivan Reitman was 5 years old when his family emigrated from Czechoslovakia to Canada in 1951. He did his early film work in Canada, but his major films were made in the U.S. In Canada, as a producer and director, he played a major role in the careers of *Second City* (Chicago- and Toronto-based) performers, including Bill Murray, Dan Aykroyd, and John Belushi. Murray would make a big splash on the screen in the Reitman-directed *Meatballs*, while Belushi would do the same in Reitman's *National Lampoon's Animal House*. Both Aykroyd and Murray also appeared in Reitman's supernatural spoof *Ghostbusters*. The eccentric Ghostbusters mythology became part of the 1980s culture, spinning off a hit single, merchandise, and a

cartoon series. For Broadway, Reitman produced *The Magic Show* starring Doug Henning; for Off-Broadway and a subsequent year-long tour, he produced *The National Lampoon Show*.

REMNICK, DAVID

The New Yorker, 20 West 43rd St., New York, NY 10036-7440 (212) 840-3800

Remnick is a prominent journalist. For career credentials consult the portion of this book entitled "Biographees by Profession" in the Appendix. Within this portion, the list "Journalists" describes requirements for inclusion in this volume.

RENDELL, EDWARD GENE

Office of the Mayor, Room 215 City Hall, Philadelphia, PA 19107 (215) 688 2181
BORN: 1944, New York City. ACHIEVEMENTS: recipient Man of the Year Award, Veteran's of Foreign Wars, 1980; Distinguished Public Service Award, Pennsylvania County Detectives Association, 1981; mayor of Philadelphia; district attorney, Philadelphia. STUDIED: University of Pennsylvania, 1965; Villanova Law School, 1968.

After graduating from law school, Rendell worked at the Philadelphia District Attorney's Office. In 1977 he ran for district attorney, beat the incumbent in the primary, and went on to become the youngest Philadelphia district attorney in the city's history.

U.S. Attorney General Janet Reno.

He was re-elected in 1981. After an unsuccessful primary attempt to unseat incumbent mayor W. Wilson Goode in 1987, Rendell ran for mayor again in 1991 and was elected mayor with 68 percent of the vote. Rendell took office in a city that was facing near bankruptcy. He restored fiscal stability by negotiating new collective bargaining agreements, winning favorable labor agreement arbitration awards, increasing tax revenue collection efforts, contracting out city services, and implementing management and productivity initiatives.

RENO, JANET

Office of the Attorney General, 10th & Constitution Ave., Washington, D.C. 20530 (202) 514-2001

BORN: 1938, Miami, Fla. ACHIEVEMENTS: First female U.S. attorney general; state attorney for Dade County, Fla. STUDIED: Cornell University; Harvard University, LL.B., 1963

Janet Reno, the first female U.S. attorney general, received her law degree from Harvard Law School in 1963. After graduation Reno practiced law in Miami with a number of firms. She was named staff director of the Florida House Judiciary Committee in 1971. She accepted a position in the Dade County State Attorney's Office in 1973, and was appointed state attorney for Dade County in 1978. She was elected to the position in November 1978, and was re-elected four more times. Reno was nominated U.S. attorney general by President Bill Clinton, and confirmed by the U.S. Senate on March 12, 1993.

RHODES, MARY

P. O. Box 9277, Corpus Christi, TX 78469 (512) 880- 3100
ACHIEVEMENTS: Mayor, Corpus Christi, Texas; council member, Corpus Christi, Texas.

In her second term as the mayor of Corpus Christi, Texas, Mary Rhodes got her start in city government when she was appointed to the Corpus Christi Planning Council. Shortly thereafter, Rhodes was elected to the city council as an at-large council member in 1987, and ultimately served two, two-year terms. She was first elected mayor in April, 1991, and was re-elected in April, 1993. Rhodes has participated in a number of civic and professional organizations such as the United Way, League of Women Voters, and the City Council of Parent/Teacher Associations. She places a high priority on law enforcement and youth, attending DARE graduations, and is a member of Mayors United on Safety, Crime, and Law Enforcement.

RICCIARDI, LAWRENCE R.

RJR Nabisco Inc., 1301 Ave. Of The Americas, New York, NY 10019
BORN: 1941 ACHIEVEMENTS: Member of the Association of the Bar of the City of New York. STUDIED: Fordham University, B.A., 1962; Columbia University, J.D., 1965; Stanford University, executive program, 1978.

Before joining Nabisco in 1989 as executive vice-president and general counsel, Lawrence Ricciardi served as executive vice president and general counsel of American Express Travel Related Services, Inc. His first stint with Nabisco was as co-chairman and director.

RICE, ANN

c/o Alfred A. Knopf, Inc., 201 E. 50th St., New York, NY 10022
BORN: 1941, New Orleans. ACHIEVEMENTS: Best-selling novelist. STUDIED: Texas Women's University, student; San Francisco State College, B.A., M.A.; University of California at Berkeley.
Named Howard Allen O'Brien after her father, Rice legally changed her name around 1947. She began her career as a popular vampire and erotica author after stints as waitress, cook, and insurance underwriter. She quickly gained a vast cult audience with her sado-masochistic sex novels such as *Beauty's Punishment* in 1984, and her supernatural stories such as *Vampire Chronicles* in 1989. She also writes mainstream novels using the pen names Anne Rampling and A.N. Roquelaure.

RICE, NORMAN

Office of the Mayor, 600 Fourth Avenue, Seattle, WA 98104-1873 (206) 684-4000
BORN: 1943, Denver. ACHIEVEMENTS: The first African- American mayor in Seattle, elected 1989, re-elected 1993. STUDIED: University of Washington, B.S. in communications and M.P.A in public administration.
When Mayor Norm Rice was elected in 1989, he became Seattle's first African-American mayor. He was re-elected in 1993 with 67 percent of the vote. During his administration, public school enrollment increased dramatically, reversing a 30-year trend, and student achievement improved; greater diversity of race and gender were introduced at all levels of city government positions; and Seattle was named by *Fortune* magazine as America's number one city for business in 1992. Rice also served 11 years on the Seattle City Council; chaired the U.S. Conference of Mayors Committee on Youth, Families and Education; and co-chaired the National League of Cities Task Force on Children and Education. He was also elected as a Trustee of the U.S. Conference of Mayors, and serves on the Intergovernmental Policy Advisory Committee to the U.S. Trade Representative.

RICHARDSON, BILL

U.S. House of Representatives, Room 156, Washington, D.C. 20515 (202) 225-7660
Richardson is a prominent political leader. For career credentials consult the portion of this book entitled "Biographees by Profession" in the Appendix. Within this portion, the list "Political Leaders" describes requirements for inclusion in this volume.

RICHIE, LIONEL B. JR.

Columbia/CBS, 51 West 52nd St., New York, NY 10019 (212) 975-4321

BORN: 1949, Tuskegee, Ala. ACHIEVEMENTS: Grammy award, Best Pop Vocal-Male, Truly, 1982; Grammy, Album of the Year, Can't Slow Down, 1984; Grammy, Endless Love (duet with Diana Ross), 1982; Grammy, Best Song and Record of the Year, We Are The World, 1985; Academy Award, Best Song, Say You, Say Me, 1985 Country Songwriter's Award, Three Times a Lady, 1978. STUDIED: Tuskegee University, B.S. economics, 1971, MusD (honorary), 1985; Boston College, MusD (honorary), 1986.
While in college Lionel Richie and a group of college friends formed the band, The Commodores. The band's first album, *Machine Gun*, was an instant success because of its instrumental rhythm-and-blues disco sound. The Commodores' growth in popularity had a great deal to do with Richie's melodious ballads and sensuous singing style. In 1978, the song, *Three Times a Lady*, brought Richie a country songwriter's award, demonstrating that soul and country music share common roots. Richie wrote and produced hits for other artists, notably *Lady*, 1980, for Kenny Rogers, and the music for *Endless Love*, 1981, which he performed with Diana Ross. After leaving the Commodores, Richie produced, wrote, sang, and played piano on his solo debut album, *Lionel Richie*, 1982. That album and the next one, *Can't Slow Down*, 1983, combined, sold 20 million copies worldwide. In 1985 Richie and Michael Jackson co-wrote the hunger relief song *We Are the World*. Richie also wrote songs for the films *White Nights* (*Say You, Say Me*, and *The Color Purple* (*Miss Celie's Blues*). Richie's third album, *Dancing on the Ceiling*, 1986, sold more than three million copies in the United States alone.

RICHTER, BURTON

Stanford Linear Accelerator Center, P.O. Box 4349, Palo Alto, CA 94309
BORN: 1931, Brooklyn. ACHIEVEMENTS: Nobel Prize in Physics (shared with Samuel C.C. Ting, both U.S.), 1976; Ernesto Orlando Lawrence Medal. STUDIED: Massachusetts Institute of Technology.
The existence of a fourth type of quark (up, down, strange, and charmed) was first observed in 1974 by the team of Burton Richter and Samuel Ting, and has been called "the greatest discovery ever in the field of particle physics". Their finding was of a subatomic particle three times heavier than the atom's proton, with a life span 10,000 times longer than could be predicted by discoveries prior to theirs, and led to drastic changes in quark theories. Both men disagreed as to what to name their new particle discovery, Richter opting for "psi" and Ting for "J," so their published announcement called it "J/psi".

RIDGE, TOM

Commonwealth of Pennsylvania, Office of the Governor, Harrisburg, PA
BORN: 1945, Munhall, Pa. STUDIED: Harvard, B.A., government studies; Dickinson College, J.D., law.
After one year in college, Gov. Ridge found himself in Vietnam as an infantry staff sergeant. He would be twice decorated for bravery before returning home to finally win his doctor-of-law degree. While serving as assistant district attorney in Erie, Pa., he ran for the U.S. House and overcame a 35,000 voter advantage

held by the Democrats to begin a five-term tenure as a congressman. Known as a tough and independent voice for Western Pennsylvania, Ridge helped write laws benefitting his state's troubled inner cities, building affordable housing, and delivering quality care and programs for the nation's veterans. The governor's race in 1995 marked the first time he had run for state-wide office.

RIEGLE, DONALD W., JR.

U.S. Senate, 105 SDOB, Washington, D.C. 20501-2201 (202) 224-4822

Riegle, Jr. is a prominent political leader. For career credentials consult the portion of this book entitled "Biographees by Profession" in the Appendix. Within this portion, the list "Political Leaders" describes requirements for inclusion in this volume.

RILEY, RICHARD WILSON

Department of Education, 400 Maryland Ave., SW, Washington, D.C. 20202 (202) 401-3000

BORN: 1933, Greenville, S.C. ACHIEVEMENTS: U.S. Secretary of Education; governor of South Carolina. STUDIED: Furman University, A.B., political science, 1954; University of South Carolina, LL.B., 1959.

Riley served in the U.S. Navy from 1954 through 1956. He served four years as a South Carolina state representative, 1963-67, ten years as a state senator, 1967-77, and eight years as the Governor of South Carolina, 1978-86. Riley was nominated to the post of U.S. Secretary of Education by President Bill Clinton on December 21, 1992, and was confirmed by unanimous consent on January 21, 1993.

RINES, ROBERT

13 Spaulding St., Concord NH 03301-2571

BORN: 1922, Boston. ACHIEVEMENTS: Invented High-resolution Image-scanning Radar and Sonar; recipient Civilian Distinguished Service award from U.S. Army, 1976, Inventions citation, President Jimmy Carter and U.S. Commerce Department, 1980, N.H. High Tech. Entrepreneur award, 1989; Beyond Peace award, 1989, Bangladesh; Distinguished Service award, 1990; inducted into the National Inventors Hall of Fame, 1994. STUDIED: M.I.T.,

B.S. Physics, 1942; Georgetown University, JJD, 1947; Chiao Tung University in the Republic of China, Ph.D., 1972; New England College of Law, D.J., 1974.

Robert Rines holds over 60 patents that have been used for both war and peace. Inventions based on his patents underlie all of the high-definition image-scanning radar used in early-warning weapons fire and control systems during the Persian Gulf War. In peace time his inventions were used to locate the Titanic and the Bismark. His scanning systems have also revolutionized the medical field, allowing non-invasive ultrasound imaging of internal organs. In 1972 he performed a sonar search to locate the Loch Ness monster. The search resulted in images of a large flipper and body, but the results were inconclusive. He founded the Academy of Applied Science and helped establish a patent system in mainland China that encourages inventions. In 1973 he founded the Franklin Pierce Law Center in New Hampshire where he still resides. He has also written music for on- and off-Broadway shows.

RIORDAN, RICHARD J.

City Hall, 200 N. Spring St., Los Angeles, CA 90012 (213) 485-2121

Riordan is a prominent political leader and mayor of Los Angeles, the successor of Mayor Tom Bradley.

RIPLEY, ALEXANDRA

c/o Warner Books, 666 Fifth Ave., New York, NY 10103 (212) 484-2900

BORN: 1934, Charleston, S.C.

Author Alexandra Ripley.

STUDIED: Vassar, B.A., Russian major.

In 1986, Margaret Mitchell's two nephews and their lawyers, representing the author's estate, began a search for somebody to write a sequel to *Gone with the Wind*. After interviewing 11 women and one man they selected Alexandra Ripley, author of three Southern historical novels. A call from the William Morris Agency, which also represents the Mitchell estate, found the one-time ghostwriter for neurosurgeons willing to attempt the formidable task. Until then, she had worked in the advertising department of *Life* magazine in New York, for Air France in Washington, D.C., and at several odd jobs while writing three failed books. Her fourth book, and her first historical novel, *Charleston*, put her on a road that took her to *Scarlett:*

The Sequel to Margaret Mitchell's Gone with the Wind, as her book would be called. She received $25,000 from the estate after submitting an outline; two years later the book brought in a winning bid of $4.94 million at a publishing auction. For the next 18 months Ripley poured over historical documents, wandered over the settings she planned to use—Savannah, Charleston, and Ireland—and re-read *Gone with the Wind* six times, even copying 200 pages in longhand to get the feel of Mitchell's style. Stormy sessions with her editors over a first draft delayed publication of the book a year. When it finally came out, in September 1991, the advance sale totaled 900,000 copies, while reviewers almost universally condemned it as trash. Before *Scarlett* had been in the stores a week, its publisher, Warner Books, was printing 50,000 copies a day and Ripley had taken the podium at the Southeastern Booksellers Association to complain about the way writers are treated by the publishing industry. Three months later the book reached the top of The *New York Times* best-seller list where it would remain for 16 weeks, even as CBS led a group of investors in buying television rights for a reported $8 to $10 million. In November, according to the 1992 Current Biography Yearbook, Ripley signed 10,000 copies of Scarlett and developed tendonitis and carpal tunnel syndrome.

RITTER, JOHN SOUTHWORTH

Robert Myman, 11777 San Vincente Blvd., Los Angeles, CA 90049.
BORN: 1948, Burbank, Calif. ACHIEVEMENTS: Emmy Award, Best Actor in a Comedy Series, and Golden Globe Award, Best Actor in a Television Comedy Series, both for Three's Company, 1984. STUDIED: University of Southern California, B.A., 1971; studied at Harvey Lembeck Comedy Workshop and Mary Carver Studio.
John Ritter has been a staple on film and television since the early 1970s. His first television series was *The Waltons,* 1972-76, where he played the part of the Reverend Matthew Fordwicke. He gained fame for his portrayal of Jack Tripper in the situation comedy series *Three's Company,* 1977-84. His next series was *Three's a Crowd,* 1984-85, which didn't achieve nearly the success as the original series *Three's Company.* Ritter didn't limit himself entirely to series performances. He also appeared in numerous television movies, specials, and episodes. In addition to television, Ritter has appeared in many films, including *The Stone Killer,* 1973, *Wholly Moses!,* 1980, and *Skin Deep,* 1989. Ritter was honored with the 1,768th star on the Hollywood Walk of Fame, right next to his father, the country western singer, Tex Ritter.

RIVERA, CHITA

c/o Armando Rivera, 825 Columbus Ave., New York, NY 10002
BORN: 1933, Washington, D.C. ACHIEVEMENTS: Antoinette Perry Award, Best Actress in a Musical, The Rink, 1984; inducted into the Televi-

sion *Academy Hall of Fame, 1985. STUDIED: Trained at The American School of Ballet, 1950-51.*
Chita Rivera has appeared on the stage throughout the world. Her Broadway debut was as a dancer in *Guys and Dolls,* 1950, at the 46th Street Theatre. Her London debut was in *West Side Story,* 1958, playing the part of Anita at Her Majesty's Theatre. Rivera was a regular on Broadway, playing parts in the plays *Can-Can,* 1953; *Seventh Heaven,* 1955; *West Side Story,* 1957; *Bye Bye Birdie,* 1960; *Chicago,* 1975; *The Rink,* 1984; and *Jerry's Girls,* 1985-86. She has participated on nationwide stage tours in *Sweet Charity,* 1967 to 1968; and *Kiss Me Kate,* 1974. In addition to her stage career, Rivera has performed in nightclubs throughout the world, including Grand Finale in New York City, and Studio One in Los Angeles.

RIVERA, GERALDO

Geraldo Investigative News Group, 555 W. 57th st., New York, NY 10019
BORN: 1943, New York City. ACHIEVEMENTS: Author, five books including Exposing Myself; host of major television talk show. STUDIED: University of Arizona, B.S., journalism; Brooklyn Law School, J.D., law; University of Pennsylvania, postgrad.
He began his career as an antipoverty lawyer in New York City from 1968 until 1970. He gained his first taste of fame for an expose of a state home for the retarded while working on a local TV station. Climbing onward, he joined ABC and did pieces for *20/20.* When given his own show in 1987, Rivera founded a new milieu-tabloid journalism, featuring many sordid individuals and subjects. On at least one occasion he engaged in a fist fight with a guest. Rivera is the author of five books, his most recent being *Exposing Myself,* published in 1992.

RIVERS, LARRY

92 Little Plains Rd., Southampton, NY 11968
BORN: 1923. ACHIEVEMENTS: Third Prize, Corcoran Gallery of Art; collections: Metropolitan Museum of Art; Corcoran Gallery of Art; exhibitions: Whitney Museum of American Art; Museum of Modern Art. STUDIED: Hans Hofmann School of Fine Arts; New York University
A versatile artist, Larry Rivers was first a jazz musician and also designed sets for plays. In the 1950s he combined influences from abstract expressionism with figurative elements, and put together vague terms with precise details in undefined spatial planes. In 1960, with growing Pop tendencies, he began to employ mixed media in works featuring commercial and historical visual cliches such as *Dutch Masters and Cigars II,* a cigar box with a rendition of Rembrandt's *Syndics* on the cover. His multiple views of a single subject recall montage, and an interest in the coincidences between words and images make him akin to Pop Art, but a painterly treatment sets him apart from the anonymous styles of Pop. To Rivers, the method of execution is more important than the subject itself. Media have included figural sculpture in wood, metal and plexiglass; collage; printing; and shaped-canvas constructions.

ROBERTS, BARBARA

Office of the Governor, State Capitol, Rm. 254, Salem, OR 97310 (503) 378-3111

Roberts is a prominent political leader. For career credentials consult the portion of this book entitled "Biographees by Profession" in the Appendix. Within this portion, the list "Political Leaders" describes requirements for inclusion in this volume.

ROBERTS, CORINNE ("COKIE") BOGGS

ABC News, 1717 DeSalle St., NW, Washington, D.C. 20036

BORN: 1943, New Orleans, La. ACHIEVEMENTS: Edward R. Murrow Award, Corporation for National Broadcasting for Outstanding Contributions to Public Radio; Mother of the Year, National Mother's Day Committee, and honors from the National Organization for Working Women, National Women's Political Caucus, and Georgetown University. STUDIED: Wellesley College, B.A., political science.

Roberts grew up in a Democratic household headed by father Rep. (Thomas) Hale Boggs, who was killed in a plane crash in Alaska in 1972. Her mother, Corinne Morrison (Claiborne) Boggs, was elected to take the congressman's seat. At age 15 Roberts edited her high school student newspaper. After graduation from Wellesley she took her first television job hosting a show on a local Washington, D.C., station. After two years at the station she married Steven Roberts, a correspondent for The *New York Times*, and moved to Manhattan, later following her husband's career moves to Athens, Greece. In Athens she worked as a stringer for CBS News radio, winning recognition for a report she made on the coup that toppled George Papadopoulos' military junta. Roberts joined National Public Radio when the couple returned home in 1977. Her work on PBS television show *The Lawmakers* and as regular congressional correspondent on the *Mac-Neil/Lehrer NewsHour* caught the attention of ABC. She began appearing on the program *This Week with David Brinkley*, alongside regulars Sam Donaldson and George Will. Roberts is known not only for her Washington savvy, but as an intelligent and resolutely nonpartisan journalist with a sense of humor and the ability to joust with her peers on even terms.

ROBERTS, JULIA

International Creative Management, 40 West 57th St., New York, NY 10019

BORN: 1967, Smyrna, Ga. ACHIEVEMENTS: Golden Globe Award, Best Supporting Actress, Steel Magnolias, 1990; Golden Globe Award, Best Actress in a Comedy, Pretty Woman, 1991.

Julia Roberts is relatively new to the entertainment industry, but she has already made a significant impact. Though she had originally wanted to be a veterinarian, the acting tradition runs deep in her family. Roberts is the daughter of the proprietors of an acting workshop; her brother, Eric, and sister, Lisa, also act in movies. She debuted on television in the series, *Crime Story*. However, she has found her greatest success to date in films, winning awards almost right from the start. She was nominated for an Independent Spirit Award for best actress in 1988 for her work in *Mystic Pizza*. Just a year later she won a Golden Globe Award for best supporting actress in *Steel Magnolias*. Her role in *Pretty Woman*, in 1990, earned her both an Academy Award nomination for best actress and a Golden Globe Award for best actress in a musical or comedy. More recently, her work in *The Pelican Brief*, again earned her critical praise.

ROBERTS, RICHARD J.

Cold Spring Harbor Laboratory, P.O. Box 100, Cold Spring Harbor, NY 11724 (516) 367-8388

BORN: 1943, Derby (England). ACHIEVEMENTS: Nobel Prize for Physiology or Medicine (with Phillip A. Sharp), 1993. STUDIED: Sheffield University, England, B.S., Ph.D., science.

After three years as a research fellow at Harvard, from 1969 to 1972, new emigre to the U.S. Richard Roberts joined the Cold Spring Harbor Laboratory in Cold Spring Harbor, New York, where he led research in identifying enzymes. In 1977 he helped revolutionize molecular biology by discovering "split genes," spinoffs from messages on DNA strands that heretofore were thought to be unbroken and continuous. He received the Nobel award for this discovery 16 years later, along with Phillip A. Sharp, who had made the same observation independently in the same year at Massachusetts Institute of Technology.

ROCKEFELLER, JOHN D., IV

SH-109 Hart Bldg., Washington, D.C. 20510-4802 (202) 224-6472

BORN: 1937, New York City. ACHIEVEMENTS: W.Va. secretary of state, 1969-73; president of W. Va. Wesleyan College 1974-77; W.Va. governor, 1977-85. STUDIED: Harvard University., B.A., far eastern languages and history, 1961.

John Rockefeller's service as a VISTA worker brought him to West Virginia in 1964 and he never left the Mountain State. He served two years in its House of Delegates (1966-68), then four as secretary of state, and later, after a stint as a college president, he served as governor to his beloved state. He reached the U.S. Senate in 1984, serving as chairman of the Pepper Commission, and authoring legislation that reformed Medicare, expanded Medicaid, and preserved health benefits for retired coal miners. He has also served on the Veteran's Affairs, Finance and Commerce, Science, and Transportation Committees, and as chairman of the National Commission on Children.

ROHRER, HINRICH

IBM Research Division, One Old Orchard Rd., Armonk NY (1800) 426-4968

BORN: June 6, 1933, Buchs (Switzerland). ACHIEVEMENTS: Invented the scanning tunneling microscope; Nobel Prize for physics 1986; King Faisal International Prize for Science; Hewlett-Packard Europhysics Prize; inducted into the National Inventors Hall of Fame, 1994. STUDIED: Swiss Federal Institute of Technology, 1960.

In 1963 Hinrich Rohrer joined IBM. He began his work on the scanning tunneling microscope at IBMUs Zurich Division Research Laboratory, along with Gerd Karl Binning. Five years after building the microscope, Dr. Binnig and Dr. Rohrer received the Nobel Prize for physics. Prior to their invention, optical systems were limited by the wavelength of light. The scanning tunneling microscope allowed for individual atoms to be viewed.

ROKER, AL

NBC-TV, 30 Rockefeller Plaza, New York, NY 10112
ACHIEVEMENTS: Best Weatherman, 1985, (New York Magazine); American Meteorological Society's Seal of Approval. STUDIED: State University of New York at Oswego.
Roker, weatherman for the *Today Show*, also reports the weather for WNBC-TV, the NBC owned station in New York. In 1985 he unveiled state-of-the-art forecasting equipment including Doppler radar and computer graphics, now common to most major stations and the networks. His career began in 1974 at WTVH-TV in Syracuse, N.Y., where he was a weatherman and graphic artist. After working at several stations, including Cleveland's NBC affiliate WKYC-TV, he joined WNBC as the weekend weatherman in 1983.

ROMER, ROY

State of Colorado Executive Chambers, 136 State Capital, Denver CO 80203-1792 (303) 866-2471
BORN: 1928, Garden City, Kan. ACHIEVEMENTS: First chairman of the National Education Goals Panel where he developed the first national education report card. STUDIED: Colorado State University, B.S. agriculture economics, 1950; University of Colorado, Boulder, L.L.B., 1952; Yale University, program in ethics, social policy and theology, 1954.
Romer will serve as the 39th governor of Colorado until January, 1999. He served from 1977-1987 as Colorado state treasurer. He was a member of the Colorado House from 1958-1962, and a member of the Colorado Senate from 1962-1966. Romer is chairman of the Education Commission of the States, and a past chairman of the National Governors' Association. He developed a portion of Colorado's Centennial Airport, owned and operated Colorado Flying Academy.

ROONEY, ANDREW (ANDY) A.

CBS News/60 Minutes, 555 West 57th St. New York, NY 10019
BORN: 1919, Albany, N.Y. ACHIEVEMENTS: Recipient Awards for Best Written Television Documentary, Writers Guild of America, 1966, 1968, 1971, 1975, 1976; Emmy Awards, 1968, 1978, 1981, 1982. STUDIED: Colgate University, 1942.
After reporting for the Army newspaper *Stars & Stripes* during World War II, and later writing for a series of radio and television programs, Andy Rooney began to contribute regular three-minute personal essays to the CBS program *60 Minutes* in 1972. His wry, and sometimes cantankerous, views about seemingly mundane aspects of everyday life struck a chord, and sometimes a nerve, with viewers. He started a news-paper column in 1979, and collected his essays in a series of books, including *A Few Minutes with Andy Rooney*, 1981; *More by Andy Rooney*, 1982; *Pieces of My Mind*, 1984; *Word for Word*, 1986; *Not That You Asked*, 1989 and *Sweet and Sour*, 1992.

ROSALDO, RENATO

Stanford University, Department of Anthropology, Building 110, Stanford, CA 94305
BORN: 1941, Champaign, Ill. ACHIEVEMENTS: Harry Benda Prize, Association for Asian Studies; Mellon Professor of Interdisciplinary Studies. STUDIED: Harvard College, B.A., Anthropology; Harvard University, Ph.D., Anthropology.
Renato Rosaldo has spent his entire career at Stanford University, first joining its faculty as assistant professor in 1970. Six years later he became an associate professor, and in 1985 a full professor. In 1992, the university appointed him Lucie Stern Professor in the Social Sciences. His book, *Ilongot Headhunting 1883-1974*, about a farming and fishing people who live in small barrios on islands clustered around the central Philippines, received a Harry Benda Prize. He also is author of a second book, *Culture and Truth*.

ROSEANNE

Hal Ray, William Morris Agency, 151 El Camino Blvd., Los Angeles, CA 90048 (310) 859-4000
BORN: 1952, Salt Lake City, Utah ACHIEVEMENTS: Golden Globe Award, Best Actress in a Comedy Series, 1993; Emmy Award, Best Actress in a Comedy Series, both for Roseanne, 1993.
Roseanne left high school to hitchhike cross-country and finally ended her journey at a Colorado artists' colony, at the age of 18. Later in life, she developed a raw, raunchy style of comedy and appeared at clubs and auditoriums throughout the United States. In 1988 she began the television series *Roseanne*, playing the title role, Roseanne Conner. The show has gained notoriety by dealing with subjects considered too controversial for prime time television. Withstanding the controversy, *Roseanne* won both a Golden Globe Award and an Emmy Award for best comedy series in 1993. Her film debut came in 1989, when she played the role of Ruth Patchett in *She Devil*. Always one to poke fun at the accepted norm, Roseanne stunned baseball fans nationwide in 1990 when she grabbed her crotch and spit on the ground, imitating the body language of a baseball player, while attempting to sing the national anthem at a San Diego baseball game.

ROSENQUIST, JAMES

Box 4, 420 W. Broadway, Aripeka, FL 33502
BORN: 1933. ACHIEVEMENTS: Torcuato di Tella International Prize, Buenos Aires; collections: Metropolitan Museum of Art; Museum of Modern Art; exhibitions: Museum of Modern Art; Solomon R. Guggenheim Museum. STUDIED: Art Students League .
James Rosenquist's early work was abstract, but employment as a Times Square billboard painter in the late 1950s led to the application of commercial art imagery, when he produced paintings in day-glo colors that resembled randomly arranged advertising frag-

ments like the different layers of a billboard. These Pop works were made by splicing blow-ups of commercial motifs and then creating for them a new context, sometimes readable and other times elusive to the viewer. His interest in depicting "visual inflation" continued in montages incorporating such modern materials as neon, plexiglass, plastic and Mylar in freestanding constructions, murals and picture-assemblages.

ROSENTHAL, RACHEL

2847 S. Robertson Blvd., Los Angeles, CA 90034
BORN: 1926, Paris (France) ACHIEVEMENTS: NEA Fellowship; exhibitions: The Woman's Building, Los Angeles; Franklin Furnace, New York City. STUDIED: New School of Social Research, New York City; Sorbonne, Paris.
Rosenthal comes from a multiple background of visual art, dance and theater. She studied art with Hans Hoffman, dance with Merce Cunningham, and theatre with Jean-Louis Barrarlt and Erwin Piscator. In 1956 she founded Instant Theatre, an experimental theater group based in Los Angeles, and in the late 1960s she emerged as a sculptor and one of the leaders of the women's art movement. It was in 1975 that she switched to performance art, and since then she has focused on that art form. Early performances took the shape of personal, autobiographical exorcisms with allusions to ancient ritual, Zen Buddhism and healing rites. Recent solo performances, as in *Traps*, encompass all humankind in the exorcisms. With great sensitivity to the power of the dramatic persona, and with surprising visual images, she presents intimate, poetic pieces addressing social and political problems and offering hope.

ROSS, DIANA

RTC Management, P.O. Box 1683, New York, NY 10185
BORN: 1944, Detroit. ACHIEVEMENTS: Billboard, Cash Box and Record World awards as world's outstanding singer; Grammy Award, 1970; Antoinette Perry Award, 1977; Academy Award nomination, Best Actress, Lady Sings the Blues, 1972; Golden Globe Award, 1972; Rock and Roll Hall of Fame, 1988.
As a teenager in Detroit, Diana Ross joined the Primettes, an all-girl group formed by Motown's music mogul Berry Gordy. The Primettes became the Supremes, and Ross became the lead singer, recording numerous hit singles with the group. As Ross' popularity surged, the group was renamed Diana Ross and the Supremes, and in 1969 she left to pursue a solo career. In 1970 she released her debut solo album *Diana Ross*. During the 1970s she appeared in numerous films including, *Lady Sings the Blues*, 1972, for which she received a Academy Award nomination, *Mahogany*, 1975, and *The Wiz*, 1978. Her autobiography, *Secrets of a Sparrow*, was published in 1993, and revealed her secret relationship with Motown president Berry Gordy. Ross continues to appear in sold-out concerts, and in 1994 she made her television acting debut in the TV movie *Out of the Darkness*.

ROSTOW, WALT WHITMAN

1 Wildwind Point, Austin, TX 78746
BORN: 1916, New York City. ACHIEVEMENTS: Former Chairman, U.S. State Department Policy Planning Council. STUDIED: Yale University, B.A., Ph.D., economics.
Walt Rostow was a member of President John F. Kennedy's inner circle from 1961 to 1963 as the President's special adviser, and chairman of the Policy Planning Council at the State Department from 1961 to 1966. He was a strong interventionist in Vietnam under President Lyndon B. Johnson. Later he resumed teaching at the University of Texas, polishing up his expertise in British economics history and in his theory that all societies pass through five stages of economic growth.

ROSTROPOVICH, MSTISLAV

National Symphony Orchestra, Kennedy Center, Washington, D.C. 20566
BORN: 1927, Baku, (USSR). Achievements : Stalin Prize; Lenin Prize; People's Artist of USSR; Officer Legion of Honor, France; Fellow, Royal College of Music; KBE, 1987. STUDIED: Moscow Conservatory
Since his debut in the USSR in 1941, Mstislav Rostropovich has received over 30 honorary degrees from colleges including: Oxford, Cambridge, Yale, Harvard, Trinity University (Dublin), and St. Andrews University (Scotland). In 1977 he was named music director of the National Symphony Orchestra in Washington, D.C. He premiered the Shostakovich cello sonata, concertos by Bliss, Lutoslawaki Christobel Halffter in 1986 and 1992. Opera engagements include, *The Queen of Spades* at San Francisco, and *Eugene Onegin* at Aldeburgh. He conducted Prokofiev's *The Duenna* at the Royal Academy of Music, London, 1991. His recordings include: compact discs of Beethoven's *Triple Concerto*, and Dvorak's cello concerto, with the Berlin Philharmonic Orchestra; Britten's cello symphony, Debussy and Schubert sonatas (Decca); Dutilleux and Lutoslawski concertos (EMI); Mozart flute quartets (CBS); and Boris Godunov (Erato).

ROTH, WILLIAM V.

U.S. Senate, 104 SHOB, Washington, D.C. 20510-0801 (202) 224-2441
Roth is a prominent political leader. For career credentials consult the portion of this book entitled "Biographees by Profession" in the Appendix. Within this portion, the list "Political Leaders" describes requirements for inclusion in this volume.

ROWLAND, JOHN G.

State of Connecticut Executive Chambers, Hartford, CT 06106 (203) 566-4840
BORN: 1958, Waterbury, Conn. ACHIEVEMENTS: youngest person ever elected to governor of Connecticut; received the Watchdog of the Treasury Award. STUDIED: Villanova University.
Gov. John Rowland, a Republican, is Connecticut's 86th governor, and at 37, the youngest person to hold that office. He began his political career in 1980, win-

ning a seat in the Connecticut State Legislature. After only one term as a state legislator, he was named House Minority Whip. In 1984 he was elected to the U. S. House of Representatives, and won re-election in 1986 and 1988. While serving in Congress, he was the first Connecticut member to be named to the Armed Services committee in 20 years. He also served on the Intelligence and Veterans' Affairs Committees, the House Select Committee on Narcotics Abuse and Control, and the House Republican Anti-Drug Task Force. For his efforts against unnecessary government spending, he received the "Watchdog of the Treasury" award. In 1992 he was President Bush's Connecticut campaign chairman. Governor Rowland's family has lived in Connecticut for over 200 years, and has a 50-year tradition of public service.

ROYKO, MIKE

The Chicago Tribune, 435 N. Michigan Ave., Chicago, IL 60611-4022 (312) 222-3232
BORN: 1932, Chicago. ACHIEVEMENTS: Pulitzer Prize for commentary, 1972. STUDIED: Wright Junior College.
Mike Royko's journalistic training began when he was 20 years old and editing his U.S. Air Force base newspaper. The *City News Bureau* of Chicago picked him up in 1956 as an assistant city editor. In 1959 the *Chicago Daily News* hired him as a general assignment reporter, a position he held until 1976 when the *Chicago Sun-Times* gave him his first column. In 1984 he moved to *The Chicago Tribune* where he remains today. While always geared to his Chicago constituency, his column manages to deal with many national crises. It is frequently reprinted in major dailies around the country, and anthologies of his work have sold well in book form. Royko has authored several books including; *Up Against It*, 1967; *I May Be Wrong but I Doubt It*, 1968; *Boss: Richard J. Daley of Chicago*, 1971; *Stats Grobnik and Some Other Friends*, 1973; *Sez Who? Sez Me*, 1982; *Like I was Sayin*, 1989; and *Dr. Kookie, You're Right*.

RUBIN, BENJAMIN

NCIPLA, Suite 203, 2001 Jefferson Davis Hwy., Arlington, VA 22202 (703) 415-0780
BORN: 1917, New York City. ACHIEVEMENTS: Invented the bifurcated vaccination needle; inducted into the National Inventors Hall of Fame, 1992. STUDIED: City College of New York, B.S., biology-chemistry; Virginia Polytechnic Institute, M.S., biology; Yale University, Ph.D., microbiology, 1947
Dr. Benjamin Rubin did extensive work at Schenley Research, Yale University, Brookhaven National laboratory, Syntex Corporation, Baylor University College of Medicine and the University of Texas before joining Wyeth Laboratories in 1965. While at Wyeth, he began working on alternatives to conventional needles. Taking a sewing machine needle, he grounded the eyelet into a fork-shape (bifurcated), and developed the bifurcated vaccination needle. This invention allowed natives in the most remote places to administer smallpox vaccinations. The World Health Assembly de-

clared smallpox defeated in 1980. Dr. Rubin also holds patents in radiation devices, vaccines, steroid chemistry and microbiology.

RUBIN, ROBERT E.

The White House, Washington, D.C., 20500
BORN: 1938, New York City. ACHIEVEMENTS: Assistant to President Bill Clinton for Economic Policy, 1993-. STUDIED: Harvard University, B.A. (summa cum laude), 1960; London School of Economics, 1960-61; Yale University, LL.B., 1964.
Robert Rubin has been involved in economics for most of his professional career. After graduating from Yale University in 1964, Rubin took a position as an associate for Cleary, Gottlieb, Steen & Hamilton, of New York City. In 1966, he moved to Goldman Sachs & Co., also of New York. Although he began as an associate at Goldman Sachs, he had risen to co-senior partner by 1992. Rubin has been active in many civic and political activities, especially in the 1980s and early 1990s. He was a member of the President's Advisory Committee for Trade Negotiations, in Washington, D.C., from 1980 to 1982. In 1983 and 1984, he was a member of the finance committee for the New York campaign of Mondale for President. From 1989 until 1992, Rubin was on the advisory committee for international capital markets of the Federal Reserve Bank of New York. He was appointed an economic advisor to President Bill Clinton in 1993.

RUBIN, STEPHEN EDWARD

Doubleday, 1540 Broadway, New York, NY 10036 (212) 354-6500
BORN: 1941, New York City. STUDIED: New York University, B.A.; Boston University, M.S.
Stephen Rubin began as a freelance writer. Founder and director of the magazine *Writers Bloc* in 1976, then editor of the magazine *Vanity Fair*, he became executive editor of Doubleday's Bantam Books in 1984 and editorial director in 1985. In 1990 he became president and publisher of the Doubleday division of Bantam Doubleday Dell Publishing Group, which found itself in dire straits because of the loss of prominent authors, including Stephen King. Under Rubin, best-selling authors were acquired, including Bill Moyers (*Healing and the Mind*), the hard cover novels of John Grisham, Laura Esquivel (*Like Water for Chocolate*), and Jane Hamilton (*A Map of the World*), which turned the publishing giant around during the next five years. The Doubleday Group rewarded Rubin with an appointment to chairman and chief executive officer of Bantam Doubleday Dell's International Division, which earns about 20 percent of its operating profits in book sales outside the United States.

RUSCHA, EDWARD JOSEPH

1024 3/4 N. Western Ave., Hollywood, CA 90029
BORN: 1937. ACHIEVEMENTS: NEA Grant; Guggenheim Fellowship; collections: Museum of Modern Art, New York City; Los Angeles County Museum of Art; exhibitions: Whitney Museum, New York City; San Francisco Museum of Modern Art. STUDIED: Chouinard Art Institute.

Edward Ruscha's early Pop paintings are hyper-realistic depictions of garages—some on fire—and other buildings. A humorous series describes proper word and name usage. *Every Building on the Sunset Strip* was just that, in a montage showing both sides of the street. He is known for books of photographs of ordinary things, such as *Twenty-six Gasoline Stations* and *Real Estate Opportunities*, in which typography and pictures are combined to make a cohesive whole. Text is eliminated. They are simply reproduced snapshots. The books do not "house a collection of art photographs—they are technical data like industrial photography," according to Ruscha.

RUSSELL, GEORGE ALLAN

c/o Concepts, 1770 Massachusetts Ave., Suite 182, Cambridge, MA 02140
BORN: 1923, Cincinnati. ACHIEVEMENTS: Composer/author, The Lydian Chromatic Concept of Tonal Organization. STUDIED: Wilberforce University High School.

Drawn to both jazz and classical music in his youth, George Russell composed in a variety of styles that usually rebounded from his African-American tradition. He greatly influenced musical theory in his book *The Lydian Chromatic Concept of Tonal Organization*, a subject he has also taught in the U.S. and foreign countries since 1953.

SAFER, MORLEY

CBS News, 524 West 57th St., New York, NY 10019
BORN: 1931, Toronto (Canada). ACHIEVEMENTS: Author Flashbacks: On Returning to Vietnam, 1990; French Ministry of Culture's "Chevalier dans l'order des Arts et des Lettres," 1995. STUDIED: University of Western Ontario.

Safer began his career as a print journalist in Ontario, but was swept into the world of television news by the Canadian Broadcast Company (CBC) in 1955. He quickly became a foreign correspondent, and then began producing the *CBC News Magazine*. He was assigned to the CBC London bureau in 1961, and in 1964 joined the CBS News where he worked ever since. He made his name with graphic coverage of the war in Vietnam before returning to London as bureau chief and finally joining *60 Minutes* in 1970.

SAFIRE, WILLIAM

The New York Times, 229 West 43rd Street, New York, NY 10036 (212) 556-1234.
BORN: 1929, New York City. ACHIEVEMENTS: Speechwriter/special assistant to President Richard Nixon; author, Plunging Into Politics, 1964; You Could Look it Up, 1988; In Love with Norma Loquendi, 1993. STUDIED: Syracuse University.

William Safire began as the Europe and Middle East correspondent for WNBC-TV in 1949, only to be drafted by the Army in 1952 and assigned to army public relations until his discharge in 1954. In 1955 he began working as a vice-president for a public relations firm, but left in 1960 when he founded his own. His largest client was then-President Nixon for whom he wrote political speeches. This experience led the *New York Times* to offer him his own column, *Essay*, in 1973. He has also written the *On Language* column for the *New York Times Magazine* since 1979, and authored several books on his experiences.

SAGE, DENNIS

Phoenix Symphony Orchestra, 6328 North Seventh St., Phoenix, AZ 85014 (602) 277-7291
Sage is a prominent concert master and conductor of the Phoenix Symphony Orchestra.

SAHLINS, MARSHALL DAVID

University of Chicago, Department of Anthropology, 5836-46 Greenwood Ave., Chicago, IL 60637
BORN: 1930, Chicago. ACHIEVEMENTS: Author, Evolution and Culture, and Culture and Practical Reason. STUDIED: University of Michigan, B.A., anthropology; Columbia University, Ph.D., anthropology.

While teaching at the Universities of Michigan and Chicago, Sahlins made a major advance in oceanic ethnography, which deals with descriptions of various oceanic cultures. He also studied and wrote about cultural evolution and economic anthropology in such works as *Evolution and Culture*, 1960 and *Culture and Practical Reason*, 1976.

SAJAK, PAT

Merv Griffin Productions, 1541 N. Vine St., Los Angeles, CA
BORN: 1946, Chicago. ACHIEVEMENTS: People's Choice Award (shared with Johnny Carson), Proctor & Gamble Productions; Emmy Award, Game Show Host for Wheel of Fortune; four Emmy nominations. STUDIED: Columbia College, Chicago.

Sajak, a one-time hotel desk clerk, weatherman in Los Angeles, and disk jockey for the Armed Forces Radio in Vietnam, is best known as host on the game show *Wheel of Fortune* since 1982. But his years of working in the medium include an extensive list of acting credits as well as host of many specials. He has appeared in two movies, *Jack Paar is Alive and Well*, and as a Buffalo, N.Y. anchor person in *Airplane II—The Sequel*. Sajak has hosted Macy's Thanksgiving Day Parade two times, the *Emmy Daytime Awards*, the Tournament of Roses Parade in 1986 and 1987, *American Bandstand's 40th Anniversary Special*, and the Bugs Bunny's 50th birthday show, *Happy Birthday Bugs: 50 Looney Years*.

SAKS, GENE

271 Central Park West, New York, NY
Saks is a prominent dramatic artist. For career credentials consult the portion of this book entitled "Notable Americans by Profession" in the Appendix. Within this portion, the list "Dramatic Artists" describes requirements for inclusion in this volume.

SAMUELSON, PAUL ANTHONY

Massachusetts Institute of Technology, Department of Economics E52383C, Cambridge, MA 02139

BORN: 1915, Gary, Ind. ACHIEVEMENTS: Nobel Prize in Economic Science, 1970; Harvard's David A. Wells Award; first winner of the John Bates Clark Medal of the American Economics Association; Albert Einstein Medal; President of the American Econometric Society; books, Economics, Linear Programming and Economic Activity (with Robert Dorfman and Robert Solow). STUDIED: University of Chicago, Harvard University.

A giant among giants in his field, Paul Samuelson wrote his first paper at the age of 23 while still a graduate student at Harvard. Over the next 45 years he averaged almost one technical paper a month, which made up five, fat books when gathered under the title *Collected Scientific Papers* and published in successive volumes ending in 1983. His treatise, *Economics*, made him one of the most successful authors of books on economists. It has been translated in a dozen languages, including Russian, and its sales have no equal in anything ever published on economics. His subjects are wideranging, touching fundamental concepts and theories in almost every branch of economics: international trade; production, growth, and capital theory; financial analysis; economic history; and macroeconomics, which deals with the general aspects of economies as a whole. Though known as a liberal, Samuelson carefully steps around contentious subjects, letting his more militant colleagues bear the brunt of scholarly rage for any misstep, while he remains a careful moderate in his political views. But such centrist positions invite some members of his profession, some of whom call him an intellectual gymnast. But just as many, if not more, regard him as one of the founders of mainstream economics, which they admiringly label "the age of Samuelson."

SANCHEZ, SONIA

Temple University, Professor of English, 1701 N. Broad St., Philadelphia, PA 19122
BORN: 1934, Birmingham, Ala. STUDIED: Hunter College, B.A.
Sonia Sanchez's poetry is known for its persuasive and metaphorical substance as illustrated in *Homegirls and Handgrenades*. She has also written plays, short stories, children's books, and has edited African-American anthologies. Besides teaching and writing, she is a black nationalist and activist. She has taught as Temple University and several other institutions since 1977.

SANDERS, WAYNE R.

Kimberly-Clark Corporation, P.O. Box 619100, Dallas, TX 75261
BORN: 1947, Chicago, Ill. ACHIEVEMENTS: Board of trustees Lawrence University, Appleton. STUDIED: Illinois Institute of Technology, B.C.E., 1969; Marquette University, M.B.A., 1972.
Wayne Sanders joined Kimberly-Clark, a world leader in the consumer goods sector, in 1975 as a senior financial analyst. After performing well in various business planning positions, he took over as the vice-president of strategic planning for the company's Canadian branch. With steady velocity he spent the latter half of the 80s climbing to various high-level positions within the company, and has been the chairman and chief executive officer since 1991.

SANGER, DAVID E.

The New York Times, 229 West 43rd St., New York, NY 10036 (212) 556-1234
Sanger is a prominent journalist. For career credentials consult the portion of this book entitled "Notable Americans by Profession" in the Appendix. Within this portion, the list "Journalists" describes requirements for inclusion in this volume.

SAPIEJEWSKI, ROMAN

Bose Corporation, The Mountain, Framington, MA 01701 (508) 879-7330
ACHIEVEMENTS: Co-developer of the NoiseBuster.
Roman Sapiejewski and David Claybaugh are the men behind the NoiseBuster, an invention that drowns out unwelcome noise. Sapiejewski is an engineer at Noise Cancellation Technologies. Claybaugh is director of engineering development for the same firm. The NoiseBuster is comprised of two microphones that sample background noise at the range of 30 to 1,200 hertz (cycles per second). What the mikes hear is relayed to a computer chip that signals the user's stereo headset speakers to generate noise exactly opposite to the offending waveform, thus cancelling the original sound. The equipment has a built in safety factor: The low range of sound the set picks up does not seal off higher-pitched sounds such as phone calls, alarms, or voices. Also contributing to the NoiseBuster were engineers Dan Gaugher and Amar Bose.

SARANDON, SUSAN

International Creative Management, 8899 Beverly Blvd., Los Angeles, CA 90048
BORN: 1946, New York City. ACHIEVEMENTS: Academy Award nomination, Best Actress, for Atlantic City, 1981; Academy Award nomination, Best Actress, Golden Globe Award nomination, Best Actress in a Drama, both for Thelma and Louise, 1992. STUDIED: Catholic University of America, B.A., drama and English, 1968.
Best known for her part in *Thelma and Louise*, the 1991 blockbuster hit, Susan Sarandon toiled for years to achieve her current success. One of nine children, she went to Catholic schools right through college, raising money to pay her college expenses by doing office work and housecleaning. Sarandon's first successful role in a movie was in *Joe*, which premiered in 1970. In 1975 she appeared in the cult classic, *The Rocky Horror Picture Show*. Sarandon appeared frequently in movies and television shows during the 1970s, 1980s, and 1990s, including the 1987 hit, *The Witches of Eastwick*, and *Bull Durham* in 1988.

SARETT, LEWIS HASTINGS

c/o NCIPLA, Suite 203, 2001 Jefferson Davis Hwy., Arlington, VA 22202

BORN: 1917, Champaign, Ill. ACHIEVEMENTS: Produced first synthetic cortisone. STUDIED: Northwestern University, B.A., chemistry; Princeton University, Ph.D., chemistry.

Lewis Sarett prepared the first synthetic cortisone in 1944 while working as a chemist at Merck Research Laboratories in Rahway, N.J. He was 27 years old at the time, and not long before had graduated from Princeton. In his career at Merck he collaborated on more than 100 technical papers and patents, rising to senior vice president for science and technology.

SASSER, JIM

U.S. Senate, 363 SROB, Washington, D.C. 20510-4201 (202) 224-3344

Sasser is a prominent political leader. For career credentials consult the portion of this book entitled "Notable Americans by Profession" in the Appendix. Within this portion, the list "Political Leaders" describes requirements for inclusion in this volume.

SAUNDERS, RAYMOND JENNINGS

6007 Rock Ridge Blvd., Oakland, CA 94618

BORN: 1934. ACHIEVEMENTS: Guggenheim Fellowship; NEA Fellowship; collections: Museum of Modern Art, New York City; Whitney Museum, New York City; exhibitions: San Francisco Museum of Modern Art; Oakland Museum. STUDIED: Pennsylvania Academy of the Fine Arts; University of Pennsylvania; Carnegie Institute of Technology; California College of Arts and Crafts

In Raymond Saunders' works, loose brushstrokes and large color fields of abstract expressionism are often combined with Pop images, such as cartoon characters, stenciled letters or numbers, and graffiti to create a variety of humorous and enigmatic works reflecting personal experiences and Black history in an urban environment. During the 1960s, he did not produce art of protest, but rather was more interested in the art of genre. His media have also included collage and assemblage, as well as watercolor, as in *Suite of Flowers*.

SAVAGE, M. SUSAN

Office of the Mayor, 200 Civic Center, Tulsa, OK 74103 (918) 596-7777

BORN: 1956. ACHIEVEMENTS: Tulsa's first woman mayor; elected twice to the office. EDUCATION: Beaverside College, Penn.

Savage got her hands-on experience in public service as the administrative assistant to former Tulsa Mayor Rodger Randle in 1988. In that post she served on city board and commissions, including the Citizens Crime Commission, which she headed for 10 years. When former Mayor Randle resigned in 1992 to become president of the University Center at Tulsa, Savage stepped in as interim mayor. A month later, she defeated 53 candidates in an election to complete Randle's term. In 1994, she was re-elected with 58 percent of the vote. Her term ends in 1998. Savage is the daughter of Federal Judge Royce Savage; she is married and has two daughters of her own.

SCALIA, ANTONIN

Supreme Court of the United States, One First St. N.E., Washington, D.C. 20543 (202) 479-3000

BORN: 1936, Trenton, N.J. ACHIEVEMENTS: Sheldon fellow, Harvard University. STUDIED: University of Fribourg (Switzerland), Georgetown University, B.A., 1957; Harvard University, LL.B., 1960.

Scalia, the father of nine children, practiced corporate law for six years, and then became a professor of law at the University of Virginia in 1967. From 1971 to 1972 he served as general counsel, Office of Telecommunications Policy, Executive Office of the President. Scalia was nominated by President Reagan to the U.S. Court of Appeals for the District of Columbia Circuit in 1982. In 1986 Reagan nominated Scalia as associate justice, Supreme Court of the United States. He took the oath of office on September 26, 1986.

SCANGA, ITALO

7127 Olivetas, La Jolla, CA 92037

BORN: 1932. ACHIEVEMENTS: Cassandra Foundation Grant; NEA Grant; collections: Los Angeles County Museum of Art; Oakland Museum; exhibitions: Dorothy Goldeen Gallery, Santa Monica; Whitney Museum, New York City. STUDIED: Michigan State University.

Scanga was born in Italy, settled in America in 1947 and served in the U.S. Army. After formal study in sculpture, he began to employ mixed media, including found objects, to create installations that present "unresolved cultural value cohabiting the integrated structure." For example, room-sized presentations display religious kitsch resembling icons, sprinkled with red paint, hung near the floor. Urns containing grains or spices such as chili powder are to be smelled or tasted as the viewer kneels to see a painting of Christ or the Madonna. Menacing farm implements often lean against the wall, and dried herbs are hung from the ceiling. Thus he creates a kind of shrine using the imagery of martyrdom typical to poor households in Italy. His complicated iconography points to the disparity between the violent suffering of martyrs and the religious devotional images that glorify the pain, creating a new kind of provocative folklore.

SCHAFER, EDWARD T.

600 E. Boulevard, Bismarck, ND 58505 (701) 224-2200

BORN: 1946, Bismarck, N.D. ACHIEVEMENTS: Governor, State of North Dakota; president, Gold Seal Company. STUDIED: University of North Dakota, B.A., business administration, 1969; University of Denver, M.B/A, 1970.

Edward Schafer began working in the mailroom of the Gold Seal Company, founded by his father, at the age of 14. After graduating from the University of Denver with an M.B.A. degree, Schafer worked in several management divisions of the family business. In 1978 he was elected president of the company. Under his leadership over the next seven years, the company saw a 42 percent increase in sales, and the net worth of the company tripled. Schafer was elected governor of North Dakota in 1992. Schafer is active in the National Governors Association, serving as co-chairman of the

Taskforce on State Management, and as a member on the Welfare Reform Leadership Team.

SCHAWLOW, ARTHUR LEONARD

Stanford University, Department of Physics, Stanford, CA 94305
BORN: Mt. Vernon, N.Y. ACHIEVEMENTS: Nobel Prize in Physics (shared with Nicolaas Bloembergen), 1981; Ballantine Medal, Franklin Institute; Thomas Young Medal and Prize, Institution of Physics and Physics Society of London; Liebmann Prize, Institute of Electrical and Electronic Engineers; Frederick Ives Medal, Optical Society of America. STUDIED: University of Toronto, Canada.

Arthur L. Schawlow, Kai M. Siegbahn of Sweden, and Nicholaas Bloembergen helped push back the boundaries of laser spectroscopy (measuring wavelengths and intensities of a spectrum of light, or radiation from any source), which permits the investigation of complex forms of matter not observed previously. Shortly after the first lasers were made, they were called "an invention looking for a use." Today the colaureates' work on the intricacies of the interaction of light with matter extended the uses of lasers in numerous areas of physics, chemistry, and biology, including pollution monitoring. Besides garnering the Nobel Prize with Nicolaas Bloembergen, Arthur Schawlow also worked in maser development (the progenitor of the laser) and then extended the maser principle to optics.

SCHIEFFER, BOB

CBS News, 524 West 57th St., New York, NY 10019
Schieffer is a prominent journalist with CBS news and one of the principle reporters on the *CBS Evening News with Dan Rather*. He frequently anchors the program when rather is unavailable, as well as the weekend evening news.

SCHIRRA, WALTER MARTY, JR.

PO Box 73, Rancho Santa Fe, CA 92067
BORN: 1923, Hackensack, N.J. ACHIEVEMENTS: Space missions: Mercury 8, commander, Gemini 6A, commander Apollo 7; medals: Distinguished Flying Cross, Korean War. STUDIED: U.S. Naval Academy, B.S., 1945.

After he graduated from the U.S. Naval Academy, Schirra went on to receive flight training. On exchange with the U.S. Air Force, he flew 90 combat missions in Korea, which earned him the Distinguished Flying Cross. He became a test pilot and worked on the Sidewinder air-to-air missile project before becoming one of the original seven astronauts in 1959. He orbited the Earth six times on the spacecraft Mercury 8, inside the Sigma 7 space capsule, and splashed down less than five miles from the recovery ship. He and pilot Thomas Stafford took part in the first space rendezvous of two manned spacecraft while on board Gemini 6A by rendezvousing with Gemini 7. He commanded the first flight of the Apollo command service module, Apollo 7, in 1968.

SCHLESINGER, FRANK

732 17th Street NW, Washington, D.C. 20006

BORN: 1925. ACHIEVEMENTS: Fellow, AIA; Architectural Record Award, 1960, 1974; Distinguished Designer Fellowship, National Endowment for the Arts; notable works: 1301 Pennsylvania Avenue, Washington, D.C.; Rochester Waterfront Crossroads Plaza, Rochester, N.Y. STUDIED: Harvard University.

Schlesinger argues that Modernism is not dead. Instead, the artificial homogeneity of the last era has given way to a more informed and equally valid diversity of approaches and techniques. A distinguished teacher, Schlesinger has simultaneously directed a professional practice which has garnered more than 30 design awards in the last quarter century. In 1977 he became associated with the Pennsylvania Avenue Development Corporation, a government agency charged with refurbishing and development the blocks adjacent to the White House in Washington, D.C. His unimposing curtain-walled mid-rise at 1301 Pennsylvania Avenue, completed in 1981, was the first office building in what looks like a major pulse of expansion. His 1984 National Place—a mixed-use complex funded by Marriott Corporation and the Quadrangle Development Corporation, and designed in collaboration with Mitchell/Giourgola—was the only entry in a national competition which proposed to preserve the landmark National Theater.

SCHLESINGER, ARTHUR MEIER JR.

CUNY, 33 W 42nd St., New York, NY 10036-8003
BORN: 1917, Columbus, Ohio. ACHIEVEMENTS: Pulitzer Prize for History, The Age of Jackson, 1946; Pulitzer Prize for Biography, A Thousand Days, 1966. STUDIED: Harvard University, B.A. summa cum laude, 1938; em. Society of Fellow, 1939-1942; postgrad, (Henry fellow), Cambridge University, 1938-39.

Historian Schlesinger is a professor at the City University of New York, a position he has held since 1966. He was a professor at Harvard from 1954 to 1961 and special assistant to President John F. Kennedy from 1961 to 1964. He won two Pulitzer prizes for his books on American political history: The Age of Jackson, and A Thousand Days. Other books Schlesinger has written include: The Age of Roosevelt (3 volumes), 1957-60; The Imperial Presidency, 1973; Robert Kennedy and His Times, 1978, and The Disuniting of America, 1972.

SCHMALENSEE, RICHARD LEE

4417 Chalfont Place, Bethesda, MD 20816
Schmalensee is a prominent economist. For career credentials consult the portion of this book entitled "Notable Americans by Profession" in the Appendix. Within this portion, the list "Economists" describes requirements for inclusion in this volume.

SCHMEMANN, SERGE

The New York Times, 229 West 43rd St., New York, NY 10036 (212) 556-1234
The grandson of an exiled Russian nobleman, Serge Schmemann, *The New York Times'* Moscow correspondent shows a deep knowledge of Russia and flavors his dispatches with tinges of pre-revolution

nostalgia. Visiting a town near his grandfather's former estate, he finds a youth passing a political gathering. Studying the gathering, the youth shouts, "I'm going to vote for Yeltsin" in Yeltsin's battle with parliament. Schmemann points out that the new Russian constitution has been amended more than 300 times and still is riddled with contradictions. And the Caspian republic of Azerbaijan in the two years since it gained independence has known war, coups and pogroms, corruption, intrigue, and the fugitive promise of oil wealth. Throughout his reports, he remains a cool, erudite commentator on the travails of his ancestors' birthplace.

SCHMOKE, KURT L.

Office of the Mayor, 250 City Hall, Baltimore, MD 21202 (410) 396-3835
BORN: 1949, Baltimore. ACHIEVEMENTS: Rhodes Scholar. STUDIED: Yale University, B.A., history, 1971; Harvard University, law, 1976.
After college Schmoke entered private practice in Baltimore, and, in 1977, joined President Carter's White House Domestic Policy staff. He returned to Baltimore in 1978 as assistant United States attorney. Schmoke was elected state's attorney for Baltimore City in 1982. He served in this position until his election as mayor of Baltimore on Nov. 3, 1987. In 1991 Mayor Schmoke was re-elected to a second term. His goal as mayor is to make education, public safety, and the environment a top priority of city government.

SCHNABEL, JULIAN

24 East Twentieth St., New York, NY 10003
BORN: 1951. ACHIEVEMENTS: Collections: Whitney Museum of American Art; exhibitions: Whitney Museum Biennial; Royal Academy of Art, London. STUDIED: University of Houston; Whitney Independent Study Program
Part of a developing European and American conceptual movement of painting, ranging from the totally abstract to a combination of abstraction and figuration, Julian Schnabel works in the figurative vein, operating within the constructivist collage tradition of Pablo Picasso's creations of 1908-1914. Since his recent emergence as a gallery artist, he has intrigued and puzzled the art world with his enigmatic language. His crude intensity has been described as "overkill" and "ugly," even by his admirers. Large-scale, ponderous figurations are expressionistic, sometimes chaotic, and violent images in oil with such additions as fiberglass, broken crockery and encrustations of plastic.

SCHNEIDER, WILLIAM

New York Times, 229 West 43rd St., New York, NY 10036 (212) 556123
ACHIEVEMENTS: Resident fellow, American Enterprise Institute; professor of Government, Harvard University; contributor, The Atlantic, Public Opinion; "Political Pulse" columnist, National Journal, political analyst, CNN.

Schneider is an insightful commentator on national and world affairs who writes for the New York Times. His material is frequently reprinted in newspapers throughout the U.S.

SCHORER, JANE

Des Moines Register, 715 Locust St., Box 957, Des Moines, IA 50304 (515) 284-8000
Schorer is a prominent journalist. For career credentials consult the portion of this book entitled "Notable Americans by Profession" in the Appendix. Within this portion, the list "Journalists" describes requirements for inclusion in this volume.

SCHRIEFFER, JOHN ROBERT

Florida State University, NHMFL, 1800 E. Paul Dirac Dr., Tallahassee, FL 32306
BORN: 1931, Oak Park, Ill. ACHIEVEMENTS: Nobel Prize in Physics (shared with Leon N. Cooper and the late John Bardeen), 1972; Buckley Prize, Comstock Prize, National Academy of Sciences; John Ericksson Medal, American Society of Swedish Engineers; National Medal of Science. STUDIED: Massachusetts Institute of Technology; University of Illinois.
Proving that electrical resistance in certain metals vanishes far above absolute zero (the temperature at which substances possess no thermal energy, equal to -273.15 degrees Celsius, or -459.67 degrees Fahrenheit), John Schrieffer and his colaureates, the late John Bardeen and Leon Cooper, stimulated much work on superconductivity in physics. Their research showed that, at low temperatures, electrons in a conductor could act in bound pairs, called "Cooper pairs," an action which results in no electrical resistance to the flow of electrons through solids. The discovery that there are materials that are superconductive at hundreds of degrees above absolute zero has since revolutionized the production and transmission of electrical energy.

SCHROEDER, PATRICIA

U.S. House of Representatives, 2208 RHOB, Washington, D.C., 20515-0601 (202) 225-4431
BORN: 1940, Portland, Ore. ACHIEVEMENTS: Co-chair of Gary Hart's 1984 presidential campaign. STUDIED: University of Minnesota, B.A., 1961; Harvard University, law degree, 1964.
A vocal champion of women's rights, Patricia Schroeder began her professional life as a field attorney for the National Labor Relations Board in 1964. Before her election to Congress, in 1972, Schroeder was chief counsel to the Colorado chapter of Planned Parenthood. She has been a backer of many liberal causes, including the Equal Rights Amendment, and was a strong opponent of the Vietnam War. Schroeder was the senior woman in the 103rd Congress, and the third-ranking Democrat on the House Armed Services Committee. She has been highly critical of sexual harassment in the military, and voted to permit female pilots to fly combat missions. In 1995 she announced that she will not run for re-election.

SCHULTZ, THEODORE W.

University of Chicago, Department of Economics, 1126 E. 59th St., Chicago, IL 60637

BORN: 1902, Arlington, S.D. ACHIEVEMENTS: Nobel Prize in Economic Science (shared with W. Arthur Lewis), 1979; Francis A. Walker Medal, American Economic Association; Leonard Elmhirst Medal, International Agricultural Economic Association; many honorary degrees from universities in both North and South America, and a member of many academic bodies around the world. STUDIED: South Dakota State College, Graduate School of Agriculture, Brookings S.D., University of Wisconsin.

Born in a German farming community, the future Nobel Prize winner made agriculture his major in college. In quick succession after winning a bachelor's degree, Schultz earned a master's two years later and a doctorate two years after that. Taking a teaching post at Iowa State College, his career then opened up before him when he popularized the then-new "human capital theory"— the investment a nation makes in its productive workers—in an address to the American Economic Association. He followed this by drawing attention to the new "economics of the family," associated with Gary Becker and the University of Chicago, which, exploring the division of labor among members of a family, parted company with conventional economists who treated the family as a one-person consumption unit, leaving the rest of family studies up to social scientists. Moving to the University of Chicago in 1943, his agricultural interests burst into bloom. In four years he published four critical books on American agriculture leading up to *The Economic Organization of Agriculture*, which would become a major textbook in the field. *Transforming Traditional Agriculture* announced his interest in the Third World, which would be cited by the Nobel economics committee in Stockholm for firming up his award in 1979. The one constant theme in successive books on the agricultural problems of poor countries is that rural poverty in the Third World is related to a pro-urban bias toward development, which seeks rapid industrialization that inevitably condemns farmers to mere subsistence production.

SCHWAB, CHARLES R.

101 Montgomery St., San Francisco, CA 94104

ACHIEVEMENTS: Founder, Charles Schwab & Company. STUDIED: Stanford University, M.B.A.

After graduation Charles R. Schwab went to work for the securities industry. He opened his own brokerage firm in 1971. By 1972 he employed 12 people and had about 2000 clients. At about the same time, the Securities & Exchange Commission changed the rules of the game, and instituted a system where investors were free to negotiate commissions with brokers. Schwab adopted the new system and changed his way of doing business at once. He established a system of discount pricing for fast trades, without the usual research or tips provided by most other brokerages. In 1982 Charles Schwab & Company was purchased by the BankAmerica Corporation for $53 million.

SCHWANTER, JOSEPH

21 Overbrook Rd., Rochester, NY 14624

Schwanter is a prominent composer. For career credentials consult the portion of this book entitled "Notable Americans by Profession" in the Appendix. Within this portion, the list "Composers" describes requirements for inclusion in this volume.

sis

SCHWARTZ, CARL

13872 Pine Villa Ln. S.E., Ft. Myers, FL 33912

BORN: 1935. ACHIEVEMENTS: Logan Medal, Art Institute of Chicago; Purchase Prize, Illinois State Museum; collections: British Museum, London; Smithsonian Institute, Washington, D.C.; exhibitions: Art Institute of Chicago; Cultural Center, Chicago. STUDIED: School of the Art Institute, Chicago.

Schwartz works deal primarily with landscapes. His current work continues to reflect his long-time interest in the effects of light on his imagery, and in this, while he categorizes himself a realist, he works within the Impressionist tradition. Indeed, he cites Cezanne and Monet as his major influences. He works full time in his Florida studio, painting from sketches and photographs of the lilly ponds and foliage in the nearby lagoons and surrounding environs. Time and time again, he is attracted to water imagery, an interest exemplified in painting "Wet Woodland" and "Bubbling Stream." In addition to his acrylic paintings (occasionally he works in watercolor, rarely in oil), he also produces hand-pulled limited edition stone lithographs.

SCHWARTZ, MELVIN

Brookhaven National Laboratories, Building 510 P, Upton, NY 11973

BORN: 1932, New York City. ACHIEVEMENTS: Nobel Prize in Physics, (shared with Leon M. Lederman and Jack Steinberger), 1988; Hughes Prize; Guggenheim Fellowship. STUDIED: Columbia University.

The Melvin Schwartz team's discovery, which confirmed the reality of quarks, was based on the bombardment of the light metal beryllium with the subatomic particle proton, which produced neutrinos, which are elementary particles having little or no mass, but under the bombardment produce a beam. The beam in turn led the researchers to discovery of a second neutrino associated with the mumeson, one of the particles that glue all particles in an atom together. The team's "breakthrough" work had far-reaching effects on fundamental particle theories. Today the beams are routinely produced in machines called "meson factories" for further study exploring the structure of matter as well as for radiological therapy.

SCHWARZ, GERARD

Los Angeles Chamber Orchestra, 285 West Green St., Pasadena, CA 91105 (213) 796-2200

Schwarz is a prominent concert master. For career credentials consult the portion of this book entitled

"Notable Americans by Profession" in the Appendix. Within this portion, the list "Concert Masters" describes requirements for inclusion in this volume.

SCOTT, MARION

UCLA Dance Department, Los Angeles, CA 90024 (213) 825-3951
BORN: 1922, Chicago. ACHIEVEMENTS: Notable ballets: Pastorale; Museum Piece; Afflicted Children; Bacchanale; Dilemma; Jump! Jump!; Life Begins on Childhood Wings; A Celebration for Percussion and Dance; He That Has Time to Mourn Has Time to Mend; Mysterium; Invitation. STUDIED: Bennington College; Martha Graham, Doris Humphrey, Charles Weidman schools for modern dance, and a variety of teachers in ballet.
A choreographer while still a dancer in her mid-20s, Marion Scott's career has been devoted as much to furthering the craft in others as it has been to producing her own work. An influential teacher at the High School of Performing Arts, she also teaches dance and composition at the University of California at Los Angeles. Her first works were presented for performances at the Choreographers' Workshop, founded to offer recitals to dancers who wanted to try out single titles without the stress of producing entire concerts. Later she became a founding member of Contemporary Dance Productions, which offers talented new choreographers a stage for their work, and has presented several of her own works on its programs.

SCOTT, NATHAN A. JR.

University of Virginia, Department of Religious Studies, 1419 Hilltop Rd., Charlottesville, VA 22903
ACHIEVEMENTS: Fellow, American Academy of Arts and Sciences. STUDIED: University of Michigan, B.A.; Union Theological Seminary, M.A., Divinity; Columbia University, Ph.D, Religion; many honorary degrees.
Appointed Dean of the Chapel at Virginia Union University soon after graduation from Union Theological Seminary, Nathan Scott completed his studies toward a doctorate in religion and then became a professor of theology and literature at the University of Chicago. He remained at Chicago for 16 years, moving to the University of Virginia in 1976 where he was professor emeritus of religious studies and professor emeritus of English until his retirement in 1990. Author of 25 books and contributor to 42, he served as vice president and then president of the American Academy of Religion.

SCUTT, DER

Der Scutt Architect, 244 Fifth Avenue, New York, NY 10001 (212) 725-2300
BORN: 1934. ACHIEVEMENTS: Fellow, Illuminating Engineering Society; Architectural Record Award of Excellence, 1970, 1974, 1975; E.F. Gruth Award, 1970; notable works: Trump Tower, New York City; Continental Center Corporate Headquarters, New York City; West Houston Street Hotel, New York City. STUDIED: Yale University.
When he began his practice, Der Scutt pledged to involve himself only with monumental, important projects. He didn't establish his own practice for nearly two decades, but in the intervening years he apprenticed to some of the Modern movement's greatest masters: Philip Johnson, Vincent Kling, Edward Fureli Stone, Paul Rudolph and Ely Kahn. In 1981 he emerged as a mature, commanding talent. His first solo commissions reflected an obvious delight in inspiring and motivating the occupants of his buildings with bold, opulent spaces, sometimes stretching the limits of budget and decorum in the process. Early designs had revealed a deep interest in the aesthetic and practical psychological effects of lighting. Lighting is a key factor in worker efficiency and user enjoyment in any space, he believes, and lighting sources should be completely integrated with architectural form. His particular fondness for the steel and glass skyscraper comes from its unique ability to capture natural light, even in Manhattan's concrete canyons. The rippling, striated, mirrored-glass facade of his 58-story Trump Tower in New York City is at once an eloquent repudiation of the "raw," unmodeled envelopes of neighboring Brutalist towers, and an impassioned effort to catch and capture the transforming rays of the sun.

SEAWELL, DONALD R.

510 East 84th St., New York, NY 10028
Seawell is a prominent dramatic artist. For career credentials consult the portion of this book entitled "Notable Americans by Profession" in the Appendix. Within this portion, the list "Dramatic Artists" describes requirements for inclusion in this volume.

SEESKIN, KENNETH R.

Department of Philosophy, Northwestern University, 1818 Hinman Ave., Evanston, IL 60201
BORN: 1947, Skokie, Ill. ACHIEVEMENTS: Phi Beta Kappa; Danforth Fellow; Tew Prize in the Humanities, Yale University; Cooper Prize in Greek Philosophy, Yale University; Outstanding Teacher Award, Northwestern University; Fellow, Foundation of Jewish Studies, and many other awards. STUDIED: Northwestern University, B.A.; Yale University, M.A., philosophy, Ph.D., philosophy.
Beginning at age 25, as an assistant professor of philosophy on his graduation from Yale in 1972, Kenneth Seeskin has spent his entire career at Northwestern University. As assistant professor he won the Cooper Prize in Greek Philosophy and an award from his school for outstanding teaching. He was an associate professor from 1978 to 1988, during which time he became chair of the department of philosophy at Northwestern, a position he still holds. In 1987 he became director of the school's Jewish Studies Program and continued in that role when he became a full professor in 1988. He presently is Charles Deering McCormick Professor of Teaching Excellence. In addition to his teaching, Seeskin is editor of the *State University of New York's Press Series in Jewish Philosophy.* Author of four books, Seeskin has also contributed articles to more than a score of professional journals, in the United States and abroad, and many critical reviews of philosophers and philosophical subjects.

SEGAL, GEORGE

Davidsons Mill Rd., New Brunswick, NJ 08901
BORN: 1924. ACHIEVEMENTS: Walter K. Gutman Foundation Award; First Prize, Art Institute of Chicago; collections: Museum of Modern Art; Art Institute of Chicago; exhibitions: Whitney Museum of American Art; Art Institute of Chicago. Education: New York University; Rutgers University.

First a figurative painter in 1956, George Segal gained recognition two years later with experiments in plaster sculptures made of chicken wire and burlap, molds from live models placed in "environments" containing real objects such as chairs, tables, beds, baths, ladders, and traffic lights. His medium changed to the casting of plaster of Paris directly from the human form, producing hollow molds which looked as if they might still hold the bodies inside, like mummies in eternal imprisonment. These sculptures have always been melancholy depictions of people in isolation, alienated from one another.

SEGER, BOB

c/o Capitol Records Inc., 1750 N. Vine St., Hollywood, CA 90228
Seger is a prominent vocalist. For career credentials consult the portion of this book entitled "Notable Americans by Profession" in the Appendix. Within this portion, the list "Vocalists" describes requirements for inclusion in this volume.

SEINFELD, JERRY

Bantam Books, 666 Fifth Avenue, New York NY 10103
(212) 765-6500
BORN: 1955, Brooklyn, N.Y. ACHIEVEMENTS: Emmy, Best Comedy Series, Seinfeld, 1993; Golden Globe, Best Actor in a Comedy Series, Seinfeld, 1994. STUDIED: Queens College
When Seinfeld first appeared on stage, he was a bundle of nerves and could only mumble a few unintelligible words before walking off the stage. To force himself to succeed as a comedian, he sought dead-end jobs, including selling jewelry on New York streets and light bulbs over the telephone. In 1976 he made his stand-up debut at Catch a Rising Star in Manhattan. He won the American Comedy Award for the Funniest Male in 1988. In addition to his popular TV sitcom *Seinfeld*, his book *Seinlanguage* was a best seller in 1993.

SELLECK, THOMAS

McCartt, Oreck, and Barrett, 10390 Santa Monica Blvd., Los Angeles, CA 90025
BORN: 1945, Detroit. ACHIEVEMENTS: Emmy and Golden Globe Awards, Outstanding Lead Actor in a Drama Series, Magnum P.I., 1984. STUDIED: Attended the University of Southern California.
Selleck shot to fame when he played the title role, Thomas Magnum, in the television series *Magnum P.I.*, 1980. Filmed on scenic locations, *Magnum P.I.* featured Selleck in mystery dramas each week. Prior to *Magnum P.I.*, Selleck played the role of Lance White in another drama series, *The Rockford Files*. Selleck also appeared in the television movies *The*

Concrete Cowboys, 1979; *The Sacketts*, 1979; *Shadow Riders*, 1982; and *Divorce Wars: A Love Story*, 1982. His principal film appearances include *The Seven Minutes*, 1971; *Daughters of Satan*, 1972; *Midway*, 1976; *Coma*, 1978; *High Road to China*, 1983; and the title role in *Lassiter*, 1984.

SERNA, JOE JR.

205 City Hall, 915 I Street, Sacramento, CA 95814
(916) 264 5407
BORN: Stockton, Calif. ACHIEVEMENTS: Economic Development Leadership Award, National Council of Urban Economic Development. STUDIED: Sacramento State College, B.A., social science/government, 1966; post-grad, University of California, Davis.
Serna began his career as a sheet metal worker and attended college at Sacramento State College. After college Serna entered the Peace Corps, and worked as a community development volunteer in Guatemala. Serna was elected to the Sacramento City Council in 1981. He chaired the Budget and Finance Committee from 1981 to 1989 and the Transportation and Community Development Committee from 1989 to 1991. Serna became the mayor of Sacramento in November, 1992.

SERRA, RICHARD

P.O. Box 645 Canal St. Station, New York, NY 10013
BORN: 1939. ACHIEVEMENTS: Skowhegan Medal Collections, Museum of Modern Art, New York City, Whitney Museum; exhibitions: University Art Museum, Berkeley; Margo Leavin Gallery, Los Angeles. STUDIED: University of California, Santa Barbara; Yale University.
An interest in process art and the quality of materials led Richard Serra to produce sculptures utilizing neon tubes, rubber, metal slabs and molten lead. The first of several *splash-pieces* was conducted in 1968, in which molten lead was flung onto the bottom of a wall. The next year, large metal sheets were leaned against each other, exploring aspects of gravity in the *Prop* series. In the '70s his site sculptures integrated the landscape with sculptural elements like cement or metal sheeting, in order, according to Serra, "to find an awareness of physicality in time, space and motion. . . one's relation to the breadth of the land." He has also engaged in graphics work and filmmaking.

SESSIONS, ROGER HUNTINGTON

63 Stanworth Lane, Princeton, NJ 08540
Sessions is a prominent composer. For career credentials consult the portion of this book entitled "Notable Americans by Profession" in the Appendix. Within this portion, the list "Composers" describes requirements for inclusion in this volume.

SHAIN, HAROLD

Newsweek, Inc., 444 Madison Ave., New York, NY 10022-6999 (212) 350-4000
Shain is a prominent publisher. For career credentials consult the portion of this book entitled "Notable Americans by Profession" in the Appendix. Within

this portion, the list "Publishers" describes requirements for inclusion in this volume.

SHALALA, DONNA

Department of Health & Human Services, 200 Independence Ave. SW, Washington, D.C. 20201 (202) 690-7000

BORN: 1941, Cleveland. ACHIEVEMENTS: Rresident, Hunter College, 1979; chancellor, University of Wisconsin. STUDIED: Western College for Women, B.A.; Syracuse University, M.A., Ph.D.

Donna Shalala has been an active university administrator since she finished her college career. With degrees in urban studies and social sciences, Shalala began her career in academics in New York City. She was appointed president of Hunter College in 1979, where she greatly increased the number of women and minority administrators. In the late 1980s and early 1990s, Shalala, as chancellor of the University of Wisconsin, aggressively worked to reduce racial tensions, stop underage drinking, build a better football team, and raise the number of minority students and faculty at the institution. In 1988 President Clinton appointed her Secretary of Health and Human Services. Among her accomplishments in that post was to convince the French manufacturer of RU-486, a drug used to induce abortions, to donate its U.S. patent rights to a nonprofit organization. Roussel-Uclaf gave those rights to the Population Council in 1994.

SHALES, TOM

The Washington Post, 1150 15th St. NW, Washington, D.C., 20071. (202) 334-6000

BORN: 1948, Elgin, Ill. ACHIEVEMENTS: Author On The Air!; co-author, The American Film Heritage. STUDIED: American University, B.S., journalism, 1973.

Shales joined the *D.C. Examiner* as their entertainment writer before moving to the *Washington Post* in 1977 to become their television critic and entertainment columnist. He can also be heard on National Public Radio as the film critic of the *Morning Edition*, a position he's held since 1979. His reviews are carried by many major dailies, and are frequently reprinted in *The Los Angeles Times* television guide. He is the author on *On The Air!*, and co-author of *The American Film Heritage*.

SHALIKASHVILI, JOHN MALCHASE DAVID

Office of the Secretary, Pentagon, Washington, D.C. 20301-1155 (703) 545-6700

BORN: 1936, Warsaw (Poland). ACHIEVEMENTS: Appointed chairman of the Joint Chiefs of Staff, 1993. STUDIED: U.S. Army, Officer's Candidate School. o

Joint Chief of Staff General "Shali," as he is called by fellow military personnel, immigrated to the United States from Poland in 1952. He enlisted in the U.S. Army in 1958, and advanced through the ranks, becoming a full general in 1992. As NATO commander stationed in Brussels from 1992-1993, he supervised NATO airstrike preparations during the war in Bosnia. After the Persian Gulf war, he directed the crea-

tion of a safe zone for the Kurds in northern Iraq. In August 1993 this career U.S. Army officer was appointed chairman of the Joint Chiefs of Staff, during a time of transition for the U.S. military.

SHARP, PHILLIP ALLAN

Massachusetts Institute of Technology Center for Cancer Research, 40 Ames St., Room B17 529B, Cambridge, MA 02139

BORN: 1944, Falmouth, Ky. ACHIEVEMENTS: Nobel Prize for Physiology or Medicine, 1993 (with Richard J. Roberts). STUDIED: Union College, Barbourville, Kentucky, B.A., biology; University of Illinois, Ph.D., biology; California Institute of Technology, diploma.

Working on the family farm helped pay the tuition for Phillip Sharp at Union College. After acquiring his doctorate at the University of Illinois he joined the Cold Spring Harbor Laboratory in Cold Spring Harbor, New York. In 1974 he moved to the Massachusetts Institute of Technology, where he directed the Center for Cancer Research. In 1977 he discovered the "split gene," which proved that the DNA strand is not continuous as scientists had believed, and he eventually became a Nobel awardee with Richard J. Roberts, who had made the same discovery the same year. In 1978 Sharp helped found Biogen, a Cambridge, Mass., producer of interferon. In 1990, deciding that he preferred teaching and research, he declined the presidency of MIT.

SHARPE, JAMES

City Hall, 920 Broad St., Newark, NJ 07102 (201) 733-6400

Sharpe is a prominent political leader in New Jersey and the mayor of Newark.

SHARPE, WILLIAM FORSYTH

Stanford University, Department of Economics, Stanford, CA 94305

BORN: 1934, Cambridge, Mass. ACHIEVEMENTS: Nobel Prize in Economic Science (with Harry M. Markowitz and Merton H. Miller) 1990. STUDIED: University of California at Los Angeles, B.A., M.A., Ph.D., economics.

Investment management analysis is his forte, but William Sharpe is especially known for a model he constructed on capital asset pricing. He has taught at Stanford's Graduate School of Business for 25 years, and is the Timken Professor of Finance there. The Nobel awards committee pointed out that the work of Sharpe and his conferees provided new ways of measuring the risks and rewards of investments, and for more accurately valuing corporate stocks and bonds.

SHATZEL, COL. R. D.

Office of the Secretary, Pentagon, Washington, D.C. 20301-1155 (703) 545-6700

Shatzel, USA is a prominent military leader. For career credentials consult the portion of this book entitled "Notable Americans by Profession" in the

Appendix. Within this portion, the list "Military Leaders" describes requirements for inclusion in this volume.

SHAW, BREWSTER HOPKINSON, JR

Director, Space Shuttle Operations, L.B. Johnson Space Center, Houston TX 77058
BORN: 1945, Cass City, Miss. ACHIEVEMENTS: Colonel USAF; piloted the STS-9, 1983 space mission; commander of the STS 61-B, 1985, and STS-28, 1989 space missions. STUDIED: University of Wisconsin, B.S., engineering mechanics, 1968; University of Wisconsin, M.S. engineering mechanics, 1969.
Starting out as a test pilot for the U.S. Air Force at the Test Pilot School at Edwards AFB in California., Shaw joined the eighth group of astronauts selected in 1978. Colonel Shaw was the commander of the STS-28 mission, which was a classified Department of Defense mission. He left the astronaut corps in 1993 to become director of space operations at the Johnson Space Center.

SHAW, BERNARD

CNN, 111 Massachusetts Ave., NW, Washington, D.C. 20001
BORN: 1940, Chicago. ACHIEVEMENTS: Award for Cable Excellence (ACE) for Best News Anchor; National Association of Television Arts and Sciences News and Documentary; Emmy Award for Outstanding Coverage of a Single Breaking News Story (Beijing, China's Tiananmen Square student riots); STUDIED: University of Illinois.
Shaw quit college when Westinghouse Broadcasting Company offered him a job in the nation's capital. Previously he reported for Westinghouse station WIND in Chicago, distinguishing himself with coverage of the Martin Luther King assassination and its aftermath in 1968. In Washington he covered the White House for three years before joining CBS News. During his six years with CBS he covered the White House, the State Department, the Pentagon, and the Supreme Court. His biggest feat was securing an interview with President Nixon associate John Mitchell during the Watergate scandal which led to Nixon's resignation. Shaw moved to ABC in 1977 as Latin American correspondent and covered the Jonestown massacre, where 900 members of the Jim Jones cult committed mass suicide; interviewed Cuban president Fidel Castro; and covered the Nicaraguan revolution. In 1980 he joined the fledgling 24-hour, all-news cable network CNN as chief anchor, which was to grow to more than 21 bureaus broadcasting in 80 countries in 10 years. His landmark work with CNN to date was his coverage of the Persian Gulf War, the highlight of which, with colleagues Peter Arnett and John Holliman, was their broadcasts of the American bombing of Baghdad. For 16 1/2 hours the three men offered the world the only live coverage of the event, broadcasting from the ninth floor of the AlRashid hotel—later called "the center of hell" by Shaw—until Iraqi officials shut down the phone line they were using after they lost visual transcription.

SHAW, ROBERT

Atlanta Symphony Orchestra, 1280 Peachtree St., NE, Atlanta, GA 30399 (404) 898-1182
Shaw is a prominent concert master. For career credentials consult the portion of this book entitled "Notable Americans by Profession" in the Appendix. Within this portion, the list "Concert Masters" describes requirements for inclusion in this volume.

SHAW, SANDY

c/o Warner Books, Inc., 666 Fifth Avenue, New York, NY 10103 (212) 484-2900
Shaw is a prominent author. For career credentials consult the portion of this book entitled "Notable Americans by Profession" in the Appendix. Within this portion, the list "Authors" describes requirements for inclusion in this volume.

SHEEHY, GAIL HENION

c/o Random House, 201 E. 50th St., New York, NY 10022
BORN: 1937, Mamaroneck, N.Y. ACHIEVEMENTS: Best-selling author, Passages, New Passages. STUDIED: University of Vermont, B.S.; Columbia University, fellow, journalism.
Gail Sheehy's career in newspapers and magazines has perfectly suited her for translating the often untranslatable and peculiar character of scholastic or professional writing into the general language of the broad public. The result has been more than a dozen bestsellers such as *Passages: Predictable Crises of Adult Life* in 1976, named by a Library of Congress survey as one of the most influential books of our times; *Pathfinders* in 1981; and *The Silent Passage*, in 1992. She spent three years as a feature writer for the *New York Herald Tribune* from 1963 to 1966 and 11 years as an editor for the *New York* magazine from 1966 to 1977. She left that job after the success of *Passages*. Her latest book, *New Passages: Mapping Your Life Across Time*, released in 1995, maps out the new frontier of "second adulthood" in middle life.

SHELDON, SIDNEY

c/o William Morrow, 105 Madison Ave., New York, NY 10016
BORN: 1917, Chicago. ACHIEVEMENTS: Academy Award, The Bachelor and the Bobby Soxer, 1947; Antoinette Perry Award, Redhead, 1959. STUDIED: Northwestern University.
A prolific playwright, screen writer and novelist, Sidney Sheldon won an Oscar for Best Screenplay for *The Bachelor and the Bobby Soxer* in 1947, and a Tony for *Redhead* in 1959. He created the television series *The Patty Duke Show*, 1963-1966, and *I Dream of Jeannie*, 1965-1969. In 1970, at the age of 53, he published his first novel, a psychological thriller titled *The Naked Face*, which was nominated for an Edgar Award by the Mystery Writers of America. Since then, he has written a series of best-selling novels including *The Other Side of Midnight*, 1974, and *Bloodline*, 1977. In the

1980s many of his novels were adapted for motion picures.

SHEPARD, ALAN BARTLETT, JR.

c/o NASA, L.B. Johnson Space Center, Houston, TX 77058 (713) 483-0123

BORN: 1923, East Derry, N.H. ACHIEVEMENTS: Space missions: Mercury 3, first U.S. astronaut in space, commander Apollo 14. STUDIED: U.S. Naval Academy, B.S., 1944.

Alan Shepard was a U.S. Navy test pilot when NASA selected him as one of the first seven astronauts in 1959. He was the first American to reach outer space when he flew on the Mercury 3 spacecraft, inside the Freedom 7 space capsule. The flight was a suborbital trip that lasted 15 minutes, reaching an altitude of 116.5 miles. He fell victim to an inner-ear disorder that kept him from later flights until a surgical correction in 1969. In 1971, he commanded Apollo 14, the third manned mission to reach the moon. He and lunar module pilot Edgar Mitchell explored the lunar surface for 4-1/2 hours during the 33 hours they were on the moon. He was the chief of the Astronaut Office between 1963 and 1969, and again between 1971 and his retirement in 1974. He retired from the Navy as a rear admiral.

SHEPARD, SAM

International Creative Management, 8942 Wilshire Blvd., Beverly Hills, CA 90211

BORN: 1943, Fort Sheridan, Ill. Boeing CEO Frank Shrontz.
ACHIEVEMENTS: Pulitzer Prize, Buried Child, 1979; Obie Award, 1979; Academy Award nomination, Best Supporting Actor, The Right Stuff, 1984. STUDIED: Mount San Antonio Junior College, 1960-1961.

After jobs in his youth that ranged from stable hand and orange picker in California to waiter and musician in New York City, Sam Shepard produced his first full-length play, *La Turista*, 1967, at age 23. In some 40 plays since then, he has considered "theater and writing to be a home where I bring the adventures of my life and sort them out." His dramas include *Mad Dog Blues*, 1971; *The Tooth of Crime*, 1973; *Angel City*,

1977; *Curse of the Starving Class*, 1976; and *A Lie of the Mind*, 1985. He wrote the screenplay for the film version of his play *Fool for Love*, 1983, and also appeared in the picture. His other screenplays include *Zabriskie Point*, 1970, and *Paris, Texas*, 1984. Shepard was nominated for an Academy Award in 1984 for his work in the film *The Right Stuff*, and he has appeared in other hit films including *Steel Magnolias*, 1989 and *The Pelican Brief*, 1993.

SHERWIN, ELTON JR.

International Business Machines, Old Orchard Rd., Armonk, NY 10504 (914) 765-1900

ACHIEVEMENTS: Developed IBM's Personal Dictation System

The esoteric computer speech recognition system used for years in expensive laboratory settings reached desktop operators in 1994 with IBM's Personal Dictation System. Developed by Elton Sherman Jr., manager of IBM's Strategic Development in Speech Recognition, the system consists of software, a microphone, a card that drives the speech adapter, and a vocabulary of up to 32,000 words. It sells for under $1,000. The Personal Dictation System works by listening to the user read, analyzing the way one pronounces words. It then converts the sounds into typewritten words or computer commands. It learns a little more about the speaker's style each time it is used, and the user corrects errors as they appear.

SHIPLER, DAVID K.

The New York Times, 229 West 43rd St., New York, NY 10036 (212) 556-1234

Shipler is a prominent journalist. For career credentials consult the portion of this book entitled "Notable Americans by Profession" in the Appendix. Within this portion, the list "Journalists" describes requirements for inclusion in this volume.

SHRONTZ, FRANK ANDERSON

Boeing Company, P.O. Box 3707, 7755 E. Marginal Way S, Seattle, WA 98108

BORN: 1931, Boise, Idaho. ACHIEVEMENTS: Board of directors for the Strategic and International Studies, 1986; member of the Business Roundtable; member of the Advisory Board at the Stanford Business School. STUDIED: University of Idaho, LL.B., 1954; Harvard University, M.B.A., 1958; Stanford University, 1969-70.

Boeing CEO rank Shrontz started working with the company in 1958. He left in 1973, when he was appointed assistant secretary of the Air Force. In 1976, that position launched him to assistant secretary of defense. He rejoined Boeing in 1977 as a corporate vice president in charge of contract administration and planning. He was elected chief executive officer of Boeing in 1986 and became chairman in 1988. He also serves as a board member at Citicorp, Boise Cascade Corporation, and the 3M Company.

SHULTZ, PETER

University of California, Department of Chemistry, Berkeley, CA 94720

BORN: 1942, Brooklyn, N.Y. ACHIEVEMENTS: designed and produced optical fiber (along with Robert Maurer and Donald Keck); inducted into the National Inventors Hall of Fame, 1993. STUDIED: Rutgers University, B.S., 1964; Ph.D. in ceramics, 1967.

Dr. Peter Schultz began his career at Corning in 1967 as a senior ceramicist. In a collaborative effort with Donald Keck and Robert Maurer, they invented the optical fiber used in modern telecommunications. In 1970 the trio designed and produced an optical fiber with low optical losses. The reduction of light loss removed the 20-decibels-per-kilometer barrier, enabling the widespread use of the optical fiber in telecommunications. The trio's discoveries helped commercialize the optical fiber, thus ushering in the telecommunications industry.

SIDEY, HUGH

Time, Rockefeller Center, New York, NY 100201

BORN: 1927, Greenfield, Iowa. ACHIEVEMENTS: Correspondent, Life, 1955-1958; correspondent, Time; 1958-1966, columnist, 1966-1969, chief contributing editor, 1969-1978, Washington contributing editor, "The Presidency". STUDIED: Iowa State University, 1950, BS

Sidey, a senior writer for *Time* magazine, frequently writes the "Presidency" and "America" columns for the magazine. He is a career journalist for Time, Inc., and has therefore built his career around reporting on world events for their various magazines. He is regarded as one of the insiders in Washington journalism and often scoops other reporters on major breaking stories. He is especially well-known for his *Time* essays that focus on contemporary issues.

SIEGEL, BERNIE S.

c/o Harper Collins, 10 East 53rd St., New York, NY 10022 (212) 207-7759

Siegel is a prominent author. For career credentials consult the portion of this book entitled "Notable Americans by Profession" in the Appendix. Within this portion, the list "Authors" describes requirements for inclusion in this volume.

SILAS, C. J.

Phillips Petroleum Company, 1237 Adams Building, Bartlesville, OK 74004 (918) 661-5460

BORN: 1932, Miami, Fla. ACHIEVEMENTS: Commander, Order of St. Olaf, Norway; Athletic Hall of Fame, Georgia Institute of Technology, Former Scholar-Athlete Total Person Award; Oklahoma Business Hall of Fame. STUDIED: Georgia Institute of Technology, B.S., chemical engineering.

C. J. Silas began his 40-year career with Phillips Petroleum in the company's natural gas and gas liquid divisions. His road to company president and chairman began with his appointment as managing director of the Europe-Africa division. The new division announced a major departure for Phillips. Until that time, Phillips was a domestic oil company with most of its exploration and production facilities located in the Southwestern United States. Silas played a major role in the development of North Sea oil and directed the building of the largest European petroleum terminal in Teeside, England, before becoming chief executive officer. He retired in 1994 at age 62.

SILVER, RON

ICM, c/o Sam Cohn, 40 West 57th Street, New York, NY 10019

BORN: 1946, New York City. ACHIEVEMENTS: Antoinette Perry Award, Leading Actor in a Play, Speed-the-Plow, 1988. STUDIED: State University College at Buffalo, N.Y., B.A.; St. John's University, M.A.; trained for acting at Herbert Berghof Studios and at the Actors' Studio.

Silver made his stage debut in 1971, appearing in *Kaspar* and *Public Insult*, a double billing. His off-Broadway debut was as Pepe Hernandez, in *El Grande de Coca-Cola*, 1972, at the Mercer Arts Center in New York City. He arrived on Broadway playing at the Ethel Barrymore Theatre in *Hurly Burly*, 1984-1985. Silver played in the television series *The Mac Davis Show*, 1976; *Rhoda*, 1976-78; *Dear Detective*, 1979; *The Stockard Channing Show*, 1980; and *Baker's Dozen*, 1982. He also appeared in the mini-series *Kane and Able* in 1985, *The Billionaire Boys Club* in 1987 and *Reversal of Fortune* in 1990.

SILVERSTEIN, SHELBY (SHEL)

c/o Harper Collins Publishing Company, 10 E. 53rd St., New York, NY 10022

BORN: 1932, Chicago. ACHIEVEMENTS: Author, best-selling children's books, A Light in the Attic, and The Giving Tree.

A cartoonist on the Pacific edition of the U.S. Army newspaper *Stars and Stripes* in the 1950s, Shel Silverstein served his hitch in the armed forces and returned to New York City and Greenwich Village. He caught the attention of children's editor Ursula Nordstrom of Harper & Row who persuaded him to write books. He has published 18 books for readers of all ages but principally for the children's market, among them his first book *The Giving Tree* in 1964, which has since sold more than one million copies. His third volume,

A Light in the Attic, a collection of poems and drawings written for children, oddly climbed to the top of the 1981 *New York Times* adult fiction best-seller list, which it occupied for several weeks. His country western songs include *A Boy Named Sue* which reached No. 1 on the charts. A frequent contributor of cartoons and writings in *Playboy* magazine, he continues to write, compose, play music, draw cartoons and refuse to give interviews since several reviewers have called his work superficial and commercial.

SILVESTRI, MARTIN

c/o Polydor Records, Inc., 810 Seventh Avenue, New York, NY 10019 (212) 399-7075
Silvestri is a prominent composer. For career credentials consult the portion of this book entitled "Notable Americans by Profession" in the Appendix. Within this portion, the list "Composers" describes requirements for inclusion in this volume.

SIMKO, RICHARD

Information Storage Devices, San Jose, CA.
ACHIEVEMENTS: developed Direct Analog Storage Technology.
Richard Simko's development of Direct Analog Storage Technology (DAST) may usher in a new wave of recording devices. DAST is a new computer chip that stores human voice and other sound information directly, without the digitalization other computer devices rely on. Each chip is a self-contained recorder or answering machine, and it retains information even when cut from a power source. This new technology will likely spawn developments, such as talking aids for the blind, pagers with voice messages instead of bleeps or buzzers, and talking medical equipment.

SIMON, NEIL

c/o G. DaSilva, No. 400, 10100 Santa Monica Blvd., Los Angeles, CA 90067
Simon is a prominent dramatic artist. For career credentials consult the portion of this book entitled "Notable Americans by Profession" in the Appendix. Within this portion, the list "Dramatic Artists" describes requirements for inclusion in this volume.

SIMON, HERBERT A.

Carnegie Mellon University, Department of Psychology, Schenley Park, Pittsburgh, PA 15213
BORN: 1916, Milwaukee, Wis. ACHIEVEMENTS: Nobel Prize in Economic Science, 1978; Award for Distinguished Scientific Contributions, American Psychological Association; distinguished fellow, American Economic Association; Administrative Award, American College of Hospital Administrators; Dow Jones Award; National Medal of Science; Chairman, many scientific organizations; many other awards both in U.S. and abroad. STUDIED: University of Chicago; Honorary doctorates: Yale University, Marquette University, Columbia University, University of Michigan, University Paul Valery, France, among many received.
Simon has spent his professional lifetime deconstructing the decision-making process within economic organizations. In Simon's analogy, the "economic man" is like the chess player faced with millions of alternative possibilities in every move, but instead of attempting to examine those alternatives, he seizes on promising patterns and lines of play. Simon holds that economists dealing with institutional decision-making and administrative behavior likewise depend on similar rules of thumb, which he calls unrealistic. They are, in fact, "bounded" by ignorance of an uncertain future and by the costs involved in obtaining data about alternative opportunities. They do as well as they can with what they have, and afterwards gradually adjust these levels upward or downward, depending on whether the outcome exceeds or falls short of expectations. One of his books on the subject, *Administrative Behavior,* has become a standard text the world over on business management and administration, thus his award from the American College of Hospital Administrators. Because of his studies in human behavior in its multitudinous variations and in automation in management, he is regarded by psychologists as a psychologist, by computer scientists as a computer scientist, and by economists as an economist.

SIMON, PAUL

462 Dirksen Senate Office Building, Washington, D.C.., 20510-2152 (202) 224-2152
BORN: 1928, Eugene, Ore. ACHIEVEMENTS: Special agent of the Counter Intelligence Corps, 1951-53, 39 honorary degrees, 15 books including Lovejoy: Martyr to Freedom, 1964; The Tongue-Tied American, 1980; Letters to the President, 1994. STUDIED: Dana College, 1946-48.
Sen. Simon's passion for writing flared early when, at 19, he purchased the first of 15 newspapers he would own and operate in his journalistic career. He served in both the Illinois House and Senate, helping to develop a community college system for his state, before serving as lieutenant governor in 1968. He entered the U.S. House of Representatives in 1974, where he sponsored the legislation that created the National Center for Missing and Exploited Children, before his 1984 election to the U.S. Senate. In the 103rd Congress he served on committees for the Budget, Foreign Relations, Indian Affairs and Judiciary, Labor and Human Resources, while also maintaining his 45-year-old newspaper column, *P.S. Washington.* In 1995 he announced that he will not run for re-election.

SIMON, PAUL

Warner Brothers Records, 3 East 54th St., New York, NY 10022 (212) 832-0600
BORN: 1941, Newark, N.J. ACHIEVEMENTS: Grammy (with Art Garfunkel), Record of the Year, Best Pop Performance-Duo or Group,Mrs. Robinson, 1968; Grammy, Best Soundtrack, The Graduate (with Dave Grusin), 1968; Grammy (with Art Garfunkel), Record of the Year, Album of the Year, Song of the Year, Best Rock/Contemporary Song, Bridge Over Troubled Water, 1970; Grammy, Album of the Year, Best Pop Vocal-Male, Still Crazy After All These Years, 1975; Grammy, Album of the Year,Graceland, 1986; Emmy, Best Writing in a Comedy, Variety or Music Special, The Paul Simon Special, 1978; inducted into the Rock and Roll Hall

of Fame (with Art Garfunkel), 1990. STUDIED: Queens College, B.A.; Brooklyn Law School, post-grad.

Paul Simon's solo career has been even more diverse and complex than his earlier career with Art Garfunkel. His albums have been consistently rich, with rhythms borrowed from reggae, gospel, jazz, rock, folk, African and Brazilian music, and from traditional pop. Simon has experimented on each solo album with different approaches, but at the same time has not abandoned his distinctive, melodic songwriting style. During the 1970s, his albums were consistent best sellers—all three of his solo albums reached the Top Five and his live album went gold. Since the award-winning 1986 album, *Graceland*, Simon has produced eight albums, including the retrospective *1964-1993*. In 1990 Simon, along with Art Garfunkel, was inducted into the Rock and Roll Hall of Fame

SIMPSON, ALAN K.

U.S. Senate, Room 229, Washington, D.C. 20510 (202) 224-2708
Simpson is a prominent political leader. For career credentials consult the portion of this book entitled "Notable Americans by Profession" in the Appendix. Within this portion, the list "Political Leaders" describes requirements for inclusion in this volume.

SINATRA, FRANCIS (FRANK) ALBERT

Sinatra Enterprises, Goldwyn Studios., 1041 N. Formosa, Los Angeles, CA 90046
BORN: 1915, Hoboken, N.J. ACHIEVEMENTS: Special Academy Award, 1945; Academy Award, Supporting Actor, From Here to Eternity, 1953; Grammy, Best Album, Come Dance with Me, 1959; Grammy, Best Album, September of My Years, 1965; Grammy, Best Album, Moonlight, 1966; Grammy, Record of the Year, Moonlight, 1966; Grammy, Best Male Vocalist, 1959, 1965, 1966; Emmy, Outstanding Musical Special, Frank Sinatra: A Man and His Music, 1965; Presidential Medal of Freedom, 1985. STUDIED: Attended Drake Institute.

"Old Blue Eyes," as he is effectionately known, became a pop-music icon in the early 1940s. Frank Sinatra's appearances caused mass hysteria among his fans. Sinatra had no formal vocal training, but his sophisticated vocal style set him apart from other singers of his era. He begged Columbia Pictures to let him have the role as Maggio in the 1953 film *From Here to Eternity*, for which his performance won an Oscar. As a part of the Hollywood "rat pack," he starred in several films with Peter Lawford, Sammy Davis Jr., and Dean Martin. Other memorable films include *Guys and Dolls*, 1955; *High Society*, 1956; *Some Came Running*, 1958; and *The Manchurian Candidate*, 1962. In 1971 Sinatra announced his retirement, however by 1974 he began performing again. Throughout the early 90s he performed at live concerts. In 1992 and 1994 he recorded his "Duet Series," in which—by the miracle of electronic dubbing—he sang with major artists including Gladys Knight and Stevie Wonder. In 1995, in honor of his 80th birthday, he released his CD album, *80th—Live Concert*.

SINGER, CAROLE BAYER

c/o Columbia/CBS, 51 West 52nd St., New York, NY 10019 (212) 975-4321
Singer is a prominent composer. For career credentials consult the portion of this book entitled "Notable Americans by Profession" in the Appendix. Within this portion, the list "Composers" describes requirements for inclusion in this volume.

SINNOT-ARMSTRONG, WALTER P.

Department of Philosophy, Dartmouth College, 6305 Thornton Hall, Hanover, NH, 03755 (603) 646-2386
BORN: 1955, Memphis, Tenn. ACHIEVEMENTS: Published numerous articles in top philosophy journals. STUDIED: Yale University, Ph.D., philosophy, 1982, Whiting Fellowship; Amherst College, Phi Beta Kappa, summa cum laude, Lamprecht Fellowship, 1977.

Sinnot-Armstrong began his teaching career at Dartmouth College and is currently the chairman of the philosophy department there. In 1993, he was promoted to full professor. He has been a visiting professor at the Johns Hopkins University and Edinburgh University. Sinnot-Armstrong is the director of two Humanities Institutes, *Constitutional Interpretation* and *Moral Knowledge*. He has written six books in the last eight years; the most current one is *Moral Epistemology*.

SISKIND, AARON

15 Elm Way, Providence, RI 02906 (401) 267-1234
BORN: 1903. ACHIEVEMENTS: Gold Star of Merit, Philadelphia College of Art; Guggenheim Fellowship; collections: Museum of Modern Art; Metropolitan Museum of Art. STUDIED: College of the City of New York.

Without any formal training, he went on to create a social documentary series which included *Harlem Document* and *The Bowery*. Seven years later, more interested in the geometric beauty of architectural cityscapes, he abandoned formal concepts of perspective and space. Influenced by the Abstract Impressionist movement and the artists who became his steady friends, he began to explore the expressive possibilities of pure form. Experimenting with close-up abstractions of isolated objects, such as urban walls, battered stone, cracking paint and graffiti, compositions transcend the realm of ordinary reality, creating an experience in their own right. A frontrunner in the evolution of contemporary photography, he joined Harry Callahan at the Institute of Design in Chicago where he taught for 20 years, influencing the work of countless students.

SISLER, WILLIAM P.

Harvard University Press, 79 Garden St., Cambridge, MA 02138-1499 (617) 495-2600
Sisler is a prominent publisher. For career credentials consult the portion of this book entitled "Notable Americans by Profession" in the Appendix. Within this portion, the list "Publishers" describes requirements for inclusion in this volume.

SKERRIT, TOM

Guttman and Pam, 8500 Wilshire Blvd., Suite 811, Beverly Hills, CA 90211
BORN: 1933, Detroit. ACHIEVEMENTS: Emmy, Best Actor in a Drama Series, Picket Fences, 1993. STUDIED: Wayne State University and University of California at Los Angeles.
Tom Skerrit began acting in the early 1960s, finding his greatest success in movies, both in the theater and on television. Skerrit's first film appearance was as Corporal Showalter in *War Hunt*, in 1962. During the filming of *War Hunt*, Skerrit met Robert Redford, who, like Skerrit, was an unknown at the time. Thirty years later, Skerrit and Redford were reunited on the set of *A River Runs Through It*. In the intervening years, Skerrit appeared in some memorable movies, most often playing professionals and military men. Among the many parts Skerrit has played are, Dr. Duke Forrest in the 1970 hit, *M*A*S*H*; Sheriff George Bannerman in *The Dead Zone*, in 1983; and Major Logan in *Opposing Force*, in 1987. He is currently starring in the leading role in the television serious *Picket Fences*.

SLATKIN, LEONARD

St. Louis Symphony Orchestra, 718 N. Grand Blvd., St. Louis, MO 63103 (314) 533-2500
Slatkin, son of concert master Felix Slatkin, is the conductor of the St. Louis Symphony Orchestra. In 1995 he announced he will be leaving the post.

SLOYAN, PATRICK J.

Newsweek, 444 Madison Ave., New York, NY 10022 (212) 350-4000
Sloyan is a prominent journalist. For career credentials consult the portion of this book entitled "Notable Americans by Profession" in the Appendix. Within this portion, the list "Journalists" describes requirements for inclusion in this volume.

SMITH, FREDERICK W.

P O Box 727, Memphis, TN 94104
ACHIEVEMENTS: Founder, Federal Express Corporation. STUDIED: Yale University.
The concept of a coast-to-coast, overnight delivery system for small parcels and documents occurred to Frederick Smith while he studied economics at Yale University. He wrote a paper proposing a company consisting of an independent airline and truck fleet that would operate nationwide, delivering its cargo from dusk to dawn. Smith only received a C on his paper, but his idea did not die. After leaving Yale, Smith was able to nurture his idea and convert it to reality. His dream, The Federal Express Corporation, is the leading overnight express delivery service in the nation. The Federal Express Corporation now employs more than 25,000 people and has revenues in excess of $1 billion.

SMITH, HAMILTON OTHANEL

Johns Hopkins Medical School, Baltimore, MD 21205
BORN: 1931, New York City. ACHIEVEMENTS: Nobel Prize in Physiology or Medicine (shared with Daniel Nathans and Werner Arber, Switzerland), 1978; Guggenhein Fellow.
Daniel Nathans and Hamilton Smith, working cooperatively on the same problem and progressing with work done earlier by the Swiss Werner Arber, developed enzymes that can be used to study genetic organization and to manipulate DNA for genetic engineering. The enzymes, or "chemical knives," can cut certain DNA chains carrying viruses, perhaps, thus curbing their activity. Nathans also described a DNA technique—later to be the subject of much controversy—about the future role of genetic engineering. Smith purified and characterized the first "chemical knife" from a form of influenza, and applied the knife in experiments.

SMITH, HARRY

CBS-TV, 524 West 57th Street, New York, NY 10019
BORN:: 1951, Lansing, IL.
Smith began with CBS in 1986 as a Dallas-based reporter and one year later became a correspondent for the *CBS News With Dan Rather*. The early part of his career he worked as a radio host and disc jockey before entering television in 1981 as a talk show host for KRMA, a public station in Denver. Smith has co-anchored *CBS This Morning* since it premiered in 1987. He covered the 1988 and 1992 National Conventions for the show, as well as the aftermath of Hurricane Hugo and the Oklahoma City bombing on April 19, 1995. In Saudi Arabia he dispatched live reports on the Gulf War for a month. He originated *CBS This Morning* broadcasts from Japan and Cuba and was the weekday morning co-host for the the Albertville and Lillehammer Olympics in 1992 and 1994 respectively. His reports have appeared on *CBS News Sunday Morning* and the CBS news magazine *48 Hours*.

SMITH, MARTIN CRUZ

Random House, 201 E. 50th St., New York, NY 10022 (212) 751-2600
BORN: 1942, Pa. ACHIEVEMENTS: Best-selling author, Gorky Park, 1981. STUDIED: University of Pennsylvania.
Smith, who has used a serious of pen names, wrote for the Associated Press and *For Men Only* magazine before turning to novels. With his best-seller *Gorky Park*, published in 1981, Smith began a series of detective novels set in Russia. His other books include *Nightwing, The Analogue Bullet,* and *Stallion Gate,* 1987.

SMITS, JIMMY

c/o David Eidenberg, STE Representation, 211 S. Beverly Drive, #201, Beverly Hills, CA 90211

BORN: 1955, Brooklyn, N.Y. ACHIEVEMENTS: Emmy Award, Best Supporting Actor, Drama Series, L.A. Law, 1989-1990 STUDIED: Brooklyn College, B.A.; Cornell University, M.F.A.

Jimmy Smits is the co-lead in the television police drama *NYPD Blue*. His gritty acting, along with the daring story line, has made the series an instant success. Before *NYPD Blue*, Smits appeared in *Miami Vice*, 1984; *L. A. Law*, 1986; *Rockabye*, 1986; *The Highwayman*, 1987; and *Dangerous Affection*, 1987. He is also active on the stage, having appeared in *Hamlet*, 1982; *Little Victories*, 1983; *Buck*, 1983; *The Ballad of Soapy Smith*, 1984; and *Native Speech*, 1985. When he has the time, Smits works for his local community as an organizer.

SMUIN, MICHAEL

c/o Samuel Liff-William Morris Agency, 1350 Avenue of the Americas, New York, NY 10019 (212) 586-5100
ACHIEVEMENTS: Antoinette Perry Award, Anything Goes!, 1988.

Early in his career, Michael Smuin danced with the American Ballet Theater. He worked as artistic director of the San Francisco Ballet, but was let go after artistic differences with board members of the company. His leaning toward show dance, abhorred by some in ballet, is probably his strongest asset. Other opportunities, such as Hollywood, Broadway, and theater and opera in San Francisco, have kept him busy since leaving the San Francisco Ballet. Smuin choreographed the Broadway productions of *Shogun* and *Sophisticated Ladies*, and won a Tony Award for *Anything Goes!*, produced in 1988. Smuin is again running his own dance company, Smuin Ballets/SF, which has enjoyed strong booking throughout the world.

SNELL, GEORGE DAVIS

Harvard Medical School, Boston, MA 02115
BORN: 1903, Bradford, Maine. ACHIEVEMENTS: Nobel Prize in Physiology or Medicine (shared with Baruj Benacerraf, U.S., and Jean Dausset, France), 1980; Bertner Foundation Award; Griffin Award, Animal Care Panel; Gregor Mendel Award, Czechoslovak Academy of Sciences; Gairdner Foundation Award; Wolf Prize; National Institute for Arthritis and Infectious Diseases, National Cancer Institute. STUDIED: Dartmouth University; Harvard University.

George Snell's work on how the structure of cells relates to organ transplants and disease brought him the Nobel award at age 77. His research began with mutations in mice and progressed to the breeding of mice that were genetically identical except for a single genetic area. He found 10 sites that controlled graft resistance, but one was paramount in determining graft acceptance. That site was worked on by his colaureates as well.

SNYDER, RICHARD EDWARD

Macmillan, Inc., 866 Third Ave., New York, NY 10022.
BORN: 1933, New York City. STUDIED: Tufts University, B.A.

Snyder began his career in publishing in 1958 as marketing director for Doubleday & Company, moving up to sales director in 1960. Soon after, Simon & Schuster lured him away, and made him sales director. He spent the next 30 years with Simon & Schuster. He moved through successive ranks finally achieving chief executive officer and chairman of the board in 1981. He retained those positions until 1994, as he oversaw the company's transformation into a multi-billion dollar publishing entity. In February, 1994, Viacom, Inc., took over Simon & Schuster and soon after, Macmillan, where he is now at the helm of their new sister company. Snyder is a founding director of the National Book Awards, co-chairman of the PEN Benefit, and a member of several boards of directors.

SYNDER, SOLOMON HALBERT

Johns Hopkins Medical School Department of Neuroscience, 725 Wolf St., Baltimore, MD 21205
BORN: 1938, Washington, D.C. ACHIEVEMENTS: Director, Johns Hopkins University School of Medicine's Neuroscience Department. STUDIED: Georgetown University, cum laude M.D.; many honorary degrees.

Joining Johns Hopkins University School of Medicine in 1965, Solomon Snyder has remained there for more than 30 years, becoming director of neuroscience in 1980. His contributions to his field include opening the way to many advances in molecular neuroscience after having identified receptors for neurotransmitters (drugs that transmit nerve impulses to another nerve, muscle, or gland), and explaining the actions of mood-altering drugs.

SNYDER, WILLIAM

Dallas Morning News, Box 655237, Dallas, TX 75265-5237 (214) 977-8222

Snyder is a prominent journalist. For career credentials consult the portion of this book entitled "Notable Americans by Profession" in the Appendix. Within this portion, the list "Journalists" describes requirements for inclusion in this volume.

SOKOLOFF, LOUIS

U.S.P.H.S., NIH Bldg. 36, Rm. 1A-05, Bethesda, MD 20205

Sokoloff is a prominent physician. For career credentials consult the portion of this book entitled "Notable Americans by Profession" in the Appendix. Within this portion, the list "Physicians" describes requirements for inclusion in this volume.

SOKOLOW, ANNA

1 Christopher St., New York, NY 10014 (212) 929-5043
BORN: 1915, Hartford, Conn. ACHIEVEMENTS: Notable ballets: Slaughter of the Innocents; Lyric Suite; Session for Six; Rooms; Songs of a Semite; Memories; Tribute; Homage to Federico Garcia Lorca; Ride the Culture Loop. STUDIED: Bennington School of Dance, Vermont; Martha Graham school.

Intense, honest, brutally frank, Anna Sokolow has devoted her career to speaking out through dance against social discontent and human savagery. Her work casts a satirical eye on such topical subjects as assassinations, bombings of civilians, the drudgery and cruelty of poorly paid labor, and the plight of Jewish refugees, with the themes of loneliness, despair, and hate overriding the subject matter. During a sojourn in Mexico, which began with a six-week engagement in Mexico City, she founded The Blue Dove (La Paloma Azul), introducing Mexican dancers to modern ballet. She formed another long international alliance in Israel in 1953 when she accepted an invitation to teach an Israeli dance group and to help found the Lyric Theatre in Tel Aviv. She has since returned to Israel 20 times to teach or direct, feeling that, as in Mexico, she and her penetrating work are appreciated more than they are at home.

SOLOMONS, GUS JR.

The Solomons Company Dance, 889 Broadway, New York, NY 10003 (212) 477-1321
BORN: 1940, Boston. ACHIEVEMENTS: Notable ballets: as dancer: Winterbranch; Variations; How to Pass, Kick, Fall, and Run; as choreographer: Kinesia for Woman and Man; The Ground is Warm and Cool; Ecce Homo; Kinesia for Five; Neon; CITYMOTIONSPACEGAME; Stoneflesh. STUDIED: Boston Conservatory of Music, no degree; Massachusetts Institute of Technology, B.A., architecture, 1962.
Solomons often employs quixotic and paradoxical scores, decors, and gesture systems. These are exemplified by his frequent allusions in his work to architecture, which he studied at MIT, and mathematics, an offshoot of his part-time job of creating crossword puzzles for the Off Off Broadway trade paper *Other Stages*. An inventive and off-beat talent, he has choreographed numbers games such as *Par: Tournament*; solos with audience noises to accompany dancer (*Kinesia for Five*); dances performed in silence (*Ad Hoc Transit*); and dances made for specific environments, as New York City streets and plazas (*Hits & Runs*). He has taught at various universities, was dean at the California Institute of the Arts in Valencia, Spain, and has been a frequent panelist for the National Endowment for the Arts.

SOLOW, ROBERT M.

Massachusetts Institute of Technology, Department of Economics, Cambridge, MA 02139
BORN: 1924, New York City. ACHIEVEMENTS: Nobel Prize in Economic Science, 1987; chairman, Board of Directors, Federal Reserve Bank, Boston; John Bates Clark Medal, American Economic Association; president, Econometric Association and American Economic Association; fellow, Cambridge University, Society of Fellows, Harvard, Center for Advanced Study in Behavioral Sciences, American Academy of Arts and Sciences. STUDIED: Harvard University; honorary doctorates: Brown University, Tulane University, Dartmouth University, University of Geneva, University of Glasgow, among more than a dozen received.
When the U.S. economy was dominated by small firms and by farmers, economists talked little about economic growth. As large corporations began dominating the American scene, attention to growth developed. When it became clear that U.S. households were gaining income and personal investments, into this unexplored path Solow made seminal contributions to the theory of economic growth. One of his classic writings, *Technical Change and the Aggregate*

Production Function, led to an outpouring of work by his peers attempting to separate the contributions to growth in labor and capital from those of technical change. He went on to create models of growth, showing that capital growth depended not on growth in size but also on the age of the corporation, with new capital goods counting more than old capital goods. Solow has gone on to become a frequent and instructive popularizer of the works of others, with side forays against people in his field who belittle the achievements of mainstream economics.

SONDHEIM, STEPHEN

Flora Roberts Inc., 157 West 57th St., New York, NY 10019
BORN: 1930, New York City. ACHIEVEMENTS: Pulitzer Prize, Best Play, Sunday in the Park with George, 1985; Grammy, Best Cast /Show Album, Company, 1970; Grammy, Best Cast Show Album, A Little Night Music, 1973; Grammy, Song of the Year, Send in the Clowns, 1975; Grammy, Best Cast Show Album, Sweeny Todd, 1979; Grammy, Best Cast Show Album, Sunday in the Park with George, 1984; Grammy, Best Cast show Album, West Side Story, 1985; Grammy, Best Cast Show Album, Follies in Concert, 1986; Grammy, Best Cast Show Album, Into the Woods, 1988; Academy Award, Best Song, Sooner or Later (I Always Get My Man), 1990; Antoinette Perry Award, Best Score, Company, 1971; Antoinette Perry Award, Best Score Follies, 1972; Antoinette Perry Award, Best Score, A Little Night Music, 1973; Antoinette Perry Award, Best Score, Sweeney Todd, 1979; Antoinette Perry Award, Best Score, Into the Woods, 1988. STUDIED: Williams College, B.A., 1950.
Sondheim left home at the age of 15, and was taken in by lyricist Oscar Hammerstein II. While living with Hammerstein, Sondheim learned how to structure songs. Sondheim first gained recognition with his lyrics for *West Side Story*. His subsequent credits as lyricist and composer include *A Funny Thing Happened on the Way to the Forum*, 1962; *A Little Night Music*, 1973; *Sweeney Todd*, 1979; *Sunday in the Park with George*, 1984; and the folktale-based *Into the Woods*, 1987. Sondheim's versatility is also suggested by his Academy-Award winning songs for the film *Dick Tracy*, 1990. In 1992 he rejected the NEA's Medal of Art's Award, because he felt the agency is "a symbol of censorship and repression rather than encouragement and support."

SOUTER, DAVID HACKETT

Supreme Court of the United States, One First St. N.E., Washington, D.C. 20543 (202) 479-3000
BORN: 1939, Melrose, Mass. ACHIEVEMENTS: Rhodes Scholar, Phi Beta Kappa. STUDIED: Harvard University, A.B., 1961; Harvard University, LL.B., 1966; Oxford University, M.A., 1989.
Souter practiced law for two years with the firm Orr and Reno in New Hampshire, and then entered public service. He was attorney general of New Hampshire from 1976-1978. He became a state trial judge in New Hampshire in 1978, and in 1983 became associate justice for the New Hampshire Supreme Court. In 1990 Souter served as a U.S. Court of Appeals judge for the First Circuit, and just two months later was nominated as associate justice for the Supreme Court of the United States by President Bush.

SPECTER, ARLEN

BORN: 1930, Wichita, Kan. ACHIEVEMENTS: Editor, Yale Law Journal; assistant counsel, Warren Commission; STUDIED: University of Pennsylvania, 1951; Yale Law School, 1956.

Arlen Specter's two years in the Air Force Office of Special Investigations during the Korean War prepared him well for his future appointment as an assistant counsel to the Warren Commission. While investigating President John Kennedy's assassination, Specter helped develop the single bullet theory. His first elected office was district attorney of Philadelphia in 1965, and he was re-elected in 1969. In 1980 he was elected to the U.S. Senate where he crafted the Armed Career Criminal Act, the Terrorist Prosecution Act and the Missing Children's Assistance Act. He is a member of several committees including Appropriations, Intelligence, Judiciary and Veteran's Affairs. Specter announced his candidacy for the 1996 Republican presidential primary to fight what he considers dangerous intrusions from the religious right into his party's platform. By year's end, he dropped out of the race.

SPERRY, ROGER WOLCOTT

Harvard Medical School, Boston, MA 02115
BORN: 1913, Hartford, Conn. ACHIEVEMENTS: Nobel Prize in Physiology or Medicine (shared with David Hunter Hubel, U.S., and Torsten N. Wiesel, Sweden), 1981; Oberlin College Alumni Citation; Howard Crosby Warren Medal, Society for Experimental Psychology; Distinguished Scientist/Contribution Award, American Psychological Association; William Thompson Wakeman Research Award, National Paraplegic Foundation; Passano Award, Passano Foundation; Karl Lashley Award; American Philosophical Society; Albert Lasker Award, Albert and Mary Lasker Foundation; Ralph Gerard Prize; Wolf Foundation Prize. STUDIED: Oberlin College, Ohio; University of Chicago.

It was Roger Sperry's research that separated and identified the functions of the left and right hemispheres of the brain, but his Nobel citation also honored his 40-year dedication to achieving an understanding of the conscious processes and functions of the brain. Sperry's work after the Nobel award concentrated on the emotional and social components of the two-sided brain.

SPINDLER, MICHAEL H.

Apple Computer, 20525 Mariani Blvd., Cupertino, CA 95014 (408) 996-1010
Spindler is a prominent business leader. For career credentials consult the portion of this book entitled "Notable Americans by Profession" in the Appendix. Within this portion, the list "Business Leaders" describes requirements for inclusion in this volume.

SPRINGSTEEN, BRUCE

Premier Talent Agency, 3 East 54th St., New York, NY 10022
BORN: 1949, Freehold, N.J. ACHIEVEMENTS: Grammy, Best Recording for Children, In Harmony 2 (with others), 1982; Grammy, Best Rock Vocal, Dancing in the Dark, 1984; Grammy, Best Rock Vocal, Tunnel of Love, 1987; Academy Award, Best Song, Streets of Philadelphia, 1994. STUDIED: Attended Ocean Community College.

Bruce Springsteen's songs explore the American experience and reflect his kinship with the working class. In 1973 he formed the E Street Band, and made his debut with the album *Greetings from Ashbury Park*. Springsteen became popular with the 1975 album *Born to Run*. His popularity surged with the 1984 album *Born in the U.S.A.* In 1986 he declined a $12 million dollar offer from Lee Iaccoa to use his signature song *Born in the U.S.A.* in Chrysler commercials. Among his other albums are *Darkness on the Edge of Town*, 1978; *The River*, 1980; *Nebraska*, 1982; *Tunnel of Love*, 1987; and *Lucky Town* and *Human Touch*, 1992. Springsteen won the Grammy for Best Song in 1994 for *Streets of Philadelphia*.

SPRINKEL, BERYL

20140 St. Andrews Dr., Olympia Fields, IL 60461
BORN: 1923, Richmond, Mo. ACHIEVEMENTS: Alumni Leadership and Service Award, University of Chicago; Hamilton Bolton Prize, Financial Analysts Association; Merit Citation, University of Missouri; Alexander Hamilton Award, U.S. Treasury Department. STUDIED: Northwest Missouri State University, University of Oregon, University of Missouri, Northwestern University, University of Chicago; honorary doctorates, DePaul University and St. Michael's College.

Called by his critics contentious, blunt, and narrow minded, Beryl Sprinkel has had more than his share of battles in the field of economics. After years of association with Harris Bank of Chicago, he was called by President Reagan to join economists Norman Ture, a Washington consultant, and Paul Craig Roberts, another Washington supplysider (those who espouse the theory that reducing taxes encourages business investment, hence boosting the economy). The three policies advocated by the troika were lower tax rates, less government, and more control of money growth, with the goal being to reinvigorate the economy by increasing savings, expanding the private economy, and stabilizing the growth of the national economy. In opposition, which has sometimes been called "uproarious," Sprinkel argued instead that the monetariast doctrine (changes in the money supply decide the direction of a nation's economy), a policy then pursued by the Federal Reserve, would lead to a temporary shrinkage of the real economy. Time proved him correct. Other fights were fought in the international ring, first against Europe's complaint that U.S. interest rates were too high and its dollar overvalued. His strenuous response that Europe was too preoccupied with U.S. interest rates and that France, especially, should get its own economic policies in order, brought forth from the *London Financial Times* the title of "the arch bad guy" of the international scene. Finally, he told Japan to open up its capital markets to foreign competition and to allow the yen to play a larger international role to remove some of the pressures on the U.S. dollar.

STAFFORD, JOHN ROGERS

American Home Products Corporation, 685 3rd Ave., New York, NY 10017

BORN: 1937, Harrisburg, Pa. ACHIEVEMENTS: Board of trustees U.S. Council for International Business; recipient of the John Bell Larner First Scholar Award, George Washington University Law School, 1962; Outstanding Alumnus Award, 1981. STUDIED: Dickinson College, A.B., 1959; George Washington University, LL.B., 1962.

John Stafford joined American Home Products, a pharmaceutical and household products company, as an attorney in 1970 after working for law firms in Washington, D.C., and New Jersey. He was named the chairman and chief executive officer of the $8 billion manufacturer in 1986.

STAFFORD, THOMAS PATTEN

Stafford, Burke, and Hecker, Inc., 1006 Cameron St., Alexandria, VA 22314

BORN: 1930, Weatherford, Okla. ACHIEVEMENTS: space missions: pilot Gemini 6A, commander Gemini 9A, commander Apollo 10, U.S. commander Apollo-Soyuz Test Project. STUDIED: U.S. Naval Academy, B.S., 1952.

After he graduated from the Naval Academy, Thomas Stafford transferred to the U.S. Air Force. NASA selected him as an astronaut in 1962, and his first space flight put him onboard Gemini 6A in 1965 as pilot of the first rendezvous of two manned spacecraft in space. He commanded Gemini 9A, and, with pilot Eugene Cernan, he performed more rendezvous tests. He and Cernan teamed up again in 1969 on Apollo 10 in the lunar excursion module, and flew within 9.26 miles of the moon's surface on the last test mission before the first manned moon landing. In 1975, he commanded the U.S. Apollo spacecraft during the Apollo-Soyuz Test Project, the first international space mission. Afterwards, he returned to duty in the Air Force, and eventually became the Air Force deputy chief of staff for research and development.

STAPLETON, JOAN M.

The *New Republic*, 1220 19th St., NW., Washington, D.C., 20036 (202) 331-7494

ACHIEVEMENTS: First woman to head the New Republic. STUDIED: Graduated University of Virginia-Charlottesville.

President of the *New Republic*, Stapleton has been with the publication for 15 years. She was the magazine's publisher since 1988. Early on she served as manager of advertising, sales operations and marketing for the *New Republic*. The *New Republic* credits her for successfully obtaining corporate as well as smaller advertisers for the magazine. Stapleton also performs as a jazz and cabaret singer. She has appeared at the Kennedy Center, Georgetown University and around the nation's capital. In addition to her music, Stapleton is active in several charitable and professional organizations.

STEEL, DANIELLE

Delacorte Press, 666 5th Ave., New York, NY 10105 (212) 765-6500

BORN: 1947, New York City. ACHIEVEMENTS: Best-selling novelist. STUDIED: Lycee Francais; attended Parsons School of Design; New York University.

Born in New York City, Danielle Steel was educated in France and worked in public relations and advertising before publishing her first book *Going Home*, in 1973. During the next two decades, she wrote more than 30 best-sellers while having nine children from four marriages, three to ex-convicts. Her novels include *The Ring*, 1980; *Remembrance*, 1981; *Changes*, 1983; *Full Circle*, 1984; *Secrets*, 1985, and *Daddy*, 1989.

STEELE, JAMES B.

The Philadelphia Inquirer, 400 N. Broad St., Philadelphia, PA 19130-4015 (215) 854-5900

Steele is a prominent journalist. For career credentials consult the portion of this book entitled "Notable Americans by Profession" in the Appendix. Within this portion, the list "Journalists" describes requirements for inclusion in this volume.

STEERE, WILLIAM CAMPBELL JR.

Pfizer Inc., 235 W. 42nd St., New York, NY 10017

BORN: 1936, Ann Arbor, Mich. ACHIEVEMENTS: Served on board of directors at Texaco, New York University Medical Center, Minerals Techs. Inc., Federal Reserve Bank of New York; trustee New York Botanical Garden. STUDIED: Stanford University, B.S. 1959.

William Steere Jr. began his career as a medical service representative in 1959 for Pfizer, a pharmaceuticals manufacturer. After moving through sales management and domestic product management, Steere became director of marketing for Pfizer Latin America in 1969. Throughout the next two decades, he ascended to various leadership positions until he was named president in 1986, and then chief executive officer in 1992.

STEIN, HERBERT

Council of Economic Advisors, Old Executive Office Bld., Washington, D.C. 20500

Stein is a prominent economist and author. The son of Ben Stein, also a notable economist, he, as well as his father, have advised contemporary presidents and played a part in formulating public policies since the Nixon administration.

STEINBERGER, JACK

European Center for Nuclear Research, CH 1211, Geneva, Switzerland

BORN: 1921, Bad Kissingen (Germany) ACHIEVEMENTS: Nobel Prize in Physics (shared with Leon M. Lederman and Melvin Schwartz), 1988; Director, European Center for Nuclear Research; Medal of Science. STUDIED: University of Chicago.

Jack Steinberger, a naturalized American, was part of a team which confirmed the reality of quarks. Their discovery was based on the bombardment of the light metal beryllium with the subatomic particle proton, which produced neutrinos, elementary particles having little or no mass, but under the bombardment produced a beam. The beam in turn led the researchers to discovery of a second neutrino associated with the mumeson, one of the particles that glue all particles in an atom together. The team's "breakthrough" work had far-reaching effects on fundamental particle theories, and today the beams are routinely produced in machines called "meson factories" for the purposes of further study and radiological therapy.

STEINEM, GLORIA

c/o Ms Magazine, 119 W. 40th St., New York, NY 10018 BORN: 1934, Toledo, Ohio. ACHIEVEMENTS: Cofounder: Women's Action Alliance, National Women's Political Caucus, New York and Ms Magazines; author: A Thousand Indias, 1957; Outrageous Acts and Everyday Rebellions, 1983; Moving Beyond Words, 1994; collaborator, The Beach Book, 1963. STUDIED: Smith College, magna cum laude, 1956.

Steinem emerged from a transient, financially insecure childhood to become a symbol of American feminism. Upon graduation from college, she left for India on a fellowship. Finding her studies lacking, she traveled, wrote free-lance articles and the guidebook, *A Thousand Indias.* Two years later she returned to the U.S. and worked as co-director of the Independent Research Service in Cambridge, Mass. Steinem's first job as a U.S. journalist came in 1960, when she was hired as a writer for *Help!,* a political satire magazine. She went on to publish pieces in *Esquire, Vogue, Glamour,* among other media. After a short stint as a scriptwriter in 1968, Steinem began writing a weekly political column for *New York* magazine, which she helped found. In the late 1960s, Steinem was active in the presidential bids of Eugene McCarthy and Robert F. Kennedy. It was during this period that she became immersed in feminism. Thought by many to be articulate and attractive, she quickly was catapulted into the public arena as a feminist spokesperson. By the end of 1971, she was instrumental in the founding of the National Women's Political Caucus and *Ms,* magazine. While editing *Ms,* Steinem continued her role as a political activist and lobbied for the never-ratified Equal Rights Amendment and served on the National Committee on the Observance of International Women's Year in 1977. In the 1980s she published a collection of essays and journal entries and a biography of Marilyn Monroe that was published in 1986. In 1994, the year she turned 60, she published, *Moving Beyond Words,* a collection of essays that included a piece on aging women. The book was not well received by some literary critics. Steinem continues to be tapped by media interviewers as a spokesperson for her generation of feminists.

STELLA, FRANK

17 Jones St., New York, NY 10021
BORN: 1936. ACHIEVEMENTS: First Prize, International Biennial Exhibition of Paintings, Tokyo; collections: Museum of Modern Art; Whitney Museum of American Art; exhibitions: Museum of Modern Art; Whitney Museum of American Art. STUDIED: Phillips Academy; Princeton University.

Frank Stella's first show in the late 1950s was a group of black canvases in which parallel bands, surrounded by bare canvas, echoed or opposed the direction of the frame's edges. Metallic or fluorescent pigments emphasized the artificiality of the work. A prolific painter, he worked on several series of metallic paintings of geometric shapes. These massive canvases were followed by other similar series, using stripes of color outlined in white, and later zigzags, arcs, and other shapes, in fluorescent polychrome. In the 1970s he was still employing flat, synthetic hues on large canvases, but the idea of structure had become more complex. Colors change value as one's eyes move across the paintings, the shapes and colors interacting in a constant state of flux.

STERN, HOWARD

Simon & Schuster, 1230 Avenue of the Americas, New York, NY 10020 (212) 698-7000
BORN: 1954, New York City. ACHIEVEMENTS: Popular and controversial radio personality. STUDIED: Boston University.

Renowned for shocking his radio listeners with earthy interviews and salacious commentary, Howard Stern's autobiography, *Private Parts,* 1993, was a best seller. Through a blend of sex and satire, the so-called "shock jock" first gained notoriety in 1982, and soon became one of the most popular personalities on radio. The risque content of his programs offended some listeners, and they complained to the Federal Communications Commission, triggering a long battle between him and the government. His 1995 book, *Miss America,* was a number-one bestseller.

STERN, ROBERT A.M.

Robert A.M. Stern Architects, 200 W. 72nd Street, New York, NY 10023 (212) 246-1980
BORN: 1939. ACHIEVEMENTS: Fellow, AIA; National Honor Award, AIA, 1980, 1985; Award of Merit, housing, 1977; notable works: Point West Place Office Building, Framingham, Mass.; Cohn House, Martha's Vineyard, Mass. STUDIED: Yale University.

A widely influential critic, author and teacher, Robert Stern has only recently devoted his primary energies to design. He remains an articulate spokesman for the Grays, a group of Postmodern architects and academics who believe that architecture is, at base, a communicating art, that ornamentation isn't an affront to otherwise functional designs, and that referring to the history of architecture and deferring to surrounding structures both can strengthen designs. His buildings share a pronounced historicism and a disdain for revealing structural elements. His corporate commissions, most notably his Point West Place in Framingham, Mass., share much with the recent institutional work of Michael Graves and to a lesser extent Philip Johnson. Point West Place is a modified horizontal glass box, accented with bright ribbons of primary color and accessed through a large arching concrete block facade which dominates the center of the primary elevation, behind the portico. It evokes the grand entrances of early twentieth-century rail stations and municipal buildings.

STEVENS, JOHN PAUL

Supreme Court of the United States, One First St. N.E., Washington, D.C. 20543 (202) 479-3000
BORN: 1920, Chicago. ACHIEVEMENTS: Phi Beta Kappa, Psi Upsilon. STUDIED: University of Chicago, A.B., English literature, 1941; Northwestern University Juris Doctor, 1947.
Stevens served in the United States Navy during World War II, and earned the Bronze Star. After the war Stevens entered Northwestern University, and received his J.D. degree, graduating magna cum laude in 1947. He served as clerk to the Honorable Wiley Rutledge, associate justice to the Supreme Court of the United States from October 1947 through July 1948. The next several years were spent in private practice and as a lecturer at Northwestern University and the University of Chicago Law Schools. In 1970 Stevens was nominated to the U.S. Court of Appeals for the Seventh District by President Richard Nixon. He was nominated by President Gerald Ford, and confirmed by the U.S. Senate, as associate justice of the United States Supreme Court in 1975.

STEVENS, ROGER L.

1501 Broadway, New York, NY 10036
Stevens is a prominent dramatic artist. For career credentials consult the portion of this book entitled "Notable Americans by Profession" in the Appendix. Within this portion, the list "Dramatic Artists" describes requirements for inclusion in this volume.

STEWART, JAMES B.

The Wall Street Journal, 200 Liberty Street, New York, NY 10281 (212) 416-2000
BORN: 1952, Quincy, Ill. ACHIEVEMENTS: Pulitzer Prize for Explanatory Journalism, 1987. STUDIED: DePauw University, B.A., history, 1973; Harvard, J.D., 1976.
With his law degree in hand, James Stewart joined Cravath, Swain and Moore in their New York offices. He worked as a lawyer from 1976 until 1979, and then became executive editor of *American Lawyer* until 1983. He became a legal writer for *The Wall Street Journal* from 1983 until 1988, and "Page One" editor from 1988 to 1992. From 1993 to the present, Stewart has been a reporter for *The New Yorker* and still found time to author *Den of Thieves*.

STIGLER, GEORGE

University of Chicago, Graduate School of Business, 1101 E. 58th St., Chicago 60637
BORN: 1911, Renton, Wash. ACHIEVEMENTS: Nobel Prize in Economic Science, 1982; president, American Economic Association, History of Economics Society; National Bureau of Economic Research; member: National Bureau of Economic Research. STUDIED: University of Washington, Northwestern University, University of Chicago; honorary doctorates from five American and European universities.

In addition to being awarded a Nobel Prize in 1982 for his work on government regulations and the functioning of industry in the economy, George Stigler is an essayist of the first magnitude: urbane, eminently readable, often witty. *Information in the Marketplace*, one of his most original essays, broke the ground for all subsequent work on "search models" for unemployment, stating simply that it is a voluntary spell of unemployment while the jobsearcher seeks the best rate of pay. In fact, there is no such thing as one rate of pay for any one job, but a multiple of pay rates so that the jobseeker has first an information problem to solve. Another article, *The Kinky Oligopoly Demand Curve and Rigid Prices*, states that industries made up of a few firms will rarely change prices, a conclusion that has troubled writers on the subject ever since. Again, he warns against government agencies that supposedly regulate the price and investment policies of public utilities in the public interest for acting instead on the side of the producers, that being a logical result of public regulation—a conclusion he carries forward in studies of one U.S. regulatory agency after another. His article, *The Politics of Political Economists*, which concludes that economists' study of politics inevitably drives them to conservatism, has set off endless debates.

STIRITZ, WILLIAM P.

Ralston-Purina Co., Checkerboard Square, St. Louis, MO 63164 (314) 982-1000
Stiritz is a prominent business leader. For career credentials consult the portion of this book entitled "Notable Americans by Profession" in the Appendix. Within this portion, the list "Business Leaders" describes requirements for inclusion in this volume.

STOCKMAN, DAVID A.

Harper Collins, 10 E. 53rd St., New York, NY 10022 (212) 207-7759
BORN: 1946, Camp Hood, Texas. ACHIEVEMENTS: U.S. congressman, budget director in the Reagan administration. STUDIED: Michigan State University, 1968.
As President Reagan's budget director from 1981 to 1985, David Stockman was a key policy maker in the administration's thrust to cut taxes and reduce welfare spending. Though considered a very effective budget director and respected for his extensive knowledge of the budgeting process, he embarrassed the administration by publicly expressing his reservations concerning its economic policies. He resigned in 1985 and wrote a highly critical book in 1986, *The Triumph of Politics: Why the Reagan Revolution Failed*. Before joining the Reagan administration, he was a Republican congressman from Michigan, 1976-1980.

STONE, CHUCK

UNC, School of Journalism, 101 Howell Hall, 021A, Chapel Hill, NC 27599
BORN: 1924, St. Louis. ACHIEVEMENTS: Excellence-in-Teaching Award, University of Delaware, 1989, and University of North Carolina, 1992; Na-

tional Association of Black Journalists Lifetime Achievement Award, 1992. *STUDIED: Wesleyan University, A.B., 1948; University of Chicago, M.A., 1951.*

Chuck Stone has pursued many different career paths over the years. He was a regular columnist at the *Philadelphia Daily News* and a nationally syndicated journalist. During the reigns of Mayors Frank Rizzo and Wilson Goode in Philadelphia, Stone often battled against what he perceived to be a corrupt, racist, and inept city government. Stone was also active in education as a visiting professor at various schools. He was an English professor at the University of Delaware from 1984 until 1991. In 1991 he was named the Walter Spearman Professor at North Carolina's School of Journalism and Mass Communications. For his work as a journalism professor, Stone received the Free Spirit Award from the Freedom Forum in 1994.

STORNETTA, SCOTT

Bell Communications Research Inc., 290 W. Mt. Pleasant Ave., Livingston, NJ 07039 (201) 740-3000
ACHIEVEMENTS: Developed the Digital Time Stamp computer security system.

Scott Stornetta has provided some security for computer users. Computer thieves, forgers, and counterfeiters are foiled when confronted with machines installed with the Digital Time Stamp, a creation of Stornetta and Stuart Haber. Both men are researchers at Bellcore, a research and engineering company. The electronic notary system is based on cryptography, Haber's field, and enhanced with work by Stornetta. A small piece of a document is generated by a mathematical procedure that creates a unique digital fingerprint of the whole document based on a chain composed of the letters, numbers, graphics, and symbols in the document. Changing even one character in the original changes the chain's unique value. To check the authenticity of a document's time stamp requires only a recomputation of the values in the chain and comparing the results on file with the time stamper. Additional security is provided by altering the chain each week and publishing it in a garbled series of numbers and letters under "Public and Commercial Notices" in The New York Times.

STRAUS, ROGER W.

Farrar, Straus, & Giroux, 19 Union Sq., West, New York, NY 10003 (212) 741-6900
Straus is a prominent publisher. For career credentials consult the portion of this book entitled "Notable Americans by Profession" in the Appendix. Within this portion, the list "Publishers" describes requirements for inclusion in this volume.

STREEP, MERYL

International Creative Management, 40 West 57th St., New York, NY 10019
BORN: 1949, Summit, N.J. ACHIEVEMENTS: Emmy Award, Best Actress in a Limited Series, Holocaust, 1978; Academy Award and Golden Globe Award, Best Supporting Actress, Kramer vs. Kramer, 1979; Academy Award,

Best Actress, Sophie's Choice, 1982. STUDIED: Vassar College, B.A., 1971; Yale University, M.F.A., 1975.

Meryl Streep is an acclaimed actress on the stage, silver screen, and television. On stage she has appeared in both New York Shakespeare Festival productions and on Broadway. She has starred in numerous made-for-television movies, and won an Emmy Award as best actress in the miniseries *Holocaust*. Among her many film credits are *The Deer Hunter*, 1978; *The Seduction of Joe Tynan*, 1979; *The French Lieutenant's Woman*, 1981; *Still of the Night*, 1982; *Silkwood*, 1983; and *Out of Africa*, 1985. She has won two Academy Awards: Best Supporting Actress in *Kramer vs. Kramer*, and Best Actress in *Sophie's Choice*.

STREIBER, WHITLEY

c/o William Morrow and Company, 105 Madison Avenue, New York, NY 10016 (212) 889-3050
Streiber is a prominent author. For career credentials consult the portion of this book entitled "Notable Americans by Profession" in the Appendix. Within this portion, the list "Authors" describes requirements for inclusion in this volume.

STREISAND, BARBRA

Creative Artists Agency, 1888 Century Park E., Los Angeles, CA 90028
BORN: 1942, Brooklyn, N.Y. ACHIEVEMENTS: Emmy, Outstanding Program Achievement, My Name is Barbra, 1965; Academy Award, Best Actress, Funny Girl, 1968; Academy Award, Best Song (co-recipient), Evergreen, 1976; Grammy Awards, Best Female Pop Vocalist, 1963-1965, 1977, 1986; Grammy, Best Songwriter (with Paul Williams), 1977; Antoinette Perry Special Award, 1970. STUDIED: Attended Yeshiva University.

By the end of 1989, Streisand had amassed more platinum records than any other recording artist. Streisand's entertainment career began in the mid-1960s when she started singing in New York City nightclubs. She got her first big break when she appeared in the Broadway musical *I Can Get it For You Wholesale*. Not long after, she garnered the starring role in the Broadway musical *Funny Girl* and later starred in the film version of the show. As musical tastes moved toward younger audiences in the 1970s, Streisand adapted by singing more rock-oriented material. However, she found her greatest popularity during that period singing contemporary ballads, such as the theme song for her hit movie *The Way We Were*. Although she did few recordings in the 1980s, Streisand went back to her roots in 1985 to create *The Broadway Album*, her most popular album to date.

STROTHMAN, WENDY J.

Beacon Press, 25 Beacon Street, Boston, MA 01208 (617) 742-2110
ACHIEVEMENTS: Director, Beacon Press; vice president and publisher at Houghton Mifflin Co. STUDIED: Brown University, B.A., 1972; attended Radcliffe College's publishing procedures course.

Although Strothman graduated from college with a degree in Russian studies, her career path has taken a different course. Early in her publishing career, she was assistant director of the University of Chicago Press. In 1983 she was hired as director of Beacon Press. A liberal Unitarian publisher, Beacon Press was very successful under Strothman's leadership. Two titles in particular, *The Measure of Our Success*, by Marian Wright Edelman, 1992 and *Race Matters*, by Cornell West, also in 1992, were Beacon's first best sellers in 40 years. In 1995 Strothman was hired by Houghton Mifflin Co. as vice president and publisher of the adult trade and reference division.

STRUTTON, LARRY D.

Rocky Mountain News, 400 W. Colfax Ave., Denver, CO 80204 (303) 892-5000
BORN: 1940, Colorado Springs, Colo. ACHIEVEMENTS: President, publisher and chief executive officer of the Rocky Mountain News. STUDIED: Emily Griffith Electronics School, A.A., electrical engineering; Metropolitan State College of Denver, B.S., business management; Harvard University, Advanced Management Program.
Starting his newspaper career in 1961 as a linotype operator on a local paper, Larry Strutton worked on the paper three years before moving to the *Rocky Mountain News*, in Denver, as production director. He remained in Denver for the next 16 years, taking time out to acquire the education necessary for the higher management roles he saw ahead. His next stop was the *Detroit Free Press*, serving as vice president of operations and advertising. Not long after, he joined the *Los Angeles Times* as vice president of operations in 1981. Finally, Strutton returned to where he began his career 26 years earlier, the *Rocky Mountain News*, as president, publisher, and chief executive officer.

STYRON, WILLIAM

12 Rucum Rd., Roxbury, CT 06783
BORN: 1924, Newport News, Va. ACHIEVEMENTS: Pulitzer Prize, The Confessions of Nat Turner, 1968; American Book Award, Sophie's Choice, 1980. STUDIED: Christ Church School; Davidson College; Duke University, A.B., 1947; Litt. D, 1968; Davidson College, Litt .D (Honorary), 1986.
William Styron's fictionalized account of the slave rebellion of 1831, *The Confessions of Nat Turner*, won him the Pulitzer Prize for literature in 1968. His other books included *Lie Down in Darkness*, 1951, about a Southern family in decline; *The Long March*, 1957; *Set This House on Fire*, 1960; *Sophie's Choice*, 1959, a novel about a concentration-camp survivor that won the American Book Award in 1980; *Darkness Visible*, 1990, a memoir of his own depression, and *A Tide Water Morning*, 1993.

SUAU, ANTHONY

c/o Black Star, 450 Park Ave., New York, NY 10016
BORN: 1956. ACHIEVEMENTS: Pulitzer Prize, 1984. STUDIED: Rochester Institute of Technology.
Suau first gained national attention with a series of photographs documenting the plight of famine victims in Ethiopia. Suau took a leave of absence from the *Denver Post* to cover the story, and the images he brought back helped shock an indifferent nation out of its complacency. "Wherever I looked I saw people dying," said Suau. "The inhumanity of the situation was overwhelming." His photographs gave a boost to U.S. relief efforts and eventually earned Suau the Pulitzer Prize.

SULLIVAN, GEN. GORDON

Office of the Secretary, The Pentagon, Washington, D.C. 20301 (703) 545-6700
BORN: 1937, Quincy, Mass. ACHIEVEMENTS: Army Chief of Staff, 1991 to 1995; among his many decorations are the Bronze Star, Purple Heart, Legion of Merit, Combat Infantryman Badge, and Army Commendation Medal with oak leaf cluster. STUDIED: Norwich University, Northfield, Vt., B.A., history; University of New Hampshire, M.A., political science; U.S. Army Command General Staff College; U.S. Army War College.
Gen. Gordon Sullivan entered the U.S. Army as a second lieutenant in an armored division, and 32 years and many citations and stations later became Army Chief of Staff. He served in post-war Korea, as an assistant civil guard and self-defense adviser in Vietnam, and for three assignments through the late 60s to the late 80s in Europe. In the interim, he returned to Vietnam for two years. Called to Washington as deputy chief of staff for operations and plans in 1988, Sullivan became vice chief of staff in the Office of the Chief of Staff the next year. Sullivan was Army Chief of Staff from 1991 until 1995, when he retired.

SULZBERGER, ARTHUR OCHS

The New York Times, 229 West 43rd St., New York, NY 10036 (212) 556-1234
BORN: 1926, New York City. ACHIEVEMENTS: Columbia Journalism Award; many honorary degrees from American universities. STUDIED: Columbia University, B.A.; Dartmouth, LL.D; Bard College.
With the exception of one year spent at the *Milwaukee Journal*, Sulzberger spent his entire career at the *Times*, with time out for service with the Marine Corps in World War II and Korea. He has been chairman and chief executive officer of the *New York Times* since 1973. He became publisher of the newspaper in 1963, after his father moved from publisher to chairman of the board in 1961. His grandfather, Adolph S. Ochs, bought the paper when it was close to bankruptcy in 1896 and was its publisher until 1935. He worked as a city reporter and as a foreign correspondent in Paris, Rome, and London. Sulzberger is co-chairman of the *International Herald Tribune* and an independent trustee of the Reuters Founders Share Company, a group that oversees the reliability, independence, and freedom from bias of the Reuters News Agency.

SUMMERALL, PAT

Fox Broadcasting Company, 205 East 67th Street, New York, NY 10021
ACHIEVEMENTS: Professional football player, television sportscaster.
Summerall was born with a deformity that made a career in professional sports an unlikely future. His right foot was oriented backward. Doctors corrected

the deformity by breaking his shin and turning the foot around. Summerall attended the University of Arkansas on a basketball and football scholarship. After college, Summerall was signed by the Chicago Cardinals as a tight end in 1952. In 1957 Summerall was traded to the New York Giants and played for them until he retired in 1961. After leaving football, Summerall worked for CBS, giving five-minute daily sportscasts. By 1962 he was one of the first ex-football players giving play-by-play analysis on television.

SUMMERS, CAROL

133 Prospect Ct., Santa Cruz, CA 95065
BORN: 1925. ACHIEVEMENTS: Louis C. Tiffany Foundation Fellowships; Guggenheim Fellowship; collections: Metropolitan Museum of Art; Corcoran Gallery of Art; exhibitions: Museum of Modern Art, New York City; San Francisco Museum of Modern Art. STUDIED: Bard College.

Carol Summers' early woodcuts featured abstract biomorphic shapes. After 1958, she applied preliminary rough sketches in ink and brayer to paper before the final print was made. During the 1960s, her images of domestic life in cubist space, as in *Bon Appetit*, were more recognizable. The artist is known for her simplified landscapes and mountainscapes. Sometimes color is printed on the back of the paper for the desired color effect. Large and simple landscapes are multicolored, each element saturated with color. Some of these woodcuts are executed in a technique similar to rubbings.

SUNDQUIST, DON

State Capitol, Nashville, TN 37243 (615) 741-2001
BORN: 1936, Moline, Ill. ACHIEVEMENTS: Chairman, Young Republican National Federation.

A quotation summarizes the Governor of Tennessee's approach to politics: "We want to get the government out of people's business and the people into the business of government." To that end, through 12 years as a U.S. congressman, he held nearly 100 town meetings and stayed close to his constituents. "In Touch with Tennessee" is the slogan he vows will guide him as governor. Howard Baker, former Senate Majority leader, White House Chief of Staff, and Sundquist's role model and close personal friend, urged him to run for governor after the congressman had served six terms. As the state's 47th governor, Sundquist plans to reduce crime, reform welfare, aid education, and spur economic development.

SWINGER, JULIAN SEYMOUR

UCLA, Dept. of Physics, 405 Hilgard Ave., Los Angeles, CA 90024

Swinger is a prominent scientist. For career credentials consult the portion of this book entitled "Notable Americans by Profession" in the Appendix. Within this portion, the list "Scientists" describes requirements for inclusion in this volume.

SYMINGTON, FIFE

1700 West Washington, Phoenix AZ 85007 (602) 542-4331
BORN: 1945, New York City. ACHIEVEMENTS: Received the Bronze Star medal for his service during the Vietnam War. STUDIED: B.A. Harvard University, 1968.

Fife Symington was a real estate developer until he ran for Arizona Governor in 1991 and won an unprecedented special runoff general election. He was reelected in 1994 to another four-year term. Some of his special programs include Project Intervention, a multi-million dollar grant program to help reclaim Arizona neighborhoods, and The Border Volunteer Corps, a volunteer program that improves the quality of life along the Arizona-Mexico border. He has organized a volunteer clean-up effort, the largest of any metropolitan area in U.S. history. Governor Symington has also served as chair of the Western's Governors' Association from 1992 until 1993, and vice chair of the Committee on Natural Resources for the National Governors Association during 1993 until 1994.

TAMARKIN, BOB

503 W. Briar Place, Chicago IL 60657
BORN: 1938, St. Louis. ACHIEVEMENTS: Three-time nominee, Pulitzer Prize, Best-selling Books: New Gastsbys, 1985; The Leader Within, 1993, The Merc, 1993. Co-executive Producer, White Mile (HBO made-for-TV movie). STUDIED: Washington University, B.A., 1960; University of Missouri, Masters in Journalism, 1962.

Tamarkin, author of more than 10 books, has worked as an investigative reporter and foreign correspondent for the *Chicago Daily News* and *Wall Street Journal*. While authoring his books, he frequently contributes to numerous publications including the *New York Times Sunday Magazine*, *Fortune*, the *Los Angeles Times*, and the *Washington Post*. Early in his career he was a reporter for Fairchild Publications and left to become founder of *Generation*, a magazine for young professionals. He was a foreign correspondent for the *Chicago Daily News* in the 1970s serving in Vietnam, Africa, India and Lebanon. He served as Midwest bureau chief of *Forbes* in the 1980s and later developed various books and periodicals for several Chicago publishers. Today Tamarkin is one of the nation's most published business authors, writing on derivatives, commodities, and investing.

TAN, AMY

c/o Putnam Berkley Group, 200 Madison Avenue, New York, NY 10016 (212)-951-8400
BORN: 1952, Oakland, Calif. ACHIEVEMENTS: Commonwealth Club Gold Award for Fiction, Bay Area Book Reviewers Award for Best Fiction, nomination for National Book Critics Circle Award for Best Novel, all 1989, all for The Joy Luck Club, Putnam, 1989. STUDIED: San Jose State, B.A., 1973, M.A., 1974; University of California, post graduate study, 1974-1976.

A former consultant to programs for disabled children, Amy Tan began her writing career as a reporter, managing editor, and associate publisher for *Emergency Room Reports*. In 1983 Tan became a free-lance technical writer. In short order, her workaholic nature resulted in 90-hour work weeks, with little time left over for a personal life. Tan tried to change her habits through psychological counseling, but quit when her therapist revealed a tendency to fall asleep during counseling sessions. Tan devised her own therapy, taking jazz piano lessons and writing fiction. Her first novel, *The Joy Luck Club*, Putnam, 1989, was both a commercial and literary success. Tan followed up with a second book, *The Kitchen God's Wife*, Putnam, 1991, considered by many to surpass the standard set by her first novel.

TANNER, TONY

BORN: 1932, Hillingdon (England). ACHIEVEMENTS: Lyricist, author (of book based on) The Snow Queen, 1953. STUDIED: Webber-Douglas School, England.

Tanner spent the early years of his career acting, directing, and playwriting in England, including a role in *Stop the World—I Want to Get Off.* He moved into the New York City stage scene in 1968 as a director and actor in productions staged mostly off-Broadway. His film work, done mostly in England, included *Stop the World—I Want to Get Off* for Warner Brothers. His writings include the book and lyrics for the musical *The Snow Queen*, presented in Sheffield, England in 1953.

Author Amy Tan.

TAUBE, HENRY

Stanford University, Department of Chemistry, Stanford, CA 94305

BORN: 1915, Neudorf, Saskatchewan (Canada). ACHIEVEMENTS: Nobel Prize in chemistry, 1983; Harrison Howe Award; Chandler Medal, Columbia University; Kirkwood Award, Yale University and American Chemical Society; Distinguished Service in Advancement of Inorganic Chemistry Award; National Medal of Science; Monsanto Company Award; Welch Award; Priestley Medal. STUDIED: University of Saskatchewan; University of California.

The metals industry became more productive and rich by Taube's answer to the question of how negatively charged electrons move, especially in metal complexes, from one molecule to another in chemical reactions. His answer was an important step forward in metallurgy, one of the youngest sciences but one of the oldest arts, in the science's ultimate aim to be so exact as to predict the behavior of a new metal and to say where and how best it can be used. Taube, a naturalized American, has also studied the transfer of electrons in the formation of rust and other oxidizations.

TAYLOR, JEFF

Kansas City Star, 1729 Grand Avenue, Kansas City, MO 64108 (816) 234-4141

Taylor is a prominent journalist. For career credentials consult the portion of this book entitled "Notable Americans by Profession" in the Appendix. Within this portion, the list "Journalists" describes requirements for inclusion in this volume.

TAYLOR, JOSEPH HOOTON, JR.

Princeton University, Physics Department, Princeton, NJ 08544

Taylor is a prominent scientist. For career credentials consult the portion of this book entitled "Notable Americans by Profession" in the Appendix. Within this portion, the list "Scientists" describes requirements for inclusion in this volume.

TAYLOR, PAUL

Paul Taylor Dance Company, 552 Broadway, New York, NY 10012 (212) 431-5562

BORN: 1930, Allegheny, Pa. ACHIEVEMENTS: Notable ballets: Epic; Three Epitaphs; Panorama; Esplanade; Insects and Heroes; Scudorama; Poetry in Motion; Airs; Arden Court; Aureole; Orbs; Big Bertha; So Long Eden; American Genesis. STUDIED: Syracuse University, Connecticut College, Juilliard School of Music, no degrees; Martha Graham, Metropolitan Opera Ballet schools.

Combining a blend of wit, athleticism, and rebelliousness, Taylor's work has evolved into a sunny style of strong but essentially lyric movements. His tendency to create roles for big and bulky dancers—he stands over six-feet tall and was a swimmer at Syracuse University while he majored in painting—gives his writing bounce and compactness as he contrasts walking, running, skipping, and hopping steps. He has choreographed complete stillness, the sound of rain, the voice of a telephone operator, with each reflecting his strong interest in movement, but often leaving critics limp. He also shows a bitter streak in such works as *Big Bertha*, where he virtually destroys an all-American family at an amusement park visit that leads to rape and death. Twyla Tharp and Dan Wagoner both danced for Taylor before founding their own companies. In 1962 Taylor's troupe represented the U.S. at the International Theatre Festival in Paris, where Taylor won the top award for choreography, recognizing his fertile, imaginative, musical, and often humorous choreographic talents.

TAYLOR, PETER H.

Random House, 201 E. 50th St., New York, NY 10022 (212) 751-2600
BORN: 1917, Trenton, Tenn. ACHIEVEMENTS: Pulitzer Prize, A Summons to Memphis, 1986. STUDIED: Kenyon College
Primarily a short-story writer, Peter Taylor's fiction explored urban middle-class life and social change in the South, especially in the Tennessee cities of Memphis and his native Nashville. His stories include *The Scoutmaster, The Old Forest, The Death of a Kinsman,* and *A Very Long Fourth.* His work, *Collected Stories,* was published in 1969. His only novel, *A Summons to Memphis,* written in 1986, won a Pulitzer Prize.

TAYLOR, RICHARD E.

Stanford Linear Accelerator Center, P.O. Box 4349, Palo Alto, CA 94309
BORN: 1929, Medicine Hat (Canada). ACHIEVEMENTS: Nobel Prize in Physics, 1988; STUDIED: University of Alberta, Canada; Stanford University.
Taylor, a naturalized American, has been a researcher for the Boursier Laboratory in France and the Lawrence Laboratory, in California. Presently he is a physics professor at Stanford University where he conducts research on quarks. His 1988 Nobel Prize is shared with Jerome Friedman, and Henry Way Kendall. For futher information on his findings and subsequent award-winning research consult the entry of Henry Way Kendall in which it is described.

TAYLOR, WILLIAM

The Boston Globe, 135 Morrissey Blvd., Boston, MA 02107-3310 (617) 929-2935
Taylor is a prominent publisher. For career credentials consult the portion of this book entitled "Notable Americans by Profession" in the Appendix. Within this portion, the list "Publishers" describes requirements for inclusion in this volume.

TELLEP, DANIEL MICHAEL

Lockheed Corp., 4500 Park, Granada Calabasas, CA 91399
BORN: 1931, Forest Park, Pa. ACHIEVEMENTS: Tower Award San, Jose State University, 1985; Aerospace Laurels Award, Aviation Week and Space Technology, 1993; fellow AIAA, Lawrence Sperry Award, 1964; Missile Systems Award 1986. STUDIED: University of California at Berkeley, B.S., 1954, M.S., 1955; Harvard University, Advanced Management Program, 1971.

After taking control of Lockheed in 1989, Daniel Tellep is largely credited with guiding the $13 billion company through the lull that struck the defense industry shortly thereafter. He joined the company, which specializes in missiles and space systems, in 1955 as a scientist. Tellep became vice president in 1983 and president in 1986 before becoming the chief executive in 1989. In 1993, he was the primary player in the $1.5 billion purchase of General Dynamics, a deal which made Lockheed the world's biggest builder of fighter planes.

TEMKO, NED

The Christian Science Monitor, 1 Norway St., Boston, MA 02115 (617) 450-2000
Temko is a prominent journalist. For career credentials consult the portion of this book entitled "Notable Americans by Profession" in the Appendix. Within this portion, the list "Journalists" describes requirements for inclusion in this volume.

TETLEY, GLEN

15 West 9th St., New York, NY 10011 (212) 475-4604
BORN: 1926, Cleveland, Ohio. ACHIEVEMENTS: Notable ballets: Birds of Sorrow; Pierrot Lunaire; Sargossa; Ricercare; Embrace Tiger and Return to Mountain; Fieldmass; Mythical Hunters; Rag Dances; Strophe Antistrophe; Daphnis and Chloe; Contradances; The Tempest. STUDIED: Franklin and Marshall College, Lancaster, Pa.; Columbia Medical School, B.S., 1948; Tanya Holm, Antony Tudor, Margaret Craske schools.
After a wide-ranging career as a dancer, performing in Broadway shows, on television, with various ballet companies, and at the New York City Opera, Glen Tetley turned to choreography. Most of his work has been done for a series of European ballet companies, including the Royal Danish Ballet and the Royal Ballet in Britain. He often employs original scenic elements to offset the intensity and outright sensuality of his nonstop movements, and at other times works with movement systems themselves. The first choreographer to blend modern dance and ballet, and thus a pioneer in the dance world, he has often been scolded by American dance critics as being too mannered and strenuous.

THARP, TWYLA

PMK 1776 Broadway, New York, NY 10019 (212) 582-1111
BORN: 1941, Portland, Ind. ACHIEVEMENTS: Notable ballets: The Fugue; Eight Jelly Rolls; The Bix Pieces; Nine Sinatra Songs; Baker's Dozen; Deuce Coupe; Push Comes to Shove; Bach Parthia; Brahms/Handel; As Time Goes By. STUDIED: Pomona College, Claremont, Cal.; Barnard College, B.A., art history, 1963; American Ballet Theatre, Richard Thomas, Barbara Fallis, Martha Graham, Paul Taylor, Carolyn Brown schools.
Twyla Tharp burst on the American dance scene in the early 1970s. Climbing out of an early, stiffly structural period with mathematically based works usually performed in silence, Tharp began packing her suites in the 1970s with floppy, scrambling, squiggling stage contortions filled with comedy and sassiness. Joining the Joffrey Ballet in 1973, she constructed Deuce

Coupe, with the Beach Boys crooning as the dancers strutted. She became the first American choreographer to showcase Mikhail Baryshnikov at American Ballet Theater, (ABT) with *Push Comes to Shove*. The combination of the Russian showing his comedic talents as he cavorts with ABT ballerinas and Tharp's racy composition resulted in the most talked about ballet of the decade and its title became a phrase used nationwide. Tharp has embraced video with enthusiasm, filming her stage work as well as many original pieces, and feature films, choreographing dances for *Hair, White Nights, Amadeus*, and *Ragtime*. With her own company, and new mix of modern and traditional dance movements, she continues to look for new ways to meld emotion into dance, ever conscious of the fact that dancing does not need to be severe and stern to be serious.

THIEBAUD, WAYNE

1617 7th Ave., Sacramento, CA 95818
BORN: 1920. ACHIEVEMENTS: Member, American Academy and Institute of Arts and Letters; academician, National Academy of Design; collections: San Francisco Museum of Modern Art; Metropolitan Museum of Art, New York City; exhibitions: San Francisco Museum of Modern Art; Arts Club of Chicago. STUDIED: California State, Sacramento.
Before formal art training, Wayne Thiebaud worked as a cartoonist, a designer and an advertising art director—experiences that have influenced his paintings. With thickly applied paint, variations of images of single-food items and other products, are repeated in bright colors and artificial light. Realistic representations have also included lone figures on white backgrounds executed in a style reminiscent of advertising images. An alliance with the Pop movement is evident throughout his work, although his style characteristically incorporates a more realistic approach. He continues to teach art and has received numerous pedagogical awards, including special citations from the College Art Association and the National Association of Schools of Art and Design. He has also been awarded honorary Doctorates of Fine Arts from the California College of Arts and Crafts, Dickenson College and the San Francisco School of Fine Arts.

THIEROT, RICHARD

San Francisco Chronicle, 901 Mission St., San Francisco, CA 94103-2988 (415) 777-1111
Thierot is a prominent publisher. For career credentials consult the portion of this book entitled "Notable Americans by Profession" in the Appendix. Within this portion, the list "Publishers" describes requirements for inclusion in this volume.

THOMAS, CAL

The Los Angeles Times, Times Mirror Square, Los Angeles, CA 90012-3645. (213)237-5000
BORN: 1942, Washington, D.C. ACHIEVEMENTS: Author, Uncommon Sense, 1990. STUDIED: American University, B.A., English literature, 1968.
Thomas worked for NBC News from 1961-1965, taking a break to obtain his degree in English literature, and

returning to the newsroom for KPRC-TV in Houston from 1968-69, and for NBC News from 1969-73. He returned to KPRC-TV from 1973-77. In 1985 he became a Washington commentator for WTTG-TV and a commentator for National Public Radio, both positions he continues to hold. His columns are syndicated by the *Los Angeles Times*, and he has authored several books delving into his politically conservative and Christian philosophies including *Uncommon Sense* in 1990.

THOMAS, JUSTICE CLARENCE

Supreme Court of the United States, One First St. N.E., Washington, DC 20543 (202) 479-3000
BORN: 1948, Savannah, Ga. ACHIEVEMENTS: Associate justice, U.S. Supreme Court, chairman, U.S. Equal Employment Opportunity Commission. STUDIED: Holy Cross College, A.B., 1971; Yale University, J.D., 1974.
Thomas' first government position was as Assistant Attorney General of Missouri, from 1974 through 1977. He was assistant secretary for civil rights at the U.S. Department of Education from 1981 through 1982, and then chairman of the federal Equal Employment Opportunity Commission from 1982 through 1989. It was during this period of his life that he became known as a candid, black conservative opposed to minority preference programs. He was nominated by President Bush to the U.S. Court of Appeals for the District of Columbia in 1990, and in 1991, Bush nominated Thomas as associate justice of the United States Supreme Court. His pending appointment was contested when one of his employees at EEOC, Anita Hill, accused him of sexual harassment. A subsequent televised hearing before a Senate committee is generally regarded as a significant development in bringing the issue of sexual harassment into the public consciousness. Despite the controversial hearing, Thomas won the appointment.

THOMAS, EDWARD DONNALL

Brigham & Women's Hospital, 75 Francis St., Boston, MA 02115
BORN: 1920, Mart, Texas. ACHIEVEMENTS: Nobel Prize in Physiology or Medicine (shared with Joseph E. Murray), 1990. STUDIED: University of Texas; Harvard University.
Thirty-one years after publishing his first paper, at age 39, on the subject of bone-marrow transplants, Thomas won the Nobel Prize by his continuing dedication to the subject. Specifically, his citation hailed his proof to all doubters that the lives of dying patients could be saved with transplanted organs. His recognition principally involved work with bone-marrow transplants in the treatment of leukemia. He also worked in the areas of hematology (diseases of the blood and bloodforming organs), biochemical medicine, and irradiation biology.

THOMAS, MICHAEL TILSON

Davies Symphony Hall, San Francisco, CA, 94102

BORN: 1944, Los Angeles. ACHIEVEMENTS: Winner of the Koussevitzky Prize, Conductor of the Year given by Musical America. STUDIED: University of Southern California.

At age 19 Thomas was named music director of the Young Musicians Foundation Debut Orchestra. In 1969, he was appointed assistant conductor of Boston Symphony Orchestra, and, in the same year, made his New York Debut with the Boston Symphony after replacing ailing music director William Steinberg in mid-concert—an event which triggered the comparison between him and his mentor Leonard Bernstein. Though he has yet to match the famed composer's persona or output, Thomas shares the same devotion to Copland, Stravinsky and Ives. His interpretations favor objectivity and elegance, and his commitment to American music remains strong, as evidenced by his restoration of Gershwin musicals and concert works to their original scoring during a run with the Los Angeles Philharmonic in the 1980s. Beginning in 1987, he led the London Symphony Orchestra on tour through Europe, Japan, and the U.S. In September, 1995, he accepted the post of music director with the San Francisco Symphony.

Symphony conductor Michael Tilson Thomas.

THOMPSON, RICHARD

U.S. News & World Report, 2400 N St., NW., Washington, DC 20037-1153 (202) 955-2000

Thompson is a prominent publisher. For career credentials consult the portion of this book entitled "Notable Americans by Profession" in the Appendix. Within this portion, the list "Publishers" describes requirements for inclusion in this volume.

THOMPSON, TOMMY G.

Office of the Governor, E. State Capitol, Rm. 115, Madison, WI 53707-7863 (608) 266-1212
BORN: 1941, Elroy, Wis. ACHIEVEMENTS: Elected to Wisconsin State Assembly, 1966, at age 24; first governor elected to a third term. STUDIED: University of Wisconsin-Madison, B.S., political science, 1963, and law degree, 1966.

In 1986, Gov. Tommy Thompson was the only Republican gubernatorial candidate in the nation to defeat an incumbent Democrat. He returned to office in 1990 by the largest victory in a non-presidential year since the Great Depression. In 1994 he became the first governor in Wisconsin's history to be elected to a third term. Key areas of initiatives under his administration include welfare reform, education, environmental protection and trade, and the first parental school choice program in the nation. He served as chairman of the Republican Governor's Association, the Midwestern Governor's Conference, and the council of Great Lakes Governors. Gov. Thompson assumed the chairmanship of the National Governor's Association in August, 1995.

THURMOND, J. STROM

Senate Office Building, Washington, D.C. 20310
BORN: 1902, Edgefield, S.C. ACHIEVEMENTS: Youngest circuit judge in South Carolina; U.S. Senator since 1955; military decorations: Legion of Merit with oak leaf cluster; Bronze Star, Purple Heart, Congressional Medal of Honor, among others. EDUCATION: Clemson College, B.S.; 14 honorary degrees; law school by correspondence course, passed bar in 1930.

Strom Thurmond, 94, began his professional life as a school teacher in South Carolina's public schools. His public life began as a member of the Edgefield County School board and included city and county attorney, state senator (1933-38), and circuit judge (1938-46), although he took leave from the bench to enlist in the army during WWII. Thurmond served in the Army as part of the 82nd airborne division during the invasion of Europe and was later transferred to the Philippines. He was highly decorated for his military efforts. In 1948, while he was governor of South Carolina, he was the presidential candidate for the Southern States' Rights ticket, whose platform opposed federal intervention in state affairs and the civil rights program. He denied being a white supremacist but maintained that it was up to the states, not the federal government, to handle racial problems. In 1957, two years after becoming a U.S. Senator, Thurmond gained the notorious record of the longest individual filibuster, 24 hours, 18 min., against the Civil Rights Act of 1957. He later became a Republican and was a delegate to three of the party's national conventions. Forty-one years later, Thurmond continues to represent South Carolina in the U.S. Senate.

TIGERMAN, STANLEY

Tigerman, Fugman, McCurry Architects, 444 N. Wells Street 2C, Chicago, IL 60610 (312) 644-5880
BORN: 1930. ACHIEVEMENTS: Award of Merit, AIA, 1970; Progressive Architecture Award, 1980; Masonry Institute Award, 1982; notable works: Hard Rock Cafe, Chicago; Illinois Regional Library for the Blind and Physically Handicapped, Chicago; "Animal Crackers" (Blender House), Highland Park, Ill. STUDIED: Yale University.
Stanley Tigerman's work is perhaps an architectural analog to the Pop Art of the 1960s and early 1970s. He is best known for a group of fancifully and often self-descriptively titled projects: Kosher Kitchen of a Suburban Jewish-American Princess, Hot Dog House and Zipper Townhouses are among his residential oeuvre. He shocks as often as he amuses; his Daisy House is in the shape of a human phallus, and his proposed Catholic cathedral included a series of confessional boxes which resembled the stalls of a public men's room. For all his whimsy and irreverence, his career has been far from frivolous. In the early 1970s he brought new energy and finesse to Chicago's public housing pool with his largely vernacular designs for indigent and low-income low-rises. Later he addressed Third-World poverty in a series of Bangladesh development efforts. Even in the heyday of Miesian minimalism, his eclectic architecture won favor as well as comment. His recent work is moving toward large, simplified neo-classical spaces: solid yet theatrical. The low, boxy facade of his Chicago Hard Rock Cafe, for example, is broken by a huge palladian window/doorway, and capped with a central domed rotunda.

TILLINGER, JOHN

William Morris Agency, 1350 Avenue of the Americas, New York, NY 10019
BORN: 1939. ACHIEVEMENTS: Antoinette Perry Award nomination, Best Director, Loot, 1986. STUDIED: Old Vic School, Bristol (England).
An actor, director and playwright, John Tillinger was nominated for a Tony Award for his direction of *Loot*, 1986. His other directing assignments included *A Call from the East*, 1981; *The Golden Age*, 1983; *Serenading Louie*, 1984; *Corpse!*, 1986; and *Sweet Sue*, 1986; as well as numerous stage productions at the Long Wharf Theater, New Haven, Conn. His acting credits include the films *Resurrection*, 1980, and *A Little Sex*, and television's *The Adams Chronicles*, 1975, on PBS.

TOBIN, JAMES

Yale University, Department of Economics, P.O. Box 1972, New Haven, CT 06520
BORN: 1919, Champaign, Ill. ACHIEVEMENTS: Nobel Prize in Economic Science, 1981; John Bates Clark Medal, American Economic Association; president, Econometric Society, American Economic Association. STUDIED: Harvard University; honorary degrees from five American and European universities.
The last of the prominent American Keynesians, Tobin has spent a major part of his career salvaging and updating the theories, doctrines, and policies of the British economist whose basic idea was the old law of supply and demand of a particular commodity extended to explain national output and inflation. His treatise, *A General Equilibrium Approach to Monetary Theory*, concluded that interest rates were only one of the elements altering the rates of unemployment and inflation, and not the most important one at that. In essence, according to Tobin, the ultimate element is the relationship of equities and debts of wealth owners as measured by their stock market portfolios, and the replacement cost on the asset side at current prices. At the center of his work, almost entirely laid down in articles in professional journals, is this concept of asset holding and its influence on spending and saving by families and businesses. He explicated the application of the concept in a long series of papers since 1955, which subsequently figured heavily in the branch of economics called the Theory of Finance.

TODD, BRUCE M.

7629 Rockpoint Drive, Austin, TX 78731 (512) 499-2250
ACHIEVEMENTS: Mayor of Austin, Texas; presidential appointee to Advisory Commission on Intergovernmental Relations. STUDIED: University of Texas, B.B.A. in accounting.
Bruce M. Todd is employed as a certified public accountant, a career he started in 1974. He was formerly a partner in the firm Mueller, Todd and Company, and is presently a senior consultant with Glass & Company in Austin, Texas. Todd was elected a Travis County commissioner in 1987, and was re-elected in 1991. He became the mayor of Austin on June 15, 1991. Todd has held a number of positions in the U.S. Conference of Mayors, including the Advisory Board, Legislative-Action Committee, National Unfunded Mandates Task Force, and as chair of the Standing Committee on Education, Jobs, and Family.

TOLES, TOM

The Buffalo News, 1 News Plaza, Box 100, Buffalo, NY 14240 (716) 849-3434
Toles is a prominent journalist. For career credentials consult the portion of this book entitled "Notable Americans by Profession" in the Appendix. Within this portion, the list "Journalists" describes requirements for inclusion in this volume.

TOMLIN, LILY

P.O. Box 27700, Los Angeles, CA 90027
BORN: 1939, Detroit. ACHIEVEMENTS: Emmy Award, Best Variety, Music, or Comedy Special, 1973; Special Antoinette Perry Award, Appearing Nitely, 1977; Antoinette Perry Award, Best Actress in a Play, The Search for Signs of Intelligent Life in the Universe, 1986; Grammy Award, Best Comedy Recording, This Is a Recording, 1971; Emmy award, Best Variety, Music, or Comedy Special, Lily Tomlin, 1973; Emmy award, Best Variety Program, Lily: Sold Out, 1981. STUDIED: Wayne State University; studied mime with Paul Curtis; studied acting with Peggy Feury.

Best known for her portrayal of the acerbic telephone operator, Ernestine, and the precocious, little Edith Ann, Lily Tomlin has successfully crossed the line from comedy to drama during her many years as a performer. Tomlin began performing in the mid-1960s in the nightclubs of New York City, on television commercials and, from time to time, on television shows. Between 1969 and 1972, she was a regular on the television show, *Rowan and Martin's Laugh-In*, where viewers first became acquainted with her characters, Ernestine and Edith Ann. Through the 1970s, Tomlin appeared in several television specials and the Broadway comedy review, *Appearing Nitely*. In the meantime, she also began appearing in movies playing serious roles, including *Nashville*, in 1975; *Moment by Moment*, in 1978; and *All of Me*, in 1984. Tomlin returned to Broadway in 1985 with her one-woman show, *The Search for Signs of Intelligent Life in the Universe*.

TONEGAWA, SUSUMU

Massachusetts Institute of Technology, Department of Physics, Cambridge, MA 02139
BORN: 1939, Nagoya (Japan). ACHIEVEMENTS: Nobel Prize in Physiology or Medicine, 1987; Cloetta Prize; Avery Landsteiner Prize; Louisa Gross Horwitz Prize; Gairdner Award; Bunka Kunsho Order of Culture, Japan; Robert Koch Prize; BristolMyers Award; Albert Lasker Award, Albert and Mary Lasker Foundation. STUDIED: Kyoto Imperial University, Japan; University of California at San Diego.

The first Japanese recipient of the Nobel Prize in Physiology and Medicine, and a naturalized American, Susumu Tonegawa discovered how the body can suddenly marshall its immune defenses against millions of different disease agents it has never dealt with before. His "genetic principle for production of antibody diversity" solved the puzzle of how the human body can manufacture a great amount of antibodies from a limited number of genes in order to respond to various invasive conditions. The immune system's cells reorganized the genes to produce an antibody whose unique structure selectively attacks the specific condition.

TOOKER, GARY L.

Motorola Inc., 1303 East Algonquin Rd., Schaumberg, IL 90196 (708) 576-5000
Gary Tooker joined Motorola Inc. in 1962. He spent his early years with the company working his way through the hierarchy of the semiconductor products group.

Tooker rose to the position of general manager of the Semiconductor Products Sector in 1981. He was elected chief corporate staff officer of Motorola in 1986, and in 1988 was promoted again to chief operating officer. Tooker, with two other senior officers of Motorola, was part of a three-member executive triumvirate. With the departure of one member, George Fisher, Tooker was given sole possession of the CEO position, with the added title of vice chairman.

TORME, MEL

Triad Artists, 9200 Sunset Blvd., #823, Los Angeles, CA 90069
BORN: 1925, Chicago. ACHIEVEMENTS: Grammy, Best Jazz Vocal-Male, An Evening with George Shearing and Mel Torme, 1982; Grammy, Best Jazz Vocal-Male Top Drawer, 1983.

Mel Torme has had a long and colorful career in show business. Best known for his exceptional voice and his acting in movies and on television, Torme got started as a professional singer at the age of 3. He began acting and composing music professionally in his teens. Torme played drums and sang in Chico Marx's band in the early 1940s and later formed his own vocal ensemble, called the Mel Tones. The ensemble toured with Artie Shaw's band. He established himself in the late 1940s and 1950s as a solo singer. Torme has also written a novel, an autobiography, a work on Judy Garland, and a biography of his close friend and coworker, Buddy Rich.

TOWNES, CHARLES HARD

University of California, Department of Physics, Berkeley, CA 94720
BORN: 1915, Greenville, S.C. ACHIEVEMENTS: Invented the Maser (microwave amplification by simulated emission of radiation); inducted into the National Inventors Hall of Fame, 1976.

In 1939 Charles Townes joined Bell telephone Laboratories, Inc. and worked on radar bombing systems during WW II. In 1948 he became a faculty member at Columbia University. While at Columbia he invented the maser, or microwave amplification by simulated emission of radiation, in 1953. His maser invention was soon followed by the laser and both were used in radar communications, astronomy, navigation, atomic clocks, surgery and industry. Townes served as vice-president and director of research from 1959 to 1961 for the appointed provost and professor of physics at Massachusetts Institute of Technology.

TRIBBLE, GUY

NeXT, Inc., 900 Chesapeake Dr., Redwood City, CA 94063
ACHIEVEMENTS: Developed new system for creation of computer programs.

Tribble, a software engineer at NeXT, Inc., developed a program that leapfrogged over the old complicated programming codes. Tribble's development tool made life easier for software designers. The old codes are replaced in Tribble's system with easily worked windows and buttons, enabling creation of new programs with ease.

TROTMAN, ALEXANDER J.

Ford Motor Co., The American Road, Dearborn, Michigan 48121

BORN: 1933, Middlesex (England). ACHIEVEMENTS: Navigator for the Royal Air Force from 1951-1955. STUDIED: Mich. State University, M.B.A., 1972.

Alexander Trotman made his entrance into the Ford Motor Company 38 years ago as a multi-faceted professional. He performed a variety of functions until 1971, when he became the director of sales and marketing planning. Trotman oversaw the truck operations for Ford in Europe and presided over Ford Asia-Pacific Inc., as well as other overseas divisions. He's been president of the company since 1993.

TRUELL, PETER

The Wall Street Journal, 200 Liberty St., New York, NY 10281 (212) 416-2000

Truell is a prominent journalist. For career credentials consult the portion of this book entitled "Notable Americans by Profession" in the Appendix. Within this portion, the list "Journalists" describes requirements for inclusion in this volume.

Astronaut Richard Harrison Truly.

TRUITTE, JAMES

854 Rue de la Paix, Cincinnati, OH 45220 (513) 559-1999

BORN: 1925, Chicago, Ill. ACHIEVEMENTS: Notable ballets: Mirror, Mirror; With Timbrel and Dance Praise His Name; Variegations; Bagatelles; Guernica; The Mole People; The Sins of Russell Cade. STUDIED: University of California at Los Angeles, no degree; Janet Collins, Carmelita Maracchi, Lester Horton schools.

Most of Truitte's choreography shows the profound effect one of his teachers, Lester Horton—who maintained a theater and studio in Los Angeles—had on his career. And in his choreography he has gone out of his way to repay the debt. An example is his ballet *Variegations*, where the vocabulary of dancing techniques are highlighted rather than a story or plot line, resulting in an elastic portrayal of sustained strength and control. In homage to his teacher, Truitte presented the work to familiarize the audience with Horton's techniques when the Alvin Ailey company, which he had joined in 1960, visited London in 1964. In addition to ballet, Truitte helped Horton on the film *South Sea Woman*, and went on himself to stage dances for the film, *The Sins of Rachel Cade.*

TRULY, RICHARD HARRISON

NASA, Office of the Administration, 400 Maryland Ave. SW, Washington, DC 20546

BORN: 1937, Fayette, Miss. ACHIEVEMENTS: Space missions: STS-2 and STS-8 space shuttle missions. STUDIED: Georgia Institute of Technology, B.S., aeronautical engineering, 1959.

Truly joined the U.S. Navy after graduation from college, and was assigned as a flight instructor and a pilot on aircraft carriers. He advanced to the rank of rear admiral and transferred to NASA's astronaut corps after the Air Force cancelled its Manned Orbital Laboratory program. Truly flew space shuttle test flights in 1977, then was the pilot on the STS-2 space shuttle mission aboard the shuttle Columbia, its second flight. He commanded the STS-8 space shuttle mission in the shuttle Challenger. Truly left NASA to run the Navy Space Command, but returned to NASA after the 1986 Challenger explosion, to take charge of the space shuttle program. He became the NASA administrator in 1986, the first astronaut to do so. He resigned in 1992 over a dispute with the President's administration about the future of the space program.

TRUMP, DONALD J.

Random House, 201 E. 50th St., New York, NY 10022 (212) 751-2600

BORN: 1946, New York City. ACHIEVEMENTS: Flamboyant real estate developer; best-selling author, Art of the Deal, 1988. STUDIED: Fordham University; University of Pennsylvania Wharton School of Finance, economics, 1968.

As a high-flying developer and celebrity in New York City, whose fortunes rose and then fell in tandem with the real estate marketplace, Donald Trump was emblematic of the economic and social extravagances of the 1980s. After graduating from college, he joined his father's real estate business, and shifted its focus from middle-income apartment complexes in the New York borough of Queens to big, attention-getting projects in Manhattan. He branched out into casino and airline investments before narrowly avoiding bankruptcy in the 1990s. His reputation as a shrewd negotiator contributed to the success of his book, *Art of the Deal.*

TUCKER, JIM GUY

Office of the Governor, State Capitol, Little Rock, AR 72201 (501) 682-2345
BORN: 1943, Little Rock, Ark. ACHIEVEMENTS: Served in the United States Marine Corps Reserves. STUDIED: Harvard University, B.A., University of Arkansas, J.D.
The 43rd governor of Arkansas was elected to a four-year term in 1994. Gov. Jim Tucker has served as governor since 1992, after filling the unexpired term of then President-elect Bill Clinton. His public service career includes two years as a prosecuting attorney for the Sixth Judicial District (1970-1972); two terms as Arkansas attorney general (1972-1976); two years as a member of congress (1976-1978) and lieutenant governor (1990). As governor he convened the first state-wide crime summit and the first summit focusing on prevention of youth crime.

TUNE, TOMMY

International Creative Management, 40 West 57th St., New York, NY 10019
Tune is a prominent dramatic artist, dancer and choreographer. For career credentials consult the portion of this book entitled "Notable Americans by Profession" in the Appendix. Within this portion, the list "Dramatic Artists" describes requirements for inclusion in this volume.

TURNER, KATHLEEN

Gersh Agency Inc., 122 N. Canon Dr., Beverly Hills, CA, 90210
BORN: 1954 Springfield, Mo. ACHIEVEMENTS: Golden Globe Award, Best Actress in a Musical or Comedy, Romancing the Stone, 1984; Golden Globe Award, Best Actress in a Comedy, Prizzi's Honor, 1986; Academy Award, Best Actress, Peggy Sue Got Married, 1987. STUDIED: Southwest Missouri State University, University of Maryland, M.F.A., 1977, Central School of Speech and Drama, London.
Turner began her acting career on the stage in the play, *Gemini*, in 1978, but has worked primarily in film. Turner is the daughter of a U.S. foreign service officer. While she grew up, she lived with her family in Cuba, Venezuela, Canada and Washington, D.C. Turner has appeared in many popular movies, however she is probably best known for playing the title role in *Peggy Sue Got Married*. She made her film debut in *Body Heat*, in 1981, and has starred opposite Michael Douglas and Danny DeVito in a number of movies, including *Romancing the Stone*, in 1984, *The Jewel of the Nile*, in 1985, and *The War of the Roses*, in 1989.

TURNER, MARK ANTHONY

Asst. Dean for Business Affairs, University of Cincinnati, Cincinnati, OH 45221
BORN: 1951, Lynch, Ky. ACHIEVEMENTS: Ford Foundation Scholarship, 1973; assistant dean, Univ. College, University of Cincinnati. STUDIED: University of Kentucky Southeast Community College, A.A., 1972; Western Kentucky University, B.S., 1974.
After college, Turner rapidly established himself in the accounting field. In 1974 he worked for Deloitte, Haskins, and Sells as a senior assistant. In 1978 he moved on, becoming a senior consultant for the Business Resource Center. Next, Turner was a senior consultant-auditor for Arthur Young & Company in 1980. Finally, in 1982, Turner took a position as assistant dean at University College, University of Cincinnati. Turner is also active in community affairs, founding the Cincinnati Chapter of the National Association of Black Accountants in 1980. He also served as treasurer of the Bond Hill Community Council, and was a consultant to the Sickle Cell Awareness Group of Greater Cincinnati.

TURNER, (TED) ROBERT EDWARD III

One CNN Center., Box 105366, Atlanta, GA, 30348 (404) 827-1700
BORN: 1938, Cincinnati. ACHIEVEMENTS: Time magazine's "Man of the Year", 1991. STUDIED: Brown University
Turner inherited his father's failing billboard business in 1963, after his father committed suicide. In 1970 he purchased WTBS, a declining UHF television station in Atlanta. By 1975 Turner had turned the station around and was making a profit. He accomplished this by transmitting sports and low cost entertainment programs via satellite to cable systems around the country, turning WTBS into the nation's first "superstation". In 1980 Turner started the Cable News Network (CNN), the first all-news television station. CNN received international acclaim for its coverage of the Persian Gulf War, 1990-91.

TURNER, TINA

Capitol Records, 1750 N. Vine St., Hollywood, CA 90028 (213) 462-6252
BORN: 1939, Nutbush Borough, Tenn. ACHIEVEMENTS: Grammy, Best R&B Duo, Proud Mary (with Ike Turner), 1972; Grammy, Record of the Year and Best Pop Vocal Female, What's Love Got To Do With It?, 1984; Grammy, Best Rock Vocal of the Year, Better Be Good to Me, 1985; Grammy, Best Rock Vocal of the Year, One of the Living, 1986; Grammy, Best Rock Vocal of the Year, Back Where You Started, 1986; Grammy, Best Rock Vocal of the Year, Tina, Live in Europe, 1988.
Annie Mae Bullock joined Ike Turner and the Kings of Rhythm in 1956, married Ike Turner that same year and changed her name to Tina Turner. Their debut song, *Fool in Love*, was released in 1960. They were

more successful overseas than in the U.S., and, in 1966, they had a number one song in Britain, *River Deep and Mountain High*. The success of this song gave them the chance to open for the Rolling Stones in 1969. In the early 1970s, they began having success in the United States with hits such as *Proud Mary*, which won a Grammy. After the breakup of her marriage, Turner's career declined and concert promoters would not book her for performances for several years. In 1984 the album *Private Dancer* established her as a leading rock singer and earned her three Grammys. In 1991 she was inducted into the Rock and Roll Hall of Fame. Turner's autobiography *I, Tina*, was made into the 1993 movie *What's Love Got to Do with It?*

TUROW, SCOTT

Carlin, Nath, and Rosenthal, Sears Tower, Suite 8000, Chicago, IL 60606

BORN: 1949, Chicago. ACHIEVEMENTS: Writing Award, College English Association and Book-of-the-Month Club, 1970; Silver Dagger Award, Crime Writers Association, 1988, for Presumed Innocent, Farrar, Straus, 1987. STUDIED: Amherst College, B.A., 1970; Stanford University, M.A., 1974; Harvard University, J.D., 1978.

A former prosecutor for the Chicago U..S. Attorney's office, and a partner in a Chicago law firm, Turow flunked freshman English at New Trier High, but in time became editor of the high school newspaper. Turow attended Amherst College as an English major, where he began to write short stories and novels. Turow then went to Stanford University, where he taught and worked on the novel *The Way Things Are*. When he tried to market the novel, Turow met nothing but rejection. It was then that he decided to become an attorney. While serving as a prosecutor for the U.S. Attorney's office in Chicago, Turow began work on his first published novel, *Presumed Innocent*, Farrar, Straus, 1987. The novel was a huge success, both as a novel and a movie. Turlow's second book, *The Burden of Proof*, Farrar, Straus, 1990, was equally successful.

TYLER, ANNE

222 Tunbridge Rd., Baltimore, MD 21212

Tyler is a prominent author. For career credentials consult the portion of this book entitled "Notable Americans by Profession" in the Appendix. Within this portion, the list "Authors" describes requirements for inclusion in this volume.

TYRRELL, R. EMMETT JR.

The American Spectator, 1101 N. Highland St., Arlington, VA 22210 (703) 243-3733

Tyrrell's is regarded as an irreverent columnist characterized by hard sleuthing to support his libertarian-conservative views.

TYSON, LAURA D'ANDREA

Council of Economic Advisors, Old Executive Office Building, Washington D.C. 20500

BORN: 1947, Bayonne, N.J. ACHIEVEMENTS: Chief economic advisor to U.S. President Bill Clinton. STUDIED: Smith College, B.A., 1969; Massachusetts Institute of Technology, Ph.D., 1974.

Laura D'Andrea Tyson showed an affinity for mathematics at an early age. She graduated first in her class at Holy Trinity High School and was named "Miss Scholastic" at a local Junior Miss pageant. She changed her major from math to economics while at Smith College, where she earned her bachelor's degree. Tyson continued her education and earned her Ph.D. in economics at MIT. After college Tyson taught economics, first at Princeton University, then at the University of California, Berkeley. While at Berkeley, Tyson received Berkeley's Distinguished Teaching Award. In 1992, Tyson was tapped by the Clinton election campaign to advise on economic strategy. After his election, Clinton nominated Tyson to head the President's Council of Economic Advisors. In 1995 Tyson was named head of the National Economic Council, filling the vacancy left by Robert E. Rubin, who took over as secretary of treasury.

UHRY, ALFRED

Flora Roberts, 157 W. 57th St., New York, NY 10019

BORN: 1939, Atlanta. ACHIEVEMENTS: Pulitzer Prize, 1988, Academy Award, Best Screenplay, 1990, both for Driving Miss Daisy. STUDIED: Brown University, 1988.

Alfred Uhry's early work was primarily as a lyricist and librettist for a series of musicals. He was nominated for a Tony Award for *The Robber Bridegroom*, 1976. A dozen years later, his first and only full-length play, *Driving Miss Daisy*, 1987, won the Pulitzer Prize, and in 1990 he won an Academy Award for the film screenplay. The play, based on his childhood in Atlanta, and his grandmother's chauffeur of 25 years, is an understated study of people striving to maintain their equilibrium in an environment of prejudice and change.

ULRICH, LAUREL THATCHER

University of New Hampshire, Department of History, Durham, NH 03824 (603) 862-1764

BORN: Sugar City, Idaho. ACHIEVEMENTS: Bancroft Prize, History. STUDIED: University of New Hampshire, B.A., M.A., Ph.D.

Ulrich married a professor of chemical engineering who taught at the University of New Hampshire. She managed to obtain her B.A., M.A., and Ph.D. while raising five children. Her first book, *Good Wives: Image and Reality in the Lives of Women in Northern New England, 1650-1750*, Knopf, 1982, was published during this period. The book, based on the diary of an early New England midwife, explored the daily lives of the pioneers in the New England area. In 1985 Ulrich began teaching in a tenure-track position at the University of New Hampshire's history department, and in 1991 she won the Bancroft Prize for History.

UNRUH, JAMES A.

Unisys Corporation, P.O. Box 500, A2-15, Blue Bell, PA 19424 (215) 986-4011

ACHIEVEMENTS: CEO and chairman, Unisys; on the Board of Directors of Ameritech. STUDIED: Jamestown College, bachelor's degree; University of Denver, M.B.A.

Unruh has a long history of experience running high-tech companies. In 1980 he became vice president of finance at Memorex. He retained his position when Memorex was absorbed by Burroughs. In 1986 the Sperry Corporation merged with Burroughs and Unruh became an executive vice president of the merged company. In 1989 Unruh was named president and chief operating officer of Unisys. Unruh was promoted again in 1990, when he assumed the position of chief executive officer and chairman of the company. As CEO, Unruh led a restructuring and financial turnaround of Unisys. In 1995, Unruh was named to the Board of Directors of Ameritech, one of the world's largest communications companies.

UPDIKE, JOHN HOYER

Beverly Farms, MA 01915
BORN: 1932, Shillington, Pa. ACHIEVEMENTS: Pulitzer Prize, Rabbit is Rich, 1982. STUDIED: Harvard College, B.A., 1954; Ruskin School of Drawing and Fine Art at Oxford, 1954-55.

John Updike was a staff writer for the *New Yorker* magazine for two years before moving to Massachusetts in 1957 to write novels, poems and short stories. Known for his literary craftsmanship and exploration of middle class manners and mores, his novels are grouped around memorable characters like Henry Bech in *Bech: A Book*, 1970, and *Bech is Back*, 1982. His four *Rabbit* novels include *Rabbit Run*, 1960; *Rabbit Redux*, 1971; and *Rabbit is Rich*, 1981, which earned him the Pulitzer Prize. His other novels include *A Month of Sundays*, 1975; *Roger's Version*, 1986; *S*, 1988; and *Memories of the Ford Administration*, 1992.

URBANOWSKI, FRANK

MIT Press, 55 Hayward St., Cambridge, MA 02142
(617) 253-5646
BORN: 1936, Baltimore, Md. ACHIEVEMENTS: STUDIED: Virginia Polytechnic Institute, B.S., engineering; New School for Social Research; Columbia University.

The turnaround of MIT Press from a struggling university publishing house to the second largest in dollar volume among six competitors was led by Frank Urbanowski, its present director. With experience since 1962 in the college divisions of Ronald Press Company of New York, the MacMillan Company, Glencoe Press, in Beverly Hills Calif., and Princeton University Press, Urbanowski joined MIT in 1976. He guided the company's growth from $3 million to $17 million annually in the 1990s. Along the way he brought MIT Press into the modern age of computer science and artificial intelligence, and added an architecture series, which won the first Publisher's Achievement Award from the American Institute of Architects in 1982. The company concentrates on a "core list" of disciplines in its publishing efforts. Currently the list includes: environment, economics, computer science, architecture and design, and science, technology, and society. Urbanowski directs the publication of 180 hardcover and 80 paperback titles a year.

VALENTI, CARL

The Wall Street Journal, 200 Liberty St., New York, NY 10281-1099 (212) 416-2000
Valenti is a prominent publisher. For career credentials consult the portion of this book entitled "Notable Americans by Profession" in the Appendix. Within this portion, the list "Publishers" describes requirements for inclusion in this volume.

VAGELOS, PINDAROS ROY

Merck & Company, Inc., Box 100, 1 Merck Dr., White House Station, NJ 08889
BORN: 1929, Westfield, N.J. ACHIEVEMENTS: Chairman, Merck & Co. STUDIED: University of Pennsylvania, B.A., premed; Columbia University, M.D., medicine; many honorary degrees.

Dr. Vagelos was a successful surgeon at the National Institutes of Health from 1956 until 1966, and then an educator at Washington University School of Medicine in St. Louis, from 1966 until 1975. Joining Merck, Sharp & Dohme as president in 1976, another talent emerged: that of persuading top research scientists to join Merck, where they discovered many major drugs. Vagelos became president and chief executive officer of the company, now Merck & Company, in 1985, and chairman in 1986.

VARMUS, HAROLD ELIOT

University of California at San Francisco, 1001 Portrero Ave., San Francisco, CA 94110
BORN: 1939, Oceanside, N.Y. ACHIEVEMENTS: Nobel Prize in Physiology or Medicine (shared with John Michael Bishop), 1989; Albert Lasker Award, Albert and Mary Lasker Foundation; Passano Award, Passano Foundation; Alfred Sloan Award; Armand Hammer Prize; Shubitz Prize. STUDIED: Amherst College; Harvard University, Columbia University.

A discovery in cancer development that affected all future research on the normal growth of cells and the growth of tumors won the Nobel Prize for Harold Varmus and his colaureate. The pair discovered that the cancer-causing genes associated with a virus (oncogenes) did not come from the viral genes themselves, but resulted from altered cellular cells (proto-oncogenes) the virus had picked up.

VENTURI, ROBERT

Venturi, Rauch and Scott Brown, 4236 Main Street, Philadelphia, PA 19127
BORN: 1925. ACHIEVEMENTS: FAIA; Design Award, Progressive Architecture, 1967; Honor Award and Medal National AIA; notable works: Guild House, Philadelphia; Vanna Venturi House, Philadelphia; Wu Hall, Princeton University, Princeton, N.J. STUDIED: Princeton University.

Robert Venturi is one of the nation's most vehement and incisive polemicists for architectural pluralism and pragmatic realism, and one of the most energetic and imitated builders of the post-war epoch. His landmark work *Complexity and Contradiction in Architecture*, 1967, laid firm intellectual ground for a move past the idealized, exclusive credo of American functionalism, and toward an eclectic, unfussy "architecture that works." "Main street," he has written, "is almost night." There is more to be learned from the chaotic, often rococo building legacy of the baby boom, he argues in *Learning From Las Vegas*, than the stark, cool towers of the International School: "Less," he says, "is a bore." The "ordinary" structures that middle class America has built for itself, he believes are vastly more functional than the majority of academic modernist efforts, in that they attend to creative comforts without embarrassment or pretension. Surprisingly, he rejects the conscious historicism of the post-modern camp, and works toward an architecture that will embody the functionalistic rigor of modernism, while dispensing with its hidden minimalistic agenda. His 1960 Guild House, an apartment complex for the elderly, for instance, was worked analytically from the real needs and concerns of the housebound occupants. The polite symmetry of the main facade is sacrificed to ungainly rows of large, industrial window units to draw the sun and facilitate street watching.

VICCELLO, LT. GEN. HENRY, JR.

Office of the Secretary, Pentagon, Washington, DC 20301-1155 (703) 545-6700
Viccello is a prominent military leader and general in the United States Air Force. For career credentials consult the portion of this book entitled "Notable Americans by Profession" in the Appendix. Within this portion, the list "Military Leaders" describes requirements for inclusion in this volume.

VINGE, JOAN D.

26 Douglas Rd., Chappaqua, NY 10514
Vinge is a prominent author. For career credentials consult the portion of this book entitled "Notable Americans by Profession" in the Appendix. Within this portion, the list "Authors" describes requirements for inclusion in this volume.

VINROOT, RICHARD A.

325 Cherokee Place, Charlotte, NC 28207 (704) 336-2244
BORN: 1941, Charlotte, N.C. ACHIEVEMENTS: Mayor of Charlotte, NC; Bronze Star, U.S. Army, 1968. STUDIED: University of North Carolina-Chapel Hill, B.S., 1963; University of North Carolina-Chapel Hill, J.D., 1966.
After completing his education, Vinroot entered the U.S. Army in 1967, saw service in Vietnam, and won a Bronze Star in 1968. Vinroot returned to Charlotte after his military service and joined the law firm Robinson, Bradshaw, & Hinson in 1969. Vinroot, a member of the Mecklenburg County Republican Party,

started his political career as a member of the Charlotte City Council in 1983. He served as a council member until 1991, when he was elected Mayor.

VISE, DAVID A.

The Washington Post, 1150 15th St., NW., Washington, DC 20071 (202) 334-6000
Vise is a prominent journalist. For career credentials consult the portion of this book entitled "Notable Americans by Profession" in the Appendix. Within this portion, the list "Journalists" describes requirements for inclusion in this volume.

VOINOVICH, GEORGE V.

State of Ohio, Office of the Governor, Columbus, OH 43266
BORN: 1936, Cleveland, Ohio. ACHIEVEMENTS: Outstanding Public Service Award, National Association of Public Officials; All-Pro City Management Team, City and State magazine; member, National Governors' Association Executive Committee, Committee on Human Resources. STUDIED: Ohio University, B.A., government; Ohio State University, J.D., law; Ohio University, LL.D (honorary).
After 10 years as mayor of Cleveland, Republican George Voinovich became the 65th governor of Ohio, and received his second term in 1995. He is noted for aggressively creating jobs, reforming the educational system, assisting families and children, and tightening up state government. In his first term he cut government costs and held Ohio's budget to its lowest growth rate in 25 years. Among his major credits were stopping the drilling for oil in Lake Erie, and being the prime mover behind the creation of the Ohio Environmental Protection Agency.

VOULKOS, PETER

951 62nd St., Oakland, CA 94608
BORN: 1924. ACHIEVEMENTS: Guggenheim Fellowship; Creative Arts Award for Sculpture, Brandeis University; collections: Museum of Modern Art, New York City; Whitney Museum, New York City; exhibitions: Oakland Museum; San Francisco Museum of Modern Art. STUDIED: Montana State University; California College of Arts and Crafts.
Peter Voulkos was an abstract expressionist painter in the 1950s, but after studying ceramics he turned to sculpture, helping to revolutionize the use of clay by freeing it from its limits as a craft. An abstract style in naturally-colored fired clay suggested innumerable possibilities for the medium and inspired many of his pupils. As an educator, he has wielded a good deal of influence, inspiring the "Funk Art" of Robert Arneson and James Melchert, among others. While a teacher at Berkeley, he made small-scale metal pieces that led to large outdoor sculptures such as the 30-foot-high untitled bronze commissioned by the San Francisco Hall of Justice. The three-year project is an example of the continuous energy in his work, a sturdy tower inhabited by twisting and turning organic bronze forms.

WAGONER, DAN

c/o Dan Wagoner and Dancers, 476 Broadway, 4th Floor, New York, NY 10013 (212) 334-1880

BORN: 1932, Springfield, W.Va. ACHIEVEMENTS: Notable ballets: An Occasion for Some Revolutionary Gestures; Spiked Sonata; Brambles; Changing Your Mind; Seven Tears. STUDIED: West Virginia University, B.S., pharmacy, 1955; Connecticut College summer dance school; Martha Graham Dance School.

A farm boy, and the last of ten children, Dan Wagoner became a full-time dancer only after graduating from college with a degree in pharmacy. Subsequently, dancing with Paul Taylor, Merce Cunningham, and Martha Graham, he carried their influences throughout his career, with Cunningham's random structure and Taylor's mordant view of modern city life perfectly supplementing Wagoner's love of his farmland roots. He formed his own small group in 1969 and has choreographed for it ever since, using music,—for example intricate piano variations on *Yankee Doodle Dandy*,—to highlight the sense of community always found in his work. After staging a number of works for British companies and with one of his pieces, *Changing Your Mind*, entering the repertory of London Contemporary Dance Theatre, in 1988 he accepted the post of artistic director of the theater.

WALKER, ALICE M

G.K. Hall, 70 Lincoln St., Boston, MA 02111

BORN: 1944, Eatonton, Ga. ACHIEVEMENTS: Pulitzer Prize, The Color Purple, 1982. STUDIED: Spelman College, 1961-1963; Sarah Lawrence College, B.A., 1965.

Walker's poetry, short stories and novels vividly depict the lives of southern blacks. Born into a sharecropper family in Georgia, she registered voters in the civil rights movement while in college. Those experiences were the basis for her novels *The Third Life of Grange Copeland*, 1970, and *Meridian*, 1976, and for her collection of stories about black women *In Love and Trouble*, 1973. She won the Pulitzer Prize for literature for her third novel *The Color Purple*, 1982, which was made into a film in 1985. Her later novels include *The Temple of My Familiar*, 1989, and *Possessing the Secret Joy*, 1992.

WALKER, NORMAN

200 West 79th St., New York, NY 10024 (212) 799-9123

BORN: 1934, New York City. ACHIEVEMENTS: Notable ballets: Four Cantos; Crossed Encounter; Baroque Concerto; Cowboy in Black; Splendors and Obscurities; Clear Song After Rain; Reflections (for television); Triondo di Afrodite; A Certain Slant of Light; A Broken Twig. STUDIED: New York School of Performing Arts, City Colleges of New York, B.A., drama, 1956; May O'Donnell, Gertrude Shurr, Robert Joffrey, Fernand Nault, Martha Graham, Valentina Pereyaslavec schools.

Widely known and respected for his solos and duets, which show his lyrical talent and keen dramatic sense, Norman Walker is also a popular teacher whose first assignment was with the School of Performing Arts in 1956. That same year he took a two-year leave from the school for service in the U.S. Army, during which he became a featured dancer in Army shows. He has danced and choreographed in musicals staged by the Summer Dance Festival at Utah State University, and the troupe he formed in 1960 has appeared three times at the Jacob's Pillow Dance Festival. He currently is a member of the Department of Performing Arts at Delphi University in Garden City, New York.

WALLACE, (MIKE) MYRON LEON

CBS News 524 West 57th St., New York, NY 10019

BORN: 1918, Brookline, Mass. ACHIEVEMENTS: Author, Mike Wallace Asks, 1958; Close Encounters, 1984. STUDIED: University of Michigan, 1939.

Right out of college Mike Wallace's distinct voice led him to a career in radio as an announcer and actor before the intervention of World War II. After the war he worked successfully in Chicago and New York on a series of talk shows for both radio and the emerging medium of television, before becoming a special correspondent for CBS. It was there, in 1968, that he was offered the chance to co-edit and anchor what would become the most respected news hour in television history, *60 Minutes*. Since then his aggressive interviewing style has been admired as well as copied by many less successful news shows.

WALLOP, MALCOLM

U.S. Senate, 237 SROB, Washington, DC 20510-5001 (202) 224-6441

Wallop is a prominent political leader. For career credentials consult the portion of this book entitled "Notable Americans by Profession" in the Appendix. Within this portion, the list "Political Leaders" describes requirements for inclusion in this volume.

WALLER, ROBERT JAMES

c/o Warner Books, Inc., 666 Fifth Avenue, New York, NY

BORN: 1939, Rockford, Iowa. STUDIED: University of Iowa, student; University of Northern Iowa, B.A., mathematics, economics; Indiana University, Ph.D., economics.

Waller was a 52-year-old professor at a little-known college in Iowa in 1991. A bolt of creative lightning struck him on a visit to Madison County, Iowa. The next day he started writing a story that would become, in one critic's estimation a "yuppie women's porno" novel, *The Bridges of Madison County*. He wrote continuously for fourteen days, showed the finished novel to friends—one of whom passed it on to a New York agent—and soon received a $32,000 advance from Warner Books for the right to publish. The book, about a four-day affair between a married woman and a photographer, at the conclusion of which the woman, though deeply in love with the photographer, dutifully decides to remain with her husband, came out and leaped onto the best-seller lists almost at once. By November 1993 it had sold more than 4.1 million copies. In addition to *Bridges*, Waller has written three books of essays and stories, and another novel, *Slow Waltz in Cedar Bend*, which soon was outselling *Bridges* two to one, although the books carry similar story lines, settings, and characters. He has also recorded a 10-song album for Atlantic, *The Ballads of Madison County*, four songs of which were written by him.

WALSH, MICHAEL

Tenneco Inc., Tenneco Building, Houston, TX 66002 (713) 757-2131

Walsh is a prominent business leader. For career credentials consult the portion of this book entitled "Notable Americans by Profession" in the Appendix. Within this portion, the list "Business Leaders" describes requirements for inclusion in this volume.

WALTERS, BARBARA

Barwell Productions, 825 7th Ave. Fl 3, New York, NY 10019-6014
BORN: 1931, Boston. ACHIEVEMENTS: Author How to Talk with Practically Anybody about Practically Anything; Television Academy of Arts & Sciences Emmy Award, 1975; Overseas Press Club President's Award, 1988; Woman of the Year in Communications, 1974; named to the Television Academy Hall of Fame, 1990; International Women's Media Foundation Lifetime Achievement Award, 1992. STUDIED: Sarah Lawrence College, 1953.

Though best known for her successful *Barbara Walters Specials*, which began running on the ABC network in 1976, Walters began her career as a writer for NBC's

Author Robert James Waller.

Today Show in 1961. Ten years later she was given her own show, but her real fame came in 1976 when she switched to ABC and became the first woman to co-anchor an evening newscast at the unheard of salary of $1 million a year. Her co-anchor position with Harry Reasoner failed, however, and she joined *20/20* in 1979 opposite Hugh Downs, who had been her boss at the *Today Show* 14 years earlier.

WALTERS, DAVID

Office of the Governor, State Capitol, Rm. 212, Oklahoma City, OK 73105 (405) 521-2342

Gov. Walters of Oklahoma is a prominent political leader. For career credentials consult the portion of this book entitled "Notable Americans by Profession" in the Appendix. Within this portion, the list "Political Leaders" describes requirements for inclusion in this volume.

WARD, GEOFFREY CHAMPION

1 West 85th St., New York, NY 10024
BORN: 1940, Newark, Ohio. ACHIEVEMENTS: Christopher Award, The Christophers; National Book Critic Award; Francis Parkman Prize, Society of American Historians; Biography Prize, Los Angeles Times; Ohiona Award; Writers Guild of America Award; Emmy Award (with others), Individual Achievement in Informational Programming; New England Booksellers Award; American Book Award. STUDIED: Oberlin College, B.A., history.

Geoffrey Ward is a celebrated Public Broadcasting consultant and writer, author of eight books, and co-founder and editor of the magazine *Audience* in Boston. Ward began his career as a writer for Encyclopedia Britannica in Chicago, at age 24, and became picture editor before moving to *Reader's Digest* in 1968, as art director and writer in the General Books Division. After four years at *Audience*, he became managing editor of *American Heritage* magazine in 1976, and editor in 1978. He has been the "Life and Times" columnist for the magazine since 1982. Hooking up with PBS in 1991, he became senior creative consultant for *The American Experience* episodes: *Coney Island, The Donner Party, FDR*, in which he appeared, *Duke Ellington*, and *The Kennedys*. He worked on the PBS series *The Civil War, Baseball* with Ken Burns, and the specials *The Statue of Liberty, Huey Long, Thomas Hart Benton, Lindbergh, Nixon, Empire of the Air: The Men Who Made Radio*, and *George Marshall and the American Century*. Among his eight books are *A First-Class Temperament: The Emergence of Franklin Roosevelt; The Civil War*, with Ken and Ric Burns; *American Originals: The Private Lives of Some Singular Men and Women*; and, with Ken Burns, *Baseball: An Illustrated History*.

WARNER, JOHN WILLIAM

2225 Russell Senate Office Building, Washington, DC 20510-4601 (202) 224-2023
BORN: 1927, Amherst County, Va. ACHIEVEMENTS: Secretary of the Navy, 1972-1974. STUDIED: Washington and Lee University, B.S., 1949; University of Virginia Law School, 1953.
A veteran of both the U.S. Navy and Marine Corps, John Warner has been deeply involved in issues of national defense and foreign policy, but is perhaps most widely known for his brief marriage to the actress Elizabeth Taylor. Warner won election to the U.S. Senate from Virginia in 1978, and is the second-most senior member of the Armed Services Committee. Outside the Senate he has served in a number of special assignments for national security, including representing the Department of Defense at the Law of the Sea talks, co-chairman of the Nunn-Warner Working Group on Nuclear Risk Reduction, and leadership of the U.S delegation to the Incidents at Sea Conference with the Soviet Navy in 1972.

WARNES, JENNIFER

RCA Records, 1133 Sixth Ave., New York, NY 10019 (212) 930-4000
BORN: 1947, Orange County, Calif. ACHIEVEMENTS: Grammy (with Joe Cocker), Best Pop Vocal-Duo or Group, Up Where We Belong; Grammy (with Bill Medley), Best Pop Vocal-Duo or Group, (I've Had) the Time of My Life, 1987.
With 25 years of professional singing to her credit, Jennifer Warnes is best known for her Grammy award winning duet, *Up Where We Belong*, which she sang with Joe Cocker in the soundtrack for the movie *An Officer and a Gentleman*. In the 1960s, she starred in the Los Angeles production of *Hair*, and was a regular on the hit television show *The Smothers Brothers Comedy Hour*. In addition to her Grammy, Warnes also won praise in 1987 for her solo renditions of Leonard Cohen's songs on her album *Famous Blue Raincoat*, and for her duet with former Righteous Brother Bill Medley, *(I've Had) the Time of My Life*, from the film *Dirty Dancing*.

WASHINGTON, DENZEL

Sandy Rice PMK, Public Relations Inc., 955 S. Carillo, Suite 200, Los Angeles, CA 90048
BORN: 1954, Mt. Vernon, N.Y. ACHIEVEMENTS: Golden Globe Award, Best Supporting Actor, Glory, 1989, Academy Award, Best Supporting Actor, Glory, 1990. STUDIED: Fordham University, B.A. in journalism; American Conservatory Theatre, San Francisco, studied acting with Wynn Handman, N.Y.
Denzel Washington worked as a drama instructor before deciding to become an actor himself. He acted in several television movies in the late 1970s before debuting in the movie, *Carbon Copy* in 1981. Washington played Dr. Phillip Chandler from 1982 until 1988 on the television series, *St. Elsewhere*. In the mean-

time, Washington established himself as a movie actor of merit with many success on the silver screen, including parts in *A Soldier's Story*, in 1984, *Glory*, and *Mo' Better Blues*, in 1990. In 1992, Washington played the title role in Spike Lee's movie, *Malcolm X*, a role he had originally played on Broadway in the play, *When the Chickens Came Home to Roost*, in 1981. Now an established box-office draw, Washington has appeared in the hit films *Philadelphia* (1993), *The Pelican Brief* (1993), *Ricochet* (1993), and *Crimson Tide* (1995). Washington is a sports enthusiast and coaches his son's little league team.

WASSERSTEIN, WENDY

International Creative Management, 40 W. 57th St., New York, NY 10019
BORN: 1950, New York City. ACHIEVEMENTS: Antoinette Perry Award and Pulitzer Prize, Best Play, The Heidi Chronicles, 1989. STUDIED: Mount Holyoke College, B.A., 1971; City University of New York, M.A., 1973; Yale University School of Drama, M.F.A., 1976.
Wendy Wasserstein's 1989 drama *The Heidi Chronicles*, about a single woman searching for identity in society and life, won the Pulitzer and Tony awards for best play, and established her as an advocate of women's causes. Feminist concerns and the search for identity are themes in most of her plays, which include *Uncommon Women and Others*, 1977; *Isn't It Romantic*, 1983; *Tender Offer*, 1983; *Miami*, 1986; *Smart Women/Brilliant Choices in Urban Blight*, 1988; and *The Sisters Rosensweig*, 1992. She also authored a television play, *The Sorrows of Gin*, in 1979.

WATERMAN, ROBERT H. JR.

c/o Harper, 10 East 53rd. St., New York, NY 10022 (212) 207-7000
ACHIEVEMENTS: Co-author of In Search of Excellence: Lessons from America's Best Run Companies. STUDIED: Colorado School of Mines, engineering; Stanford University, M.B.A.
Robert Waterman Jr. left McKinsey and Co., where he had risen to the position of senior director, in 1986. After leaving McKinsey and Co., Waterman became chairman of Waterman & Miller Inc., and later The Waterman Group Inc., a research, writing, and consulting business. In addition to his consulting business, Waterman is co-author of the best-seller *In Search of Excellence: Lessons from America's Best Run Companies*. Waterman also authored *The Renewal Factor: How the Best Get and Keep the Competitive Edge* and *Adhocracy: The Power to Change*. In 1990 Waterman became a director of ASK Computer Systems, which provides management information systems to manufacturing companies.

WEAVER, SIGOURNEY

International Creative Management, 40 West 57th St., New York, NY 10012
BORN: 1949, New York City. ACHIEVEMENTS: Golden Globe Award, Best Actress, Gorillas in the Mist, 1989; Golden Globe Award, Best Supporting Actress, Working Girl, 1989. STUDIED: Sarah Lawrence College; Stanford University, B.A., English, 1971; Yale University, M.A., drama, 1974.

Sigourney Weaver captured the imaginations of moviegoers in 1979 when she was pursued by the ultimate space monster in *Alien*. Originally named Susan, Weaver took her stage name from a character in *The Great Gatsby*. The daughter of Sylvester Weaver, a television executive, and Elizabeth Inglis, an actress, Weaver began acting professionally in the early 1970s. She has been a member of several California theater groups and acted in television commercials. Although she has won her greatest critical praise for her 1988 role in *Gorillas in the Mist*, she is probably better known for her work in the science fiction/fantasy genre. Weaver repeated her success with *Alien* in two sequels: *Aliens*, in 1986, and *Alien 3*, in 1992, which she also co-produced. She is also well known for her role as Dana Barrett in the movies, *Ghostbusters*, in 1984, and *Ghostbusters II*, in 1989.

WEBB, WELLINGTON E.

City-County Bldg., 1437 Bannock St., Rm. 350, Denver, CO 80202 (303) 430-2400

Webb is a prominent political leader. For career credentials consult the portion of this book entitled "Notable Americans by Profession" in the Appendix. Within this portion, the list "Political Leaders" describes requirements for inclusion in this volume.

WEESE, HARRY MOHR

Harry Weese and Associates, 10 West Hubbard Street, Chicago, IL 60610 312) 467-7030
BORN: 1915, Chicago. ACHIEVEMENTS: FAIA; Merit Award, American Society of Landscape Architects, 1981; Merit Award, AIA, D.C. Chapter, 1983; notable works: Hawaii State Capitol, Honolulu (with Belt, Lemmon and Lo); United States Court of Claims Building, Washington, D.C.; George Washington University, Washington, D.C. STUDIED: M.I.T.

Although he has often argued that the main responsibility of architecture is innovation, Harry Weese's own work is typified by a thorough, perfectionist attention to design details. His success derives from his willingness to suspend all technical and aesthetic preconceptions and approach each design problem freshly. His 1967 renovation of Louis Sullivan and Dankmar Adler's landmark Auditorium Theater in his native Chicago launched a long and distinguished career as a preservationist. His gift for designing and reworking dignified, substantial public buildings led to his appointment as chief architect for Washington D.C.'s rail transit system. The fundamental challenge of that commission, he felt, was to establish a uniform and quickly identifiable style for the system's wide variety of terminals. This style would extend beyond mere cosmetics to include the commuter's entire sequence of experiences. His ingenious solution was to design a set of functional station sub-units which individual designers could shuffle as needed, and so create custom yet cost-effective terminals.

WEGMAN, WILLIAM

431 E. Sixth St., New York, NY

BORN: 1943. ACHIEVEMENTS: Fellowship, John Simon Guggenheim Memorial Foundation; National Endowment for the Arts grant; collections: Museum of Modern Art; Whitney Museum of American Art; exhibitions: Museum of Modern Art; Whitney Museum Biennial. STUDIED: Massachusetts College of Art, Boston; University of Illinois.

William Wegman's video tapes, drawings and photographs are humorous, often parody works, characterized by informality and deliberate artlessness. *Madam I'm Adam*, for example, in 1970, was a "visual palindrome"—two identical photographs, one printed backwards. In 1975 he began a four-year series of black-and-white over-exposed or under-exposed photographs, with comments drawn directly on the prints. He is known for photographs and video tapes which feature his dog, Man Ray, which some say was his alter ego, in comical costumes and situations. He made large-scale color Polaroid prints of Man Ray, which were published in a book in 1982, the year the dog died, entitled *Man's Best Friend*.

WEIDENBAUM, MURRAY LEW

Washington University Center for the Study of American Business, 1 Brookings Dr., Box 1208, St. Louis, MO 63130
BORN: 1927, Bronx, N.Y. ACHIEVEMENTS: Edward Mallinckrodt Distinguished University Professor, Washington University, St. Louis; director, Center for the Study of American Business; Townshend Harris Medal, City College Alumni Association; Alexander Hamilton Medal, U.S. Department of the Treasury; director, NASA Economic Research Program; chairman, Council of Economic Advisers. STUDIED: City College of New York, Columbia University, Princeton University.

An economist who likes to write, Weidenbaum has many interests: the federal budget, government bailouts of business, the military, and government regulations. He wrote early in his writing career that budget reform fails because the public does not understand either the budgetary system or how government programs are funded, reviewed, and controlled. He maintains that bailouts of troubled companies by the government increases federal borrowing and raises interest rates, while eliminating businesses' risks and costs. On the military, he holds that military power no longer is an effective weapon because modern weaponry is so destructive. Government regulations, he believes, hamper business, encourage inflation and raise the prices of goods and services to the consumer. As a corollary to these theories, Weidenbaum has also taken an interest in government planning He and Linda Rockwood revealed their govenmental theories in an article in a paper entitled *Corporate Planning Versus Government Planning*. They wrote that although executives are familiar with governmental plans, they are so complicated that most members of Congress fail to understand them. The authors conclude that since government cannot manage itself well, they cannot successfully plan the economy.

WEIL, CYNTHIA

c/o MCA Records, Inc., 70 Universal City Plaza, Universal City, CA 91608 (213) 508-4000

Weil is a prominent composer. For career credentials consult the portion of this book entitled "Notable Americans by Profession" in the Appendix. Within this portion, the list "Composers" describes requirements for inclusion in this volume.

WEIL, LOUIS A. III

Phoenix Newspapers, Inc., 120 East Van Buren St., Phoenix, AZ 85004 (602) 271-7300
BORN: 1941, Grand Rapids, Mich. ACHIEVEMENTS: Honorary doctor of letters degrees, Mercy College, Dobbs Ferry, N.Y., Grand Valley State University, Allendale, Mich. STUDIED: Indiana University, B.A., English.
Once a U.S. Naval officer stationed in Ethiopia, Louis Weill III is now publisher and chief executive officer of *The Arizona Republic*. He began his 29-year career in newspapering in 1966 at the *Port Huron (Mich.) Times Herald*, where he worked in circulation and advertising for two years. He next joined the *Lafayette (Ind.) Journal & Courier* as personnel director. He then became publisher of the *Journal & Courier* and remained there until the paper was sold to Gannet Company, Inc. After six years in the Gannet corporate fold he was named president of the *Detroit News*, later becoming president and publisher. In 1989 he became publisher of *Time* magazine He returned to the newspaper business in 1991, when he took up his present post at *The Arizona Republic*. Among many memberships in civic groups, Weil serves on the Cronkite Endowment board of trustees. The endowment is a part of the Walter Cronkite School of Journalism and Telecommunications at Arizona State University.

WEILL, SANFORD I.

65 East 55th St., New York, NY 10022
BORN: Brooklyn, N.Y. ACHIEVEMENTS: Co-founder, Shearson Lehman Brothers. STUDIED: Cornell University.
In 1955, while a senior at Cornell University, Sanford Weill suffered two serious setbacks. First, he had a personal family crisis. Then, all the brokerage firms he had applied to rejected him. Weill took a job as a messenger for Bear, Stearns & Company. The next year they hired him as a stockbroker. By 1960 Weill saved enough to form a partnership in investment banking and brokerage. In 1967 the partnership purchased a money management company. Weill continued to progress until 1974, when he acquired Shearson, Hammill & Company. Shearson was finally bought by the American Express Company in 1980 for $930 million.

WEINBERG, STEVEN

University of Texas, Department of Astronomy, Austin, TX
BORN: 1933, New York City. ACHIEVEMENTS: Nobel Prize in Physics (shared with Sheldon Isaac Glashow and Abdus Salam, Pakistan), 1979; J.R. Oppenheimer Prize; Dannie Heineman Prize, American Physical Society; American Institute of Physics Prize; U.S. Steel Foundation Science Writing Prize; Elliott Cresson Medal, Franklin Institute. STUDIED: Harvard University; California Institute of Technology.
Co-creater of the Weinberg-Salam theory on electromagnetic interaction between elementary particles, Steven Weinberg was awarded the Nobel prize with Abdus Salam and Sheldon Isaac Glashow. Glashow extended the theory by defining a new characteristic to the unity the team discovered between an electromagnetic force and a "weak" nuclear force—a feeble short-range force responsible for radioactive decay in some atomic nuclei. Glashow's concept, that both are facets of the same phenomena, a phenomena he named "charm," has been widely used since in work on the quark theory.

WEINER, TIM

Philadelphia Inquirer, 400 N. Broad St., Philadelphia, PA 19130-4015 (215) 854-2000
Weiner is a prominent journalist. For career credentials consult the portion of this book entitled "Notable Americans by Profession" in the Appendix. Within this portion, the list "Journalists" describes requirements for inclusion in this volume.

WELCH, JOHN FRANCIS JR.

General Electric Company, 3135 Easton Turnpike, Fairfield, CT 06431
BORN: 1935, Salem, Mass. ACHIEVEMENTS: CEO, General Electric Co. STUDIED: University of Massachusetts, B.S., chemical engineering; University of Illinois, M.S., Ph.D., chemical engineering.
John Welch Jr. is celebrated in the business world for taking General Electric, a fat and flabby industrial giant, and turning it into an organization known for its initiative. Named GE's chairman and chief executive officer in 1981 at age 46, he was the youngest ever to hold those positions at GE. Once at the helm, he mandated that the company be number one or two in everything it did in plastics, materials, and consumer goods and services. Anything that failed to perform was sold, resulting in 132,000 layoffs, 73 plant closings, more than 200 sales of products or businesses, and only one acquisition, RCA in 1985.

WELD, WILLIAM F.

Executive Department, State House, Boston, MA 02133 (617) 727-3600
BORN: 1945, Smithtown, N.Y. ACHIEVEMENTS: Governor of Massachusetts, U.S. Attorney for Massachusetts. STUDIED: Harvard College, 1966; Oxford University, 1967; Harvard Law School, 1970.
After graduating from Harvard Law School in 1970, Bill Weld worked as a law clerk with the state of Massachusett's Supreme Judicial Court. A year later he entered private practice with the firm Hill & Barlow in Boston. In 1974 Weld was associate minority council to the U.S. House Judiciary Committee during the Watergate impeachment inquiry. Weld was named U.S. Attorney for Massachusetts in 1981 by Ronald Reagan. As U.S. Attorney, Weld won impressive conviction rates in political corruption cases, convicted and jailed leaders of the Boston Mafia, and imposed fines on several banks for money laundering. Weld was appointed U.S. Assistant Attorney General, in charge

of the Criminal Division, by Ronald Reagan in 1986. Weld was elected governor of Massachusetts in 1990, and was re-elected to a second term in 1994.

WELDON, BARBARA

6131 Romany Dr., San Diego, CA 92120
BORN: 1931. ACHIEVEMENTS: W.A. Paton Prize, National Academy of Design; San Diego Watercolor Society, 1st Award; collections: San Diego Museum of Art; Bank of America World Headquarters, San Francisco; exhibitions: San Diego Museum of Art; Laguna Beach Museum of Art. STUDIED: San Diego State University; University of California, San Diego
Weldon is primarily a non-representational painter and also a printmaker. Her earlier works are on paper, with many lyrical, transparent watercolor washes and layers of rice-paper collage. Among her influences are Matisse, Hofmann, Diebenkorn and Rauschenberg. Recent mixed-media collage paintings use a grid pattern, and occasionally figuration. Many of the newer works are large-scale canvases, but she also continues to work on rag papers. Portions of earlier paintings and intaglios frequently appear in the layers of collage in recent paintings. Work since 1985 includes the *Tango* series, utilizing a reductive palette of black and silver; the *Soniat* series, named for a restored mansion she visited in New Orleans; and the *Firebird* series, containing brilliant colors in shapes resembling feathered forms in beige fields.

WELTY, EUDORA

1119 Pinehurst St., Jackson, MS
BORN: 1909, Jackson, Miss. ACHIEVEMENTS: Pulitzer Prize, The Optimist's Daughter, 1972; Medal of Freedom, 1980. STUDIED: Mississippi State College for Women, University of Wisconsin, Columbia Graduate School of Business.
Eudora Welty's writings, typically set in Mississippi, explore either complex family relationships or isolated lives. She has published seven volumes of short stories, including *The Golden Apples*, 1949; *The Bride of the Innisfallen*, 1955; and *A Sweet Devouring*, 1969. However, she is best known for her novels such as *Delta Wedding*, 1946; *Losing Battles*, 1970; and the Pulitzer Prize-winning *The Optimist's Daughter*, 1972. She was awarded the Presidential Medal of Freedom in 1980, when she published her collected stories. Her autobiography, *One Writer's Beginnings*, was published in 1984.

WENDT, GEORGE

Brillstein Company, 9200 Sunset Blvd., Rm 428, Los Angeles, CA 90069
BORN: 1948, Chicago. ACHIEVEMENTS: Emmy Award nominations, Best Supporting Actor, Cheers. STUDIED: Rockhurst College, economics, 1971.
George Wendt is an alumni of the *Cheers* television series. Playing the part of Norm Peterson, Wendt appeared on the series from 1982 until the final episode. Wendt was a member of the Second City improvisational comedy troupe for six years, honing his skills in comedy. In addition to *Cheers* he also appeared in the series *Making the Grade*, 1982. Wendt played parts in the films *Somewhere In Time*, 1980; *My Bodyguard*,

1980; *Airplane II: The Sequel*, 1982; *Dreamscape*, 1984; *Fletch*, 1984; *Thief of Hearts*, 1984; and others. He also played the part of Mr. Sweeney in the television movie *The Rating Game*, 1984.

WESCOTT, ROBERT

Council of Economic Advisors, Old Executive Office Bld., Washington, DC 20500
Wescott is a prominent economist. For career credentials consult the portion of this book entitled "Notable Americans by Profession" in the Appendix. Within this portion, the list "Economists" describes requirements for inclusion in this volume.

WESTON, BRETT

228 Vista Verde, Box 694, Carmel Valley, CA 93924
BORN: 1911. ACHIEVEMENTS: Fellowship, John Simon Guggenheim Memorial Foundation; collections: Museum of Modern Art; San Francisco Museum of Modern Art; exhibitions: San Francisco Museum of Modern Art.
Brett Weston began photographing at age 13, while on a trip in Mexico with his father, the well-known photographer Edward Weston. Afterwards he learned photography from his father, with whom he shared a studio from 1928 until 1935. Abstracts of nature and landscapes are large-format silver prints. Although primarily influenced by his father, Brett Weston's photographs have more of a sharp tonality than his father's.

WESTON, COLE

c/o Weston Gallery, P.O. Box 655, Sixth Ave., Carmel CA 93921
BORN: 1919. ACHIEVEMENTS: Collections: Philadelphia Museum of Art; Fogg Art Museum; exhibitions: Witkin Gallery; Focus Gallery. STUDIED: Cornish Institute.
Cole Weston began a photographic career in the U.S. Navy, then worked for *Life* magazine. In 1946 he began working with his father, photographer Edward Weston, until the latter's death in 1958. Executor of Edward's estate, he has since spent a great deal of time printing his father's negatives. Influenced by the work of his father and brother Brett, his photographs continue Weston's concerns, with views of Point Lobos and Big Sur country. He, however, works in color, rendering sensuous landscapes in subdued and delicate earth tones. These large-format dye transfer prints are in precisely sharp focus. He has produced very few black-and-white photographs.

WETTIG, PATRICIA

c/o Barkin, Perren, Schwager, 5855 Topanga Canyon, Suite 410, Woodland Hills 91367 (818)719-9020
BORN: 1951, Cincinnati. ACHIEVEMENTS: Emmy Award, Best Supporting Actress in a Drama, thirtysomething, 1988; Emmy Award, Best Actress in a Drama, thirtysomething, 1990; Golden Globe Award, Best Actress in a Drama, thirtysomething, 1990. STUDIED: Graduated from Temple University, attended Ohio Wesleyan University and University of Aberdeen, Scotland.

Patricia Wettig is an actress with experience on the stage, television, and in films. Wettig is a veteran of the stage, making her Broadway debut in 1980 at the Circle Repertory Theatre in the play *Innocent Thoughts, Harmless Intentions*. She appeared at the Circle Repertory Theatre in many plays throughout 1980 and 1981, including *The Woolgatherer, Childe Byron, A Tale Told, Threads,* and *The Diviners*. Wettig played the parts of Joanne McFadden and Joanne Morrison in the television series *St. Elsewhere* (1986-87). She began the series *thirtysomething* in 1987, playing the part of Nancy Weston. She continued in the series until 1991, winning two Emmy Awards and a Golden Globe. After thirtysomething she appeared in *St. Elsewhere, L.A. Law* and other television shows including a Stephen King made-for-TV movie, *Langoliers*, aired in 1995.

WHITE, BETTY

William Morris Agency, 151 El Camino, Beverly Hills, CA 90212
BORN: 1922, Oak Park, Ill. ACHIEVEMENTS: Emmy Awards, The Mary Tyler Moore Show, 1975 and 1976; Daytime Emmy, Just Men, 1982.
Betty White began her acting career on radio, playing parts in *The FBI, The Great Gildersleeve,* and *Blondie*. She came to television early on, playing in the series *Life with Elizabeth*, 1953-55. She followed this early effort with the television series *Date with the Angels,* 1957-58; *The Betty White Show,* 1957; *The Mary Tyler Moore Show,* 1973-77; *The Betty White Show,* 1977-78; *Mama's Family,* 1983-84; and, finally, as the innocent Rose in *The Golden Girls*, on the air since 1985. White was also a regular in summer-stock stage acting, appearing in the plays *Guys and Dolls, Take Me Along, The King and I,* and *Hello Dolly*. She is also very active in animal rights as a director of the Greater Los Angeles Zoo Association, and as a member of the American Humane Association.

WHITE, KARYN

c/o Warner Brothers Records, 3300 Warner Blvd., Burbank, CA 91510 (818) 846-9090
White is a prominent vocalist. For career credentials consult the portion of this book entitled "Notable Americans by Profession" in the Appendix. Within this portion, the list "Vocalists" describes requirements for inclusion in this volume.

WHITE, MICHAEL R.

City Hall, 601 Lakeside Avenue, Cleveland, OH 44114 (216) 664-2220
BORN: 1951, Cleveland. ACHIEVEMENTS: Mayor, Cleveland; Board of Trustees, U.S. Conference of Mayors. STUDIED: Ohio State University, B.A., education, 1973; M.P.A, public administration, 1974.
Michael White began his public service as aide to Columbus, Ohio Mayor Tom Moody. He returned to Cleveland in 1977, and was elected to the Cleveland City Council. He was chair of the Community Development Committee and also served on the Finance Com-

mittee. In 1984 White was appointed to the Ohio State Senate. He was re-elected to the Senate for a full term in 1986. While in the Senate, White served on the Judiciary, Ways and Means, Rules, and Health and Human Services committees. White was elected mayor of Cleveland in 1990 and 1994. He has focused his administration on public safety, education, economic and job development, neighborhood revitalization, and race relations.

WHITE, RICHARD

University of Washington, Department of History, Seattle, WA 98195 (206) 543-5790
ACHIEVEMENTS: Professor of history, University of Washington, Seattle, Wash. STUDIED: University of California, Santa Cruz, Ph.D., History.
White, a professor of history at the University of Washington, attended college during the turbulent 1960s. White admits to being influenced by the consciousness raising and crusades for social justice during these years. After graduation, he migrated to the Pacific Northwest to be among the Native American people at Frank's Landing. White began studying Indian treaties, which led to his Ph.D. in history. White is a proponent of the "New Western History" movement, called revisionist history by some. His textbook, *Your Misfortune is None of My Own*, University of Oklahoma Press, presents his view of recent Western history, and displays a darker view of the American West than what has traditionally been taught.

WHITE, VANNA

Merv Griffin Productions, 1541 N. Vine St., Los Angeles, CA 90028
White is a prominent television personality. For career credentials consult the portion of this book entitled "Notable Americans by Profession" in the Appendix. Within this portion, the list "Television Personalities" describes requirements for inclusion in this volume.

WHITMAN, CHRISTINE TODD

State House, Office of Governor, Trenton, NJ.
BORN: 1941, Oldwick, N.J. ACHIEVEMENTS: Member, Community Foundation of New Jersey, National Council on Crime and Delinquency, Somerset County Board of Social Services, North New Jersey Transportation Coordinating Somerset County Planning Board. STUDIED: Wheaton College, Norton, Mass., B.A., government.
A Republican National Committee worker after graduation from college, the daughter of politically prominent parents was elected to the Hunterton, N.J. County Board in 1982. At this post she helped open the county's first homeless shelter and created an open-space program. Tapped by Gov. Tom Kean in 1988, she became president of the New Jersey Board of Public Utilities. A failed race for the U.S. Senate in 1990 followed, and after her defeat she remained politically oriented by writing a newspaper column and hosting a radio show. In 1993 she became the first woman in the Garden State's history to win its highest office, governor.

WHITWAN, DAVID RAY

Whirlpool Corp., 2000 M-63 North Benton Harbor, MI 49022

BORN: 1942, Stanley, Wis. ACHIEVEMENTS: Fellow Aspen Institute; president of the board directors, The Soup Kitchen; member of the National Council Housing Industry; served as captain in the U.S. Army. STUDIED: University of Wisconsin, B.S., 1967.

David Whitwan began his career with Whirlpool in 1975 as a general manager of sales in the Southern California division. He spent the next decade in various marketing and leadership positions until 1987, when he became Whirlpool's chief executive officer and chairman.

WIESEL, TORSTEN N.

Harvard Medical School, Boston, MA 02115

Wiesel is a prominent physician. For career credentials consult the portion of this book entitled "Notable Americans by Profession" in the Appendix. Within this portion, the list "Physicians" describes requirements for inclusion in this volume.

WILEY, WILLIAM T.

615 Main St., Sausalito, CA 94965

BORN: 1937. ACHIEVEMENTS: Purchase Prize, Whitney Museum; William H. Bartels Prize, Art Institute of Chicago; collections: Museum of Modern Art, New York City; Los Angeles County Museum of Art; exhibitions: Museum of Modern Art, New York City; Art Institute of Chicago. STUDIED: San Francisco Art Institute.

William Wiley's early paintings are expressionistic and full of mysterious symbols. He gained recognition in the mid-1960s as a California Funk artist, painting images of minutiae related to surrealism and dada. Verbal puns accompany fragments of letters, logs and notebooks in collages and constructions. Objects such as feathers, string, rope, and branches—suggesting American Indian artifacts—and children's games of cowboys and Indians are incorporated into three-dimensional works that reveal a love for the American West. Imaginative drawings, such as *The Balance is Not So Far Away From the Good Old Daze*, are meticulously drawn and show infinite spatial planes, imaginary charts and metaphysical objects.

WILKINS, ROGER WOOD

George Mason University, 4400 University Dr., Fairfax, VA 22030

BORN: 1932, Kansas City, Mo. ACHIEVEMENTS: Roger Baldwin Civil Liberties Award, New York Civil Liberties Union; chairman: Pulitzer Prize Board. STUDIED: University of Michigan, B.A., pre-law, J.D., law; honorary degrees from the University of Michigan, Georgetown University Law School, Central Michigan University, Wilberforce University, and the Union of Experimenting Universities.

The nephew of Roy Wilkins, a former executive secretary of the NAACP, Wilkins practiced international law after earning his doctorate in 1956. After passage of the Civil Rights Act of 1966, LeRoy Collins—admin- istrator of the Community Relations Service, an organization formed under the act to defuse and prevent urban riots—tapped Wilkins to run the branch. President Lyndon Johnson soon moved the Community Relations Service from Commerce to the Justice Department, promoting Wilkins to the rank of assistant attorney general in which Wilkins became known as Johnson's chief troubleshooter on racial problems. He later became an officer of the Ford Foundation, then, in 1972, a member of the *Washington Post* editorial staff. The *Post* won a Pulitzer Prize in 1973, with Wilkins cited for his editorials on the Watergate scandal. He subsequently wrote editorials and columns for the *New York Times* and the now defunct *Washington Star*. Wilkins wrote a book, *A Man's Life: An Autobiography*, co-edited *Quiet Riots: Race and Poverty In the United States*, and has contributed to many other publications. Since 1987 he has been the Clarence J. Robinson Professor of History at George Mason University.

WILL, GEORGE F.

c/o Washington Post, 1150 15th St. NW, Washington, DC 20071

BORN: 1941, Champaign, Ill. ACHIEVEMENTS: Political analyst; Pulitzer Prize, 1977. STUDIED: Trinity College, B.A., 1962; Oxford University, 1962-1964; Princeton University, Ph.D., 1964.

George Will taught political science and was a Senate aide before becoming Washington editor of the *National Review* in 1972, a columnist for the *Washington Post* in 1973, a contributing editor of *Newsweek* magazine and a regular on public affairs television programs. Known for his measured conservative analysis, he received the Pulitzer Prize for commentary in 1977. His books include: *The Pursuit of Virtue and Other Tory Notions*, 1982; *Statecraft as Soulcraft: What Government Does*, 1983; *Men at Work: The Craft of Baseball*, 1990; and *Restoration: Congress, Term Limits and the Recovery of Deliberative Democracy*, 1992.

WILLE, LOIS

The *Chicago Tribune*, 435 N. Michigan Ave., Chicago, IL 60611 (312) 222-3232

ACHIEVEMENTS: Two Pultizer Prizes; eight Peter Lisago rAwards for Editorial Writing, Chicago Headline Club.

Lois Wille started her journalism career with the *Chicago Daily News* in 1956. Handling a wide variety of assignments, she won her first Pulitzer Prize for public service in 1963 for a series of articles that exposed state and local public health services' refusal to provide birth-control information and services to impoverished women. In 1978 Wille assumed the job of editorial page editor for the *Chicago Sun-Times*. Wille changed papers again in 1984, when she accepted the position of associate editorial page editor at the *Chicago Tribune*. In 1989 Wille received her second Pulitzer Prize, this time for editorial writing. Wille has also won eight Peter Lisagor Awards for editorial writing from the Chicago Headline Club. Wille retired from the *Chicago Tribune* on May 3, 1991.

WILLIAMS, JOHN ALFRED

Rutgers University, Department of English, 175 University Ave., Newark, NJ
BORN: 1925, Jackson, Miss. ACHIEVEMENTS: Author, !Click Song. STUDIED: Syracuse University, B.A.; Southeastern Massachusetts University, L.L.D., law.

After leaving school John Williams worked for a county welfare department, drifted into public relations, and spent two years in television and radio in New York City and Hollywood. For four years he worked for a variety of publishing houses in Manhattan, then taught at numerous institutions, and spent two years in Africa as a correspondent for Newsweek. He has written nonfiction and many novels, some under the pen name J. Dennis Gregory, and is known as a champion of civil rights, as is demonstrated in his book, !Click Song, published in 1982.

WILLIAMS, JOHN TOWNER

Michael Gorgaine, Gorfaine/Schwartz, 3301 Barham Blvd. Suite 201, Los Angeles, CA 90068
BORN: 1932, Flushing, N.J. ACHIEVEMENTS: Emmy, Heidi, 1969; Emmy, Jane Eyre, 1971; Academy Award, Best Musical Adaptation, Fiddler on the Roof, 1971; Academy Award, Grammy Jaws, 1976; Academy Award, three Grammy awards, Star Wars, 1977; two Grammy Awards, Close Encounters of the Third Kind, 1977; two Grammy Awards, Superman, 1978; two Grammy Awards, The Empire Strikes Back, 1980; Grammy, Raiders of the Lost Ark, 1981; Academy Award, Best Original Score, Grammy, E.T., 1982; Academy Award, Best Original Score, Schindler's List, 1993. STUDIED:: UCLA; private studies with Madame Rosina Lhvinne, N.Y.C; honorary degrees: Berklee College of Music, Northeastern University, Tufts University, University of Southern California, Boston University, New England Conservatory of Music, Providence College.
For more than 30 years, Williams has been one of the country's most creative and prolific film music composers. His father was a jazz drummer and symphony orchestra percussionist. Williams' success in a variety of musical idioms—jazz, pop, classical—reflects his father's influence. His first movie score was for Because They're Young, 1960. Since then, Williams has composed and arranged music for more than 50 motion pictures, including The Reivers, 1969; Jaws, 1975; Star Wars and Close Encounters of the Third Kind, both in 1977; Superman, 1978; Raiders of the Lost Ark, 1981; and E.T: The Extra Terrestrial, 1982. Williams, who also has written chamber music, concertos, and a symphony, succeeded Arthur Fiedler as conductor of the Boston Pops Orchestra in 1980, a post he held for more than ten years.

WILLIAMS, ROBIN

Creative Artists Agency, 9830 Wilshire Blvd., Beverly Hills, CA 90212
BORN: 1951, Chicago. ACHIEVEMENTS: Grammy, Best Comedy Recording, Reality...What a Concept, 1979; Grammy, Best Comedy Recording, Good Morning, Vietnam, 1978; Grammy, Best Recording for Children, Pecos Bill, 1988; Golden Globe, Best Actor in a Comedy Series, Mork and Mindy, 1979; Emmy, Best Individual Performance in a Variety or Music Program, A Carol Burnett Special, 1987; Emmy, Best Individual Performance in a Variety or Music Program, ABC Presents a Royal Gala, 1988; Golden Globe, Best Actor in a Comedy, The Fisher King, 1992; Golden Globe, Special Achievement, Aladdin, 1993; Golden Globe, Best Actor in a Comedy, Mrs. Doubtfire, 1994. STUDIED: Attended Claremont Men's College and College of Marin; The Julliard School, Speech and Drama, 1973-1976.
While attending the Julliard School in New York, Robin Williams studied with John Houseman and worked as a street mime to supplement his income. Later, he moved to San Francisco and appeared in clubs in the area including, Holy City Zoo, Intersection, the Great American Music Hall and The Boardinghouse. He performed as a stand-up comedian in Los Angeles comedy clubs, becoming a regular at The Comedy Store, Improvisation and The Ice House. In 1977 he made his TV debut on Laugh-In and wrote and performed on the Richard Pryor Show. A guest appearance on Happy Days as Mork from Ork spun off his signature series Mork and Mindy. Williams major film credits include; Popeye, The World According to Garp, Moscow on the Hudson, Good Morning Vietnam, Dead Poet's Society, Cadillac Man, Awakenings, The Fisher King, Hook, Toys, Aladdin (as the voice of the genie), and Mrs. Doubtfire. Williams co-founded the Comic Relief charities, along with Whoppi Goldberg and Billy Crystal. Williams annually appears in televised benefits for the oranization. In 1996 he was the first actor to star in two films that grossed over $100 million—Jumanji and The Birdcage

WILLIAMS, VANESSA

Wing Records, 8335 Sunset Blvd., Los Angeles, Ca 90069 (213) 656-3003
BORN: 1963, New York City. STUDIED: Syracuse University.
Williams first rose to prominence in 1984 as the first African-American woman to win the coveted title of Miss America. However, after being forced to relinquish her crown amid a highly publicized scandal, she took off to rebuild her image as well as her career. In 1988, with her first album, The Right Stuff, Williams burst on the scene with the top 10 R&B hit Dreamin, causing the music industry to take note of the talented singer. Taking the skills she honed while a musical theater major at Syracuse University, she took to the Broadway stage as the lead in Kiss of the Spider Woman. Williams has also appeared in many other television and movie roles. Although she has received many accolades for her acting abilities, she has received the most acclaim as a vocalist. Her 1991 hit, Save The Best For Last, reached the top 10 on both the R&B and Pop charts, thus catapulting her to crossover status. She later recorded two albums: The Right Stuff and The Comfort zone. In 1995 she was the voice of Pocahontas, an animated film of the same name.

WILLIS, BRUCE

Triad Artists Inc., 10100 Santa Monica Blvd., 16th Floor, Los Angeles, CA 90067

BORN: 1955, (Germany) ACHIEVEMENTS: Emmy Award, Outstanding Lead Actor in a Drama Series, Moonlighting, 1987; Golden Globe Award, Best Performance by an Actor in a Television Series, Comedy/Musical, Moonlighting, 1987. STUDIED: Montclair State College.

Bruce Willis initially rose to popularity on the television series, *Moonlighting*, which ran from 1985 until 1989. Born in Germany, Willis worked for a short time at a chemical company, a nuclear power plant and also as a security guard before embarking on a career in entertainment. While establishing himself as a performer, he acted in commercials for Seagram's Golden Wine Coolers and Levi's 501 Jeans. Willis debuted on film in *Blind Date*, in 1987. From then on, he has worked primarily in movies. His portrayal of John McClane in *Die Hard*, in 1988, and *Die Hard II: Die Harder*, in 1990, provided Willis much popular recognition. Willis is also an accomplished singer and has appeared in that capacity on numerous television specials.

WILLIS, BRIG. GEN. MARY C.

Office of the Secretary, Pentagon, Washington, DC 20301-1155 (703) 545-6700
Willis,is a prominent military leader and the highest reanking woman in the U.S. Army. For career credentials consult the portion of this book entitled "Notable Americans by Profession" in the Appendix. Within this portion, the list "Military Leaders" describes requirements for inclusion in this volume.

WILSON, KENNETH GEDDES

Ohio State University, Department of Physics, Columbus, Ohio
BORN: 1936, Waltham, Mass. ACHIEVEMENTS: Nobel Prize in Physics, 1982; fellow, Harvard University, Ford Foundation; Heineman Prize; Boltzmann Medal; Franklin Medal; Eringer Medal. STUDIED: Harvard University; California Institute of Technology.

Honored by the Nobel physics committee "for his theory for critical phenomena in connection with phase transition," Kenneth Wilson joins a very select group of physicists who operate far out on the edge of chaos. Known as a quiet physics professor at Cornell University, who seemed never to produce anything, the question of his tenure was up in the air. Those who knew him, however, gambled that eventually he would produce and persuaded the administration to keep him. Almost overnight a flood of papers came out, one of which brought him the Nobel Prize. The paper concerned "phase transition," the point at which ice turns to water or water turns to vapor. The exact point where the transition occurs is called the critical point. It is this point at which seemingly random and unpredictable configurations occur, pointing to a hopeless understanding of the system. Wilson's calculations demonstrated the surprising conclusion that far from being chaotic, critical point phenomena have an underlying mathematical order. This "order out of chaos," where matter has the innate ability to self-organize itself out of chaos, has since been found in weather systems, insect populations, lasers, electrical and chemical reactions, even in dripping water taps and the spirals made by cigarette smoke, and is the subject of a distinctive branch of what is called the "New Physics" describes requirements for inclusion in this volume.

WILSON, LANFORD EUGENE

Hill and Wang, 19 Union Square West, New York, NY 10003
BORN: 1937, Lebanon, Mo. ACHIEVEMENTS: Pulitzer Prize, The 5th of July, 1980. STUDIED: Southwest Missouri State College, 1955-1956; San Diego State College, 1956-1957; University of Chicago, 1957-1958.

Lanford Wilson's plays deal with the conflict between traditional values and modern pressures, as in his drama *The Hot l Baltimore*, 1973, that contrasts the values of the old and young in the deteriorating Hotel Baltimore, whose sign has lost its "e." In his Pulitzer Prize-winning play *The 5th of July*, 1978, another building symbolized the conflict between past and present as the sale of a house is intertwined with the evolution of politics in the 1960s. His other plays include *Talley and Son*, 1985; *Talley's Folly*, 1979 and *Angels Fall*, 1983.

WILSON, PETE

State Capitol, 1st Floor, Sacramento, California 95814; Phone (916) 445-2841
BORN: 1933, Lake Forest, Ill. ACHIEVEMENTS: Member, California General Assembly 1967-1971, mayor of San Diego 1971-1983, U.S. Senate 1983-1991, governor of California, 1990. STUDIED: Yale University, B.A., 1955; University of California Berkeley, J.D., 1962.

Gov. Pete Wilson has spent 27 years in public service. He served in the Marine Corps from 1955 to 1958 and practiced law for five years before entering politics. His first office was in the California General Assembly from 1967 to 1971, after which he ran for mayor of San Diego. He held the post of mayor for 12 years, serving from 1971 to 1983. In 1983 the California Republican won a U.S. Senate seat where he represented the State of California for two terms. In 1990 he became Governor of California. In 1995, he declared as a Republican candidate for U.S. President in the 1996 Republican primary. Shortly thereafter he quit the race.

WILSON, ROBERT WOODROW

AT&T Bell Laboratories, HOH L239, Holmdel, NJ 07733
BORN: 1936, Houston, Texas. ACHIEVEMENTS: Nobel Prize in Physics (shared with Arno A. Penzias and Piotr L. Kapitsa), 1978; Henry Draper Medal, Royal Astronomy Society; Herschel Medal, National Academy of Sciences. STUDIED: Rice University, Texas; California Institute of Technology.

Two scientific theories about the creation of the universe have been hotly debated since Edwin Hubble first proposed, in 1929, that we live in a constantly expanding universe. In one, the "big bang" theory, Hubble and other radio astronomers postulated that all matter and all energy were once a single primeval atom, from which it has been expanding since an explosion 20 billion years ago. In the contrary "Steady

State" theory, scientists believe the universe has continually expanded until it collapsed upon itself, the collapse compensated for by the constant creation of new universes. Robert Wilson and Arno Penzias laid the "Steady State" theory to rest with their work in microwave radio detection, which found for the first time—and by accident—a hundredfold excess of radiation than that coming from all known scientifically measured sources, which with temperature and wave length calculations factored in, would support the "big bang" theory. If further evidence develops along this line, scientists believe the team's discovery will have been as important as Hubble's theory itself.

WILSON, WILLIAM JULIUS

University of Chicago, Department of Sociology, 1126 E. 59th St., Chicago, IL 60637

BORN: 1935, Derry Township, Pa. ACHIEVEMENTS: Author, Power, Racism and Privilege. STUDIED: Wilberforce University, B.A., sociology; Bowling Green State, M.A., sociology; Washington State University, Ph.D., sociology; many honorary degrees.

As a faculty member at the University of Chicago since 1971, William Wilson has studied the ghetto poor and the cycles of poverty in the U.S. He has also developed programs in Chicago to help African-Americans. His major works are *Power, Racism and Privilege*, 1973; *Through Different Eyes*, 1973; and *The Truly Disadvantaged*, 1987.

WINGER, DEBRA

P.M.K. Public Relations, 8436 W. 3rd St., Rm. 650, Los Angeles, CA 90048

Winger is a prominent actress. Her first major role was as Sissy, the leading lady in *Urban Cowboy* in which she played opposed John Travolta. For career credentials consult the portion of this book entitled "Notable Americans by Profession" in the Appendix. Within this portion, the list "Actors" describes requirements for inclusion in this volume.

WINFREY, OPRAH GAIL

Harpo Inc., 1058 W. Washington Blvd., Chicago, IL 60609 (312) 633-1000

BORN: 1954, Nashville, Tenn. ACHIEVEMENTS: Emmy, Best Host of a Talk Show, The Oprah Winfrey Show, 1987, 1991, 1992. STUDIED: :Tennessee State University.

America's queen of talk shows reigns as one of the most powerful women in entertainment. Winfrey's personal wealth has been estimated at $250 million, and she consistently ranks in the top five of the *Forbes Magazine* list of top earners in the entertainment industry. She is the only African-American woman in history to own a television and film studio, Harpo Productions, where her talk show is produced, along with other prime-time specials and film projects. Winfrey's talk show is the highest-rated in syndication history, reaching roughly 15 million viewers a day in the United States alone. Her gift of gab was recognized early. When she was 12 years old she won $500 for a speech she gave at church. A winning speech in

an oratorical contest won her a scholarship to Tennessee State University. While in college she read afternoon newscasts for a local Nashville radio station, and in her sophomore year, she became co-anchor of the evening news at the local TV station. After graduation she moved to Baltimore and worked as a reporter and co-anchor at WJZ-TV, the ABC affiliate. A year later she became the host of *Baltimore is Talking*. The producer of the show sent in a tape of Winfrey to WLS-TV in Chicago, and she was hired as anchor of *A.M. Chicago*, a half-hour morning talk show. After only one month the show's ratings were even with Donahue, and three months later it was leading. In 1983 *A.M. Chicago* was renamed *The Oprah Winfrey Show* and expanded to an hour. Also during this year Quincy Jones cast Oprah as Sophia in *The Color Purple* for which she was nominated for an Academy Award. A year later she appeared in another film *Native Son*. After her movie appearances her popularity rose, and King World bought the syndication rights to air her talk-show in 138 cities, a record for first-time syndication. Winfrey also contributes millions to charitable organizations and has championed causes to help the nation's children.

WINTER, ALAN

Cambridge University Press, 40 West 20th St., New York, NY 10011-4211 (212) 924-3900

Winter is a prominent publisher. For career credentials consult the portion of this book entitled "Notable Americans by Profession" in the Appendix. Within this portion, the list "Publishers" describes requirements for inclusion in this volume.

WINTERS, JONATHAN

Triad Artists, Inc., 10100 Santa Monica Blvd., Los Angeles, CA 90067

Winters is a prominent actor. For career credentials consult the portion of this book entitled "Notable Americans by Profession" in the Appendix. Within this portion, the list "Actors" describes requirements for inclusion in this volume.

WOLFE, (TOM) THOMAS KENNERLY JR.

Farrar, Straus & Giroux, Inc., 19 Union Square West, New York, NY 10003

BORN: 1931, Richmond, Va. ACHIEVEMENTS: Best-selling novelist, essayist and journalist. STUDIED: Washington and Lee University, Yale University, Ph.D., American studies.

In magazine articles and in books about popular culture, Tom Wolfe popularized the new journalistic technique of employing novelistic literary devices to present facts in new and compelling guises. Among his books are: *The Kandy-Kolored Tangerine-Flake Streamline Baby*, 1965; *The Electric Kool-Aid Acid Test*, 1968; and *The Right Stuff*, 1979. His commentaries include *The Painted Word*, 1975, on art, and *From Bauhaus to Our House*, on architecture. His only novel, *The Bonfire of the Vanities*, 1987, a satire on avarice in New York City, was a best seller.

WOLFF, NELSON W.

Office of the Mayor, 100 Military Plaza, San Antonio, TX 78205 (210) 299-7060

Wolff is a prominent political leader. For career credentials consult the portion of this book entitled "Notable Americans by Profession" in the Appendix. Within this portion, the list "Political Leaders" describes requirements for inclusion in this volume.

WONDER, (STEVIE) STEVELAND MORRIS

Tamla Records, 6255 Sunset Blvd., Los Angeles, CA 90028 (213) 468-3454

BORN: 1950, Saginaw, Mich. ACHIEVEMENTS: Grammy Awards for singles, I Wish, 1977; Boogie on Reggae woman, 1975; You are the Sunshine of My Life, 1974; Superstition, 1974; Living for the City, 1975; Grammy awards for albums, Innervisions, 1974; Fulfillingness' First Finale, 1975; Songs in the Key of Life, 1977; Academy Award and Golden Globe, I Just Called to Say I Love You, single from the movie The Woman in Red, 1984; Songwriters Hall of Fame, 1982; Rock and Roll Hall of Fame, 1989; recipient Nelson Mandela Courage Award, 1991. STUDIED: attended public schools in Detroit until age 12, then transferred to the Michigan School for the Blind.

When 11-year-old Steveland Morris auditioned for Motown records, in 1962, he demonstrated his enormous talent by playing every instrument in the studio. Berry Gordy, the president of Motown, immediately signed him and changed his name to Stevie Wonder. A year later he had his first number-one hit single *Fingertips*. Within the next two years, "Little Stevie Wonder," was one of Motown's brightest stars, recording a string of hit records for the next nine years, most of which he wrote himself. In 1971 his recording contract expired with Motown, and Wonder negotiated for his own record label, total artistic control and the rights to his music, a fight which he won. Wonder's music in the 1970s marked a new era in R & B music. He created socially conscious songs, addressing such social issues as racism, apartheid and poverty. He is the recipient of sixteen Grammy Awards, more than any other Motown artist, and an Oscar for the song *I Just Called To Say I Love You*, the hit song from the movie *The Women in Red*. In 1982 he was inducted into the Songwriters Hall of Fame, and in 1989 he entered the Rock and Roll Hall of Fame. Wonder has worked tirelessly for social issues, and in 1991 he received the Nelson Mandela Courage Award.

WONG, B. D.

Agency for the Performing Arts, 888 Seventh Ave., New York, NY 10019

BORN: 1962, San Francisco ACHIEVEMENTS: Antoinette Perry Award, Best Featured Actor, M. Butterfly, 1988. STUDIED: acting with Don Hotton, voice with Tony McDowell.

Although B. D. Wong is relatively new on the scene, he is making his mark. Wong is best known for his 1988 performance in *M. Butterfly*, for which he won a Tony award. He began his acting career with a role in *Androcles and the Lion*, in 1982, at the Town Hall in New York City. He also appeared as Ariel in *The Tempest*, in 1989, at the Roundabout Theatre in New York. Wong's first movie role was a boy on the street in *The*

Karate Kid II, in 1986. More recently he has appeared as James Lew in *Mystery Date*, and Howard Weinstein in *Father of the Bride*, in 1991.

WONG, WILLIE

55 North Center Street, P. O. Box 1466, Mesa, AZ 85211 (602) 644-2388

BORN: 1948, Mesa, Ariz. ACHIEVEMENTS: Mayor, Mesa, Ariz.; Outstanding Young Man of 1989, Mesa Leadership, Training & Development Association. STUDIED: Arizona State University.

Willie Wong has been active in Mesa, Ariz., city government most of his life. He has been on the Board of Directors of the Southwest Public Recycling Association, the Child Crisis Center, and the YMCA. Wong served as a member of the Economic Development Advisory Board, the MAG Regional Council, and the League of Arizona Cities and Towns. He served two terms as a member of the city council, from June, 1986 through October, 1991 when he resigned from the council to run for mayor. He was elected mayor of Mesa and began his term of office on June 1, 1992. In addition to his duties as mayor, Wong is president of a local auto parts company.

WOOD, TOM

Atlanta Constitution, 72 Marietta St., NW., Atlanta, GA 30303-2899 (404) 572-5151

Wood is a prominent publisher. For career credentials consult the portion of this book entitled "Notable Americans by Profession" in the Appendix. Within this portion, the list "Publishers" describes requirements for inclusion in this volume.

WOODWARD, (BOB) ROBERT UPSHUR

The Washington Post, 1150 15th St., NW, Washington, D.C. 20005

BORN: 1943, Geneva, Ill. ACHIEVEMENTS: Pulitzer Prize, in connection with uncovering the Watergate scandal; numerous other awards. STUDIED:: Yale University, B.A., journalism.

Woodward will long be remembered, along with his colleague, Carl Bernstein, for their sensational unmasking and coverage of the Watergate scandal and coverup. The team's investigation helped bring down the administration of President Nixon and won the *Washington Post* a Pulitzer Prize for meritorious public service, in 1973 as well as almost every major journalistic prize in 1973. Woodward became assistant managing editor of the paper in 1981 and has written controversial "insider" books such as *The Brethren*, with Scott Armstrong, in 1979, *Wired* in 1984, and *The Commanders* in 1991.

WOOLARD, EDGAR S., JR.

Du Pont, 1007 N Market St, Wilmington, DE 19898

BORN: 1934, Washington, N.C. ACHIEVEMENTS: board of directors: N.C. Textile Foundation, Citicorp, IBM Corp.; Joint Council on Economic Education. STUDIED:: N.C. State University, B.S., 1956.

Woolard began with Du Pont as an industrial engineer in 1956 and worked in virtually every facet of the company's engineering and marketing sects. He was named chairman in 1989.

WOOLSEY, JAMES R., JR.

CIA, Washington, D.C., 20001 (703) 482-1100
BORN: 1941, Tulsa, Okla. ACHIEVEMENTS: Delegate at large, Soviet Arms Talks, 1983-86; Regent, Smithsonian Institution, 1989-93. STUDIED: Stanford University, B.A. (with great distinction), 1963; Oxford University (England), Rhodes Scholar, M.A., 1965; Yale University, LL.B., 1968.
James Woolsey began working in government right out of law school. After graduation, in 1968, Woolsey served in the Army until 1970, working as a program analyst for the secretary of defense. During that period, Woolsey advised the U.S. delegation to the Strategic Arms Limitation Talks, held in Helsinki and Vienna in 1969 and 1970. He continued working in defense-related government jobs through the early 1970s. Woolsey left government service in 1973 to join the law firm Shea & Gardner, of Washington, D.C. However he continued work with government. Woolsey was a delegate at large for the Soviet Arms Talks, held in Geneva from 1983 to 1986, and a member of the President's Commission on Strategic Forces, from 1983 until 1984. He was appointed director of the Central Intelligence Agency by President Bill Clinton, in 1993.

WRIGHT, STEVEN

Agency for the Performing Arts, Inc., 888 Seventh Ave. New York, NY 10106.
BORN: 1955, New York, N.Y. ACHIEVEMENTS: Academy Award (with Dean Parisot), Best Live Action Film, Short Subject, The Appointments of Dennis Jennings, 1988. STUDIED:: Emerson College, B.A.
A former parking attendant, Steven Wright began working as a stand-up comedian in 1979 performing mainly in New England. In 1982 he began making public appearances nationwide and made his national debut on the Tonight Show where he appeared nine times from 1982 to 1986. Wright appeared in his own HBO special, On Location: Steven Wright, Comic Relief specials and Saturday Night Live. His film appearances include: Desperately Seeking Susan, where he portrayed Larry Tilman, D.D.S., Stars and Bars, Coffee and Cigarettes, and Men of Respect. In 1985 he recorded a comedy album I have a Pony. Besides his Oscar winning television script, The Appointments of Dennis Jennings, he also wrote the screenplay for Coffee and Cigarettes and the script for Wicker Chairs and Gravity.

WUDUNN, SHERYL

The New York Times, 229 West 43rd St., New York, NY 10046 (212) 556-1234
BORN: 1959, New York City. ACHIEVEMENTS: Pulitzer Prize, 1990; Overseas Press Club Award, 1990; George Polk Award, 1989. STUDIED: Princeton University, M.P.A., 1988; Harvard Business School, Harvard, M.B.A., 1986, graduated Cornell University, B.A., European history, 1981.
Sheryl WuDunn started at the New York Times in 1989 as a correspondent in the Beijing bureau. It was there that she received a Pulitzer Prize, won jointly with her husband Nicholas Kristof (also a Times journalist), for international coverage of Tiananmen Square. In December of 1994, she joined the Tokyo bureau where she is a foreign correspondent. WuDunn also worked at the South China Post and interned at the Miami Herald, the Wall Street Journal, and Reuters, while completing graduate work in business. WuDunn has traveled extensively throughout Asia and Europe. She speaks French, German, and Chinese (Mandarin). WuDunn has won three major awards for her coverage of China.

YAMASAKI, MINORU

Minoru Yamasaki and Associates, 350 West Big Beaver Road, Troy, MI 48084 (313) 689-3500
BORN: 1912. ACHIEVEMENTS: fellow, AIA; fellow, American Academy of Arts and Sciences; Design Award, Progressive Architecture, 1956; notable works: World Trade Center, New York City; Eastern Airlines Terminal, Logan International Airport, Boston; World Trade Center, Bangkok, Thailand. STUDIED: New York University.
Minuro Yamasaki's work is a study in contradictions. He has often professed that man is happiest in an environment of soft, delicate, humanely proportioned elements. Yet he typically works on a monumental scale, in rough, unyielding materials. He advocates a place for Oriental serenity in Occidental architecture, yet his best known "mega-creations" are profoundly imposing, even overwhelming. His 1974 World Trade Center in New York was briefly the world's tallest occupied building and is still gargantuan by any measure. To distance the Center from the brute verticality of New York's mid-town skyline, he designed a tapering window scheme in which parallel columns separating the windows smoothly curve together as they reach the roof. This subtle closure, especially when viewed from ground level at intermediate distance, is meant to suggest a great gothic "sky-arch," and soften the hard angles and uncompromised mass of the twin rectangular towers. It's a startling place to find such notes of grace. "Dramatic Artists"

YEAGER, CHARLES (CHUCK) ELWOOD Jr.

P.O. Box 128, Cedar Ridge, CA 95924;
BORN: 1923, Myra, W.V. ACHIEVEMENTS: First person to travel faster than the speed of sound, 1947.
As an World War II fighter pilot based in England, Chuck Yeager flew 64 missions and shot down 13 German aircraft. After the war, he became a flight instructor and test pilot and began flying the experimental X-1 rocket research aircraft. On Oct. 14, 1947, he flew the X-1 to a speed of more than 670 mph at an altitude of 40,000 feet, thus breaking the "sound barrier" of 662 m.p.h. In 1953 he set another world speed record, flying the Bell X-1A at more than twice the speed of sound. He later commanded the Air Force Aerospace Research Flight School and the 4th Fighter Bomber Wing. Yeager retired in 1973 as a brigadier general and wrote two autobiographies, Yeager, 1985, and Press On, 1988.

YOUNG, JAYNE

The Atlantic Monthly, 1290 6th Ave., New York, NY 10104
ACHIEVEMENTS: Member of Advertising Women of New York. STUDIED: Hunter College, B.A. in English literature.
In January of 1993, Jayne Young became *The Atlantic Monthly's* first female publisher. After having joined the magazine as an advertising sales director in 1986, she was appointed to the position of associate publisher in 1987. Since then she has not only steered the magazine to a 31 percent increase in advertising pages, but has also played a leading role in reinforcing its position as an influential force in both the political and public spheres. During her tenure as publisher, The Roper Organization has recognized the magazine as one of the foremost industry leaders in the consumer publications field. Young's workshops and seminars on the many facets of advertising are featured prominently on *Folio Magazine's* national publishing conferences.

Publisher Jayne Young.

YOUNG, JOHN WATTS

c/o NASA, L.B. Johnson Space Center, Houston, TX 77058 (713) 483-0123.
BORN: 1930, San Francisco. ACHIEVEMENTS: Space missions: Gemini 3 (copilot), Gemini 10 (commander), Apollo 10 (command module pilot), Apollo 16 (commander), STS-1 and STS-9 space shuttle missions (commander). STUDIED: Georgia Institute of Technology, B.S., Aeronautical Engineering, 1952.
NASA selected John Young as an astronaut in 1962, when he was a U.S. Navy test pilot. He was the copilot on Gemini 3 in 1965. Young commanded Gemini 10 in 1966, in which he and pilot Michael Collins rendezvoused with two Agena rockets and docked with another. In 1969 he was the command module pilot on Apollo 10. Young walked on the moon in 1972, as commander of Apollo 16. He and Charles Duke stayed on the lunar surface for 71 hours, with more than 20 hours spent walking outside the lunar module. In 1981

he commanded the shuttle *Columbia* on its first mission, STS-1, into space. He also commanded the *Columbia* on the STS-9 space shuttle mission in 1983. Young was chief of NASA's Astronaut Office from 1975 to 1987.

ZAHN, PAULA

CBS-TV, 524 West 57th Street, New York, NY 10019
BORN: 1956, Omaha, NE. ACHIEVEMENTS: One of 1992's National Mothers of the Year; Newscaster of the Year, 1983, the American Women in Radio and Television; Emmy, Reporting; Emmy, Outstanding Coverage of a Continuing News Story. STUDIED: Stephens College, B.A., Journalism.
Before taking over as co-anchor with Harry Smith for *CBS This Morning* in 1990, Zahn was a co-anchor of *ABC's World News This Morning* and contributed features to *Good Morning America*. Her ABC career began in 1987 as anchor of *The Health Show*. Previously Zahn was an Emmy-award-winning reporter at KFMB-TV in San Diego and at KCBS-TV in Los Angeles. Her career trajectory has included anchoring and reporting stints with WNEV in Boston, and KPRC-TV in Houston, where she received a National Commission on Working Women Broadcasting Award in 1982. She garnered her latest Emmy in 1994 for her reportage on the mainstreaming of the mentally handicapped. Away from the newsroom, she made her Carnegie Hall debut as a cellist with the New York Pops orchestra in 1992. In 1995, she was awarded a citation by the Beth Israel Medical Center in New York City for her efforts in the battle against breast cancer.

ZAHN, TIMOTHY

c/o Bantam, 666 Fifth Avenue, New York, NY 10103 (212) 765-6500
BORN: 1951, Chicago. ACHIEVEMENTS: Hugo Award for Best Novella, for Cascade Point, 1984; Hugo Award nomination, for Return to the Fold,

1985. STUDIED: Michigan State University, B.A., 1973; University of Illinois at Urbana-Champaign, M.A., 1975; graduate study, 1975-1980.

Timothy Zahn started writing science fiction while working toward his Ph.D. in physics at the University of Illinois. In July, 1979, his doctoral thesis advisor died, causing a complete disruption to his doctoral project. Rather than start over again, Zahn decided to try writing full time. In his first year he sold nine stories, giving him the motivation to continue writing. Zahn is now a prolific writer of science fiction stories and novels. His interest in advanced technology and warcraft is apparent in a number of his books, such as the *Blackcollar* novels and the *Cobra* series. Zahn has received numerous Hugo Award nominations and received a Hugo Award for Best Novella in 1984 for *Cascade Point.*

ZAKS, JERRY

Lincoln Center Theater, 150 W. 65th St., New York, NY 10023
BORN: 1946, Stuttgart (Germany).
In the 1970s, Jerry Zaks acted in 1972's popular *Grease* and in *Tally's Folly.* By the 1980s he had turned to directing as well as continuing to act. In 1985 he won the prestigious Obie Award for directing *The Foreigner* and *The Marriage of Bette and Boo.*

ZANE, ARNIE

Bill T. Jones/Arnie Zane & Company, 853 Broadway, Suite 1706, New York, NY 10003 (212) 477-1850
Zane is a prominent dancer. For career credentials consult the portion of this book entitled "Notable Americans by Profession" in the Appendix. Within this portion, the list "Dancers" describes requirements for inclusion in this volume.

ZINDEL, PAUL

c/o HarperCollins, 10 East 53rd St., New York, NY 10022
Zindel is a prominent dramatic artist. For career credentials consult the portion of this book entitled "Notable Americans by Profession" in the Appendix. Within this portion, the list "Dramatic Artists" describes requirements for inclusion in this volume.

ZUCCHINO, DAVID

The *Philadelphia Inquirer*, 400 N. Broad St., Philadelphia, PA, 19130 (215) 854-2000
BORN: 1951. ACHIEVEMENTS: Three-time Pulitzer Prize finalist (1985, 1989, 1995); Overseas Press Club Award, 1988; Pulitzer Prize 1989; National Association of Black Journalists Award, 1989; Best News Story of 1994, Associated Press Managing Editors Association, 1994; Investigative Reporting Award, Society of Professional Journalists, 1994.
Currently the chief of correspondents, David Zucchino has been with the *Philadelphia Inquirer* since 1982. He joined as Middle East bureau chief, then moved on to projects reporter from 1985 to 1986. In 1986, he became Africa bureau chief in Nairobi and then held the same position in Johannesburg. His writing about the state of emergency in South Africa won him a Pulitzer and got him a nomination for another. During the Persian Gulf War, he wrote about military affairs in Washington, D.C. He also has covered gangs and drug trafficking in inner-city Philadelphia.

ACTORS

Criteria: Actors who received major American awards for their achievements which include: (1) those who received an Academy award since 1979 for Best Actor, Best Actress, Best Supporting Actor, or Best Supporting Actress; (2) those who received an Academy Award nomination and are major American motion pictures stars; (3) other at-large cinema performers who have starred in numerous major motion pictures; (4) those who received an Emmy Award for Best Actor or Best Actress for a comic or dramatic series since 1980 and were prominent celebrities; (5) other at-large performers on major American television shows and (6) those who received a Tony Award for Best Actor, Best Actress, Best Actor in a Leading Role, Best Actress in a Leading Role, Best Actor in a Musical, or Best Actress in a Musical since 1985 and were prominent stage-celebrities who starred in major American theatrical productions.

Alda, Alan
Alice, Mary
Alley, Kirstie
Arthur, Beatrice
Baker, Kathy
Bates, Kathy
Bergen, Candice
Busfield, Timothy
Caldwell, L. Scott
Channing, Stockard
Cher
Close, Glenn
Costner, Kevin
Cruise, Tom
Danson, Ted
Davis, Geena
Delany, Dana
Deniro, Robert
Devito, Danny
Douglas, Michael
Duvall, Robert
Eastwood, Clint
Falk, Peter
Field, Sally
Ford, Harrison
Foster, Jodie
Gaines, Boyd
Getty, Estelle
Gleason, Joanna
Goldberg, Whoopi
Goodman, John
Gossett, Louis Jr.
Grammer, Kelsey
Hackman, Eugene (Gene)
Hanks, Tom
Harrelson, Woody
Hepburn, Katherine
Hirsch, Judd
Hoffman, Dustin
Hunter, Holly

Hurt, William
Huston, Angelica
Hutton, Timothy
Ivey, Judith
Jeter, Michael
Jones, James
Jones, Tommy
Kahn, Madeline
Kaye, Judy
Kline, Kevin
Lange, Jessica
Lansbury, Angela
Larroquette, John
Lavin, Linda
Leibman, Ron
Lowe, Chad
MacLaine, Shirley
Madonna, (Ciccone)
Malkovich, John
Martin, Andrea
McClanahan, Rue
McCutcheon, James
Metcalf, Laurie
Midler, Bette
Miller, Barry
Nelson, Craig
Neuwirth, Bebe
Newman, Paul
Nicholson, Jack
Olmos, Edward
Pacino, Alfredo (Al)
Palance, Jack
Perlman, Rhea
Pesci, Joe
Peters, Bernadette
Pfeiffer, Michelle
Presley, Priscilla
Prince, Faith
Randolph, John
Redford, Charles
Rivera, Chita
Roberts, Julia
Sarandon, Susan
Selleck, Thomas
Silver, Ron
Skerrit, Tom
Smits, Jimmy
Streep, Meryl
Tomlin, Lily
Turner, Kathleen
Washington, Denzel
Weaver, Sigourney
Wendt, George
White, Betty
Willis, Bruce
Winger, Debra
Winters, Jonathan
Wong, B.

ARCHITECTS

Criteria: Architects were chosen from the following categories: (1) Those who have designed major American landmarks (2) Those who have won numerous national honors awarded by the American Institute of Architects.

Beeby, William Jr.
Blake, Peter
Booth, Laurence
Brubaker, Charles William

Burgee, John
Cavaglieri, Giorgio
Freed, James Ingo
Gehry, Frank O.
Goldberg, Bertrand
Graham, Bruce
Graves, Michael
Greenberg, Allan
Gwathmey, Charles
Hellmuth, George Francis
Jahn, Helmut
Johnson, Philip Cortelyou
Keating, Richard
Knowles, Edward Frank
Kohn, Eugene A.
Kolb, Keith R.
Lawton, Herbert T.
Meier, Richard Alan
Morgan, William
Nagle, James L.
Obata, Gyo
Pedersen, William
Pei, Ieoh Ming
Pelli, Cesar
Pereira, William Leonard
Schlesinger, Frank
Scutt, Der
Stern, Robert A.M.
Tigerman, Stanley
Venturi, Robert
Weese, Harry Mohr
Yamasaki, Minoru

ARTISTS

Criteria: Artists who have been featured in one-person shows at major metropolitan museums or nationally recognized art museums (e.g. the Whitney Museum of American Art, the Amon Carter Museum, et al).

Andre, Carl
Appel, Karel
Arneson, Robert
Artschwager, Richard Ernst
Baldessari, John Anthony
Bartlett, Jennifer Losch
Benglis, Lynda
Brown, Frederick J.
Brown, Roger
Chicago, Judy
Conklin, William
De Forest, Roy Dean
de Kooning, Willem
Delap, Tony
Diebenkorn, Richard
Diehl, Guy Louis
Dill, Guy Girard
Dill, Laddie John
DiSuvero, Mark
Engel, Morris
Fine, Jud
Flavin, Dan
Francis, Sam
Frankenthaler, Helen
Garabedian, Charles
Golub, Leon Albert
Gorman, R.C.
Hanson, Duane
Hockney, David
Hunt, Richard Howard

Impiglia, Giancarlo
Irwin, Robert
Johns, Jasper
Kelly, Ellsworth
Koons, Jeff
Kosuth, Joseph
Lichtenstein, Roy
Longo, Robert
Max, Peter
Noland, Kenneth C.
Oldenburg, Claus Thure
Olendorf, Bill
Paschke, Edward F.
Pearlstein, Philip
Raffael, Joseph
Ramos, Melvin
Rauschenberg, Robert
Reilly, Jack
Rivers, Larry
Rosenquist, James
Rosenthal, Rachel
Ruscha, Edward
Saunders, Raymond
Scanga, Italo
Schnabel, Julian
Schwartz, Carl
Segal, George
Serra, Richard
Stella, Frank
Summers, Carol
Thielbaud, Wayne
Voulkos, Peter
Wegman, William
Weldon, Barbra
Wiley, William

ASTRONAUTS

Criteria: Astronauts were selected from the following categories: (1) Commanders of American space missions; (2) those who have become important figures in NASA administration, rocket research, or the defense industry, and (3) other astronauts who were crew member of prominent American space missions.

Aldrin, Edwin Eugene
Anders, William
Armstrong, Neil
Bolden, Charles Frank Jr.
Borman, Frank
Brandenstein, Daniel
Brand, Vance
Cameron, Kenneth
Carr, Gerald
Casper, John
Cernan, Eugene
Conrad, Charles Pete Jr.
Cooper, Leroy Gordon Jr.
Covey, Richard
Crippen, Robert
Fullerton, Charles
Gibson, ("Hoot") Robert
Grabe, Ronald
Gregory, Frederick
Hartsfield, Henry
Hauck, Frederick "Rick"
Lovell, James
Mattingly, Thomas

McDivitt, James
Schirra, Walter Jr.
Shaw, Brewster Hopkinson
Shepard, Alan
Stafford, Thomas
Truly, Richard
Young, John

AUTHORS

Criteria: Authors were selected from the following categories: (1) those who have received a Pulitzer Prize for fiction since 1970; (2) those who have received a Nobel Prize for Literature, and (3) those whose books were number-one best-sellers since 1980 (both fiction and non-fiction) according to *the New York Times.*

Batra, Ravi
Bellow, Saul
Bennett, William John
Bly, Robert
Bombeck, Erma
Bradford, Barbara
Bugliosi, Vincent
Buscaglia, Leonardo
Caro, Robert
Carter, Steven Lisle
Clancy, Thomas L. Jr.
Clark, Mary
Clavell, James
Collier, Peter
Crichton, John
Dershowitz, Allan Morton
Eadie, Betty
Eddings, David
Estes, Clarissa
Fonda, Jane
Fulghum, Robert
Grisham, John
Halberstam, David
Heymann, C.
Hijuelos, Oscar
Irving, John
Jakes, John
Keillor, Garrison
Kelley, Kitty
Kennedy, William
King, Stephen
Kleinfield, Nathan
  Richard (Sonny)
Koch, Edward
Koontz, Dean
Krantz, Judith
Kuralt, Charles
Limbaugh, Rush
Ludlum, Robert
Lurie, Alison
Mailer, Norman
Manchester, William
Mazel, Judy
McGinniss, Joe
McMurtry, Larry
McPherson, James
Michener, James
Morrison, Toni
Naisbitt, John
O'Rourke, P.

Pearson, Durk
Peters, Thomas
Phillips, Julia
Puzo, Mario
Redfield, James
Regan, Donald
Rice, Anne
Ripley, Alexandra
Shaw, Sandy
Sheehy, Gail
Sheldon, Sidney
Siegel, Bernie
Silverstein, Shelby
Smith, Martin
Steel, Danielle
Steinem, Gloria
Stern, Howard
Stockman, David
Streiber, Whitley
Styron, William, Jr.
Tan, Amy
Taylor, Peter
Turow, Scott
Tyler, Anne
Updike, John
Vinge, Joan
Walker, Alice
Waller, Robert
Ward, Geoffrey
Waterman, Robert H. Jr.
Welty, Eudora
Wolfe, Thomas
Yeager, Charles
Zahn, Timothy

BUSINESS LEADERS

Criteria: Business Leaders were selected from the following categories: (1) CEOs of the largest American corporations and (2) influential entrepreneurs whose companies are not necessarily among the largest in the U.S., but are major forces within their industries (i.e. Microsoft Corp., Turner Broadcasting Systems, et al).

Allaire, Paul
Allen, Martin
Alley, William
Anderson, J.
Andreas, Dwayne
Arledge, David
Artzt, Edwin
Ash, Mary
Atwater, H. Brewster, Jr.
Augustine, Norman
Beall, Donald
Becherer, Hans
Bloch, Henry
Bryan, John
Campbell, Robert
Carney, Frank
Carrol, Philip
Cook, Lodwrick
Creighton, John W. Jr.
Daniell, Robert
Decrane, Alfred C.
Dell, Michael
Derr, K.

Desimone, L.
Drew, Ernest
Eaton, Robert
Fisher, George
Fletcher, Philip
Fuller, Lawrence H.
Gates, William
Gault, Stanley
Georges, John
Gerstner, Louis Vincent
Gibbons, Fred
Goizueta, Robert
Gorman, Joseph
Grove, Andrew
Hall, John
Hall, R.
Hardymon, James
Heimbold, Charles Andreas Jr.
Hewlett, William
Hughs, Mark
Iacocca, (Lee) Lido A.
Irani, Ray
Jobs, Steven
Jordan, Michael
Junkins, Jerry
Knight, Charles
Knight, Philip
Larsen, Ralph
Lazarus, Charles
Loucks, Vernon, Jr.
Mahoney, Richard
Mark, Reuben
McDonnell, John
McGowan, William
Miles, Michael
Monaghan, Thomas
Murdoch, Rupert
Murphy, Thomas
Murray, Allen
O'Reilly, Anthony
Olsen, Kenneth
Palmer, Robert
Pfeiffer, Eckhard
Picard, Dennis
Platt, Lewis
Popoff, Frank
Raos, John
Raymond, Lee
Ricciardi, Lawrence
Ritter, John Southworth
Sanders, Wayne
Schwab, Charles
Shrontz, Frank
Silas, C.
Smith, Frederick
Spindler, Michael
Stafford, John
Steere, William
Stiritz, William
Tooker, Gary
Trotman, Alexander
Trump, Donald
Turner, Robert
  Edward (Ted) III
Unruh, James
Vagelos, Pindaros Roy
Walsh, Michael
Weill, Sanford
Welch, John
Whitwan, David Ray
Woolard, Edgar S. Jr.

COMEDIANS

Criteria: Comedians were selected from the following categories: (1) those who play leading roles on popular American television series; (2) those who have won a Grammy Award for the Best Spoken Comedy Album since 1985; (3) those who frequently star in major comedic motion pictures, and (4) other prominent comedians who regularly appear on television.

Akroyd, Dan
Carlin, George
Carson, Johnny
Carvey, Dana
Chase, Chevy
Cosby, Bill
Crystal, Billy
Dangerfield, Rodney
Hope, Bob
Leno, Jay
Letterman, David
Martin, Steve
Murphy, Eddie
Murray, Bill
Newhart, Bob
O'Brien, Conan
Piscopo, Joseph
Roseanne
Seinfeld, Jerry
Williams, Robin
Wright, Steven

COMPOSERS

Criteria: Composers were selected from those who have won a Grammy award since 1985 for: (1) Best Contemporary Composition; (2) Best Song Written Specifically for a Motion Picture or Television; (3) Best Instrumental Composition for a Motion Picture or Television; (4) Best Musical Show Album, and (5) Song of the Year.

Babbitt, Milton Byron
Bacharach, Burt
Carter, Elliott
Coleman, Cy
Corea, Chick
Corigliano, John
Elfman, Danny
Foster, David
Glass, Philip
Gordon, Irving
Gould, Morton
Grusin, Dave
Hamlisch, (Marvin)
  Frederick M.
Henley, Don
Henley, Larry
Holmes, Rupert
Horner, James
Jackson, Michael
Jarreau, Al
Jennings, Will
Mann, Barry
Marsalis, Wynton

Masser, Michael
Mays, Lyle
McFerrin, Bobby
Metheny, Patrick Bruce
Miller, Roger
Morricone, Ennio
Newman, Randy
Penderecki, Krzystof
Post, Mike
Reich, Steve
Richie, Lionel
Schwanter, Joseph
Sessions, Roger
Silvestri, Martin
Simon, Paul
Singer, Carole
Sondheim, Stephen
Weil, Cynthia
Williams, John

CULTURAL INFLUENTIALS

Criteria: Cultural Influentials include prominent: (1) *Symphony Conductors* including conductors of major metropolitan orchestras. (2) *Educators* including recipients of the Guggenheim Fellowship since 1992; (3) *Historians* including recipients of the Pulitzer Prize for history since 1988; (4) *Philosophers* who are most often cited in major reference works about philosophy, and (5) *Religious Leaders* of mainstream religions in the United States.

Angelou, Maya
Baker, Houston A. Jr.
Barenboim, Daniel
Beck, Lewis
Berry, Mary
Boorstin, Daniel
Card, Claudia
Chapman, Morris H.
Chisholm, Roderick
Chomsky, Avram
Comer, James
Danto, Arthur
Darity, William A.
Daye, Charles
Demaria, Robert, Jr.
Dohnanyi, Christoph Von
Epps, Edgar
Evans, Slayton
Falwell, Rev. Jerry
Farrakhan, Rev. Louis
Gates, Henry Louis Jr.
Gellmann, Murray
Gert, Bernard
Giordano, John
Gomes, Peter
Gorovitz, Samuel
Graham, Rev. Billy
Greer, Thomas
Groves, Harry
Hamilton, Charles
Hickey, Cardinal James
Jones, Quincy

Kennan, George
Klugh, Earl
Knight, Franklin
Lewis, David
Maslin, Rabbi Simeon J.
Morrow, John
Moskos, Charles
O'Connor, John
Ozawa, Seiji
Painter, Nell
Rampersand, Arnold
Rosaldo, Renato
Rostropovich, Mstislav
Russell, George
Sage, Dennis
Sahlins, Marshall
Sanchez, Sonia
Schlesinger, Arthur Meier Jr.
Schwarz, Gerard
Scott, Nathan
Seeskin, Kenneth
Shaw, Robert
Sinnot-Armstrong, Walter P.
Slatkin, Leonard
Stone, Chuck
Thomas, Michael Tilson
Turner, Mark
Tyrrell, R.
Ulrich, Laurel
White, Richard
Wilkins, Roger
Wilson, William

DANCERS

Criteria: Dancers were selected from the following categories: (1) choreographers who have received nominations for the Tony Award since 1980, and (2) Prominent dancers/choreographers and dance personalities who have appeared in major productions on the American stage.

Alum, Manuel
Anthony, Mary
Baryshnikov, Mikhail
Brown, Trisha
Butler, John
Catterson, Pat
Charlip, Remy
Cunningham, Merce
Currier, Ruth
Dunn, Douglas
Erdman, Jean
Farber, Viola
Feld, Eliot
Field, Ron
Foreman, Laura
Garth, Midi
Griffin, Rodney
Halprin, Anna
Hoving, Lucas
Jones, Bill
King, Eleanor
Koner, Pauline
Lamhut, Phyllis
Lang, Pearl
Lewitzky, Bella
Louis, Murray

Lubovitch, Lar
Martins, Peter
Maslow, Sophie
McKayle, Donald
Meehan, Nancy
Moore, Jack
Muller, Jennifer
Nagrin, Daniel
Neville, Phoebe
Newman, Rosalind
Nikolais, Alwin
Perez, Rudy
Posin, Kathryn
Redlich, Don
Scott, Marion
Smuin, Michael
Sokolow, Anna
Solomons, Gus Jr.
Taylor, Paul
Tetley, Glen
Tharp, Twyla
Truitte, James
Wagoner, Dan
Walker, Norman
Zane, Arnie

DRAMATIC ARTISTS

Criteria: Dramatic Artists were chosen from the following categories: (1) *Playwrights* who have received a Pulitzer Prize for drama since 1960; (2) *Directors* who have been nominated for a Tony Award since 1980, and (3) *Arrangers* who have been nominated for a Tony award since 1980.

Albee, Edward F.
Allen, Woody
Azenberg, Emanuel
Bernhardt, Melvin
Charnin, Martin
Cristofer, Michael
Davidson, Gordon
Feist, Gene
Flatt, Ernest
Fuller, Charles, Jr.
Gersten, Bernard
Gilroy, Frank
Gordone, Charles
Gregory, Don
Henley, Beth
Hines, Gregory
Kahn, Michael
Kushner, Tony
Lapine, James
Layton, Joe
Maltby, Richard, Jr.
Mamet, David
Mason, Marshall
Matalon, Vivian
Mauceri, John
Miller, Arthur
Mosel, Ted
Nederlander, James
Nichols, Mike
Norman, Marsha
Nugent, Nelle
Prince, Harold
Quintero, Jose

Reitman, Ivan
Saks, Gene
Seawell, Donald
Shepard, Sam
Simon, Neil
Stevens, Roger
Tanner, Tony
Tillinger, John
Tune, Tommy
Uhry, Alfred
Wasserstein, Wendy
Wilson, Lanford
Zaks, Jerry
Zindel, Paul

ECONOMISTS

Criteria: Economists were chosen from the following categories: (1) recipients of a Nobel Prize for Economic Sciences; (2) members of the Council of Economic Advisors during the Reagen, Bush, and Clinton administrations; (3) other prominent economists who have advised U.S. presidents, and (4) economists who have written major theories on economics that are traditionally taught at U.S. colleges and universities.

Arrow, Kenneth
Baumol, William
Becker, Gary
Bergson, Abram
Blinder, Allan
Boskin, Michael
Buchanan, James
Debreu, Gerard
Domar, Evsey
Feldstein, Martin
Fogel, Robert
Friedman, Milton
Greenspan, Alan
Jordan, Jerry
Kindleberger, Charles P. Ii
Klein, Lawrence
Leontief, Wassily
Markowitz, Harry
Miller, Merton
Modigliani, Franco
Moore, Thomas
Musgrave, Richard
Niskanen, William A.
North, Douglass C.
Pace, Arrow Kenneth
Poole, William
Rostow, Walt
Samuelson, Paul
Schmalensee, Richard
Schultz, Theodore
Sharpe, William
Simon, Herbert
Solow, Robert
Sprinkel, Beryl
Stein, Herbert
Stigler, George
Tobin, James
Tyson, Laura
Weidenbaum, Murray
Wescott, Robert

EDITORS & PUBLISHERS

Criteria: Editors and publishers were chosen from the following categories: (1) publishers of major commercial book publishing houses; (2) editors and publishers of major regional, metropolitan, and national newspapers; (3) editors and publishers of popular and influential magazines, and (4) publishers of prominent university presses (with an output of more than 100 titles per year).

Ackerman, John
Anderson, Bill
Applebaum, Irwyn
Bauer, Virginia
Blethen, Frank
Buckley, William F., Jr.
Cook, David T.
Cooper, Roger
Craig, George
Curley, Tom
Darehshori, Nader
Day, Colin
Dionne, Joseph
Douglas, Netty
Egen, Maureen
Eiger, Richard William
Elletin, Michael
Famighetti, Robert Joseph
Friedman, Jane
German, William
Giles, Robert
Goellner, J.
Gompertz, Mark
Graham, Donald
Grann, Phyllis E.
Hagelstein, Robert
Hall, Robert
Hayes, James
Hayward, Charles
Johnson, Richard
Kaiser, Robert
Kalikow, Peter
Laventhol, David
Lee, Tony
Lifvendahl, Harold
Lippencott, Walter, Jr.
Lipsey, Stanford
Long, Elizabeth Valk
MacArthur, John
Machaskee, Alex
Madigan, John
Mayer, Peter
Miller, Robert
Moore, John
Nyren, Neil
Osborne, Burl
Page, Robert
Parkinson, Roger
Patten, John
Penniman, Nicholas
Phelps, Ashton, Jr.
Philipson, Morris
Pittman, H.
Pope, Norris
Pulliam, Eugene
Purcell, Patrick

Quinson, Bruno
Rubin, Robert
Rubin, Stephen
Shain, Harold
Sisler, William
Snyder, Richard
Stapleton, Joan
Straus, Roger
Strothman, Wendy
Strutton, Larry
Sulzberger, Arthur
Taylor, William
Thierot, Richard
Thompson, Richard
Urbanowski, Frank
Valenti, Carl
Weil, Louis
Winter, Alan
Wood, Tom
Young, Jayne

INVENTORS

Criteria: Inventors were chosen from the following categories: (1) living members of the National Inventors Hall of Fame in Akron, Ohio, and (2) various inventors prominently cited in major lay-scientific journals.

Baker, Al
Beckman, Arnold
Berlin, Sanford
Bose, Amar
Butterworth, William
Camras, Marvin
Claybaugh, David
Colton, Frank
Conover, Lloyd
Coppley, Jack
Damadian, Dr. Raymond
Dichting, Doug
Djerassi, Carl
Durant, Dr. Graham
Elahian, Kamran
Elion, Gertrude
Erickson, Jerry
Fabel, George
Fergason, James
Finley, James
Gallagher, Dennis
Gandhi, Haren
Ganellin, Dr. Charon Robin
Gardner, John
Gauger, Dan
Gehrels, Neil
Glier, Michael
Gould, Gordon
Greatbatch, Wilson
Greene, Leonard
Gulotta, Joseph
Haber, Stuart
Hall, Robert
Hanford, William
Hiller, James
Holler, Mark
Hussey, Kevin
Keck, Donald
Kilby, Jack
Kolff, Willem
Kroo, Ilan
Kuntman, Daryal

Lakerveld, Harry
Landers, Sam
Ledley, Dr. Robert
Ligon, Thomas
Logan, Andrew
Lutz, Jim
MacHover, Tod
Maiman, Theodore
Maurer, Robert
McMillan, Larry
Millman, Irving
Morganti, Steven
Naef, Derick
Olsen, Kenneth
Palermo, Peter
Parker, Louis
Parsons, John
Poole, Ronald
Rines, Robert
Rohrer, Hinrich
Rubin, Benjamin
Sapiejewski, Roman
Sarett, Lewis
Sherwin, Elton Jr.
Shultz, Peter
Simko, Richard
Stornetta, Scott
Tribble, Guy

JOURNALISTS

Criteria: Journalists were chosen from the following categories: (1) recipients of a Pulitzer Prize for journalism since 1988; (2) journalists who regularly cover major national and international news for eminent U.S. metropolitan newspapers and magazines; (3) nationally syndicated columnists, and (4) prominent television and radio reporters and anchorpersons.

Abelson, Alan
Abrahim, Youssef M.
Angier, Natalie
Baker, Russell
Baquet, Dean
Barry, Dave
Blitzer, Wolf
Blumenthal, Sidney
Bradley, Edward
Braver, Rita
Brinkley, David
Broder, David
Brokaw, Thomas
Brooke, James
Buchanan, Patrick
Clines, Francis
Coll, Steve
Darlin, Damon
Dedman, Bill
Dietrich, Bill
Donaldson, Samuel
Echikson, William
Edsall, Thomas
Evans, Rowland
Fields, Suzanne
Friedman, Thomas
Gaines, William
Glassman, James
Grenier, Richard

Gwinn, Mary
Healy, Jane
Hume, Brit
Ibrahim, Youssef
Jennings, Peter
Keller, Bill
Kinsley, Michael
Koppel, Ted
Kristof, Nicholas
Lapinski, Ann
Malone, Don
Mansfield, Stephanie
McGraw, Mike
Mitchell, Andrea
Moyers, Bill D.
Mudd, Roger
Murphy, Carlyle Marie
Murray, Jim
Musbruger, Brent
Nalder, Eric
Novak, Robert
Page, Clarence
Pfaff, William
Quindlen, Anna
Raines, Howell
Raspberry, William J.
Rather, Dan
Remnick, David
Roberts, Corinne (Cokie) Boggs
Rooney, Andrew
Royko, Mike
Safire, William
Sanger, David
Schieffer, Bob
Schmemann, Serge
Schneider, William
Schorer, Jane
Shales, Tom
Shaw, Bernard
Shipler, David
Sidey, Hugh
Sloyan, Patrick
Snyder, William
Steele, James
Stewart, James
Tamarkin, Bob
Taylor, Jeff
Temko, Ned
Thomas, Cal
Toles, Tom
Truell, Peter
Vise, David
Wallace, Myron (Mike)
Walters, Barbara
Weiner, Tim
Wille, Lois
Will, George
Woodward, Robert
Wudunn, Sheryl
Zucchino, David

MILITARY LEADERS

Criteria: Military Leaders were chosen from the following categories: (1) Chairman of the Joint Chiefs of Staff in the U.S. military; (2) leaders of the Army, Navy, Air Force, and Marine Corps; (3) other members of the JCS, and (4) others leaders at the divisional-command level in the U.S. Military.

Brandtner, Lt. Gen. M.L.
Hearney, Gen. Richard D.
Jeremiah, Adm. David E.
Kelso, Adm. Frank B. Ii
Krulak, Gen. Charles C.
Lautenbacher, Rear Adm. C. Conrad Jr.
Macke, Vice Adm. Richard C.
McCaffrey, Gen. Barry R.
McPeak, Gen. Merrill A.
Mears, Lt. Gen. Gary H.
Mundy, Gen. C. E.
O'Neill, Lt. Gen. Malcolm R.
Ostovich, Rudolph
Reimer, Gen. Dennis J.
Shalikashvili, Gen. John
Shatzel, Col. R.D.
Sullivan, Gen. Gordon
Viccello, Henry
Willis, Brig. Gen. Mary C.

PHOTOGRAPHERS

Criteria: Photographers were chosen from the following categories: (1) those who have shown their work at one-person shows at major U.S. museums, and (2) Corporate/industrial photographers who have contributed work regularly to major U.S. magazines (including advertising).

Avedon, Richard
Caponigro, Paul
Dickinson, Eleanor Creekmore
Dickman, James
Dominis, John
Duncan, David
Dykinga, Jack
Eggelston, William
Feininger, Andreas B.L.
Gray, Mitchell
Groover, Jan
Grossfeld, Stan
Leibovitz, Annie
Meyerowitz, Joel
Penn, Irving
Siskind, Aaron
Suau, Anthony
Weston, Brett
Weston, Cole

PHYSICIANS

Criteria: Physicians were chosen from the following categories: (1) recipients of a Nobel Prize for Medical Sciences and Physiology since 1975, and (2) Recipients of the Albert Tasker Award for Medical Research (clinical and basic) since 1975.

Austrian, Robert
Beierwaltes, William
Benacerraf, Baruj
Blumberg, Baruch
Brady, Roscoe

Bray, George
Brown, Michael
Cohen, Stanley
Dixon, Frank
Elster, Allen
Finn, Ronald
Freda, Vincent
Gajdusek, Daniel
Gallo, Robert
Goldstein, Joseph
Gorman, John
Gotschlich, Emil, Jr.
Guillemin, Roger
Herzog, David
Hubel, David
Kandel, Eric
Mountcastle, Vernon, Jr.
Murray, Joseph
Nathans, Daniel
Pendergrass, Henry
Petersdorf, Robert
Potter, Michael
Roberts, Richard
Sharp, Phillip
Smith, Hamilton
Snell, George
Snyder, Solomon
Sokoloff, Louis
Sperry, Roger
Thomas, Edward Donnall
Tonegawa, Susumu
Varmus, Harold
Wiesel, Torsten

POLITICAL LEADERS

Criteria: Political Leaders were chosen from the following categories: (1) state governors; (2) mayors of the seventy largest cities; (3) majority and minority leaders of both the House and the Senate; (4) majority and minority chairpersons of important House and Senate committees; (5) other prominent federal legislators; (6) living Presidents and vicepresidents, and (7) members of President Clinton's cabinet.

Abramson, Jerry
Agnew, Spiro
Allen, George, Jr.
Allen, Joan
Almond, Lincoln
Andrews, M.D.
Archer, Dennis
Arrington, Jr., Richard
Austin, Ed
Babbitt, Bruce
Barry, Marion Jr.
Barthelemy, Sidney
Bartlett, Steve
Batt, Philip E.
Baucus, Max
Bayh, Evan
Beasley, David M.
Belton, Sharon
Biden, Joseph Robinette Jr.
Bingaman, Jeff
Bonior, David E.
Bosley, Freeman R., Jr.
Boxer, Barbara

Bradley, Bill
Branstad, Terry E.
Breaux, John
Bredesen, Philip
Breyer, Stephen
Broadfoot, Elma
Brooks, Jack
Brown, Jesse
Brown, Ronald
Bush, George
Byrd, Robert C.
Campbell, Bill
Caperton, Gaston
Carlson, Arne
Carnahan, Mel
Carper, Thomas R.
Carter, James Earl
Cayetano, Benjamin J.
Chafee, John H.
Chavez, Martin
Chiles, Lawton
Christopher, Warren
Cisneros, Henry
Clark, Steve
Clayton, Eva
Cleaver, Emanuel Ii
Clinton, President (Bill) William Jefferson
Cohen, William S.
Coleman, Norm
Conyers, John
Craig, Larry E.
D'amato, Alfonse
Daley, Richard
Daly, Tom
Danforth, John
Daub, Hal
Dean, Howard
Deconcini, Dennis
Dellums, Ronald V.
Dingell, John
Dodd, Christopher J.
Dole, Robert J.
Domenici, Pete
Durbin, Richard
Edgar, Jim
Edwards, Chet
Engler, John
Fasi, Frank
Feingold, Russ
Finkbeiner, Carleton
Fink, Tom
Fischer, David J.
Fish, Hamiliton, Jr.
Ford, William David
Ford, Gerald, R. Jr.
Fordice, Kirk
Francis, Larry
Freedman, Sandra
Frist, Bill
Frost, Martin
Gephardt, Richard A.
Geringer, Jim
Gibbons, Sam
Gingrich, Newton Leroy
Ginsburg, Ruth
Giuliani, Rudolph
Glendening, Parris N.
Glenn, John Jr.
Glickman, Dan
Golding, Susan
Goldsmith, Stephen
Gonzalez, Henry

Gore, Vice President Albert Jr.
Gorton, Slade
Graham, Bob
Grams, Rod
Granger, Kay
Grassley, Chuck
Graves, Bill
Greene, Richard E.
Hamilton, Lee
Hammer, Susan W.
Harkin, Tom
Harris, Elihu
Hatch, Orrin
Hatfield, Mark
Helms, Jesse Alexander
Herenton, W. W.
Hollings, Ernest
Hunt, James
Isaac, Robert
James, Forest Hood
James, Sharpe
Janklow, William J.
Jeffords, Marion
Johnson, Gary
Johnson, William
Johnston, J. Bennett
Jones, Brereton
Jordan, Frank
Kassebaum, Nancy
Katz, Vera
Kell, Ernie
Kemp, Jack
Kempthorne, Dirk
Kennedy, Edward M.
Kennedy, Joseph P. III
Kennelly, Barbara
Kerrey, Robert
Knowles, Tony
Kyl, Jon
Lanier, Robert
Lashutka, Gregory S.
Leahy, Patrick
Leavitt, Michael O.
Lewis, Joseph
Lieberman, Joseph
Loveridge, Ronald
Lowry, Mike
Lugar, Richard
Masiello, Anthony
McKernan, John R.
Menino, Thomas
Merrill, Stephen
Mfume, Kweisi
Michel, Robert Henry
Miller, Pam
Miller, Robert
Miller, Zell
Mitchell, George
Mondale, Walter
Moseley-Braun, Carol
Moynihan, Daniel
Murkowski, Frank
Murphy, Tom
Murray, Patty
Nelson, E. Benjamin
Norick, Ronald
Norquist, John
Nunn, Samuel Augustus Jr.
O'Connor, Sandra
O'Leary, Hazel
Oberndorf, Meyera E.
Obey, David R.

Panetta, Leon
Pataki, George E.
Patterson, Jim
Pell, Claiborne
Pena, Federico F.
Perot, Henry Ross
Perry, William
Pressler, Larry
Pulido, Miguela A.
Qualls, Roxanne
Quayle, James Danforth (Dan)
Racicot, Marc
Rangel, Charles B.
Reagan, Ronald
Rehnquist, William
Reich, Robert
Rendell, Edward
Reno, Janet
Rhodes, Mary
Rice, Norman
Richardson, Bill
Ridge, Tom
Riegle, Donald, Jr.
Riley, Richard
Riordan, Richard
Roberts, Barbara
Rockefeller, John
Romer, Roy
Roth, William
Rowland, John
Rubin, Robert
Sasser, Jim
Savage, M.
Scalia, Antonin
Schafer, Edward
Schmoke, Kurt
Schroeder, Patricia
Serna, Joe Jr.
Shalala, Donna
Sharpe, James
Simon, Paul
Simon, Paul (Sen.)
Simpson, Alan
Souter, David
Specter, Arlen
Stevens, John
Sundquist, Don
Symington, Fife
Thompson, Tommy
Thurmond, J. Strom
Todd, Bruce
Tucker, Jim
Vinroot, Richard
Voinovich, George V.
Wallop, Malcolm
Walters, David
Warner, John
Webb, Wellington
Weld, William

White, Michael
Whitman, Christie
Wilson, Pete
Wolff, Nelson
Wong, Willie
Woolsey, James

SCIENTISTS

Criteria: Scientists were chosen from the following categories: (1) recipients of a Nobel Prize for Chemistry since 1970, and (2) recipients of a Nobel Prize for Physics since 1970.

Altman, Sidney
Anderson, Philip
Anfinsen, Christian
Berg, Paul
Bishop, John Michael
Bloembergen, Nicholaas
Brown (Brovarnik), Herbert Charles
Chandrasekhar, Subrahmanyan
Cooper, Leon
Corey, Elias
Cram, Donald
Cronin, James
Dehmelt, Hans
Fitch, Val
Fowler, William
Friedman, Jerome
Giaever, Ivar
Gilbert, Walter
Glashow, Sheldon
Hauptman, Jerome A.
Herschbach, Dudley
Hitchings, George Herbert
Hoffman, Roald
Karle, Jerome
Kendall, Henry
Lederman, Leon
Lipscomb, William Nunn Jr.
Marcus, Rudolph
Merrifield, Robert
Mullis, Kary
Penzias, Arno
Ramsey, Norman
Richter, Burton
Schawlow, Arthur
Schrieffer, John
Schwartz, Melvin
Steinberger, Jack
Swinger, Julian
Taube, Henry
Taylor, Joseph H.
Taylor, Richard

Townes, Charles
Weinberg, Steven
Wilson, Kenneth
Wilson, Robert

TELEVISION PERSONALITIES

Criteria: Television Personalities were chosen from the following categories: (1) hosts of nationally syndicated American talk shows; (2) hosts of popular American game shows; (3) sports announcers of nationally broadcast sporting events; (4) other prominent American television personalities not included on the list of Actors, Journalists, or Comedians, and (5) anchorpersons and weatherpersons at network television morning shows.

Albert, Marv
Barker, Robert
Caray, Harry
Christian, Spenser
Costas, (Bob) Robert Quinlan
Couric, (Katie) Katherine
Dierdorf, Dan
Donahue, (Phil) Philip John
Enberg, Dick
Gibson, Charles
Gifford, Frank
Gumbel, Bryant
Jackson, Keith
King, Larry
Lunden, Joan
Madden, Earl John
McEwen, Mark
Povich, (Maury) Maurice Richard
Raphael, Sally
Rivera, Geraldo
Roker, Al
Safer, Morely
Sajak, Pat
Smith, Harry
Summerall, Pat
White, Vanna
Winfrey, Oprah
Zahn, Paula

VOCALISTS

Criteria: Vocalists who received major American awards for their achievements from the following

categories: (1) singers who have had "Number One Songs in the U.S." since 1980 according to *Billboard* magazine's pop chart; (2) singers who have received a Grammy Award for Song of the Year since 1985, and (3) other prominent singers in traditional genres of American music who frequently perform on the American stage and television specials.

Abdul, Paula
Bennett, Tony
Bolton, Michael
Brown, Bobby
Carey, Mariah
Cash, Johnny
Ciccone, Madonna
Clapton, Eric
Denver, John
Diamond, Neil
Estefan, Gloria
Franklin, Aretha
Grant, Amy
Jackson, Michael
Hornsby, Bruce
Houston, Whitney
Ingram, James
Jackson, Janet
Joel, Billy
Labelle, Patti
Lauper, Cyndi
Lewis, Huey
Loggins, Kenny
Manilow, Barry
Marx, Richard
Medley, Bill
Mellencamp, John
Miller, Steve
Ocean, Billy
Parton, Dolly
Prince, (the artist formerly known as)
Raitt, Bonnie
Ross, Diana
Seger, Bob
Sinatra, Frank
Springsteen, Bruce
Streisand, Barbra
Torme, Mel
Turner, Tina
Warnes, Jennifer
White, Karyn
Williams, Vanessa
Wonder, (Stevie) Steveland